1,000,000 Books
are available to read at

Forgotten Books

www.ForgottenBooks.com

Read online
Download PDF
Purchase in print

ISBN 978-1-5279-3196-1
PIBN 10925317

This book is a reproduction of an important historical work. Forgotten Books uses state-of-the-art technology to digitally reconstruct the work, preserving the original format whilst repairing imperfections present in the aged copy. In rare cases, an imperfection in the original, such as a blemish or missing page, may be replicated in our edition. We do, however, repair the vast majority of imperfections successfully; any imperfections that remain are intentionally left to preserve the state of such historical works.

Forgotten Books is a registered trademark of FB &c Ltd.
Copyright © 2018 FB &c Ltd.
FB &c Ltd, Dalton House, 60 Windsor Avenue, London, SW19 2RR.
Company number 08720141. Registered in England and Wales.

For support please visit www.forgottenbooks.com

1 MONTH OF FREE READING

at

www.ForgottenBooks.com

By purchasing this book you are eligible for one month membership to ForgottenBooks.com, giving you unlimited access to our entire collection of over 1,000,000 titles via our web site and mobile apps.

To claim your free month visit:
www.forgottenbooks.com/free925317

* Offer is valid for 45 days from date of purchase. Terms and conditions apply.

English
Français
Deutsche
Italiano
Español
Português

www.forgottenbooks.com

Mythology Photography **Fiction** Fishing Christianity **Art** Cooking Essays Buddhism Freemasonry Medicine **Biology** Music **Ancient Egypt** Evolution Carpentry Physics Dance Geology **Mathematics** Fitness Shakespeare **Folklore** Yoga Marketing **Confidence** Immortality Biographies Poetry **Psychology** Witchcraft Electronics Chemistry History **Law** Accounting **Philosophy** Anthropology Alchemy Drama Quantum Mechanics Atheism Sexual Health **Ancient History Entrepreneurship** Languages Sport Paleontology Needlework Islam **Metaphysics** Investment Archaeology Parenting Statistics Criminology **Motivational**

University of the State of New York

Extension Bulletin

No. 10   October 1895

EXTENSION OF UNIVERSITY TEACHING
IN
ENGLAND AND AMERICA

A STUDY IN PRACTICAL PEDAGOGICS

By James E. Russell, Ph. D.

Professor of Philosophy and Pedagogy in the University of Colorado
Late special commissioner of the University of the State of New York to visit European schools and report on their methods

An annotated German translation of this bulletin under the title *Die Volks-Hochschulen in England und Amerika* by Otto Wilhelm Beyer is published by R. Voigtländer, Leipzig. 1895.

	PAGE		PAGE
Salient features of educational progress in England and America	148	Courses and methods in the extension of university teaching	208
Rise and development of university extension in England	161	Results of 21 years of progress	220
Spread of the extension movement to America and other countries	176	Pedagogic considerations in the extension of university teaching	237
Organization of university extension work	188	Bibliography	246
		Index	248

ALBANY
UNIVERSITY OF THE STATE OF NEW YORK
1895

Price 15 cents

Regents

ANSON JUDD UPSON, D. D., LL. D., L. H. D., *Chancellor*
WILLIAM CROSWELL DOANE, D. D., LL. D., *Vice-Chancellor*
LEVI P. MORTON, LL. D., Governor   ⎫
CHARLES T. SAXTON, LL. D., Lieutenant-Governor ⎬ *Ex officio*
JOHN PALMER, Secretary of State   ⎪
CHARLES R. SKINNER, M. A., LL. D., Sup't of Pub. Inst. ⎭

In order of election by the legislature

YEAR
1873	MARTIN I. TOWNSEND, M. A., LL. D.	Troy
1874	ANSON JUDD UPSON, D. D., LL. D., L. H. D.	Glens Falls
1876	WILLIAM L. BOSTWICK, M. A.	Ithaca
1877	CHAUNCEY M. DEPEW, LL. D.	New York
1877	CHARLES E. FITCH, LL. B., M. A., L. H. D.	Rochester
1877	ORRIS H. WARREN, D. D.	Syracuse
1878	WHITELAW REID, LL. D.	New York
1881	WILLIAM H. WATSON, M. A., M. D.	Utica
1881	HENRY E. TURNER	Lowville
1883	ST CLAIR MCKELWAY, LL. D.	Brooklyn
1885	HAMILTON HARRIS, LL. D.	Albany
1885	DANIEL BEACH, Ph. D., LL. D.	Watkins
1888	CARROLL E. SMITH	Syracuse
1890	PLINY T. SEXTON, LL. D.	Palmyra
1890	T. GUILFORD SMITH, M. A., C. E.	Buffalo
1892	WILLIAM CROSWELL DOANE, D. D., LL. D.	Albany
1893	LEWIS A. STIMSON, B. A., M. D.	New York
1894	SYLVESTER MALONE	Brooklyn
1895	ALBERT VANDER VEER, M. D., Ph. D.	Albany

Elected by the regents

1888	MELVIL DEWEY, M. A., *Secretary*	Albany

University of the State of New York

Extension Bulletin

No. 10　October 1895

EXTENSION OF UNIVERSITY TEACHING IN ENGLAND AND AMERICA

A STUDY IN PRACTICAL PEDAGOGICS

By James E. Russell, Ph. D.

Professor of Philosophy and Pedagogy in the University of Colorado

Late special commissioner of the University of the State of New York to visit European schools and report on their methods

---

In July 1893, on recommendation of some of the leading members of convocation, the regents appointed Prin. James E. Russell, then of New York but now professor of pedagogy in the University of Colorado, a special commissioner to visit European educational institutions and report on whatever he might find of most importance to educational institutions in New York. He had no instruction as to the topic but was left to select it after making his investigation.

The subject which he found most useful is that great movement known as university extension, which has clearly taken a prominent place in modern education. His report treats this important matter so fairly, broadly and ably that it is deemed important to print it for the use of those in the state of New York who in recent years have become deeply interested in extension work. In this form it will be a most convenient manual for those who wish to understand clearly this modern movement.

MELVIL DEWEY, *Secretary*

INTRODUCTION
SALIENT FEATURES OF EDUCATIONAL PROGRESS IN ENGLAND AND AMERICA

University extension, a term in current use in England since about 1850, has of late come to designate a new and powerful movement in education. It means to-day the extension of university teaching to persons of any class or condition who are unable to pursue a course of study in residence. The guiding principle throughout is that men and women while busily engaged in the affairs of life are capable of doing systematic intellectual work of an order worthy of university recognition and support, and that to study *during* one's life-work is a nobler conception than to study *for* one's life-work.

The rapid progress of this movement, specially during the past five years, in which time it has come to assume almost international importance, is sufficient warrant for a careful pedagogic account of the aims and methods involved. Such a study, however, must first consider the general conditions under which new forces in systematic education arise and the special circumstances which should make so radical a movement possible and popular among English-speaking people.

Conditions of educational reform. Educational reforms are progressive and powerful in proportion as they harmonize with the spirit of the times, and only when they satisfy legitimate needs of the times do they assume permanent form. Old customs are dropped off as their usefulness disappears and new ones take their places. The evolution in the educational world is largely determined by those gravely important forces which find their expression in the political, industrial, social and intellectual life of a people. Granted an ideal aim — the perfection of human character, the promotion of happiness, the regeneration of the race, or whatever it may be — the *form* of the resultant system will depend on the controlling forces inherent in the national life. The corollary of this principle is equally true; that by painful steps and slow must each people work out its own educational destiny. A foreign importation, however strong, will rarely thrive as well as in its native soil.

1 *Political.* A stern political necessity forced on Sparta a system of education which to this day is synonymous with all that is hard and severe in training. Athens recognized no such overpowering constraint and accordingly adopted quite a different mode of fitting her young men for citizenship. The words of Friedrich Wilhelm 3 — *Der Staat muss durch geistige Krafte ersetzen, was er an physischen verloren hat* — breathe the spirit that makes possible great national systems of education. The subsequent development in Prussia is proof sufficient of what political expediency can effect when spurred to its best by patriotic fears.

2 *Industrial.* A potent force, because closely linked with a nation's prosperity, is manifest in the prevailing tendencies of industrial activity. The invention of machinery has revolutionized the customs of ages. The manufactured article, which to day is a product of many machines and of the labor of many hands, was once produced by a master workman. The apprentice system is becoming obsolete because the times demand mechanics, highly intelligent machines, instead of craftsmen, masters of their art. Manual training and trade schools, which till recent years would have been anachronisms, are getting to be a necessity. New fields of investigation are daily opened in the ever increasing competition in business.

The rivalry between Genoa and Venice for the carrying trade of the east, created a demand for training in seamanship and commercial education which resulted in the finding of a new continent and the creation of an international competition little dreamed of when the fall of Constantinople forced Genoese adventurers to take service under other flags. A similar expansion of commercial interest in modern times has given rise to the importunate demand for the *Realbildung*, a demand as truly in accord with the spirit of the times as that for classical scholarship during the age of humanism.

3 *Social.* A change in the social life of a people modifies previously existing ideals The composition and density of population, the relations of man to man and of class to class, the respect for law and order, the strength of moral and religious faith, these and many more are interrelated forces of vital importance in the social order, and give it character. The ideals of protestant Ger-

many are not those of the 15th century. The educational reforms in France under the first empire could have had no weight in the reign of Louis 16. The school system of modern Japan is devised to satisfy conditions which had no existence in 1854 when Perry opened her ports to western commerce and civilization. In every century there has been an extension of educational advantages precisely in proportion as the people have secured additional power in the state. The growth of democracy is a fact not to be gainsaid and the influence of the democratic spirit on every phase of social development is one of the predominating characteristics of the 19th century.

4 *Intellectual.* The introduction of new subjects of study discloses another field for investigation and demands a distinct following in the learned world. True it may be that only a few are directly interested in the new pursuit but indirectly the whole civilized world may share in the results. Of such a power was the revival of Greek art and literature in the 15th and 16th centuries, a movement whose beneficent influence in molding our modern life is beyond calculation If one would be convinced of the reality and virility of humanistic ideals in the educational system of the times let him study the curriculum of any standard higher school in Christendom.

The possibilities of knowledge have been enormously extended within the present century. The progress of natural science has been phenomenal within a period of 50 years. A new literature has sprung up devoted to the theory and practical application of natural laws, while the scientific spirit has given new vigor to intellectual pursuits long enervated by a romantic idealism. Even in classical study, within the sacred precincts of humanism, this new power has given strength of purpose and accuracy in detail hitherto unknown. Its influence on the times is certainly not less marked than that other movement which broke the reign of the dark ages.

Scientific progress in 19th century. 15 years of this century had passed before we had a steamboat and 30 years before a locomotive drew the first passenger train in England. The spinning-jenny, the power loom and cotton gin, though invented earlier, came into use as steam power became more practicable; and with the steam engine to furnish the power both for manufacture and transportation, England's bountiful stores of coal and iron were drawn on to supply the world's markets. The invention of the telegraph in conjunction with quick and easy means of communication provided the conditions favorable for the growth of the newspaper. The growing importance of electricity in the mechanic arts testifies too, to the wonderful results of inventive genius. During the 20 years preceding 1850, it is said, more patents were issued in England than for two centuries and a half before, and since 1870, a period not of revolution but of progress, a conservative estimate makes the reduction in the hours of labor due to improved machinery, not less than 25 per cent.[a]

Resulting changes in social and industrial life. The social condition of the country resulting from the abrupt change from the old order to the new was something appalling. Increasing density of population in industrial centers adding to the miseries of life, women and children pressed into factory service and forced to compete with men under conditions unsanitary and immoral in the extreme, hours of labor mercilessly long and wages at the starvation point — such was the background of the social life of the times. Class distinctions were becoming increasingly more marked. Workingmen's societies and trades unions were formed to make the separation more complete.

Philanthropic movements. The progress of industrial activity brought benefits, however, as well as ills. The press and the spread of cheap literature tended to promote a better understanding of class differences and to alleviate the most obnoxious forms of industrial oppression Philanthropic spirits were not lacking who, learning of the people's wants from personal contact, plead their cause from the pulpit and the platform. Sporadic attempts were made for the practical betterment of the lower classes from the beginning of the century, but with meager results beyond the founding of a few local lecture courses, lyceums and mercantile libraries, and "peoples' colleges" in Nottingham and Sheffield.[b] In the early '50s, F: D. Maurice, Rev. Charles

---

[a] The steam-power of the U S was reckoned in 1888 as equivalent in working-power to 161,833,000 men See Mulhall *Growth of American industries and wealth*, p 70

[b] Ruskin was a teacher in one of these colleges "One of the most remarkable art teachers in England at the present time was, first his pupil, afterward his successor, there."

Kingsley and others began the Christian socialist movement, of which a leading aim was the establishment of social settlements — headquarters for the dissemination of good influence in the community, centers to which the people could look for personal assistance and encouragement. In 1854 Maurice founded a college for workingmen in London, and in 1867 Edward Denison, a young Oxford man imbued with the scientific spirit, took up his residence among the poor of the east end that he might study their condition at first hand.[a] ' Arnold Toynbee followed him a few years later and in the short period before his early death in 1883, succeeded in inaugurating a philanthropic and educational work which is admirably carried on at Toynbee Hall, an institution established in his memory

London has many such settlements, and the movement is spreading to other cities. In America highly educated men and women, university graduates, are using similar organizations for the promotion of a better understanding of social problems.[b] Cooperative associations of workingmen, an outgrowth of the same movement, have been formed not only for the material improvement of their members but for the elevation of the popular standards of moral and intellectual life From such beginnings, the principles of practical Christianity have found acceptance within a period of 40 years among all English-speaking people It is rarely questioned nowadays that the best way to help the masses is to help them to help themselves; that mere giving is of no avail unless the recipient is taught to take higher views of life.

Political changes in England. Without wars at home or external constraint, political changes of deepest significance have taken place in England within the memory of men now living. Under the reforms of 1832 the balance of power went over from the landed aristocracy into the hands of the middle class. The progress of industry based on mechanical invention brought to the front the interests of a new class against which king and nobility strove in vain. A year later, parliament chartered the first railway into London, despite the dismal predictions of the

---

[a] E. B 5 200-6, R. of rs. 3.593-98.   [b] U E. W. 3·102-12

of London, with the assistance of Sir Stafford Northcote, Prof. Max Müller and other distinguished scholars[a] The college of preceptors and the society of arts had previously made experiments in local examinations but now for the first time the universities assumed to guide directly, as well as indirectly, the educational interests of the country. Hard on this radical change of policy followed internal changes which permitted students to matriculate at the universities without becoming members of a college, thus materially reducing the expenses of residence. Another decade of progress saw courses of study broadened and deepened, a scheme matured for the extension of university teaching to those outside the universities, and an increase in the number of provincial colleges from three in 1871 to 14 in 1884.

Cardinal points in the century's progress. No particular acumen is required of one familiar with English history to note the cardinal points in the century's progress. At regular recurring intervals of about 20 years decisive steps have been taken in politics under the stimulus of changing conditions in the industrial and social life, and each instance has inaugurated a corresponding epoch in the progress of education.

1830 The principle of state aid was first recognized in the early '30s, but grants were made only to voluntary schools for children of the middle classes. That this measure should follow within two years the extension of political rights to the middle classes, and that it should be simultaneous with the first fruits of steam propulsion, is, to say the least, suggestive. Two

1850 decades later the leaven had permeated the whole lump. The telegraph, the press, cheap literature, Christian socialism and free trade are teaching the lessons of national unity and social brotherhood. This period is marked, too, by the beginning of the movement for industrial schools and popular education; the universities are being reformed, taken out of the hands of the few

1870 and drafted into the national service. Another 20 years pass; political changes have included the workingman in the electorate, educated men are beginning to concern themselves

---

[a] Acland, T D Some account of the origin and objects of the new Oxford examinations for the title of associate in arts and certificates for the year 1858. London. 1858.

The growth of the democratic spirit is exhibited in every important legislative act. Class distinctions, so far as subject to official action, are gradually disappearing; even the separation of church from state and the reorganization of the house of lords are mooted questions. At each step new tasks are set before the educationist and public sympathy warmly supports every suggestion that offers reasonable promise of efficiency.

University reforms Oxford and Cambridge have ranked for centuries among the chief sources of intellectual life in England, and to these venerable institutions the nation has looked for light in the critical period of its educational transaction. In 1850, as the modern ideas began to take shape, the universities were veritable cloisters, graduation from which was conditioned by subscription to the tenets of the church of England.[a] Only men of wealth could enjoy the luxury of a university education.[b] Five years before, however, an address had been presented to the hebdomadal board of the University of Oxford[c] praying for the admission of "talented and well-conditioned young men, however poor, provided they shall be prepared to benefit by its education."[d]

The matter was taken up in parliament and on the report of a royal commission the religious disabilities were removed in the early '50s, and as a method of reducing expenses, it was suggested that the universities might properly found professional chairs in the large cities where students could do a part of the work required in a degree course. The Oxford university commission declined to approve the scheme of local professorships, and little good came from several other similar proposals made at about the same time, save that indirectly the universities were induced tacitly to acknowledge that they owed a duty to the nation at large.

Local examinations. The first important move was in 1857 when Oxford, and afterward Cambridge, adopted a system of local examinations in secondary studies which had been organized voluntarily by Sir Thomas Acland and Dr Temple, afterward headmaster of Rugby and now bishop

---

[a] Whitaker's almanack, 1891, p 639-42 [b] Camb. s. m Rept. p 11.
[c] Oxford university commission. Report. 1852. [d] Mackinder & Sadler, p. 2.

year following a parliamentary commission was appointed to inquire into the state of popular education but, as though much needed to be said, no report was made till 1861.

Certain suggestive facts were not far to seek. Every one knew that illiteracy was dense, but few could realize that of the marriages in the years 1841-45, as shown by official records, 32.6 per cent of the men and 48.9 per cent of the women were unable to sign their own names to the marriage register. In 1850, with a total population of about 18,000,000, there were only 1844 schools under inspection and these were but half full, the attendance being 197,578, with accommodations for 370,948. Not 20 per cent of pupils enrolled could read, but few more could write and less than "two per cent had mastered arithmetic as far as the rule of three."[a]

Founding of a free-school system. A new code was issued in 1862 but real progress seemed to wait on political expediency. The seven great public schools of England were reformed in 1869 by act of parliament in a way greatly to extend their usefulness among the upper and middle classes. The science and art department of South Kensington has done most important service within a restricted field, but by the act of 1870 an elementary education was put within reach of every child in the kingdom. It created a new public school under control of a local board and in part supported by local taxation, with provisions for free tuition of all too poor to pay. This was the beginning of state education for the people. Later amendments, notably in 1889-90, have done still more, till at present it may be said that the elementary schools of England are free to all and lavishly supported. In 1870 the number of schools under inspection had increased to 8986 with 1,255,083 pupils in attendance; in 1890 the schools numbered 19,498 with an average attendance of nearly 4,000,000. State grants have grown from £20,000 in 1834, and £150,303 in 1864, to £6,500,000 in 1894. No words more eloquent could be spoken than the simple recital of these facts.

The parallel courses of political and educational reforms in England are something more than a coincidence. Both have been controlled and directed by forces inherent in the national life.

---

[a] Sharpless. *English education*, p. 8.

landlords that the substitution of steam for horse-power would be the "curse and ruin of England." But railroads multiplied. The press was becoming increasingly more influential. The forces which were driving classes apart were also promoting the cause of national unity. Slowly the idea grew that questions of political policy were better settled when the interests of all were consulted than of any special class. The corn laws of 1846, and the spread of free trade notions, indicate the strength of the democratic spirit The American declaration of independence and the French revolution were bearing fruit on English soil. That sentiment which in 1833 freed all slaves in British dominions and reached its climax 30 years later in the bloody war between the states, may well claim a similar origin. The old English belief in the virtue of liberty could not check political reform midway in its course. After 15 years of direct agitation, the workingmen of England took their place in 1867 by the side of the middle and upper classes as members of the body politic. Subsequent legislation has added to their power and still further extended privileges which once were the prerogatives of a few.

Progress in education. Political responsibilities, as well as philanthropic ideals, demand increasing educational facilities. The growing power of the middle classes in the early years of the century brought about some changes before 1820 in the management of the higher schools and compelled the admission of science, art and modern languages into the curriculum. In 1834, two years after the reform act, the first direct annual grant for the promotion of public education was made. Five years later a committee of the privy council on education was instituted for purposes of supervision and distribution of state money. In 1857 an act was passed providing for the establishment of industrial schools. The work of Maurice and Kingsley was beginning to be felt in all circles of society. Simultaneously with the growth of the movement for the admission of the lower classes to the electorate the idea of education for *all* the people began to make headway. Resolutions which were adopted at an educational conference held in London in 1857 under the presidency of the prince consort, put the case squarely before the country. The with social problems, a national system of elementary education is established and the universities go out of their way to extend their benefits to the country at large. Finally now, in the '90s, with political privileges still further extended and the principle of "home rule" a matter of parliamentary agitation, with fresh local and national legislation for restriction of hours of labor and alleviation of industrial oppression, it is to be noted that educational progress is once more promoted by legislation, the first of consequence since 1870.

1890

The intermediate education act for Wales, 1889, was the first official recognition on the part of government of "the need of systematic and organized provision of secondary schools by public money,"[a] and now in the present year (1894) the plan is perfected by the founding of a Welsh university which may be approached in regular steps from the lowest schools. In 1890 absolutely free education in the elementary grades was provided by enactment and a new code followed which has wonderfully stimulated both day and evening schools. Technical training has received an unexpected stimulus in the diversion of a large sum, proceeds of the extra tax on spirits, to the purpose of education. The universities are growing more liberal as is evidenced by the expansion of the curriculum, the offering of summer courses and the admission of women. A new teaching university for London has recently been proposed by a committee of government. Even now a royal commission is formulating a comprehensive system of intermediate education to bridge over the gulf between the lower schools and the universities hitherto occupied by a heterogeneous mass of institutions and organizations, endowed or private. In the words of the minister of education:[b] "The country is slowly making up its mind that, whatever the wealthy part of the community may do, provision of a 'public kind shall be made for all those in the middle class or the working class who demand an education above the elementary schools, cheap, effective and close to their doors, with some public guarantee of its efficiency."

Conditions in America. The peculiar conditions existing in America differentiate the new world from the old. The United

---

[a] Acland *and* Smith, *Studies in secondary education*, p 107
[b] Acland *and* Smith, *Studies in secondary education*, p. 307.

States is a land of paradoxes, educational as well as political. A high order of intelligence, a widespread interest in education, a magnificent free school system leading those who will even to the universities, stand opposed to the powers of darkness embodied in millions of recently liberated slaves whose very presence is a constant incentive to race prejudice, and in an ever-increasing immigrant population, many of whom know government only as a means of repression, and all of whom are in a degree possessed of social, political and moral ideas wholly disparate with American life. The nation's need for education is pressing, an education suited to the people of every class and of all ages, an education capable of converting some very raw material into decent, self-respecting, patriotic citizenship.

That some rather crude attempts have been made to solve the educational problem is not to be gainsaid, but without repeated trial and many a failure no lasting progress could be made. America is not Europe; it is not England; the experience of the old world can be helpful in the new only by way of suggestion. Further, if a republican government were to wait till settled conditions permitted the organization of an ideal educational system, it would probably cease to be republican. It is only by unrestricted voluntary effort supplemented by every form of state activity that a new country can hope to make sure progress. The one great advantage is that there are no traditions to respect, nothing to retard advance save a false philosophy which under education gradually merges into a better.

Democracy and higher education. The one important question, about which a century of dispute has waged, is a necessary outcome of the extreme democratic notions embodied in the declaration of independence. If all men are equal it is no business of the state to make them unequal; what the state gives to one it must give to all. Slowly public opinion has come to recognize that it is not inconsistent with republican ideas to grant the *privilege* of the higher training to all who are capable of getting benefit from it; but that it is the *duty* of the state to grant such privileges is a theory not yet unhesitatingly accepted. No one doubts the necessity of education in advance of the elementary for the well-being of the nation and the cause of humanity.

This paradox, a conscious element in the life of the people, has stimulated private munificence to a degree unparalleled elsewhere; it has given rise to great numbers of organizations directly or indirectly engaged in the spread of truth and righteousness; and in a way most earnestly to be desired, it has emphasized the personal responsibility of the individual in his quest for knowledge.

Lyceum system. For 50 years after the formation of the Union, schools of all grades were ridiculously inadequate. The lack of systematic instruction, however, begot other educational advantages of the greatest importance in the national life. Early in the century a system of popular lectures came into vogue and for many years the ablest statesmen, the most distinguished scholars, clergymen and men of letters, used the public platform as the most efficient means of reaching the people.[a] By the lyceum system Wendell Phillips and the abolitionists were enabled to reach the hearts of the north and to force on the conflict with slavery. The cause of temperance and other moral issues were ably supported by popular lecturers. Sometimes courses of lectures were given and specially in the cities efforts were made to interest the working classes. In New Haven regular courses in natural science were instituted for mechanics as early as 1831 by certain professors of Yale college.[b] Later the plan was carried to Hartford, then to Lowell, Salem and Boston. The Lowell institute, a people's college in Boston, is the outcome of this idea.

Agriculture and the mechanic arts. With the founding of a school of science in connection with Yale college in 1847, regular instruction for the people of the community was incorporated. Particular attention was given to scientific agriculture and the spread of scientific ideas among farmers. From this beginning the movement has spread till every state has its agricultural experiment station and some organized scheme for practical training in husbandry.[c] Closely following Yale's success in rousing an interest in rural affairs, and undoubtedly influenced

---

[a] E B 5.206–7; R. of rs. 3 598–99.   [b] E. B 5 206; R. of rs 3 598.
[c] E B 5.206–9; R. of rs. 3 599–600.

by it, came the only important federal grant ever made for purposes of higher education.[a] In the darkest days of the civil war, when the north realized most keenly that strength in arms depends quite as much on an intelligent soldiery as on material resources, congress made an enormous grant of public lands to the several states — "30,000 acres for each senator and representative"— on condition that the proceeds should be used in the support of at least one college in which, without excluding other scientific and classical studies, military tactics, agriculture and the mechanic arts should be taught On this foundation many of the states have established universities with low fees or free tuition to all. The important consideration is that a system of free schools has been developed in most of the newer states continuing from the primary grades to the university and that the state university by virtue of its position is able to utilize the entire system in furthering any educational project that meets with general approbation.

Summer schools. Another feature worthy of mention in connection with the progress of republican ideals in education is the American summer school. It is said that Prof. Louis Agassiz made the first experiment in 1873 by giving a course for students and teachers of zoology. Soon afterward a religious assembly accustomed to meet yearly at Chautauqua lake in New York resolved itself into a summer school. In 1878 a regular course of home study was added to supplement and continue the summer work.[b] The best talent in American universities has been drawn on to supply the teaching, and laboratories, lecture halls— one of them seating nearly 8,000 people — and equipment have been lavishly supplied For six weeks each summer Chautauqua is the most unique if not the largest university in the world. It has hundreds of branches in different parts of the Union and its phenomenal success has induced nearly all the leading universities to offer summer courses for the benefit of those who can not attend their regular sessions.

Spirit of the times. During the greater part of this century the intellectual forces of English and American life have been

---

[a] The Morrill land grant of 1862, was supplemented by special grants in 1889 and 1891
[b] E. B. 5:809-15; R. of rs. 8:600-4.

profoundly influenced by the universal acceptance of the truths of natural science. The progress of mechanical invention, with the consequent revolution in the industrial and social orders, has impressed on people of all classes a wholesome appreciation of that knowledge whose attribute is power; it has bestowed an attitude of mind which wonderfully facilitates the acquisition of new ideas but in domains beyond concrete apprehension, open alike to truth and error. Time and again experience has demonstrated that intellectual ability is not a monopoly of one class, even of those trained in the schools; nor is genius so abundant or so entirely engaged in right service that the nation can afford to dispense with that which bears not the marks of wealth and social rank. Slowly English-speaking people have come to recognize the principle that a man has rights of more worth than political privileges; that good citizenship presupposes good citizens. If, as Emerson says, "the world exists for the education of each man," Ezra Cornell did the cause of humanity a good service in writing as the motto of the great New York university which bears his name, "I would found an institution where any person can find instruction in any study."

RISE AND DEVELOPMENT OF UNIVERSITY EXTENSION IN ENGLAND

The change of public opinion in England consequent on the inauguration of the universities local examinations in 1857 was decidedly marked. An eagerness for knowledge hitherto unknown characterized the middle classes and generous gifts of money were freely made from private sources to further the work undertaken by the universities. It was indeed an examination epoch; even state support of elementary schools was based on results of examinations. Those directly concerned in the preparation of pupils for university tests soon learned that good teaching was the one essential prerequisite of a good examination. For the first time, too, in their official capacities the universities made no distinctions of sex[a] and it is noteworthy that from this beginning has arisen practical freedom for women in all educational privileges of the United Kingdom.

---

[a] Girls were first admitted to the Cambridge locals in 1867 and to the Oxford locals in 1870.

Origin of university extension. The second and decisive step in university extension was taken by James Stuart, fellow of Trinity college, Cambridge, in the fall of 1867. He was invited by an association of ladies, mostly school-teachers, to lecture to them in the north of England on the art of teaching.[a] Mr Stuart with characteristic modesty and practical foresight suggested that "as a thing is often best described by showing a piece of it," it might be better to practise the art than to theorize about it. The suggestion was well received and a course of eight lectures on astronomy was given in Leeds, Sheffield, Manchester and Liverpool. For two months Mr Stuart made the rounds of these four cities each week lecturing to some 600 pupils.[b]

His methods were an innovation in several respects. First, he refused to deliver either a single lecture or a series of lectures on disconnected themes. He was "vexed with the insufficiency of the single lecture system which prevailed in connection with mechanics institutes and literary societies." The satisfaction of general curiosity on a popular subject was in his eyes too low an aim; his efforts should be directed toward doing something well. To this end he devised a method of assisting his hearers in note-taking; at each lecture the pupils were provided with a syllabus "which was intended to be a sample of the notes which they should take, whose skeleton might be filled up by them afterward to recall the thread of the lecture."[b] Not only were the ladies who were his hearers unaccustomed to note-taking but they were equally helpless in oral examination. It was to avoid this difficulty that he prepared printed questions to be answered in writing at home. These were forwarded to Mr Stuart by post in time for him to return them with the necessary corrections and comments at the next lecture.

While Mr Stuart was still lecturing in the north of England he was asked by Mr Moorsom, one of the officials of the Crewe railway works, to give a single lecture to his workingmen. Mr Stuart says: "The lecture was on the meteors and received an advertisement, wholly unexpected but exceedingly effective, from the great meteor shower of the preceding evening, in consequence of which the audience was remarkably large and a greater interest taken in the subject than probably would otherwise have mani-

[a] Mackinder & Sadler, p. 18.   [b] U. E. W. 2:74.

fested itself."[a] The result was that a course of six lectures on astronomy was given here in the following summer. This course was repeated in the autumn of 1868 before the Equitable pioneers society of Rochdale, "a great cooperative association of workingmen of honored name in the economic history of England.[b] At this time there arose one more distinctive feature of university extension work as since carried on, viz the class. In writing the weekly papers, many pupils found there were difficulties which neither the lecture nor the syllabus made clear to them; personal contact with the teacher, therefore, became a necessity not only to impress truths already outlined but to assist earnest students to a further application of the fundamental principles. A special hour was set aside for purely conversational teaching It proved so valuable educationally and so efficient in arousing enthusiasm that it has ever since been found indispensable.

Early efforts. During the next three years Mr Stuart and a few friends whom he had interested in the scheme were engaged in keeping up courses of study already begun among teachers and artisans of north England, but it was getting more apparent with each year that the societies could not afford to retain capable men permanently in their service and few university professors were willing to undertake this extra work involving not a little special preparation and tiresome railway journeys. The first solution attempted was to organize a "peripatetic cooperate university" among workingmen's associations which would assure employment for a few special lectures Mr Stuart earnestly sought to further this plan by making a tour among cooperative societies with the aim of founding a union pledged to the support of the new undertaking, but his efforts were unsuccessful. At about this time new strength was added by a union of Nottingham, Leicester and Derby for the purpose of securing courses of lectures, but with growing local enthusiasm, the inherent weakness of the plan, a lack of central organization, became the more apparent. Finally, on November 23, 1871, Mr Stuart submitted to the University of Cambridge a proposal

---

[a] U. E. W. 2:74. [b] U. E. W. 2:75.

whereby the new movement should be adopted by the university and become an integral part of its system.*

Proposition to Cambridge. The experience of four years among the people had given Prof. Stuart a right to speak authoritatively and enabled him to outline a course of action. He had no doubt that a demand for education was widespread, but would the universities supply it? "I believe," he wrote, "that it is incumbent on us to supply it and I believe that some such system, which will carry the benefits of the university through the country, is necessary, in order to retain the university in that position with respect to the education of the country which it has hitherto held, and to continue in its hands that permeating influence which it is desirable that it should possess." The highest law of the land had but lately declared the universities to be national institutions. This step, he urged, would tend to realize the rights of the nation and in return, the university would experience benefits commensurate with the value of the giving. It is not altogether a lack of funds that keeps many earnest students away from the university; residence, he pointed out, is only for those "who can procure some years of continuous leisure, which is far harder to get than the requisite money." The recent organization of the elementary schools was destined to sow the seeds of learning broadcast over the land; shall the field be left uncultivated till it becomes a national danger? There must be teaching, and that of the right kind; only the best of teachers are called to the work. The universities are able to meet the demand; they alone have the teachers and possess the necessary prestige which will allay all suspicions of superficiality or of proselyting motives.

Special arguments. This letter of Prof Stuart's, since famous both as a declaration of rights and prophecy of the future, was ably supported by memorials addressed to Cambridge university from the centers in which he had done his work;—from women's educational associations, committees of industrial and cooperative societies, mechanics institutes and provincial cities.[b] Not-

---

[a] Stuart, James *A letter on university extension* (see U E. W 1 52-54) [b] Roberts, p. 94.

tingham, through her mayor and leading citizens, urged the claim of the workingmen and the great opportunities awaiting the right teachers in promulgating sound views on political and social questions. Birmingham emphasized the value of a full course of study, periodical examinations and some sort of recognition by the university. Others showed that what was most wanted was systematic instruction, continuous throughout a series of courses and extending even over a number of years. "We wish to state clearly," said Crewe, "that we are not wishing for more examinations, but for a better teaching and educating power." The senate of the university appointed a syndicate to consider these memorials, which, after a thorough inquiry into the merits of the demand for university lectures, reported in favor of making the experiment, on condition that the local authorities should bear the necessary expenses. Arguments in opposition were not wanting. The expense of maintaining a central organization at the university would be considerable and it was feared that if university privileges were taken to the people the number of students in residence might diminish, thus cutting off financial support at both ends. Therefore a period of trial was the only solution.

First regular courses. The first courses given by Cambridge were at Nottingham, Derby and Leicester on political economy, mechanics and English literature; all three lecturers were fellows of Trinity college.[a] The prescribed regulations for each course included: (1) a weekly lecture for 12 weeks; (2) a printed syllabus; (3) a weekly written exercise to be corrected and returned by the teacher; (4) a class in connection with each lecture; and (5) a new requirement — "written examinations to be held at the conclusion of each course by examiners appointed by the syndicate, and certificates to be granted to the candidates who manifest sufficient merit in these examinations."

The movement, which was already recognized as the most promising form of university extension, found popular support in the national agitation which had changed the character of the universities and had given birth to a new conception of governmental responsibilities in education. Three classes of people, in the opinion of extension enthusiasts, were still unprovided for, and to these — women, young men of business and working people — they would carry university privileges. Their aim was ambitious, "too ambitious" as Prof Stuart afterward acknowledged,[a] and it was most discouraging to find that local centers begrudged the outlay for parallel courses suited to the needs of all classes. Even in the larger towns it proved to be a more serious matter to raise funds than had been expected and in most small towns it was simply impossible. A more serious disappointment was experienced when distinct efforts were first made to push the movement. In nearly every place a few persons could be interested, but the majority of those on whom the leaders thought to rely for support were either indifferent or hypercritical. The fact was clear that the public was not yet ready spontaneously to put pet theories into practice; but the best proof of the inherent strength of the movement and of the devotion of its leaders is shown in the steady progress achieved, despite all hindrances and disappointments.

Extension work in London. Some three years after the movement took definite form in Cambridge it was proposed to extend it to London. At a public meeting held at the Mansion house in June 1875 under the presidency of the then lord mayor it was resolved on motion of the Hon. G. J. Goschen, M. P., "that the principle of the Cambridge university extension scheme be applied to London, and that the various educational institutions of the metropolis be requested to cooperate in an endeavor so to apply it."[b] The fact that London had no teaching university somewhat complicated matters; university extension with the university left out was an anomaly to be considered. A fortunate solution, however, was devised, one that has given no little strength and stability to the movement and that in a way most needed. In harmony with the spirit of the resolution, all the leading educational institutions of London, including University and King's colleges, Birkbeck institute, Royal institution and Workingmen's college, warmly supported the scheme.

---

a Inaugural address to the second summer meeting of university extension students in Oxford, 1889.
b Roberts, p. 77.

In 1876 the London society for the extension of university teaching was formed and entered on a most successful career under the presidency of Mr Goschen. The character of instruction given under the auspices of the London society is specially guaranteed by a joint board composed of representatives of the universities of Cambridge, Oxford and London which nominates all its lecturers and examiners. The greatest possible concentration consistent with effective cooperation in the educational work of existing institutions is the particular contribution of the London society to the theory of university extension.

The first courses organized in London were not exceptionally successful because they were arranged in connection with city colleges, which made it the more difficult to overcome popular prejudice. Increased attendance was secured by working through special committees and using local halls. London, following the example of Cambridge, has been pledged from the beginning to long courses and when possible, to courses in sequence. Of the special features of the work mention will be made later, but at this point it may be noted that scholarly work even among artisans has not been considered at all impossible.

Oxford courses The attention of Oxford was first called to university extension in 1877 by Prof. Benjamin Jowett, late master of Balliol, famous as one of the most noted scholars of recent years in England. He not only pointed out what was being done elsewhere in "secondary adult education," but suggested two practical schemes for its adoption by Oxford He would have a permanent secretary for the new department paid by the university and would extend "the tenure of non-resident fellowships . . . in the case of persons lecturing or holding professorships in large towns." The next year the university organized a department for the extension of university teaching in connection with their local examinations and appointed as the first secretary Mr Arthur Acland, son of Sir Thomas Acland who was the founder of the examination scheme[a] From the start the work met with indifferent success. It lingered along a year or two and was at length for the time abandoned. Whether Oxford met with unusual difficulties or failed to

---

[a] Mackinder & Sadler, p. 29–32.

appreciate the need of the missionary spirit is not entirely clear. In many towns the time was not yet ripe for such a movement; the smaller centers, however anxious for teaching, could not afford the expense of the long courses then generally in vogue. The financial question was the pressing one. The fees could not be lowered and at the same time retain the best lecturers; without distinguished teachers there could be no assurance of successful continuity in the work. When Oxford revived her activity in 1885, she deliberately cut the knot which had proved so troublesome. It was said in substance that if centers could not pay for 12 lectures in sequence they might have shorter courses, preferably of six lectures. The result was that the Oxford department advanced by leaps and bounds. The second year of trial showed 50 centers with 67 courses and an average attendance of 9908 as against 22 centers with 27 courses (attendance not recorded) in 1885-86. Thus is seen how important a factor the financial problem was; it is to be observed, too, that Oxford's solution was at the expense of educational opportunities. The end, however, has long since justified the means, and full atonement has been gained by arranging a series of short courses in sequence or by making pioneer lectures the opening wedge for substantial work which at the beginning would have seemed impossible.

New methods. Oxford early made other valuable contributions to the general plan. The lecture, syllabus and class were counted good in themselves, but a lecture on literature to be found only in books or on sciences dependent on recorded researches, a syllabus which gives only an outline and which is intended to inspire the pupil to independent study, the results of which may be discussed in class, all these are half worthless without the necessary books. And what average town can supply a decent reference list of the standard works on any special topic? Together with the teacher and the syllabus Oxford determined to send out a library. And as the teacher traveled from place to place in successive terms the books went with him and earned the name of the traveling library. This feature, reasonable and necessary as it was, was looked on as a startling innovation; but it came to stay.

Another of Oxford's devices to extend university influence was the summer meeting which was introduced in 1888. Cambridge had already made the experiment in 1885 and 1887 of bringing a few of her best pupils from local centers to continue special work at the university during the long vacation. Oxford's plan was immediately successful both in attracting large numbers of students from a busy life to a place rich in tradition and conducive to quiet study, and in enlisting the services of famous teachers surrounded with their working appliances who could not fail to imbue their hearers with a wealth of new ideas.

Dark days. The darkest days of university extension in England were from 1880-85. The number of students in Cambridge centers sunk from over 12,000 in 1875 to about 3500 in 1881, a number not much in excess of the first year's enrolment. Oxford gave up the task. A main cause, the financial burden, has already been mentioned, but more significant was a flagging of public interest. Many had been attracted by curiosity who, when the work became serious, had no inclination to continue it; the boundless enthusiasm, too, of the early leaders caused them to plan too rapid advance in a scheme by no means simple. It was a hard lesson for the friends of the movement on the one hand to learn that the average man cared little for his estrangement from the university, that he was not much troubled by his ignorance; and on the other hand for intelligent work-a-day people to learn that what they needed most was systematic training in educational lines rather than miscellaneous entertainment even in the guise of lectures.

Extension courses among miners. It was at this period when fond hopes were being daily wrecked, that a strenuous effort was put forth to effect some permanent organization among Northumberland miners. Courses on political economy, begun in 1879 in certain Tyneside towns, had aroused great local interest. The audiences were very mixed as is shown by the final examination, in which the highest place was taken by a working miner and the second by a lady, a daughter of a wealthy manufacturer and member of parliament for the borough.[a] The

---

[a] Roberts, p. 28.

result so encouraged the workingmen that, during the following summer, a committee, including the prize-winner, made a tour of the mining district and added five villages to the Cambridge list, with an aggregate attendance at the lectures of over 1300 working miners. The movement spread rapidly, and courses in English literature and history, geology, mining, chemistry and physical geography were soon called for. The men entered heartily into the work and Dr Roberts, who was frequently among them, speaks in the highest terms of their achievement. Subjects apparently not in keeping with the daily life of the community found enthusiastic and capable students. Of the students themselves he says: " The sturdy intelligence of the pitmen, their determined earnestness, the appreciative and responsive way in which they listened, the downright straightforwardness of their speech, all this it is impossible fully to express."[a] But every effort to induce the labor organization to support the work from their common funds was a failure; their leaders were not of a stamp to yield easily to influences which must eventually have undermined their power. Successful as the work in Northumberland had been and with many strong and vigorous centers as its result, the great strike of 1887 left almost no material trace of eight years of progress. In the face of starvation and with loss of many of the most earnest students who left the locality to seek work elsewhere, the centers were long unable to think of intellectual improvement.

Technical education grant. It has been demonstrated once and again that university extension thrives best in centers composed mostly of ladies and of well-to-do people of the middle classes. These have the leisure to devote some time each day to study and besides can afford the expense entailed from a course of lectures by the ablest teachers. Thus being able to help themselves, circumstances favor them through the enthusiasm inspired by men whose services may not be commanded by less favored centers. The masses must first be put on their feet and helped to stand besides. No more fortunate windfall has come to the movement than the appropriation by the government in 1890 of £750,000 for purposes of technical education. The grant

---

[a] Roberts, p. 23.

is applied by the county councils in each county in whatever way seems to them most meet. No restrictions are put on the local committees beyond the mere definition of what constitutes technical instruction. It "shall mean instruction in the *principles of science and art* applicable to industries, and in the application of special branches of science and art to specific industries and employments. It shall not include the teaching the practice of any trade, industry or employment." In a word the act aims at the improvement of industries through a higher intelligence among artisans on fundamental scientific principles. The unexpected diversion of so large a sum of money from the original purpose into educational channels demanded greater familiarity with educational matters and a wider acquaintance with the industrial needs of rural communities than were then accessible or indeed ascertained. In the work of educational experiment university extension organizers were already in the field; men trained in the universities or familiar with local needs Some counties at once made liberal appropriations for the support of extension courses in all subjects but history and literature. Others planned systematic training, generally by university men, for the elementary teachers of their respective districts, with ultimate aim of carrying on the technical instruction independently of outside aid. The success of a scheme so lacking in essentials of organization and so dependent on local caprice could hardly be remarkable in itself; but what is of consequence is the indirect influence of the highest educational centers of the country on the industrial training of the remotest rural districts. The policy of applying the university extension plan to so ignoble a purpose as teaching village audiences "the diseases of plants, the principles of drainage, and the comparative merits of rival manures," has been vigorously assailed even by good friends of the general movement On the other hand, Mr Sadler, secretary of the Oxford delegacy, declares that it is the duty of the universities to see to it that what was intended as a national blessing should not prove to be a national curse. "A narrowly conceived technical education," he writes, "inspired by no wide conception of the general principles which underlie science and art, would tend to sterilize rather than to increase the national power of adjusting industrial methods to changing needs" So it is that university extension lecturers have found an entrance to out-of way places and there spread abroad the new gospel of salvation to those who will but study. Inasmuch as the technical instruction act includes all trades, industries and employments as objects of its solicitation, a means is thereby given university representatives to reach classes hitherto inaccessible. To a certain extent it has solved the perplexing financial problem of reaching the masses; its best results, however, are those foreseen only by a few; viz the indirect connection with the universities and an experience which will more carefully husband future grants [a]

Centers affiliated to Cambridge. The onus of continuing university extension work, it will be observed, falls on the local center; the university organizations serve their functions in directing and stimulating local efforts. It is highly important, therefore, that some sort of permanency be assured in order to attract and retain a class of earnest students. If a course of lectures systematically conducted on the extension plan is an advance, pedagogically considered, over the old lyceum system, just so surely is a series of courses in harmonious sequence an advance over the single course. The university of Cambridge early recognized this need and in 1886 secured the powers under a new statute of extending to local centers under special conditions, the privileges of affiliation. The idea was borrowed from a custom some time previously introduced of granting local colleges certain advantages. Cambridge went a step further and said in effect to local committees: If you have a body of earnest students prepared to undertake a three years' course of study under our teachers and can guarantee the necessary financial foundation, we will approve of your work as though done in residence and to that extent will consider you part of the university. The requirements insist on eight full courses of 12 lectures each with class work (six courses from natural, physical and mathematical science and two from history, economics, literature, etc. or vice versa) and examination at the end of each course. The student that completes such a course and besides satisfies the university of proficiency in elementary mathematics, Latin and some other

---

[a] U. E. J. 4.23-25; U. E. 2:151-57, 231-39.

language may consider himself "affiliated to the university of Cambridge;" and if he chooses to reside in the university he may take an honors degree in two years instead of three.

Newcastle was the first center to avail itself of the privileges of the new scheme. Contrary to expectations the number of students as well as the general audiences at once increased. This success led other strong centers to follow till at the present time there are five centers affiliated to the university of Cambridge. It was not expected that many would make these local courses stepping stones to the university, nevertheless in the last Cambridge natural science tripos "one of the few women who obtained a place in the first class" did one third of her work *in absentia* in an affiliated center.[a] But the university stamp thus put upon local effort was of decided importance. Cambridge settled in the affirmative the disputed question whether or not classes of busy, work-a-day people could do any educational work worthy of university recognition.

University extension colleges. The Oxford university extension delegacy, not to be outdone in careful organization, took a still more important step in 1892. Assisted by Christ Church, a wealthy and most influential Oxford college, the delegacy united all the various educational bodies in and near Reading with the local university extension association of the town. The title "University extension college" was conferred on the new organization and Christ Church, Oxford, undertook in a single act to supply efficient supervision, to assure a certain income and to place the institution in close connection with itself by setting aside a fellowship for the principal of the new college.

From private subscription and town and government grants the college has secured suitable buildings and equipment for carrying on genuine collegiate work. Workingmen have become interested in the evening classes and have themselves done not a little to further the success of this "people's college." The extent of the work may be inferred from the annual expenses which now amount to about £3,000; its teachers, about 20 in all, are largely drawn from Oxford. A somewhat similar plan was entered into six months later between the town of Exeter and

---

[a] Internat. U. E. cong. Rept. p. 79-80.

the university of Cambridge. The university syndicate likewise stands in close relations with the new extension college through the medium of the principal to whose salary it contributes. A certain dignity attaches thereby to local efforts and the results already attained seem to justify the experiment.

Gresham university commission. The sketch of the progress of university extension in England would be incomplete without some reference to the report of the commission appointed by government on a teaching university for London. The recommendations are for the union of most of the institutions for higher education in London into a great university of six faculties In the multiplicity of details university extension is not omitted. The plan, as suggested in the report of Feb. 24, 1894, is to charge a standing board with the oversight and direction of extension work and to provide for recognition of such work in the regular university degree courses, as the senate, on recommendation of the academic council, may determine to be of correspondent value. This report by the most influential royal commission on education in recent years is strikingly indicative of the signs of the times.

Change of public sentiment. A few years since the university extension movement was considered as unworthy of serious concern in truly educational circles; it was at first pronounced incapable of more than momentary success, founded as it was on a misconception of the demands of the people and pushed by inexperienced enthusiasts who could not be expected to possess either practical common sense or administrative ability. Other good men believed with the *St James gazette* which greeted the founding of Birkbeck institute for workingmen a half century before in these words: "A scheme more completely adapted for the destruction of this empire could not have been invented by the author of evil himself." The movement, however, despite all opposition and without government support has waxed increasingly stronger; it has penetrated all parts of England and Wales, has passed over the boundaries into Scotland and across the channel to Ireland, has crossed the seas to America, to Asia, Africa and Australia — in short it extends to all parts of the world where the English language is spoken or where English influence reaches. In England alone nearly 700 courses were given last year attended by an aggregate of over 57,000 persons. The beneficent influence of the movement both on the trend of higher education and on the life of the people is attested by the highest authorities. The little band of enthusiasts of 15 or 20 years ago of whom so little was expected are no longer unknown.

Promoters of university extension in England. The first secretary of the Oxford delegacy, Mr Arthur Acland, is now minister of education; the home secretary, Mr Asquith, has been a lecturer of the London society; the marquis of Ripon was a leading spirit in organizing the work in London; Mr Morley, chief secretary for Ireland, has taken part in extension lecturing; the president of the board of trade, Mr Bryce, who is the chairman of the royal commission now considering the organization of secondary education in England, has been an ardent advocate of the movement from the beginning and still takes active interest in furthering the work; — so much for the present [1894] liberal government. Among other friends of the movement of not less honored rank are: Prof James Stuart, now an influential member of parliament, but as enthusiastic as in the days of circuit lecturing in Northumberland; Right Hon. G. J. Goschen, ex-chancellor of the exchequer and for years president of the London society; Mr H. Llewellyn Smith, for many years an Oxford lecturer, now commissioner for labor; Prof R. C. Jebb, "the foremost Greek scholar of England;" the noted biologist, Prof. Patrick Geddes, heart of the movement in Scotland; the duke of Devonshire, Prof Max Müller, Lord Playfair, Messrs R. D. Roberts, M. E. Sadler, Arthur Berry, respectively secretaries of the London, Oxford and Cambridge organizations,[a] Prof. R. G. Moulton, and many others, who need no introduction to those familiar with educational affairs in the United Kingdom. A movement which commands such support at home must have its lessons for educationists the world over. The following chapter traces its development in America and other countries.

---

[a] Since this was written Dr Roberts has succeeded Mr Berry at Cambridge, J A R Marriott has succeeded Mr Sadler, who has been appointed "Director of inquiries and reports," a new post in the education department, and Dr C. W Kimmins has been made secretary of the London society.

SPREAD OF THE EXTENSION MOVEMENT TO AMERICA AND OTHER COUNTRIES

Prof. H. B. Adams of Johns Hopkins university, who had been for some time interested in a system of popular lectures in and about the city of Baltimore, laid the English scheme of university extension before the American library association in session at the Thousand Islands in 1887. He urged that no better agency existed for its introduction into America than through the public libraries. A librarian's duty does not end with giving out books; the public must be taught how and what to read.

First course in Buffalo. Prof. Adams' appeal bore immediate fruit. Mr J. N. Larned, librarian of the Buffalo, N. Y. library, found, in widening the influence of his work, that university extension provided precisely the right means for utilizing the class rooms in his library. On recommendation of Prof. Adams, Dr E. W. Bemis was chosen as lecturer and in the winter of 1887-88 gave the first extension course in America. He dealt with the economic questions of the day in 12 lectures accompanied by a printed syllabus and class discussions. As Dr Bemis had no other engagements he resided the full three months in Buffalo and spent a portion of each day at the public library assisting those who needed special help and directing their reading. Full reports of each lecture were given in the city papers and much interest was aroused by the presence of men representing many phases of political and economic theory. So decided was the success of this first course that a local organization was formed for the study of political economy, which has since become a branch of the American economic association.

Adopted by Chautauqua. In the summer of 1888 university extension was preached by two Johns Hopkins men at the Chautauqua summer school. Bishop Vincent, chancellor of the Chautauqua institution, from visits to England in 1880 and 1886 had become deeply interested in the extension movement and was resolved to add it to the Chautauqua work. Under the stimulus of Prof. Adams and his colleague a plan was drawn up, approved and printed. Dr W. R. Harper, professor in Yale university and director of the Chautauqua college of liberal arts, was a member of the approving committee; from this beginning dates his interest in the movement which found its perfect expression in his unique organization of the University of Chicago.

The Chautauqua prospectus, which was spread far and wide, undoubtedly influenced to no small degree later developments in America. The objects proposed were: (1) A revival in the United States of the original idea of a university as a voluntary association of students and itinerant lecturers for higher education by means of systematic courses of local lectures on special subjects; (2) the promotion of good citizenship by the popular study of social science, economics, history, literature, political ethics and the science of government, in continuous and progressive courses, under the guidance of competent teachers; (3) courses of instructive lectures on natural science; (4) cooperation with American colleges and other institutions of learning in order to supplement their work by university extension courses; (5) affiliations with public libraries, mechanics institutes, lyceums, labor unions, gilds, young men's Christian associations, Chautauqua literary and scientific circles; (6) the higher education of the American people by the organization of the most intelligent and progressive local forces.[a]

In Brooklyn. In the same year the teachers of Brooklyn under the leadership of Mr S. T. Stewart proposed to unite certain features of English extension work with the Chautauqua reading courses. In the preparation of syllabuses and for the general direction of this work some of the leading professors of Harvard, Yale, Columbia and Princeton took part. Prominent educators sanctioned the movement and a little later the lecture feature was added, Pres. Eliot and Com'r Harris being among the first to give assistance.

Movement in New York. New York takes pride in the fact that the first five significant steps in extension history in America were all in the Empire state; viz, the library meeting at the Thousand Islands, the work at Buffalo, Chautauqua, Brook-

---

[a] E B 5·212, R. of rs. 8:602.

lyn and at the capital in connection with the regents. New York also claims the distinction of being the first state in the world to make university extension an integral part of its educational system. This step was singularly favored by the state's method of school control, now more than a century in practice.[a]

At the university convocation in Albany in July, 1888, Melvil Dewey, then chief librarian and professor of library economy in Columbia college but a few months later appointed secretary of the University of the state and also director of the state library, discussed university extension with reference to the public libraries A year afterward Sec. Dewey again addressed convocation on the subject and urged its adoption. A committee was appointed to report on a scheme for carrying on the work, "including a plan for lending to communities, for use during university extension courses, suitable libraries, collections, apparatus and illustrations." At the convocation of 1890 a committee of college presidents was appointed to confer with the regents; this committee reported in February, 1891, that it seemed desirable that the regents establish a system of university extension subject to state supervision and examination. The committee emphasized the necessity of maintaining a high standard which could only be assured if the state department worked through the colleges and universities On this recommendation a department of university extension was immediately established and it was resolved to apply to the state legislature for funds to carry it on. A joint hearing of both houses was secured late in March

---

[a] By legislative enactment of May 1, 1784, since three times revised and extended, all institutions for higher education in the state including high schools, academies, professional schools, colleges, universities with the state museum and the state library and its affiliated branches— in all over 500 institutions — are incorporated parts of the "University of the State of New York" This so-called university, which antedates by several years and is admitted by Frenchmen to have served as a model for the first Napoleon's University of France and which in reality is a state department of education, is governed by a board of regents charged with the extension, direction and supervision of the higher education of the state The regents have power to incorporate, and to alter or repeal the charters of educational institutions in the University; to distribute to them all funds granted by the state for their use, to inspect their workings and require annual reports under oath to establish examinations as to attainments in learning, and to confer certificates, diplomas and degrees Once a year a convocation of the regents and representatives of the institutions of the University is held at the capitol in Albany. The actual work of the board is carried on by the secretary assisted by a corps of inspectors and examiners The work of the University is divided into five departments. (1) administrative, (2) examinations, (3) extension, including the promotion and wider extension of opportunities and facilities for education; (4) state library, including all incorporated public libraries and a school for the training of librarians; (5) state museum designed to promote public interest in art and science.

State aid at which many prominent educators and professional men urged the expediency of state aid. The press of the state regardless of party lines vigorously championed the new movement. The result was an unanimity of opinion quite unusual in matters of state appropriation. On April 14th the bill passed the senate without a dissenting voice; the next day it was reported favorably in the assembly and the day following was passed unanimously; on University day, May 1, the anniversary of the original charter in 1784, Gov. Hill gave his approval. With a rapidity which might seem to indicate desperate straits, the state government gave its assent to a measure appropriating $10,000 for organizing university extension under the University. The law stipulated that no part of this money should be applied in payment of expenses or services of lecturers; the regents may direct the work, issue publications and syllabuses, designate lecturers, examine candidates, in short they may do everything but bear local expenses.[a]

Traveling libraries. Under most favorable auspices university extension gained a foothold in New York, where it has since made steady progress. The special feature of the work has been the development of the library system in all its branches, on which the department expends $25.000 annually. Besides free public libraries, for which local support must be assured, the regents have organized over 100[b] traveling libraries and are adding new ones to the list as rapidly as the public libraries division can prepare them. These collections of 50 to 100 of the best books on a wide range of topics are loaned for six months at a time not only to extension centers but to any responsible organization or community within the state. A fee is paid to cover cost of transportation, cataloging, etc. On similar terms scientific apparatus, lantern slides or other illustrative material needed by the centers may be procured from the regents. This outpouring of educative material from the central reservoirs of the state into every stirring hamlet is a noteworthy and practical extension of the means to higher culture. The peculiar strength of the New York system, however, is for most states impracticable because of the lack of efficient central organization. On the contrary

---

[a] E. B. 1:8-12.   [b] Nov. 1, 1895.

there can be no doubt that progress in extension teaching is retarded in New York by dearth of independent teachers, stafflecturers who can give their entire time to the organization and direction of local effort. Legal restrictions in this case undoubtedly render difficult of attainment the very ends for which state aid was granted. It is the peculiar privilege of democracy, however, to be inconsistent even to the extent of defeating its own purposes.

Special difficulties. In launching the new educational scheme in America obstacles were encountered against which English experience was of slight avail. Instead of two great universities, venerable in years and powerful both in wealth of national tradition and in abundance of material resource, there is in the United States a variety of smaller and weaker institutions In no sense could the adoption of the movement even by several of the strongest universities be termed national; indeed the size of the country would restrict the extension of any one institution to a very limited field. No university has an excess of learned men on its staff; no instructor even in the humblest rank who is not overworked. As yet America has no "learned proletariat."

In Philadelphia. Early in 1890 Provost Pepper of the University of Pennsylvania began public agitation of the question in Philadelphia. In June a preliminary organization was formed, whose secretary, Mr George Henderson, was sent to England to study the movement there. His report made on his return put the case definitely, and just at this juncture fortune favored the Philadelphians in sending to them Prof. R: G. Moulton, one of the most experienced of the Cambridge extension lecturers. His eloquence and zealous faith in the new movement, at once made him a veritable apostle to the Americans, a title which he has since earned many times over. In November a public meeting was held which so quickened local sentiment that financial support was readily pledged and a season of work begun which numbered 40 courses with an attendance of 50,000 persons, thus "surpassing all English records." Within a few months a more extensive organization was formed at Philadelphia which was incorporated under the name of "the American society for the extension of university teaching" with the original Philadelphia society as its first branch. Prominent citizens of Philadelphia, many of them business men, guaranteed the necessary funds for the corporation which is made up of representatives of all colleges and universities connected with the society in extension teaching. This organization, which closely resembles the London society, is the most influential society engaged in the work in the eastern states.

Need of good teachers. The Philadelphia society early experienced the difficulty above mentioned of enlisting capable university teachers. To meet growing needs the entire services of two able men were secured in 1891-92 in addition to the regular list of instructors from colleges and universities. The next year the number of these so-called "staff-lecturers" was increased to four and for the present year the services of six are required. These men devote their entire time to the work, lecturing, organizing and assisting new centers, conducting the society publications, etc. It is perhaps the best contribution of the Philadelphia society to the general project that it has insisted on having teachers trained for the work.

Training for extension workers. In October, 1892, the corporation opened a seminary in connection with the University of Pennsylvania and the Wharton school of political science for training of extension lecturers and organizers. The object was not only to supply teachers for the Philadelphia society but to enable other organizations and universities in any part of the country to secure capable teachers fully conversant with the best methods and qualified to practise them. The experiment seems to have been fully justified and bids fair to become an object lesson of importance to those interested in promoting higher education in the schools.

The work in Chicago. One of the best organized extension centers in America is in Chicago, where work was begun by Dr W: F: Poole of the Newberry library, who in common with other librarians got his inspiration from Prof. Adams. The final impulse was given, however, by the founding of Chicago university. Pres. Harper's purpose was not to organize a university merely to compete with older institutions; he intended the Chicago university to seek out its own field and work therein. To Pres. Harper, who was already familiar with Chautauqua methods and who was thoroughly convinced of the national need of more and better higher education, "no demand was more evident and more evidently unprovided for than that the universities should extend their influence beyond their own premises and offer to intelligent men and women throughout the country whatever of university advantages they can use."[a] In the new university, therefore, one of the four grand coordinate divisions was assigned to university extension It has its own separate faculty and special administrative officers. The department is not a mere adjunct of the university; it is as much a part of the university as any other division and has its own most excellent equipment

Chicago university. Appropriating to its own use the results of English experience and such American innovations as the teachers seminary and an extension library system, the Chicago department added two new features: (1) correspondence-teaching, and (2) special class-teaching on Saturdays and week-day evenings By correspondence with the teacher a student in any part of the world may carry on regular and systematic study *in absentia* and yet be a matriculated student of the university. The special evening and Saturday classes, which are confined naturally to Chicago and its suburbs, have proved to be a most satisfactory feature. The nature of the work is the same as within university walls save that it is more prolonged. In this way, or by correspondence study, a student may do one half of the undergraduate, or one third of the doctorate work.

Chicago university was opened October 2, 1892, and on that very day Prof. R: G. Moulton of Cambridge, England, began the first extension course A full corps of teachers was soon in the field and before December 15 000 persons were in attendance on the course lectures The united efforts of a faculty recruited from the ablest teachers in England and America have roused the country for hundreds of miles about Chicago to a realization of what the movement is The experience of two years has modified some points of view, but in the main the work

[a] U E 3.245-51.

at Chicago has showed constant progress and illustrates without doubt the pedagogic high-water mark of university extension in the world.

Extension work in other states. The three central organizations, above described, New York, Philadelphia and Chicago, are the most important in America. There are other interesting experiments in progress which would seek to combine the advantages of state supervision and public support with the stability that comes only from close connection with a live university. For example, in Ohio, Indiana, Illinois, Michigan, Wisconsin, Minnesota, Iowa, Kansas, Missouri and California the movement has been taken up by the state universities. Some of these states have supported for several years systematic courses in agriculture and kindred subjects for the better training of their farmers Notably in Wisconsin was the system so perfect that the state university found it an easy matter to extend special privileges through its extension department to all parts of the state. The state university of Minnesota has long maintained close relations with the engineers of Minneapolis and St Paul, even to giving regular instruction to hundreds of workingmen in no wise connected with the university A complete system of farmers institutes, as in Wisconsin, has also been in operation long enough to pave the way for a more extended plan of university extension. In point of time Brown university in Rhode Island was the first to incorporate the extension system as a part of its regular work. A director was appointed from the faculty in June, 1891, and all preparations were made to enter active service the following semester. At first no effort was made to attract large audiences, in fact the university avoided all over-stimulus; small classes and hard study were the special features of the work. However, in his last report, 1893, Pres. Andrews in speaking of the work during the past year, notes the "substantial and unexpected increase" in the number of students. School teachers, business men and young people are attracted to the work and "a large proportion are workingmen." The subjects offered are history, literature, science, economics and mechanical drawing (wholly class work). Teachers are instructed to teach; that is, "carefully explain, expound, repeat, illustrate and catechize"[a]

---

[a] E. B. 5.230.

Colleges interested. Among the other colleges and universities which are now engaged in university extension may be mentioned Bowdoin and Colby in Maine, Colgate and Rochester in New York, Rutgers in New Jersey, Cincinnati in Ohio, and Trinity college in Connecticut. In January, 1892, Ohio formed a special state organization, and in the following April the Connecticut association became a state branch of the American society, Philadelphia. Other societies, as at Cleveland, Ohio, and Atlanta, Georgia, are in the field, all concerned more or less actively in promoting what they believe to be university extension. Some of them have made serious errors. Teachers have been commissioned independently of the universities, whose qualifications are, to say the least, questionable; it has sometimes been overlooked that university extension without a university to extend is an anomaly in word and fact [a] The history of the movement in England suggests that a period of rest or even retrogression may be expected after the first hot blood has cooled, but thus far there has been steady progress all along the line. The effects of the hard times during the past year and a half have been serious in some localities, but it may be fairly assumed that the work of university extension has not suffered more than other forms of higher education.

The work in Canada. A Canadian society was formed in November 1891, on the model of the American society, Philadelphia, but for some reason the progress has not been commensurate with that in the United States. There are several flourishing centers that find able teachers among the university men, of whom Prof. Cox, "one of the most brilliant and successful of the Cambridge science lecturers," is a leading spirit.

In Australia. University extension has become "one of the regular educational agencies of Australia and its friends are active and increasing."[b] The University of Melbourne undertook extension teaching in 1890 and has been most active in promoting the work throughout Victoria and in the neighboring colonies. In 1893 it maintained seven local centers with more than 1000 students. The bureau publishes a monthly

---

[a] Camb. s. m. Rept. p. 31.　　　　[b] U. E. B. 1.75.

journal which holds high rank among university extension publications. In New South Wales a special board has charge of the work which extends even into Queensland; some 500 students are in attendance. New Zealand is likewise interested in the movement. The government has given state aid to university extension in Sydney, a precedent which is being urged on the governments of other colonies. In Africa the work was begun at the Cape of Good Hope by Mr Bensly, another Cambridge lecturer, whose missionary efforts have borne good fruit. In short the good reports of university extension have carried its fame wherever the English language is spoken; the circle of the globe is completed with its introduction into India under the sponsorship of the university of Madras.

In Norway and Sweden. From England the movement has crossed over to Norway and Sweden. In 1892 Prof. Dr J. Mourley Vold attended the university extension summer meeting in Oxford in order to study the methods. His report, printed in pamphlet-form, gave the first impulse toward making the Scandinavian universities truly national. The following year a summer school was held at the University of Upsala, Sweden, which was attended by about 400 school teachers and others from all parts of the country. The meeting lasted two weeks, during which time about 100 lectures were given [a] This past summer (1894) such meetings were held in several Scandinavian universities — Christiania, Lund, Helsingfors and others. It is not, however, the extraordinary interest shown in the summer university sessions that is of most significance, but the fact that through the medium of university extension the national high schools are being connected with the universities. For more than 25 years the "folkhöjskoler" have supplied the higher training for the great body of the people.[b] Originating in Denmark as early as 1844, these schools first took prominent rank after the disastrous war with Germany in 1864. The aim was to give young men and women practical training in practical affairs and to inspire them with patriotic and religious ideals. With some modifications these schools passed over into Scandi-

---

[a] U. E. J 4 104   [b] Healey.

navia where they have been well supported by the people but entirely without university recognition. With the beginning of extension courses these schools have become natural centers for university work.[a] Through them the highest scholarship of the land finds ready communication with the people and a means of influence of unusual power. It is said that the movement has the support of the state and "a grant from public funds would probably be forthcoming for the purpose if desired."[b]

In Belgium. In Belgium a beginning had been made in the fall of 1892 at Ghent, the national university, with courses of free or very cheap lectures. Teachers, merchants and workingmen were attracted to the work which consisted of 20 lectures on Dutch literature and 10 each on German and English literatures Courses in botany were afterward arranged for the summer. In March, 1893, a society was formed in Brussels for the extension of university teaching. The leaders of the movement were professors of the *Université libré de Bruxelles*, one of whom M. Léon Leclère, had studied the development and methods of university extension in England and reported his findings in the *Revue universitaire* for January, 1893. The rules of the society stipulate that no one may be commissioned as teacher who is not connected with the university The work is based on the lecture, syllabus and class as in England but the weekly written exercise is dropped out. Centers have been formed in all the large towns of Belgium. For the past year[c] 25 courses are reported at 13 towns with a total attendance of nearly 4000. The subjects were in order of popularity, history, sociology, physiology and hygiene, zoology, law, palaeontology and agricultural chemistry. The progress already made is beyond the most sanguine hopes of the founders of the movement. Difficulties are reported, specially those of oral communication arising from the fact that most of the university professors speak only French, or at most the literary Flemish, neither of which is intelligible to the average Flemish audience. It is further hinted that the Brussels society is in the hands of politicians — "several (of the promoters) are socialists; almost all the others determined radicals." If this be true, it is

---

[a] U E. J. 4:105. [b] Internat U. E. cong. Rept p 73
[c] See *Revue universitaire*, June 15, 1894, for annual report of university extension in Belgium.

the first instance of partizan propaganda under guise of university extension. Such a charge, if applicable to the actions of a few, can not be imputed to the great majority of those interested in the work. The report for 1893-94 is sufficient proof of the general tendency and it shows where the popular interest is; of the 25 courses reported, only five were on sociologic or economic subjects.[a]

On the continent. University extension, beyond the exceptions already noted, has made no considerable progress on the continent. Three pioneer courses were given last winter to English residents in Montreux and two in Lausanne. It is intended in 1894-95 to continue the work in these two "English winter colonies" and to establish courses in Switzerland and on the Riviera. The influence of such centers, however, must remain exceedingly limited, and the use of the English language takes away what little value might accrue to the communities from a well conducted object lesson in their midst. The French government has commissioned agents to study the movement in England.[b] The Italian department of education sent representatives, one of them a professor in the University of Rome, to the university extension congress held in London, June 22-23, 1894. A professor of the University of Moscow, who was sent to Cambridge in the summer of 1893, was authorized to report on the practicability of starting a university extension movement in Russia. The University of Vienna, on petition of the Peoples' education society, has formulated a practical scheme of cooperation in educational work throughout the city. Sporadic efforts to extend university teaching may be found here and there in other places on the continent, but neither in method nor in result do they correspond to the English ideals. In process of growth, however, it is to be expected that the branches will become in-

---

[a] Since this writing a conference "of critical importance to the movement in Belgium" was held at Brussels, Jan 20, '95 " The real point at issue was whether the Brussels university extension society should adopt the full method of the English system — lectures, followed by classes, accompanied by essay work and leading up to a final examination — or drift into a mere lecture-agency for the supply of more or less isolated addresses on different subjects. The battle was fought with spirit and pertinacity But at last the English idea prevailed, and the Brussels committee and its secretary Mr Hirsch will have the satisfaction of feeling that their work, instead of being doomed to early failure, has been systematized and strengthened by the conference " O. G 5 47.

[b] Camb. a. m. Rept. p. 30.

creasingly differentiated from the parent stem. The principles of university extension are susceptible of many and varied interpretations; they are not inconsistent with any established order whose highest aim is the common weal. The particular interests of a nation (to mention no smaller unit) and its special needs, political, economic, intellectual and religious, predetermine the limits of the movement and unalterably fix its character.

ORGANIZATION OF UNIVERSITY EXTENSION WORK

Leaders in the extension of university teaching one and all emphasize the principle that the movement exists primarily for the sake of its students, a truism too often lost sight of in more conservative schemes of higher education. It is as important in the organization of the system that the needs of each particular community and of its various social and industrial classes be thoroughly understood as that there should be somewhere a board of experts charged with the supervision of the work and the maintenance of a definite standard of scholarship. For the fulfilment of the latter requirement it appears that the universities, or organizations working with or through universities, are the best means, but university men can know comparatively little of local conditions or of the needs of a class whose daily life belongs to a world entirely separated from that of the scholar. For these reasons, the success of university extension is directly proportional to the completeness with which local managers understand their environment and to the persistency and diplomacy displayed in uniting all factions in striving toward the common end.

First steps toward a local center. University extension is contagious; it is neither of spontaneous generation nor is it absorbed with food or drink. Its origin in a town may generally be traced to a single person, who, having experience of its workings elsewhere, determines to secure it at home. A few friends are interested, or perhaps some local society takes it up. Correspondence is opened with the secretary of the nearest central organization and publications are secured giving a history of the movement, its aims, methods, expenses and other general information. A volunteer committee undertakes to enlist the sympathy of the clergy, of the board of education and the heads of schools, of employers of labor and of labor organizations; in short to secure the cooperation of as many representative men as possible. The next step, unless the movement is supported by some association strong enough to take risks, is to have the mayor or chairman of the school board call a public meeting. The central organization sends a representative, if requested, who can plead the cause of better education for the people; some intelligent workingman has been requested to consider the educational needs of his class; a representative business man will present the results of his study on the practicability of forming a local center and its financial management; still others, probably clergymen and teachers, will speak of the benefit to accrue directly to those who enter on the work and indirectly to the town by having such a center in their midst It is resolved to form a society; a constitution with by-laws is adopted; provisional officers are chosen; and those in the audience interested in the movement are requested to fill up the blanks previously distributed pledging themselves to pay certain amounts annually in return for the privileges of membership.

Securing funds. A meeting of the new center is held at an early date when special committees are elected and a definite choice is made of the subject for the introductory course of study. In response to the request of the local committee the central organization designates a lecturer. From this time on everything is definite; the managers know precisely what course will be given and by whom; the expense, and the number of tickets that must be sold in order to meet it. A certain amount may be relied on from the annual dues, and possibly there is also a guarantee subscription fund which may be drawn on in case of final deficit. In almost every case, however, the financial success of the undertaking depends on the sale of special admission tickets. It is at this stage that the faith of the leader is most tried. Some who would gladly avail themselves of the opportunities offered can not pay the regular rates; others who, as all the town know, are most likely to receive special benefit, show no interest; and there are some public-spirited, educated men, on whom the promoters of university extension thought to rely, who will have nothing to do with it and who take no pains to conceal their disapprobation of such seemingly superficial means of education. At such a crisis the fate of many a center has been decided by a single person, often a lady, who, as member of the committee or as local secretary, was determined to see the matter through; by house to house visits, judicious advertising in all the town papers and the spread of posters, personal appeals to labor leaders and the officers of local associations, her efforts are finally crowned with success and the course is assured without debt.

Choice of secretary. An efficient secretary is the heart and soul of the local center. With the launching of the scheme his work has only begun. Theoretically the management includes a committee representative of all classes participating in the work, but such a committee is of value only when under the direction of an able secretary. He must make all arrangements for the lectures, he must receive the lecturer and acquaint him with the local conditions, he should keep a record of each meeting and make all announcements, he has charge of the library; in short the secretary stands as a mediator between the central organization represented in the teacher, and the students of the local center. This requires some special knowledge of the history of the university extension movement and its pedagogic methods on the one hand, and on the other tact in the management of men, a correct appreciation of students' difficulties and ready sympathy in assisting them.[a]

Formation of a permanent center. With the conclusion of the first course new problems arise, more serious than any hitherto encountered. It is after all a comparatively simple matter to secure pledges and sell tickets enough for a single course; the rub comes when it is proposed to effect a permanent organization. Some of the first students, impelled only by curiosity, have fallen by the way-side; others have no inclination to repeat the experience. A small band remains faithful. It is enthusiastic and willing to make considerable personal sacrifice to continue the work, but it is noted that individual preferences have become strongly marked during the introductory course, usually on some topic of general interest, and it becomes

---
[a] U. E. W. 1 22-25.

less easy to select a topic for the succeeding course. Some come chiefly to be interested and others wish to do scholarly work in definite lines The student with literary tastes finds no use for geology and few of the ladies are likely to express a preference for economics, a subject of intense interest to many men. Small centers, too, find special difficulties in retaining their financial support. The curiosity to hear of some new thing may no longer be turned to account, while conflicting rumors of the value of the work tend to develop a factional spirit in the town. The local secretary, however, assisted now by a corps of students personally interested, can work wonders; few centers with a good secretary have ever given up the work at the conclusion of a successful introductory course.

Possibilities in large towns. Small centers with no external means of support are obliged to compromise on many points to save themselves from extinction. Centers in large towns have decided advantages. Granted sufficient funds they can inaugurate a system of two or three concurrent courses on subjects which will interest all classes; lectures may be given afternoons to ladies and people of leisure and repeated evenings of the same days at reduced rates to workingmen. Courses in sequence extending over several years are possible; an English center may become an affiliated branch of the extension department of Cambridge university; and, finally, it is not impossible for a local center to develop into a veritable people's university college. In any event the first effort of a center permanently established is to induce an interest in earnest and prolonged study in definite lines. Local conditions occasionally favor this plan. A good public library provided with classrooms makes an admirable nucleus for permanent operations; in large cities special foundations, as Toynbee hall, a social settlement in London, or Young men's Christian associations are often utilized. The experience of Reading and Exeter in England seems to indicate the possibility of fusing several such permanent associations into a corporate institution charged with the higher educational interests of the people. With suitable headquarters and substantial support assured it appears to be no more difficult to arrange for courses in sequence for three or four years than for six months.

The London society has specially developed this phase of the work, of which more at length in the following chapter.

University extension colleges. Mr Sadler, secretary to the Oxford delegacy, and Mr Mackinder, principal of the university extension college at Reading, have given particular study to the practicability of securing permanent foundations. Their plans for central headquarters call for an expenditure of about £3,000 for a building "containing two lecture rooms, one designed for a large audience, the second for a smaller class; a students reference library; a small laboratory; an office for the local secretary and a caretaker's house." "A further outlay of £500," it is estimated, "would furnish the nucleus of the students library, and equip the laboratory and lecture rooms with educational apparatus. A yearly expenditure of £600 would provide all the teaching (by the itinerant staff of lecturers, three or four of whom would visit the college in each week of the session) and pay the local secretary's clerk and caretaker."[a] It is proposed, should private munificence fail to supply the necessary funds, that the annual expenses be divided equally between the students, the city and the government. Few centers, however, can hope either for so magnificent a gift of fortune or for state aid; the many must seek for more practical ways of reducing expenses and increasing the number of scholars and the quality of scholarship.

Ways of reducing expenses. There are two factors which conspire to make rates abnormally high: first, the traveling expenses of the lecturer in going out to a single center, specially in the United States, are often no inconsiderable item; second, a staff-lecturer wholly dependent on extension work for an income must have higher fees than would be necessary could he be guaranteed permanent employment. The first difficulty is in part overcome when a number of centers near each other take the same lecturer on successive days. Such a circuit on the weekly

1 lecture circuit lecture plan may comprise six towns and thus reduce to a minimum the extra expenses which are shared in common. In Pennsylvania where bi-weekly lectures are more common

---

Mackinder & Sadler p. 123-24.

a 12-town circuit is reported; Dr W. Clarke Robinson in delivering 72 lectures in the fall of 1893 traveled 5817 miles.[a] He also lectured in practically the same circuit during the winter and spring terms of 1894. Every effort is being made both in England and America to group towns with convenient railway connections into circuits, in the belief that it is for the best interests of neighboring centers to be in touch with each other but specially to secure reduced rates to the several centers. It is a more difficult matter to insure permanency of employment to the lecturer. The practical outcome of English experience is a tendency to federate all the centers in a given district, or county, and to place a secretary in charge of the whole [b] The London society, although usually counted as one of the four English central organizations, is in reality a district association dependent on the universities. There were in 1891 four similar federations among the counties and of late others have been added but their success has not been marked. The one thing needful — a need which will in time be satisfied — is that the secretary of a district association should be an extension lecturer with fixed salary who could devote his entire time to the work of organization and teaching within his district.[c] In return for the assurance of a fixed income the centers would secure more teaching than under present arrangements and besides enjoy the advantages of having a more systematic organization and a responsible head. The founding of a memorial lectureship at Toynbee hall, London, suggests the possibility of private foundations for the support of district secretaries. Prof. Stuart prophesied 15 years ago that a system of federated centers would grow up which would employ not only a

a district associations

---

[a] U E. B 1 44. [b] Mackinder & Sadler, p 49-53
[c] Since this writing a member of the Oxford delegacy has given £600 to provide for the appointment of two "superintendents or directors of university extension teaching (for three years each) in certain districts where railway communications make combined effort natural and easy" The donor makes the following suggestions "It is felt that such directors should be nominated by the university authorities (preferably after private consultation with some of the more experienced organizers resident in the districts concerned), and should serve for a short term of years, as their influence would depend on their becoming familiar with local conditions and personally acquainted with the teachers and others closely concerned with education in the district Their first duties would lie in the direction of forming lecture-circuits to be served by one lecturer at a time, in promoting sequence of studies, and in encouraging the establishment of classes for systematic work alongside of, or between, the lecture courses."

permanent secretary, or principal, but a full staff of peripatetic teachers as well.[a] The recent county council grants show the expediency of having a central board of responsible experts familiar with the educational needs of the districts and qualified to direct the instruction.

Tendency to centralization. The historical development of university extension in England has tended rather to hinder than to advance the formation of district associations. For more than 10 years Cambridge carried on the work alone, save for the city of London and a limited district about Oxford; but with the inauguration of shorter and more popular courses by Oxford in 1885 new centers sprang up all over England joining themselves to Oxford. From this time on, all England, one may say, has been competed for by the two universities and of late a third one, Victoria, has begun work in the northern counties. Gradually the methods are becoming uniform and with increasing harmony a better and more economically administered system will arise. So long as university extension continues to be a missionary movement — and when it ceases to be missionary further extension will be out of the question — its strength will lie in the efficiency of the central organizations and in the zealous loyalty of its leaders.

Methods of central control. Mention has already been made of the main centers both in England and America but in summary it may be pointed out that in England the universities maintain full control, indirectly to be sure in London, but even here we may expect consolidation with the new teaching university, when it is established. It was reported at the recent university extension congress in London that the following five schemes are in active operation:[b]

"1 *By university commission.* At Oxford the movement is managed by a delegacy of 21 members, at Cambridge by a syndicate of 18 members which has charge of the local examinations also, and at Victoria by a committee of the general board of studies, 14 in number, 11 of whom are lecturers At Oxford

---

[a] Roberts, p. 75. [b] Internat. U. E cong. Rept. p. 24-25.

six delegates are or have been lecturers. At Cambridge two syndics have been lecturers, and two elected representatives of the present lecturers have seats on 'the lectures committee' of the syndicate, which considers questions connected with the local lectures and reports on them to the syndicate.

2 *As part of university work.* At Chicago the work 'is managed by a special division of the university, coordinate with other divisions,' and 'the executive officers of instruction of the university extension division constitute a faculty for the discussion and general oversight of the activities of this division.' In the University of the State of New York[a] the work is in charge of a committee of the regents, and at the state university of Minnesota it is in the hands of 'a committee appointed annually from the general faculty of the university.'

3 *By university boards.* At Melbourne and at Sydney the central authority is a university board. The Sydney board received early in 1894 power 'to enlarge itself from 12 members to 18 at most, by adding during the year any persons who take a strong interest in forwarding university extension.'

4 *By independent societies.* The constitution of the London society is comprehensive. Out of the 34 members of the council, 12 represent educational institutions and three are local secretaries. Side by side with the council there is a universities' joint board, consisting of three representatives appointed by each of the universities of Oxford, Cambridge and London. The American society for the extension of university teaching, which has its headquarters at Philadelphia, is an incorporated society, which elects annually members of a board of directors.

5 *By representative committees.* At Cincinnati the governing committee is composed of representatives from the university faculty, the teachers of the high schools and the students. In nearly all the smaller organizations the central authority consists of a few local professors, who are in most cases the lecturers, and of a few of the leading citizens of the district."

---

[a] The University of the State of New York has a distinct department for its extension work, coordinate with the administrative, examination, library and museum departments. Each of the five departments has a standing committee of regents entrusted with its immediate supervision.

Functions of central organizations. The chief functions of the central organizat'on are to promote the progress of university extension, to supply competent lecturers and suitable apparatus including syllabuses to local centers, to devise courses of study with final examinations and to award suitable certificates to students satisfying prescribed conditions of scholarship. The progress of the movement is promoted indirectly whenever the work of any center is successfully conducted. Each central office, however, takes special pains to provide publications, tracts, circulars, monthly journals, etc. for the explanation of its work and methods. The periodical literature devoted to university extension is already formidable. The London society began the publication of a monthly magazine, the *University extension journal*, in February 1890 and the *Oxford university extension gazette* was started in August of the same year[a]; the Philadelphia society publishes two[b] excellent monthly magazines, the *University extension bulletin* devoted chiefly to news, and *University extension*, an ably conducted journal of pedagogy; Chicago university publishes the *University extension world*, an excellent journal now issued quarterly and practically superseding the *University extension magazine*, formerly published by the Chicago society; the Melbourne university extension journal was also published quarterly from Dec. 1892 to Dec. 1894, in the interests of the work in Australasia; and the New York department issues official bulletins from time to time. Besides these there are local papers for the spread of university extension news. Nearly all of the main centers send out post-free circulars of instruction and historical tracts sufficient to initiate the movement at a local center. Lists of lecturers and their subjects, the names and addresses of local secretaries, information on courses of study, examinations and award of certificates, are supplied on request.

Work included under university extension. The conception of a traveling library and of movable apparatus for science teaching was a happy thought. The central office has become a veritable library, museum and laboratory clearing-house. The

---
[a] These two journals were replaced in October 1895 by the *University extension journal*, published under official sanction of the Oxford, Cambridge, London and Victoria university extension authorities.
[b] Replaced, March 1895, by the *Citizen*, a monthly issue devoted to university extension in its widest sense.

tendency in university extension work to include within its province more than the formal lecture course has led to a corresponding increase in the duties of the central office. New York has dropped the term "university" in view of the fact that the aim of her department is to extend "opportunities and facilities for education" without distinction of grade; Summer schools (both Chautauqua and the Catholic summer school of America are incorporated in the New York department), public traveling libraries and teaching by correspondence are all considered worthy of promotion. Chicago university divides the work of university extension into five departments each in charge of a secretary responsible to the head director: (1) The lecture-study department has charge of the work carried on at local centers by a university lecturer with the aid of syllabuses, class, written exercises, etc. This department is concerned with what is usually considered the main work of university extension. Besides this there is (2) a vigorous correspondence department which assists individual students in any part of the world either directly through its secretary or indirectly by putting them in correspondence with university specialists; (3) a class work department in charge of evening and Saturday classes of matriculated students in and about Chicago; (4) a library department which sends out special libraries or books as required; and (5) a district organization and teachers training department.[a]

Selection of teachers. The most delicate and yet most responsible duty devolving on the main centers is the selection of competent teachers. Not every scholar is a teacher and not every teacher is or can become a successful university extension lecturer. The qualifications are various and exacting. An independent movement, working very often in the face of popular distrust and opposition, can risk no experiments with local centers. And what is required of this new species? First, he must have a physical constitution strong enough to bear the fatigue of long journeys in the most inclement season of the year and to withstand the dangers of daily change in food and lodgings. Mr Marriott, an English lecturer[b], has traveled over 50,000 miles in the last five or six years in order to deliver about 1,500 lectures; Dr Robinson of the American society traveled, it is estimated, during the winter of 1893-94, over 16,000 miles in delivering

---

[a] U E 2.245-51.   [b] Since March 25, 1895, secretary of the Oxford delegacy.

three courses of 72 lectures each in his 12-town circuit. The second requirement of the lecturer is that he be a scholar, not necessarily a specialist, but a man of learning and broad culture. To a firm grasp of the subject he must add the missionary spirit which finds as much satisfaction in broadening the realm of knowledge as in pursuing his researches to ever increasing depths. His function is not merely to impart instruction but to stimulate men to think and study for themselves. He must be a man of keen imagination and ready powers of adaptation in order to understand the needs of his audience and to supply that fund of concrete illustration without which all popular teaching is meaningless. He must be sympathetic and patient, knowing that to wound the feelings of a sensitive student, however crude and awkward, defeats the purpose of his teachings. In a word, the desirable extension lecturer is a gentleman, as well as a scholar and a teacher, and it is not the least of his qualifications that he possesses a goodly amount of executive ability joined to unbounded faith in the work and worth of university extension[a].

It is, indeed, little wonder that many able men, conscientious scholars, even noted teachers in academic circles, should hesitate to enter on a work so peculiarly exacting in all its requirements; and when in addition the dangers and hardships of incessant travel and hard work on small or uncertain salaries are considered, some conception may be found of the difficulties encountered by centers in securing and retaining good teachers. The most remarkable thing in the history of the movement is the fidelity of its chief lecturers. Some of them — nearly all those whose names would be first mentioned — have given up lucrative and life-long positions in order to enter on a missionary life, and the ranks are daily being recruited with men anxious to take the places of those worn out in the service.

Training of teachers. There is great danger, it is recognized, specially in the United States, of commissioning men who fulfil every requirement but those of scholarship and moral earnestness. There are quacks in every profession and it is in the interests of self-preservation that university extension teachers, specially staff lecturers, should be in every respect qualified. In America only Philadelphia and Chicago have lecturers engaged solely in the work; New York offers a long list of volunteers from her

---

[a] Mackinder & Sadler, p 103-12.

schools and colleges, trusting to the principle of natural selection and the survival of the fittest. It is certain that wherever the universities are not in immediate control there is danger of superficiality; the man of ready speech may succeed at first in furthering his own interests, but unless he have true culture to impart, the outcome is ultimately disastrous. Oxford requires in addition to a university degree special recommendations of the candidate's attainments and ability to speak in public; next he must submit a syllabus of the course which he proposes to give; the whole or part of this course is given to a private audience without fee, and at each step his work is criticized and amendments suggested if need be; finally, if accepted, he visits a center and studies the work actually in operation under guidance of an experienced teacher. Cambridge applies similar checks thus assuring reasonable protection to the movement in England. The American society (Philadelphia) and the extension department of the University of Chicago undertake to train men of special attainments in the theory and practice of extension teaching. The Philadelphia seminary started Oct. 1892, with seven members, each of whom carried on graduate work in his particular line besides the special pedagogics of university extension.[a] The success of this venture is highly encouraging, and with the strong seminaries in the United States, friends of the movement may hope for a higher standard of scholarship and better educational results than are at present possible.

Cost of a lecture course. The expenses of a course of university extension lectures, a matter of vital importance to both lecturer and local center, fall under three heads: (1) fee payable to the main center, including payment to lecturer, 50 to 60 copies of the printed syllabus, examination, certificates, etc.[b] (2) lecturer's traveling expenses; loan of traveling library and illustrative apparatus; (3) local expenses for rent of hall and class room and for printing and advertising.

In England. Oxford's fee for a course of 12 lectures is generally £42 12s. Staff lecturers receive higher fees The Cambridge syndicate sets the following scale for teacher's fees in 12-week

[a] U. E B 1 91
[b] There is no fee payable to the New York extension department; syllabuses are sold at cost of paper and presswork, and the lecturer's fee is usually paid to him directly by the center, though if preferred it may be paid through the central office.

courses: staff lecturers, £50; regular lecturers, £45; junior lecturers, £35. When the lecturer repeats a day course in the evening, the charge for the two is a fee and a half. Centers grouped by fours secure staff lecturers for £46 and regular lecturers for £41 5s. Short trial courses cost about £25 for six lectures. The expenses classed under (2) and (3) vary greatly according to the grouping of the centers, their distance from the main center, and local advantages. For these Oxford estimates a total of £9, when a lecture-room can be obtained free of cost For long courses at centers connected with Cambridge and Oxford a total of £60 – £70 is not an unreasonable estimate; for the London, Victoria and Scotch university extension courses, about £10 less.

In America. Rates in America are somewhat higher owing specially to the increase in the item of traveling expenses. The official report of Dr Robinson's 12 town circuit, six lectures in each town, is instructive. Following is a summary: "2044 persons in the aggregate attended each lecture; 1482 persons remained for each of the class discussions; 243 students did the paper work on each lecture; $2124.83 were raised by the sale of tickets; $1885.68 were spent in carrying out the course of instruction in the 12 different towns; seven towns had a surplus amounting in all to $332.05; four towns had a deficit amounting to $92.90; leaving a net total surplus in the circuit of $239.15. The average amount raised by each town was $193.16; the average total cost to each town (including lecture fee, lecturer's expenses, rent, light, heat, janitor and printing) was $171.42. The total net cost of the course to each town was $153.05."[a]

Expenses of chief central organizations. The last annual report of the London society, dated Nov. 18, 1893, shows an income of £5400 18s. 10d, of which £3661 2s. 8d. came from local centers, the balance being made up from subscriptions and grants from public bodies. The expenses were for lecturers, examinations, certificates, etc. £4268 8s. 8d.; for management, etc £1008 2s. 5d.; for miscellaneous expenses, £123 12s. This is an increase of about £350 in income over the previous year and of £500 in payment to teachers.[b] In comparison with Oxford and Cam-

[a] U E B 144
[b] The annual report of the London society for 1893-94 shows an increase in income of £400 and in payment to teachers, etc of £246 over the previous year.

bridge these figures are considerably smaller; London maintained in 1892-93 only 16 short and 120 long courses, while Cambridge gave 78 short and 155 long courses and Oxford 151 short and 87 long courses. We may infer, therefore, that the universities expend from one third to one half more than the London society.[a] During the same year the Philadelphia society on a basis of less than one half the number of lectures given in London, received from local centers $18,514.92, which paid lecturers' fees and teaching expenses and left a balance of $1,119.50 to the society Other expenses were for the summer meeting, $2158.74, special classes in civics, $600, printing and publication, $2752 67, library, $622.09, management, etc. $8276 66. The total outlay for the year amounted to about $40,000 of which more than $5000 was raised by a tax of 75% on a fund guaranteed by 60 citizens of Philadelphia.[b]

Enough has been said to show that the expenses of general management are heavy, and the organization, whether university or independent society, must be exceptionally strong to withstand the heavy drain On the other hand the rates to centers can not be reduced if the present standard of scholarship is to be maintained. The desire to extend the privileges of university extension to centers at present unable to bear the cost has brought about in England an appeal for support from the government and serious consideration of a possible place for university extension in the national scheme for secondary education now being studied by a royal commission. The leaders of the movement have realized the utter hopelessness of asking for state aid or other governmental recognition without some show of national organization. The tendency to federate local centers into circuits, and these again into districts, suggests the possibility of dividing all England into federated districts directed by the different universities and represented in a national council. What England does will later on be of practical value for the work in America and other countries.

An international conference. The international character of university extension was amply demonstrated by the congress held in London, June 22-23, 1894. The occasion of this meeting was the 21st anniversary of the origin of the movement in Cam-

[a] The report of the Oxford delegacy for the year ending August 31, 1894, shows a total income of £10,999 9s [b] Report dated Dec. 31, 1893.

bridge; and besides, the recommendations of the commission on a teaching university for London and the recent appointment of a parliamentary commission to report on a national system of secondary education made the time appropriate for the summing up of past experiences and the interchange of views on a general policy for the future. About 600 delegates were present representing all the chief central organizations conducting university extension in the world, the local centers of the United Kingdom, the British universities and local colleges and the education ministries of Great Britain and of several colonies and foreign countries. Representatives were appointed by the following university extension organizations outside the United Kingdom: the Brussels society; the American society, Philadelphia; and the universities of Chicago, Melbourne, New Brunswick, New York, Minnesota, Madras, Sydney, and Queen's (Kingston, Canada). The governments officially represented were Great Britain, Italy, Norway and Sweden, Nova Scotia, New Zealand, Natal, Queensland and South Australia. The sessions were presided over in turn by the marquis of Salisbury, K. G., chancellor of the University of Oxford, the duke of Devonshire, K. G., chancellor of the University of Cambridge, and Lord Herschell, chancellor of the University of London. An assembly more thoroughly representative of all phases of educational work has probably never met in England and the honor done to university extension by the presence of the chancellors of England's three great universities, who never before took a common part in a university ceremonial, and by the reception given the delegates at the Mansion house by the lord mayor of London, are evidences of the moral strength of the movement in England.

Recommendations. Three committees presented reports to the congress dealing with the educational character of the work, the essentials of organization and its relation to the universities and the state.[a] These reports framed by experienced extension teachers and university professors, and unanimously adopted by the congress, form an admirable summary of the results already secured and of the hopes entertained for the future. They point the way to a federation of university extension centers in England which shall work in harmony with established schools and higher institutions of learning and which shall in no wise

---

[a] Internat. U. E cong Rept. p. 17-37.

antagonize, but rather supplement all other means of education. They suggest a national subsidy "to the central authorities toward the general expenses of their administration, and to enable them to retain the permanent services of experienced lecturers." A small grant — the thousandth part of what is spent annually on elementary education — would serve to perfect the organization of university extension work and constitute it a veritable part of the national system of education. How near the day of federation and representative central government may be is problematic. The announcement of a joint commission of the four central organizations for the revision and correlation of the several standards is offset by the report of a falling off in the number of district associations. Without state aid there must be ups and downs; with it stability and uniformity at least could be assured.

Outlook in America. The outlook for systematic organization in America is very obscure. Every day it becomes more apparent that English precedents can not be found for every emergency that arises. The progress of the movement may continue but it must be partially in new lines. A better elementary school system, the highly mixed population, the higher social status of workingmen, fewer densely populated districts, long railway distances, all these differentiate American methods from the English. The numerous central societies already in existence, and others forming, show conclusively that as yet no one plan has been found suitable to all parts of the country. It is more than likely, if university extension is to become a permanent feature of the educational system, that this process of differentiation will continue after the American fashion till the need of union becomes too strong to be resisted. Such an event is highly improbable; the most that friends of the movement can hope for, is state supervision and a national acceptance of high ideals in aims and standards.

COURSES AND METHODS IN THE EXTENSION OF UNIVERSITY TEACHING

Objects of university extension. University extension "has for its objects the extension of knowledge among people too old to go to school and unable to give their entire time to study; the cultivating of habits of useful reading, correct thinking and right conduct; the awakening and stimulating of intellectual life; all for the purpose of making better citizens, inducing social progress and rendering the conditions of society at large more interesting and enjoyable for its members."[a] The aim is not to produce critical scholars, nor to induce persons of average ability to forsake satisfactory means of livelihood for callings in which they could find only disappointments; it is rather to inspire busy people, those whose lifework is already fixed, with higher ideals of life and a nobler conception of their work. University extension seeks to stimulate a desire for self-culture by guiding men and women to a better employment of their leisure hours. It offers: (1) "education by means of systematic courses of lectures and class instruction in the subjects usually taught at high schools and universities;" (2) "illustrated lectures and classes in literature, art, and science, with the purpose of teaching the appreciation of the beautiful and rendering life more interesting and enjoyable;" (3) "lectures and classes in history, civics, and economics, with the purpose of aiding the citizen in studying the problems of free government and modern life, and of encouraging a sense of responsibility, habits of sound thinking and right conduct."[b]

The leaders of the movement to-day have clearly before them two main objects: (1) to create a desire for intellectual nourishment and (2) to satisfy that desire in an orderly and thorough manner. The former implies that the means must be attractive in form and popular in content; in the latter the criterion is sound educational work conducted on a pedagogic basis. Some years of strife on questions of ways and means have been passed in England. One party, led by Cambridge, has stood firm against all popular encroachments on the dignity of university extension work, holding that not less than 12 weeks should be counted a "course" and the ideal should be a series of courses in sequence. Oxford on the other hand contended that shorter courses, generally of six weeks, were all that many centers could afford, and if they chanced to be attractive so much the better. The London society has in a measure reconciled the factions by showing that

---

[a] Statement by the board of directors of the American society for the extension of university teaching U E B 1 114
[b] U E B 1 113.

both are right; that the short, popular pioneer course is the best means of interesting large audiences, among which will be found a few honest students eagerly seeking for light; and with a body of earnest students all things are possible — long courses, courses in sequence, even a complete curriculum of study.

What constitutes a pioneer course depends, aside from its length, on local conditions and the personality of the lecturer; it appeals to the audience through any medium that touches their feelings, be it Greek literature, domestic economy or modern art. To select from such a motley crowd a band of volunteers, and lead them despite opposing obstacles into that wider realm of understanding whose possession is power, is the work of a master.

Pedagogic methods The pedagogic methods of university extension, in themselves neither new nor startling, have particular value in their rational combination and in the systematic precision with which they are applied to all phases of the work. The corner-stone of the system is the efficient, enthusiastic teacher who wields the power that only the spoken word can give. The printed syllabus puts clearly the main points of the lesson and suggests how the interest roused by the speaker's words may best be satisfied; this is the best thought of the teacher put in the clearest form. There is also an hour for quiet conversation; this enables the pupil to bring forward his difficulties and shows the teacher his own weak points; it is helpful for both alike inasmuch as it establishes a more sympathetic relationship. Inspired by the lecturer to independent research, and assisted by syllabus and class, the pupil is ready to produce something be it ever so little; once a week he is expected to write out his conclusions in concise form and submit them to the criticism of the teacher. A few words of advice written in the margin or short discussions in class serve to put the beginner right and to encourage him for the future.

Lecture. The lecture is about an hour in length and is given usually at weekly intervals. In short courses, i. e. courses of six lectures or less, it is not unusual (specially in the United States) to have biweekly meetings. The methods of illustration and explanation will vary with the subjects and preferences of the teachers. One "likes a sloped desk about four feet high;"

another " prefers to speak from a platform, and requires no desk or table." A lecturer on art " likes a large table on which to place books, photographs or sketches, a blackboard for drawings, and conveniences for hanging diagrams, etc.; also necessary arrangements for oxyhydrogen lantern." For geography are required " a blackboard and colored chalks, lantern and screen, and a table for experiments." To illustrate lectures in chemistry the teacher " likes a common deal table at least eight feet long, two buckets, and a blackboard. Gas and water supply preferred, but not necessary. Platform if available."[a] In the larger cities it is usually possible for science lecturers to secure equipped laboratories and access to collections. In botany, geology, etc. field work is encouraged and many teachers announce that in case of a circuit being formed they will reside in the district in order to lead in field or laboratory research.

The lecture itself is for inspiration; the chief function of the teacher is to direct the awakened ambitions of his students. In literary, historical and economic study, books are the best resort, and in coming to them the average person who is not a student by avocation knows not what to do. Methods of study are foreign to him; he is not able even to read with profit. Dr T: J. Lawrence, a noted lecturer both in England and America, says: " My own experience has shown me that many an earnest student needs direction as to the tools to work with, and the way to use them, far more than incitement to industry or information as to the details of the subject." In case there is a public library within reach the lecturer will advise with the librarian in order that the latter may direct the students' readings during the week. If a traveling library is the only resource, it devolves all the more on the teacher to indicate what to read and how to make it useful. He must show his pupil how to advance step by step from the simple to the complex, from concrete and obviously simple facts to difficult abstract conclusions. He must teach the value of broad views and impartial judgment; he must demonstrate that the principles of law and order, of right and equity, transcend the creed of partizans or the tenets of popular conception.

---

[a] Arrangements preferred by Oxford lecturers (See Oxford university, University extension lectures, March 1894, p 45-46.)

"Firstly, secondly and lastly he is a teacher; and if he ceases to teach he is little better than a walking and talking fraud."[a]

Syllabus. The printed syllabus is the teacher's best thought and judgment on methods of studying the subject, condensed into few pages and arranged in clear, concise, systematic form. Prof. H: W. Rolfe, a Philadelphia lecturer, says: "The task of the syllabus is to reconcile as well as may be two somewhat conflicting requirements; the necessity of so guiding the student that he shall not find it easy to be superficial, and the no less imperative necessity of leaving him so free from guidance that he shall be forced to be somewhat independent and original in his work" It is now generally conceded that Prof. Stuart's original plan of making it an abstract of the lecture is surpassed by the broader conception of the teacher's function. The typical syllabus will give an outline of each lecture, usually with short selections from various authorities or references to exact pages in standard works, a complete working bibliography of the subject and series of questions for class discussion and essay themes.

Paper work. The written work on topics suggested in the syllabus is naturally enough confined to the minority. Many who attempt it, fail because of lack of previous training; others treat the theme most superficially; some others, however, produce a study of real merit. The usual plan is to set a question which demands further reading in line with the lecture. Those who believe with Prof. W: H. Mace of Syracuse university and one of the leading New York lecturers, that most general themes, no matter how valuable in themselves, are too indefinite for beginners, content themselves with an argumentative topic dealing with precise facts. This well done, always leading from the particular to the general, gives valuable training in logical thinking.

Class. The essay must be sent to the lecturer by post "not later than the third day before the next lecture" in order that it may be read and criticized in time for discussion in class. The serious difficulties of the student will appear most clearly in the written work. A lecturer writes: "When I am examining a

---

[a] U. E J. 4 56.

student's exercise, I make a point of noting down everything that is at all out of the common. It may be a misunderstanding; it may be a brilliant saying; I get a great many of them. It may be some unexpected side light on the matter from some person who has special experience. And I take care that the whole class has the full benefit of what everybody has said. I do not mention names; everything that is sent in is received in sacred confidence. But, I assure you, it is an immense stimulus to a student, very often a shy, quiet person, to hear some remark he has put in his paper quoted to the whole class, even without his name, and to see the start of admiration over the whole room. And we are often equally indebted to people who make a mistake; a good, rattling mistake serves to clear up a matter for a lot of people who are too hazy to make the mistake themselves. Besides, mistakes are good preparation for further teaching." At the conclusion of the course all students " who have attended two thirds of the classes following each lecture and have written for the lecturer answers to two thirds of the questions set by him " are entitled to admission to the examination.

Examination. These examinations, which are always in writing and about three hours long, are set by specially appointed university examiners and forwarded under seal to some responsible person at the center, who acts as the university representative and vouches for the integrity of the test. Certificates of two grades, ordinary and in honors, are awarded to successful candidates; the joint recommendation of examiner and lecturer, however, determines the awards of certificates of distinction. In England no certificates are granted for courses of less than 10 to 12 lectures, though Oxford will give examinations and a statement of results for a course of not less than six lectures. In America the unit is generally a six-lecture course; New York, however, insists on courses of 10 and her examinations are free to all.[a]

---

[a] In general well-behaved persons of any age and of any social rank are admitted to the lecture courses An effort is made, however, to exclude children of school age The following official notice has recently been issued by the London society: "The council and universities' joint board again desire to remind local committees, students and others that the society's lectures are not intended for those of school age; and, by the regulations of the board, lecturers are not required to correct the papers of students under 15 years of age, nor are such entitled to enter for the examination and obtain certificates."

Certificates. University extension students, it appears, are not unlike their more orthodox brethren in laying much store on testimonials of proficiency. Four to five different grades are recognized by the English universities according to the number of courses followed. The London society grants a so called "sessional certificate" for two long courses and a short summer course, representing about nine months' work; the next award is based on examination following an approved sequence of 75 to 100 lectures, representing about three years' work; the highest grade is the certificate which in addition to those preceding requires an examination in elementary mathematics and two languages and which admits to the second year of the university course.[a]

Benefits of examinations. The examination system plays a minor part in university extension work, nevertheless it has proved to be of value indirectly in inducing more consecutive study. The number of centers and of students in London increased rapidly on the adoption of the sessional certificates in 1889–90; of 16 two-term courses in progress that year, eight were supplemented by the summer term in order to qualify for the new certificate. So it has been with each new testimonial offered; though comparatively few have been able to reach the highest grades, many have been induced to follow more systematic work than they otherwise would have done. This is a main condition of success in university extension work. So long as attendance is voluntary and the choice of subjects rests with the

---

[a] The recent London congress approved the following table of suggested departments, courses and certificates (See Internat U. E. cong Rept. p. 89):

First or short course department

1 Pioneer lectures	No paper work and no examinations.
2 Short courses of from six to nine lectures	Paper work and examinations but no university certificate

Second or certificate course department

1 Courses of 10 or 12 lectures, and linked courses of six lectu es	Terminal certificate
2 Courses of 24 lectures, and linked courses including at least 24 lectures, forming a sessional course	Sessional certificate, ordinary and in honors
3 Linked sessional courses extending over three consecutive years	Vice-chancellor's certificate, ordinary and in honors
4 The requirements for the vice-chancellor's certificate, plus the requirements for the vice-chancellor's certificate in honors, the two having been fulfilled in different branches of study	The title of associate of the university.

local centers, there will be those who join the classes only to be amused. And "if Shakspere gets sandwiched between electricity and Praxiteles, what does it matter?" The most pressing need of the day is to convert enthusiasts for the nonce into earnest, life long students, and the wisest leaders of the extension movement have striven earnestly to meet this need. The award of certificates by university authority based on the results of examinations given by university examiners and on university standards has served admirably to give a tangible aim to consecutive study.

Continuation schemes. Besides examinations, some plan is necessary to keep pupils together for a series of years so that their interest may not flag for lack of competition.

1 *Students associations.* One of the earliest continuation schemes was begun in the early '80s in a mining village of north England. A course on mining had been given and at its conclusion a students' association was formed to continue the work.[a] The members brought together their little stores of books for a reference library and agreed to meet one evening a week for study. Soon afterward they determined to devote another evening a week to land-surveying. Prof. Stuart sketched out a course of study and recommended text-books. Not only did these miners study the manipulation of surveying instruments but they set themselves earnestly to acquire a knowledge of simple geometric principles bearing on the subject. From midwinter to August they carried on their study under direction of a leader selected from their own number. In their free time they did practical field-work with chain, cross-staff and compass, working out the problems at home and discussing them in class.

This pioneer association gained in membership from year to year; it lived through the disastrous strike of 1887 "holding their two meetings a week as usual, one being devoted to the study of arithmetic and the other to English grammar"[b] and has since joined with its work in science a long series of courses in literature. Its success was so marked and its purpose so laudable that the plan has been widely adopted. The mere fact of organization with a definite aim in view, the cooperation with other educational schemes, and the utilizing of existing local resources in

---

[a] Roberts, p. 39–47. [b] Backworth students association Report, 1888

teachers, books and apparatus, are all valuable adjuncts of university extension work. The objects to be attained are admirably stated in a recent announcement of the Gresham college students association, London:

Aims of associations "(1) to encourage and maintain an interest in the university extension lectures given at the Gresham college centre; (2) to encourage continuous study and original work, especially during the vacations; (3) to support the council of the London society for the extension of university teaching in securing the arrangement of courses in regular sequence throughout the year; (4) to increase the attendance at the lectures and the proportion of earnest students doing regular work for the lecturer; (5) to hold meetings, scientific, literary, and social; (6) to arrange excursions, historical, scientific, etc. during the summer months. The subscription of 2s. 6d. per annum entitles each member to attend all meetings and excursions, and to receive the *University extension journal* post free. Those who are at present attending the lectures at Gresham college, or who hold certificates of the London society for the extension of university teaching in connection with any center, are eligible as members."

2 *Home reading circles*. Many small centers can not afford more than one course of lectures a year, but through cooperation the work may be carried on continuously. In consideration of such cases a system of home reading circles has been formed with the distinct aim of supplementing the regular extension work. Some of the readings are intended as a preparation for certain lecture courses arranged so that after a period of special study the lectures may complete the topic. Oxford offers a special set of six printed lectures for workingmen, with full references to standard works, arranged in a form convenient for home study or for use in class. The series deals with the economic position of the working classes in England and was prepared by Mr A. H. D. Acland, now [1894] minister of education in the Gladstonian government.[a] The total cost of a set of

---

[a] The course is on the worker and his welfare, and the subjects of the lectures are as follows: (1) A retrospect, free trade in commerce and labor; association and intelligence. (2) Association and cooperation, friendly societies; trade unions and cooperative societies. (3) The intelligence of the worker; technical and commercial education in England and abroad The education of citizens. (4) Cooperative production. (5) Industrial partnership. (6) Pauperism.

lectures and a loan collection of reference books is £2 4s. 6d.; for 10 sets of lectures alone £1. A more extensive plan is that offered in connection with the Chautauqua reading circles in America, which includes printed lecture courses in literature, social science and art by the foremost scholars of the country.

How conducted

The main object of the home reading circles, as conducted by the Oxford delegacy, is to make the work of the local centers continuous and to provide so far as possible university supervision; in other words an effort is made to establish a bond of permanency between the local centers and the university. The syllabuses are prepared by university men, mostly extension lecturers, and give an outline of readings for three months with complete references, hints for study, essay topics, etc. On payment of 7s. to 10s. each, the members of the circle individually have the right of communicating with the writer of the syllabus six times. "Such communications may take the form of questions which the leader will briefly answer; or of essays, which the leader will return with short comments. One or two questions requiring brief answers may be appended to each essay."[a] An ingenious device by which the membership ticket, printed on adhesive paper and perforated, may be divided into six stamps, one of which is affixed to each communication sent to the leader, assures complete protection to both parties. Additional stamps may be bought for 1s. 3d. each.

3 *Correspondence teaching.* A method of correspondence teaching has grown up in the United States with some of the characteristics of the Oxford system but on the whole intended to bring the individual student under the direct tutelage of the university professor. The University of Chicago, as has been already noted, offers to students *in absentia* courses of study in any department.[b] For a stipulated fee the student may correspond with his teacher, have his exercises corrected, essays criticized and thus carry on independent research under the direction of a master.

---

[a] Oxford university Home-reading circles, 1893, p 4.
[b] "The correspondence-teaching department [of the University of Chicago] has a constituency extending from Maine and Canada to the Sandwich Islands. One of its students is an Arizona ranchman studying Arabic by correspondence, another, a school teacher in the Hawaiian Islands, studying Sanskrit; and another, a member of the standing army in Arizona."— Prof. N Butler, jr, U. E 3.249.

4 *Special classes.* A more comprehensive plan of extending actual university teaching is through "class courses." In England it has resulted from a desire manifested in several centers to supplement lecture courses in Greek history and literature by class study of the Greek language. So hazardous a scheme was considered impracticable at first but with the support of the Hellenic society several classes in Greek have been successfully carried on. Other languages have been added and several subjects of natural science. Students entering these classes must be above school age, and before receiving certificates must have studied "the history, literature, philosophy or art of the nation whose language is studied in class." The teachers are specialists approved by university authorities. "Each course of instruction must comprise at least 36 classes, each of not less than one and one half hour's duration, and accompanied by the writing of an exercise by the student." In science special stress is laid on laboratory practice. In America outside class teaching has been strongly supported by many colleges and universities as the most effective means within their reach of maintaining a high standard in extension work. The universities of Cincinnati and Chicago, Boston institute of technology and Brown university have maintained for two years or more a large number of evening and Saturday classes. The Boston institute offers special courses for teachers extending over two years. Brown university gives biology and botany on Saturday afternoons. "The courses offered by the University of Cincinnati during the past year were Horace, Hebrew, Greek, archeology, English and French literatures, history, analytic geometry, physics, chemistry, biology, graphical statics, astronomy and geology. Many extended through the year; all at least one term. In 1892-93 Chicago offered 51 courses; 20 classes were organized with attendance varying from four to 50. During the past year the number of classes was doubled. It is reported from Chicago that the results attained in general subjects, i. e. such as require no extensive library collection or work-room, are as good as in the university classes. In history, economics and sociology the students *in absentia* being more mature and better prepared for the work than the regular students, their unbounded enthusiasm in the subject chosen carries them safely over difficulties arising from inex-

perience in methods of study. A year ago the American society first offered to the citizens of Philadelphia and adjacent towns instruction in any branch of collegiate study at a nominal price. The courses consisted of 10 weekly lessons. Particular attention was given to the subjects of civics for which a special fund had been provided. The first term showed an enrolment of 600 in 12 classes in civics, 120 in two classes in history, and 300 in five classes in literature. During the winter the number of classes was increased to 30. The experiment was of such a practical nature and so eminently desirable from a political standpoint that it can no longer be omitted from the university extension system.

5 *Summer schools*. No more serious charge has been brought against university extension methods than that no provision is made for continued residence amid university surroundings. It is urged that the corner-stone of an educational system is the living contact of mind with mind, the teacher with the student and student with student. University life is as essential as university study; the two may not be separated in the quest for general culture. The leaders in extension teaching are not indifferent to the defects in their own methods nor do they depreciate the importance of university residence in a scheme of liberal education. The fact is that for the great majority of extension students such advantages, if offered, could not be utilized. Local centers must work out their own destinies with a minimum of outside aid.

a Advantages. The moral support and encouragement on which every center depends come mainly from two sources: (1) from the teacher, who brings with him at each visit something of the university spirit and in whose wisdom and personality are embodied all the ideals of the little group; and (2) from those more fortunate members who can themselves come in contact with many university men in a university environment. For many years local centers depended wholly on itinerant lecturers, but since the origin of university summer meetings, a more powerful influence has been at work. It is possible that the direct educational benefits of summer courses have been too much lauded but it would certainly be difficult to overestimate their indirect influence on local centers.

b Origin in America. Summer meetings have long been a custom in America. Chautauqua has become a university with an extraordinarily long vacation at a time when orthodox institutions are open. Its rapid progress, however, has not passed unnoticed, the direct result of which has been the founding of a summer school in connection with very many of the leading colleges and universities. The new Chicago university, which is nothing if not liberal, has deliberately added a fourth term thus keeping its work practically in continuous operation. Teachers and all who will are invited to avail themselves of the privileges offered in the summer term. During the past summer 150 courses were offered by 70 members of the faculty; the attendance reached 540, "a large proportion of the matriculates being teachers."

c Spread in England. The fact that the English universities stood half the year idle while local extension centers were in direct need of more stimulus than the lecturers could give, led in 1888 to an adoption by Oxford of the American plan of summer meetings. Beneficial effects were at once perceived. University professors who could not take up circuit work cheerfully gave themselves to their vacation classes; apparatus, books and laboratory stores were accessible to an extent impossible elsewhere; and, finally, the advantages of social intercourse between town and gown and of the strength of purpose begot of strong hearts in the midst of traditions inseparably linked with England's greatness, were influences at once more powerful and more efficient for the cause of popular education than any step hitherto taken in university extension. Cambridge has since 1885 in a small way encouraged the best students of her local centers to spend a few weeks of the summer in quiet study at the university, a policy which she still adheres to. The larger popular meeting is peculiarly Oxonian, although it was held at Cambridge in 1893 and will be held there again in 1896 and each alternate year thereafter.

Directly following the first summer meeting in Oxford a considerable fund was collected for awards of scholarships to worthy students who might wish to attend the next summer course. The scholarships were awarded on competitive essays assigned at the conclusion of the winter term, and among the winners were " two carpenters, two clerks, a fustian weaver, a dockyard artisan and three elementary school teachers."[a] In 1890 more than 20 such grants were made of which six went to workingmen and four to teachers in elementary schools. At the present time in addition to a main fund of some £182, granted in £10, £5 and £1 scholarships, there are many special grants made by local societies and friends of the movement. The special object in granting these prizes is to enable workingmen and members of small country circles to broaden their intellectual horizon and to take home to their comrades new views of the dignity of the work in which all are engaged. A gratifying result has been the voluntary subscription for scholarships made by artisans in the interest of their own centers; no better testimony could be adduced to show the attitude of even the weakest local centers toward the university advances

d Courses offered. In 1891 Oxford introduced the plan of devoting the greater part of the summer course to a particular period of history and studying that period from every point of view. A sequence of 72 lectures and classes were given on medieval history, literature, architecture and economics. The following year the special topic was the renaissance and reformation. During the past summer the 17th century was studied, to be followed in 1895 by similar courses on the 18th century. In this way an effort is made to secure greater unity in the summer work and at the same time to suggest a logical system of study to all centers following Oxford's leadership.

The 1894 summer meeting at Oxford was in session from July 27 to Aug. 24, and for the convenience of those unable to spend the entire month the work was arranged for two parts each complete in itself. The program was as follows:

(1) "The history, literature, etc. of the 17th century. Lectures will, if possible, be given by 28 professors, on the following subjects: the Laudian movement; the puritan revolution; the restoration; Wallenstein; Richelieu; Mazarin, and Colbert;

---

[a] Oxford *Report*, 1890

the economic history of the period; the influence of Holland; Herrick, Milton, Bunyan, Dryden; the pilgrim fathers; George Fox; Descartes, Hobbes, Spinoza and Locke; Pascal, Molière, Bossuet; Galileo, Harvey, Newton; Rubens, Vandyke, Velasquez, Rembrandt; Grotius; the architecture and music of the 17th century"

(2) "The life and duties of the citizen (a course specially designed to follow the syllabus in the continuation school code, 1893) by nine professors. Lectures will be given on municipal government, poor law, factory and public health legislation; the civil service; India, the colonies and dependencies; social and industrial organizations; trade unions, cooperative and friendly societies; public education; the law of contract; and the growth of English political institutions, local and central."

(3) The Greek language and literature: two courses of lectures and two classes in language work.

(4) Astronomy, anthropology, geology, hygiene, chemistry; one course each with practical work.

(5) Science and art of education: courses by four teachers in psychology, theory of education (with special reference to class teaching with criticism lessons), German educational science (by Prof. W. Rein, Jena), school hygiene and practical lessons on preparation of experiments, use of lantern, etc.

(6) Economics and industrial history; courses by six lecturers.

(7) History of Oxford; five illustrative lectures and numerous visits to colleges, etc.

(8) Special classes in art, music, wood carving, photography, shorthand, dramatic recitals, debates, conversaziones; visits to places in the neighborhood of Oxford connected with the history of the 17th century, etc.

e Expenses. The university professors and extension teachers engaged in the regular work numbered about 60 besides the instructors required for the special classes. Tickets cost £1 10s. for the whole meeting, or £1 for either part; special classes and laboratory fees were extra. The attendance at the first part was limited to 1000 and to 600 at the second part. All reports agree in stating that the meeting was in every way by far the most satisfactory of any yet held in England.[a]

f In Cambridge. The summer courses at Cambridge in 1894 which were held from Aug. 7-28 were open only to holders of the Cambridge local lecture certificates and the numbers were restricted to 50 in chemistry and 30 in all other classes. The work was nearly all of an advanced nature and intended for earnest students. Courses were arranged, but not all were called for, (1) in science: chemistry, physics, astronomy and hygiene; (2) in history: English reformation and French revolution; and (3) in literature: Shakspere and the Elizabethan dramatists. The fee for any course was two guineas or for two courses, three guineas.

g In Philadelphia. Popular summer schools are so numerous in America that no addition to the number from university extension organizers is necessary. The Philadelphia summer meeting in 1894, therefore, was devoted to special advanced studies in pedagogy, American history, economics and sociology. The principles and practice of the Herbartians was ably presented during the month of July. In national history special courses were given by several university professors and at the conclusion of the meeting a pilgrimage was made to Boston, visiting all points of importance connected with Washington's military operations. But the great feature of the meeting was the work in economics. Lectures were given three hours a day for four weeks by the most noted specialists of the country representing seven different colleges and universities. The work was intended " primarily for students and teachers of economics,

---

[a] "The sixth summer meeting of university extension and other students at Oxford, which was brought to a close on Saturday, has proved a complete success. This year, there has been a marked increase in the number of students entering themselves for the special classes. In the education class more than twice as many entered as were contemplated as possible. The same remark applies to the class for the study of Greek, while those devoted to economics, anthropology, hygiene, chemistry, and geology have all been up to their previous numbers, though the work done in each has been more advanced. So keen was the desire for instruction in Greek that it was found necessary to hold the first class at a quarter past seven in the morning, and with intervals the study has been pursued until seven or eight in the evening. The experiment of dealing with a limited period of history — this year the 17th century — from all points, political, economic, artistic, philosophic, religious, and literary, and intrusting each to a specialist was an undoubted success. The class in education has also been very well attended. Mr Wells, of Wadham college, who examined the Greek class, has sent in a report congratulating Mr Gibson and the class on the excellent work done, the result having exceeded the most sanguine expectations."— *The Times*, London, Aug 27, 1894.

rather than for the diffusion of elementary knowledge." There were courses on the distribution of wealth, political finance, the relations of economics and politics, and of economics and sociology, the Ricardian system, the theory of dynamic economics, etc. No similar gathering of scientific men has ever been held in America for the interchange of ideas in so systematic a way; it was a meeting of scholars in which the program permitted each man instead of the usual short hour for the reading of a paper a full month for the presentation of his best thought in his own way.

h Foreign criticism. The summer meeting has come to stay. It has justified its existence, if in no other way, by bringing the universities into closer relations with the people, in sending out to the remotest parts of the land something of that "sweetness and light" which comes only with higher ideals of life and duty. Unsought and unbiased testimony on this point comes from Prof. J. Mourley Vold, a Norwegian, who visited Oxford in the summer of 1892 and in whose report on university extension this statement occurs: "If you ask me for my general impression of the meeting, I can only exclaim: What attention, what enthusiasm during the lectures, what energy in the work, what interest, humor, and tolerance in discussions, what gaiety in the conversations and on the excursions; briefly, what life, what health and vivacity! I should be tempted to compare the meeting with an old Greek festival"

And after a month in such an environment the student returns to his home, conscious perhaps for the first time in his life of his own littleness but resolved to be a nobler man and a better neighbor. Some perhaps with over-weening confidence will misapply the lesson learned and pride themselves on their accomplishment, but were every movement to cease when hypocrites abound, there would be little organized effort for good in the world. That the good outweighs the bad in every phase of university extension work is confidently asserted by hundreds of men who best know what is being done. The presence of a few enthusiastic students in any town or village assures the success of the local center and if there be no such center one is pretty sure to be organized. And so the movement spreads.

RESULTS OF 21 YEARS OF PROGRESS

The influence of any movement which affects the life of a people can not be measured in mathematical units. Statistics, like oracles, lend themselves all too readily to the arbitrary interpretation of biased inquirers. But with whatever predilections we observe the progress of university extension there is one conclusion which all must reach: the movement is no longer a nonentity; it has attained proportions which make it of national, if not international, importance.

Direct results. There are in England alone nearly 400 centers organized for university extension work. The Cambridge syndicate offers for 1894-95 some 315 different courses by 64 teachers; 179 courses are in literature, history, economics and art, and 136 courses in natural, mathematical and physical science. Oxford has 60 lecturers, 16 being "staff lecturers" offering 432 courses, 282 in arts and 150 in science. The Philadelphia society has six staff lecturers who devote their entire time to teaching and four more, available for circuit work. The total teaching-force numbers 78 with courses amounting to 194.[a] New York offers 221 courses by 119 teachers representing 11 colleges and 23 academies and professional schools.[b] In Chicago there were 30 centers doing active work last year besides 73 others in Illinois or adjoining states connected with Chicago university or local colleges.

It is difficult to estimate the amount of money expended yearly in university extension work even in England. A careful reckoning made in 1891 estimated the total cost at £21,850 on a basis of 464 courses.[c] If the same ratio holds now the annual expenditure in England alone amounts to more than £30,000.

---

[a] U E B 1 131

[b] "There are 33 centers in the state. Owing to the financial stringency this year (1893-94), only 20 have been active In these 31 courses were given The estimated total attendance at lectures was 50,499 and at classes 22,590 13 examinations have been given for which there were 106 candidates, of whom 94 passed. There were six courses on electricity, seven on American history, seven on litera'ure, three on geology and four on economics There might have been a great many more courses on economics but it is impossible to find enough capable men who have time to do the lecturing In most centers the effort to reach the working classes has not been altogether successful, as, in fact, it has not been anywhere in this country "—Letter from Miss Myrtilla Avery, director s assistant, Extension department, New York

[c] Mackinder & Sadler, p. 90-95.

Statistics. The following table, prepared for the London congress, shows the work of the chief English and the three chief American organizations for the session 1892-93, being the last for which complete figures are attainable :[a]

	No of short courses	Courses of 10 or more lectures	Total number of courses	Attendance	Workers of weekly papers	Passed the final examination
Oxford	151	87	288	28,051	2714	1295
Cambridge	78	155	233	15,824	2565	1730
London	16	120	139	13,374	1958	1281
Victoria			59	4,900	472	
Philadelphia	107	1	108	18,822	429	888
Chicago	122	0	122	24,822	725	486
New York [b]	0	34	34	3,667	223	142

a STATISTICS OF UNIVERSITY EXTENSION IN ENGLAND

	No of centers	No of courses	Av attendance at lectures	Av attendance at class	Av no of weekly papers	No examined
CAMBRIDGE						
1881-82	29	43	3,406	2100	832	502
1884-85	57	73	7,259	4152	1592	1093
1887-88	74	96	9,509	4653	1975	1531
1889-90	85	125	11,595	54.5	2458	1733
1891-92	296	329	18,779	8873	3360	2645
1893-94	114	136	10,617	4332	2085	1478
						(Certificates awarded)
OXFORD						
1885-86	23	27	not recorded			25
1887-88	59	82	13,036			590
1889-90	109	148	17,904			927
1891-92	c279	d398	e37,969			f2315
1893-94	g169	h2.9	i23,308	(f) 7000	2123	j1314
LONDON						
1884-85		63	(Entries) 5,195		808	405
1887-88		80	7,150		1204	859
1889-90		130	12,923		1972	1350
1891-92		131	11,597		1799	1281
1893-94		152	15,665		2186	1553

b The extension department of New York has from the first laid less stress than any of the other central offices on the lecture system and has given greater attention than any other to the establishment of free public libraries, the circulation among scattered communities of traveling libraries, the formation of reading circles, study clubs and other agencies for university extension Its activity and work therefore can not be judged by the statistics of lecture courses. These it believes in heartily, but considers them as only one of many excellent agencies for advancing education among the people at large The summary of its plan of work is sent free to all applicants and will make clear the broad lines on which the department is organized and for which it has contended from the first.

c Including 157 centers organized by county councils
d Including 221 courses organized by county councils
e Including 8608 at centers organized by county councils
f Including 1028 at centers organized by county councils
g Including 54 centers organized by county councils
h Including 58 courses organized by county councils
i Including 2675 at centers organized by county councils.
j Including 272 at centers organized by county councils

Returns for 1893-94 show a falling off both in attendance and number of courses. In America generally it is attributed to the prevailing financial depression and the distractions, specially in Chicago, of the Columbian exposition. The artificial stimulus given to the work in England under grants from the county councils has reached its reaction. The many science classes throughout the country with free tuition or extremely small fees give no place for similar courses from the universities and besides make it difficult to maintain courses in arts. "Not only have literature and history thus suffered, but courses on branches of science not of obviously practical utility (such as astronomy) have tended to be displaced by more 'technical' subjects."[a]

Pedagogic progress. Steady progress is being made in London, however, and in all large towns where parallel courses on a variety of subjects can be supported. The most notable gain of all is in the number of courses arranged in sequence. No other fact shows so well the tendency toward more scholarly methods. The London society arranged in 1888-89, 10 courses extending over two consecutive terms and four over three terms; in 1890-91, 16 two-term courses and six three-term; in 1892-93, 34 two term and 25 three term courses. "Out of the total of 139 courses 53 only were isolated; each of the other 86 was arranged in definite connection with either one or two other courses at the same center."[b] Among Oxford centers the average length of term has increased from eight and one half weeks in 1888 to 14 weeks in 1893. An increasing number of students in London has obtained the sessional certificate for nine months of continuous study. In 1889, 12 were awarded; in 1890, 60; in 1891, 94, and in 1893 the number reached 124.

Distribution of work. The distribution of the work among the different subjects makes an interesting commentary. In

---

[a] Cambridge university — Local examinations and lectures syndicate Annual report, v 20 1893, p. 11.

[b] London society for extension of university teaching Report for 1893 The report for 1894, makes a still better showing: "Out of a total of 152 courses only 40 were isolated, each of the remaining 112 formed part of an educational sequence."

1890-91 the work of the three chief English organizations was divided as follows:[a]

	History and political economy	Literature and art	Natural science
Oxford	95	33	64
Cambridge	33	32	70
London	31	39	57
	159	104	191

In the 59 centers in London in 1892-93, 55 courses were given in natural and physical science, 39 in literature, 23 in history, nine in economics, six in architecture, and seven in philosophy.[b] The program for the winter term, 1894, of the university extension college at Reading, includes physical geography, the Homeric poems, English history of the 18th century, chemistry (four courses), electricity, biology and botany (three courses); the first three courses were of 12, the others of 24 lectures each. Of the results of this work the government inspector of the science and art department speaks in the highest terms and pronounces it "of a thoroughly practical and efficient character"[c] The courses in sequence in London during 1892-93 were distributed as follows: 15 in science, five in English literature, two in Plato's *Republic*, eight in history and political economy, one in architecture, two in Dante's *Purgatorio* and *Paradiso* (the latter read in the original). The special fact of note in these figures is the remarkable equilibrium everywhere maintained between scientific, literary and historical studies.

Indirect results. The indirect consequences of the extension of university teaching are not so easily reduced to paper, but

---

[a] Mackinder & Sadler, p. 63

[b] London society for extension of university teaching. Report for 1893. The report for 1894 makes a still better showing "Out of a total of 152 courses only 40 were isolated, each of the remaining 112 formed part of an educational sequence"

[c] Under date of April 30, 1894, he writes "This school is doing a unique work. The literary and historical work is blended in a most satisfactory manner with the technical and scientific. The organization seems to be quite perfect The blending of the university extension departmental systems has succeeded, and there are apparently not many difficulties in working the two systems together" O. G. 4·105.

those effects which play no part in statistics, concerning primarily only the individual, his habits and ideals of life, and tending to improve society by making its units better — such are in reality the genuine aims of university extension. Statistics of courses, attendance and examinations, teachers and the amount of money expended in the work, are very definite facts but not the only ones. It is more desirable to know what efficiency can be claimed for the work from an educational point of view, what influence it has on the well-being of its disciples and how far it benefits society by reaching classes excluded from ordinary educational advantages.

EFFICIENCY OF UNIVERSITY EXTENSION TEACHING

No one claims that all extension work is good; not all school work is good nor is the teaching within the university faultless. A glance at the list of English extension lecturers, however, dispels all doubts of the high academic distinction of the staff. Certain it is that no corps of teachers in the country stands on a higher level. Prof. Vold's impression of the summer meeting has been cited; other impartial witnesses speak highly of university extension methods. The French ministry of education commissioned M. Espinas, "a distinguished professor in the faculty of Bordeaux" to report on the movement in England; the results of his study are published in the March and April, 1892, numbers of the *Revue internationale de l'enseignement*. In a work published this present year by another Frenchman, M. Max Leclerc, the attitude of the students is thus described: "Le sérieux, l'ardeur avec lesquels ses auditeurs écoutent et profitent, la précision de leur langage, sont admirables." Of the lecturer M. Leclerc has this to say: "Il discute avec un véritable esprit scientifique les sources, les points douteux, les objections."[a]

Disinterested criticism

Reports of examiners. The official reports of the university examiners are worthy of consideration inasmuch as the standard on which they base their judgment is the same as required of regular university students.[b] The Rev. A. H. Johnson, a distin-

---

[a] Leclerc, Max. *L'education et la société en Angleterre; l'education des classes moyennes et dirigeantes en Angleterre.* Paris, 1894.
[b] Sadler, M E. Facts about university extension (see 19th cent. 36 371-82).

guished tutor and examiner of Oxford, says of papers in history: "A large proportion of them would be fully up to our second class standard, while some few would reach that of a first class." Dr A. Whitelegge, Oxford examiner in hygiene says: "The papers referred to me have been usually good and often excellent, and I am satisfied that the knowledge gained by the students who enter for the final examinations is no mere smattering, but an intelligent acquaintance with the essentials of the subject." Selections from examiners' reports made to the London society a year or two ago read as follows: "Much of the work done in science is of a very high quality, such, indeed, as I should have been pleased to receive from honor students in Cambridge; I have constantly selected certain answers of the best extension students in political economy in order to show them to my pupils here (Cambridge) as models of what an answer should be" A distinguished Greek scholar makes this comment on his class in the *Iliad*: "I have no doubt, so far as the best of my students were concerned, they were much superior to the average passman both in intelligence and application."

Guaranteed by all universities of England and Wales. A further proof of the efficiency of the university extension work is that every university in England is engaged in it. The new University of Wales is expressly authorized by its charter to recognize extension work in the principality. The Gresham university commissioners report: "We have received much valuable evidence on the subject, and we have no doubt that the university extension system deserves the encouragement of the university, and under favorable conditions may be a useful supplement to its work, as bringing under the direct influence of university study many students who would otherwise have remained outside that influence." Mr Sadler refers thus to the significance of the recent London congress: "The chancellors of the universities of Oxford, Cambridge and London do not often express themselves in public on matters of university policy, still more rarely do they act together in concert. It was, therefore, a memorable event when the three chancellors consented to take the unusual, if not unprecedented, step of presiding in succession over the three sittings of a conference summoned to celebrate the coming of age of university extension and to further its educational aims." Lord Salisbury, late prime minister of England, said on that occasion: "I appear here as connected with the University of Oxford . . . in order to testify to the warm sympathy which I know exists between the university which I have the honor on this occasion to represent and this most successful and advancing movement. It is one with which all who are concerned in the common weal and the common progress of our country and our people must sympathize if it is attended by the success which by all promise and all appearance is likely to wait on the efforts which you have made."[a]

INFLUENCE OF EXTENSION STUDY ON INDIVIDUALS AND SOCIETY

No test can be universally applied in estimating the direct value of the work, but probable inferences may be very legitimately drawn from certain known facts. The remarkable spread of the movement during the past 10 years is not entirely due to the missionary zeal of its leaders or the curiosity of the populace to see or hear some new thing. If it were, how then explain the steadfastness through years of trial which many a small and weak center has shown in the pursuit of knowledge? The case of Backworth, already cited, is to the point. Here in a small colliery village the work has been carried on continuously for more than 10 years by a little group of miners. Their secretary was present at the London congress last June and spoke with authority on local organization and the benefits of students associations. From a course in mining and land surveying, their association has come to include a section for science and another for literature; both are actively employed and the secretary announced that "in a few weeks more a class to study French was to be commenced. A member of the Tyneside students association had kindly consented to teach and conduct the class free of charge. Each of these sub-divisions brought in new members, who would not have joined if the students had confined their studies to one particular branch alone. . . The students themselves showed unmistakable signs of improvement. Any one attending meetings in his center might observe the difference between the discussions now and those that used to take place. The most backward now were more advanced

Results among artisans

---

[a] Internat. U. E cong Rept. p 41

than those who were considered to be very learned formerly. This was mainly due to the influence of university extension lectures."[a] So much for a small center and one of the poorest financially. Others more favored, as has been mentioned in this chapter, are now engaged on their second three years' course of continuous study. The only conclusion from such evidence is that a genuine demand for educational advantages exists among these people, else their ardor would be less persistent. They find a pleasure in intellectual exercise which tempts them ever further in its pursuit.

Increases desire for good reading. Probably the first experience of those who fall under the spell of the higher study is a desire for more and better reading. From many centers it is reported that the circulation of public library books has been radically altered under the influence of university extension courses One librarian reports that a single year of extension work reduced the demand for works of fiction from 90% to less than 70% of all books drawn.[b] In several cases in England, university extension students have taken a leading part in local movements for the establishment of free libraries. Scarcely a center is established without access to a public library that does not at once proceed to collect works for the common advantage which in turn form the nucleus for larger collections. In New York the largest division of the extension department is devoted solely to promoting general library interests of the state. This division, which is coordinate with that controlling extension teaching, expends annually $25,000 for the benefit of free public libraries on condition that local support be given in each case to an amount equal to the state apportionment. The committee which first recommended the adoption of university extension by New York state anticipated this effect: "Its operation," it is stated, "will hasten recognition of the need of and create a demand for local public libraries, until, in time, no area of population throughout the state will be beyond convenient access to the garnered wisdom of the past and the best thought of the present. Such libraries will become the homes and centers of university extension work, and will soon require librarians trained for wider usefulness than that of mere custodians of books."[c]

---

[a] Internat. U. E. cong. Rept. p. 91.   [b] E. B. 4.161.   [c] E. B. 1:11.

Adverse criticism. In any matter dealing largely with subjective experiences it is no great task so to adjust one's premises that any conclusion whatsoever may be reached. University extension lends itself with equal freedom to the sneers of its opponents and to the praises of its friends. A recent writer[a] undertakes to show that "from the beginning it has trodden learning under foot." He maintains that "not a single habit fostered by learning is taught to the victims of this new-invented debauch " Even Mr Moulton has "preached the gospel of the attic drama to thousands who knew not the shape of Greece upon the maps.   To artisans and housemaids he carried the message of Sophocles and Aristophanes. Once it was the fashion for the decent navvy to pride himself that he had no book learning. To-day he is anxiously scraping acquaintance with the masterpieces of Greek literature." Of the summer meetings this caustic writer says: "For three weeks at a time the universities are invaded by a mob of intellectual debauchees. . . The learning of all the ages is crammed into a fortnight .   . and the distended ones return to their homes battered beyond recognition, and firmly convinced that they have enjoyed in three weeks all the privileges of a university career."

Those who, like this gentleman, see in university extension only "the shallow optimism of democracy expressing itself in a blind enthusiasm" will agree with him in condemning every effort that does not respect the divine limitations of the people; they see no virtue save in the aristocracy of birth and of culture. Even the appreciation of " art and literature must remain aristocratic and exclusive unto the end of time   . The people never had, and never can have, the smallest interest in its privileges and penalties."

A favorable report. On the other hand the pastor of a small New England church in describing the results of a course on modern European history which was carried on in his village under great difficulties four months of the year, can not speak highly enough of the new life and stimulus roused among his

---

[a] Whibley, Charles. Farce of university extension (see 19th cent 36 306-10).

people. He concludes: "10 years of such courses, and what a large education would be won! Men and women would be looking out from our New England hills and valleys over the whole world, scandals and petty localisms would lose their charm, spirituality would be enriched, preaching from the pulpit would appeal to greater sensitiveness, the kingdom of God would be advanced; for it is not only in the spectacular movements of metropolitan Christianity, but as certainly in the quiet work of the village church, 'not with observation,' that the kingdom comes."[a]

Between these two witnesses to the practical value of study among common people the reader must take his choice or find a middle ground. One represents the optimism, the other the pessimism, one the liberalism, the other the conservatism, of the times; and it is with these two opposing forces that university extension has to reckon.

WHO BENEFITS BY EXTENSION TEACHING

No class distinctions. Prof. Stuart, the father of the movement, said on a recent occasion, "Continuous and systematic contact between those persons (who could not go to the universities) and persons who had been trained under the discipline and with the traditions of university education, continuous and systematic contact between them and all sections of our people, rich and poor, men and women alike, was the idea which animated us."[b] Time has more than satisfied the expectations of those early leaders. In one respect there has been disappointment. Except in particular instances comparatively little progress has been made in dealing with separate classes; the most successful centers are those in which class distinctions are disregarded. In afternoon lectures, as might be expected, the attendance is largely of ladies. Evening lectures, save in certain industrial districts, invariably attract highly mixed audiences: professional men, shop-keepers and artisans; both sexes, individually and by families; the well to-do and the very poor; university graduates and men of no schooling whatever. Even the earnest students are scarcely more homogeneous. Of 58 candidates who took an

---

[a] George, Rev E A., The institutional village church (see Outlook, 50 343-44)
[b] Internat. U. E. cong Rept. p 60.

Mixed audiences examination in political economy at Nottingham, 31 were men and 27 women. "Of the men, four were students, five artisans, four warehousemen, nine clerks and shopkeepers, six large manufacturers, one schoolmaster and two unknown; of the women, seven were daughters of manufacturers, two of a minister, 12 of tradesmen and six were milliners."[a] Another instance cited by the same writers gives the social position of 330 persons in the south of England who attended an afternoon and evening course given by Mr R. G. Moulton on 'Greek tragedy," as follows: "About two thirds of this number were persons in easy circumstances, who paid 10s. 6d. for the course, while 93 were admitted at a reduced charge, and were described as follows: teachers in private, middle class and high schools, 31; private governesses, 23; elementary school teachers, 13; pupils in schools, 11; employees in houses of business, 10; artisans, 4; domestic servant, 1." One more case: "In an examination recently held in a lecture-center, among those to whom were awarded certificates of distinction were a national schoolmistress, a young lawyer, a plumber and a railway signalman."[b]

Work among special classes. The reader must not infer, however from what is said above, that special classes are not interested in extension work or that every effort to reach the masses has been a failure. Small centers, specially those in rural districts, must remain mixed because of financial inability to serve different classes, and parallel courses for general audiences, to say nothing of courses for workingmen or men of this or that profession, are with difficulty carried on save in the largest towns. But wherever possible, special courses have been arranged. From Chicago comes the announcement that Prof. E. W. Bemis will organize a class from the clergymen of the city to study the labor movement. "It is intended," the circular reads, "to make the course very practical, touching upon many questions which confront all city pastors and which call for serious study by our clergy."[c] The alumni of the University of California living in Sacramento have formed a local center for the purpose of carrying on regular lecture studies in connection with their

---

[a] Roberts, p. 14-15. [b] Oxford university — Extension lectures. Annual report, 1890.
[c] U. E. W. 3 126-27.

alma mater. The work was begun with a course on political economy. An electrical workers union of New York city, 400 strong, has organized courses for its members in subjects allied to their daily work.[a] Many such instances might be cited to show that special classes can be interested in the work, but in America at least workingmen have given no essential support to the movement.

English artisans The artisans of England are more stable and better organized than the working classes in America. They are Englishmen too, and not a mixture of every race under the sun. The feverish unrest and the sport of fortune, so prominent in colonial life, play a minor role among a people long accustomed to make the best of life as they find it It is among English artisans, therefore, and particularly among those who are life-workers in fields remote from commercial influence that university extension work has been most warmly received. In the mining region of the north country the best work has been done. In many towns along the Tyne there have been continuous courses for many years. The pitmen have their own committees and make their own arrangements with the central organizations. The thought given to study not only affords a healthful recreation but equips the learner for independent judgment on matters affecting the well-being of his class. As a delegate from a mining center pointed out to the London congress: " It must be remembered that the platform in England is free to all and that there is always an army of orators, socialists, anarchists, agitators, and demagogues of all shades of social and political opinions, not always well informed or highly cultured, going about lecturing and speech-making, and trying to force their theories and fancies upon the public."[b] From this the speaker argued the wisdom of giving to as many as possible of his people a better intellectual equipment that they might reason on these matters for themselves.

Rarely does a lecturer leave such a center. it is said, without finding some workingman who has spent the little leisure of his life in the pursuit of some favorite study. Now it is a man of south England, who, while learning to read when past 30 years

---

[a] U. E. B. 1:47.   [b] Internat. U. E cong. Rept. p 91.

of age, had familiarized himself with most standard works on astronomy and who by careful saving had procured himself a telescope that he might still further pursue his studies; he writes to the lecturer: "I feel somewhat ashamed of my ignorance when in the society of the more educated of those I see sitting at your evening lectures. I am trying to overcome that feeling so that I may not lose the first opportunity I have ever had, and perhaps will be the only one I shall ever get, of testing the correctness of my astronomical conceptions "[a] Another case is that of a man who began to work underground at nine years of age but by dint of perseverance "acquired a masterly knowledge of certain branches of English literature." Two others under the stimulus of university extension work became very able local geologists and expert paleontologists of the carboniferous period. The coal-measures, one may imagine, are to them no longer the forbidding pit but nature's own book of secrets to whose interpretation, every hour of homely toil adds new incentives to life and suggests indefinite possibilities worth striving for.

London workingmen. In London it has been possible from private subscription or charitable foundations to provide courses of study for the people at mere nominal rates. Workingmen have been quick to avail themselves of these privileges and much of the growth noticeable in the London society since 1891 is attributable to these courses for artisans. The numbers of foreigners in London and the density of the population in certain districts have led university extension lecturers to preach first of all the gospel of cleanliness and right living. Special courses on hygiene and domestic economy have particular value. In America the needs of the foreign classes in the great cities are very marked and special pains are being taken to meet their wants. First of all is a knowledge of the duties of a citizenship which is thrust on them; very few have ever had any share in civil government and to many the very name of government carries with it memories bitter and hateful. For these Philadelphia maintains special classes in civics, and, for centers unfamiliar with English, lectures are offered in the Russian, Polish and German languages. The Chicago university extension depart-

---

[a] Roberts, p 33-37.

ment goes a step farther and offers for the present year courses in German, French, Italian, Russian, Scandinavian and Spanish; and has appointed as staff lecturer an eminent Scandinavian scholar who will devote himself to the interests of the Swedes and Norwegians of the great northwest.

Farmers. Another special class which is being directly influenced by the university spirit is composed of the farmers. There is scarcely a state of the Union which does not maintain some system of extension work directly applicable to agricultural wants. In England the technical education act extends its aid to every hamlet in the land. The part of the university, it is getting to be clear, is not to impart training in handicraft even under the stimulus of state grants, but rather to see that the instruction given does not produce "more harm than good by stereotyping present methods instead of leaving the powers of rapid and intelligent adaptation to ever changing conditions."

The fact that "a man needs knowledge, not only as a means of livelihood, but as a means of life," is the guiding principle of university extension. The training which discloses to the student no new conceptions of the dignity of labor and of the richness and variety of life even under humble circumstances is unworthy the name of education. The pith of the matter can hardly be better stated than has been done in an open letter addressed by two workingmen to English cooperative societies urging on them the general adoption of university extension. "What we particularly need," they state, "is to break up this notion (that unless knowledge in some way affects our incomes it is not worth the trouble of acquiring) and create a sympathy with and desire for knowledge, because it broadens life, heightens pleasure and puts us in communication with the best that has been said and thought and known."

General conclusions. The foregoing sketch of the development and present organization of the university extension system leads to certain conclusions of weight in the consideration of the movement as a whole.

1 *Popular demand for higher education.* There is clearly a demand on the people's part for something of the higher cul-

ture. In every community there are men and women anxious to keep up some form of study for the sake of their own intellectual life. To such as these the extension of university teaching comes as a boon of which every advantage is most eagerly accepted and profitably enjoyed. There are others whose strength would be turned into channels of questionable benefit to themselves and to society were they not attracted to the harmless, if not stimulating, occupations suggested by extension methods

2 *Universities can supply demand.* It has been demonstrated that the universities can supply the teaching force and means of supervision requisite for bringing certain phases of the higher culture within reach of those who can not themselves seek it at the fountain head. The universities can do this, too, without perversion of their highest interests; nay they must find inspiration and renewed vigor in the very process of conveying to an expectant constituency those forces which make for culture and righteousness. Unless it be true that the higher institutions of learning exist for the privileged few, the benefits that proceed indirectly from cloistered retreats are not to be compared with the active influence that may be exerted when citizen and scholar stand shoulder to shoulder in the promotion of the common weal.

3 *Progress limited by lack of financial support.* The one great hindrance, however, to the progress of the movement and that which most limits its educational influence, is the lack of sufficient financial support. Workingmen with an income of but a few shillings a week and with a family to support can not pay the usual rate of five or 10 shillings a course. Rural centers must content themselves with reading circles or correspondence teaching. The great majority of centers, even those on permanent foundations, must continue to " sandwich Shakspere between electricity and Praxiteles " in order to retain paying members of varying tastes. Only in towns of considerable size can parallel courses be maintained for the benefit of students interested in different lines of study. Still more difficult is it to support attractive courses for the masses, for those who would find pleasure in intellectual pursuits if they were not forced to seek it in centers frequented by those of a higher social status and among surroundings repugnant to personal pride. But

further there is the teacher to consider. Few men with the proper equipment can be induced to devote their life-work to the precarious profession of itinerant lecturer in which salaries range from £825 in England, and $4500 in America, down to absolute zero, the lower limit being oftener reached than the higher. Few men have the strength to endure the fatiguing journeys necessitated in circuit work among centers too poor to organize properly. District associations can not be maintained for lack of funds to support a permanent secretary. In brief, the best work of university extension is limited, its highest ideals rendered unattainable, because there is no foundation on which teachers can take their stand and feel themselves secure; there is no assurance that when the people ask for bread they will not receive a stone

4 *Movement must remain voluntary.* The movement from its inception has been voluntary and so must it remain. Paradoxical as it may seem this characteristic is at once its weakness and its strength. Local centers may have erred in choice of subject, they may have selected the Attic drama instead of hygiene and domestic economy; by failure to cooperate with their next-town neighbors, they may have spent a goodly sum for railway travel that might have been better applied; all this they may have done and more, but what would have been the result had the university said "Take this course just as it is and in just this way and by this teacher, or nothing?" Compulsory higher education is an anomaly that needs no explanation. State inspection which looks to success in examinations, governmental grants based on attendance or any other tangible result, regulations in the interest of a more symmetric system and for facility in central management, are in the nature of things opposed to those interests based on personal freedom. *Lehrfreiheit* is an essential of university education. If some choose a lesser good in place of a greater, the conclusion does not follow that what they secure is necessarily bad. In fact it may be doubted if the system of university extension could long endure with state paid teachers or a constituency assisted to such a degree as to make self-help no longer necessary. It rests to-day on a purely missionary basis; its strength is that it brings to

earnest, self-sacrificing students that power which can be appreciated and properly used only by those who are, or can become, interested in truth for its own sake

5 *Necessary element of a democratic educational system.* Finally, the permanency of this great educational movement is dependent on economic laws deeper and more profound than the enthusiastic encomiums of its friends or the drastic criticisms of those who oppose it. If by judicious management coupled with precisely the right degree of financial support the system could be extended to every community that wishes it, there would still be uppermost that most important question, "To what end"? The answer will be returned in terms of each man's philosophy; the final decision will be dictated according to the spirit of the times. Those who sniff danger in every wind that blows the people any good, who see in every concession made to a strong and rising democracy a menace to the state and to civilization, will view with alarm the progress of any movement that tends to put increased power into the hands of many. There are others, too, with the deepest interest in humanity who fear the consequences of pressing on every one a higher education, which few at best can enjoy and which for the many may be only the means of wakening hopes and aspirations beyond the possibility of fulfilment. Another party sees in universal education, in the extension of the higher culture to every inquiring mind, the only efficient means — the *only* means worthy of an enlightened age — of combating successfully the direst influences pervading the social fabric of the time. What is needed, from this point of view, is an education that will produce a greatness of character commensurate with the responsibilities of modern political life, an education that will vouchsafe a strength of patriotic purpose unassailable by conniving politicians or prating demagogues, an education impregnated with the highest ideals of life and abounding in the noblest conceptions of man's duty to his fellow-man. If the extension of university teaching, considered as a whole, contributes to these highest ends it becomes an essential factor in a national system of education. It needs no further apology.

PEDAGOGIC CONSIDERATIONS IN THE EXTENSION OF UNIVERSITY TEACHING

Conception of education. Education is a means to an end, not an end in itself. Popular disregard of this very patent distinction leads to endless confusion in the consideration of pedagogic matters. Departments of education, when they systemize the schools to the extent of crushing out all individuality on the pupil's part, are not wholly guiltless of promoting such misconceptions. State and society intensify the error when they permit considerations of civil and social rank to become identified with the completion of successive steps in the school curriculum. When intelligent people talk of getting their education at this or that institution, or when they send their daughters to "finishing" schools, it is little wonder that false ideas should arise, that the ends of education should become confounded with the means.

In all education there is one necessary presupposition — a person to be educated, a mind responsive to influences. It is equally certain that the educational process is one of development. Development of some kind being assured, the determining factors are the individual and the forces which beset him. The overpowering necessity of establishing harmony between the individual and his surroundings determines directly or indirectly the whole of his conscious life. The mind is receptive, it gets impressions and yields itself to the influences of its environment, but it is also active, and reacts on its environment; it thinks, feels and wills. Whatever view is accepted of the relative worth of internal and external forces in education, individuality is always presupposed. It follows that what is acquired is conditioned by the temperament of the individual and by the content of thought already at hand.

Education conditioned by subjective receptivity. If the educational process is the evolution of an individual mind, a concrete, subjective process, it becomes evident that influences are good or bad, strong or weak, precisely in so far as they enter into the inner life and determine its character. It is nothing to me that potent forces exist if they exist merely for others; for me personally they are neither potent nor forces. What matters it that my surroundings are mean and degrading in the eyes of the world if for me they are pure and elevating? What avail is it that an atmosphere of culture and refinement is about me if all that I breathe in be debasing? It is the use that is made of opportunities, not opportunities themselves, that counts.

Commonplace as such argument is, a logical application of its principles would dispel many popular delusions and revise some accepted pedagogic theories. Education is not entirely a matter of schooling, of tutorial skill or personal influence; it need not be dependent on blind chance, nor is it solely the result of voluntary effort under purely subjective conditions.

Education not confined to school days. The development of the higher life is continuous from birth to death, if, indeed, any limits whatsoever can be postulated. "One is never too old to learn" means that one's education is never completed. Each mind steadfast enough to assimilate and inform its own impressions advances consciously or unconsciously toward definite ends. It may be possible that circumstances over which the individual can have no control undesignedly determine a course from which there is no turning, but experience offers the reasonable hope of attaining definite ends when personal inclination and external influence are favorable. It is on this basis that educational systems must stand. Schools and teachers are humble instruments for lending symmetry and direction to the mental development of the young. So, too, family and social relations, professional and industrial life, the church, press and theater, duties of citizenship, nature—all these are educative forces and exert an influence more or less marked according as the learner's mind is inclined to receive and apply them. The school of life is the one great educational institution. Its greatest teachers are those means by which the largest number of individual minds are turned toward that goal which they instinctively recognize as highest. It is immaterial whether these means, these teachers, are persons or things. The only language which they speak is a spiritual one, intelligible only to those who can apprehend it, of worth solely to those who apply it.

Function of school training. No discredit is cast on the schools by the fact that they are not the be-all and end-all of edu cation It is enough that they ease the path of the learner at a critical age and start him in the right direction. They may well rejoice in unrestricted access to the accumulated knowledge of the centuries and in their abilities to place it temptingly before youthful minds. Further, it is granted to men, specially men of the schools, so to modify the learner's environment, to select and systemize the influences which play on him, that his development will approximate a designed form Herein lies the secret of the teacher's power, and it is a power not to be underestimated. The mistake comes when it is asserted that schoolmen are the only teachers and that orthodox "seats of learning" are the only educational institutions. As long as children are born into family and social relations, as long as the young instinctively sit at the feet of their elders, as long as books and nature are accessible, so long will there be teachers and pupils outside the schools. It is the hight of absurdity to judge of a man's education by the school through which he has passed, as if in any case development ceased with the schooldays. The artisan who spends his days at the bench, the miner living for the most part underground or the business man engrossed in the duties of his calling, may, indeed, have had very little schooling, but it does not follow that he is uneducated. Nor does the fact that a man bears a university degree infallibly bespeak the highest culture. Results of education may not be reckoned in units of time ; least of all by such objective standards as the world generally applies. On pedagogic grounds, therefore, no means of education should be excluded simply because of variance from established precedents. The possibility of systematically directing the mental-spiritual development of the individual beyond the days of childhood is an important contribution to modern pedagogy.

Interest of the state in education. One consideration outweighs all others from the view-point of society and the state: the persistency and continuity of the educational process. It is not a question of education or no education, but rather of a true or a false education. The units composing the body politic undergo continual development. Some are carefully brought under influences of a nature best calculated to fit them for commanding positions in the world. To the select few the state looks for the formation and execution of her laws; society beholds in them the supporters of the moral order and the guardians of her cherished institutions. The successful workings of such an organization presuppose leaders possessed of a high order of statesmanship and a constituency at all times submissive and tractable. That such conditions should be found in a democratic age is not to be expected save on the hypothesis that the masses are educated to a high sense of personal responsibility in furthering the common weal. There is no question that the masses are being educated; but how? The one extreme discloses homes destitute of every vestige of refinement, social relations of which the predominating characteristics are envy, lust and crime, industrial oppression that intensifies the horrors of the struggle for existence; it offers, too, the leadership of ignorant, prating demagogues, designing politicians and malcontents of every class whose crafty selfishness is paralleled only by their tenacity of purpose. These are the powers of darkness. Such is the environment of a considerable part of the social body. No one, however, looks for uniformity in this world. A personality all his own is every man's birthright, but its worth is conditioned by the source from which it draws its strength.

Insufficiency of school training. Now, what is the state doing? The great majority of citizens are in school considerably less than eight years; an insignificant minority pass on to university training. Those who can neither read nor write far outnumber the learned few. This means for the many a knowledge of reading and writing with some exercise in elementary reasoning. It is not impossible that during this process so good a foundation should be laid that nothing could afterward shake the superstructure, but experience teaches that the man is not always what was promised in the boy. The most enthusiastic supporters of the elementary schools, or of schools of any grade, will hardly claim that a "universal education" has proved to be the panacea for all ills, civic and social, as was so confidently predicted a few decades ago. Is it reasonable to hope for peace when an unscrupulous and hungry mob stands armed at the doors? We have given the masses intellectual weapons of no small caliber, but without practical directions for their use. Shall we stand idly by while hostile leaders train these forces to conduct a bitter warfare against us? It may fairly be doubted if after all it is prudent to teach men to read but to take no pains that they read what is good, or having trained them to reason if it is right to withhold that knowledge from which alone sound conclusions can be drawn. If it is worth while to *begin* the training of citizens for popular self government, surely hearty encouragement should be extended to every effort that helps to bring that process to a sound fruition. The church and press, benevolent and charitable organizations, circulating libraries, social settlements and the like, are earnestly striving to increase the sum total of right thinking and pure living, but in the multiplicity of forces some unifying agent is essential to the best results. It matters little what that agent is if it appeals to the individual on his own grounds. The spirit of the genuine teacher must be present showing the learner how to arrange his mental store, how to convert it into power. To the man who can read, it should teach the right use of the newspaper and periodical; it should give him a discriminating sense in the selection of books and assist him to a right use of their contents; it should help him to understand nature better, to attain to nobler conceptions of the true and the beautiful; and to all who will hear, it should speak of peace and good-will among men and of steadfast adherence to the highest principles of faith and reason. On mere prudential grounds society dare not dispense with any means, howsoever humble, that tends to increase the general culture.

Interest of the university in popular education. The university, standing at the head of the school system and guaranteeing the character and validity of all that is the subject of instruction in schools of every grade, is and must remain the most influential means of culture in modern society. All other educative forces appeal to the university for indorsement. Here are learned men devoting their lives to the extension of the limits of knowledge; here "any person can find instruction in any study." The progress of civilization is to no small extent conditioned by the unrestricted search for truth and freedom in its promulgation. History tells all too clearly the story of the oppression of the scholar and its baneful effects; it tells too that other story of progress and discovery under the banner of *Lehrfreiheit.*

The university has reached its present position of honor and usefulness, it must be conceded, under the patronage of a few liberal-minded men who have occupied at critical times places of influence in the state. If the modern university exists for the favored few, it is as certainly true that the favored few have made the university. At every step there has been opposition and often it has come from sources least expected. Men of rank, so-called educated men, have earnestly striven to impede the progress of truth for no better reason than that it did not appeal to them as true or because it conflicted with their temporary interests Shortsightedness and intolerance are weaknesses of human nature. A man's judgment is oftener warped by the little that he thinks he knows than by the combined wisdom of all other men besides. Heresy trials and courts of inquiry exhibit plainly enough the natural inclination even at the present day to distrust the power of truth to win its way in triumph over error.

Dangers in democracy. In the light of experience the query may well be raised as to the probable effects on the organs of higher education consequent on the balance of power in the state going over to the people. It is clear that men unacquainted with the history of civilization can have no definite basis for the exercise of right judgment in those matters of most concern to the scholar, and where reason fails and the spirit of the times is equivocal it is presumptuous to hope that men will long maintain faith in virtues which transcend their powers of comprehension. Abstract reasoning and patient research are not of a nature to appeal seriously to persons whose only measure of honest work is muscular fatigue. A hundred years of American history show with what reluctance a popular government comes to the support of higher schools and how great is the inclination to make the curricula conform to an apparent practical point of view. The average man is slow of persuasion that the university benefits all classes; that "of all forms of government a democracy has most to gain from higher education and most to lose from its neglect."

The danger that besets the university, and indirectly all formal education, in the spread of democracy is by no means illusory. When the popular will becomes the voice of the state no institution dependent on public support or tolerance can long endure if actively engaged in opposing the wishes of the people. No ruling power gracefully assents to flat contradiction or views without anxiety the operation of forces concerned in undermining the seat of authority.

The remedy. Among English-speaking peoples, where democracy becomes annually more pronounced, there is but one recourse remaining; the popular will must be made to conform to the public good. We can not dispense with any legitimate means of culture, least of all with the sources of the deepest influences in the national life. The higher education must be retained in its integrity. Motives of expediency and common sense alike dictate a careful consideration of present conditions with a view to reasonable adjustment to future requirements. In so far as the university considers the needs only of a special class, thus fostering on the one hand false notions of education and on the other a hypocritical contempt for the practical life of the people, so far must it be reformed; in so far as university teaching is sacrificed to original investigation, or the spirit of research dulled in the effort to become popular, so far is reorganization a necessity; both are legitimate functions and of equal worth. If the university entertains the idea that its mission transcends the ordinary affairs of life, that those who would approach it should put off their shoes as a sign that the place whereon they stand is holy ground, the modern spirit suggests a rude awakening. The university exists for the individual, society, the nation; it should set no higher aim than to inspire ordinary mortals with love for "the truth that makes men free." It dares no longer remain a sequestered "seat of learning" absorbed in the petty interests of its own little world. The university must so far identify itself with the life of the people as to understand their wants that it may the better utilize their energy. The future of the higher education is doomed unless its promoters come to recognize the inexorableness of the moral injunction resting on those to whom much has been given. Democracy becomes tolerant of learning only when it is taught to respect the past services of higher education, to appreciate its present worth in concrete form and to have faith in its honesty of purpose for the future.

University extension and the spirit of the times. The principles of university extension, it needs hardly be asserted, harmonize to a remarkable degree with the spirit of the times. The movement refuses to recognize a monopoly of culture. It makes a broad distinction between mere learning and true culture, between the preparation which enables one to do something and the spiritual development whose aim is to be something. It aims to systemize and reduce to concrete terms those educational forces which stand in closest relation to the individual; it strives to give him such mastery over his environment, such insight into its unalterable requirements, as will make him a desirable member of society, truly appreciative of that which lies within his sphere and tolerant of all that extends beyond it. Its standards are purely relative. There is no prescribed course, no highest degree, no graduating class. To substitute a more definite aim for the vague unrest pervading unoccupied minds, to neutralize the evil effects of bad teachings by a forcible presentation of the truth, to inspire men with warmer emotions, higher impulses, nobler ambitions — these are its legitimate functions.

Limits of the movement. Beneficent and praiseworthy as may be its virtues, there are bounds beyond which the movement must not pass. It is much to be feared that in the flush of first victory its leaders may be tempted to enter on campaigns for which they are ill fitted and in which they must suffer heavy loss. University extension teaching is no substitute for school training. It can never take the place of the church any more than it can hope to supersede the press or family. It should offer no royal road to learning, nor pose as a short cut to the university. The cloud on the horizon — already larger than a man's hand — bodes a coming storm if the question of certificates and degrees becomes increasingly more prominent. Recognition of honest worth is not debasing, but it is both debasing and demoralizing to judge the results of university extension teaching by the absolute standards of the schools. There is no doubt that such tests can be applied, there are presumably grounds for asserting that extension students occasionally attain to high grades of scholarship, but if the hope of material reward be the student's chief inducement it were better that he spare his pains. It would be no less a blunder to array university extension against the schools than to despoil the integrity of university degrees by impressing them into an alien service. Better have fewer courses and smaller attendance than foster overmuch confidence in a show of learning.

Future possibilities. The promoters of this new movement in education are engaged in no simple task. In its final analysis their aim is no other than to harmonize sound educational methods with the democratic tendencies of the age. The possibilities which lie before them may well inspire to heroic effort and beget a zeal akin to religious fervor. But two decades of progress make only a beginning The obstacles which have been overcome are merely preparatory to those yet to be surmounted. The problems on which the destiny of the movement hangs still await solution. Chief among these, because based on a popular misconception of the nature of culture, is the vulgar demand for knowledge which can be measured in materialistic units. With a fidelity worthy of imitation among a wider circle of educators, university extension teachers, however, maintain that culture has no cash value, that education together with religion belongs to the permanent interests of life The motto of the London society is its creed: "Man needs knowledge, not only as a means of livelihood, but as a means of life." It remains to be seen whether democracy will accept this in its integrity as an article of its faith.

APPENDIX

The writer desires to express his obligations to the secretaries of the principal extension organizations in England and America for assistance given him in the collection of material for this study in practical pedagogics; he is specially indebted to M. E. Sadler, secretary of the Oxford university extension delegacy, and to Melvil Dewey, secretary of the University of the State of New York and director of the extension department, for criticism and verification of parts of the manuscript. The authorities cited in the following bibliography of recent literature on the subject have been supplemented by personal experience, by information contained in circulars of instruction, official announcements, secretaries' reports and other documents issued by the various main centers, by press notices and by correspondence with persons engaged in the work.

December, 1894.

BIBLIOGRAPHY

Adams, H. B. Progress of university extension. (University of the State of New York. Extension bulletin 5: 179–84. Reprinted from Cong. 25 Ag 92.)

—— University extension and its leaders. (University of the State of New York. Extension bulletin, 5: 199–225 Reprinted from Review of reviews 3: 593–609.)

American society for the extension of university teaching. Proceedings of the 1st annual meeting of the national conference on university extension held in Phil. Dec. 29–31, 1891. 292 p O Phil. 1892.

Boughton, Willis. University extension (see Arena 4: 452–5E).

Cambridge university. Report of a conference on university work under the county councils.

—— Report of the 4th summer meeting. Camb. 1893.

—— Report on instruction given in technical science under county councils. v. 3. Camb. 1893.

Collins, J. C. The ideal university (see 19th cent. 80: 243–54).

—— The universities in contact with the people (see 19th cent. 26: 561–83).

Dewey, Melvil. New York's part in university extension. (University of the State of New York. Extension circular. no. 7. Alb. 1891. Reprinted from Critic 16: 90.)

Extension bulletins. no. 1–7, O. Alb. 1891–94.

BIBLIOGRAPHY

Healey, E. Educational systems of Sweden, Norway and Denmark. Lond. 1892. Healey

International university extension congress. Report of proceedings. O. Lond. 1894. Intern U E. Rept

James, G: F. Handbook of university extension; 2d ed. enl. with an introd. by E. J. James. 421 p. O. Phil. 1893.

Mackinder, H. J. *and* Sadler, M. E. University extension, past, present and future. Ed. 3 enl. 144 p. D. Lond. 1891. Macki & Sadl

Mullaney, J: F. University extension of the Catholic summer school (*see* Am. Cath. q. 18· 166–75).

Oxford university extension gazette. v 1–5, Q Ox. 1890–95. O. G.

Palmer, G. H. Doubts about university extension (*see* Atlan. 69. 367–74).

Playfair, Lyon, *baron*, and others. Aspects of modern study; being university extension addresses. 187 p. D. N. Y. 1894.

Roberts, R. D. Eighteen years of university extension. Ed. 2. Camb. 1894. Robe

Sadler, M. E. Facts about university extension (*see* 19th cent. 36: 371–82).

Stuart, L. E. Facts about university extension (*see* 19th cent. 36: 383–88).

University extension. v. 1–4, O. Phil. 1891–94. U E

University extension bulletin. v. 1, Q. Phil. 1893–94. U E B

University extension journal. v. 1–5, Q Lond. 1890–95. U. E. J

University extension world. v. 1, Q. v. 2–4, O. Chic 1891–94. U. E.

Whibley, Charles. The farce of university extension (*see* 19th cent. 36: 203–10, 598–603).

INDEX

The superior figure tells the exact place on the page in ninths, e. g. 185² means two ninths of the way down page 185. Dates are printed in italics.

Acland, Arthur, first secretary of Oxford dep't of extension teaching, 167⁹, lectures for workingmen, 211⁹.
Adams, H. B., appeal for extension work before American library association, 176¹.
Africa, extension work, 185².
Agassiz, Louis, founder of summer schools, 160⁵
Agriculture, extension work, 233², scientific instruction in, 159⁸–60⁵
America, educational progress, 157⁹–61⁵, growth of extension work, 176–84⁸, outlook for extension movement, 203⁵, statistics, 221².
American society for the extension of university teaching, formation, 180⁹–81². *See also* Philadelphia.
Australia, extension work, 184⁸–85², 195⁶.
Austria, extension work, 187⁸.

Belgium, extension work, 186²–87⁹.
Bemis, E. W., course at Buffalo, 176⁵
Bibliography of extension literature, 246⁵–47.
Books *see* Reading, Traveling libraries.
Boston institute of technology, *see* Massachusetts institute of technology.
Bowdoin college, interest in extension work, 184².
Brooklyn, early extension work, 177⁷.
Brown university, cooperation with extension movement, 183⁷, 213⁵.
Brussels, conference at, 187⁹.

Buffalo library, first course in America at, 176².

California, extension work in state university, 183³.
Cambridge university, reforms in, 155²–56⁴, local examinations adopted, 155⁶–56⁴, Prof. Stuart's appeal to, 164¹; first courses given by, 165⁶, affiliated centers, 172³–73⁵; management of extension work, 194⁸–95¹; summer school, 215⁷, 218¹
Canada, extension work, 184⁶
Centers, organization, 188⁸–92¹, expenses, 189⁵–90², 192¹–94², 199⁷–201⁹; choice of secretary, 190², federated, 193⁴–94².
Central organizations, early efforts toward, 163²–65⁵, expenses, 200⁸–1⁹; functions, 196¹, methods of control, 194⁷–96¹; possible aids, 191⁷, tendencies, 194⁹; in Chicago, 182³–in New York, 178¹–79⁹.
Certificate, *see* Credentials
Chautauqua university, extension movement, 176⁶–77⁸, summer school, 166⁶.
Chicago, extension movement, 181⁸–83¹. *See also* University of Chicago
Christian socialist movement 152¹.
Cincinnati university, interest in extension work, 184², 213⁶; system of control, 195⁹–96¹.
Circuit plan, 192⁸–93⁴.
Class, 207⁹–8⁵; introduction in extension work, 163².
Class courses, 182⁵, 213¹–14².

Colby university, interest in extension work, 184².
Colgate university, interest in extension work, 184².
Colleges interested in extension movement, 184¹. *See also* University extension colleges.
Conference, international, on university extension, 201⁹-2⁶; recommendations, 202⁶-3⁵
Continuation of extension work, various methods, 210²-19⁹.
Cooperative associations of workingmen, 152⁵; peripatetic cooperative university, 163⁷.
Correspondence teaching, 182⁸, 212⁵.
Courses, admission to, 208⁹; circuit plan, 192⁶-93⁴; concurrent, 191⁵; expenses, 189⁸-90², 192⁷-94², 199⁷-201⁹, earliest given, 162⁸, 165⁶; improved methods, 222⁴-2₃⁹, among miners, 169⁶-70⁷; number in England during *1894*, 175¹; in sequence, 191⁸, for special classes, 230⁵-33⁵, offered in summer schools, 216⁵-19⁵. *See also* Class; Class courses, Examinations, Lectures, Paper work; Syllabus.
Courses and methods in the extension of university teaching, 203-19.
Credentials, 203⁷, 20ɔ¹, 245¹.

Denison, Edward, work among London poor, 152².
Denmark, connection of schools with extension work, 185⁹-86².
Dewey, Melvil, interest in extension movement, 178²; acknowledgments to, 246².

Education, conception of, 237¹-38², century's progress, 156⁴-57⁹, influences affecting progress, 148⁵-50⁸, influence of university, 241⁸-44², should extend beyond school days, 238⁸-39⁸; importance to state, 239⁶-41⁸, 243⁸-44²; state aid to, 153⁷-54⁵, 157⁸, 158⁷-59⁶. *See also* Public school system, Technical education.
Educational progress in England and America, 148-61.

England, annual expenditures for extension work, 220⁸, courses given during *1894*, 175¹, development of university extension, 161-75; founders of university extension, 175²; number of centers, 220⁴; political changes, 152⁶-53⁵, progress of education in, 150⁹-7⁹, statistics of extension work, 221⁴.
Espinas, M, commissioned to report on extension movement, 224⁶.
Examinations, 208⁵, value, 161⁸, 209⁵-10². *See also* Local examinations.
Examiners, reports, 224⁹-25⁵.
Expenses, 189⁸-90², 192⁷-94², 199⁷-201⁹.
Extension centers, *see* Centers.
Extension colleges, 173⁵-74², 192¹.
Extension courses, *see* Courses.
Extension lectures, *see* Lectures.
Extension literature, bibliography, 246⁵-47, periodicals, 196⁴.
Extension movement, aim, 203⁹-5², 244², change of public sentiment, 174⁵-75²; dark days, 169²; a factor in democratic educational system, 236¹; need of financial support, 234⁵-35⁴; founders in England, 175²; meaning 148¹; origin, 162¹-64¹; pedagogic considerations, 237-45, possibilities, 245⁵; results of 21 years of progress, 220-36, in Africa, 185²; in Australia, 184⁸-85⁴, in continental Europe, 185⁴-88²; in England, progress, 161-75,
in America, difficulties, 180², growth, 176-84⁸; outlook, 203⁵.
Extension teachers, *see* Teachers.
Extension teaching, *see* Teaching.
Extension work, class distinctions disregarded, 229⁵-30⁵; criticism, 228¹-29⁵; efficiency of, 224⁴-26³, expenditures in England, 220⁸, influence on individuals and society, 226²-29⁵; connection with libraries, 176², 206⁷, 227⁴, limitations, 244⁸-45⁵, means of continuation, 210²-19⁹, organization, 188-208; state aid to, 179¹-203¹, various features, 196⁹-97⁶, must remain voluntary, 235⁴-36¹.

Farmers, extension work for, 159⁶-60⁵, 233²

Fees, lecturers, 199²-200², 235¹.
Founders of extension movement in England, 175².
France, extension movement in, 187², investigation of extension movement by Ministry of education, 224⁶.
Free schools, *see* Public schools

Ghent, extension work at university, 186⁵.
Gresham college students' association, object, 211¹
Gresham university commission, 174²

Harper, W· R., extension work, 176⁹-77¹, 182¹.
Higher education, demand for, 233²-34⁵, relation to state, 158⁷-59², 286², necessity of in democratic government, 242⁵-44².
Home reading circles, 211⁶-12⁷.

Illinois, extension work in state university, 183³.
Illiteracy in England, statistics, 154².
Indiana, extension work in state university, 183³.
Industrial activity, progress, 149³, 150⁹-51⁵.
Industrial education, appropriation for, 170⁷-72².
Industrial schools, establishment in England, 153⁶.
International conference on university extension, 201⁹-2⁸, recommendations, 202⁸-3⁵
Iowa, extension work in state university, 183³
Italy, interest in extension work, 187⁶

Kansas, extension work in state university, 183³.
Kingsley, Charles, founding of Christian socialist movement, 152¹
Knowledge, increased possibilities, 150⁴.

Leclerc, Max, quoted, 224⁸
Lecturers, *see* Teachers.
Lectures, 205⁹-7¹; course vs single lecture, 162⁴, 172⁴. *See also* Courses, Lyceum system

Legislative appropriations for extension work, 179¹
Libraries, connection with extension work, 176², 206⁷, 227⁴. *See also* Traveling libraries
Literature of extension movement, 196²; bibliography, 246⁵-47.
Local examinations adopted by Oxford and Cambridge, 155⁵-56⁴.
London, workingmen's college in, 152², extension work in, 166⁵-67⁵; union of educational institutions recommended, 174², courses for workingmen, 232⁵
London society for the extension of university teaching formed, 167¹; scheme of control, 195⁶.
Lyceum system, 159².

Massachusetts institute of technology, cooperation with extension work, 216⁶.
Maurice, F· D , founding of Christian socialist movement, 151⁹-52²
Mechanic arts, education in, 159⁸-60⁵.
Melbourne university extension journal, 196¹.
Methods in extension teaching, 20⁷-19.
Michigan, extension work in state university, 183³
Miners, extension work among, 169⁸-70¹, 210⁵, 226⁵-27², 231⁵
Minnesota, extension work in, 185⁵
Missouri, extension work in state university, 183³
Morrill land grant, 160¹.
Moulton, R. G., extension work in America, 180⁷, 182⁸

New York, progress of extension movement in, 177⁹-80², library extension work, 179⁵, 227⁶, organization of extension work, 195²; number of centers, 220⁹, special features, 221⁷.
New Zealand, interest in extension work, 185²
Norway, extension work in, 185⁴-86².
Note-taking in extension courses, 162⁵.
Nottingham, early educational efforts, 151⁹.

University of the State of New York

Object. The object of the University as defined by law is to encourage and promote education in advance of the common elementary branches. Its field includes not only the work of academies, colleges, universities, professional and technical schools but also educational work connected with libraries, museums, university extension courses and similar agencies.

The University is a supervisory and administrative, not a teaching institution. It is a state department and at the same time a federation of more than 500 institutions of higher and secondary education.

Government. The University is governed and all its corporate powers exercised by 19 elective regents and by the governor, lieutenant-governor, secretary of state and superintendent of public instruction who are *ex officio* regents. Regents are elected in the same manner as United States senators; they are unsalaried and are the only public officers in New York chosen for life.

The elective officers are a chancellor and a vice-chancellor who serve without salary, and a secretary.

The secretary, under official bonds for $10,000, is responsible for the safe keeping and proper use of the University seal and of the books, records and other property in charge of the regents, and for the proper administration and discipline of its various offices and departments.

Powers and duties. Beside many other important powers and duties, the regents have power to incorporate, and to alter or revoke the charters of universities, colleges, academies, libraries, museums, or other educational institutions; to distribute to them funds granted by the state for their use; to inspect their workings and require annual reports under oath of their presiding officers; to establish examinations as to attainments in learning and confer on successful candidates suitable certificates, diplomas and degrees, and to confer honorary degrees.

They apportion annually an academic fund of $106,000, part for buying books and apparatus for academies and high schools raising an equal amount for the same purpose, and the remainder on the basis of attendance and the results of instruction as shown by satisfactory completion of prescribed courses for which the regents examinations afford the official test. They also expend annually $25,000 for the benefit of free public libraries.

Regents meetings. Regular quarterly meetings are held on the fourth Thursdays of November, February and May. Special meetings are held whenever business requires.

Convocation. The University convocation of the regents and the officers of institutions in the University, for consideration of subjects of mutual interest, has been held annually since 1863 in the senate chamber in Albany. Convocation meets on the last Wednesday, Thursday and Friday in June.

Though primarily a New York meeting, nearly all questions discussed are of equal interest outside the state. Its reputation as the most important higher educational meeting of the country has in the past few years drawn to it many eminent educators not residents of New York, who are most cordially welcomed and share fully in all discussions. It elects each year a council of five to represent it in intervals between meetings. Its proceedings issued annually are of great value in all educational libraries.

University of the State of New York

Departments

1 Administrative (Regents office) — including incorporation, supervision, inspection, reports, legislation, finances and all other work not assigned to another department.

Duplicate division. This is a state clearing house, to which any institution in the University may send books or apparatus which it no longer requires and select from it in return an equal value suited to its locality and needs.

2 Examination — including preacademic, law student, medical, dental and veterinary student, academic, higher, law, medical, dental, veterinary, library, extension and any other examinations conducted by the regents, and also credentials or degrees conferred on examination.

The examinations are conducted as the best lever for securing better work from teachers and more systematic and continuous study from students, and as the best means of detecting and eliminating inefficient teachers or methods. They cover 130 subjects and require 1,500,000 question papers annually, and are held the week ending the last Friday in January and March and the third Friday in June, in the 502 academies and high schools in the University and also at various central points where there are 10 or more candidates.

3 Extension — including summer, vacation, evening and correspondence schools and other forms of extension teaching, lecture courses, study clubs, reading circles and other agencies for the promotion and wider extension of opportunities and facilities for education, specially for those unable to attend the usual teaching institutions

Public libraries division. To promote the general library interests of the state, which through it expends $25,000 a year for the benefit of free public libraries. Under its charge are the traveling libraries for lending to local libraries or to communities not yet having permanent libraries.

The most important factor of the extension movement is provision of the best reading for all citizens by means of traveling, home and capitol libraries and annotated lists through the public libraries division.

4 State library — including state law, medical, and education libraries, library school, bibliographic publications, lending books to students and similar library interests.

Library school. The law authorizes the state library to give to any librarian, assistant, or other person interested in any library in the state, instruction and assistance in organizing and administering libraries. Students receive from the state library staff, in return for services rendered to the library during their two years' course, careful training in cataloging, classification and all other duties of professional librarianship.

5 State museum — including all scientific specimens and collections, works of art, objects of historic interest and similar property appropriate to a general museum, if owned by the state and not placed in other custody by a specific law; also the research department carried on by the state geologist and paleontologist, botanist and entomologist, and all similar scientific interests of the University.

registration ....
es ....
....
....
....
....
rganizations aiding study clubs .. ..
clubs. ....
clubs of New York in order of registration .
red................................
....
....
....
....

ALBANY
NIVERSITY OF THE STATE OF NEW YORK
1895

Regents

Anson Judd Upson, D. D., LL. D., L. H. D., *Chancellor*
William Croswell Doane, D. D., LL. D., *Vice-Chancellor*
Levi P. Morton, LL. D., Governor ⎫
Charles T. Saxton, LL. D., Lieutenant-Governor ⎪
John Palmer, Secretary of State ⎬ *Ex officio*
Charles R. Skinner, M. A., LL. D., Sup't of Pub. Inst. ⎭

In order of election by the legislature

YEAR
1873	Martin I. Townsend, M. A., LL. D.	Troy
1874	Anson Judd Upson, D. D., LL. D., L. H. D.	Glens Falls
1876	William L. Bostwick, M. A.	Ithaca
1877	Chauncey M. Depew, LL. D.	New York
1877	Charles E. Fitch, LL. B., M. A., L. H. D.	Rochester
1877	Orris H. Warren, D. D.	Syracuse
1878	Whitelaw Reid, LL. D.	New York
1881	William H. Watson, M. A., M. D.	Utica
1881	Henry E. Turner	Lowville
1883	St Clair McKelway, LL. D.	Brooklyn
1885	Hamilton Harris, LL. D.	Albany
1885	Daniel Beach, Ph. D., LL. D.	Watkins
1888	Carroll E. Smith	Syracuse
1890	Pliny T. Sexton, LL. D.	Palmyra
1890	T. Guilford Smith, M. A., C. E.	Buffalo
1892	William Croswell Doane, D. D., LL. D.	Albany
1893	Lewis A. Stimson, B. A., M. D.	New York
1894	Sylvester Malone	Brooklyn
1895	Albert Vander Veer, M. D., Ph. D.	Albany

Elected by the regents

1888	Melvil Dewey, M. A., *Secretary*	Albany

University of the State of New York

Extension Bulletin
No. 11   November 1895

STUDY CLUBS

The extension department of the University of the State of New York includes all registered agencies for higher education outside the regular teaching institutions, i. e. schools, academies, colleges. So cordial has been the welcome given to the effort to make education available to all, that the number of agencies for home study organized in the past 10 years marks the decade as an epoch in educational development. Much of the work however is desultory and unorganized. In many places it has entirely or partly failed for lack of systematic local efforts   No standards are set because none have existed and there has been lack of incentives to raise the work to higher grade.

In this line the great work of Chautauqua is too well known to need more than a reference. By outlining courses and requiring reports it has made systematic home study possible and has proved that such work can accomplish definite educational results, a theory by no means generally received a quarter of a century ago. Since this is now an admitted principle in the science of education no explanation is necessary for the statement that the University through its extension department recognizes home study as a distinct phase of its work.

The club division of the extension department includes study clubs, which expect of their members study, reading and usually some writing on the subject, during the interval between meetings; and reading circles, whose members are following the same systematic course of reading with more or less frequent meetings for discussion of the matter read. Many without time or inclination to undertake the work of a study club would be glad to engage in such a course, which may be registered with the same privileges as a study club. As the plan of work is the same for both sections, it is discussed under the general name of clubs.

Plan of work. The work of the division is to encourage the formation or to find out the existence of New York clubs for systematic study, and after registering them, to put at their disposal the various helps provided for them by the University.

The local work is sometimes directed by a lecturer or specialist on the subject studied but each club is entirely free to follow its own bent without leadership from outside. Most clubs however prefer if possible to have at least a few lectures on their subject by some one specially qualified. The relation of the department to the local organization is purely advisory and administrative, binding together the work of similar organizations throughout the state. In this way the experiments and conclusions of all may be focalized, and the best methods made available with a minimum expenditure of labor. By making known experiences shown in the reports, the energy now dissipated in working on problems already solved by other clubs may be utilized in more satisfactory ways. From time to time the department will issue bulletins giving statistics of work done by similar organizations at home and abroad, tabulated for comparison, together with details of progress and suggestions for more efficient work in the various lines of study pursued. Added to the recognized advantages of organized effort are the more definite privileges of registration, including loans of books, maps, pictures and apparatus, traveling libraries, exchanges, examinations, credentials and similar rights of regents centers.

Certificates of registration are issued under the University seal, clubs are recorded and numbered in order of establishment, a letter following the number indicating the extent of work undertaken. Clubs maintaining one course a year are marked E; two courses D; three or four courses C; five to nine courses B; and the largest and most active clubs maintaining 10 or more courses annually are marked A. Every club which on inspection is found to maintain at least the minimum standard required will receive a certificate stating that it is officially registered as study club no. . . This stamps the work as of superior grade, prompting the best to maintain their standing and inducing weaker organizations to raise their work at least to the minimum required for registration.

Requirements for registration. Not less than 10 weeks' work on the same general subject entitles to registration on the University lists. The provision of continued study on one subject prevents the waste of thought and energy common in clubs which take up a topic one week only to drive it out of mind the next by one totally different. 10 weeks of such desultory work are full of suggestions and impressions but so confused as to discourage the student from proceeding further. Worse than this, he has lost the thought development and mental culture which follow persistent investigation of a subject in its varied phases and beyond its surface ideas. This rare quality which every one feels is infinitely more to be desired than the mere acquisition of facts has no place in a plan which provides only for superficial study of constantly varying subjects.

The justification for selecting different topics for each week's study is that it gives entertaining variety and provides a subject for each meeting in which some members of the club are specially interested. Lord Playfair gives an amusing example of this effort to please all in a single course by quoting the program of the Mechanics' institute for 1845. It was as follows: "Wit and humor, with comic songs; Women, treated in a novel manner; Legerdemain and spirit rapping; The devil (with illustrations); The heavenly bodies in the stellar system; Palestine and the Holy Land; Speeches by eminent friends of education, interspersed with music, to be followed by a ball. Price for the whole 2s. 6d. Refreshments in the anteroom." The absurdity of this marvelous collection appeals to all, but it is only in a lesser degree that all variety programs lack true educational value. Yet this is the point hardest to impress on local managers who with the best of motives neutralize much of the educational value of their work by catering to the demand which results in the "variety hall" entertainments so much deplored by intelligent friends of music and the drama.

This criticism would not necessarily apply to those clubs whose subject is "Current topics," for this ought not to mean study of isolated subjects having no connection with each other. The study of recent movements and events is synthetic, bringing out causes and effects and the interrelation of the incidents of modern progress.

Besides the approved course of study, the only requirements for registration are that each club must have at least five members and must annually report its work on blanks supplied by the department. There are no registration fees. Clubs are advised to elect their officers and decide on the course of study in the spring so that the report may include the names of officers for the following year and the application for the traveling library, thus avoiding delay when the club is ready to begin work.

Guides for study. While holding the policy of non-interference, the department is always glad to give any practicable help in planning the program or in suggesting methods of study. While we do not offer to lay out entire courses of study for clubs, assistance over difficult points will be given and syllabuses will be lent from the duplicate collection to give further suggestions or to serve as the program for the club. Where the club does not wish to assume the responsibility of planning the work, extension syllabuses may be bought at cost of paper and press work, i. e. two cents for each eight pages. These syllabuses are used by lecturers at extension centers and contain for each of the 10 lectures an analysis of the lecture, references to books and periodicals, and topics for papers. These full notes in the hands of each member of the club have been found very satisfactory aids to thorough study. Sample copies for selection will be sent free to each registered club unless no syllabus on the subject chosen is available from our files, when the club will if possible be referred to some other central organization which has published a syllabus on the subject.

Traveling libraries. Study club libraries are made up from our extension and duplicate collections, of which since the books are constantly changing, we have only a card catalog. The printed finding lists of the traveling libraries for general reading will however be sent to suggest recent desirable books to clubs wishing to prepare their own list; if desired, the library will be made up for the club by the department. In either case the program of study must be sent in advance, to be used by the book board of the state library in approving the list recommended and so preventing any but the best books and most satisfactory editions from being sent. In a few subjects, traveling libraries of the 25 or 50 best books on the subject are already prepared, and when possible these should be taken, to avoid delay in buying other books.

These libraries will be supplied only for subjects on which at least five members of the club agree to study during not less than 10 weeks. As it does not belong to this plan to supply general reading, every book is expected to be of service to the student of the subject either for information, inspiration or illustration.

The fee for a library of 100 volumes is $5; for 75 volumes, $4; for 50 volumes, $3; and for 25 volumes, $2. The University pays transportation on club libraries only when the club agrees to form itself into a public library committee, keeping all the regents rules for public libraries in regard to hours of opening, records, etc, as outlined in the circular on traveling libraries. When circulation or reference is in any way restricted the club pays transportation.

A blank for application for a traveling library, containing also forms for trustees and librarians agreements, is supplied and this should be signed and forwarded with the fee in advance. To avoid delay, the application should be made at least six weeks before the date set for beginning the year's work.

Oak book cases are supplied without extra charge but as some clubs do not need them, they are not sent unless requested.

Loans. Apparatus, lantern slides, photographs or other illustrative material needed by clubs is lent as far as it is available, on payment of fees corresponding to those paid for traveling libraries.

Registered clubs may borrow from the state library not exceeding 10 volumes at once for use at a single meeting. The books will be sent by express on the day before the meeting at which they are to be used and must be returned on the day following. No fee is charged, but the club pays transportation.

Exchanges. Books, apparatus or other material bought by a club and no longer needed will if practicable be exchanged with another club for an equivalent. Values will be determined without charge by a disinterested appraiser. The club pays for packing and transportation both ways.

Examinations. An extension examination will be given under regents rules, on application of five members. Candidates must have been present at not less than two thirds of the meetings and have done the allotted work. Before the date of the examination, the secretary must forward to the department, a list of candidates eligible to the examination on these conditions. The examination will be based on the outline of study submitted by the secretary and passcards will be awarded to successful candidates.

Constitution. The constitution properly gives the essential rules as to name and object, members, officers, meetings and amendments. Experience proves it wise to make the organization simple and avoid multiplying officers, committees or rules. Usually the secretary is the active working member, though a good president should not only preside and represent the club officially but should be an active executive officer. It is better to elect a judicious executive board and let them attend to nearly all the detail business of the club, as interest in literary or similar work is dulled by introducing much routine or miscellaneous business at the meetings.

Many literary and study clubs have been wrecked by the effort of different members to outdo each other in refreshments served to the club when meeting at their respective homes. It seems almost impossible to prevent this when elaborate refreshments are permitted. The result is that club meetings become a burden, and in many cases the dissolution of an otherwise promising club can be traced to this apparently trifling matter. The best results have come from a by-law positively forbidding any refreshments whatever at club meetings. In other cases the club has been sufficiently protected by a by-law strictly limiting such refreshments to sandwiches and coffee, or something equally simple, so that there is no opportunity for an expensive or troublesome feature. The omission of refreshments also enables members to go home at an earlier hour and so removes another difficulty.

Two forms for constitution are here printed as suggesting a good model. Details should be put in the form of by-laws.

[*Suggested form*]

1 *Name.* This organization shall be called
2 *Object.* Its object shall be
3 *Officers.* A president, two vice presidents, secretary and treasurer shall be elected by ballot at the annual meeting or when a vacancy occurs, and shall hold office till the close of the meeting at which their successors are elected.

4 *Duties of officers.* The president, or in his absence a vice-president, shall preside at all meetings of the club and have general supervision of its interests.

The secretary shall have charge of club correspondence and keep an accurate record of all business transacted by the club or its executive board, and shall have charge of the books, photographs, apparatus and other club property, and shall prepare for approval of the board the annual report to the University.

The treasurer shall collect and have charge of all funds, disburse them only as voted by the executive board, and at the annual meeting, and whenever directed by the board, shall report all receipts and payments, with date, purpose and amount, and with proper vouchers.

5 *Executive board.* The officers of the club shall be the executive board with power to appoint committees and in intervals between club meetings by unanimous vote of the board to take any action in behalf of the club not inconsistent with the constitution and by-laws.

Within one month after the annual meeting the executive board shall announce the course of study for the following year. At the annual election the board shall present at least two names for each office, but members shall not be limited to these nominations.

6 *Members.* Members may be elected by ballot at any regular meeting if recommended to the club by the executive board. Five votes shall reject any candidate. Each member shall pay to the treasurer an annual fee of   , and membership shall be limited to   members.

Club members may be elected at any business meeting by unanimous vote of the members present.

7 *Meetings.* Regular meetings of the club shall be held   . The annual business meeting for election of officers

shall be held at the close of the year's program when called by the board.

8 *Quorum*. A majority of the members of the club or board shall be a quorum.

9 *Amendments*. This constitution may be altered by a two-thirds vote at two successive meetings, if all members have been notified of the proposed change in the call for the second meeting

---

The following constitution which has worked well is also printed as suggesting a good model.

CONSTITUTION OF THE SATURDAY CLUB
Name and object

1 This organization shall be called the Saturday club.

2 Its object shall be the study of literature and the literary and social entertainment of its members.

Officers

3 The officers shall be a president, vice-president, secretary and treasurer, elected by separate ballots at each annual meeting.

4 The executive board shall be the president and four members appointed by him and confirmed by the club.

5 The secretary shall record all proceedings and those present at each meeting of the club, have charge of its books, papers and correspondence, give three days notice of the annual meeting, with a request for prompt notice if membership is not to continue, and notify members of elections, appointments or other matters requiring personal attention.

6 The treasurer shall have charge of, and record all receipts and disbursements, with date, purpose and amount, pay money only on order of the executive board, and report to each annual meeting.

7 The executive board shall prepare the program, provide places for meetings, assign parts to members, giving at least two weeks notice, receive and in case of vacancies propose the names of all candidates for membership, call needed special meetings and act for the club in the intervals between meetings subject to the approval of the club at the next regular meeting.

Members

8 The number of members shall not exceed 40, not counting memberships resigned or withdrawn by the club, and shall include only those duly elected and who signed the annual pledge for the current year.

9 In case of vacancy, any candidate reported by the executive board may be elected by a two thirds ballot of those present.

10 Each member shall annually pay a fee of 50 cents and sign this pledge:

We the undersigned agree to support and abide by the constitution and rules of the Saturday club; and in order to maintain its good standing and general welfare, we hereby pledge ourselves to perform all duties assigned us by the executive board, or to provide a substitute, unless excused by the committee.

Meetings

11 The annual meeting for organization shall be held the third Saturday of September and the regular literary meetings on the third Saturday of October and every alternate Saturday thereafter till May 1.

12 All meetings shall be at 7.30 p. m., and shall be called to order for business at precisely 7.45 p. m.

13 A majority of the active members shall constitute a quorum for transacting business, but the members present at any meeting duly called shall be a quorum for carrying out its program of exercises.

14 All business shall be done in accordance with the parliamentary rules in Cushing's *Manual*.

Amendments

15 This constitution may be amended or suspended only by a two-thirds vote of the entire membership, or a unanimous vote of those present at a legal meeting.

Blanks for statistics are sent to all clubs, circles and lecture courses in the state known to the department, and from the returns is decided whether the work done by each is of such a grade as to entitle it to the indorsement implied in formal registration by the University.

All are urged to reach at least the minimum standard required for registration, and it is highly desirable that every club maintaining a course of study worthy of registration should secure it.

The department however interprets its duties broadly and will gladly be of any practicable service to organized effort outside those registered, assisting so far as is in its power all efforts toward creditable work in extending educational opportunities more widely.

ADMINISTRATIVE ORGANIZATIONS AIDING STUDY CLUBS

Following are brief accounts of various agencies for aiding the work of study clubs prepared by those familiar with the plan of work used. Many clubs unable to find proper local leaders will gladly avail themselves of these opportunities of working under capable direction

CHAUTAUQUA LITERARY AND SCIENTIFIC CIRCLE

Among the many organizations which have sprung into life during recent years, perhaps none has been more signally successful in bringing help to hard pressed humanity than the famous Chautauqua reading circle. For 17 years the C. L. S. C. has offered each year a definite plan of study. The course has been historical, literary and scientific, and each year's work has formed part of a four years' scheme which each reader is urged to carry through, and whose purpose may be summed up in the words "a broad outlook." Thus in four years are considered Greek, Roman, French, German, English and American history, literature and art, with such of the sciences as may be presented in readable form and made clear to the average student. Supplementing the required books is a monthly magazine, the *Chautauquan*, which contains certain required articles by the best writers of the day, on subjects related to the year's work. One department of the magazine is devoted to notes on the required readings, review questions, programs for circles, reports, etc. so that the reader who must often do his work far away from encyclopedia or dictionary may find in his magazine explanations of unusual words, pronunciation of proper names and similar helps. A new and most valuable feature of the magazine is the department of current history and opinion, which keeps every reader in touch with the world about him.

The phenomenal success of the Chautauqua circle has been due to the fact that its plan has been broad enough to appeal to people of most diverse tastes and that its methods of work are of the simplest possible character. No entrance examination frightens away the aspiring but timid inquirer, and no examination is required at any time during the course. A membership book sent to every member who pays the enrolment fee of 10 cents gives much valuable aid. The one purpose of the society is to enable busy people to make the most of their opportunities for self-culture, and those whose interest has been aroused by a given subject are, through supplementary courses, enabled to pursue such a subject as a specialty. The year 1895-96 in the course of the reading circle is known as the American year, as the subjects studied relate chiefly to American history and progress. The circle has a membership reaching into every part of the world, and the effectiveness of the plan is indicated by an enrolment of nearly a quarter of a million members during the 17 years of its history.

The members of the C. L. S. C. carry on their work as individuals, or in groups called local circles. The latter plan has many advantages, and members are urged to form local organizations wherever it is possible. All members are however enrolled at the central office as individuals, and the solitary student may attain to equal honor with the more favored local circle reader. The circle has no hard and fast rules to restrict its progress; its workings are most flexible in their nature, and in its general plan and specific courses it is able to adapt itself continually to the needs of the times. Individuals in every walk of life have found its systematic and comprehensive course a great stimulus to literary activity, and weary and often discouraged toilers have gained daily inspiration from a work which emphasizes the truth so well expressed by Matthew Arnold that "Life is not a having and a getting, but a being and a becoming."— KATE F KIMBALL, *Secretary*

GROWTH OF CATHOLIC READING CIRCLES

It is now somewhat over 30 years since Father Hecker, assisted by intelligent workers among the laity, established a free circulating library for the scholars of St Paul's Sunday-school in New

York city. No expense was spared to get the best books. The object kept in view was to provide for the intellectual needs not only of the little children attending school, but also to encourage the love for good reading among the young folks. Library cards, finished on one side with white silicate, were arranged containing 15 books, of which 10 were selected from writers of fiction and five from biography, history, or entertaining books of adventure and travel. At least one book devoted to the life of a saint, or some explanation of religious truth, was assigned to each set. These cards, with the titles of 15 books and the names of their authors, were distributed on Sunday during the recitation of the catechism lesson. Under the guidance of the teachers, scholars made a choice of the books By the aid of a number for each book the librarians easily kept the account of the circulation. For the return of books every two weeks the class was held accountable as well as the individual. This rule directed attention in a public manner to the delinquents who were promptly admonished by their own classmates.

Not to mention other obvious advantages, it may be claimed that this method of supplying books gave the teachers an excellent opportunity to elicit conversation about favorite authors, and to make the library a potent influence in the mental growth and character-building of their scholars. Each class became in reality a miniature reading circle, with the teachers in charge, assisted by the librarians, and under the personal supervision of the Rev. Director. From the graduates of St Paul's Sunday-school trained in this way during their early days came the first members of a catholic reading circle for women, in the year 1886. It was named in honor of Frederic Ozanam, the gifted friend of Lacordaire, the leader of young men in work for the poor, who won conquests for the faith in the field of literature within the 19th century. The object proposed for the Ozanam reading circle was the improvement of its members in literary taste by meeting together once a week in an informal and friendly way to talk about books — giving prominence always to catholic authors — to take part in reading aloud some of the best specimens of magazine literature, and to aid one another by the discussion of current topics. At that time, less than 10 years ago, no society could be found in existence intended to provide for catholic young women equal intellectual advantages, such as were secured for young men by parish lyceums and literary unions . . .

Rumors have been heard that some objection was made to the reading circle movement because of its recent origin. As in the case of the young man who promised to try to get older every day, this objection will shortly be removed by time. The underlying principle of cooperation in all departments of human activity may be traced a long way back in history. No one can doubt that a union of intellectual forces extending from the Atlantic to the Pacific, or vice versa, could develop a bulwark of strength for catholic literature in the United States. Any one desiring the sanction of hoary antiquity for the modern reading circle can find it at the University of Paris in the days of St Thomas Aquinas, when students made notes of his profound lectures and afterward read them aloud to their friends at the family gathering.

A description of a meeting may give some idea of the work done in the Ozanam reading circle. The exercises begin with the reading of the minutes of the previous meeting. These minutes are not presented in tabular form, but are rather a description of the part each member had in the proceedings. This is followed by quotations containing good, wholesome thoughts that impress the members in the course of their readings; an entire evening has often been devoted to one catholic author. The readings are selected from the literary standpoint; standard periodicals are frequently consulted. For instance, every month at least one selection from the *Catholic world* is rendered. The members subscribe to this magazine and circulate it weekly, so that each member in turn is supplied with a copy. Original writings have taken the form of letters to the circle, essays, and reviews of popular books, or impressions of particular works. Sometimes the whole time of the meeting has been devoted to one special subject or one celebrated character. All efforts have tended in some way to acquaint the members with catholic history and catholic literature. No attempt is made to educate professional readers, but to cultivate expression chiefly as a means of bringing out the spirit and thought of the author . . .

Compared with the condition of things that formerly existed, the progress of the past 10 years is exceedingly gratifying, though much remains yet to be accomplished. The continued existence of the *Catholic reading circle review*, published at Youngstown, Ohio, is undoubtedly the best evidence that has been given of the energy developed within the reading circle movement. With a noble ambition rarely found among young men, Mr Warren E Mosher made heroic sacrifices in starting and sustaining it to the present time. Every one who knows the difficulties he has had to encounter must wish him success beyond his most sanguine expectations . . .

A very large share of the success which has attended the summer school at Lake Champlain may be claimed for the members of catholic reading circles. From the circles of the west, it may be confidently predicted, the Columbian catholic summer school at Madison will derive enthusiastic workers, eager for self-improvement and the intellectual advancement of their fellow catholics. — REV. THOMAS MCMILLAN in the *Catholic world*, Aug. 1895

COLUMBIAN READING UNION

On December 5, 1891, 14 former pupils of Mount St Vincent met to form the reading circle " Pupils of the holy see," the object of which was to be a study of the history of the church, and of catholic literature in general. At the meetings church history questions are asked and answered, and the new section announced. Besides church history questions, there are distributed general and period questions, the latter embracing the period under consideration The members answer these at the next meeting. Then the *résumé* of the book of the month, a sketch of its author's life, or both, are read; and some musical selection follows. A novelty is the writing and reading by each member, in turn, of the current events of the previous month, gleaned from a judicious perusal of the daily papers. From this arise discussions on various subjects which occasionally arouse the members to a high degree of enthusiasm.

The 14 members soon increased, and a branch was formed in Newburg, N. Y. Other branches followed, and associate circles, under the same title, Pupils of the holy see, now may be found in Savannah, Ga., Lancaster, Pa, Middletown and Poughkeepsie, N. Y. The present number of members is more than 150.

As the numbers increased so also did the desire for active literary work. During the second season the circle took up the works of such English women writers as Jane Austen and Lady Fullerton Next came a period in which were studied some catholic authors of France: Lacordaire, Montalembert, Lamartine and Ozanam.

During the past winter the members have been intent on the Oxford movement. At this point, during the month of March, the Pupils of the holy see invited their friends to a lecture on Cardinal Newman, a rare literary treat, delivered by Henry Austin Adams, a recent convert to the catholic faith. It was the crowning point of success for the members of the circle and their friends. During the coming fall and winter Mr Adams will deliver to the circle his course of literary lectures and the members have the prospect of his guidance, as he has graciously consented to become the director of the Pupils of the holy see.— From the *Catholic world*, Aug. 1895

TEACHERS INTERNATIONAL READING CIRCLE

The Teachers international reading circle was organized to furnish assistance and guidance to teachers wishing to pursue a course of professional reading and study.

The outline of the course, which was prepared by Dr William T Harris, is based on the International education series, edited by Dr William T. Harris, and published by Appleton & co., New York. This series, which comprises many of the most valuable works in educational literature, is classified by Dr Harris under four heads: history of education; criticism of existing methods; theory of education; practice.

Three years has been adopted as the working basis of time but the full course of reading has been subdivided into a brief course of three books a year, an advanced course of five books and the complete course of seven books.

Monthly syllabuses are issued containing topics and questions designed to suggest the most systematic method of study. The correspondence work consists in preparing written work to be forwarded to the secretary of the circle. The preparation of this written work is considered of more value for reading circle purposes than examination, and no examination is given unless specially desired.

When the written work prescribed for a year in either course is satisfactorily completed, a certificate for that year is issued.

A final certificate or diploma is issued when the three years' course is completed.

There are no membership fees and the only expense to members is the cost of the books, which are purchased as required for use.

SOCIETY TO ENCOURAGE STUDIES AT HOME

The Society to encourage studies at home, organized in 1873, was the first of the American correspondence societies of which there are now so many. The yearly fee is $3. The teachers give their services. As many of them are college graduates, or have had experience in schools, the work in their hands, with the system and method established by the committee and pursued with improvements for over 20 years, is thorough and reliable. The subjects of study are six: history, science, art, and the German, French and English literatures. These large departments are subdivided so that nearly 30 courses are offered to students. Monthly reports are expected from each pupil and the work is tested by written examinations. No diplomas are given.

Originally the work was to be carried on only with individual students, but of late a constantly increasing number of applications has come from clubs consisting on the average of a little over 10 members. The work is done through correspondence with the club secretary, who alone pays the fee, much as in the case of an individual, as she sends in monthly reports, adding specimens of papers written by the members and accounts of discussions or difficulties. The teacher plans the work in advance, giving topics for essays and for general and individual study. As a rule these clubs do excellent work, and the different members show thoughtfulness and industry. Occasionally however there are clubs where the chief desire is to do many things at once, and combine music, history and conversation in one short evening. For these the society can do little and mutual disappointment is the only result.

The clubs represent all parts of the country, Texas, California, Minnesota and New England being the extreme points. History, art and literature are the favorite studies. During the past winter, 88 members of clubs have studied Shakspere, and have done thorough work. Others have taken a course of foreign travel, visiting many foreign cities and galleries by the aid of photographs and books. One club studying the history of medieval art, through the winter, annually turns its attention in spring to ornithology and the habits of the returning birds.

Altogether clubs now form an important part of the work of the society and the fact that a club taking one subject and having but one correspondent pays but one individual fee should be observed; the addition of another subject which requires another correspondent however requires another fee.

The lending library and the circulating collection of photographs add to the value of the work.

Circulars setting forth the subjects of study and general rules with other documents may be had by application to the secretary at 41 Marlborough st, Boston, Mass.

To make clear the methods used by the society a page from the syllabus on ancient history is here reprinted.

Lesson 3

Chaldaea, 2200–1500. Babylonia, 2245–538. Assyria, 1150–650 B. C

Syllabus: A nomadic people, probably Turanian, settled the region of the Tigris and Euphrates; they were called Accadians; they intermarried with the Semitic tribes that supplanted them and so were founded Chaldaea and the empires of Assyria and Babylonia. Their wandering life led to the study of astrology and astronomy; this probably influenced their religion; their gods were sun and planet creations, generally of revengeful nature. Semitic thought tended toward monotheism. The Babylonians invented symbolic writing; they were peaceful, the Assyrians were warriors and traders.

Subjects for essays: Cuneiform writing, its nature and revelations. Compare the Assyrians and the Babylonians.

Subjects

Mesopotamia, its inhabitants and geography

The legendary founder of Chaldaea, astronomy, astrology

The Accadians, beginning of Babylonia, the Semitic conquest

The first Assyrian empire, Tiglath Pileser 1, Assur-natsir-pal Shalmaneser; Nineveh

The second Assyrian empire, Tiglath Pileser 2, Conquest of Babylonia, Sargon 2, overthrow of Hittites, Sennacherib, Conquests of Egypt, Assur-bani-pal

Conquest of Assyria, by Babylonia and Media
Babylonian empire, Nebuchadnezzar, Babylon
Persian conquest of Assyria and Babylonia
Religion of Accadians, modification by Semites
Literature, libraries, writing, science, art

Text-books

Ragozin, Z. A. Story of Chaldaea } Stories of the nations
Ragozin, Z. A. Story of Assyria
Sayce. Ancient empires of the east
Quackenbos. Ancient literature.

Auxiliary books

A Sayce, A. H. Social life among the Assyrians and Babylo- } Fresh lights
           nians   on
A Sayce, A. H. Assyria, its princes, priests and people } Bible races
A Layard, A. H Nineveh and Babylon Harper. Ill. *Out of print*
A The Bible; stories of Abraham, Daniel, Jonah
B Rawlinson, George Five great monarchies
B Maspero, G. Life in ancient Egypt and Assyria, tr. Appleton, $1.50
B Perrot and Chipiez History of art in Chaldaea and Assyria. 2 vols. Ill. Armstrong. $15 50.

Miss A. E. Ticknor, *Secretary*

HOME CULTURE CLUBS [a]

I thought that it might be of interest, specially to those that are not now in college, yet are in sympathy with all its concerns, to know something of a movement in the town which has enlisted a large number of college girls as its supporters. I refer to the home culture clubs.

They were established here in 1886 by Geo. W. Cable. As their name implies they are essentially clubs for home work, meeting from week to week at the houses of the various members. Thus the leaders and members are brought into a closer relationship than would be the case if they were obliged to meet in the rooms belonging to the organization. Much is learned of a person by a few glimpses into his home life, and a bond of sympathy is established which is of great value. For it is desired that the relations between the members should not be that of a teacher to a pupil or a pupil to a teacher, but rather that of fellow-learners and fellow-workers toward one another.

---

[a] This article and the one following supplement Miss Moffatt's account of the present condition of the organization.

As most of the members are persons with little leisure at their command the work must necessarily be light in its requirements and yet give free scope for any further study that any one may wish to do by himself. Therefore the clubs usually meet for only an hour's session, upon some fixed day, every week.

To keep the clubs advised of one another's doings and stimulated by one another's progress, reports are issued every two weeks and furnished to each member. In these reports are given the names of the books read by each club in meeting and outside, also the number of pages read and any remarks the leader may make on the work of his club. Often there is a pleasant spirit of rivalry between two or more clubs which spurs them on to do much more and much better reading than they might otherwise.

Perhaps I can in no way give you a better idea of the inside life of the clubs than by telling you what my own has been doing during the year. It includes six young, unmarried women; a good number for easy fellowship and spirited work. We called ourselves a country club; for at the beginning of the year each girl chose some country as her special field for study. She was to treat it in any way she liked, taking up only one phase, as art or literature, or touching upon all. It was necessary to give such latitude, for they were not trained sufficiently to deal with too narrow a subject. Every once in six weeks, as her turn came around, each member was to furnish the entertainment for the evening. She could get others to read extracts for her or help her in other ways, but the planning and the responsibility were hers. The girls took hold of the plan with much zest and have carried it through the winter with the same spirit Much to my surprise many of them have written papers showing not a little care and thought. For the first 15 minutes of the hour we discussed current events, hoping thus to awaken interest in judicious newspaper reading. We followed the progress of the anti lottery movement and the Hill boom with not a little enthusiasm.

One feels that it is impossible to form any exact ideas as to the results of the work. One can sum up the number of books read and note the interest taken during the year, but they are nothing but bare facts and represent but a small part of what has been accomplished. The greatest good has, doubtless, been done in a way that is least apparent, and where, perhaps, one least expected it. The benefit gained is by no means wholly on one side; the leaders as well as the other members feel that their sympathies have been widened by the opportunities which this club has afforded.—C Isabel Baker, in *Alpha quar.* Smith college, June, 1892

A Home culture club is any group of persons, however small, meeting periodically in the homes of its members for the purpose of cultivating the intellectual and social sides of life, and which sends a record of its proceedings to the general secretary of the Home culture clubs. Each club is suppled with printed postal cards, free of charge, if so desired, with blanks for members in attendance, amount of work done, etc. to be filled out and forwarded after each meeting. These reports are tabulated and printed monthly in the *Letter*, which is distributed to all, and constitutes the bond holding them together. Each club is a self-governed body, making its own rules, choosing its own pursuit, and deciding the amount of work to be done. It has no connection with the other clubs, except through the exchange of experiences in the *Letter*. The central office lays no requirements on the clubs except that they keep it informed of their methods, successes and failures. There are no demands made for money. A club may contribute as generously as it chooses to the financial support of the clubs, or it may give nothing. Each club is furnished with a "penny treasury," into which it drops as much or as little as it chooses, at each meeting. These are opened at stated intervals, and the contents sent to the general secretary.

The central office holds itself in readiness to give a club as much attentive supervision and advice as it asks for and no more. In some clubs every meeting is outlined by the general secretary. In others the general plan and all details are arranged by the club members without consulting the general secretary.

It will be plain that there may be, as there is, wide variety in the quantity and quality of the work done and in the attainments of the members of the various clubs. The spirit of the movement is democratic, and excludes no one on account of the importance or the humbleness of his social status. Almost all ranks and all ages are represented in the total membership. Some clubs are composed of highly educated men and women of more or less local distinction; other clubs, perhaps in the same town, draw their members from those obscure planes of social life where hard labor and illiteracy are often the cause and consequence of each other. Some are rich and some are poor. There is no incongruity in this association, the differences are of degree, not of kind. Both are working, either directly or indirectly, toward the same end, the cultivation of themselves and of the home

Astronomy, arithmetic, art history, Bible, botany, biology, bookkeeping, biography, civil government, drawing, dramatics, current events, elocution, French, German, geography, geology, gymnastics, household arts, histories (of countries, great men, great movements and great events). literature, language, music, mechanics, mathematics, natural history, penmanship, political economy, public questions, reading, spelling and travel have all been chosen as club pursuits, and suggestions along these lines, based on the experiences of the clubs and consultations with authorities on the various topics, are in the secretary's hands for the use of clubs desiring them.

The purpose of the general organization is to secure for individual clubs the freedom to follow their own choice in the matter of pursuits, and to give them at the same time the stimulation that comes of organization, concerted action, and outside resources. It thus meets the needs of a number of persons who do not find themselves in line with the many other well known plans for intelligent recreation or for study. Perhaps one of these plans may require more time than they can give, or a special hour that is not their own. The schedule of another may not include the topics they wish to take up. The benefits of another may be exclusively for some special class to which they do not belong, or it may require the absence of a member of the home circle whose absence means loss to other members, a mother or father, an elder son or daughter. Still other plans require a fresher mind than they can bring to anything after a hard day's work in the shop, mill, store, counting-room or kitchen. Moreover, most if not all of these plans involve pledges, fees and forfeits, and there are many who do not wish to add to the necessary obligations of life an avoidable allegiance to some highly organized system, especially when seeking recreation. Lastly, there is a large number of people who have an instinctive dislike of formality, and are impatient of any form of restraint or direction. To all of these it is an advantage to belong to something that will stimulate and suggest and at the same time leave them unhampered. By the Home culture plan, each receives the stimulus of weekly meetings with a few people all interested in the same thing. Each has the advantage of seeing, through the monthly reports, what all the others are doing, and each feels that he must do something worthy, since whatever he does goes into print for the benefit of all the others. All are engaged in the same common end — their own growth as individuals and the cultivation of their homes — and it is good for all that there are wide differences in the attainments of the various members. Each club, by meeting regularly, getting as much good as it can from its meetings, and reporting them promptly, may be sure that it is a helpful unit in a movement which is broadening, and doing good to others whom they do not and can not know personally.

In order to meet the requirements of so many people of so many sorts, it follows that the actual organization of the clubs must be extremely simple. They have found no need for constitution or by-laws, and have few traditions.

A Home culture club may or may not be philanthropic in its intention. That is, it may be started with the intention of seeking pleasure and benefit or of bestowing it. The club that unites these principles is most likely to succeed. It has behind it the stimulation of self-interest and the inspiration that comes of unselfish effort for others.

There are two kinds of persons who may be very helpful to each other. They may be loosely classified as those who have had "advantages" and those who have not. There is every year an increasing number of people who find themselves equipped with an expensive education and who do not see any immediate practical use to which it may be put. Within walking distance of them there is apt to be abundant opportunity to make it useful to others. There are many individuals, sometimes whole families, who, in the hand to hand struggle for a bare livelihood, have little time left to indulge their natural taste for good literature. It takes time to go to the public library, and reaching there they scarcely know what to ask for. Then there are others who have no idea at all of the world of rest and pleasure that lies between the covers of a book. Still others find that the necessity of beginning early to earn a livelihood has deprived them of the chance to lay the foundations of a good common education, or to follow as far as they wish some favorite study With a little help from some one who has more leisure and is more constantly in contact with books, all of these may find an entirely new value in life.

There are everywhere ambitions to be gratified or stimulated, narrow outlooks to be broadened, isolation to be relieved, coveted companionship to be offered. This can not be done effectually by any system of class treatment or special legislation, no matter how benevolent. It must be done by the individual for the individual, and by mutual consent. Each instance where this is being done may seem a small thing in itself, but it is all helping in the solution of one of the great problems of the world's politics, a better understanding between people whose advantages have not been equal. We may be sure that neither is giving the other a benefit without receiving one in return. A knowledge of books is exchanged for knowledge of life. This relation does away with mutual condescension, and permanent groundwork for mutual understanding is established. This is not theory, it is a fact proven daily in some of the Home culture clubs.

Silent influences are the most potent, and it may be safely affirmed that one third of the actual work of the clubs does not find its way into print. What we do for each other we wish to do in quiet, friendly fellowship. A quotation from a thesis by a divinity student of Yale might serve as a summary of this division of the subject:

"There is no formal connection, no president, no committees, no general motto in an ancient or modern language, no certificate, no summer school degrees, no fireworks, no national council, no long procession of bewildering initials. The work is as quiet as it is effective, and partakes largely of the genial spirit so characteristic of the author of *Old Creole days, Bonaventure,* and the *Grandissimes.*"

In answer to the question, "How shall I start a club?" I should say, first of all, begin at once. The hardest thing to do in starting a club is to bring it out of the future into the present.

Select from the people you come in contact with in the various relations of life two or three people who may possibly be willing to give one hour a week to some profitable pleasure. Ask each to ask some friend. This gives each a share in the formation of the club, and insures a certain amount of congeniality. Members can be selected from two points of view, those who will be an advantage to the club, and those to whom the club will be an advantage. It is well to have both represented. If material for a club can not be found among one's nearer friends, if those who are first bidden will not come to the feast, there are plenty of guests to be found in the highways, and experience has shown that very few come without the wedding garment. Appoint a time for the first meeting at the most convenient home. Suggest the thing that you would like best yourself, music, literature, art, science, history, current events, poetry, whatever you may wish to know more about. It is likely that others will have the same desire. If the others show a preference for something else, discuss freely, and get everybody's opinion on the relative merits of the subjects proposed. If, as is much more likely, it is found that all want to do something, but nobody knows exactly what, do not at first fix definitely upon a program, but let the subject or work be chosen from week to week. While undecided as to what the final pursuit of the club shall be, it is a good idea to use the magazines. They are designed to meet all tastes. If desirable, the general secretary can be consulted. Try to give each member some part in the club. Doubtful definitions, references and obscure points can be divided among the members, being careful to avoid burdening tired or busy people. Try to get all the members to realize their individual importance in the club and the value of their attendance. Do whatever may be done, even at some sacrifice of other values, to secure good attendance. The only difficulty which a club can not survive is the absence of its members. All others settle themselves with time and experience. As questions arise which the clubs find it hard to determine, the experience of the general secretary can be consulted, and suggestions used or rejected, as seems advisable for the interest of the club.

Leaders and members must be prepared for discouragements. Some meetings will be bright and some dull. The burden of the work may fall upon a few, as it is apt to do in progressive work of any kind. Results may seem small, and opportunities too limited for some or too much neglected by others. But it must always be remembered that the growth of our minds and hearts is, like that of our bodies, an unconscious process. Long spaces of time must elapse between measurements, and we must judge what we have learned by what we might not have learned. Honest effort in any direction is always worth while. "The only sure way to fail is not to try."— From the *Home culture club letter*, Sept. 1893

The Home culture clubs are an association of small groups of persons scattered over the country but mainly in and near Northampton, Massachusetts, who meet in their own homes for improvement of themselves and the home and for recreation. Among the 500 members enrolled this year are persons of all ages, both sexes, and every degree of culture from the adult who can not read and write, to the college professor. The feature of the Home culture club idea which differentiates it from many organized and unorganized plans of home study, is that the clubs were designed by their founder, George W. Cable, "to establish and maintain the offices of friendship and neighborship, between diverse elements of society, which the ordinary discrepancies of life and the movement of affairs tend to separate or to antagonize." It may happen, therefore, that a single club may count among its members a laborer who writes a cross for his name, a college graduate, a mechanic who works 10 hours a day for a bare livelihood, a man of means, a clerk and a millhand. These persons who ordinarily would not meet except possibly in the unpropitious relations of business, are usually brought together by some one person whose insight enables him to see the value of the association in that particular instance and who has the unselfish courage to risk failure in the attempt. The relation is a difficult one to establish and maintain and the basis of the union must be real, not sentimental. The club members must come together for some purpose recognized by all as more tangible than the spiritual value, great though that may be. They may meet to secure various points of view on some sociologic questions, to study the history of their town or the best interests of their neighborhood, or to pursue some favorite study. It will be evident that the spirit of the Home culture club is furthest removed from "exclusive" in the offensive sense of the word. It is necessary to exclude only those who are so tactless as to bring into the club those distinctions of private social position which may be perfectly proper outside the club. The true Home culture club proposes at the outset to ignore superficial class distinctions and to bring together in the club relation those who may receive or bestow benefit in the association. It is not a charitable enterprise. No one expects to bestow a benefit without receiving one in return. The student, for instance, exchanges his knowledge of books for the workingman's knowledge of life.

A club may be large or small as circumstances determine. Several valuable "clubs" have only two members. Since the club meets in the homes of its members, usually in rotation, it is seldom larger than the seating capacity of the smallest room at the command of the group. The meetings have something of the democratic freedom from social entanglements implied in the word club, and something of the personal friendliness which can not fail to be born of the gracious exchange of private hospitality.

The general organization of the clubs is exceedingly simple and elastic. This is of course necessary in a movement made up of such varied elements. The central office lays no obligation on its members except to require of them weekly reports of their condition. Blanks are furnished free for this purpose. Courses of study, rules, amount and character of work done, the fees even, are all voluntary, each club deciding for itself or in counsel with the general secretary. The central office however lays itself under obligation to supply practical schedules of work, to plan meetings, to suggest methods of forming and conducting clubs, in short to hold itself in readiness to assist whenever called on. To this end it keeps in close touch with educational institutions and similar movements throughout the country and there is constantly on file in the secretary's office valuable plans of work which are at the disposal of all who apply for them.

The clubs are held together by the exchange of their experiences in the *Home-culture club letters* published monthly. Another bond is the inspiring consciousness that they are all working together, each person in his own home, each club in its own neighborhood, toward the solution of the great problem, how to bring about a better understanding between those whose advantages have not been equal. The individuals of the various groups may seldom or never see each other face to face but they are encouraged and inspired by the thought that others perhaps widely separated by geographic or social spaces join with them in spirit for mutual uplift and for the enlargement of the gracious influences of the home.— ADELINE MOFFAT, *General secretary*

REPORT OF THE ROUND ROBIN READING CLUB

This organization, having its center in Philadelphia, opened its work January, 1894, and already has members in 25 states and one territory, and some abroad. The system does not conflict with, or supplement that of any other organization; its intention being to work on a distinctive basis of its own. The readers whose needs it seeks to supply, are not primarily those whose object is simply to gain mental training and some information from a designated course of reading, but rather those whose needs are defined and specific, and who desire necessary guidance through literature relating to their chosen subject. Here then is the starting point of the Round Robin system: As the title denotes, it follows the old "Round Robin" petition in regarding all subjects as in a circle, giving each a position of equal value, leaving to the reader the choice of what shall be his object and his work. The first information sought from members relates to their preferences in subjects, and facilities for obtaining books. There are now over 40 courses in use, all made on request, frequently three and four on the same subject, but varying in treatment as the reader may require. Sometimes the character of the work is graduate, sometimes juvenile. Each course is prepared by a specialist, who continues interest in the work, criticizes papers, gives advice, and is ready in any way to assist the members. The Round Robin has no books of its own. It uses the best literature wherever it is to be found, and always seeks to make a good study of one subject, or epoch, rather than take a superficial view of many. In history it seeks the fiction, essays, biography, drama and poetry connected with the period under consideration, makes suggestions for study, and in a "foreword" to each schedule describes the varying uses of the books and the comparative value of the writers. The same system is in use for individual readers and classes, except that classes have arrangements made for their meetings. For these, programs are prepared, in which readings are selected and subjects for papers and discussion suggested, the whole work being mapped out clearly and logically. Each member of a class receives a schedule for home work similar to that given the individual reader, and no pains are spared to induce him to keep up this connected reading so that he may not rely, as is so often the case, on the meetings, for information on the subject of study. In arranging the work the year is divided into two periods of six months each, members entering at any time except during July and August when names are registered but no schedules supplied.

The selection of subjects by the members is often interesting. The author most in request for special work is Shakspere, often only one play being desired The most popular subjects are: Before going to Europe, the English drama, Ruskin, The mother and her child, English and French history, American literature. France is the favorite country for history alone, and England for literature. American literature ranks well, but American history is not much in request, the Columbian year having apparently exhausted the interest; readers who take it however desire to study it thoroughly. Spain, from 711 to 1492, is always a favorite, perhaps because its history is such a wonderful romance, while all the literature relating to it seems to have caught picturesque qualities of style that become fascinating. Browning has never secured one reader, while Ruskin has a very large number. Last winter in Philadelphia, a Venice section connected with Mr Hudson Shaw's historical lectures was successfully carried through, and this summer a course in Greek literature made by two of the leading lecturers, is offered to students of the university extension summer school for preparatory or supplementary reading. In the same city, next winter, a class will be formed to study Shakspere in connection with readings by Horace Howard Furness, Hudson Shaw and Louis C. Elson

The unusual and unexpected interest taken in the Round Robin seems to prove that our people do not, as has so often been asserted, care only for superficial and alien culture, but that a large number recognize very definite needs, and are eager for assistance from scholars willing to work for readers at a distance from the centers of education. The readers come from every class, many being bread-winners who have their evenings only; others are foreigners desiring a knowledge of English literature, teachers training for special work, lecturers, boys and girls not attending school, graduates and a large number who read for pleasure and general improvement. — LOUISE STOCKTON, *Director*

NATIONAL YOUNG FOLKS' READING CIRCLE

The National young folks' reading circle was organized in 1888. Its central office is in Chicago, and S. R. Winchell, principal of the Winchell academy, Evanston, is manager. It has been called the Children's Chautauqua. The courses of reading may be followed by individuals or by local circles. Its leading object is "to encourage and promote the reading of good books by children and adults." Its officers select each year a list of the best books adapted to different ages, and group their titles under different headings, such as history, literature, science, travel, etc. It also offers courses in art and pedagogy for adults.

Permanent membership is secured by the payment of 50 cents, annual membership by paying 25 cents. Partial certificates are given as often as the reading of a book is completed, and an annual certificate, when all the required books of any course for one year have been completed. A diploma is awarded on the completion of a four years' course. Each course contains three or four titles each year. Charters are granted to local circles when applied for.

The lists for 1894-95 are divided into three grades: junior, for children 12 years old and under; middle, for children from 13 to 16; and senior, for adults. The junior grade contains three courses of three books each; the middle grade has eight courses of three or four books each; and the senior grade has 11 courses of three or four books each. No examinations are required but a certificate that the books have been read, signed, in case of minors, by parent or teacher, must be submitted.

The board of directors consists of Albert R. Sabin, assistant superintendent of public schools in Chicago, *president;* L. R. Halsey, New York, *secretary;* S. R. Winchell, Evanston, *treasurer and manager;* A. E. Winship, Boston; Richard Edwards, Bloomington, Illinois; and J. W. Stearns, Madison, Wisconsin. Among the counselors are Rev. Lyman Abbott, Dr John Bascom, Mrs Mary A. Livermore, Prof. Edward S. Joynes, Mrs Alice Freeman

Palmer, Louise M. Hodgkins, and other men and women well known in different parts of the country.

An important and valuable feature of the work recently undertaken by this association is that of high school extension, so-called This is intended to aid children or adults to carry forward a systematic and thorough course of study at home. For aid in accomplishing this, a small additional fee is charged, to cover actual expenses in printing and instruction Outlines are furnished for daily work, and by frequent reports and criticisms a given subject is completed and an examination given, with a certificate. It is expected that these certificates will receive recognition from the schools and thus enable students to prepare for college and still remain at home a part of the time.

Local circles of the National young folks' reading circle have been formed in all parts of the United States, specially in Maine, Massachusetts, South Carolina, Michigan, Illinois, Wisconsin, Iowa, Minnesota and California According to the scheme of organization, there are local circles with leaders, district secretaries, county secretaries, and state secretaries. Provision is also made for summer assemblies, with lectures by prominent people. Circulars of information may be obtained from the manager, by inclosing a two cent stamp.

NATIONAL HOME-READING UNION

The object of the National home reading union of England is to promote systematic reading, recreative and instructive, among young and old, as a means of continued education. The union consists of four sections: introductory, young people's, general course and special courses. Courses of reading and monthly magazines containing introductions to the prescribed books, answers to questions and other helps are published by the union.

The union aims to organize its members into reading circles, each circle consisting of five or more members working under guidance of a leader. Besides the educational advantage of association there is a pecuniary saving, the subscription being reduced 6d. per annum and the purchase of books can thus be divided among members

The courses prepared for young people include reading in history and biography, literature, romance, travel and citizenship, arranged in three lists, required, supplementary and recommended books. These courses aim not only to extend knowledge but to inculcate a love for the study of poetry, natural science and history and thus to develop high ideals of life. To obtain a certificate six required books, chosen from at least three groups, must be read during the year. The annual fee for this section is 1s. 6d. to individual members.

The general course is intended for working men and women, members of the working-class organizations as cooperative societies, trade unions and social clubs. It is also adapted to the needs of those wishing to acquire the rudiments of several sub jects before taking up their detailed study. The book list has two divisions, required and supplementary, and certificates are awarded on the same conditions as those of the young people's section. The annual fee is 2s.

The special courses are intended to cover the chief branches of a liberal education. Each of the special courses contains three lists of books: required, all of which must be read to secure a certificate; recommended; and reference. The annual fee is 3s. 6d.

While each year's work in each of the courses is complete in itself, th se who make their reading continuous and connected will find in the special courses of the N. H. R. U. a substitute for a university education. Examinations are not part of the ordinary work of the union though they will be given when desired by a sufficient number who are willing to pay a fee to cover the cost.

Summer assemblies are organized and held in places of historic interest or in localities offering peculiar facilities for the study of geology, botany and natural history. The object is to illustrate the year's work and give a vivid and realistic interest.

The central office is at Surrey House, Victoria Embankment, London, W. C.

AUSTRALASIAN HOME READING UNION

The Australasian home reading union was formed in January 1892 by members of the literature section of the Australasian association for the advancement of science.

Its object and methods are the same as those of the National home-reading union of England, the plan including courses of reading and study in science, history and literature. The books chosen for the courses are divided into two classes, required and recommended.

Any two or three readers may form themselves into a circle, all circles in the same town or suburb forming a group, which holds periodical meetings and is controlled by a board chosen by its members. The groups in each colony form a section of the Australasian home reading union. The presidents and secretaries of the sections, the president of the union, the general secretary and the editor of the journal constitute the general council in which the government of the union is vested. A monthly journal, the *Australasian home reader*, is published by the union giving information in regard to the progress of the work, answers to questions, and papers.

SOCIAL SETTLEMENT CLUBS

So much of the work at college settlements is conducted by means of clubs as being the most flexible yet binding form of organization for the results aimed at, that an outline of the club work in a few of the settlements is given.

DENISON HOUSE

The club work of Denison house is most compactly shown in the following schedule:

Monday, 4 p. m.	Current topics
Monday evening	Art class; gymnastic class
	Federal labor union
	Garment workers union.
Tuesday, 4–5 p. m.	Library and stamps savings bank; girls embroidery club
Tuesday evening	Social science club
Wednesday, 4–5:30 p. m.	Little girls sewing club
Wednesday evening	American basket weavers club; club of older boys
Thursday, 4–5 p. m.	Club of little boys
Friday, 3–5 p. m.	Mothers meetings
Friday evening	Class in penmanship; singing class; dramatic club
Saturday, 9:30–11 a. m.	Kitchen garden club
Saturday, 2–3 p. m.	Club of little children
Saturday, 3:30–5 p. m.	Basket weaving club
Saturday, 4–5 p. m.	Girls embroidery club

Every club given in the above schedule has held weekly meetings, with the exception of the Federal labor union, the Social science club, and the Mothers meetings. It will easily be seen that, omitting the three last mentioned clubs, an average of three clubs a day is included under the activities of Denison house.

The classes in the above schedule may be called both social and educational in form and in aim. The social and educational progress is furthered by the underlying thought of each club, that is, the idea of organization.

Organization as applied to club life is a rather comprehensive term, embracing in its meaning the thoughts of self-government and self support, which are of themselves an inspiration to social, educational and moral uplift.

Each club is under the personal supervision of at least one resident and one or more outside workers, as the case may require. This method of leadership has always proved productive of excellent results.

Although club life is not a distinctive feature of the activities of Denison house, it is perhaps one of its most obvious attractions, and hence lends itself the most readily to descriptive detail.

The club work which began with "the play school" of a Saturday afternoon for the small children at large in Tyler street, has developed, as has been seen by the schedule, into a regular system of weekly meetings including over 250 people, old and young.

It is on bank and library days that we see the largest number of our younger neighbors. They come eagerly and voraciously to the circulating library to demand "war-books" and "fairytales." Occasionally, a quiet wide-eyed child asks in a timid whisper for "Longfeller's po'try book" or "Lo'ell's pomes." Books are actually worn out with much reading and new contributions to our modest collection are hailed with the greatest glee by both residents and library children.

The very little children, both boys and girls, between the ages of three and 10 are gathered together on Saturday afternoons for an hour of play. Games and toys of all sorts are placed on a long table, round which gather the children and the "gameladies," as our young neighbors have styled the young women who assist at this function.

Another club, of boys alone, meets on Thursday afternoon, also for game-playing and a half-hour's attention to wonderful stories told by the resident in charge.

Two other boys' clubs are practising the art of basket-weaving. These clubs have grown in interest and skill till they may be said to be largely self supporting. From the first almost shapeless shells of reeds there have been gradually evolved baskets of which both teachers and pupils may be proud.

Each boy is allowed to have for himself one out of every three baskets. The two others are sold to defray the expenses of the reeds. Both these clubs are organized societies and at meetings strict accounts are required of each office holder.

Girls of corresponding age have been formed into an afternoon sewing class. This is also a well organized club, paying weekly dues to defray, in a nominal way, the cost of the sewing materials. The girls have been successful in making articles of use both for themselves and for others, without being taught any particular system of instruction. It is hoped that next year may see some severer work done.

Another club of girls exists in a Kitchen garden which is a valuable form of training for children who get little or no instruction or even encouragement from their mothers in respect to the housewifely arts. There has been included in this year's course instruction in bed-making, dusting, dish-washing, and table setting and clearing.

With the Kitchen garden, we have passed from the children's clubs as such, and come now to the clubs for our young men and women. For almost three years six or seven boys, now almost young men, have met with one of our residents to talk of the inventions and discoveries of different periods of history and to collect bits of information about famous men. We can not but hope that this three years' devotion to the club and its work is the beginning of a permanent relation between these boys and the settlement.

Two girls' embroidery classes, whose members are of the same age as these boys, meet for a quiet hour's reading and work. It is astonishing to note how fast both reading and sewing progress during an hour's application.

An enthusiastic and expert gymnast who was in residence during the last winter, organized a class in gymnastics during her visit. The club is composed almost wholly of the young women of the immediate neighborhood and is one of our most popular classes. The social character of this club is fully as pronounced as its educational side. The healthful activity which the exercises produce seems to show itself in an increased social feeling, and we feel that the girls have come to understand both themselves and all other people a little better for these meetings.

Some of the young women in the gymnastic class have also been members of a singing and dramatic club. Several choruses and solos from modern operas with some of the old ballads have been studied to great advantage; for these girls have good voices, needing only cultivation of the right character. After the course of singing lessons, a study of dramatic expression, according to Delsarte, was given, the results of which bore very pleasant fruit in Mr Howells' *Mouse-trap*. That the study of Mr Howells' farces is a profitable affair for people whose experience has been wholly along popular lines has been at least partially demonstrated in the evident sympathy with the spirit of the text shown by all the young actors. The interpretation was such as college-bred girls need not have been ashamed to have given. Indeed, I have seen this same farce rendered much less felicitously by college undergraduates.

A class of young tailoresses, members of the Garment makers union, is studying penmanship and the lost art of letter-writing. The eagerness with which all suggestions have been received after the first reticences of the young women over what seemed to them unpardonable ignorance has proved a great inspiration to the residents acting as teachers

The Mothers meetings of this year have been among our signal victories. An average of 20 mothers come to these fortnightly gatherings which consist of music from piano, voice or violin, and of practical informal talks on home topics. Miss Wiltsie and Miss Fisher, Dr Emma Call, Miss Lucia Ames and Mrs Ellen Richards of the Mass. institute of technology have all given valuable suggestions from out rich experiences.

After the talks a social hour is enjoyed by all members, who seem to take pride in cooperating with the idea of the meetings in any way pointed out to them.

It has come to our knowledge from time to time that the mothers have been trying to carry out in their homes the suggestions given to them in hygienic clothing, cooking, care of children and beauty in the homes.

In the late fall, close on the edge of winter, two series of purely educational work were undertaken. One was a class in current topics, consisting of lectures on events of the times given by Wellesley professors and teachers; the other was an art class consisting of a course of lectures on Florentine art. The rare illustrations of each particular school of painting, lent to us by the Boston art museum, added definitely to the interpretative suggestions of the lectures. These classes were attended largely by the teachers of the neighboring public schools, by many young working women and by the residents.

The house further seeks the union, or at least the sympathetic cooperation of men and women of so-called leisure with the men and women of toil.

With that end in view, the social science club was formed. As Miss Helena S. Dudley, the head worker of the home says in her annual report: "To offer common ground where earnest people of various classes may, through freer intercourse, gain fuller sympathy, is certainly one legitimate function of a settlement. We are encouraged to hope that Denison house may exercise this function in the future by the surprising welcome accorded us by some of the prominent working men of Boston and by the warm faith that they have expressed in us."

The social science club has fulfilled, in good measure, these hopes. Papers have been read on the social problem in England, the social problem in France, Restriction of immigration, German socialism, Ethics of trade-unions, English vs American trade-unions, Contract labor. We have on our list of guests eminent professional men and women, prominent trade unionists and labor men and women, many students of the industrial problem, all of whom are coming better to comprehend and to take advantage of the differing points of view represented by the members of such a club.

In March 1894 a federal labor union was organized by one of our working men friends. It consists of wage earners, professional people, and of students of sociology. This union stands for organization among women workers, for improvement in the condition of workers, for education among all classes regarding the labor movement, for sympathetic appreciation of the moral ends to which the labor movement stands committed. Its most important functions have been its monthly open meetings, its reorganization of the garment workers, its enlisting of public sympathy and the consequent material support in behalf of the striking shoe-workers of Haverhill and its efforts toward furthering arbitration in the case of the pending strike of the Hyde Park rubber-workers.

The membership of the Garment workers' union has risen to such large figures, almost 700, that the meetings are no longer held at the house. The union hires a room of its own, and holds there its weekly meetings. The strength of the union is constantly demonstrated in the respect and prompt redress with which its complaints and grievances are met by the shops in which the women work. Its value to its members consists in training in parliamentary rule, in formal expression of ideas, in sympathy and knowledge of the life-conditions of others, and in education in matters pertaining to the industrial problem.

It has seemed permissible to include in an account of club life the definite efforts toward organization in a different sense, because they are more directly representative of the work of Denison house. The words of the first circular report of the work in the Boston college settlement were indeed prophetic: "It now seems to us that our leading interests at Denison house will be two-fold. If we use the larger phrases, university extension and the organization of labor it is not because we dare feel that we have much power to help, but because we know that we have great desire."

Of our relation to the labor movement and its practical results we have spoken, but of university extension as such we have said nothing; and this is because we have borne but little fruit in the way of university extension. The whole of this phase of the work however is to pass into the hands of a resident thoroughly competent to organize such an affair, and classes in any subject desired are to be formed. It would seem that in a program varying with the desire of the student, appreciable results must be secured, and since we thoroughly believe that the best intellectual progress is attainable only when there exists, on the part of the instructor, a complete sympathy with the temperament of each student, we shall strive to make the educational part of our work inhere in the social life that we have always inspired and encouraged.

We wish to make of our club members real friends, for it is only as we gain in friendship with club members that we can hope to know what are their deeper needs, their higher aspirations.— MABEL WARREN SANFRD

UNIVERSITY SETTLEMENT SOCIETY, NEW YORK

University settlement, 26 Delancey st., was started at 146 Forsyth st. in 1887, and transferred to the present location in 1891. The settlement includes 11 clubs, graded according to age and sex. Members of the youngest clubs are from six to 10; others are from 10 to 12, 12 to 14, 14 to 17, 18 to 25. There are clubs of both boys and girls for these ages and a peoples club composed of men and women. The bond of the clubs is, of course, social; the first educational purpose is physical culture. Our youngest boys clubs meet in the afternoon immediately after school and their first need is a general limbering up. We have thorough gymnastic courses bringing the muscles into play and aiming both to arouse those who are dulled by sitting in overcrowded and badly ventilated school-rooms and to quiet those whose nerves are over excited and strained by the same conditions. Lighter relaxation of the same sort is arranged for girls The result is a reasonable amount of good order and attentiveness during the club meeting. In clubs of older members gymnastic exercise is provided to serve the same purpose for those who have spent the day in shops or factories.

Next, we teach order and government. Our clubs, even the youngest, elect their own officers and manage their own affairs. The younger clubs are supplied with directors who assist and exercise a veto power if necessary. At these business meetings all the interests of the club are discussed within parliamentary limits, and the officers of the club are expected to preserve good order and promote an interest in the affairs of the club. Three of our younger boys' clubs have military drill. We are in doubt as to the value of this, but have consented to it because the boys wished it. Nearly all our girls clubs organize as sewing classes for part of their sessions, and naturally in all our work the industrial feature is prominent.

One club has taken up the study of history and another mythology; these two are the only ones not confined to the study of strictly practical matters, such as drawing, stenography and bookkeeping.

The young men are interested in civic matters, and one club has devoted itself to the sanitary conditions of the district. A club of young women has had conferences on hygiene as a proper supplement to previous courses in gymnastics and physical training. The average membership of our clubs is 30. Quarterly conferences of all the clubs are held, to which reports are presented and there is opportunity for a free discussion and criticisms of the clubs and the entire work of the house.

EAST SIDE HOUSE, NEW YORK

The Webster free circulating library, with 5294 volumes and a circulation of 19,200 in 1894, is our largest and, probably, most valuable line of work. The circulation is 95% among children.

A kindergarten of 25 children is held daily except Saturdays and Sundays. The kindergartner conducts, also, a Girls goodwill club on Tuesday afternoons (average attendance 15) and a Mothers meeting once a month.

In the kindergarten hall a Sunday-school is held on Sunday afternoons. The children are generally of foreign born parents. The average attendance is 30.

Lectures, talks, concerts, dramatic entertainments, etc. are the rule on Monday evenings from October to May.

A Young women's club, numbering 33, average attendance 17, meets once a week in the evening. The first intention is recreation, but besides dancing, games and general sociability, it takes up readings and discussions of the topics of the day. The tone of this club, except for an exclusive disposition among its members, is excellent.

A dancing class, of all ages under 40 and of both sexes, meets one evening of each week. This is greatly enjoyed and very popular. Each member pays 40 cents a month.

A singing class taught by the tonic sol fa system is held one night in the week. This is one of our best courses. With the dancing class, it affords peculiar opportunities for spreading good social influences far beyond the evenings and the members. The same may be said of the Young women's club. A literary society, of men from 20 to 45 years of age, holds weekly meetings from September to June. Debates, announced a month in advance, are often opened by fellows of Columbia college. The discussions that follow are exceedingly interesting. The residents of the house are members of the society and participate in the discussions sufficiently to influence generous treatment of the subjects and, personally, in a manner to secure the confidence and good fellowship of the outsiders.

An association for good citizenship, the East end improvement association, working with the departments of health, street cleaning and police, meets once a week, average attendance 19, monthly dues 15 cents. The members are householders and other neighbors from 24 to 70 years of age. This is, perhaps, the most evidently practical line of work done in our settlement.

A Boys club meeting once a week and using the gymnasium, is taught calisthenics and has debates, stories, games, etc; a fine body of boys, 43 in number, average attendance 21, weekly dues 5 cents

Besides these clubs and classes, the regular daily users of the house rooms, gymnasium, billiard room, grounds and baths are from 100 to 125 men, 18 to 25 years of age, to whom the privileges of the house are open from 6 to 11 p. m. The association is known as the Colleagues of the East side house. The following reprint explains the relationship between this body of men and the house. It is the plan and hope of kind and intelligent *cooperation*. The men pay 45 cents a month for colleagueship

DECLARATION OF COLLEAGUESHIP IN THE EAST SIDE HOUSE

We, the undersigned, desiring to become, and hereby becoming, Colleagues of the East side house, attest our accordance with the purposes of the house, which are (1) to promote better understanding and social interchange between people regardless of circumstances in life, (2) to furnish opportunities and leadership for cooperation in educational and recreative advancement, and (3) to induce and conduct intelligent combination for the health, cleanliness and good order of our neighborhood; and we hereby promise and agree to act among ourselves and with the East side house to secure agreeable and beneficial fellowship and good government for all parties jointly concerned in this association.

We have knowledge of the rules adopted by the managers of the house, as declared in connection herewith, and we concur in the same, and will endeavor, individually and collectively to have such regulations observed without resort to the authority of the resident manager of the house.

The influences at work are personal, those of character. Those with whom we work must find in their hosts and leaders justice, probity, manliness and the love of fellow-men, or the work goes for naught. Our neighbors are not to be patronized nor coddled. They demand one's own self, just as one is, without attempt to come down or diplomatically to adjust oneself in manners, words or anything else to them differently situated. — CLARENCE GORDON, *Secretary and resident manager*

WHITTIER HOUSE

Whittier house is a social settlement situated in the midst of the densely populated district of Jersey City. In common with other institutions of a similar kind, it aims to help all in need by improving their circumstances, alleviating as far as possible their distress, and by placing before them new motives and higher ideals to fit them for the responsibilities of life. The policy pursued is to reach as many as possible, not allowing differences of class or religion to be a barrier to any department of the work. Consequently the work is not confined to the very lowest classes as such, but reaches forward to the better class of working men and their families. It endeavors to show all with whom it comes in contact how to better their own condition and not, as has been inferred by some, by indiscriminate charity, further to complicate the problem of the relation of the masses as such to the social movement. The work is yet young but is prospering and rapidly gaining confidence of the people which it aims to reach. The instruments employed are practically the same as are in use in other settlements. During the year 26 classes and clubs have met regularly at the Whittier house, 174 Grand st. These clubs and classes include men, women and children studying German, elocution, literature, art, vocal and instrumental music, dressmaking, plain sewing, physiology and hygiene and dancing. In the clubs the subjects vary from evening to evening as seems wise to the worker in charge. In addition to the work of instruction there are also departments connected with Whittier house which are of direct practical benefit to those who avail themselves of the opportunities offered. These consist of a resident physician, a poor man's lawyer, and a penny provident fund. From such an enumeration ought not to be omitted the free kindergarten, which is the first to be established in this city. 30 or 40 children attend this school daily and receive the benefits of professional instruction.

The results of the work are visible in many ways. The hearty cooperation of the people among whom we labor, their eagerness to receive instruction, the improvement seen in the regular frequenters of Whittier house both as a class and as individuals, all constitute a part of the results of the work which are full of encouragement to those who are trying to contribute their share toward the elevation of the masses from the present physical, mental and moral degradation.

LOS ANGELES SETTLEMENTS ASSOCIATION

This association was organized in February 1894 by the Los Angeles branch of the Collegiate alumnae association. The idea is, as the work grows to form small settlements in different parts of the city. At present the work is carried on in Sonoratown, decidedly the worst part of the city, peopled by a mixture of foreign elements. The Little men's club of 24 boys from five to eight years old is composed of Mexicans, Italians, French, German, English, Spanish and even Arabians. The club method of work is chosen as being most natural and least restricted.

Boys clubs, of 12 members only, can do fine work. When the number is limited, it is like a family; with the increase in members, the social side is less prominent and certainly individual help decreases. In "La primavera" the aim is an understanding of true civics — and first a knowledge of the various departments of the city's government; e. g. one member of the club takes up the fire department, studying it in detail and reading a paper before the club. One question, not to be overlooked, is: What does La primavera think of the departments considered. The answer in many cases might be very instructive. In fact, there is nothing equal to first-hand-knowledge on these points.

The use of parliamentary practice is very obvious. It develops those who take part in it, and in some instances leads club members to visit the city's council meetings and see for themselves just how the city's life is controlled. Such study makes toward good citizenship and a purer ballot, and ought to be a part of each club's life.

The members of the Health protective league are chosen from our immediate neighborhood. This touches the physical life of every house in the block and even beyond.— M. B. FOSTER

An outline of the club work of the association follows:

Monday 9–12 a. m. Kindergarten. Two teachers. 20 children, from three to five years old.

3–5 p. m. Isabella club. Two workers. 12 girls, from 12 to 18 years of age. Embroidery, crocheting, reading and singing.

3–5 p. m. Marguerite club. Two workers. Over 30 girls, from five to 12 years old. Plain sewing, music and games.

8–10 p. m. La primavera club. Young men, from 18 to 25 years old. Two workers. Parliamentary practice. Study of city government (all departments). Singing class.

Tuesday 9–12 a. m. Kindergarten.

8–10 p. m. Tuesday night club. Three workers. Boys from 14 to 18 years old. Parliamentary practice and travel letter-writing.

Wednesday 9–12 a. m. Kindergarten.

3–5 p. m. El club esperanza. Two workers. Young women. Letter-writing, spelling, lectures on hygiene, music.

3–5 p. m. Mothers' meeting. An occasional lecture and tea-drinking. Very irregular in attendance.

Thursday 9–12 a. m. Kindergarten.
    4–6 p. m. Little men's club. Three workers. 24 little boys, from five to eight years old. Scrap-books, drawing, basket-making, marching and round games.
    8–10 p. m. Lincoln club. Four workers. Young men, 16 to 18 years old. Basket-making, wood-carving, letter-writing, music and games.

Friday 9–12 a. m. Kindergarten.
    3–5 p. m. Washington club. Two workers. About 20 boys, from eight to 14 years old. Games of all sorts and music.

BERTHA LEBUS

 Allied to social settlement work is that of the working girls clubs, which though well known by name, are often not fully understood. That their relation to similar work may be made clear, Miss Grace H. Dodge has sent the following account.

WORKING GIRLS CLUBS

 12 years ago a small group of young women representing various phases of life learned to know each other and to appreciate each other's needs From their talks, the first New York Working girls club started. Its aims and objects soon became those of many others, and the following is a condensed summary now generally adopted as indicating the movement:

 A Working girls society or club is an organization formed among busy girls and young women, to secure, by cooperation, means of self-support, opportunities for social intercourse, and development of higher and nobler aims. To this end pleasant rooms are furnished where members can pass the evening, classes organized for mutual improvement and enjoyment, circulating libraries established and cooperative measures fostered, which are for the benefit of members. Members must be over 14 years of age. They must pay an initiation fee of 25 cents, and monthly dues of from 15 to 25 cents.

 Their advantages are free use of rooms, library, piano and writing materials, privilege of consulting the club physician, access to musical drill, lectures, talks and entertainments, sewing and embroidery classes, and penny-provident fund; by paying class fee, privilege of joining dress making, cooking, millinery, school extension and other pay classes.

The clubs are governed by the members for the members. Officers are chosen from the membership of the clubs, and are elected by ballot. Matters of business are presented at monthly business meetings, and decided by a majority vote. All questions arising as to the government of the clubs are carefully discussed and settled in the same way.

The following is the usual list of officers: president, vice-president, secretary, assistant secretary, treasurer, assistant, librarian, or steward. Many clubs have a council, consisting of 12 members, including the six officers. The six members who are not officers are elected by ballot, and hold office two years. This council has general charge and control of the funds and property of the club.

As far as possible, the clubs are supported by monthly dues, entertainments provided by the members, where small admission fees are required, and fairs or sales of fancy and useful articles, made or contributed by members.

From the above it will be seen that there are many societies known as Working girls clubs which in the New York acceptation of the term should not receive the name. Thus, there are those governed by boards of managers, advisory councils, etc. such as the Young women's Christian association, the Girls friendly society, various industrial and educational unions, and many others under the auspices of the Women's Christian temperance union and different churches. These are generally sectarian in character. Second, there are organizations such as labor unions, fraternity circles, etc all of which have some sociologic object. Between, come the Working girls clubs governed as are those connected with the New York association. These are usually composed of young women mainly dependent on their own exertions, quickened by contact and experience into sympathy with those who combine for personal advantage or advancement Often too conservative to take active part in such movements, they are usually conversant with the aims and methods of labor unions, and are very frequently members of benefit societies, organized by companies for those employed in trades. Such thinkers and workers are readily drawn to cooperate with women of leisure in movements where individualism is cherished, but are not so easily attracted to bodies with strongly defined characteristics, such as church societies. The clubs being self-governed, each member has an equal right to direct its expenditures, and an equal responsibility in procuring and receiving the necessary funds.

Clubs greatly differ in size and variety of life. One meets only once a week in a hired room and has but 25 members; another has its own suite of rooms, 300 members, many classes and constantly changing interests. An officer says: " Methods must and do differ greatly, but the spirit which animates us all is the same. Our beautiful ideal takes to itself different forms, and indeed opens to us all new possibilities every year. Recreation, class work and literary interests with us are considered as means to an end. Perhaps the shortest way of stating what we should feel it necessary to keep if we should be obliged to prune away many valuable growths is to pronounce this one word as our key note, *character*. We would keep the opportunity to learn to value character in ourselves and in others. This it is which we claim to do in whatever form we may for the time being clothe our purpose."

The educational advantages in the strict sense of the word are not great, but a general education based on common sense and contact is secured. An important factor in the education of individuals and the development of club life is the Practical talks. They for the most part deal with practical, everyday subjects, for these are the topics of study of those busily engaged in routine work. A leader is selected whose duty is simply to bring out the ideas of those present, and to aid them in focusing these thoughts, either in a verbal summary or a written paper, longer or shorter. Following are some of the topics given in one club:

In what way can women obtain, for the same work, the same wages as men? Is there any danger that men's salaries will be cut down to what women receive?

Is our present school system the best possible? What changes would you propose?

What do we like most in the newspaper of the present? What features would we eliminate, if we could do as we liked?.

Are cheap books a help or hindrance to gaining knowledge? What are our favorite authors?

Does a woman gain a broader education by associating with men, as well as women?

Education before and after marriage.

How shall we teach patriotism?

What do we mean by the terms womanly and unwomanly?

Is economy wealth? What is true economy?

How can we train our judgment to make love stronger than sentimentality?

What should be the relation of business women to each other?

What is the ideal family life?

What qualities in women have most influenced our lives?

A member of one such Talk night whose trade is that of a silk weaver says: "Why do we love our Practical talks so much and how are they of value to us? Because Practical talks give us a better idea of the value of time more than anything else can, for the reason that we learn to think quickly and speak readily, and the friction puts our ideas into definite shape, so that almost before we are aware of it, we have been able to put into words the very ideas we never thought would see the light of day, partly because they were not developed and partly because there is no other outlet than the Practical talks. We forget ourselves and in such moments our hidden selves shine forth and unconsciouly we sometimes make an impression we would find hard to eradicate; many a strong quiet character has been discovered in just that way. In Practical talks nothing is glossed over, we are living our lives and our talk therefore must come from our practical experience to be worth much. Hereby plain facts are talked out and we find that what we value will not come to us in life without the hard work beforehand. Every experience however small it may seem is going to be of use to us; nothing is wasted, nor can we foresee how soon we may find it most useful. Practical talks is an education that can not be found in either schools or colleges, it is an education in life and living, which all people however they may be situated in life need."

There have been various outgrowths of the club movement. The domestic circles consist of young married women, former club members and friends, who meet weekly to gain ideas about practical matters affecting their homes. Babies and young children are brought and enjoy toys, while the mothers listen to lectures or discuss given topics.

The Junior clubs are inside organizations, consisting of girls under 15 who are too young for the club proper. They use the rooms once a week, pay 10 cents for monthly dues, and generally have separate officers and constitution, the older club members cooperating with them.

There are various organizations for helping others, such as Lend a hand, Benefit, Loan closet, Visiting, Work and the general Mutual benefit fund, whose members pay monthly dues and receive benefits during sickness or in case of death a given sum.

The summer gives opportunities for vacations and outings, and to meet this need the association has the use of three houses, where members can spend their vacations. Two of these, Holiday house and Holiday harbor, are at Miller's place, Long Island. The third, Brookside cottage, is at Mountainville, New York. Club members pay railroad fares and three dollars a week for board. Arrangements are also made for excursions, picnics and short outings to many neighboring localities, for which reduced rates are secured on boats or trains, and leaders for the parties provided.

There have been the following associations formed since the New York body in 1886: Brooklyn association of working girls societies, organized October 1888; Massachusetts association of working girls societies, organized February 1 89; Connecticut association of working girls societies, organized May 1891; and Philadelphia association of working women's societies, organized April 1892.

Chicago is starting one, and yet these united bodies do not properly represent the movement. There are clubs and societies all over the country. The clubs represent We, Us and company, and in the company only working girls and women are allowed; one might say, wage-earning girls. Some have received their wages in advance; that is, money and responsibility have come to them through birth, inheritance and surroundings. These owe it in h,nor more than all others to work out their wages in loving, hearty, faithful services, first to God, then to their fellow sisters. All together they rouse themselves, learn methods and ways, and then by cooperation secure results. — GRACE H. DODGE

REGISTERED STUDY CLUBS OF NEW YORK

These are arranged in order of registration. The accounts were either prepared by members of the clubs or compiled from available statements issued by the club.

HOME CULTURE CLUB, LITTLE FALLS

The Home culture club reports a membership of 16 with an average attendance of 14. Biweekly meetings are held and French history was the subject of study for 1894. Colonial history will be studied during 1895-96.

GRADUATES ASSOCIATION OF THE BUFFALO SEMINARY

This association was organized March 22, 1876 and incorporated by the legislature of New York September 5, 1884.

The membership, which is limited to those holding the diploma of the Buffalo female academy, is 175. The object of the society is mutual improvement in art, literature, history, music and science and the advancement of the interests of the Buffalo female academy. Weekly meetings are held on Friday afternoons at the chapter house from November to April.

During the winter of 1893 an extension course of 10 lectures on physical geology was given by Prof. H. D. Fairchild of Rochester university.

MONDAY AFTERNOON STUDY CLASS, GLOVERSVILLE

In 1886 Mrs Nellie G. Avery invited a few ladies to meet at her home to form a literary class for mutual improvement and such intellectual recreation as would naturally proceed from such an organization. Only four were present, but it was decided to limit membership to 20 and to hold meetings every Monday at 2:30 p. m. during six months of the year. The election of a president and secretary and the adoption of a brief and simple constitution completed the organization of this class which has for nine years done excellent work with zeal and fidelity.

This band of busy women, without exception women with household and family cares, has followed with little variation the programs arranged by a topic committee, appointed each year by the president, as follows: 1886–87 Germany; 1887–88 France; 1888–89 British Isles; 1889–90 Contemporaneous history of Europe, 16th century; 1890–91 Contemporaneous history of the 17th century; 1891–92 Contemporaneous history of the 18th century, Outline history of art; 1892–93 Contemporaneous history of Europe and America 1800–50, Outline history of art in Europe and America; 1893–94 Japan, Gleanings from modern history; 1894–95 Mexico, Selected readings, literary and scientific.

We have no treasury or treasurer, any incidental expenses being paid by assessment. The Free library of Gloversville supplies us with all needed books for study and reference. The president appoints a critic for each meeting, and criticisms of pronunciation which we have found highly beneficial, follow each reading.

In the spring of 1893 by invitation of Sorosis, we prepared a folio for exhibit at the Columbian exhibition. By earnest endeavor we have sought for intellectual advancement, and feel that our time has been well spent.—MRS W. F. STEELE, *Secretary*

WEDNESDAY MORNING CURRENT TOPIC CLUB, ROME

This club, soon to begin its third year, has fully demonstrated the need of such a club in this city. We are regularly organized with president, vice-president, secretary and treasurer, constitution and by-laws. Special committees are appointed on membership, lectures and for general business of the society. Membership is limited to 50. There is an annual election of officers and to fill vacancies in membership. Among our number are women not only of literary tastes and ability, but also women on whom devolve many other social and domestic duties. A number of our younger members are fresh from college and school.

We are divided into 10 groups of five members. Each group chooses a chairman and assumes the charge of two meetings in the year according to the Kalendar. At every regular meeting some time is set apart for discussing current topics, book reviews, etc.

Last year our subject was the history, literature and art of France and Scotland. The special art committee gave us some delightful mornings on French art. We had a lecture on Burns and Scotland, finely illustrated, which the friends of the club also enjoyed. One meeting was devoted to listening to Scotch ballads sung most delightfully by a charming Scotch woman.

The coming year promises still greater results. The study of the 19th century in England and colonial history has been decided on. We are to have a local habitation in the Jervis library building, the club furnishing a room. More lectures and papers by men and women outside the city are looked forward to A distinct feeling of interest and enthusiasm in the welfare of the club prevails, which promises a rich harvest of mental improvement to all.

FORTNIGHTLY, JAMESTOWN

This club was organized in 1894 with a membership of 65. French history, the renaissance, the revolution, the consulate and empire with contemporary history, was the subject of study for the first year. The course closed with a brilliant lecture on Napoleon by Mrs Helen Barrett Montgomery of Rochester. The work of the second year was on Italy, medieval and modern. Lectures were given by Mrs Montgomery on Dante's *Divine comedy* and by Mr Henry Clapp of Boston on Shakspere's *Twelfth night*.

At each meeting two major papers are read with four to six minor ones of five minutes each. Occasionally the major papers are in the form of a discussion and a general discussion always follows the regular program.

HIGHLAND PARK LITERARY CLUB, BUFFALO

The Highland park literary club is a band of 35 neighbors in the Parkside district of Buffalo. The officers are president, vice-president, recording secretary, corresponding secretary and treasurer, elected by ballot at the annual business meeting.

Any woman pledging herself to accept any office to which she may be called and to perform all work assigned her, may be admitted to membership, which is limited to 50. The name of any woman may be proposed by any member of the club at any regular meeting. The candidate for membership, after signing an application, stating her intention to obey the constitution, may be balloted for at any following meeting.

The club holds one meeting for work, on Tuesday at 10 a. m. of each week from October 1 to about April 1. The last meeting of the season is known as the annual business meeting. Annual dues are one dollar, payable at the annual meeting. At this meeting is given the program for the ensuing year and the work assigned to members. The officers of the society, with any other members of the club, usually two, whom the president may appoint, constitute the executive committee, which meets by order of the president or of the club, and has general direction of affairs, authorizes expenditures, and plans the literary program for the year. Other committees may be appointed by the president.

After the executive committee, the first in importance is the program committee, the duty of which is to ascertain, weeks in advance, that papers are forthcoming. This season only one member failed to do her allotted work, and this was due to severe illness.

The membership committee looks after new members and delinquents, and the reception committee attends to the physical needs of the club.

In November 1894 a traveling library of books on our subject was sent to the club by the University. This has been a constant source of profit and delight, and we heartily recommend that each study club of the state avail itself of the privilege.

Our only social gathering during the past year was a luncheon at the Genesee hotel, given in honor of Mrs Ednah D. Cheney, who was attending the mid-year conference of the Association for the advancement of women. We were favored in having also Mrs Julia Ward Howe, Mrs Frances Stewart Parker of Chicago and Mrs Henrietta L. Woolcott. Mrs Cheney gave a half-hour talk on Some artistic points, which was followed by graceful and appropriate remarks by most of the out-of-town guests and by several of the club members.

We have completed our third year and our purpose to improve by study is stronger than ever before; to this we have added a desire to stand as a unit of strength in the vicinity, for progress in all directions. A society of three years standing can hardly discover results; rather are they felt to be growing, as the purposes are taking deeper hold and steadily throwing out influence in every direction.

EVERY MONDAY CLUB, GLOVERSVILLE

The Every Monday club was organized five years ago and is now composed of 12 active members, the size of the club being limited to that number. The regular meetings occupy two hours every Monday afternoon between the first of October and the last of March, with the exception of two weeks at the holidays, and are held at the homes of the members as their names occur on the roll.

At each meeting the roll is called by the secretary, and every member is expected to respond to her name by giving an item of general interest, a current event or information of an historical or of a scientific nature.

A topic committee is appointed by the president, and it is its duty to arrange the program to be used by the club during the succeeding year. Each member prepares three papers and reads them at the meetings of the club.

During the season of 1894-95 the Every Monday club considered American history to the close of the revolutionary war, following as an outline for their papers, the syllabuses on the subject which have been issued by the Extension department of the University of the State of New York. The result has proved to be most gratifying, for with the aid of the syllabuses the papers have been better arranged and more comprehensive than ever before

If the entire two hours is not occupied by the papers which have been prepared, the remainder of the time is devoted to supplementary reading. During the last season, besides miscellaneous articles from current magazines the club has read the paper on "Napoleon" written by Miss Ida Tarbell and published in *McClure's magazine.*

In the five years of its existence the Every Monday club has never been in a more prosperous condition than it is at the present time, and during the season that is approaching the members are desirous of devoting themselves more earnestly to the acquirement of a broader and deeper culture.— ELLEN G. KINGSLEY, *Secretary*

TRAVELERS-AT-HOME CLUB, SARATOGA

The Travelers at-home club of Saratoga Springs was organized in October 1892 and at the close of our third season's work we can happily say that our last six months' work has been most successful, not only in regularity of meetings but in increased study and research. Our aim has been not to make our club literary only, but as nearly as possible to make members feel that they were actually traveling amid the varied scenes described or viewing the riches of famous galleries. Our meetings are held weekly at members' homes from 10:30 a. m. to 12:30 p. m. the first hour being given to a paper or a talk on the route of the day, the next half hour to light refreshment and social chat and the final half hour to general discussion of the topics of the day's route.

Officers consist of president, vice-president, secretary and courier, librarian and treasurer. The courier maps out the line of travel for each week's paper, and also has acted as illustrator. Our work has been profusely illustrated with engravings, photographs, paintings, etchings, choice ceramics, rare books, etc. Invaluable aid has been given by the large number of wood-cuts which could be drawn from, for the best wood-cut is by no means to be despised when mounted on heavy manila paper with a wide margin.

The headings or main points of the weekly papers are given out as far as possible in alphabetic order of members' names and two or more weeks have been allowed for their preparation. This short time has been found imperative to keep to an unbroken line of travel and as a rule when a longer time than two weeks has been given for preparation the writer of the paper has rarely done any work on it, till within the last week or two of her time.

The work of our club can be expressed in two words, research and condensation; one of our mottoes is: "He who eats the kernel, must not complain of cracking the nut." In two seasons' work of six months each our field of travel was in England whence we crossed the channel to France, where our last season's work has been of no less interest. The club voted to continue travel in France next year.

One of the most valuable rules of our club has been that each member should furnish the courier with a list of volumes she was willing to lend for the club's use. For our English travels this placed over 300 books at the disposal of the club, and for France about 150, many of them being rare and valuable. These books were not to be called for unless unavailable at our town libraries. The second year the club had two subscriptions in the Mercantile library of New York but labored under the great disadvantage of an incomplete catalog. Returning, almost discouraged, after an interview at the Mercantile library, the courier saw in a newspaper an account of the traveling libraries of the University of the State of New York, and action was at once taken which provided us with the needed books for our study.

An interesting rule has been that all members absent from town during four successive meetings should write to the club describing points of interest visited. Many delightful letters have resulted, telling not only of the literature, music, art and science of our own country but of the greater wealth of the older countries This rule has since been modified to allow instead of a letter, a gift of 50 cents for each month's absence, the sum to go toward our book fund. Our annual dues are $1. Bädeker's and Hare's guides are owned by the club, all other books being obtained from members and libraries. A booklet has been published each year giving a brief outline of our work. At no meeting has the paper for the day failed to be ready and even in a blizzard seven members were present at the meeting. Our membership is limited to 20, which we find quite large enough for thorough work. — ANNA MARSEILLES, *Secretary*

SHAKSPERE UNIVERSITY EXTENSION CLUB, SYRACUSE

This club was organized in November, 1894, with a membership of 15 busy young women resident at the Syracuse Women's Christian association. During the previous winter we had studied the *Merchant of Venice* and *Hamlet*, using questions arranged by Mrs Jessie K. Curtis in her syllabus printed by the University of the State of New York. This study was so interesting that we continued last winter with *Romeo and Juliet* and the *Tempest*.

Meetings were held each Friday evening from 7:45 to 9 o'clock, with often an extra half hour spent in lively discussion greatly enjoyed by all. After roll call, time was allowed for transaction of business, after which the lesson text was read and questions answered round the class. Only half a lesson was assigned for each recitation, as with our limited time for study we found frequent reviews of the whole necessary to keep up interest Then followed a lecture by our instructor, Mrs Minnie S. Fisher, to whose tireless efforts in behalf of our club we owe much.

Our constitution provided that only those residing at the home were eligible to membership and each member was expected to attend each meeting unless detained by some obligation or illness. In case no reasonable excuse could be given a fine of five cents was imposed. To defray expenses a membership fee of 25 cents was required.

As a unifying influence and promoter of mutual interest, healthful home feeling and self-culture without burdensome restraint, we regard our club as very successful. One of its happiest results is the development of a taste for good reading, for all spare moments were utilized in reading matter pertaining to our study, whereas they would otherwise have been spent on light literature.— M. Eliza Trapp, *Secretary*

WEDNESDAY CLUB, SYRACUSE

The Wednesday club was organized November 20, 1887, and now has 30 active and seven honorary members. Its objects are both intellectual and social Meetings are held biweekly from October to April For the present year a program on France has been arranged, embracing its earliest history through the period of Louis 14.— E. F. Loomis, *Secretary*

TRAINING CLASS OF THE BUFFALO FREE KINDERGARTEN ASSOCIATION

As its name implies, the purpose of this class, or school, is to prepare its students for kindergarten teaching. The regular course of study includes kindergarten theory and practice, child study, history of education and psychology. In addition to this there are brief courses in literature, art and natural history. Each student is required to present abstracts of lessons and lectures and at least two formal papers. While some text-books are used, many books are needed for reference, comparison and supplementary study. From January to the close of the year, in June, the class had the use of a traveling library of 100 volumes. This proved to be of great value in broadening the line of study, and in turning to good account the leisure reading of the students, by making easily accessible books on subjects kindred to those pursued in the regular course —ELLA C. ELDER, *Superintendent*

HISTORICAL CLUB, CAMDEN

The Historical club of Camden was organized in 1884 with 15 members. Weekly meetings are held during 26 weeks, beginning the first Monday in October, for the study of some country with special attention to its history and literature During 1894-95, India has been the subject of study; papers have been prepared, readings given from poems of Sir Edwin Arnold and from *Lalla Rookh*. The program closes with a discussion of current topics followed by criticism of pronunciation. — L. J. ALDRICH, *President*

SOCIETY TO PROMOTE USEFUL READING, SCHENECTADY

A number of ladies, feeling the need of stimulating the mental culture of young women after school life has ended, of inducing them to perfect or extend the knowledge already acquired and of furnishing necessary books for systematic rather than desultory reading, associated themselves together as an executive committee and adopted the title Society to promote useful reading, as most expressive of the objec s in view. A small loan library was started for the use of the members, courses of reading were arranged in the several departments of history, literature and art, each under the supervision of ladies of the executive committee. Classes were also formed under competent instructors for young women who desired to pursue advanced work in certain college studies and arrangements made through the college authorities for test examinations, with certificates of the work accomplished, somewhat on the Cambridge plan in England.

During the past four years a number of young women, many of them teachers in our public schools, have availed themselves of these advantages and now hold certificates testifying of their work in geology, physiology, metaphysics, moral science and architecture The testimony of the superintendent of the public schools to the beneficent results of such work among several of his teachers, is most satisfactory. For four years past the society as a whole has devoted itself to study of the centuries, including their history, literature, art and world-wide relations. Last winter the subject considered was the early middle ages closing with the 12th century. Once a week throughout the winter, papers on subjects which had been arranged early in the year were presented before the society by the several members of the executive committee, including once a month a consideration of the topics of the times.

The benefits of the society are open to any lady on the payment of a small annual fee. The funds so accumulated are mainly devoted to the increase of the library, which now numbers 600 volumes. During the past winter our facilities have been increased by the use of a traveling library. The average number of members during the past 18 years has been over 50.

MONDAY CLUB, WARSAW

The papers during the course of study on French history have given evidence of careful thought in preparation and have been exceedingly entertaining and helpful. 28 meetings have been held during the year with an average attendance of 24, including guests from several states. The smallest number present at any meeting was on February 4th when there were only 11 and the largest on March 25th when 60 witnessed the presentation of Molière's comedy *Les precieuses ridicules*, charmingly given by seven members of the club A new and decidedly interesting feature of the last year's course of study has been the half hour devoted once each month to consideration of current topics, and such subjects as the simplification of housekeeping, physical culture and dress reform. Mrs Maud Humphrey, delegate from the Monday club to the General federation of woman's clubs convention in Philadelphia, gave a report of that meeting, and Mrs Alice Gardiner and Mrs Gouinlock gave accounts of the conference held in New York for the formation of a state federation, at which they were present representing this club.

It has been the custom of the club to have one or more out-of-town lecturers during the season, but this year the funds in the treasury have been used in beautifying our rooms.

The following are the officers of the club: Mrs Maud Humphrey, *president;* Mrs W. C. Gouinlock, *vice-president;* Mrs Carolin Bristol Beardslee, *secretary ;* Miss Anna Holmes, *treasurer.—*
CAROLIN BRISTOL BEARDSLEE, *Secretary*

SOCIETY FOR THE STUDY OF CHILD NATURE, NEW YORK

History. This society, though first organized in 1890, traces its origin to an earlier date. In 1888, several ladies met at stated times to discuss questions of interest in the education of their children. It was their purpose originally to devote their attention mainly to stories adapted to telling and reading to children; but the work could not be restricted to these limits and the idea forced itself on them, that their subject should be studied not in a hap-hazard manner, but seriously, in the spirit of the true student, seeking for knowledge with a desire to learn the truth.

In 1889, five ladies met once a week regularly from November to May. They planned a course of reading, and were deeply impressed with the thoughts that were revealed to them. In 1890, new members were invited to join in the work, and it was then that a name was adopted for the society and definite methods for conducting its affairs decided. The membership of the new society was limited to 35, which number has since been maintained as its limit.

Organization. The plans of organization are based on cooperation. The officers and executive council plan the work, but all members unite in reading the authors prescribed, and in discussing the text at the meetings, while individual members, appointed by the president, prepare papers relating to the text. The papers do not always represent the original thought of the writer; in many instances they consist of the opinion of persons of accredited authority, due acknowledgment being made to the author quoted. They generally comprise comments on the allotted text, or on such parts of it as appealed most forcibly to the attention of the writer of the paper. In sanctioning an opinion given in the text, or in refuting it, she will call to her aid, if necessary, an authority on the subject; frequently, however, relying on her own opinions or judgment, and challenging the opinions of others.

Business methods. The business methods of the society are as follows: The president calls the meeting to order; the secretary reads the minutes of the preceding meeting; notices or special business matters that do not consume a great amount of time are disposed of and then the paper for the day is read. When there is no paper, the text that has been read is cursorily reviewed, followed by discussions or questions on the text or on the paper, or on both. Often these discussions furnish subject-matter for papers at future meetings, and sometimes two sides of a subject are presented by different members. When possible, a thoughtful presentation of opinion, as exemplified in a paper, is preferred to an impromptu expression of ideas

The question-box is next referred to. It was instituted as a means of presenting questions anonymously, where the direct manner of inquiry might be a matter of delicacy, perhaps compromising the questioner or some member of her family. Then the text for the following meeting is assigned, and adjournment follows after a session of one and one half hours, generally too short a period to satisfy the members

Purpose. The purpose of the society is to study the child in its physical, mental and moral nature, and to enable mothers to understand their duties and to perform them intelligently.

Literary methods. The society began its work with a study of *Emile* by Rousseau, a paper on the life of Rousseau being read as an introduction. The entire season, November 1890–May 1891, was devoted to this work and to discussions and questions suggested. 17 papers were prepared by as many members on various portions of the text; e. g On the teaching of several languages to young children; On methods of instruction; On clothing and physical culture.

Discussions. The discussions and questions coming under this text may be indicated as follows:

Moral sense in children. Does it exist early? How can it be influenced?

Should implicit obedience be enforced in children?

How can a true idea of property be conveyed to the child, while its disposal of property is circumscribed by parental authority?

Falsehood from a moral aspect.
Punishments.
The sense of duty.
Rewards.
Should the child be made familiar with the destruction of life? Is cruelty engendered by such knowledge? Should the child see death in any form?
Importance of attention to detail.
Amount of personal attention the mother should vouchsafe her child.
Is the time devoted to young children stultifying to the mental growth of the mother?
Is it right that the children monopolize the mother's attention to such an extent, that other members of the family, say the father, may be at a disadvantage?
Authority of older children over younger. The feelings such authority arouses in each.
Approbation as an element in education.
Discouragement of rivalry as an incentive.
Good manners. The importance of form or address in the child's demeanor.
Toys.

Collateral reading. The collateral reading at meetings during this same year consisted of: An article by Dr G. Stanley Hall on The imaginative aspect of falsehood; Several translations from Prof. Waitz's *Pedagogy;* Preyer on *The senses and the will;* Uffelmann on *Domestic hygiene of the child;* Dr Elizabeth Blackwell on *Moral education of children.* A list of books was also recommended for parents and children respectively.

Auxiliary work In addition to the work specified, much help was derived from various magazines and publications recommended The society subscribed to several educational journals, which were circulated among the members. Invitations were extended to the society to attend lectures on various topics. The society had one speaker give an address on physical culture, and a class was formed to take instruction in this branch of development. A paper, written by one of the members, on The value of making scientific observations of children was read, and with some additions was published in pamphlet form later.

Subsequent work. The work of the first year has been continued on the same plans, but only an outline of this can be given here.

The following books have been studied carefully: Locke's *Education*, Richter's *Levana*, Spencer's *Education*, Adler's *Moral instruction of children*, Radestock's *Habit*. Lectures on The punishment of children by Prof. Adler were read at meetings and discussed.

As an introduction to *Levana* Ruskin's *Advice to readers* was read. Biographies of men and women representing the thought or the work in line with the aims of our society were read.

Lectures have been given before the society on: Principles underlying the ethical training of the child by Prof. J. Allen; Child nature by Dr Stanton Coit; Ethical aspect of civic life by Mrs C. Neymann; Physical care of the child by Dr Dorning; Influence of tenement house environment on the child by Jacob Riis.

Many subjects have been brought before the society in the form of questions and discussions; but to enumerate them would involve explanations that would increase the scope of this account beyond its desired limits. Indeed a report of our work can comprise only such parts of it as is possible to give in outline. Much remains untold, which can not be so treated, but which exerts a strong influence on the work itself.

Results. Of results it is difficult to speak. We know that interest has been awakened in the subject of child-study. Our society has been requested to give assistance in organizing similar societies in four states, in one instance the officers being invited to attend and lead the first meeting. Several universities have also placed themselves in communication with our society, in order to ascertain our mode of study and purpose. Notably the departments of psychology and pedagogy of Clark university have shown interest in our work; and our plan of study for the season of 1895–1896 includes a careful consideration of the syllabuses published by Dr G. Stanley Hall, and sent to our society. These syllabuses have been distributed among members, and the questions are to be answered and discussed.

One great hindrance to rapid progress in our work rises from the fact that we seem to be pioneers in the particular direction which we have chosen; for as a rule the child is an object of scientific experiment, while we study it as a human being, and meet with great difficulty in getting help in our work from books or from individuals, treating the study from this point of view.

In closing this account of our society, mention must be made of the great advantage derived by our members, from the personal contact of a number of mothers, all serious in their desire for enlightenment on this most important subject. The insight into human nature disclosed through such association, is in itself a most valuable adjunct of our work. The questions propounded are an indication of the needs presenting themselves to parents in all aspects of the education of their children.

The discussions reveal the attitude of those who undertake the consideration of the questions; and both questions and discussions prove to be the key to the results which we see and feel about us, good as well as bad. — LILLIE W. SALIGSBERG, *Secretary*

STUDY CLUB, OAKFIELD

The Study club was organized November 5, 1894 with a membership of 16. The object of the club is the study of history and literature. French history was chosen as the study for the first year. At each meeting one or more papers are read, a general discussion follows, after which the oral topics in the program have special notice, forming the basis for a more extended study of the period — GEORGIA W. RATHBONE, *Secretary*

TRAVELERS CLUB, MIDDLETOWN

This club of women was started in the spring of 1889, and was organized with the object of becoming thoroughly acquainted with our own country and others, and to study the lives of the eminent men and women whose history is connected with the places under consideration.

The club started with nine members and the few changes have been occasioned by absence and illness. We have met with unfailing interest fortnightly, from October till June of each year, at the homes of the different members of the club. Till 1893, we had no nominal officers, but at that time we organized more formally and sent some papers to the world's fair. Since then we have had a president and secretary, their term of office lasting for one season only. Up to that time the exercises had been conducted by the member of the club at whose house we were meeting.

We have traveled through Italy, France, Germany and England. Last winter we had a library from the extension department of the University of the State of New York, on Holland and Spain, and have spent one afternoon each week in study under direction of the University. It has been our most successful and interesting season, marked by unflagging interest and regular attendance. We have never had many original papers. but have been content with compilation, discussion and readings. There have been several entertainments for the club and its friends, including a reading and concert in 1891, a talk in 1892, some teas, and a trip to Lake Mohonk.

FORTNIGHTLY CLUB, WORCESTER

This club was organized in 1890 as a woman's club, limited by its constitution to 18 members. Meetings are held weekly instead of fortnightly as at first proposed, but the name Fortnightly club is retained.

The officers are president, vice-president, secretary and treasurer, committees for extra work being appointed by the president as they are needed. Our meetings are conducted according to usual parliamentary practices, an unwritten law of our society being, that no one shall refuse to do or attempt to do, anything that is required of her

Our literary work has followed the Chautauqua course. We select such books as seem best suited to our needs, and they are read by two members appointed the evening previous By the aid of maps, dictionaries and encyclopedias the subjects are studied broadly, are freely discussed and often reviewed at the next meeting by questions prepared by readers. Frequently, characters in our reading are written on by members, and these excellent papers, prepared after much study and reading, are of great benefit. All members are supplied with paper and criticisms are freely made. It is not intended that any errors in pronunciation shall slip by. After the special subjects, current events are taken up, thus keeping the club in touch with progress both at home and abroad. Outside of regular work many articles of interest are read from the best magazines Social life is by no means ignored, the club occasionally entertaining its friends with music, papers and readings, ending with a collation.

Our purpose is to continue and increase our knowledge of history, biography and literature; to know what has been done and is being done in science and art; to keep out of the rut of daily cares that engulf so many women and to broaden and enlarge our own intellectual powers for our own happiness and the benefit of others.

The results of our endeavors have been very satisfactory. We can see a great deal more to do, but that, of itself, is hopeful. To be satisfied might be to cease our efforts; as it is, our only purpose is to do better work and more of it.— ADELAIDE C. MARTIN, *Secretary*

MONDAY EVENING CLASS, GENESEO

The Monday evening class of Geneseo met for the first time in September 1882. Time throws a dimness over the causes that led the half dozen ladies to meet at the home of the one who has been our guiding star ever since. There must have been a desire in our minds for some systematic study, and this wish we were able to gratify, since the first president of the Ebell society of Oakland, California, Miss Mary K. Culbertson, had come to reside in our midst, and would lead the class. Class it has always been, the organization never aspiring to the name of club. Each Monday evening from September to June, the parlor of one of the members has been the meeting place. From the few that composed the first gathering, the number grew until it was necessary to limit membership to 18. A few honorary members have been added, who take no part in the study, but attend on special occasions.

We have the usual officers, president, vice-president, secretary and treasurer, but not even an election day, and no one knows the length of her term of office. There is usually about $1 in the treasury, collected in annual dues of 10 cents from each member, just to make us feel we are a monied institution.

During the 13 years Shakspere was read for two years, then different countries were taken up. Following this we gave several years to the history, art and literature of England. This afforded us ample field for study and papers. Art in general and American history came up for attention before the great exposition. At present we have just finished the first of a three years' course in the history, art and philosophy of Germany. An evening program consists of the roll call answered by quotations, the recitation of the history of the particular time we are studying, one or more papers on some person or event, and frequently extracts from the literature of the time. Every fourth evening is devoted to current events in charge of the vice-president.

Our aim in the beginning was rather indefinite and the passing years, while they have intensified the general desire for improvement, have wrought no change. Results are as varied as are the members of our class. The least studious have gained much by their presence at the regular meetings; all have learned the value of systematic study of the 19th century. We more justly measure men and women of our own time when compared with those of other centuries and are able to take a broader and more comprehensive view of art, literature and the history of our world.

One of the most delightful outcomes of our gathering is the warm personal interest felt by those who are occupied in the same line of thought, and the love and gratitude felt for our leader of the past 13 years.

By invitation of Sorosis, the M. E. C. fulfilled the requirements necessary and was given a place at the exposition of 1893, among the representative woman's clubs.— *Prepared by committee*

TRINITY METHODIST CHURCH READING CLUB, ALBANY

This club was organized for the study of sociology, using as a special text-book Washington Gladden's *Tools and the man*. Readings were followed by discussion led by the director, Dr Brundage.

UNIVERSITY EXTENSION STUDY CLUB, OGDENSBURG

The desire for foreign travel seems inherent in Americans whether through a natural curiosity to investigate, or an intuitive longing for culture It has been said that the hope of our ambitious countryman is fulfilled when he has amassed wealth sufficient to indulge in a trip to Europe. "The world belongs to him who has seen it," said Seneca; "but he who would make his travels delightful, must first make himself delightful" There is therefore a decided movement to repair the disadvantages of imperfect preparation in the studies of history and the classics, and the lack of appreciation of art in its different forms.

A cynic says that clubs and circles are for the accumulation of superficial information, and the unloading of it on others, without much individual absorption, but we are absolved from such a charge. At the close of our first year of study, though no descriptions can approach the reality, the earnest and applied efforts of our club members have furnished us with word-pictures that have the advantage of all save an actual visit.

Our club, which proudly enrolled itself as a branch of the Extension department of the University of the State of New York, owes its being to the inspiration of Mrs S. H. Palmer, its efficient and energetic president. It was organized with 20 members, the limit for the coming year, now being increased to 25, and was called a study club at present working on Great Britain.

"We Americans are said to have been born busy," and though we refute that assertion, yet we are born with the fear of not being busy; as those gifted with intelligence and leisure feel their responsibility, and provide for the good use of each hour. "This," says Charles Dudley Warner, "is conscientiousness in women, not restlessness." That the name is verified is proved by the successful results of our efforts. Such enthusiasm for study has not manifested itself since our school days. The excellent itinerary prepared by our executive committee includes a careful study of the physical geography of England, its history ancient and modern, its classic authors, architecture, art and antiquities. We gratefully acknowledge the attention given our program, by the directors of the Extension department, in the selection of books, specially chosen with regard to the preparation of papers assigned. A printed program with respective subjects, dates and writers was furnished each member, and was faithfully adhered to, in accordance with the rules of a constitution, signed by each one.

Some of our members have had the advantage of visiting the places described by them, and this, with the additional charm of literary gifts, has given special delight to others less favored. Under the auspices of the club, an illustrated lecture was given on points of interest that we had visited in our studies, the proceeds of which, were presented to our new public library fund. Thus have we made our travels interesting, even though, like those of the Vicar of Wakefield, all our adventures are by our own fireside. The vivid and accurate descriptions, the poring over maps, plans, and pictures, which have been drawn and furnished with painstaking care by those who preside at the meetings, have helped us to see more than we should, perhaps, perceive for ourselves

Those familiar with the beauties of England have enjoyed reviewing delightful memories, and as a preparation for a tour abroad, the benefit is incalculable. We have learned to know the rich woods and smiling fields, the castles and cathedrals, the many spots immortalized in history. How pleasant the journey down the Thames, the visit to Oxford with its colleges, the small towns, teeming with human interest and historical associations, as are all those about Warwickshire; the great cathedral towns, 'then London! the greatest sight in itself, where one loses one's self, as an atom among millions."

Our interest is unabated, but summer fitly leaves us in the peaceful Isle of Wight, at the Shrine of Tennyson, beloved by Americans, as by his loyal countrymen, who have preserved his laureate crown, without a wearer, since his loss.

So keenly have we enjoyed the travel talks, that our entire party has planned a continuation of these easy journeyings; and will, next season, visit the north of England, and the wild, romantic scenes of Scotland, Ireland and Wales. — HARRIET FRANK, *Secretary*

HELI STUDY CLUB, JOHNSTOWN

The Heli society was organized as a reading circle, its plan of work being to take up authors and miscellaneous subjects devoting one meeting to each. In 1894 the subject of study was the 15th century. 18 regular meetings were held and thorough work done.

WOMAN'S CLUB, ONEONTA

The Woman's club of Oneonta was organized February 13, 1894, with 111 members and incorporated under the laws of the state of New York, September 7th. At the close of the first year the 200 membership limit had been reached, and a suite of rooms was rented consisting of an auditorium seating about 200, a handsome parlor, a reception room, a large, well lighted reading-room and a class-room The reading-room is supplied with the best periodicals and had also two of the state traveling libraries during the year. The class-room is fitted with all necessary appliances for class work.

On account of its size the club is divided into classes, members choosing the lines of study desired. With the exception of the languages, classes are conducted by members of the club with weekly meetings in all but parliamentary usage which meets monthly. The French classes in charge of Prof. E. F. Bacon of the state normal school have made satisfactory progress specially in conversation. The club is fortunate in having among its members, members of the faculty of the state normal school.

Classes have been maintained in English literature, French history, current topics, botany, harmony and composition, parliamentary usage, cooking, physical culture, ladies chorus and a mandolin and guitar club. Every class has been a decided success with increasing interest each month. Through July and August the regular work is suspended, though the rooms are accessible at all times to members. A monthly reception is held in the parlors, four ladies being appointed hostesses each time.

The first Tuesday evening of each month is devoted to a musical and literary entertainment for the whole club, the last one of the year being a review of the work in all of its divisions. These evenings have revealed much unsuspected talent and each month has given something fresh, bright and instructive. A committee has in charge the arranging of a systematic plan for the musical and literary evenings of the winter of 1895–96, leaving only a part of the evening for a miscellaneous program.— Mrs Nellie Howe Miller, *Secretary*

SATURDAY CLUB, SCHUYLERVILLE

The Saturday club was organized by eight ladies of Schuylerville, with two objects in view: one, the exchanging of magazines, the other a course of reading preparatory to travel in Scotland, England and France. We had a traveling library of 25 volumes, and following Badeker, studied the principal cities with reference to historic interest, art, and particularly as connected with lives of prominent authors. We also read some historic fiction, the lives of George Eliot, Ruskin and Carlyle Much reading was done outside the club.

Regular meetings are held on Saturday from three to six. An hour and a half is spent in reading, followed by a discussion of articles read, or of general literature. At the close, five o'clock tea is served.

The officers consist of president, vice-president, secretary and treasurer. There were no fees except in payment of library charges. The club was voted by all to be both delightful and instructive.— HELEN MAY KNOX, *Secretary* .

EAST SIDE STUDY CLASS, TROY

This class was formed a little over five years ago, by three ladies who regretted that so much that had been learned in school was slowly but surely slipping away. They thought a systematic course of reading would be beneficial and invited nine friends to join, deciding that 12 would be a good working number. Shaw's *New history of English literature* was chosen as a basis of study, the lessons being enlarged by taking up the principal works of each author. The meetings were held bimonthly. The reading and study were done at home and results brought to the class. One winter was spent on Shakspere, the history of each play studied being taken up and quotations learned. Most of the topics were made out by members of the class, with the exception of the study of Robert Browning, when the *Study class*, by Anna McMahan, was used as a partial guide. In addition, a course of lectures on Browning and other English authors was given at the Emma Willard seminary After three years, a *Guide to the study of 19th century authors*, by Louise Manning Hodgkins, was taken up and used with good results. In the study of John Ruskin further help was desired, and a six months' course on Ruskin as an art critic was obtained from the Round Robin reading club, of Philadelphia. This course necessitated the use of more books than were owned by the class, and a traveling library was obtained. A small fee is collected each year by the treasurer as a fund for needed books and supplies. In the study of Ruskin there is a schedule for home reading, and programs for the 12 meetings. Papers on subjects pertaining to the lesson for the day were read, besides selections from other authors, followed by a discussion of the whole subject.

The meetings are very much enjoyed. No member would willingly give up her place, and when one is obliged to do so she is still an honorary member, and has the first chance of again becoming a working member when a vacancy occurs Most of our number are busy people, still the lessons are invariably well prepared, and all feel that by means of this class they have gained what they could not have accomplished in any other way — CHARLOTTE E HARRISON, *Secretary*

EVERY SATURDAY NIGHT CLUB, WATERVILLE

16 ladies of Waterville met Dec. 4th, 1886 to form a society for mutual intellectual advancement and improvement. Membership was limited to 16, and weekly meetings were to be held at homes of members; and the society named Every Saturday night club. The first few meetings were devoted to reading one of Shakspere's plays and selections from Ruskin.

The society then decided to take up a course of English literature, beginning with the early Anglo-Saxon, and five years were spent on that subject, taking the more noted authors and the history of their time, with numerous selections from their writings The work was profitable and pleasant, both to those who had had courses of study, and to others to whom it brought the benefits they had missed earlier in life.

In October 1891 our membership having been decreased by death and removal, eight new members were invited to join. The society then decided to study Spain, its history, literature, art and customs, including the bearing of the discoveries of Columbus on our country. Our guide was Fiske's *Discovery of America*. This course continued during two years. The work of 1894-95 was on the history of Greece.— ELLEN REYNOLDS WRIGHT, *Vice-president*

WESTCHESTER WOMAN'S CLUB, MT VERNON

The Westchester woman's club was organized in response to a call sent out by five ladies who had grown tired of filling their leisure with afternoon whist and the desultory reading of literary societies. Among those who responded were some who felt that the active interest they had taken in our city affairs had been too often wasted for want of organized support, and they would gladly join the club if one of its objects would be to further the higher interests of our city. We decided that at our first club meeting we would discuss "For what am I here?" and that the answers should as far as possible form the objects of our organization. It happened that Sunday's *Herald* published a sketch of the Middlesex club at Lowell, which appealed to the ladies as so simple in its plan and so inspiring in its aims that we wrote them at once, and on their lines laid the basis of our club. With the opening of the new year we had 76 charter members, a printed constitution and had engaged a hall for our biweekly regular meetings. The membership has divided itself into seven sections: sociology, education, hospitality, literature, history, science and art. Under the first two the members have begun to put our Bureau of charities on a better basis, and to help in the wise enforcement of the new school act. We have three study classes in sculpture, history and pedagogy, which meet at members' houses. These classes have enrolled with the University and have traveling libraries. We have also classes in physical culture and we expect to lengthen the 10 weeks of consecutive study, the minimum requirement for registration in the University, to a full year on each of these subjects.— MARTHA F. GAY, *President*

Educational section. This section is presided over by a chairman, who chooses four other ladies as the committee to plan the work for the year. Seventeen members enrolled in this section which meets bimonthly on Thursday afternoons, from two to half past three, to study the newest methods of school work and the most approved ways of school government, always keeping in view the needs of our public schools.

We have a comprehensive library of pedagogic books, sent from the University under which the club is organized; the books bear on education, mental, physical and moral. One or two members write short papers on books read since the last meeting and which treat particularly the point under discussion; then follows an informal exchange of thought in which all members present take part.

Four months were spent in this work when we called for volunteers to visit our five public schools and report on the work done and on the methods in vogue. In many instances they compared most favorably with the ideas of the best educators, and again we found room for improvement specially in the methods of appointing teachers, whose qualifications in some cases did not conform to the law of the state regarding city schools. Our board of education however seemed willing to remedy this and raise the standard of examinations to agree with that required in other cities. We hope in the future to be of still greater service to our public schools.— ALMA D. KITTEL, *Chairman*

SATURDAY CLASS, BUFFALO

The Saturday class is with perhaps one exception, the oldest organization of the kind in the city, having been formed October 2d, 1876. It consists of 25 women, who meet on Saturday afternoons through the winter, to rest and refresh themselves by comparing notes on certain lines of study which occupy them more or less during the entire year. Each one prepares a paper once a year, which is certainly of great value to herself, since it necessitates long and careful reading in one direction and also teaches her how to value the work of her associates. With scarcely any rules or by-laws, working quietly, without publicity, for nearly 20 years, with an interest which has never abated, the class of 1895 is as full of life and energy as the original of 1876. The one requisite for membership is love for the work and this is fully proved by the large average attendance, it being a rare occurrence when a member is absent except from necessity. That the work of such a class is superficial may be true, and none can better realize how imperfect and incomplete it is than those who are engaged in it. Nevertheless with all its imperfections, this class has been an inspiration and blessing to its members by diverting them into broader paths and enlarging their too limited horizon.

There have been but three presidents in the course of its existence, and their influence has always been strictly conservative. The attempt to introduce topics of the day and political questions was not popular with the majority, the members not caring to become a debating society, representing as they do all sides of political and religious questions. From year to year the work has grown and the interest in study has increased. The scope of subjects has been enlarged and what was first intended more strictly as a study of art, has grown into more general study of each country in its literary, artistic and general history.

The first course was on architecture in India, Greece and Rome, followed by Byzantine, Saracenic, early Gothic and Norman; by 1881 the subjects were more miscellaneous, archeologic, social and political, and the following outline shows the sequence in thought between the yearly subjects of study:

1882-83, Egypt; its history, religions and literature.
1883-84, American history; early settlements and colonial life.
1884-85, American institutions, history and literature.
1885-86, England, studied by counties, with descriptions of the cathedrals, scenery and literary men connected with each locality.
1886-87, Italy from the 13th to the end of the 16th century.
1887-88, Parallel history of Europe in the 17th century.
1888-89, Literature and character studies of the 18th century.
1889-90, 18th century, continued
1890-91, 19th century topics.
1891-92, Literature, history and art in England in 19th century
1892-93, Spain; its literature, history and art.
1893-94, Germany; its history and literature.
1894-95, Germany; its history, art and literature.
1895-96, Greece.

CALEDONIAN CLUB, PORTVILLE

The Caledonian club, an organization of 20 members, has just completed its second year's work. It is composed of ladies only, the majority of whom are married. Three directors plan the year's work, and at the beginning of the season furnish each member with a program covering the work of the entire year. Each member, on joining, pledges herself to write articles or take part in discussions, whenever invited by the club. A unique feature is that there are no dues and no treasurer.

Last year this club took up the study of Scotland, its history and literature. There was some trouble in obtaining books on the very early history of Scotland as we were not then aware of the provisions for such needs made by New York state in its traveling libraries. We meet once in two weeks and at each meeting three topics are assigned, on one of which a paper must be written, the other topics being discussed from brief notes only. The remaining time is spent in informal discussion of all the topics of the meeting, each member being at liberty to bring in any additional fact or item pertinent to the subject. Newspaper clippings and suitable magazine articles are sometimes read but never to the exclusion of the regular program.

In 1895 the topic of study will be England, her history and literature, beginning with the Norman conquest and closing with Elizabeth's reign. Interest in the work has been well sustained, though membership involves considerable time and mental effort.—Mrs Eva A. H. Barnes, *Secretary*

FORTNIGHTLY CLUB, POTSDAM

The Fortnightly club may be considered an outgrowth of the Chautauqua idea; a number of ladies and gentlemen who had formed a literary and scientific circle and completed the four years' course, wished to continue systematic study in some profitable and connected line. The president of the circle, Frederic M. Heath, issued a call for persons interested in the formation of a literary club to meet at his residence and the result was the Fortnightly club meeting on alternate Monday evenings at the homes of the members. The original membership included seven gentlemen, their wives, and 12 other ladies, 26 in all. Mr Heath was elected president, and unanimously reelected for four years and it was with extreme reluctance that the club at that time accepted Mr Heath's refusal of the office on account of the prospect of his removal from town. The success of the club during these first four years may be said to be mainly due to the wise and disinterested management of the president, who gave so marked an example of punctuality and regularity, being absent from the meetings of the club only three times in four years. His careful study of the subject of the evening was always a source of inspiration, and his remarks so candid and forceful were equally an incentive to impartial discussion. Great credit is also due the club members for their perseverance and enthusiasm. We doubt if any other club can show a finer record in this respect, being held together for six years only by harmonious consent and genuine interest in the work. It was thought best at the beginning to have as slight an organization as possible, the officers consisting only of a president, vice-president and committee on program. No secretary even was considered necessary, a mode of procedure afterward justly regarded as a mistake, for if some of the members had not kept records for their own use and pleasure, the early history of the club would have been lost; and the Fortnightly club would now recommend from its own experience that any club in organizing should start with all the requirements and restrictions which the circumstances seem to demand; to institute changes is at best a somewhat hazardous proceeding. No formal constitution was adopted, only a simple statement of the work proposed being signed by each member as a declaration of good faith in assuming the duties. This pledge is as follows:

The object of the Fortnightly club is the study of good literature, and we whose names are signed beneath, join it with the intention of attending its meetings with regularity and of doing the work assigned when not prevented by more urgent duties.

The work of the club has been from the first distinctively literary, the first four years being occupied with a cursory study of English authors from Chaucer to the present time, a grand total of 80 authors, studied with as much thoroughness as the character of organizations such as ours permits. Several of Shakspere's plays were read entire, the characters being assigned and the readings given with more or less action. Milton's *Masque of Comus* was read in the same way; also Goldsmith's *She stoops to conquer*. Three months were spent in study of the Waverley novels, taking them up in their order historically. The set programs are varied with quotations, reviews, songs, recitations, character-sketches, exhibition of portraits, autograph letters, pictures and photographs as occasion offers. The committee on program consists of three members appointed for three months who arrange for the exercises each evening, the selection of authors to be studied being usually made by the club. The regular meetings begin with September and close with June and are held fortnightly on Monday evenings from half past seven until half past nine.

An amusing incident in connection with the history of the club is the anomalous fact of its representation in the exhibit of literary clubs in the woman's building at the world's fair, 1893. About the time that statistics of women's literary clubs were called for, the personnel of the Fortnightly club had changed in a marked degree. Removals from town and other causes over which our gentlemen members presumably had no control, for we are loth to ascribe it to any lack of interest in the work of the club, had reduced their numbers to proportions "small and beautifully less," till but two men besides Mr Heath could in any sense be styled regular members, and the president was often the only gentleman in attendance, as he was for a long time the only one always present. The number of members remaining substantially the same, the proportion of lady members was so much in excess of the gentlemen as to give the club a somewhat appropriate if left-handed right to a place in an exhibit of women's clubs. The end seemed to justify the means, and the vice-president, Mrs Mary B. Stowell, wrote an article on the Origin, history and purpose of the Fortnightly club and prepared the folio, special programs, copies of original articles, etc. called for by the world's fair committee; and this folio may now be seen preserved in the archives at Albany The club did not seek to fly under false colors, but it was carefully explained that the club had gentlemen members and a gentleman as president, but for the reasons above stated wished a representation. Whether it was that the men became jealous of the assumption of woman's control, or from a more commendable motive, that was the only year in which it would have been possible for the ladies to "steal the club"; the ranks began to fill up, and now the membership, though much larger, includes a larger proportion of men than ever before.

The Fortnightly club believes that the association of men and women together in study club work is of mutual advantage; viewed from the different standpoints of each, from business, professional and social outlooks, each subject under discussion reveals its many-sidedness, and is viewed impartially and without prejudice. The importance of a literary club as an educational center in any town can hardly be over-estimated. A club whose members are persons of widely different opportunities and occupations meets with a common interest and aim — intellectual improvement, and however limited the time for study, to be kept to a connected line of work is invaluable and saves for profitable study the minutes and half-hours that would otherwise be frittered away in light reading or utterly wasted; the mind is kept stimulated to exertion by contact with other minds and the advantages of a higher education are measurably secured. Acquaintance with literature is the basis of culture and the source of lasting enjoyment.

The past two years have been occupied with the study of American authors: a rapid review of the colonial and revolutionary periods, a more extended study of Bryant, Hawthorne and Longfellow and during the last year, a thorough study of Emerson, Lowell and Holmes. Their works have been largely read by the members, several complete sets of their books were purchased, and the year's study has been found extremely interesting and profitable.

Prof. Stansbury Norse, for the last two years the able and efficient president, introduced a feature which has proved of great value, has stimulated interest in the club, and appreciation of its work; namely, a course of lectures by members of the club. By courtesy of the authorities of the normal school these lectures have been delivered in Normal hall which though seating 500 persons has at times been filled. This course of lectures is entirely complimentary, tickets of admission being furnished by the club to their friends. The lectures were all of a high order and elicited great commendation. The course for 1894 was as follows:

1 Edgar Allan Poe, Frederic M. Heath.
2 Discussion of *Looking backward*, Prof Stansbury Norse.
3 All history a preparation for the American republic, Rev. C. H. Guile.
4 Henry David Thoreau, Prof. Edward W. Flagg.

The course for 1895 was as follows:

Fall of Paris in 1871, with American lessons, Rev. C. H. Guile.
Wendell Phillips, Prof. C. F. Simpson.
Literary and musical entertainment, Miss Esterly and Phœnix club.
Origin and influence of poetry, Prof. Stansbury Norse.
Problems of life in the Greek and English dramas, Prof. Edward W. Flagg.

Health culture, a review of recent work, F M. Heath.

At the close of the sixth year we feel that the club may congratulate itself on the fact that the membership is larger than at any previous time in its history, and also on the punctuality and regularity of attendance which continued to the last in spite of the allurements of summer evenings. The true spirit of unity, literary exactness and zeal is rapidly growing, and we feel that there is every promise of still better things in the future. The Fortnightly club is on a firm basis, it has an assured place among the cultural institutions with which Potsdam is so highly favored, and we believe that it will become an increasing power as a center for intellectual growth and spiritual quickening.

The connection with the university extension movement has been a stimulus, and the loan of the traveling library makes it possible to take up the subject of study chosen for next year, Italy, its history, literature and art. Stimulated by these helpful influences we have also the happiness of knowing that we have ourselves been a source of inspiration to others; a club in a neighboring town has modeled itself after our plan, using our programs, which have been printed each fortnight by courtesy of R E Sumner, a charter member and editor of the *St Lawrence Herald*. These programs have also been made the basis of home-study by persons in town who have been unable to attend the meetings of the club.

It may be thought that the club is not made sufficiently recreative but such is not the case. The club believes that intellectual benefit is to be first considered, and everything is arranged to that end, the feast of reason being the only feasting that is allowed at the regular meetings; but there is during each session a short intermission which is fully improved in social intercourse, and after each lecture this past winter there was a social hour in honor of the lecturer at the home of some member, when refreshments were served, and these occasions were greatly enjoyed. By invitation of Mr and Mrs Heath the club twice signalized the completion of the year's work by an entertainment at their residence when in addition to a literary program, a collation was spread. At the close of other years there have been club-picnics till this has become an established institution. Romantic spots on the beautiful Racquette river have been selected and gala-days enjoyed by the members and their families, the bountiful dinner being supplemented by toasts and other literary exercises.

It has been thought best in view of the increasing numbers to work on a somewhat more restricted plan, and a constitution was adopted April 20, 1895, which will go into effect at the beginning of another year. It is believed that this constitution while not excluding any diligent and conscientious worker will give to the membership greater efficiency and power.— Mrs Mary B. Stowell, *Secretary*

ROUND ROBIN READING CLUB, OXFORD

This club was organized in January 1895 as a branch of the Round Robin reading club of Philadelphia. As the outgrowth of an earnest desire for definite and systematic study of literature, it has, in its first half year's course, agreeably demonstrated the possibilities of the Round Robin system. It has a limited membership of 15, with a local board of officers who are responsible to the central bureau in Philadelphia for its literary and business management.

Carefully prepared schedules on the course elected, are issued to each member, who is privileged at any time to submit the results of her work to an examiner, previously assigned; this direct, personal guidance being a distinctive feature of the system. The meetings, which are fortnightly, are varied by selections, original papers, discussions and special topics.

Among a variety of papers thus far offered on our subject, Five representative American writers, the following have been of special interest: Condition of American literature when the Knickerbocker history was written; Home life of the Brook Farm association; Puritan element in Hawthorne's works; Longfellow and Bryant as poets of nature; Longfellow as household poet; Longfellow as dramatist, with biographic sketches of the authors studied, Irving, Poe, Hawthorne, Longfellow and Holmes.

The Round Robin is of comparatively recent organization, but its rapid growth and popularity already testify to its unique place among modern educational movements. Its founder, Miss Louise Stockton, of Philadelphia, needs no introduction to those acquainted with the brilliant record of the New century club, with which, as an officer, she has been identified since its formation in 1877. Herself an author of special charm, she is farther distinguished as the sister of a famous American novelist. Under her personal direction, it is needless to add that the Round Robin enjoys peculiar privileges, while it has received the endorsement of men and women everywhere prominent in the field of letters.

By its methods, in touch with the broadest culture of the day, it is able to offer unusual advantages for home study. The best results of thought and research, to the exclusion of unnecessary matter, are collected for the student, and a wide range of collateral reading is offered, thus presenting the subject from many points of view.

The Oxford branch of the Round Robin, in common with others, enjoys the provision of the state of New York by which loan libraries of carefully selected books are furnished for the use of its registered study-clubs and extension centers.

This club begins its second course of study October 10th, 1895, on the English drama and Shakspere.— ELIZABETH MYGATT HYDE, Secretary

AZARIAS READING CIRCLE, SYRACUSE

The organization of each new reading circle is hailed with pleasure by all lovers of progress and culture. A continued increase of these institutions marks their long felt necessity, and denotes as well the permanence of their establishment. While the excellent work accomplished in reading circles recommends itself to all centers of advancing civilization and refinement, a spontaneous desire of self improvement causes them, as if magically, to spring into existence on every side.

The Azarias reading circle, of Syracuse, was organized by the Rev. John F. Mullany, of that city in October 1894, he himself serving as its first moderator. The character of this circle is strictly and exclusively of a literary nature, and weekly meetings are held from October to June. The manner of conducting the meetings was such that entirely satisfactory results were secured. The curriculum consisted principally of English history and literature with brief essays on current topics, sketches and biographies as secondary branches. In both subjects one common author was adopted and followed as a class book, while other authors on the same subject were recommended and procured by members as books of reference. A catalog in which proportionate lessons for each meeting were assigned, was carefully prepared by a board of studies and given to each member of the circle. The same prospectus contained two courses of lectures which were delivered during the year, one by members of the circle to the circle, the other by outside talent to the general public of the city of Syracuse. The first course provided two lectures each month for the members of the circle, the subject serving generally as a review of the studies discussed at the two previous meetings or as a preparation for two subsequent sessions. The public lectures were given under the auspices of the Azarias reading circle, at the expense of the members, the object of the lectures being to make known the organization and to invite new members.

Scholarly lectures were given by Rev. Joseph H. McMahon, of St Patrick's cathedral, New York, Col. Richard Malcolm Johnston, of Baltimore, and others. As a result of these evidences of the high aims of the Azarias reading circle the establishment of many new circles in the city of Syracuse and its surroundings may be expected.

The only qualification for membership is a desire for self-improvement and a degree of education sufficient to follow with advantage the assigned course of studies. The membership of the Azarias reading circle is limited to 35, the directors favoring the formation of new circles rather than admission of too many persons into one circle. Church history will form the principal study in the Azarias circle this year with a study of the history of languages or the history of music or of architecture as a probable secondary branch.— Rev. Joseph Wilmes

METHOD CLASS, TROY

This class, consisting of five teachers in the kindergarten of the Froebel school, held weekly meetings during the winter of 1895 for the study of kindergarten methods. The plan of work was preparation for the daily lessons in the kindergarten and the meetings were informal. The traveling library was placed in the schoolroom and the books were in constant use both by teachers and pupils. The interest thus aroused led to the purchase by the class of 50 selected books. The Froebel school has been discontinued but the meetings of the Method class will be held in 1896 in connection with the Emma Willard school.

SHAKESPEARE CLUB, PHOENIX

This club of 18 members, meeting weekly was organized in January, 1895, and commenced the study of *Hamlet*, using the syllabus and lectures prepared by Mrs Jessie K. Curtis, of Syracuse. After each act has been studied, Mrs Curtis' lecture is read by the club president.

ART READING CLUB, GENEVA

This club has for its object the study of art both ancient and modern. It was organized in 1889; its number is limited to 25 with an average attendance of 15. Meetings are held weekly commencing with the annual meeting the last Thursday in September and continuing till the last of June. Last winter was devoted to French art, a large portion of the time being given to the artists of the Barbison school

How to judge a picture and *Art for art's sake* by Van Dyke were read in the club as a lesson and thoroughly enjoyed and appreciated by all.— E. S. BELL, *Secretary*

ART CIRCLE, GENEVA

This club has for its object the study of ancient and modern art. The study year begins the first Wednesday in October and ends the last Wednesday in May. Meetings are weekly and each member in turn prepares the lesson for the day from the various works on art to which the circle has access.

The class, limited in number to 18, has been organized two years and has spent its time on the study of Italian art. This month the circle begins the study of Dutch art. Photographs of the best painting of each artist are secured and shown each week with the corresponding reading. We have thoroughly appreciated the books sent from Albany last spring, and hope we may enjoy the same privilege in the future.—ROSE WALTHAM NESTER, *President*

WEDNESDAY MORNING ART CLASS, WATERTOWN

The Wednesday morning art class of Watertown was organized in December 1892, at an informal meeting of a few ladies interested in the study of art. Its constitution is of the simplest and the membership is limited to 21. The membership fee is $1.

Topics are assigned by the president to each member of the class, and papers are prepared on these topics, two or three being read at each meeting. The class meets fortnightly at the homes of its members. As a guide for study, Farrar's *Art topics* is used. Sculpture was studied the first winter; since then architecture has been the subject of study. Last winter, after a study of definitions and technical terms, the time was devoted to ancient Egyptian, Asiatic, and classic Greek architecture. This winter Roman, early Christian, Gothic and renaissance architecture will be taken up. Before the existence of the traveling libraries was known the class bought a share in the Athenæum library of Watertown, entitling it to the use of their art books. Finding these inadequate, the club registered in the Extension department of the University of the State of New York and secured a traveling library which has been most helpful.— MRS W. H. CAMP, *Secretary*

EAST SIDE LITERARY SOCIETY, NEW YORK

The East Side literary society was organized in 1894 to develop literary tastes and further the power of debating, and study of current topics. At present there are eight honorary and 17 active members, a majority of whom are connected with the university settlement society, at the foot of 76th st. and East river, where the East Side literary society meets. Any man over 18 years of age is eligible for membership; the initiation fee being 25 cents and the dues 5 cents weekly. Meetings are held every Thursday from 8 to 10:30 p. m. The officers of the society are a president, secretary, treasurer and critic, all of whom are elected for a term of four months. An executive committee composed of the officers of the society, arrange the order of exercise, subject to the approval of the society. One fourth of the active members constitute a quorum. The meetings are opened by the election of a chairman, who presides over the assembly for that evening; in this way, each member has a chance to become acquainted with the duties of that office. This method has proved very successful, satisfying every one, and causing no discord among members. The chairman who has been elected appoints the debaters for the following week. 20 minutes are allowed for discussion of a clause in the constitution of the United States. An essay on some current topic is then read by one of the members, with 15 minutes allowed for discussion. The debate of the evening follows, the four appointed speakers leading. Eight minutes are allowed for the affirmative and five for refutation. Voluntary debating on either side is permitted after the appointed speakers have concluded. A vote is then taken on the merits and arguments of the question, a record being kept of results. The critic sums up and criticizes the exercises of the evening, including the arguments of the debate. When the society has a specialist to open the debate, he gives, first, the explanation of the question; second, the arguments pro and con; third, the arguments which he deems most important and to which he desires the debaters to confine themselves. After the debate, he gives his opinion on the merit of the arguments and the question.

The debates thus opened were as follows:

1 Resolved that corporations be compelled by law to abide by an 8 hour working day; Prof. F. H. Giddings, Columbia college.

2 Resolved that lynching is justifiable; ex-Pres. J. F. Crowell, Trinity college, N. C.

3 Resolved that trusts are beneficial to the community; W. S. Hill, Chicago university.

4 Resolved that strikes are beneficial to the workingman; W. S. Ufford, Columbia college.

5 Resolved that a protective tariff is beneficial to the people; C. S. Crook, Columbia college.

Hon. Everett P. Wheeler, a member of the society, opened the debate on: Resolved that senators be elected by the people; and Arthur Morgan Day, also of the society, opened the debate on: Resolved that we favor a bimetallic system.

While the work of the society has been very interesting to the members, it did not lead to any result beyond giving an idea of the question. In future it is the intention of the society to devote about 12 weeks to one question, in this way hoping to receive a permanent and lasting benefit.— EDWARD A. WEISS, *Secretary*

NEIGHBORHOOD CLUB, ONEIDA

The Neighborhood club was organized in November 1894 for systematic and continued reading in connection with the Extension lectures on American history delivered by Prof. G. W. Smith of Colgate university.

The club consisted of nine ladies, who met once a week for a season of two hours following the course of reading outlined in Prof. Smith's syllabus.

TRAVELERS' CLUB, OLEAN

In 1884, 20 women met and formed the Travelers' club of Olean. At first the meetings were informal, a chairman being chosen at each meeting to preside, but at the end of three months it seemed wise to organize permanently, and a president, first and second vice-presidents, and a secretary were elected and a constitution was framed and adopted. To this list of officers a treasurer and corresponding secretary have since been added. These six, elected annually, with a topic committee appointed by the president, constitute the officers. The expenses of the club are defrayed by an annual fee of one dollar from each member.

The meetings are held every alternate Tuesday afternoon at the homes of the members and it became necessary very early in the history of the club to limit the number of members to 30. Each of these 30 members is expected to write two articles yearly, unless prevented by some good reason. Failures to comply with this rule have been very few and the penalty, forfeiture of membership for two consecutive failures, has never been imposed. On withdrawing from the club, a member has the privilege of naming her successor, subject, of course, to approval of the club; otherwise, the opportunity of proposing a new member is given to members alphabetically.

The club decides by ballot the country to be studied the following year, and on the topic committee devolves the duty of going over the ground and arranging and assigning topics alphabetically. For several years appointments were made only four weeks in advance, but in 1890 a list of topics for the whole year was put in the hands of each member. It was such an improvement on the old method that the little books containing the order of subjects have come to be a necessity.

The object of the Travelers' club as stated in the constitution is " the study of the geography and the general history of different countries and the interchange of ideas on the same." With this object in view we have turned our attention to Spain and Portugal, France, the British Isles, Italy, Germany, Holland and Belgium, the United States of America and Mexico. Some of these countries have been so interesting, that it has required two years to do them even partial justice. This was notably true of our own country to which we devoted two years and three months. It is the purpose of the club to spend at least two years on the present subject of study, Egypt. The mysteries of ancient Egypt which have already been brought to light by Egyptologists, as well as those which remain to be discovered and explained, are proving a most fascinating study and to some of us at least, Egypt "seemeth best of all."

At the beginning of the present year, to facilitate "the interchange of ideas" a new plan was adopted and a discussion was substituted for the third and last paper on the program. The subject of the discussion is in the line of the topic of study except at every third meeting when it is current events. The leader of the discussion is appointed by the topic committee and has the privilege of choosing one or two assistants. All of the members are expected to participate in the discussion and they do so more readily than seemed possible when the subject was first broached.

In October 1893, the Travelers' club joined the General federation of women's clubs for two years It is pleasant to feel that the history of the club during the 11 years of its existence has been one of progress; that we know more about the earth and its inhabitants than we did 11 years ago; that this knowledge has enlarged our ideas and broadened our sympathies. But we have other worlds to conquer, and shall not cease our wanderings till all lands have been visited and some of them, it may be, have been revisited.

The present officers are: Mrs F. R. Eaton, *president;* Miss Anna R. Danforth, *1st vice-president;* Mrs C. D. Clarke, *2d vice-president;* Miss Mary D. Bartlett, *clerk;* Mrs W. H. Mandeville, *treasurer;* Mrs W. H. Horner, *corresponding secretary.*— MARY D. BARTLETT

CHARLTON READING CIRCLE

"And where may Charlton be?" I hear the reader ask. Like the territory of which Caesar wrote in his commentaries, it is far distant from the culture and refinement of the province, so that merchants resort to it less frequently, and bring those things which tend to weaken the mind. It enjoys the unenviable reputation of being without electric lights, telephone, or railroad, but its proud boast is that here was born the first superintendent of public instruction of New York state, as well as the only speaker of the house of representatives New York has ever furnished. Perhaps the shadow of their greatness still hovers over us but at least we have here a lively, wide awake reading circle now 13 years old.

The beginning was modest in the extreme, about a dozen meeting to study American history, with Higginson's *Young folks' history of the United States* as the text-book. The aim at first was, more particularly, to arouse an interest in good reading among young people, who ought to care for such things, but were somewhat indifferent. To make the meetings attractive to that class, we spent about half the evening in reading and study, and the remainder in social intercourse. In those early days, the prime movers in the affair humbled themselves in their efforts to make literature attractive to those who would not be attracted by it; we awoke one day to the fact that other things are of more importance in a reading circle than numbers, and that nothing can more effectually dampen the ardor of the few enthusiastic ones than two or three bored and yawning members, present only out of deference to the wishes of friends. From that time on the reading circle was conducted for the benefit of those seeking mental culture, not for those who would not accept it when thrust on them. This does not mean that the meetings are stiff and formal. Up to the moment of opening there is a busy hum of conversation, and after opening we are not less lively, but our conversation is directed to the subject under investigation, the freest discussion being allowed. It is customary with us to give a public notice each year of our reorganization, at which time all interested are invited to meet with us. We no longer have to entreat persons to join our circle, but those who would make desirable members apply to us for admission. This first meeting is in October, when a temporary chairman is chosen, the subject of study for the season is decided on, and other business transacted. The chairman appoints a committee of three to formulate a plan for the winter's work, after which we adjourn for two weeks to give the committee time for their work. The committee goes over the subject thoroughly, and makes a schedule giving the topics and the names of a committee responsible for the program on the given evening. The chairman of each program committee acts as presiding officer and in this way each member presides over at least one meeting during the winter. Care is taken, in arranging these committees, that one having had experience in making an evening's program be placed with the less experienced or newer members, and that committees be assigned subjects for which they have some particular fitness. The schedule is so arranged that each member serves, as nearly as may be, the same number of times. The success of our evening's program may seem to depend too largely on the committee for that evening, but though some meetings are more interesting than others, no member of a committee has ever failed to do his work, or, in case of sickness or unavoidable absence, to see that it was done by another.

The committee of three, spoken of above, give merely a sketch of the work for each evening. Their schedule having been accepted by the circle, they are released from further duty. It now becomes the work of each program committee in turn to give their attention to the subject assigned. They meet a week or two before the evening on which they are to serve, decide on the manner in which the topic shall be treated, select the most important points, and at the next regular meeting apportion parts for investigation, essays and debates. As one circle is not large, each person usually has some work assigned, the result of which he gives either orally or in writing as the committee may request or he may prefer. In addition, all are supposed to have a general knowledge of the topic under discussion, and the more original a committee, the more interesting and instructive the evening's work.

There are many devices for varying the program Occasionally we have a debate; at other times a quiz; again we have examinations of previous work, when, occasionally, some simple prize is offered to the one having the highest per cent. Again we have a spelling match, the words selected being those used in describing a campaign we have just been studying. On another evening we may be asked to write a stanza or two of verse describing the life and character of some author previously studied, and whose name has been handed us on a slip of paper. These are trifles, but they add zest and animation to an evening's entertainment, and certainly are not without an educational value. They are merely side-issues, however, and usually are thrown in toward the close of the evening, as dessert follows dinner.

The first half-hour of our meeting is always occupied by questions on current topics. Each member prepares a question at home. The slips of paper on which they are written are collected, drawn by the different members, and, if possible, each one answers the question he draws. If he is unable to do this, any one in the circle may answer it. If all others fail, the one who wrote the question gives the answer. Occasionally a person asks a question for information, and may not know the answer himself; in that case, if none of the circle have the desired information at hand, we appoint a committee to investigate. We find this exercise of great value, for we no longer read even the daily paper in a careless way.

Soon after we organized, it was proposed to place in our constitution a clause making the writing of essays obligatory on members. Several so violently opposed this that the proposition was abandoned. Two months later one of the most violent opposers of the "essay plank" of her own accord read before the circle a well-written essay, though perhaps she did not give it so dignified a name. She found that what she had to say could be better said in that way than in any other, and since then members have cheerfully done the work assigned, to the best of their ability.

The choice of a subject for the winter has always been troublesome. After the first course in American history, which is one of the best for a club just starting, we took the regular Chautauqua course for three years. We have studied English and American literature, in both cases bringing in history and geography. We have traveled over England, Scotland, Ireland, France and Italy. In our travels we also studied the lives of illustrious men and women who were in any way connected with the places visited.

One winter we studied the "15 decisive battles of the world," spending at least an evening on each. This demanded considerable attention to contemporaneous history, making a very full course of study, but none the less interesting on that account. It is surprising how latent talent will develop as occasion requires We found we needed maps and could not afford to buy them. Not one member only, but at least one third of the club drew on paper or slated cloth maps of which they need not be ashamed, thus bringing more vividly before the eyes of the class positions of places or of armies, and so making the study, on the evening for which they were responsible, more practical and beneficial.

We have been somewhat handicapped in our work for lack of a reference library. That has also influenced us in our choice of a subject. Certain subjects that we should have liked to study, we could not on account of the small supply of suitable books. There is no public library in the place, but we were surprised to find the rich stores of information tucked away in some garret or old forgotten chest. Something to the point can always be found in old magazines. Those who have no encyclopedias borrow them of their neighbors, when necessary; and members of the committee who assign topics try to see that proper books are available for study. With the advent of the traveling libraries dawned a brighter day for the smaller villages, where the establishing of a public library seems impracticable. Members of our circle pay $1 a year, which we at first spent for books bearing on the subject studied. Each person kept his book two weeks, then passed it to the one whose name appeared in the list next below his. In that way each one had the reading of all the books. At the end of the winter the books were divided among the members. When the traveling libraries were ready, Charlton was the first place to apply for one and the Charlton reading circle furnished the money. From that time to the present we have paid the requisite sum for two libraries each year, and given 100 readers an opportunity to enjoy valuable books, which many of them otherwise never would have seen. The remainder of our money we have spent for magazines, which the members of the circle have in turn. This year we subscribed for five magazines, the *Century*, the *Forum*, the *Popular science monthly*, *Blackwood*, and the *Nineteenth century*. We are not entirely satisfied with this plan, some of the magazines being of necessity several months old before they have made their rounds.

The social event of the season is the annual supper of the reading circle given by its members at Christmas time, when all former members are invited and others whom we desire specially to honor.

Our meetings are held weekly during about seven months of the year at the homes of members. We believe that attendance will be more regular and interest greater if meetings are held weekly than would be the case if they were less frequent.

Our reading circle has been a development; we attempted last winter what we should not have dared attempt before, and next year we shall dare attempt even more. It has been our ambition to have a course of extension lectures, and this we shall accomplish in the future. Our continued existence is an assured fact, so we need no longer plan for the hour or the day, but for the years that are to come. Had it not been for the preparatory work of the reading circle, I doubt if we would have availed ourselves of the advantages offered by the traveling libraries. Our youngest members go out into the world with some knowledge of the riches stored in books and eager for mental improvement. They connect themselves with other clubs for purposes of study, and when such clubs do not exist, they call them into being. A young man, who took his first lessons in our circle a few years ago, is now president of a flourishing Brooklyn club of nearly 200 members.

Where reading clubs are possible, study need not end with school days; nor minds be allowed to rust and decay just when, after years of training, they have become capable of doing the work for which they were designed.— MARY E. CALLAGHAN, *Secretary*

WOMEN'S LITERARY CLUB, DUNKIRK

10 years ago 27 women banded for "the pursuit of study as a means of intellectual culture and general improvement." This was the outcome of a course of parlor lectures on English history given by Miss E. C. Lapham whose earnestness and enthusiasm stimulated the faint-hearted to crystallize their desires into ac-

tion. A program of work for the ensuing year was prepared by Miss Lapham, the study being that of English history and literature, conducted by means of essays and discussions. After three years spent on England, the land of the shamrock received our attention. We spent one year among its bogs and lakes, alternately heated with indignation at the eviction system and its landlords, or brimming with sympathy for the poor Irish peasant. From Ireland we came next to our own "land of the free," where, after two years' study of its history and literature beginning with prehistoric America, our patriotism was still unsatisfied and a supplementary year's study was added We then visited *la belle* France, where for two years we were interested and fasci-' nated by the wonderful characters as they passed in review before us; Louis 14, the indomitable Richelieu, Napoleon, down through all the changes of that most changeful nation to the day of Sadi-Carnot. Last year we began a two years' study of German history and literature with which most interesting work we shall be occupied through the winter of 1895-9). We are an incorporated club with membership limited to 50, since at present we hold our meetings at the homes of the members. We were incorporated in 1889, and have the nucleus of a building fund with which some day, when it shall have grown to goodly increase, we hope to make for ourselves a club house. We are members of the New York State federation of women's clubs sending a delegate to the convention which met in New York last November for organization. We have an executive committee formed of the president, two vice-presidents, corresponding secretary, recording secretary, treasurer and two auditors. Our dues are $1 a year. We meet every Tuesday from October to March. Our regular meetings are varied by the business meeting which occurs in March at which officers are elected for the coming year, reports of outgoing officers read, dues paid, the work for the ensuing year assigned to different members and other necessary business transacted. Two critics are also chosen on that day or within a week, by each of the members, to criticize her paper, lead in discussion and be with her generally responsible for the success of the day on which she reads her paper. A very pleasant feature of the year is the mid-winter evening meeting and also the evening meeting in the spring at the close of the club year, to which guests are usually invited, a literary and musical program carried out, refreshments served, toasts given and the social element introduced. The club has issued two women's calendars one in 1890 and one in 1891. These pretty booklets were very successful and brought to the club much commendation as well as a substantial pecuniary return. During our 10 years' existence public lectures have been given under auspices of the club, and also home entertainments for the purpose of enlarging our much cherished building fund.

Our plan of work, our business methods, our purposes, and results have been asked for; three I have tried to give, the last— who can tell? Organization, for a common interest and purpose has brought to us as to all, greater sympathy, leniency in judgment, a broader outlook, greater power of concentration of thought, power also of giving that thought expression, more confidence and self-possession. It has developed latent gifts, enabling each to bring to the common storehouse of good, that in which she is most successful. If our club has so helped its members, who can trace how far its influence has reached, through the enriching and sweetening of the homes brought under their sway.— Sarah B. Driggs

UNITY CLUB, ALBANY

The Unity club is a group of about 50 persons who come together to study the Bible in the light of higher criticism. The purpose is to examine all the facts in a reverent but scientific spirit. The Bible is studied historically as the literature of the people of Israel. The era of the great prophets of the 8th century B. C. forms the starting point of study. The state library supplied 100 volumes of the best and most recent literature on the subject

The club meets every week. Certain books which bear on the particular subject of the evening have been recommended by the leader at the previous meeting, so that the exercises of the evening are of the nature of a free parliament The leader opens the discussion by a half hour lecture; then as many as are interested participate in the discussion. In order that all phases of the subject may receive proper attention particular questions which require special study are previously assigned to different individuals.

A small fee sufficient to cover all necessary expenses is imposed on all regular members. The average attendance at the meetings of the club has been 38.— Rev. WILLIAM MILTON BRUNDAGE, *President*

CLIO CLUB, NEW YORK

Clio was organized October 1, 1888 and on February 14, 1895 was incorporated as the Clio club of New York city. The club is composed of 50 active members who meet every Monday afternoon from October to May. Authors and their works are studied. The one in charge of the program for the day reads an original paper or gives a talk on the life and works of the author under discussion after which about six members previously notified read selections from his works Current topic meetings are also held at which papers are read. At the social meetings, guests are invited and a talk or reading given by some noted man or woman.—MRS A. J. SHIPMAN, *Secretary*

COLUMBIAN CLUB, GROTON

The Columbian club was organized in 1892 and now has a membership of 19. At first the work of the club was desultory, embracing a variety of subjects but it has gradually developed into connected work with very satisfactory results. The increase in attendance and interest is noticeable.

In the fall of 1894, the club became associated with the Boston Society to encourage studies at home and commenced the study of ancient history. The great benefit derived from this society has been the list of valuable reference books which they furnish on each subject.

The following program, for a meeting devoted to *King Lear*, shows the character of the work done :

Roll call was responded to with quotations.
Paper : History of the drama.
Paper : Historic legend of Lear and his three daughters.
Paper : Drama of King Lear.
Character sketches of Lear, Earl of Kent, Cordelia, Goneril and Regan and the Earl of Gloster
Booth's and Irving's interpretations of the character of Lear.
Readings selected from the play.

Discussion of the chief aim of the play, the lessons it teaches, and its morality.

A review of current topics is a feature of every meeting of our club in addition to the work laid down in the program, each member giving what has most interested her. The study of Wallace's *Prince of India*, with special relation to contemporary history and religions, occupied 14 weeks, the following papers being presented:

Biography of Gen. Le v Wallace; Legend of the Wandering Jew; The crusades; Byzantine empire; Turkish empire; The Epicureans; Growth of the Christian religion; Religion of Buddha; Religion of Zoroaster; Religion of Confucius; Astrology; History of the Jews.

At each meeting some member gave a synopsis of a portion of the story, and two papers were read, followed by a discussion and explanation of obscure allusions or references.—Mrs C. O. Rhodes, *Secretary*

FORTNIGHTLY CLUB, BROOKLYN

The object of this club is to encourage literary work and arouse an interest in questions of the day. The plan of work is prepared by the executive committee, composed of the president, vice-president and one member appointed by the president.

The first year, 1894–95, 12 meetings were devoted to the study of Spain and two evenings to debate on questions of general interest.

CIVIC LEAGUE OF THE WOMAN'S INSTITUTE, YONKERS

The Civic league is a department of the Woman's institute, organized under action of the trustees January 22, 1895, for the promotion of an interest in and study of civic affairs by means of lectures, classes, special libraries, etc. It endeavors by active cooperation with the city and other authorities to promote a higher public spirit and better social order.

In accordance with the by-laws of the institute, the following officers of the league were appointed: Miss Mary Marshall Butler, *chairman;* Mrs William Sharman, *secretary;* Miss Harriet A. Butler, *treasurer.*

Any woman interested in the objects of the Civic league may become a member by payment of $1 annually, which entitles her to attend the regular meetings, to serve on the section committee; to enter the classes, to use the library, etc.

Section committees. In order to develop the work of the league most actively and efficiently in various localities, the city has been divided into sections, in each of which there is a committee composed of the members living in that section. The leader of each committee is appointed by the chairman of the league. It is the duty of each section committee to study the needs of its particular locality and to devise the best methods for advancing the objects of the league there, and to report through its leader at the general meetings.

While each committee may appoint its own place and time of meeting and is free to plan its own methods of work, no new work is to be undertaken nor any expense incurred for which the league would be responsible, without the approval of the officers of the league; and all matters that call for cooperation of the city authorities must be communicated in writing to the secretary of the league for official action. The officers and section leaders shall meet on the call of the chairman to confer as to best methods of advancing the league and to plan new work.

It will be seen that the object of the league is two-fold, educational and cooperative. It does not desire to duplicate work but to arouse a united and enlightened public sentiment in civic matters which will benefit existing societies.

Besides the general meetings in the Institute hall, classes for study on civic subjects will be organized and the social parlor at the institute arranged as a reading-room with books of reference on civic subjects. A course of five lectures on the government of the United States will be given by Miss Jane Slocum beginning November 1, 1895.

The practical work already taken up is cooperation with the city authorities toward cleaner streets and better conditions of public health, prevention of cruelty to animals and the introduction of instruction in civic matters in the public, parochial and private schools and the circulation of the cards relating to the city ordinances issued by the board of public works and police.

SOCIETY FOR POLITICAL STUDY, NEW YORK

In April 1885 a committee was appointed by the Woman Suffrage league of New York to organize the following autumn a society for the study of the government of our country. A call was sent to women belonging to the league and also to other societies of women, to meet at the residence of Miss Hannah Allen, 36 Irving place, November 16, 1885. About 30 women responded to the call and organized the Society for political study. Municipal and state government, its officers and departments, were the subjects of study during the first year.

The next year we took up the national government, the papers including a history of the constitution, and the different administrations with the important events in each.

In the years following there have been papers on the leading questions of the day, such as the tariff, protection, free trade, reconstruction, reciprocity, annexation of Canada, international copyright, telegraphs and railroads nationalized, bimetallism, banking system. We have also had papers on education, political economy and historical matters, the history of commerce and of slavery and of the different political parties. One year was devoted to the study of South American republics and other small republics. Last year we again devoted to the study of municipal affairs, commencing with the city charter. Next year subjects are taken from the new state constitution. Meetings will be held at 144 Madison avenue at 3 o'clock Tuesdays, beginning October 15.

Some of the interesting features of our meetings are that the papers are all written by members; after the reading of the paper one of the members is called to the chair, so that each one has an opportunity to preside. The papers are discussed and an opportunity given for the study of parliamentary practice.— EMILY L. WAKEMAN

MONDAY EVENING CLUB, WESTFIELD

Like most study clubs throughout the country, the Monday evening club is an organization of women. It belongs both to the General federation of women's clubs and to the New York State federation of women's clubs In membership it is limited to 40 active and 10 associate members. During eight months of the year it holds weekly literary meetings and gives occasional social entertainments. The club has not a house of its own, but rents large, pleasant rooms in the center of the village.

Besides the regular officers, the club annually elects a critic and standing committees on literature, entertainment and rooms.

The literature committee chooses the subject for the year's work, prepares the outline, and assigns topics to the active members. Each member has a printed copy of the year's program, and besides preparing her own particular part of the work, is supposed in her reading to follow the entire course. Most of the members prepare written papers on their topics. Some, however, speak with the aid of a few notes only, and some with no notes whatever. The latter courses have been encouraged as tending to give self-reliance and readiness. In debates and discussions papers are generally discarded as the speakers warm up to their subjects. One interesting feature of the meetings is the roll-call, at which, instead of responding "present," members will at one meeting give quotations from some particular author, at another, a current event; or an "item of interest." In this way each member is made to take part, at least in a small way, in every meeting. The club is thoroughly business-like and adheres strictly to parliamentary rules.

During a period of 15 years various courses of study have been taken. The club has been a "travelers' club." It has studied English literature and American constitutional history, and the last two years it has devoted to Our country. This coming year French literature of the 17th and 18th centuries is to be taken up.

By way of social entertainment the club occasionally concludes its regular literary meetings with informal "afternoon tea." Several times during the year more elaborate entertainments are given, to which guests outside the club are invited. These social meetings are of a literary or musical character. Sometimes a short play is given, or some distinguished guest or member of the club makes a short address The most successful entertainment of this year was a banquet given on Washington's birthday. Old-time costumes were worn, and prominent men and women of the revolutionary period were personated. The patriotic and appropriate toasts of the evening were gracefully and cleverly responded to by club members and a few chosen guests.

Of the results of the club's work it is difficult to speak accurately. The knowledge gained of the subjects studied is, of course, one good and definite result. However, there are other and better results of a more intangible nature. The club and its members have acted and reacted on each other with a steady growth and development. From a small and informal reading circle the club has grown to be an important and recognized literary force in the village. Many of the members have not had the advantages of higher education and the club has helped to bring them out from narrow, uninteresting lives into touch with the literary activity of the world. It has furnished an impetus to those who would not work by themselves and has awakened a desire for deeper reading and study. . The best results of the club's work may perhaps be described not as its literary attainments, but as an improved attitude toward literature not only among its members, but throughout the entire village.— FRANCES PATTERSON FAUST

FORTNIGHTLY CULTURE CLUB, MEDINA

The Fortnightly culture club of Medina was organized in 1891. Its object is the literary and social culture of its members. Meetings are held fortnightly from October 1 to May 1, and the work is done under direction of the Boston Society to encourage studies at home.

The club is composed of 25 busy women who have not time for a large amount of work, so subjects are chosen best adapted to the needs of such a club. General American literature was the subject for 1894-95, and the present year we are studying five American authors, Cooper, Parkman, Whittier, Hawthorne and Holmes. The lives of these writers, different phases of their work and reviews of some of their productions are presented in papers or informal talks. Other features of the work are the answering to roll call with quotations from the author of the evening, the discussion of current events and criticisms of the pronunciation and use of words.— LENA G. BOWEN, *Secretary*

NINETEENTH CENTURY CLUB, HAVERSTRAW

This club, organized in 1893, has a membership of 17. Meetings are held on alternate Tuesday afternoons and a carefully prepared program is carried out, consisting of quotations, a paper, readings and conversation on some assigned topic. English authors were studied in 1894-95 and German history will be the subject for 1895-96.

SATURDAY CLUB, LOCKPORT

The Saturday club of Lockport began its existence January 25, 1890, and grew out of a course of lectures delivered the preceding winter, by Mrs Spalding Evans, who became the first president of the club. These lectures on French and English history having been given on Saturday, the club became the Saturday club, a modest as well as a commemorative name.

During the first year of its existence the Saturday club was considered an experiment, but before the first year was over sufficient interest and enthusiasm had been aroused to assure its success as a literary club. During the first year meetings were held weekly, but since that time the work has been begun earlier, and meetings have been held fortnightly. This arrangement has been found more satisfactory, in case of unavoidable changes. It is usually arranged that 12 meetings shall be held, so that the close of the season shall come some time in April. No refreshments are allowed, except at the last meeting, when the hostess is at liberty to serve tea and cake, with ices or some trifling dainty of that sort. A woman wise in her generation, the immortal Harriet Beecher Stowe once said, that refreshments were the rock on which many a literary society had foundered. The Saturday club has kept this sage maxim well in mind, and has therefore carefully frowned down any attempts to introduce refreshments of even the slightest kind, till the work for the year is over, and the last paper read.

During the first year topics of papers were left to the individual taste of each writer, and were mostly biographical in character. The second year the time was divided between the stage, famous dramatists ancient and modern, famous players, etc., and a consideration of foreign cities, looked at from various points of view, both historically and as seen by modern tourists.

The third year was devoted to study of Germany, considered with regard to its history, literature, religion, social institutions, art-treasures, philosophy, and even its legends. Two afternoons were also given up to German music, able papers being read on the subject of the lives of the most famous German musicians, and fine selections of their music being rendered. In this year also was introduced the custom of having a small annual fee of 25 cents, to cover expense of well printed programs, notices in papers, etc.

The fourth year of its work, the Saturday club took up the study of Italy, in the same way that Germany was studied during the preceding year; Rome, Venice, Milan, Florence, with other famous cities, and the great deeds done in them, and the great men who there lived and died, made a most interesting subject of literary work.

The fifth year was given to study of American history and literature, with two afternoons devoted to American music and musicians. Much patriotic feeling was aroused, and deep interest manifested in our native land, its struggles and trials and its later development and success.

The sixth year took the 18th century as the ground work of study, that time of changing ideas, of shifting principles, of new philosophies and philosophers, and of great musicians. This interesting time evoked a most entertaining series of papers, in which almost every notable event was touched on, from the days of Queen Anne to those of Napoleon Bonaparte.

While not aiming to accomplish any great literary work the Saturday club may justly feel that it has brought forward for consideration of its members very many subjects both interesting and instructive, while much ability hitherto hidden has been brought to light. A greater confidence, both in reading before the club and in writing articles, has been observed as time has gone by. Many women, who, during the first year, hesitated about accepting any part of the literary work of the club, have since that time, written and read most interesting papers, and if as great improvement should be observed in the work of the coming years, the Saturday club may yet hope to stand foremost in the ranks among literary clubs.— Mrs M. A. B. Evans

EMERSON CLUB, MOUNT VERNON

The first meeting of the Emerson club was held October 1, 1895. The program adopted by the club is one prepared by William C. Gannett, and published by the National bureau of unity clubs, Boston. Twelve meetings will be devoted to the study of Emerson's first series of essays.

FREDONIA SOCIETY FOR THE STUDY OF ART

The society was organized in 1884 for the purpose of promoting a knowledge of artists and their works and cultivating true artistic taste.

After several years the membership had increased so largely that it was deemed advisable to divide the club into sections, limited in number to 25 members. There are now three sections, A, B and C, containing 65 members and studying respectively architecture, painting and sculpture.

Each section elects its own chairman, secretary and treasurer, the chairmen of the sections constituting the vice-presidents of the society, taking precedence in order as the sections are formed.

A president, secretary and treasurer are each year elected by the whole society and with the officers of the various sections form an executive committee.

The line of work followed is that laid out in Dr Farrar's *Art topics*. Papers are prepared by the members and read at the monthly meetings. One or two general meetings are held during the year when various art topics are discussed.

The society owns a number of standard art books and a good collection of photographs.— F. B. Pratt, *Secretary*

FREDONIA SHAKSPERE CLUB

The club was organized in 1885 to study the writings of Shakspere together with any line of work helpful in the accomplishment of that purpose. The plays were read in chronologic order and carefully studied, with discussion of the text, papers being read on subjects suggested by the plays. The history of dramatic art from the early Greek drama to the Elizabethan period was studied during 1894-95 and Elizabethan dramatists will be the subject for 1895-96. The club is striving "To show how much of Shakspere shines in the great men, his contemporaries, and how far in his divine mind and manners he surpasses them and all mankind."— Mrs A. D. Dana, *Secretary*

NEW CENTURY CLUB, UTICA

The New century club was incorporated under the laws of the state of New York December 13, 1893. By December 1894 the membership of the club was 250. This rapid increase in membership and the growth of the work of the various committees, specially the kitchen garden work, made the purchase of a home necessary. On May 1, 1895, the house 253 Genesee st. with a lot in the rear on which an auditorium is to be built, was purchased, the club thus incurring a debt of $16,000. This the members expect to pay by the issue of interest-bearing bonds redeemable after 10 and within 30 years.

The object of the club is to create an organized center of action among women for educational, social and philanthropic work. The 15 standing committees are on education, kitchen-garden, literature, government and history, science, economics, current topics, the home, music, art, hospitality, criticism, purchasing, printing and finance.

During the year 1894-95 three study classes were formed within the club; a class of 20 in physical culture under direction of Mrs F E. Davies; a class of 12 in social science who made the Chautauqua extension lectures by Prof. A. W. Small the basis of their work; and a class for the critical study of Browning's *Sordello* under leadership of Miss Irene Sargent. A housekeeper's club was also organized by the home committee for the study of domestic science.

Kitchen-garden classes with a membership of 60 children held their meetings in the club house. The mothers of many of these children attend the mothers classes held every two weeks by the committee on economics.

A class for the study of English literature has been formed for the coming year and lectures will be given by Mrs Mary B. Hedges; also a class in civil government using Fiske's *Civil government* as a text-book.

LITERARY CLUB OF THE CHURCH OF THE MESSIAH, BUFFALO

The Literary club of the Church of the Messiah is essentially a history club, and was organized in 1880. The club has spent three years on American history, literature and art, three on English, two each on French and German, and one year each on Ireland, Spain, Italy and Greece, with a brief study of their literature and art.

The original aim of the club was to foster a taste for systematic reading, and the improvement from year to year in all branches of its work, shows that the policy of a systematic course of study was a wise one.

The membership has grown from 46 to 165, of whom 50 are elected, and the waiting list is always large. There are also five honorary members.

The club issues for each course a calendar of topics and reference list, which last year included a list of magazine articles. The meetings are held in the church parlors, Wednesday afternoons from November to April.

At each session, one or more short papers are read, followed by an informal discussion in which the progress of civilization, the politics, and a contrast with other nations for the same period, are frequent topics These discussions are interesting, and are a fine test of the personal interest of the members, and of the extent of their reading.

The coming winter's work is the study of Egypt, its history and antiquities. An archeological committee will report from week to week on the subject for study. A new departure is the registering of the club with the Extension department of New York, and our facilities for work will be much greater, with the use of a traveling library of 100 volumes, specially selected for our course of study, and duplicating many which are in our large Buffalo libraries, but which will be much called for during the season.— LURA NEWMAN, *Secretary*

CATHEDRAL LIBRARY READING CIRCLES, NEW YORK

These circles, of which there are two, numbering altogether about 50 members, were established respectively in 1889 and 1892. The first circle was begun as a Magazine club, but by general consent was, almost immediately after its inception, continued as a study club in the strict sense of the word. The second circle was the outcome of the first session of the Catholic summer school held in New London. The object of these circles is to direct systematically the reading of its members in chosen lines. They aim at securing the best results from the time and energy spent in reading. Desultory reading is discouraged and definite courses of reading are insisted on. Thoroughness is thus obtained. The mind is benefited by the training. Knowledge becomes accurate. The special object of these circles is to direct the reading of its members in catholic lines, developing sympathy with catholic thought, teaching an appreciation of the breadth and beauty of catholic truth, stimulating an interest in catholic literature by suggesting its wealth. These ends are attained mainly by courses of historical reading, and that historical reading is chiefly ecclesiastical, as the history of the church is coextensive with the history of modern nations, and includes a discussion of the great questions that engage men's attention. Variety is secured by occasional courses of reading in literature, always treated from the catholic point of view.

The method pursued is simple but effective. The director, who is a priest, prepares a systematic course of reading on the subject selected. At the meetings the relative importance and the purpose of the books mentioned in this course are pointed out. The course itself admits of election on the part of the members, allowing them to read as deeply as they choose on the subject proposed. The courses of historical reading have been commended by so able a critic as Brother Azarias in his little volume on *Books and reading*. After indicating the best way of studying the history of a people, he states that the method therein described by him is that followed by the Cathedral library reading circles of New York.[a] The Cathedral free circulating library supplies the books indicated in the course, withdrawing them from general circulation so that the members can pursue their reading without interruption. The members pledge themselves to read for at least 15 minutes daily, in some of the books of the course. Voluntary failure is visited with a self-imposed fine determined in advance by the will of the circle.

Each member is required to note on a slip provided for the purpose, whether the required time for reading has been spent each day, stating in case of omission whether the same was voluntary or involuntary, adding the amount of fine in the former event; indicating also the book, and the number of pages read. These reports, together with the accumulated fines, are handed to the secretary at each meeting.

Meetings are held once a month from October to June inclusive. At these meetings the purpose and scope of the course is explained by the director, who suggests broadly the line of

---
a *Books and reading*, p 12-'8

investigation to be pursued and states current objections to the views or principles dominating the course. An appreciation of the different authors and questions involved is given, and special lines on subsidiary questions are indicated. Incidentally papers treating of some of these special topics are read by members who have been designated in advance, and the general subject under consideration then follows. Questions that have been previously proposed in writing are answered by the director. The routine business ended, the remainder of the time is devoted to social enjoyment.

The motto of the circle is " *Nulla dies sine linca* " as indicative of its method and work. Its colors are the papal colors, gold and white.

Each circle is governed by a director (who is the same for both) a president, a secretary and a treasurer. The director supervises in all its details the intellectual work of the circle, prepares the different courses, etc. He inspects and signs the reports before they are returned to the members.

The president, usually appointed by the director, presides at all the meetings of the circle, and directs its business workings, superintends the circulation of books, etc. The secretary notifies the members of the time and place of meetings, collects the monthly reports and gives them to the director; collects the fines and transmits them to the treasurer. The treasurer collects the dues and keeps an account of the finances of the circle.

There is an initiation fee and an annual fee, the amount of which is determined by the circle. The money obtained by these fees is given to the Cathedral library for the purchase of the books used in the different courses. The expenses for postage, stationery, etc. are met by a tax levied whenever necessary

Public lectures are given from time to time under the auspices of the circle. The subjects of these lectures are in the line of reading done by the circle, and in some instances many of the lecturer's notes have been prepared by members of the circle, who are supposed to be familiar with the admirable manual of Brother Azarias, *Books and reading*, which serves as a guide in the method of reading. The following courses of reading have been pursued by these two circles since their inception: Gregory 7, and the reformation of the 11th century; the crusades; the reformers of the 13th century, St Dominic and St Francis; Thomas Becket; Tennyson; Longfellow; modern catholic novelists; some recent secular novels; Christopher Columbus and the discovery of America. The course in scripture pursued last year by both these circles was found to be specially interesting as it was both critical and literary. The subject chosen, namely, the book of Job, was admirably adapted to give an insight into the rich literary treasures contained in the Bible. At the conclusion of the session the following questions were proposed to the members, and the answers were exceedingly satisfactory, showing that much intelligent work had been accomplished during the year.

1 State the most probable opinion as to the authorship of the book of Job; as to the time at which it was written; and as to whether it is to be regarded as a true history or a parable.

2 State the geographical situation that best corresponds with the location described in the opening chapters of Job.

3 State the reasons (1) for its literary excellence; (2) for its being considered the epic of the Hebrew race; also indicate how it differs from the epics of the Greeks and Latins and show how the difference was to be expected.

4 State briefly the argument of the poem and indicate its structural divisions.

5 What is the best interpretation of the words rendered in the Vulgate CXIX, verse 25, "For I know that my Redeemer liveth, and in the last day I shall rise out of the earth"? verse 26 "And I shall be clothed again with my skin and in my flesh and I shall see my God." On what grounds can you defend that interpretation?

6 Indicate the precise force of the word rendered "Redeemer" in verse 25 and show why it can not be restricted to its primary meaning in this passage.

7 By what reasons can you prove that XIX, verses 23 and 24 must refer to verses 25 and following?

8 How do you explain that Job was not guilty of sin in his malediction of the day of his birth?

9 What was the relative position of Job and his friends in each of the three circles of the debate?

10 How was the conduct of Job's friends the supreme trial of his patience?

2 Maccabees C. XII, 43 and following, is used as a scriptural proof of the dogma of purgatory and the utility of prayers for the dead. Its strength as an argument is denied by biblical protestants on the ground that the 2 Maccabees is not a canonical book therefore has no divine authority. Indicate the arguments for the canonicity of this book as recognized by the Roman catholic church Show also that the argument is strong even if the inspiration of the book were not admitted

When the circles were reading the course on the reformers of the 13th century, it was found that in order to make them fully acquainted with the great work accomplished by St Thomas of Aquinas, it would be necessary to instruct them in the principles of scholastic philosophy. Accordingly, lectures were given every week on mental philosophy to familiarize them with the scholastic terms. These lectures were very well attended. It is proposed during the coming term to carry on a threefold course, historical, literary and scriptural. The subject of the historical course will be Joan of Arc and her times, the literary course will embrace the current books of essays, and the scriptural course will deal with the Gospel of St John.— Joseph H. McMahon

HISTORICAL CONVERSATION CLUB, ALBION

The subjects studied by the club are historical; i. e. history with the many kindred subjects suggested by it, as art, architecture, biography, politics and philosophy. A conversational method of work is adopted at the meetings and discussion is encouraged. Topics are assigned early in the year so that time is given for preparation and excellent work is done.

Four years have been spent on American history and the present year the club will return to the study of the earliest civilizations.

The club has existed 17 years and has accomplished much intellectually and socially, though results in these lines are due also to the Albion historical club, which is older and equally successful.

CARDINAL NEWMAN READING CIRCLE, DUNKIRK

The circle holds weekly meetings from September to July and during 1894-95 devoted 18 meetings to the study of ancient

Greece. One paper is read at each meeting and this is followed by a discussion of the subject led by the literary director. Each essayist selects a member of the circle to criticize her paper and to be with her responsible, for the program of the evening on which it is read.

The officers of the club are a chairman, an assistant chairman, a secretary and a librarian. The pastor or any other priest designed by him is the literary director.

JUDEAN CLUB, ROCHESTER

The Judean club was organized August 13, 1895 with the object of advancing its members in the knowledge of Jewish history and literature and of creating among them a spirit of unity and friendship.

The club is managed by an executive council consisting of the officers, president, vice-president, secretary and treasurer and three members appointed by the president. The council arranges all the exercises, invites speakers and recommends the purchase of all literature. Weekly meetings will be held from September to June and the study of different periods of Jewish history will be taken up systematically.

SALAMANCA SALMAGUNDI SOCIETY

This society was organized in 1890 with a limited membership of 30. Various topics were studied the first year after which systematic work was begun in English history and literature lasting through the year. American history and literature were then studied for two years and French history is the subject for 1895-96. The programs consist of readings, papers and discussions in which each member is expected to be ready to assist. All papers are limited to 20 minutes. Weekly meetings are held from October to March.

LADIES LITERARY CLUB, MASSENA

The Ladies literary club was organized in October 1893 with a membership of 15, which has gradually increased to 30. American authors and their works were studied two years; English authors will be the subject of study for 1895-96. The programs consist of quotations from the author under discussion, followed by biography, brief sketch of works, reading of selections or recitation; if a novelist, a reproduction of the author's best book with either vocal or instrumental music.

The meetings are held at the homes of members biweekly from October 15 to May 15.— DORA WORDEN, *Secretary*

MONDAY CLUB, CATSKILL

The association of ladies called the Monday club originated in a Historical society, which had been in existence for several years. Many changes having occurred both in the membership and in the plan of work, several of the members decided to form a new club, which should be strictly a study club. The membership of the new club was limited to 20 and informal meetings were to be held every Monday evening. German history was chosen as the subject of the first year, 1894-95, and topics were taken from the program of a similar club in Buffalo. The topics were drawn and a paper not less than 30 minutes long, was written by each member and followed by discussion. Many well written papers, both instructive and entertaining, were read during the winter. For the winter of 1895-96 the subject selected is Spain. The officers of the society are president, secretary and treasurer and an executive committee of three which chooses the subject of study, subject to approval of the club.— MRS F. B. WEY, *President*

COTERIE, FAYETTEVILLE

The Coterie of Fayetteville is an outgrowth of a Shakspere club which after a few winters of successful work was merged into this ladies literary society October 26, 1885. Its membership is limited to 25 active and five honorary members. The object of the society is mutual improvement and a united effort toward a higher social and intellectual life. At its beginning the Coterie attempted only the study of art, commencing with the Italian school of painting England, its history, literature and art have since been studied During the present winter the readings are on Holland. For two years current events have been introduced with good success. Among the pleasant features of the work are social evenings when friends are invited to share in the literary treat. The entertainment may be in the form of a lecture given by outside talent for the reading of some standard play by members of the society, or the evening may be devoted to some particular author.— Mrs F. J. House, *Secretary*

FULTON READING CIRCLE

The Fulton reading circle was organized in 1876 and has for nearly 20 years pursued a course of study that has broadened and deepened from winter to winter. At first study was some. what desultory, but at length it was thought wiser to concentrate on some continuous theme.

The history and literature of France were reviewed somewhat curiously for two years; then for nine consecutive winters followed a thorough study of English history and literature. The personal history of English authors, extracts from their best works and reviews of their books, have been the most successful means of making the circle familiar with the riches of the English tongue.

German history and literature, studied according to similar methods, have been the subjects for the past winter. Among the topics taken up were the *Nibelungen Lied*, the minnesingers and the meistersingers; early song and hymn writers; the mystics and humanists; studies in the life and times of Luther; leading characters and campaigns in the 30 years' war. Famous castles, cathedrals and towns connected with these themes have been studied with the aid of illustrations, poetry and all else obtainable relating to them. Instead of written articles we avail ourselves of the most readable productions of the best authors.

The members of the club take this opportunity to express their appreciation of the benefit derived from the traveling library of 25 volumes relating to Germany, furnished by the state. These books to which we could not otherwise have had access have added greatly to the interest of our work.

The membership is limited to 25 ladies. Meetings of two hours duration are held weekly, from October to May. A reading committee selects and assigns the work and its members are seldom changed. All business details are arranged by an executive committee of the six officers of the circle.

CLUBS NOT REGISTERED

Accounts of a few clubs not yet registered are appended, because of their interest as typical clubs.

FROEBEL SOCIETY, BROOKLYN

The Froebel society of Brooklyn has for its object "the advancement of educational interests, and the promotion of self-culture and mutual helpfulness among its members." It was originated by a few earnest mothers, who desired so to understand the principles of education, that the home and school life of their children might become complementary parts of one scheme.

During the 11 years of its existence it has acquired a membership of nearly 100, and has joined both the general and state federations of women's clubs. This presupposes the usual complement of officers, a constitution and by-laws, regular meetings, and a business-like conduct of affairs.

Several years ago it adopted a committee system, arranging its work under five heads; i. e. art, education, home, literature and science. Each member is expected to join and work with one of these committees. Each committee, in rotation, is required to furnish the program for a regular meeting of the society. The program must include at least one original paper, by a member, bearing on the subject which the committee has in charge. It is also desired that one paper shall deal with the subject in its relation to the training of children.

Regular meetings are held on the first Monday of each month from October to June inclusive. The program of the May meeting was in the hands of the home committee, and will illustrate the usual plan of procedure. After the call to order, and the transaction of preliminary business, a paper was read on Music in the home. It urged that every child be given a certain amount of musical training, that singing be encouraged, and that music be considered a necessity in the home, rather than a luxury. A paper on Hospitality followed. True hospitality was defined, handicaps to hospitality dealt with and a history of the ways in which hospitality finds expression in different countries, was given. A reading from Dickens' *Christmas carol* brought out the fine contrast between the hospitable instincts of Scrooge the miser, and Bob Cratchit, his humble clerk. Following this was a lively discussion of the present and local methods of showing hospitality, and a considerable number of "helps over hard places" were brought to light. The program closed with a short paper on the necessity of encouraging or limiting, as the case might be, the hospitable proclivities of children.

At the preceding meeting for April, the program was under the direction of the committee on education. This committee gave, in two papers, the results of its investigations on the desirability of the classical as compared with the scientific course of study in colleges. The value of manual training for children received careful consideration. Discussion brought out the merits and demerits of our public school system, and called attention to the several technical and trades schools within visiting distance, special notice being given to the fine work accomplished in the new Manual training school for boys, in our own city.

Our recording secretary's report shows that during the past year we have had 17 or more papers from our own members, four papers from members of sister clubs, and two lectures by well known educators. We frequently introduce music and recitations into these monthly programs.

In addition to its regular meetings, the society holds three business meetings at stated times, one of them the annual meeting, at which reports are presented by each of its officers, the chairman of its board of trustees and advisory board, and by the chairman of each standing committee.

It also gives three evening socials during the year, when music, readings, addresses and light refreshments are offered for the entertainment of guests. The social event of the year is an annual reunion, where a supper followed by toasts, is the main feature.

In the earlier years of its history, the Froebel society arranged each year for courses of lectures on chosen themes, to be given before its members; e. g. the Red Cross course on home nursing and hygiene and one year 20 lectures were given on the kindergarten. The club has also had 12 lectures on the principles of art and two lectures setting forth the respective merits of the tonic sol fa, and the Holt methods of teaching music.

History claimed our attention in six lectures on nation making, six on the workingman in history and a course on the history of our own times. We had also a Shaksperian course, and one on the evolution of the English press.

The necessity for providing these lecture courses is not so great since the systematic arrangement of our work into committees. Apart from the general club work, there is now special committee work. The committees choose their chairmen annually, and adopt their own plan of study. They usually meet fortnightly.

The wonderful opportunities for culture which grow out of residence in a great educational center are open to all our members. They do not depend on the club life for general enlargement, but they find it invaluable as an aid in the training of their children.

The history of the Froebel society is so closely interwoven with that of Froebel academy, that mention of the latter must be made. The academy was opened in September 1883. It undertook to provide a system of education which should carry Froebel's principles through every grade. The Froebel society was organized in the following April, its membership consisting of the mothers and teachers of the pupils of the academy. They held that the union of the father, mother and teacher in the education of the child, justified the hope of the best possible results. Throughout the 11 years of its existence, this has been the central idea.

The Froebel society holds its meetings and sociables in the Academy building. It is represented in the management of the school by an advisory board of five ladies elected by the society from among its members. This board visits the Froebel academy regularly and frequently, and also visits other schools in Brooklyn and neighboring cities.

The society does not confine its interests to the Froebel academy alone but urges the establishment of free kindergartens, and is friendly to all branches of educational work. Its income is derived from dues and initiation fees. These are kept low, $2 being the annual dues and $1 the initiation fee. With no expense for club-rooms, the need of funds is not great. A special assessment for the annual supper, or for extra lecture courses, meets every necessity.

The business matters of the society are in the hands of a board of nine trustees, elected to serve for three years, one third of them retiring each year. The list of officers for 1895-96 is as follows: Sadie W. Taylor, *president;* Deborah L. Read, *vice-president;* Clara O. Wright, *recording secretary;* Mary C. Willard, *corresponding secretary;* H. Estelle Hartich, *treasurer.* — SADIE W. TAYLOR, *President*

INGLESIDE, BROOKLYN

The Ingleside, a small home club, was organized in March 1885. The original membership of 13 was soon increased to 20, and is still limited to that number.

The object of the club is the mutual improvement of its members and their advancement in all branches of history and literature. Their meetings are held in private parlors, twice a month, from October to May, and two hours given to readings and discussion.

The first five years of the club were spent in the study of American literature, and very thorough work was accomplished. Lives and sketches of authors were written, their books reviewed and selections read, while several talks from well known lecturers formed a pleasant feature of the work.

It was natural to turn from the literature of our country to the country itself, and study the times and events that made so many of our authors statesmen; therefore American history was the next subject chosen. Bryant and Gay's *United States history* was taken for a text-book, papers written, home readings faithfully followed, and two years spent in this work.

From our own republic to that of France was but a step, and a year proved none too long for a comparison between the two countries. In connection with the history of France, a study was also made of the literature, language, art, music and architecture, and thus a comprehensive view of the whole was obtained.

The last two years' work has been given to modern literature including novels, short stories, political economy, history and essays. Sketches and criticisms were written, and selections read. The aim of the club work has been to draw out the individuality and originality of its members, and so much discussion and many papers have been required. During the past winter a course of lectures on modern literature has been given to the club and its friends, by Mrs Garretson of New York, which proved very enjoyable.

Another feature of the club work has been the study of current events, each member taking a certain country, and reporting once a month on the progress of history, politics, literature and art within its borders.

The Ingleside has a constitution and by-laws, and the arrangement of work is in the hands of an executive board of five together with the officers. The club believes in rotation of office, each member serving in her turn. The present officers are: Mrs DeWitt V D. Reiley, *president;* Mrs Freeman Clarkson, *vice-president;* Mrs Henry Manning Wells, *secretary;* Mrs G. Newton Ferris, *treasurer.*

COLUMBIA LITERARY CIRCLE, BROOKLYN

The Columbia literary circle of Brooklyn was founded October 1889, and true to its name, adopted as a course of study American history and literature, gathering material from every available source.

Meetings were held fortnightly, and the plan of devoting the first hour to study and the second to entertainment, selected by several committees, usually relating, as far as practicable, to the appointed evening's subject, has shown itself one of the cementing features of affiliation In the season of 1889–90 the mooted subject Indian, with all his *pros* and *cons*, was studied. His education, extermination, civilization, myths and folk-lore were treated in such interesting papers that possibly the winter's study influenced one of the charter members, Miss D. B. Dodge, to devote her life to missionary work in that field. Prehistoric America, with accompanying essays and talks on mound-builders of the northwest, southwest, Ohio and Mississippi valleys; hieroglyphs and migration of the Toltecs; prehistoric mining; Pueblo Indians; the cliff dwellers, and many others, was found to be "an undiscovered country" full of delight and wonder. History and ruins of Mexico; the ancient races and ruins of Yucatan and Central America; the land of the Incas and conquest of Peru were all touched on in that year's work. This may sound as dry and unattractive as the old bones and Indian curios kindly loaned by Dr Hunt and others for our edification, but our club paper, the

Prehistoric galvanizer, from which the versatile and long-serving editor still darts shafts of wit, not prehistoric, but quite up to A. D. 1895, and the relative literary and musical quota of each evening gave no possibility for "all work" making "Jack a dull boy."

American literature, beginning with colonial writers and taking in order the prominent lives and works of those who with brains and pens have helped make our country's history, was the next study. A Longfellow evening, on the anniversary of the poet's birthday, is recalled, an interesting feature of which was a monologue by the president, Mrs Walsh, who introduced into a charming commentary on the poet's wonderful adaptation to all the varied moods of nature and humanity, a number of his poems set to music.

In the season of 1893-94 the study of Iceland was taken up, its ancient autonomy, history and literature, religious customs, traditions and myths, its geology, geography, entomology, mineralogy, botany, commerce, laws, schools, rise and evident decline, were investigated. Greenland was next studiously explored and made specially interesting by a private lecture delivered by Dr Cook, a member of the Peary expedition.

In 1894-95, Alaska was similarly studied. In connection with this work, letters from members of the circle, pseudo-travelers in Iceland and Alaska, have been entertaining and instructive. The composite novels "Sergius Paulus, or Broken-the-shovel-off," and "Karolina, or the Ice maiden of Reykjavik," grew, chapter by chapter with increasing interest; and the bright serial "A story of Alaska," by Mrs C. A. Nelson is still "to be continued in our next."

The Columbia literary circle was represented at the world's fair, as one of the women's literary clubs of New York state by a folio exhibit.

A literary club which is about to enter its seventh year of existence has earned its own excuse for being, and this short sketch of work accomplished may be inspiriting to clubs of like caliber, equally unknown to fame.— JULIA SEDGWICK KING

LADIES SCOTTISH CLUB, ROCHESTER

The Ladies Scottish club now completing its fifth year was organized purely as a social club, with no fees, dues or restrictions of any nature. Officers were elected simply as a matter of convenience. During the first year two or three cases of want and destitution were laid before the club by individual members, thus giving the club a quasi-benevolent character it was never designed to have. The futility of such aid as the club with its small membership could give, suggested the idea of endowing a Scotch bed in one of the city hospitals.

The second year the club reorganized with two distinct objects, the social feature predominant and the bed endowment as the cherished dream of its originator. This made necessary an annual membership fee of $1 for the bed fund, all other expenses being willing offerings from the members.

The third year in addition to the membership fee each member paid 10 cents monthly, one half to be appropriated to the current expenses of the club and the other half to be at the disposal of the benevolent committee.

For the first four years the literary work was of a varied and desultory nature, being introduced more for the sake of variety than study. In the spring of 1894 it was decided to pursue a systematic course of study for the following year, and the history of Scotland from ancient times to the union was determined on. This plan worked admirably. Our active membership is small, and without exception each one has done personal work to promote the interests of the meetings. The papers have shown a great deal of study and research, and consequently have benefited all.

By the plan pursued last year a chairman was appointed for each evening, and she with her committee took entire charge of the evening, furnishing the papers, music, etc. Next year a tour of Scotland has been determined on and separate topics assigned individual members. At each meeting, 10 minutes will be devoted to the discussion of current events.

The growth of the club has been very gradual; commencing with seven members it now numbers 50. Our treasurer's report shows that the bed endowment fund has increased to $501.95, and while the social or literary element may seem to predominate, the object and aim of the club now is the endowment of a hospital bed.— PAULINE MORTON, M. D.

CHAUTAUQUA JUNIOR OUTLOOK CLUB

This club was formed at Chautauqua in 1895 by Miss Helen A. Bainbridge of New York city and had a membership of 100. Girls from eight to 16 were occupied from two to four hours a day, five days in the week, with study and outdoor amusements. The nature study lessons included talks in geology and botany and simple experiments in chemistry and physics. There was also regular work in the gymnasium besides lessons in rowing, bathing and swimming. Many prominent speakers and singers entertained the club in the club room and at the close of the season the children themselves gave an entertainment with singing, recitations and illustrations of their kitchen-garden work.— GRACE EASTMAN

SYLLABUSES

LIST OF SYLLABUSES PRINTED BY THE UNIVERSITY AND NOW AVAILABLE FOR THE USE OF STUDY CLUBS

Price to registered clubs 2 cents for each 8 pages; single copies at prices specified.

Jenks, J. W. *Professor of history of political and municipal institutions and international law, Cornell University.* Practical economic questions. 60p. Jan. 1892. *Price* 15 *cents.*

Pt 1 Reading list, 21p Pt. 2 Syllabus, 39p

Mace, W: H. *Professor of history and political science, Syracuse University.* American revolution. 72p. Jan. 1892. *Price* 15 *cents.*

38p appendix of reprints of original documents

Boyesen, H. H. *Late professor of Germanic languages and literature, Columbia College.* English literature. 28p. Jan. 1892. *Price* 10 *cents.*

Rees, J: K. *Professor of astronomy, Columbia College.* Popular astronomy. 8p. Mar. 1892. *Price* 5 *cents.*

Curtis, Mrs J. K. American literature. 24p. Sept. 1892. *Price* 5 *cents.*

Mace, W: H. *Professor of history and political science, Syracuse University.* American constitution. 76p. Sept. 1892. *Price* 20 *cents.*

38p. appendix of reprints of original documents

Warren, H: P. *Principal of Albany Academy.* Colonial history of America. 36p. Oct. 1892. *Price 10 cents.*

Harding, S: B. *Instructor in history and geography, Workingman's School of the Society for Ethical Culture, New York city.* American history, 1781–1829. 64p. Oct. 1892. *Price 15 cents*
21p. app•ndix of reprints of original documents

Jackson, A. V. W. *Adjunct professor of the English language and literature, Columbia College.* The English language and its history. 16p. Oct. 1892. *Price 5 cents.*

Cohn, Adolphe. *Professor of the romance languages and literatures, Columbia College* History of France, from the French revolution to the first establishment of the third republic, 1789–1875. 16p. Nov. 1892. *Price 5 cents.*

Ross, E: A. *Associate professor of political economy and finance, Cornell University.* Present day economic reforms. 28p. Dec. 1892. *Price 10 cents.*

Spence, A.. M. *Vice-principal of Saratoga high school and lecturer on literature in the Saratoga Athenæum.* Critical study of authors of to-day. 16p. Dec 1892. *Price 5 cents.*

Turk, M. H. *White professor of the English language and literature, Hobart College.* Introduction to the study of English literature. 32p. Jan. 1893. *Price 10 cents.*

Curtis, Mrs J. K. Macbeth and King Lear. 24p. Jan. 1893. *Price 5 cents.*

Mills, H. E. *Associate professor of history and economics, Vassar College.* Practical economic questions. 52p. Jan. 1893. *Price 15 cents.*

Price, T: R. *Professor of the English language and literature, Columbia College;* Woodberry, G: E: *Professor of literature, Columbia College,* and Jackson, A. V. W. *Adjunct professor of the English language and literature, Columbia College.* The English drama; its rise and development to the closing of the theaters (1640). 20p. Jan. 1893. *Price 5 cents.*

Hudson, G: H: *Vice principal, State Normal and Training School, Plattsburg.* Zoology from the modern standpoint of animal biology. 28p. Feb. 1893. *Price 10 cents.*

Crawshaw, W. H. *Professor of English literature, Colgate University.* English literature. 32p. Feb. 1893. *Price 10 cents.*

Kaiser, Arthur. Discovery of America: period of discovery; land and people discovered and the discoverers 28p. Feb. 1893. *Price 10 cents.*

Burton, H: F. *Professor of Latin, University of Rochester.* Ancient Roman life. 16p. Sept. 1893. *Price 5 cents.*

Forbes, G: M. *Professor of Greek and logic, University of Rochester.* Monetary science. 28p. Sept. 1893. *Price 10 cents.*

Jackson, A. V. W. *Adjunct professor of the English language and literature and instructor in the Iranian languages, Columbia College.* Some masterpieces of English literature 16p. Sept. 1893. *Price 5 cents.*

Fitch, C: E. *Regent of the University.* Civil and religious liberty in America. 20p. Dec. 1893. *Price 5 cents.*

Onderdonk, A. F. *Physics and natural science, Albany high school.* Electricity. 28p. Oct. 1893. *Price 10 cents.*

Curtis, Mrs J. K. Hamlet and Merchant of Venice. 36p. Oct. 1893. *Price 10 cents.*

Jenks, J. W. *Professor of political, municipal and social institutions, Cornell University.* Economic legislation. 24p. Dec. 1893. (Half course. Five lectures.) *Price 5 cents.*

Smith, G: W: *Professor of history, Colgate University.* Practical economic questions. Dec. 1893.

Boyesen, H. H. Late *Professor of Germanic languages and literature, Columbia College.* Medieval German literature. 12p. Nov. 1893. *Price 5 cents.*

Sears, Mrs F. . G. The making of France. 8p. Nov. 1893. (Half course. Five lectures.) *Price 5 cents.*

Truax, J. R. *Professor of rhetoric, English language and literature, Union College.* Studies in English literature. Dec. 1893.

Forbes, Charles, M. D. Electricity. 32p. Dec. 1893. *Price* 10 *cents*.

Brigham, A. P. *Professor of geology and natural history, Colgate University.* Geology and scenery of New York. 24p. Dec. 1893. *Price* 5 *cents*.

Mace, W: H *Professor of history and political science, Syracuse University.* Development of the nation. 60p Dec. 1893. *Price* 15 *cents*.
_{20p appendix of reprints of original documents.}

Arey, A. L. *Sciences, Rochester Free Academy.* Various forces of nature as related to modern life. 36p. Jan. 1894. *Price* 10 *cents*.

Bennett, C: E. *Professor of Latin language and literature, Cornell University.* Private life of the Romans. 12p. Jan. 1894. *Price* 5 *cents*.

Electricity. Under direction of Columbia college. Feb. 1894. (Half course. Five lectures.)

Jenks, J. W. *Professor of political economy, civil and social institutions, Cornell University.* Political methods. 32p. Mar. 1894. *Price* 10 *cents*.

Waterman, H. B. *Oriental lecturer, Chautauqua.* Nations of the orient. 20p. July 1894. *Price* 5 *cents*.

Forbes, G: M. *Professor of Greek and logic, University of Rochester.* Money, banking and the silver question. 36p. Oct. 1894. *Price* 10 *cents*.

Weatherly, U. G. Comparative politics. 40p. Ap. 1895. *Price* 10 *cents*.

Smith, G: W: *Professor of history, Colgate University.* Early American history. 48p. Oct. 1894. *Price* 10 *cents*.

Scott, W. B. *Professor of geology, Princeton College.* Geology. 16p. Oct. 1894. *Price* 5 *cents*.

Crawshaw, W: H: *Professor of English literature, Colgate University.* The English novel. 32p. Jan. 1895. *Price* 10 *cents*.

Curtis, Mrs J. K. Romeo and Juliet and the Tempest. 28p. Dec. 1894. *Price* 10 *cents*.

Hamlin, A. D. F. *Adjunct-Professor of architecture, Columbia College, School of Mines.* History of architectural styles. 16p Dec. 1894. *Price 5 cents*

Mace, W: H. *Professor of history and political science, Syracuse University.* The civil war and some of its problems. 52p. Jan. 1895. *Price 15 cents.*

Wickes, W: K. *Principal of Syracuse High School.* American history. 12p. Jan. 1895. *Price 5 cents.*

Smith, G: W: *Professor of history, Colgate University.* American colonial history. Feb. 1895.

Gilmore, J. H. *Professor of rhetoric and English, University of Rochester.* American poetry. 20p. Jan. 1895. *Price 5 cents.*

Montgomery, Mrs Helen Barrett. Life in old Florence. 32p. Feb. 1895. *Price 10 cents.*

Curtis, Mrs Jessie K. Julius Caesar. 40p. Sept. 1895. *Price 10 cents.*

Hodges, G: C. *Instructor in science, Utica Free Academy.* Electricity up to date. 20p. Sept. 1895. *Price 5 cents.*

Mrs Jessie K. Curtis has had stenciled in large clear type easily read, lectures to accompany her syllabuses on *Macbeth* and *King Lear* (10 lectures) and on *Julius Caesar* (10 lectures). These lectures have been somewhat extensively used by Shakspere clubs and excellent work has been done by their aid. All questions of the syllabus are answered in the lectures and Mrs Curtis will correspond with the clubs suggesting methods of work that she has found effectual in her own classes.

The lectures on *Julius Caesar* give a careful study of the era and the man historically considered, as well as the drama. Several clubs in Shakspere study have already selected this as their winter's work. The lectures on *Macbeth* and *King Lear* will be lent for $15; those on *Julius Caesar*, for $10.

Mrs Curtis has also a few type written lectures on *Hamlet* and *Merchant of Venice* (11 lectures) and on *Romeo and Juliet* and the *Tempest* (10 lectures). Terms for these will be arranged by correspondence.

OUTLINES OF STUDY

The most elaborate and systematic course of study for clubs which has come to the department was arranged for the Clio club of Palmyra, N. Y. for the winter of 1891-92 and is founded on Fisher's *Outlines of universal history*. It is designed to give a bird's-eye view of the subject, preparatory to subsequent study of history in greater detail. Such preliminary general survey of the historical field is helpful in showing relations of parts to the whole, making clearer the comparative significance of events of different epochs. The 80-page program is printed on one side of linen paper, so that notes may be inserted at each meeting.

The society for the study of Child nature, of New York, has included in its report for 1890-92 many valuable suggestions for clubs studying educational subjects The work for 1890-91 was based on a thorough study of Rousseau's *Emile* and in 1891-92 selections from Locke, Richter, Spencer, Adler and others were discussed. The outline as given includes not only the plan of work but in some cases the conclusions reached by the club. The report will be sent free to those interested in the subject, on application to the secretary, Mrs L. W. Seligsberg, 1023 Park av., New York.

The National bureau of Unity clubs, 25 Beacon street, Boston, Mass., has published a useful series of study outlines for clubs. The outline for study of Emerson, selected by the Emerson club of Mount Vernon, contains a list of books for club use; suggested methods of study and an outline for 12 meetings; at the end is an additional list of books for more general reading.

From our large collection of programs the following are reprinted as suggestive to other clubs. In many cases the program is printed as issued, but quotations have often been omitted as well as reviews, business meetings, etc If a program is adopted or largely copied by another club, the results of valuable experience can often be utilized by writing to the secretary of the club originating the program. For the same reason all clubs using any of the outlines here printed are asked to inform the department in order that future clubs may communicate with them if desirable.

Subj. no. 170   ETHICS

Woman's ethical club, Rochester

1891–92

1 Barbarisms in modern life
    Inhumanities toward servants
    Inhumanities of tradesmen
    Treatment of criminals
    Cruelties to animals encouraged by fashion and custom
    Barbarisms in dress and house decoration
2 Ethics of business relations
    Duties of women as consumers
    Shopping, bargaining and smuggling
    Training of girls in business methods
    Consumers' leagues; are they objectionable?
    Cooperation; why does it fail in housekeeping?
    Economics of charity
3 Cooperation in the home
    In business and finance
    In the employments of the home
    In reading and study
    In hospitality and amusements
    Between employers and employed
4 Coeducation in colleges
    Objects of college education
    Character and demeanor of boys and girls at college
    Intellectual training
    Moral aspect
    Physical considerations
    Professional schools
    Mutual influence of boys and girls in their education
5 Ethics of the use of time
    Healthful and useful work
    Physical development
    Intellectual development
    Reading
    Time given to amusements; pastime, diversion, recreation

6 Ethics of the arts
    Origin and purpose of the arts imply ethical relations
    Ethical qualities in the arts
    National conditions favorable to their development
    Art education
    National art the culmination of national life

Subj. no. 720 ARCHITECTURE, SCULPTURE AND OUTLINE HISTORY FROM PREHISTORIC TIMES

Highland Park literary club, Buffalo
1895–96

1 Egypt: an outline of its history and architecture
2 Egyptian sculpture
    Memphitic period
    Theban period
  Asiatic architecture
3 Architecture of ancient Greece
  Grecian sculpture
    Prehistoric period
    Early archaic period
4 Architecture of ancient Greece (*continued*)
    Doric: the Parthenon
    Ionic
    Corinthian
    Symposium: inferences on the styles of the three orders
5 Architecture of ancient Greece (*continued*)
    Influence of the theater on architecture and sculpture
  Grecian sculpture (*continued*)
  Influence of the games
    Schools of Argos and Sikyon
    Schools of Aegina
6 Grecian sculpture (*continued*)
    Early Attic school
    Calamis, Pythagoras, Myron
    Temple of Theseus
7 History of Greece: outline from earliest times to Roman conquest
8 Grecian sculpture (*continued*)
    Phidias: the Parthenon
    Alcamenes: temple of Zeus

9 Grecian sculpture (*continued*)
    Acropolis
    Phigalian marbles
    Polycleitos of Argos
10 Grecian sculpture (*continued*)
    Attic school
    Praxiteles
    Peloponnesian school
11 Grecian sculpture (*continued*)
    Historic sketch of Pergamus
    Art and acropolis of Pergamus
    School of Rhodes
    Venus de Milo, Apollo Belvidere, the Nikes, Tiber, Ariadne
12 Historic outline of early Italy; and comparison of national traits of Romans, Etrurians and Greeks
    Architecture, Etruscan
    Sculpture, Etruscan
13 Historic outline of the Roman conquest of Greece
    Works of Attic artists in Rome
    Asiatic-Greek sculptors in Rome
14 Roman architecture: great engineering and architectural works of Rome
15 Roman sculpture
    Pasiteles and his school
    Monumental sculptures
    Descriptions and definitions in church architecture
16 Comparison of Christian and pagan basilicas
    Sculptures of the early Christian centuries
    Byzantine architecture, and its influence on Italian sculpture
17 Romanesque architecture
    History, description and select examples
    The Romanesque in England
18 Italian sculpture
    The three Pisanos
    Orcagna, Nina, Balduccio
    Influence of the Pisan school
    Sienese school

19 Gothic architecture: its origin, description, influence and select examples
20 Florentine school of sculpture
    The goldsmith's art in Italy
    Lorenzo Ghiberti
    Donatello
    Luca della Robbia
21 Florentine school of sculpture (*continued*)
    Pollajuolo, Verocchio
    Mino (da Fiesole)
    Benedetto (da Majano)
    Tuscan monumental tombs
22 Sculpture in upper Italy
    Matteo Civitale, the Certosa at Pavia
    Antonio Amadeo
  The later renaissance
    Andrea Sansovino, Jacopo Tatti
    Michael Angelo
23 Italian sculpture (*continued*)
    Benvenuto Cellini
    Giovanni da Bologna
    Lorenzo Bernini
    Winkelmann, Lessing
    Flaxman
24 Renaissance architecture: its spread over Europe
    Influence and examples
25 Italian sculpture, third revival
    Canova
    Thorwaldsen
26 Saracenic architecture

Subj. no. 822 33   SHAKSPERE

Fredonia Shakspere club

1890–91

ANALYSIS FOR USE IN PREPARATION OF PAPERS

Chronological proofs, external and internal
Outline of plot; on what does it turn ?
Condition of the text as to correctness

What of the title? its rank as compared with other plays of the same period
How long a time is comprised in the action?
Analyze the two central characters
By what individual characteristics are the people grouped around them distinguished?
What by-play in the drama?
What of its poetic excellence?
What proportion of end-stopped lines, rhymes, extra syllables, etc?
Questions for constant use in study of the plays
Read one scene, then review, any member being called on for explanation
Point out and give full explanation of:
1 All classical and mythological allusions
2 All scriptural allusions and parallels
3 All figures of speech
4 All allusions to customs and occasions now obsolete
5 All obsolete words
6 All parallel passages in other plays
7 All references to works of other authors
8 All historical or geographical allusions

TWELFTH NIGHT

1 Paper: *Twelfth night* and kindred festivals
  Reading, act 1; discussion
2 Paper: Friendship as portrayed by Shakspere
  Reading, act 2; discussion
3 Paper: The clown in history and literature
  Act 3, to "enter Sir Andrew Aguecheek," scene 4
4 Paper: Stage history of the play, *Twelfth night*
  Conclude act 3 and read act 4
5 Reading, act 5
  Paper: Review of the play
  Report of critic

TROILUS AND CRESSIDA

6 Paper: Homer
  Read act 1 to scene 3; discussion
7 Conclude act 1 and read act 2 to scene 2. Special discussion of text as compared with selections from earliest plays

8 Paper: The heroic age
Reading, conclude act 2
9 Read act 3 to "enter Achilles and Patroclus"
Discussion
10 Conversation: Ancient Troy, researches and discoveries
Conclude act 3 and read act 4 to scene 4
11 Paper: Home life of the Greeks
Conclude act 4; discussion
Critic's report
12 Reading, act 5
Review paper, Troilus and Cressida

OTHELLO

13 Preliminary paper
Read act 1 to "enter Brabantio," scene 3
14 Paper: Venice and the Turks
Read to conclusion of act 1; discussion
15 Paper: Cyprus
Read act 2 to "re-enter Othello and attendants," scene 3
16 Talk: The Moors of to-day
Conclude act 2 and read act 3 to scene 2
17 Paper: Venetian school of painting
Read act 3, scenes 2-3; discussion
18 Conclude acts 3 and 4; discussion
Report of critic
19 Paper: Othello and Iago, a comparative study
Reading, act 5

ALL'S WELL THAT ENDS WELL

20 Paper: The political relations of France and Italy in the 16th century
Reading, act 1; discussion
21 Paper: Italian literature of the 16th century
Act 2 to scene 4; discussion
22 Paper: Personal reminiscences of Florence
Reading, finish act 2, and act 3 to scene 5
23 Conclude act 3 and read act 4; discussion
Critic's report
24 Reading, act 5
Review paper, All's well that ends well
Annual reports

Subj. no. 822 33   DRAMATIC ART
Fredonia Shakspere club 1894-95

Wisdom is the supreme part of happiness; and reverence toward the gods must be inviolate.—*Sophocles*

1 Greek dramatic art
  Paper: Sources and early forms of Greek literature
  Five-minute talks on early Greek authors
  Read from *Comedy of errors*
2 Paper: Conditions necessary for development of the national drama
  Sub-topics: How were these conditions fulfilled in Greece?
    What in the nature of the Greeks was peculiarly favorable for the production of the drama?
  Read from *Comedy of errors*
3 Paper: Origin of the drama in Greece
  Sub topics: What is tragedy?
    The chorus; its importance in the ancient drama
  Read from *Comedy of errors*
4 Paper: Sketch of Aeschylus
  Read *Prometheus bound*
5 Comparative study of Eumenides and Hamlet
6 Paper: Sophocles and his writings
  Read *Antigone*
  Talk: Representations of the tragedy in America
7 Paper: Comparison of Euripides with his predecessors
  Read *Alcestis;* Compare the character of Admetus and Othello
8 Paper: Characteristics of the Greek drama as distinct from the modern
  Read *Oedipus tyrannus*, and selections from *King Lear*
9 Paper: Classical unities of action, time and place
  Sub-topics: Which of these alone can be regarded as an absolute art principle?
    Illustrate from Shakspere and the Greek
    Show how both in Shakspere and the Greek tragedies, action and plot are subordinate to the delineation of human motive and passion
10 Paper: Nemesis, the cardinal idea in Greek tragedy
   Illustrate with selections from *Macbeth* and *Richard 3*

11 Paper: Origin of comedy and its relations to the god Dionysus
Sub-topic: Greek mythology and its influence on the lives of the people
12 Paper: Aristophanes as a poet of the fancy
Selections from comedies of Aristophanes
13 Read *Midsummer night's dream* and compare with the comedies of Aristophanes
14 Alexandrian period
Paper: Art of Menander
Paper: The new comedy; decadence of the Greek drama, and a sketch of Philemon
Discussion
15 Graeco Roman period
Paper: The Roman drama, as created by Plautus and Terence
Sub-topics: Sketch of Seneca as a dramatist
Why was there no Roman tragic drama?
Short talks on Horace, Virgil and Lucretius
Account of plays of Plautus and Terence as given in western colleges
16 Paper: Origin and development of mystery and morality plays throughout Europe
Read and comment on miracle plays
Talk: The troubadours
17 Paper: The drama in Italy in the 15th and 16th centuries compared with English drama of the same period
Short papers on Ariosto, Trissino, Macchiavelli and Aritino
18 Paper: Development of dramatic art in Spain in the 16th century
Sub-topic: Plot and manner of treatment of the tragedy of Numantia
Compare cervantes with Shakspere
19 Paper: Comparison of the pre-Elizabethan period with that preceding the Greek drama
The four schools of tragedy: the antique, or classical; Gothic or romantic; French or rhetorical; German or paradoxical; discussion
20 Read morality play, and interlude
Skelton's *Magnificence*
Marriage of wit and wisdom
General discussion

21 First dramatic period in England
  Read *Ralph Roister Doister*, the earliest English comedy; *Ferrex and Porrex*, the earliest English tragedy
  General discussion
22 Immediate predecessors of Shakspere
  Short papers on Lyly, Peele and Greene, with extracts from their plays
  Read *Love's labour's lost*
23 Paper: Christopher Marlowe
  Read *Dr Faustus* and compare with Göthe's *Faust*
24 General discussion of the year's work
  Annual reports

PHASES OF CHARACTER AND PASSION IN MODERN FICTION
Eliot society of Church of the Messiah, St Louis, Mo.
1890–91

1 The rogue.— W. E. Norris
  Tom Heywood: Humanity's overestimation of weak or selfish good nature
2 The nether-world.— George Gissing
  All the characters: Ignorance of the means, relations and ethics of life
3 A little journey in the world.— C. D. Warner
  Margaret Debree: Disintegration of character by luxury and success
4 Crime and punishment.— Dostoyevsky
  Raskolnikof: Remorse
5 April hopes.— W. D. Howells
  Alice Pasmer and Dan. Mavering: Restricted conscientiousness and lack of definite ideals
6 Dimitri Roudine.— Tourgenieff
  Dimitri Roudine: Excess of ideals without the foundation of intelligent self-control
7 Marie Bashkirtseff
  Marie: Intense and undisciplined psychic consciousness and vitality
8 An enemy of society.— Henrik Ibsen
  Hovstadt Burgomaster, etc.: False standards of society
9 The mayor of Casterbridge.— Thomas Hardy
  Michael Henchard: A result of competition

10 The deemster.—Hall Caine
   Dan Mylrea: Anger
11 Anne.—Constance F. Woolson
   Anne: Love
12 The Peckster professorship.—J. P. Quincy
   Professor Hargrave: The courage of one's conviction

Subj no. 913 32   **ANCIENT EGYPT**
           Travelers club, Olean
                THE OLD EMPIRE

Dynasty 1–6

" We'll eat the lotus of the Nile"

1 The land of the lotus flower: Geography, climate
  Ancient Egyptians
  Current events; discussion

   "Hail to thee, O Nile
      Thou showest thyself in this land
      Coming in peace, giving life to Egypt."

2 The Nile
  Menes and the earlier dynastic kings
  Hieroglyphics and literature
  Discussion

   " O'er Memphis site the turbaned robber strays,
      Each wall is razed, each pillared shrine o'erthrown "

3 The pyramid builders
  Memphis, its glory and ruins
  Form of government; discussion

   "The labor of an age in piled stones."

4 Pyramids and sphynx
  Condition of women 4000 years ago
  Current events; discussion

Dynasty 6–12

"The hundred gated queen, tho' fallen, grand."

·5 Reign of Amenemhat
  Thebes. The twin colossi
  Military aggrandizement; discussion

THE MIDDLE EMPIRE
Dynasty 12–18

"Now there was a famine in the land of Canaan and Abram went down into Egypt to sojourn there."

6 Sojourn of the Israelites in Egypt
  Usurtasen 1, his temple and obelisks
  Amenemhat 3; Lake Moeris, Labyrinth, Fayoum; discussion

"Marvelous things did He in the sight of their fathers in the land of Egypt, in the fields of Zoan."

7 Hyksos reign
  History of Tanis
  Current events; discussion

THE NEW EMPIRE
Dynasty 18–21

"Like ships that sailed for sunny isles."

8 Queen Hatasu and her fleet
  Thothmes 3
  Manners and customs; discussion

"Whited sepulchers, which indeed appear beautiful outward, but within are full of dead men's bones"

9 Bubastis
  Temples and temple service
  The lost arts; discussion

"High on his cart Sesostris struck my view,
  Whom sceptered slaves in golden harness drew."

10 Rameses 2
  A fete day 33 centuries ago
  Current events; discussion

"I will sing unto the Lord for He has triumphed gloriously, the horse and his rider hath He thrown into the sea."

11 The Pharaoh of the Exodus and his son
  The Ramesseum
  Moses; discussion

"Who has not heard where Egypt's realms are named,
  What monster gods her frantic sons have framed?"

12 Egyptian deities
Decline of Egypt under the Ramessides
Scientific knowledge of the Egyptians; discussion

Dynasty 21, to 332 B. C.

"For there is music wherever there is harmony, order or proportion."

13 Music and musical instruments
Abydos
Heliopolis
Current events; discussion

"The land shadowing with wings which is beyond the rivers of Ethiopia."

14 Ethiopian invasion
Karnak and Luxor
Domestic architecture and house furnishings; discussion

"Know ye the land where the cypress and myrtle,
Are emblems of deeds that are done in their clime,
Where the rage of the vulture, the love of the turtle,
Now melt into sorrow, now madden to crime?"

15 Fauna and flora
The last Pharaoh
Funeral rites and ceremonies; discussion

"A sword shall come upon Egypt and her foundations shall be broken down."

16 Cambyses and the Persian conquest
Mummies and the art of embalming
Current events; discussion

"Why may not imagination trace the noble dust of Alexander?"

17 Alexander the Great in Egypt
Alexandria
Spoiling the Egyptians; discussion

Subj. no 913.38 GREECE ITS HISTORY AND LITERATURE
Saturday class, Buffalo
1895-96

1 The land and the people
2 Legendary or heroic age; Homer
3 Religion of the Greeks; mythology and games

4 Age of constitutional changes and of colonization
5 Epic poetry
6 Greco-Persian wars
7 Plato
8 Splendor of Athens. Age of Pericles
9 Architecture; the hill of the Acropolis
10 Peloponnesian war; its results
11 Socrates
12 Spartan and Theban supremacy
13 Sculpture and painting
14 Greek drama. Tragedy. Aeschylus. Sophocles and Euripides
15 Greek drama. Comedy. Aristophanes
16 Macedonian supremacy. Empire of Alexander
17 Schools of philosophy; Epicurus
18 Education. Civil and domestic life
19 Aristotle
20 Architecture; the Parthenon
21 Achaean league
22 Greek oratory: Demosthenes
23 Historians: Herodotus, Thucydides, Xenophon
24 Men of science: Euclid, Archimedes

Subj. no. 914.2   ENGLAND
University extension study club, Ogdensburg
1894-95

1 Physical geography of England; Liverpool, Chester, Roman remains
2 Birmingham, Warwick, Leamington
3 Kenilworth, Coventry
4 Rugby; an English public school
5 Stratford on-Avon, Charlecote, Shottery
6 Evesham, Cheltenham, Gloucester, Cirencester Cumner hall, Cuddesden, Hughenden manor, and minor points along the Thames
7 Oxford; the six older colleges
8 Remaining colleges of Oxford; halls, etc. Outline of the Tractarian movement
9 Woodstock, Blenheim, Henley, Eton college, following the Thames

10 Windsor castle, Albert memorial chapel, Magna Charta island
11 Hampton court, Bushy park, Twickenham, Kew, etc.
12 Old London
13 St Paul's cathedral
14 Outline sketch of Westminster abbey and principal monuments of north transept and nave
15 Westminster abbey: poet's corner and south transept
16 Westminster abbey: choir and chapels
17 Westminster abbey: cloisters, crypt, chapter house, deanery, Jerusalem chamber and Westminster school
18 St Margaret's church, Westminster hall, parliament buildings
19 Tower of London
20 Hyde park, St James palace and park, Buckingham palace, Holland house
21 St Savior's church, Lambeth palace, temple, British museum, Greenwich
22 Rochester cathedral, Canterbury cathedral, Streatham, Brighton, Arundel castle, Chichester
23 Portsmouth, Isle of Wight, Ryde, Sandown, Shanklin, Ventnor
24 Bonchurch, Newport, Carisbrook castle, Yarmouth, Cowes, Haslemere, Wimbledon, Southampton

Subj no. 930 ANCIENT HISTORY

Historical conversation club, Albion

1895-96

1 Commercial, intellectual and moral influence of the east on the west
  Valleys of the Tigris and Euphrates and their commerce
2 Chaldean civilization
  Great Assyria, its kings, cities and learning
3 Assyrian art
  Land of Palestine before and to the time of Abraham
4 The Hittites
  Cities of the caravan routes
5 Palestine in the time of the judges, its divisions into kingdoms and its great kings

6 Social and domestic life and state of learning in Palestine from the conquest by Joshua to the Babylonish captivity
Phoenicia and its influence on the religion of the Jews
7 Relations of Assyria and Egypt
8 Jewish captivity in Babylon
Rise of the Medio-Persian empire
9 Sacred books and epics of Persia
Early Greek migrations to Asia Minor, Ionian influence
10 Legendary invasion of the east by the west. The *Iliad* and *Odyssey*
11 Persian invasion of the west, Darius and Xerxes
Relations of Greece and Persia from defeat of Xerxes to the conquest of Alexander
12 Divisions and kingdoms of Asia Minor to Alexander's conquest; civilizations, religion, kings, etc.
Greek conquest of the east, Alexander the Great
13 Founding of commercial centers established by Alexander and their history
Divisions of Alexander's kingdom. Downfall of western power in the east
14 Commercial and literary centers in Egypt in the time of Ptolemys
The *Talmud*
15 The *Septuagint*
Roman conquests in the east
Turanian invasions of Europe
16 Dependence of the cities of the Mediterranean on eastern countries
Etruscan influence on Roman and Italian art
17 Strife for commercial supremacy on the Mediterranean from first Punic war to the time of Pompey
Arabs and Mahomet
18 Mahometan occupation of the east, its influence on art, literature and commerce
19 Medieval travelers and missionaries, true and false reports of countries, peoples
Mahometan occupation of India and conversion of people
20 Commercial, intellectual and moral influence of the west on the east

Subj. no. 937   **ROMAN HISTORY**

Historical club, Ilion

1893-94

" She sits among the eternal hills,
Their crown, thrice glorious and dear,
Her voice is as a thousand tongues
Of silver fountains, gurgling clear."— *Julia Ward Howe*

1 Map of Italy (physical features)
Italy in early times
Early inhabitants
Primitive civilization of the Latins
Early government
Outline map of early Rome
Kingly period of Rome
Lucius Junius Brutus' oration over the body of Lucretia

· Reference books

History of Rome, v. 1	Mommsen
Early Rome	Ihne
History of Rome, v. 1-2	Merivale
Epitome of Roman history	L. A. Florus
Early Roman law	E. C. Clark
City of Rome	Dyer
History of Rome	Leighton

"The Tarpian rock, the citadel
Of great and glorious Rome, queen of the earth,
So far renown'd, and with the spoils enriched of nations."— *Milton*

2 Great names of early Rome: Brutus, Horatius, Coriolanus, Cincinnatus
Horatius at the bridge
Social troubles
Secession
Office of tribune
Laws of the 12 tables
Story of Virginia
Gaulish invasion
Fate of Virginia

Reference books

Plutarch's lives	Shakspere
Coriolanus	Ihne
Early Rome	Macaulay
Lays of ancient Rome	Creighton
History of Rome	Gilman
The story of the nations	

> " Great Carthage is laid low. Scarcely can eye
> Trace where she stood with all her mighty crowd:
> For cities die; kingdoms and nations die,
> A little sand and grass is all their shroud."—*Tasso*

3 Conquest of Italy
  Greece
  Appian way
  Carthage
    Nature of the Carthaginian empire
    Constitution of Carthage
    Relative strength of Rome and Carthage

Reference books

History of Rome	Creighton
History of Rome	Le'ghton
History of Rome	Liddell
Walks in Rome	Hare
Six months in Italy	Hillard
Rome and Carthage	Smith
Story of the nations	Gilman

> " In that elder day, to be a Roman
> Was greater than a King !"— *M R. Mitford*

4 First Punic war
    Regulus
    Hamilcar
  Second Punic war
    Hannibal
    Scipio Africanus
    Archimedes
  Third Punic war
    Cato
    Cornelia
  Old Romans at home

Reference books

Rome and Carthage	Smith
History of Rome, v. 2	Mommsen
History of Hannibal, the Carthaginian	J. Abbott
Story of the nations	Gilman
History of Rome	C. M. Yonge
History of Rome	E M. Sewell

"Where his rude hut by the Danube lay
There were his young barbarians all at play;
There was their Dacian mother, he, their sire,
Butcher'd to make a Roman holiday!"—*Byron*

5 A Roman triumph
  Mythology
  Civil dissensions to the Mithridatic war
  Mithridatic war to the first triumvirate
  Massacres of the Roman amphitheater
  Spartacus to the gladiators

Reference books

Mythology of ancient Greece and Italy	Keightley
History of Rome	Creighton
The Gracchi, Marius and Sulla	Beesly
Story of the nations	Gilman
Roman triumvirate	Merivale
Compend of history of Rome	Paterculus
Cosmopolitan, v. 13	

"Tully, most e'oquent, most sage
  Of all the Roman race
That deck the past or present age,
  Or future days may grace."—*Hon G. Lamb*

6 Cicero
  Julius Caesar
  Mark Antony's oration in the Forum
7 Julius Caesar

"This was the noblest Roman of them all:
All the conspirators, save only he,
Did that they did in envy of great Caesar;
He, only, in a general honest thought,
And common good to all, made one of them.
His life was gentle; and the elements
So mix'd in him, that nature might stand up,
And say to all the world '*This was a man!*'"—*Shakspere*

> "Rome, for empire far renowned,
>   Tramples on a thousand states;
> Soon her pride shall kiss the ground
>   Hark! the Gaul is at the gates!"— *Cowper*

8 Public works and buildings.
  First triumvirate.
  Last days of the republic.
  Cleopatra

Reference books

Early empire	W. W Capes
Six months in Italy	Hillard
City of Rome	Dyer
History of the Romans, v. 1–2	Merivale
Roman triumvirate	Merivale
History of Rome, v. 4	Mommsen
Characteristics of women (Cleopatra)	Mrs Jameson
Cleopatra	George Ebers
Life of Cleopatra	Abbott

9 Antony and Cleopatra

> "We, ignorant of ourselves,
> Beg often our own harms, which the wise powers
> Deny us for our good; so find we profit
> By losing of our prayers."— *Antony and Cleopatra*

> "Along the sacred way
> Hither the triumph came, and, winding round
> With acclamation, and the martial clang
> Of instruments, and cars laden with spoil,
> Stopped at the sacred stair that then appeared,
> Then thro' the darkness broke, ample, star-bright,
> As tho' it led to heaven."— *Rogers*

10 Contemporaneous history at 88 B. C.
  Belshazzar's feast
  Carcer Momertinus
  Cloaca maxima
  Circus maximus
  Oration against Catiline
  Catiline's defiance

Reference books

Jewish war	Josephus
Egypt and Sinai	Rev. D. A. Randall
Dictionary of Greek and Roman antiquities	Anthon
Caesar	Froude
City of Rome	Dyer
Walks in Rome	Hare
Compend of history of Rome	Paterculus

"Simple, erect, severe, austere, sublime —
Shrine of all saints and temple of all gods."—*Byron*

11 Military organization
  Principal events of Gaulish campaigns
  "Baths of Caracalla," from Turner and H. H.
  Pantheon
  Augustus Caesar
  In ancient Italy

Reference books

History of Rome	Leighton
City of Rome	Dyer
Early empire	W. W. Capes
Bits of travel	H. H.
Roman days	Viktor Rydberg
Society in Rome under the Caesars	Inge
Six months in Italy	Hillard
Gallus, or Roman scenes in time of Augustus	Becker
Italy: Rome and Naples	Taine
History of Rome	Merivale

"Alas, for Earth! for never shall we see
That brightness in her eye she bore when Rome was free."—*Byron*

12 Mausoleum of Augustus
  Basilica Julia
  Campus Martius
  Maecenas and Agrippa
  Golden age of literature
  Description of imperial Rome, Milton: *Paradise regained*
  Tiberius
  Caligula
  Claudius

	Reference books
City of Rome	Dyer
Handbook of universal literature	Botta
Roman poets of the Augustan age	Sellar
Handbook of classic literature	C. A. White
Eighteen Christian centuries	Jas. White
Early empire	W. W. Capes
Ben Hur	Wallace

"Nero, the synonym of all that is vile and cruel.

13 Nero
Women of the last Caesars
Galba, Otho and Vitellius
Vespasian and his works
Fall of Jerusalem and dispersion of the Jews

	Reference books
Nero	Eckstein
Early Christianity	F. W. Farrar
Imperial purple	Edgar Saltus
History of Nero	Abbott
Early empire	W. W. Capes
Society in Rome under the Caesars	Inge
City of Rome	Dyer
History of early Rome	Josephus
Story of the Jews under Roman rule	Morrison
Jewish war	Josephus
Story of the Jews	Hosmer

" As when mighty Rome's spectators meet
In the full theatre's capacious seat,
At once, by secret pipes and channels fed,
Rich tinctures gush from every antique head;
At once ten thousand saffron currents flow,
And rain their odors on the crowd below."—*Rowe:* Lucan, bk 9

14 The coliseum
Titus; Pompeii: Herculaneum
Ancient Rome; Pompeii
The Roman soldier
Domitian

	Reference books
Roba di Roma, v. 1	W. W. Story
Roman empire	Gibbon
Wonders of Pompeii	Monnier
Last days of Pompeii	Bulwer

Buried cities of Campania	Adams
Imperial purple	Edgar Saltus
Ancient cities	Wright
Early empire	W. W. Capes

> " Rome, with her palaces and towers,
>   By us unwished, unreft,
>   Her homely huts and woodland bowers
>   To Britain might have left ,
>   Worthless to you their wealth must be,
>   But dear to us, for they were free !"—*Barton*

15 Nerva
    Trajan
    Hadrian
    Trajan's forum and column
    Castle of St Angelo
    Caractacus
    Antoninus Pius
    Marcus Aurelius

Reference books

Eighteen Christian centuries	Jas. White
Roman days	Viktor Rydberg
Age of the Antonines	W. W. Capes
Castle St Angelo	W. W. Story
Marcus Aurelius Antoninus	Watson
Seekers after God	F. W. Farrar
Six months in Italy	Hillard

> " O city of prophets and martyrs!
>   O shrines of the sainted dead!
>   When, when shall the living day-spring
>   Once more on your towers be spread?"— *H. B. Stowe*

16 Polycarp and Justin Martyr
    Emperors, 180 — 270
    Commodus in the arena
    Emperors, 270 — 306
    Extracts from *Zenobia*

Reference books

Book of martyrs	John Fox
History of Christianity, v. 2	Milman
Eighteen Christian centuries	White
History of Rome	Merivale
History of Rome	Gibbon
Zenobia	Wm. Ware

> " While stands the coliseum, Rome shall stand;
> When falls the coliseum, Rome shall fall.
> And when Rome falls, the world."— *Byron*

17 Constantine the Great
  History from Constantine to the fall of Rome, A. D. 476
  Conversation
18 Selection
  Catacombs
  The last fight in the arena
  Baths of Caracalla (statues excavated)

Reference books

History of Christianity, v. 2	Milman
Decline and fall of the Roman empire	Gibbon
City of Rome	Dyer
Catacombs of Rome	Withrow
Museum of antiquity	
Roba di Roma	W. W. Story
Book of golden deeds	C. M. Yonge

> " Majesty,
> Power, glory, strength and beauty, all are aisled
> In this eternal ark of worship undefiled."— *Byron*

19 St Peter
  Guido Reni
  Vatican
  The marble prophecy
  A morning in the Etruscan museum in the vatican

Reference books

Six months in Italy	Hillard
Walks in Rome	Hare
Italian sights and papal principles	Jarves
History of art	Clement
Italian schools of painting, v. 2	Kugler
Bits of travel	H. H.

> " Art was his world, and he was Art's anointed king.

20 Raphael and his works
  Extracts: " Capitoline museum "
  Michelangelo Buonarroti
  Sistine chapel
  Tasso's tomb
  History of sculpture

	Reference books
Artist biographies	Sweetser
Raphael	Grimm
Memoirs of Italian painters	Mrs Jameson
Old Italian masters	Stillman
Painters, sculptors and engravers	Waters
Michelangelo	Clement
History of sculpture	Wilhelm Luebke
Elementary history of art	D'Anvers
Renaissance in Italy	Symonds
History of ancient sculpture	Lucy M. Mitchell

21 Cultivation is as necessary to the mind as food to the body.— *Cicero*

Subj. no. 937 ROMAN HISTORY—FROM EARLIEST TIMES TO 476 A. D.

Monday club, Warsaw

1892-93

1 Geography of Italy. Ancient population. Political and religious organization
2 Legendary history of the kings. Publius Valerius
3 Legendary wars. Character of the people. Patricians and plebeians. Origin of tribunes. Cincinnatus Horatius
4 Gaulish invasion. Brennus. Notable works of kingly and republican Rome. Coriolanus, elder Brutus
5 Plebeian oppression and victory. Democracy. Pyrrhus
6 Roman jurisprudence
7 Carthage. Sketch from foundation to first Punic war
8 First Punic war. Hannibal, Scipio
9 Second and third Punic wars. Cato, Fabius
10 Beginnings of Latin literature. Ennius, Plautus, Cato, Terence. Signs of corruption
11 The Gracchi. Agrarian laws
12 Oligarchy, democracy, Sulla, Marius. Jugurthine and Mithridatic wars. Rise of Pompey
13 Latin literature. Cicero, Lucretius, Cornelius, Nepos, Sallust, Varro
14 First and second triumvirates
15 The reign of Augustus. Imperial constitution
16 Reigns of Tiberius, Caligula and Claudius
17 Emperors from Nero to Domitian. Seneca, his life and works

18 Poets of the Augustan age. Virgil, Horace, Ovid
19 Nerva, Trajan, Hadrian, Antoninus Pius
20 Marcus Aurelius and Epictetus. Oratory of the Augustan age
21 Architecture and art of the Augustan age and first century
22 Social life and education under the empire
23 Commodus to Claudius. Aurelian. Fall of Palmyra. Zenobia, Longinus
24 Diocletian to Gratian. Establishment, abolition and reestablishment of Christianity
25 Theodosius the Great to fall of western Roman empire, 476 A. D.

Subj no. 938   ANCIENT GREECE
Every Saturday night club, Waterville
1894-95

1 Reading from Hall Caine's *Shakespeare as a novelist;* from Eclectic magazine
2 Geography of ancient Greece. Legends of gods and men. Voyage of the Argonauts. The Seven against Thebes.
3 Society in the heroic age of Greece. Grecian mythology. Mrs Browning's *The dead Pan*
4 Homeric period. Introduction, with selections from *Iliad* and *Odyssey*
5 Shakespeare's *Troilus and Cressida*, with introductions and criticisms. Reading of Tennyson's *Oenone*
6 Reading the play, *Troilus and Cressida*. Reading, Mrs Browning's paraphrase on Homer, *Hector and Andromache*. Paper: One touch of nature makes the whole world kin
7 Schliemann's excavations in ancient Troy. Paper: "Helen's ornaments"
8 Schliemann's excavations in ancient Mycenae and Tiryns
9 Dawn of history. Eastern provinces. Western provinces. The Peloponnesus. Attica. The Hellenic colonies. Early literature, social and religious bonds
10 Historic period. The Persian wars, Persia. First Persian invasion, Marathon. Second Persian invasion, Thermopylae, Artemisium. Paper: "What was won at Marathon?"
11 The Persian wars, Salamis. Results of the battle. Expulsion of the Persians. Contemporaneous wars in Sicily. Paper: Music of the early Greeks

History of Italy. Story of the Goths. Bradley. Theodoric the Goth. Hodgkin.
The Guelphs and Ghibellines. En. Brit.
The makers of Florence. Oliphant. The history of Venice. Adams.
Childe Harold. Byron. The Monk of the Aventine. Eckstein.
Saint Francis of Assisi. Mrs Oliphant.

Story of Spain. E. E. Hale. Moors in Spain Lane-Poole.
Spanish ballads. Lockhart.

The life of Mahomet Sir William Muir. Irving Carlyle.
Mahomet and Islam. The Caliphate, its rise. Decline and fall. Muir.
Story of the Saracens. Gilman.
Jerusalem, the city of Herod and Saladin. Besant and Palmer.

Story of Norway. Boyesen. Mythology of the north Bulfinch.
Knights and sea kings. Erling the Bold. Ballantyne. Sintram. Fouque.
Story of Russia. Morfill. Story of Turkey. Lane-Poole.
Story of the Jews Hosmer. Jerusalem delivered. Tasso.
Poets and poetry of Europe. Poems of places. Longfellow.
Introduction to Gothic architecture. Parker. History of architecture. Ferguson.
Church buildings in the middle ages. Elliot. Norton.
Guilds. Music. Guido of Arrezzo. Funeral customs. Folk-lore. En. Brit.

Subj. no. 941 SCOTTISH HISTORY FROM ANCIENT TIMES TILL THE UNION

Ladies Scottish club, Rochester
1894–95

"The marshalled array of imperial Rome
Essayed thy proud spirit in vain."

1 Period, to 80 A. D.

Aboriginal period. Invasion of Romans. Introduction of Christianity

"Ours is no sapling, chance-sown by the fountain."

2 Period, 80 to 843

Formation of government. Administration of justice. Bishopric of Glasgow

"Tread light where our battlefields lie,
Each spot is a warrior's grave."

3 Period, 843 to 1286

Kenneth McAlpine's conquest. Feudal system. Norman influence on the Scotch language

"Dumfoundered the English were a', were a'."

9 Supplemental　　　Age of chivalry. King Arthur
　　　　　　　　　　Feudal system
　　　　　　　　　　The crusades
　　　　　　　　　　Christian kingdom of Jerusalem
　　　　　　　　　　The Mongols
　　　　　　　　　　Literature. Religious drama
　　　　　　　　　　Bards and minnesingers
　　　　　　　　　　Art. Architecture

HISTORY AND LITERATURE

Decline and fall of the Roman empire. Gibbon.
Fall of Rome and rise of the nationalities. Sheppard.
General sketch of history. Freeman. Middle ages. Menzie. Emerton. Duruy.
The crusades. Cox. Morris. Studies of feudalism. Bell.
Civilization in the middle ages. Adams. Curious myths. Baring-Gould.
Monks of the west. Montalembert. Legends of the monastic orders. Jameson.
Popular romances of the middle ages. Cox and Jones.
History of civilization. Guizot. Holy Roman empire. Bryce.

Story of Germany. Baring-Gould. Lewis. Yonge.
St Boniface and the conversion of the Germans. Mrs Hope.
Story of Siegfried. The Nibelungenlied.
Sidonia the sorceress. Meinhold. The story of Hungary. Vambery.

History of France. White. Kirkland. Masson. Yonge.
History of Latin Christianity. Milman.
Historical monuments of France. Hunnewell.
The little duke. Yonge. Sacred and legendary art. Jameson.
Count Robert of Paris. Scott.
St Bernard. Storrs. Philip Augustus. James.
In his name. E. E. Hale.

History of England. Green. Hume. Freeman. Yonge.
Legends of King Arthur. Bulfinch. The faerie queene. Spenser.
Idyls of the king. Tennyson. The vision of Sir Launfal. Lowell.
Alfred the Great. Hughes. Pauli. Queens before the conquest. Hall.
Harold. Bulwer. Hereward. Kingsley. William the Conqueror. Abbott.
Short history of the Norman conquest. Freeman. Decisive battles. Creasy.
Early Plantagenets. Stubbs Life and times of Thomas Becket. Froude.
Richard I. White. The betrothed. The talisman. Ivanhoe. Scott.
Maud and Miriam. MacKeever. Blondel. Rice. Her Majesty's tower. Dixon.
England's chronicle in stone. Hunnewell.
History of Scotland. Mackenzie. Tales of a grandfather. Scott.
The story of Ireland. Hon. Emily Lawless.

29 Rise of Macedonia. Sacred wars. Paper: Character of the first Hellenism

Subj. no. 940.1   EARLY MIDDLE AGES

Society to promote useful reading, Schenectady

1 Introduction to early middle ages
    Clovis
    Charlemagne
    Treaty of Verdun
2 Germany
    Otho 1. Henry 4
    Free cities. Guilds
    Frederic Barbarossa
3 France
    The Normans
    Hugh Capet and the Capetian line
    Louis 6. Philip Augustus
    Growth of the French kingdom
4 England
    Saxon Period: Alfred the Great
    Edward the Confessor
    Norman Period: William 1
    Early Plantagenets: Henry 2
    Thomas a Becket. Richard 1
5 Italy
    Theodoric the Goth
    The Lombards
    The popes. The church
    The Guelphs and Ghibellines
    The kingdom of Sicily
6 The Eastern empire
    Justinian
    The Magyars. The Turks
    The Alexandrine school
    The Greek church
    Anna Comnena
7 Spain and Portugal
    The Gothic Kingdom. The Cid
    The Moorish kingdom
    Independence of Portugal
8 Mohammedanism
    Mohammed
    His successors
    Story of the Saracens
    Literature. Art
    Jerusalem of Saladin

12 Athenian supremacy to the Peloponnesian war. Paper: Attic salt
13 Peloponnesian wars
14 Shakespeare's *Timon of Athens*. Introduction. Reading the play
15 Literature, art and architecture of Athens during the golden age. Paper: The Athens of Pericles
16 Spartan period. State of Hellas after the Peloponnesian war. Cyrus and the 10,000. Early decline of the Spartan's rule. The war against the Persians. Paper: Spartan heroism
17 Spartan period continued to the liberation of Thebes. Condition of the Hellenic world at the close of Spartan supremacy. Thebes
18 Some great lawgivers of ancient Greece: Minos, Lycurgus, Solon and others. Paper: The constitution of Solon
19 Some great statesmen of ancient Greece: Clisthenes, Aristides, Pericles and others. Paper: Hellenic patriotism and politics
20 Some great generals of ancient Greece: Miltiades, Epaminondas, Alexander and others. Paper: The tactics of Epaminondas at Leuktra
21 Some great orators of ancient Greece: Demosthenes, Pericles, Aeschines. Paper: The influence of oratory in ancient Greece
22 Some great dramatists of ancient Greece: Aeschylus, Sophocles, Euripides. Paper: The Greek drama
23 Aeschylus, *Prometheus bound*. Reading the drama. Selections from translations
24 Sophocles' *Oedipus tyrannus*. Reading a translation
25 Some great philosophers of ancient Greece: Socrates, Plato, Aristotle and others. Selections from writings. Paper: Influence of Aristotle's philosophy on mediæval learning and religious dogma
26 Some historians of ancient Greece: Herodotus, Thucydides, Xenophon, with selections
27 Some great artists of ancient Greece: Phidias, Praxiteles, Apelles. Paper: Characteristics of Greek sculpture. Paper: The Elgin marbles
28 Rise of Theban power. Culmination of Theban power

4 Period, 1286 to 1388

*Contest of Bruce and Baliol for the crown. William Wallace.
Bannockburn*

"Hear'st thou," he said, "the loud acclaim
With which they shout the Douglas name."

5 Period, 1400 to 1542

James 1 the poet king. House of Douglas. First kirk of Scotland

"For Scotland and Mary on with speed,
Now, now is the time and the hour of need."

6 Period, 1542 to 1587

*Mary, Queen of Scots. Beginning of the reformation. Edinburgh
university founded*

"O, God! give me Scotland, or I die!"

7 Period, 1542 to 1587

*Reformation and its effects on the Scottish people. The first
covenant. John Knox*

"The thistle spreads its thorny leaf
To keep the rose from harm."

8 Period, 1587 to 1707

*James 6 and 1. Crowned King of England, Scotland, and Ireland.
Last Scottish parliament*

"Now let us take a kind farewell,
Gude night, an' joy be wi' you a.'"

Subj. no. 941   A JOURNEY THROUGH SCOTLAND
Ladies Scottish club, Rochester, 1895–96

"Elements each other greeting,
Gifts and power attend your meeting."

1 Scottish days and superstitions
  Scottish days: St Andrew's, Halloween, Hogmana, etc.
  Reading, *Tam O'Shanter.*
    Folk-lore
        "Let Glasgow flourish."
2 Glasgow
  Ancient landmarks
  Commercial interests
  Municipal government
  Reminiscences

"The sun has gane down o'er the lofty Ben Lomond
And left the red clouds to preside o'er the scene."

3 Lochs Long and Lomond
  The Trossachs and Loch Katrine
  Reading, *Lady of the lake*, canto 1
  Reminiscences

> " The bulwark of the north,
>   Gray Stirling with her towers and town.'

4 Stirling
  Bannockburn
  Linlithgow
  Reminiscences

> " Prosperity to Edinburgh wi' every risin' sun,
>   And blessin's be on Edinburgh till time his race has run."

5 Edinburgh, past and present
  Intellectual supremacy
  Places of historical interest
  Reminiscences

> " And far beneath in lustre wan,
>   Old Melros' rose, and fair Tweed ran,
>   Like some tall rock with lichens gray
>   Seemed dimly huge the dark abbaye."

6 Melrose and Abbotsford
  Hawthornden and Roslyn
  Dunfermline
  Reminiscences

> " Flow on, lovely Dee, flow on thou sweet river,
>   Thy banks, purest stream, shall be dear to me ever."

7 The granite city
  The banks of Dee
  Arbroath
  Reminiscences

> " There are brave Duinnewassels three thousand times three
>   Will cry, ' Hey for the bonnets o' Bonnie Dundee.' "

8 Dundee
  Perth
  St Andrews
  Reminiscences

> " The land where the strains of grey Ossian were framed,
>   The land of fair Selma, the land of Fingal."

9 Physical features and traditions of the highlands
  The isle of the west and north
  Highland literature
    " Auld Ayr, wham ne'er a town surpasses
    For honest men and bonnie lasses."
10 The home of Burns
  Banks o' Doon
  Reading : the *Brigs of Ayr*
  Reminiscences
    " O, sing to me the auld Scotch sangs."
11 Scotch ballads
    " Freen's ! gie's your advice ! we'll follow your counsel."
12 Annual election of officers
    " Health, peace and prosperity
    Wait on us a'."

Subj. no. 941.5   IRELAND AND THE IRISH
Literary club of the church of the Messiah, Buffalo
1887–88

GEOGRAPHY
1 The Emerald isle
2 Principal cities : Dublin, Cork, Galway, Limerick
3 Lakes of Killarney

HISTORY
4 Ancient Ireland to the time of Henry 2
5 Early Irish church
6 Conflict between protestantism and papacy
7 Cromwell in Ireland
8 Holiday reception
9 The parliament
10 Orators and statesmen :   Grattan, Emmet, O'Connell, Curran
11 The union and movement for repeal
12 Coercion versus home rule

SOCIOLOGY
13 Education
14 Conversation : Manners and customs
15 Irish industries
16 Present condition of the people

17 Poets and poetry
18 Prose writers

Subj. no. 942

LITERATURE

ENGLAND

Historical club, Ilion

1894-95

" That pale, that white-faced shore;
Whose foot spurns back the ocean's roaring tides."—*Shakspere*

1 America to Great Britain
  Map of early Britain
  Prehistoric times
    Stone age
    Bronze age
    Iron age
  St George and the dragon
  Legendary history
  The druids

Reference books

History of the English people	Green
Old English history	Freeman
Story of early Britain	A. J. Church
English traits	Emerson
Imperial island	Hunnewell
Reliques, v. 2	Percy
Age of fable, ch. 84	Bulfinch
Prehistoric times	Lubbock

" Then, sad relief, from the bleak coast that hears
The German ocean roar, deep-blooming, strong,
And yellow-haired, the blue-eyed Saxon came."

2 Map of Roman Britain
  Britain under Roman rule
    Boadicea
    Saxon rule, 449-871
    Alfred the Great
    Dunstan, the Politician-priest

Reference books

History of England, v. 1	Hume
Alfred the Great	T. Hughes
Beacon lights of history, v. 2	Lord

History of England, v. 1-2 — Knight
Dragon and the raven — Henty
Imperial island — Hunnewell
Alfred, king of England — Abbott

"In other countries, the struggle has been to gain liberty; in England to preserve it."—*Alison*

3 Map
   Danish invasion and restoration of the Saxons
   Condition of England before the Norman conquest
   King Canute and his nobles
   William the Conqueror
   Burial of William the Conqueror

Reference books

Harold, last of the Saxon kings — Bulwer
Hereward — Kingsley
Story of the Normans — Jewett
Development of English literature — Welsh
Cinque ports — Burrows
History of the English people, v. 1 — Green
History of the Norman conquest — Freeman

"I do love these ancient ruins:
   We never tread upon them but we set
   Our feet upon some reverend history.
   . . . But all things have their end."—*The duchess of Malfi*

4 Canterbury cathedral
   Oxford
   Feudalism
       Origin
           Extent and duration
           Classes of people
       Advantages
       Disadvantages
   Westminster abbey
   Tower of London

Reference books

English cathedrals — Mrs Schuyler Van Rensselaer
The southern empire (Oxford) — Morton
The feudal system, v. 2 — Lord
Imperial island — Hunnewell
Tower of London — Ainsworth
Abbeys and castles of England and Wales, v. 3 — Timbs and Gunn

"Becket had all the dauntlessness, none of the meekness of the martyr."
—*Milman*

5 William Rufus, Henry 1, Stephen and Matilda
  Map
  Henry 2
  Thomas à Becket
  Selection from Thomas à Becket by Tennyson

Reference books

William Rufus	Freeman
Early Plantagenets	Stubbs
History of the English people	Green
Beacon lights of history, v. 2	Lord
Modern Europe, v. 1	Russell
Eighteen Christian centuries	White
History of England, v. 1	Hume

"A famous man is Robin Hood
 The English ballad-singer's joy."—*Wordsworth*

6 Robin Hood and Allan-a-dale
  Richard 1
  Coeur de Lion at the bier of his father.—*Mrs Hemans*
  The crusades
      Characteristics and causes
      First crusade
      Second crusade
      Third crusade
      Later crusades
      Results

Reference books

Ivanhoe, Talisman, Betrothed	Sir Walter Scott
Crusades of Richard I	T. A. Archer
Crusades	G. W Coxe
Middle ages	Hallam
Matilda, Princess of England	Mme. S. Cottin
History of France v 1	Guizot

"A knight without truth, a king without justice, a Christian without faith.'

7 John (Lackland)
      Contest with the pope
        Magna charta
  History of Prince Arthur.—*Dickens*
  Henry 3
  Rise of the house of commons
  A visit to the house of commons in the 19th century

OUTLINES OF STUDY

	Reference books
King John	Shakspere
Magna Charta stories	Gilman
History of England, v 1	Hume
History of England, v. 1-2	Knight
Modern history	Russell
Eighteen Christian centuries	White

"Scots wha' ha'e wi' Wallace bled."—*Burns*

8 Early monasteries
   Edward 1
   Ballad of Eleanor
   William Wallace
   Banishment of the Jews

	Reference books
Legends of the monastic orders	Mrs Jameson
Edward I	Tout
History of England, v 2	Hume
Scottish chiefs	Jane Porter
Jews of Angevin England	Jacobs
History of the English people, v. 1	Green
Modern Europe	Russell
Eighteen Christian centuries	White

"— That Mars of men,
The black prince Edward, 'gainst the French who then
At Cressy field had no more years than you."—*Ben Jonson*

9 Edward 2
   The heart of the Bruce.—*Aytoun*
   Edward 3
   Commencement of hundred years' war and history of the Black Prince
   Battle of Crécy

	Reference books
Cameos from English history, v. 1	C. M. Yonge
Days of Bruce	Aguilar
Edward III	Warburton
Siege of Calais	C. M. Yonge
History of the middle ages	Menzies
History of England, v. 2	Hume
History of England, v. 1-2	Knight

"The whole of heraldry and of chivalry is in courtesy."—*Emerson*

10 Siege of Calais
   Chivalry and military orders
   Richard 2
   Selections from Richard 2
   Religion of the middle ages
       Mendicant friars
       Roger Bacon

   Reference books

Age of chivalry	Bulfinch
Heroes of chivalry	
Military and religious life in the middle ages	Lacroix
Middle ages	Hallam
Beacon lights of history, v. 2	Lord
Richard II	Shakspere
History of England, v. 2	Green
History of England, v. 2	Hume

> "The Morning-star of song, who made
>   His music heard below;
> Dan Chaucer, the first warbler, whose sweet breath
>   Preluded those melodious bursts, that fill
> The spacious times of great Elizabeth
>   With sounds that echo still."—*Tennyson*

11 Rise of English literature
   Chaucer. Father of English poetry
   Selection from the *Canterbury tales*
   Education and architecture
   Old London bridge

   Reference books

English literature	Taine
Renaissance and reformation	Lord
Abbeys and castles of England and Wales	Timbs and Gunn
Development of English literature, v. 1	Welsh
English men of letters	
History of the English people, v. 8	Green

> "God's most dreaded instrument,
>   In working out a pure intent,
>   Is man—arrayed for mutual slaughter."—*Wordsworth*

12 Henry 4
   Selection from *Henry 4*
   Henry 5
   Ballad of Agincourt
   Persecution of the Lollards

Reference books

Houses of Lancaster and York	Gairdner
History of England, v. 2	Hume
Cameos from English history, v. 2	C. M. Yonge
History of England, v. 1-2	Knight
History of the English people, v. 3	Green

"—Warwick, peace,
Proud setter up and puller down of kings!"—*Shakspere*

13 Henry 6 and Margaret of Anjou
   Selection from Henry 6
   Joan of Arc
   Joan of Arc's farewell to home
   Feudal barons

Reference books

History of Margaret of Anjou	Abbott
Queens of England, v. 1	Strickland
Joan of Arc	Tuckey
Last of the barons	Bulwer
Great women	Lord
Shakespeare's Heroines	
Joan, the Maid	Mrs Charles
Wars of the Roses, v. 3	C. M. Yonge
Eighteen Christian centuries	White

"The art preservative of all arts, and preservative of liberty no less."

14 Edward 4
   Richard of Gloster.—*J. G. Saxe*
   Edward 5 and Richard 3
   "Death of the two princes"
   Wars of the roses

Reference books

Wars of the roses	C. M. Yonge
History of the middle ages	Menzies
Anne of Geierstein	Scott
History of England, v. 2	Hume
History of England, v. 1-2	Knight

"Then, since the heavens have shap'd my body so,
Let hell make crookt my mind to answer."— *Richard 3*

15 Richard 3

" My conscience hath a thousand several tongues,
   And every tongue brings in a several tale;
   And every tale condemns me for a villain."

"The world owes some of its greatest debts to men from whose memory it recoils."— *William Stubbs*

16 Henry 7
   Court of star chamber
   Selection from *Henry* 8
   Henry 8
   Edinburgh after Flodden.— *Aytoun*

	Reference books
Early Tudors	Moberly
Star chamber	Ainsworth
Life of Henry VIII	Herbert
Henry VIII	Shakspere
Portraits of persons, v. 1	Lodge
Divorce of Catharine of Aragon	Froude
History of England, v. 8	Hume
History of England, v. 1_2	Knight

> "O Cromwell, Cromwell,
> Had I but served my God with half the zeal
> I served my king, he would not in mine age
> Have left me naked to mine enemies."— *Shakspere*

17 Cardinal Wolsey
   Fall of Wolsey.— *Shakspere*
   Suppression of the monasteries and its effects
   Field of the cloth of gold.— *C. M. Yonge*
   Sir Thomas More

	Reference books
Cardinal Wolsey	Creighton
Portraits of persons	Lodge
Household of Sir Thomas More	Rathbone
History of England, v. 3	Hume
History of England, v. 3_4	Knight
History of the English people, v. 3	Green
Constitutional history of England, v. 1	Hallam

> "Tell your master if there were as many devils at Worms as tiles on its roofs, I would enter."— *Luther*

18 Catharine Parr
   Martin Luther and the English reformation
   Monk and knight
   Characteristic men of the day
      Thomas Cromwell
      Cranmer
      Fisher
      Latimer
      Tyndale
      Erasmus
   Selection from the *Schonberg-Cotta family*

	Reference books
Henry VIII and his court	Mundt
English reformation	Geike
Renaissance and reformation	Lord
History of the church of England	Perry
Portraits of persons	Lodge

"After my death, you will find Calais written on my heart."— *Queen Mary*

19 Edward 6
    Lady Jane Grey and Roger Ascham
    Queen Mary
    Calais
    Martyrs of the Tudor period

	Reference books
History of the English people, v. 3	Green
Abbeys and castles of England and Wales	Timbs and Gunn
Queens of England, v. 2	Strickland
Lives of celebrated female sovereigns	Mrs Jameson
History of France, v. 2	Guizot
History of England, v. 3	Hume
History of England, v. 1-2	Knight

"Though I have but the feeble body of a woman, I have the heart of a king, and of a king of England, too."— *Queen Elizabeth*

20 In the tower.— *Susan Coolidge*
    Elizabeth
    Mary, Queen of Scots
    Two queens in Westminster
    Leicester
    Essex
    Raleigh
    Spanish armada

	Reference books
Age of Elizabeth	Creighton
Kenilworth	Scott
Great women, v. 5	Lord
Queens of England, v. 3-4	Strickland
History of England, v. 3-4	Hume
History of the English people, v. 3	Green
History of England, v. 3-4	Knight

"Some there are,
By their good works, exalted, lofty minds
And meditative, author of delight
And happiness, which to the end of time
Will live, and spread, and kindle."— *Wordsworth*

21 Elizabethan age of literature; dissertation
   Edmund Spenser
   Sir Philip Sidney
   Marlowe
   Ben Jonson
   Beaumont and Fletcher
   Hooker
   Francis Bacon
   Rise of the English drama

Reference books

Age of Elizabeth	Creighton
Literature of the age of Elizabeth	Whipple
Elizabethan literature	Hazlitt
Beaumont and Fletcher	Leigh Hunt
English men of letters	

"Triumph, my Britain, thou hast one to show,
   To whom all scenes of Europe homage owe."— *Ben Jonson*

22 A day with Shakspere
   Stratford-on-Avon
   Shakspere
   Discussion of Hamlet
   The great cryptogram

"Shakspere is of no age. He speaks a language which thrills in our blood in spite of the separation of two hundred years. His thoughts, passions, feelings, strains of fancy, all are of this day as they were of his own; and his genius may be contemporary with the mind of every generation for a thousand years to come."— *Prof. Wilson*

Subj. no. 942   **GREAT BRITAIN AND IRELAND**
University extension study club, Ogdensburg
1895-96

1 English architecture
2 Kent and Sussex. The Weald, Margate, Ramsgate, Richborough, the Cinque ports, Dover, Folkestone, Maidstone, the Medway, Penshurst, Tunbridge wells, Hastings, Battle abbey, the south downs

3 Surrey, Hants, Berks and Wilts. The downs, Guildford, the mole, Dorking, Epsom, Reigate, Bearwood, Reading, White Horse hill, Basingstoke, Silchester, Winchester, the new forest, Beaulieu abbey, Salisbury, Stonehenge
4 The channel islands. History, language and characteristics. Guernsey, St Peter port, Alderney and Sark, Jersey, St Helier's
5 Dorset and Somerset. Dorset coast, Bournemouth, Corfe castle, Dorchester, Portland island, Isle of Athelney, Sedgemoor, the Cheddar cliffs, Glastonbury Wells, Bath, Clevedon
6 Devon. Tiverton, Exeter and its cathedral, south coast, Torquay, Dartmouth. Dartmoor, Plymouth, Eddystone light, north coast, Exmoor, Bideford, Clovelly
7 Cornwall. Tintagel, Land's end, the lizard, Mount's bay, St Michael's mount, Penzance, St Just and its Celtic antiquities, the Scilly isles, Falmouth, Pendennis castle, Truro, Polperro, the Lynher, Saltash
8 Old Chelsea; its literary and artistic associations
9 Worcester and the valley of the Wye. Worcester cathedral, Malvern hills, Hereford, Ludlow castle, Ross, Forest of Dean, Monmouth, Raglan castle, Offa's Dyke, Tintern abbey, Chepstow, the Monnow
10 Valley of the Usk and Southern Wales. Abergavenny, Llanthony abbey, Black mountains, Newport, Carleon, Cardiff, Swansea, Caermarthen, Milford Haven, St David's
11 North Wales. Aberystwyth, Dolgelly, Llangollen, Port Madoc, Bettws-y-Coed, Snowdon, Beddgelert, Llanberis, Caernarvon castle, Bangor, the Bridges, Isle of Anglesey, Holyhead, Conway castle, the Dee
12 Lancashire and the Isle of Man. Manchester, ship canal, Lancaster, Furness abbey. History and characteristics of the Isle of Man. Castle Rushen, Peel castle
13 Lake country. Kendal, Penrith, Eden Hall, Windermere, Ambleside, Rydal Water, Grasmere, Keswick, Derwentwater, Lake poets
14 Art galleries of London
15 Harrow, Audley End, St Albans, Bedford, Elstow, Northampton, Fotheringay, Leicester, Bosworth field, Edgehill, Naseby

16 Cambridge and its colleges
17 Fen country and eastern counties. Isle of Ely, Ely cathedral, Peterborough, Bury St Edmonds, Norwich, Boston, Lincoln
18 Central England. Peak of Derbyshire, Haddon Hall, Chatsworth, Hardwicke Hall, Derby, Stafford, Walsall, Alton Towers, Mansfield
19 Western Yorkshire. Sheffield, Leeds, Kirkstall abbey, Bolton abbey, the Strid, Bradford Keighley, Haworth, Selby, Harrogate, Knaresborough, Ripon, Fountains abbey, Middleham castle, Richmond castle
20 Yorkshire, in the east and north riding. Hull, Scarborough, Whitby, York, Northallerton, Jervaulx abbey, Barnard castle
21 Durham, Northumberland and the Border castles. Durham, its cathedral and castle, Alnwick castle, Newcastle, Lindisfarne island, Berwick on-Tweed, Roman wall, Carlisle, Brougham castle
22 Outline of Scottish history; Edinburgh
23 Melrose abbey, Dryburgh, Stirling castle, Bannockburn, Loch Lomond, Loch Katrine, The Trossachs
24 Glasgow, Ayr, Dumfries, Paisley, Hamilton, Bothwell, the Hebrides, Iona, Staffa
25 Dundee, Perth, Dunkeld, Montrose, Aberdeen, Braemar, Inverness
26 Abbotsford and Sir Walter Scott
27 Ireland. Physical geography and outline history. Queenstown, Cork, Blarney castle, Killarney, and its lakes
28 Ireland. Limerick, Kilkenny, Dublin, County of Wicklow, Belfast, Londonderry, Giant's causeway

Subj. no. 942   **EARLY ENGLISH HISTORY**

Wednesday club, Syracuse

1893–94

1 England under the Britons and Romans
  Roman art in Briton
2 Teutonic conquest
    Poem, Alfred the Harper.—*Sterling*
  Current events

3 How the Saxons lived
   Macbeth, act 1
4 Norman conquest
   Bayeux tapestry
   "A Norman lady"
5 Effect of the conquest on England
   Music
   Macbeth, act 2
6   Music
   Pottery
   Music

PLANTAGENETS

7 Henry 2; Richard 2; John; Henry 3
   Macbeth, act 3
8 Edwards 1, 2, 3; Richard 2
   Music
   Macbeth, act 4
9 Rise in modern literature and change in the English language
   Music
   Selections from Chaucer
10 War of the Roses
   Music
   Macbeth, act 5

TUDORS

11 Tudor monarchs — Henry 7 and 8
   Westminster Abbey.— *Hawthorne*
   Current events
12 Reformation in England
   Music
   Condition of the known world in the 16th century
   Music
13 Edward 6, Mary 1 and Lady Jane Grey
   Poem, Queen Mary.— *Tennyson*
14 Elizabeth; events of her reign; attitude toward the church of Rome
   Music
   Selections from Spenser's *Faerie queene*
15 Social manners and customs of the Elizabethan era
   Current events

16 Era of the new learning or The golden age of literature
    (Prose writers)
   Poem, After a lecture on More.— *Holmes*
       Election of officers
17 English drama
       Poem, Ode to Shakspere.— *Sprague*
   Current events, Music
18 Poets of the " Golden age "
   Intellectual development of the English people

Subj. no. 942.08   VICTORIAN ERA
            Hamilton Fortnightly club
                    1895-96

 1 England in 1837
   Early life of Victoria and of the Prince Consort
   Lake poets
   Discussion
 2 High church leaders
   Chartism
   Charles Kingsley
   Discussion
 3 Earlier troubles in Ireland
   The Brontë sisters
   Charles Dickens
 4 Anti-corn law league and free trade
   (Richard Cobden and John Bright)
   Prince Albert and the exhibition of 1851
   William Makepeace Thackeray
   Discussion
 5 Crimean war
   Alfred Tennyson
   Thomas Carlyle
   Discussion
 6 Indian mutiny and consequent changes
   George Eliot
   The Brownings
 7 Progress in mechanic arts
   Extension of suffrage and education
   Charles Darwin
   Discussion

8 John Ruskin
  Pre-Raphaelite movement
  Rossetti family
  Discussion
9 John Henry Newman and Romanism in England
  Leaders in the broad church movement
  The Arnold family
10 Home rule in Ireland
  Benjamin Disraeli
  William Ewart Gladstone
  Discussion
11 The eastern question
  Growth of the colonies
  Essayists
  Discussion
12 Philosophers: Herbert Spencer, John Stuart Mill, James Martineau
  David Livingstone
  English women in politics
13 Reform in municipal government
  Philanthropic work in East London
  Robert Louis Stevenson
  Discussion
14 Trades' unions and socialism
  Historians
  Minor poets
  Discussion
15 Ceramic art in England
  Popular painters
  Girton and Newnham

Books of reference

Short history of our own times	Justin McCarthy
Epoch of reform	Justin McCarthy
Reign of Queen Victoria	Ward
Fifty years ago	Walter Besant
Life of the Prince Consort	Theodor Martin
England in the nineteenth century	E. W. Latimer
The Victorian poets	Edmund C. Stedman
History of England	Molesworth
London	Walter Besant

All sorts and conditions of men — Walter Besant
Literary landmarks of London — Lawrence Hutton
Memories of old friends — Caroline Fox
Our old home — Nathaniel Hawthorne
Miss Marjoriebanks — Mrs Oliphant
Victorian age of English literature — Mrs Oliphant
Municipal government in Great Britain — Albert Shaw
The history of trades' unionism — Sidney and Beatrice Webb
Practical socialism — Samuel A. Barrett
Socialism and social reform — Richard T. Ely
Marcella — Mrs Humphry Ward

Cyclopedias, magazines and reviews
Biographies and works of the authors mentioned in the calendar

Subj. no. 943 GERMANY: ITS LITERATURE AND HISTORY

Saturday class, Buffalo

1893–94

1. Ancient Germans. Confederation of tribes. St Boniface and the introduction of Christianity
2. Charlemagne and his times. Feudalism. Schools and clergy
3. Saxon and Franconian emperors. Hildebrand and Henry 4
4. The Hohenstaufen
5. Political condition of Germany during the interregnum. The Hanseatic league
6. Earliest monuments of German literature. Myths and epics. Minnesingers
7. Rise of the house of Hapsburg. Swiss league
8. German civilization in the 14th and 15th centuries. National reform. The Vehm Gericht
9. Mystery plays and beginning of the drama. Meistersingers and revival of learning
10. Sigismund and the reforming councils. The Hussite war
11. Maximilian, the last of the knights. End of the middle ages
12. German Switzerland: its great religious houses
13. Luther. Literature of the reformation
14. Gustavus Adolphus. Wallenstein and Ferdinand
15. Louis 14 and the house of Hapsburg
16. German life in the 17th century. Literary societies and the schools of poetry
17. Great castles

18 The Hohenzollern. Rise of Prussia
19 Frederick and the seven years' war
20 Lessing
21 Rise of Austria. Maria Theresa and Kaunitz
22 Prussia's fall. French domination. End of the Holy Roman empire
23 Wars of liberation. Stein and Scharnhorst
24 Struggle in the Tyrol
25 Effects of the French revolution in German literature and politics. Unfinished problems of the 18th century

Subj. no. 943 GERMANY: ITS LITERATURE AND HISTORY

Saturday class, Buffalo

1894–95

1 Stein and Scharnhorst, Founding of the Germanic confederation
2 The revolutions of 1848, Frederic William 4
3 Jean Paul Friedrich Richter
4 German philosophers
5 The absorption of Schleswig and Holstein, Prussia and Austria
6 Austria in Italy
7 Göthe
8 The universities
9 Founding of the new empire, William 1 and Bismarck
10 Catholics in Germany, Anti-catholic legislation
11 Socialism, its growth and strength
12 The schools and education
13 Germany's defenses
14 Berlin, old and new
15 Church and state, German theologians
16 Israelites in Germany, Anti-semitic movement
17 Modern art: schools of Munich and Düsseldorf
18 Vienna, Prague and Budapest
19 German science and scientists
20 Four kings
21 Modern writers: historians, poets, novelists
22 Historic cities of Saxony: Dresden, Leipsic, Altenburg

23 Charitable institutions and philanthropic work
24 Social orders and social life
25 Germany's friends and allies, The triple alliance

Subj. no 943 GERMAN HISTORY AND LITERATURE
Women's literary club, Dunkirk
1894-95

1 Geology and ethnology through the great migration
2 Mythology
3 Invasion of Rome and her influence on Teutonic life
Charlemagne in Germany
4 Saxon dynasty
Magyars
5 Emperors of the house of Franconia
Feudalism
6 Hohenstaufen dynasty
Hanseatic league

MEDIEVAL LITERATURE

7 Origin and development of the German language
Ballads, songs of Hildebrand
8 Minnesingers
Niebelungenlied, Gudrun
Parzival, Isolde, Tristan
9 The great interregnum
The rise of the Hapsburgs to the reformation

LATER MEDIEVAL LITERATURE

10 Meistersingers
Invention of printing
Literature from 1300 to the reformation
11 Meister Eckhart
Johann Huss, Jerome of Prague
12 Luther and his times
Character and home life of Luther
13 Mid-winter evening meeting
German Christmas carnival
14 Other religious reformers: Zwingli, Melanchthon, Hutton
15 Karl 5

16 Wood carving and sculpture
Architecture
17 Art: Flemish, German, Dutch
18 The 30 years' war
Peace of Westphalia
19 Founding of the German universities
Influence of Holland on German civilization
20 Decline of the Hapsburg monarchy
Peace of Ryswick
21 Rise of Prussia
22 Frederick the Great and his times
23 Science and philosophy
 Gesner to Linnaeus
 Copernicus to Kepler
 Boehm to Leibnitz
24 Bach, Handel, Haydn, Mozart
25 Annual meeting
Evening meeting. The Rhine and its legends

Subj no. 944   **FRENCH HISTORY AND LITERATURE**
Women's literary club, Dunkirk
1892–93

FOREIGN RULE

1 "All Gaul"

MEROVINGIAN KINGS

2 Beginnings of modern France

AUSTRASIAN KINGS

3 Reign of Charlemagne
4 Norman invasion
Separation from the empire and rise of a kingdom

CAPETIAN KINGS

5 Political and social conditions
Feudalism
The Crusades

HOUSE OF VALOIS

6 Foreign relations and growth of civilization
7 Rise of the Huguenots
The France of Catherine de Medici

MIDDLE AGES

8 Early literature
  Troubadours and Trouvères
  Marie de France
  Froissart
  Villon
  Comines

THE RENAISSANCE

9 Rabelais
  Calvin
  Montaigne
10 Marot
  Ronsard
  Malherbe
  Amyot
  Brantome

HOUSE OF BOURBON

11 Henry 4 and his policy
12 Administration of Richelieu
13 Evening meeting
  Gothic art and architecture
14 Louis 14: " L'état c'est moi "
15 State of the people in the reign of Louis 15

LITERATURE OF THE 17TH CENTURY

16 L'hotel de Rambouillet
  Duchesse de Longueville
  Princesse de Condé
  Mme de Sablé
  Mme de La Fayette
  Marquis de Montausier
  Voiture, Balzac
  Les précieux et les précieuses
  Mlle de Scudéri
17 Corneille
  Racine
18 Molière
19 Descartes
  Pascal

20 Fénelon
La Rochefoucauld
La Bruyère
Madame Guion
21 Bossuet
Fléchier
Bourdaloue
Massillon
22 La Fontaine
Madame de Sévigné
Boileau

LITERATURE OF THE 18TH CENTURY

23 Montesquieu
Buffon
J. J. Rousseau
24 Voltaire
25 Annual meeting
Evening meeting, Jeanne d'Arc

Subj. no. 944   FRENCH HISTORY AND LITERATURE
Women's literary club, Dunkirk
1893-94

1 Structure of society
2 Louis 16. Ministers and court
3 Administration of finance
The states general, Turgot
Necker, Colonne
4 What influence if any did the independence of the American colonies have on the French revolution?
5 The constituent assembly
Mirabeau
The Bastile
6 The national convention
The Gironde. The mountain
Madame Roland
7 Reign of terror
Charlotte Corday, Robespierre
Marat, Danton
The Marseillaise
8 The English, American and French revolutions: A comparison from the present point of view

9 The civil and military career of Napoleon
　Directorate, consulate
　Empire
10 Napoleon and Josephine
　Madame de Rémusat
11 Talleyrand
　Sismondi
12 Madame de Stael and Corinne
13 Madame Récamier
　Chateaubriand
　Béranger
14 The restoration
　Charles 10
　Louis Philippe
15 Comte
　Cousin
　Cuvier
　Discussion: French academy; University of France; Sorbonne
16 Guizot
　Michelet
　La Place
　Discussion: College of France; Academy of science
17 Revolution of 1848
　Lamartine
　Journalism
18 De Musset
　Sainte Beuve
　Balzac
19 The Dumas
　Eugène Sue
　Thierry
20 Napoleon 3
　Maximilien and Carlotta
21 Victor Hugo
　George Sand
22 Republic of to-day
　Thiers, MacMahon
　Grévy, Gambetta

23 Renan
   Daudet
   Sardou
24 Annual meeting
   Evening meeting, Peasant life

Subj. no. 944   FRENCH HISTORY
Study club, Oakfield
1894-95

1 Beginnings of French history
   Paper: Origin of the empire
   Oral topics: Clovis
                Pepin
                Charles Martel
                Origin of language and its early influence on literature
2 Empire of Charlemagne and the Carlovingian line
   Paper: Charlemagne, his empire and character
   Oral topics: His service to education
                Feudalism
                The church
3 House of Capet
   Paper: Capetian kings
   Oral topics: The truce of God
                The three dukes of Normandy
                Norman conquest
4 House of Capet
   Paper: The crusades
   Oral topic: Hildebrand
   Paper: Early lyrics of the middle ages
   Oral topic: The church and the drama
5 House of Valois
   Paper: The hundred years' war with England
   Oral topics: Early rulers to Louis 11
                Joan of Arc
                Results of the hundred years' war
6 House of Valois
   Paper: Louis 11
   Oral topics: Charles the Bold
                The renaissance and reformation
   Paper: Writers of the renaissance

7 House of Valois
    Paper: Civil and religious wars
    Oral topics: Charles 9 and Catherine de Medici
                The Huguenots
                Massacre of St Bartholomew
8 House of Bourbon
    Paper: Henry of Navarre and the edict of Nantes
    Paper: Richelieu, his character and policy
    Reading: *Henry of Navarre*
9 House of Bourbon
    Paper: Louis 14 and his wars
    Oral topics: Court life
                Augustan age of French literature
                Revocation of the edict of Nantes
10 House of Bourbon
    Paper: Events leading to the revolution
    Paper: Louis 16 and Marie Antoinette
    Oral topic: Literature of the period and its influence
11 The revolution
    Paper: Leaders of the revolution
    Oral topics: Madame de Stael
                Storming of the Bastile
    Readings: *Tale of two cities*
                Carlyle's *French revolution*
12 Reign of terror and the republic
    Paper: Reign of terror
    Reading: Victor Hugo's '93
    Oral topics: Girondists
                Marie Antoinette and her execution
13 The empire
    Paper: Napoleon Bonaparte, his life and character
    Paper: Napoleon and his campaigns
    Oral topics: Battle of Marengo
                Battle of Trafalgar
                Battle of Jena
                Retreat from Moscow
                Battle of Leipsic
                Battle of Waterloo
    Reading: *Vanity fair*

14 Paper: The restoration
   Oral topics: Louis 18
      Charles 10
      Louis Philippe
      Guizot
15 Second revolution and second empire
   Paper: Republic of '48
   Oral topic: Napoleon 3
   Paper: Franco-Prussian war
   Oral topic: Battle of Sedan and Napoleon 3 made prisoner
16 Third republic
   Paper: Siege of Paris and founding of the third republic
   Oral topics: Gambetta
      Grévy
      Thiers
      MacMahon
      Carnot
17 Paper: Victor Hugo as a poet and novelist
   Oral topics: Some other French novelists
      Paris, old and new

Subj. no. 944   FRENCH HISTORY AND LITERATURE

Salamanca Salmagundi society

1 Map of Gaul with explanations
  Paper: The dawn of France
  Reading: "The ladies of long ago (François Villon)
  Music, piano solo
  Paper: The Merovingian kings
  Paper: Charlemagne and his reign
  Reading: "Song of Roland" (Theroulde)

2 Paper: Beginnings of modern France, 987
  Reading: "Literature in Gaul from 6th to 8th centuries" (Guizot)
  Paper: Results of foreign invasions
  Music, instrumental duet
  Reading: "Peter the Hermit and the crusades" (Joseph Francois Michaud)
  Paper: Feudalism, and political and social conditions

3 Paper: The early communes and the third estate, 1270-1328
Reading: "Friar Thomas and his reforming crusade" (De Monstrelet)
Paper: The hundred years' war
Music
Reading: selection from "The Maid of Orleans" (Robert Southey)
Debate: Resolved, That Jeanne d' Arc was inspired

4 Paper: Kaleidoscope royal, 1328-1515
Reading: The Huguenots
Paper: Religious reformation in France
Music, male quartette
Reading: "Character of Louis 11" (Philippe de Comines)
Paper: Catherine de Medici and her times
Discussion

5 Paper: Henry 4 and his policy
Reading: "Richelieu" (selected from Dumas)
Paper: Louis 14 and 15
Music, piano solo
Reading: "Mazarin" (selected from Dumas)
Topic: Famous women of these times
Discussion

6 Paper: Voltaire and the encyclopedists
Reading: "Gil Blas and the robbers" (Le Sage)
Paper: Louis 16 and his courtiers
Music, instrumental duet
Topic: Marie Antoinette
Discussion
Paper: Condition of the people and attempted reforms
Discussion

7 Paper: Causes of the revolution
Discussion
Reading: "A night of terror" (Paul Louis Courier)
Paper: The administration of finance, Turgot, Necker, Colonne
Music, piano solo

Reading: "The youth of Mme Maintenon," selection (Arsene Houssaye)
Topic: Marie Jean Paul Roch Yves Gilbert Motier, Marquis de Lafayette
Discussion

8 Paper: The national assembly
Topic: Mirabeau and the Bastile
Discussion
Reading: "Man with the iron mask"
Music, piano solo
Paper: The national convention
Reading: "Madame Roland"
Paper: The Gironde, the mountain

9 Paper: The reign of terror
Reading: Selected from "Zanoni" (Bulwer-Lytton)
Topic: Marat, Robespierre and Danton
Discussion
Music: "Marseillaise hymn"
Paper: Literature under Louis 16
Reading: Selected from "Charlotte Corday" (Lamartine)

10 Paper: The English, American and French revolutions, a comparison from the present point of view
Reading: "Friar Lubin" (Clement Marot)
Paper: Napoleon, a character sketch
Music, instrumental duet
Reading: "Personal manners of Napoleon" (Pierre Lanfrey)
Paper: Military career of Napoleon
Reading: "The night before Waterloo" (Victor Hugo)

11 Paper: The directorate, the consulate, the empire
Discussion
Reading: "The little man all in gray" (Béranger)
Paper: Napoleon and Josephine
Discussion
Reading: "Marrying for the sake of a dog" (Saintine)
Music

12 Paper: Franco-Russian war
Discussion
Reading: "The burning of Moscow" (J. S. C. Abbott)
Music
Paper: Talleyrand and Sismondi
Discussion
Reading: "Retreat from Moscow" (J. S. C. Abbott)

13 Paper: Capitulation of Paris and abdication of Napoleon
Reading: "Utterances of Napoleon"
Paper: The restoration
Music, instrumental duet
Topic: England's treatment of Napoleon
Discussion
Reading: "Napoleon at St Helena" (Marquis de las Casas)

14 Paper: Charles 10
Reading: "How Aesop brought back his master's wife" (Sir L'Estrange)
Paper: Madame de Stael and Corinne
Music
Reading: "Corinne at the Capitol" (Madame de Stael)
Paper: Noted French scientists
Discussion

15 Paper: Louis Philippe
Reading: "Toussaint L'Ouverture" (Wendell Phillips)
Paper: Revolution of 1848
Music
Reading: "To Diane de Poitiers" (Clement Marot), "To Mary Stuart" (Pierre de Ronsard), "To Madame du Chatelet" (Voltaire)
Paper: The French academy and Sorbonne
Discussion

16 Paper: Napoleon 3
Reading: "Arago's presentation to Napoleon 1" (Dominique Francois Arago)
Paper: Maximilian and Carlotta
Music, piano solo
Reading: "Lisette in Attic cell" (Pierre Jean Béranger)
Paper: Noted French historians
Discussion

17 Paper: The second empire, 1852-70
  Reading: "The Kings of France"
  Music, piano solo
  Paper: Victor Hugo and his works
  Reading: selected from "Les Miserables" (Victor Hugo)
  Topic: Famous women, George Sand, Mme Rémusat, Mme Récamier
  Discussion

18 Paper: Siege of Paris, 1870-71
  Discussion
  Reading: selected from "Tale of two cities" (Charles Dickens)
  Paper: The commune
  Music, guitar solo
  Reading: "The three great ties of humanity" (Massillon)
  Paper: Noted French preachers

19 Paper: Noted marshals of France
  Discussion
  Reading: "A Picture of wild nature on the Mississippi" (Chateaubriand)
  Paper: French poets and dramatists
  Discussion
  Music, piano solo
  Reading: "The French and Anglo-Saxon races compared" (William Edward Lecky)
  Paper: American artists in France

20 Paper: The republic of to-day
  Reading: "Causes of the downfall of Rome" (Montesquieu)
  Music, piano solo
  Paper: The College of France and the Academy of science
  Discussion
  Reading: "John Law and the Mississippi bubble" (Thiers)
  Topic: Famous French leaders, Thiers, Grévy, Gambetta, Carnot, Périer
  Discussion

21 Paper: Development of the French navy
   Reading: "The exiles of Siberia" (Mme Cotton)
   Paper: French novelists
   Discussion
   Music, piano solo
   Reading: Fable, selected (La Fontaine)
   Paper: Works of Alexander Dumas
   Discussion

22 Paper: Financial and social condition of France
   Discussion
   Reading: "The prison of La Force in 1839" (Eugène Sue)
   Music
   Paper: Paris
   Reading: "Royal amusements at Fontainebleau" (Dumas)
   Topic: Versailles and Fontainebleau
   Discussion

23 Paper: French architecture
   Discussion
   Reading: "The palaces of Genoa" (Janin)
   Paper: French artists of to-day and their works
   Music, piano solo
   Reading: Description of the Latin Quartier, selected from "Trilby" (Du Maurier)
   Paper: Sculpture
   Topic: Peasant life
   Discussion

Subj. no. 945 STUDIES IN ITALY FROM THE 13TH TO THE END OF THE 16TH CENTURY

Saturday class, Buffalo
1886–87

1 Italy in the 13th century
2 Republic of Florence and its government during the latter part of the 13th and first half of the 14th century
3 Minor Italian republics
4 Masters in art, ending with Giotto and his immediate school
5 Dante

6 Petrarch and Boccaccio
7 Life and time of Cosmo de Medici
8 Literature in the time of Lorenzo de Medici
9 Savonarola and religious condition of Italy
10 Art from Ghiberti to Raphael
11 Michael Angelo and Raphael
12 Italian life and customs in the time of Michael Angelo
13 Tasso and Ariosto
14 Macchiavelli
15 Troubadours, romancers and ballad-singers, and development of the Italian opera and drama
16 Italian industries, exclusive of the fine arts
17 Milan and Lionardo da Vinci
18 Italian universities and academies
19 Progress of the mathematical and physical sciences; Galileo and other leaders
20 Distinguished popes
21 Venice, its early art and architecture
22 Venice, its government, sources of prosperity and causes of its decline
23 Titian and the decline of art
24 Italy at the close of the 16th century

Subj. no. 945   ITALY: MEDIEVAL, MODERN
Fortnightly, Jamestown

MEDIEVAL ITALY

1 History: General view from the time of Charlemagne to Barbarossa
The Tuscan tongue
Medieval civilization
Feudalism
Chivalry

MEDIEVAL ITALY

2 Frederick 1: Barbarossa, 1121-1190
The Lombard league
Power of the popes
Guelphs and Ghibellines
The despots
Five rival powers: Florence, Venice, Milan, Naples, Rome

FLORENCE

3 House of Medici
  The podesta
  Account of the great plague
  Giovanni Boccaccio, 1313-1375
  Dominican monks
  Macchiavelli, 1469-1527
  Brothers of the Misericordia
  Michael Angelo, 1475-1563

FLORENCE

4 Dante Alighieri, 1265-1321
    His youth
    His public life
    His exile
  Pictures of Florentine life in the 14th century
  The Borgia
  The Cenci
  Savonarola, 1452-1498
  Discussion: Epicureans, Platonic school

VENICE

5 The Islanders
  The doges
      Enrico Dandolo, the blind doge, 1110-1205
  Venetian school of painters
  Council of ten
  Venice in her glory, 13th century
  Marco Polo, 1254-1324
  Medieval commerce
  Contrast between Florentine and Venetian character

MILAN

6 Surrender to Barbarossa
  Dynasty of the Visconti and Sforza families
  Dukes of Milan
  Leonardo da Vinci, 1452-1519
  Battle of Pavia
  Spanish rule
  Condottieri, the Italian mercenaries
  Wealth of Milan

NAPLES
7 Revolt of the barons under Ferdinand
Invasion of Italy by Charles 8 of France
Revival of vernacular literature
Ariosto, 1474–1533
Herculaneum and Pompeii, the cities of antiquity and their life
Neapolitan beggars
ROME
8 Petrarch, 1304–1374
The inquisition
Rienzi, the last of the tribunes, 1312–1354
Popes of the renaissance
Sack of Rome
Italian peasantry
ROME
9 Noble families: Orsini, Colonna, Doria, Savelli
Raphael, 1483–1520
Franciscan friars
Order of Jesuits
Tasso, 1544–1595
Italian festivals
Roman street music
MODERN ITALY
10 Napoleonic era
   Congress of Vienna
Papal supremacy
Revolution of 1848
Mazzini (the prophet), 1805–1872
Cavour (the statesman), 1810–1861
Garibaldi (the soldier), 1807–1882
The House of Savoy
   King Victor Emmanuel, 1820–1878
United Italy

Subj. no. 945   ITALY: ANCIENT AND MODERN
Fortnightly club, Potsdam
1895–96

1 A day in ancient Rome
The old Romans at home
Greco-Roman art
Roman reading and writing
Roman writers of comedy: Plautus; Terence

2 Quotations from *Meditations of Marcus Antoninus*
Beginnings of Christianity
The coliseum and its associations
Influence of Christianity on literature, art and architecture
The catacombs
Early Italian art
Great Roman satirists: Horace; Juvenal
Mosaic work from which oil painting received its impetus

3 Charlemagne in Italy
Rise of the papal power
Italian sculpture from Christian era to renaissance (Nicolo Pisano)
Roman orators
Giotto, "the true regenerator of art"
Fra Angelico da Fiesole
Influence of the crusades on commerce

4 Monastic institutions, the home of literature and art
Books and libraries
Great sculptors of the 15th century: Ghiberti; Della Robbia; Donatello
Universities and schools
Leonardo da Vinci
Early Italian poets

5 Table talk. Concerning Dante
Italy at the time of Dante's birth
Life of Dante. Part first
Review of *Vita nuova*
The under world in Homer, Virgil and Dante
Divina commedia, Inferno
Ruskin on the scenery of Dante's *Inferno*

6 Quotations from Dante
Life of Dante. Part second
Contemporaries of Dante
Divina commedia. Purgatorio
Divina commedia. Paradiso
The angels of Milton and Dante
Masaccio. The new departure in painting

7 Italian renaissance
  Petrarch, " the forerunner of the renaissance "
  Michael Angelo; personal history; as a writer
  Great inventions and discoveries of the 15th century
  Macchiavelli
  Michael Angelo as a sculptor
  Ariosto
8 History of Florence
  Florence the Beautiful
  Academy
  Pitti gallery
  House of Medici
  Palaces
  Stirring times of Savonarola
9 Famous men of Florence
  Cameos and mosaics
  Cathedrals
  Ponte Vecchio
  Reading, *Giotto's tower*
  Uffizi gallery
  Boccaccio
10 Venice
  Venetian boats
  Grand canal
  Bellini family
  Industrial arts of Venice
  Venetian printing press
  Titian
11 St Mark's
  Paul Veronese and Giorgione
  Rialto and Bridge of sighs
  Ducal palace
  Tintoretto
  Venetian life
  Academy of fine arts
12 Naples and its bay
  The museum
  Virgil and his home
  Mt Vesuvius
  Pompeii and Herculaneum

  Characteristics of the different schools of Italian painting
13 Rome of to-day
  St Peter's
  Museums
  Raphael
  Churches
  Castle of St Angelo
14 Vatican
  Sistine chapel
  Sculpture in the vatican
  Raphael's Stanze in the vatican
  Picture gallery
  Raphael's Loggia
15 Roman palaces and villas
  Famous ghetto of Rome
  Ruins of ancient Rome
  Correggio
  Beatrice Cenci
  Raphael's Madonnas
  Vittoria Colonna
  Tasso
16 History of Italy prior to 1815
  Rambles among Italian hills
  Bernini
  Drama and dramatists
  Milan cathedral
  Congress of Vienna
  Street life in Naples
  Language and literature
  Italian art of to day

17 United Italy, 1815-1871
   Novels and novelists
   Minor cathedrals
   Mazzini
   Reading, *The disciples*
   Canova
   Italian church music
18 Maps of Italy
   Lakes of Italy
   Historians and scientists
   Studios of Italy
   Italian opera and opera writers
   Natural resources
   Metastasio
   Great Italian singers
19 Pius 9
   Papal manufactory of mosaics
   Theater

Protestant churches and missions
Reading, *The song of Italy*
Garibaldi
Italian architecture since 1600
20 Victor Emmanuel 2
   Government, army and navy
   Sicily and Sardinia
   Reading *Super flumina Babylonis*
   Cavour
   Genoa
21 Humbert and Marguerite
   Universities and schools
   Leo 13
   Giosue Carducci
   Capri and Sorrento
   Industry and commerce

Subj. no. 946   SPAIN, ITS LITERATURE, HISTORY AND ART

Saturday class, Buffalo
1892-93

1 The Iberians, Roman Spain and the Goths
2 Cordova and her Caliphate
3 Moorish civilization
4 Saracenic art
5 Christian Spain and the perpetual crusade
6 The *Cid* and early Castilian literature
7 Ferdinand and Isabella
8 Columbus
9 Spain under Charles 5
10 The Spanish inquisition
11 Conquest and colonization; Mexico, Peru, Chili
12 Italian school of poetry; Boscan, Garcillasco, Mendosa
13 Rise of Portugal
14 Philip 2 and the invincible armada

15 Christian architecture in Spain
16 Revolt of the Netherlands
17 Spanish painters
18 Cervantes and Spanish fiction
19 Lope de Vega and Calderon. Spanish drama and theater
20 Spain under the Bourbons
21 Napoleon and the peninsula
22 The revival and progress of Spanish literature
23 Gibraltar
24 Education, language and races
25 Constitutional Spain; Spain of to-day

Subj. no. 973   **AMERICAN HISTORY**

Medina Culture club

1893-94

"Every noble life leaves the fibre of it interwoven forever in the work of the world."

1 Declaration of independence
    American flag
    Darkest hour of the revolution
    Lord Cornwallis
    Peace of Paris
2 The confederation
    Benjamin Franklin
    Thomas Paine
    Continental currency
    What was the English idea of government typified in colonial America
3 Constitution or the Philadelphia convention of 1787
    The *Federalist*
    Ordinances of 1787
    French revolution
    Compare the American with the English form of government
    Political parties
4 George Washington
    Alexander Hamilton

Modes of travel
Population of the country
Number and distribution
Foreign relations of the United States
Whiskey rebellion of 1794
Political parties
5 Thomas Jefferson
John Adams
X. Y. Z. papers
Alien and sedition laws
Purchase of Louisiana
Robert Fulton
Political parties
6 Causes and results of the war of 1812
James Madison
Tecumseh — Red Eagle
Hartford convention
Henry letters
Political parties
7 James Monroe or the Missouri compromise and the Monroe doctrine
Ohio, the first fields of the ordinances of 1787
Purchase of Florida
John Quincy Adams
Henry Clay
High tariff of 1828
Political parties
8 History of the United States bank
Andrew Jackson
John C. Calhoun
Tariff; — Financial panic
Mormonism
Growth of the west
Political parties
9 Effects of the railway and telegraph on our life
John Tyler
Dorr rebellion
Ashburton treaty
Whigs and democrats
Political parties

10 Annexation of Texas (including Mexican war)
   James K. Polk
   Elias Howe
   Wilmot proviso
   Oregon question
   Treaty with China
   Political parties
11 Charles Sumner
   Zachary Taylor
   Compromise of 1850
   Kansas-Nebraska act
   Gadsden purchase
   Cuba — Ostend manifesto
   Clayton Bulwer treaty
   Political parties
12 Growth and influence of slavery
   James Buchanan
   John Brown
   Homestead bill
   Business panic of 1857
   Frederick Douglas
   Political parties
13 Causes and results of the civil war
   Jefferson Davis
   Abraham Lincoln and emancipation proclamation
   Freedman's bureau
   Finances
   Political parties
14 Ulysses S. Grant
   Andrew Johnson
   Immigration
   Business panic of 1873
   Reconstruction
   Treaty with England
   Political parties
15 Rutherford B. Hayes
   Greenbacks — Effect on national debt
   Silver bill

Indian policy
Specie payment
Political parties
16 James A. Garfield
Chester A. Arthur
Civil service reform
Arctic expeditions
The Chinese
Refunding public debt
Political parties
17 United States influence abroad
Grover Cleveland
Benjamin Harrison
Congress of the three Americas
International copyright
James G. Blaine
Political parties
18 Social condition of the American people
Art in the United States
American press
Woman suffrage
Frances E. Willard
Political parties

Subj. no. 973   AMERICA

Monday evening club, Westfield
1894-95

1 What Americanism means
    Responsive roll call (current events)
2 Story of the constitution
    History of the U. S. flag
    Responses (quotations from framers of constitution)
3 Our treaties with other nations
    Study of nationalities
    Responses (wit of nationalities)
4 Leading events of each administration to the present
    Parliaments of the world
    Responses (cablegrams)

5 How bills become laws
    Day in congress
    Responses (name and motto of some state)
6 United States supreme court
    Postal service
    Discussion: Resolved that the study of history is more important than the study of literature
    Responses (current events)
7 Banking system
    Numismatics
    Responses (items of interest)
8 Philanthropists
    Orators
    Responses (quotations from orators)
9 United States navy
    Lighthouses
    Reading
    Responses (miscellaneous)
10 Eminent women of the period
    Social evolution
    Responses (quotations from women)
11 Cliff dwellers
    Jesuits in America
    Discussion: Who had the better right to our territories, English or French?
    Responses (current events)
12 Swedish colonies in America
    Exploring expeditions
    Responses (miscellaneous)
13 Our ships on the lakes and seas
    A glimpse of our neighbor, Canada
    Club discussion: Which of the United States is the most civilized?
    Responses (current events)
14 Quakers
    Scotch-Irish in America
    Responses (quotations from Whittier)
15 American caricaturists
    Papers of to-day

Discussion: Does the newspaper meet the intellectual needs of the people ?
Responses (proverbs from Franklin)
16 Scientific developments of the century
Aluminum and its uses
Responses (current events)
17 Precious stones
Petrifactions
Responses (miscellaneous)
18 Great manufacturing cities
Glass workers
Silk culture
Responses (current events)
19 The drama and its origin
Influence of Greek architecture in the U. S.
Responses (quotations from Shakspere)
20 Women as official inspectors
Hospital sketches
Responses (quotations from Oliver Wendell Holmes)
21 Educational progress in America
Art at the world's fair
Responses (bright sayings of children)
22 Women's clubs and what they are doing for women
Book review
Responses (miscellaneous)
Discussion by club: Novel reading has done more harm than good
23 Transcendentalism in America
Libraries of the United States
Responses (quotations from Emerson)
24 Recreation as a source of culture
The most popular novels in America
Discussion: Influence of fairy tales on children
Responses (current events)
25 Famous letter writers
Responses (quotations from letter writers)
26 Popular education in citizenship
American railways
Responses (miscellaneous)

27 Concentration of capital
    Social life in America and England
    Discussion: Who is the best contributor to literature, the scientist, the historian, the novelist or the poet?
    Responses (quotations from Maurier)
28 Poem (original)
    Reminiscences of '94 and '95
29 Business meeting

CLUBS IN

	PLACE	Name	Year organised	Beginning	Closing
1	Albany	Sesame book and reading club	1882		
2		Trinity methodist church reading club	1894	N	F
3		Unity club	1895	S	My
4		Williams' (Mrs) Friday morning club	1887		
5	Albion	Albion historical club	1870	N	Mr
6		Historical conversation club	1878	N	Ap
7	Auburn	Fortnightly club	1884	O	Ap
8	Belmont	Belmont literary and historical society	1885	O	Je
9	Binghamton	Fortnightly			
10	Brooklyn	Associate alumnae of Packer coll. inst.	1878		
11		Brooklyn heights seminary club	1885	N	My
12		Cambridge club	1890	O	My
13		Columbia literary circle	1889		
14		Fact club	1880		
15		Fenelon reading circle	1890		
16		Field's (Mrs) literary club	1884	D	My
17		Fortnightly club	1894	N	My
18		Friday afternoon club	1888	O	Ap
19		Froebel society	1884	O	Je
20		History class	1868		
21		Motley club	1889	O	Je
22		Our history class	1877		
23		Philosophian literary & scientific circle			
24		Photereone club	1882	O	My
25		Portia reading club	1879	O	Je
26		Woman's club	1869	O	My
27		Women's health protective ass'n	1890	O	Je
28	Buffalo	Catholic fortnightly reading circle	1889	O	My
29		Das Kränzchen		O	Je
30		Graduates ass'n of the Buffalo seminary	1867	N	Ap
31		Hawthorne club			
32		Highland Park literary club		O	Ap
33		Lit club of the Church of the Messiah	1880	N	Ap
34		Monday class	1885	S	Ap
35		Saturn club			
36		Saturday class	1876	O	Ap
37		Saturday morning club	1888		
38		Train'g class of Buff free kind ass'n	1891	S	Je
39		University club			
40		Woman's investigating club	1888	O	Je
41	Camden	Historical club	1884	O	Ap
42	Canandaigua	Backus' (Mrs) literary club	1876		
43	Cannonsville	Merry delvers			
44	Carthage	Shakespeare club		O	Ap
45	Catskill	Monday club	1894	N	Mr

NEW YORK

No.	Frequency	T'tal no. of papers	T'tal no. of readings	Subjects of study with number of meetings devoted to each	
					1
....	Biweekly	....	....	Sociology and the great cities of the world	2
....	Weekly	....	....	Critical Bible study, literature, sociology ..	3
					4
17	Weekly	....	....	American history	5
20	Weekly ..	0	0	American history.	6
....	Biweekly..	..	....	German history ...	7
....	Weekly . .				8
....	....				9
....	....				10
....	Biweekly. ..				11
....	Biweekly. ..				12
....	Biweekly. ..				13
....	Biweekly. ..				14
					15
....	Monthly	..	..		16
....	Biweekly....	16	16	Spain (12)........	17
....	Biweekly....				18
...	Monthly .	17	....	Art, education, literature, science	19
....	....	....	....	England.	20
					21
....	Biweekly .				22
....	....				23
....	Biweekly. ..				24
....	Biweekly. ..				25
....	Biweekly.. ..			Miscellaneous..	26
14	Monthly . .			Questions relative to the city's health, cleanliness and beauty	27
....	Biweekly. ..	..	..	Spanish history and literature	28
19	Biwe-kly	..	..	Art topics	29
21	Weekly ..	21	21	Conventions at Chicago (6), American art (1), Library (2), Physical geology (10).	30
....	Biweekly. ..				31
28	Weekly	24	....	History of art (24)	32
25	Weekly	28		Greece	33
....	Weekly ...			England in the 18th century............	34
....	....				35
25	Weekly	25	....	Germany.	36
25	....				37
?108	Triweekly ..			Kindergarten theory (36), Psychology (36), History of education, etc....	38
					39
....	Biweekly.. .				40
25	W(ekly			Japan (2); China (5), Amer. lit. (11), India (7)	41
....	....				42
....	....				43
26	Weekly	12	12	Shakspere	44
20	Weekly	20	0	Spain........	45

460   UNIVERSITY OF THE STATE OF NEW YORK

CLUBS IN NEW

| | MEMBERS || AVERAGE ATTENDANCE || NO VOLS. IN LIBRARY || FEES ||
	Men	Women	Men	Women	Circulating	Reference	Entrance	Annual
1								
2	6	20	5	18	0	0	0	0
3	20	20						
4		80						
5	20	32			0	0	0	0
6	16	32	8	18	0	0	0	$ 50
7		80					0	50
8		47					$2	1
9								
10								
11							1	1
12		47						1
13							25	
14		22						
15								
16		84					5	10
17		19		16	0	0	0	2 50
18		22						
19		94		50			1	2
20		14						
21		15						
22								
23								
24		20						
25		15						
26		200		?100	0	0	15	5
27		600		800	0	0	1	1
28								1
29		15		18	100		0	1
30		175		?40	0	0	5	2
31		14						
32		80		?20	0	0	0	1
33		167		80			0	1
34		25						25
35								
36		25		17	0	0	0	1
37		20						1
38		24		21	0	0	0	35
39								
40		67					2	1
41		15		12	0	0	0	0
42								
43								
44		12		9	0	0	0	75
45		20		18	0	0	0	50

YORK (continued)

Secretary		
Name	Address	
		1
G: T. Waterman	119 Hamilton st. Albany, N. Y	2
G: T. Waterman	119 Hamilton st. Albany, N. Y	3
		4
Miss A. E. Sears	Albion, N. Y	5
Mrs W. G. Swan	Albion, N. Y	6
Miss H.. C. Woodruff	Auburn, N. Y	7
Mrs F. G. Horner	Belmont, N. Y	8
		9
		10
Mrs K. P. Von Der Smith		11
Miss S. A. Loomis		12
Miss M. E. Duncan		13
Mrs J. A. Radcliffe		14
Miss C. F. Hennessy		15
		16
Miss Bertha Cook	195 Calyer st. Brooklyn, N. Y	17
Mrs W. H. Burger		18
Mrs J: N. Wright	317 Jefferson av. Brooklyn, N. Y	19
		20
Mrs Alonzo Gaubert		21
		22
		23
Mrs C: F. Towner		24
Mrs J. A. Sperry		25
Mrs H: T. Wing	152 Clinton st. Brooklyn, N. Y	26
Mrs Edwin Atwell	1088 Dean st. Brooklyn, N. Y	27
Miss Ellen Coffey		28
Miss Helena Werner	1188 Main st. Buffalo, N. Y	29
Miss F. A. Hawkins	278 Hudson st. Buffalo, N. Y	30
		31
Mrs E: P. Aspinwall	185 Summit av. Buffalo, N Y	32
Miss Lura Newman	168 College st. Buffalo, N. Y	33
Mrs Frank G. Wheeler	589 Breckinridge st. Buffalo, N. Y	34
		35
Mrs H: R. Howland	217 Summer st. Buffalo, N, Y	36
Miss Hattie Caldwell		37
Miss E. C. Elder	211 Highland av. Buffalo, N. Y	38
		39
Miss E. S. Brooks		40
Mrs E. C. Case	Camden, N. Y	41
		42
		43
Miss F. E. Kellogg	Carthage, N. Y	44
Mrs F. H. Osborn	Catskill, N. Y	45

CLUBS IN NEW

	PLACE	Name	Year organized	Beginning	Closing
46	Cattaraugus	C. L. S. C.		O	My
47	Charlton	Charlton reading circle	1888	N	Ap
48	Corning	Corning Clionian circle	1881	S	Je
49	Cortland	Corlonor fraternity	1878		
50		Ladies literary club	1880		
51	Dunkirk	Cardinal Newman reading circle	1893	S	Je
52		Women's literary club	1885	O	Mr
53	East Randolph	East Randolph historical and lit. soc	1894	S	My
54	Elma	Shakespeare club			
55	Elmira	Elmira theological and literary society	1878	Ja	D
56	Fayetteville	Coterie	1885	S	Je
57		Philomath	1884		
58	Flatbush	Ingleside	1885	S	Je
59	Flushing	Good citizenship league	1891	O	My
60	Fort Plain	Bryant literary society			
61	Frankfort	E. Schuyler literary club			
62	Fredonia	Shakspere club	1895	O	Mr
63		Society for the study of art	1884	S	Je
64	Friendship	Ladies literary society	1885		
65	Fulton	Fortnightly Shakespeare club		O	Je
66		Fulton reading circle		O	Ap
67		Fulton Shakespeare society		O	Ap
68	Geneseo	Monday evening class	1882	S	Je
69	Geneva	Art circle	1893	O	My
70		Art reading club of Geneva	1889	O	Jl
71	Gloversville	Every Monday club		O	Mr
72		Monday afternoon study class		N	Mr
73	Groton	Columbian club	1892	Ja	D
74		Fortnightly club	1894	O	Ap
75	Hamilton	Laurie club	1894	Ja	My
76	Haverstraw	Nineteenth century club	1893	O	My
77	Herkimer	Progressive club	1894	O	My
78	Hornellsville	The Forum	1891	S	Je
79	Horseheads	Miscellany searchers	1892	Ja	
80	Hudson	Fortnightly club	1888	N	Ap
81	Ilion	Historical club	1893	N	My
82		Travelers club	1890	S	My
83	Jamaica	Woman's club of Jamaica	1883	O	Je
84	Jamestown	Fortnightly	1894	N	Mr
85	Johnstown	Aldine club	1881		
86		Heli		O	Je
87	Little Falls	Home culture club		N	
88	Lockport	Saturday club	1890	N	Ap
89	Massena	Ladies literary club	1893	O	My
90	Medina	Fortnightly culture club	1891	O	Je

YORK (continued)

No.	Frequency	Total no. of papers	Total no. of readings	Subjects of study with number of meetings devoted to each	
29	Weekly	57	84	Countries of Europe..................................	46
? 20	Weekly			English writers (16).................................	47
38	Weekly			General history (32); English literature (28)..	48
....				....	49
....	Biweekly			....	50
24	Weekly	17	8	Ancient Greece (18).................................	51
26	Weekly	42	0	German history and literature (25).............	52
14	Biweekly			Greek and Roman hist (14); Lit., cur. topics	53
....				....	54
11	Monthly			....	55
....	Biweekly			Holland...	56
26	Biweekly			....	57
....	Biweekly			....	58
16	Biweekly			Miscellaneous..	59
....				....	60
					61
24	Weekly	20	18	Shakspere...	62
23	Monthly	90	...	Art..	63
...	Weekly			....	64
25	Biweekly			Shakspere...	65
25	Weekly			English literature (25).............................	66
15	Biweekly			Shakspere...	67
? 36	Weekly			General history (29)..............................	68
...	Weekly			Italian art...	69
40	Weekly			French art...	70
24	Weekly	105	0	American history...................................	71
19	Weekly	40	18	Mexico (18)..	72
27	Biweekly	26	2	Prince of India (7); Prehistoric man (5); Ancient Egypt (4).....................................	73
15	Biweekly	45	...	American history and literature..................	74
6	Semimonthly			Educational topics...................................	75
17	Biweekly	17	84	England..	76
14	Semimonthly	42	0	French history.......................................	77
40	Weekly	2	1	Current topics.......................................	78
...	Biweekly			....	79
...	Biweekly			....	80
26	Weekly	68	30	English history.....................................	81
...				Germany...	82
9	Monthly			Miscellaneous..	83
18	Biweekly			Italy, medieval and modern (10)................	84
...	Weekly			....	85
18	Biweekly			15th century...	86
? 15	Biweekly	? 3	...	French history.......................................	87
...	Biweekly	24	...	18th century...	88
15	Biweekly			American authors...................................	89
19	Biweekly	101	...	American history...................................	90

CLUBS IN NEW

	MEMBERS		AVERAGE ATTENDANCE		NO VOLS IN LIBRARY		FEES	
	Men	Women	Men	Women	Circulating	Reference	Entrance	Annual
46								
47	2	18	2	11	0	0	0	$1
48		20		15	0	0	0	0
49								
50		80						
51		17			12		0	50
52		43		27	0	0	$1	1
53	11	14			0	0	0	0
54								
55	36		30		0	0	1	50
56		80		18	0	0	0	25
57		80						25
58		20						1
59		170		?75	0	0	1	2
60								
61								
62		12		11	0	0	1	1
63		72		36	10	10	50	50
64		24						
65		25		20	0	0	0	0
66		25		15	0	0	0	0
67		20		16	0	0	0	?
68		18		18	0	0	0	10
69		18						
70		18		12	20	20	3	2
71		10		7	0	0	0	0
72		19		18	0	0	0	0
73		15		9	0	10	50	1
74		40		27	0	0	0	1
75	45	15	35	7	0	0	0	0
76		17		11	0	0	50	50
77		35		20	0	0	1	1
78	?22		?22		0	0	50	1
79								1
80		50						1
81		29		21	0	0	50	1
82							50	50
83		80		20	0	0	1	1
84		65			6844	2268	0	2
85		25					25	
86		24		15	0	0	0	65
87	1	15	1	18	0	0	0	0
88		75		40	0	0	0	25
89		30		?25	0	0	0	0
90		22		10	0	0	0	50

YORK (continued)

Name	Secretary Address	
Mrs Oakes	Cattaraugus, N. Y.	46
Miss M. E. Callaghan	Charlton, N. Y.	47
Mrs J: H. Way	Corning, N. Y.	48
		49
Miss S. M. Adams	Cortland, N. Y.	50
Miss Ruth Driggs	508 Eagle st. Dunkirk, N. Y.	51
Mrs Charlotte Hequembourg	786 Central av. Dunkirk, N. Y.	52
Miss M. E. Weeden	East Randolph, N. Y.	53
		54
Rev. J. R. Robinson	Painted Post, N. Y.	55
Miss J. E. House	Fayetteville, N. Y.	56
Mrs S. S. Pratt	Fayetteville, N. Y.	57
Miss S. S. Walden	Flatbush, N. Y.	58
Mrs Foster Crowell	140 Barclay st Flushing, L. I., N. Y.	59
		60
		61
Mrs Anna McK. Dana	Fredonia, N. Y.	62
Mrs C. S. Clothier	Fredonia, N. Y.	63
Mrs K. W. Ingham	Friendship, N. Y.	64
Mrs E. H. French	Fulton, N Y.	65
Mrs E. R Redhead	Fulton, N. Y.	66
Mrs E. E. Morrill	Fulton, N. Y.	67
Mrs Maria W. C. Goodwin	Geneseo, N. Y.	68
Miss R. W Nester, pres	Geneva, N Y	69
Mrs L B. Bell	Geneva, N Y.	70
Miss E. G. Kingsley	187 Bleecker st Gloversville, N. Y.	71
Mrs W F. Steele	79 Broad st Gloversville, N. Y.	72
Mrs C: O Rhodes	Groton, N, Y.	73
Mrs J. B Grant	Hamilton, N. Y.	74
H. D Winters	Hamilton, N Y.	75
Mrs M. F. Washburn	Haverstraw, N Y.	76
Miss R. M. Dutton	Herkimer, N. Y.	77
William Davis	Hornellsville, N. Y.	78
		79
Mrs J. R. Cady	Hudson, N. Y.	80
Miss K. E. Moran	Ilion, N. Y.	81
Mrs M. E. Draper	Ilion, N. Y.	82
Miss A. F Belknap	Jamaica, L. I., N. Y.	83
Mrs H. W. Tew	Prospect st. Jamestown, N. Y.	84
Miss Gertrude McEwen Kelly	Johnstown, N. Y	85
Miss C. E. Benter	Gloversville, N. Y.	86
Miss Anna Suell	Lansing st. Little Falls, N. Y.	87
Miss F L. Van Valkenburgh	Lockport, N Y	88
Mrs Dora Worden	Massena, N. Y.	89
Miss Lena Bowen	Medina, N. Y.	90

	PLACE	Name	Year organized	Beginning	Closing
91	Middletown	Travelers club	1889	O	Je
92	Mount Vernon	Emerson club	1895	O	
93		Westchester woman's club	1894	D	O
94	New Brighton	Fortnightly club	1890	O	My
95	New Utrecht	Winter club	1890	O	Je
96	New York	Cathedral library reading circle	1889	O	Je
97		Causeries du lundi	1880		
98		Clio club	1888	O	My
99		Drawing room club, ladies branch	1884		
100		East Side literary society	1894		
101		Meridian	1886	N	My
102		Mount Holyoke alumnae ass'n	1886		
103		Ozanum reading circle	1886		
104		Philomathean society	1871		
105		Post Parliament	1894	O	Mr
106		St Ursula club	1895		
107		Society for political study	1886	O	Ap
108		Society for the study of child nature	1890	N	My
109		Sorosis	1868		
110		Wednesday afternoon club	1888		
111	Oakfield	Study club	1894	D	Je
112	Ogdensburg	University extension study club	1894	D	My
113		Alpha branch of Univ. exten. study club	1894	O	Je
114	Olean	Travelers club	1884	O	Ap
115	Oneida	Neighborhood club	1894	N	
116	Oneonta	Agonian fraternity, Beta chapter	1892		
117		Clionian fraternity, Beta chapter	1890		
118		Woman's club	1894	S	Je
119	Oxford	Round Robin reading club, no 16	1895	Ja	Jl
120	Palmyra	Clio club			
121	Phoenix	Shakespeare club	1895	Ja	
122	Pike	Emersonian reading club	1879	O	Je
123	Portville	Caledonian club	1893	O	My
124	Port Washington	Port Washington woman's club	1892	Ja	Ja
125	Potsdam	Fortnightly club	1889	S	Je
126	Rensselaer co	Rensselaer county farmers club	1888	N	Je
127	Rochester	Browning club	1884		
128		Catholic reading circle	1889	O	Je
129		Fortnightly ignorance club	1881		
130		Judean club	1895	S	Je
131		Ladies Scottish club	1889	N	My
132		Roundabout club	1885	S	My
133		Woman's ethical club	1889	N	Ap
134	Rome	Current topic club		O	My
135	Rushford	Historical class			

YORK (continued)

No.	Frequency	Total no. of papers	Total no. of readings	Subjects of study with number of meetings devoted to each	
16	Biweekly			Holland, Belgium, France and Spain	91
12	Biweekly	12		Emerson	92
24	Biweekly			Art, Education, history, literature.	93
16	Biweekly	16		Miscellaneous	94
	Biweekly				95
24	Semimonthly	2		Book of Job (24)	96
					97
84	Weekly	84	204	Authors and their works	98
					99
	Weekly	8	8	Social problems of the day	100
7	Monthly	7			101
2					102
	Weekly				103
	Weekly				104
12	Semimonthly			Parliamentary law	105
	Biweekly				106
24	Weekly	22			107
? 20	Weekly	? 12	12	Child nature	108
	Semimonthly				109
				A century of science	110
17	Biweekly	23	5	French history (17)	111
25	Weekly	25		England (24)	112
20	Biweekly	20		English history	113
18	Biweekly	84	34	Ancient Egypt (17)	114
? 12	Weekly			American history	115
					116
					117
24	Weekly			Cook'g, cur top., Eng. & Am. lit., Fr & Ger., French hist., Orchestra and harmony, Parliamentary usage, Phys. cult., Voice cult..	118
12	Biweekly	10	86	Six representative American writers	119
					120
	Weekly			Hamlet	121
	Biweekly	? 22		American literature (20)	122
12	Biweekly	12	12	History and literature of England	123
	Weekly			Miscellaneous	124
22	Biweekly	19	18	American authors and their works (18)	125
10	Monthly	8	0	Modes of farming	126
					127
	Biweekly				128
	Biweekly				129
40	Weekly			Jewish history and literature	130
14	Biweekly			Scottish history (8)	131
21		20	20	Miscellaneous	132
6	Monthly				133
	Weekly			France and Scotland	134
					135

| | MEMBERS || AVERAGE ATTENDANCE || NO. VOLS. IN LIBRARY || FEES ||
	Men	Women	Men	Women	Circulating	Reference	Entrance	Annual
91		10		5	0	0	0	?
92	4	4			0	0	$10	
93		74		?	0	0	5	$3
94		34		18	0	0	0	1
95		40					1	1
96		15		12			1	2
97								
98		50		? 25	0	0	5	3
99							15	12
100	26		17				25	.05 w'kly
101		? 80		? 18				1
102		130		100	0	0	1	1
103								
104	•						50	.20 m'thly
105		47		25	0	8	5	1
106								50
107		235		100-150	0	0	50	50
108		85		18	0	0	2	2 50
109		298					25	5
110		93					3	3
111	7	8	6	7	0	0	0	0
112		20			0	0	0	50
113		20			0	0	0	50
114		30		22	0	50	0	1
115		9		7	0	0	0	0
116							1	1 50
117							1	1
118		175		100	0	100	2 50	5
119		12		? 10	80	80	50	1
120								
121		18		15	0	0	0	0
122		34		18	200		25	25
123		18		9	0	0	0	0
124		30		18	575		2	2
125	10	25			0	0	0	0
126	140		75		0	0	25	25
127								
128		114						50
129		50						
130	25		20		0	0	25	2
131	5	54			30	0	1	1
132		20		14			50	50
133							25	25
134		50		35	0	0	0	1
135								

YORK (*continued*)

SECRETARY		
Name	Address	
Mrs Charles Clark	Linden av. Middletown, N. Y	91
H H Robbins	240 S 10th av. Mount Vernon, N. Y	92
Mrs J. S. Wood	185 S. 2d av. Mount Vernon, N. Y	93
Mrs William Tompkins	12 Boyd Hill, Stapleton, S. I., N. Y	94
Mrs H A. Bogert		95
Miss Elizabeth M. Murphy	128 East 50th st. New York	96
Mrs H: C. Howells		97
Mrs A. J Shipman	55 Lenox av. New York	98
Miss E C. Davis		99
E: A. Weiss	408 E. 75th st. New York	100
Mrs H M Miller	628 Hancock st. Brooklyn, N. Y	101
Mrs S. W. Cleaveland	45 W 50th st. New York	102
		103
Miss Ellen de Koster		104
Mrs Holbrook	128 W. 59th st. New York	105
		106
Mrs Minnie Chapin	66 Madison av New York	107
Mrs L Seligsberg	1028 Park av. New York	108
Mrs E. V. Townsend	218 W 44th st. New York	109
Miss L.. T Caldwell		110
Miss G W Rathbone	Oakfield, N. Y	111
Miss Harriet Frank	64 Greene st. Ogdensburg, N Y	112
Miss V M. Hamilton	283 Ford st Ogdensburg, N. Y	113
Miss M.. D Bartlett	Olean, N Y	114
Mrs S H Goodwin	28 Grove st. Oneida, N Y	115
Miss E J Mathews	Oneonta, N Y	116
Miss Helen King	Oneonta, N. Y	117
Mrs N. H. Miller	291 Main st Oneonta, N. Y	118
Miss E.. M. Hyde	Oxford, N Y	119
		120
Miss Mary Gleason	Phœnix, N. Y	121
Mrs C B. Ryder	Pike, N. Y	122
Mrs E A H. Barnes	Portville, N. Y.	123
Mrs A. G Cornwell	Port Washington, N. Y	124
Mrs T. B. Stowell	Potsdam, N. Y	125
O. J Lewis	Schodack Center, N. Y	126
		127
Sabina Curran		128
Mrs J M. Parker		129
Louis Lipsky	91 Chatham st. Rochester, N. Y.	130
Miss Katherine Ross	74 East av. Rochester, N. Y.	131
Miss Harriett Farrar	898 Lake av. Rochester, N. Y	132
Mrs A M. Mosscrop		133
Miss Barton	N. George st. Rome, N. Y	134
		135

	PLACE	Name	Year organised	Beginning	Closing
136	Salamanca	Olla Podrida	1891	N	Mr
137		Salamanca salmagundi society	1890	O	Mr
138	Sangerfield	Travelers club			
139	Saratoga	Travelers-at-home-club	1892	O	Ap
140	Schenectady	Society to promote useful reading	1877	N	Mr
141	Schuylerville	Saturday club	1894	Ja	Jl
142	Seneca Falls	Seneca Falls Shakespeare society	1888		
143	Silver Creek	Silver Creek study club	1894	S	Je
144	Syracuse	Azarias reading circle	1894	N	Je
145		Current topic club (morning class)	1890		
146		" (afternoon class)			
147		Portfolio club		O	Ap
148		Roman ramblers club			
149		Shakspere university extension class	1893	O	Ap
150		Wednesday club	1887	O	Ap
151	Troy	East side study class	1889	O	Je
152		Method class	1895	F	
153	Utica	New century club	1893	S	Je
154		Wednesday morning club	1882		
155	Warsaw	Monday club	1891	O	My
156		Political equality club	1891	S	My
157	Watertown	Current topics club	1894	N	My
158		Wednesday morning art class	1892	O	Je
159	Waterville	Every Saturday night club	1886	O	My
160	Westfield	Monday evening club	1888	O	My
161	Worcester	Fortnightly club	1890	O	Je
162		John Lord literary society	1885		
163	Yonkers	Civic League of the Woman's institute	1895	Mr	
164		Fortnightly club	1888	N	Ap

YORK (continued)

No.	Frequency	Total no. of papers	Total no of readings	Subjects of study with number of meetings devoted to each	
21	Weekly	27	27	French history..	186
26	Weekly	92	50	French history and literature (25)..	187
					188
25	Weekly	..	..	France	189
...	Weekly	14	6	Middle ages.	140
24	Weekly	...	...	Cities of Gt. Brit (12), Cities of Fr & Ger. (12)	141
..	Weekly	...	...		142
37	Weekly	15	...	French revolution ..	143
27	Weekly	27	...	Development of old Eng. thought (9); Eng. lit (9), Eng. hist (21), Eng. poetry (19)....	144
...	...	...	...	...	145
					146
26	Weekly	28	6	History and literature of Scotland (25).....	147
...	...	...	...	...	148
22	Weekly	...	...	Romeo and Juliet (11), The tempest (11)	149
18	Biweekly	23	8	Hamlet and Merchant of Venice	150
19	Biweekly	1	254	English literature (19), Ruskin (12)	151
..	Weekly	...	...	Pedagogic methods	152
52	Weekly	100	...	Browning (12), Social science (15)........	153
...	Weekly	...	...		154
39	Weekly	44	...	History of France (27)	155
22	Biweekly	? 20	...		156
12	Biweekly	12	...	Travel through England (12)...............	157
16	Biweekly	? 64	0	Architecture (16).........................	158
30	Weekly	16	30	Greece (30)	159
30	Weekly	55	10	Amer. history (14); Miscellaneous subjects (14)	160
33	Weekly	...	...	C L S. C. topics	161
...	Weekly	...	...		162
? 9	Monthly	...	...		163
18	Biweekly	...	...		164

CLUBS IN NEW

	MEMBERS		AVERAGE ATTENDANCE		NO VOLS IN LIBRARY		FEES	
	Men	Women	Men	Women	Circulating	Reference	Entrance	Annual
136	......	27	......	20	0	0	$1	$1
137	8	22	......	......	......	......	......	......
138	......	......	......	......	......	......	......	......
139	......	20	......	12	......	......	......	1
140	......	75	......	40	600	......	0	1
141	......	8	......	7	0	0	0	88
142	......	......	......	......	......	......	......	......
143	6	6	3	6	1767	......	0	0
144	7	20	5	15	0	0	0	0
145	......	......	......	......	......	......	......	......
146	......	......	......	......	......	......	......	......
147	......	30	......	22	0	0	0	2
148	......	......	......	......	......	......	......	......
149	......	12	......	......	0	0	......	20
150	......	30	......	28	26	0	0	1
151	......	12	......	9	0	0	0	25
152	......	5	......	......	......	......	......	......
153	......	269	......	?100	224	......	......	10
154	......	20	......	......	......	......	......	......
155	......	68	......	85	0	0	0	1
156	6	45	1	25	6	0	50	50
157	......	16	......	10	50	50	0	50
158	......	21	......	15	0	0	1	......
159	......	16	......	14	0	0	0	25
160	......	50	......	25	0	0	1	1
161	......	18	......	18	0	0	25	25
162	......	......	......	......	......	......	......	......
163	......	82	......	......	0	0	0	1
164	17	17	......	......	......	......	1	1

YORK (concluded)

Name	Secretary Address	
Mrs Jennie Swan	Salamanca, N. Y.	136
Miss Carrie A. De Nike	Salamanca, N. Y.	137
Miss Catherine Livermore	Sangerfield, N. Y.	138
Miss Anna Marseilles	88 Circular st Saratoga Springs, N. Y.	139
Mrs William Wells	Union college, Schenectady, N. Y.	140
Miss H M. Knox	Schuylerville, N. Y.	141
		142
Miss E. E. Montgomery	Silver Creek, N Y	143
Miss C. T Dunn	700 Bear st. Syracuse, N Y	144
Mrs S. B. Larned		145
Mrs F. P. Denison		146
Mrs W. E. Gilbert	Onondaga Valley, N. Y.	147
		148
Miss M. E. Trapp	518 S Salina st Syracuse, N. Y	149
Mrs H. E. Clark	504 Bear st Syracuse, N. Y	150
Miss C E Harrison	Linden av. Troy, N. Y.	151
Miss E. H. Angell	33 Second st Troy, N. Y.	152
Mrs M. A. Mitchell	258 Genesee st Utica, N. Y	153
Mrs Wallace Clarke		154
Mrs N. S. Beardslee	Warsaw, N. Y.	155
Mrs Jennie Harris	Warsaw, N. Y	156
Miss F. G. Olin	Stone st. Watertown, N. Y	157
Mrs W. H. Camp	26 Clinton st. Watertown, N. Y	158
Mrs C. B. Peck	Waterville, N. Y.	159
Mrs A. F. Mason	Westfield, N. Y.	160
Mrs A. L. Emmons	Worcester, N. Y	161
		162
Mrs William Sharman	6 Hawthorne av. Yonkers, N. Y	163
Mrs J. R. Brevoort		164

CLUBS OUTSIDE

	PLACE	Name	Year organized	Time of Beginning	Closing
	Massachusetts				
165	Newtonville	Every Saturday club	1870	O	Mr
166	Pittsfield	Wednesday morning club	1879	Je	D
	Pennsylvania				
167	Braddock	Woman's club of Braddock	1893	O	My
168	Philadelphia	R'd Robin read. club of New cent club	1895	Ja	Mr
169		Round Robin reading club, no. 14	1895	Ja	Ap
	New Jersey				
170	Burlington	Round Robin reading club, no. 17	1895	Ap	D
	Missouri				
171	St Louis	Eliot soc. of the Church of the Messiah			
172		Literary class of Unity club	1888	O	Mr
173		Novel club	1886	N	My
174		Social science club	1893	D	My
175		Wednesday club	1889	O	My
	Wyoming				
176	Laramie	Alpha	1889	O	Je

NEW YORK

No.	Frequency	Total no. of papers	Total no. of readings	Subjects of study with number of meetings devoted to each	
15	Biweekly..	....	..	Ruskin's art teaching (6); Sociology (6)	165
?12	Biweekly..	....	..	Miscellaneous	166
16	Biweekly.....	....	.	Grecian history....	167
6	Bimonthly ...	12	27	....	168
13	Weekly	8	30	Art and literature of Venice	169
12	Biweekly.. .	...	....	Paris (6), London (6)	170
....	....	....	..	....	171
12	Biweekly.....	?48	8	King Lear (4); Agamemnon (4), Henry 8 (4)	172
12	Biweekly.....	?86	0	Human nature as portrayed in the mod novel	173
16	....	?16	0	Ethical, economic & reformatory questions..	174
17	Biweekly.. .	12	0	Art (7), Education (7), Science (7), Cur. topics (11); Social economics (7), Lit. and hist. (7)	175
16	Biweekly. ..	14	14	Early English drama	176

CLUBS OUTSIDE

| | MEMBERS || AVERAGE ATTENDANCE || NO VOLS. IN LIBRARY || FEES ||
	Men	Women	Men	Women	Circulating	Reference	Entrance	Annual
165	25	15	? 20	? 10	0	0	0	$1
166		250		78	0	0	$1	1
167		85		25			1	2
168		58		39	0	0		
169		22		18	0	0	50	5
170		15			0	0	18 75	
171								
172	20	25			0	0	0	1
173	30	40			0	0	0	1
174	88	118	? 50	? 75	0	0	0	1
175		200		75	0	24	10	10
176		14		18	0	0	0	0

NEW YORK

Secretary		
Name	Address	
Mrs Winfield S. Slocum	Newtonville, Mass	165
Mrs W. F. Colt	South st. Pittsfield, Mass	166
Mrs Grant Anderson	Braddock, Pa	167
Mrs Wilbur F. Litch	1507 Walnut st. Philadelphia, Pa	168
Miss H. C. Stockton	4218 Chester av. Philadelphia, Pa	169
M. H. Gangewer	Burlington, N. J	170
		171
Mrs E. C. Rowse	10 Benton Place, St Louis, Mo	172
Mrs C H. Stone	5562 Clemens av. St Louis, Mo	173
Mrs A. H. Blaisdell	4048 Westminster Place, St Louis, Mo	174
Mrs F. D. Lee	3916 Bell av St Louis, Mo	175
Miss E L. Jackson	Laramie, Wyoming	176

INDEX

The superior figure points to the exact place on the page in ninths, e g. 278²
means two ninths of the way down page 278. Dates are printed in italics.

Adams, H: A., lectures, 273³
Administrative organizations aiding study clubs, 268-90
Albany, *see* Study clubs, statistics; Trinity methodist church reading club; Unity club.
Albion, *see* Historical conversation club, Albion.
Aldrich, L. J., report of Camden historical club, 315².
America, *see* United States, history.
American constitution, syllabus by W· H Mace, 378⁹
American literature, syllabus by Mrs J K. Curtis, 378⁸.
American poetry, syllabus by J. H. Gilmore, 882⁴.
American revolution, syllabus by W: H. Mace, 378⁶.
Apparatus, loans and exchanges, 263⁸-64¹
Architectural styles, syllabus by A. D. F Hamlin, 882¹, outline of study, 885²-87⁸.
Arey, A. L., Various forces of nature as related to modern life, syllabus, 881².
Art, Fredonia society for the study of; report, 861¹, statistics, 462-65.
Art circle, Geneva, report, 841⁵; statistics, 462-65.
Art class, Watertown, report, 841⁹-42⁵, statistics, 470-78.
Art reading club, Geneva, report, 841³; statistics, 463-65.
Astronomy, syllabus by J: K. Rees, 878⁸.
Australasian home reading union, report, 289⁸-90³

Azarias reading circle, Syracuse, report, 889⁵-40⁴; statistics, 470-78.

Baker, C. I., report on Home culture clubs, 276⁶-76⁵.
Barnes, Mrs E A. H , report on Caledonian club, 832⁸-83³.
Bartlett, M.. D., report of Travelers club, 844²-45⁹.
Beardslee, C. B., report of Monday club, Warsaw, 816⁵-17².
Bell, E S , report of Art reading club, 841³.
Bennett, C: E., Private life of the Romans, syllabus, 881⁴.
Books, loans from state library, 268⁸; exchanges between clubs, 263⁹-64¹; traveling libraries loaned to study clubs, 262⁹-68⁸.
Boston college settlement, *see* Denison house.
Bowen, L. G., report of Fortnightly culture club, 358⁵.
Boyesen, H. H., English literature, syllabus, 878¹, Medieval German literature, syllabus, 880⁸.
Brigham, A. P., Geology and scenery of New York, syllabus, 881¹.
Brooklyn association of working girls societies, 806⁶.
Brooklyn, *see also* Columbia literary circle; Fortnightly club, Froebel society, Ingleside; Study clubs, statistics.
Brundage, W: M., report of Unity club, 852⁶-58¹.
Buffalo free kindergarten association, report of the training class, 814⁸-15²; statistics, 458-61.

Buffalo seminary, *see* Graduates association of the Buffalo seminary.
Buffalo, *see also* Highland park literary club; Literary club of the Church of the Messiah; Saturday class, Study clubs, statistics
Bulletins on study clubs, 260⁶.
Burton, H: F, Ancient Roman life, syllabus, 380².

Cable, G: W., founder of home culture clubs, 276⁵; quoted, 283⁶.
Caledonian club, Portville, report, 332⁷-33⁸, statistics, 466-69.
Callaghan, M. E., report of Charlton reading circle, 345⁹-50⁸.
Camden, *see* Historical club, Camden.
Camp, Mrs W. H, report of Wednesday morning art class, 341⁹-42⁵.
Cardinal Newman reading circle, Dunkirk, report, 367⁹-68², statistics, 462-65.
Cathedral library reading circles, New York, report, 363⁷-67⁵, statistics, 466-69.
Catholic reading circle review, 272¹
Catholic reading circles, growth, 269⁹-78⁴
Catholic world, 271¹; extracts, 269⁹-78⁴.
Catskill, *see* Monday club, Catskill, Study clubs, statistics
Certificates of registration, 260⁶-61¹.
Charlton reading circle, report, 345⁹-50⁸; statistics, 462-65
Chautauqua junior outlook club, report, 378¹.
Chautauqua literary and scientific circle, report, 268⁴-69⁵.
Chautauqua university, educational influence, 259⁵.
Chautauquan, 268⁷.
Chicago, proposed association of working girls societies, 306⁹.
Child nature, books on study of, 319⁶, 320³; report of Society for study, 317² 21⁵, 333⁴, statistics, 466-69.
Children's Chautauqua, report, 287⁹.
Church history, study, 272⁵
Citizenship clubs, 296⁸, 298⁴, 300⁹-1¹.

Civic league of the woman's institute, Yonkers, report, 354⁸-55⁹; statistics, 470-73
Civil and religious liberty in America, syllabus by C· E. Fitch, 380⁵.
Clio club, New York, report, 353², statistics, 466-69
Clio club, Palmyra, course of study, 333¹; statistics, 466-69
Cohn, Adolphe, History of France, syllabus, 879⁴
College settlements, reports, 290⁴-96², 300⁶-2⁴.
Colonial history of America, syllabus by H: P. Warren, 379¹.
Columbia literary circle, Brooklyn, report, 375⁴-76⁹; statistics, 458-61.
Columbian catholic summer school at Madison, 272⁸
Columbian club, Groton, report, 353⁵-54⁵; statistics, 462-65
Columbian reading union, report, 272⁵-73⁴.
Connecticut association of working girls societies, 306⁸.
Constitutions, suggested forms for study clubs, 264³-68².
Coterie, Fayetteville, report, 369⁷-70¹; statistics, 462-65.
Courses of study, 262⁵, 268⁶, 269⁴, 288⁹-89⁶. *See also* Outlines of study; Study clubs, statistics, Syllabuses.
Crawshaw, W: H, English li·erature, syllabus, 380², English novel, syllabus, 381⁹.
Current topics clubs, 261⁹-62¹.
Curtis, Mrs J. K, American literature, syllabus, 378⁸, Hamlet and Merchant of Venice, syllabus, 380⁶, Julius Caesar, syllabus, 382⁵, Macbeth and King Lear, syllabus, 379⁷, Romeo and Juliet and the Tempest, syllabus, 381⁹, lectures and fees, 382⁶.

Dana, Mrs A D., report of Fredonia Shakspere club, 361⁶.
Denison house, report, 290⁵-96⁹.
Discovery of America, syllabus by Arthur Kaiser, 3£0².
Dodge, G H., report of working girls' clubs, 302⁵-7⁹.

Dramatic art, outline of study, 390¹-92³. *See also* English drama.
Driggs, S.. B , report of Women's literary club, 350⁸-52⁶.
Dudley, H. S., quoted, 294⁵.
Dunkirk, *see* Cardinal Newman reading circle, Women's literary club.

East side house, New York, report, 29⁴-99⁵.
East side literary society, New York, report, 342⁸-43⁹; statistics, 466-69.
East side study class, Troy, report, 328⁴-29⁴, statistics, 470-73.
Eastman, Grace, report of Chautauqua junior outlook club, 378¹.
Economics, Economic legislation, syllabus by J. W Jenks, 380⁷, Economic questions, syllabus by J. W. Jenks, 378⁵; Economic questions, syllabus by H. E Mills, 379¹, Economic questions, syllabus by G: W· Smith, 380⁷; Economic reforms, syllabus by E. A. Ross, 379⁵. *See also* Money.
Educational work undertaken by study clubs, 33₀⁷-31⁸. *See also* Kindergarten methods
Egypt, ancient, outline of study, 393⁸-95⁸
Elder, E. C., report of the training class of the Buffalo free kindergarten association, 314⁶-15².
Electricity, syllabuses; for course under direction of Columbia college, 381⁵; by Charles Forbes, 381¹, by G· C Hodges, 382⁶, by A. F. Onderdonk, 380⁶.
Eliot society of Church of the Messiah, St Louis, outline of study, 392⁴-93³; statistics, 474-77
Emerson club, Mt Vernon, report, 360²; statistics, 466-69.
England, outlines of study, 396⁷-97⁵, 416²-24⁸, 426⁸-30², National home reading union, report, 288⁶-89⁶. *See also* Great Britain.
English drama, syllabus, 379⁸. *See also* Shakspere.
English language and its history, syllabus, by A. V. W. Jackson, 879².

English literature, syllabuses, by H. H. Boyesen, 378⁷, by W: H. Crawshaw, 380²; by A. V. W. Jackson, 380⁴; by J. R. Truax, 380⁶; by M. H. Turk, 379⁴. *See also* English drama; English novel.
English novel, syllabus by W: H. Crawshaw, 881⁹. *See also* Fiction.
Ethics, outline of study, 884¹-85².
Evans, Mrs M. A. B., report of the Saturday club, 359⁸-60⁸.
Every Monday club, Gloversville, report, 311²-12¹; statistics, 462-65.
Every Saturday night club, Waterville, report, 329⁴, outline of study, 408³-10¹; statistics, 470-73.
Examinations, 264¹.
Exchanges, system of, 263⁹-64¹.
Extension bulletins, *see* Bulletins.
Extension department, scope of work, 259².
Extension work, for high school pupils, 288¹, in Boston college settlement, 295⁸-96¹.
Faust, F. P., report of Monday evening club, 356⁸-58⁸.
Fayetteville, *see* Coterie, Fayetteville, Study clubs, statistics.
Fees, for apparatus, etc., 263⁶; for traveling libraries, 263⁴.
Fiction, phases of character in, outline of study, 392⁴-93². *See also* English novel.
Fitch, C. E , Civil and religious liberty in America, syllabus, 380⁵.
Forbes, Charles, Electricity, syllabus, 381¹.
Forbes, G· M., Monetary science, syllabus, 380⁴, money, banking and the silver question, syllabus, 881⁶
Fortnightly, Jamestown, report, 309⁵, outline of study, 445⁶-47⁶, statistics, 462-65.
Fortnightly club, Brooklyn, report, 354⁵; statistics, 458-61.
Fortnightly club, Hamilton, outline of study, 428²-30².
Fortnightly club, Potsdam, report, 338⁴-38⁹, outline of study, 447⁶-50⁵; statistics, 466-69.

Fortnightly club, Worcester, report, 322⁵-28⁵; statistics, 470-78.
Fortnightly culture club, Medina, report, 358⁵; outline of study, 451⁴-54⁷, statistics, 462-65.
Foster, M. B, report of Los Angeles settlements association, 300⁵-1⁴.
France, history, outline of study, 433⁵-44⁶; syllabus by Adolphe Cohn, 379⁴; syllabus by Mrs F . G. Sears, 380⁹; history and literature, outline of study, 433⁵-37³, 439⁵-44⁶.
Frank, Harriet, report of University extension study club, 324⁴-26⁶.
Fredonia Shakspere club, report, 361⁶; outline of study, 387⁸-92³; statistics, 462-65
Fredonia society for the study of art, report, 361¹, statistics, 462-65
Froebel society, Brooklyn, report, 371²-74², statistics, 458-61.
Fulton reading circle, report, 370²; statistics, 462-65.

Gay, M. F., report of Westchester woman's club, 329²-30⁷.
Geneseo, see Monday evening class, Geneseo
Geneva, see Art circle, Geneva; Art reading club, Geneva; Study clubs, statistics.
Geology, syllabus by W. B Scott, 381⁶, geology and scenery of New York, syllabus by A. P. Brigham, 881¹.
Germany, literature, syllabus by H. H. Boyesen, 380⁸; history and literature, outline of study, 430⁴-33⁵.
Gilmore, J. H , American poetry, syllabus, 382⁴.
Gloversville, see Every Monday club, Monday afternoon study class.
Gordon, Clarence, report on East side house, 297⁴-99⁵.
Graduates association of the Buffalo seminary, report, 207⁵ ; statistics, 458-61.
Great Britain, outline of study, 424³-26⁸ See also England.

Greece, history, outline of study, 408²-10¹; history and literature, outline of study, 395²-96⁶.
Groton, see Columbian club; Study clubs, statistics.

Hall, G. S., syllabuses, 320⁹-21¹.
Hamilton fortnightly club, outline of study, 428²-30³.
Hamlet and Merchant of Venice, syllabus by Mrs J K Curtis, 380⁶.
Hamlin, A. D. F., History of architectural styles, syllabus, 382¹.
Harding, S. B., American history, 1781-1829, syllabus, 379¹.
Harris, W: T , outlines course for teachers, 273⁶.
Harrison, C.. E., report of East side study class, 328⁴-29⁴.
Haverstraw, see Nineteenth century club.
Hecker, Father, Sunday school library, 269⁹-70⁷
Heli study club, Johnstown, report, 326⁹; statistics, 462-65.
High school extension, 288¹.
Highland park literary club, Buffalo, report, 309⁸-11², outline of study, 385²-87⁶, statistics, 458-61.
Historical club, Camden, report, 315³, statistics, 458-61.
Historical club, Ilion, outlines of study, 399¹-407², 416²-24⁶; statistics, 462-65.
Historical conversation club, Albion; report, 367⁶; outline of study, 397¹-98⁹; statistics, 458-61.
History, syllabus on Nations of the orient, 881⁶, prehistoric, outline of study, 385²-87⁸; ancient , outline of study, 397¹-98. See also America; England; Egypt; France; Germany; Greece; Ireland; Italy; Middle ages; Roman history; Scotland; Spain.
Hodges, G: E., Electricity up to date, syllabus, 382⁶.
Home culture club, Little Falls, report, 307⁴; statistics, 462-65.
Home culture club letter, 278⁶, 284⁹; extract, 278²-83².

Home culture clubs, aims, 279⁵-80⁵, 283²; definition, 278³, 283³; democratic spirit, 278³-79³, 280⁵-81⁰, 283⁵-84⁴, 284⁰-85³; establishment, 276⁵; number of members, 283⁴, 284⁴; methods of work, 277⁴, 278³, 282¹; organization, 280⁵, 281⁰-82⁰, 284⁰; reports, 276⁰-85³; subjects, 279³.
Home study, organization, 259⁴.
Home study, society to encourage, report, 274³-76⁰; methods, 275⁵-76⁵.
House, Mrs F. J., report of Coterie, Fayetteville, 369⁷-70¹.
Hudson, G: H:, Zoology from modern standpoint of animal biology, syllabus, 380¹.
Hyde, E M., report of Round Robin reading club, 388³-39⁵.

Ingleside, Brooklyn, report, 374²-75⁴.
Ilion, see Historical club, Ilion, Study clubs, statistics.
International education series, 278⁶.
Ireland, outline of study, 415⁵-16¹, 424⁵-26⁵.
Italy, history; outline of study, 444⁵-50⁵; Life in old Florence, syllabus, 382⁵.

Jackson, A. V. W., English drama, syllabus, 379³; English language and its history, syllabus, 379³, Some masterpieces of English literature, syllabus, 380⁴
Jamestown, see Fortnightly, Jamestown.
Jenks, J. W., Economic legislation, syllabus, 380⁷; Political methods, syllabus, 381⁵; Practical economic questions, syllabus, 378⁵.
Jersey City, Whittier house; report, 299⁵-300⁵.
Johnstown, see Heli study club; Study clubs, statistics.
Judean club, Rochester, report, 368³; statistics, 466-69.
Julius Caesar, syllabus by Mrs J. K. Curtis, 382⁵.

Kaiser, Arthur, Discovery of America, syllabus, 380⁰.

Kimball, K F., report of Chautauqua literary and scientific circle, 268⁴-69⁵.
Kindergarten association, Buffalo, report of the training class, 314²-15³; statistics, 458-61.
Kindergarten association. See also Froebel society.
Kindergarten methods, study of, 340⁵-41¹.
King, J. S., report of Columbia literary circle, 375⁴-76⁰.
Kingsley, E. G., report of Every Monday club, 311³-12¹.
Kittel, A. D, report of educational section of Westchester woman's club, 380⁷-81².
Knox, H. M., report of Saturday club, 327⁰-28⁴.

Labor union at Boston college settlement, 294⁰-95³.
Ladies literary club, Massena, report, 368⁵-69⁵.
Ladies Scottish club, Rochester, report, 376⁰-77⁰; outline of study, 412⁶-15⁴, statistics, 466-69.
Language, see English language.
Lantern slides, loans and exchanges, 263⁷-64¹
Libraries, see Sunday school libraries; Traveling libraries
Literary club of the Church of the Messiah, Buffalo, report, 362⁵-63³; outline of study, 415⁵-16¹, statistics, 458-61.
Literature, Critical study of authors of to-day, syllabus, 379⁵. See also American literature; English literature, Dramatic art; Fiction; France; Germany; Greece, Shakspere.
Little Falls, see Home culture club; Study clubs, statistics.
Loans to study clubs, 262⁰-63⁰.
Lockport, see Saturday club.
Loomis, E. F., report of Wednesday club, 314⁶.
Los Angeles settlements association, 300⁵-2⁵.

Macbeth and King Lear, syllabus by Mrs J. K. Curtis, 379⁷.

Mace, W: H , American constitution, syllabus, 378³; American revolution, syllabus, 878⁴, The civil war and some of its problems, syllabus, 882², Development of the nation, syllabus, 381².

McMahon, J. H., report of Cathedral library reading circles, 363¹-67⁵.

McMillan, Thomas, on Catholic reading circles, 269⁹-72⁴.

Madison, Columbian catholic summer school, 272³.

Marseilles, Anna, report of Travelers-at-home club, 312²-18⁶.

Martin, A. C , report of Worcester fortnightly club, 322⁵-23⁵.

Massachusetts association of working girls societies, 806⁹.

Massena, Ladies literary club, report, 368⁸-69².

Medina, see Fortnightly culture club, Medina.

Method class, Troy, report, 340⁸-41¹, statistics, 470-73.

Middle ages, outline of study, 410¹-12⁵

Middletown, see Travelers club, Middletown

Miller, Mrs N H , report of Woman's club, 327¹

Mills, H E., Practical economic questions, syllabus, 879⁷

Moffat, Adeline, report on Home culture club, 283³-85².

Monday afternoon study class, Gloversville, report, 307⁸-8⁶, statistics, 462-65

Monday club, Catskill, report, 369², statistics, 458-61

Monday club. Warsaw, report, 316⁵-17²; outline of study, 407⁴-8³; statistics, 470-73.

Monday evening class, Geneseo, report, 323⁵-24³, statistics, 462-65.

Monday evening club, Westfield, report, 356⁸-58⁵, outline of study, 454⁷-57, statistics, 470-73.

Money, Monetary science, syllabus, 380⁴, Money, banking and the silver question, syllabus, 381⁷

Montgomery, Mrs Helen Barrett, Life in old Florence, syllabus, 382⁵.

Morton, Pauline, report of Ladies Scottish club, 376⁹-77⁹.

Mount Vernon, see Emerson club; Westchester woman's club.

National bureau of Unity clubs, outlines of study, 888⁴.

National home-reading union of England, report, 288⁶-89².

National young folks reading circle, report, 287³-88⁶.

Nations of the orient, syllabus by H. B. Waterman, 381⁶.

Neighborhood club, Oneida, report, 343⁹-44², statistics, 466-69.

Nester, R. W., report of Art circle, 341⁵.

New century club, Utica, report, 361¹-62⁶, statistics, 470-73.

New York working girls club, report, 802⁵-7⁹.

New York, see also Cathedral library reading circles; Clio club; East side house; East side literary society; Society for political study; Society for the study of child nature; Study clubs, statistics, University settlement society

Newman, Lura, report of Literary club of the Church of the Messiah, 362⁶-63⁶.

Nineteenth century club, Haverstraw, report, 358²-59¹; statistics, 463-65.

Northampton Home culture clubs, 288⁴.

Oakfield, see Study club, Oakfield.

Ogdensburg, see Study clubs, statistics; University extension study club.

Olean, see Travelers club.

Onderdonk, A. F., Electricity, syllabus, 380⁶.

Oneida, see Neighborhood club.

Oneonta, see Study clubs, statistics; Woman's club, Oneonta.

Organizations aiding study clubs, 268-90.

Outlines of study, 388-457.

Oxford, see Round Robin reading club.

Ozanam reading circle, 270⁸-71⁹.

INDEX TO STUDY CLUBS 485

Palmyra, see Clio club, Palmyra.
Phases of character and passion in modern fiction, outline of study, 392⁴-93².
Philadelphia association of working girls societies, 306⁹.
Phoenix, see Shakespeare club, Phoenix.
Photographs, loans and exchanges, 263⁷-64¹.
Physics, syllabus on forces of nature, 881².
Political study, report of the New York society, 856¹; statistics, 466-69.
Politics, Comparative politics, syllabus, 881⁷; Political methods, syllabus, 881⁵.
Portville, see Caledonian club.
Potsdam, see Fortnightly club, Potsdam.
Pratt, F.. B., report of Fredonia society for the study of art, 861¹.
Price, T: R., English drama, syllabus, 879.⁹
Pupils of the holy see, 272⁵-73⁴

Rathbone, G. W., report of Oakfield study club, 321⁵.
Reading circles, plan of work, 259⁸-60¹, reports, 268⁴-90³, Antiquity, 271³. See also Study clubs
Rees, J: K, Popular astronomy, syllabus, 378⁸.
Refreshments at club meetings, 264⁶, 359⁵.
Registered study clubs of New York, reports, 307-70.
Registration, certificates, 260⁸-61¹, requirements, 261²-62⁴.
Rhodes, Mrs C. O.. report of Columbian club, 353⁵-54⁵.
Rochester, see Judean club; Ladies Scottish club, Study clubs, statistics. Woman's ethical club.
Roman history, outline of study, 399¹-408², Ancient Roman life, syllabus, 380⁶; Private life of the Romans, syllabus, 381⁴.
Rome, see Wednesday morning current topic club.
Romeo and Juliet and The tempest, syllabus by Mrs J. K. Curtis, 381⁹

Ross, E: A., Present day economic reforms, syllabus, 379⁵.
Round Robin reading club, report, 285²-87³
Round Robin reading club, Oxford, report, 338²-39⁵, statistics, 466-69.
St Louis, see Eliot society of Church of the Messiah, Study clubs, statistics.
St Paul's Sunday school library, 269⁶-70⁷.
Salamanca salmagundi society, report, 368⁶; outline of study, 439⁵-44⁶; statistics, 470-73
Salamanca, see also Study clubs, statistics.
Saratoga, see Travelers-at-home club.
Saturday class, Buffalo, report, 331³-32⁶, outlines of study, 395³-96⁶, 430⁴-32¹, 444³-45⁶, 450⁵-51², statistics, 458-61.
Saturday club, constitution, 266⁴-67⁸.
Saturday club, Lockport, report, 359²-60⁸; statistics, 462-65.
Saturday club, Schuylerville, report, 327²-28⁴, statistics, 470-73
Schenectady, see Society to promote useful reading.
Schuylerville, see Saturday club, Schuylerville
Scotland, outline of study, 412⁶-15⁴. See also Great Britain.
Scott, W. B., Geology, syllabus, 881¹.
Sculpture, outline of study, 385³-87⁶.
Sears, Mrs F G, The making of France, syllabus, 380⁹.
Seligsberg, L W, report of Society for the study of child nature, 317²-21⁵.
Shakespeare club, Phoenix, report, 341¹, statistics, 466-69.
Shakspere, lectures by Mrs J. K. Curtis on, 382⁶; outline of study, 387³-92³; syllabuses; on Hamlet and Merchant of Venice, 380⁶; on Julius Caesar, 382⁵, on Macbeth and King Lear, 379⁷; on Romeo and Juliet and The tempest, 381⁹.
Shakspere club, Fredonia, report, 361⁶; outlines of study, 387³-92³; statistics, 462-65
Shakspere university extension club, Syracuse, report, 313⁸-14⁵, statistics, 470-73.

Shipman, Mrs A. J., report of Clio club, 358².
Smith, G: W:, Practical economic questions, syllabus, 380⁷; Early American history, syllabus, 381²; American colonial history, syllabus, 382³.
Social science club, 294⁵.
Social settlement clubs, reports, 290⁴-302⁵. *See also* Working girls clubs
Society for political study, New York, report, 356¹; statistics, 466–69.
Society for the study of art, Fredonia, report, 361¹; statistics, 462–65.
Society for the study of child nature, New York, report, 317²-21³, 388⁴; statistics, 466-69.
Society to encourage studies at home, report, 274²-76⁵; methods, 275⁵-76⁵.
Society to promote useful reading, Schenectady, report, 315⁵-16²; outline of study, 410¹-12⁵; statistics, 470–78.
Spain, outline of study, 450⁵-51².
Spence, A. M., Critical study of authors of to-day, syllabus, 379⁵.
Statistics, of study clubs in New York, 458–78; of study clubs outside of New York, 474–77.
Steele, Mrs W. F., report of Monday afternoon study club, 307³-8⁴.
Stockton, Louise, founder of Round Robin reading club, 388²-89²; report on Round Robin reading club, 285²-87².
Stowell, Mrs M.. B, report of Fortnightly club, 388⁴-89³.
Study, outlines of, 388–457.
Study club, Oakfield, report, 321⁵; outline of study, 437²-39⁵, statistics, 466–69
Study club division, distinctive work, 259³-61², 267⁸-68⁹.
Study clubs, administrative organizations aiding, 268–90, assistance from extension department, 260¹, 262⁵, 267⁸-68⁹; assistance from Society to encourage study at home, 274⁵-75², constitutions, 264²-68²; course vs single lecture, 261²; executive board, 265⁵, 266⁶; membership, 265³, 267¹; meetings, 265²-66¹, 267⁴; officers, 265³, 266⁵; simplicity of organization, 264⁴; outline of work, 259²; rank by extent of work, 260⁶; certificates of registration, 260²-61¹; requirements for registration, 261²-62⁴; reports of registered clubs, 307–70; reports of clubs not registered, 371–78; statistics, 458–77. *See also* Current topics clubs; Home culture clubs.
Subjects, advantages of continuous study, 261²; unrelated, 261⁵. *See also* Outlines of study; Study clubs, statistics; Syllabuses.
Sunday school library at St Paul's, 269⁹-70⁷.
Syllabuses, 262⁶; lists with prices, 378–82.
Syracuse, *see* Azarias reading circle; Shakspere university extension club; Study clubs, statistics; Wednesday club, Syracuse.
Systematic study, advantage of, 261⁹.

Taylor, S. W., report of Froebel society, 371²-74²
Teachers international reading circle, report, 278⁴-74¹.
Ticknor, A. E., report on Society to encourage home study, 274²-76⁵.
Training class of the Buffalo free kindergarten association, report, 314³-15²; statistics, 458–61.
Trapp, M E., report of Shakspere university extension club, 318⁸-14⁸.
Travelers-at-home club, Saratoga, report, 312²-13⁸; statistics, 470–78.
Travelers club, Middletown, report, 321³-22⁵; statistics, 466–69.
Travelers club, Olean, report, 344²-45²; outline of study, 393²-95²; statistics, 466–69
Travelers clubs. *See also* England; Saturday club, Schuylerville; University extension study club, Ogdensburg.
Traveling libraries, loans to study clubs, 262⁶-63⁷.
Trinity Methodist church reading club, Albany, 324⁶; statistics, 458–61.

Troy, see East side study class; Method class.

Truax, J. R., Studies in English literature, syllabus, 380⁹.

Turk, M. H., Introduction to the study of English literature, syllabus, 379⁶.

United States, outline of study, 454⁷-57; history; outline of study, 451⁴-54⁷;
syllabuses; on American history, 882³; on Civil and religious liberty in America, 880⁵; on Development of the nation, 881³; on Discovery of America, 880²; on Early American history, 881⁸; on Colonial history, 379¹, 882², on American revolution, 878⁶; on The civil war, 882². See also American constitution.

Unity club, Albany, report, 852⁶-53¹; statistics, 458-61.

Unity clubs, National bureau of; outlines of study, 388⁶.

University extension study club, Ogdensburg, report, 324²-26³; outlines of study, 896⁷-97⁴, 424³-26³; statistics, 466-69.

University extension, see also Extension.

University settlement society, New York, report, 296⁹-97⁴.

Utica, see New century club; Study clubs, statistics.

Wakeman, E. L., report of Society for political study, 856¹.

Warren, H: P., Colonial history of America, syllabus, 879¹.

Warsaw, see Monday club, Warsaw; Study clubs, statistics

Waterman, H. B., Nations of the orient, syllabus, 881⁶.

Watertown, see Study clubs, statistics; Wednesday morning art class.

Waterville, see Every Saturday night club.

Weatherly, U. G., Comparative politics, syllabus, 881⁷.

Webster free circulating library, 297⁵.

Wednesday club, Syracuse, report, 814⁵; outline of study, 426²-28³; statistics, 470-73.

Wednesday morning art class, Watertown, report, 841⁹-42⁵; statistics, 470-73.

Wednesday morning current topic club, Rome, report, 308⁷-9⁵; statistics, 466-69.

Weiss, E: A., report of East side literary society, 842³-43⁹.

Westchester woman's club, Mt Vernon, report, 829²-81¹; statistics, 466-69.

Westfield, see Monday evening club, Westfield.

Wey, Mrs F. B., report of Catskill Monday club, 869⁹.

Whittier house, Jersey City, report, 299⁵-300⁵.

Wickes, W: K., American history, syllabus, 382³.

Wilmes, Joseph, report of Azarias reading circle, 889¹-40⁶.

Winchell, S. R., manager of National young folks reading circle, 287⁹.

Woman's club, Oneonta, report, 827¹; statistics, 466-69.

Woman's ethical club, Rochester, outline of study, 884¹-85³; statistics, 466-69.

Woman's institute, Yonkers, report of the Civic league, 354²-55²; statistics, 470-73.

Women's literary club, Dunkirk, report, 850⁹-52⁶; outlines of study, 432³-37³; statistics, 462-65.

Woodberry, G:E., English drama, syllabus, 379⁸.

Worcester, see Fortnightly club; Study clubs, statistics.

Worden, Dora, report of Ladies literary club, 868³-69².

Working girls clubs, report, 302⁵-7⁷.

Wright, E. R., report of Every Saturday night club, 329⁴.

Yonkers, Woman's institute, see Woman's institute, Yonkers.

Zoology, syllabus by G: H: Hudson, 880¹.

University of the State of New York

Object. The object of the University as defined by law is to encourage and promote education in advance of the common elementary branches. Its field includes not only the work of academies, colleges, universities, professional and technical schools but also educational work connected with libraries, museums, university extension courses and similar agencies.

The University is a supervisory and administrative, not a teaching institution. It is a state department and at the same time a federation of more than 500 institutions of higher and secondary education.

Government. The University is governed and all its corporate powers exercised by 19 elective regents and by the governor, lieutenant-governor, secretary of state and superintendent of public instruction who are *ex officio* regents. Regents are elected in the same manner as United States senators; they are unsalaried and are the only public officers in New York chosen for life.

The elective officers are a chancellor and a vice-chancellor who serve without salary, and a secretary.

The secretary, under official bonds for $10,000, is responsible for the safe keeping and proper use of the University seal and of the books, records and other property in charge of the regents, and for the proper administration and discipline of its various offices and departments.

Powers and duties. Beside many other important powers and duties, the regents have power to incorporate, and to alter or revoke the charters of universities, colleges, academies, libraries, museums, or other educational institutions; to distribute to them funds granted by the state for their use; to inspect their workings and require annual reports under oath of their presiding officers; to establish examinations as to attainments in learning and confer on successful candidates suitable certificates, diplomas and degrees, and to confer honorary degrees.

They apportion annually an academic fund of $106,000, part for buying books and apparatus for academies and high schools raising an equal amount for the same purpose, and the remainder on the basis of attendance and the results of instruction as shown by satisfactory completion of prescribed courses for which the regents examinations afford the official test. They also expend annually $25,000 for the benefit of free public libraries.

Regents meetings. Regular quarterly meetings are held on the fourth Thursdays of November, February and May. Special meetings are held whenever business requires.

Convocation. The University convocation of the regents and the officers of institutions in the University, for consideration of subjects of mutual interest, has been held annually since 1863 in the senate chamber in Albany. Convocation meets on the last Wednesday, Thursday and Friday in June.

Though primarily a New York meeting, nearly all questions discussed are of equal interest outside the state. Its reputation as the most important higher educational meeting of the country has in the past few years drawn to it many eminent educators not residents of New York, who are most cordially welcomed and share fully in all discussions. It elects each year a council of five to represent it in intervals between meetings. Its proceedings issued annually are of great value in all educational libraries.

University of the State of New York

Departments

1 Administrative (Regents office) — including incorporation, supervision, inspection, reports, legislation, finances and all other work not assigned to another department.

Duplicate division. This is a state clearing house, to which any institution in the University may send books or apparatus which it no longer requires and select from it in return an equal value suited to its locality and needs.

2 Examination — including preacademic, law student, medical, dental and veterinary student, academic, higher, law, medical, dental, veterinary, library, extension and any other examinations conducted by the regents, and also credentials or degrees conferred on examination.

The examinations are conducted as the best lever for securing better work from teachers and more systematic and continuous study from students, and as the best means of detecting and eliminating inefficient teachers or methods. They cover 130 subjects and require 1,500,000 question papers annually, and are held the week ending the last Friday in January and March and the third Friday in June, in the 502 academies and high schools in the University and also at various central points where there are 10 or more candidates.

3 Extension — including summer, vacation, evening and correspondence schools and other forms of extension teaching, lecture courses, study clubs, reading circles and other agencies for the promotion and wider extension of opportunities and facilities for education, specially for those unable to attend the usual teaching institutions.

Public libraries division. To promote the general library interests of the state, which through it expends $25,000 a year for the benefit of free public libraries. Under its charge are the traveling libraries for lending to local libraries or to communities not yet having permanent libraries.

The most important factor of the extension movement is provision of the best reading for all citizens by means of traveling, home and capitol libraries and annotated lists through the public libraries division.

4 State library — including state law, medical, and education libraries, library school, bibliographic publications, lending books to students and similar library interests.

Library school. The law authorizes the state library to give to any librarian, assistant, or other person interested in any library in the state, instruction and assistance in organizing and administering libraries. Students receive from the state library staff, in return for services rendered to the library during their two years' course, careful training in cataloging, classification and all other duties of professional librarianship.

5 State museum — including all scientific specimens and collections, works of art, objects of historic interest and similar property appropriate to a general museum, if owned by the state and not placed in other custody by a specific law; also the research department carried on by the state geologist and paleontologist, botanist and entomologist, and all similar scientific interests of the University.

University of the State of New York

Extension Bulletin

No. 12   October 1895

REPORT OF

EXTENSION DEPARTMENT, 1894

	PAGE		PAGE
Public libraries division	8	Lecturers added	27
Statistics	8	Names withdrawn	36
Inspection	8	Courses withdrawn	37
Organization of new libraries	5	Biblical study	87
Libraries chartered during the year	7	University extension in the colleges	38
Public libraries under state supervision	8	University extension conferences	40
Apportionment of public library money	8	Sociologic courses	41
		Libraries and university extension	43
Traveling libraries	9		
Rules	10	Summer school division	44
Use	18	Study club division	45
Summary of use	18	Institutes	48
Extension teaching division	19	Extension exhibit	52
Regents centers	19	Publications	52
Statistics	21	Use of printed matter outside the state	55
Students clubs for regents centers	25	University extension literature	55
Extension teachers	27	Index	65

ALBANY

UNIVERSITY OF THE STATE OF NEW YORK

1895

E25m-O95-2000   Price 10 cents

Regents

ANSON JUDD UPSON, D. D., LL. D., L. H. D., *Chancellor*
WILLIAM CROSWELL DOANE, D. D., LL. D., *Vice-Chancellor*
LEVI P. MORTON, LL. D., Governor ⎫
CHARLES T. SAXTON, LL. D., Lieutenant-Governor ⎬ *Ex officio*
JOHN PALMER, Secretary of State ⎮
CHARLES R. SKINNER, M. A., LL. D., Sup't of Pub. Inst. ⎭

In order of election by the legislature

YEAR
1873 MARTIN I. TOWNSEND, M. A., LL. D. - - Troy
1874 ANSON JUDD UPSON, D. D., LL. D., L. H. D. - Glens Falls
1876 WILLIAM L. BOSTWICK, M. A. - - - Ithaca
1877 CHAUNCEY M. DEPEW, LL. D. - - - - New York
1877 CHARLES E. FITCH, LL. B., M. A., L. H. D. - Rochester
1877 ORRIS H. WARREN, D. D. - - - - - Syracuse
1878 WHITELAW REID, LL. D. - - - - New York
1881 WILLIAM H. WATSON, M. A., M. D. - - - Utica
1881 HENRY E. TURNER - - - - - Lowville
1883 ST CLAIR MCKELWAY, LL. D. - - - - Brooklyn
1885 HAMILTON HARRIS, LL. D. - - - - Albany
1885 DANIEL BEACH, Ph. D., LL. D. - - - - Watkins
1888 CARROLL E. SMITH - - - - - Syracuse
1890 PLINY T. SEXTON, LL. D. - - - - - Palmyra
1890 T. GUILFORD SMITH, M. A., C. E. - - - Buffalo
1892 WILLIAM CROSWELL DOANE, D. D., LL. D. - Albany
1893 LEWIS A. STIMSON, B. A., M. D. - - - New York
1894 SYLVESTER MALONE - - - - - Brooklyn
1895 ALBERT VANDER VEER, M. D., Ph. D. - - Albany

Elected by the regents

1888 MELVIL DEWEY, M. A., *Secretary* - - Albany

University of the State of New York

Extension Bulletin

No. 12   October, 1895

REPORT OF EXTENSION DEPARTMENT
FOR THE YEAR ENDING SEPTEMBER 30, 1894

PUBLIC LIBRARIES DIVISION

Statistics. Blanks were sent to 1015 libraries in the state to obtain reports for the year ending 30 June 1894. From the returns 704 were found to contain 300 or more volumes each and these reports are published in the bulletin of statistics of New York libraries. Many of those addressed were found to have no real existence as libraries. Many failed to report, even after repeated application. These returns will be made as much more complete and satisfactory in the future as the material supplied by the libraries allows.

Inspection. From Oct. 1, 1893, to Sept. 30, 1894, the inspector, William R. Eastman, visited 62 libraries in 27 different counties. When called to make official inspection and consult with trustees and others respecting the establishment and development of libraries, he improved the opportunity to call on other libraries in the immediate neighborhood though not connected with the University. In several instances these visits have resulted in renewed library interest and subsequent relations to the University. The following are the libraries visited:

- [a] Auburn, Seymour library
- [a] Bath, Davenport free library
- Boonville, Erwin library
- [a] Brooklyn, Eastern district library

---

[a] Not connected with the University.

Brooklyn, Pratt institute library
a Brooklyn, Union for Christian work library
Camden library
Claverack free library
Corinth union school library
Dansville public library
Dansville union school library
Dolgeville academy library
a Dolgeville union school library
Fort Hamilton free library
Fort Plain free library
Gilbertsville free library
a Great Neck library
a Great Neck union school library
Jamestown high school library
Jamestown, James Prendergast free library
a Keene Heights library club
Keene Valley public library
Lake Placid public library
Liberty circulating library
Liberty public library
Little Falls union school library
a Matteawan, Howland circulating library
Mohawk public library
Nassau free library
New York, Bryson library, Teachers college
a New York, Maimonides library
a New York, Peck memorial library
a New York, Riverside association library
New York, St Agnes free library
a New York, Washington Heights free library
New York, Webster free library
New York, Y. W. C. A. library
North Tonawanda public library
Nyack library
Oneida union school library
Oyster Bay peoples library
a Oyster Bay union school library

---

a Not connected with the University.

- [a] Peekskill, Field library
- Philmont public library
- Pocantico Hills lyceum
- Poughkeepsie library
- Rockville Center public library
- Rome, Y. M. C. A. library
- [a] Saranac Lake, Adirondack library
- Saugerties public library
- Schuylerville public library
- Sidney union school library
- Springville public library
- [a] Tarrytown lyceum library
- Tarrytown union school library
- Tivoli public library
- Tonawanda public library
- Troy, Young women's association library
- [a] Wappinger's Falls, Grinnell library
- [a] Watkins library
- Wellsville public library
- Yonkers women's institute

Organization of new libraries. Three libraries already incorporated under general laws, two others chartered under special acts of the legislature and one incorporated institute containing a free library were admitted to the University. 12 absolute and 14 provisional library charters were granted by the regents. Of these 26,

- 10 were established by school authorities
- 3 by school districts
- 3 by village trustees
- 2 by common councils of cities
- 5 by library associations
- 1 by private gift
- 1 by a public meeting of citizens
- 1 by the rector of a church

These new organizations involved the transfer of 13 existing school district libraries, containing 36,400 volumes. In five cases there was no previously existing library.

---

[a] Not connected with the University.

Of these 26 libraries, trustees are chosen for
- 8 by the local board of education
- 4 by the voters of school districts
- 2 by mayors of cities with the consent of the common council
- 2 by village trustees
- 7 by the library trustees themselves
- 2 by contributors of $1 each during the preceding year

and for 1 the managers of another library are trustees.

Adding to these the libraries previously chartered by the regents we have a total of 53 libraries, of which
- 25 were established by school authorities
- 6 by school districts
- 5 by village trustees
- 3 by common councils of cities
- 10 by library associations
- 2 by private gift
- 1 by public meeting of citizens
- 1 by the rector of a church

Trustees are chosen for
- 13 by the local board of education
- 17 by the voters of the school districts
- 2 by mayors of cities
- 2 by village trustees
- 2 by the voters of a village
- 12 by the library trustees themselves
- 3 by contributors of $1 each
- 1 by an individual benefactor

and for 1 the managers of another library are trustees.

In three cases *ex officio* trustees have been added to those appointed as above.

The number of trustees for a library varies greatly. Out of 53 libraries
- 16 have 3 trustees each
- 21 " 5 "
- 3 " 6 "
- 5 " 7 "
- 1 has 8 trustees
- 3 have 9 trustees each

1 has 10 trustees
1 " 12 "
1 " 13 "
1 " 17 "

Libraries and institute chartered, admitted and registered during the year ending September 30, 1894

Post-office	Libraries	Vols.	Property
1 Arkport	Arkport public library *p*		$200
2 Dansville	Dansville public library	2,450	1,500
3 Fort Hamilton	Fort Hamilton free library	900	1,100
4 Fort Plain	Fort Plain free library	862	800
5 Glen Haven	Glen Haven public library *p*		80
6 Havana	Havana free library *p*	600	418
7 Ilion	Ilion district library	155	1,050
8 Joshua's Rock	Mountainside free library *p*		80
9 Keene Valley	Keene Valley public library *p*	400	519
10 Lake Placid	Lake Placid public library	1,000	1,650
11 Liberty	Liberty public library *p*	275	400
12 Madalin	Tivoli public library *p*	100	140
13 Mohawk	Mohawk public library *p*	619	675
14 Morristown	Morristown free library *p*		60
15 New York	St Agnes free library	972	1,350
16 North Tonawanda	North Tonawanda public library	1 250	1,300
17 Ogdensburg	Ogdensburg public library	3,000	8,500
18 Philmont	Philmont public library *p*	452	407
19 Plattsburg	Plattsburg public library *p*		200
20 Port Henry	Sherman free library	4,200	19,545
21 Rockville Center	Rockville Center public library *p*	500	500
22 Saugerties	Saugerties public library	1,000	800
23 Springville	Springville public library *p*	1,825	{ 800 *a*750
24 Syracuse	Syracuse central library	26,000	40,000
25 Tonawanda	Tonawanda public library	900	1,000
26 Wellsville	Wellsville public library *p*	900	665
	Total	48,860	$79,489
Admitted with existing charters			
1 Boonville	Erwin library and institute	1,858	*$34,575
2 Buffalo	Grosvenor public library	37,000	254,540
3 Claverack	Claverack free library and reading room	710	4,217
4 Jamestown	James Prendergast library association	8,847	201,800
5 Nyack	Nyack library	3,000	4,700
6 Yonkers	Women's institute of Yonkers	2,000	50,000
	Total	53,415	$549,832
Registered			
1 New York	Y. W. C. A. library	22,000	$15,000
33	Grand total	123,775	$644,271

p Provisional charter   *a Held in trust.*

The total number of volumes in charge of the public libraries division Sept. 30, 1894 was 14,121, distributed as follows:

General libraries

No.						
1	100 v.		5 sets contain	500 v.
2	" "		5 " "	500
3	" "		5 " "	500
4	" "		2 " "	200
5	" "		5 " "	500
6	" "		5 " "	500
7	" "		5 " "	500
8	" "		2 " "	200
9	" "		2 " "	200
10	" "		8 " "	800
11	50 "		10 " "	500
12	" "		10 " "	500
13	" "		10 " "	500
14	" "		10 " "	500
15	" "		10 " "	500
16	102 "		5 " "	510
17	50 "		5 " "	250
18	" "		5 " "	250

General libraries, 109 sets contain   7,910 v.

Subject libraries

Economics	subj. no. 880	25 v.	5 sets contain 125 v.
"	" " 880	50 "	5 " " 250 "
Agriculture	" " 680	33 "	5 " " 165 "
"	" " 680	60 "	5 " " 300 "
In literature	" " 800	57 "	10 " " 570 "
In Amer. liter.	" " 820	26 "	5 " " 180 "
French history	" " 944	45 "	3 " " 135 "
U. S. history	" " 978	20 "	4 " " 80 "
"	" " 978	43 "	6 " " 258 "

Subject libraries, 48 sets contain   2,013 v.
For extension purposes and for lending to institutions in the University   4,198 v.

Total   14,121 v.

Rules. The rules for the loan of these libraries have been revised and are now as follows:

Rules for the loan of libraries

1 On satisfactory guarantee that all regents rules will be complied with, a traveling library may be lent to any public library under visitation of the regents on application of its trustees.

2 Under like conditions a traveling library may be lent to a community on application of 25 resident taxpayers or of the officers of an extension center, club, course or circle, if registered by the regents; provided that the applicants also agree that as soon as public interest will warrant such action, they will take steps to establish a free public library as provided in laws of 1892, ch. 378, § 36. The applicants shall name a responsible owner of real estate, to act as trustee of said library and he must become personally responsible for any loss or injury beyond reasonable

wear. This trustee shall designate a suitable person to be librarian

3 A fee of $5 for 100 or $3 for 50 volumes shall be paid in advance for suitable cases, printed catalogs, necessary blanks and records, and transportation both ways If the right to borrow books is to be limited to members of a center or club, a double fee must be paid, i. e only 50 volumes for $5 or 25 for $3 will be sent.

4 Such precaution shall be taken in packing as to guard effectively against injury in transportation.

5 Notes, corrections of the press, or marks of any kind on books belonging to the library are unconditionally forbidden. Borrowing trustees will be held responsible for all losses or injuries beyond reasonable wear, however caused.

6 The traveling library shall not be kept longer than six months after its reception, except by special permission. It may be exchanged for another on the same terms and these exchanges may continue as long as the regents rules are observed.

7 The librarian shall care for the books while under his control and circulate them in accordance with the regents rules, and shall make such reports respecting their use as the regents may require

8 For wilful violation of any library rule the director of the state library may suspend the privilege of state loans till the case is considered by the regents committee.

Annotated lists of libraries will be sent on request, and inquiries for information or advice will be promptly answered if directed to Public libraries department, State Library, Albany, N. Y.

MELVIL DEWEY, *Director*

An extension of the privilege was authorized by the regents June 5, 1894, as shown by the following extract from their minutes.

Lending traveling libraries. § 14 and 47 of the University law authorize the regents to lend books under such rules as they may think expedient. During the summer many villages return their traveling libraries and wait till fall to order new ones. This leaves idle for two or three months several thousand volumes carefully selected as best adapted to advancing that form of education in charge of the extension department. On February 9, 1893, the regents authorized the loan of these books to any reading circle, club or other organization registered and under inspection; and such organizations have properly first claim. Books not required by them, however, might in some cases be doing excellent work, if lent to responsible persons who would in turn be willing to supervise their circulation and pay a fee sufficient to cover expenses and the wear of the books.

Voted, That by permission of the secretary traveling libraries may be lent to persons making a deposit to cover their value or furnishing satisfactory guarantee of responsibility and paying such fee as shall be found necessary to cover loss and injuries, provided that no fee shall be charged for the use of the books, that such loans shall not be made when they would interfere with the claims of libraries or other registered organizations of the University, and that preference shall be given to applicants who will make them most valuable educationally.

The following rules were prepared for carrying out this action:

Traveling libraries, not required for immediate use to meet applications under rules 1 and 2 for lending, may be lent on approval of the director for free use in any part of the state on the following terms.

1 The borrower shall guarantee the safe return of the books either by furnishing a satisfactory indorsement with his application or by making a deposit of $100 for 100 volumes, or $50 for 50, to be refunded on their return.

2 The borrower shall pay the usual fee of $5 for 100 volumes or $3 for 50, or $2 a month for 100 volumes or $1 a month for 50.

3 The borrower shall pay transportation both ways.

4 The usual supply of catalogs, cards and cases will be furnished.

5 The usual rules for circulation as printed in the catalogs need not be observed; but no charge shall be made for the use of books.

6 After three months any such library shall be returned to the state library on two weeks notice that it is wanted for use elsewhere.

The following circular was issued:

FREE TRAVELING LIBRARIES
Choice reading for the summer months

By recent action of the regents of the University of the State of New York, traveling libraries of 100 volumes each are offered to responsible borrowers for a limited time at the cost of transportation and the trifling fee of $2 a month or $5 for the season. The books are carefully selected from recent publications, are fresh and popular in character and cover the various classes of literature. One hundred of these libraries have been in use the past year in different parts of the state and the demand is steadily growing.

Such a library for the free use of guests is a very attractive feature in any summer resort. The small fee may be paid either by the proprietor or by some of the more permanent guests. If this notice is posted, those interested in having the very best reading available for rainy days and evenings, are sure to find a way for meeting the trifling expense.

Application blanks, explanatory circulars and sample annotated catalogs of the libraries available may be had free from the Public libraries department, State library, Albany, N. Y.

MELVIL DEWEY
Director

Use. During the year 102 libraries have been lent.

46 were sent to 34 public libraries, including those of 10 regents academies.

35 "   "   27 groups of taxpayers
19 "   "   15 University extension centers
2 "   "   2 other borrowers under new rule
___
102 "   "   78 places

Three places, Havana, Plattsburg and Wellsville, in which libraries were first obtained by petition of taxpayers, now have chartered public libraries

Of the 18 general libraries, 109 sets were provided. In 20 months, from February, 1893, when the first library was lent, there have been 58 libraries used once,   for 58 issues

22 "   "   twice,   " 44   "
6 "   "   three times, " 18   "
___   ___
86 "   "   for   120 "

These 120 issues carried out 9750 volumes. 100 of these with 8350 volumes have come back without loss. The six months circulation of 100 volumes has varied from 66 to 609, with an average of 275. The total circulation was 23,951, of which 12,646 were fiction. The readers were 7111, an average of about 3⅓ books to each reader. The highest average in one place was 7.1 books to a reader. The largest circulation of single books in one place was as follows

Plympton.	Little sister of Wilfred	25 readers
Stoddard.	On the old frontier	25 "
King.	Between the lines	24 "
Munroe.	Campmates	23 '
Tourgée.	A son of old Harry	22 '
Wilkins.	Jane Field	21 '
———	Pot of gold	' 20 '
Johnson.	Country school	20 ··

Of the nine subject libraries, 48 sets were provided. 26 had been sent out previous to Oct. 1, 1894, and 17 returned with 566 volumes. These show a circulation of 413 with 132 readers Some of these were used by study clubs and in connection with University extension lectures under circumstances in which no satisfactory statistics of use could be secured.

Of the 19 libraries sent to extension centers, and the two sent to individual borrowers no returns of use have been made.

A further account of the traveling library system and its working will be found in an article prepared by the inspector, and printed in the *Forum* for January, 1895.

Details are shown in the following tables:

Traveling libraries sent Oct 1, 1893—Sept. 30, 1894 to

Free libraries		25 taxpayers		Extension centers, etc.	
Addison		Adams Center		Attica	
Albany	2 libs	Amityville		Chautauqua	2 libs.
Andover		Aquebogue		Dobbs Ferry	
Ballston		Charlton	2 libs	Little Falls	
Canajoharie	2 "	Clinton		Lockport	
Canandaigua		Fort Hill		Mount Vernon	
De Ruyter		Glen		New York, Columbia coll.	
Ellenville	2 "	Glendale		Oneida	
Fort Plain	2 "	Hannibal	2 "	Owego	
Jamestown		Harkness		Rome	
Joshua's Rock		Havana		Salem	
Keene Valley	2 "	Hoosick		Tarrytown	
Lake Placid		Jefferson		Utica	2 libs.
Lansingburg	2 "	Melrose	2 "	Waverly	2 "
Liberty		Meriden		Yonkers	2 "
Liverpool		Monticello			
Lowville	2 "	Pattersonville			
Madison		Peru	2 "	19	
Morristown	2 "	Philadelphia			
Nassau	2 "	Plattsburg	4 "		
New Rochelle		Prince's Bay			
No. G'nbush dist 6,	2 "	Prohibition Park	2 "		
North Tonawanda	2 "	Reed's Corners		To individuals	
Ogdensburg	2 "	Rensselaerville			
Pocantico Hills		Riga			
Pompey		Sodus			
Rome		Wellsville		in Buffalo	
Schuylerville				in Lewiston	
Spencer					
Tonawanda					
Trumansburg				2	
Utica					
Waverly					
Westport					
46		35		21	
				35	
				46	
				103	

The table which follows shows the use of each library since the first issue Feb. 8, 1893, including those given in the report of 1893.

Traveling libraries sent previous to October 1, 1894

Lib. no.	Place	Sent	Returned	How obtained	No. of readers	Circulation Total	Circulation Fiction	Average books per reader	Highest circulation of 1 book
1	Chariton	8 F 93	12 Ag 93	Pet	68	446	192	6.5	15
1	Canandaigua	17 Ag 93	19 F 94	Un sch	105	504	289	4.8	19
1	Riga	20 F 94	1 N 94	Pet	33	215	112	6.5	10
1a	Fort Plain	11 F 93	17 Ag 93	Pet	49	162	72	3.3	11
1a	DeRuyter	3 O 93	19 Mr 94	Un sch	62	364	230	5.8	14
1b	Glendale	13 O 93	10 Ap 94	Pet	24	117	45	4.8	8
1b	Hoosick	17 S 94	6 F 95	Pet	18	90	42	5	5
1c	Utica	1 N 93	17 My 94	Pub lib	86	201	113	2.3	8
1c	Morristown	24 S 94		Pub lib					
1d	Glen	20 N 93	22 O 94	Pet	48	166	80	3.5	9
					488	2228	1175	4.5	
2	Dundee	8 F 93	18 Jl 93	Un. sch.	29	99	55	2.5	8
2	Keene Valley	14 N 93	28 My 94	Pub lib.	55	165	89	3	11
2a	Canandaigua	11 F 93	12 Ag 93	Un. sch.	105	374	195	3.5	15
2a	Fort Plain	21 Ag 93	7 Mr 94	Pet	37	189	68	5.1	11
2b	Lowville	24 O 93	23 Je 94	Acad	46	249	130	5.4	12
2b	Melrose	21 Ag 94		Pet					
2c	Madison	6 N 93	23 My 94	Un sch	56	327	213	6.3	23
2d	Tonawanda	8 D 93	14 Je 94	Pub lib.	?41	113	69	2.7	8
					379	1546	819	4	
3	Onondaga Valley	21 F 93	28 Jl 93	Acad	60	156	82	3.2	7
3	Pompey	24 O 93	3 Ja 94	Un. sch.	76	290		3.8	
3a	Harkness	8 F 93	12 Ag 93	Pet	61	269	168	4.7	12
3a	Meriden	3 O 93	10 Ap 94	P.t	61	275	128	4.5	10
3a	Peru	24 Jl 94	11 Ja 95	Pet	56	200	130	3.5	8
3b	Philadelphia	6 D 93	18 Je 94	Pet	64	242	102	3.7	10
3c	Havana	31 O 93	18 My 94	Pet	166	609	317	3.6	24
3c	Hannibal	3 Jl 94	19 Ja 95	Pet	39	190	123	4.9	10
3d	Plattsburg	21 N 93	27 Mr 94	Pet	117	378	207	3.2	16
3d	Liberty	8 My 94	26 N 94	Pub lib.	92	239	151	2.6	10
					792	2688	1360	3.4	
4	Jordanville	17 Mr 93	22 S 93	Pet	91	339	127	3.7	14
4	Adams Center	20 O 93	16 Ap 94	Pet	30	91	47	3	8
4	New Rochelle	16 Jl 94	18 F 95	Pub. lib	64	143	110	2.2	13
4a	So Bethlehem	26 Ap 93	4 D 93	Pet	35	136	78	3.6	7
4a	Peru	2 Ja 94	11 Jl 94	Pet	107	490	260	4.6	19
					327	1199	652	3.6	
5	Port Jervis	27 F 93	21 S 93	Pub lib	28	66	55	2.3	8
5	Spencer	10 O 93	10 Ap 94	Un sch	71	243	140	4.3	14
5	Addison	11 My 94	29 O 94	Pub lib	35	81	53	2.3	8
5a	Albany F. L.	14 Jl 93	15 Ja 94	Pub lib	50	162	64	3.2	9
5a	Canandaigua	15 F 94	17 Ag 94	Un sch	101	476	167	4.7	15
5c	Rensselaerville	21 Mr 94	25 S 94	Pet	22	195	66	8.8	8
5d	Rome	18 S 94	8 Ap 95	Pub lib					
					307	1322	545	4.3	
6	Pompey	21 F 93	Ag 93	Un sch	75	208	93	2.7	11
6	Onondaga Valley	20 S 93	7 N 94	Acad	174	449	159	2.6	22
6a	Plattsburg	20 My 93	17 N 93	Pet	102	344	150	3.4	12
6a	Aquabogue	5 Ap 94	11 O 94	Pet	43	273	158	6.3	12
					394	1274	565	3.2	

r16   UNIVERSITY OF THE STATE OF NEW YORK

Traveling libraries sent previous to October 1, 1894 (*continued*)

Lib no.	Place	Sent	Returned	How obtained	No. of readers	Total	Fiction	Average books per reader	High at circulation of 1 book
7	Ballston	27 F 93	1 S 93	Pub lib	?115	301	152	2.6	14
7	Prohibition Park	10 Ja 94	26 Jl 94	Pet	39	156	65	4	8
7a	Trumansburg	31 O 93	2 Je 94	Pub lib	100	204	162	2	15
7b	Melrose	20 Ja 94	17 Ag 94	Pet	39	156	65	4	9
7b	Amityville	1 S 94	25 Mr 95	Pet					
7c	Albany	17 Ja 94	24 S 94	Pub. lib	109	310	134	3	15
7d	Nassau	29 My 94	29 D 94	Pub lib	64	295	185	4 6	12
					466	1422	714	3	
8	Spencer	6 Ap 93	20 O 93	Un sch.	no cds	159	82	2 2	7
8	Chariton	18 O 93	10 Ap 94	Pet	42	3.1	172	7.1	16
8	Prince's Bay	24 My 94	29 O 94	Pet	59	378	200	5.4	14
8a	Canajoharie	12 O 93	18 Mr 94	Pet	15	22	8	1 5	8
8a	Harkness	17 O 93	20 Ap 94	Pet	?15	137	91	4 1	12
					149	1025	553	5.7	
9	Havana	6 Ap 93	7 O 93	Pet	94	302	161	3 2	15
9	Hannibal	20 D 93	2 Jl 94	Pet	89	379	167	4.2	18
9a	Prohibition Park	27 Jl 94		Pet					
					183	681	328	3.7	
10	Lansingburg	13 F 93	Ag 93	Un sch.	85	379	196	4.5	16
10	Westport	17 Ag 93	21 F 94	Pub lib	129	458	280	3.5	17
10	Monticello	5 Ap 94	8 O 94	Pet	44	181	127	4 2	12
10a	Medina	21 F 93	Ag 93	Un sch.	?41	112	68	2.8	8
10a	Ellenville	26 Ag 93	28 F 94	Pub. lib.	135	348	164	3 8	17
10b	Plattsburg	28 Mr 94	4 S 94	Pet	?254	500	268	1.9	17
10c	Canaan	6 Je 93	26 D 93	Pub lib	75	288	197	8.8	14
10c	Morristown	20 F 94	20 S 94	Pub lib.	88	449	275	5 1	16
10d	No Greenbush	7 Jl 93	5 Ja 94	Pub. lib.	74	202	113	2.7	11
10d	Clinton	10 Ja 94	17 Ja 94	Pet	117	584	207	4 9	20
10e	Ogdensburg	20 D 93	27 Je 94	Pub lib	206	598	378	2 8	25
10f	Liverpool	20 D 93	30 Je 94	Pub lib	46	209	122	4.5	12
10g	No Tonawanda	8 Ja 94	11 Jl 94	Pub lib	90	383	212	4 2	15
					1339	4704	2709	3.4	
11	Lansingburg	19 O 93	23 Ap 94	Acad	59	216	66	3.6	12
11	Lowville	1 S 94		Acad					
11a	Harkness	17 O 93	20 Ap 94	Pet	36	92	65	2.5	10
11b	Wellsville	13 D 93	18 Ja 95	Pet		203	84		12
11c	Nassau	21 N 93	22 My 94	Pub lib	68	338	118	4.9	
11d	Fort Hill	4 Ja 94	17 Jl 94	Pet	30	125	65	4.2	11
11e	No Greenbush	18 Ja 94	23 Jl 94	Pub lib	38	86	31	2.2	7
11f	Jefferson	20 Ja 94	17 Ag 94	Pet	30	55	27	1 8	4
11g	Ballston	22 Ja 94	7 Ag 94	Pub lib	100	219	130	2 2	16
11h	Fort Plain	26 F 94	12 S 94	Pub lib	57	141	63	2 5	10
11i	Patersonville	3 F 94	19 Ja 95	Pet		123	70		14
					418	1395	730	3.3	
12	Plattsburg	14 F 94	31 Jl 94	Pet	?254	263	146	1	16
12a	No Greenbush	18 Ja 94	23 Jl 94	Pub lib	64	124	87	1 9	12
12b	Ballston	22 Ja 94	7 Ag 94	Pub lib	?125	246	164	1 9	21
12c	Fort Plain	26 F 94	12 S 94	Pub lib	72	168	105	2.3	14
12d	Ellenville	24 F 94	7 S 94	Pub lib	142	233	149	1.6	14
12e	Chariton	18 Ap 94	19 O 94	Pet	44	220	122	5	15
12f	Buffalo	12 Je 94	20 O 94	Person			56		8
12i	Lake Placid	11 Jl 94	25 Ja 95	Pub lib		148	81		12
					701	1402	886	2	
13	Canajoharie	26 Mr 94	2 O 94	Un sch.	48	143	69	2.9	12
13a	Sodus	4 My 94	28 N 94	Pet	84	34	162	8 8	18
13b	Jamstown	21 My 94		Pub lib					
13c	Ellenville	26 F 94	7 S 94	Pub lib	146	289	196	1.9	25
13c	Fort Plain	13 S 94		Pub lib					
13d	Westport	10 Mr 94	4 O 94	Pub lib	102	240	115	2.3	12
13e	Niagara Falls	15 Je 94	6 O 94	Person					

REPORT OF EXTENSION DEPARTMENT, 1894   r17

Traveling libraries sent previous to October 1, 1894 (*concluded*)

Lib. no.	Place	Sent	Returned	How obtained	No. of readers	CIRCULATION Total	Fiction	Average books per reader	Highest circulation of 1 book
13f	Schuylerville	2 Ag 94		Pub. lib					
13g	Pocantico Hills	30 Jl 94		Pub lib					
13h	Plattsburg	1 Ag 94	19 F 95	Pet					
13i	No Greenbush	28 Ag 94		Pub lib					
					380	986	473	2.6	
14	Charlton	13 Ap 94	19 O 94	Pet	41	191	115	4 8	15
14a	Jamestown	22 My 94		Pub. lib					
14b	Westport	10 Mr 94	4 O 94	Pub lib	100	233	136	2 3	12
14c	Sodus	4 My 94	28 N 94	Pet	78	312	163	4 2	17
14d	Niagara Falls	15 Je 94	6 O 94	Person					
14e	Lansingburg	6 Jl 94	21 Ja 95	Acad	83	242	1'0	2.9	15
14f	Lake Placid	11 Jl 94	25 Ja 95	Pub lib		161	83		11
14g	Schuylerville	2 Ag 94		Pub lib					
14h	Ogdensburg	13 Jl 94	25 Ja 95	Pub lib	174	309	156	1.7	20
14i	No. Greenbush	23 Ag 94		Pub lib					
					474	1447	753	3	
15	Lansingburg	6 Jl 94	21 Ja 95	Acad	84	293	100	3.5	15
15a	Buffalo	12 Je 94	10 O 94	Person			89		6
15b	Ogdensburg	13 Jl 94	15 Ja 95	Pub lib	178	339	185	1.9	18
15c	Ellenville	7 S 94	4 Ap 95	Pub lib					
15d	Fort Plain	12 S 94	1 Ap 95	Pub lib					
					262	632	384	2.4	
16	Joshua's Rock	9 Ag 94		Pub lib					
16a	Keene Valley	5 S 94		Pub lib					
16c	Albany	26 S 94	27 Mr 95	Pub lib					
18a	Ellenville	7 S 94	4 Ap 95	Pub lib					
3301	Chautauqua	2 Jl 94	29 Ag 94	U. X					
330k	Canajoharie	12 O 93	13 Mr 94	Pet	30	27		.9	9
330o	Lansingburg	19 O 93	23 Ap 93	Acad	15	23		1.5	7
330o	Rome	20 N 93	18 Mr 94	U X					
330p	Oneida	11 D 93	30 O 94	U. X					
					45	50		1.1	
630j	No Tonawanda	23 My 94		Pub lib		20		1.6	
630k	Jefferson	20 Ja 94	17 Ag 94	Pet	12	23		3 9	5
630o	Reed's Corners	5 s 94	17 Ag 94	Pet	6	46		5.1	3
630p	Fort Hill	4 Ja 94	17 Jl 94	Pet	9	45		8 2	6
630q	Nassau	21 N 93	22 My 94	Pub lib	14	50			5
630r	Pattersonville	3 F 94	19 Ja 95	Pet		2		1	7
630s	Canajoharie	26 Mr 94	2 O 94	Un sch	2				2
					43	186		4.3	
800i	Lowville	1 S 94		Acad					
800j	Andover	21 S 94		Acad					
800k	Waverly	29 S 94		Un sch					
800o	Waverly	29 S 94		Un sch					
810p	Waverly	19 S 94		Un sch					
944i	Wellsville	13 D 93	18 Ja 95	Pet		69			8
944j	Chautauqua	2 Jl 94	29 Ag 94	U X					
973j	Chautauqua	2 Jl 94	29 Ag 94	U. X					
973k	Canajoharie	12 O 93	13 Mr 93	Pet					
973k	Pocantico Hills	30 Jl 94		Pub lib					
973o	Pattersonville	3 F 94	19 Ja 95			73			
973p	Lansingburg	19 O 93	23 Ap 94	Acad	24	41		1.9	9
973q	Nassau	21 N 93	22 My 94	Pub lib	16	31		1 9	7
973r	Reed's Corners	5 F 94	17 Ag 94	Pet	4	7		1.7	4
					44	158		3.6	

Summary of use of traveling libraries to October 1, 1894, 20 months

GENERAL LIBRARIES

Library number	Sets	Sent	Ret'd	Circulation of volumes in 6 months					Readers
				Least	Largest	Average	Total	Fiction	
100 volume libraries 1...	5	10	9	90	504	247	2,228	1,175	488
2...	5	8	7	99	374	221	1,546	819	379
3...	5	10	10	186	609	269	2,688	1,360	792
4...	2	5	5	91	490	240	1,199	652	327
5...	5	7	6	66	476	220	1,322	545	307
6...	5	4	4	208	449	318	1,274	565	394
7...	5	7	6	156	310	237	1,422	714	466
8...	2	5	5	137	378	205	1,025	558	151
9...	2	8	2	302	379	340	681	328	183
10...	8	18	13	122	598	362	4,704	2,709	1,389
Total	44	72	67	66	609	270	18,089	9,420	4,876
50 volume libraries 11...	10	11	10	55	388	189	1,895	730	418
12...	10	8	8	124	268	175	1,402	886	701
13...	10	10	5	143	314	197	986	478	380
14...	10	10	7	161	312	207	1,447	758	474
15...	10	5	3	293	339	311	632	384	262
100 vol. 16...	5	8	.	..	.....	....	......	......	......
50 vol. 17...	5	..	.	..	.....	....	......	......	......
18...	5	1	.	..	.....	....	......	......	......
Total	65	48	33	55	339	177	5,862	3,226	2,235
Total of all	109	120	100	55	609	275	23,591	12,646	7,111

SUBJECT LIBRARIES

Library number	Vols	Sets	Sent	Ret'd	Circulation				Readers
					Least	Largest	Average	Total	
Economics
380......	25	5	3	3	...	28	......	......	15
380......	50	5	2	2	...	27	......	......	80
Agriculture
630......	33	5	5	5	2	50	33	166	31
630......	60	5	2	1	..	20	......	20	12
Literature
800......	57	10	8	..	....	.	..	..	......
American literature
820......	26	5	2	..	....	.....	......	......	......
French history
944......	45	2	2	..	.	69	......	69	......
U. S. history
973......	20	4	4	4	4	76	40	158	44
973......	43	6	3	2	....	......	......	......	......
	....	47	26	17	....	......	......	413	132

No statistics of the use of the University extension libraries have been kept.

EXTENSION TEACHING DIVISION

Regents centers. Though the financial stringency in New York as elsewhere has interfered with the work of some centers, yet the fact that so many courses were given with so large an attendance shows the local appreciation of the value of extension work. At a time when people must economize, the movements soonest affected will probably be those resting on mental and moral obligations. For this reason extension workers feared that the winter of 1893-94 would be disastrous for extension work. That their fears were not realized is proved by the comparative statistics shown below.

Comparative statistics

YEAR	No. of active centers	No. of courses	Total attendance at lectures	Total attendance at classes	% of total attendance at class	Total no. of papers written	No of examinations	ANSWER PAPERS Written	Accepted	% accepted	% of total attendance taking examination	% of class attendance taking examination	No. of bi-weekly courses
1892-93	25	34	33,670	13,190	29	2,532	21	157	141	90	.4	1	3
1893-94	20	31	50,489	22,591	45	1,270	13	106	94	89	.2	.5	4

During 1892-93 only five more centers were active and three more courses were given than in 1893-94. Of the 33 centers enrolled on the list, 13 failed to resume extension lectures, though this by no means indicates that extension work was abandoned. In Albion, for example, instead of the two courses hitherto maintained each year, the Columbian association was formed with about 250 members and a subscription of $5000. The association maintains a free reading room, library, gymnasium and evening and Saturday classes. For an outline of the work of the association see *Regents bulletin*, no. 27, p. 103-5. Of the 31 courses given during the year eight were on science (five of these on electricity), eight on literature, seven on American history, four on economics, two on Roman life and one each on French history and the English language.

Five new centers were formed during the year: Columbia college, Dobbs Ferry, Oneida, Utica and Waverly. Some members of the Syracuse Portfolio club united with other residents of Syracuse and formed the Syracuse center, to study the same subject (Shakspere), the Portfolio club dropping from the University lists.

The work of the Columbia college center was intended for electric workers and almost all members of the center were practical electricians. Each lecture was given by a noted specialist on the subject, but Mr W. H. Freedman, of Columbia, had charge of the class and paper work and managed the course. The same plan was followed by Yonkers in its electricity course, Prof. A. V. W. Jackson, of Columbia, the president of the center, taking charge of the class and paper work. The lecturers and subjects of the course in the Columbia college center were :

C. O. Mailloux, consulting electrical engineer, Batteries;

Louis Bell, Thomson-Houston electric co., Dynamos and motors, alternating;

S. S. Wheeler, president, Crocker-Wheeler electric co., Dynamos and motors, direct;

A. E. Kennelly, Edison laboratory, Newark, Electric measurements;

Prof F. B Crocker, Columbia college, Electric lighting;

T. C. Martin, editor *Electrical engineer*, Street railways;

Nikola Tesla,[a] Electric engineer and inventor, Power;

William Maver, jr, Telegraphy;

J J. Carty, Metropolitan telephone and telegraph co., Telephone;

William Maver, jr, Electric alarms and signals.

The lecturers and courses at Yonkers were:

Prof. William Hallock, Columbia college, Fundamental principles and measurements;

Prof. F. B. Crocker, Columbia college, Dynamos and motors;

Prof. W. L Robb, Trinity college, Hartford, Electric lighting;

Prof. M. I. Pupin, Columbia college, Alternating current phenomena;

J. J. Carty, Metropolitan telephone and telegraph co, Telephone and telegraph.

---

[a] Omitted because of lecturer's illness.

Statistics of regents centers 1894

Centers	SUBJECT	Lecturer	No of lectures	Lectures	Class	Study club	Total no. of papers written	Examined	Passed	Passed with honor
Albany	{ Electricity	A. F Onderdonk	10	146	26		57	9	8	4
	{ Some masterpieces of English literature	A. V. W Jackson	10	388	359		45	2	1	
Attica	American history	C: E. Fitch	10	74	46	35	4			
Batavia	American history	C: E. Fitch	10	121	20	7	5			
Binghamton	{ Economic legislation	J W. Jenks	5	a						
	{ French history	Mrs F . G. Sears	6	a						
Buffalo	Physical geology	H. L. Fairchild	5	190	100		3			
Columbia college	Various forces of nature as related to modern life	A. L Arey	10	83	34		45			3
Dobbs Ferry	Electricity	Specialists	10	231	62		116	20	18	9
Lockport	Some masterpieces of English literature	A. V. W. Jackson	10	184	81		50	8	8	
Medina	English literature	J. H. Gilmore	10	164	98		186	9	9	8
	American history	C E. Fitch	10	105						
Mount Vernon	{ English language	A. V. W. Jackson	10	121	115		34	6	5	:8
	{ English, Italian and Spanish literature	{ A V. W Jackson (4 lectures) C: S. Smith (7 lectures)	11	125	119					:2
Oneida	Current economic questions	G: W. Smith	9	334	180					
Owego	{ English literature	J H. Gilmore	10	275	50		42	7	6	:3
	{ Ancient Roman life	H: F. Burton	10	400			41	6	5	8
Rochester	{ Monetary science	G. M Forbes	10	250	260			8	4	4
	{ Electricity	Charles Forbes	10	327	240		75		:9	:9
	{ Electricity and related forms of energy	Charles Forbes	10	125	75					
	Development of the nation	W: H. Mace	13	321	252		885	20	19	11

a No report received.

Statistics of regents centers, 1894 (*continued*)

Centers	SUBJECT	Lecturer	No. of lectures	Lectures	Class	Study club	Total no. of papers written	Examined	Passed	Passed with honor
Rome	Current economic questions	G. W. Smith	10	164	68		50	5	5	3
Salem	Studies in English literature	J. R. Truax	10	58	22		95	5	5	4
Syracuse	Hamlet and Merchant of Venice	Mrs J. K. Curtis	10	28	28	7	2	6	6	
Tarrytown	American politics	L. P. Powell	6	80	21	4	9			
Utica {	American history	C. E. Fitch	10	189	89	50	28			
{	Geology and scenery of New York	A. P. Brigham	10	143	33	42	29			
Waverly {	American history	C. E. Fitch	10	203			13			
{	Private life of the Romans	C. E. Bennett	5	233			12			
Yonkers {	German literature	H. H. Boyesen	10	236				5	5	2
{	Electricity	Specialists	5	205	29					

Further details of the work of the centers in 1893-94 are given in *Regents bulletin*, no. 27, p 102-17. The two reports following were received too late for insertion in that bulletin.

Salem center no. 16. The course on English literature by Prof. J. R. Truax of Union university was held in Bancroft public library beginning December 8, 1893. The extension library was used largely not only by members but by others not students. The librarian and library committee of the public library noticed the increased number of books of reference and criticism now drawn from the library and the literature teacher in the public school said the lectures were of great benefit to her pupils.

The center has enjoyed great unanimity, the one aim of all being to secure the best interests of the center. Much less difficulty was experienced in raising the required amount this year than last, through the liberality of Rev. Father J. F. Donohoe, who gave for the benefit of the center a lecture on the World's fair. At the end of the course there was a surplus of $ 00 in the treasury, which greatly encouraged future efforts. Much of our prosperity is due to our good fortune in securing so earnest and enthusiastic an instructor as Prof. Truax The center also wishes to thank the regents department for the interest they have shown in the work of the center.— MABEL GIBSON, *Secretary*

Utica center no. 30 The course of lectures on "Civil and religious liberty in America," delivered in Utica in the autumn of 1893, by Regent Charles E. Fitch, was followed by a course on "The geology and scenery of the Empire state" by Prof. Albert P. Brigham, of Colgate university.

Lectures were delivered on 10 successive Monday evenings, beginning January 15, 1894. These were held in Association hall, the use of which was kindly given by the Young men's Christian association at the actual cost of warming and lighting.

The lectures were very much enjoyed. They were clear and simple and thoroughly scientific while yet sufficiently popular. The geologic history of our state was ably treated, and the dependence of the scenery of the present on the physical geography of the remote past was made evident. The hearers were pleased with the unaffected self possession of the speaker, who made the lectures seem much like classes. Five of the lectures were illustrated by the stereopticon, some of which were very beautiful. The attendance was about 150.

Nearly half of the audience remained for the after-meetings at which questions were asked. In answering these Prof. Brigham amplified the lectures considerably.

The class, which was held before the lectures, had an average attendance of 33. Its members were enthusiastic in their appreciation of Prof. Brigham's efforts. Many gained a satisfactory outline knowledge of geology, and all acquired an interest in the subject which will doubtless affect their future reading.

The traveling library was used more than those we have had in connection with previous courses.

The books were placed in the public library. On an average five were taken out daily, and there were readers at the table nearly always during library hours.

22 papers were handed to the lecturer, who was well satisfied with their quality. He criticized them before the class, reading such extracts as seemed to him useful.

There was a small students club, with an average attendance of about four. It met seven times during the course, and three or four times after the lectures were over. In this club all the papers were read and discussed in an informal way. The members gave one another accounts of articles or chapters in which they had been interested, and often brought extracts to read to one another. In this way a number of books from the traveling library, several short treatises of Prof. Brigham's, and some magazine articles were reviewed.

The board had fully intended to have an examination on the work of the course, but was unwilling to ask for it unless the center should prove itself entitled to the privilege. The papers, however, came in very slowly, as most of those who were reading preferred not to put their notes into definite form till the course was over. To oblige these Prof. Brigham kindly offered to accept papers up to the end of the year. But some students postponed writing the papers till the others were quite out of the spirit of the course and declined to take an examination. Therefore no extra papers were sent in. In this, the center will attempt to do better another year, having learned that it is wise to require all papers to be ready before the last lecture — IDA J. BUTCHER, *Secretary*

Students clubs for regents centers.[a] One of the greatest needs of university extension is earnest and systematic student work, not only during the course itself but after its completion. This will lift the whole movement above the plane of lecture courses and entertainments, establish it as a powerful educational factor and repel the unjust criticism that it interests but does not instruct, that it rouses enthusiasm but fails to impart permanent benefits. The best means known for inducing continuous study is the organization of a students club. During the course the lecturer is the students' safest guide, and much of the work is necessarily of an individual nature affording comparatively little scope for intercourse with others ; but both during the course and specially after it, the club has an important part in suggesting and stimulating thought, in encouraging interchange of opinions, in creating an *esprit de corps* and in broadening the field of vision. The ways and means of organizing this phase of the work demand the careful consideration of all those interested in the success of the extension movement.

Students clubs fall naturally into three divisions : those organized before, during and after the course of lectures. While the club which begins active work in advance of the lectures can achieve far the best results, frequently interest does not warrant organization in the early years of the work. When practicable, it should be done ; when not, the club should be formed at the first opportunity after the lectures begin, when interest is fresh and when the bent may be received largely from the lecturer himself, who can suggest topics for discussion, outline home work, and possibly arrange to be sometimes present at the club meetings. In this way the club is started more efficiently than if all planning and directing were left to local leaders, who may be entirely inexperienced in this kind of work.

If circumstances make it wiser to have only regular class and paper work during the course, the club is sometimes organized at the close of the course, when much aid may still be received from the lecturer, who will usually outline a course of reading and suggest methods for successful work.

At all centers where it is decided to organize a students club, local managers should rouse interest in much the same way as when the course itself is started. (See handbook, *Local organization*.) The matter must be brought before the community both by public announcements and personal visits. Regular attendants at the lectures should always be fully informed of the proposed work, and all existing literary, scientific or other educational societies invited to cooperate in the movement. A good room can almost always be obtained free.

The following by laws may suggest a suitable form of organization :

1 *Name*. This organization shall be called   extension students club [*or*   club, if a shorter name is preferred.

---

a Printed separately in handbook size.

If general in its sco pe the name "students" or "study club," prefixed by the name of the place, is good. If the work is limited it is well to show it in the name by prefixing to "club," social science, science, art, literature, history or whatever explains its field]

2 *Object.* Its object shall be cooperation among attendants on extension courses in the study of the subjects chosen by the center.

3 *Officers.* Its officers shall be a president, vice president, and a secretary who shall also act as treasurer. They shall be elected by ballot at the first regular meeting of each year or when a vacancy occurs, and shall hold office till their successors are elected. These officers shall form a standing committee, with authority to transact any necessary business for the club, to appoint committees and to arrange programs for meetings and home study.

4 *Members.* The standing committee may elect any person a member by unanimous vote.

5 *Meetings.* The meetings of the club shall be held on each [or alternate]   day evening at   o'clock, beginning with the first [or second, third or fourth]   day of [give month] each year [or beginning the first .. day after the opening of the extension course]

6 *Fees.* The annual fee of 25c shall be payable to the secretary at the first regular meeting of each club year, which shall be the same as the state academic year, August 1 to July 31 Money shall be expended only by vote of the club or by unanimous vote of the standing committee.

7 *Amendments* These by laws may be altered by majority vote at two successive meetings, if all members have been notified of the proposed change.

It is generally advisable during the course to conduct work suggested by the lectures, with discussions or debates on topics for papers or other allied subjects   Clubs continued after the end of the course usually secure the best results by following up the work of the course; e g. social science clubs may debate subjects partially discussed during the course; historical clubs may take up the period following that which they have been studying, and literary clubs may consider authors contemporary with those studied during the course. At club meetings discussions while thrown open to all are best opened and closed by appointed leaders   Interested students are usually willing to join the discussion if it is thoroughly understood that the utmost freedom is allowed. Those who shrink from a discussion may frequently be induced to prepare papers or essays, for which it is generally best to have a time limit, both to encourage condensed and accurate statement and to discourage those who are never more delighted than when wearying a patient audience.

For the periods between meetings a definite amount of reading should be laid out if possible by the lecturer, who best understands the students' needs and how to meet them. Specific work for individuals should be planned by the standing committee. The ultimate aim however of the whole work is to insure that systematic study which so closely affects the whole movement. All interested in educational extension are urged to consider seriously the formation of these clubs, and when started, to register them early with the extension department that all may have the practical benefits of organized effort. The department specially asks for reports, suggestions and plans of work from educational clubs of any sort and in any place. It will issue from time to time a special bulletin on study clubs, giving the experience in other states and countries as well as that in New York The bulletin will be sent to any who cooperate in advancing general interests by contributing their own experience.

Extension teachers. 125 lecturers offering 229 courses are now registered on the University lists. Since the last report (Mar. 1, 1894) 15 lecturers and 35 courses have been added and 12 lecturers and 22 courses have been dropped. Prof W: H Mace of Syracuse university has given nine 10-lecture courses in regents centers, the largest number yet given by a single lecturer in New York. Those who have given five or over are: Regent Charles E. Fitch, Prof. A. V. W. Jackson of Columbia and Mrs Jessie K. Curtis. Prof. J. II. Gilmore of Rochester and Prof. G: W: Smith of Colgate have each given four and Prof. J. W. Jenks of Cornell has given three.

A revised list of lecturers was issued in June as Circular 31, but is not reprinted as the last report contained the list then in use. The following changes have been made since the last report:

LECTURERS ADDED

Frederic Bancroft, Ph. D., Metropolitan club, Washington, D. C.

B. A. Amherst 1882, Ph D. Columbia 1885, lecturer on American history, Amherst 1888; librarian Department of state 1888-92; lecturer on American diplomacy, Johns Hopkins 1892-93, American history, Barnard college 1893, American diplomacy, Columbia school of political science 1890-92; American history, Columbia 1892- , author *A study of the negro in politics*, 1885, *Life of William H. Seward* (in preparation); contributor to *Political science quarterly, Atlantic monthly, Harper's weekly*, etc , member American historical association.

Epoch of disunion and reconstruction 1849-77.

R. K. Duncan, B. A. *Instructor in science,* Auburn high school, Auburn, N. Y.

<small>B. A. University of Toronto 1892, fellow Clark university, Worceste-, Mass. 1892-93, instructor in science, Auburn high school 1891-</small>

Heredity: 1 Ourselves and our inheritance; 2 Nature of life; 3 Immortality of micro-organisms; 4 Origin of death; 5 Physiology of a cell; 6 Continuity of the germ-plasm; 7 Are the characteristics we acquire during life transmitted to our children; 8 Influence of natural selection; 9 Rival theories; 10 The hope of the race

Modern doctrine of evolution: 1 "The first morning of creation wrote what the last dawn of reckoning shall read;" 2-4 Evidences of organic evolution: from morphology; from embryology; from paleontology; 5 Natural selection; the fittest survives, the weakest goes to the wall; 6 Are the effects of use and disuse inherited; 7 Relation of mind to matter; 8 Mental evolution; 9 Cosmic evolution; 10 Destiny of the race.

William H. Good, B. A., LL. B. *Lecturer,* University of the city of New York, Law school.

<small>B. A. St Francis Xavier 1889; LL. B University of the city of New York 1892, teacher in primary schools 1890-91, lecturer on legal instruments in common use in litigation, University of the city of New York, Law school 1892-; author Treasure trove, article in *American and English encyclopedia of law,* v. 25.</small>

Christianity as an element in New York civil law: 1 Confusion of civil law and religion; 2 Their separation in legal development; 3 How far the civil law of to-day follows any system of morals; 4 Indications that state laws assume belief in a Christian God; 5 Indications that state laws rest on no religious system; 6 Points of interference between civil law and Christian morality; 7 Penal measures and institutions; 8 Domestic relations; 9 Theories of public instruction; 10 Theory of prohibitive, restrictive and sumptuary regulations.

Present legal status of women: 1 Historical outline of legal theories regarding women; 2 Principal disadvantages of women, present and past; 3 Reasons for legal privileges and exemptions enjoyed by women; 4 Contract of marriage; 5 Legal rights and duties of wife; 6 Parent and child, household law, schools; 7 Woman as citizen and voter; 8 Eligibility of women to public office; 9 Women in penal law; 10 Trend of legal reforms.

H. Newman Lawrence. 34 W. 19th st., New York.

> Graduate in electric engineering, City and gilds of London (Eng) technical college, 1885; instructor in mathematics to evening classes, City and gilds of London technical college 1887-89, lecturer on electricity, Institute of medical electricity and Grafton college, London 1889-93, member Institution electrical engineers, England; fellow American electro-therapeutic association, joint author of *Manual of electro-therapeutics*, author of *Electricity and the body*, papers read before the British association for the advancement of science, and other scientific societies

Electricity in relation to health: 1 Electric energy and work; 2 Batteries and dynamos; 3 Measurements and measuring instruments; 4 Electro chemic and electro-physiologic action; 5 Induction coils and currents of high potential and frequency; 6 Resistance of the human body; 7 Electric dangers; 8 Electricity in medicine and surgery; 9 Hygienic uses of electricity; 10 Electric cooking.

Electricity in the home: 1 Electric energy and work; 2 Batteries and supply from street mains; 3 Electric bells and indicators; 4 Electric light; 5 Protection from fire; 6 Electromotors and domestic machinery; 7 Telephones; 8 Thief and fire alarms; 9 Electricity as a disinfectant; 10 Electric cooking.

Electricity in the service of man · 1 Electric energy and work; 2 Electromagnetism; 3 Electric generators; 4 Induction coils; 5 Measurements and measuring instruments; 6 Electric light; 7 Electric telegraph and bell signals; 8 Telephones; 9 Electric traction; 10 Electricity in medicine and surgery.

William P. McKenzie, B. A. *Instructor in English and rhetoric*, University of Rochester, Rochester, N. Y.

> B A University of Toronto 1884; graduate Knox college, Toronto 1889; post-graduate Auburn seminary 1890, author *Songs of the human*, *Voices and undertones*.

Scottish writers: 1-2 Robert Burns; 3 Burns and Scottish song; 4-5 Scott; 6-7 Carlyle; 8 Successors of Chaucer; 9 Ossian; 10 General.

W. H. Perry, B. A. *Vice-principal* Lowville academy, Lowville, N. Y.

B A Syracuse university

American revolution.

Jacques W. Redway. *Geographer*, 39 E. 4th st, Mt Vernon, N. Y.

Fellow Royal geographical society, member Engineers club, author of a series of school geographies. *Physical geography of the United States, Treatise of physiography, Modern facts and ancient fancies in geography*, the *Landfall of Columbus* and other papers, formerly editor-in-chief of *Goldthwaite's geographical magazine*, contributor to various cyclopedias

Physiography; earth sculpture: 1 How rocks are formed; age of the earth; 2 Mountains, plains and plateaus; earth sculpture; 3 Volcanos and earthquakes; 4 Lakes and the lessons they teach; 5 Rivers; 6 Glaciers and glacial phenomena; 7 Ocean waters and their movements; 8 The atmosphere and its movements; storms and weather gaging; 9 Physical geography of the United States, an application; 10 Effects and results of geography on human history.

P. C. Reynolds, Rochester, N Y.

Practical farmer and horticulturist, secretary Western New York farmers club, Western New York horticultural society, editor *American rural home*, member American pomological society.

Improved agriculture: 1 Soil; origin and composition; 2 Vegetable life; how plants grow and feed; 3 Mixed husbandry; obstacles to overcome; 4 How to grow large crops and maintain fertility; 5 Making, preserving and applying manures; 6 Horticulture; garden vegetables and market gardening; 7 Horticulture; production of fruits; 8 Dairying for milk, butter and cheese; 9 Stock breeding; feeding and rearing of stock; 10 Making farm life attractive.

Calvin W. Rice, B. S. *Assistant engineer*, power and mining depaitment, General electric co., Schenectady, N. Y.

B. S. Massachusetts institute of technology, 1890.

William H. Scudder, M. A. Norwich, N. Y.

B. A. Rutgers 1878, M. A. 1881; member American academy of political and social science.

Prehistoric America: 1 Pre-Columbian America; general survey; 2 Mound builders; mounds and shell banks; 3 Mound builders; arts, manufactures, mining; 4 Pueblos; 5 Cliff-dwellers; 6 Prehistoric northern races; Alaska, Greenland; 7 Prehistoric characteristics of the Pacific coast; 8 North American Indians; 9 Prehistoric characteristics of Mexico and Central America; 10 Antiquity and unity of prehistoric Americans.

A. Trumbull Seymour, B. L. 1295 Broadway, New York.

B. L. Cornell 1892, principal high school, Bristol, N. H.; instructor Newton, N. J. collegiate institute, special student at Harvard, summer 1893.

Political institutions (stereopticon): 1 Political machines in Europe and America; 2 Functions of the executive in Europe and America; 3 Character and composition of national legislatures in Europe and America; 4 Judicial systems of Europe and America; 5 Local government of France; 6 Local government of Germany; 7 Local government of England; 8 Local government of other European countries; 9–10 Municipal government.

Henry B. Waterman, LL. B., B. D. *Oriental lecturer*, summer assembly, Chautauqua, N. Y.

B. A. Yale 1863; LL. B University of Chicago 1865, B. D. Newton seminary, Mass. 1869, secretary London Palestine exploration fund.

Nations of the Orient: 1 China; 2 Japan; 3 India; 4 Egypt; 5 Palestine; 6 People and customs; 7 Some resting places of Bible history; 8 Progress of Palestine exploration; 9 Persia; 10 Ottoman empire.

Ulysses G. Weatherly, Ph. D. 18 Hazen st., Ithaca, N. Y.

B A. Colgate 1890; Ph D Cornell 1894, principal Marathon academy 1890-91; graduate student in history and political science, Cornell 1891-93, President White fellow in modern history, Cornell 1893-94; student at Heidelberg and Leipzig universities 1893-94.

Historical and comparative politics: 1 Some typical political theories; 2 Forms of government; 3 Constitutional government; 4 Government of England; 5 German empire and Prussia; 6 Government of France; 7 Federal and cantonal government in Switzerland; 8 Government of the U. S.; 9 Government of cities; 10 Socialism as related to the state.

Schuyler Skaats Wheeler, Sc. D. 159 W. 48th st., New York.

Hobart honorary on electric theses Columbia 1888, member American society civil engineers, American society mechanical engineers, American institute electrical engineers, Crocker-Wheeler electric co.; author numerous articles in the *Technical press*, two supplements to *Harper's weekly*, *Practical management motors and dynamos*.

Dynamos and motors.

Norman Wilde, M. A, Ph. D. *Assistant in philosophy*, Columbia college, New York.

B A. Columbia 1889, M. A 1890, Ph D. 1894; university student in philosophy, Columbia 1889-91, Berlin university, Germany 1891-93, Harvard 1893-94, assistant in philosophy, Columbia 1894- ; author *Friedrich Heinrich Jacobi, a study in the origin of German realism*

The spirit of modern civilization: 1 The medieval church; 2 Medieval science; 3 Medieval art; 4 Causes of the renaissance; 5 The new science and literature; 6 The new art; 7 The reformation; 8 18th century enlightenment and its causes; 9 Literature and art of the 18th century; 10 French revolution and modern reconstruction.

NEW COURSES OFFERED

Albert L. Arey, C. E. *Instructor in physics*, Rochester free academy, Rochester, N. Y.

Electricity and magnetism.

Rolla C. Carpenter, M. M. E. *Professor of experimental engineering*, Cornell university, Ithaca, N. Y.
Manual training.
The steam engine.

Adolphe Cohn, LL. B., M. A. *Professor of Romance languages and literatures*, Columbia college, New York.
History of French literature: 1 Formation of the French language; 2 Medieval poetry: historical poems on Charlemagne; 3 Medieval poetry: Arthurian romances; 4 Medieval chroniclers: Froissart; 5 Renaissance: Calvin, Rabelais, Montaigne; 6 Classic period: Descartes, Corneille; 7 Classic period: Racine, Bossuet; 8 Classic period: Molière; 9 18th century: the reforming spirit, Voltaire; 10 19th century: romanticism, Victor Hugo.

Herman L. Fairchild, B S. *Professor of geology and natural history*, University of Rochester, Rochester, N. Y.
Economic geology.
Historical geology: 1 Review of physical geology, methods of correlation, general view of the earth's history; 2 Archaean and Cambrian ages; 3 Lower Silurian age; 4 Upper Silurian age; 5 Devonian age; 6 Carboniferous age; 7 Reptilian age; 8 Mammalian age; 9 Quaternary age; 10 Prehistoric man.

Charles E. Fitch, LL. B., M. A. Rochester, N. Y.
European statesmen of the 19th century: 1 Talleyrand; 2 Pitt; 3 Stein; 4 Metternich; 5 Gortschakoff; 6 Thiers; 7 Cavour; 8 Kossuth; 9 Bismarck; 10 Gladstone.

Charles Forbes, M. D.   289 West av., Rochester, N. Y.
Physics.
Sanitary science.

Joseph H. Gilmore, M. A., Ph. D. *Professor of rhetoric and English*, University of Rochester, Rochester, N. Y.
American poetry.
Recent English poetry with special reference to Tennyson and Browning.
Shakspere.
Poetry of the Bible with special reference to the book of Job.

Samuel B. Harding, M. A.

Basis of the English constitution: Ancient Germanic character and governmental ideas; English government of the Anglo Saxon period; changes effected by Norman conquest; innovations of Henry 2; misgovernment of John, the great charter and its reissues; rise of parliament and the legislation of Edward 1; summary of local and central government at close of middle ages.

Formation of the American union $1760_{-}81$: Sketches of the English colonies in 1760; American *vs* English ideas of the constitution of the empire; Stamp act and passive resistance of $1761_{-}66$; Townshend acts and beginning of revolution; Continental congresses; Declaration of independence; early plans of union; formation and adoption of articles of confederation.

Jeremiah W. Jenks, Ph. D. *Professor of political economy, civil and social institutions,* Cornell university, Ithaca, N. Y.

Political methods: 1 Fundamental principles of politics; 2 Political parties; 3 Representation; 4 Methods of making nominations to elective offices; 5 Elective methods; 6 Legislative methods; 7 The work of the executive; 8 Municipal government; 9 State governments; 10 Settlement of international disputes.

William P. Mason, C. E., B. S., M. D. *Professor of analytic chemistry,* Rensselaer polytechnic institute, Troy, N. Y.

Methods of water analysis.

Relations between water supply and disease.

Frederick J. H. Merrill, Ph. D. *Director* New York state museum, Albany, N. Y.

Mineral resources of New York.

Mineral resources of the United States.

Mrs Fanny Gordon Sears, Binghamton, N. Y.

English literature through Elizabethan era.

Medieval France.

Florence C. Sherwood, Emerson college of oratory, Boston, Mass.
Evolution of expression.
Physical culture
Voice : 1 Effect of diaphragm and abdominal muscles on voice; 2 Right use of voice in its relation to health; 3 Relation of pitch to resonance applied to voice; 4 Relation of the voice to the emotions; 5 Relation of the voice to the intellect; 6 Influence of the imagination on the voice; 7–10 (*Topics not yet decided*).

Frank Smalley, M. A., Ph. D. *Professor of Latin language and literature*, Syracuse university, Syracuse, N. Y.
Roman biography: 1 Romulus; 2 Tarquinius Superbus; 3 Hannibal; 4 Caius Gracchus; 5 Caesar; 6 Cicero; 7 Augustus; 8 Nero; 9 Diocletian; 10 Constantine the Great.

S. R. Stoddard, Glens Falls, N. Y.
Southward to the summer land.

Charles W. Tooke, M. A. Columbia college, New York.
New York constitutional history: development of the colony under the Dutch and English and the evolution of the principles embodied in the constitution of 1777 (10 *lectures*).
New York constitutional history: political history of the state from the revolution to the present time, with special emphasis on the work of the constitutional conventions of 1777, 1821, 1867 and 1894 (10 *lectures*).

Milton Haight Turk, M. A., Ph. D. *Horace White professor of the English language and literature*, Hobart college, Geneva, N. Y.
Introduction to the study of English literature: 1 Beginnings of the literature; epochs of the later literature; 2 The
- English novel: Richardson to Scott; 3 The English novel: Dickens, Thackeray, George Eliot; 4 18th century prose; 5 Poetry of Spenser, Milton, Dryden, Pope; 6 Poetry from Cowper to Keats; 7 Origin and early history of the

English drama; 8 Shakspere: his life and the progress of his work; 9-10 Suggestions toward a useful study of Shakspere's plays.

English literature before Chaucer: 1 The English literature, its origin and growth; 2 The Anglo-Saxons, their history and culture; 3 Beowulf and minor heathen poems; 4 Caedmon and the Caedmonic poems; 5 Cynewulf and his fellows; 6 Oldest English prose; Alfred the Great, his assistants and his successors; 7 Anglo Saxon chronicle and other chronicles; 8 Norman conquest and the English people, language and literature; 9 The long transition to Chaucer; 10 Chaucer as the poet of the new English.

English prose in the hands of its masters; 1 Unformed prose of Bacon, Milton and their compeers; 2 Formed prose begun by Temple and Dryden, established by Addison and Steele; 3 Swift, the master of satire; 4 Prose seeks new fields; beginnings of the novel; 5 Fielding, the master novelist; 6 Johnson, the master of conversation; Burke; 7 Lamb, De Quincey and the great tribe of contributors; 8 Macaulay and Carlyle; 9 Thackeray, the 19th century master of the novel; 10 Ruskin and Arnold, critical prose of our day.

19th century poetry: 1 Glance at Elizabethan and 18th century poetry to the death of Pope; 2 Beginnings of the romantic movement in Thomson, Collins, Gray; rise of the new school in Cowper; 3 French revolution and our poetry; "The great name of Burns;" 4-5 Lake district: Wordsworth, what he believed and what he accomplished; Coleridge; 6 Byron and Shelley; 7 Keats; Tennyson; 8-9 Robert Browning; Mrs Browning; 10 Matthew Arnold and certain poets of our day.

Burt G. Wilder, B. S., M. D. *Professor of physiology, comparative anatomy and zoology*, Cornell university, Ithaca, N. Y.
Uses and abuses of the cat.

NAMES WITHDRAWN

Jerome Allen, Ph D. Professor of pedagogy, University of the city of New York. Died 1894.

N. Lloyd Andrews, Ph. D, LL. D. Professor of Greek language and literature, Colgate university, Hamilton, N. Y.

Charles C. Brown, C. E.   City engineer, Indianapolis.
J. L Davies, Utica, N. Y.
Charles O. Dewey, Ph. D.   ex-Principal Central high school, Binghamton, N. Y.
Sarah Frances Pellet, M A.   Binghamton, N. Y.
Edward Alsworth Ross, Ph. D.   Professor of political economy, Leland Stanford, jr university.
Gertrude Parker Spalding, B. S.   Cleveland, Ohio.
Lewis Swift, Ph. D.   California.
T. B. Stowell, M. A., Ph. D.   Principal State normal and training school, Potsdam, N. Y.
Beverly E Warner, M. A.   Louisiana.
Wardner Williams, Mus. M., Ph. D.   University of Chicago.
W. W. Willoughby, Ph. D.   458 La. av. N. W. Washington, D C.

COURSES WITHDRAWN

Physical geography by Prof. H. L. Fairchild.

Classic period of German literature, German literature from the crusades to the reformation, and German literature of the 19th century by Prof. R. W. Moore.

English prose fiction, and Shakspere and the Elizabethan drama by Prof. J. R Truax.

Romantic school in French literature by Prof. C: H. Thurber.

Medieval history by Prof. H. E. Mills.

Noted women of the middle ages by F. C. Sherwood.

Biblical study.   To those who recognize the beauty of Biblical literature and the interest of Biblical history, the renaissance of Bible study is one of the most gratifying of recent literary awakenings. The cooperation of the New York university extension department with the American institute of sacred literature (see *Regents bulletin* no. 27, p. 91-92) is a step toward making more general, systematic Biblical study under expert guidance.

The organization of courses is recommended in connection with churches and Sunday schools, either in place of one of the services or at a special meeting on Sunday afternoon. New life would be infused into many churches by thus utilizing the research and culture of skilled professors whose whole time is spent in Biblical study and allied topics. In churches where the pastor can so adjust his time as to permit it, such work might be conducted by him in person, though it will usually be found more satisfactory, where funds will permit, to have a specialist from another locality. In places distant from colleges or seminaries there will often be found neighboring pastors able to conduct successfully such work in other churches.

University extension in the colleges. Every friend of the modern movement which promises to do so much in extending the influence of the colleges and universities is delighted to see the rapidity with which the leading institutions of the country are showing their interest in the new work, but there seems to be grave danger that strength and resources will be wasted by establishing too many departments. There is almost sure to be some earnest man in every faculty whose sense of local pride is so great that he will strenuously urge the institution to create a distinct extension department, rather than join with some other institution which has already started the work. As a result, we shall shortly have five times too many organizations undertaking to carry the great detail and expense of organization and administration, and shall be expending on the means, time and money that are sadly needed for the end.

This work to be successful must be thoroughly organized and must be managed with great skill from central offices. College professors will be taxed to the utmost if they give the required instruction unhampered with business details, for which few have any taste and perhaps as few have any peculiar fitness. The great problem before university extension in this country is to secure enough competent teachers, and no greater mistake is conceivable than that of using a considerable part of the energy of this all too small company of teachers on administrative details which could be done as well, or better, by men and women wholly unqualified for lecturing. The economic consideration is equally strong. This work can not be done well without a somewhat elaborate organization and staff, and the effort of one or two men in a single institution to duplicate all the necessary machinery is bound to result in failure, or at best in only indifferent success. Our country is so large that we probably need more than the three or four central offices which are sufficient for Great Britain, but at most an administrative center for each state would be ample provision In short, we are in danger of repeating the same mistake that is made in establishing many weak, struggling universities instead of a few really well-equipped and efficient institutions; and the difficulty is that the local pride and jealousy of certain institutions, often the weakest, make them unwilling to unite with others in securing what all admit to be the desideratum. It would seem for various reasons that the natural center in many states would be the state university, where that is at all a strong and representative institution, as in Michigan, Wisconsin, Minnesota, California, Kansas, etc. or, if there should be no state university, that the oldest or strongest institution of the state, if there is one preeminently so recognized, should be the center for the new work, and that all the other colleges of the state should loyally support the general movement by furnishing lecturers from their faculties. The state institution seems to be the natural representative of the state movement, and besides that, it would be the natural center from which to spend most wisely and efficiently any appropriations to be secured from the legislature.

Another evil likely to spring from the existence of too many centers is the cheapening of standards caused by an unworthy competition among weak institutions anxious to roll up a large list of students. The success of the movement is largely dependent on maintenance of proper standards not only among neighboring colleges and throughout the entire state, but in different parts of the country and abroad. In the extension centers of England there is keen appreciation of the importance of maintaining what might be termed an international standard, so that the words university extension should not be degraded and made ridiculous by being applied to work of a low grade.

New York is fortunate in having two colleges with regularly organized extension departments working in direct connection with the central body at Albany. They are Colgate, where Prof. Ralph W. Thomas is organizer, and Rochester, whose secretary is J. E. Whitney. Each works within its own territory and usually places members of its own faculty in its centers. A similar department is in formation at Hobart college, Geneva. In addition to his position as secretary of the Rochester university extension department, and of the Rochester local center,

Mr Whitney is also the authorized representative in western New York of the University. As such he organizes new and inspects old centers, and gives any needed help or advice to local managers in his district. See *Regents bulletin* no. 27, p. 90.

University extension conferences. Two general conferences were held during the year. The first, held in March at Chicago university, reached only workers in the Mississippi valley, but many interesting facts were reported which were of value to all engaged in the work. A brief summary of this meeting was given in *Regents bulletin* no. 27, p. 121.

One of the most widely known meetings of the year was the University extension congress held in London in June to celebrate the "coming-of age" of university extension. The report of the University delegate, James Russell Parsons, jr is in *Regents bulletin* no. 27, p. 133-41.

On receiving the official report of proceedings the following circular was sent to secretaries of registered centers and clubs, lecturers on the university list and others interested in extension work:

University of the State of New York
Extension Department

REPORT OF THE UNIVERSITY EXTENSION CONGRESS, LONDON, JUNE 22-23, 1894

The recent congress in London to celebrate the "coming-of-age" of university extension in England was full of interest not only to extension students and workers but to all who are watching the trend of education. A *resumé* by the University delegate, James Russell Parsons, jr, was given in *Regents bulletin* no. 27, which was sent you in September. The official report of the proceedings has now been delivered in America. It contains, in addition to the papers and discussions of the three sessions, the tabulated returns from the several committees appointed in advance, to correspond with the extension boards of the world as to methods of work, both educational and financial, the relation of the movement to state and local authorities, the recognition given to extension work by colleges and universities in the form of certificates and degrees, and other topics of interest in the comparative study of the movement. There is also a list of delegates to the congress and a five-page appendix containing remarks from delegates who did not speak on their special topics for lack of time. The report of 102 pages will be mailed to any one specially interested in extension work on receipt of 16 cents, the price of the pamphlet at wholesale in London.

Melvil Dewey
Director

Albany, N. Y.

Sociologic courses. Extension work during the past year has been characterized by special activity in such practical subjects as civics, good government, health, hygiene, etc. Not only are extension methods suited to such study, but work of this kind finds the extension organization specially adapted to its purpose. The schools can serve the coming generation by giving their pupils right sociologic notions, but for the enfranchised citizen there has been no agency to counteract the stump speeches of demagogues and local partizans except the pulpit, which is often felt not to be the place for such discussions and certainly fails to reach a large majority of the class who are in greatest need of information and instruction in social science. Particularly in Philadelphia has this movement succeeded with all classes of citizens, including many of foreign birth ignorant not only of American institutions and civilization but of the principles which underlie them. Through the efforts of several public spirited citizens a fund was placed at the disposal of the Philadelphia university extension society, by which class courses were established for the study of civics. These class courses continue during 10 instead of six weeks, which is the unit course of the Philadelphia society; informal talks instead of lectures are given and a text-book is used instead of the syllabus. Besides this the fee for the course is considerably less than for a lecture course.

Philadelphia hygiene classes. About the same time Dr Charles Spivak, convinced that the squalor and disease of the tenement-house districts were due rather to ignorance than to laziness, organized some classes among the immigrant population and personally explained to them the laws underlying health. To some classes Dr Spivak lectured in their own language and even when speaking in English, his acquaintance with various European languages enabled him to make his lectures attractive and intelligible to his foreign-born audiences. The following description of the intellectual awakening which is taking place among the various nationalities included in our immigrant population is given by Dr Spivak in the Philadelphia *University extension bulletin*, v. 1, p. 5:

"It is said that one half of the world does not know how the other half lives, and this usually referred to the squalor, misery and intellectual poverty of the other half. The foreigner comes in for the greatest share in that half, as a matter of course. But in reality the foreigner is very little known. He is mainly depicted by the reporter, but very little described by the sociologist. Half of the world does not know what an intense intellectual activity is going on in the other half. There exists among the foreigners a craving for knowledge, a thirst for the acquirement of new ideas and a desire for an intellectual development which is perfectly astonishing. The civilizing influence of the United States on the foreigners can be measured by the periodical literature which they publish in their respective languages. There are many ex-subjects, now free citizens, who read nothing but their prayer book while in their old country, and after having tasted from the fruits of the trees growing in Uncle Sam's garden, have acquired the habit of reading. You can see the Italian fruit vender read his paper at his stand, the Pole enjoying his weekly at the dinner recess, and the Hun absorbed in a publication on a Sunday morning — none of them have ever seen a newspaper in their native villages. I know many a foreigner who has learned to read his own language only after he came over to this country. Some nationalities maintain more publications in this country than the whole of the nations in their old country. The Jews living in Russia number upwards of 5,000,000 and they have only one daily, two weeklies, and one monthly; while the number of Russian Jews residing in this country is about 200,000 and they can boast of one daily, 13 weeklies and two monthlies There is not a nationality here that has not a newspaper, a dramatic club, a literary society, a beneficial organization, etc. to satisfy its growing moral, physical and intellectual wants."

Philadelphia civics classes. The funds at the society's disposal enables it to reduce the fee in the civics courses, to $1 for each student enrolled, the minimum fee for each class being $25 and the maximum $75. 19 civics classes were organized, one without fees and composed entirely of Russian Hebrews. The interest shown by the poorer and less cultured classes was very encouraging and of the certificates given for class-work about half were awarded to negroes and Russian Jews. The highest percentage of candidates passing the examination was in a class composed of young negroes. The work was based on Fiske's *Civil government in the U. S.* To those unfamiliar with that book the topics studied will suggest the ground covered:

1 Our interest in politics
2 Our civil service
3 Taxation and government
4 Township and county government
5 Problems of city government
6 State governments
7 Government by constitutions
8 Party government
9 Our national executive and judiciary
10 Congressional and cabinet government

At the end of the course one member said, "I shall read the newspapers now with my eyes open."

Connecticut school of sociology. Another promising plan is a school of sociology in connection with the Connecticut society for educational extension at Hartford. The reason given for founding this school is that "present social conditions require more concentrated scientific investigation than they have yet received." The school is not limited to civic or hygienic problems, but takes up the more complex questions of social science, including social evils and their remedies, capital and labor, treatment of criminals and increase of vice. The curriculum will cover three years, the first beginning in October, 1894, and deals with the philosophy of sociology, including the evolution of the family considered biologically, legally, theologically and ethically; the status of woman; domestic economy; food, shelter and dress historically and sanitarily considered, sanitary science, growth of cities. A college diploma or its equivalent is required for matriculation, but special students may take the course on payment of the tuition fee. If successful, the school will create a new profession, whose experts will be qualified to deal with social problems intelligently and scientifically, relegating to their deserved obscurity the "social quacks" now so anxious to administer their remedies and so ignorant of the true causes of the disease.

Libraries and university extension. Every librarian is urged to keep careful statistics of the use of books on subjects taken up by extension centers. Such statistics in England have shown results beyond the hopes of the most sanguine friends of extension teaching; e. g. in one case the use of fiction, which had been 90 % of the total circulation, fell to 60 %, while the reading of books on extension subjects correspondingly increased. In order to work out this problem successfully we must study carefully the results of various experiments, and among all the active coworkers in university extension, the public librarian easily stands first.

Recognizing this, the following circular has been sent with explanatory circulars, to those in charge of libraries in the University:

To the librarian:

The fact that the library is the real corner-stone of extension work and the means of starting so many successful centers, suggests that your interest in the movement will lead you to present its claims to those of your community who are interested in educational work. Few have the public librarian's opportunity to study educational needs and possibilities, for the public library is the natural center of all educational work outside the schools. The librarian best knows who are interested and willing to foster interest in others. He has practical opportunities for improving and extending educational efforts to organize among ambitious students a movement to systemize their work. The inclosed circulars give a general idea of the New York extension system which besides local centers, summer and evening schools and correspondence teaching, includes study clubs, reading circles and lecture courses

In organizing and conducting the work the department will give all possible assistance.

MELVIL DEWEY
Director

SUMMER SCHOOL DIVISION

The growing interest in this work is shown by the great demand for the first bulletin on this subject, which has proved to be the most popular of the extension bulletins. Constant calls for copies have come not only from educators but from home students and others engaged in business or professions other than that of pedagogy. The demand for the bulletin justified the orginal plan of an annual issue and the second number [a] sum-

---

[a] The demand for copies was so urgent that the second edition was printed and bound with this report (See *Extension bulletin*, no 9).

marizes the methods and results of the work of 1894 and announces future plans.

There are 18 New York summer schools on the University lists. Their names and locations are:

Cascadilla summer school, Ithaca
Catholic summer school of America, Plattsburg
· Catskill summer school of art, Ellenville
Central N. Y. summer school, Tully Lake Chautauqua
Columbia college
    Summer school in practical mining (various places)
    Summer school in geology (various places)
    Summer school in surveying, Litchfield, Conn.
    Summer school in practical geodesy (various places)
Cornell university summer school, Ithaca
Lake George assembly
Long Beach Chautauqua
Point o' Woods Chautauqua
National summer school of methods, Glens Falls
Natural science camp, Canandaigua
Port Leyden summer school
Prohibition Park summer school
Round Lake institute
Shinnecock Hills summer school of art, Southampton, L. I.
Summer vacation meeting, Keene

STUDY CLUB DIVISION

Four clubs working at least 10 weeks on one subject were registered. Details are given in the following table:

NAME	Location	No. members	Average attendance	Meetings held how often	No. meetings	Subjects of study
Home culture club	Little Falls	16	14	bi-weekly	15	French history
Gradua'es association of the Buffalo seminary	Buffalo	175	40	weekly	21	Conventions at Chicago (6) Miscellaneous (3) Physical geology (10)
Current topic club	Rome	50	25	weekly	20?	Hist. lit. & art of France and Scotland
Monday afternoon study class	Gloversville	20	13	weekly	23	Japan and modern history

The course in physical geology at Buffalo was led by Prof. H. L. Fairchild of Rochester and consisted of the lectures belonging to his university extension course supplemented by reading and study on the part of club members.

A blank for statistics and application for registration was sent to all New York study clubs, reading circles and lecture courses known to the department, with the following circular, printed in handbook size:

ORGANIZATIONS FOR HOME STUDY

In addition to regents centers, the extension department of the University of the State of New York includes all registered agencies for higher education outside the regular teaching institutions; i. e. schools, academies, colleges. So cordial has been the welcome given to the effort to make education available to all, that the number of agencies for home study organized in the past 10 years marks the decade as an epoch in educational development. The state of New York has not only done its full share of such work but again sustains its claim to leadership. It is the first state or country to organize a distinct extension department to supervise and promote such work, and was a half century in advance of all the states in establishing the system of school district libraries. Added to this honor it had the first extension center in America (Buffalo 1887-88) and was also the birthplace of the first independent woman's club in the world (Sorosis, New York city, 1868). It has also the two national organizations for summer, vacation and home study, Chautauqua and the Catholic summer school of America. In almost all cases, however, the work is still desultory and unorganized. In many places it has entirely or partly failed for lack of systematic local efforts. No standards are set because none have existed and there has been lack of incentives to raise the work to higher grade.

In this line the great work of Chautauqua is too well known to need more than a reference. By outlining courses and requiring reports it has made possible systematic home study and has proved that such work can accomplish definite educational results, a theory by no means generally received a quarter of a century ago. Since this is now an admitted principle in the science of education no explanation is necessary for the statement that the University through its extension department recognizes home study as a distinct phase of its work.

Registry. The usual forms of organization are study clubs, reading circles and lecture courses. In each case not less than 10 weeks work on the same general subject entitles to registration on the University lists. The provision of continued study on one subject prevents the waste of thought and energy common in clubs which take up a topic one week only to drive it out of mind the next by one totally different. 10 weeks of such work are full of suggestions and impressions but so confused as to discourage the student from proceeding further. Worse than this, he has lost the thought development and mental culture which follow persistent investigation of a subject in its varied phases and beyond its surface ideas. This rare quality which every one feels is infinitely more to be desired than the mere acquisition of facts has no place in a plan which provides only for superficial study of constantly varying subjects.

The justification for selecting different topics for each week's study is that it gives entertaining variety and provides a subject for each meeting in which some members of the club are specially interested. Lord Playfair gives an amusing example of this effort to please all in a single course by quoting the program of the Mechanics' institute for 1845. It was as follows: "Wit and humor, with comic songs; Women, treated in a novel manner; Legerdemain and spirit rapping; The devil (with illustrations); The heavenly bodies in the stellar system; Palestine and the Holy Land; Speeches by eminent friends of education, interspersed with music, to be followed by a ball. Price for the whole 2s. 6d. Refreshments in the anteroom." The absurdity of this marvelous collection appeals to all, but it is only in a lesser degree that all variety programs lack true educational value. Yet this is the point hardest to impress on local managers who with the best of motives neutralize much of the educational value of their work by catering to the demand which results in the "variety hall" entertainments so much deplored by intelligent friends of music and the drama.

This criticism would not of course apply to those clubs whose subject is "Current topics," for this does not mean study of isolated subjects having no connection with each other. The study of recent movements and events is necessarily synthetic, bringing out causes and effects and the interrelation of the incidents of modern progress.

Besides the approved course of study, the only requirements for registration are that each organization must have at least five members and must report its work annually to the department. There are no registration fees.

The relation of the department to the local organization is purely advisory and administrative, binding together the work of similar organizations throughout the state. In this way the experiments and conclusions of all may be focalized, and the best methods made available with a minimum expenditure of labor. From time to time the department will issue bulletins giving statistics of work done by similar organizations at home and abroad, tabulated for comparison, together with details of progress and suggestions for more efficient work in the various lines of study pursued. Added to the recognized advantages of organized effort are the more definite privileges of registration, including loans, traveling libraries, exchanges, examinations, credentials and similar rights of regents centers.

Certificates of registration for each of the three forms of work are issued under the University seal. This stamps the work as of superior grade, prompting the best to maintain their standing

Photography, J. Foster Flagg, C. E.
Physics, Samuel Sheldon.
Political science, John A. Taylor.
Psychology, Frederick W. Osborn, M. A.
Zoology, John Mickelborough.

The department of law was also organized during the season and courses of lectures were given on subjects of interest to lawyers, including addresses on state, national and international law.

A description of the biologic laboratory at Cold Spring Harbor is given in *Extension bulletin* no. 9, p. 31.

The Brooklyn art school was established by a joint action of the Brooklyn art association and the department of art of the institute. For description of the Shinnecock Hills summer school of art, located at Southampton-by-the-sea, see *Extension bulletin* no. 9, p. 37; the Catskill summer school of art is described on page 43 of the same bulletin.

The Woman's institute of Yonkers is an active educational center, maintaining in its building a library and various classes and clubs for the intellectual development of its constituency. Its library report is given in the report of the library division but the club work is tabulated below:

REPORT OF EXTENSION DEPARTMENT, 1894

Institute day classes 1893-94

NAME	Instructor	Time	Hours	Total no. of lessons	Total no. entered	Aggregate attendance	Average attendance	Teacher's attendance	Aggregate of visitors attendance	Aggregate attendance practice lesson	Committee attendance
Callsthenic class	Mrs Belle Morris	Monday a. m.	2	25	20	480	10	23	......	......	......
Plain sewing class	Miss Johnson	Tuesday a. m.	2	35	12	151	4	35	......	......	......
Embroidery class	Miss Johnson	Friday a. m.	2	34	15	97	3	34	......	......	......
Cooking class	Miss Johnson	Saturday a. m.	2	23	25	176	8	23	......	......	......

Institute club classes for self-supporting women

Callsthenic class	Mrs Belle Morris	Monday evening	2	29	27	467	13	29	2157	143	64
Plain sewing class	Miss Johnson	Monday evening	2	28	35	163	7	23	......	......	......
Cooking class	Miss Johnson	Tuesday evening	2	38	40	411	12	32	......	......	......
Dressmaking class	Mrs Jones and Miss Howes	Tuesday evening	2	38	30	326	10	60	......	......	......
Millinery class	Miss Charlton	Thursday evening	2	26	11	90	3	26	......	......	......
Library class	Educational class committee	Thursday evening	1½	25	33	156	6	40	......	......	66
Embroidery and home decoration class	Miss Johnson	Friday evening	2	33	45	356	11	33	......	......	......

Young girls' classes

| Relief sewing class for unemployed girls | Volunteer teachers | Tuesday afternoons | 2 | 20 | 68 | 325 | 16 | 60 | ...... | ...... | ...... |
| Kitchen garden class | Miss Parsons | Friday afternoons | 2 | 12 | 20 | 138 | 11 | 12 | ...... | ...... | ...... |

The treasurer reports a balance of $159.13 in the treasury at the close of the fiscal year, 30 Ap 1894.

Extension exhibit. This valuable collection is steadily increasing. Everything received is labeled and protected from injury as carefully as possible. Circulars, syllabuses and other pamphlets are on the state library shelves. The following circular is sent to any society or individual issuing material suited for this exhibit and the greatest kindness has uniformly been shown in contributing publications asked for:

University of the State of New York
Extension Department

DEAR SIR: The comparative extension exhibit shown at the Columbian exposition was placed in charge of this department and included American and foreign bulletins, circulars, syllabuses, administrative blanks, forms and everything available in print of interest to extension workers. This entire exhibit is now permanently deposited here as an extension museum, representing the various plans and methods of different organizations. The hundreds of syllabuses show side by side the different treatment of the same topic by various extension lecturers, while closely classed administrative forms facilitate comparative study of methods of organization, supervision, examinations and records. The state has provided fireproof rooms having every comfort and convenience for readers, to whom they are open from 8 a. m. to 10 p. m. throughout the year, including holidays and vacations. Unequaled facilities are therefore afforded to all, and books and pamphlets are made widely useful to special investigators. In exchange for gifts, an equivalent in our publications, of which a list is inclosed, will be sent if desired. Will you not send to this important collection the items below?

MELVIL DEWEY
Director

Publications. The following have been issued since the last report:

Regents bulletins. Large 8°, 25 x 17.5 cm. Alb. 1891 — date.
Price to advance subscribers, 50 cents a volume.

Extension teaching (Extension no. 7). 72p. July 1894. *Price* 10 *cents.*
Specific suggestions from experience, to aid extension teachers in securing best results. Contains report on London extension conference of June 1894 by the University delegate.

Summer schools (Extension no. 8). 84p. Aug. 1894. Replaced by revised edition, Bulletin 9.

> Summary of purpose, courses and equipment of summer schools and other agencies for vacation study in this country and abroad.

Extension circulars. Large 8°, 25 x 17.5 cm. Alb. 1892 — date.

How to get most help from extension courses. 2p. 12°. Feb. 1894.

> Suggestions for using to best advantage syllabus, references, class, paper work and examination.

Lists of extension teachers. 56p. June 1894.

> Revised to June 1894.
> This circular is not reprinted but changes in the list of lecturers and courses as printed in the last report are indicated on p. r27-37.

Extensi n syllabuses. 12°. Alb. 1892 — date.

> Outlines of courses given under direction of the University of the State of New York, containing selected lists of authorities on the subjects treated. *Price to registered centers or clubs 2 cents for each 8 pages; single copies at prices specified.*

Fitch, ⟨ : E. *Regent of the University.* Civil and religious liberty in America. 20p. Dec. 1893. *Price 5 cents.*

Onderdonk, A. F. *Physics and natural science, Albany high school.* Electricity. 28p. Oct. 1893. *Price 10 cents.*

Curtis, Mrs J. K. Hamlet and Merchant of Venice. 36p. Oct. 1893. *Price 10 cents.*

Jenks, J. W. *Professor of political, municipal and social institutions, Cornell University.* Economic legislation. 24p. Dec. 1893. (Half course. Five lectures.) *Price 5 cents.*

Smith, G: W: *Professor of history, Colgate University.* Practical economic questions. Dec. 1893. *Out of print.*

Boyesen, H. H. *Professor of Germanic languages and literature, Columbia College.* Medieval German literature. 12p. Nov. 1893. *Price 5 cents.*

Sears, Mrs F. . G. The making of France. 8p. Nov. 1893. (Half course. Five lectures.) *Price 5 cents.*

Truax, J. R. *Professor of rhetoric, English language and literature, Union College.* Studies in English literature. Dec. 1893.

Forbes, Charles, M. D. Electricity. 32p. Dec. 1893. *Price* 10 *cents.*

Brigham, A. P. *Professor of geology and natural history, Colgate University.* Geology and scenery of New York. 24p. Dec. 1893. *Price* 5 *cents.*

Mace, W: H. *Professor of history and political science.* Development of the nation. 60p. Dec. 1893. *Price* 15 *cents.*

20p. appendix of reprints of original documents.

Arey, A. L. *Sciences, Rochester Free Academy.* Various forces of nature as related to modern life. 36p. Jan. 1894. *Price* 10 *cents*

Bennett, C: E. ' *Professor of Latin language and literature, Cornell University.* Private life of the Romans. 12p. Jan. 1894. *Price* 5 *cents.*

Electricity. Under direction of Columbia college. Feb. 1894. (Half course. Five lectures.)

Jenks, J. W. *Professor of political economy, civil and social institutions, Cornell University.* Political methods. 32p. Mar. 1894. *Price* 10 *cents.*

Waterman, H. B. *Oriental lecturer, Chautauqua.* Nations of the orient. 20p. July 1894. *Price* 5 *cents.*

University handbooks. Postal size, 7¼ x 12¼ cm. Alb. 1893.

Price in quantities, 1 cent for each 16 pages or less. Single copies postpaid, 5 cents.

Extension department.

Contents Local organization. Students clubs for regents centers. Organizations for home study.

Local organization is not reprinted as it is a revision of Circular 25 (see *Regents bulletin* no 24, p 1466-50)
Students clubs for regents centers is reprinted on p. r25-27 and *Organizations for home study* on p r46-48

Public libraries division.

Contents: State aid to libraries; Traveling libraries.

Traveling library finding lists. Annotated class lists of libraries for lending to local libraries, communities or extension centers. 7½ x 12½ cm. *Price 2 cents each.*

Lists 1–10; 100 miscellaneous volumes each.

Lists 11–15, 17, 18, 21; 50 miscellaneous volumes each.

List 16, Mountainside library; 102 miscellaneous volumes selected by Edward Eggleston.

Economics; one list of 50 and one of 25 volumes.

Agriculture; one list of 60 and one of 33 volumes.

French history; one list of 45 volumes.

United States history; one list of 43 and one of 20 volumes.

Regents reading course in literature; one list of 57 volumes.

Regents reading course in English and American literature; one list of 26 volumes.

Use of printed matter outside the state. Constant inquiries are made as to whether our circulars, pamphlets and other printed matter are available except in New York. It would clearly be improper that New York should pay expenses of educational work in other states, but it costs nothing to allow those outside the state to use matter which has been prepared and put in type for use in New York. We therefore furnish it freely to all applicants willing to pay cost of paper and press work. This enables small extension societies and centers to secure documents needed, for much less than they themselves could print small editions, and we gladly render this service, which is subject to no criticism from even the most selfish tax payer.

University extension literature. There are now three American, one Australian and two English magazines devoted solely to university extension. The Philadelphia society has two monthlies, *University extension* and the *University extension bulletin.*[a] The first has in each number three or four long articles and a few editorials on some phase of modern education or allied topics; the other is devoted mainly to the news side, noting changes and

---

[a] Now combined in one monthly, the *Citizen.*

developments, announcing new plans and including one or two short discussions of methods or accounts of experiences and results at various centers.

The *University extension world*, published by the Chicago society, was till last summer a monthly but with the July number, the first of v. 4, it became a quarterly, subordinating the news items though its articles deal with the later events or developments of extension work. It is printed on coated paper in clear type, well leaded, and with wide margins. Its illustrations add greatly to the favorable impression produced by the magazine as a whole.

The London *University extension journal* is the organ of the London society and since Cambridge has no journal of its own, seems to be the unofficial representative of that university. The *Oxford university extension gazette*, which has served as the model of the Philadelphia *University extension bulletin*, already described, is the organ of the Oxford society. The two English journals are published monthly and though very similar in character, by appearing at different times are able to cover different fields and both are therefore valuable to American extension students.[a]

The *Melbourne university extension journal* is a quarterly record of university extension news in Australia, Tasmania and New Zealand.[b] The reports from local centers are of unusual interest.

Of all single articles on the subject in the general magazines during the year none has excited more discussion than "The farce of university extension," which appeared in the August number of the *Nineteenth century*. A real service was done to the cause by calling out such admirable replies as those by Mr M. E. Sadler and Mrs James Stuart in the September number of the same review. Some excellent editorials on the subject have also appeared in American newspapers. The following selections are reprinted:

Under the condemnatory caption, "The farce of university extension," a writer in the current *Nineteenth century* renders his verdict

---

[a] Both replaced Oct 1895 by the *University extension journal*, edited by a joint board representing the Oxford, Cambridge, London and Victoria university extension authorities.
[b] Discontinued Dec. 1894.

upon the 21 years' work of university extension in England. As university extension is at present being vigorously promoted in this country, and appeals to the people as something which directly concerns them, it will be of interest to examine the grounds of this caustic criticism.

If the tone of the writer were less satirical and more judicial, one would be inspired with greater confidence in his fairness of observation and opinion. Plainly he is a tory with a grievance and his point of view explains his hostile attitude. He rates university extension as a democratic device, that of itself being sufficient condemnation. His contention is that it deceives the public with false hopes of attaining the unattainable, cheapens culture, degrades learning by making the credulous and ignorant lower classes believe they can share in its heritage and promotes superficiality and restlessness. Worst of all, this evil of associating Greek tragedy and a housemaid — "monstrous association!" — and all the other sins of extension, are committed in the name and with the sanction of Oxford and Cambridge. In this he sees a ruinous surrender to democracy. By their newly devised extension summer schools the universities, he thinks, are aiming at "a cheapjack popularity," have dishonored the "resort of a leisured culture" and converted "their cloistered colleges into so many crystal palaces of cheap and easy learning." With such changes as these coming from one who declares that learning is and must remain the exclusive possession of the cultured few, and that there is no reason for the existence of the universities if "the unlettered are given their share in the privileges and patronage of learning," we need have small concern. The writer's conception of the aim of university extension is perverted and absurdly narrow, as is also his conception of the legitimate function of the universities. The spreading of intelligence among the masses has no place in his perception. Doubtless he could see nothing but danger to government and evil to themselves, in such courses of lectures on law and the relations of capital and labor, on political economy and sociology, as Dr Lawrence (a learned Cambridge lecturer, who was for a year in the extension work at the University of Chicago) gave, year after year, to thousands of English miners and mill-workers. What right have such as these, forsooth, to aspire to knowledge? That the English extension lecturers have given their hearers the idea that they could "exhaust each province of knowledge in three lectures," we are not ready to believe.

The only charge which merits consideration is that of superficiality. This is unquestionably the peril attendant upon the extension movement in this country. The work here is in its experimental stages and it is too early to pronounce judgment upon its character and value. These will depend upon its thoroughness or the want of it. There is no doubt with us that it is advantageous to have the best possible educational facilities opened to the largest possible number of persons. That a housemaid should attend a course of lectures on Greek tragedy does not shock our sensibilities. But it does concern the promoters of university extension in America to see to it that the lecture courses do not degenerate into the merely popular lyceum entertainment, ministering to the greed for some new form of amusement, rather than to the mental quickening of the people. The difficulties in the way of securing continuity and concentration are pointed out by our critic So long as the local centers select the subjects and lecturers, it will be impossible to avoid such confusing combinations of courses as geology and the classical drama, land surveying and Shakspere, electricity and art. Centers will, like pulpit committees, seek that which promises to "draw" the best. The educational feature thus becomes secondary to the financial. The lecturer assumes more importance than the subject, while study, as a motive, comes in third if at all. Here is the critical point in the problem.

We believe however that university extension meets a demand and a need in this country and that it has a future of usefulness. It does not pretend to give the masses such scholarship as is to be obtained by the college course. It does put within reach the results of learning in its various branches; it brings the people into contact with scholarly instructors; it stimulates to reading and research those who are open to such stimulus; it offers facilities for self-culture to thousands of people young and old, who are by daily occupation shut away from school advantages; and this is very much to do, if it accomplish nothing more. University extension rightly conducted, no more fosters superficiality or self-conceit of knowledge than does any other educational instrumentality. And we see no reason as yet to doubt that this educational movement will prove a factor of moment in the mental and social advancement of our people — *Watchman*, Boston, 30 August, 1894

In a somewhat caustic article in the *Nineteenth century*, Mr Charles Whibley ridicules the movement which for the last 21 years in England has gone by the name of "university extension." He calls it a "farce," and is evidently very angry with it. Beginning with the instance of "an adventurous housemaid" who had the temerity, in company with

23 private governesses, 10 employees and four artisans, to attend a course of lectures on Greek tragedy, he goes on to make merry with the whole business of trying to get a university education in any other way but that of leisured calm, and in which the whole life is devoted to learning. He has no fancy for popular lectures in which "Shakspere is sandwiched between electricity and Praxiteles," or where " a slice of chemistry shall be placed delicately between twin crusts of Gothic architecture and the reign of the Stuarts." He says that not a single habit fostered by learning was taught to the victims of this "new-invented debauch." Indeed, he says that it is impossible to consider the movement without recognizing that from the beginning it has trodden learning under foot, and that it has "violated every principle of sound research or amiable culture that Oxford and Cambridge are pledged to respect " He pours contempt on the summer festival, when for three weeks at a time the "universities are invaded by a mob of intellectual debauchees, whose ambition is greater than their stomach, and who sit them down to an orgy of information which is warranted to leave the stoutest with a mental dyspepsia."

Mr Whibley's article is a very pungent one and there is a good deal of truth in what he says. If it should tend to take some of the conceit out of mere smatterers who when they have gotten hold of a little knowledge talk as if they were authorities, its results will be beneficial. Shallow and flippant students are a great nuisance, for they never realize how very little they know. We can readily understand how distasteful the talk of such persons must be to a scholar of Mr Whibley's caliber. He narrates how a workman once said to him, "Which do you prefer, 'Omer or Hossian?" And when Mr Whibley's "astonished silence" gave him encouragement, the bold artisan said, "Hossian's my man, he's much better at nature." "Straightway," says the writer, "I recognized a victim of the extension, and reflected how far honester a citizen would he have been had he attempted to understand only such topics as were within his reach." Now here, we not only recognize the old exclusive spirit of learning which in days gone by divided mankind into two distinct bodies of unlearned pariahs on the one hand and learned high-caste people on the other, but we perceive an utterly fallacious and gratuitous assertion. Mr Whibley is reluctant to see that the days of "benefit of clergy," when the ability to read a Latin book sometimes saved a man from merited punishment, have entirely passed away. He was evidently angry to find that his plumber had ever heard of "'Omer" or "Hossian," and he jumps to the conclusion that such a man can not be "honest," or, at all events, that he would be a good deal honester if he let learning alone altogether. But there is no reason why a plumber should wipe a joint or mend a tap any the worse from knowing that there was such a poet as Homer and because he had heard of Ossian. He might even be tolerably well acquainted with these writings without becoming deteriorated as a tradesman If Mr Whibley had possessed the savoir-faire of a man of the world instead of the inability to disclose himself except in a limited circle, which is common in many learned persons, he might have responded with a scientific appreciation of what the plumber was doing. "Astonished silence" under the circumstances was simply bad manners and gaucherie. The workman was the better gentleman of the two. Operating in classical regions, he did his best to talk on classical subjects. But he could not overcome the unfortunate dumbness which is frequently one of the accompaniments of learning. As to Mr Whibley's article, it shows that he is too strongly prejudiced in favor of the exclusiveness and aristocracy of learning to be received as an impartial judge on the merits or demerits of university extension.— *Mail*, Toronto, Ont. 23 August, 1894

The Paterson (N. J.) *Press* has lately published a series of excellent articles on university extension, edited by the secretary of the Paterson scientific and literary association. A few extracts are printed from these and other similar articles which have appeared so frequently during the year as fair indexes of the growing public sentiment.

There was once a time when any progressive community which wished to place the opportunity for higher education within reach of more than the very limited number of its citizens whose means permitted a long residence away from home, found no other way of doing so than by the endowment of a college in its own midst. At present such a community organizes a university extension local center. It finds that the universities are willing to send out competent lecturers on any subject recognized as a regular college discipline. It finds that it can secure a sequence of courses in the same subject, or, if it prefers it, can have a taste of various subjects by selecting a course, say, in natural science, then one in history or political science or literature. It finds that a complete scheme of higher education by non-resident lecturers has been inaugurated, and that it has been already thoroughly tested; that it provides for examination and certifies results; and that for the individual student it involves but very little expense.

The enormous advantage of the present situation over the earlier one is that the newer system adapts itself to the amount of work to be done and to the amount of money available for such educational work at any particular point. To establish or endow a small college was once praiseworthy, for each such institution can boast that half or more than half its students would not have been educated at any distant university. But there is little doubt that the amount necessary to provide the plant and the very meager support which is grudgingly given these institutions would, if applied to the support of university extension courses, yield far more valuable educational results. We are not casting a slur upon any existing institution or any town which, in its desire to promote the cause of higher education, has established and supports a center of learning however weak. But we would raise the question whether, in view of the rapid and permanent development of university extension within the past two years, it is not well to consider the advisability of bringing the higher education to our own doors by means of these more economical and more effective channels. No supporter of university extension work claims that it is possible to make scholars or to produce investigators by six lecture courses. But experience shows that it is possible by university extension instruction to raise the line of living by creating an interest in higher things. Much more can be accomplished in a scholarly direction than one would suppose who has not taken the trouble to examine carefully what has been actually achieved.

Many who have been prevented by the circumstances of their lives from taking up any formal college work, have found on enrolling for an extension course that they are nevertheless in entire sympathy with students of the higher subjects, and that they have latent powers of which they had been unconscious. Many whose period of formal study has long been closed have found that their slumbering interest in literature or science or history is easily rekindled by the new spark and have reproached themselves for their neglect of books and of scholarly discussion. It is no small matter to set an entire community talking about new subjects, to elevate the general tone of conversation and discussion. Yet this has been done in scores of centers by the instructive lectures and the vigorous discussions provided in extension courses.
—*Press*, Paterson, N. J. 1 November, 1894

The university extension movement has been criticized both as attempting too much and as doing too little. It is said that to present the fruits of higher education to people who have had little or no preliminary training is to build upon spongy ground a structure which becomes distorted and dangerous. On the other hand, complaint is made that the teaching does not sufficiently reach those whose lives might be brightened and inspired by an awakening to intellectual life. Both these criticisms are more or less just, but it is evident that to attempt to satisfy one set of critics would be to fall lower in the opinion of the other.

Again, it has been alleged that owing to lack of continuity in the teaching and of proper standards to which the work of students must conform, university extension differs little from the old lyceum lecture system. In some cases this seems to be very nearly the truth; but the lyceum lecture was not a bad thing in its way, and in general, the newer system is more serious, has more continuity, and exacts more from students. The mere fact that those who attend the courses are thought of, and think of themselves, as students, is significant; and this idea is enforced by the classes that follow the lectures, in which, for half or three-quarters of an hour, there is free interchange of questions and answers between the lecturer and his audience. If there is not a very great amount of study or collateral reading, it is not so much through the fault of instructors or of the system as because it is impossible under the conditions that exist to exercise any great amount of control in these matters. While it is true that in most cases only a minority of those who attend lectures prepare essays or pass examinations, the fact remains that many do, and it must be remembered that such tests can not be insisted upon, much as they may be urged, without seriously limiting the number brought within the influence of the teaching It is hard in our day and country to believe that people can be kept from discontent by keeping them in ignorance. Especially among the uncultivated, ideas of happiness are associated with increased wealth and physical ease or pleasure; not envy of culture, but of comfort or luxury, is the common cause of discontent. Is it not better, in view of the fact, that in these days, education is not only a harmless but an inexpensive gratification, to offer it freely to all who can find in it either pleasure or the hope of progress? Luxury and the power of money are too apparent to allow them to remain the only gods before the people. There may be danger in the presumption that comes of a little knowledge, but, thanks to the public schools and the press, there is a little knowledge everywhere. It is perhaps less dangerous to add to it under the direction of university men than to leave it to the nurture of the literature of the news stand. — *Press*, Paterson, N. J. 14 November, 1894

There is nothing that is more encouraging in the work of spreading and perfecting university extension teaching among the people than the constant inspiration and impetus which it affords to other lines of educational work and to almost all phases of social improvement. A successful course of extension lectures in a village or town invigorates every educational organization therein; it increases the activity and renews the zeal of members of societies and clubs whose chief purpose is social improvement.

Browning and Shakspere societies are started or receive new life because of the renewed interest generated by a course of lectures on literature. Churches are quickened in their work. Working men's clubs and organizations become energetic in their desire to promote their own and the community's welfare because of lectures on history, economics, or civics. Libraries are not infrequently started because of the needs of the extension students; and in every case where one exists in the center the demand upon it is increased many times by extension courses. And, finally, the activity and usefulness of our higher institutions of learning are increased many times because of their interest in the work, and also, be it said, because they may have a slight dread that the excellence of the extension work may reflect upon their own or draw students from them. — *Times*, Bethlehem, Pa. 12 November, 1894

There are many who can read books but can not read nature. They do not know the meaning of the strata in the rocks, or the migration of the birds Their local history is little known, or even if known from books is not associated with the mountain, the river, the village, of the locality which might be invested with a double interest if its history were more accura ely known. One important function which a university extension seems well adapted to perform is this linking of the information of the books with the results of intelligent personal observation. The rock which has been entirely dumb may be made to speak in an intelligible voice. The valley which has been only a material environment, a place to live in, may be made to furnish food to man's thoughts.

Every glance into the wood or field, when once the attention of the student has been fixed upon the attempt to understand nature, will reveal some new secret or recall some significant fact. University extension is designed to accomplish such results as these for busy people. The man of leisure it is true may seek culture in travel, in association with congenial spirits wherever they may be. The fortunate young woman or man may undertake a regular college course confident of being brought into contact with at least one or two of those strong natures who always exert an influence over those who know them.— *Times*, Bethlehem, Pa. 16 November, 1894

INDEX

The superior figure points to the exact place on the page in ninths; e. g. r55⁴ means four ninths of the way down page r55. Dates are printed in italics.

Agriculture, list of books, r55⁴.
Albion Columbian association, *see* Columbian association, Albion.
Albion extension center, work, r19⁷.
American institute of sacred literature, cooperation with Extension department, r37⁸.
Apportionment of public library money, r8⁴-9⁷
Arey, A. L., Various forces of nature as related to modern life, syllabus, r54⁴.
Art schools, r50⁴.

Bennett, C: E, Private life of the Romans, syllabus, r54⁵.
Bethlehem, Pa., *Times*, articles on university extension, r63¹-64.
Biblical study, extension courses, r37⁷-38².
Books, most popular in traveling libraries, r18⁶. *See also* Traveling libraries; Volumes
Boston *Watchman*, reply to Charles Whibley, r56⁹-58⁸.
Boyesen, H. H, Medieval German literature, syllabus, r53⁹.
Brigham, A. P., course in Utica, r23⁷, Geology and scenery of New York, syllabus, r54².
Brooklyn art school, r50⁴
Brooklyn institute, report, r49¹-50², biologic laboratory, r50².
Buffalo extension center, first in America, r46⁵.
Bulletin on study clubs, r27⁴

Catholic summer school of America, r46⁵.

Centers, comparison with work of preceding year, r19¹, details of work, r23¹, first in America, r46⁵; formed during year, r19⁹-20¹, statistics, r19⁸, r21-22, use of traveling libraries, r11⁷, r14².
Certificates of registration, r47¹-48¹.
Charters granted to libraries, r5⁴-r6⁴, r7²
Chautauqua university, r46⁵.
Circular, on extension exhibit, r52², on London extension congress, r40⁵-41¹, on relation of libraries to university extension, r44⁴.
Citizen, r55⁹.
Citizenship, training in, r41⁸
Civics classes, r41⁷, r42⁵-43⁴.
Civil and religious liberty in America, by C: E. Fitch, r5⁵.
Clubs, *see* Student clubs, Study clubs; Woman's club.
Cold Spring Harbor, biologic laboratory, r50².
Colgate university, cooperation in extension work, r39⁸
Colleges, connection with extension work, r38⁹-40¹.
Columbia college center, lectures and subjects, r19⁹-20⁸, statistics, r21.
Columbian association at Albion, r19⁷; report, r45⁹.
Conference of extension workers, at University of Chicago, r40²; at London, r40⁴.
Connecticut school of sociology, r43⁵.
Courses, added since March 1, *1894*, r82⁹-36⁹; withdrawn, r87⁴; on sociologic subjects, r41⁹-43⁹. *See also* Lecture courses.

Criticism of extension work, r56⁸-64.
Current topics club, r47⁵.
Curtis, Mrs J K, courses given by, r27⁶, Hamlet and Merchant of Venice, syllabus. r53⁷.

Development of the nation, syllabus by W: H. Mace, r54³
Dobbs Ferry center, formation, r19⁹; statistics, r21.
Donohoe, Rev. J. F., lecture for benefit of Salem center, r28⁴.

Eastman, W: R , libraries inspected by, r8⁷-5⁵, article in *Forum*, r14⁵.
Economic legislation, syllabus by J W. Jenks, r53⁶.
Economic questions, syllabus by G: W: Smith, r53⁹.
Economics, lists of books, r53⁶, r55³
Electricity syllabuses; by A. F. Onderdonk, r53⁶; by Charles Forbes, r54¹, of course under direction of Columbia college, r54⁴.
English literature, studies in, by J. R. Truax, r54¹.
Extension centers, *see* Centers.
Extension conferences, r40²-41¹.
Extension courses, *see* Courses.
Extension department, lectures and courses, r27⁴-36⁹; cooperation with American institute of sacred literature, r37⁶; scope of work, r46⁹, publications, r52⁸-55⁰.
Extension exhibit, r52¹.
Extension literature, periodicals, r55⁸-56⁷.
Extension teachers, *see* Lecturers.
Extension teaching division, report, r19-64.
Extension work, in the colleges, r38²-40¹, necessity of organization, r38⁵; administrative centers, r38⁵-40¹, criticisms, r56⁸-64.

Farce of university extension, magazine article, r56⁸-60⁵
Fitch, C: E., courses given by, r27⁶. syllabus, Civil and religious liberty in America, r53⁸.
Forbes, Charles, syllabus Electricity r54¹.

Forces of nature as related to modern life, by A. L. Arey, r54⁴
Foreign population, reached by extension movement, r41⁵-48⁴.
Forum, article on traveling library system, r14⁹.
France. Making of, syllabus by Mrs F.. G Sears, r5₀⁰.
Freedman, W. H., manager of course at Columbia, r20².
French history, list of books, r55⁴.

Geology and scenery of New York, syllabus by A. P. Brigham, r54⁹.
German literature, Medieval; syllabus by H H Boyesen, r53⁹.
Gilmore, J. H., courses given by, r27⁶.

Hamlet and Merchant of Venice, syllabus by Mrs J. K Curtis, r53⁷.
Hartford, extension work in, r43⁵.
Hobart college, cooperation in extension work, r39⁹.
Home study, organization, r46²-48⁶; selection of subjects, r46⁸-47⁶.
Hygiene classes, r41⁸.

Inspection of libraries, r37-5⁵.
Institute day classes, statistics, r51.
Institute, reports, r48⁹-51⁹.

Jackson, A. V. W., manager of course at Yonkers, r20²; courses given by, r27⁶.
Jenks, J. W, courses given by, r27⁶; syllabus, Economic legislation, r53⁸, syllabus, Political methods, r54⁶.

Lecture courses. registration, r46⁸, r47⁷, substitution for extension courses, r48⁶
Lecturers, during *1894*, r21-22, added to list since Mar 1, *1894* r2 ₁-32⁹; withdrawn from list, r3,⁹-⁵7⁴, difficulty in providing, r38⁷, at C lumbia college center, r20⁴, at Yonkers, r20⁸
Libraries, apportionments for, r6⁴-9⁷; charters granted, r5⁶-r6⁵, charters, admissions and registrations during *1894*. r7⁹, inspections, r3⁷-₅⁵, number under state supervision, r5¹; organization, r5⁵-7²; relation to exten-

sion work, r28³, r24⁴, r43³-44³; statistics, r8⁵, choice of trustees, r6¹; number of trustees, r6³. *See also* School district libraries; Traveling libraries.

Literature, regents reading courses in, r55⁵; of extension movement, r55⁵-56⁹.

London extension congress, r40³-41¹.

Mace, W. H., courses given by, r27⁵; syllabus, Development of the nation, r54³.

Making of France, syllabus by Mrs F.. G. Sears, r53⁹.

Medieval German literature, syllabus by H. H. Boyesen, r53⁹.

Melbourne university extension journal, r56⁶.

Merchant of Venice, syllabus by Mrs J. K. Curtis, r53⁷.

Nations of the orient, syllabus by H. B. Waterman, r54⁷.

New York, colleges interested in extension work, r39³-40¹; educational leadership, r46³.

Newspaper articles on university extension, r56²-64.

Nineteenth century articles on extension work, r56⁵-60⁵.

Onderdonk, A. F., syllabus, Electricity, r53⁶.

Oneida extension center, formation, r19³; statistics, r21.

Organization of libraries, r5⁵-7⁵.

Oxford university extension gazette, r56⁴.

Parsons, J. R. jr, delegate to London extension congress, r40⁴

Paterson (N. J) *Press*, articles on university extension, r60⁵-63¹.

Philadelphia, extension work among foreign classes, r41⁵-43⁴.

Political methods, syllabus by J W. Jenks, r54⁶.

Private life of the Romans, syllabus by C. E. Bennett, r54⁵.

Public libraries division, report r8-18; publications, r54⁹-55⁴.

Publications of extension department, r52⁸-55³, charges for, r55⁴.

Reading circles, loan of traveling libraries to, r11⁹, registration, r46⁸, r47⁷; assistance offered, r48⁵. *See also* Home study.

Reading courses in literature, r55⁵

Registration, of lecture courses, r46⁸, r47⁷, of reading circles, r46⁸, r47⁷; of study clubs, r46⁸, r47⁷.

Rochester university, cooperation in extension work, r39⁸.

Romans, Private life of, syllabus by C: E. Bennett, r54⁵.

Sadler, M. E., reply to Charles Whibley, r56⁹.

Salem extension center, report, r28⁹. *See also* Centers, statistics.

School district libraries, transfer, r5⁹; establishment, r46⁴.

Sears, Mrs F G., syllabus, Making of France, r53⁹.

Shinnecock Hills summer school of art, r50⁵.

Smith, G: W:, courses given by, r27⁶, syllabus, Practical economic questions, r53⁶

Sociologic courses, r41⁹-43⁹.

Sorosis, first woman's club, r46⁹.

Spivak, Dr Charles. work in Philadelphia, r41⁸.

Standards in extension work, r39⁴.

State universities should be center for extension work, r39³.

Statistics of extension centers, r19⁸, r21-22; of Institute day classes, r51; of libraries, r3⁵, of traveling libraries, r18³-18⁹.

Stuart, Mrs James, reply to Charles Whibley, r56⁹.

Student clubs, r25-27⁴; at Utica, r24⁵. organization, r25⁴, by-laws, r25⁹-26⁷.

Study club division, report, r45⁷-48⁸.

Study clubs, special bulletin on, r27⁴; statistics, r45⁸; registration, r46⁸, r47⁷; direction of work, r48¹, fees for traveling libraries, r48⁸. *See also* Current topics club, Home study.

Subjects during *1894*, r21-22.

Summer resorts, loan of traveling libraries to, r12⁹.
Summer schools, r44⁸-45⁷.
Sunday schools, courses in Bible study, r37².
Syracuse center, formation, r19⁹; statistics, r22.
Syracuse Portfolio club, r19⁹-20¹.

Teachers, *see* Lecturers.
Thomas, R. W., organizer of extension work, r39⁸.
Toronto *Mail*, reply to Charles Whibley, r58⁸-60⁵.
Traveling libraries, additions to, r9⁷; circulation, r13⁶-14¹, r15¹-18⁹; fees, r48²; finding lists, r55¹; rules for loan, r10⁷-18¹, loans to individuals, r11⁵-18¹, r14⁹; readers, r18⁷, r15¹-18⁹; subject libraries, r10⁵, r13²-14¹, r17⁵, r18⁸, statistics of use, r13²-18⁹, use at extension centers, r11⁷, r14⁹, r23³, r24⁵; number of volumes, r10¹.
Traveling library system, article in *Forum*, r14⁹.
Truax, J. R., course at Salem, r23²; syllabus, Studies in English literature, r54¹.
Trustees, library, r6¹-7¹.
United States history, syllabus by W: H. Mace, r54²; traveling library list of books, r55⁴.

University extension, *see* Extension.
University extension, r55⁹-56¹.
University extension bulletin, r55⁹-56¹, r56⁵; extract, r42¹.
University extension journal, r56².
University extension world, r56².
Utica extension center, formation, r19⁹; statistics, r22; report, r23⁶-24⁹.

Volumes, number in Public libraries division, r10¹.

Waterman, H. B., syllabus, Nations of the orient, r54⁷.
Waverly extension center, formation, r19⁹; statistics, r22.
Whibley, Charles, criticisms, r56⁹-60⁵.
Whitney, J. E., organizer of extension work, r39⁸-40¹.
Woman's club, first in America, r46⁵.
Woman's institute of Yonkers, r50⁴.
World's fair, extension department exhibit, r52¹.

Yonkers extension course, lecturers and courses, r20², r20⁵; statistics, r22.
Yonkers woman's institute, *see* Woman's institute of Yonkers.

University of the State of New York

Object. The object of the University as defined by law is to encourage and promote education in advance of the common elementary branches. Its field includes not only the work of academies, colleges, universities, professional and technical schools but also educational work connected with libraries, museums, university extension courses and similar agencies.

The University is a supervisory and administrative, not a teaching institution. It is a state department and at the same time a federation of more than 500 institutions of higher and secondary education.

Government. The University is governed and all its corporate powers exercised by 19 elective regents and by the governor, lieutenant-governor, secretary of state and superintendent of public instruction who are *ex officio* regents. Regents are elected in the same manner as United States senators; they are unsalaried and are the only public officers in New York chosen for life.

The elective officers are a chancellor and a vice-chancellor who serve without salary, and a secretary.

The secretary, under official bonds for $10,000, is responsible for the safe keeping and proper use of the University seal and of the books, records and other property in charge of the regents, and for the proper administration and discipline of its various offices and departments.

Powers and duties. Beside many other important powers and duties, the regents have power to incorporate, and to alter or revoke the charters of universities, colleges, academies, libraries, museums, or other educational institutions; to distribute to them funds granted by the state for their use; to inspect their workings and require annual reports under oath of their presiding officers; to establish examinations as to attainments in learning and confer on successful candidates suitable certificates, diplomas and degrees, and to confer honorary degrees.

They apportion annually an academic fund of $106,000, part for buying books and apparatus for academies and high schools raising an equal amount for the same purpose, and the remainder on the basis of attendance and the results of instruction as shown by satisfactory completion of prescribed courses for which the regents examinations afford the official test. They also expend annually $25,000 for the benefit of free public libraries.

Regents meetings. Regular quarterly meetings are held on the fourth Thursdays of November, February and May. Special meetings are held whenever business requires.

Convocation. The University convocation of the regents and the officers of institutions in the University, for consideration of subjects of mutual interest, has been held annually since 1863 in the senate chamber in Albany. Convocation meets on the last Wednesday, Thursday and Friday in June.

Though primarily a New York meeting, nearly all questions discussed are of equal interest outside the state. Its reputation as the most important higher educational meeting of the country has in the past few years drawn to it many eminent educators not residents of New York, who are most cordially welcomed and share fully in all discussions. It elects each year a council of five to represent it in intervals between meetings. Its proceedings issued annually are of great value in all educational libraries.

University of the State of New York

Departments

1 Administrative (Regents office) — including incorporation, supervision, inspection, reports, legislation, finances and all other work not assigned to another department.

Duplicate division. This is a state clearing house, to which any institution in the University may send books or apparatus which it no longer requires and select from it in return an equal value suited to its locality and needs.

2 Examination — including preacademic, law student, medical, dental and veterinary student, academic, higher, law, medical, dental, veterinary, library, extension and any other examinations conducted by the regents, and also credentials or degrees conferred on examination.

The examinations are conducted as the best lever for securing better work from teachers and more systematic and continuous study from students, and as the best means of detecting and eliminating inefficient teachers or methods. They cover 130 subjects and require 1,500,000 question papers annually, and are held the week ending the last Friday in January and March and the third Friday in June, in the 503 academies and high schools in the University and also at various central points where there are 10 or more candidates.

3 Extension — including summer, vacation, evening and correspondence schools and other forms of extension teaching, lecture courses, study clubs, reading circles and other agencies for the promotion and wider extension of opportunities and facilities for education, specially for those unable to attend the usual teaching institutions.

Public libraries division. To promote the general library interests of the state, which through it expends $35,000 a year for the benefit of free public libraries. Under its charge are the traveling libraries for lending to local libraries or to communities not yet having permanent libraries.

The most important factor of the extension movement is provision of the best reading for all citizens by means of traveling, home and capitol libraries and annotated lists through the public libraries division.

4 State library — including state law, medical, and education libraries, library school, bibliographic publications, lending books to students and similar library interests.

Library school. The law authorizes the state library to give to any librarian, assistant, or other person interested in any library in the state, instruction and assistance in organizing and administering libraries. Students receive from the state library staff, in return for services rendered to the library during their two years' course, careful training in cataloging, classification and all other duties of professional librarianship.

5 State museum — including all scientific specimens and collections, works of art, objects of historic interest and similar property appropriate to a general museum, if owned by the state and not placed in other custody by a specific law; also the research department carried on by the state geologist and paleontologist, botanist and entomologist, and all similar scientific interests of the University.

University of the State of New York

Extension Bulletin

No. 13   May 1896

SUMMER SCHOOLS

First annual supplement

	PAGE		PAGE
Introduction	3	University extension summer meeting	37
Schools in New York		Marienfeld summer camp	41
Columbia college	6	University of Virginia	41
Chautauqua	7	Florida Chautauqua	42
Round Lake	9	Catholic winter school of America	42
National summer school	10	Western reserve university	45
Silver Lake	11	Cook county normal school	45
Biological laboratory of Brooklyn institute	12	Chicago Commons school of social economics	45
Natural science camp	13	Biol. exp. station of the Univ. of Illinois	48
Brooklyn institute summer schools of art	13	Bay View	49
Catholic summer school of America	14	Alma college summer school	49
Central New York summer school	15	University of Michigan	50
Cornell University	16	Grand Rapids summer school	50
Port Leyden	17	Western secretarial institute	51
Cayuga lake	17	University of Wisconsin	52
Long Island Chautauqua	17	Columbian Catholic summer school	53
Prohibition Park	17	Summer school for physical training	53
Clinton classical school	18	University of Minnesota	54
New York university	18	Des Moines summer school of methods	54
University of Buffalo	19	Drake university	55
Summer class in geology	21	University of Missouri	55
New York state library school	22	Fairmount Chautauqua	55
Metropolitan normal art summer school	23	University of California	56
Saratoga atheneum summer school	23	Pacific coast students conference	56
Teachers college, New York	25	**Foreign schools**	
Other American schools		Summer school of science for the Atlantic provinces of Canada	57
Eastern New England Chautauqua	28	Edinburgh summer meeting	57
Greenacre summer school	29	Cambridge university	59
N. H. coll. of agriculture and the mech. arts	29	Oxford summer meeting	59
Harvard summer school	30	Lectures for clergy	60
Harvard summer school of physical training	31	Ancoats Brotherhood	60
H. E. Holt normal institute of vocal harmony	32	L. A. U. K. summer school	61
Sauveur coll. of lang. and the Amh. sum. sch.	33	London school of economics and pol. sci.	62
Marthas Vineyard summer institute	33	National home-reading union	62
Marine biological laboratory	34	Alliance Française	63
New England Chau. Sunday school assembly	35	Modern language holiday courses	63
School of applied ethics	36	**Statistics, 1895**	65
Clark university	36	**Index**	83
Wellesley summer school	37		

ALBANY

UNIVERSITY OF THE STATE OF NEW YORK

1896

E8gm–My96–2000   Price 10 cents

Regents

Anson Judd Upson, D.D., LL. D., L. H. D., *Chancellor*
William Croswell Doane, D. D., LL. D., *Vice-Chancellor*
Levi P. Morton, LL. D., Governor
Charles T. Saxton, LL. D., Lieutenant-Governor ⎫
John Palmer, Secretary of State   ⎬ *Ex officio*
Charles R. Skinner, M. A., LL. D., Sup't Pub. Instr'n ⎭

In order of election by the legislature

ELECTED
1873 Martin I. Townsend, M. A., LL. D. - - Troy
1874 Anson Judd Upson, D.D., LL. D., L. H. D. - Glens Falls
1876 William L. Bostwick, M. A. - - - - Ithaca
1877 Chauncey M. Depew, LL. D. - - - - New York
1877 Charles E Fitch, LL. B., M. A., L. H. D. - Rochester
1877 Orris H. Warren, D. D. - - - - - Syracuse
1878 Whitelaw Reid, LL. D. - - - - - New York
1881 William H. Watson, M. A., M. D. - - Utica
1881 Henry E. Turner - - - - - - Lowville
1883 St Clair McKelway, LL. D. - - - - Brooklyn
1885 Hamilton Harris, Ph. D., LL. D. - - - Albany
1885 Daniel Beach, Ph. D., LL. D. - - - - Watkins
1888 Carroll E. Smith, LL. D. - - - - Syracuse
1890 Pliny T. Sexton, LL. D. - - - - - Palmyra
1890 T. Guilford Smith, M. A., C. E. - - - Buffalo
1892 William Croswell Doane, D. D., LL. D. - Albany
1893 Lewis A. Stimson, B. A., M. D. - - - New York
1894 Sylvester Malone - - - - - - Brooklyn
1895 Albert Vander Veer, M. D., Ph. D. - - Albany

Elected by the Regents
1888 Melvil Dewey, M. A., *Secretary* - - - - Albany

University of the State of New York

Extension Bulletin

No. 13 May 1896

SUMMER SCHOOLS

First annual supplement

The first bulletin of the extension department on summer schools was issued in 1894, giving detailed information on the most important summer schools in the United States and foreign countries from which official reports could be secured. As the edition proved entirely inadequate to the unexpectedly great demand, the bulletin was reprinted in 1895 with large additions as Extension bulletin 9. This bulletin supplements that of 1895, containing statistics of the 1895 sessions and announcements for 1896 as far as obtainable up to the time of printing, and also a few historical accounts which were not available last year.

During the year, the New York school law has been amended to provide summer institutes for the training of common-school teachers. The law directs that the superintendent of public instruction shall arrange for three such institutes, each lasting at least three weeks, and appropriates $6,000 annually to cover expenses. Glens Falls, Chautauqua and Thousand Island Park have been chosen as the locations for these institutes in 1896. The courses will continue from July 15 to Aug. 7, and at the close, the uniform examinations for teachers' certificates will be given, as provided in the amendment. Admission and all advantages are free to every teacher in the state and also to those preparing to enter the profession.

The plan for giving state aid to summer schools for common-school teachers was suggested and briefly outlined in the article by Sup't Sherman Williams, printed in the summer school bulletin of 1895. (See *Extension bulletin* no. 9, p. 13)

All registered summer schools in the state are entitled to the traveling libraries and similar privileges of the University, as accorded to study clubs. Libraries of general reading, prepared to lend to public libraries and not needed during the summer months, may be had during the session. In addition, special subject libraries for use of classes will be made up and lent. Juvenile books for clubs can also be supplied, to a limited extent.

The extension of the universities through their summer schools is well brought out by Charles B. Bliss of the New York university school of pedagogy, in an article published in the *School journal* for May 2, 1896, which is here reprinted

UNIVERSITY SUMMER COURSES

In one direction, university extension work is advancing in this country as fast as its most ardent supporters could desire. The number of summer courses offered in the universities is increasing every year, while the number of teachers and others who avail themselves of this opportunity for advanced work is increasing still more rapidly It is impossible to give exact figures in reference to this growth, owing to the rapid changes and the incomplete character of many of the reports In his report for 1894, the commissioner of education gives the names of 48 colleges and universities which have summer courses, also of 28 summer schools not connected with other educational institutions Some of these universities offer summer courses in only one subject, and in some of the colleges the work is of an elementary character. But perhaps a dozen of the best universities of the land are offering regular university courses during the summer, the instruction being given by members of the faculty and the entire equipment of the university being placed at the disposal of the students

This work began at Harvard over 20 years ago But it is only during the last four or five years that the present rapid development has been going on At Harvard the number of courses has been largely increased, and during the last four years the average number of students enrolled has been over 500 At Cornell, summer courses were begun in 1892, with an attendance of 115. Since then the numbers have increased to 275. At the first summer session of the University of Michigan in 1894, there were 91 students and 16 instructors Last year there were 191 students and 25 instructors. This summer 41 instructors offer 101 courses These three instances are representative of what is taking place in all the universities that have undertaken the work.

Most of the universities are in substantial agreement as to the aims and methods of summer work These have been determined by the circumstances and conditions which have led to the development of the summer courses. All courses are open to women as well as men They are intended primarily for teachers and others desiring to do advanced work who are unable to enter the other departments of the university

Instruction is given by members of the university faculty. The libraries, laboratories, museums, and other equipment of the university are placed at the disposal of the students The usual length of the session is six weeks Satisfactory progress can not be made in much less time, and a much longer session makes too large an inroad upon the summer vacation Students are urged to confine their work to one subject, and in some cases the same course is continued over several years. So far as possible, every opportunity and encouragement is given for independent work in addition to the regular courses Where the work done is equivalent to that required in corresponding courses in other departments, due credit for the same is given by the university

The work accomplished depends to a certain extent upon the individual student and his previous preparation But by concentrating the attention upon one subject, under the direction of an able instructor, more can often be accomplished in six weeks than in a college course of two or three hours a week extending throughout the year. In all cases the student gains an insight into the spirit and methods of university work, becomes more or less familiar with the literature of the subject, and is better prepared for further work.

Now that the movement is taking place on so large a scale, it seems strange that it did not begin sooner. The expensive plants of our universities have been lying idle during the summer At the same time the entire body of teachers have been enjoying a long vacation, many of them willing and anxious to prepare themselves for better work in the coming year

This movement has already begun to play an important part in solving one of the most vital questions of the present time, namely, that of raising the standard of the teaching profession It is second only in importance to the establishing by the universities of professional schools of pedagogy on a par with those of law and medicine To those who are qualified for this work and who are willing to devote one, two or three years to a course in a professional school, the universities can offer nothing better. But unfortunately not many are able to make so great a sacrifice To those who can not do this, as well as to those who desire to work only in special lines, the universities offer summer courses What this offer means to the great body of teachers can only be understood by those who know something of the advantages of university work. All the accumulated equipment of many years, the endowments, the libraries, the laboratories, the training and experience of the instructors is for the time placed at the command of the student, all for a fee not exceeding five dollars a week.

As to summer work in general, it is the universal testimony, of those who have tried it, that six weeks of work with new surroundings and new associations, is not exhausting On the contrary the complete change of work is restful. The work of the teacher is not laborious above that of the other professions that they require so much longer vacations. The vacations are on account of the pupil rather than for the sake of the teacher But the teacher is fortunate indeed above the members of the other professions in having so great freedom during the pleasantest months of the year, and with these new opportunities for improvement open to them they may easily make the long vacation a most important factor in our school system.

The great increase in the number of summer schools shows that in spite of objections, they meet a present need. The Woman's education association of Boston has this year established several scholarships for summer school work. During 1896, these scholarships will be offered chiefly for the course in physical geography given by Prof. Davis of Harvard university. The committee in charge finds that a much larger sum than is now at their disposal could be used to advantage and asks that contributions be sent to Mrs R. H. Richards, Institute of technology, Boston, Mass.

The arrangement of New York schools is in order of founding; others are in the same order under the state or country in which they are located. When no other authority is assigned, the facts given are taken from official circulars. Some schools have so little change in the character of their programs for 1896 that no entry is made here, but the reports for the last session will be found summarized in the tables at the end.

SCHOOLS IN NEW YORK

COLUMBIA COLLEGE

Summer school in surveying. Attendance at this summer school is required of students in the three upper classes in the school of engineering The headquarters are at Camp Columbia near Morris, Conn. Students of the second class will assemble July 25, third-class students on July 18, and members of the fourth class on August 29 Conditioned students are not allowed to attend

Summer school in practical geodesy. Seniors in the school of engineering are required to take this summer course in charge of Prof. J. K. Rees. The class will assemble on June 1 at Columbia college. Part of the work will be done at the observatory and the remainder in the field.

CHAUTAUQUA

Synoptic view of the Chautauqua system, in effect January 1, 1896

Summer lectures and classes

Assembly department

1 *Courses of lectures* Consecutive lectures on a single subject by specialists.
2 *Lectures, addresses, sermons*, on a variety of subjects by distinguished speakers
3 *Music*. Organ and piano recitals, orchestral concerts, vocal and instrumental concerts by grand chorus, soloists, quartets and orchestra.
4 *Entertainments* Stereopticon lectures, readings, tableaux, illustrations, fireworks, tennis tournaments, regattas, athletic games, etc
5 *Clubs and classes* for people of various ages and tastes:
   Free kindergarten for children
   Little people's class for Bible lessons
   Boys and girls' class for Bible study
   Primary chorus, for children under 10
   Young people's glee club.
   Boys' club, for boys between eight and 16
   Intermediate class. Bible study
   Chautauqua country club, for young men
   Junior outlook club, girls seven to 15.
   Outlook club, girls over 15
   Woman s club
   German club for students of German
   Ministerial club
   Sunday school normal class for Sunday school teachers

Collegiate department

1 *School of modern languages and literatures:* French, German, etc
2 *School of ancient languages and literatures:* Assyrian, Hebrew Greek and Latin.
3 *School of English* · Language, rhetoric and literature
4 *School of mathematics and science* Mathematics, geology, physics, chemistry, biology
5 *School of social sciences* History, economics, political science, sociology
6 *School of philosophy and pedagogy* Psychology, philosophy, principles of education, general and special methods
7 *School of sacred literature* In English and in the oriental languages
8 *School of fine arts* Art history and technical instruction
9 *School of music*. Harmony, counterpoint, analysis, practice
10 *School of expression* Physiology and psychology of expression
11 *School of physical education* Anatomy, physiology, anthropometry, gymnastics as an art
12 *School of practical arts* China decoration, wood-carving, clay modeling, stenography, type-writing, bookkeeping, cookery

Announcement, 1896 Pedagogy will receive special attention at the session of 1896, under direction of Walter L Hervey, president of Teachers college, New York. In general and special pedagogy, 14 courses are offered, and addresses and courses of lectures will be given by Prof. Nicholas Murray Butler, Prof. William L Bryan, Prof.John Dewey, Sup't F. Treudley, Sup't Charles R Skinner and others. Kindergartners will have the benefit of observing the work of expert teachers in the daily sessions of the two kindergartens.

Professors W. D McClintock of the University of Chicago, W. M. Baskerville of Vanderbilt university, E. H. Lewis of Lewis institute, Chicago, and Mrs P. L. McClintock of Chicago, will conduct the work in the School of English. A weekly conference on the teaching of English literature will be open to all members of the college

In the School of classical languages, professors Alfred M. Wilson of the University of Nebraska and William W. Bishop of Northwestern university will offer instruction in Latin and Greek.

Prof John W. Perrin of Allegheny college offers courses in the history of Europe in the 19th century and in economics; George E. Vincent of the University of Chicago, on the province of sociology and social psychology. The schools of sacred literature will be in charge of Pres. William R. Harper, Professors D. A McClenahan, E L. Curtis, F. K. Sanders and Shailer Mathews. The work includes courses in Hebrew, New testament Greek and the English Bible.

In connection with the usual technical instruction of the School of fine arts, a course on art history and criticism will be given by A. T. Van Laer of New York. The courses in the Chautauqua school of expression include literary and dramatic interpretation and mental teaching and practice in rendering by S. H. Clark of the University of Chicago, and philosophy and technic of gesture by Mrs Emily M. Bishop. The following well known readers will be at Chautauqua in 1896: George Riddle, Miss Ida Benfey, Hannibal Williams, Leland T. Powers, and S. H. Clark.

Over 60 lecturers are engaged among whom are Pres. Eliot of Harvard, Pres. Andrews of Brown, Pres Harper of the University of Chicago, Dr George Adam Smith of Glasgow. Scotland, Prof. Joseph Agar Beet, of Wesleyan college, Richmond, Eng., Rev Charles Aked, of Liverpool, Eng., Prof. Nicholas Murray Butler of Columbia, Lieut. Robert E. Peary, Rev. George A. Gordon of Boston and Prof. Homer B Sprague of New York.

The department of music, which is in charge of Dr H. R. Palmer of New York, provides frequent concerts and recitals

The first meeting of instructors and students will be held Saturday, July 11, and the various departments will be organized on the same day. Examinations will be held at the close of the session, August 19-21, and passcards will be issued to successful candidates by the University of the State of New York.

ROUND LAKE

The session of 1896 begins at Round Lake, N. Y., with the opening of the art school June 21. Mr Hugo Breul of New York is director of the work in art and will give daily lessons in drawing and painting from casts, still life, landscape and the living figures. 20 lectures on art and archeology will be given at the George West museum.

The school of music under direction of Miss Lillie Berg of New York will open July 1 and continue six weeks. In the school of languages instruction is given in French, German and Italian by Prof. L. V. Zucchi, who uses the celebrated Berlitz method.

The third session of the Eastern New York summer school for teachers will be held from July 15-August 13. The courses offered are college preparatory, preparatory course for state certificates, preparatory courses for first, second and third grade certificates, courses in physical culture and school music, and in kindergarten and primary methods. July 14 will be observed as educational day when representatives from the state department, regents office and state normal schools will be present

The first session at Round Lake of the New York school of expression will be held July 6-August 15. The principals are Mrs Genevieve Stebbins and Mr F. Townsend Southwick. The work includes practical Delsartism, elocution, oratory, physical culture and dramatic art. Classes will be formed for teachers of elocution, public readers and speakers and for beginners

The ministers institute opens July 27 and closes August 15. The departments of the institute are pastoral theology, Hebrew, Greek, oratory and archeology. Classes for both beginners and advanced students will be formed in Hebrew and Greek.

The Round Lake musical association announces that the festival of 1896 will include four grand concerts at which the Germania orchestra of Boston will appear.

An assembly department has also been formed with classes for little people, a normal class and a graduate class.

NATIONAL SUMMER SCHOOL

The courses of study offered by the National summer school have been reorganized into four departments: the professional training department for experienced teachers; the training class department for instructors of teachers training classes; the academic department for teachers wishing to make a specialty of some one subject, the drill and review department for students who wish to prepare themselves for examination, specially for the New York first grade examination.

The following courses are offered for the session of 1896, beginning July 14 and ending Aug. 3.

Professional training department

Psychology and pedagogy—Dr Richard G. Boone	20 lectures
Primary work and lessons—Anna K. Eggleston	20 lessons
Methods in arithmetic—Sup't George I. Aldrich	8 lectures
Elocution—Prof Henry L. Southwick	4 lectures
Advanced reading—Sup't George I Aldrich	5 lectures
Literature in primary and grammar schools—Supervisor R. C. Metcalf	5 lectures
School management—Supervisor R C Metcalf	5 lectures
Methods in history—Prin. W. F Gordy	8 lectures
Methods in geography—Prin. Charles F. King	8 lectures
Historical lectures—Regent Charles E Fitch	10 lectures
Natural history—Prof. Austin C. Apgar	2 lectures

Training class department

Organization and management of teachers training classes—A. S Downing, Supervisor of teachers training classes	5 lectures
History and philosophy of education and art of questioning—Prin. E. D. Merriman	15 lectures
Psychology—Dr Richard Boone	10 lectures
Methods—Gertrude Bacon	15 lessons
Drawing—Gratia Rice	15 lessons

Academic department

Drawing, primary, grammar, and high school courses—H P. Smith,
  Ella Richardson, E M Groome . 15 lessons each
Manual training—Mrs E. A. Nye .... 15 lessons
Botany—Prof. Austin C. Apgar .. . . 15 lessons
Elocution—Prof Henry L. Southwick ... . . . 30 lessons
Physical training—Fredric A Metcalf .. .. 15 lessons
School made apparatus—Henry R. Russell . . .. 15 lessons
Physics and chemistry—Henry R Russell .... 15 lessons
Penmanship—Howard Champlin .. .. 15 lessons
Vocal music, four courses—E W Newton ...... 15 lessons each
Kindergarten work and methods, two courses—Caroline Haven 15 lessons each

Drill and review department

Natural science—Prin W D Johnson with assistant 15 lessons each subject
Arithmetic and algebra—Prin. George Winslow .... 15 lessons each
Bookkeeping—Prin. E G Lantman. . . .. 15 lessons
Plane geometry, civil government and school law—Prin H T
  Morrow . .. . 15 lessons each
Geography—Anna Stone .... 15 lessons
History and current topics—Prin Ernest Smith . .... 15 lessons each
Composition, rhetoric, grammar and analysis—Sup't A. Hall
  Burdick .... 15 lessons each
Drawing—Florence B Himes .... 15 lessons
Methods and school economy—Anna K Eggleston . ... 15 lessons
Philosophy of education—Prin E. D Merriman . . 15 lectures

The time of recitations or lectures varies from 35 minutes to an hour. No examinations are given and the only certificates granted are for attendance

The usual series of evening entertainments, readings, lectures, concerts, etc. is provided. The sessions of the summer school are held in the public school and Y. M. C. A. buildings.— SHERMAN WILLIAMS, *Manager*

SILVER LAKE

Announcements for 1896 include a camp meeting, July 7-12; a Good government congress, July 13-16; National Epworth league assembly, July 16-26; Silver Lake assembly, July 27-Aug. 20; International Christian workers assembly, August 21-28; Silver Lake summer university, July 17-Aug. 20. At the Good government congress under direction of Prof. Frank Parsons of Boston, addresses will be made by Prof. Richard T. Ely, Pres Anthony Comstock, Prof. Edward W. Bemis, Theodore Roosevelt, Prof. John Commons, Miss Diana Hirschler and Mrs Annie L Diggs.

The National Epworth league assembly for the United States will be directed by Dr Edwin A. Schell. There will be schools of Bible study, church music and history, instruction in the various departments of league work and popular lectures and entertainments.

During the Silver Lake assembly which follows, a popular program of lectures and conferences will be carried out. A special feature is the musical festival continuing for three days.

The summer university of which Rev. John P. Ashley is president is an outgrowth of the summer schools and includes the following departments music, directed by Perley Dunn Aldrich of Rochester, who will give a university extension course on the History of music; languages; physical training, in charge of B. B Brown of Yale university and G. W. Bush of Western Maryland college; expression; English Bible, art, photography; practical business, and conference studies with classes in kindergarten, mathematics, history, literature, philosophy. Genesee Wesleyan seminary has charge of classes in history, literature, mathematics, languages, art and commercial training. Further information may be had from the sup't of instruction, Rev. Ward Platt, 226 Averill av. Rochester, N. Y.

BIOLOGICAL LABORATORY OF BROOKLYN INSTITUTE

The 1896 session will be held during the months of July and August, beginning July 6

Courses are given in

1 Comparative embryology, by Prof H. T. Fernald.
   Designed for advanced students
2 Elementary zoology, by Prof H. S. Pratt.
   Teachers course, though no preliminary training is required.
3 Cryptogamic botany.
4 Bacteriology.
   Designed specially for medical students

Opportunities are offered for special botanical work and for original research. A course of popular evening lectures will be given to members of the laboratory and friends of the school.

NATURAL SCIENCE CAMP

The encampment of 1896 will begin July 1. The regular term lasts six weeks, but may be extended to August 26 for those desiring to remain if there is sufficient demand. Besides the educational features, which include instruction in geology, entomology, taxidermy, sketching and photography, opportunity is offered for all kinds of outdoor sports and training is given in athletics, boxing, swimming and horseback riding.

The daily routine is as follows·

Reveille	6:15 A M	Swimming call	4	P. M.
Assembly (roll call)	6.35 "	Recall	4:45	"
First call for breakfast	6:55 "	First call for supper	5:25	"
Breakfast call	7 "	Supper call	5.30	'
School call (expeditions start)	8 "	Drill call	6:25	'
		Assembly (for drill)	6:30	"
Swimming call	11 "	Dress parade	7	'
Recall	11.45 "	Adjutant's call	7:02	'
First call for dinner	12:25 P. M	Retreat	7:05	'
Dinner call	12:30 "	Tattoo	9	'
School call	2	Taps (lights out)	9:30	"

BROOKLYN INSTITUTE SUMMER SCHOOLS OF ART

Belle Island. This school, formerly known as the Old Lyme summer school of art, located at Old Lyme, Conn. held its 1895 session at Belle Island, near So. Norwalk, Conn The situation proved so satisfactory that the 1896 session will also be held there, from June to October.

Catskill. The session of 1896 will be held at Napanoch, a village situated at the foot of the Catskills. The class will open June 21 and continue through the summer with Mr George M. Reevs as instructor. Information may be had from Miss Harriet S. Peck, 100 Willow st. Brooklyn, N. Y.

Shinnecock Hills. The next session of this school will be held from June 1 to Oct. 1, under direction of William M. Chase. The school is located near Southampton, L. I.

For further information regarding these schools address Brooklyn Institute of arts and sciences, 502 Fulton st. Brooklyn, N. Y.

CATHOLIC SUMMER SCHOOL OF AMERICA

The fifth session of the school at Plattsburg will be held from July 12 to Aug. 16, 1896. The circulars call attention to the increase of interest in this form of educational extension among Roman catholics during the four years since this school opened Not only has this venture proved a success but two other schools have been established, the Columbian catholic summer school at Madison, Wis. and the winter school at New Orleans. In addition, a school for the Pacific coast is also contemplated.

Since last summer the Champlain club has been formed, open to Roman catholic men over 20. It is proposed to buy the administration building from the summer school, so that the club may have a home this summer. State houses are also to be erected, and the Philadelphia cottage is now in process of construction.

The program for the 1896 session is as follows:

1st week
  1 Conde B. Pallen, Philosophy of literature........ 5 lectures
  2 Rev. Hugh T. Henry, History of English literature 5 lectures
                Evening lectures—illustrated
  3 Rev. J. Driscoll, D. D., Christian archeology..... 4 lectures
  4 Marc F. Vallette, Mexico...................... 1 lecture
  5 S. R. Stoddard, Pictured Adirondacks.......... 1 lecture

2d week
  1 Rev. James F. Loughlin, D. D., Ecclesiastical history ... ... 5 lectures
  2 Charles G. Herbermann, Early German literature.. 5 lectures
                Evening lectures
  3 Sidney Woollette, Shaksperian recitals..........
  4 Hon. Morgan J. O'Brien, subject to be announced.

3d week
  1 Rev. Edward A. Pace, D. D., Empirical psychology 5 lectures
  2 Rev. James A. Doonan, Metaphysics........... 5 lectures

Evening lectures

3 Rev. Henry G. Ganss, Music.................. 4 lectures
4 Rev. Andrew E. Breen, D. D., Galileo.......... 1 lecture

4th week

1 Rev. Francis W. Howard, Political economy...... 5 lectures
2 Rev. T. J. A. Freeman, Physics... ... . 5 lectures

Evening lectures

3 Richard Malcolm Johnston, Evolution of the essay 4 lectures
4 John F. Waters, Hawthorne.................. 1 lecture

5th week

1 Rev. Hermann J. Heuser, Sacred scripture....... 5 lectures
2 Rev. Charles Warren Currier, American history... 5 lectures

Evening lectures

3 Rev. Peter O'Callaghan, Some phases of New England life ... ... 2 lectures
4 Hon. Judge Curren, Sir John Thompson......... 1 lecture
5 Sir William Hingston, Our northern climate and how it affects us......................... 1 lecture
6 D. J. Stafford, D. D., subjects to be announced.... 2 lectures

The completed list will include 75 lectures. The board of studies has also arranged a course of five dogmatic sermons for morning services, in sequence with the course in apologetics of last session. There will be no formal sermons at Sunday evening services, but the board will arrange a course of five popular instructions on the common objects employed in Roman catholic worship.

CENTRAL NEW YORK SUMMER SCHOOL

The fourth annual session will be held at Assembly Park, Tully Lake, July 21-Aug. 12.

The officers of the school are:

President, C. W. Evans, M. A., Elmira high school; secretary and treasurer, T H. Armstrong, Friendship academy; superintendent of instruction, J. H. Carfrey, M. Ph., sup't of schools, Naugatuck, Conn.; manager, W. E. Stillwell, Tully union school.

Five courses are offered Courses A, B, C, are preparatory for the third, second and first grade certificates, course E prepares for state certificates, and course F for teachers training classes. In each course instruction is given in drawing, vocal music, kindergarten and primary work. Special courses are also offered in piano-forte, elocution, physical training, kindergarten, primary work and vocal music. The fees for the different courses vary from $4 to $5.

Free tuition may be secured by organizing clubs of at least six members If clubs of 10 or more are organized, 10 per cent of the tuition of the excess over six will be paid to the organizer.

At the close of the school a Chautauqua assembly will be held, Aug. 14-31.

CORNELL UNIVERSITY

The following courses are offered for the session of 1896, which begins July 6 and closes August 15:

Greek, 2 courses	Chemistry, 10 courses
Latin, 2 "	Botany, 3 courses
German, 3 "	Drawing and art, 5 courses
Romance languages, 4 courses	Mechanical drawing and designing, 3 courses
English, 2 courses	
History, 1 course	Experimental engineering, 4 courses
Mathematics, 13 courses	
Physics, 9 courses	

The work is specially adapted to teachers and advanced students. Certificates of attendance and satisfactory work are granted. Addresses are given before the school by the president and professors of the university and others. Sage college will be open for the accommodation of students during the session of 1896.

Summer law school. The courses offered by the Law school are:

1 Contracts } Prof Huffcutt
2 Torts
3 Crimes
4 Code of procedure } Prof Pound
5 Real property } Prof W. A. Finch
6 Wills
7 Equity } Prof Hardon
8 Evidence

Three lectures will be given daily and the law library of 25,000 volumes will be accessible to students.

PORT LEYDEN

The design of this school is to aid teachers in passing the uniform state examinations. So far as possible conflict of recitation hours is avoided, so that teachers may take any desired course. The term is from July 27 to August 14 and the tuition fee is $3.

CAYUGA LAKE

The third session of the Cayuga lake summer school will be held in the Ithaca high school, beginning July 20, 1896. As before, there will be two departments of study·

1 Professional training department for teachers who wish to familiarize themselves with the best methods of teaching;

2 Academic department, offering courses to those preparing for state teachers examinations.

Tuition is $4 for each course. General lectures on pedagogic topics have been arranged for all registered members of the school, and also a series of entertainments and excursions to neighboring points of interest.

LONG ISLAND CHAUTAUQUA

A special school of modern languages is held under the auspices of the Long Island Chautauqua at Point o' Woods, L. I. Besides courses in mathematics, art, ancient languages, music, history and political economy, Chautauqua exercises are held every summer and a variety of concerts and lectures are given without charge. The fees are $10 for one course and $5 for each additional course. The session for 1896 is open July 1-Oct. 1.

PROHIBITION PARK

The Park is beautifully situated on the woodland hills of Staten Island, 125 feet above the sea. The summer assembly is held annually under the auspices of the National prohibition camp ground association and has an attendance of from 500 to 2500 people.

The season of 1896 opens May 30 and closes September 29. The program includes lectures and addresses, readings, concerts and conferences. Prof. W. C. Peckham, of Adelphi academy, Brooklyn, will give a lecture on the Rontgen rays, Lieut. R. E. Peary will describe his explorations in Greenland and I. K. Funk will lecture on How a dictionary is made.

CLINTON CLASSICAL SCHOOL

The session for 1896 opens June 25 and closes September 3. The location of the school at Peekskill on the Hudson gives opportunity for visiting interesting and historic points in the vicinity. Excursions will be made to West Point, Washington's headquarters at Newburg, the state military encampment and the many mountain lakes, on one of which the boys will camp for two weeks. The reputation of the school for thorough work is well established and the summer course is so arranged as to combine recreation with a reasonable and definite amount of study

Special advantages are offered pupils from Spain, Cuba and Mexico desiring to study idiomatic English. To reach these students the circular of the summer school has been translated into Spanish.

NEW YORK UNIVERSITY

The results of the first summer session at New York university were so satisfactory that the work will be continued and increased in 1896. The session will begin July 6 and end August 14. 28 courses are offered by professors and instructors of the university in mathematics, chemistry, biology, experimental psychology, comparative study of systems of education, Latin, Semitic languages, German, French, economics and physical training.

The summer school work when equivalent to corresponding courses in the university and the school of pedagogy will be credited toward a degree. The courses in comparative study of systems of education and experimental psychology may be taken as part of the regular work in the school of pedagogy. The official prospectus for 1896 accompanies this bulletin.

UNIVERSITY OF BUFFALO
Summer school of pedagogy

The summer school under the auspices of the School of pedagogy, Buffalo, will be devoted entirely to professional work during its two weeks session, July 13-24. The mornings will be given to round tables and lectures, the afternoons to debates on important pedagogic questions. There will also be two evening lectures. The program for the morning sessions is as follows·

Dr Ida C. Bender, School of pedagogy, Buffalo
  Primary work
Pres. John W. Cook, State normal school, Normal, Ill.
  Arithmetic in the grades
John W. Hall, Franklin school, Buffalo
  Subject matter in U. S. history
L. H. Galbreath, State normal school, Winona, Minn.
  Correlation
Dr Woods Hutchinson, Univ. of Iowa, and School of pedagogy, Buffalo
  1 Important types in biology
  2 *a* Birth of experience
    b Cell republic
    c March of muscle
    d Biologic basis of education
Prof. William James, Harvard university
  Mind and environment
  Instinctive impulses and habits
  Association and memory
  Interest and attention
  Will
F. M. McMurry, School of pedagogy, Buffalo
  Laws underlying methods of teaching
Herbert G. Lord, School of pedagogy, Buffalo
  Statesmen of the 19th century
  Literature
Mrs Lida B McMurry, State normal school, Normal, Ill.
  Nature study

M V. O'Shea, School of pedagogy, Buffalo
  Educational psychology
  Child-study
C: A McMurry, State normal school, Normal, Ill.
  Literature suitable for common school grades
  Aim of education, and relative value of studies
Sup't W. S. Sutton, Houston, Texas
  School management
C. C. Van Liew. State normal school, Normal, Ill.
  Child-study
  Reading
  Leaders and subjects for the afternoon discussions are:
Prof. Nicholas Murray Butler, Columbia university
  Study of history of education
Pres. Charles DeGarmo, Swarthmore college
  Essential elements in good character
William James, Harvard university
  Formal training of the mind
John W Cook, State normal school, Normal, Ill.
  How to hold boys longer in school
Sup't W. S. Sutton, Houston, Texas
  Courses of pedagogic study for a corps of city teachers
C A. McMurry, State normal school, Normal, Ill.
  Isolation vs unification of studies
M. V. O'Shea, School of pedagogy, Buffalo
  Relation of child-study to practical teaching
C. C. Van Liew, State normal school, Normal, Ill.
  Culture epochs theory
Prof J. W Jenks, Cornell university
  Training for citizenship
F. M McMurry, School of pedagogy, Buffalo
  Established laws of teaching

Students may be present at these discussions, but are not expected to take part, except by special arrangement

The following evening lectures will be given:
Monday, July 13, Pres. Chas DeGarmo, Swarthmore college
  Culture epochs in education

Thursday, July 23, Prof J. W Jenks, Cornell university
Relation of educational to social reform

The whole program is arranged so that specialization in a high degree may be accomplished, and the plan of debates in the afternoon assures a vividness and thoroughness not heretofore surpassed. Added to the unusually large amount of professional work, are the advantages of meeting so many eminent educators from different sections of the country.

Tuition for the courses will be $6 for one week and $10 for two weeks Those who take partial courses will pay 50 cents for each round table, lecture or discussion that they attend. Suitable boarding places will be recommended on application to F. M. McMurry, School of pedagogy, Buffalo, N. Y.

SUMMER CLASS IN GEOLOGY

At the request of several teachers Prof. Irving P. Bishop of the Buffalo state normal school will conduct a class of men over the western New York section. The route selected will cross the outcrops of all rocks lying between the upper Medina and the top of the Portage group, and will afford an opportunity of studying the character of the different strata, their thickness and relation to each other. Features of economic interest, such as gas-wells, stone-quarries, and manufactories of lime, cement, and clay products will be visited and inspected. Special attention will also be paid to glacial action and its effects on the rocks in the vicinity of Buffalo, and to the erosive effects of streams and other agencies which have shaped the physical features of this region.

The following program, which may be varied somewhat if necessary, will give an outline of each day's work:

1st day. The Niagara gorge from Lewiston to the falls. A study of the stratigraphy, of the recession of the falls, and of their geologic history.

2d day. The rocks of the Salina period including the water-lime group.

3d day. The Onondaga and corniferous limestones and the Marcellus shale.

4th day. The Hamilton shales. These are very fossiliferous and afford excellent opportunities for collecting.

5th day. The lower Portage rocks.

6th day. The upper Portage rocks.

The class will be limited in number to 15. The conductor's fee will be $7 for each member. Railroad and car fare will probably not exceed a dollar for each day. Board will cost from one to three dollars a day according to quality.

Since it is expected that many of those entering the class will be teachers, it is proposed to conduct this excursion either during the last week in June or in the week immediately following the National educational association meeting held in Buffalo July 7-10.

NEW YORK STATE LIBRARY SCHOOL
[Reprinted from Summer school bulletin, 1895]

The first summer session of the New York state library school will begin July 7, 1896 and will last five weeks. After the very heavy year's work of the regular faculty they can not undertake detailed instruction of the summer class. They will however give certain lectures and will select for the direct conduct of the school, graduates who from their library course and experience seem best adapted to this peculiar work. The summer faculty will have every facility of the school and such assistance as is practicable. At the close of the course regents examinations will be given, and certificates stating that the summer course has been completed will be awarded to successful candidates. Students will have free use of the state library as well as the bibliothecal museum and other collections belonging to the Library school. Obviously five weeks will allow study only of the simplest methods and most elementary work included in the 80 weeks of the full course, which is found hardly long enough for the work. Simple cataloging, classification, accessioning, shelf-listing, loan systems and some elementary work in bibliography and library economy will be taken up.

As this summer course is given at the urgent request of library assistants who can not leave their position for the full course, they will have preference in admission, and there will probably be no vacancies for those without library experience as a basis for the short five weeks' course. As the number of desks is limited, early application should be made. Only those who hold credentials for the completion of a full four-year academic or high school course, or its equivalent, will be admitted to the summer session. For those engaged in library work in the state of New York, and who meet the requirements for admission, instruction will be provided without charge as part of the work of the public libraries division. To all others meeting the conditions for admission the fee will be $20 for the five weeks' course.

METROPOLITAN NORMAL ART SUMMER SCHOOL

A four weeks' session beginning July 13 will be held this summer in New York city in the building of the New York university on Washington square. Further information may be had from Langdon S. Thompson, 12 Park street, Jersey city, N. J.

SARATOGA ATHENEUM SUMMER SCHOOLS

The popular lectures conducted last summer at Saratoga Springs were attended so widely that in planning for a repetition of the course this year, a permanent summer school has been organized. Union college and the Hartford theological seminary have both established summer courses to be given at Saratoga.

Classes will be held in the high school building from July 6-August 14, and will be open to men and women without examination, but the faculty will not admit any who are clearly unprepared for the instruction. Except where definitely stated, the work will be of the same character as that done in college during the academic year. Each course will consist of five exercises a week and will count as a three-hour course for one term at Union college. Special provision will be made for students who are preparing for college entrance examinations.

The faculty and courses of study are:

Latin, Mr Edwards	Mathematics, Prof Patterson
Greek, Mr Bennett	Physics, Prof Wright
German } Ass't Prof Pepper Spanish }	Botany } Prof Stoller Biology }
French, Mr Mosher	Engineering, Prof Landreth
English language } Prof Truax and literature }	Physical education, Dr Linhart
	Psychology and } Prof Hoffman ethics }
Rhetoric and } Prof Hale composition }	

The courses offered by the Hartford school of theology, while intended for students of theology of all degrees of attainment, will include several which will be attractive to thoughtful laymen. The program will include:

1 Hebrew and English Bible courses by Prof. Harlan Creelman of Yale. This department will be carried on in conjunction with the American institute of sacred literature of which Dr Creelman is a member and the authorized representative. Three courses will be offered: *a*) Elementary course in Hebrew; *b*) Advanced course in Hebrew; *c*) English Bible course.

2 Ancient Israel among the nations, by Prof. J. F. McCurdy of the University of Toronto, six lectures.

3 New testament literature, by Prof. E. P. Gould of the Episcopal divinity school, Philadelphia, six lectures.

4 The Christian church and the Roman empire, by Prof. Henry Ferguson of Trinity college, Hartford, six lectures.

5 The Roman catacombs, by Prof. Charles C. Stearns of Hartford theological seminary.

6 The medieval church. Arrangements for this course are being made with a professor of the Catholic university, Washington.

7 Four centuries of English hymns, by Prof. Waldo S. Pratt of Hartford theological seminary.

8 Present theological tendencies, by Prof. J. H. W. Stuckenberg of Cambridge, Mass.

9 Some phases of the religious life of New England, 1620-1896, by Rev. George Leon Walker of Hartford.

Besides the courses in charge of Union college and the Hartford theological seminary, a series of lectures will be arranged corresponding to the assembly program at the various Chautauquas. This will include three lectures by Louis C. Elson, the musical lecturer and illustrator; a political symposium, during which prominent speakers of both parties will address the attendants at the summer school; three lectures by Bishop Perry of Iowa on early American history, and other lectures by Bishop Newman, Mrs E H. Walworth, William R. French and Gen. J. B. Gordon. These are to be followed by a grand concert, for which the committee is completing arrangements.

TEACHERS COLLEGE, NEW YORK

A summer school of manual training will be held at Teachers college, Morningside hights, New York, for five weeks from July 6-Aug 8, under management of the directors of the department of manual training and art education of Teachers college. This school has been established in response to a demand for instruction in drawing and manual training during the summer vacation The aim of the school will be to furnish such excellent facilities for the work and such thorough instruction that it will become a summer headquarters for teachers and supervisors of manual training and drawing. With this in view, special effort has been made to select as instructors in the several courses, men who are not only teachers of reputation, but masters of the arts they are to impart.

The following courses of instruction will be offered manual training for elementary schools, mechanical drawing, freehand drawing and painting, wood-carving, forging, wood-joinery, wood-turning and pattern making.

Each course of instruction named below is intended to occupy the entire work-time of the student, six days in the week, for five weeks. All work will be rated as in the regular classes of the same grade at Teachers college. The amount of work done by students receiving a passing mark will be equivalent to that done in a course in the same subject during an entire year in one of the regular college courses, and the faculty of the college will credit it as such to students who are, or shall become, candidates for the Teachers college diploma.

The Macy manual arts building will be occupied by the summer school. This building completely equipped was given to Teachers college by Mrs Josiah Macy, as a memorial to her husband. It is 147 feet long, 71 feet wide and five stories high, including a well lighted basement. The machinery, tools, cases and furniture constituting the equipment, have been selected with special reference to the requirements of manual training and art work. The library in this building contains many books, pamphlets, periodicals, photographs and reports of great value to students of manual training and art education. In the museum and scattered through the work rooms are vases, reliefs, models, carvings and casts. The purpose has been to make the building and its equipment complete and in every way adapted to its use.

The following courses of lectures will be given by members of the teaching staff, and will be open to all students in the summer school. Whenever possible, these will be illustrated by blackboard sketches, models and lantern photographs.

Four lectures by Prof. Bennett.
- July 8 The manual training idea in education: its origin and development.
- July 10 Some lessons we may learn from a study of the Russian system and the Swedish sloyd.
- July 13 Manual training in America. Brief history, the manual training high school, manual training in the elementary schools.
- July 15 Four principles of teaching applied to manual training.

Three lectures by Mr Hall.
- July 17 The aim and scope of art education.
- July 20 Pictorial drawing. The best means of teaching it in a school; artistic composition.
- July 22 Design. How much can be taught; its relation to house furnishing, dress, etc.

Two lectures by Prof. Mason.
- July 24 Principles of orthographic projection. First angle method; third angle method.

July 27 Working drawings. Their use; principles involved; methods of teaching.

Two lectures by Mr Vroom.

July 29 Wood and its use in construction.

July 31 Constructive design.

Two lectures by Prof. Mason.

Aug. 3 Some general principles that should be considered in planning a manual training school building.

Aug. 5 Equipment of a room for wood-working.

A number of conferences, open to all students, will be conducted by the instructors in charge of the various courses. These will take place on days when there are no lectures. The subjects will be such as may be suggested by the lectures and the daily work, the students being allowed to select.

The school will be in session six days of each week for five weeks. The program for each day will be the following

9- 9 15 Chapel exercises and announcements.

9.15-11 15 Demonstration lesson or lecture and work under the eye of the instructor.

11.15-12 15 General lecture or conference.

12.15- 1.30 Luncheon.

1.30- 3 Afternoon practice.

As regards location, Teachers college enjoys many of the advantages of both country and city. It is situated on a high point of land between Riverside and Morningside parks, just across 120th st. from the new site of Columbia university, and only a few blocks north of the site of the cathedral of St John the Divine. In this commanding position on the " American acropolis " it overlooks Central park on the southeast; the Harlem river and Long Island sound on the northeast, and the Grant monument, the Hudson river and the Palisades on the northwest. It is near many points of historic interest; Fort Lee, Fort Washington and Harlem plains are in sight. A few minutes by railway brings one to Tarrytown and a few hours by boat to West Point and Newburg.

It is, too, within easy reach of the Metropolitan museum of art and the American museum of natural history. 40 minutes by elevated train takes one to the greatest shopping center in America, and a few minutes more lands one at Battery park from which point he can embark for Brooklyn, Bedloe's island, Staten island, Coney island and many of the numerous seashore resorts along the New Jersey and Long Island shores.

Another attraction is the many miles of excellent roads for bicycling in the region round about Riverside drive, the Boulevard, Central park, upper Fifth av. and the roads to Washington bridge are the haunts of thousands of New York wheelmen on summer evenings. It takes but 35 minutes by ferry and wheel to go to Englewood cliffs above the Palisades on the New Jersey side of the river, from which point the noble Hudson may be viewed for miles up and down

For the accommodation of students in the summer school, the Teachers college hall will be open from July 1 to August 8. This is a new building designed specially for the accommodation of students, is on high ground, three minutes' walk from the Macy manual arts building and faces the new site of Columbia university.

It is important that those who expect to attend the summer school should notify the director of their intention not later than June 20. In case there should be less than eight applicants for instruction in any given course, the management will not feel under obligation to carry it on.

For circulars or further information, address Charles A. Bennett, Teachers college, Morningside hights, 120th street, West, New York.

OTHER AMERICAN SCHOOLS
EASTERN NEW ENGLAND CHAUTAUQUA

The Eastern New England Chautauqua and Biblical institute at Ocean park, Maine, will open its session for 1896 on July 20 and close August 7.

The Biblical institute will be in charge of Rev. J. A. Howe, D. D., dean of Cobb divinity school of Bates college, and Prof. K. Bachelder of the department of Greek and English literature of Hillsdale college There will be a young people's normal Bible class, a children's normal Bible class and a normal mission class. The department of oratory and physical culture will be in charge of Miss Sadai Prescott Porter of Emerson college of oratory, Boston. The art course will be conducted by Miss Luella I. Ainger of Sutton, Vt. The musical department is in charge of Prof. A. P. Briggs assisted by Mrs Martha Dana Shepard, pianist. There will be a series of excellent lectures and concerts for the assembly program.—E. W. PORTER, *Chairman assembly committee*

GREENACRE

The session of 1896 will open July 1 with a Peace conference, to be followed July 6 with a conference on Comparative religion conducted by Rev. F. Huberty James of England Later conferences are· July 13, Education; July 20, The home, conducted by Mrs Ellen A. Richardson; July 27, Anthropology, conducted by Rev. Duren J. H. Ward, August 3, Evolution, by Dr Lewis G. Janes; August 10, Nature, by Hamilton W. Mabie; August 17, Art; August 24, Sociology. The lectures will be given four times a week, with two evening discussions —MISS SARAH J FARMER, *Secretary*

In connection with the Greenacre lectures, Miss Mary H. Burnham, of the Burnham school of music, New York, will conduct a summer school of music from July 1 to August 5. The course will include two piano lessons a week, class lessons in musical analysis, harmony, concentration, ear training, talks on teaching, acoustics and Beethoven analysis. The fee for the entire course is $25.

NEW HAMPSHIRE COLLEGE OF AGRICULTURE AND THE MECHANIC ARTS

The third annual session for 1896 will occupy the four weeks between July 6 and August 1. Laboratory courses are offered in zoology and botany, elementary entomology, systematic botany, and in the collection and cultivation of specimens for biologic study; the last designed specially for teachers of botany and zoology.

To meet the need of teachers of natural history who wish to study higher cryptogams and flowering plants, a course in systematic botany is offered by Miss Flora S. Beane. Prof. Weed will conduct a course in systematic and biologic entomology, supplemented by as much field work as each student has time for.

Three or four hours daily will be given to laboratory work, animal forms being studied in the morning and plant forms in the afternoon. In addition, a number of more elaborate lectures on biologic topics will be given by instructors in the college.

HARVARD SUMMER SCHOOL

During the summer of 1896, courses will be given as follows·

English, 5 courses
  Composition, 2 courses
  Language and literature, 3 courses
German, 2 courses
French, 2 courses
Latin, for teachers
Education and teaching.
  History and principles of education
  Psychology for teachers
  School hygiene and study of children
  Methods of teaching geometry and algebra
Mathematics, 3 courses:
  Solid geometry
  Trigonometry
  Plane analytic geometry

Engineering, 3 courses.
  Drafting and descriptive geometry
  Land surveying
  Railway engineering
  Freehand drawing
  History and theory of the fine arts
Physics, 2 courses
Chemistry, 4 courses.
  Fundamental principles of chemistry
  Qualitative analysis
  Quantitative analysis
  Organic chemistry
Botany, 2 courses
  Vegetable morphology and floral analysis
  Physiology of phanerogams

Geology, 3 courses:
  Elementary geology
  Geologic field work, 2 courses
Physiography, 2 courses

Physiology and hygiene for teachers
Physical training, 2 courses
Courses at the medical school
Courses at the dental school

A library of all the recent text-books has been provided so that students may examine the comparative merits of those on a given subject. Students have access to the college library, the museum of comparative zoology, the Peabody museum, the Semitic museum and the mineralogic collection.

HARVARD SUMMER SCHOOL OF PHYSICAL TRAINING

The increased attendance at the course on physical training since it was established in 1887 has made it necessary to raise the standard and define the methods more clearly. Though the course is primarily designed for teachers, it is also open to all students. The exercises are conducted at the Hemenway gymnasium on the adjoining grounds, and in the lecture halls of the university.

The theoretical work of the course consists of lectures and practical talks, with illustrations on the following subjects:

Applied anatomy
Elementary and experimental physiology
Personal hygiene
Physical training
First aid to the injured
Anthropometry
Growth of children
Physical examinations and diagnosis
Physical basis of mental life
Physical exercise in the treatment of spinal curvature
Diseases of women and their treatment through physical agencies
Testing for normal vision and hearing
Massage

The following exercises comprise the practical work of the course:
  Free movements
  Calisthenics
  Light gymnastics
  Military drill
  Methods of conducting squad, class or division exercises
  Gymnastic games
  Delsarte movements and relaxing exercises
  Swedish gymnastics
  Heavy gymnastics
  Track and field athletics
  Boxing
  Fencing
  Rowing
  Swimming
  Voice training
  Special exercises on developing appliances

The session of 1896 will begin July 3 and end August 8. In the study of anthropometry special attention will be given to practice in plotting from Dr Sargent's new charts, which were exhibited at the World's fair.

Opportunities will also be given for learning of some of the most recent tests in experimental physiology and psychology, directing class exercises, conducting athletic meetings and studying the modern methods of selecting and training men for participation in various field games and athletic events. Marching calisthenics and exercises adapted to the use of public schools will be a special feature of the work.

The fee for the full course is $50; for practice or theory, alone, $25.

H. E HOLT NORMAL INSTITUTE OF VOCAL HARMONY

The 13th annual session will be held July 14-31, at Lexington, on the Boston and Lowell railroad, 10 miles from Boston.

While the work was originally designed for teachers in public schools, the scope has been so broadened that it now embraces the whole subject of vocal training from an educational standpoint. The course covers three sessions of the school. At its close, diplomas are awarded to those who successfully pass the examination An advanced course is arranged for graduates. Fee for the term, $20

SAUVEUR COLLEGE OF LANGUAGES AND THE AMHERST SUMMER SCHOOL

Since 1894 these two schools have held their sessions together at Amherst college. The 21st session will open at Amherst July 6 and close August 14.

There will be classes for beginners and advanced students in French, German, Italian, Spanish, Latin, Greek and Hebrew.

Dr L. Sauveur, Mlle A. Villeré, Mlle Emma Morhard and Mme P. P. Myer will be in charge of the French department Dr Wilhelm Bernhardt and Prof. Friedrich Karl Brede of German, Prof. T. E. Comba of Italian and Spanish, Prof. J. H Dillard of Latin, Prof J P. Leotsakos of Greek, and Rev David Sprague of Hebrew.

Besides the regular classes there will be six French lectures, five German lectures and six lectures on Dante (in English). Prof. Dillard will lecture on Cicero, Horace and the younger Pliny, and Prof. Leotsakos will give two illustrated lectures in English on Greece of old and Greece of to-day.

The classes in English literature will be conducted by Dr William J. Rolfe This course is intended to be practical both for teachers and students, though interesting and profitable to others. One or more plays of Shakspere and selections from other authors will be read in connection with the lectures. Instruction in mathematics will be given by Clinton Clark of the Rutgers college preparatory school and a practical course in library economy is offered by W. I. Fletcher, librarian of Amherst college. Lessons in out-door sketching in oil and water colors, and in drawing from casts will be given by Miss Lucy C. Hitchcock of the art department of Smith college

MARTHAS VINEYARD SUMMER INSTITUTE

The 19th annual session of Marthas Vineyard summer institute will be held at Cottage City, Mass. beginning July 13. The School of methods with 30 instructors offers an elementary and a high school course for teachers and all interested in educational work. The session will continue four weeks.

A general course in pedagogy and psychology open to all members of the institute will be given by Prof. John Dewey, Prof. M. G. Brumbaugh, J. W. Dickinson, Frank A. Hill, William Hawley Smith, W. S. Monroe, Rev. A. E. Winship and Prin. Everett Schwartz.

The academic department with 29 instructors offers courses in botany, form, drawing and color, English literature, French, German, history and civil government, Latin and Greek, mathematics, microscopy, music, nature study and elementary science, photography, physics and chemistry, painting, physical culture and sloyd The academic department will be in session five weeks.

A school of elocution and oratory will be conducted by the faculty of the Emerson college of oratory, Boston.

MARINE BIOLOGICAL LABORATORY

Courses of instruction consisting of lectures and laboratory work are given in zoology, botany, embryology and physiology. The work is arranged for students, teachers of science and investigators.

Of the 40 private laboratories for investigators 22 are used for zoology, 8 for physiology and 10 for botany These rooms are rented at $100 to colleges, societies or individuals There are also general laboratories for the use of students engaged in special research under supervision of the director and for advanced courses preparatory to investigation.

The total number in attendance in 1895 was 199. The number of investigators in zoology was 34; in physiology, 6, in botany, 2. Of these 13 had instruction in zoology, 2 in physiology and 6 in botany. 35 attended the course in embryology, 85 the introductory course in zoology and 16 the introductory course in botany The number of institutions represented at the 1895 session was 85.

In 1894 a Biological association was formed to aid in securing funds for founding a biological station as a national center of research in every department of biology

The season of 1896 opens June 1 and closes October 1. Dr Lillie of the University of Michigan and Dr Strong of Columbia will conduct the laboratory work in embryology. The course also includes lectures and seminar work under the director. The class is limited to 18.

The course for teachers and students in zoology includes a study of the typical marine animals by lectures, laboratory work and collecting excursions. Lectures are given every morning and collecting excursions made on Wednesdays and Saturdays.

The work is arranged as follows.

July 1-2 Protozoa; July 3-9 Coelenterata; July 10-11 Platodes; July 13-17 Vermes; July 18-24 Mollusca; July 25-30 Echinodermata; July 31-Aug. 8 Crustacea; Aug. 9-12 Tunicata.

Dr J. E. Humphrey of Johns Hopkins university and G. T. Moore, jr of Harvard will conduct the work in cryptogamic botany. Dr Humphrey will give a course of lectures on the various groups of plants from the standpoint of comparative morphology.

The course in phanerogamic botany will consist of lectures and laboratory instruction on the development and comparative anatomy of flowering plants with methods of observing, preserving and preparing objects. There will also be special classes for advanced and research students in botany.

Tables are reserved for those prepared to do original work in zoology and botany and special subjects for investigation will be assigned. Evening lectures on biologic subjects of general interest will be given. The fee for each course is $50. Further information may be had from the secretary, Mrs A. P. Williams, 23 Marlborough st. Boston, Mass.

NEW ENGLAND CHAUTAUQUA SUNDAY-SCHOOL ASSEMBLY

The 18th assembly will be held July 20-August 1, 1896 at South Framingham, Mass. Daily classes will be conducted in the following departments: Bible normal, by Rev. J. L. Hurlbut; Sunday-school normal, by Prof. George W. Pease; music, by Prof. Charles E. Boyd; physical culture and elocution, by Miss Emily Robinson;

C. L. S. C., by Rev. J L. Hurlbut; New testament Greek, by Dean Alfred A. Wright, temperance, by Mrs Abby T. Rolfe; Browning's poetry, by Charles Malloy. There will be three lectures daily, besides special conferences, reunions and entertainments

SCHOOL OF APPLIED ETHICS

Owing to proposed changes in the organization and plan of work of the school, no session will be held in 1896, but it is expected that an attractive location will be found and arrangements made for an important session in 1897. A new constitution is in preparation which will increase the scope of the work, and the school will be incorporated under the laws of Massachusetts The sessions held at Plymouth have been well attended by clergymen, college instructors, teachers and special students, and as a result of the lectures valuable additions have been made to ethic and pedagogic literature.

CLARK UNIVERSITY

The summer school at Clark university offers much that is new and valuable in the line of psychology and child-study. The school will open July 13 and close July 25. In psychology, child-study, physiology and neurology, pedagogy, language and history of curriculums and anthropology, 96 hours of instruction will be given. Much of Dr G. Stanley Hall's course on child-study is based on answers to the questions in his printed syllabuses which have been sent out widely during the last two years. The work is entirely new and will be of special interest to professors and students of psychology and teachers of all grades.

Topics are as follows: Food and appetites of children; Fears in childhood and youth; Anger; Friendship and love in childhood and youth; Old age, disease and death; Laughing, fun, wit, tickling; Toys, playthings and games; Dolls; Common automatisms, nerve signs, etc.; Common traits and habits; Folk-lore among children; Spontaneous feelings toward objects of nature; Religious nature, experience and training of children; Moral defects and moral education; Exceptional and peculiar children; Musical education, Kindergarten; Arithmetic, counting; Child-study in general.

A special course of evening lectures will be given which is free for members of the school. The fee is $12 a week or $20 for the course of two weeks.

WELLESLEY SUMMER SCHOOL

A private summer school was held last year at Wellesley college, but as it was not widely advertised only a few students were in attendance. This year the plan has been enlarged and the following subjects will be offered by members of the Wellesley college faculty:

Natural history, Mr A. P. Morse, curator of Zoological museum.
History, Associate-Prof. Elizabeth K. Kendall.
German, Miss Elsbeth Muller.
French, Miss Hélène J. Roth.
Greek and Latin, Dr Helen L. Webster.

The fee for each course in history and language is $12; for natural science, $13-$20. Classes will meet in College hall, and library and laboratories will be open to students.

UNIVERSITY EXTENSION SUMMER MEETING

The American society for the extension of university teaching will hold its fourth summer meeting in the buildings of the University of Pennsylvania, West Philadelphia, July 6-31, 1896. There are five departments, as follows:

Department A, Literature and history. This department is intended to be of interest to all adult students. The present year is the second in the cycle of study begun in 1895, which will cover five or more years, each devoted to one of the specially important and attractive periods of the world's history. In the first year of this course a study was made of Greek life and thought, and in the present session the subject is Life and thought of ancient Rome. The subjects which are most prominent are Roman law and institutions in the ancient and modern world, to be discussed in a course of 10 lectures by Prof. Munroe Smith of Columbia university; and the Relations between the Roman empire and early Christianity, to be discussed in two courses, one of 10 lectures by Rev. Thomas J. Shahan, D. D., professor of early ecclesiastical history in the Catholic university of America, and another of five lectures by Rev William Bayard Hale, of Middleboro, Mass , lecturer of the American society. Other courses, mainly of five lectures each, are on the Principate, an elementary introduction to the study of the constitutional history of the Roman empire, by Prof. Elmer Truesdell Merrill, Wesleyan university; Roman historiography, by Prof. Alfred Gudeman, University of Pennsylvania, Scenes from the private life of the Romans, by Prof. Tracy Peck, Yale university; Roman poetry in the Augustan age, by Prof. Clement L. Smith, Harvard university, Philosophy in Rome, by Prof. William A. Hammond, Cornell university; Influence of Latin literature and language on English, by Dr Clarence Griffin Child; Special Roman studies, by Prof. William Cranston Lawton; Gibbon's *Decline and fall of the Roman empire*, by Prof. Dana C. Munro of the University of Pennsylvania, and special lectures or classes by Prof. Henry Gibbons, Dr Homer B. Sprague, Dr Ernest Riess, Prof. William Henry Goodyear and Mr Hilaire Belloc, Oxford university. The latter will also deliver the inaugural lecture of the summer meeting on the Roman basis of our civilization on Monday evening, July 6.

Department B, Psychology. This department will provide a course of 20 lectures and three laboratory courses, all under charge of Prof. Lightner Witmer, director of the psychologic laboratory in the University of Pennsylvania, and lecturer in physiologic psychology in Bryn Mawr college. These courses are specially suitable for teachers, physicians and students of those branches of economics and sociology which have a psychologic basis. The instruction offered does not require nor presuppose any special training in psychology. The work will appeal to special students of psychology, however, as well as to beginners, because of the use that will be made of experimentation and demonstration. The lectures and laboratory courses combined present an outline of psychologic principles and methods that will be found to be of material service to those preparing themselves to give instruction along similar lines in colleges and normal schools, or as institute lecturers.

Department C, Music. Besides the courses heretofore offered by Dr Hugh A. Clarke in harmony and counterpoint, there will be an extended course on the principles of music analysis by Mr Thomas W. Surette of Baltimore, dealing with pianoforte sonata, church music, and the opera. This work will be introduced by a lecture-recital on Parsifal on the evening of July 7.

Department D, Science. The lectures and laboratory work of the courses in the department of science have been arranged with a view to the special needs of teachers. They will suggest much new material for study in the school-room, give information concerning the best and most modern methods of using it for nature study, and also such technical training in the use of the microscope and other instruments as will enable those who complete the course to continue their work in the university. The lectures in the various courses will be fully illustrated by natural objects, charts, diagrams and lantern. The laboratories and equipment of the university are placed fully at the disposal of the department for the use of students, and unusually good facilities are thus afforded at a merely nominal cost. The courses deal with biologic and chemical subjects as follows: Evolution and distribution of flowering plants, by Dr Benjamin L. Robinson of Harvard university; Timber trees in health and decay, by Dr John M. Macfarlane of the University of Pennsylvania; the Natural history of field and garden plants, by Dr J. W. Harshberger of the University of Pennsylvania; Natural products, by Dr William P. Wilson of the Philadelphia museums; Life history of insects, by Dr S. C. Schmucker of the West Chester normal school; Fungous diseases of plants, by Prof. Byron D. Halstead of the New Jersey agricultural college experiment station; Principles of chemistry, by Dr M. E. Pennington of the University of Pennsylvania; Chemistry of the soils, by Prof. William Frear of the Pennsylvania state college; Chemistry and economy of food and nutrition, by Prof. W. O. Atwater of Wesleyan university; Chemistry of food, by Dr F. G. Benedict of Wesleyan university; Proper correlation of nature studies, by Mrs L. L. W. Wilson; and the Chemist as an agent of human progress, by Dr Vickers Oberholtzer.

Department E, Mathematics. Instruction in mathematics will embrace such topics in the higher branches of that science as are called for by students in attendance. There will be courses adapted to the needs of teachers in secondary and grammar schools, as well as those more advanced for instructors in colleges and high schools and for advanced students of mathematics. A new course is offered this year by Dr Isaac J. Schwatt on Methods of teaching mathematics.

In addition to the five regular departments outlined above there will be a popular evening course on the French revolution, by Mr Hilaire Belloc of Oxford university.

The registration fee for department tickets is $10; for inclusive tickets, $15. The unique feature of the present meeting is that a special fund of $1000 has been subscribed by persons interested in the public school system of Pennsylvania to enable the university extension society to give to the teachers of the commonwealth a special rebate in the registration fee. The inclusive ticket, because of this fund, is given to Pennsylvania teachers for $5. The trunk line association has consented to give the ordinary convention rates —one and one third fare for the round trip—so that the total expense of attending the summer meeting is very materially reduced without any corresponding reduction in the quality or character of the program.

The summer meeting is held for the purpose of giving to university extension and other students the privilege of a month's residence at a great university, with instruction under the favorable conditions supplied by libraries, laboratories and other university facilities, and the presence of a number of eminent specialists in each branch of study pursued. Incidentally those who attend the summer meeting will have an excellent opportunity to visit the very large number of places in and near Philadelphia which have interesting historical associations, and to become acquainted with a city, which, with a population smaller than Chicago or New York, has a larger number of dwellings than both of those cities combined, and which has a larger number of churches in proportion to its population than any other city in the world. By picnics and excursions frequent opportunity is given for breaking the routine of lectures, and for becoming acquainted with the beautiful park and suburbs of the city. Full information of the different departments of the summer meeting, may be obtained from Edward T. Devine, *Director*, 111 S. 15th st., Philadelphia, Pa.—EDWARD T. DEVINE

MARIENFELD SUMMER CAMP

The summer camp is located in the beautiful region of the upper Delaware, about a mile from Milford, Pa. A house and farm of 200 acres have been selected for the use of the camp and a delightful country life during July and August is promised the boy campers. The camp will be in charge of Dr C. Hanford Henderson, Charles A. Gilchrist and Philip H. Goepp.

An opportunity to pursue special lines of study and to prepare for college entrance examination will be given, though the course is entirely flexible and study is limited to the hours of 9 to 12 a. m.

The following subjects are offered:

1 Humanistic group: English, German, French, Greek, Latin, history, logic and ethics.

2 Mathematics: geometry, algebra, arithmetic, trigonometry, analytics, calculus, mechanics and surveying.

3 Science physical geography, natural history, physics, chemistry, geology and astronomy.

4 Art. music, sketching and wood-work.

Boating, bathing, cycling, horseback riding and all out-door sports will form the main occupation of the day, the educational work being secondary. Candidates for admission may be from nine to 20 years of age and must be reasonably free from moral, mental and physical defects. The fee for the summer is $150 payable in advance.

UNIVERSITY OF VIRGINIA
Summer law lectures

Prof. John C. Minor, the founder and conductor of the summer law lectures, died in 1895 but the work will be continued as nearly as possible on the original plan. The lectures are divided into three classes:

Class 1 includes elementary law, principal and agent, husband and wife, parent and child, guardian and ward, contracts, personal property, wills, probate and administration.

Class 2 is designed for more advanced students and includes lectures on common law and equity pleading and practice, real estate and the law of corporations.

Class 3, which is for Virginia students and practitioners only, is offered for the first time. The Virginia statutes as contained in the code of 1887 and subsequent acts of assembly will form the subject of the course.

Classes 1-2 begin July 1 and continue two months; class 3 begins July 15 and ends August 15. The fee for class 1 is $50; for class 2, $50; for class 3, $25; for any two classes, $60 and for the full course $65.

A special course of 30 lectures on Evidence and mercantile law is offered by James B. Green of the University of Virginia, beginning July 2. The fee is $15.

FLORIDA CHAUTAUQUA

The 12th annual session, held February 20-March 18, was marked by great enthusiasm and success; an attractive program of lectures and concerts was presented. The round tables were unusually successful and helpful.

CATHOLIC WINTER SCHOOL OF AMERICA

The Catholic winter school of America, which held its first session during the present year in the quaint and historic city of New Orleans from February 20 to March 14, is an outcome of the needs of the catholic people of the south. It has two elder sister schools known as the Catholic summer school of America, located at Plattsburg, N. Y., and the Columbian catholic summer school of Madison, Wis. It is the purpose and desire of the founders and promoters of the Catholic winter school of New Orleans to do intellectually for catholics of the south what the schools of the east and west are doing for the catholic people of the north.

The idea of establishing a course of university extension lectures among catholics of the south—for practically these catholic summer and winter school lectures are university extension lectures on the very broadest plan—first found lodgment in the brain and heart of Rev. Dr Mullany of Syracuse, N. Y. and through the sympathy and cooperation of the progressive archbishop of New Orleans, Most Rev. Dr Janssens, Very Rev. F. V. Nugent and many others of the clergy as well as prominent laymen of that city, the idea took root, flowered and became a crystalized fact.

The inauguration of the lecture course, which took place in Tulane hall February 16, was marked by the presence of their eminences Cardinal Gibbons and Satolli, nearly all the bishops of the south, many of the leading state and city functionaries and a large gathering of the clergy and laity. Addresses of welcome were delivered by Most Rev. Dr Janssens, Judge Parlange, representing the governor of Louisiana, and Mayor Fitzpatrick. The Catholic winter school of the south had a most enthusiastic and auspicious opening.

During the session three lectures were delivered each day; the morning lecture at half past 10, the afternoon lecture at four o'clock and the evening lecture at eight. The attendance in general was good, varying of course with the attractiveness of subjects and speakers. The fact that more than 2000 registered and that there was an aggregate attendance of some 25,000 during the three weeks' course is ample testimony to the success of the school. Nor did the interest subside in any way as the session began to draw to a close. The lecturers were from various parts of the United States and in many instances possessed national reputations as writers, speakers and specialists. Among those who shared in the lecture program were Cardinals Gibbons and Satolli, Rt Rev. J. J. Keane, D. D., Rector of the Catholic university of Washington, Rev. Martin S. Brennan of the Kenrick seminary, St Louis, Mo., Rev. A. B. Langlois of St Martensville, La., Prof. Richard Malcolm Johnston the southern novelist, of Baltimore, Md., Rev. Dr Zahm, the noted scientist of Notre Dame university, Ind., Rev. Morgan M. Sheedy, a clever and scholarly young priest of Altoona, Pa., Conde B. Pallen, the well known journalist and *litterateur* of St Louis, Mo., Brother Baldwin of St Joseph's normal school, Amawalk, N.Y., Hon.

R. Graham Frost of St Louis, Mo., Rev. Wm. Power of Spring Hill college, Ala., Prof. Alcée Fortier of Tulane university, New Orleans, Rev. J: F. Mullany of Syracuse, N. Y. and Miss Eliza Allen Starr the eminent art critic of Chicago.

The lectures covered a wide range of subjects and included botany, astronomy, history, rhetoric, English literature, Italian literature, social and economic problems, pedagogy, ethics, biology and art. The able series of lectures on pedagogy by Brother Baldwin drew out large audiences made up chiefly of teachers from the various religious communities as well as from the public and high schools of the city. The sisters and brothers of the various teaching orders in New Orleans manifested throughout the course the keenest and most constant interest in the Catholic winter school proving by their attendance and that of their pupils as well, that as educators and students they are alive to the advantages offered by this phase of the university extension movement.

Financially the Catholic winter school was able to meet all obligations, a very necessary feature of its success. Life membership in the school has been fixed at $100, an annual patron's ticket at $10 and single admission at 25 cents.

The school is conducted under the auspices of the board of directors of the Society of the Holy Spirit, of which Most Rev. Francis Janssens, D. D., archbishop of New Orleans, is honorary president, Judge Frank McGloin, president, A. J. Doizé, secretary, and George W. Young, treasurer. These are aided by an auxiliary board of which the following are the chief members. Very Rev. F. V. Nugent, Very Rev. J. H. Blenk, Rev. E J. Fallon, Rev. J. F. Lambert, I. H. Stauffer, Prof. Alcée Fortier, A. H. Flemming, John T. Gibbons, Chas. A. Fricke, John W. Fairfax and J. J. McLoughlin.

The promoters and patrons of the Catholic winter school believe that education is a life work; that the mind should be developed, the will trained and the affections of the heart purified by the noblest influences of religion, science and art, not alone for five or 10 academic years but during the span of man's earthly life, while throbbing heart and throbbing brain beat to the divine music of each wheeling year.

All true education glorifies God through the soul, advances civilization, promotes the happiness of both the individual and society, and places man on a higher plane that he may reach toward the stars. The Catholic winter school of the south aims in its humble way to promote the great cause of true education by inculcating principles which form the basis of right living and right thinking. It has chosen as its permanent home a great city full of historic memories of the past and throbbing hopes of the future, whose people are as generous as they are gifted and as brave as they are true. — THOMAS O'HAGAN

WESTERN RESERVE UNIVERSITY

A summer school of theology open to all was held for 10 days beginning July 8, 1895 in the buildings of Adelbert college of Western reserve university at Cleveland. About 40 lectures were given. Among the lecturers were: Prin. Fairbairn of Oxford, Eng., Pres. Strong of Rochester, Prof. McGiffert of Union, Rev. Dr George A. Gordon of Boston, Rev. David N. Beach of Cambridge, Rev. A. H. Bradford and Rev. B. W. Bacon of Oswego. The representation of attendance was wide, Massachusetts, Vermont, Ontario, New York, Pennsylvania, Indiana, Illinois, Minnesota and Tennessee being represented.

The professors of Adelbert college of Western reserve university also gave summer courses in 1895 and have arranged a summer course for 1896.

COOK COUNTY NORMAL SCHOOL

The Cook county normal summer school will be held for three weeks beginning July 13, 1896.

The model school will be in session two hours each day and will be free to all who take any of the regular courses. The teachers in charge of this school will illustrate the work given in all the other departments.

CHICAGO COMMONS SCHOOL OF SOCIAL ECONOMICS

The Chicago Commons school of social economics is nearly if not quite a unique manifestation of the social settlement movement. It is a part of the regular and permanent activity of "Chicago Commons," a settlement located in the 17th ward of the city of Chicago, in the midst of a neglected population of 30,000 people, of many nationalities, the Scandinavian predominating. The regular work of the settlement includes the usual friendly neighborhood visiting, the educational classes, clubs, musical classes, choruses and private lessons, civic and political unification, specially in the activities of the 17th ward council of the civic federation; sanitary inspection, industrial and economic studies and conferences representing all classes, philanthropic inquiry and ministration and the publication of a monthly paper known as *Chicago Commons*. The School of social economics is the name given to the occasional (thus far semi-annual) gathering at the Commons, for conference, discussion and study, of workers in economic and social fields, from all parts of this country and from England. Three sessions have thus far been held. The first was in April, 1895, with Percy Alden of Mansfield house, London and the Rev. A. Holden Byles of London, the originator of the " Pleasant Sunday afternoon " services, as the most notable speakers. The second, or summer session, in the last week of August, was specially successful, and permanently established the school by attracting a large attendance including some of the best known social and religious workers. The list of speakers included Miss Jane Addams of Hull house; Prof. George D. Herron of Iowa college; Mr Robert A. Woods of Andover house, Boston; Rev. Dr Josiah Strong, secretary of the Evangelical alliance; Rev. W. E. McLennan of Epworth house, Chicago, a leading worker and student of socio-religious conditions in Chicago, and Prof. Graham Taylor, warden of Chicago Commons, and professor of Christian sociology in Chicago theological seminary.

The third session, the spring session of 1896, is just concluded as this bulletin goes to press. Its general subject was " The social function of education," and the school teachers and educators of the vicinity of Chicago responded warmly to the opportunity to hear so many leading authorities on educational problems. The speakers and their subjects were as follows

Prof. Albion W. Small, Ph D., head professor of sociology. University of Chicago: Relation of pedagogics and sociology.

H. H. Belfield, director Chicago manual training school· Social value of industrial training.

Prof. George H. Mead, Ph. D., assistant professor of philosophy, University of Chicago: Bearing of embryological development on a theory of education; Relation of play to education.

Rev. D. M Fisk, Ph. D., associate pastor First congregational church, Toledo, Ohio: Plea for the recognition of the whole nature. Education *of* life; Method of culture, Education *by* life; The goal of culture, Education *for* life.

Miss Josephine C. Locke, superintendent of art instruction, Chicago public schools· The need of beauty.

Miss Amalie Hofer, editor the *Kindergarten magazine*, Chicago: Socializing influences in education.

Col. Francis W. Parker, principal Cook county normal school: The ideal school; Ethics in the common schools.

Ethics in the common schools.

Rev. J. B. Silcox, pastor Leavitt street congregational church, Chicago: Relation of our churches to our schools.

Leslie Lewis, assistant superintendent Chicago public schools: Claim of the public schools on the people.

Rev. W. E. McLennan, pastor M. E. Church, Berwyn, Ill.: Appeal of our city's life to the public schools.

Pres. George A. Gates, D. D., Iowa college, Grinnell, Iowa. Education for the kingdom of God; The teacher as a trainer for service.

Prof. W. B Chamberlain, M. A., professor of elocution and sacred music, Chicago theological seminary. Social value of training in sacred music

Prof. W. L. Tomlins, Tomlins' musical institute, Chicago: Social function of music.

Prof. Graham Taylor, professor of Christian sociology, Chicago theological seminary. Progress of the practical purpose in education.

John P. Gavit, Chicago Commons, formerly city editor of the *Hartford post:* The newspaper as a social educator.

The autumn session of the school will be held, probably in the first or second week of September, and there will be an extraordinarily able representation of thinkers of many schools, to discuss the topic " Social reconstruction: Are the principles of the Sermon on the mount a sufficient basis ? "

No charge is made for attendance at the school, the lecturers usually gladly giving their services; the small amount needed to defray necessary expenses is raised by the willing subscriptions of those taking advantage of the privileges of the school.

This school of social economics is essentially a popular institution; so much so that there is no effort to raise or to lower the tone of the subjects or discussions to suit any so-called stratum of society. The subjects are believed to be important for the social welfare, and every effort is made to have them treated in the most valuable way, by the best speakers attainable. The result is that all classes are represented in the audiences, and workingmen and college professors, ministers, women and artisans meet in the same room, and on the platform of common humanity and with a feeling of common interest in vital problems, discuss the papers and addresses. It is felt that these sessions are permanently profitable in many ways and much thought and labor is expended in the effort to make them pay the largest return of inspiration and instruction to those who attend, many coming long distances to do so.

Chicago Commons is at 140 North Union st., and information regarding the School of social economics or any other department of its work is gladly furnished to all interested inquirers — JOHN P. GAVIT

BIOLOGICAL EXPERIMENT STATION OF THE UNIVERSITY OF ILLINOIS

During the months of June, July and August, a limited number of students will be received at the newly equipped biological station of the University of Illinois. The station is established on the Illinois river with principal headquarters at Havana, 40 miles below Peoria. The situation is beautiful and unusually attractive.

The floating laboratory boat is 60x20 feet and is furnished with fixed and movable tables, cases of shelves, sinks and aquaria and also with kitchen equipment. Additional rooms in the town are provided with the usual equipment for biologic work and a working library of about 150 volumes.

As only 16 persons in addition to the station force can be accommodated no one but independent investigators and students who have had experience in zoologic or botanical work will be received. No restriction is placed on the lines of zoologic or botanical work to be pursued and no provision is made for formal instruction. A biologic club will be formed and regular meetings held for conference discussion and lectures by the station force or by visiting specialists.

A fee of $5 a month is charged and rooms and board can be obtained in the town for $4 or $5 a week.

BAY VIEW

The Bay View summer university embraces seven thoroughly organized and equipped departments, comprising the college, conservatory of music, and schools of methods, art, physical culture and Bible.

The work is under the direction of Dr J. M. Coulter of Chicago university and has a faculty of over 40 instructors from leading colleges. The 1896 session will be held July 8-Aug. 12.

ALMA COLLEGE

The eighth teachers summer school and review term will be held at Alma, Mich., for six weeks beginning June 29. In addition to the common branches, classes will be formed in history, civil government, school law, school management, pedagogy, bookkeeping, calisthenics, algebra, rhetoric, literature, political economy, Latin, French, German and the sciences.

Students will have free use of the library of 24,000 volumes, the physical, chemical and biologic laboratories, the museum and a large and well equipped gymnasium. Credit will be given in the college for summer school work. The fee for the term of six weeks is $5.

UNIVERSITY OF MICHIGAN

The second session of the summer school of law will be held June 29-August 21, 1896. The work is intended as a review of leading topics of law and will consist of lectures and daily recitations from text-books. Two courses on elocution and one on Shaksperian reading are also offered. The work is arranged in two classes, one of first year and the other of second year subjects, requiring three hours of class-room work daily for each class. Students will receive certificates of attendance, and requirements for admission to the law department of the university will be modified in favor of those who have completed the summer school course.

The following free lectures will be given: Judicial system of the Jews, Trial of Jesus, from a lawyer's standpoint Magna charta, Right of the teacher to inflict corporal punishment.

GRAND RAPIDS SUMMER SCHOOL FOR KINDERGARTEN STUDY

The course offered is the same as that given in the Grand Rapids kindergarten training school and includes the study of the gifts, occupations, songs, games, stories and Fröbel's book *Mutter und kose lieder*. Advanced classes may have in addition Fröbel's *Education of man*, Susan Blow's *Symbolic education* and Hailman's *History of pedagogy*. Daily practice work in kindergartens is given.

Mrs Lucretia W. Treat, Maria E. Barker, Sophia Holdridge and Carrie May Huse, prominent kindergarten workers from Grand Rapids, Utica and Albany, will conduct the work. Two lectures are offered, one by Henry W. Blake of Springfield, Mass, on the Life of Fröbel and one by M. Helen Jennings of Grand Rapids, on Science work.

When by attendance for several summers students have completed the full nine months' course, a certificate is granted, for an eight months' advanced course, a diploma is given. Students may enter for elementary or advanced courses of study.

The term is from July 6 to Aug. 29; tuition for two months is $15 and for one week, $2.

WESTERN SECRETARIAL INSTITUTE

The summer courses of instruction for secretaries and physical directors at Lake Geneva, Wis. will be essentially the same for the summer of 1896 as for 1895. One notable addition, however, is three courses of studies in the books of the Bible by Prof. Wilbert W. White, Ph. D., of the Chicago Bible institute. Each course will consist of 10 lessons and will be complete in itself. The books studied will be the gospel of John, the prophecies of Isaiah and the epistle to the Romans. The lecture and recitation method will be combined, and students will be assisted in their study by the use of printed syllabuses. These studies will open July 27 and close August 14.

Other sessions are held on the grounds of the Western secretarial institute during the summer. A brief notice of these, with a word concerning the general purpose of the institute, is appended.

The Western secretarial institute, which holds summer sessions on its grounds at Lake Geneva, Wis., is the oldest association educational institution in existence. Its short sessions, coming at the vacation season, are adapted to the circumstances of the volunteer association worker or the paid worker who can not take the longer course of the training school, or, having taken it, desire to supplement it by further study.

The equipment of the institute has recently been very materially increased by new athletic grounds. Athletics, therefore, as well as gymnastics and aquatics are now well provided for.

Three sessions are held each summer:

1 The College students conference, identical in its plan and purpose with the famous Northfield conference held under the patronage of Mr Moody. The well understood purpose of this meeting is " to deepen the spiritual life of college men, to train them for leadership in organized Christian work among students, and to open up the possibilities of Christian service which await them after graduation." First held in 1890, this gathering has had a very marked and wholesome influence on the religious life of the colleges of the west

2 The institute program proper, held the first two weeks of August. This is the program participated in more than any other by the older secretaries and physical directors. Conference and instruc-

tion are combined with recreation and good fellowship Its combination of recreative and educative features lends to this annual session an attractiveness and a value that are highly appreciated and warmly commended by all who attend. A strong course of Biblical lectures is a principal feature of the program.

3 The Summer school for secretaries and physical directors offers instruction in subjects germane to the work of the officers. The session opens about the middle of July and continues one month. The Bible, association history and management, Christian evidences, church history, anatomy, physiology, gymnastics, athletics and aquatics are among the subjects taught. Instruction is given by competent specialists. To young men contemplating the work, or to those already in it who desire greater effectiveness, these brief summer sessions are helpful and stimulating.—JOHN W. HANSEL, *General secretary*

UNIVERSITY OF WISCONSIN

The ninth annual session of the Wisconsin summer school will be held at the university for six weeks, from July 6 to August 14, 1896 37 courses of instruction will be offered in 14 departments. Instruction will be given in psychology and pedagogy by Prof. J. W. Stearns; in English literature, by Prof. J. C. Freeman; in history, by Prof. F. J. Turner; in German, by Mrs Abbie F. Eaton; in mathematics, by Prof. C. S. Slichter; in surveying and astronomy, by Prof. L. S. Smith; in botany, by Prof. C. R. Barnes; in physiology and zoology, by Prof. E. A. Birge; in chemistry, by Prof. W. W. Daniels; in histology, by E. P. Carlton; in geology and physical geography, by E. R. Buckley. In all of the laboratory courses assistance will be provided so that the laboratory will be open the greater part of the day.

Special attention is called to the course on Library science, to be given by Miss Katharine L. Sharp, director of the Library school at the Armour institute, Chicago. This course is made possible by the generosity of Senator James H. Stout, of Menomonie. It will continue six weeks during the present year and will be designed to meet the needs of librarians in the smaller libraries. The rapid increase of interest in libraries in the state of Wisconsin makes this course peculiarly useful and it is hoped that it will be largely attended.

The work of the summer school will be credited as work done in the university wherever the subjects are of the same grade as the university courses. Persons wishing to enter the university will find the mathematics or elementary science a most useful introduction to university work. Teachers will find the courses useful as general reviews of the subjects offered, and special attention will be given to adapting the courses to their needs.

The school is supported mainly by the tuition fees, which are $15 for the session.

Rooms can be obtained for from 75 cents to $1 a week, and if a sufficient number of persons apply, a club will be formed for the benefit of students, in which the cost of board will be from $2.25 to $2.50 a week. Rooms and board can be obtained for from $5 to $6 a week in families. Those who desire to avail themselves of the lower priced rooms are advised to apply to the director of the school at an early date. Accommodations will be found for persons applying in this manner. Circulars of the school are now issued and can be obtained on application to Prof. J. W. Stearns at the university.— Reprinted from University of Wisconsin *Bulletin for editors*

COLUMBIAN CATHOLIC SUMMER SCHOOL

An executive committee of this school located at Madison, Wis. has been appointed by Bishop Messmer, president, and the school will be incorporated under the laws of Wisconsin.

Plans are in progress to erect a large auditorium in Madison at the corner of West Main and Fairchild st., to accommodate the increased attendance. One of the many attractive courses announced is a series of afternoon lectures by Conde B. Pallen of St Louis.

SUMMER SCHOOL FOR PHYSICAL TRAINING

This school is held under the auspices of the North-American gymnastic union at the Normal school of gymnastics, Milwaukee, Wis. A six weeks course is announced for 1896 from June 29 to

August 8. The object of the school is to give teachers and students an opportunity to study German gymnastics.

The course includes theory and practice of gymnastics, anatomy and physiology, orthopedics, mechanical therapeutics, massage and anthropometry, systems, methods, applied physiology and hygiene, history of gymnastics, informal talks, psychology, fencing, wrestling, boxing and swimming. The following is the daily program.

Swimming 6:30-7.30	Gymnastics 2-3
Lectures 8:30-10	Fencing 3-4
Gymnastics 10-12	Boxing and wrestling 4-5:30

The fee for the full course is $25, for the special course, which consists of fencing, wrestling, boxing and swimming, $30.

UNIVERSITY OF MINNESOTA

The session for 1896 opens July 27, and closes August 21; registration will close July 29, after which students will not be admitted. As instruction is in university and elementary sections, opportunity is given for meeting individual preferences. The subjects are those of the university curriculum; in addition, a course in methods is offered. Examinations for first and second grade certificates provided by the state superintendent of public instruction, will be held during the fourth week of the summer school.

The educational congresses, which are business meetings of representative persons in the three leading departments of the educational system, are appointed for August 18-21. They will not interfere with class work, but any teachers may attend the meetings.

Special courses of lectures to be given daily in the chapel will be announced at the opening of the school.

DES MOINES SUMMER SCHOOL OF METHODS

The seventh session of the Des Moines summer school of methods will be held in the West Des Moines high school building July 6-31, 1896. The corps of instructors has been increased and additional courses in grammar school methods will be offered.

DRAKE UNIVERSITY SUMMER LATIN SCHOOL

The sixth session will be held during the nine weeks beginning June 22, at Drake university, Des Moines, Iowa. Each class is expected to do a year's work and will recite two consecutive hours daily.

The courses laid out for the three classes are as follows:

1 First Latin book, Caesar, book 2;
2 Caesar, three books, Cicero, four orations;
3 Virgil, six books, Ovid, 1500 lines.

UNIVERSITY OF MISSOURI

Summer school of science. During 1895 courses in biology, physics and chemistry were established by law to prepare teachers to give instruction in those branches in the high schools of the state and specially those connected with the university. Special attention will be given to laboratory work, particularly details of equipment and care of supplies and apparatus, so that teachers may make the best use of the means and appliances at their disposal. The work of the summer school will not be counted toward the degree of the university but will be recognized as satisfying conditions for entrance to the freshman class. There is no fee for tuition or supplies.

Summer school of language. These courses are private enterprises and in this respect differ from the Summer school of science. Conditioned students in the university may make up work in these summer classes by special arrangement with the professors. Courses are offered in English, Latin, Greek, German and French. The fee for each course is $10.

FAIRMOUNT CHAUTAUQUA

The first assembly at Fairmount Park, Kansas City, Mo. will be held May 30-June 14.

The program includes the usual Chautauquà assembly topics. The Children's normal course and the Sunday-school normal classes will be conducted by Mrs Wilbur F. Crafts, the department of physical education, by Prof. Edward B. Warman ; music, by Prof.

C. C. Case; the ministers' institute and Bible exposition, by Dr M. M. Parkhurst. C. L. S. C. round tables will be held daily directed by Mrs Mary H. Gardner, Rev. G. M. Brown, field secretary of the C. L. S. C., Dr W. L. Davidson and others.

Gen. John B. Gordon, Dr T. DeWitt Talmage, Bishop John H. Vincent, Prof. W. H. Dana and other eminent lecturers will be present.

UNIVERSITY OF CALIFORNIA

The course in chemistry which has been given during the last four years will be repeated in 1896, beginning June 10 and closing July 20.

During the vacation at the end of junior year, all students in mining spend about four weeks in systematic study of practical mining, taking notes and making sketches of processes observed and preparing a full report to be presented at the opening of the term.

The Biological laboratory will devote its summer session to making explorations in San Francisco bay.

PACIFIC COAST STUDENTS CONFERENCE

The first Pacific coast students conference will be held at Elim Grove, Cazadero, Cal., May 22-31, 1896 under direction of the college department of the international committee of the Y. M. C. A.

The purpose is to train college men for leadership in organized Christian work and the plans indicate a gathering notable in the history of the colleges of the Pacific coast

The work of the assembly will be carried on through Bible classes, conferences of Y. M. C. A. presidents, a missionary institute under leadership of George Sherwood Eddy with a series of lectures on the development of missionary interest, life-work conferences or informal evening meetings, delegation meetings and personal interviews. At least one platform meeting will be held daily. The afternoons will be devoted exclusively to athletics and recreation.

FOREIGN SCHOOLS

SUMMER SCHOOL OF SCIENCE FOR THE ATLANTIC PROVINCES OF CANADA

The 10th session of the school will be held at Parrsboro', N. S., July 9-24. The picturesque situation of Parrsboro' on the Partridge Island river has proved to be also so advantageous for scientific study that it has been suggested as the permanent location of the school.

Courses are offered in botany, chemistry. meteorology, mineralogy, physics, physiology and hygiene, zoology and entomology, civics, elocution, English literature, kindergarten, music and psychology.

The examinations in science will cover the prescribed text-book and lectures, and practical and original work with the collections, mountings and apparatus. Certificates will be awarded after examination. Evening meetings will be devoted to discussion of the subjects of the curriculum.

EDINBURGH SUMMER MEETING

Ten years ago, courses of seaside zoology and garden botany were arranged to be held in Edinburgh during August, so that they might be available for teachers and others who had only the vacation to devote to study. The moving spirit in organizing these classes was Patrick Geddes, now professor of botany in University college, Dundee. The actual teachers were, in zoology, J. Arthur Thomson, joint-author with Prof. Geddes of the *Evolution of sex*, and in botany, G F. Scott Elliot, who has since been best known as an unwearying traveler and student of natural history in Africa The classes were attended by about 25 students and the experiment was considered successful.

In the next three years the classes were held at Granton marine station, near Edinburgh, and the numbers continued to increase. During these years, botany and zoology continued to be the main subjects of instruction, the courses being made parallel. In 1889 and 1890 a general course of lectures was delivered by Prof Geddes in the morning, dealing with the application of the idea of evolution to social as well as to biologic studies. In 1891, most of the classes were held in Edinburgh, near the first of the residential houses for students which Prof. Geddes has arranged as University hall. Next year the summer meeting was largely extended, many more courses of lectures were offered and there was a gratifying increase in the number of students who came to take advantage of them.

From 1893 till 1895, the meeting has been held in the normal school of the training college and has been greatly assisted in its work by grants of money from the town council. The number of courses offered has been greatly increased specially in philosophy and social science, in history and in geography. Many more students have come in each year as the meeting became better known.

The summer meeting of 1896 will number among its lecturers, Prof. Geddes, Mr Thomson and Mr Scott Elliot, the three associated with it in its first year. Lectures will also be delivered by Elisée Reclus, the veteran geographer; Prof. Rein of Jena, the distinguished exponent of the educational theories of Herbart; Dr R. M. Wenley, the new head of the department of philosophy in the University of Michigan; Paul Desjardins of Paris, author of *Le devoir présent*, and others. The studio of the old Edinburgh school of art will be open under the direction of Miss Hay for the study of Celtic ornament. Popular lectures and musical recitals, managed by Mrs Kennedy Fraser, are held in the evenings. A daily paper, the *Interpreter*, is published during the meeting giving summaries and notes of the previous day's lectures and containing all special announcements. Numerous excursions to places near and far are arranged to illustrate generally the courses of contemporary social evolution of history and of geography. This year the summer meeting has obtained a permanent home in the Outlook Tower, now being arranged as a geographic museum. In it the office of the meeting and several of the lecture rooms are situated.

The fees for the whole meeting (Aug. 3-29) are £3 3s.; for any fortnight, £1 11s. 6d. Board can be had in the houses of University hall at 25s. weekly.

Any further information may be obtained from the secretary. Outlook tower, University hall, Edinburgh. The program of the meeting will be sent post free for 7d.—T R MARR, *Secretary*

CAMBRIDGE UNIVERSITY

The summer meeting for 1896 will open July 30 with a lecture on William Pitt the son, by Dr Butler, master of Trinity college. The plan of work covers a general course of 12 lectures dealing with the influence on modern life of Greek and Roman literature, art, philosophy and civilization; systematic courses on evolution, economics, art, and the history of Europe in the 19th century, with special reference to the formation of the German empire, and the unification of Italy; Early progress of English poetry; laboratory courses in botany, zoology and chemistry; shorter courses on the Great days of Spain, Dissolution of the monasteries, Monastic institutions of East Anglia, Some problems of species, Anthropology, the Herbartian system by Prof. Rein of Jena, Germany, and Relation of the Herbartian doctrine to English education by Dr J. J. Findlay. If a sufficient number of students desire it. special classes may be formed for the study of languages.

The systematic courses and laboratory demonstrations will be held as far as possible on Mondays, Tuesdays, Thursdays and Fridays so that special lectures, conferences and excursions may be arranged on Wednesdays and Saturdays.

Lectures will be given by the divinity professors, and by Dr Jebb, Dr Cunningham, Dr Lawrence, M E. Sadler, J. Churton Collins, Dr Mandello of Budapest, Dr C. W. Kimmins, Mr I. Gollancz, Dr Waldstein and others.

The fee for the whole meeting will be £1 10s.

OXFORD SUMMER MEETING

There will be no summer meeting at Oxford in 1896 in accordance with the plan of alternating the university extension summer gatherings between Oxford and Cambridge.

The session of 1897 will be held at Oxford in August. The chief subjects of study will be the history, literature, art and economics of the revolutionary era, 1789-1848, the lectures being in direct sequence to those given in 1895.

LECTURES TO CLERGY

Lectures to clergy which have been given at Oxford for the last three years will this year be given at Durham, July 13-25, 1896.

The program includes the following subjects: pastoral work, the book of Job, church law, history of the church of Durham, history of religion, doctrine of the Trinity in the creed and in the New testament, doctrine of grace, the church and social problems, epistle to the Romans Additional afternoon and evening lectures are also promised. The cathedral and abbey buildings will be accessible to all attendants at the lectures, and arrangements will be made for visits to places of interest in the neighborhood. The fee is £1 for the whole time, or 15s. for either week.

ANCOATS BROTHERHOOD

Ancoats Brotherhood, an organization in the old workshop part of Manchester, England, has in charge a variety of agencies for the education and recreation of its members. Sunday afternoon lectures were commenced in 1882 by Sir Henry Roscoe and met with such success that they have been continued. The list of lecturers now includes Mrs Fawcett, Rev. Hudson Shaw, Prof. R: G. Moulton, William Morris, Walter Crane, and others. The lectures are free and the audience varies from 400 to 1000.

In 1885 extension work was started with a course of lectures by M. E. Sadler and a book stall was established where good cheap editions of standard works could be obtained. Several years later the recreation department of summer outings and rambles was instituted. This is self-supporting.

The summer program for 1896 opened March 1 with a lecture on the Good and evil of the factory system by Joseph Nasmith. Mr Belloc lectured on France and England of the last century, Industrial and political changes of this century in France and England and the French and English ways of solving modern problems Other lecturers were Dr Annie Anderson, Miss Olivia Rossetti and Mr Frank Hoy. An Easter trip to Holland was arranged and visits made to Rotterdam, Amsterdam, the Hague and Scheveningen, Dordrecht and on the return a visit to Cambridge.

The rambles begin in May and are arranged as follows: May 10 Bowdon, for Castle Mills; May 17 Kersal Moor, garden " at home"; June 7 garden " at home "; June 14 Birch Vale over Chinley Head, return by valley through Bugsworth to New Mills; June 21 Cheadle Hulme, garden " at home "; June 27-29 Lake District; July 4 Miss Barlow's garden " at home "; July 12 Marple,Chadkirk valley; July 19 Derbyshire, Hathersage, Grindleford bridge, Eyam; July 26 Boggart Hole clough, Oliver's clough; August 9 Dunford bridge, Holmfirth and Woodhead.

L. A U. K. SUMMER SCHOOL

The fourth session of this summer meeting will be held in London in June. Following is the draft program of lectures, demonstrations and visits:

Monday, June 15

7.30 p. m. Reception in the rooms of the association, 20 Hanover sq. London, W.

8 p. m. Inaugural address by Charles Welch, chairman of committee.

8.30 p. m. Lecture: Bookbinding and the book beautiful, by T. J. Cobden Sanderson.

Tuesday, June 16

10.30 a. m. Visit to the British museum.

3 p. m. Lecture: History of the development of the printed book, by E. Gordon Duff.

8.30 p. m. Lecture : The bibliographical description of a book, by E. Gordon Duff.

Wednesday, June 17

10.30 a. m. Visit to the Guildhall library by invitation of W. O. Clough, chairman of library committee.

11 a. m. Demonstration of cataloging (illustrated by appliances) by E. M. Barrajo.

12.30 p. m. Visit to the type foundry of Sir Charles Reed and sons, Fann street, Aldersgate.

3 p. m. Visit to Sion college library, Thames embankment, with a demonstration of classification and shelf arrangement, by Rev. W. H. Milman.

7.30 p. m. Things heard and seen; an open discussion by members of the summer school.

8.30 p. m. Lecture: Modern English literature, by R. Garnett.

Thursday, June 18

10.30 a. m. Visit to Tate central library, Brixton, S. W.; lecture, Library buildings, by F. J. Burgoyne.

12.15 p. m. Visit to the Battersea central public library, Lavender Hill, S. W., by invitation of L. Inkster.

8.30 p. m. Lecture: Modern English literature, by T. F. Hobson.

Friday, June 20

Examination.

Particulars of each lecture will be found in the syllabus which will be forwarded to intending students on application. Further information may be had from W. E. Doubleday, 48 Priory road, London, N. W., Eng.

LONDON SCHOOL OF ECONOMICS AND POLITICAL SCIENCE

The first summer meeting of this school will be held July 31-Aug. 14 at Toynbee hall, Whitechapel. The object is to give opportunities for study of economic questions during the long vacation, and through informal conferences to help those who have studied without guidance. The fee will be £1.

NATIONAL HOME READING UNION

The summer assembly of the national home reading union will be held at Chester, England, June 27-July 6 under the presidency of the duke of Westminster. Lectures on various scientific and historic subjects will be delivered.

The fee will be 7s. 6d. to members of the union and 10s. 6d. to others.

ALLIANCE FRANÇAISE

During the months of July and August, 1896, vacation courses in French will be conducted in Paris for foreign professors and for foreigners wishing to increase their knowledge of the language, literature, institutions and arts of France.

The courses are under the patronage of MM Gréard, Lavisse, Claretie, members of the French academy; Michel Bréal, member of the institute; Gaston Paris and L. Léger, professors in the College of France; Gen. Parmentier, general of division; M. Bardoux, senator; M. LeMyre de Vilers, deputy; M. Foncin, inspector-general of public instruction; Franck Puaux, member of the superior council for the colonies; A. Colin, publisher; F. Brunot, master of lectures at the Sarbonne; and G. Monod, master of lectures in the École normale.

The courses will be given in two series; the first, from July 2 to Aug. 1, and the second from Aug. 1 to 31. Ladies are admitted to all lectures. The courses of each series will consist of 28 lessons on the French language, classic literature, contemporary literature, elocution and French pronunciation, in classes arranged both for elementary and advanced students; 12 lessons on the institutions of modern France, political, social and educational organizations, 12 visits to the museums, monuments and works of art in the galleries of Paris and the neighborhood, and an excursion to Rouen. 24 conversation classes arranged for groups of 12 students will be held every evening from 8 30 to 9.30.

An examination will be given at the end of each series of classes; an advanced diploma will be awarded to those who show that they can not only speak and understand the French language but are capable of teaching it to a foreigner, and an elementary diploma to those who can speak and understand the language.

For information address Alliance française, 45, rue de Grenelle, Paris.

MODERN LANGUAGE HOLIDAY COURSES

Jena. Two courses are given every summer; the first for German schoolmasters, and the second intended chiefly for foreign teachers wishing to study German. These courses are increasing in popularity and have been attended by more than 200 teachers. The session will be held Aug. 3-23, 1896, and the subjects of study will be the natural sciences, German language and history, pedagogy and philosophy.

The matriculation fee is 5 marks [about $1.25]. For each 12-lecture course in special subjects the fee is 15 marks; for a 6-lecture course, 7 marks 50 pf. For language courses, including 24 appointments, the fee is 30 marks. Board can be had at about 25 marks a week.

Caen. Similar provision for the study of French is made at Caen, Normandy. Besides the Easter and summer sessions, a Christmas course of 12 days was arranged for 1895 to be held at Paris, under the same auspices.

STATISTICS 1895

Reports of 1895 sessions only are included in the following tables. Schools whose first session is in 1896 are reported in their proper places in the pages preceding.

In the column headed Subjects of study, " Chautauqua assembly topics" means the subjects commonly taught at the various Chautauquas; e. g. physical culture, elocution, art, music, W. C. T. U. methods, Sunday school normal subjects, kindergarten, cooking, with sometimes the addition of lectures on literature or science. Schools which give instruction in the common branches, usually include courses in methods of teaching each subject.

College preparatory topics are those of high schools, implying that the work is with special reference to college entrance requirements.

EXPLANATION OF ABBREVIATIONS

* preceding statements means approximately

a = assembly	mater. med = materia medica
anat = anatomy	math = mathematics
Bib = Bible study	mech eng = mechanical engineering
biol = biology	mus = music
chem = chemistry	ora = oratory
econ = economics	norm = normal
eloc = elocution	p c = physical culture
geod = geodesy	path = pathology
geol = geology	ped = pedagogy
hist = history	phys = physiology
inst = institute	psych = psychology
kind = kindergarten	s. m. = summer meeting
lang = language	s. s. = summer school
lib. econ = library economy	sci = science
lit = literature	surv = surveying

	NAME	Place	Year founded	Opening
1	Acton Park assembly	Acton Park, Ind.	1882	26 Jl
2	Alma college summer school	Alma, Mich.	1889	8 Jl
3	Am inst of norm meth East. session	Providence, R I.	1890	16 Jl
4	" " Western session.	Highland Park, Ill.	1891	6 Ag
5	Amer. society univ exten. s m	Philadelphia, Pa	1893	1 Jl
6	Atlanta assembly	Atlanta, Ga.	1893	25 Je
7	Atlantic prov of Can s s. of science	Amherst, N. S.	1887	3 Jl
8	Baker university summer school.	Baldwin, Kan.	1893	
9	Bay View summer university	Bay View, Mich.	1885	17 Jl
10	Beatrice Chautauqua assembly.	Beatrice, Neb.	1887	19 Je
11	Belle Island summer school of art	South Norwalk, Conn	1894	15 Je
12	Black Hills assembly	Black Hills, S D.	1890	2 Jl
13	Bowdoin college summer courses.	Brunswick, Me	1895	9 Jl
14	Brooklyn inst biological laboratory	Cold Spring Harbor, N Y	1889	
15	Caen holiday course for teachers.	Caen, France	1894	15 Ap
16	" "	"		8 Ag
17	California univ. physical laboratory.	Berkeley, Cal		5 Je
18	" S s. of marine biology	San Pedro, Cal	1892	15 Je
19	Cascadilla summer school	Ithaca, N Y	1891	6 Jl
20	Catholic s. s. of America.	Plattsburg, N. Y.	1892	7 Jl
21	Catholic winter school of America	New Orleans, La	1896	26 F
22	Catskill school of art	Cos Cob, Conn	1891	11 Je
23	Cayuga Lake summer school	Ithaca, N Y.	1894	15 Jl
24	Central New York summer school	Tully Lake, N Y.	1892	23 Jl
25	Chautauqua col. of liberal arts	Chautauqua, N Y	1875	6 Jl
26	Chicago commons s. of social econ.	Chicago, Ill	1894	22 Ap
27	" "	"		22 Ag
28	Clark university summer school	Worcester, Mass	1892	15 Jl
29	Clinton classical school	Peekskill, N Y.	1895	25 Je
30	Colorado s. s of sci phil. and lang	Colorado Springs, Col.	1892	15 Jl
31	Columbia college summer schools	Various places	1877	
32	Columbian catholic summer school	Madison, Wis.	1894	14 Jl
33	Connecticut s s for teachers	Norwich, Conn	1891	9 Jl
34	Connecticut valley assembly	Northampton, Mass.	1887	16 Jl
35	Cook county normal summer school	Chicago, Ill.	1893	15 Jl
36	Cornell university summer school	Ithaca, N. Y.	1892	8 Jl
37	" Summer law school	Ithaca, N Y		8 Jl
38	Cotuit summer school	Cotuit, Mass	1895	9 Jl
39	Cumberland valley assembly.	Harrisburg, Pa.	1886	24 Jl
40	Denver normal and prep school	Denver, Col.	1893	10 Je
41	Des Moines s s. of methods	Des Moines, Iowa	1890	8 Jl
42	Detroit Lake interstate assembly.	Detroit Lake, Minn	1893	3 Jl
43	Devils' Lake assembly	Devils' Lake, N D	1892	28 Je
44	Drake univ summer Latin school	Des Moines, Ia	1891	24 Je
45	Eastern Maine assembly	Northport, Me.	1893	14 Ag

STATISTICS OF SUMMER SCHOOLS, 1895

Closing	Students	Visitors	States	Countries	Subjects of study	
	ATTENDANTS		**REPRESENTATION**			
19 Ag	....	....	....	...	Chautauqua assembly topics.....	1
2 Ag..	33	....	1	...	General	2
2 Ag..	120	30	15	...	Music, drawing, penmanship, p c....	3
23 Ag .	100	....	7	...	Vocal music, drawing.........	4
28 Jl..	225	?500	....	...	General	5
9 Jl .	....	....	....	...	Chautauqua assembly topics.	6
18 Jl..	98	?200	...	Can	Sci. Eng. lit. mus. eloc. econ. ped. psych.	7
	....	....	....	...	General................	8
14 Ag .	787	....	12	...	General	9
4 Jl .	....	....	....	...	Chautauqua assembly topics......	10
15 S .	....	....	....	...	Art	11
12 Jl .	....	....	....	...	Chautauqua assembly topics.....	12
13 Ag	12	....	....	...	Chemistry, physics, biology......	13
	....	....	....	...	Science	14
27 Ap .	20	....	....	Gt.Br.	French language and history.....	15
28 Ag .	70	....	....	Gt.Br.	"	16
17 Jl .	....	....	....	...	Physics, chemistry..........	17
5 Ag .	....	....	....	...	Biology...............	18
11 S .	....	....	....	...	College preparatory..........	19
18 Ag .	?1200	?500	21	...	General	20
14 Mr .	1500	?1000	....	...	General	21
10 S .	....	....	....	...	Art	22
5 Ag .	....	....	....	...	Common branches..........	23
30 Ag .	100	....	5	...	General	24
16 Ag .	1741	....	....	...	General	25
29 Ap .	....	....	....	...	Social science	26
29 Ag .	1500	....	....	...	"	27
27 Jl .	200	....	....	...	Pedagogy, psychology, child-study...	28
3 S...	10	....	....	7 Mex	College preparatory..........	29
9 Ag..	559	250	?33	Can	General	30
....	....	....	....	...	Mining, geol. surv. geod. biol. mech. eng	31
4 Ag .	....	....	....	...	General..............	32
25 Jl .	781	....	10	...	General	33
26 Jl .	....	....	....	...	Chautauqua assembly topics......	34
5 Ag .	500	250	26	3	General..............	35
16 Ag .	234	....	29	6	General..........	36
2 S...	41	....	16	2	Law	37
2 S...	....	....	....	...	College preparatory	38
31 Jl .	....	....	....	...	Chautauqua assembly topics	39
27 Jl .	190	....	8	...	General..............	40
2 Ag .	.	....	....	...	General	41
31 Jl .	....	....	....	...	Chautauqua assembly topics......	42
22 Jl .	....	....	....	...	Chautauqua assembly topics......	43
23 Ag .	42	....	5	...	Latin	44
22 Ag	....	....	....	...	Chautauqua assembly topics......	45

5

68   UNIVERSITY OF THE STATE OF NEW YORK

	Lecturers	Lectures	Recitations	EXTENSION COURSES Subjects	EXTENSION COURSES Lecturers	Buildings	Entrance	FEES Full course	FEES Single course
1									
2	3	..	18			Alma college		$5	
3	10	108	325			Brown univ		55	$15
4	6	18	175			North-west mil.acad		25	15
5	40	352				Univ. of Pa.		15	2
6									
7	14	155	20					2 50	2
8						University		15	5
9	45						$6		6
10									
11								8–15 a mo.	
12									
13	4					College		20	10
14						5		20	
15	2	24	24					£2 10s	£1 1
16	4	54	54					£3 10s	£2 5s
17									
18									
19	4		200			Wait hall		$75	$30
20	27	103						10	
21	15	54						10	1
22								8–15 a mo.	
23						Ithaca high school			
24	18		28			3		7	3 7
25	62	73	480	16	16	13		a	
26									
27									
28	8					University		20	12
29	3							100	
30	33							10	5
31	16								
32								5	
33	42	?250						5	
34									
35	13	97	172			Normal school		12	3
36	32					University	1		10–35
37	4					University		35	
38								15–25	
39									
40		120	415					10	
41									
42									
43									
44	4		270			University		15	15
45									

a Fees vary in each dep't

Single lecture	Name	Address	
....	Mrs J D Gatch	Lawrenceburg, Ind.	1
....	J T Northon	Alma, Mich	2
....	F. D. Beattys	31 E 17th st. New York	3
....	Robert Fores i an	262 Wabash av Chicago, Ill	4
$ 50	E. T Devine	111 S. 15th st. Phil. Pa.	5
....	Rev W Shaw, pres		6
....	J D Seaman	Charlottetown, P E Island	7
....	G. W. Martin	Baldwin, Kan	8
.25	J· M Hall	Flint, Mich.	9
....	A. R Dempster, pres.		10
....	J H Boston	203 Montague st Brooklyn, N. Y	11
....	E E. Clough, pres.		12
....	L. A Lee	Brunswick, Me	13
....	F. W Hooper	502 Fulton st Brooklyn, N Y	14
....	J. Richards	Gram sch. Stoke Newington, Lon N.Eng	15
	"		16
....	E R. Drew	Oakland, Cal	17
....	W. E. Ritter	2222 Durant av Berkeley, Cal.	18
....	C V Parsell	Ithaca, N Y.	19
.25	W. E. Mosher	123 E 50th st. New York	20
.25	A. H Fleming	938 Royal st New Orleans, La	21
....	Miss H S. Peck	100 Willow st Brooklyn, N. Y.	22
....	F. D. Boynton	Ithaca, N Y	23
.20	T. H Armstrong	Friendship, N. Y.	24
....	W. A Duncan	Syracuse, N. Y	25
....	Miss M. E. Colman	140 N Union st Chicago, Ill.	26
...	"	"	27
.50	L N. Wilson	Worcester, Mass.	28
....	Robert McCord	Peekskill, N Y	29
.50	P K Pattison	Colorado Springs, Col.	30
....	W H. H Beebe	Columbia college, N Y	31
.25	H. J Desmond	Wisconsin bldg Milwaukee, Wis	32
....	C D Hine	Hartford, Conn	33
....	Dr W L. Davidson	Cuyahoga Falls, O	34
....	I B Meyers	6953 Eggleston av. Station O, Chicago, Ill	35
....	D F. Hoy	Ithaca, N. Y	36
..	"		37
....	C E Fish	Cotuit, Mass.	38
....	A A Line, sup't	Carlisle, Pa.	39
....	Fred Dick, pres	Denver, Col.	40
....	C W Martindale	Webster City, Ia	41
....	Dr S J Hill, pres		42
....	Ir Eugene May, sup't		43
....	C O Denny	1090 25th st Des Moines, Ia	44
....	G D Lindsay, pres.		45

	NAME	Place	Year founded	Opening
46	Eastern New Eng. Chautauqua	Ocean Park, Me.	1881	29 Jl
47	Edinburgh summer meeting	Edinburgh, Scotland	1887	5 Ag
48	Florida Chautauqua	De Funiak Springs, Fla.	1886	20 F
49	Gearhart Park Chaut. assembly	Gearhart Park, Or		10 Jl
50	Geneva univ vacation courses	Geneva, Switzerland		15 Jl
51	" "	"		1 O
52	Georgia Chautauqua assembly	Albany, Ga	1888	31 Mr
53	Glenmore sch. for the culture sci.	Keene, N Y	1891	
54	Grand Rapids kindergarten train sch	Grand Rapids, Mich	1892	5 Jl
55	Greenacre assembly	Eliot, Me	1894	4 Jl
56	Grindelwald conference	Grindelwald, Switzerland	1892	
57	H E Holt norm inst of vocal har	Tufts College, Mass	1883	
58	Hackley Park assembly	Hackley Park, Mich	1891	20 Jl
59	Harvard s s of physical training	Cambridge, Mass	1887	
60	Harvard univ summer school	Cambridge, Mass	1874	6 Jl
61	Hedding assembly	East Epping, N. H	1886	5 Ag
62	Hopkins seaside laboratory	Pacific Grove, Cal	1892	17 Je
63	Hull house college extension s. s.	Rockford, Ill	1891	6 Jl
64	Illinois university summer school	Urbana, Ill	1894	17 Je
65	Indiana state normal school	Terre Haute, Ind.	1894	1 Jl
66	Indiana university summer school	Bloomington, Ind	1890	25 Je
67	Iowa Chautauqua assembly	Colfax, Iowa	1889	9 Jl
68	Iowa school of the kingdom	Grinnell, Ia	1895	26 Je
69	Island Park assembly	Rome City, Ind	1878	31 Jl
70	Jena holiday course for teachers	Jena, Germany	1893	5 Ag
71	Kentucky Chautauqua assembly	Lexington, Ky	1886	2 Jl
72	Knox college summer school	Galesburg, Ill.	1894	17 Je
73	L A U K. summer school	London, Eng	1893	24 Je
74	Lake Forest college summer session	Lake Forest, Ill	1895	18 Je
75	Lake Geneva conf Inter Y. W C A	Lake Geneva, Wis	1891	12 Jl
76	Lake Geneva students conference	Lake Geneva, Wis	1891	
77	Lake George assembly	Lake George as'bly, N. Y		
78	Lake Madison Chautauqua s. school	Lake Madison, S D	1891	9 Jl
79	Lakeside summer school	Lakeside, O	1877	11 Jl
80	Leland Stanford, jr, university	Palo Alto, Cal	1894	3 Je
81	Long Beach Chaut assembly	Long Beach, Cal	1884	13 Jl
82	Long Beach summer parliament	Long Beach, L I, N Y	1894	4 Jl
83	Long Island Chautauqua	Point o' Woods, L I., N.Y	1894	4 Jl
84	Marine biological laboratory	Woods Holl, Mass	1888	1 My
85	Marthas Vineyard summer institute	Cottage City, Mass	1878	8 Jl
86	Mass inst of technology s school	Boston, Mass	1888	Je
87	Michigan univ summer school	Ann Arbor, Mich	1894	8 Jl
88	Summer school of law	Ann Arbor, Mich		
89	Mid-summer school	Owego, N Y	1891	
90	Minnesota university summer school	Minneapolis, Minn	1892	29 Jl

Closing	Students	Visitors	States	Countries	Subjects of study	
8 Ag.	....	....	...	...	Chautauqua assembly topics.	46
31 Ag	100	30	...	5	Social science	47
20 Mr	....	....	...	...	Chautauqua assembly topics. ...	48
21 Ag	....	....	...	...	Common branches	49
31 Ag	177	....	...	12	French language and literature	50
20 O..	....	....	...	...	"	51
7 Ap..	450	1000	10	...	Chautauqua assembly topics	52
....	....	....	...	...	Social science	53
31 Ag	47	25-30	10	Can	Kindergarten	54
31 Ag	150-600	....	...	...	Social science	55
....	....	....	...	...	Christian sociology.	56
....	100	....	...	...	Vocal harmony...........	57
5 Ag..	....	....	...	...	Chautauqua assembly topics	58
....	90	1500	24	Eng	Physical culture	59
15 Ag	601	....	...	...	General............	60
24 Ag.	....	....	...	...	Music, art, French, Bible study	61
27 Jl..	44	....	...	...	Science	62
10 Ag.	75	....	...	...	Science, language, needlework	63
15 Jl..	....	....	...	...	General	64
2 Ag..	202	....	2	...	General	65
26 Jl..	....	....	...	...	General	66
23 Jl..	200	....	6	...	Chautauqua assembly topics.....	67
3 Jl..	....	....	...	...	Christian sociology	68
14 Ag.	....	....	...	...	Chautauqua assembly topics ...	69
25 Ag.	80	....	...	6	German lang and hist, pedagogy, sci .	70
12 Jl..	....	....	...	...	Chautauqua assembly topics	71
22 Jl..	....	....	...	...	General	72
29 Je..	....	....	...	...	Library economy	73
10 Ag.	33	....	6	...	General............	74
16 Jl..	227	12	15	...	Y. W C A topics	75
....	319	....	...	...	Bible	76
....	....	....	...	...	Chautauqua assembly topics	77
23 Jl..	140	?60	4	...	General	78
11 Ag	40	....	...	...	Chautauqua assembly topics ...	79
....	....	....	...	...	General	80
10 Ag.	200	1500	...	...	Chautauqua assembly topics	81
20 Ag.	....	....	...	...	Chautauqua assembly topics	82
2 S	....	....	...	...	General..........	83
1 O..	199	....	22	...	Science	84
....	725	....	39	...	General	85
Jl..	....	....	...	...	General	86
16 Ag.	191	....	21	4	General	87
....	....	....	...	...	Law ...	88
....	230	....	5	...	General	89
23 Ag.	1217	....	...	...	General	90

	Lecturers	Lectures	Recitations	Subjects	Lecturers	Buildings	Entrance	Full course	Single course
				EXTENSION COURSES				FEES	
46	10	..	..	..	..	5........	..	$2	..
47	25	139	..	..	..	4........	..	£3 3s	10s 6d
48	..	..	..	..	..	Assembly buildings	..	..	..
49	..	..	..	..	..		..	..	..
50	..	..	60	..	..		..	30fr	..
51	..	..	36	..	..		..	15fr	..
52	..	..	..	..	..		..	$2	..
53	..	..	..	..	..		..	..	..
54	4	14	83	..	..		..	12 50	$12 50
55	59	69	..	..	..		..	..	..
56	..	..	..	..	..		..	..	..
57	..	..	..	..	..		..	20	..
58	..	..	..	..	..		..	..	..
59	22	..	..	..	..	Hemenway gymnas.	..	50	25
60	66	984	..	..	..	University	..	..	20
61	..	..	..	..	..		..	..	..
62	6	42	..	..	..	2........	..	15-25	..
63	10	..	..	..	..		..	..	..
64	..	..	..	..	..	University	..	10	..
65	4	..	416	..	..	Normal school	$10	10	10
66	..	..	..	..	..	University	..	10	5
67	26	39	32	..	..		.25	2	1
68	14	..	..	..	..	Iowa college	..	..	..
69	20	32	75	..	..	5........	..	2.50	..
70	12	48	..	..	..		5 marks	..	15 marks
71	100	..	..	..	..		..	..	..
72	..	..	..	..	..		..	10	$5
73	8	8	..	..	..		..	..	..
74	5	..	..	..	..	College..	..	20	20
75	13	..	..	..	..		..	5	..
76	..	..	..	..	..		..	..	..
77	..	..	..	..	..		..	5	..
78	7	123	..	..	..		..	3	1 per week
79	5	..	..	..	..	7........	..	5	..
80	23	..	..	..	..	University	..	..	5-35
81	20	40	100	..	..	7........	$2 50	6	2 5
82	..	50	..	..	..		..	3	..
83	..	..	..	..	..		..	..	..
84	17	..	..	..	..	4........	..	50	..
85	..	..	..	..	..		1	15	7
86	..	..	..	..	..		..	25	..
87	26	..	?930	..	..	University	..	30	15
88	..	..	..	..	..	University	..	35	4
89	14	765	..	..	..		..	4.50-8	5-8
90	40	1006	..	a..	..	University	1	a5-6	..

a Free to Minnesota students

STATISTICS OF SUMMER SCHOOLS, 1895

Fees (Single lecture)	Secretary Name	Address	
$ 25	E W. Porter	85 Central st. Peabody, Mass	46
....	T. R. Marr	Outlook Tower, Univ hall, Edinb'h, Scot	47
....	Dr W L Davidson, sup't.	Cuyahoga Falls, O.	48
....			49
....	Prof Bernard Bouvier	10, Bourg-de-Four, Geneva, Switzerland	50
....	"	"	51
....	H. M. McIntosh	Albany, Ga.	52
.50	Thomas Davidson	Keene, N. Y.	53
....	Clara Wheeler	117 Barclay st Grand Rapids, Mich	54
....	Miss S.. J. Farmer	Eliot, Me	55
....	Henry Riches	5 Endsleigh Gardens, London, N W.	56
....	Mrs H. E Holt	Box 109, Lexington, Mass	57
....	Dr H. W. Bolton, pres		58
....	Dr D. A. Sargent	Cambridge, Mass.	59
....	M. Chamberlain	Cambridge, Mass.	60
....	O. S Baketel, sup't		61
....	O. P. Jenkins	Stanford university, Cal	62
....	Miss Jane Addams	Hull House, Chicago, Ill.	63
....	David Kinley	Urbana, Ill.	64
....	R. G. Gillum	Terre Haute, Ind.	65
....	S. C Davisson	Bloomington, Ind.	66
.25	P. H. Cragan	Colfax, Ia.	67
....	G. D Herron, prin	Grinnell, Ia	68
....	C S Stroup	La Grange, Ind	69
....	Dr W. Rein	Jena, Thuringen, Germany	70
....	Dr W. L Davidson, sup't	Cuyahoga Falls, O	71
....	J: H Finley	Galesburg, Ill.	72
....	W. E Doubleday	48 Priory road, Lond. N. W. Eng.	73
....	Malcolm McNeill	Lake Forest, Ill.	74
....	Miss C B. Wilson	R. 1301-2 Vene'n bld. 34 Wash'n st. Chi. Ill	75
....	C C. Michener	40 E. 23d st. New York	76
....	D. S Sanford, pres.	Lake George assembly, N. Y.	77
....	H. E. Kratz	Sioux City, Ia.	78
....	S R Gill	Lakeside, O	79
....	O L. Elliott	Stanford university, Cal.	80
.25-.50	Prof. G. R. Crow	1012 W. 7th st. Los Angeles, Cal.	81
.25	S. H Berry	502 Fulton st. Brooklyn, N. Y.	82
....	C. F. Kroeh	Hoboken, N. J	83
....	Mrs A. P. Williams	23 Marlborough st. Boston, Mass.	84
....	A C Boyden	Bridgewater, Mass.	85
....	H. W. Tyler	Mass. inst of technology, Boston, Mass	86
....	E H Mensel	28 Monroe st. Ann Arbor, Mich.	87
....	E F. Johnson	31 N. University av. Ann Arbor, Mich.	88
....	G: R. Winslow	2 Bevier st. Binghamton, N. Y.	89
....	D. L. Kiehle	Univ. of Minnesota, Minneapolis, Minn.	90

UNIVERSITY OF THE STATE OF NEW YORK

	NAME	Place	Year founded	Opening
91	Mississippi Chautauqua assembly	Crystal Springs, Miss	1895	18 Jl
92	Missouri univ s. s of languages	Columbia, Mo		10 Je
93	Summer school of science	Columbia, Mo	1895	27 My
94	Monona Lake assembly	Madison, Wis	1880	23 Jl
95	Monteagle summer schools	Monteagle, Tenn	1882	4 Jl
96	Mountain Chautauqua assembly	Mountain Lake Park, Md	1883	7 Ag
97	National home reading union	Leamington Spa, Eng	1889	29 Je
98	National Prohibition Park	Prohibition P'k, S I, N.Y.	1891	
99	National summer school	Glens Falls	1882	16 Jl
100	Natural science camp	Canandaigua, N. Y.	1890	3 Jl
101	Nebraska Chautauqua assembly	Crete, Neb	1882	3 Jl
102	Neff college of oratory	Hamilton, N. Y.	1893	21 Je
103	New Eng Chaut Sunday-school a	So Framingham, Mass	1879	23 Jl
104	New Hampshire coll. s. s. of biology	Durham, N. H	1894	8 Jl
105	New Hampshire summer institute	Plymouth, N H.	1893	15 Ag
106	New York university summer school	New York	1895	9 Jl
107	Normal school of gymnastics	Milwaukee, Wis	1895	1 Jl
108	North Carolina university s school	Chapel Hill, N. C.	1894	25 Je
109	Northeast Georgia Chaut. assembly	Demorest, Ga	1893	1 Ag
110	Northern New Eng. Sunday-school a	Freyeburg, Me	1882	23 Jl
111	Northfield conf Internat. Y W C A	Northfield, Mass	1893	20 Jl
112	Oak Island Beach summer school	Oak Beach, N. Y	1895	1 Jl
113	Oberlin s. s of Christian sociology	Oberlin, O.	1895	22 Je
114	Ocean City assembly	Ocean City, N J.		31 Jl
115	Ocean Grove assembly	Ocean Grove, N J.	1884	
116	Old Lyme summer school of art	Belle Isl., S Norwalk, Ct	1894	
117	Ottawa Chautauqua assembly	Ottawa, Kan	1878	17 Je
118	Oxford lectures for clergy	Oxford, Eng		15 Jl
119	Oxford univ extension sum meeting.	Oxford, Eng	1888	1 Ag
120	Pacific coast assembly		1880	2 Jl
120a	Pacific Grove Chaut assembly	Pacific Grove, Cal.	1878	8 Jl
121	Pennsylvania Chautauqua	Mt Gretna Park, Pa.	1892	1 Jl
122	Piasa Bluffs assembly	Alton, Ill.	1887	25 Jl
123	Port Leyden summer school	Port Leyden, N Y	1891	
124	Rock River assembly	Dixon, Ill.	1888	30 Jl
125	Rocky Mountain Chautauqua assem'y	Glen Park, Col.	1886	11 Jl
126	Rogerville confer Internat Y W C.A	Rogerville, Tenn.	1895	7 Je
127	Round Lake summer institute	Round Lake, N. Y.	1887	23 Je
128	Eastern N Y s s for teachers	Round Lake, N. Y.	1894	16 Jl
129	Saratoga summer lectures	Saratoga Springs, N Y.	1895	30 Jl
130	Sauveur coll of lang & Amherst s s	Amherst, Mass	1876	1 Jl
131	School of applied ethics	Plymouth, Mass	1891	7 Jl
132	Shasta assembly	Shasta, Col	1895	16 Jl
133	Shinnecock Hills sum sch of art	Southampton, L I, N. Y	1890	1 Je
134	Silver Lake summer university	Silver Lake, N Y	1887	1 Jl
135	Southern Oregon Chaut. assembly	Ashland, Or	1893	10 Jl

STATISTICS OF SUMMER SCHOOLS, 1895

Closing	Students	Visitors	States	Countries	Subjects of study	
28 Jl					Chautauqua assembly topics.	91
20 Jl					Eng, Latin, Greek, French, German	92
17 Ag					Biology, physics, chemistry	93
21 Ag					Chautauqua assembly topics	94
24 Ag	200				General	95
27 Ag					Chaut. assembly topics, stenog. photog	96
8 Jl	500			4	Science, history	97
		500-2500				98
6 Ag					Pedagogy, common branches	99
28 Ag	129	?700	6		Science, sketching, physical culture	100
13 Jl					Chautauqua assembly topics	101
1 Ag	85			6 Can	Oratory, voice culture	102
5 Ag		2000 d'ly			Chautauqua assembly topics	103
5 Ag	19		6		Botany, zoology	104
29 Ag	164			6 Alas	General	105
17 Ag	25	25	6		General	106
10 Ag	21		7		Gymnastics	107
17 Jl	140	?100			General	108
12 Ag					Chautauqua assembly topics	109
10 Ag	150	250			Chautauqua assembly topics	110
30 Jl	204	50	18		Y W C. A. topics	111
30 Ag					General	112
29 Je					Christian sociology	113
2 Ag					Chautauqua assembly topics	114
	200	5000			Bible	115
					Art	116
28 Je					Chautauqua assembly topics	117
27 Jl					Theology	118
26 Ag	653			13	General	119
13 Jl					Chautauqua assembly topics	120
21 Jl	100	750			Chautauqua assembly topics	12
1 Ag					General	121
22 Ag					Art, music, kindergarten	122
					Preparatory for teachers examinations	123
15 Ag					Chautauqua assembly topics	124
1 Ag	60	300			Chautauqua assembly topics	125
17 Je	30	7	10	4	Y W. C. A. topics	126
22 Ag	200	2080			Lang. mus. ora. Bib. hist. art. kind	127
10 Ag	92				General	128
30 Ag		300-700			Religions, ethnology, geology, sociology	129
9 Ag	171	? 50		21 Can	Lan. sci. Eng. lit. lib.econ. art, math. p.c.	130
9 Ag	100	? 100			Econ ethics, religion, education	131
21 Jl					Chautauqua assembly topics	132
1 O					Art	133
1 S	?300	?5000			General	134
19 Jl					Chautauqua assembly topics	135

	Lecturers	Lectures	Recitations	EXTENSION COURSES Subjects	Lecturers	Buildings	FEES Entrance	Full course	Single course
91									
92	6					University			$10
93	5					University		a	
94								$2	
95	20	152						10	4
96									
97	12	21						7a	
98									
99								$20	7-14
100	16	151	100					64	
101									
102	5	30	80			Colgate acad		40	
103		77				4	$2 50		
104	2					Thompson Hall		10	
105	10	98							
106	7					University		25	
107	9	272				Normal school		30	25
108	20					University	1	5	
109	12							1 50	
110	9	60				2		2	
111	11							5	
112									
113								5	
114									
115	9		21			3			
116									
117									
118	17	? 40				Examinat'ns schools		£1	15s
119						Examinat'ns schools			3
120									
120a	12	86				2			
121									
122									
123								$3	
124									
125	10			Eng. hist.& lit.	1	4		2 50	
126	9							4	
127	28	30	68			6			
128	10							9	$3
129	4	20							
130	20	258	852			Amherst coll		20	12
131	33	? 80						20	10
132									
133								32-80	
134	45	149	660	4	4	7	3		1-10
135	5	18			1		.25	1 50	

b Free to Missouri teachers

STATISTICS OF SUMMER SCHOOLS, 1895

FEES	SECRETARY		
Single lecture	Name	Address	
....	Bishop C B Galloway ...	....	91
....	Miss Mary Iglehart	Columbia, Mo	92
....	M L Lipscomb, prin	Columbia, Mo	93
....	J E Moseley	Madison, Wis	94
....	J I D Hinds	Lebanon, Tenn.	95
....	Dr W L Davidson, sup't	Cuyahoga Falls, O	96
1s	Miss M. C Mondy ...	Surrey House, Vic emb'k't, Lon W C Eng	97
....	C L. Haskell, sup't	West New Brighton, S I , N Y	98
....	J A Holden	Glens Falls, N Y	99
....	A L. Arey	229 Averill av Rochester, N. Y	100
...	W Scott, D.D sup't	....	101
$ .50	H F Yale	1414 Arch st. Philadelphia, Pa ...	102
....	G H Clarke	Malden, Mass	103
....	C M Weed	Durham, N H	104
....	Fred Gowing	Concord, N H	105
....	C · B. Bliss	University hights, New York city ...	106
....	W · A Stecher ...	3d and Chestnut st. St Louis, Mo ...	107
....	E A Alderman ...	Chapel Hill, N C	108
.25	A. A Stafford ...	Demorest, Ga	109
.25	N W Edson	First national bank, Portland, Me....	110
....	Miss C. B Wilson	R. 1301-2 Vene'n bld 34 Wash'n st Chi Ill	111
....	Rev J D Long	Babylon, L. I , N Y......	112
....	Z W Holbrook ...	475 Dearborn av Chicago, Ill.	113
....	Rev B C Ogden, pres .	Mantua, N J.	114
....	B B Loomis	Canajoharie, N. Y..........	115
....	J H Boston	203 Montague st Brooklyn, N Y ...	116
....	Sandford Topping	Ottawa Kan	117
....	Rev Dr Robertson	Bishop Hatfield's hall, Durham, Eng	118
....	J A R Marriott	Examinations schools Oxford, Eng	119
....	Dr A C Hirst, sup't		120
....	Mrs E J Dawson	San Jose, Cal	120a
....	Rev E S Hagen	Lebanon, Pa	121
....	L Halleck, pres		122
...	C D Hill	Port Leyden, N Y. ...	123
....	Rev W H Hartman	Dixon, Ill	124
.25	T M Priestly, pres	University Park, Col.	125
....	Miss C B Wilson	R. 1301-2 Vene'n bld. 34 Wash'n st Chi Ill	126
..	Dr H C Farrar ...	433 Clinton av Albany, N Y ...	127
....	W U. Hinman	Stillwater, N Y .	128
...	D. F Ritchie	98 Circular st Saratoga Springs, N Y	129
.50	W L Montague	Amherst, Mass	130
.50	S. B Weston	1305 Arch st Philadelphia, Pa. ...	131
....	Thomas Filben, sup't....		132
...	W M Chase, director ...	51 W 10th st New York ...	133
....	Rev. Ward Platt ...	226 Averill av. Rochester, N. Y.	134
.25	Mrs C. R. Minkler	Ashland, Or	135

	NAME	Place	Year founded	Opening
136	Southern students conference	Knoxville, Tenn.	1892	14 Je
137	Summer school of science	Kingston, Canada	1894	10 Jl
138	Summer vacation meeting	Keene, N. Y.	1894	
139	Texas Chautauqua assembly	Georgetown, Tex.	1888	4 Jl
140	Upsala summer meeting	Upsala, Sweden	1893	
141	Virginia summer school of methods	Bedford City, Va.	1889	24 Je
142	Virginia university s s of law	Charlottesville, Va.	1870	
143	Sum. sch. of medicine (private)	Charlottesville, Va	1891	
144	Sum class in chem. (private)	Charlottesville, Va.		
145	Viroqua assembly	Viroqua, Wis	1895	18 Ag
146	Waseca Chautauqua assembly	Waseca, Minn	1885	9 Jl
147	Waterloo Chautauqua assembly	Waterloo, Ia	1892	20 Je
148	Wellesley summer school	Wellesley, Mass.	1895	
149	Western reserve univ summer school	Cleveland, O.	1895	29 Je
150	Sum. school of theology	Cleveland, O.	1895	8 Jl
151	West. secretarial inst Y M C A.	Lake Geneva, Wis.	1884	17 Jl
152	College students conference			21 Je
153	Institute program			1 Ag
154	Institute summer school			17 Jl
155	Willamette Valley assembly	Willamette Valley, Or.	1894	10 Jl
156	Winfield Chautauqua assembly	Winfield, Kan	1891	18 Je
157	Winona presbyterian assembly	L'keside Pk, Warsaw, Ind.	1895	
158	Wisconsin summer school	Madison, Wis	1887	
159	World's student conference	Northfield, Mass.	1866	

STATISTICS OF SUMMER SCHOOLS, 1895

Closing	Students	Visitors	States	Counties	Subjects of study	
23 Je	145	? 20			Y. M. C. A topics	136
7 Ag					Science	137
					Nature	138
18 Jl					Chautauqua assembly topics	139
						140
19 Jl					Pedagogy, common branches	141
	66		22		Law	142
	21		9		Anat. chem phys hist. path mater. med.	143
					Chemistry	144
22 Ag					History, literature, astronomy	145
25 Jl					Chautauqua assembly topics	146
4 Jl					Chautauqua assembly topics	147
					Mathematics, philosophy	148
25 Jl	15				General	149
18 Jl				9 Can	Theology	150
17 Ag	50	? 500	13		Y. M. C. A. topics	151
30 Je						152
14 Ag						153
17 Ag						154
20 Jl					Chautauqua assembly topics	155
28 Je	300	100			Chautauqua assembly topics	156
						157
					General	158
					Bible	159

(Column headers: OF / ATTENDANTS / REPRESENTATION)

	Lecturers	Lectures	Recitations	Extension Courses Subjects	Extension Courses Lecturers	Buildings	Entrance	Full course	Single course
136	? 16	. .	. .	. .	. .	. .	. .	$6	. .
137	. .	. .	. .	. .	. .	Queens univ.	$1	4	. .
138	. .	. .	. .	. .	. .	. .	. .	. .	. .
139	. .	. .	. .	. .	. .	. .	. .	4	. .
140	. .	. .	. .	. .	. .	. .	. .	. .	. .
141	. .	. .	. .	. .	. .	Randolph-Macon ac.	. .	5	. .
142	2	100	100	. .	. .	University	. .	65	$50
143	6	120	144	. .	. .	University	. .	120	40
144	. .	. .	. .	. .	. .	. .	. .	. .	. .
145	. .	. .	. .	. .	. .	. .	. .	. .	. .
146	. .	. .	. .	. .	. .	. .	. .	. .	. .
147	. .	. .	. .	. .	. .	2 . .	3	3	. .
148	. .	. .	. .	. .	. .	. .	. .	. .	. .
149	5	. .	. .	. .	. .	Adelbert college	. .	20	10
150	7	40	. .	. .	. .	Adelbert college.	. .	. .	. .
151	9	80	260	. .	. .	6 . .	3	. .	⁂
152	. .	. .	. .	. .	. .	. .	. .	. .	. .
153	. .	. .	. .	. .	. .	. .	. .	. .	. .
154	. .	. .	. .	. .	. .	. .	. .	. .	. .
155	. .	. .	. .	. .	. .	. .	. .	. .	. .
156	8	67	62	. .	. .	3 . .	1	1	.50
157	. .	. .	. .	. .	. .	. .	. .	. .	. .
158	. .	. .	. .	. .	. .	2 . .	. .	10	. .
159	. .	. .	. .	. .	. .	. .	. .	. .	. .

FEES	SECRETARY		
Single lecture	Name	Address	
....	H P Andersen, treasurer	Asheville, N C	136
....	William Mason........	School of mining, Kingston, Canada	137
....	E E Moore	109 E 45th st New York	138
....	Rev D W Gerhard....	131 S Duke st Lancaster, Pa	139
....	H Hjarne.........	University of Upsala, Upsala, Sweden	140
....	W A Jenkins	Portsmouth, Va	141
....	R C Minor	University station, Charlottesville, Va	142
....	Dr W A Lambeth	University station, Charlottesville, Va	143
....	....	....	144
....	Rev J S Parker	....	145
..	James Quirk........	....	146
$ .50	F J. Sessions	Waterloo, Ia.	147
....	Dr Helen L. Webster....	Wellesley, Mass	148
.50	F M Warren.......	Adelbert college, Cleveland, O	149
....	C F Thwing.......	Cleveland, O	150
....	J W Hansel.......	709 Association bldg. Chicago, Ill	151
....	....	....	152
....	....	....	153
....	....	....	154
....	Col R. A. Miller, pres	....	155
.25	A. H Limerick......	Winfield, Kan.	156
....	Rev Dr Johnson	....	157
....	E A Birge	Madison, Wis	158
....	C. S Cooper	40 E. 23d st. New York	159

INDEX

The superior figure tells the exact place on the page in ninths, e. g. 65^4 means four-ninths of the way down page 65. Dates are printed in italics.

Abbreviations, explanation, 65^4.
Algebra, *see* Mathematics.
Alliance française, 63^1.
Alma college, summer school, 49^7. *See also* Summer schools, statistics.
American society university extension summer meeting, 37^6–41^2. *See also* Summer schools, statistics.
Amherst summer school, *see* Sauveur college of languages and the Amherst summer schools.
Anatomy, at Harvard summer school of physical training, 31^7; at Western secretarial institute, 52^8; at Summer school for physical training, 54^2.
Ancoats Brotherhood, 60^5–61^2.
Anthropology, at Greenacre summer school, 29^4; at Clark university, 36^6.
Anthropometry, at Harvard summer school of physical training, 31^8; at Summer school for physical training, 54^2.
Appropriation for summer institutes, 3^8.
Aquatics, at Western secretarial institute, 51^7, 52^8.
Archeology, at Round Lake, 9^9; at Catholic summer school, 14^6.
Arithmetic, *see* Mathematics.
Art, at Bay View, 49^5; at Belle Island summer school, 13^7; at Cambridge (Eng.) university, 59^2; at Catholic winter school of America, 44^2; at Catskill summer school, 13^8; at Chautauqua, 7^6, 8^6; at Cornell university, 16^5; at Eastern New England Chautauqua, 29^2; at Edinburgh summer meeting, 58^5; at Greenacre summer school, 29^5; at Harvard summer school, 30^5, at Long Island Chautauqua, 17^7; at Marienfeld summer camp, 41^7; at Metropolitan normal art summer school, 23^5; at Round Lake, 9^2; at Sauveur college of languages and the Amherst summer school, 33^8: at Shinnecock Hills summer school, 13^9–14^2; at Silver Lake, 12^5. *See also* Summer schools, statistics.
Assyrian language, at Chautauqua. 7^8.
Astronomy, at Catholic winter school of America, 44^2; at University of Wisconsin, 52^7.
Athletics, at Natural science camp, 13^2; at Harvard summer school of physical training, 32^8; at Western secretarial institute, 51^6, 52^8; at Pacific coast students conference, 56^9. *See also* Physical culture.

Bacteriology, at Biological laboratory of Brooklyn institute, 12^9.
Bathing, at Marienfeld summer camp, 41^7.
Bay View, summer university, 49^5 *See also* Summer schools, statistics.
Belle Island summer school of art, 13^7. *See also* Summer schools, statistics
Bible study, at Bay View, 49^5; at Chautauqua, 7^5, 8^5; at Durham (Eng) 6^1; at Eastern New England Chautauqua, 28^9–29^1; at Fairmount Chautauqua, 56^1; at New England Chautauqua Sunday-school assembly, 35^9; at Saratoga atheneum summer schools, 24^4; at Silver Lake, 12^2; at Western secretarial institute, 51^2, 52^8. *See also* Summer schools, statistics.
Biblical institute at Ocean Park, 28^8–29^1.
Bicycling, *see* Cycling.
Biological association, at Marine biological laboratory, 34^9.
Biological experiment station of the University of Illinois. 48^8–49^4.

6

Biological laboratory of Brooklyn institute, *see* Brooklyn institute biological laboratory
Biological laboratory of University of California, 56[5]
Biology, at Biological experiment station of the University of Illinois, 48[8]–49[3]; at Catholic winter school of America, 44[2]; at Chautauqua, 7[4], at Marine biological laboratory, 34[5]–35[8]; at New Hampshire college of agriculture and the mechanic arts, 29[9]–30[1]; at New York university, 18[8]; at Saratoga atheneum summer schools, 24[2], at University of Buffalo, 19[5]; at University of Missouri, 55[4]. *See also* Summer schools statistics.
Bliss, C: B., article on University summer courses, 4[5]–6[2].
Board, price of, at Biological experiment station of the University of Illinois, 49[3], at Edinburgh summer meeting, 58[8]; at Jena, 64[2]; at University of Wisconsin, 53[5].
Boating, at Marienfeld summer camp, 41[7]
Bookkeeping, at National summer school, 11[4]; at Alma college, 49[8].
Botany, at Biological experiment station of the University of Illinois, 49[2]; at Biological laboratory of Brooklyn institute, 12[8]; at Cambridge (Eng) university, 59[3], at Canada summer school of science, 57[3]; at Catholic winter school of America, 44[2]; at Cornell university, 16[5]; at Edinburgh summer meeting, 57[6], at Harvard summer school, 30[5]; at Marine biological laboratory, 34[5]–35[8], at Marthas Vineyard summer institute, 34[8], at National summer school, 11[1], at New Hampshire college of agriculture and the mechanic arts, 29[9]–30[1], at Saratoga atheneum summer schools, 24[2]; at University of Wisconsin, 52[7]. *See also* Summer schools, statistics.
Boxing, at Natural science camp, 13[2]; at Summer school for physical training, 54[2]; at Harvard summer school of Physical training, 32[4].
Brooklyn institute, Biological laboratory, 12[7]. *See also* Summer schools, statistics.
Brooklyn institute summer schools of art, 13[7]–14[3].

Browning's poetry, at New England Chautauqua Sunday-school assembly, 36[1].
Buffalo university, *see* University of Buffalo.
Business methods, at Silver Lake, 12[5]

Caen, sessions for the study of French, 64[3].
California, University of, *see* University of California.
Calisthenics, *see* Physical culture
Cambridge (Eng) university, summer meeting, 59[1].
Canada summer school of science, *see* Summer school of science
Canandaigua, natural science camp at, 13[1].
Catholic summer school of America, 14[2]–15[8], program, 14[5]–15[5]. *See also* Catholic winter school of America, Columbian catholic summer school; Summer schools, statistics.
Catholic winter school of America, 42[7]–45[8]; directors, 44[6]. *See also* Summer schools, statistics.
Catskill summer school of art, 13[8]. *See also* Summer schools, statistics.
Cayuga Lake summer school, 17[2]. *See also* Summer schools, statistics.
Cazadero, students conference at, 56[6].
Central New York summer school, 15[8]–16[4]. *See also* Summer schools, statistics
Certificates for teaching at University of Minnesota, 54[5].
Champlain club, 14[5].
Chautauqua, summer institute at, 3[8].
Chautauqua summer school, 7[2]–9[2]; announcement, *1896*, 7[8]–9[2]; assembly department, 7[3]; collegiate department, 7[3]; lecturers, 7[8]–8[9]; regents examinations at, 9[1]
Chautauqua, *see also* Eastern New England Chautauqua, Fairmount Chautauqua, Florida Chautauqua; Long Island Chautauqua; New England Chautauqua Sunday-school assembly.
Chemistry. at Cambridge (Eng.) university, 59[3]; at Canada summer school of science, 57[3], at Chautauqua, 7[4], at Cornell university, 16[5], at Harvard summer school, 30[5]; at Marthas Vine-

yard summer institute, 34⁴; at National summer school, 11²; at New York university, 18⁸; at University of California, 56³; at University of Missouri, 55⁴, at University of Wisconsin, 52⁷ *See also* Summer schools, statistics.
Chester, National home reading union at, 62⁸.
Chicago Commons, 46³
Chicago Commons school of social economics, 45⁹-48⁷; lecturers, 46⁵-47⁹. *See also* Summer schools, statistics
Child-study, at University of Buffalo, 20¹; at Harvard summer school, 30⁵; at Clark university, 36⁶. *See also* Summer schools, statistics
Church history, at Catholic summer school of America, 14⁸, at Saratoga atheneum summer schools, 24⁷; at Western secretarial institute, 52³.
Civil government, at National summer school, 11⁴; at Marthas Vineyard summer institute, 34³; at Alma college, 49⁸; at Canada summer school of science, 57³ *See also* Political economy.
Clark university summer school, 36⁵-37². *See also* Summer schools, statistics.
Clergy, institute for, 9⁸; lectures to, 60¹.
Clinton classical school, 18². *See also* Summer schools, statistics
College preparation, specialty at Saratoga atheneum summer schools, 23⁹.
College students, *see* Students conferences.
Columbia college summer school, geodesy, 6⁹-7¹; surveying, 6⁸. *See also* Summer schools, statistics.
Columbian catholic summer school, 14⁴, 53⁶. *See also* Summer schools, statistics.
Composition, at National summer school, 11⁵; at Saratoga atheneum summer schools, 24³; at Harvard summer school, 30³.
Concerts, at Chautauqua, 8⁹; at Eastern New England Chautauqua, 29³; at Florida Chautauqua, 42⁶, at Long Island Chautauqua, 17⁷; at National summer school, 11⁷; at Prohibition Park, 17⁹; at Round Lake, 10¹, at Saratoga atheneum summer schools, 25³.
Cook county normal school, 45⁷. *See also* Summer schools, statistics

Cornell university summer school, 16⁴, law school, summer term, 16⁸ *See also* Summer schools, statistics.
Courses, *see* Summer schools, statistics. and special subjects.
Credentials, at Alliance française, 63⁷; at Chautauqua, 9²; at Cornell university, 16⁷, at Grand Rapids summer school for kindergarten study, 50⁸, at H E. Holt normal institute of vocal harmony, 33¹; at New York state library school, 22⁶; at Summer school of science for the Atlantic provinces of Canada, 57⁵; at University of Wisconsin, 53².
Cycling, at Marienfeld summer camp, 41⁷.

Dentistry, at Harvard summer school, 31¹
Des Moines summer school of methods, 54⁹ *See also* Summer schools, statistics.
Drake university summer Latin school, 55¹ *See also* Summer schools, statistics.
Drawing, at Central New York summer school, 16²; at Cornell university, 16⁵; at Harvard summer school, 30⁴, at Marthas Vineyard summer institute, 34³; at National summer school, 10⁹, 111. *See also* Summer schools, statistics
Durham (Eng) summer meeting, 60¹.

Eastern New England Chautauqua, 28⁸-29³. *See also* Summer schools, statistics
Eastern New York summer school for teachers, at Round Lake, 9⁵.
Economics, *see* Political economy.
Edinburgh summer meeting, 57⁵-58⁹; fees, 58⁸, price of board, 58⁸.
Education, *see* Pedagogy.
Educational congresses, at University of Minnesota, 54⁶.
Educational day at Round Lake, 9⁸
Educational theories, at National summer school, 11⁶; at New York university, 18⁸, at Greenacre summer school, 29⁴, at Harvard summer school, 30⁴.
Elocution, at Canada summer school of science, 57³, at Central New York summer school, 16², at Marthas Vineyard summer institute, 34⁴; at National

summer school, 10[6] 11[2], at New England Chautauqua Sunday-school assembly, 35[9]; at University of Michigan, 50[2]. *See also* Oratory; School of expression, Summer schools, statistics, Voice culture

Embryology, at Biological laboratory of Brooklyn institute, 12[8]; at Marine biological laboratory, 34[5]-35[2].

Engineering, at Cornell university, 16[6], at Saratoga atheneum summer schools, 24[2]; at Harvard summer school, 30[4] *See also* Geodesy; Mining; Surveying

England, summer school in, 59[1].

English, at Chautauqua, 7[4], 8[2], at Cornell university, 16[6]; at Harvard summer school, 30[3] at Marienfeld summer camp, 41[5]; at Saratoga atheneum summer schools, 24[3]; at University of Missouri, 55[7]. *See also* Summer schools, statistics.

English literature, at Canada summer school of science, 57[3]; at Catholic summer school of America, 14[6]; at Catholic winter school of America, 44[2]; at Chautauqua, 7[4], 8[2]; at L. A. U. K. summer school, 62[2], at Marthas Vineyard summer institute, 34[3]; at New England Chautauqua Sunday-school assembly, 36[1], at Saratoga atheneum summer schools, 24[2]; at Sauveur college of languages and the Amherst summer school, 33[6], at University of Wisconsin, 52[6]. *See also* Summer schools, statistics.

Entertainments, at Chautauqua, 7[4]; at National summer school, 11[7]. *See also* Concerts

Entomology, at Natural science camp, 13[3]; at New Hampshire college of agriculture and the mechanic arts, 29[9]-30[1]; at Canada summer school of science, 57[3]

Ethics, at Saratoga atheneum summer schools, 24[3]; at School of applied ethics, 36[2]; at Marienfeld summer camp, 41[5]; at Catholic winter school of America, 44[2]. *See also* Summer schools, statistics.

Evolution, at Greenacre summer school, 29[5]; at Cambridge (Eng.) university, 59[2]

Fairmount Chautauqua summer school, 55[8]-56[2].

Fees, at Alma college, 49[9]; at Biological experiment station of the University of Illinois, 49[3]; at Cambridge (Eng.) university, 59[7], at Catholic winter school of America, 44[5]; at Cayuga Lake summer school, 17[6]; at Central New York summer school, 16[2], at Clark university, 37[2]; at Durham (Eng.) Lectures to clergy, 60[3]; at Edinburgh summer meeting, 58[8]; at Grand Rapids summer school for kindergarten study, 50[9]; at Greenacre summer school, 29[8]; at H. E Holt normal institute of vocal harmony, 33[1]; at Harvard summer school of physical training, 32[8]; at Jena, 64[3]; at London school of economics and political science, 62[8]; at Long Island Chautauqua, 17[8]; at Marienfeld summer camp, 41[8], at Marine biological laboratory, 35[7]; at National home reading union, 62[9]; at New York state library school, 23[8]; at Port Leyden, 17[8]; at Summer class in geology, 22[8], at Summer school for physical training, 54[2]; at University extension summer meeting, 40[3], at University of Buffalo, 21[3]; at University of Missouri summer school of science, 55[6]; at University of Missouri summer school of language, 55[7]; at University of Virginia, 42[4], at University of Wisconsin, 53[3]; at Wellesley summer school, 37[5]. *See also* Summer schools, statistics.

Fencing, at Harvard summer school of physical training,32[4], at Summer school for physical training, 54[3].

Florida Chautauqua, winter school 42[5]. *See also* Summer schools, statistics

French, at Alliance française, 63[1]; at Alma college, 49[8]; at Caen, 64[3]; at Chautauqua, 7[3]; at Harvard summer school, 30[4], at Marienfeld summer camp, 41[5]; at Marthas Vineyard summer institute, 34[3]; at New York university, 18[8], at Round Lake, 9[4], at Saratoga atheneum summer schools, 24[3]; at Sauveur college of languages and the Amherst summer school 33[3]: at University of Missouri, 55[7]; at Wellesley summer school, 37[4]. *See also* Summer schools, statistics.

Genesee Wesleyan seminary, work at Silver Lake, 12[6].
Geodesy, summer school at Columbia college, 6[9]–7[1]. *See also* Summer schools, statistics.
Geography, at National summer school, 10[8], 11[5]; at Edinburgh summer meeting, 58[3] *See also* Physical geography.
Geology, at Chautauqua, 7[4]; at Harvard summer school, 31[1]; at Natural science camp, 13[2]; Summer class in, 21[5]–22[4]; at University of Wisconsin, 52[7]. *See also* Summer schools, statistics.
Geometry, *see* Mathematics.
German, at Alma college, 49[8]; at Chautauqua, 7[3]; at Cornell university, 16[5]; at Harvard summer school, 30[4]; at Jena, 64[1]; at Marienfeld summer camp, 41[5]; at Marthas Vineyard summer institute, 34[8]; at New York university, 18[3]; at Round Lake, 9[4]; at Saratoga atheneum summer schools, 24[1]; at Sauveur college of languages and the Amherst summer school, 33[3]; at University of Missouri, 55[7]; at University of Wisconsin, 52[6]; at Wellesley summer school, 37[4]. *See also* Summer schools, statistics.
German literature, at Catholic summer school of America, 14[7].
Glens Falls, summer institute at, 3[8].
Glens Falls summer school, *see* National Summer school.
Good government congress, 11[8]–12[1].
Grand Rapids summer school for kindergarten study, 50[5]. *See also* Summer schools, statistics.
Great Britain, summer conference in, 57[5]–62[9].
Greek, at Chautauqua, 7[4], 8[3]; at Cornell university, 16[5]; at Marienfeld summer camp, 41[5]; at Marthas Vineyard summer institute, 34[8]; at New England Chautauqua Sunday-school assembly, 36[1]; at Round Lake, 9[9]; at Saratoga atheneum summer schools, 24[1]; at Sauveur college of languages and Amherst summer school, 33[3]; at University of Missouri, 55[7]; at Wellesley summer school, 37[4]. *See also* Summer schools, statistics.
Greenacre summer school, 29[8]. *See also* Summer schools, statistics.
Gymnastics, *see* Physical culture.

H. E. Holt, normal institute of vocal harmony, 32[8]–33[1]. *See also* Summer schools, statistics.
Hartford theological seminary, summer course at Saratoga, 23[7]–24[9]; program, 24[8].
Harvard summer school, 30[8]–31[3]; library, 31[2]. *See also* Summer schools, statistics.
Harvard summer school of physical training, 31[5]–32[8]. *See also* Summer schools, statistics.
Hebrew, at Chautauqua, 7[4], 8[5]; at Round Lake, 9[9]; at Saratoga atheneum summer schools, 24[4]; at Sauveur college of languages and the Amherst summer school, 33[3].
Histology, at University of Wisconsin, 52[7].
Historical pilgrimages, 18[3], 40[8], 58[7], 61[1].
History, at Alma college, 49[8], at Cambridge (Eng.) university, 59[2]; at Catholic summer school of America, 15[4], at Catholic winter school of America, 44[2]; at Chautauqua, 7[5], 8[4]; at Cornell university, 16[6]; at Edinburgh summer meeting, 58[3]; at Long Island Chautauqua, 17[7], at Marienfeld summer camp, 41[5]; at Marthas Vineyard summer institute, 34[8]; at National summer school, 10[7]; at Oxford summer meeting, 59[9]; at Saratoga atheneum summer schools, 25[8]; at Silver Lake, 12[3]; at University extension summer meeting, 37[7]–38[6]; at University of Buffalo, 19[4]; at University of Wisconsin, 52[6]; at Wellesley summer school, 37[4]. *See also* Summer schools, statistics.
Home science, at Greenacre summer school, 29[4].
Horseback riding, at Natural science camp, 13[2]; at Marienfeld summer camp, 41[7].

Hygiene, at Harvard summer school, 30[5], at Harvard summer school of physical training, 31[7]; at Summer school for physical training, 54[2]; at Canada summer school of science, 57[8].

Illinois, University of, *see* Biological experiment station of the University of Illinois.
Instructors, *see* Lecturers.
International Christian workers assembly, 11[9].
Interpreter, 58[6].
Italian, at Round Lake, 9[4]; at Sauveur college of languages and the Amherst summer school, 33[8].
Italian literature, at Catholic winter school of America, 44[2]

Jena summer school, 63[8]–64[8].

Kindergarten methods, at Canada summer school of science, 57[8]; at Central New York summer school, 16[2], at Chautauqua, 7[5], at Grand Rapids summer school for kindergarten study, 50[8], at National summer school, 11[8], at Round Lake, 9[8]; at Silver Lake, 12[5]
See also Summer schools, statistics.

L. A. U. K. summer school, 61[4]–62[5].
See also Summer schools, statistics.
Lake Geneva students conference, 51[1].
See also Summer schools, statistics.
Languages, at Alma college, 49[8], at Cambridge (Eng) university, 59[5], at Chautauqua, 7[8], 8[2]; at Drake university summer Latin school, 55[1], at Harvard summer school, 30[4], at Jena, 64[2]; at Long Island Cnautauqua, 17[7]; at Marienfeld summer camp, 41[5], at Marthas Vineyard summer institute, 34[8], at New York university, 18[8], at Round Lake 9[5]; at Saratoga atheneum summer schools, 24[1]; at Sauveur college of languages and the Amherst summer school, 33[2]; at Silver Lake, 12[5]; at University of Missouri, 55[6]; at University of Wisconsin, 52[6], at Wellesley summer school, 37[4] *See also* Summer schools, statistics.

Latin, at Alma college, 49[8], at Chautauqua, 7[4], 8[3]; at Cornell university, 16[5], at Drake university summer Latin school, 55[1]; at Harvard summer school, 30[4]; at Marienfeld summer camp, 41[5], at Marthas Vineyard summer institute, 34[8], at New York university, 18[8]; at Saratoga atheneum summer schools, 24[1]; at Sauveur college of languages and the Amherst summer school, 33[8], at University of Missouri, 55[7], at Wellesley summer school, 37[4] *See also* Summer schools, statistics.

Law course, at Cornell summer school, 16[8]; at University of Virginia, 41[9]–42[5], at University of Michigan, 50[1] *See also* Summer schools, statistics.

Lecturers, at Alliance française, 63[2]; at Ancoats Brotherhood, 60[5]; at Bay View, 49[5]; at Biological laboratory of Brooklyn institute, 12[8]; at Cambridge (Eng.) university, 59[6]; at Catholic summer school of America, 14[6]–15[6]; at Catholic winter school of America, 43[8]–44[1], at Catskill summer school of art, 13[8]; at Chautauqua summer school, 7[8]–8[9]; at Chicago Commons school of social economics, 46[5]–47[9], at Columbian catholic summer school, 53[8]; at Cornell summer law school, 16[8]; at Eastern New England Chautauqua, 28[8]–29[3], at Edinburgh summer meeting, 58[4]; at Fairmount Chautauqua, 55[9]–56[2]; at Grand Rapids summer school for kindergarten study, 50[8]; at Greenacre summer school, 29[4], at L. A. U. K. summer school, 61[5]–62[4]; at Marine biological laboratory, 35[1]; at Marthas Vineyard summer institute, 34[2], at National summer school, 10[6]–11[6]; at New England Chautauqua Sunday-school assembly, 35[8]–36[2]; at New Hampshire college of agriculture and the mechanic arts, 30[1]; at Prohibition Park, 18[1]; at Round Lake, 9[3]; at Saratoga atheneum summer schools, 24[1]–25[3]; at Sauveur college of languages and the Amherst summer school, 33[3]; at Shinnecock Hills summer school of art, 14[1]; at Silver Lake, 11[8]–12[6]; at Teachers college summer schools, 26[5]–27[8], at University extension summer

meeting, 38²-40⁸, at University of Buffalo, 19²-21¹; at University of Wisconsin, 52⁵; at Wellesley summer school, 37⁴; at Western Reserve university, 45⁵; at Western secretarial institute, 51². *See also* Summer schools, statistics.
Lectures to clergy, 60¹.
Libraries, for summer schools 4².
Library economy, at New York state library school 22⁵-23⁴; at Sauveur college of languages and the Amherst summer school, 33⁸; at University of Wisconsin, 52⁸-53¹; at L. A. U. K. summer school, 61³-62⁵. *See also* Summer schools, statistics.
Literature courses, at Alma college, 49⁸; at Catholic summer school of America, 14⁶; at Chautauqua, 7³; at Harvard summer school, 30⁴; at Silver Lake, 12⁵; at University extension summer meeting, 37⁷-38⁶; at University of Buffalo, 19⁹. *See also* English literature; German literature; Sacred literature; Summer schools, statistics.
Logic, at Marienfeld summer camp, 41⁵.
London school of economics and political science, 62⁶
Long Island Chautauqua, 17⁶. *See also* Summer schools, statistics.

Macy manual arts building, 26¹
Madison, Wis, Columbian catholic summer school at, 14³, 53⁷
Manchester (Eng.) Ancoats Brotherhood, 60⁵-61¹.
Manual training, at National summer school, 11²; at Teachers college summer school, 25⁶ *See also* Sloyd.
Marienfeld summer camp, 41²
Marine biological laboratory, 34⁵-35⁸. *See also* Summer schools, statistics.
Marthas Vineyard summer institute, 33⁹-34⁵. *See also* Summer schools, statistics.
Massage, at Harvard summer school of physical training, 31⁹, at Summer school for physical training, 54³.
Mathematics, at Alma college, 49⁸, at Chautauqua, 7⁴; at Cornell university, 16⁶; at Harvard summer school, 30⁵; at Long Island Chautauqua, 17⁷; at Marienfeld summer camp, 41⁵: at Marthas Vineyard summer institute, 34³; at National summer school, 10⁶, 11³, at New York university, 18⁸, at Saratoga atheneum summer schools, 24¹; at Sauveur college of languages and the Amherst summer school, 33⁷; at Silver Lake, 12⁵; at University extension summer meeting, 40¹; at University of Buffalo, 19³, at University of Wisconsin, 52⁶. *See also* Summer schools, statistics.
Medicine, at Harvard summer school, 31¹.
Metaphysics, at Catholic summer school of America, 14⁹
Meteorology, at Canada summer school of science, 57³.
Metropolitan normal art summer school, 23⁵.
Michigan university, summer school of law, 50¹. *See also* Summer schools, statistics.
Microscopy, at Marthas Vineyard summer institute, 34³.
Military discipline, at Natural science camp, 13³; at Harvard summer school of physical training, 32⁸
Milwaukee, summer school for physical training at, 53⁹-54⁴
Mineralogy, at Canada summer school of science, 57³.
Mining, at University of California, 56⁴. *See also* Summer schools, statistics
Ministers institute, at Round Lake, 9⁹.
Minnesota university summer school, 54⁵. *See also* Summer schools, statistics
Missouri university summer school, 55⁸. *See also* Summer schools, statistics.
Modern language holiday courses, 63⁸-64⁵.
Music, at Bay View, 49⁵; at Canada summer school of science, 57³, at Catholic summer school of America, 15¹, at Central New York summer school, 16²; at Chautauqua 7³, 8⁹, at Eastern New England Chautauqua, 29²; at Fairmount Chautauqua, 55⁹-56¹, at Greenacre summer school, 29⁶; at Long Island Chautauqua, 17⁷; at Marienfeld Summer camp, 41⁷; at Marthas Vineyard summer institute, 34³, at New England Chautauqua Sunday-school assembly, 35⁹, at Round Lake, 9⁴; at Silver Lake, 12²; at University exten-

sion summer meeting, 39[1]. See also
Summer schools, statistics
Musical festival, at Silver Lake, 12[8].

Napanoch, summer school of art at, 13[8].
National Epworth league assembly,
11[8]–12[2].
National home reading union, 62[8]. See
also Summer schools, statistics.
National summer school, 10[2]–11[8]. See
also Summer schools, statistics.
Natural history, at National summer
school, 10[8]; at Wellesley summer
school, 37[3].
Natural science, at National summer
school, 11[8]
Natural science camp, 13[1]. See also Summer schools, statistics.
Nature study, at University of Buffalo,
19[9]; at Greenacre summer school, 29[5];
at Marthas Vineyard summer institute, 34[3].
Neurology, at Clark university, 36[6].
New England Chautauqua Sunday-school
assembly, 35[8]–36[2]. See also Summer
schools, statistics.
New Hampshire college of agriculture
and the mechanic arts, summer school,
29[8]–30[2].
New Orleans, winter school at, 14[4],
42[7]–45[8].
New York college for the training of
teachers, see Teachers college.
New York school law, provision for summer institutes, 3[7].
New York state library school, 22[8]–23[4].
New York university, summer school,
18[7]. See also Summer schools, statistics.

Ocean Park, Maine, summer assembly
at, 28[8]–29[3].
Old Lyme summer school of art, 13[7]. See
also Belle Island summer school of art;
Summer schools, statistics.
Oratory, at Round Lake, 9[9]; at Eastern
New England Chautauqua, 29[1]; at
Marthas Vineyard summer institute,
34[4]. See also Elocution; School of
expression; Summer schools, statistics.
Orthopedics, at Summer school for physical training, 54[2]

Oxford university extension summer
meeting, 59[8]. See also Summer schools,
statistics.

Pacific coast students conference, 56[6].
Painting, at Marthas Vineyard summer
institute, 34[4]. See also Art.
Paris, Alliance française, 63[1]; winter
school in, 64[5].
Parrsboro', summer school at, 57[1].
Pedagogy, at Alma college, 49[8]; at Catholic winter school of America, 44[2]; at
Cayuga Lake, 17[2]; at Chautauqua, 7[8]–
8[1]; at Clark university, 36[6]; at Des
Moines summer school of methods, 54[9];
at Harvard summer school, 30[4]; at
Jena, 64[1]; at Marthas Vineyard summer institute, 34[1], at National summer
school, 10[5], 11[6]; at New York university, 18[9]; at University of Buffalo, 19[1]–
21[4]; at University of Wisconsin, 52[6].
See also Summer schools, statistics.
Peekskill, Clinton classical school at, 18[2].
Penmanship, at National summer school,
11[2]. See also Summer schools, statistics.
Philosophy, at Chautauqua, 7[5]; at Silver
Lake, 12[5]; at Edinburgh summer meeting, 58[3]; at Jena, 64[1]. See also Summer schools, statistics.
Photography, at Silver Lake, 12[5]; at
Natural science camp, 13[2]; at Marthas
Vineyard summer institute, 34[8]. See
also Summer schools, statistics.
Physical culture, at Alma college, 49[8];
at Bay View, 49[5], at Central New
York summer school, 16[2], at Chautauqua, 7[7], at Eastern New England
Chautauqua, 29[1]; at Fairmount Chautauqua, 55[9]; at Harvard summer
school, 31[1]; at Harvard summer
school of physical training 31[4]–32[5]; at
Marthas Vineyard summer institute,
34[4]; at National summer school, 11[2];
at New England Chautauqua Sunday-school assembly, 35[9]; at New York
university, 18[8]; at Round Lake, 9[6]; at
Saratoga atheneum summer schools,
24[3]; at Silver Lake, 12[5]; at Summer
school for physical training, 53[9]–54[4];
at Western secretarial institute, 51[7]–52[3].
See also Athletics; Summer schools,
statistics.

Physical geography, at University of Wisconsin, 52⁷.
Physics, at Canada summer school of science, 57⁸; at Catholic summer school of America, 15²; at Chautauqua, 7⁴; at Cornell university, 16⁶; at Harvard summer school, 30⁵; at Marthas Vineyard summer institute, 34⁴; at National summer school, 11²; at Saratoga atheneum summer schools, 24¹; at University of Missouri, 55⁴. *See also* Summer schools, statistics.
Physiography, at Harvard summer school, 31².
Physiology, at Canada summer school of science. 57²; at Clark university, 36⁶; at Harvard summer school, 31¹; at Harvard summer school of physical training, 31⁷; at Marine biological laboratory, 34⁵; at Summer school for physical training, 54²; at University of Wisconsin, 52⁷; at Western secretarial institute, 52⁸.
Plattsburg, summer school at, 14².
Political economy, at Alma college, 49⁸; at Cambridge (Eng.) university, 59²; at Catholic summer school of America, 15²; at Catholic winter school of America, 44²; at Chautauqua, 7⁵, 8⁴; at London school of economics and political science, 62⁶; at Long Island Chautauqua, 17⁷; at New York university, 18⁸ *See also* Civil government; Summer schools, statistics.
Political science, at London school of economics and political science, 62⁶.
Port Leyden summer school, 17¹. *See also* Summer schools, statistics.
Prohibition Park, 17⁸-18¹.
Psychology, at Canada summer school of science, 57⁸; at Catholic summer school of America, 14⁹; at Chautauqua, 7⁵, 8⁴; at Clark university, 36⁶; at Harvard summer school, 30⁵; at Marthas Vineyard summer institute, 34¹; at National summer school, 10⁵; at New York university, 18⁸; at Saratoga atheneum summer schools, 24⁸; at Summer school for physical training, 54²; at University extension summer meeting, 38⁶-39¹; at University of Buffalo, 19⁶, 20¹; at University of Wisconsin, 52⁶. *See also* Summer schools, statistics.
Public instruction, Dep't of, supervision of summer institutes, 3⁸.

Regents examinations, at Chautauqua, 9¹; at New York state library school, 22⁶.
Religions, study of at Greenacre summer school, 29⁴.
Rhetoric, at Saratoga atheneum summer schools, 24²; at Catholic winter school of America, 44²; at Alma college, 49⁸.
Röntgen rays, lecture on, 18¹.
Romance languages, at Cornell university, 16⁵.
Round Lake musical association, 9¹.
Round Lake summer institute, 9²-10²; assembly department, 10¹. *See also* Summer schools, statistics.
Round tables, at Fairmount Chautauqua, 56²; at Florida Chautauqua, 42⁶.
Rowing, at Harvard summer school of physical training, 32⁴.

Sacred literature, at Chautauqua, 7⁵, 8⁵. *See also* Bible study.
Saratoga atheneum summer schools, 23⁶-25⁸.
Sauveur college of languages and the Amherst summer school, 33². *See also* Summer schools, statistics.
Scholarships for summer school work, 6².
School journal, article on University summer courses, 4⁵-6².
School law, at Alma college, 49⁸; at National summer school, 11⁵; provision for summer institutes, 3⁷ *See also* New York school law.
School of applied ethics, 36². *See also* summer schools, statistics.
School of expression, at Chautauqua, 7⁷, 8⁶; at Round Lake, 9⁸; at Silver Lake, 12⁶. *See also* Elocution, Oratory.
Science courses, at Alma college, 49⁸; at Biological laboratory of Brooklyn institute, 12⁸; at Canada summer school of science, 57¹; at Catholic summer school of America, 14⁹-15²; at Chautauqua, 7⁴; at Cornell university, 16⁵, at Edinburgh summer meeting, 57⁸-58⁴; at Jena, 64¹; at Marienfeld summer camp, 41⁶; at

Marine biological laboratory, 34[5]-35[8]; at Marthas Vineyard summer institute, 34[3]; at National summer school, 10[5]; at Natural science camp, 13[2]; at New Hampshire college of agriculture and the mechanic arts 29[8]; at New York university, 18[6]; at Saratoga atheneum summer schools, 24[1]; at University extension summer meeting, 39[3]; at University of Buffalo, 19[4]; at University of Missouri, 55[3]; at University of Wisconsin, 52[7] *See also* Summer schools, statistics

Scotland, summer school in, 57[5]-58[9].

Semitic languages, at New York university, 18[8].

Shaksperian reading, at Catholic summer school of America, 14[8]; at University of Michigan, 50[2].

Shinnecock Hills summer school of art, 13[2]-14[2]. *See also* Summer schools, statistics.

Silver Lake, summer university, announcements for *1896*, 11[8]-12[6]. *See also* Summer schools, statistics.

Sketching, at Natural science camp, 13[2] *See also* Art.

Sloyd, at Marthas Vineyard summer institute, 34[4] *See also* Manual training.

Sociology, at Greenacre summer school, 29[5], at Chicago Commons school of social economics, 46[1]; at Edinburgh summer meeting, 58[3]; at Chautauqua, 7[5], 8[4] *See also* Political economy; Summer schools, statistics.

South Framingham, summer assembly at, 35[8]

Spanish, at Saratoga atheneum summer schools, 24[2]; at Sauveur college of languages and the Amherst summer school, 33[3].

State aid, to summer institutes, 3[7].

Staten Island summer assembly, 17[8]

Statistics, tables, 65[1].

Stout, J H., aid for course on library science, 52[9].

Students conferences at Lake Geneva, 51[7]; Pacific coast, 56[5].

Summer class in geology, 21[5]-22[4]

Summer institutes, appropriation, 3[8]; length of course, 3[8]. *See also* Summer schools.

Summer school for physical training, 53[a]-54[4], program, 54[2]

Summer school of science, 57[1]. *See also* Summer schools, statistics.

Summer schools, privileges, 4[1]; average length of session, 5[8]; statistics, 65[1]-81[7]. *See also* Summer institutes.

Sunday-school assembly at South Framingham, 35[8]-36[2]

Surveying, summer school at Columbia college, 6[8]; at Harvard summer school, 30[4]; at Marienfeld summer camp, 41[6]; at University of Wisconsin, 52[7]. *See also* Summer schools, statistics.

Swimming, at Natural science camp, 13[2]; at Hartford summer school of physical training, 32[6]; at Summer school for physical training, 54[3].

Taxidermy, at Natural science camp, 13[2].

Teachers, summer school for, 9[5]; National summer school for, 10[2]-11[8]. *See also* Lecturers.

Teachers college, summer school, 25[4]-28[7]; lectures, 26[5]-27[4]; program, 27[5]; location, 27[6]-28[4].

Teaching, *see* Pedagogy.

Teaching profession, standard raised, 5[7].

Temperance, at New England Chautauqua Sunday-school assembly, 36[1].

Theology, at Round Lake, 9[9]; at Saratoga atheneum summer schools, 24[4]; at Western Reserve university, 45[4]; at Western secretarial institute, 52[8]. *See also* Summer schools, statistics.

Therapeutics, at Summer school for physical training, 54[3]

Thousand Island Park, summer institute at, 3[8].

Tully Lake summer school, 15[8]-16[4].

Union college, summer course at Saratoga, 23[7]-24[9]

University extension summer meeting, *see* American society university extension summer meeting

University of Buffalo, summer school of pedagogy, 19[1]-21[4].

University of California, summer school, 56[3].

University of Illinois, Biological experiment station, 48[8]–49[4].
University of Michigan, *see* Michigan university.
University of Minnesota. *see* Minnesota university.
University of Missouri, *see* Missouri university.
University of the city of New York, *see* New York university.
University of Virginia, *see* Virginia university.
University of Wisconsin, *see* Wisconsin summer school.
University summer courses, C: B. Bliss on, 4[5]-6[2].

Virginia university, summer school of law, 41[9]–42[5]. *See also* Summer schools, statistics.
Voice culture, at National summer school, 11[2]; at Central New York summer school, 16[2]; at Harvard summer school of physical training, 32[5]; at H. E. Holt normal institute of vocal harmony, 32[8]–33[1]. *See also* Summer schools, statistics.

Wellesley summer school, 37[2]. *See also* Summer schools, statistics.

West Philadelphia, summer meeting at, 37[7]–41[2].
Western Reserve university, summer session, 45[8]. *See also* Summer schools, statistics.
Western secretarial institute, 51[1]–52[4]. *See also* Summer schools, statistics.
Whitechapel, school of economics and political science at, 62[6].
Williams, Sherman, article on state aid to summer schools, 4[1].
Wisconsin, summer school, 52[4]–53[6] *See also* Summer schools, statistics.
Woman's education association of Boston, scholarships for summer school work, 6[3].
Wrestling, at Summer school for physical training, 54[2]

Y. M. C A. students conferences, 56[7].

Zoology, at Biological experiment station of the University of Illinois, 49[2]; at Biological laboratory of Brooklyn institute, 12[8], at Cambridge (Eng.) university, 59[3]; at Canada summer school of science, 57[8]; at Edinburgh summer meeting, 57[5]; at Marine biological laboratory, 34[5]–35[8]; at New Hampshire college of agriculture and the mechanic arts, 29[9], at University of Wisconsin, 52[7] *See also* Summer schools, statistics.

University of the State of New York

Object. The object of the University as defined by law is to encourage and promote education in advance of the common elementary branches. Its field includes not only the work of academies, colleges, universities, professional and technical schools, but also educational work connected with libraries, museums, university extension courses and similar agencies.

The University is a supervisory and administrative, not a teaching institution. It is a state department and at the same time a federation of 640 institutions of higher and secondary education.

Government. The University is governed and all its corporate powers exercised by 19 elective regents and by the governor, lieutenant-governor, secretary of state and superintendent of public instruction who are *ex officio* regents. Regents are elected in the same manner as United States senators; they are unsalaried and are the only public officers in New York chosen for life.

The elective officers are a chancellor and a vice-chancellor, who serve without salary, and a secretary. The secretary is the executive and financial officer, is under official bonds for $10,000, is responsible for the safe keeping and proper use of the University seal and of the books, records and other property in charge of the regents, and for the proper administration and discipline of its various offices and departments.

Powers and duties. Besides many other important powers and duties, the regents have power to incorporate, and to alter or revoke the charters of universities, colleges, academies, libraries, museums, or other educational institutions; to distribute to them funds granted by the state for their use; to inspect their workings and require annual reports under oath of their presiding officers, to establish examinations as to attainments in learning and confer on successful candidates suitable certificates, diplomas and degrees, and to confer honorary degrees

They apportion annually an academic fund of $106,000, part for buying books and apparatus for academies and high schools raising an equal amount for the same purpose, and the remainder on the basis of attendance and the results of instruction as shown by satisfactory completion of prescribed courses for which the regents examinations afford the official test. Each school of academic grade also receives $100 yearly. The regents also expend annually $25,000 for the benefit of free public libraries.

Regents meetings. Regular meetings are held on the third Thursdays of October, December and March, and in June during convocation week. The executive committee, consisting of the chancellor, vice-chancellor and the chairmen of the six standing committees, meets the third Thursday of each month from October to June.

Convocation. The University convocation of the regents and the officers of institutions in the University, for consideration of subjects of mutual interest, has been held annually since 1863 in the senate chamber in Albany. It meets the last Wednesday, Thursday and Friday of June.

Though primarily a New York meeting, nearly all questions discussed are of equal interest outside the state. Its reputation as the most important higher educational meeting of the country has in the past few years drawn to it many eminent educators not residents of New York, who are most cordially welcomed and share fully in all discussions. It elects each year a council of five to represent it in intervals between meetings Its proceedings, issued annually, are of great value in all educational libraries.

Departments

1 Administrative (Regents office)—including incorporation, supervision, inspection, reports, legislation, finances and all other work not assigned to another department.

Duplicate division. This is a state clearing house, to which any institution in the University may send books or apparatus which it no longer requires, and select from it in return an equal value suited to its locality and needs.

2 Examination—including preacademic, law student, medical, dental and veterinary student, academic, higher, law, medical, dental, veterinary, library, extension and any other examinations conducted by the regents, and also credentials or degrees conferred on examination.

The examinations are conducted as the best lever for securing better work from teachers and more systematic and continuous study from students, and as the best means of detecting and eliminating inefficient teachers or methods. They cover 130 subjects and require 1,500,000 question papers annually, and are held the week ending the last Friday in January and March and the third Friday in June, in the 540 academies and high schools in the University and also at various central points where there are 10 or more candidates.

3 Extension—including summer, vacation, evening and correspondence schools and other forms of extension teaching, lecture courses, study clubs, reading circles and other agencies for the promotion and wider extension of opportunities and facilities for education, specially for those unable to attend the usual teaching institutions.

Public libraries division. To promote the general library interests of the state, which through it apportions and expends $25,000 a year for the benefit of free public libraries. Under its charge are the traveling libraries for lending to local libraries or to communities not yet having permanent libraries.

The most important factor of the extension movement is provision of the best reading for all citizens by means of traveling, home and capitol libraries and annotated lists through the public libraries division.

4 State library—including general law, medical, and education libraries, library school, bibliographic publications, lending books to students and similar library interests.

Library school. The law authorizes the state library to give instruction and assistance in organizing and administering libraries. Students receive from the state library staff, in return for services rendered to the library during their two years' course, careful training in library economy, bibliography, cataloging, classification and other duties of professional librarianship.

5 State museum—including all scientific specimens and collections, works of art, objects of historic interest and similar property appropriate to a general museum, if owned by the state and not placed in other custody by a specific law; also the research department carried on by the state geologist and paleontologist, botanist and entomologist, and all similar scientific interests of the University.

SS LIST

OF A

COMMENDED FOR SCHOOLS

PAGE		P.
99	Literature (*continued*)	
101	English literature	
101	English poetry and drama	
101	English essays and miscellany	
101	German and classic literature	
101	Fiction	
102	History	
102	General	
102	Travel	
102	General	
103	Atlases and gazetteers	
103	Antiquities	
103	Europe	
103	Asia	
103	Africa	
103	America	
104	Arctic regions	
104	Biography	
104	Collective	
104	Individual	
104	Ancient history	
104	History of Europe and Asia	
105	History of America	
105	Regents reading courses	

Regents
SEPTEMBER 1896

Anson Judd Upson, D. D., LL. D., L. H. D., *Chancellor*
William Croswell Doane, D. D., LL. D., *Vice-Chancellor*
Levi P. Morton, LL. D., Governor ⎫
Charles T. Saxton, LL. D., Lieutenant-Governor ⎬ *Ex officio*
John Palmer, Secretary of State ⎪
Charles R. Skinner, M. A., LL. D., Sup't Pub. Inst. ⎭

In order of election by the legislature

ELECTED
1873 Martin I. Townsend, M. A., LL. D. - - Troy
1874 Anson Judd Upson, D. D., LL. D., L. H. D. - Glens Falls
1876 William L. Bostwick, M. A. - - - - Ithaca
1877 Chauncey M. Depew, LL. D. - - - - New York
1877 Charles E. Fitch, LL. B., M. A., L. H. D. - Rochester
1877 Orris H. Warren, D. D. - - - - Syracuse
1878 Whitelaw Reid, LL. D. - - - - New York
1881 William H. Watson, M. A., M. D. - - - Utica
1881 Henry E. Turner - - - - - Lowville
1883 St Clair McKelway, LL. D. - - - - Brooklyn
1885 Hamilton Harris, Ph. D., LL. D. - - - Albany
1885 Daniel Beach, Ph. D., LL. D. - - - Watkins
1888 Carroll E. Smith, LL. D. - - - - Syracuse
1890 Pliny T. Sexton, LL. D. - - - - Palmyra
1890 T. Guilford Smith, M. A., C. E. - - - Buffalo
1892 William Croswell Doane, D. D., LL. D. - Albany
1893 Lewis A. Stimson, B. A., M. D. - - - New York
1894 Sylvester Malone - - - - - Brooklyn
1895 Albert Vander Veer, M. D., Ph. D. - - Albany

Elected by the regents
1888 Melvil Dewey, M. A., *Secretary* - - - Albany

EDITOR'S NOTE

This list provides books to the amount of $500, assuming that an average discount of one third will be secured, except in case of a few books marked *net* and specially allowed for. Wherever there is opportunity for choice, editions have been carefully selected. Considerations of economy have debarred mention of many excellent editions, but have not induced the recommendation of poor print, paper or editing. An occasional note gives information about more expensive editions or fuller treatises which would be desirable could they be afforded, but which can not be substituted without exceeding the $500 limit or excluding something else. Where alternatives are suggested in the main list, as in case of cyclopedias, translations of Homer, etc. provision has been made for buying the more expensive work, but not for both. When more than one edition is mentioned, the first is the one reckoned. Amounts in headings represent list prices and do not include alternatives.

Certain series of miscellaneous standard literature, which appear frequently on the list and are sometimes brought into comparison, perhaps need brief description. The volumes of the Riverside literature series (Houghton) are 12mos printed in clear, medium sized type on good opaque paper and bound in brown linen. They are also bound in paper and boards, but only the cloth binding is quoted on this list. The Riverside school library (Houghton) volumes are generally printed from the same plates as the Riverside literature series, on somewhat finer paper and bound in red half leather. The World's classics (Putnam) are less expensive reissues of the well-known Knickerbocker nuggets. The type, though not large, is clear, the page well spaced, and the paper is good. They are neatly bound small 16mos. The Elia series (Putnam) are larger 16mos, admirable in type and paper, with gilt top and rough edges. These series, with Longman's English classics, Leach's Students series of English classics, Macmillan's School editions, and others of recognized value, may be depended on as evenly good. To know one is to be assured of the quality of all. Unfortunately this is not always true of special editions and series, the uniformity sometimes consisting only in binding and price. Of the Stratford edition of Irving certain volumes are desirable while others are poor. The Crowell Standard library, uncommonly satisfactory for the price in many instances, is very unequal and sometimes decidedly inferior. It has been recommended on this list only after examination of the individual volume.

Books marked *a* aggregate a selection costing $200. If to these the books marked *b* are added, the amount will reach $300. This selection merely suggests probable first needs in case it is impracticable to buy all on the list, but it does not imply that these books are superior in quality. It is of course impossible to make a limited list which shall perfectly meet diverse needs. A German dictionary or an advanced chemistry may be almost useless in one school and absolutely necessary in another. Variations must be made to suit the requirements of special courses and the interests of the community. The resources of the school must also be considered. It is hoped that these briefer selections will meet the average requirements fairly well and that the full list will furnish suggestions for special wants.

University of the State of New York

Extension Bulletin

No. 14   September 1896

CLASS LIST

OF A

$500 LIBRARY RECOMMENDED FOR SCHOOLS

GENERAL REFERENCE BOOKS ($48.75)
Burt, M.. E.. Literary landmarks. Houghton 75c.

Cyclopedias
a Johnson's universal cyclopaedia. 8v. 1894-95. Appleton $48 *net*.
or
Chambers's encyclopaedia. 10v. 1892-93. Lippincott $30.

PSYCHOLOGY AND ETHICS ($5)
Sully, James. Outlines of psychology. Appleton $2.50.
a Gilman, N. P. & Jackson, E: P. Conduct as a fine art. Houghton $1.50.
Smiles, Samuel. Duty. Harper $1.

MYTHOLOGY ($1.50)
a Guerber, H. A. Myths of Greece and Rome. Amer. bk co. $1.50.

SOCIOLOGY ($17.30)
a Nordhoff, Charles. Politics for young Americans. Amer. bk co. 75c.
Fiske, John. American political ideas. Harper $1.
b Johnston, Alexander. History of American politics. Holt 80c.
Bowker, R: R. Economics for the people. Harper 75c.

Perry, A. L.   Political economy.   Scribner $2.50.
a Walker, F. A.   Political economy.   Holt $2.   (Amer. sci. ser. advanced course)
Gilman, N: P.   Profit sharing between employer and employee. Houghton $1.75.
Riis, J. A.   Children of the poor.   Scribner $1.25.
a Brooks, E. S.   Century book for young Americans.   Century $1.50.
a Bryce, James.   American commonwealth.   2v.   Macmillan $4.
Dawes, A.. L.   How we are governed.   Ginn $1.

Education ($13.25)

a Williams, S: G.   History of modern education.   Bardeen $1.50.
a Compayré, Gabriel.   Lectures on teaching.   Heath $1.75.
Fitch, J. G.   Lectures on teaching.   Macmillan $1.
b Page, D. P.   Theory and practice of teaching.   Amer. bk co. $1.
Skinner, C: R. *ed.*   Arbor day manual.   Weed, Parsons & Co. $2.50.
White, E. E.   School management.   Amer. bk co. $1.
Parker, F. W.   How to study geography.   Appleton $1.50.   (Internat. educ. ser.)
a Harrison, Elizabeth.   Study of child nature.   Chic. kindergarten training school $1.
Poulsson, Emilie.   In the child's world.   Milton Bradley co. $2.

Self culture ($6.50)

a Chester, Eliza, *pseud.*   Chats with girls on self culture.   Dodd $1.25.
a Hale, E: E.   How to do it.   Roberts $1.
b Mathews, William.   Getting on in the world.   Griggs $1.50.
Munger, T. T.   On the threshold.   Houghton $1.
Smiles, Samuel.   Self-help.   Harper $1.
Chester, Eliza.   Girls and women.   Houghton 75c.

Legends and fairy tales ($5.75)

a Grimm, J. L; & W; K;   Household stories; tr. from the German by Lucy Crane.   Macmillan $2.
Lang, Andrew, *ed.*   Blue fairy book.   Longmans $2.
Jacobs, Joseph.   More English fairy tales.   Putnam $1.75.

DICTIONARIES AND SYNONYMS ($32.62)

a **Webster's international dictionary** of the English language.   Merriam $10.62.
Crabb, George.   English synonymes.   Harper $1.25.

Whitney's German dictionary. Holt $2 *net.*
Gasc, Ferdinand. French and English and English and French dictionary. Holt $2.25 *net.*

For fuller German and French dictionaries we recommend the Thieme-Preusser German dictionary, Haendcke & Lehmkuhl, $4.25, or Flügel's dictionary, English-German, 2 v. German-English, 1 v. Westerman $16 50, Smith, Hamilton & Legros' International English and French dictionary, 2 v Fouraut, $6.50. American importers will sell at the above prices.

Harpers' Latin dictionary. Harper $6.50.
Lewis' Elementary Latin dictionary, Harper $2 is excellent.
Liddell & Scott's Greek-English lexicon. Harper $10.

SCIENCE ($54.59)
General ($5.50)

a **Burroughs, John.** Locusts and wild honey. Houghton $1 25.
Torrey, Bradford. The foot-path way. Houghton $1.25.
a **Buckley, A. B.** Fairy-land of science. Appleton $1.50.
b —— Through magic glasses. Appleton $1.50.

Astronomy ($5)

a **Ball,** *Sir* **R. S.** Star-land. Ginn $1 *net.*
Proctor, R: A. Other worlds than ours. Appleton $1.75.
Young, C. A. General astronomy. Ginn $2.25.

Physics and electricity ($7.75)

Deschanel's physics; tr. and ed. by J. D. Everett. Appleton $5.75.
Cumming, Linnaeus. Electricity treated experimentally. Longmans $1.50.
a **Meadowcroft, W: H.** A B C of electricity. U. S. bk co. 50c.

Chemistry ($2.80)

Remsen, Ira. Inorganic chemistry. Holt $2 80 *net.* (Amer. sci. ser. advanced course.)

Geology and physical geography ($12.43)

b **Dana, J. D.** Manual of geology. Amer. bk co. $5.
b **Frye, A. E.** Brooks and brook basins. Ginn 58c.
Guyot, Arnold. Earth and man. Scribner $1.75.
a **Herrick, S. B.** Earth in past ages. Harper 60c.
Kingsley, Charles. Madam How and Lady Why. Macmillan 50c. (School ed.)
b **Shaler, N. S.** Aspects of the earth. Scribner $2.50.
Tyndall, John. Forms of water. Appleton $1.50.

Biology, botany and zoology ($21.11)

Drummond, Henry. Ascent of man. Pott $2.
Morley, M. W. Song of life. McClurg $1.25.
Dana, *Mrs* W. S. How to know the wild flowers. Scribner $1.75.
a Gray, Asa. Lessons and manual of botany. Amer. bk co. $2.16.
a Newell, J. H. Outline lessons in botany. 2 v. Ginn $1.30.
   pt. 1 From seed to leaf.
   pt. 2 Flower and fruit.
b Miller, Olive Thorne, *pseud*. Little folks in feathers and fur. Dutton $2.50.
a Packard, A. S. Zoology. Holt $2.40 *net*. (Amer. sci. ser. advanced course.)
b Comstock, J. H. & A. B. Manual for the study of insects. Comstock pub. co. $3.75.
b Noel, Maurice. Buz. Holt $1.
a Chapman, F. M. Handbook of birds of eastern North America. Appleton $3.

PHYSIOLOGY AND HYGIENE ($3.20)

a Martin, H. N. The human body. Holt $2.20 *net*. (Amer. sci. ser. advanced course.)
b Blaikie, William. How to get strong and how to stay so. Harper $1.

BUSINESS ($.30)

Emery, M. S. Every-day business. Lee 30c.

ART AND SPORTS ($14.80)

Hamerton, P. G. Thoughts about art. Roberts $2.
Goodyear, W. H. History of art. Barnes $2 80 *net*.
Leland, C; G. Manual of wood-carving. Scribner $1.75.
Miller, L. W. Essentials of perspective. Scribner $1.50.
a Walker, William. Handbook of drawing. Scribner $1.75.
Adams, W. I. L. Amateur photography. Baker & Taylor $1.
b Beard, D. C. American boys' handy book. Scribner $2.
b Beard, Lina & A. B. American girls' handy book. Scribner $2.

LITERATURE ($207.75)

Histories and compendiums ($7.50)

Botta, *Mrs* A. C. (Lynch). Handbook of universal literature. Houghton $2.

Brewer, E. C.   Dictionary of phrase and fable.   Lippincott $2.50.
b Bartlett, John.   Familiar quotations.   Little $3.

American poetry ($9)

Bryant, W: C.   Poetical works.   Appleton $1.50.   (Household ed.)
Holmes, O. W.   Poetical works.   Houghton $2.   (Cambridge ed.)
a Longfellow, H: W.   Complete poetical works.   Houghton, $2. (Cambridge ed.)
a Lowell, J. R.   Poetical works.   Houghton $1.50.   (Household ed.)
a Whittier, J: G.   Complete poetical works.   Houghton $2.   (Cambridge ed.)

The Cambridge editions of Holmes, Longfellow and Whittier are the only one volume editions complete with latest revisions. Contain also biographic sketches.

American essays and miscellany ($15.50)

b Curtis, G: W;   From the Easy chair.   Harper $1.
a Emerson, R. W.   Essays; 1st and 2d series.   Houghton $1 (Popular ed.)
—— Representative men, *with* Nature, lectures and addresses. 2 v in 1. Houghton $1.   (Popular ed.)
b Lowell, J. R.   My study windows.   Houghton $2.
Repplier, Agnes.   Points of view.   Houghton $1.25.
a Holmes, O. W.   Autocrat of the breakfast table.   Houghton 50c. (Riverside literature ser. no 81); 60c. (Riverside school lib.); $1.50 (Riverside ed.)
Irving, Washington.   Alhambra.   Crowell $1.   (Standard lib.)
—— —— ed. by W: L. Phelps.   Putnam $1.   (Students' ed.)
b —— Knickerbocker.   Putnam $1.25.   (Stratford ed.)
a —— Sketch book.   Putnam $1.25.   (Stratford ed)
—— —— ed. by W: L. Phelps.   Putnam $1.   (Students' ed.)

G. P. Putnam's sons publish several editions of Irving of very unequal merit. The special volumes issued in the Students' ed are printed from new plates and are excellent. The Hudson ed complete, at $1.50 a vol and the Stratford ed. of *Knickerbocker* and the *Sketch book*, $1 25 each, may be recommended for library use.

Warner, C: D.   Backlog studies.   Houghton $1.   (Riverside Aldine ser.)
b —— My summer in a garden.   Houghton $1.   (Riverside Aldine ser.)
b Mitchell, D. G.   Reveries of a bachelor.   Scribner 75c.   (New Edgewood ed.)
a Thoreau, H: D: Walden.   Houghton $1.50.

English literature ($12)

a **Chambers's cyclopaedia** of English literature. 2 v. Lippincott $7.
b **Gosse, Edmund.** History of 18th century literature. Macmillan $1. (Students' ed.)
a **Nicoll, H: J.** Landmarks of English literature. Appleton $1.50.
b **Saintsbury, George.** History of Elizabethan literature. Macmillan $1. (Students' ed.)
—— History of 19th century literature. Macmillan $1.50.

English poetry and drama ($27.50)

a **Bryant, W: C.** *ed.* New library of poetry and song. Fords $5.
Henley, W: E. *ed.* Lyra heroica. Scribner $1 25.
Ward, T: H. *ed.* English poets. 4 v. Macmillan $4.
a **Whittier, J: G.** *ed.* Child life. Houghton $2.
Chaucer, Geoffrey. The students Chaucer; being a complete edition of his works, ed. by W. W. Skeat. Macmillan $1.75 *net*. (Globe ed.)
a **Milton, John.** Poetical works. Macmillan $1.75. (Globe ed.)
b **Scott,** *Sir* **Walter.** Poetical works. Macmillan $1.75. (Globe ed.)
Spenser, Edmund. Complete works. Macmillan $1.75 (Globe ed.)
a **Tennyson, Alfred.** Works. Macmillan $1.75. (Globe ed.)
Complete, with authorized revisions Gives Idyls of the king in order of Tennyson's final arrangement.
b **Wordsworth, William.** Complete poetical works. Crowell $1. (Standard ed.)
a **Shakspere, William.** Works; v. 1, Comedies, v. 2, Histories; v. 3, Tragedies. Macmillan $1.75 *each*. 3 v. $5. (Victoria ed.)
The most satisfactory cheap edition Follows text of Globe edition Good sized, clear type, excellent paper, lines not numbered. Attention is also called to:
—— New variorum edition of Shakespeare, ed. by H. H. Furness. Lippincott, v. 1-10, $4 *each*.
Presents results of an exhaustive collation of texts and gives a full selection of commentary. Invaluable to students and for reference, but not desirable for reading

Now ready:

As you like it	Midsummer night's dream
Hamlet (2 v.)	Othello
King Lear	Romeo and Juliet
Macbeth	The tempest
Merchant of Venice	

—— Works; ed. by Richard Grant White. 6 v. Houghton. $10. (Riverside ed.)
Excellent in text, notes, type and paper. Very desirable for school or home reading.

Shakspere William. Works, ed. by W. G. Clark and W. A. Wright. Macmillan $1.75. (Globe ed.)

Probably best one volume edition. Type too fine but clear and not worn. Paper very thin but good; text excellent; lines numbered.

Separate plays expurgated for school use:
Edited by W: J. Rolfe. Harper *paper* 40c.; *cloth* 56c.
Edited by H: N. Hudson. Ginn *paper* 30c.; *cloth* 45c. (New school Shakspere.)
Edited by Brainerd Kellogg. Maynard 30c. (English classics.)

a **Lamb, Charles & Mary.** Tales from Shakespeare. Ginn 50c. (Classics for children.)
—— —— Houghton 50c. (Riverside literature ser. no. 64-66), 60c. (Riverside school lib.)

English essays and miscellany ($15.60)

a **Addison, Joseph.** Sir Roger de Coverley papers. Leach 35c. (Students' ser. of Eng. classics.)

Arnold, Matthew. Essays in criticism. ser. 1. Macmillan $1.50.

Brown, John. Spare hours. ser. 1. Houghton $1.

b **Carlyle, Thomas.** Critical and miscellaneous essays. 2 v. Houghton $3.50. (Popular ed.)

De Quincey, Thomas. Confessions of an English opium eater. Putnam 50c. (World's classics.)

Hamerton, P. G. Intellectual life. Roberts $2.

b **Lamb, Charles.** Essays of Elia. 2 v. Putnam $1. (World's classics.)

Also published in 2 v. $2 in Putnam's admirably executed Elia series

b **Macaulay, T: B.** Critical, historical and miscellaneous essays. 3 v. Houghton $3.75. (Riverside ed.)

a **Ruskin, John.** Sesame and lilies. Putnam 50c. (World's classics.)
—— —— Maynard $1.50. (Brantwood ed.)

b **Thackeray, W: M.** Four Georges; English humorists. Houghton $1.50. (Illus library ed.)

German and classic literature ($6.50)

Taylor, Bayard. Studies in German literature. Putnam $2.

Church, A. J: Stories from Virgil. Dodd $1

b —— Stories from Homer. Dodd $1

a **Homer.** Iliad; tr. by W: C. Bryant. Houghton $2.50. (Roslyn ed.
or
—— —— tr. by Alexander Pope. 2 v. McClurg $2. (Laurel crowned verse.)
—— Iliad and Odyssey. Routledge $1.50. (Popular lib.)

Fiction ($114.15)

a **Alcott, L.. M.**   Little women.   Roberts $1.50.
b —— Under the lilacs.   Roberts $1.50.
a **Aldrich, T: B.**   Story of a bad boy.   Houghton $1.25.
—— Marjorie Daw and other people.   Houghton $1.50.
a **Andersen, H. C.**   Wonder stories told for children.   Houghton $1.
Barr, *Mrs* **A. B.**   Bow of orange ribbon.   Dodd $1.25.
Besant, Walter.   All sorts and conditions of men.   Harper $1.25.
Black, William.   Princess of Thule.   Harper $1.25.
b **Blackmore, R: D.**   Lorna Doone.   Crowell $1.   (Standard ed.)
Bronte, Charlotte.   Jane Eyre.   Crowell $1.   (Standard ed.)
Brooks, Noah.   The boy emigrants.   Scribner $1 25.
b **Bunyan, John.**   Pilgrim's progress.   Crowell 75c.   (Handy vol. ed.)
—— —— Macmillan $1.   (Golden treasury ser.)
b **Burnett,** *Mrs* **Frances (Hodgson).**   Little Lord Fauntleroy.   Scribner $2.
Bynner, E. L.   The begum's daughter.   Houghton $1.25.
b **Carroll, Lewis,** *pseud.*   Alice's adventures in Wonderland.   Macmillan $1.
Cervantes Saavedra, Miguel de.   Don Quixote; abridged and ed. by M. F. Wheaton.   Ginn 60c.   (Classics for children.)
b **Coolidge, Susan,** *pseud.*   What Katy did.   Roberts $1.25.
Cooper, J. F.   Leather-Stocking tales.   Putnam $1.25 *each* (Mohawk ed.)

    a Deerslayer   • Path finder   Prairie
    a Last of the Mohicans   Pioneers

—— Pilot.   Putnam $1.25.   (Mohawk ed.)
a —— Spy.   Putnam $1.25.   (Mohawk ed)
Craik, *Mrs* **D. M. (Mulock).**   John Halifax, gentleman.   Crowell $1.   (Standard ed.)
Crockett, S. R.   The raiders.   Macmillan $1.50.
a **Defoe, Daniel.**   Robinson Crusoe.   Houghton 60c.   (Riverside literature ser. no. 87); 60c. (Riverside school lib.)
Dickens, Charles.   Barnaby Rudge ⎫
a —— Christmas stories
a —— David Copperfield   ⎬ Macmillan $1 *each.*
b —— Nicholas Nickleby   (New popular ed.)
a —— Pickwick papers
a —— Tale of two cities *and* Edwin Drood ⎭

   These volumes are selected as best till a complete set, which is most desirable, can be afforded.

a **Dodge,** *Mrs* **Mary (Mapes).** Hans Brinker. Scribner $1.50.
Doyle, A. C. Micah Clarke Longmans $1.25.
Eggleston, Edward. Hoosier school master. Judd $1.50.
b **Eliot, George,** *pseud.* Adam Bede. Crowell $1. (Standard ed.)
b —— Romola. Crowell $1. (Standard ed.)
a —— Silas Marner. Leach 35c. (Students' ser of Eng. classics.)
Ewing, *Mrs* **J. H.** Jackanapes, Daddy Darwin's dovecot, Story of a short life. 3 v. in 1. Roberts 50c.
Frederic, Harold. In the valley. Scribner $1.50.
Gaskell, *Mrs* **E.. C.** Cranford. Crowell 75c. (Handy vol. ed.)
a **Goldsmith, Oliver.** Vicar of Wakefield. Houghton 50c. (Riverside school lib.)
—— —— Putnam 50c. (World's classics.)
b **Hale, E: E.** Man without a country and other tales Roberts $1.25.
a **Hawthorne, Nathaniel.** Marble faun. Houghton $2. (Riverside ed.)
—— Scarlet letter. Houghton $1. (Little classic ed.)
a —— House of seven gables Houghton $1. (Little classic ed)
—— Tanglewood tales. Houghton $1. (Little classic ed.)
a —— Wonder-book for girls and boys. Houghton $1. (Little classic ed.)

All Houghton's editions of Hawthorne are good. The Riverside edition, 13 v. $26, sometimes combines two or more stories in one volume; the Little classic edition 25 v. $25, occasionally gives two volumes to one work. Special volumes but not full sets can be bought in: Popular ed. $1 *each*, School ed. 40c. *each*, Salem ed 30c *each*, and in Riverside school library and Riverside literature series at varying prices.

a **Hayes, I: I.** Cast away in the cold. Lee $1.25.
b **Henty, G: A.** St George for England. Scribner $1.50.
—— With Wolfe in Canada. Scribner $1.50.
Howells, W: D. Chance acquaintance. Houghton $1.
b —— Rise of Silas Lapham. Houghton $1.50.
a **Hughes, Thomas.** Tom Brown's school days. Crowell $1. (Standard ed.)
—— —— Houghton 70c. (Riverside school lib.); 60c. (Riverside literature ser. no. 85.)
—— —— Macmillan 50c. (People's ed)
Hugo, Victor. Les misérables. 2 v. Crowell $2. (Standard ed.)
b **Jackson,** *Mrs* **Helen (Hunt).** Ramona. Roberts $1.50.
a **Jewett, S.. O.** Betty Leicester. Houghton $1.25
—— A native of Winby and other tales. Houghton $1.25.

Kingsley, Charles. Water babies. Macmillan 50c. (Macmillan's school lib.)
b —— Westward ho! Macmillan 50c. (Macmillan's school lib.)
—— Hypatia. Crowell $1. (Standard ed.)
a **Kipling, Rudyard.** Jungle book. Century $1.50.
Lytton, E: G: E. L. Bulwer-Lytton, *baron.* Last days of Pompeii. Crowell $1. (Standard ed.)
Macdonald, George. St George and St Michael. Lothrop $1.50.
a **Munroe, Kirk.** Campmates. Harper $1.25.
—— Flamingo feather. Harper $1.
Page, T: N. In Ole Virginia. Scribner $1.25.
Reade, Charles. The cloister and the hearth. Crowell $1. (Standard ed.)
Scott, *Sir* **Walter.** Fair maid of Perth
—— Guy Mannering
b —— Heart of Mid-Lothian
a —— Ivanhoe Macmillan $1.25 *each.*
a —— Kenilworth (Dryburgh ed.)
b —— Quentin Durward
a —— Rob Roy
a —— Talisman

These volumes are selected as best till a complete set, which is most desirable, can be afforded

a **Seawell, M. E.** Decatur and Somers. Appleton $1.
—— Paul Jones Appleton $1.
Sewell, Anna. Black beauty. Lothrop $1.
Stevenson, R. L. David Balfour. Scribner $1.50.
b —— Treasure island. Roberts $1.
—— Kidnapped. Scribner $1.50.
a **Stoddard, W: O.** Guert Ten Eyck. Lothrop $1.50.
—— On the old frontier. Appleton $1.50.
Stowe, *Mrs* **Harriet (Beecher).** Oldtown folks. Houghton $1.50.
a —— Uncle Tom's cabin. Houghton 60c. (Riverside literature ser. no. 88); 70c. (Riverside school lib.); $1 (Popular ed.)
a **Thackeray, W: M.** Henry Esmond
—— Newcomes Crowell $1 *each.* (Standard ed.)
—— Vanity fair

These are fairly good cheap editions of single volumes. Houghton's Illus. lib. ed. of Thackeray, complete in 22 v $1.50 *each,* is better.

a **Tomlinson, E. T.** Search for Andrew Field. Lee $1.50.
b **Wallace, Lew.** Ben-Hur. Harper $1.50.
Weyman, S. J. Gentleman of France. Longmans $1.25.
b **Whitney,** *Mrs* **A. D. T.** Summer in Leslie Goldthwaite's life. Houghton $1.25.
—— We girls. Houghton $1 25.
b **Wiggin,** *Mrs* **K.. D.** Birds' Christmas Carol. Houghton 50c.
b **Wilkins, M.. E.** New England nun and other stories. Harper $1.25.
Wyss, J ; D : Swiss family Robinson. Cassell 75c.

HISTORY

General ($18.65)

Keary, C : F. Dawn of history. Scribner $1.25.
b **Harper's book of facts**; compiled by J. H. Willsey and Charlton T. Lewis. Harper $8.

or

Haydn's dictionary of dates. Ed. 21, containing the history of the world to the autumn of 1895; by Benjamin Vincent. Putnam $6.

These books, about the same size, are both revisions of earlier editions of Haydn. Many entries are identical Harper's book of facts has more and much fuller entries on American affairs; Haydn treats foreign interests more fully and is brought more nearly to date.

Creasy, *Sir* **E : S.** Fifteen decisive battles of the world. Harper $1.
a **Morris, Charles.** Historical tales. 4 v. Lippincott $5.
a **Fisher, G: P.** Outlines of universal history. Amer. bk co. $2.40.
b **Mackenzie, Robert.** The 19th century. Nelson $1.

TRAVEL ($100)

General ($9)

Brassey, *Mrs* **Anne.** Around the world in the yacht 'Sunbeam.' Holt $2.
a **Dana, R : H :** *jr.* Two years before the mast. Houghton $1.
Darwin, Charles. What Mr Darwin saw in his voyage round the world in the ship 'Beagle.' Harper $3.
Davis, R: H. Rulers of the Mediterranean. Harper $1.25.
b **Rhoades, H ; E.** Around the world with the blue jackets. Lothrop $1.75.

Atlases and gazetteers ($21)

Ginn's classical atlas. Ginn $2.

a **Labberton, R. H.** New historical atlas and general history. Silver $2.

a **Lippincott's gazetteer of the world.** Lippincott $12.

a **Times atlas.** London *Times* office £1 net.

Page, 16½ x 11 in 173 maps on cloth-hinged stubs Fully indexed Remarkably good for price Represents eastern continent well, but inadequate for western, giving only three maps of the United States. The Appleton atlas supplements it fairly well, at small cost.

or

Rand, McNally & Co.'s Universal atlas of the world. $5.

Page 14 x 10¾ in. From new plates, more maps and much better than earlier editions. Greatly superior to the *Times atlas* for American continent, but inferior in general workmanship Its foreign maps are smaller and have fewer details Has 112 pages of historical and geographic information, better supplied elsewhere. Full index of state maps

Appleton's atlas of the United States. Appleton $1.50.
Page 10¼ x 6¾ in County maps of each state.

World-wide atlas. W. & A. K. Johnston 7s. 6d.
Page 12⅛ x 9⅛ in. 112 well engraved maps, fully indexed. Western continent meagerly treated. An alternative, not a supplement, if *Times atlas* is too costly

Antiquities ($8.50)

Guhl, E. K. & Koner, W. D. Life of the Greeks and Romans. Appleton $2 50.

Smith, William. Dictionary of antiquities; ed. by Charles Anthon. Harper $4.25.

a **Gow, James** Companion to school classics. Macmillan $1.75.

Europe ($24.50)

Aldrich, T: B. From Ponkapog to Pesth. Houghton $1.25.

James, Henry. Transatlantic sketches. Houghton $2.

a **Knox, T: W.** Boy travellers in southern Europe. Harper $3.

Warner, C: D. Roundabout journey. Houghton $1.50.

Besant, Walter. London Harper $3.

b **Hawthorne, Nathaniel.** Our old home. Houghton $1. (Little classic ed.)

a **Smith, Goldwin.** Trip to England. Macmillan 75c.

a **Winter, William.** Shakespeare's England. Macmillan 75c.

b **Whitman, Sidney.** Realm of the Habsburgs. Lovell $1.25.

Amicis, Edmondo de. Studies of Paris. Putnam $1 25.
Brown, H. F. Life on the lagoons. Macmillan $1.75.
b Howells, W: D. Italian journeys. Houghton $1.50.
b Hapgood, I. F. Russian rambles. Houghton $1.50.
a Amicis, Edmondo de. Holland and its people. Putnam $2.
b Tyndall, John. Hours of exercise in the Alps. Appleton $2.

Asia ($12)

a Allen, T: G. *jr* & Sachtleben, W: L. Across Asia on a bicycle. Century $1.50.
b Bacon, A. M. Japanese girls and women. Houghton $1.25.
Knox, T: W. Boy travellers in Japan and China. Harper $3.
—— Boy travellers in Ceylon and India. Harper $3.
b Warner, C: D. In the Levant. Houghton $2.
b Kennan, George. Tent life in Siberia. Putnam $1.25.

Africa ($9.50)

b Du Chaillu, P. B. Stories of the gorilla country. Harper $1.
Stanley, H: M. How I found Livingstone. Scribner $3.50.
a Vincent, Frank. Actual Africa. Appleton $5.

America ($12.25)

b Thaxter, *Mrs* Celia. Among the Isles of Shoals. Houghton $1.25
Warner, C: D. On horseback. Houghton $1.25.
b Custer, *Mrs* Elizabeth (Bacon). Boots and saddles. Harper $1.50.
Davis, R: H. The West from a car-window. Harper $1.25.
Ingersoll, Ernest. Knocking around the Rockies. Harper $2.
b Lummis, C: F. Some strange corners of our country. Century $1.50.
a Parkman, Francis. Oregon trail. Little $1 50. (Popular ed)
b Ford, I: N Tropical America. Scribner $2.

Arctic regions ($3.25)

Schley, W. S. & Soley, J R. Rescue of Greeley. Scribner $2.
b Schwatka, Frederick. Children of the cold. Cassell $1.25.

BIOGRAPHY ($72.15)

Collective

a Lippincott's pronouncing biographical dictionary. Lippincott $12.
b Smith, *Sir* William. Classical dictionary; revised and in part rewritten by G. E. Marindin. Appleton $6.

a Bolton, *Mrs* Sarah (Knowles). Lives of poor boys who became famous. Crowell $1.50.

b Yonge, C.. M. Book of golden deeds. Macmillan 50c. (Macmillan's school lib.)

b Bolton, *Mrs* Sarah (Knowles). Lives of girls who became famous. Crowell $1.50.

Brooks, E. S. Historic boys. Putnam $1.50.

Morley, John, *ed.* English men of letters. 13 v. Harper $1 *each*. (People's ed.)

   1 Gibbon, Shelley, Milton
   2 Defoe, Southey, Byron
   3 Pope, Dryden, Sidney
   4 Cowper, Landor, Bentley
   5 Burke, Macaulay, Fielding
   6 Johnson, Bunyan, Bacon
   7 Scott, Spenser, Dickens
   8 Hume, Swift, Sterne
   9 Chaucer, De Quincey, Lamb
10 Burns, Wordsworth, Coleridge
11 Goldsmith, Locke, Gray
12 Thackeray, Sheridan, Addison
13 Keats, Hawthorne, Carlyle

These biographies are also published separately in 39 vols. at 75c. *each*

Individual

Adams. Morse, J: T. *jr.* John Adams. Houghton $1.25. (Amer. statesmen.)

Adams. Morse, J: T. John Quincy Adams. Houghton $1.25. (Amer. statesmen.)

Alfred the Great. Hughes, Thomas. Alfred the Great. Macmillan $1.

a Columbus. Seelye, *Mrs* Elizabeth (Eggleston). Story of Columbus. Appleton $1.75.

b Curtis. Cary, Edward. George William Curtis. Houghton $1.25. (Amer. men of letters.)

b Caesar. Fowler, W. W. Julius Caesar and the foundations of the imperial system. Putnam $1.50. (Heroes of the nations.)

Cooper. Lounsbury, T: R. James Fenimore Cooper. Houghton $1.25. (Amer. men of letters.)

Emerson. Holmes, O. W. Ralph Waldo Emerson. Houghton $1.25. (Amer. men of letters.)

a **Franklin, Benjamin.** Autobiography. Houghton 50c. (Riverside school lib.)

—— —— Putnam 50c. (World's classics); $1 (Elia ser.)

Fulton. **Knox, T: W.** Robert Fulton. Putnam $1.75. (Boys' and girls' lib. of Amer. biog.)

Gustavus 2, Adolphus. **Fletcher, C: R. L.** Gustavus Adolphus and the struggle of protestantism for existence. Putnam $1.50. (Heroes of the nations.)

a Hale. **Lossing, B. J:** Two spies; Nathan Hale and John André. Appleton $2.

b Hamilton. **Lodge, H: C.** Alexander Hamilton. Houghton $1.25. (Amer. statesmen.)

Irving. **Warner, C: D.** Washington Irving. Houghton $1.25. (Amer. men of letters.)

Jackson. **Sumner, W: G.** Andrew Jackson. Houghton $1.25. (Amer. statesmen.)

b Jefferson. **Morse, J: T.** *jr* Thomas Jefferson. Houghton $1.25. (Amer. statesmen.)

a **Larcom, Lucy.** New England girlhood. Houghton 75c. (Riverside lib. for young people.)

a Lincoln. **Morse, J: T.** *jr.* Abraham Lincoln. 2 v. Houghton $2.50. (Amer statesmen.)

—— **Schurz, Carl.** Abraham Lincoln. Houghton $1.

b Livingstone. **Hughes, Thomas.** David Livingstone. Macmillan 75c. (Eng. men of action.)

Madison. **Gay, S. H.** James Madison. Houghton $1.25. (Amer. statesmen.)

Monroe. **Gilman, D. C.** James Monroe. Houghton $1.25. (Amer. statesmen)

a Napoleon 1. **Seeley, J: R.** Short history of Napoleon the first. Roberts $1.50.

Nelson. **Southey, Robert.** Life of Nelson Routledge 40c. (Universal lib. no. 34.)

Pericles. **Abbott, Evelyn.** Pericles and the golden age of Athens. Putnam $1 50. (Heroes of the nations.)

Stuyvesant. **Tuckerman, Bayard.** Peter Stuyvesant. Dodd $1. (Makers of America.)

Tecumseh. **Eggleston, Edward & Seelye,** *Mrs* **Elizabeth (Eggleston).** Tecumseh and the Shawnee prophet. Dodd $1.

a Washington. **Irving, Washington.** Life of Washington. Putnam $1.50. (Stratford ed.)

Abridged The full edition may be bought in Putnam's Hudson ed. 5 v. $7 50.

——— **Scudder, H. E.** George Washington. Houghton 50c. (Riverside school lib)

ANCIENT HISTORY ($7.38)

Horton, R. F. History of the Romans. Longmans $1.25.

a **Merivale, Charles.** General history of Rome. Longmans $2.

a **Harrison, J. A.** Story of Greece. Putnam $1 50. (Story of the nations.)

Mahaffy, J: P. Story of Alexander's empire. Putnam $1.50. (Story of the nations.)

Oman, C: W: C. History of Greece to Macedonian conquest. Rivington 4s. 6d.

HISTORY OF EUROPE AND ASIA ($34.05)

a **Coffin, C: C.** Story of liberty. Harper $3.

b **Duruy, Victor.** History of the middle ages. Holt $1.60 *net.*

Emerton, Ephraim. Introduction to the study of the middle ages. Holt $1.12 *net.*

——— Mediaeval Europe. Ginn $1.50.

Gardiner, S. R. Student's history of England. Longmans $3.

a **Green, J. R.** Short history of the English people. Harper $1.20.

Macaulay, T: B. History of England. 4 v. Houghton $5. (Popular ed.)

Bryce, James. Holy Roman empire. Macmillan $1.

b **Taylor, Bayard.** History of Germany. Appleton $1.50.

b **Creighton,** *Mrs* **L. H.** First history of France. Longmans $1 25.

Duruy, Victor. History of France Crowell $2.

b **Gardiner,** *Mrs* **B. M.** French revolution. Longmans $1. (Epochs of modern hist.)

Irving, Washington. Conquest of Granada. Putnam $1.50. (Hudson ed.)

Morfill, W: R. Story of Russia. Putnam $1.50. (Story of the nations)

Boyesen, H. H. Story of Norway. Putnam $1.50. (Story of the nations)

b **Griffis, W: E.** Brave little Holland and what she has taught us. Houghton 75c. (Riverside lib for young people.)

b **Motley, J: L.** Rise of the Dutch republic. 3 v. Harper $6.
b **Griffis, W: E.** Japan in history, folk-lore and art. Houghton 75c. (Riverside lib. for young people.)

HISTORY OF AMERICA ($68.35)

b **Drake, F. S.** Indian history for young folks. Harper $3.
b **Prescott, W: H.** Conquest of Mexico. 3 v. Lippincott $1.50. (Universal ed.)
 Parkman, Francis. Old régime in Canada. Little $1.50. (Popular ed.)
b **Brooks, E S.** Story of the American sailor. Lothrop $2.25.
 Coffin, C: C. Building the nation. Harper $3.
b **Eggleston, Edward.** First book in American history. Amer. bk co 60c.
a —— Household history of the U.S. and its people. Appleton $2.50.
a **Lodge, H: C & Roosevelt, Theodore.** Hero tales from American history. Century $1.50.
 Lossing, B. J: Cyclopaedia of U. S. history. 2 v. Harper $6.
 Sold only by subscription.
a **Fiske, John.** Discovery of America. 2 v. Houghton $4
a **Parkman, Francis.** Pioneers of France in the new world. Little $1.50. (Popular ed.)
 Coffin, C: C. Old times in the colonies. Harper $3.
 Parkman, Francis. Conspiracy of Pontiac. 2 v.
 —— Half century of conflict. 2 v.   Little $1.50
a —— Jesuits in North America in the 17th century   per v. *each*.
b —— La Salle and the discovery of the great West   (Popular ed.)
a —— Montcalm and Wolfe. 2 v.
a **Coffin, C: C.** Boys of '76. Harper $3.
a **Fiske, John.** American revolution. 2 v. Houghton $4.
b —— Critical period of American history. Houghton $2
b **Johnson, Rossiter.** History of the war of 1812-15. Dodd $1.
 Champlin, J: D. *jr.* Young folks' history of the war of the Union. Holt $2.50.
a **Johnson, Rossiter.** Short history of the war of secession. Bryan, Taylor & Co. $2.50.
b **Kieffer, H: M.** Recollections of a drummer boy. Houghton $1.50.
 Fiske, John. Beginnings of New England Houghton $2.
 Hawthorne, Nathaniel. True stories from history and biography. Houghton $1. (Little classic ed.)

a **Roberts, E. H.** New York. 2 v. Houghton $2 50. (Amer. commonwealths.)
Cooke, J: E. Stories of the old dominion. Harper $1.50.
b **Drake, S: A.** Making of the great West. Scribner $1 50.
Prescott, W: H. Conquest of Peru. 2 v. Lippincott $1. (Universal ed)

REGENTS READING COURSES

A SELECTION OF DESIRABLE EDITIONS OF BOOKS REQUIRED BY REGENTS READING COURSES IN ENGLISH AND AMERICAN LITERATURE AND IN UNITED STATES HISTORY

Economy has been an important consideration in choosing editions for library use, but much pains has been taken to avoid type and paper trying to the eyes. The editions selected seem to meet best all these requirements. Wherever possible cheap editions in paper such as students may buy have been mentioned. Many of these are excellent — notably Houghton's Riverside literature series, Maynard, Merrill & Co.'s English classics and Cassell's national library.

Abbott, J: S. C. Ferdinand de Soto. Dodd $1.25. (Amer. pioneers and patriots.)
Addison, Joseph. Sir Roger de Coverley papers. Leach 35c. (Students ser. of Eng. classics)
—— —— Houghton, 2 pts, *paper* 15c. *each;* 1 v. *cloth* 40c. (Riverside literature ser. no. 60–61)
—— —— American bk co. *boards,* 20c (Eclectic English classics.)
—— Sir Roger de Coverley *and* Spectator's club. Cassell, *paper* 10c. (Cassell's nat. lib. no. 28)
Bacon, *Sir* **Francis.** Essays *and* Colours of good and evil. Macmillan $1. (Golden treasury ser.)
—— Essays, civil and moral; selected. Maynard, *paper* 12c. (English classics, no. 3.)
Contains the essays called for by the regents reading lists.
Browning, Robert. Complete poetic and dramatic works. Houghton $3. (Cambridge ed.)
—— Blot in the scutcheon and other dramas. (Colombe's birthday *and* A soul's tragedy.) Harper, *paper* 40c.; *cloth* 56c. (Rolfe's Eng. classics.)
Bryant, W: C. Poetical works. Appleton $1.50. (Household ed.)

Bryant, W: C. Sella, Thanatopsis and other poems. Houghton, *paper* 15c. (Riverside literature ser. no. 54.)

—— Thanatopsis and other poems. Maynard, *paper* 12c. (English classics, no. 47.)

Burke, Edmund. Select works, v. 1. Macmillan $1.10 *net*. (Clarendon press ser.)

—— Present discontents. Maynard, *paper* 12c. (English classics, no. 118.)

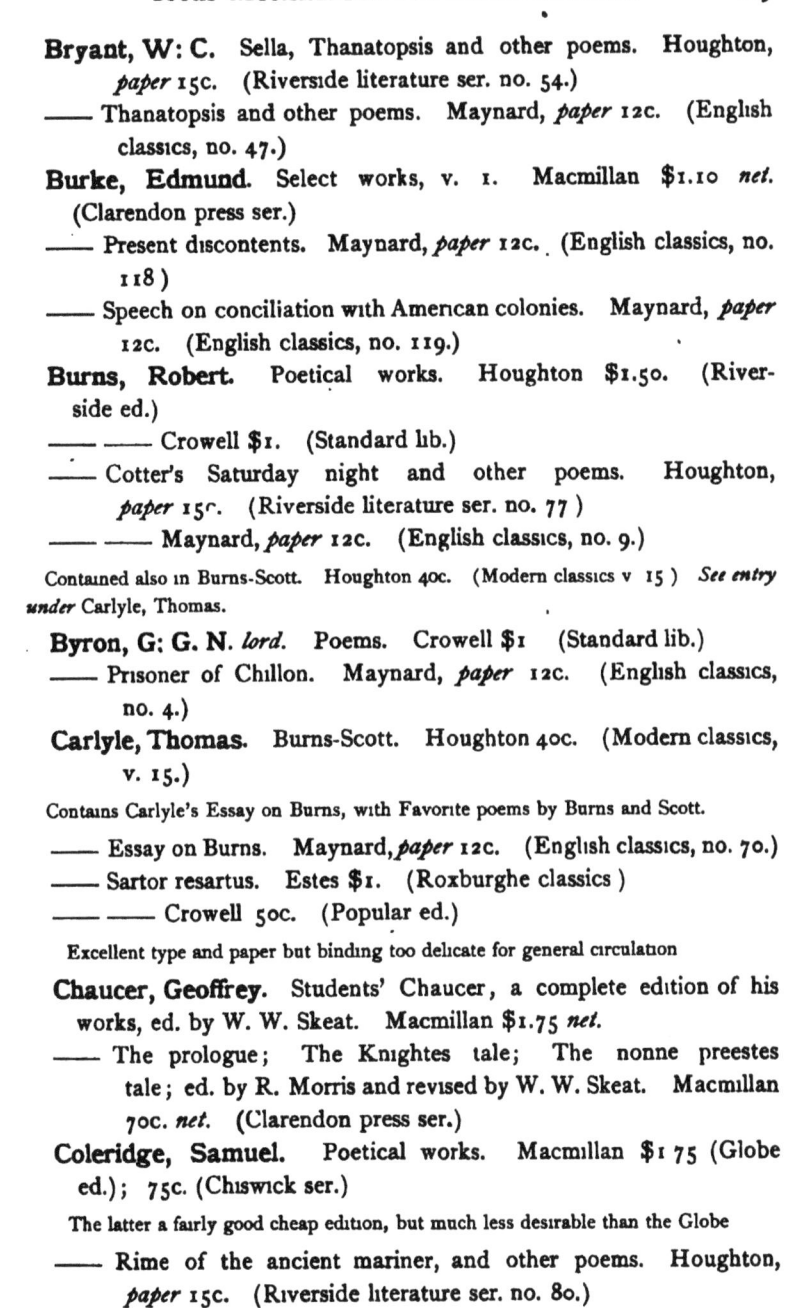

—— Speech on conciliation with American colonies. Maynard, *paper* 12c. (English classics, no. 119.)

Burns, Robert. Poetical works. Houghton $1.50. (Riverside ed.)

—— —— Crowell $1. (Standard lib.)

—— Cotter's Saturday night and other poems. Houghton, *paper* 15c. (Riverside literature ser. no. 77.)

—— —— Maynard, *paper* 12c. (English classics, no. 9.)

Contained also in Burns-Scott. Houghton 40c. (Modern classics v 15) *See entry under* Carlyle, Thomas.

Byron, G: G. N. *lord.* Poems. Crowell $1 (Standard lib.)

—— Prisoner of Chillon. Maynard, *paper* 12c. (English classics, no. 4.)

Carlyle, Thomas. Burns-Scott. Houghton 40c. (Modern classics, v. 15.)

Contains Carlyle's Essay on Burns, with Favorite poems by Burns and Scott.

—— Essay on Burns. Maynard, *paper* 12c. (English classics, no. 70.)

—— Sartor resartus. Estes $1. (Roxburghe classics)

—— —— Crowell 50c. (Popular ed.)

Excellent type and paper but binding too delicate for general circulation

Chaucer, Geoffrey. Students' Chaucer, a complete edition of his works, ed. by W. W. Skeat. Macmillan $1.75 *net*.

—— The prologue; The Knightes tale; The nonne preestes tale; ed. by R. Morris and revised by W. W. Skeat. Macmillan 70c. *net*. (Clarendon press ser.)

Coleridge, Samuel. Poetical works. Macmillan $1 75 (Globe ed.); 75c. (Chiswick ser.)

The latter a fairly good cheap edition, but much less desirable than the Globe

—— Rime of the ancient mariner, and other poems. Houghton, *paper* 15c. (Riverside literature ser. no. 80.)

Cooper, J. F. Last of the Mohicans. Putnam $1.25. (Mohawk ed.)
—— —— Burt 75c. (Burt's home lib.)
—— —— Houghton 70c. (Riverside school lib.), 60c. (Riverside literature ser. no. 95–98.)
Cowper, William. Poetical works. Macmillan $1.75. (Globe ed.)
—— The task. Harper 30c. (Harper's school classics); *paper* 20c. (Harper's half-hour ser. no. 112)
—— —— Cassell, *paper* 10c. (Cassell's nat. lib. no. 201.)
Curtis, G : W: Prue and I. Harper $1.50.
Defoe, Daniel. Journal of the plague year. Longmans 75c. (Longmans' English classics)
—— —— Maynard 24c. (English classics, double no. 154–55)
De Quincey, Thomas. Confessions of an English opium eater. Putnam 50c. (World's classics.)
—— Narrative and miscellaneous papers. Houghton $1. (Popular ed.)
Contains *Flight of a Tartar tribe*
—— Flight of a Tartar tribe. Leach 35c. (Students' ser. of Eng. classics.) *In preparation.*
Dickens, Charles. Dombey and son. Macmillan $1. (New popular ed.)
—— Tale of two cities. Macmillan $1. (New popular ed.)
—— —— Crowell $1. (Standard lib.)
Drake, S : A. Making of New England. Scribner $1.50.
Making of the great West. Scribner $1.50.
Dryden, John. Poetical works. Macmillan $1.75. (Globe ed.)
—— Poems. Cassell, *paper* 10c. (Cassell's nat. lib. no. 98)
—— Alexander's feast *and* MacFlecknoe. Maynard, *paper* 12c. (English classics, no. 39.)
Earle, *Mrs* **A. M.** Customs and fashions in old New England. Scribner $1.25.
Eliot, George, *pseud.* Romola. Crowell $1. (Standard lib.)
—— Silas Marner. Leach 35c. (Students' ser. of Eng. classics.)
—— —— Houghton, *paper* 30c.; *linen* 40c. (Riverside literature ser. no. 83.)
—— —— American bk co. *boards* 30c. (Eclectic Eng. classics.)
Emerson, R. W. Poems. Houghton $1.75 (Riverside ed.); $1.50 (Household ed.); $1.25 (Little classics.)

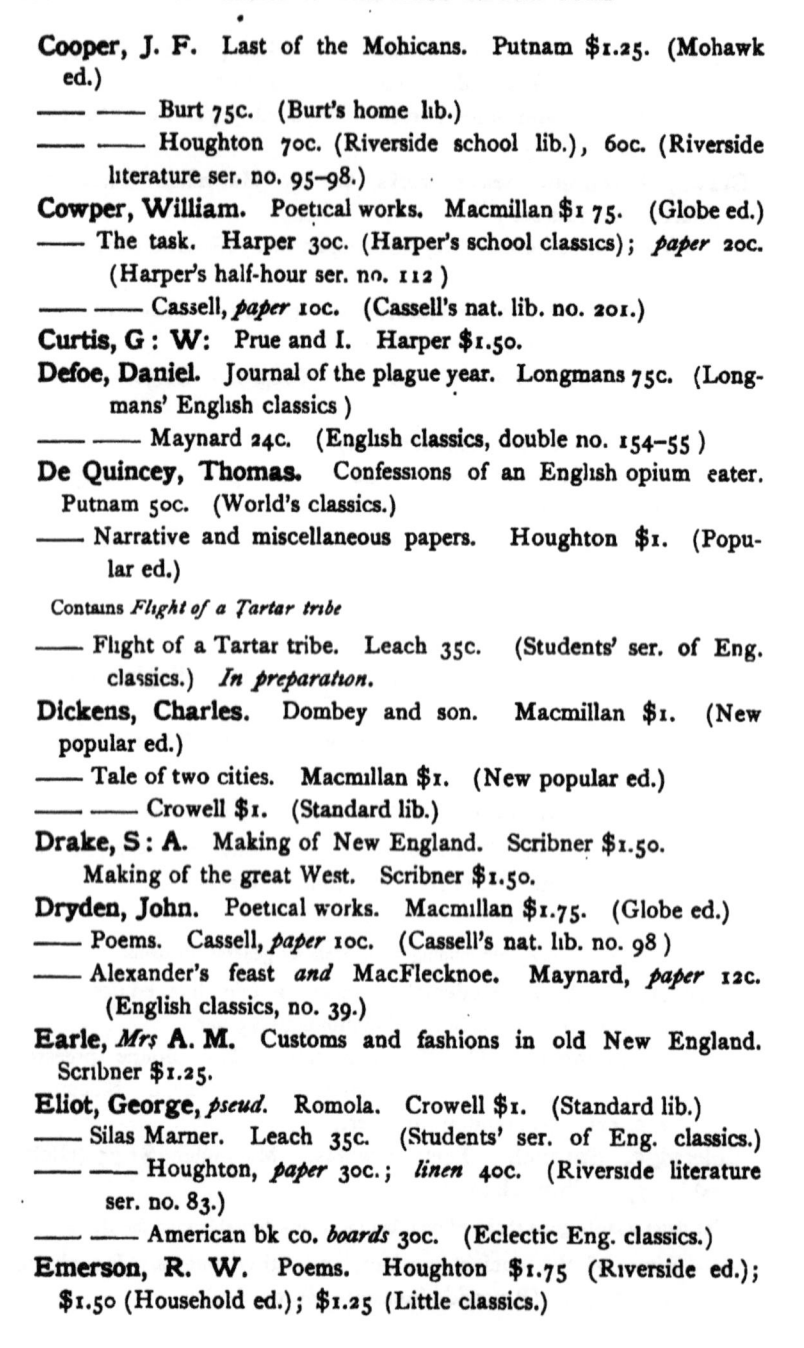

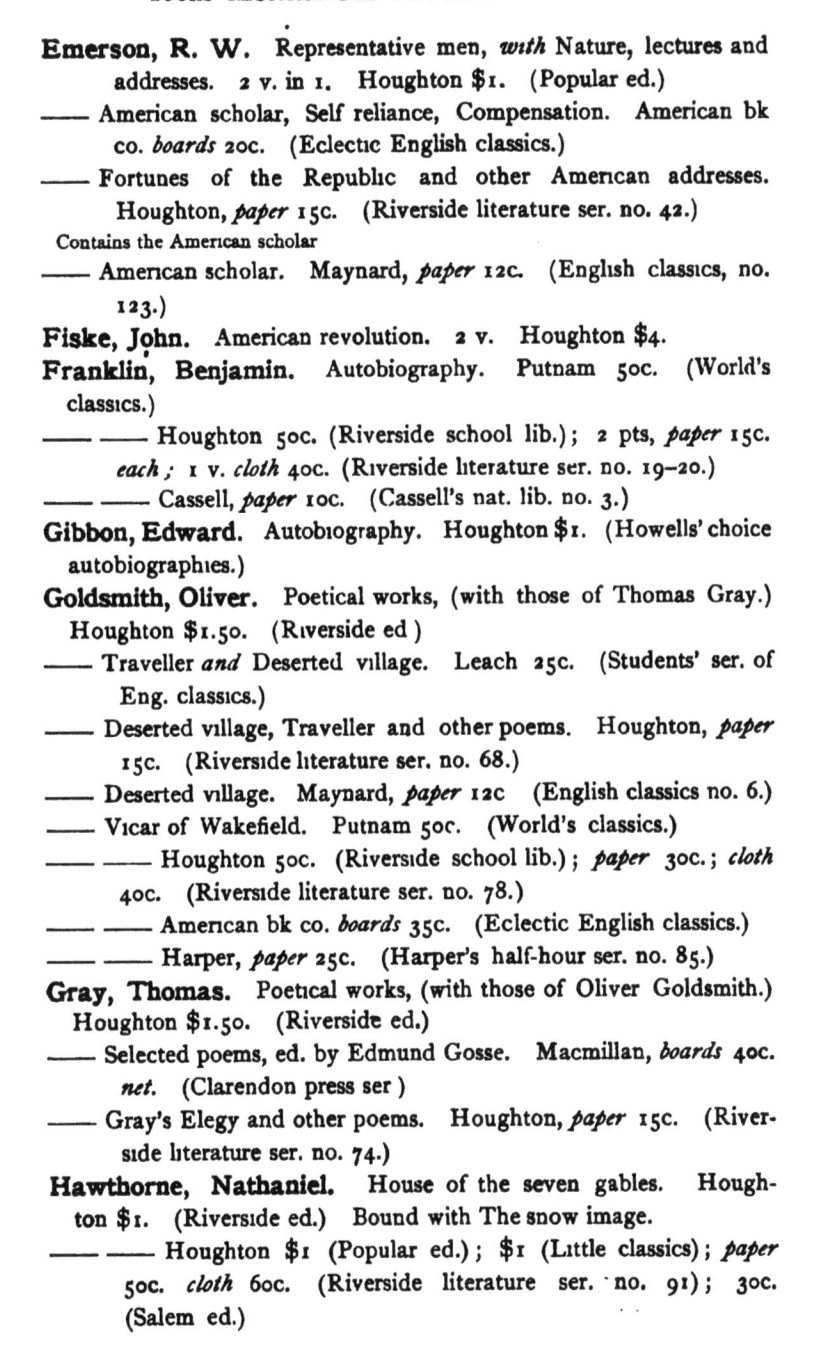

Emerson, R. W. Representative men, *with* Nature, lectures and addresses. 2 v. in 1. Houghton $1. (Popular ed.)

——— American scholar, Self reliance, Compensation. American bk co. *boards* 20c. (Eclectic English classics.)

——— Fortunes of the Republic and other American addresses. Houghton, *paper* 15c. (Riverside literature ser. no. 42.)
_{Contains the American scholar}

——— American scholar. Maynard, *paper* 12c. (English classics, no. 123.)

Fiske, John. American revolution. 2 v. Houghton $4.

Franklin, Benjamin. Autobiography. Putnam 50c. (World's classics.)

——— ——— Houghton 50c. (Riverside school lib.); 2 pts, *paper* 15c. *each;* 1 v. *cloth* 40c. (Riverside literature ser. no. 19–20.)

——— ——— Cassell, *paper* 10c. (Cassell's nat. lib. no. 3.)

Gibbon, Edward. Autobiography. Houghton $1. (Howells' choice autobiographies.)

Goldsmith, Oliver. Poetical works, (with those of Thomas Gray.) Houghton $1.50. (Riverside ed.)

——— Traveller *and* Deserted village. Leach 25c. (Students' ser. of Eng. classics.)

——— Deserted village, Traveller and other poems. Houghton, *paper* 15c. (Riverside literature ser. no. 68.)

——— Deserted village. Maynard, *paper* 12c (English classics no. 6.)

——— Vicar of Wakefield. Putnam 50c. (World's classics.)

——— ——— Houghton 50c. (Riverside school lib.); *paper* 30c.; *cloth* 40c. (Riverside literature ser. no. 78.)

——— ——— American bk co. *boards* 35c. (Eclectic English classics.)

——— ——— Harper, *paper* 25c. (Harper's half-hour ser. no. 85.)

Gray, Thomas. Poetical works, (with those of Oliver Goldsmith.) Houghton $1.50. (Riverside ed.)

——— Selected poems, ed. by Edmund Gosse. Macmillan, *boards* 40c. *net.* (Clarendon press ser.)

——— Gray's Elegy and other poems. Houghton, *paper* 15c. (Riverside literature ser. no. 74.)

Hawthorne, Nathaniel. House of the seven gables. Houghton $1. (Riverside ed.) Bound with The snow image.

——— ——— Houghton $1 (Popular ed.); $1 (Little classics); *paper* 50c. *cloth* 60c. (Riverside literature ser. no. 91); 30c. (Salem ed.)

Hawthorne, Nathaniel. Marble faun. Houghton $2 (Riverside ed.); 2 v. $2 (Little classics); 40c. (School ed.)

—— Twice-told tales. Houghton $2 (Riverside ed.); 2 v. $2 (Little classics); 40c. (School ed.); 30c. (Salem ed.)

Holmes, O. W. Autocrat of the breakfast table. Houghton $1.50 (Riverside ed.); $1.25 (Handy vol. ed.); 60c. (Riverside school lib), *paper* 45c.; *cloth* 50c. (Riverside literature ser. no. 81)

Homer. Iliad; tr. by Alexander Pope. Routledge $1.50. (Popular lib.)

Irving, Washington. Columbus. 3 v. Putnam $4.50. (Hudson ed.)

v. 3 is the Companions of Columbus.

—— —— Abridged by the author. 1 v. Putnam $1.75.

A new ed. illustrated and excellent in every respect.

—— —— Crowell $1. (Standard lib.)

Unabridged, but not including the Companions of Columbus.

—— Sketch book; ed. by W. L. Phelps. Putnam $1. (Students' ed.)

—— Essays from the Sketch book. Houghton 2 pts *paper* 15c. *each*; 1 v. *cloth* 40c. (Riverside literature ser. no. 51–52.)

Contains the Legend of Sleepy Hollow, Rip Van Winkle and other essays.

—— Legend of Sleepy Hollow. Maynard, *paper* 12c. (English classics, no 41)

—— Sketch book; selections. Maynard, *paper* 12c. (English classics, no. 31.)

Contains Rip Van Winkle.

—— Tales of a traveller; ed. by W. L. Phelps. Putnam $1. (Students' ed.)

—— —— American bk co. *boards* 50c. (Eclectic English classics.)

Johnson, Rossiter. History of the war of 1812–15. Dodd $1

—— Old French war. Dodd $1.

—— Short history of the war of secession. Bryan, Taylor & Co. $2.50.

Johnson, Samuel. Rasselas. Putnam 50c. (World's classics)

—— —— Leach 35c. (Student's ser. of Eng. classics.)

—— —— Cassell, *paper* 10c. (Cassell's nat lib. no. 191.)

Johnston, Alexander. History of American politics. Holt 80c. *net*.

Jonson, Ben. Every man in his humor. Longmans 75c.

Keats, John. Poetical works. Macmillan $1. (Golden treasury ser.)

Keats, John. Endymion and other poems. Cassell, *paper* 10c. (Cassell's nat. lib. no. 91.)
Contains the Ode on a Grecian urn.

Ladd, H. O. History of the war with Mexico. Dodd $1.

Locke, John. Conduct of the understanding. Macmillan 50c. *net.* (Clarendon press ser.)

Lodge, H: C. Alexander Hamilton. Houghton $1.25. (Amer. statesmen.)

Longfellow, H: W. Complete poetical works. Houghton $2. (Cambridge ed.)
The only one volume edition complete with latest revisions. Contains also a biographic sketch.

—— Evangeline. Leach 35c. (Students' ser. of Eng. classics.)

—— —— Houghton, *paper* 15c.; *cloth* 25c. (Riverside literature ser. no. 1.)

Lowell, J. R. Poems. Houghton $1.50. (Household ed.)

—— Vision of Sir Launfal and other pieces. Houghton, *paper* 15c. (Riverside literature ser. no. 30.)

—— —— Maynard, *paper* 12c. (English classics, no. 129.)

Macaulay, T : B. Critical, historical and miscellaneous essays. 3 v. Houghton $3.75. (Popular ed.)

—— Essay on Bacon. Harper, *paper* 25c (Harper's half-hour ser. no. 108); *cloth* 30c. (Harper's school classics.)

—— Essays on Milton and Byron. Harper 30c. (Harper's school classics.)

—— Essay on Milton. Ginn, *paper* 30c. (Annotated school classics.)

—— —— American bk co. *boards* 20c.

—— —— Maynard, *paper* 24c. (English classics, no. 102-3.)

—— Life of Samuel Johnson. Leach 25c. (Students' ser. of Eng. classics.)
Contained also, with Macaulay's Essay on Boswell's Johnson, in Johnson's *Chief lives of the poets.* Holt $1.25 *net.*

Mackenzie, Robert. America; a history. Nelson $1.

Marlowe, Christopher. Best plays. Scribner $1.25. (Mermaid ser.)

—— Dr Faustus. Routledge 40c. (Morley's universal lib.)

—— —— with notes by Wilhelm Wagner. Longmans 60c. (London ser. of Eng. classics.)

Milton, John. Areopagitica. Macmillan 75c. *net.* (Clarendon press ser.)

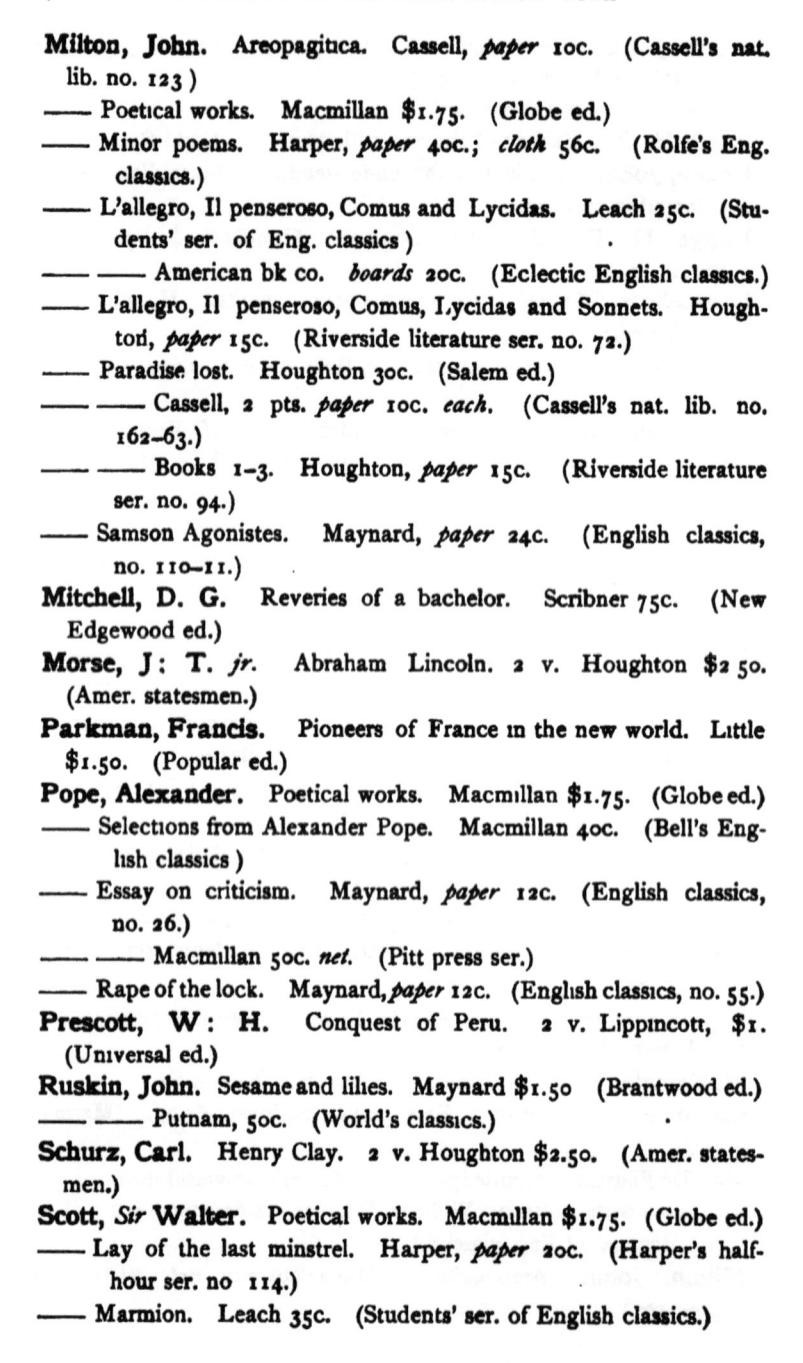

Milton, John. Areopagitica. Cassell, *paper* 10c. (Cassell's nat. lib. no. 123)
—— Poetical works. Macmillan $1.75. (Globe ed.)
—— Minor poems. Harper, *paper* 40c.; *cloth* 56c. (Rolfe's Eng. classics.)
—— L'allegro, Il penseroso, Comus and Lycidas. Leach 25c. (Students' ser. of Eng. classics)
—— —— American bk co. *boards* 20c. (Eclectic English classics.)
—— L'allegro, Il penseroso, Comus, Lycidas and Sonnets. Houghton, *paper* 15c. (Riverside literature ser. no. 72.)
—— Paradise lost. Houghton 30c. (Salem ed.)
—— —— Cassell, 2 pts. *paper* 10c. *each*. (Cassell's nat. lib. no. 162–63.)
—— —— Books 1–3. Houghton, *paper* 15c. (Riverside literature ser. no. 94.)
—— Samson Agonistes. Maynard, *paper* 24c. (English classics, no. 110–11.)
Mitchell, D. G. Reveries of a bachelor. Scribner 75c. (New Edgewood ed.)
Morse, J: T. *jr.* Abraham Lincoln. 2 v. Houghton $2.50. (Amer. statesmen.)
Parkman, Francis. Pioneers of France in the new world. Little $1.50. (Popular ed.)
Pope, Alexander. Poetical works. Macmillan $1.75. (Globe ed.)
—— Selections from Alexander Pope. Macmillan 40c. (Bell's English classics)
—— Essay on criticism. Maynard, *paper* 12c. (English classics, no. 26.)
—— —— Macmillan 50c. *net.* (Pitt press ser.)
—— Rape of the lock. Maynard, *paper* 12c. (English classics, no. 55.)
Prescott, W: H. Conquest of Peru. 2 v. Lippincott, $1. (Universal ed.)
Ruskin, John. Sesame and lilies. Maynard $1.50 (Brantwood ed.)
—— —— Putnam, 50c. (World's classics.)
Schurz, Carl. Henry Clay. 2 v. Houghton $2.50. (Amer. statesmen.)
Scott, *Sir* **Walter.** Poetical works. Macmillan $1.75. (Globe ed.)
—— Lay of the last minstrel. Harper, *paper* 20c. (Harper's half-hour ser. no 114.)
—— Marmion. Leach 35c. (Students' ser. of English classics.)

Scott, *Sir* **Walter.** Marmion. Cassell, *paper* 10c. (Cassell's nat. lib. no. 136.)

———— Marmion *and* Lord of the Isles. Macmillan 30c. (Globe readings.)

———— Kenilworth. Macmillan $1.25. (Dryburgh ed.)

———— Rob Roy. Macmillan $1.25. (Dryburgh ed.)

———— Woodstock. Macmillan $1.25 (Dryburgh ed.); 40c. (Popular ed.)

———— ———— American bk co. *boards* 60c. (Eclectic English classics.)

Shakspere, William. New variorum edition of Shakespeare, ed. by H. H. Furness. Lippincott, v. 1–10 $4 *each*.

Presents results of an exhaustive collation of texts and gives a full selection of commentary. Invaluable to students and for reference, but not desirable for reading

Now ready:

As you like it	Midsummer night's dream
Hamlet (2 v.)	Othello
King Lear	Romeo and Juliet
Macbeth	The tempest
Merchant of Venice	

———— Works, ed. by Richard Grant White. 6 v. Houghton $10. (Riverside ed.)

Excellent in text, notes, type and paper Very desirable edition for school or home reading.

———— Works; ed. by W. G. Clark and W. A. Wright. Macmillan $1.75. (Globe ed.)

Probably best one volume edition. Type too fine but clear and not worn. Paper very thin but good. Text excellent, lines numbered.

———— Works; v. 1, Comedies; v. 2, Histories; v. 3, Tragedies. Macmillan, $1.75 *each*. 3 v. $5. (Victoria ed.)

The most satisfactory cheap edition. Follows text of Globe ed Good sized, clear type, excellent paper, lines not numbered.

Separate plays expurgated for school use:

Edited by W. J. Rolfe. Harper, *paper* 40c.; *cloth* 56c.

Edited by H: N. Hudson. Ginn, *paper* 30c.; *cloth* 45c. (New school Shakespeare.)

Edited by Brainerd Kellogg. Maynard 30c. (English classics.)

The following plays are called for in the regents reading courses:

As you like it, King Lear, Macbeth, Merchant of Venice, Midsummer night's dream, Richard 3, The tempest. These may be obtained, edited by W. A. Wright, in the Clarendon press ser. Macmillan, at from 30 to 40 cents each. As you like it, Macbeth, Merchant of Venice and Midsummer night's dream are also published by the American book co *boards* 20c. *each*, and except Macbeth, still in preparation, by Longmans, 60c. *each* (English classics ser). As you like it, ed. by R. G. White, is published by Houghton in the Riverside literature ser. no. 93, *paper* 15c.

Shelley, P. B. Poetical works. Macmillan $1.75. (Globe ed.)
—— Skylark, Adonais and other poems. Maynard, *paper* 10c. (English classics, no. 85.)
Contains The cloud
—— Prometheus unbound, with Adonais, The cloud, Hymn to intellectual beauty and an exhortation. Cassell, *paper* 10c. (Cassell's nat. lib. no. 108.)

Sheridan, R: B. Dramatic works. Macmillan $1 40. (Bohn's standard lib.)
—— The school for scandal *and* The rivals. Cassell, *paper* 10c. (Cassel's nat. lib. no. 6)

Smith, Goldwin. The moral crusader, William Lloyd Garrison. Funk $1.

Southey, Robert. Life of Nelson. Ginn, *boards* 50c. (Classics for children.)
—— —— Routledge 40c. (Universal lib. no. 34.)
—— —— Cassell, *paper* 10c. (Cassell's nat. lib. no. 213.)

Spenser, Edmund. Complete works. Macmillan $1.75. (Globe ed.)
—— Faery queene, book 1; ed. by G. W. Kitchin. Macmillan 60c. *net*. (Clarendon press ser.)
—— Fairie queene, book 1; with introd. and notes by H. M. Percival. Macmillan 50c. (English classics.)
—— —— Cantos 1–2. Maynard, *paper* 12c. (English classics, no. 27.)

Swift, Jonathan. Gulliver's travels. Routledge $1. (Carisbrook lib.)
—— —— Houghton, 2 pts. *paper* 15c. *each;* 1 v. *cloth* 40c. (Riverside literature ser. no. 89–90.)
—— —— ed. for schools. Ginn, *boards* 35c. (Classics for children.)

Tennyson, Alfred. Works. Macmillan $1.75. (Globe ed.)
Complete, with authorized revisions. Gives the Idyls of the king in order of Tennyson's final arrangement
—— Enoch Arden, and other poems. Houghton, *paper* 15c. (Riverside literature ser. no. 73)
—— —— Maynard, *paper* 12c. (English classics, no. 30.)
—— In memoriam; ed. by W. J. Rolfe. Houghton 75c.
—— The princess. Houghton 75c. (Students' ed)
—— —— Leach 35c. (Students' ser. of Eng. classics.)
—— The princess, Maud, Locksley Hall *and* The talking oak. Houghton 40c. (Modern classics, school ed.)

Thackeray, W: M. Henry Esmond. Houghton $1.50. (Illus. lib. ed.)
—— —— Crowell $1. (Standard ed.)
—— The Newcomes. 2 v. Houghton $3. (Illus lib. ed.)
—— —— Crowell $1. (Standard lib.)
Thomson, James. Poems. Houghton $1.50. (Riverside ed.)
—— The seasons *and* The castle of indolence; ed. by J. L. Robertson. Macmillan $1.10 *net*.
Warner, C: D. Backlog studies. Houghton $1. (Riverside Aldine ser. no. 10.)
Webster, Daniel. Select speeches. Heath $1.50. (Heath's Eng. classics.)
—— First Bunker Hill oration, *and* Adams and Jefferson. Houghton, *paper* 15c. (Riverside literature ser. no. 56.)
—— Bunker Hill orations. Maynard, *paper* 12c. (English classics, no. 44.)
Whittier, J: G. Complete poetical works. Houghton $2. (Cambridge ed.)

The only one volume edition complete and latest revisions. Contains also a biographic sketch

—— Snowbound, Among the hills, Songs of labor and other poems. Houghton, *paper* 15c.; *cloth* 25c.; (Riverside literature ser. no. 4.)
Wordsworth, William. Complete poetical works. Crowell $1. (Standard lib.)
—— On the intimations of immortality, and other poems. Houghton, *paper* 15c. (Riverside literature ser. no. 76.)

University of the State of New York

A PROPER STANDARD FOR PUBLIC LIBRARIES

The University law of 1892 authorizes the payment of local subsidies to libraries registered by the regents as maintaining a proper library standard, and directs the apportionment of public library money under regents rules.

While the approval of any library must depend on the report of the official inspector, the following statement is issued to direct attention to the points likely to come under review.

Free public libraries to be registered by the University as maintaining a proper standard must meet the following requirements:

1 Each library must be in charge of trustees duly incorporated under state law, or must belong to an institution in the University.

2 The selection of books as a whole must be approved for literary merit and educational value, and as representing in due proportion the different classes of literature and as adapted to the wants of the community.

3 Provision for support must be sufficient for frequent addition of new books as well as to meet other current expenses.

4 The library must be open at a fixed time and in charge of a competent attendant at least one hour on three days of each week; in villages of 2,000 or more inhabitants it must be open at least two hours daily for not less than six days of each week; and in villages or cities of 10,000 or more inhabitants it must be open at least six hours daily.

To be counted as public, a college or academy library must be open at least six hours daily while classes are in session, and in vacation must be open at least one hour on each of three days of each week.

These rules do not require any library to be kept open on legal holidays or Sundays.

In special circumstances connected with starting or reorganizing a library, on approval of the regents, the requirements as to hours of opening may be modified till the library is more firmly established.

5 An accession book must be kept in which shall be recorded the date of accession, the author, title and cost of each book added. There must be besides some suitable catalogue for readers, which may be either an author index, a shelf list or a subject catalogue.

6 Books must be arranged on the shelves by some well considered system that will group subjects by themselves and place books in order in each subject. The character of the classification will depend on the size of the library and local conditions.

7 The loan system in use must provide (a) that every book lent be charged to its borrower, with the date of borrowing; (b) that the circulation of each day be recorded, with a separate statement of the number of volumes of fiction lent.

The above simple rules of business management are deemed essential to the security and usefulness of the books in any public library, and, if carefully observed, will be a guarantee to the public that the libraries are rendering valuable service in return for the aid given.

TRAVELING LIBRARIES

Extension of educational facilities. The regents may cooperate with other agencies in bringing within the reach of the people at large increased educational opportunities and facilities, by stimulating interest, recommending methods, designating suitable teachers and lecturers, lending necessary books and apparatus, conducting examinations and granting credentials and otherwise aiding such work. No money appropriated by the state for this work shall be expended in paying for services or expenses of teachers or lecturers.

Loans of books from the state. Under such rules as the regents may prescribe, they may lend from the state library, duplicate department, or from books specially given or bought for this purpose, selections of books for a limited time to any public library in this state under visitation of the regents, or to any community not yet having established such library, but which has conformed to the conditions required for such loans. (*Laws of* 1892, ch. 378, §1447.)

Under this authority many carefully prepared lists of 50 or 100 fresh and popular books suited to different communities and different classes have been issued. In some a large proportion of standard works is included; others contain only the books of a given year. About 30 per cent are works of fiction, with 10 to 20 per cent each of biography, travel and history. Popular science, sociology and general literature are well represented.

The smaller libraries may be combined with selections of 25 or 50 volumes of the best books on special subjects, adapted to the needs of extension centers, study clubs, lecture courses and reading circles.

Rules for the loan of libraries

1 On satisfactory guarantee that all regents rules will be complied with, a traveling library may be lent to any public library under visitation of the regents on application of its trustees.

2 Under like conditions a traveling library may be lent to a community on application of 25 resident taxpayers or of the officers of an extension center, club, course or circle, if registered by the regents; provided that the applicants also agree that as soon as public interest will warrant such action, they will take steps to establish a free public library as provided in laws of 1892, ch. 378, § 36. The applicants shall name a responsible owner of real estate, to act as trustee of said library and he must become personally responsible for any loss or injury beyond reasonable wear. This trustee shall designate a suitable person to be librarian.

3 A fee of $5 for 100 or $3 for 50 volumes shall be paid in advance for suitable cases, printed catalogues, necessary blanks and records, and transportation both ways. If the right to borrow books is to be limited to members of a center or club, a double fee must be paid; i. e. only 50 volumes for $5 or 25 for $3 will be sent.

4 Such precaution shall be taken in packing as to guard effectively against injury in transportation.

5 Notes, corrections of the press, or marks of any kind on books belonging to the library are unconditionally forbidden. Borrowing trustees will be held responsible for all losses or injuries beyond reasonable wear, however caused.

6 The traveling library shall not be kept longer than six months after its reception, except by special permission. It may be exchanged for another on the same terms and these exchanges may continue as long as the regents rules are observed.

7 The librarian shall care for the books while under his control and circulate them in accordance with the regents rules, and shall make such reports respecting their use as the regents may require.

8 For wilful violation of any library rule the director may suspend the privilege of state loans till the case is considered by the regents committee.

Young people's libraries

Selections of the best juvenile literature have been grouped in libraries of 25 volumes each, with annotated finding lists. The fee for one of these libraries alone is $2, but when sent with another library of 50 or 100 volumes the fee for the young people's library is $1.

Annotated lists of libraries will be sent on request, and inquiries for information or advice will be promptly answered if directed to **Public libraries division, University of the State of New York, Albany, N. Y.**

University of the State of New York

Object. The object of the University as defined by law is to encourage and promote education in advance of the common elementary branches. Its field includes not only the work of academies, colleges, universities, professional and technical schools, but also educational work connected with libraries, museums, university extension courses and similar agencies.

The University is a supervisory and administrative, not a teaching institution. It is a state department and at the same time a federation of 653 institutions of higher and secondary education.

Government. The University is governed and all its corporate powers exercised by 19 elective regents and by the governor, lieutenant-governor, secretary of state and superintendent of public instruction who are *ex officio* regents Regents are elected in the same manner as United States senators; they are unsalaried and are the only public officers in New York chosen for life.

The elective officers are a chancellor and a vice-chancellor, who serve without salary, and a secretary. The secretary is the executive and financial officer, is under official bonds for $10,000, is responsible for the safe keeping and proper use of the University seal and of the books, records and other property in charge of the regents, and for the proper administration and discipline of its various offices and departments.

Powers and duties. Besides many other important powers and duties, the regents have power to incorporate, and to alter or revoke the charters of universities, colleges, academies, libraries, museums, or other educational institutions; to distribute to them funds granted by the state for their use; to inspect their workings and require annual reports under oath of their presiding officers; to establish examinations as to attainments in learning and confer on successful candidates suitable certificates, diplomas and degrees, and to confer honorary degrees.

They apportion annually an academic fund of $106,000, part for buying books and apparatus for academies and high schools raising an equal amount for the same purpose, and the remainder on the basis of attendance and the results of instruction as shown by satisfactory completion of prescribed courses for which the regents examinations afford the official test. Each school of academic grade also receives $100 yearly. The regents also expend annually $25,000 for the benefit of free public libraries.

Regents meetings. Regular meetings are held on the third Thursdays of October, December and March, and in June during convocation week. The executive committee, consisting of the chancellor, vice-chancellor and the chairmen of the six standing committees, meets the third Thursday of each month from October to June.

Convocation. The University convocation of the regents and the officers of institutions in the University, for consideration of subjects of mutual interest, has been held annually since 1863 in the senate chamber in Albany. It meets the last Wednesday, Thursday and Friday of June.

Though primarily a New York meeting, nearly all questions discussed are of equal interest outside the state. Its reputation as the most important higher educational meeting of the country has in the past few years drawn to it many eminent educators not residents of New York, who are most cordially welcomed and share fully in all discussions. It elects each year a council of five to represent it in intervals between meetings. Its proceedings, issued annually, are of great value in all educational libraries.

Departments

1 **Administrative** (Regents office) — including incorporation, supervision, inspection, reports, legislation, finances and all other work not assigned to another department.

Duplicate division. This is a state clearing house, to which any institution in the University may send books or apparatus which it no longer requires, and select from it in return an equal value suited to its locality and needs.

2 **Examination**—including preacademic, law student, medical, dental and veterinary student, academic, higher, law, medical, dental, veterinary, library, extension and any other examinations conducted by the regents, and also credentials or degrees conferred on examination.

The examinations are conducted as the best lever for securing better work from teachers and more systematic and continuous study from students, and as the best means of detecting and eliminating inefficient teachers or methods. They cover 130 subjects and require 1,500,000 question papers annually, and are held the week ending the last Friday in January and March and the third Friday in June, in the 552 academies and high schools in the University and also at various central points where there are 10 or more candidates.

3 **Extension**—including summer, vacation, evening and correspondence schools and other forms of extension teaching, lecture courses, study clubs, reading circles and other agencies for the promotion and wider extension of opportunities and facilities for education, specially for those unable to attend the usual teaching institutions.

Public libraries division. To promote the general library interests of the state, which through it apportions and expends $25,000 a year for the benefit of free public libraries. Under its charge are the traveling libraries for lending to local libraries or to communities not yet having permanent libraries.

The most important factor of the extension movement is provision of the best reading for all citizens by means of traveling, home and capitol libraries and annotated lists through the public libraries division.

4 **State library**—including general, law, medical, and education libraries, library school, bibliographic publications, lending books to students and similar library interests.

Library school. The law authorizes the state library to give instruction and assistance in organizing and administering libraries. Students receive from the state library staff, in return for services rendered to the library during their two years' course, careful training in library economy, bibliography, cataloguing, classification and other duties of professional librarianship.

5 **State museum**—including all scientific specimens and collections, works of art, objects of historic interest and similar property appropriate to a general museum, if owned by the state and not placed in other custody by a specific law; also the research department carried on by the state geologist and paleontologist, botanist and entomologist, and all similar scientific interests of the University.

University of the State of New York

Extension Bulletin

No. 15　September 1896

CLASS LIST

OF A

$500 LIBRARY RECOMMENDED FOR SCHOOLS

SECOND EDITION, REVISED

	PAGE
Director's note	135
General reference books	137
Cyclopedias	137
Psychology and ethics	137
Mythology	137
Sociology	137
Education	138
Self culture	138
Legends and fairy tales	138
Dictionaries and synonyms	138
Science	139
General	139
Astronomy	139
Physics and electricity	139
Chemistry	139
Geology and physical geography	139
Biology, botany and zoology	140
Physiology and hygiene	140
Business	140
Art and sports	140
Literature	140
Histories and compendiums	140
American poetry	141
American essays and miscellany	141

	PAGE
Literature (*continued*)	
English literature	142
English poetry and drama	142
English essays and miscellany	143
German and classic literature	143
Fiction	144
History	147
General	147
Travel	147
General	147
Atlases and gazetteers	148
Antiquities	148
Europe	148
Asia	149
Africa	149
America	149
Arctic regions	149
Biography	149
Collective	149
Individual	150
Ancient history	152
History of Europe and Asia	152
History of America	153
Regents reading courses	154

ALBANY
UNIVERSITY OF THE STATE OF NEW YORK

E91m-N96-3000　　　1896　　　Price 5 cents

Regents

Anson Judd Upson, D. D., LL. D., L. H. D., *Chancellor*
William Croswell Doane, D. D., LL. D., *Vice-Chancellor*
Levi P. Morton, LL. D., Governor
Charles T. Saxton, LL. D., Lieutenant-Governor
John Palmer, Secretary of State
Charles R. Skinner, M. A., LL. D., Sup't Pub. Inst.
} *Ex officio*

In order of election by the legislature

ELECTED

1873 Martin I. Townsend, M. A., LL. D. - - - Troy
1874 Anson Judd Upson, D. D., LL. D., L. H. D. - Glens Falls
1877 Chauncey M. Depew, LL. D. - - - - New York
1877 Charles E. Fitch, LL. B., M. A., L. H. D. - Rochester
1877 Orris H. Warren, D. D. - - - - - Syracuse
1878 Whitelaw Reid, LL. D. - - - - New York
1881 William H. Watson, M. A., M. D. - - - Utica
1881 Henry E. Turner - - - - - Lowville
1883 St Clair McKelway, LL. D. - - - - Brooklyn
1885 Hamilton Harris, Ph. D., LL. D. - - - Albany
1885 Daniel Beach, Ph. D., LL. D. - - - - Watkins
1888 Carroll E. Smith, LL. D. - - - - Syracuse
1890 Pliny T. Sexton, LL. D. - - - - - Palmyra
1890 T. Guilford Smith, M. A., C. E. - - - Buffalo
1892 William Croswell Doane, D. D., LL. D. - - Albany
1893 Lewis A. Stimson, B. A., M. D. - - - New York
1894 Sylvester Malone - - - - - - Brooklyn
1895 Albert Vander Veer, M. D., Ph. D. - - Albany
One vacancy

Elected by the regents

1888 Melvil Dewey, M. A., *Secretary* - - - - Albany

DIRECTOR'S NOTE

This list provides books to the amount of $500, assuming that an average discount of one third will be secured, except in case of a few books marked *net* and specially allowed for. Wherever there is opportunity for choice, editions have been carefully selected. Considerations of economy have debarred mention of many excellent editions, but have not induced the recommendation of poor print, paper or editing. An occasional note gives information about more expensive editions or fuller treatises which would be desirable could they be afforded, but which can not be substituted without exceeding the $500 limit or excluding something else. Where alternatives are suggested in the main list, as in case of cyclopedias, translations of Homer, etc. provision has been made for buying the more expensive work, but not both. When more than one edition is mentioned, the first is the one reckoned. Amounts in headings represent list prices and do not include alternatives.

Certain series of miscellaneous standard literature, which appear frequently on the list and are sometimes brought into comparison, perhaps need brief description. The volumes of the Riverside literature series (Houghton) are 12mos printed in clear, medium sized type on good opaque paper and bound in brown linen. They are also bound in paper and boards, but only the cloth binding is quoted on this list. The Riverside school library (Houghton) volumes are generally printed from the same plates as the Riverside literature series, on somewhat finer paper and bound in red half leather. The World's classics (Putnam) are less expensive reissues of the well-known Knickerbocker nuggets. The type, though not large, is clear, the page well spaced, and the paper is good. They are neatly bound small 16mos. The Elia series (Putnam) are larger 16mos, admirable in type and paper, with gilt top and rough edges. These series, with Longman's English classics, Leach's Students series of English classics, Macmillan's School editions, and others of recognized value, may be depended on as evenly good. To know one is to be assured of the quality of all. Unfortunately this is not always true of special editions and series, the uniformity sometimes consisting only in binding and price. Of the Stratford edition of Irving certain volumes are desirable while others are poor. The

Crowell Standard library, uncommonly satisfactory for the price in many instances, is very unequal and sometimes decidedly inferior. It has been recommended on this list only after examination of the individual volume.

Books marked *a* aggregate a selection costing $200. If to these the books marked *b* are added, the amount will reach $300 This selection merely suggests probable first needs in case it is impracticable to buy all on the list, but it does not imply that these books are superior in quality. It is of course impossible to make a limited list which shall perfectly meet diverse needs. A German dictionary or an advanced chemistry may be almost useless in one school and absolutely necessary in another. Variations must be made to suit the requirements of special courses and the interests of the community. The resources of the school must also be considered. It is hoped that these briefer selections will meet the average requirements fairly well and that the full list will furnish suggestions for special wants.

MELVIL DEWEY
Director

University of the State of New York

Extension Bulletin

No. 15 September 1896

CLASS LIST

OF A

$500 LIBRARY RECOMMENDED FOR SCHOOLS

GENERAL REFERENCE BOOKS ($48.75)
Burt, M.. E.. Literary landmarks. Houghton 75c.

Cyclopedias
a Johnson's universal cyclopaedia. 8v. 1894-95. Appleton $48 *net*.
or
Chamber's encyclopaedia. 10v. 1892-93. Lippincott $20 *net*.

PSYCHOLOGY AND ETHICS ($5)
Sully, James. Outlines of psychology. Appleton $2.50.
a Gilman, N. P. & Jackson, E: P. Conduct as a fine art. Houghton $1.50.
Smiles, Samuel. Duty. Harper $1.

MYTHOLOGY ($1.50)
a Guerber, H. A. Myths of Greece and Rome. Amer. bk co. $1.50.

SOCIOLOGY ($17.30)
a Nordhoff, Charles. Politics for young Americans. Amer. bk co. 75c.
Fiske, John. American political ideas. Harper $1.
b Johnston, Alexander. History of American politics. Holt 80c.
Bowker, R: R. Economics for the people. Harper 75c.
Perry, A. L. Political economy Scribner $2 50.
a Walker, F. A. Political economy Holt $2. (Amer. sci. ser. advanced course.)

Gilman, N: P. Profit sharing between employer and employee. Houghton $1.75.
Riis, J. A. Children of the poor. Scribner $1.25.
a **Brooks, E. S.** Century book for young Americans. Century $1 50.
a **Bryce, James.** American commonwealth 2v. Macmillan $4.
Dawes, A.. L. How we are governed. Ginn $1.

Education ($13.25)

a **Williams, S: G.** History of modern education. Bardeen $1.50
a **Compayré, Gabriel** Lectures on teaching Heath $1.75
Fitch, J. G. Lectures on teaching Macmillan $1.
b **Page, D. P.** Theory and practice of teaching. Amer. bk co. $1.
Skinner, C: R. *ed.* Arbor day manual. Weed, Parsons & Co, $2 50
White, E. E. School management Amer. bk co $1.
Parker, F. W. How to study geography. Appleton $1 50. (Internat educ. ser.)
a **Harrison, Elizabeth.** Study of child nature Chic kindergarten training school $1.
. **Poulsson, Emilie.** In the child's world. Milton Bradley co. $2.

Self culture ($6.50)

a **Chester, Eliza,** *pseud* Chats with girls on self culture. Dodd $1.25.
a **Hale, E: E.** How to do it Roberts $1
b **Mathews, William.** Getting on in the world. Griggs $1.50.
Munger, T. T. On the threshold. Houghton $1.
Smiles, Samuel. Self-help. Harper $1.
Chester, Eliza. Girls and women. Houghton 75c.

Legends and fairy tales ($5.75)

a **Grimm, J. L; & W; K;** Household stories; tr. from the German by Lucy Crane. Macmillan $2.
Lang, Andrew, *ed* Blue fairy book Longmans $2.
Jacobs, Joseph. More English fairy tales. Putnam $1.75.

DICTIONARIES AND SYNONYMS ($32.62)

a **Webster's international dictionary** of the English language. Merriam $10.62.
Crabb, George. English synonymes. Harper $1.25.

Attention is also called to J C Fernald's *English Synonyms and antonyms,* just issued by the Funk & Wagnalls Co Its value is not yet established, but it is made on a convenient and practical plan for school use

Whitney's German dictionary. Holt $2 *net.*
Gasc, Ferdinand. French and English and English and French dictionary. Holt $2.25 *net.*

For fuller German and French dictionaries we recommend the Thieme-Preusser German dictionary, Haendcke & Lehmkuhl, $4.25, or Flugel's dictionary, English-German 2 v. German-English, 1 v. Westerman $16 50; Smith, Hamilton & Legros' International English and French dictionary, 2 v. Fouraut, $6 50. American importers will sell at the above prices.

Harpers' Latin dictionary. Harper $6 50.
Lewis' Elementary Latin dictionary, Harper $2 is excellent.
Liddell & Scott's Greek-English lexicon. Harper $10.

SCIENCE ($54.59)

General ($5.50)

a **Burroughs, John.** Locusts and wild honey. Houghton $1.25.
Torrey, Bradford. The foot-path way. Houghton $1.25.
a **Buckley, A. B.** Fairy-land of science. Appleton $1.50.
b —— Through magic glasses. Appleton $1.50.

Astronomy ($5)

a **Ball,** *Sir* **R. S.** Star-land. Ginn $1 *net.*
Proctor, R: A. Other worlds than ours. Appleton $1.75.
Young, C. A. General astronomy. Ginn $2.25.

Physics and electricity ($7.75)

Deschanel's physics; tr. and ed. by J. D. Everett. Appleton $5.75.
Cumming, Linnaeus. Electricity treated experimentally. Longmans $1.50.
a **Meadowcroft, W:¦ H.** Scholar's A B¨C of ¨electricity.¨ Amer. technical bk co. 50c.

Chemistry ($2.80)

Remsen, Ira. Inorganic chemistry. Holt $2.80 *net.* (Amer. sci. ser. advanced course.)

Geology and physical geography ($12.43)

b **Dana, J. D.** Manual of geology. Amer. bk co. $5.
b **Frye, A. E.** Brooks and brook basins. Ginn 58c.
Guyot, Arnold. Earth and man. Scribner $1.75.
a **Herrick, S. B.** Earth in past ages. Harper 60c.
Kingsley, Charles. Madam How and Lady Why. Macmillan 50c. (School ed.)
b **Shaler, N. S.** Aspects of the earth. Scribner $2.50.
Tyndall, John. Forms of water. Appleton $1.50.

Biology, botany and zoology ($21.11)

Drummond, Henry. Ascent of man. Pott $2.
Morley, M. W. Song of life. McClurg $1.25.
Dana, *Mrs* W. S. How to know the wild flowers. (Ed. 2.) Scribner $1.75.
a Gray, Asa. Lessons and manual of botany. Amer. bk co. $2.16.
a Newell, J. H. Outline lessons in botany. 2 v. Ginn $1.30
   pt 1 From seed to leaf.
   pt 2 Flower and fruit.
b Miller, Olive Thorne, *pseud.* Little folks in feathers and fur. Dutton $2.50.
a Packard, A. S. Zoology. Holt $2.40 *net*. (Amer. sci. ser. advanced course.)
b Comstock, J. H. & A. B. Manual for the study of insects. Comstock pub. co. $3.75.
b Noel, Maurice. Buz. Holt $1.
a Chapman, F. M. Handbook of birds of eastern North America. Appleton $3.

PHYSIOLOGY AND HYGIENE ($3.20)

a Martin, H. N. The human body. Holt $2.20 *net*. (Amer. sci. ser. advanced course.)
b Blaikie, William. How to get strong and how to stay so. Harper $1.

BUSINESS ($.30)

Emery, M. S. Every-day business. Lee 30c.

ART AND SPORTS ($15)

Hamerton, P. G. Thoughts about art. Roberts $2.
Goodyear, W. H. History of art. (Ed. 7.) Barnes $3.
· Leland, C: G. Manual of wood-carving. Scribner $1.75.
Miller, L. W. Essentials of perspective. Scribner $1.50.
a Walker, William. Handbook of drawing. Scribner $1.75.
Adams, W. I. L. Amateur photography. Baker & Taylor $1.
b Beard, D. C. American boys' handy book. Scribner $2.
b Beard, Lina & A. B." American girls' handy book. Scribner $2.

LITERATURE ($208.50)

Histories and compendiums ($8.50)

Botta, *Mrs* A. C. (Lynch). Handbook of universal literature. Houghton $2.

Brewer, E. C. Dictionary of phrase and fable. (New ed. enl.) Lippincott $3.50.

b **Bartlett, John.** Familiar quotations. Little $3.

American poetry ($9.50)

Bryant, W: C. Poetical works. Appleton $1.50. (Household ed.)

Holmes, O. W. Poetical works. Houghton $2. (Cambridge ed.)

a **Longfellow, H: W.** Complete poetical works. Houghton $2. (Cambridge ed.)

a **Lowell, J. R.** Poetical works. Houghton $2. (Cambridge ed.)

a **Whittier, J: G.** Complete poetical works. Houghton $2. (Cambridge ed.)

The Cambridge editions of Holmes, Longfellow, Lowell and Whittier are the only one volume editions complete with latest revisions. Contain also biographic sketches.

American essays and miscellany ($15.50)

b **Curtis, G: W:** From the Easy chair. Harper $1.

a **Emerson, R. W.** Essays, 1st and 2d series. Houghton $1. (Popular ed.)

—— Representative men, *with* Nature, lectures and addresses. 2 v. in 1. Houghton $1. (Popular ed.)

b **Lowell, J. R.** My study windows. Houghton $2.

Repplier, Agnes. Points of view. Houghton $1.25.

a **Holmes, O. W.** Autocrat of the breakfast table. Houghton 50c. *net* (Riverside literature ser. no. 81), 60c. *net* (Riverside school lib.); $1.50 (Riverside ed.)

Irving, Washington. Alhambra. Crowell $1. (Standard lib.)

—— —— ed. by W. L. Phelps. Putnam $1. (Students' ed.)

b —— Knickerbocker. Putnam $1.25. (Stratford ed.)

a —— Sketch book. Putnam $1.25. (Stratford ed.)

—— —— ed. by W. L. Phelps. Putnam $1. (Students' ed.)

G. P. Putnam's sons publish several editions of Irving of very unequal merit. The special volumes issued in the Students' ed. are printed from new plates and are excellent. The Hudson ed complete, at $1.50 a vol. and the Stratford ed. of *Knickerbocker* and the *Sketch book*, $1.25 each, may be recommended for library use.

Warner, C: D. Backlog studies. Houghton $1. (Riverside Aldine ser.)

b —— My summer in a garden. Houghton $1. (Riverside Aldine ser.)

b **Mitchell, D. G.** Reveries of a bachelor. Scribner 75c. (New Edgewood ed.)

a **Thoreau, H: D:** Walden. Houghton $1.50.

English literature ($12)

a **Chamber's cyclopaedia** of English literature. 2 v. Lippincott $7.
b **Gosse, Edmund.** History of 18th century literature. Macmillan $1. (Students' ed.)
a **Nicoll, H: J.** Landmarks of English literature. Appleton $1.50.
b **Saintsbury, George.** History of Elizabethan literature. Macmillan $1. (Students' ed.)
—— History of 19th century literature. Macmillan $1.50.

English poetry and drama ($27.50)

a **Bryant, W: C.** *ed.* New library of poetry and song. Fords $5.
b **Henley, W: E.** *ed.* Lyra heroica. Scribner $1.25.
Ward, T: H. *ed.* English poets. 4 v. Macmillan $4.
a **Whittier, J: G.** *ed.* Child life. Houghton $2.
Chaucer, Geoffrey. The students Chaucer; being a complete edition of his works, ed. by W. W. Skeat. Macmillan $1.75 *net.* (Globe ed.)
a **Milton, John.** Poetical works. Macmillan $1.75. (Globe ed.)
b **Scott,** *Sir* **Walter.** Poetical works. Macmillan $1.75. (Globe ed.)
Spenser, Edmund. Complete works. Macmillan $1.75. (Globe ed.)
a **Tennyson, Alfred.** Works. Macmillan $1.75. (Globe ed.)
Complete, with authorized revisions. Gives Idyls of the king in order of Tennyson's final arrangement.
b **Wordsworth, William.** Complete poetical works. Crowell $1. (Standard ed.)
a **Shakspere, William.** Works; v. 1, Comedies, v. 2, Histories; v. 3, Tragedies. Macmillan $1.75 *each.* 3 v. $5. (Victoria ed.)
The most satisfactory cheap edition. Follows text of Globe edition. Good sized, clear type, excellent paper, lines not numbered. Attention is also called to:
—— New variorum edition of Shakespeare, ed. by H. H. Furness. Lippincott, v. 1-10, $4 *each.*
Present results of an exhaustive collation of texts and gives a full selection of commentary. Invaluable to students and for reference, but not desirable for reading.
Now ready:

As you like it	Midsummer night's dream
Hamlet (2 v.)	Othello
King Lear	Romeo and Juliet
Macbeth	The tempest
Merchant of Venice	

—— Works; ed. by Richard Grant White. 6 v. Houghton $10. (Riverside ed.)
Excellent in text, notes, type and paper. Very desirable for school or home reading.

Shakspere, William. Works; ed. by W. G. Clark and W. A. Wright. Macmillan $1.75 (Globe ed.)
Probably best one volume edition. Type too fine but clear and not worn. Paper very thin but good; text excellent; lines numbered.
Separate plays expurgated for school use:
Edited by W: J. Rolfe. Harper *paper* 40c, *cloth* 56c.
Edited by H: N. Hudson. Ginn *paper* 30c.; *cloth* 45c. (New school Shakspere.)
Edited by Brainerd Kellogg. Maynard 30c. (English classics.)
a **Lamb, Charles & Mary.** Tales from Shakespeare. Ginn 50c. (Classics for children.)
—— —— Houghton 50c *net*. (Riverside literature ser no. 64–66); 60c *net* (Riverside school lib.)

English essays and miscellany ($15.60)

a **Addison, Joseph.** Sir Roger de Coverley papers. Leach 35c. (Students' ser. of Eng. classics.)
Arnold, Matthew. Essays in criticism. ser. 1. Macmillan $1.50.
Brown, John. Spare hours. ser. 1. Houghton $1.
b **Carlyle, Thomas.** Critical and miscellaneous essays. 2 v. Houghton $3.50. (Popular ed.)
De Quincey, Thomas. Confessions of an English opium eater. Putnam 50c. (World's classics.)
—— —— Altemus 40c. (Vademecum ser.)
Hamerton, P. G. Intellectual life. Roberts $2.
b **Lamb, Charles.** Essays of Elia. 2 v. Putnam $1. (World's classics.)
Also published in 2 v $2 in Putnam's admirably executed Elia series.
b **Macaulay, T: B.** Critical, historical and miscellaneous essays. 3 v. Houghton $3.75. (Riverside ed.)
a **Ruskin, John.** Sesame and lilies. Putnam 50c. (World's classics.)
—— —— Maynard $1.50. (Brantwood ed.)
b **Thackeray, W: M.** Four Georges, English humorists. Houghton $1.50. (Illus. library ed.)

German and classic literature ($6.50)

Taylor, Bayard. Studies in German literature. Putnam $2.
Church, A. J: Stories from Virgil. Dodd $1
b —— Stories from Homer. Dodd $1.
a **Homer.** Iliad; tr. by W. C. Bryant. Houghton $2.50. (Roslyn ed.)
or
—— —— tr. by Alexander Pope. 2 v. McClurg $2. (Laurel crowned verse.)
—— Iliad and Odyssey. Routledge $1.50. (Popular lib.)

Fiction ($113.40)

a **Alcott, L.. M.** Little women. Roberts $1.50.
b —— Under the lilacs. Roberts $1 50.
a **Aldrich, T: B.** Story of a bad boy. Houghton 70c. *net*. (Riverside school lib)
—— Marjorie Daw and other people. Houghton $1.50.
a **Andersen, H. C.** Wonder stories told for children. Houghton $1.
Barr, *Mrs* **A. B.** Bow of orange ribbon. Dodd $1 25
Besant, Walter. All sorts and conditions of men. Harper $1.25.
Black, William. Princess of Thule. Harper $1 25.
b **Blackmore, R: D.** Lorna Doone. Crowell $1. (Standard ed)
Bronte, Charlotte. Jane Eyre. Crowell $1. (Standard ed.)
Brooks, Noah. The boy emigrants. Scribner $1.25.
b **Bunyan, John.** Pilgrim's progress. Crowell 75c. (Handy vol. ed.)
—— —— Macmillan $1. (Golden treasury ser.)
b **Burnett,** *Mrs* **Frances (Hodgson).** Little Lord Fauntleroy. Scribner $2.
Bynner, E. L. The begum's daughter. Houghton $1 25.
b **Carroll, Lewis,** *pseud*. Alice's adventures in Wonderland. Macmillan $1.
Cervantes Saavedra, Miguel de. Don Quixote; abridged and ed. by M. F. Wheaton. Ginn 60c. (Classics for children.)
b **Coolidge, Susan,** *pseud*. What Katy did. Roberts $1.25.
Cooper, J. F. Leather-Stocking tales   Putnam $1.25 *each*. (Mohawk ed.)
    a Deerslayer   Pathfinder   Prairie
    a Last of the Mohicans   Pioneers
—— Pilot. Putnam $1 25. (Mohawk ed.)
a —— Spy. Putnam $1 25. (Mohawk ed.)
Craik, *Mrs* **D. M. (Mulock).** John Halifax, gentleman. Crowell $1. (Standard ed)
Crockett, S. R. The raiders. Macmillan $1.50.
a **Defoe, Daniel.** Robinson Crusoe. Houghton 60c. *net* (Riverside literature ser. no. 87); 60c. *net*. (Riverside school lib)
Dickens, Charles. Barnaby Rudge
a —— Christmas stories
a —— David Copperfield
b —— Nicholas Nickleby
a —— Pickwick papers
a —— Tale of two cities *and* Edwin Drood

Macmillan $1 *each* (New popular ed.)

These volumes are selected as the best till a complete set, which is most desirable, can be afforded.

a **Dodge,** *Mrs* **Mary (Mapes).** Hans Brinker. Scribner $1.50.
Doyle, A. C. Micah Clarke. Longmans $1.25.
Eggleston, Edward. Hoosier school master Judd $1 50.
b **Eliot, George,** *pseud.* Adam Bede. Crowell $1. (Standard ed.)
b —— Romola. Crowell $1 (Standard ed·)
a —— Silas Marner. Leach 35c. (Students' ser. of Eng. classics)
Ewing, *Mrs* **J. H.** Jackanapes; Daddy Darwin's dovecot; Story of a short life. 3 v. in 1. Roberts 50c.
Frederic, Harold. In the valley. Scribner $1 50.
Gaskell, *Mrs* **E.. C.** Cranford. Crowell 75c. (Handy vol ed.)
a **Goldsmith, Oliver.** Vicar of Wakefield. Houghton 40c. *net* (Riverside literature ser. no. 78) 50c. *net.* (Riverside school lib)
—— —— Putnam 50c. (World's classics.)
b **Hale, E: E.** Man without a country and other tales. Roberts $1.25.
a **Hawthorne, Nathaniel.** Marble faun. Houghton $2. (Riverside ed.)
—— Scarlet letter. Houghton $1. (Little classic ed)
a —— House of seven gables. Houghton $1. (Little classic ed.)
—— Tanglewood tales Houghton $1 (Little classic ed.)
a —— Wonder-book for girls and boys Houghton $1. (Little classic ed.)

All Houghton's editions of Hawthorne are good The Riverside edition, 13 v $26, sometimes combines two or more stories in one volume, the Little classic edition 25 v. $25, occasionally gives two volumes to one work. Special volumes but not full sets can be bought in Popular ed $1 *each*, School ed 40c. *each*, Salem ed 30c. *each*, and in Riverside school library and Riverside literature series at varying prices

a **Hayes, I: I.** Cast away in the cold. Lee $1.25.
b **Henty, G: A.** St George for England. Scribner $1.50
—— With Wolfe in Canada. Scribner $1 50
Howells, W: D. Chance acquaintance. Houghton $1.
b —— Rise of Silas Lapham. Houghton $1 50.
a **Hughes, Thomas.** Tom Brown's school days. Crowell $1. (Standard ed)
—— —— Houghton 60c. *net* (Riverside literature ser. no. 85), 70c. *net* (Riverside school lib)
—— —— Macmillan 50c. (People's ed.)
Hugo, Victor. Les misérables. 2 v. Crowell $2. (Standard ed.)
b **Jackson,** *Mrs* **Helen (Hunt).** Ramona. Roberts $1.50.
a **Jewett, S.. O.** Betty Leicester Houghton $1.25.
—— A native of Winby and other tales. Houghton $1.25.

Kingsley, Charles. Water babies. Macmillan 50c. (Macmillan's school lib.)
b —— Westward ho! Macmillan 50c. (Macmillan's school lib.)
—— Hypatia. Crowell $1. (Standard ed.)
a **Kipling, Rudyard.** Jungle book. Century $1.50.
Lytton, E: G: E. L. Bulwer-Lytton, *baron.* Last days of Pompeii. Crowell $1. (Standard ed.)
Macdonald, George. St George and St Michael. Lothrop $1.50.
a **Munroe, Kirk.** Campmates. Harper $1.25.
—— Flamingo feather. Harper $1.
Page, T: N. In Ole Virginia. Scribner $1.25.
Reade, Charles. The cloister and the hearth. Crowell $1. (Standard ed.)
Scott, *Sir* **Walter.** Fair maid of Perth
—— Guy Mannering
b —— Heart of Mid-Lothian
a —— Ivanhoe   } Macmillan $1.25 *each*
a —— Kenilworth   (Dryburgh ed.)
b —— Quentin Durward
a —— Rob Roy
a —— Talisman

These volumes are selected as best till a complete set, which is most desirable, can be afforded. Macmillan's new standard ed. printed from the Dryburgh plates with Dryburgh frontispiece but with no other illustrations, is sold in sets only, 25 v. $22.50.

a **Seawell, M. E.** Decatur and Somers. Appleton $1.
—— Paul Jones. Appleton $1.
Sewell, Anna. Black beauty. Lothrop $1.
Stevenson, R. L. David Balfour. Scribner $1.50.
b —— Treasure island. Roberts $1.
—— Kidnapped. Scribner $1.50.
a **Stoddard, W: O.** Guert Ten Eyck. Lothrop $1.50.
—— On the old frontier. Appleton $1.50.
Stowe, *Mrs* **Harriet (Beecher).** Oldtown folks. Houghton $1.50.
a —— Uncle Tom's cabin. Houghton 60c. *net* (Riverside literature ser. no. 88); 70c. *net* (Riverside school lib.), $1 (Popular ed.)
a **Thackeray, W: M.** Henry Esmond
—— Newcomes   } Crowell $1 *each* (Standard ed.)
—— Vanity fair

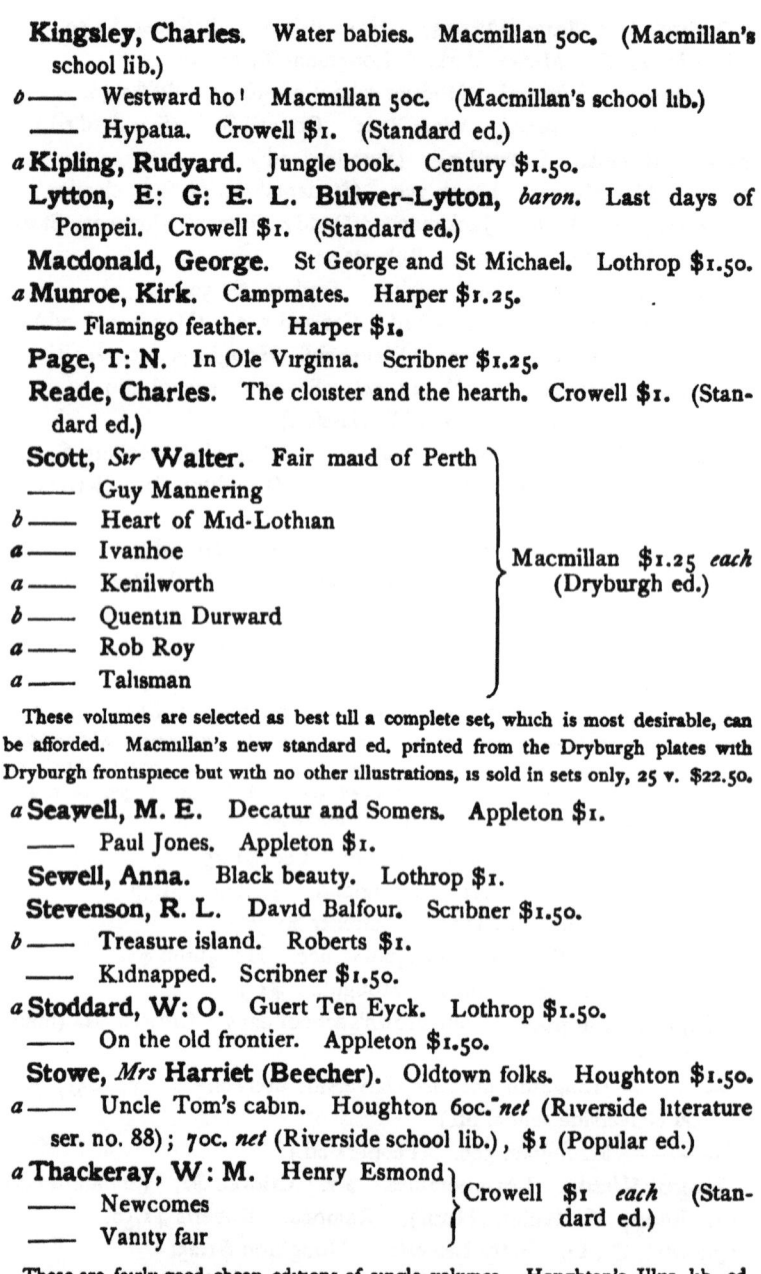

These are fairly good cheap editions of single volumes. Houghton's Illus. lib. ed. of Thackeray, complete in 22 v. $1.50 *each*, is better.

a **Tomlinson, E. T.** Search for Andrew Field. Lee $1.50.
b **Wallace, Lew.** Ben-Hur. Harper $1.50.
Weyman, S. J. Gentlemen of France. Longmans $1.25.
b **Whitney,** *Mrs* **A. D. T.** Summer in Leslie Goldthwaite's life. Houghton $1.25.
—— We girls. Houghton $1.25.
b **Wiggin,** *Mrs* **K. D.** Birds' Christmas Carol. Houghton 50c.
b **Wilkins, M. E.** New England nun and other stories. Harper $1.25.
Wyss, J. D: Swiss family Robinson Cassell 75c.

HISTORY

General ($18.65)

Keary, C: F. Dawn of history. Scribner $1.25.
b **Harper's book of facts**; compiled by J. H. Wilsey and Charlton T. Lewis. Harper $8.

or

Haydn's dictionary of dates. Ed 21, containing the history of the world to the autumn of 1895, by Benjamin Vincent. Putnam $6.

These books, about the same size, are both revisions of earlier editions of Haydn. Many entries are identical. Harper's book of facts has more and much fuller entries on American affairs, Haydn treats foreign interests more fully and is brought more nearly to date.

Creasy, *Sir* **E: S.** Fifteen decisive battles of the world Harper $1.
a **Morris, Charles.** Historical tales 4 v. Lippincott $5.
a **Fisher, G: P.** Outlines of universal history Amer. bk co. $2.40.
b **Mackenzie, Robert.** The 19th century Nelson $1

TRAVEL ($102.60)

General ($8.60)

Brassey, *Mrs* **Anne.** Around the world in the yacht 'Sunbeam.' Holt $2.
a **Dana, R: H:** *jr.* Two years before the mast. Houghton 60c. *net.* (Riverside literature ser. no. 84), 70c. *net* (Riverside school lib)
Darwin, Charles. What Mr Darwin saw in his voyage round the world in the ship 'Beagle.' Harper $3.
Davis, R: H. Rulers of the Mediterranean. Harper $1.25.
b **Rhoades, H: E.** Around the world with the blue jackets. Lothrop $1.75.

Atlases and gazetteers ($20.25)

Ginn's classical atlas. Ginn $2.
a **Labberton, R. H.** New historical atlas and general history. Silver $2.
a **Lippincott's gazetteer of the world.** Lippincott, *sheep* $8 *net*.
a **Times atlas.** London *Times* office 22s 6d. *net*.

Page, 16½ x 11 in. 173 maps on cloth-hinged stubs Fully indexed. Remarkably good for price Represents eastern continent well, but inadequate for western, giving only three maps of the United States The Appleton atlas supplements it fairly well, at small cost.

or

Rand, McNally & Co.'s Universal atlas of the world. $5.

Page, 14 x 10¾ in. From new plates, more maps and much better than earlier editions. Greatly superior to the *Times atlas* for American continent, but inferior in general workmanship. Its foreign maps are smaller and have fewer details. Has 112 pages of historical and geographic information, better supplied elsewhere Full index of state maps.

Appleton's atlas of the United States. Appleton $1.50.
Page 10¼ x 6¾ in County maps of each state.

World-wide atlas. W. & A. K. Johnston 7s. 6d.

Page, 12½x9⅝ in. 112 well engraved maps, fully indexed. Western continent meagerly treated. An alternative, not a supplement, if *Times atlas* is too costly.

Antiquities ($10.25)

Guhl, E. K. & Koner, W. D. Life of the Greeks and Romans Appleton $2.50.
b **Harper's dictionary of classical literature and antiquities.** Harper $6.
a **Gow, James.** Companion to school classics. Macmillan $1.75.

Europe ($24.50)

Aldrich, T: B. From Ponkapog to Pesth. Houghton $1.25.
James, Henry. Transatlantic sketches. Houghton $2.
a **Knox, T: W.** Boy travellers in southern Europe. Harper $3.
Warner, C: D. Roundabout journey. Houghton $1.50.
Besant, Walter. London. Harper $3.
b **Hawthorne, Nathaniel.** Our old home. Houghton $1 (Little classic ed.)
a **Smith, Goldwin.** Trip to England. Macmillan 75c.
a **Winter, William.** Shakespeare's England. Macmillan 75c.
b **Whitman, Sidney.** Realm of the Habsburgs. Lovell $1.25

Amicis, Edmondo de. Studies of Paris. Putnam $1.25.
Brown, H. F. Life on the lagoons. Macmillan $1 75.
b Howells, W: D. Italian journeys. Houghton $1.50.
b Hapgood, I. F. Russian rambles Houghton $1 50.
a Amicis, Edmondo de. Holland and its people. Putnam $2.
b Tyndall, John. Hours of exercise in the Alps. Appleton $2

Asia ($12)

a Allen, T: G. *jr* & Sachtleben, W: L. Across Asia on a bicycle. Century $1.50.
b Bacon, A. M. Japanese girls and women. Houghton $1.25.
Knox, T: W. Boy travellers in Japan and China Harper $3.
—— Boy travellers in Ceylon and India. Harper $3
b Warner, C: D. In the Levant. Houghton $2.
b Kennan, George. Tent life in Siberia. Putnam $1.25.

Africa ($9.50)

b Du Chaillu, P. B. Stories of the gorilla country. Harper $1.
Stanley, H: M. How I found Livingstone. Scribner $3.50
a Vincent, Frank. Actual Africa. Appleton $5.

America ($12.25)

b Thaxter, *Mrs* Celia. Among the Isles of Shoals. Houghton $1.25.
Warner, C: D. On horseback. Houghton $1 25.
b Custer, *Mrs* Elizabeth (Bacon). Boots and saddles. Harper $1.50.
Davis, R: H. The West from a car-window. Harper $1.25.
Ingersoll, Ernest. Knocking around the Rockies. Harper $2.
b Lummis, C: F. Some strange corners of our country. Century $1.50.
a Parkman, Francis. Oregon trail. Little $1.50. (Popular ed.)
b Ford, I: N. Tropical America. Scribner $2.

Arctic regions ($5.25)

Peary, *Mrs* J. B. My arctic journal Contemporary pub co. $2.
Schley, W. S. & Soley, J. R. Rescue of Greeley. Scribner $2.
b Schwatka, Frederick. Children of the cold. Cassell $1 25.

BIOGRAPHY ($62.15)
Collective

a Lippincott's pronouncing biographical dictionary. Lippincott, *sheep* $8 net.
a Bolton, *Mrs* Sarah (Knowles). Lives of poor boys who became famous. $1 50.

b **Yonge, C.. M.** Book of golden deeds. Macmillan 50c. (Macmillan's school lib.)

b **Bolton,** *Mrs* **Sarah (Knowles).** Lives of girls who became famous. Crowell $1.50.

Brooks, E. S. Historic boys. Putnam $1.50.

Morley, John, *ed.* English men of letters. 13 v. Harper $1 *each.* (People's ed.)

    1 Gibbon, Shelley, Milton
    2 Defoe, Southey, Byron
    3 Pope, Dryden, Sidney
    4 Cooper, Landor, Bentley
    5 Burke, Macaulay, Fielding
    6 Johnson, Bunyan, Bacon
    7 Scott, Spenser, Dickens
    8 Hume, Swift, Sterne
    9 Chaucer, De Quincey, Lamb
   10 Burns, Wordsworth, Coleridge
   11 Goldsmith, Locke, Gray
   12 Thackeray, Sheridan, Addison
   13 Keats, Hawthorne, Carlyle

These biographies are also published separately in 39 vols. at 75c. *each.*

Individual

Adams. **Morse, J: T.** *jr.* John Adams. Houghton $1.25. (Amer. statesmen.)

Adams. **Morse, J: T.** John Quincy Adams. Houghton, $1.25. (Amer statesmen.)

Alfred the Great. **Hughes, Thomas.** Alfred the Great. Macmillan $1.

b Caesar. **Fowler, W. W.** Julius Caesar and the foundations of the imperial system. Putnam $1.50. (Heroes of the nations.)

a Columbus. **Seelye,** *Mrs* **Elizabeth (Eggleston).** Story of Columbus. Appleton $1.75.

Cooper. **Lounsbury, T: R.** James Fenimore Cooper. Houghton $1.25. (Amer. men of letters.)

b Curtis. **Cary, Edward.** George William Curtis Houghton $1.25. (Amer. men of letters.)

Emerson. **Holmes, O. W.** Ralph Waldo Emerson. Houghton. $1.25. (Amer. men of letters.)

BOOKS RECOMMENDED FOR SCHOOL LIBRARIES 151

a **Franklin, Benjamin.** Autobiography. Houghton 50c. *net.* (Riverside school lib.)
—— —— Putnam 50c. (World's classics), $1 (Elia ser.)
Fulton. **Knox, T: W.** Robert Fulton. Putnam $1.75. (Boys' and girls' lib. of Amer. biog.)
Gustavus 2, Adolphus. **Fletcher, C: R. L.** Gustavus Adolphus and the struggle of protestantism for existence. Putnam $1.50. (Heroes of the nations.)
a Hale. **Lossing, B. J:** Two spies, Nathan Hale and John André. Appleton $2.
b Hamilton. **Lodge, H: C.** Alexander Hamilton. Houghton $1.25. (Amer. statesmen.)
Irving. **Warner, C: D.** Washington Irving. Houghton $1.25. (Amer. men of letters.)
Jackson. **Sumner, W: G.** Andrew Jackson. Houghton $1.25.
b Jefferson. **Morse, J: T.** *jr.* Thomas Jefferson. Houghton $1.25. (Amer. statesmen.)
a **Larcom, Lucy.** New England girlhood. Houghton 75c. (Riverside lib. for young people.)
a Lincoln. **Morse, J: T.** *jr.* Abraham Lincoln. 2 v. Houghton $2.50. (Amer. statesmen.)
—— **Schurz, Carl.** Abraham Lincoln. Houghton $1.
b Livingstone. **Hughes, Thomas.** David Livingstone. Macmillan 75c. (Eng. men of action.)
Madison. **Gay, S. H.** James Madison. Houghton $1.25. (Amer. statesmen.)
Monroe. **Gilman, D. C.** James Monroe. Houghton $1.25. (Amer. statesmen.)
a Napoleon 1. **Seeley, J: R.** Short history of Napoleon the first. Roberts $1.50.
Nelson. **Southey, Robert.** Life of Nelson. Routledge 40c. (Universal lib. no. 34.)
Pericles. **Abbot, Evelyn.** Pericles and the golden age of Athens. Putnam $1.50. (Heroes of the nations.)
Stuyvesant. **Tuckerman, Bayard.** Peter Stuyvesant. Dodd $1. (Makers of America.)
Tecumseh. **Eggleston, Edward & Seelye,** *Mrs* **Elizabeth (Eggleston).** Tecumseh and the Shawnee prophet. Dodd $1.

Washington. **Irving, Washington.** Life of Washington. Putnam $1.50. (Stratford ed.)
Abridged. The full edition may be bought in Putnam's Hudson ed. 5 v $7.50.
Scudder, H. E. George Washington. Houghton 50c. *net.* (Riverside school lib.)

ANCIENT HISTORY ($7.38)

Horton, R. F. History of the Romans. Longmans $1.25.
a **Merivale, Charles.** General history of Rome. Longmans $2.
a **Harrison, J. A.** Story of Greece. Putnam $1.50. (Story of the nations.)
Mahaffy, J: P. Story of Alexander's empire. Putnam $1.50. (Story of the nations.)
Oman, C: W: C. History of Greece to Macedonian conquest. (Rivington 4s 6d.)

HISTORY OF EUROPE AND ASIA ($34.05)

a **Coffin, C: C.** Story of liberty. Harper $3.
b **Duruy, Victor.** History of the middle ages. Holt $1.60 *net.*
Emerton, Ephraim. Introduction to the study of the middle ages. Holt $1.12 *net.*
Mediaeval Europe. Ginn $1.50.
Gardiner, S. R. Student's history of England. Longmans $3
a **Green, J. R.** Short history of the English people. Harper $1.20.
Macaulay, T: B. History of England. 4 v. Houghton $5. (Popular ed.)
Bryce, James. Holy Roman empire. Macmillan $1.
b **Taylor, Bayard.** History of Germany. Appleton $1.50.
b **Creighton,** *Mrs* **L. H.** First history of France. Longmans $1.25.
Duruy, Victor. History of France. Crowell $2.
b **Gardiner,** *Mrs* **B. M.** French revolution. Longmans $1. (Epochs of modern hist)
Irving, Washington. Conquest of Granada. Putnam $1.50. (Hudson ed.)
Morfil, W: R. Story of Russia. Putnam $1.50. (Story of the nations.)
Boyesen, H. H. Story of Norway. Putnam $1.50. (Story of the nations.)
b **Griffis, W: E.** Brave little Holland and what she has taught us. Houghton 75c. (Riverside lib. for young people.)

b Motley, J: L.   Rise of the Dutch republic. 3 v. Harper $6.
b Griffis, W: E.   Japan in history, folk-lore and art. Houghton 75c. (Riverside lib. for young people.)

HISTORY OF AMERICA ($69.60)

b Drake, F. S.   Indian history for young folks. Harper $3.
b Prescott, W: H.   Conquest of Mexico. 3 v. Lippincott $1.50. (Universal ed.)
Parkman, Francis.   Old régime in Canada. Little $1.50. (Popular ed.)
b Brooks, E. S.   Story of the American sailor. Lothrop $2.25.
Coffin, C: C.   Building the nation. Harper $3.
b Eggleston, Edward.   First book in American history. Amer. bk co. 60c.
a —— Household history of the U. S. and its people. Appleton $2.50.
a Lodge, H: C & Roosevelt, Theodore.   Hero tales from American history. Century $1.50.
Lossing, B. J: Cyclopaedia of U. S. history. 2 v. Harper $6.
   Sold only by subscription
a Fiske, John.   Discovery of America. 2 v. Houghton $4.
a Parkman, Francis.   Pioneers of France in the new world. Little $1.50. (Popular ed.)
Coffin, C: C.   Old times in the colonies. Harper $3.
Parkman, Francis   Conspiracy of Pontiac. 2 v. ⎫
—— Half century of conflict. 2 v.   ⎪ Little $1.50
a —— Jesuits in North America in the 17th century ⎬ per v. *each*
b —— La Salle and the discovery of the great West ⎪ (Popular ed.)
a —— Montcalm and Wolfe. 2 v.   ⎭
a Coffin, C: C.   Boys of '76. Harper $3.
a Fiske, John.   American revolution. 2 v. Houghton $4.
b —— Critical period of American history. Houghton $2.
b Johnson, Rossiter.   History of the war of 1812–15. Dodd $1.
Champlin, J: D. *jr.*   Young folks' history of the war of the Union. Holt $2.50.
a Johnson, Rossiter.   Short history of the war of secession. Bryan, Taylor & Co. $2.50.
b Kieffer, H: M.   Recollections of a drummer boy. Houghton $1.50.
Fiske, John.   Beginnings of New England. Houghton $2.
Hawthorne, Nathaniel.   True stories from history and biography Houghton $1. (Little classic ed.)

Earle, *Mrs* A. M. Colonial days in old New York. Scribner $1.25.
a Roberts, E. H. New York. 2 v. Houghton $2.50. (Amer. commonwealths.)
Cooke, J: E. Stories of the Old Dominion. Harper $1 50.
b Drake, S: A. Making of the great West. Scribner $1.50.
Prescott, W: H. Conquest of Peru. 2 v. Lippincott $1. (Universal ed.)

REGENTS READING COURSES

A SELECTION OF DESIRABLE EDITIONS OF BOOKS REQUIRED BY REGENTS READING COURSES IN ENGLISH AND AMERICAN LITERATURE AND IN UNITED STATES HISTORY

Economy has been an important consideration in choosing editions for library use, but much pains has been taken to avoid type and paper trying to the eyes. The editions selected seem to meet best all these requirements. Wherever possible cheap editions in paper such as students may buy have been mentioned. Many of these are excellent—notably Houghton's Riverside literature series, Maynard, Merrill & Co.'s English classics and Cassell's national library.

Abbott, J: S. C. Ferdinand de Soto. Dodd $1.25. (Amer. pioneers and patriots.)

Addison, Joseph. Sir Roger de Coverley papers. Leach 35c. (Students ser. of Eng. classics.)

—— —— Houghton, 2 pts, *paper* 15c. *each*, 1 v. *cloth* 40c. *net.* (Riverside literature ser. no. 60-61.)

—— —— American bk co. *boards*, 20c. (Eclectic English classics.)

—— Sir Roger de Coverley *and* Spectator's club. Cassell, *paper* 10c. (Cassell's nat. lib. no. 28.)

Bacon, *Sir* Francis. Essays *and* Colours of good and evil. Macmillan $1. (Golden treasury ser.)

—— Essays, civil and moral; selected. Maynard, *paper* 12c. (English classics, no. 3.)

Contains the essays called for by the regents reading lists

Browning, Robert. Complete poetic and dramatic works. Houghton $3. (Cambridge ed.)

—— Blot in the scutcheon and other dramas. (Colombe's birthday *and* A soul's tragedy.) Harper, *paper* 40c.; *cloth* 56c. (Rolfe's Eng. classics.)

Bryant, W: C. Poetical works. Appleton $1.50. (Household ed.)

Bryant, W: C. Sella, Thanatopsis and other poems. Houghton, *paper* 15c. (Riverside literature ser. no. 54.)

—— Thanatopsis and other poems. Maynard, *paper* 12c. (English classics, no. 47.)

Burke, Edmund. Select works, v. 1. Macmillan $1.10 *net*. (Clarendon press ser.)

—— Present discontents. Maynard, *paper* 12c. (English classics, no. 118.)

—— Speech on conciliation with American colonies. Maynard, *paper* 12c. (English classics, no. 119.)

Burns, Robert. Poetical works. Houghton $1.50. (Riverside ed.)

—— —— Crowell $1. (Standard lib.)

—— Cotter's Saturday night and other poems. Houghton, *paper* 15c. (Riverside literature ser. no. 77.)

—— —— Maynard, *paper* 12c. (English classics no. 9.)

Contained also in Burns-Scott. Houghton 40c. (Modern classics v. 15.) *See entry under* Carlyle, Thomas.

Byron, G: G. N. *lord.* Poems. Crowell $1. (Standard lib.)

—— Prisoner of Chillon. Maynard, *paper* 12c. (English classics, no. 4.)

Carlyle, Thomas. Burns-Scott. Houghton 40c. (Modern classics, v. 15.)

Contains Carlyle's Essay on Burns, with Favorite poems by Burns and Scott.

—— Essay on Burns. Maynard, *paper* 12c. (English classics, no. 70.)

—— Sartor resartus. Estes $1. (Roxburghe classics.)

—— —— Putnam $1.

—— —— Crowell 50c. (Popular ed.)

Excellent type and paper but binding too delicate for general circulation.

Chaucer, Geoffrey. Students' Chaucer; a complete edition of his works, ed. by W. W. Skeat. Macmillan $1.75 *net*.

—— The prologue; The knightes tale; The nonne preestes tale; ed. by R. Morris and revised by W. W. Skeat. Macmillan 70c. *net*. (Clarendon press ser.)

Coleridge, Samuel. Poetical works. Macmillan $1.75. (Globe ed.); 75c. (Chiswick ser.)

The latter a fairly good cheap edition, but much less desirable than the Globe

—— Rime of the ancient mariner, and other poems. Houghton, *paper* 15c. (Riverside literature ser. no. 80.)

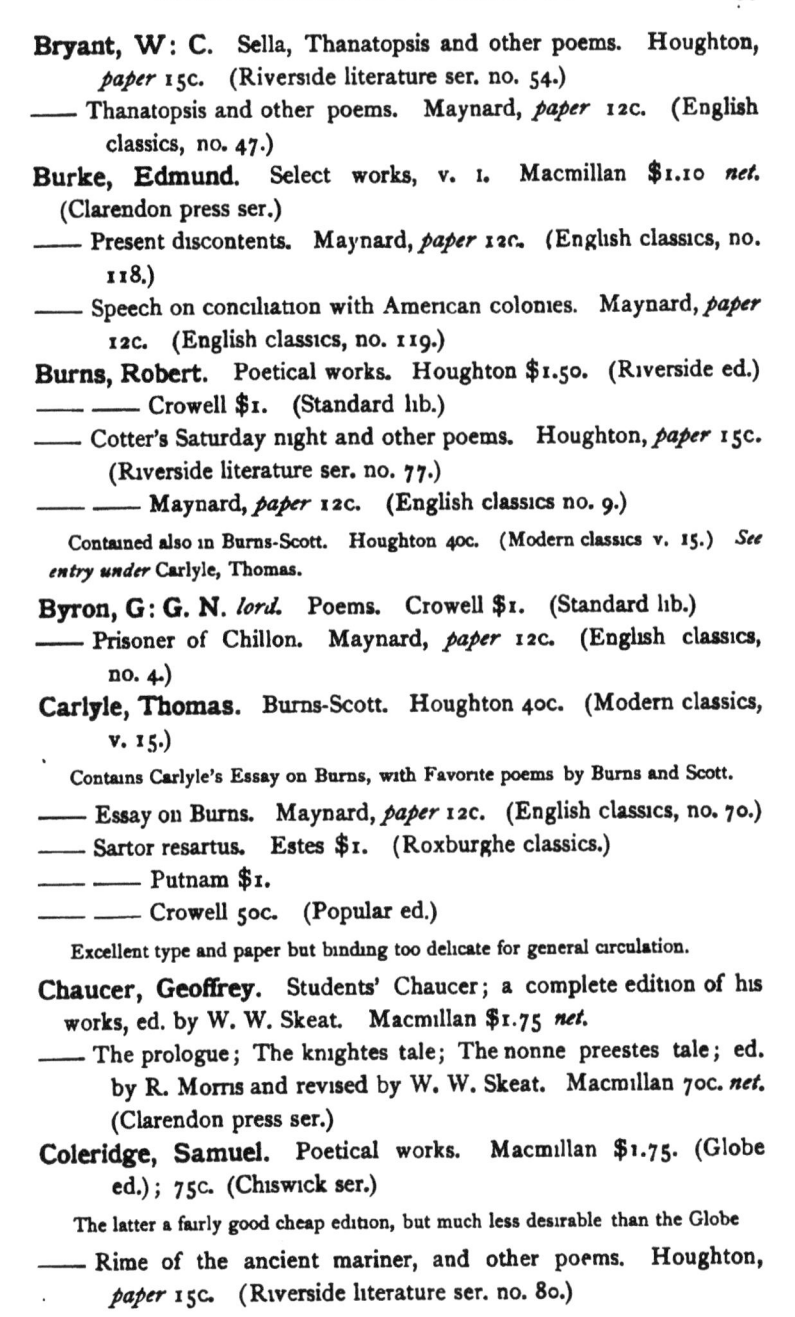

Cooper, J. F. Last of the Mohicans. Putnam $1.25. (Mohawk ed.)
—— —— Burt 75c. (Burt's home lib.)
—— —— Houghton 70c. *net.* (Riverside school lib.), 60c. *net.* (Riverside literature ser. no. 95-98.)
Cowper, William. Poetical works. Macmillan $1.75. (Globe ed.)
—— The task. Harper 30c. (Harper's school classics); *paper* 20c. (Harper's half-hour ser. no 112.)
—— —— Cassell, *paper* 10c. (Cassell nat. lib. no. 201.)
Curtis, G: W. Prue and I. Harper $1.50.
Defoe, Daniel. Journal of the plague year. Longmans 75c. (Longmans' English classics.)
—— —— Maynard 24c. (English classics, double no. 154-55.)
De Quincey, Thomas. Confessions of an English opium eater. Putnam 50c. (World's classics.)
—— —— Altemus 40c. (Vademecum ser.)
—— Narrative and miscellaneous papers. Houghton $1. (Popular ed.)
  Contains *Flight of a Tartar tribe.*
—— Flight of a Tartar tribe. Leach 35c. (Students' ser. of Eng. classics.) *In preparation.*
Dickens, Charles. Dombey and son. Macmillan $1. (New popular ed.)
—— Tale of two cities. Macmillan $1. (New popular ed)
—— —— Crowell $1. (Standard lib.)
Drake, S: A. Making of New England. Scribner $1 50.
—— Making of the great West. Scribner $1.50.
Dryden, John. Poetical works. Macmillan $1.75. (Globe ed.)
—— Poems. Cassell, *paper* 10c. (Cassell's nat. lib no. 98.)
—— Alexander's feast *and* MacFlecknoe. Maynard, *paper* 12c. (English classics, no. 39.)
Earle, *Mrs* **A. M.** Customs and fashions in old New England. Scribner $1.25.
Eliot, George, *pseud.* Romola. Crowell $1. (Standard lib.)
—— Silas Marner. Leach 35c. (Students' ser. of Eng. classics.)
—— —— Houghton, *paper* 30c. *net,* *linen* 40c. *net.* (Riverside literature ser. no. 83.)
—— —— American bk co. *boards* 30c. (Eclectic Eng. classics.)
Emerson, R. W. Poems. Houghton $1.75 (Riverside ed.); $1.50 (Household ed.); $1.25. (Little classics.)

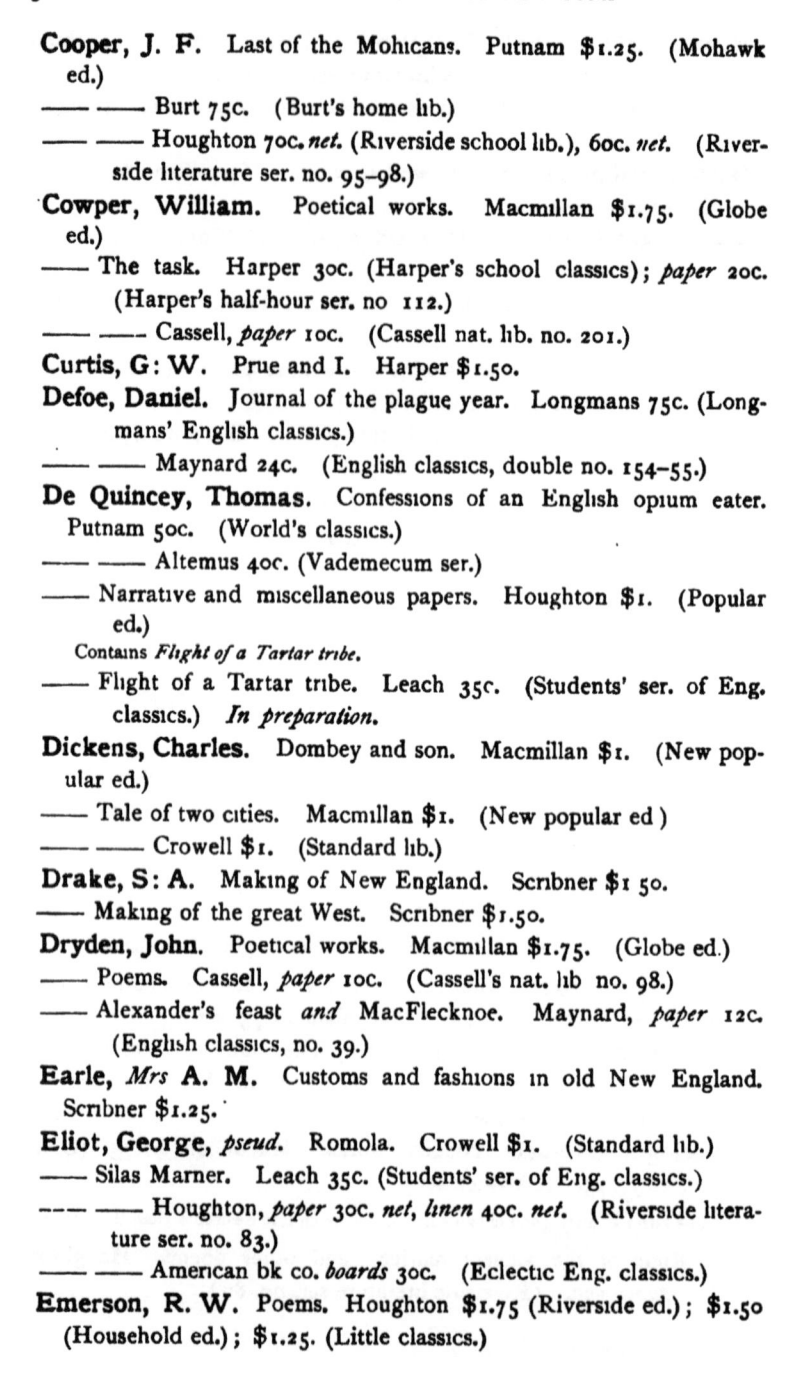

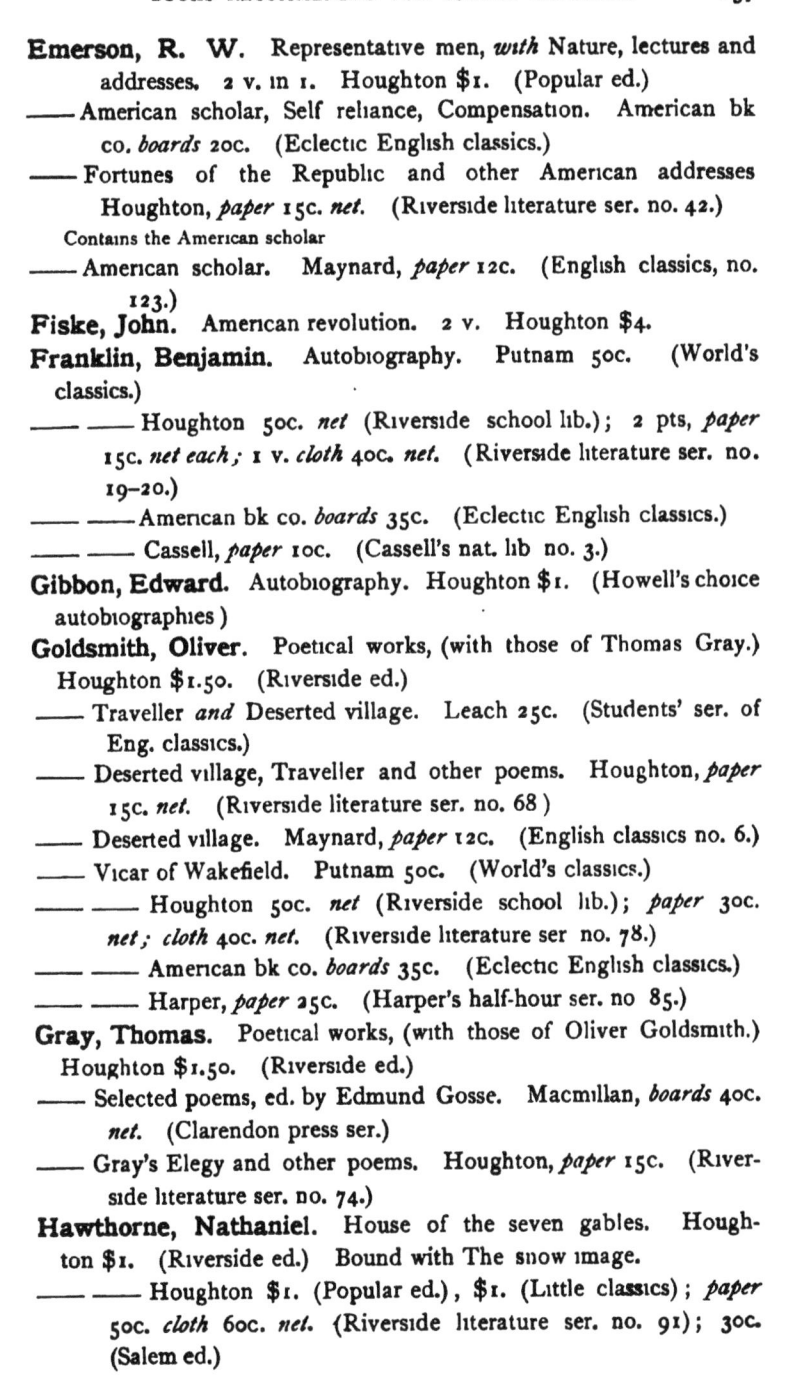

Emerson, R. W. Representative men, *with* Nature, lectures and addresses. 2 v. in 1. Houghton $1. (Popular ed.)
—— American scholar, Self reliance, Compensation. American bk co. *boards* 20c. (Eclectic English classics.)
—— Fortunes of the Republic and other American addresses Houghton, *paper* 15c. *net.* (Riverside literature ser. no. 42.)
<small>Contains the American scholar</small>
—— American scholar. Maynard, *paper* 12c. (English classics, no. 123.)
Fiske, John. American revolution. 2 v. Houghton $4.
Franklin, Benjamin. Autobiography. Putnam 50c. (World's classics.)
—— —— Houghton 50c. *net* (Riverside school lib.); 2 pts, *paper* 15c. *net each;* 1 v. *cloth* 40c. *net.* (Riverside literature ser. no. 19–20.)
—— —— American bk co. *boards* 35c. (Eclectic English classics.)
—— —— Cassell, *paper* 10c. (Cassell's nat. lib no. 3.)
Gibbon, Edward. Autobiography. Houghton $1. (Howell's choice autobiographies)
Goldsmith, Oliver. Poetical works, (with those of Thomas Gray.) Houghton $1.50. (Riverside ed.)
—— Traveller *and* Deserted village. Leach 25c. (Students' ser. of Eng. classics.)
—— Deserted village, Traveller and other poems. Houghton, *paper* 15c. *net.* (Riverside literature ser. no. 68)
—— Deserted village. Maynard, *paper* 12c. (English classics no. 6.)
—— Vicar of Wakefield. Putnam 50c. (World's classics.)
—— —— Houghton 50c. *net* (Riverside school lib.); *paper* 30c. *net;* *cloth* 40c. *net.* (Riverside literature ser no. 78.)
—— —— American bk co. *boards* 35c. (Eclectic English classics.)
—— —— Harper, *paper* 25c. (Harper's half-hour ser. no 85.)
Gray, Thomas. Poetical works, (with those of Oliver Goldsmith.) Houghton $1.50. (Riverside ed.)
—— Selected poems, ed. by Edmund Gosse. Macmillan, *boards* 40c. *net.* (Clarendon press ser.)
—— Gray's Elegy and other poems. Houghton, *paper* 15c. (Riverside literature ser. no. 74.)
Hawthorne, Nathaniel. House of the seven gables. Houghton $1. (Riverside ed.) Bound with The snow image.
—— —— Houghton $1. (Popular ed.), $1. (Little classics); *paper* 50c. *cloth* 60c. *net.* (Riverside literature ser. no. 91); 30c. (Salem ed.)

Hawthorne, Nathaniel. Marble faun. Houghton $2 (Riverside ed.); 2 v. $2 (Little classics); 40c. (School ed.)

—— Twice-told tales. Houghton $2. (Riverside ed.); 2 v. $2. (Little classics); 60c. *net.* (Riverside literature ser. no. 82); 40c. (School ed.), 30c. (Salem ed.)

Holmes, O. W. Autocrat of the breakfast table. Houghton $1.50 (Riverside ed.); $1.25 (Handy vol. ed.); 60c. *net* (Riverside school lib.), *paper* 45c. *net, cloth* 50c. *net.* (Riverside literature ser. no. 81.)

Homer. Iliad; tr. by Alexander Pope. Routledge $1.50. (Popular lib.)

Irving, Washington. Columbus. 3 v. Putnam $4.50. (Hudson ed.)

> v. 3 is the Companions of Columbus.

—— —— Abridged by the author. 1 v. Putnam $1.75.

> A new ed. illustrated and excellent in every respect.

—— —— Crowell $1. (Standard lib.)

Unabridged, but not including the Companions of Columbus.

—— Sketch book; ed. by W. L. Phelps. Putnam $1. (Students' ed.)

—— Essays from the Sketch book. Houghton 2 pts *paper* 15c. *net each*, 1 v. *cloth* 40c. *net.* (Riverside literature ser. no. 51–52.)

Contains the Legend of Sleepy Hollow, Rip Van Winkle and other essays.

—— Legend of Sleepy Hollow. Maynard, *paper* 12c. (English classics, no. 41.)

—— Sketch book; selections. Maynard, *paper* 12c. (English classics, no. 31.)

Contains Rip Van Winkle.

—— Tales of a traveller; ed. by W. L. Phelps. Putnam $1. (Students' ed.)

—— —— American bk co. *boards* 50c. (Eclectic English classics.)

Johnson, Rossiter. History of the war of 1812–15. Dodd $1.

—— Old French war. Dodd $1.

—— Short history of the war of secession. Bryan, Taylor & Co. $2.50.

Johnson, Samuel. Rasselas. Putnam 50c. (World's classics.)

—— —— Leach 35c. (Student's ser. of Eng. classics.)

—— —— Cassell, *paper* 10c. (Cassell's nat. lib. no. 191.)

Johnston, Alexander. History of American politics. Holt 80c. *net.*

Jonson, Ben. Every man in his humor. Longmans 75c.

Keats, John. Poetical works. Macmillan $1. (Golden treasury ser.)

Keats, John. Endymion and other poems. Cassell, *paper* 10c. (Cassell's nat. lib. no. 91.)

Contains the Ode on a Grecian urn

Ladd, H. O. History of the war with Mexico. Dodd $1.

Locke, John. Conduct of the understanding. Macmillan 50c. *net.* (Clarendon press ser.)

Lodge, H: C. Alexander Hamilton. Houghton $1.25. (Amer. statesmen.)

Longfellow, H: W. Complete poetical works. Houghton $2. (Cambridge ed.)

The only one volume edition complete with latest revisions. Contains also a biographic sketch.

—— Evangeline. Leach 35c. (Students' ser. of Eng. classics.)

—— —— Houghton, *paper* 15c. *net*, *cloth* 25c. *net.* (Riverside literature ser. no. 1.)

Lowell, J. R. Poems. Houghton $2. (Cambridge ed.)

The only one volume edition complete with latest revisions. Contains also a biographic sketch.

—— Vision of Sir Launfal and other pieces. Houghton, *paper* 15c. *net.* (Riverside literature ser. no. 30.)

—— —— Maynard, *paper* 12c. (English classics, no. 129.)

Macaulay, T: B. Critical, historical and miscellaneous essays. 3 v. Houghton $3.75. (Popular ed.)

—— Essay on Bacon. Harper, *paper* 25c. (Harper's half-hour ser. no. 108.), *cloth* 30c. (Harper's school classics.)

—— Essays on Milton and Byron. Harper 30c. (Harper's school classics.)

—— Essay on Milton. Ginn, *paper* 30c. (Annotated school classics.)

—— —— American bk co. *boards* 20c.

—— —— Maynard, *paper* 24c. (English classics, no. 102-3.)

—— Life of Samuel Johnson. Leach 25c. (Students' ser. of Eng. classics.)

Contained also, with Macaulay's Essay on Boswell's Johnson, in Johnson's *Chief lives of the poets* Holt $1 25 *net.*

Mackenzie, Robert. America, a history. Nelson $1.

Marlowe, Christopher. Best plays. Scribner $1.25. (Mermaid ser.)

—— Dr Faustus. Routledge 40c. (Morley's universal lib.)

—— —— with notes by Wilhelm Wagner. Longmans 60c. (London ser. of Eng. classics.)

Milton, John. Areopagitica. Macmillan 75c. *net.* (Clarendon press ser.)

Milton, John. Areopagitica. Cassell, *paper* 10c. (Cassell's nat. lib. no. 123.)
—— Poetical works. Macmillan $1.75. (Globe ed.)
—— Minor poems *and* Three books of Paradise lost. Houghton 50c. *net*. (Riverside school lib.)
—— Minor poems. Harper, *paper* 40c., *cloth* 56c. (Rolfe's Eng. classics.)
—— L'allegro, Il penseroso, Comus and Lycidas. Leach 25c. (Students' ser. of Eng. classics)
—— —— American bk co. *boards* 20c (Eclectic English classics.)
—— L'allegro, Il penseroso, Comus, Lycidas and Sonnets. Houghton, *paper* 15c *net*. (Riverside literature ser no. 72.)
—— Paradise lost. Houghton 30c (Salem ed.)
—— —— Cassell, 2 pts, *paper* 10c. *each*. (Cassell's nat lib. no. 162-63.)
—— —— Books 1-3 Houghton, *paper* 15c *net*. (Riverside literature ser. no 94)
—— Samson Agonistes. Maynard, *paper* 24c. (English classics, no. 110-11)
Mitchell, D. G. Reveries of a bachelor. Scribner 75c. (New Edgewood ed)
Morse, J: T. *jr* Abraham Lincoln 2 v. Houghton $2 50. (Amer statesmen.
Parkman, Francis. Pioneers of France in the new world. Little $1.50. (Popular ed)
Pope, Alexander. Poetical works. Macmillan $1 75. (Globe ed)
—— Selections from Alexander Pope. Macmillan 40c. (Bell's English classics.)
—— Essay on criticism. Maynard, *paper* 12c. (English classics, no. 26)
—— —— Macmillan 50c. *net*. (Pitt press ser.)
—— Rape of the lock. Maynard, *paper* 12c. (English classics, no. 55.)
Prescott, W: H. Conquest of Peru. 2 v. Lippincott $1. (Universal ed.)
Ruskin, John. Sesame and lilies. Maynard $1.50. (Brantwood ed.)
—— —— Putnam 50c. (World's classics.)
Schurz, Carl. Henry Clay. 2 v. Houghton $2 50 (Amer. statesmen.)
Scott, *Sir* **Walter.** Poetical works. Macmillan $1.75. (Globe ed.)
—— Lay of the last minstrel. Harper, *paper* 20c. (Harper's half-hour ser. no. 114.)
—— Marmion. Leach 35c (Student's ser. of English classics.)

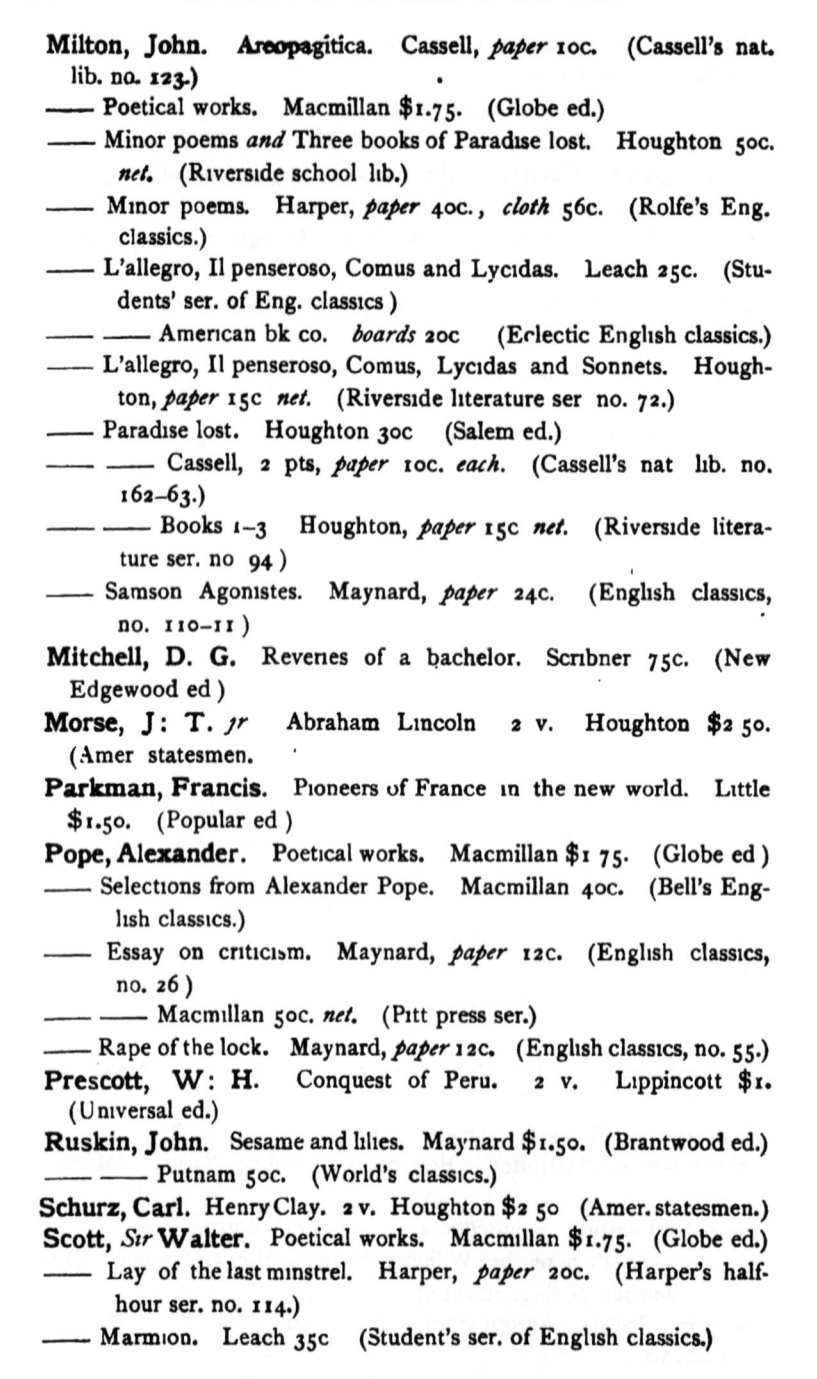

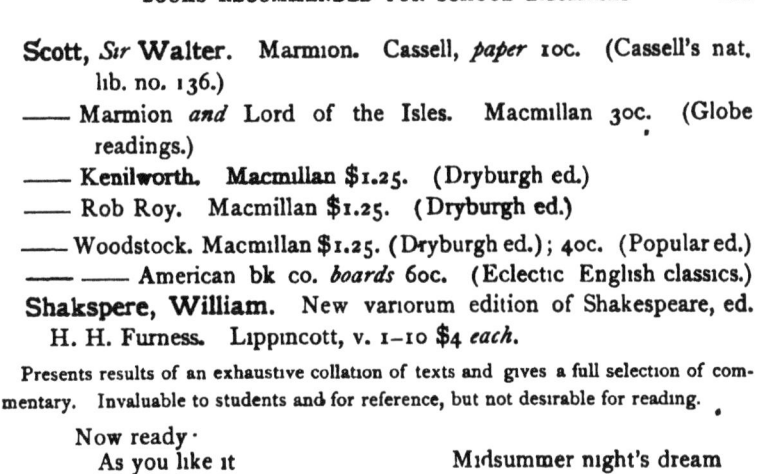

Scott, Sir Walter. Marmion. Cassell, *paper* 10c. (Cassell's nat. lib. no. 136.)

—— Marmion *and* Lord of the Isles. Macmillan 30c. (Globe readings.)

—— Kenilworth. Macmillan $1.25. (Dryburgh ed.)

—— Rob Roy. Macmillan $1.25. (Dryburgh ed.)

—— Woodstock. Macmillan $1.25. (Dryburgh ed.); 40c. (Popular ed.)

—— —— American bk co. *boards* 60c. (Eclectic English classics.)

Shakspere, William. New variorum edition of Shakespeare, ed. H. H. Furness. Lippincott, v. 1-10 $4 *each*.

Presents results of an exhaustive collation of texts and gives a full selection of commentary. Invaluable to students and for reference, but not desirable for reading.

Now ready·

As you like it
Hamlet (2 v.)
King Lear
Macbeth
Merchant of Venice
Midsummer night's dream
Othello
Romeo and Juliet
The tempest

—— Works; ed. by Richard Grant White 6 v. Houghton $10. (Riverside ed.)

Excellent in text, notes, type and paper. Very desirable edition for school or home reading.

—— Works, ed. by W. G. Clark and W. A. Wright. Macmillan $1.75. (Globe ed.)

Probably best one volume edition Type too fine but clear and not worn. Paper very thin but good Text excellent, lines numbered.

—— Works; v. 1, Comedies, v. 2, Histories; v. 3, Tragedies. Macmillan $1.75 *each*. 3 v. $5. (Victoria ed.)

The most satisfactory cheap edition. Follows text of Globe ed Good sized, clear type, excellent paper, lines not numbered

Separate plays expurgated for school use

Edited by W. J. Rolfe. Harper, *paper* 40c., *cloth* 56c.

Edited by H: N. Hudson. Ginn, *paper* 30c.; *cloth* 45c. (New school Shakespeare.)

Edited by Brainerd Kellogg. Maynard 30c. (English classics.)

The following plays are called for in the regents reading courses

As you like it, King Lear, Macbeth, Merchant of Venice, Midsummer night's dream, Richard 3, The tempest. These may be obtained, edited by W A Wright, in the Clarendon press ser. Macmillan, at from 30 to 40 cents each. As you like it, Macbeth, Merchant of Venice and Midsummer night's dream are also published by the American book co. *boards* 20c *each*, and by Longmans, 60c. *each* (English classics ser). As you like it, ed by R. G White, is published by Houghton in the Riverside literature ser no. 93, *paper* 15c *net*.

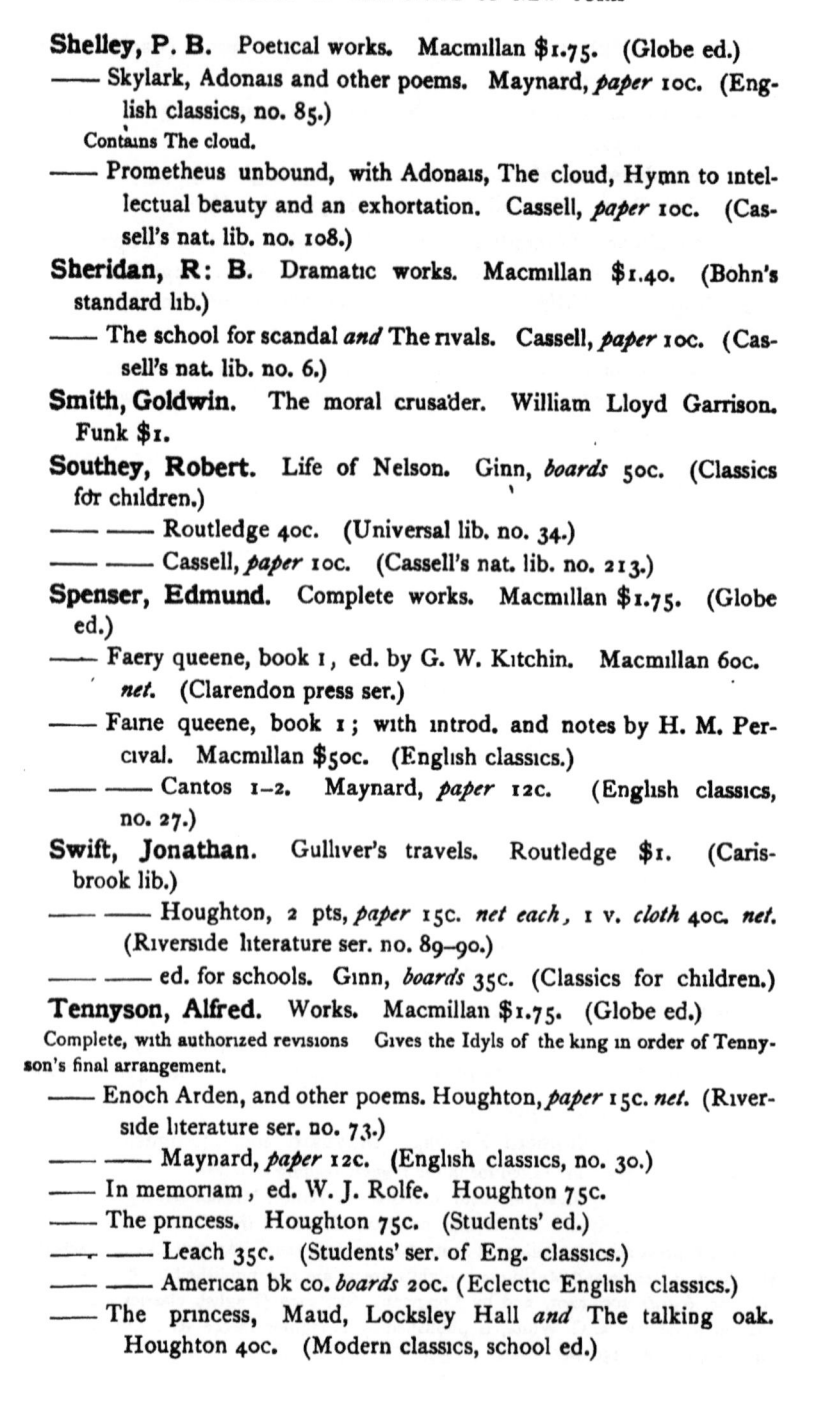

Shelley, P. B. Poetical works. Macmillan $1.75. (Globe ed.)
—— Skylark, Adonais and other poems. Maynard, *paper* 10c. (English classics, no. 85.)
Contains The cloud.
—— Prometheus unbound, with Adonais, The cloud, Hymn to intellectual beauty and an exhortation. Cassell, *paper* 10c. (Cassell's nat. lib. no. 108.)
Sheridan, R: B. Dramatic works. Macmillan $1.40. (Bohn's standard lib.)
—— The school for scandal *and* The rivals. Cassell, *paper* 10c. (Cassell's nat. lib. no. 6.)
Smith, Goldwin. The moral crusader. William Lloyd Garrison. Funk $1.
Southey, Robert. Life of Nelson. Ginn, *boards* 50c. (Classics for children.)
—— —— Routledge 40c. (Universal lib. no. 34.)
—— —— Cassell, *paper* 10c. (Cassell's nat. lib. no. 213.)
Spenser, Edmund. Complete works. Macmillan $1.75. (Globe ed.)
—— Faery queene, book 1, ed. by G. W. Kitchin. Macmillan 60c. *net*. (Clarendon press ser.)
—— Faine queene, book 1; with introd. and notes by H. M. Percival. Macmillan $.50c. (English classics.)
—— —— Cantos 1-2. Maynard, *paper* 12c. (English classics, no. 27.)
Swift, Jonathan. Gulliver's travels. Routledge $1. (Carisbrook lib.)
—— —— Houghton, 2 pts, *paper* 15c. *net each*, 1 v. *cloth* 40c. *net*. (Riverside literature ser. no. 89-90.)
—— —— ed. for schools. Ginn, *boards* 35c. (Classics for children.)
Tennyson, Alfred. Works. Macmillan $1.75. (Globe ed.)
Complete, with authorized revisions   Gives the Idyls of the king in order of Tennyson's final arrangement.
—— Enoch Arden, and other poems. Houghton, *paper* 15c. *net*. (Riverside literature ser. no. 73.)
—— —— Maynard, *paper* 12c. (English classics, no. 30.)
—— In memoriam, ed. W. J. Rolfe. Houghton 75c.
—— The princess. Houghton 75c. (Students' ed.)
—— —— Leach 35c. (Students' ser. of Eng. classics.)
—— —— American bk co. *boards* 20c. (Eclectic English classics.)
—— The princess, Maud, Locksley Hall *and* The talking oak. Houghton 40c. (Modern classics, school ed.)

Thackeray, W: M. Henry Esmond. Houghton $1.50. (Illus. lib. ed.)
—— —— Crowell $1. (Standard ed.)
—— The Newcomes. 2 v. Houghton $3. (Illus. lib. ed.)
—— —— Crowell $1. (Standard lib.)
Thomson, James. Poems. Houghton $1.50. (Riverside ed.)
—— The seasons *and* The castle of indolence; ed. by J. L. Robertson. Macmillan $1.10 *net.*
Warner, C: D. Backlog studies. Houghton $1. (Riverside Aldine ser. no. 10.)
Webster, Daniel. Select speeches. Heath $1.50 (Heath's Eng. classics.)
—— First Bunker Hill oration, *and* Adams and Jefferson. Houghton, *paper* 15c. *net.* (Riverside literature ser. no. 56.)
—— Bunker Hill orations. Maynard, *paper* 12c. (English classics, no. 44.)
Whittier, J: G. Complete poetical works. Houghton $2. (Cambridge ed.)

The only one volume edition complete and latest revisions. Contains also a biographic sketch.

—— Snowbound, Among the hills, Songs of labor and other poems. Houghton, *paper* 15c. *net; cloth* 25c. *net.* (Riverside literature ser. no. 4.)
Wordsworth, William. Complete poetical works. Crowell $1. (Standard lib.)
—— On the intimations of immortality, and other poems. Houghton, *paper* 15c. (Riverside literature ser. no. 76.)

University of the State of New York

A PROPER STANDARD FOR PUBLIC LIBRARIES

The University law of 1892 authorizes the payment of local subsidies to libraries registered by the regents as maintaining a proper library standard, and directs the apportionment of public library money under regents rules.

While the approval of any library must depend on the report of the official inspector, the following statement is issued to direct attention to the points likely to come under review.

Free public libraries to be registered by the University as maintaining a proper standard must meet the following requirements:

1 Each library must be in charge of trustees duly incorporated under state law, or must belong to an institution in the University.

2 The selection of books as a whole must be approved for literary merit and educational value, and as representing in due proportion the different classes of literature and as adapted to the wants of the community.

3 Provision for support must be sufficient for frequent addition of new books as well as to meet other current expenses.

4 The library must be open at a fixed time and in charge of a competent attendant at least one hour on three days of each week; in villages of 2,000 or more inhabitants it must be open at least two hours daily for not less than six days of each week; and in villages or cities of 10,000 or more inhabitants it must be open at least six hours daily.

To be counted as public, a college or academy library must be open at least six hours daily while classes are in session, and in vacation must be open at least one hour on each of three days of each week.

These rules do not require any library to be kept open on legal holidays or Sundays.

In special circumstances connected with starting or reorganizing a library, on approval of the regents, the requirements as to hours of opening may be modified till the library is more firmly established.

5 An accession book must be kept in which shall be recorded the date of accession, the author, title and cost of each book added. There must be besides some suitable catalogue for readers, which may be either an author index, a shelf list or a subject catalogue.

6 Books must be arranged on the shelves by some well considered system that will group subjects by themselves and place books in order in each subject. The character of the classification will depend on the size of the library and local conditions.

7 The loan system in use must provide (a) that every book lent be charged to its borrower, with the date of borrowing; (b) that the circulation of each day be recorded, with a separate statement of the number of volumes of fiction lent.

The above simple rules of business management are deemed essential to the security and usefulness of the books in any public library, and, if carefully observed, will be a guarantee to the public that the libraries are rendering valuable service in return for the aid given.

TRAVELING LIBRARIES

Extension of educational facilities. The regents may cooperate with other agencies in bringing within the reach of the people at large increased educational opportunities and facilities, by stimulating interest, recommending methods, designating suitable teachers and lecturers, lending necessary books and apparatus, conducting examinations and granting credentials and otherwise aiding such work. No money appropriated by the state for this work shall be expended in paying for services or expenses of teachers or lecturers.

Loans of books from the state. Under such rules as the regents may prescribe, they may lend from the state library, duplicate department, or from books specially given or bought for this purpose, selections of books for a limited time to any public library in this state under visitation of the regents, or to any community not yet having established such library, but which has conformed to the conditions required for such loans. (*Laws of* 1892, ch. 378, §1447.)

Under this authority many carefully prepared lists of 50 or 100 fresh and popular books suited to different communities and different classes have been issued. In some a large proportion of standard works is included; others contain only the books of a given year. About 30 per cent are works of fiction, with 10 to 20 per cent each of biography, travel and history Popular science, sociology and general literature are well represented.

The smaller libraries may be combined with selections of 25 or 50 volumes of the best books on special subjects, adapted to the needs of extension centers, study clubs, lecture courses and reading clubs.

Rules for the loan of libraries

1 On satisfactory guarantee that all regents rules will be complied with, a traveling library may be lent to any public library under visitation of the regents on application of its trustees.

2 Under like conditions a traveling library may be lent to a community on application of 25 resident taxpayers or of the officers of an extension center, club, course or circle, if registered by the regents; provided that the applicants also agree that as soon as public interest will warrant such action, they will take steps to establish a free public library as provided in laws of 1892, ch. 378, § 36. The applicants shall name a responsible owner of real estate, to act as trustee of said library and he must become personally responsible for any loss or injury beyond reasonable wear. This trustee shall designate a suitable person to be librarian.

3 A fee of $5 for 100 or $3 for 50 volumes shall be paid in advance for suitable cases, printed catalogues, necessary blanks and records, and transportation both ways. If the right to borrow books is to be limited to members of a center or club, a double fee must be paid; i. e. only 50 volumes for $5 or 25 for $3 will be sent.

4 Such precaution shall be taken in packing as to guard effectively against injury in transportation.

5 Notes, corrections of the press, or marks of any kind on books belonging to the library are unconditionally forbidden Borrowing trustees will be held responsible for all losses or injuries beyond reasonable wear, however caused.

6 The traveling library shall not be kept longer than six months after its reception, except by special permission. It may be exchanged for another on the same terms and these exchanges may continue as long as the regents rules are observed.

7 The librarian shall care for the books while under his control and circulate them in accordance with the regents rules, and shall make such reports respecting their use as the regents may require.

8 For wilful violation of any library rule the director may suspend the privilege of state loans till the case is considered by the regents committee.

Young people's libraries

Selections of the best juvenile literature have been grouped in libraries of 25 volumes each, with annotated finding lists. The fee for one of these libraries alone is $2, but when sent with another library of 50 or 100 volumes the fee for the young people's library is $1.

Annotated lists of libraries will be sent on request, and inquiries for information or advice will be promptly answered if directed to **Public libraries division, University of the State of New York, Albany, N. Y.**

University of the State of New York

Object. The object of the University as defined by law is to encourage and promote education in advance of the common elementary branches. Its field includes not only the work of academies, colleges, universities, professional and technical schools, but also educational work connected with libraries, museums, university extension courses and similar agencies.

The University is a supervisory and administrative, not a teaching institution. It is a state department and at the same time a federation of 655 institutions of higher and secondary education.

Government. The University is governed and all its corporate powers exercised by 19 elective regents and by the governor, lieutenant-governor, secretary of state and superintendent of public instruction who are *ex officio* regents. Regents are elected in the same manner as United States senators; they are unsalaried and are the only public officers in New York chosen for life.

The elective officers are a chancellor and a vice-chancellor, who serve without salary, and a secretary. The secretary is the executive and financial officer, is under official bonds for $10,000, is responsible for the safe keeping and proper use of the University seal and of the books, records and other property in charge of the regents, and for the proper administration and discipline of its various offices and departments.

Powers and duties. Besides many other important powers and duties, the regents have power to incorporate, and to alter or revoke the charters of universities, colleges, academies, libraries, museums, or other educational institutions; to distribute to them funds granted by the state for their use; to inspect their workings and require annual reports under oath of their presiding officers, to establish examinations as to attainments in learning and confer on successful candidates suitable certificates, diplomas and degrees, and to confer honorary degrees

They apportion annually an academic fund of $106,000, part for buying books and apparatus for academies and high schools raising an equal amount for the same purpose, and the remainder on the basis of attendance and the results of instruction as shown by satisfactory completion of prescribed courses for which the regents examinations afford the official test. Each school of academic grade also receives $100 yearly. The regents also expend annually $25,000 for the benefit of free public libraries.

Regents meetings. Regular meetings are held on the third Thursdays of October, December and March, and in June during convocation week. The executive committee, consisting of the chancellor, vice-chancellor and the chairmen of the six standing committees, meets the third Thursday of each month from October to June.

Convocation. The University convocation of the regents and the officers of institutions in the University, for consideration of subjects of mutual interest, has been held annually since 1863 in the senate chamber in Albany. It meets the last Wednesday, Thursday and Friday of June.

Though primarily a New York meeting, nearly all questions discussed are of equal interest outside the state. Its reputation as the most important higher educational meeting of the country has in the past few years drawn to it many eminent educators not residents of New York, who are most cordially welcomed and share fully in all discussions. It elects each year a council of five to represent it in intervals between meetings. Its proceedings, issued annually, are of great value in all educational libraries.

University of the State of New York

Departments

1 Administrative (Regents office) — including incorporation, supervision, inspection, reports, legislation, finances and all other work not assigned to another department.

Duplicate division This is a state clearing house, to which any institution in the University may send books or apparatus which it no longer requires, and select from it in return an equal value suited to its locality and needs.

2 Examination—including preacademic, law student, medical, dental and veterinary student, academic, higher, law, medical, dental, veterinary, library, extension and any other examinations conducted by the regents, and also credentials or degrees conferred on examination

The examinations are conducted as the best lever for securing better work from teachers and more systematic and continuous study from students, and as the best means of detecting and eliminating inefficient teachers or methods They cover 130 subjects and require 1,500,000 question papers annually, and are held the week ending the last Friday in January and March and the third Friday in June, in the 552 academies and high schools in the University and also at various central points where there are 10 or more candidates.

3 Extension—including summer, vacation, evening and correspondence schools and other forms of extension teaching, lecture courses, study clubs, reading circles and other agencies for the promotion and wider extension of opportunities and facilities for education, specially for those unable to attend the usual teaching institutions.

Public libraries division. To promote the general library interests of the state, which through it apportions and expends $25,000 a year for the benefit of free public libraries. Under its charge are the traveling libraries for lending to local libraries or to communities not yet having permanent libraries

The most important factor of the extension movement is provision of the best reading for all citizens by means of traveling, home and capitol libraries and annotated lists through the public libraries division.

4 State library—including general, law, medical, and education libraries, library school, bibliographic publications, lending books to students and similar library interests.

Library school. The law authorizes the state library to give instruction and assistance in organizing and administering libraries. Students receive from the state library staff, in return for services rendered to the library during their two years' course, careful training in library economy, bibliography, cataloguing, classification and other duties of professional librarianship.

5 State museum—including all scientific specimens and collections, works of art, objects of historic interest and similar property appropriate to a general museum, if owned by the state and not placed in other custody by a specific law; also the research department carried on by the state geologist and paleontologist, botanist and entomologist, and all similar scientific interests of the University.

STATISTICS OF NEW Y

	PAGE
Public libraries division	
Inspection	171
Libraries visited during year..,	172
Organization of new libraries	176
Libraries chartered during year	176
Library transfers during year	178
Change of name	178
Chartered libraries	178
Library trustees	179
Libraries admitted to the University	180
Growth of free libraries in the University	180
Registered libraries	182
Libraries under state supervision	185
Apportionment of public library money	185
Traveling libraries	188
Application blanks	189
Directions and rules	193
Volumes	196
Lost books	197
Additions	198
Sales	199
Use	199
Agriculture libraries	200
Traveling libraries sent Oct. 1, 1894– Sept. 30, 1895	201
Capitol library	206
Extension library	207
General library interests	210
Local library subsidies	210
Library council of the University	210
Library legislation	211
Library legislation in other states	212
N. Y. library ass'n and N. Y. lib. club	213
Lists of books of the year	214
New York library club	215

Publi
Am
Stati
Stat
Su
Dat
Inc
Gro
Geo

Con

The
Fre
Fre
Coll
Lav
Lib
Lib
Gift
Arr
Loa
Mis
Table
Sur
G
Li
Li

Li

C
L
Li
Inde

Regents

Anson Judd Upson, D. D., LL. D., L. H. D., *Chancellor*
William Croswell Doane, D. D., LL. D., *Vice-Chancellor*
Levi P. Morton, LL. D., Governor
Charles T. Saxton, LL. D., Lieutenant-Governor
John Palmer, Secretary of State
Charles R. Skinner, M. A., LL. D., Sup't Pub. Inst'n
} *Ex officio*

In order of election by the legislature

ELECTED
1873 Martin I. Townsend, M. A., LL. D. — Troy
1874 Anson Judd Upson, D. D., LL. D., L. H. D. — Glens Falls
1877 Chauncey M. Depew, LL. D. — New York
1877 Charles E. Fitch, LL. B., M. A., L. H. D. — Rochester
1877 Orris H. Warren, D. D. — Syracuse
1878 Whitelaw Reid, LL. D. — New York
1881 William H. Watson, M. A., M. D. — Utica
1881 Henry E. Turner — Lowville
1883 St Clair McKelway, LL. D. — Brooklyn
1885 Hamilton Harris, Ph. D., LL. D. — Albany
1885 Daniel Beach, Ph. D., LL. D. — Watkins
1888 Carroll E. Smith, LL. D. — Syracuse
1890 Pliny T. Sexton, LL. D. — Palmyra
1890 T. Guilford Smith, M. A., C. E. — Buffalo
1892 William Croswell Doane, D. D., LL. D. — Albany
1893 Lewis A. Stimson, B. A., M. D. — New York
1894 Sylvester Malone — Brooklyn
1895 Albert Vander Veer, M. D., Ph. D. — Albany
One vacancy

Elected by the regents
1888 Melvil Dewey, M. A., *Secretary* — Albany

University of the State of New York

Extension Bulletin

No. 16　October 1896

REPORT OF PUBLIC LIBRARIES DIVISION, 1895

To the regents of the University of the State of New York

I have the honor to report as follows for the year ending September 30, 1895.

Inspection. From Oct. 1, 1894 to Sept. 30, 1895 the inspector, William R. Eastman visited 115 libraries in 37 different counties. Thirty five of these libraries were not at the time connected with the University. The number of communities considering the possibility of enlarged library facilities is rapidly increasing. New institutions are less numerous than old ones putting on new life. Many of these are school district libraries asking for information respecting methods of transfer and reorganization entitling them to state aid. Some are subscription libraries desiring to become free if means of support can be found. Others are large well established libraries used both for circulation and reference and already free, but wishing to be registered as maintaining a proper library standard in order to meet the provisions of the law governing the payment of local subsidies as well as to obtain a share of public library money from the state. It is not possible to understand the local conditions and to offer the best advice without examination of the library and personal conference with those interested. These official visits, sometimes giving opportunity for public addresses, not only supply information for the guidance of the regents in giving required certificates, but serve to convey to the people visited information regarding the law and the experience of other communities. They present the best opportunity to suggest improved library methods and to stimulate and direct a new library interest in every place reached.

Some of the results of this personal work extending to all parts of the state may be traced in the tables of libraries transferred, chartered, admitted to the University and registered.

114 libraries are now under official inspection, an increase of 52 during the year.

The following libraries were visited:

Libraries visited during the year ending September 30, 1895

1 Albany, Catholic union lib.
2 Albany, Y. W. C. A. lib.
3 Alfred Center, Alfred uni. library
4 Amsterdam, lib. association
5 Arkport public library
6 *Attica, Stevens library
7 Auburn high school library
8 Auburn theological seminary library
9 Batavia, Richmond library
10 Bath Beach, New Utrecht free library
11 Binghamton high school library
12 Binghamton school library
13 *Buffalo, Catholic institute library
14 Buffalo, Grosvenor library
15 Buffalo, Historical society library
16 Buffalo library
17 *Buffalo, Otowega club lib.
18 *Buffalo, Society of natural sciences library
19 *Buffalo, University club library
20 Buffalo, University of, medical library
21 Buffalo, Women's educ. and indust. union library
22 Buffalo, Y. M. C. A. library
23 Cambridge union school library
24 Cattaraugus union school library
25 Chittenango union school library
26 Clinton, Hamilton college library
27 Cornwall-on-Hudson public library
28 Crown Point, Chapel lib.
29 Crown Point union school library
30 Dryden, Southworth library
31 Dunkirk academy library
32 *Dunkirk library association
33 Easton library
34 *Elmira, Park church library

a Not connected with the University.

35 ᵃElmira, State reformatory library
36 Flushing high school lib.
37 ᵃFlushing public library
38 Fort Edward collegiate institute library
39 Fredonia, D. R. Barker library association
40 ᵃFredonia, Normal school library
41 Glen Cove public library
42 Glen Haven public library
43 Gloversville free library
44 Hornellsville, Hornell free library
45 ᵃHuntington lib. association
46 Huntington union school library
47 ᵃIthaca, Cornell library ass'n
48 Ithaca, Cornell university library
49 Jamestown, Y. M. C. A. lib.
50 Joshua's Rock, Mountainside free library
51 Lake George free library
52 Marathon school library
53 ᵃMt Vernon school library dist. no. 1
54 Nanuet public library
55 New York, Aguilar free library, 197 E. Broadway
56 New York, Aguilar free library, 721 Lexington av.
57 ᵃNew York, American society of civil engineers' lib.
58 ᵃNew York, Boys' reading room
59 ᵃBroome street free library
60 ᵃNew York, Cathedral free library
61 ᵃNew York, College settlement library
62 New York free circulating library, Bond st. branch
63 New York free cir. lib. George Bruce mem. br.
64 New York free circulating library, Harlem branch
65 New York free circulating lib. Muhlenberg branch
66 New York free circulating lib. Ottendorfer branch
67 ᵃNew York, Harlem library
68 New York, Mechanical engineers' library
69 ᵃNew York, University settlement library
70 Newfield library
71 Newfield union school lib.
72 Niagara Falls public library
73 Niagara Falls, Suspension Bridge union school lib.
74 North Parma public library
75 ᵃNorwich circulating library
76 ᵃOlean, Forman library
77 Olean high school library
78 Oneonta public library
79 ᵃOswego city library
80 Oswego, Normal school lib.
81 ᵃOswego school library
82 Owego free library
83 Oyster Bay people's library
84 Palatine Bridge union school library

a Not connected with the University.

85 Penn Yan academy library
86 Pine Plains public library
87 Poplar Ridge, Hazard lib.
88 Randolph, Chamberlain institute library
89 ᵃRandolph, Children's Home library
90 ᵃRandolph union school lib.
91 ᵃRoslyn, Bryant circulating library
92 ᵃSalem, Bancroft public lib.
93 Salem, Washington acad. lib.
94 Sandy Hill union school lib.
95 Schenectady, Union college library
96 Schenectady union school library
97 ᵃSchenectady, Y. M. C. A. library
98 ᵃSchenectady, Y. W. C. A. library
99 Sea Cliff free library
100 ᵃSherwood library
101 ᵃShortsville, M. M. Buck library
102 ᵃSinclairville, Ladies' library
103 Sinclairville library
104 Sinclairville union school library
105 ᵃSkaneateles lib. association
106 Syracuse central library
107 Syracuse, Court of appeals library
108 Tarrytown, Young men's lyceum library
109 Trumansburg public lib.
110 ᵃWarrensburg library
111 Warrensburg union school library
112 Waterford public library
113 Waterville public library
114 Waverly union school lib.
115 West Winfield union school library

The following form is used for inspector's memoranda:

Report on

by
          library
          inspector

Year founded
Ownership or control
Support
Terms of use
Librarian
  salary
    assistants
      salaries

Building
  location
  material
  size
  owned by
  value $
Rooms
  number   size

ᵃ Not connected with the University.

story
access
light
heat
cases
shelves
arrangement
provision for growth
decoration
museum
Reading room
location
size
furniture
no. of serials
  daily
  weekly
  monthly
  quarterly
readers
Book
added last year
whole no. vols.
condition
total value
circulation last year

Class of books
  estimated vols.
  general   fine arts
  philosophy literature
  religion   fiction
  sociology   history
  philology   travel
  science   biography
  useful arts gov't docs.
      unbound
System of classification
  location of books
    fixed
    relative
Catalogue
  accession book
  shelf list
  card
  printed
Loan system
  ledger
  card
Borrowers
  no. last year
  class

.... library is open to the public
      for lending   . for reference
on Monday from   to   from   to
   Tuesday
   Wednesday
   Thursday
   Friday
   Saturday
   Sunday

Organization of new libraries. Nine absolute and 14 provisional charters were granted by the regents, involving the transfer of 16,971 volumes contained in 17 existing libraries, of which 15 belonged to school districts. In six cases there was no previously existing library. One charter was based on the transfer to a new organization of a library chartered the preceding year and one district library containing 2822 volumes was transferred to a public library chartered two years earlier. Nine libraries and one institute already incorporated under general laws were admitted to the University. 20 libraries were registered by the University as maintaining a proper standard and entitled to state aid and local subsidies. The tables which follow show the location, name, number of volumes and property of each library chartered, admitted or registered during the year. There is also a table of transfers.

Libraries and institutes chartered, admitted and registered during the year ending September 30, 1895

Chartered

	Post-office	Libraries	Vols.	Property
1	Allen's Hill	Allen's Hill free library ass'n p	255	$155
2	Bath Beach	New Utrecht free library	800	1584
3	Cornwall	Cornwall public library p	350	260
4	Cornwall-on-Hudson	Cornwall-on-Hudson public library p	811	440
5	Crown Point	Crown Point chapel library p	780	562
6	Glen Cove	Glen Cove public library p	938	450
7	Lake George	Lake George free library p	343	428
8	Lake Placid	Lake Placid public library	1200	1900
9	Nanuet	Nanuet public library p	684	383
10	Newfield	Newfield public library p	350	347
11	Niagara Falls	Niagara Falls public library	3500	2420
12	Oyster Bay	Oyster Bay people's library p	325	600
13	Pine Plains	Pine Plains free library	1800	1124
14	Schenectady	Schenectady free pub. lib. ass'n	3000	1986
15	Schuylerville	Schuylerville public library p	379	376
16	Sea Cliff	Sea Cliff public library p	....	435
17	Sidney	Sidney public library	1139	1054
18	Sinclairville	Sinclairville free library	1337	1025
19	Springfield	Springfield free library p	....	85
20	Troy	Troy children's neighb'rhood lib. p	418	507
21	Waterford	Waterford public library	2158	2030
22	Waterville	Waterville public library	1475	....
23	West Winfield	West Winfield free library p	1100	668
		Total	23,142	$18,769

p Provisional charter.

Libraries and institutes chartered, etc. (*continued*)

Admitted with existing charters

	Post-office	Libraries	Vols	Property
1	Amsterdam...	Amsterdam library ass'n.........	2140	$3682
2	Dryden.......	Southworth library ass'n.........	5365	41000
3	Easton.......	Easton library ass'n.............	490	464
4	Elizabethtown	Elizabethtown library ass'n......	1378	1650
5	Gilbertsville ..	Gilbertsville free library.........	907	9608
6	Marathon. ...	Peck memorial library ass'n......	....	6200
7	Pocantico Hills	Pocantico Hills lyceum...........	734	885
8	Poplar Ridge..	Hazard library ass'n.............	800	1825
9	Rome.........	Jervis library ass'n..............	2500	41324
10	Troy..........	Young women's ass'n of the city of Troy.....................	880	67500
		Total......................	15,194	$174,138

Registered

	Post-office	Libraries	Vols	Property
1	Albany........	Catholic union library............	1335	$2650
2	Albany........	Y. W. C. A. library of Albany....	1385	16760
3	Alfred Center .	Alfred university library.........	9232	48161.63
4	Buffalo........	Buffalo historical society library..	8000	50000
5	Buffalo......:	Buffalo library	76000	350019
6	Buffalo........	Univ. of Buffalo med dep't lib....	4948	2500
7	Buffalo........	Women's educational and industrial union library.............	584	800
8	Buffalo........	Y. M C A library of Buffalo....	6222	8839.95
9	Clinton.......	Hamilton college library..........	32860	76000
10	Fredonia	Darwin R Barker library ass'n...	4808	4000
11	Gloversville...	Gloversville free library...........	12695	30442.34
12	Jamestown....	Y M C. A. library of Jamestown	1270	7640
13	New York.....	Mechanical engineers lib. ass'n...	3500	73600
14	New York.....	N. Y free circ library............	76800	387990.33
15	New York.....	Webster free lib of East side house	4000	25542.01
16	Oswego.	Teachers library of state normal and training school.............	1200	1370
17	Randolph	Chamberlain inst. Helen Culver library	1238	3022.97
18	Rome.........	Y M. C. A library of Rome	1600	1585
19	Tarrytown ...	Young men's lyceum library of Tarrytown	3000	1115
20	Waverly.......	Waverly high school library......	1599	2336.50
		Total......................	252,276	$1,094,374.73
	Grand total	....	290,612	$1,287,281.73

Library transfers approved during the year ending September 30, 1895

	From	To	Vols
1	School dist 1, Hornellsville	Arkport public library	70
2	Bd of educ'n dist. 5, Cornwall	Cornwall public library	350
3	Bd of educ'n. dist. 4, Cornwall	Cornwall-on-Hudson pub. lib.	811
4	Bd. of educ'n dist. 1, Queensbury	Craudall free library	2822
5	Bd. of educ'n. dist. 3, Crown Point	Crown Point chapel library	43
6	Bd. of educ'n. dist. 5, Oyster Bay	Glen Cove public library	938
7	Board of educ'n., Rome	Jervis library association	
8	Lake Placid public library	Lake Placid public library	1300
9	Bd. of educ'n., Marathon	Marathon, Peck memorial lib.	225
10	Trustees sch dist. 8, Clarkstown and Orangetown	Nanuet public library	684
11	Bd of educ'n., Niagara Falls	Niagara Falls public library	3500
12	Bd. of educ'n, Schenectady	Schenectady free pub. lib. ass'n	2708
13	Bd. of educ'n., Schuylerville	Schuylerville public library	379
14	Bd. of educ'n., Sidney	Sidney public library	1137
15	First Unitarian church of Troy	Troy children's neighborh'd lib.	418
16	Bd of educ'n. dist. 1, Waterford	Waterford public library	2158
17	Bd of educ'n., Waterville	Waterville public library	1150
18	Bd. of educ'n., West Winfield	West Winfield free library	1100
		Total	19,793

Name changed. The name of the Ogden Memorial library in Walton, Delaware county, incorporated March 12, 1894, under laws of 1875, ch. 343, was, on unanimous request of its trustees, changed by vote of the regents June 26, 1895, to Wm. B. Ogden free library.

Chartered libraries. The following tables show by whom the chartered libraries of the University have been established in each of the five years and the source of election of their trustees. They indicate that more of these libraries owe both their establishment and control to the school authorities than to any other one source. Considering the district library system of the state, and the interest of school districts in the public library as the means of a broader education, this was to be expected. The influence of library associations is also evident, as well as a tendency among library trustees to keep the control as far as possible in their own hands. Many of these associations now seeking charters are opening freely to the public privileges formerly limited to subscribers.

Founding of chartered libraries for years ending September 30

Established by	1891	1892	1893	1894	1895	Total
School authorities	....	....	15	10	9	34
School districts	....	1	2	3	3	9
Village trustees	....	....	2	3	....	5
Town	....	....	....	....	1	1
Common councils	....	....	1	2	....	3
Library associations	1	....	4	4	4	13
Other associations	....	....	....	....	2	2
Public meetings	....	....	....	1	1	2
Churches	....	....	....	1	2	3
Private gifts	....	....	1	1	1	3
Total	1	1	25	25	23	75

Control of chartered libraries for years ending September 30

Trustees chosen by	1891	1892	1893	1894	1895	Total
Board of education	....	....	5	8	9	22
School trustees	....	....	....	....	1	1
School district	....	1	12	4	2	19
Village trustees	....	....	....	2	....	2
Village voters	....	....	2	....	....	2
Town	....	....	....	....	1	1
Mayor with consent of council	....	....	....	2	....	2
Library trustees	....	....	4	6	7	17
Library association	1	....	....	....	2	3
Other association	....	....	....	....	1	1
Other library	....	....	....	1	....	1
Contributors of $1 each	....	....	1	2	....	3
Individual benefactor	....	....	1	....	....	1
Total	1	1	25	25	23	75

Library trustees. In four cases ex officio trustees, as the mayor of a city, president of a school board, school superintendent and principal have been added to those appointed as above. In one case a library board includes three trustees elected by the district and two by the board of education.

The number of trustees varies greatly but the tendency is strong toward five as the best number. Among the 75 chartered libraries

 20 have 3 trustees each
 34 " 5 "
 4 " 6 "
 8 " 7 "
 1 has 8
 3 have 9

2 have 10 trustees each
1 has 12   "
1 " 13   "
1 " 17

Libraries admitted. Since the legislation of 1892, 18 incorporated libraries have been admitted to the University. Two of these the Woman's institute in Yonkers, and the Young women's association of Troy carry on so extended a work as to be properly called institutes. With classes, lectures and other educational features added to their other library work they are centers of the best influence among the self supporting women in their communities for whom they are specially planned. The property of the admitted institutions reaches a total of $746,000.

Growth of free libraries in the University. In the statistics for 1894 a table was given showing one year's growth in volumes and circulation of 28 libraries admitted to the University during the year ending September 30, 1893. The same table is here repeated with the growth added to September 30, 1895. These show a continued advance, though not at the same rapid rate as in the first year. In a few instances there was an actual decrease of circulation, but for most the increase is large, and in the aggregate the forward movement is decided. With 69,289 volumes in 1893 there was a gain of 10,625 in 1894 and of 10,644 in 1895, reaching a total of 90,558 volumes. With a circulation of 192,899 in 1893, there was a gain of 99,000 in 1894 and a further advance of 65,387 in 1895, bringing the total for these 28 libraries up to 357,289, an average circulation of 394 for each 100 volumes. The Albany free library advanced from 2300 circulation in 1894 to 6356 in 1895; Addison public library from 2438 to 5614; Belmont free library from 621 to 3371; New Rochelle public library from 3543 to 10,018; Trumansburg public library from 500 to 2340; Utica public library from 55,122 to 82,421.

Another table is given to show one year's growth of 32 libraries admitted during the year ending September 30, 1894. The increase in volumes was 15,107, in circulation 65,068. As in the first table, some libraries show a falling off of circulation, partly accounted for by the delays and inconvenience attending plans of reorganization, but the aggregate increase is large. In instances where there was no library the first year, circulations varying from 450 to 5620 are reported.

These results indicate clearly the tendency and value of the library work of the University, of which there is also abundant evidence in our correspondence. Trustees of subscription libraries made free to the public on the advice of this office have again and again expressed their astonishment and delight at the eagerness of the people to avail themselves of free library privileges.

Two years' growth of free libraries admitted to the University in year ending September 30, 1893

No.	LIBRARY	1893 Vols	1893 Circ'n	1894 Vols	1894 Circ'n	1895 Vols	1895 Circ'n
1	Addison public library	2,085	....	1,750	2,488	1,959	5,614
2	Albany free library	1,523	1,429	1,914	2,325	2,634	6,856
3	Albion public library	2,600	3,048	2,950	9,550	2,950	11,142
4	Ballston public library	375	550	856	3,244	888	6,653
5	Bay Ridge free library	2,400	7,200	2,976	9,177	3,490	12,226
6	Belmont City his soc free lib	785	720	971	621	1,368	3,871
7	Canaan public library	496	....	?513	?1,000	?555	?1,900
8	Catskill public library	1,114	825	1,291	9,830	1,074	13,718
9	Crandall free lib. (Glens Falls)	4,729	36,483	5,891	45,058	6,015	38,529
10	East Chatham public library	300	781	460	1,114	632	1,151
11	Ellenville public library	584	..	1,525	12,561	1,006	16,292
12	Green Wood pub lib (Westbury)	180	160	197	808	217	197
13	Hornell free lib (Hornellsville)	10,000	24,000	?10,000	27,085	?10,000	30,391
14	Jordanville pub lib	495	115	545	2,010	609	2,189
15	Liverpool public library	601	540	601	1,540	719	2,991
16	Lockport public library	4,956	?1,950	5,126	16,000	5,330	15,871
17	Mellenville public library	338	500	338	?820	338	266
18	Nassau free library	500	300	425	1,650	478	3,612
19	New Rochelle public library	2,105	.	1,888	3,548	2,714	10,018
20	N Greenbush dist no 6 pub lib	?90?	1,497	1,068	8,629	1,259	5,079
21	N Parma public library	301	1,054	409	1,000	643	2,787
22	Oneonta public library	2,941	15,096	3,676	16,877	4,345	19,869
23	Port Jervis free library	4,803	6,555	5,217	9,836	6,124	13,578
24	Sing Sing public library	3,218	9,207	3,283	11,896	3,537	13,716
25	Trumansburg public lib	....	....	694	500	?804	2,840
26	Utica public library	10,000	49,706	13,863	55,122	17,936	82,421
27	Westport library ass'n	1,425	375	1,408	4,795	1,426	5,590
28	Yonkers public library	9,830	31,426	10,164	33,378	10,408	31,192
	Total	69,289	192,899	79,914 69,289	291,902 192,899	90,558 79,914	357,289 291,902
	Increase for one year	.	......	10,625	99,003	10,644	65,387

One year's growth of free libraries admitted to the University in year ending September 30, 1894

No.	LIBRARY	1894 Vols.	1894 Circ'n	1895 Vols.	1895 Circ'n
1	Arkport public library	......	......	500	450
2	Claverack free library and reading room	910	700	1,000	1,500
3	Dansville public library	2,292	5,445	2,550	8,085
4	Erwin library and institute (Boonville)	2,205	5,946	2,496	6,231
5	Fort Hamilton free library	1,407	4,100	2,123	4,500
6	Fort Plain free library	965	3,262	1,023	5,627
7	Glen Haven public library	......	......	560	899
8	Grosvenor public library (Buffalo)	35,933	a	†39,000	a
9	Havana free library	547	3,693	629	4,548
10	Ilion district library	812	3,588	963	4,710
11	James Prendergast library ass'n (Jamestown)	9,112	39,867	10,045	49,194
12	Keene Valley public library	......	......	870	1,381
13	Lake Placid public library	......	......	1,103	2,818
14	Liberty public library	900	......	1,027	2,299
15	Mohawk public library	704	2,359	815	1,885
16	Morristown free library	100	41	310	1,833
17	Mountainside free library (Joshua's Rock)	......	......	337	†1,500
18	North Tonawanda public library	1,429	†6,000	1,825	5,293
19	Nyack library	3,100	18,194	3,372	;9,066
20	Ogdensburg public library	4,499	6,097	5,005	14,289
21	Philmont public library	621	2,366	810	2,903
22	Plattsburg public library	......	......	492	5,620
23	Rockville Center public library	445	55	†1,425	4,325
24	St Agnes free library (New York)	1,040	†1,067	1,832	9,225
25	Saugerties public library	†1,000	†	1,492	6,009
26	Sherman free library (Port Henry)	4,109	10,283	4,414	8,835
27	Springville public library	2,500	......	1,634	6,820
28	Syracuse central library	25,500	50,659	26,300	44,585
29	Tivoli public library (Madalin)	......	......	426	2,258
30	Tonawanda public library	1,213	1,391	1,350	1,587
31	Wellsville public library	1,084	......	1,425	†3,357
32	Woman's institute of Yonkers	2,000	6,958	2,381	5,497
	Total	104,427	172,061	119,534 / 104,427	237,129 / 172,061
	Increase	......	......	15,107	65,068

a Reference library

Registered libraries. 20 of the 21 registered libraries have been enrolled during the year. The following extract from the official minutes shows action of the regents taken June 5, 1894.

Registry of libraries. A number of libraries in the state wish to obtain local subsidies, loan libraries and public library money under the provisions of § 37, 47 and 50 of the University law but are not prepared to ask for regents charters or admission to the University. Many of these libraries are maintained in con-

nection with literary, benevolent and other corporations that do not consider a separate library organization desirable.
The conditions of the law can be met and its benefits much more widely extended by a system of inspection and registry.
It was therefore

Voted, That the regents authorize the inspection of any such library on application of its governing body, and the granting of a certificate of registry on the following terms.

[*Conditions of registry*]

Any free public library in the state of New York incorporated under a special or general law, or belonging to or controlled by any institution so incorporated, may apply to the regents of the University to be registered as maintaining a proper library standard. If approved, after official inspection, it will be so registered and a certificate given under the University seal.

The library will thereafter be subject to regents visitation and entitled to grants from public library money, to local subsidies and to the use of traveling libraries under the provisions of laws of 1892, chap. 378, § 37, 47 and 50.

[*Form*]

CERTIFICATE OF REGISTRY OF

....

Whereas application for registry of the library by the University has been received from the present trustees, namely

and

Whereas official inspection shows that they are incorporated under the laws of New York, that suitable provision has been made for rooms, furniture, books, equipment, proper maintenance and free use of the library by the public, and that all other prescribed requirements have been fully met:

Therefore, being satisfied that public interests will be promoted thereby, the regents by virtue of the authority conferred on them by law hereby register

library as maintaining a proper standard and entitled to all the privilege accorded by the regents to registered public libraries under laws of 1892, ch. 378, § 37, 47 and 50, so long as such standard shall be maintained. If, at any time, the library shall fall below the required standard and deficiencies are not remedied within 60 days after written notice from the regents, these privileges shall be withdrawn, all books received from the University shall be returned if the regents so require, this certificate shall be surrendered, and the name of the library removed from the register.

In witness whereof the regents grant under seal of the University this certificate registered as no.

The repeal of former subsidy laws, added to the wish to obtain state aid without resorting to any change of organization has called attention to these provisions for registry.

To answer numerous inquiries regarding the library standard required by the regents the following statement was issued. It is significant of the fairness with which the public libraries division represents the best library opinion and experience that this statement when brought up at an annual meeting received the unanimous indorsement of the New York library association.

A PROPER STANDARD FOR PUBLIC LIBRARIES

The University law of 1892 authorizes the payment of local subsidies to libraries registered by the regents as maintaining a proper library standard, and directs the apportionment of public library money under regents rules.

While the approval of any library must depend on the report of the official inspector, the following statement is issued to direct attention to the points likely to come under review.

Free public libraries to be registered by the University as maintaining a proper standard must meet the following requirements.

1 Each library must be in charge of trustees duly incorporated under state law, or must belong to an institution in the University.

2 The selection of books as a whole must be approved for literary merit and educational value, and as representing in due proportion the different classes of literature and as adapted to the wants of the community.

3 Provision for support must be sufficient for frequent additions of new books as well as to meet other current expenses.

4 The library must be open at a fixed time and in charge of a competent attendant at least one hour on three days of each week; in villages of 2,000 or more inhabitants it must be open at least two hours daily for not less than six days of each week; and in villages or cities of 10,000 or more inhabitants it must be open at least six hours daily.

To be counted as public, a college or academy library must be open at least six hours daily while classes are in session, and in vacation must be open at least one hour on each of three days of each week.

These rules do not require any library to be kept open on legal holidays or Sundays.

In special circumstances connected with starting or reorganizing a library, on approval of the regents, the requirements as to hours of opening may be modified till the library is more firmly established.

5 An accession book must be kept in which shall be recorded the date of accession, the author, title and cost of each book added. There must be besides some suitable catalogue for readers, which may be either an author index, a shelf list or a subject catalogue.

6 Books must be arranged on the shelves by some well considered system that will group subjects by themselves and place books in order in each subject. The character of the classification will depend on the size of the library and local conditions.

7 The loan system in use must provide (*a*) that every book lent be charged to its borrower, with date of borrowing; (*b*) that the circulation of each day·be recorded, with a separate statement of the number of volumes of fiction lent.

The above simple rules of business management are deemed essential to the security and usefulness of the books in any public library, and, if carefully observed,·will be a guarantee to the public that the libraries are rendering valuable service in return for the aid given.

MELVIL DEWEY
Director

Albany, N. Y. 15 October 1894

The list of 21 registered libraries includes some of the largest and most important circulating libraries in the state, such as the New York free circulating libraries, the Buffalo library and the Gloversville free library. They contain in all 274,000 volumes and the property held by them amounts to more than a million dollars.

Some of these libraries are free for reference only and some are technical libraries dealing with special subjects such as history, medicine, engineering and pedagogy. Whenever they were found on official inspection to be well arranged and administered and rendering valuable service to the public without charge their request for registry was granted.

Registered libraries not being members of the University are not entitled to all the privileges accorded to those that are under regents supervision.

Libraries under state supervision. The number of approved libraries now under state supervision is as follows:

Chartered 75
Admitted 18

Total 93

425 other reporting libraries connected with schools, academies and colleges in the University are also under regents supervision.

Apportionment of public library money. 10 apportionments were made during the year; in the months of October, November and December 1894, January, March, April, May, June, July and September, 1895. 107 applications were received and 105 granted for the benefit of 86 libraries. In two cases $50 was given in books.

The sums varied from $15 to $734 and the aggregate was $14,-449.03 as against $10,551.9⅄ and $6,341.74 for the two preceding years. This shows a steady increase in the demand for this form of state aid and in the number of libraries conforming to required conditions. The average was $168.01 to each library as compared with $167 and $158.50 for the two last years. In this apportionment a distinction is made between reference and circulating libraries in accordance with the following vote of the regents June 26, 1895:

Reference vs circulating library apportionments. Several libraries free for reference only have applied for public library money. They render valuable service to the public and are entitled to recognition as free libraries; but their service is not the same as that of libraries free for circulation, and therefore they can not justly receive an equal share of state aid.

Voted, That libraries open to the public for reference only, if approved on official inspection and duly registered, may receive grants of public money as free libraries, under the rules, to the amount of one half the sum raised from local sources for the same purpose.

The influence of the state bounty in raising the standard of library work is evident. In official visitation of libraries, attention is constantly called to the need of careful selection and systematic arrangement of books and effective loan systems with accurate records and accounts in every department. The value of business management is always conceded by the libraries. But when the grant of public money depends on official approval of the library in these respects an additional motive of the most practical importance is supplied. The librarian is at once roused to new effort to establish the rank of his library. New books are chosen not merely to meet the varying tastes of constituencies, but also to merit the approval of the regents. Administration becomes a study and trustees and voters are more than ever ready to supply needed facilities. Money is given by individuals and taxes are voted because the state stands ready to double the amount up to $200 a year. Results have shown that the liberality of the state is fully justified by the new interest thereby excited in library work and the improved quality of the work done. The interest of the state, which is proved by its gifts, also serves constantly to remind the people of the high educational value of the free library as a public institution, taking its true place as the necessary complement of the public school.

Public library money apportioned during the year ending September 30, 1895

1 Addison public library..	$150 00	33 Gloversville free library.	$200 00
2 Albany, Cath. union lib.	150 00	34 Hornellsville, Hornell library association.......	200 00
3 Albany free library......	200 00		
4 Albany, Y. W. C. A. lib..	77 72	35 Ilion district library.....	200 00
5 Alfred Center, Alfred university library	200 00	36 Jamestown, James Prendergast library ass'n....	200 00
6 Allen's Hill free library (In books).............	50 00	37 Jamestown, Y.M.C.A. lib.	200 00
		38 Joshua's Rock, Mountainside free library........	150 00
7 Amsterdam library ass'n.	200 00	39 Keene Valley public lib.	80 00
8 Bath Beach, New Utrecht free library............	200 00	40 Lake George free library	125 00
		41 Liberty public library ..	55 00
9 Bath-on-Hudson, North Greenbush dist. no. 6 public library..........	73 00	42 Lockport public library.	135 00
		43 Madalin, Tivoli pub. lib.	72 38
10 Bay Ridge free library..	200 00	44 Morristown public lib....	60 00
11 Belmont literary and historical society free lib..	160 00	45 Nanuet public library....	65 00
		46 New Rochelle pub. lib...	200 00
12 Boonville, Erwin library and institute............	200 00	47 New York Bryson library, Teachers college	200 00
13 Buffalo historical soc lib.	200 00	48 New York, Mechanical engineers lib. ass'n.....	100 00
14 Buffalo library..........	100 00		
15 Buffalo, Women's educati'nal and ind'str'l union	200 00	49 New York, Y. W. C. A. lib	200 00
		50 Newfield public library..	100 00
16 Buffalo Y. M. C. A. lib...	200 00	51 Niagara Falls pub. lib...	200 00
17 Catskill public library..	200 00	52 North Parma public lib.	125 00
18 Claverack free library & reading room associat'n	57 85	53 N. Tonawanda pub. lib..	200 00
		54 Ogdensburg public lib...	200 00
19 Clinton, Hamilton col. lib.	200 00	55 Oneonta public library ..	200 00
20 Cornwall public library ($50 in books)..........	75 00	56 Oswego, State normal school library..........	100 00
21 Crown Point chapel lib..	200 00	57 Oyster Bay, People's lib.	350 00
22 Dansville public library.	125 00	58 Philmont public library.	91 45
23 East Chatham pub. lib..	96 00	59 Pine Plains free library..	187 00
24 Easton public library...	200 00	60 Plattsburg public lib....	200 00
25 Elizabethtown lib. ass'n.	200 00	61 Poplar Ridge, Hazard lib.	200 00
26 Ellenville public library.	50 00	62 Port Henry, Sherman free library..................	200 00
27 Fort Hamilton free lib..	300 00		
28 Fort Plain free library...	25 00	63 Port Jervis free library..	200 00
29 Fredonia, D. R. Barker free library	100 00	64 Randolph, Chamberlain inst. library............	200 00
30 Gilbertsville free library.	200 00	65 Rockville Center public library.................	200 00
31 Glen Cove public library	200 00		
32 Glens Falls, Crandall free library................	200 00	66 Rome, Y. M. C. A. lib....	82 00
		67 Saugerties public lib....	200 00

68 Schenectady free public library	$200 00	
69 Sea Cliff public library..	200 00	
70 Sinclairville free library	200 00	
71 Sing Sing public library.	125 00	
72 Springfield free library..	80 00	
73 Springville public lib....	200 00	
74 Syracuse central library.	734 39	
75 Tarrytown lyceum lib...	200 00	
76 Tonawanda public lib...	100 00	
77 Troy children's neighborhood library	200 00	
78 Troy, Y. W. association.	$200 00	
79 Utica public library.....	350 00	
80 Waterford public lib....	50 00	
81 Waterville public lib....	200 00	
82 Waverly union school lib.	200 00	
83 Wellsville public library	200 00	
84 West Winfield free lib ..	177 24	
85 Westbury, Greenwood public library	15 00	
86 Yonkers public library ..	200 00	
Total	$14,499 03	

Summary statement of public libraries division for years ending September 30

	1891	1892	1893	1894	1895	Deduct duplicates	Total
Visits of library inspection			55	63	115		233
Libraries chartered	1	1	25	27	23	2	75
" admitted			2	6	10		18
" registered				1	20		21
" under inspection	1	1	27	34	53	2	114
Library transfers approved			20	14	18		52
Libraries receiving public library money			40	62	86		115
Money granted			$6,341.74	$10,351.92	$14,399.03		$31,092.86
Books				$200	$100		300

TRAVELING LIBRARIES

General approval of the regents novel system of traveling libraries can be found in the increasing number of applications from all parts of the state, as well as in direct statements of appreciation of the privilege, which come from small and poor libraries and specially from isolated country villages where residents are too few to make an adequate public library possible, till the taxpayers realize from experience the value of books for public use.

Appreciation of the New York law is by no means confined to citizens of this state. Frequent letters are received from public spirited citizens of other states, inquiring as to the plans in operation here. In the fall of 1894 application came from the state library of Michigan for information regarding the New York traveling library system and for aid in placing the matter before the people of that state. In response to this appeal a supply of our circulars was sent and later one of our 100 volume traveling libraries, with cases, finding lists and complete outfit showing how the same books had previously been lent to a New York community, was exhibited for three months before the Michigan legislature, the Michigan state library paying transportation both ways. As a result of these efforts the legislature of Michigan enacted a statute March 20, 1895, reorganizing the state library and establishing a system of associate libraries in the state. $2500 was appropriated for lending traveling libraries under direction of the state library committee which consists of the governor, state librarian and library committee of the two houses of the legislature.

A private traveling library enterprise has been conducted for several years by the H. Parmelee library company of Des Moines, Ia. 1000 volumes were divided into 20 sections of 50 volumes each, and each section shipped to a different town and exchanged at the end of three months. 250 sections have been sent to destinations as far distant as Washington (state) and Florida. After Jan. 1, 1896, an educational element will be introduced by supplying each 50 volume library with 10 or 20 books on some special course of reading.

The books are leather-bound and shipped in iron-bound cabinets, making the cost of the whole library of 1000 volumes about $1000. As this amount is divided among the 20 borrowing towns, the cost to each town is $50. On receipt of the new section an elaborate report is made out by the librarian and sent to the Library company in Des Moines, stating fully the condition of the outgoing and incoming sections. A small additional fee is paid each quarter to cover the cost of rebinding and replacing worn books.

Application blanks. Blanks for application for traveling libraries differ for the various bodies entitled to borrow the libraries. These fall into four groups:

1 Public libraries under visitation of the regents, in which case the trustees and librarian sign agreements;

2 Communities without public library privileges, when the application must be signed by 25 resident taxpayers, and agreements signed by a librarian and a trustee who become responsible for the proper usage and safe return of the books;

3 Organized groups of students, agreeing to study one subject during not less than 10 weeks, in which case a guarantor is required;

4 Unregistered clubs, summer hotels, business corporations or similar organizations not falling in the other groups, but having special need of libraries not otherwise available. These unregistered organizations pay transportation both ways in addition to the fee and agree to return the books at the end of three months instead of six, if they are needed elsewhere. It is impracticable also to lend them the latest libraries as they are needed for the public libraries and communities having no public library. A fuller explanation of the regulations governing the fourth form of application is given in the report of the Extension department for 1894, p. r11–13.

The blanks are here reprinted in the order given:

(*Form* 1)

TRUSTEES' APPLICATION FOR TRAVELING LIBRARY

To the Regents of the University of the State of New York

We, the trustees of
a free public library in
under visitation of the regents, hereby apply for the loan of traveling library no.   to be used by said public library. The regents rules shall be strictly observed, and we agree to return said traveling library within six months from its reception, and to make good any losses or injuries beyond reasonable wear, however occurring, while said library is in our custody.

Our librarian is

} *Trustees*

Dated at

The librarian also signs the following agreement:

LIBRARIAN'S AGREEMENT FOR TRAVELING LIBRARY

As librarian of traveling library no.   when lent to
by the regents of the University of the State of New York, I hereby agree to care properly for the books while under my control, to circulate them in accordance with the regents rules and to make any required reports respecting their use.

Librarian

Dated at
                189

(*Form 2*)

TAXPAYERS' APPLICATION FOR TRAVELING LIBRARY

To the Regents of the University of the State of New York
The undersigned, resident taxpayers of
in which there is no public library under visitation of the regents, hereby apply for the loan of a traveling library.

We name
whom we know to be a responsible owner of real estate to act for us as trustee.

We also agree that as soon as public interest wil warrant such action, we will take steps to establish a free public library, in accordance with laws of 1892, ch. 378, § 36.

(*Signatures of 25 taxpayers*)

On the reverse is printed the following certification to be signed by the town clerk:

I hereby certify that each of the 25 persons whose names are signed to the above petition is a resident taxpayer in this town.

(*Signed*)
                    Clerk of the town of
Dated at
                189

The librarian also signs the agreement preceding and the trustee signs the following agreement:

TRUSTEE'S AGREEMENT FOR TRAVELING LIBRARY

Having been named in the application of 25 resident taxpayers of   dated   18   to act as trustee of traveling

libraries lent to them by the regents of the University of the State of New York, I hereby request that traveling library no.
be sent to me. I agree to comply with the regents rules, to return the said library within six months from its reception and to be personally responsible for the same, making good any losses or injuries beyond reasonable wear, however occurring, while said library is in my custody.
    I name   to be librarian.

Dated at   *Trustee*
                   189

(*Form 3*)

APPLICATION FOR EXTENSION TRAVELING LIBRARY

To the Regents of the University of the State of New York
    We, the officers of
registered by the regents, hereby apply for a traveling library of   volumes on
to be used by { the people of / the members of
    Our librarian is

    The regents rules shall be strictly observed, and we agree to return the traveling library within six months from its reception, or at the end of the course of study if notified that it is wanted for use elsewhere, and to make good any losses or injuries beyond reasonable wear, however occurring, while the library is in our custody.

                                              } *Officers*

Dated at ....
.... 189..

    The undersigned being a resident of the state of New York owning real estate therein assessed for not less than $1000, hereby indorses the above application and agreement, and binds himself and his heirs and assigns to make good the above guarantee, to protect the public libraries division against any loss that may occur through failure of the borrowers to make good the above agreement, provided that the total responsibility shall not exceed $100.

                         ....
Dated at ....
.... 189..

    On the reverse is printed the librarian's agreement blank (see p. 191).

(*Form* 4)

BORROWER'S AGREEMENT FOR TRAVELING LIBRARY

I hereby request that traveling library no.   be sent to me for   months. I agree to comply with the regents rules, to return the said library within six months from its reception, or sooner if notified after three months that it is wanted for use elsewhere, and to be personally responsible for the same, making good any losses or injuries beyond reasonable wear, however occurring, while said library is in my custody.

....

Dated at...............
..................189..

The undersigned being a resident of the state of New York owning real estate therein assessed for not less than $1000, hereby indorses the above application and agreement, and binds himself and his heirs and assigns to make good the above guarantee, to protect the public libraries department against any loss that may occur through failure of the borrower to make good the above agreement, provided that the total responsibility shall not exceed $100.

....

Dated at......... ... .
.... .189..

The librarian's agreement is not required with this application.

Directions and rules. When the library is sent the following receipt post card is inclosed in a letter to the trustee notifying him of the manner in which the books were shipped.

[*Receipt form*]

189

Received from the University of the State of New York, Public libraries department,   books in good order, marked Traveling library no.
charging tray   and   book-cases.

(*Name*)

Trustee of

When this is received, with the signature of the trustee, it is filed for reference in case of loss or misunderstanding.

With this card is also sent a copy of the following directions, for the trustee and librarian:

GENERAL DIRECTIONS

All charges for transportation *except for local cartage* are to be paid from this office.

Unscrew the cover of the box, but not the cross pieces of cover. In unpacking the bookcases be careful not to scratch or mar the wood. The keys are in a package by themselves tacked inside the cover. Store the boxes, covers and screws in a safe, dry place.

Return the library by *freight* in the same box packed as carefully as when sent.

Retain bookcases and charging tray subject to the order of this office, if you are likely to need them for another library within six months. When cases or tray are sent away, be sure that the keys are in a package tacked inside the cover as when sent.

DIRECTIONS TO LIBRARIAN

Carefully read and observe.

Shelf arrangement. Arrange books on shelves in order of book numbers on backs.

Readers cards. See that readers cards are properly signed and if necessary, indorsed. If readers are under 16 years, cross out 16 and write actual age. Fill out all other items indicated on face of card: *surname of reader, given name, number, residence and date*, using ink if possible.

Arrange these cards in the tray alphabetically by surnames.

A numerical register of readers will be found useful in assigning consecutive numbers to avoid repeating a number.

Book cards. Each book has a book card with book number, author and title written plainly at the top. Keep this, when not in use, in its pocket inside the back cover.

Keep together in the tray arranged by book numbers all book cards belonging to books in circulation.

Charging. When a book is given out, enter in the proper columns on the book card, date of delivery and borrower's name or number and place the card in the tray.

Write on the reader's card date and number of book borrowed and return it to the file. The number is in all cases on the back of the book and also on the book plate and book card. In special subject libraries this consists of both subject and author number

If two or more libraries are in use at one time, write on the book card *both library and book number;* e. g. 11–5 or 12–15.

Do not skip any spaces or lines. When the face of a card is full, use the back. Use the card found in the book pocket till it is full, then make a new book card numbering it 'card 2.' Preserve and return 'card 1' for statistics.

Dates. Use the following method of dating and abbreviations for months:

Ja F Mr Ap My Je Jl Ag S O N D e. g. 21 Jl, 28 Ja. The year should be written at head of column.

Discharging. When a book is returned, take its book card from the tray, write date of return and replace it in the book. Write date of return also on the reader's card and return it to the file.

Renewal. To renew a book, enter its return and then charge exactly as if drawn for the first time.

Reserves. To reserve a book, write (in pencil) on its card, in the space for the next borrower, the name of the reader asking the reserve and return the card to the tray. When the book is returned, notify immediately the person for whom it is reserved and keep the book for him till the close of the first library day ending not less than 48 hours after sending the notice. If not called for within the time specified, erase the name and return the card to the book.

Overdue books. At least once a week examine readers cards for overdue books and promptly notify any one more than a week in arrears, collecting the fine on return of the book. Do not lend a book to any one having a fine unpaid.

Reports. Carefully keep and return all cards with the library to the public libraries division. If a new supply of cards is needed, send for them promptly.

Each finding list has printed in front, the following rules for circulation.

RULES FOR CIRCULATION

Books lent to a public library may be circulated in accordance with its rules provided that no charge is made for the use of books.

1 Place and time. The library shall be kept in a convenient place and be open for delivering and returning books at such times as the trustee in charge shall direct, not less than one hour on each of three days in each week, of which due public notice shall be given.

2 Readers. After signing the agreement any resident of the locality over 16 years of age may draw books as long as he complies with the rules.

AGREEMENT

Being a resident of over 16 years of age, I hereby agree, as a borrower from the New York State Traveling Libraries, to pay promptly any fines due from me for over detention of books, or for injuries of any kind beyond reasonable wear to any book while it is charged to me.

Persons less than 16 years of age, or residing outside the locality to which the library is lent, shall be entitled to the same privileges when their agreements are indorsed by the trustee. In agreements of those under 16, the actual age must be written instead of the figures 16 in the printed form.

3 Books. One volume may be drawn by each reader and kept two weeks.

4 Fines. A fine of one cent a day shall be paid for each book kept over time, and any money thus received shall be used under direction of the trustee for library expenses. No book shall be lent to any one to whom a book or an unpaid fine is charged.

5 Reserves. A reader wishing a book not at the time on the shelves may have it reserved for him at least 48 hours after its return, by giving notice to the librarian.

6 Renewal. A reader returning a book which is not reserved may renew it for two weeks.

7 Injuries. Notes, corrections of the press or marks of any kind on books belonging to the state are unconditionally forbidden; and all losses or injuries beyond reasonable wear, however caused, must be promptly adjusted to the satisfaction of the trustee by the person to whom the book is charged.

To this is added § 43-44 of the Laws of 1892, ch. 378, providing against injuries and detention of public library books, as follows:

§ 43 **Injuries to property.** Whoever intentionally injures, defaces or destroys any property belonging to or deposited in any incorporated library, reading-room, museum, or other educational institution, shall be punished by imprisonment in a state prison for not more than three years, or in a county jail for not more than one year, or by a fine of not more than $500, or by both such fine and imprisonment.

§ 44 **Detention.** Whoever wilfully detains any book, newspaper, magazine, pamphlet, manuscript or other property belonging to any public or incorporated library, reading-room, museum or other educational institution, for 30 days after notice in writing to return the same, given after the expiration of the time which by the rules of such institution, such articles or other property may be kept, shall be punished by a fine of not less than one nor more than $25, or by imprisonment in the jail not exceeding six months, and the said notice shall bear on its face a copy of this section.

Volumes. The total number of volumes accessioned in the public libraries division September 30, 1895 was 20,865; of these 123 have been sold, 55 lost and 3 worn out. The others are distributed as follows:

REPORT OF PUBLIC LIBRARIES DIVISION, 1895

General libraries

No.					
1	100 v.	5 sets contain	500 v.
2	100 "	5 "	500 "
3	100 "	4 "	400 "
4	100 "	2 "	200 "
5	100 "	4 "	400 "
6	100 "	4 "	400 "
7	100 "	5 "	500 "
8	100 "	2 "	200 "
9	100 "	2 "	200 "
10	100 "	7 "	700 "
11	50 "	9 "	450 "
12	50 "	9 "	450 "
13	50 "	10 "	500 "
14	50 "	10 "	500 "
15	50 "	10 "	500 "
16	102 "	10 "	1,020 "
17	50 "	5 "	250 "
18	50 "	5 "	258 "
19	25 "	6 "	150 "
20	25 "	6 "	150 "
21	50 "	5 "	250 "
22	25 "	6 "	150 "
23	25 "	6 "	150 "
24	50 "	5 "	250 "
25	50 "	5 "	250 "

General libraries 147 sets contain   9,270 v.

Subject libraries'

Economics	subj. no. 330	25 v.	5 sets contain	125 v.
"	" " 330	50 "	3 "	150 "
Agriculture	" " 630	33 "	5 "	165 "
"	" " 630	60 "	5 "	300 "
Literature	" " 800	58 "	10 "	580 "
American liter.	" " 820	26 "	5 "	130 "
French history	" " 944	45 "	5 "	225 "
U. S. history	" " 973	20 "	5 "	100 "
"	" " 973	46 "	6 "	276 "

Subject libraries 49 sets contain   2,051 v.
For the Capitol library... 2,229 "
Sold.. 123 "
Lost.. 55 "
Worn out.. 8 "
For extension purposes and for lending to institutions in the University 7,134 "

Total....................... 20,865 v.

Lost books. The item of 55 volumns lost would mislead unless explained. While this would be a not unreasonable margin of loss in so large a circulation as these books have had, the gratifying fact is that not a single volume has been lost in the wide circulation of the books throughout the state. 22 of the missing books were stolen from the exhibit at the world's fair, where it was impossible to combine absolute protection with as much freedom of inspection as was desirable. This price was perhaps not too great to pay for the advantages of publicity gained. The other 33 books have been lost in the capitol building where the only available place for storage was still in use by the construction department. The frequent removal of doors and windows in the course of construction and the necessary passage of workmen through the stacks, has made it impossible to protect these books from irresponsible access, and till our building is completed and the territory occupied by the regents is under their exclusive control, we shall probably have to report each year some loss.

Additions. During the year 6750 volumes have been bought for five sets each of seven new general traveling libraries, no. 19–25, and for the Capitol library, for lending to institutions in the University and for the special subject libraries made up for groups of students at registered university extension centers and study clubs.

Young people's libraries. Of the seven new general libraries, four, nos. 19, 20, 22, 23, are selections of the best juvenile literature, grouped in libraries of 25 volumes each, with annotated finding lists. The fee for one of these libraries alone is $2, but when lent with another library of 50 or 100 volumes the added fee for the young people's library is $1.

The libraries of 25 and 50 of the best books in economics were revised in June, after submitting the proposed changes to leading economists of the country. The following five books were inserted in the 50-volume lists:

Bastable, C. F. Public finance ;
Ely, R: T. Socialism and social reform ;
Hall, Ernst von. Trusts ;
Hull house. Maps and papers ;
Warner, A. G. American charities.

Those omitted were:
Barns, W: E. ed. Labor problem ;
Booth, William. In darkest England ;
Cook, W: W. Trusts ;
Cossa, Luigi. Taxation ;
Ruskin, John. Munera pulveris.

Sales. A system of exchange between the public libraries division and the duplicate department has made it desirable to sell some books from the traveling libraries. For this purpose, one set each of libraries no. 3, 5, 6, 10, 11, 12, has been broken during the year, part of the volumes having been sold and the others transferred to the extension library, where they are circulated in special collections as they bear on the various subjects of study chosen. In addition to these direct sales managed by the duplicate department, books lost by borrowers are paid for by the trustee and are entered as sold. In all sales, the following certificate, filled out for each book sold, is pasted over the book plate of the Public libraries division.

University of the State of New York

This book, no   in the

Public Libraries Accession Book

as been sold to

and is so recorded.

Director

This is a protection to the buyer and guards against the impression that state property can be held with impunity by private individuals.

Use. During the year 154 traveling libraries have been lent.

71 were sent to 34 public libraries, including those of 21 regents schools.
62 were sent to 35 groups of taxpayers.
5 " " 3 extension centers.
16 " " 9 other borrowers under special permit.
―――
154 " " 81 places.

During the year,
114 libraries were used once for 114 issues.
20 " · " " twice " 40 "
―――   ―――
134   154

Of 7545 volumes sent out and returned, the total circulation was 22,845 of which 13,762 was fiction. The readers were 4,679, an average of 5 books to each reader.

Agriculture libraries. The selections of 33 and 60 of the best books on agriculture have not been as generally used as was expected. The demand is, however, increasing and we believe that as the character of the books becomes more widely known we shall be compelled to increase the supply to meet the demand from rural communities. The following circular printed on a slip is sent in answer to letters of inquiry about traveling libraries from rural districts:

BEST BOOKS FOR FARMERS

Farmers can have good reading for themselves and their families almost for the asking.

The State Library is authorized by law to lend books to communities. A system of 'traveling libraries' has accordingly been arranged by which a collection of 100 fresh and popular books may be borrowed for six months on satisfactory guarantee against loss, and the payment of a nominal fee of $5. These will be lent without other expense to any free library under regents' supervision, or on petition of 25 taxpayers in any place which has not yet established such a library.

Many different collections of a general character have already been sent out; and several others on special subjects are now ready. Attention is specially called to the lists on *Agriculture*.

There is a choice selection of 33 books, and a larger one of 60 books covering all subjects relating to the farm. Either of these libraries will be found extremely valuable and interesting in a rural community and may be had in combination with a selection of books of a general character. If the smaller list is taken, another small list on some other subject, e. g. U. S. history, Economics, Mechanics, etc. may be added to the miscellaneous books, to make up a total of about 100 volumes.

Any that wish to take advantage of this offer should write to the Public Libraries Division, State Library, Albany, for lists and official blanks on which to make application.

MELVIL DEWEY
Director

REPORT OF PUBLIC LIBRARIES DIVISION, 1895

a Traveling libraries sent Oct. 1, 1894 — Sept. 30, 1895

Free libraries		25 taxpayers		Extension centers, etc.	
Albany	4 libs.	Albany		Chantauqua	2 libs.
Bath Beach	3 "	Amityville		Oneonta	2 "
Bath-on-Hudson	2 "	Aquebogue		Sing Sing	
Camden	2 "	Bedford Park	7 libs		
Canajoharie	5 "	Brooklyn	3 "		
Canandaigua	4 "	Burnt Hills	2 "		
Crown Point		Caledonia	3 "	3	
Ellenville		Charlton	4 "		
Fort Plain		Chestertown			
Franklin		Clinton	2 "	Borrowers	
Greenville		Cokertown			
Herkimer		Depew			
Lansingburg	2 "	Dewittville		Buffalo	5
Madison		East Durham		Lake Placid	
Morristown	3 "	Eaton		Saratoga	
Nassau	2 "	Freehold		South West Oswego	
North Tonawanda		Gansevoort		Unadilla	
Ogdensburg	2 "	Harkness			
Pocantico Hills	2 "	Marlboro	2 "	9	
Randolph		Medusa			
Rome		Morrisonville			
St Johnsville	2 "	Northport	3 "		
Saratoga		Oak Hill	3 "	Summary	
Sea Cliff	4 "	Pattersonville			
Tarrytown	3 "	Peru	3 "		
Tivoli		Piermon	2 "	Free libraries	34
Tomkins Cove		Prince's Bay	2 "	25 Taxpayers	35
Troy	2 "	Prohibition Park		Extension centers, etc.	9
Trumansburg	3 "	Rensselaerville	2 "	Borrowers	3
Waterville	2 "	Sharon Springs			
Wellsville	2 "	Sodus	3 "		
West Winfield	3 "	South Jewett		Total	81
Westport	2 "	South Westerlo			
Windsor	2 "	Vernon	3 "		
		West Stephentown			
34		35			

a Not including extension libraries

Traveling libraries sent Oct. 1, 1894 — Sept. 30, 1895

Lib. no.	PLACE	Sent	Returned	Form of application	No. of readers	CIRCULATION Total	Fiction	Average books per reader	Highest circulation of 1 book
1	Sharon Springs	26 Ja 95	2 Ag 95	Pet ..	90	381	175	4.2	10
1a	Sea Cliff	14 Ja 95	19 Jl 95	Pub lib	83	322	186	3.9	15
1b	Northport	18 Mr 95	5 S 95	Pub lib	......	183	99	....	8
1c	Chestertown	16 Ap 95	30 O 95	Pet ..	87	500	298	5.8	16
1d	Nassau	28 D 94	9 Ag 95	Pet ..	67	345	180	5.1	13
				Pub. lib.	327	1731	935	5.3	
				Person..					
2	So. West Oswego	4 Ja 95	26 Ja 95	Pet ..	66	242	123	3.7	10
2a	Northport	17 S 95	....	Pet .	......	. ..	....	....	....
2c	Depew	18 O 94	16 My 95		28	101	77	4.4	6

Traveling libraries sent Oct. 1, 1894 — Sept. 30, 1895 (*continued*)

Lib. no.	PLACE	Sent	Returned	Form of application	No. of readers	CIRCULATION Total	Fiction	Average books per reader	Highest circulation of 1 book
2d	Morrisonville	26 Ja 95	9 Ag 95	Pet	61	207	101	3.4	11
2d	Nassau	12 Ag 95		Pub lib					
					150	550	301	3.7	
3	Dewittville	13 My 95		Pet					
3b	Eaton	14 N 94	14 My 95	Pet	96	494	262	4.4	16
3c	Burnt Hills	26 Ja 95	9 Ag 95	Pet	56	279	191	4.9	16
3d	Prohibition Park	9 My 95	15 Ja 96	Pet	12	48	27	4	2
					164	751	500	4.6	
4	Prince's Bay	2 Ap 95	26 N 95	Pet	53	275	164	5.2	20
4a	Aquebogue	12 O 94	24 Ap 95	Pet	45	225	132	5	11
					98	500	296	5 1	
5a	Peru	14 Ja 95	29 Jl 95	Pet	55	206	93	3.7	11
5b	Freehold	5 F 95	16 Ag 95	Pet	38	145	62	3 8	6
5c	Harkness	16 O 95	2 My 95	Pet	31	150	70	4.8	9
					124	501	225	4.1	
6b	Tivoli	31 D 94	27 Je 95	Pub. lib.	48	132	85	3.1	10
6d	Medusa	18 F 95	3 Ja 96	Pet	40	131	96	3.3	14
					83	263	181	3.2	
7a	Peru	15 Ag 95		Pet					
7b	Amityville	1 S 94	25 Mr 95	Pet	52	211	114	4.1	11
7c	Gansevoort	29 Mr 95	7 O 95	Pet	69	273	131	4	16
7d	Rome	3 Ap 95	18 O 95	Pub. lib.	81	230	105	2.8	10
					202	714	350	3.5	
8	North Tonawanda	14 D 94	22 Je 95	Pub. lib.	39	93	40	2.4	10
8	Burnt Hills	12 Ag 95		Pet					
8a	Clinton	14 D 94	28 Ap 95	Pet	775	359	161	4.8	12
8a	Vernon	13 Je 95	14 Ja 96	Pet	71	334	227	4.7	15
					185	786	428	4.3	
9	Bedford Park	9 Ag 95		Pet					
9a	Northport	17 S 95		Pet					
10a	Bedford Park	9 Ag 95		Pet					
10b	Buffalo	22 Ja 95	10 S 95	Person					
10c	Saratoga	28 My 95	31 O 95	Person					
10d	Wellsville	28 My 95	2 Ja 96	Pub. lib.		221	162		12
10e	Prince's Bay	30 O 94	1 Ap 95	Pet	59	268	146	4.5	10
10f	Madison	20 O 94	26 Ap 95	Un sch	58	438	273	7.5	19
10g	West Winfield	27 N 94	20 Ag 95	Un. sch.	166	410	257	2.4	23
					283	1337	839	5.7	
11a	West Stephentown	21 Ja 95	26 Jl 95	Pet	33	115	46	3.5	7
11c	Westport	18 Jl 95		Pub. lib.					
11e	Canajoharie	5 Jl 95		Un. sch.					
11f	Unadilla	26 Je 95	15 Ja 96	Person		51	31		1
11g	Vernon	20 N 94	29 My 95	Pet	64	175	94	2.7	17
					97	341	171	3.5	
12	Canandaigua	18 Je 95	13 D 95	Un. sch.		302	169		19
12a	Morristown	16 Ap 95	14 Ja 96	Pub lib	71	82		1.9	12
12c	West Winfield	30 N 94	20 Ag 95	Un sch.	128	245	132	1.9	22
12e	Unadilla	26 Je 95	15 Ja 96	Person		38	29		6
12g	Oak Hill	29 Ja 95	8 Ag 95	Pet	27	53	37	1.9	6
12h	Cokertown	24 Ap 95		Pet					
					226	775	500	3.4	

REPORT OF PUBLIC LIBRARIES DIVISION, 1895

Traveling libraries sent Oct. 1, 1894 — Sept. 30, 1895 (*continued*)

Lib. no.	PLACE	Sent	Returned	Form of application	No. of readers	CIRCULATION Total	CIRCULATION Fiction	Average books per reader	Highest circulation of 1 book
13	Vernon	20 N 94	29 My 95	Pet	72	242	129	3.3	13
13b	Canandaigua	18 Je 95	13 D 95	Un. sch.	...	179	130	...	13
13c	Herkimer	7 D 94	12 Je 95	Un sch.	66	152	76	2.3	15
13e	Crown Point	3 Jl 95	13 Ja 96	Pub lib	33	109	62	3.1	9
13g	Buffalo	11 S 95		Person.					
13h	Marlboro	8 Ap 95	10 O 95	Pet		130	65		7
13i	Albany	20 Mr 95	9 O 95	Pub. lib.		119	56		9
					172	924	517	5.3	
14	Rensselaerville	16 N 94	16 My 95	Pet	18	106	54	5.9	7
14	Buffalo	7 Je 95	24 O 95	Person					
14a	Tarrytown	18 Ap 95	29 N 95	Pub. lib.		185	108		10
14b	Canandaigua	26 N 94	11 Je 95	Un. sch.	63	196	99	3.1	13
14b	Sea Cliff	15 Ag 95		Pub. lib.					
14c	West Winfield	30 N 94	20 Ag 95	Un. sch.	132	236	130	1.8	17
14d	Canajoharie	15 O 94	21 F 95	Un. sch.		201	95		10
14e	Camden	23 Ja 95	19 Ag 95	Pub. lib.		129	61		8
14f	Pocantico Hills	25 F 95	28 O 95	Pub. lib.		58	33		7
14g	Bedford Park	14 Ag 95		Pet					
14h	Albany	30 Mr 95	9 O 95	Pub. lib		128	74		10
14i	Albany	15 Ap 95	29 O 95	Pet	168	339	220		22
					381	1588	869	4.2	
15	Camden	23 Ja 95	19 Ag 95	Pub. lib		154	86		14
15a	Bath-on-Hudson	2 Mr 95	12 S 95	Pub lib	54	113	76	2.1	12
15b	Albany	30 Mr 95	9 O 95	Pub lib		76	118		14
15c	Tarrytown	18 Ap 95	29 N 95	Pub lib		196	138		16
15d	Morristown	16 Ap 95	14 Ja 96	Pub lib	77	177	102	2.3	9
15e	Rensselaerville	16 N 94	16 My 95	Pet	18	133	71	7.4	11
15e	So Jewett	22 My 95	4 D 95	Pet	19	88	57	4.6	9
15f	Sodus	14 F 95	5 S 95	Pet	88	335	197	4.1	17
15f	Buffalo	11 S 95		Person.					
15g	Canandaigua	26 N 94	11 Je 95	Un sch	70	236	140	3.4	13
15g	Canajoharie	5 Jl 95		Un. sch.					
15h	Chariton	29 O 94	1 My 95	Pet	58	296	159	5.1	15
15b	Bath Beach	8 Jl 95	16 Ja 96	Pub. lib		244	163		21
15i	Pocantico Hills	25 F 95	28 O 95	Pub. lib		68	54		6
					379	2115	1358	5.5	
16a	Brooklyn	11 My 95	24 Ja 96	Pet		200	161		9
16b	Randolph	8 N 94	25 S 95	Acad	76	256	176	3.3	10
16c	Fort Plain	3 Ap 95	7 O 95	Pub lib	80	278	180	3.5	11
16d	South Westerlo	28 N 94	31 My 95	Pet	64	508	346	6.2	20
16d	Buffalo	9 S 95		Person.					
16e	Tompkins Cove	2 Ja 95	5 Jl 95	Un. sch.		253	189		11
16f	Greenville	2 Ja 95	3 Jl 95	Acad	85	709	478	8.3	18
16g	Bath Beach	9 Ja 95	5 Jl 95	Pet		618	398		18
16g	Piermont	12 S 95		Pet					
16h	East Durham	11 Ja 95	18 Jl 95	Pet	83	583	392	7	16
16i	Pattersonville	21 Ja 95		Pet					
					388	3400	2322	8.8	
17	Trumansburg	12 Mr 95	28 O 95	Pub lib		133	109		14
17a	Albany	30 Mr 95	9 O 95	Pub. lib.		133	101		14
17b	Waterville	1 Ap 95	31 O 95	Pub lib	36	130	87	3.6	11
17c	Ellenville	6 Ap 95	8 N 95	Pub lib	127	339	210	2.7	22
17d	Ogdensburg	16 Mr 95	17 D 95	Pub lib		228	151		24
					163	963	651	5.9	
18	Caledonia	11 F 95	29 Ag 95	Pet	76	193	141	2.5	14
18	Buffalo	4 S 95		Person.					
18a	Marlboro	8 Ap 93	10 O 95	Pet	48	116	58	2.4	10
18b	Lansingburg	1 Mr 95	12 S 95	Acad	48	171	91	3.6	9
18c	Trumansburg	12 Mr 95	28 O 95	Pub lib		89	57		8
18d	Ogdensburg	16 Mr 95	17 D 95	Pub lib		218	105		19
					172	787	447	4.6	

Traveling libraries sent Oct. 1, 1894 — Sept. 30, 1895 (*concluded*)

Lib. no.	PLACE	Sent	Returned	Form of application	No. of readers	CIRCULATION Total	CIRCULATION Fiction	Average books per reader	Highest circulation of 1 book
19	Troy	15 D 94	5 D 95	Pub. lib	......	345	250	......	29
19a	Herkimer	7 D 94	12 Je 95	Un sch	57	142	110	2.5	15
19a	Chautauqua	30 Jl 95	10 S 95	E					
19b	Clinton	14 D 94	23 Ap 95	Pet	......	209	146	......	15
19b	Brooklyn	11 My 95	24 Ja 96	Pet	......	60	35	......	6
19c	Sodus	14 F 95	5 S 95	Pet	63	212	172	3.4	20
19c	Sing Sing	18 S 95		E					
19d	Canajoharie	4 Mr 95	27 Je 95	Un. sch	......	107	81	......	15
19d	Buffalo	9 S 95		Person					
					120	1075	794	9.	
20	Troy	15 D 94	5 D 95	Pub. lib	......	335	245	......	27
20a	Herkimer	7 D 94	12 Je 95	Un sch	63	181	131	2.9	15
20a	Lake Placid	13 Je 95		Person					
20b	Oak Hill	29 Ja 95	8 Ag 95	Pet	13	17	9	1.3	3
20b	Piermont	12 S 95		Pet					
20c	Caledonia	11 F 95	29 Ag 95	Pet	57	148	124	2.6	12
20d	Sodus	14 F 95	5 S 95	Pet	68	206	157	3.1	15
					201	887	666	4.4	
21	Bath-on-Hudson	2 Mr 95	12 S 95	Pub. lib.	62	144	100	2.3	23
21a	Caledonia	11 F 95	29 Ag 95	Pet	96	289	212	3.1	17
21b	Windsor	16 F 95	15 O 95	Un sch	96	314	199	3.3	17
21c	Lansingburg	1 Mr 95	12 S 95	Acad	57	174	109	3.1	10
21d	Buffalo	22 Ja 95	31 Ag 95	Person					
					311	921	620	3.	
22	Brooklyn	11 My 95	24 Ja 96	Pet	......	82	51	......	10
22a	Trumansburg	12 Mr 95	28 O 95	Pub lib	......	194	113	......	16
22b	Wellsville	28 My 95	2 Ja 96	Pub. lib.	......	214	167	......	12
22c	Tarrytown	18 Ap 95	29 N 95	Pub lib	......	185	156	......	14
22d	Morristown	16 Ap 95	14 Ja 96	Pub lib.	80	122	151	2.4	17
					80	797	638	9.1	
23a	Peru	15 Ag 95		Pet					
23b	Sea Cliff	15 Ag 95		Pub lib					
23d	Chautauqua	30 Jl 95	10 S 95	E					
24	Lake Placid	13 Je 95		Person					
24a	Buffalo	7 Je 95	24 O 95	Person					
24b	Sea Cliff	15 Ag 95		Pub. lib					
24c	Bath Beach	8 Jl 95	16 Ja 96	Pub. lib	......	205	154	......	21
24d	Westport	13 Jl 95		Pub. lib					
					......	205	154	......	
330l	Ellenville	6 D 94	29 Je 95	Pub lib	9	39	......	4.1	5
330s	Buffalo	4 S 95		Person	......	......	......	......	......
					9	39	......	4.1	
800j	Bedford Park	9 Ag 95		Pet					
800l	Canajoharie	15 O 94	27 Je 95	Un. sch	119	165	......	1.4	10
800m	St Johnsville	20 O 94	5 Jl 95	Un. sch	51	210	......	4.1	14
800n	Chariton	29 O 94	1 My 95	Pet	53	175	......	3.3	11
800n1	Oak Hill	29 Ja 95	8 Ag 95	Pet	27	49	......	1.8	5
800n2	Oneonta	14 Ja 95	27 Jl 95	E					
800n3	Windsor	16 F 95	15 O 95	Un sch	61	173	......	2.8	10
800n4	Waterville	1 Ap 95	31 O 95	Pub lib	24	37	......	1.5	9
820s	Franklin	25 Ap 95	22 N 95	Un. sch	7	9	......	1.3	3
					342	818	......	2.4	
944l	Oneonta	18 Ja 95	27 Jl 95	E					
944i	Bedford Park	9 Ag 95		Pet					
973l	St Johnsville	20 O 94	5 Jl 95	Un. sch	22	74	......	3.4	6
973l	Saratoga	28 N 94	26 Jl 95	Un. sch					
973l	Bedford Park	9 Ag 95		Pet					
					22	74	......	3.4	

REPORT OF PUBLIC LIBRARIES DIVISION, 1895   205

Summary of use of traveling libraries from Oct. 1, 1894 — Sept. 30, 1895

GENERAL LIBRARIES

Library number	Sets	Sent	Ret'd	Least	Largest	Average	Total	Fiction	Readers
1	5	5	5	183	500	346	1,731	935	327
2	5	5	3	101	242	183	550	301	150
3	4	4	3	48	424	250	751	500	164
4	2	2	2	225	275	250	500	296	98
5	4	3	3	145	206	167	501	225	124
6	4	2	2	131	132	132	263	181	83
7	5	4	3	211	273	238	714	350	202
8	2	4	3	93	359	262	786	428	185
9	2	2	....	....	....	....	....	....	....
10	7	7	6	221	438	334	1,837	839	283
11	9	5	3	51	175	114	341	171	97
12	9	6	5	38	302	155	775	500	226
13	10	7	6	102	242	154	924	517	172
14	10	12	10	58	339	176	1,588	869	381
15	10	14	12	68	335	177	2,118	1,358	379
16	10	11	8	200	709	425	3,400	2,322	388
17	5	5	5	130	339	192	963	651	163
18	5	6	5	89	218	157	787	447	172
19	6	9	7	60	345	179	1,075	794	120
20	6	7	5	17	335	177	887	666	201
21	5	5	5	144	314	230	921	620	311
22	6	5	5	82	214	159	797	638	80
23	6	3	1	....	....	....	....	....	....
24	5	5	2	....	205	....	205	154	....
25a	5	....	....	....	....	....	....	....	....
Total	142	138	109	....	....	....	21,914	13,762	4,306

a First sent in October, 1895

SUBJECT LIBRARIES

Library number	Vols.	Sets	Sent	Ret'd	Least	Largest	Average	Total	Readers

Economics

| 380 | 25 | 5 | 1 | .... | .... | .... | .... | .... | .... |
| 330 | 50 | 3 | 1 | 1 | .... | 39 | .... | 39 | 9 |

Literature

| 800 | 58 | 10 | 8 | 7 | 37 | 210 | 135 | 809 | 335 |

English and American literature

| 820 | 26 | 5 | 1 | 1 | .... | 9 | .... | 9 | 7 |

French history

| 944 | 45 | 3 | 2 | 1 | .... | .... | .... | .... | .... |

U. S. history

| 973 | 46 | 6 | 3 | 2 | .... | 74 | .... | 74 | 22 |
| Total | .... | 32 | 16 | 12 | .... | .... | .... | 931 | 373 |

Capitol library. The registration book of the capitol library was opened and the first books lent March 16, 1893. 427 borrowers are registered, 377 of whom are still entitled to draw books. Borrowers from the state library, even when not state employees, have been allowed to take one volume at a time from the capitol library. The records show that 2107 loans were made in this way before Oct. 1, 1894 and 5140 during the year ending Oct. 1, 1895. These loans are also included in the capitol library statistics.

In March 1895 the following notice printed on a card was distributed in the offices of the capitol:

CAPITOL LIBRARY

A large collection of the newest and best popular books for the free use of state employees living in Albany will be found in the north end of the main reference room of the state library.

_{Books may be borrowed for home reading on filing a recommendation from the head of the department in which the borrower is employed, and on signing the agreement to observe the rules. Blanks may be had at the library loan desk at the left of the main entrance.}

MELVIL DEWEY, *Director*

The record of loans before Oct. 1, 1895, summarized and tabulated by subjects, is here printed.

Summary of use of capitol library before Oct. 1, 1895, by subjects

	General	Philosophy	Religion	Sociology	Philology	Science	Useful arts	Fine arts	Literature	History	Total
1892-93				28		4	22	16	609	114	793
1893-94	124	7	51	97		48	53	80	4119	721	5300
1894-95	145	22	89	158	2	96	44	148	7586	1130	9420

Percentage of each subject read by borrowers from capitol library before Oct. 1, 1895

	General	Philosophy	Religion	Sociology	Philology	Science	Useful arts	Fine arts	Literature	History	Total
1892-93				3.5+		.5+	2.6+	2+	76.7+	14.3	
1893-94	2.3+	.1+	9+	1.8+		.9+	1	1.5+	77.7	13.6	
1894-95	1.5+	.2+	9+	1.6+	.ozt	1+	4+	1.5+	82.6+	11.9+	

This record shows only a small proportion of the use made of the capitol library books, which from their location on open shelves in the central reading room are very largely used by readers not entitled to take the books home. Their attractive appearance has drawn many to the state library who never came to read before and has increased greatly the number of regular readers. After becoming familiar with the capitol library shelves, readers begin to use the catalogue of the state library more intelligently and to avail themselves of its resources as a reference library. The capitol library has proved itself an important extension of the usefulness of the state library.

Extension library. No section of the work of the traveling libraries has received more general praise from taxpayers of the state than the provision by which special subject libraries are sent to groups of students so situated that without this state loan they could not continue the special work in which they are interested. Careless or desultory work is guarded against by requiring that all clubs availing themselves of this privilege shall pledge themselves to study the subject during not less than 10 consecutive weeks and the books are themselves an incentive to keeping this agreement. The limit of 10 weeks study is simply a minimum, as in almost all cases the work is continued during a much longer time. Requests have come from citizens of all the adjoining states, from Canada and from more distant states, asking the extension of the privilege beyond state limits. In such cases, while unable directly to aid such work outside our borders, we have sent a full set of our publications and blanks to be used by applicants in memorializing their own legislatures to provide for their needs as is done for citizens of New York. The work is now increasing rapidly as the date columns in the following summary will show.

Summary of use of extension books previous to Oct. 1, 1895

PLACE	Borrowing body	Subject	Vols.	Sent	Returned
Albany	Center	Economic questions	43	Ja 92	Ap 92
	"	Colonial history	28	O 92	Ja 93
	"	English literature	65	Ja 93	Ap 93
	"	Electricity	60	O 93	Ja 94
	"	English literature	103	F 94	My 94
	Club	Sociology	51	13 N 94	28 My 95
	Center	Political methods	55	Ja 95	Ap 95
	Club	Bible study	111	15 My 95	....
Albion	Center	American revolution	33	F 92	My 92
	"	" constitution	24	O 92	F 93
Attica	"	" literature	71	4 N 92	15 My 93
	"	" history	73	2 N 93	My 94
Auburn	"	" "	35	14 Mr 93	Je 93
Ballston	"	English literature	35	5 F 92	My 92
	"	" "	52	Ja 93	My 93
Batavia	"	American history	39	Ap 93	Jy 93
Binghamton	"	Economics	42	F 92	My 92
	"	Art	21	S 92	Ja 93
	"	American literature	53	F 93	My 93
	"	" revolution	36	Ap 93	Jy 93
Buffalo	Club	History of painting	104	24 N 94	16 My 95
	"	Architecture	103	18 Jl 95	....
	"	Kindergarten theory	103	4 Ja 95	29 Je 95
	"	Germany	90	29 Ag 95	....
	Center	Money, banking, etc.	54	21 N 94	29 My 95
Chautauqua	Sum. s	General	20	2 Jl 94	29 Ag 94
	"	"	461	6 Jl 95	10 S 95
Dobbs Ferry	Center	Masterpieces of English literature	61	24 O 93	15 F 94
	"	Civil and religious liberty in America	116	10 D 94	27 Mr 95
Dunkirk	Club	German hist. and lit	104	11 Jl 95	....
Fulton	"	Germany	25	27 O 94	29 My 95
Geneva	"	French art	55	7 Mr 95	31 O 95
Gloversville	Center	English literature	17	Ja 92	Ap 92
Haverstraw	Club	England	63	29 Ag 95	....
Jamestown	"	Italy	105	17 N 94	25 O 95
Johnstown	"	15th century	54	31 D 94	18 Jl 95
Little Falls	"	French history	51	13 D 93	14 My 94
Lockport	Center	American literature	84	D 93	Ja 94
	"	Development of nation	112	13 N 94	13 S 95
Lowville	"	Civil and religious liberty in America	110	21 N 94	11 Jl 95
Medina	"	English literature	75	F 93	Je 93
Middletown	Club	Holland, Belgium, France and Spain	56	19 D 94	5 Jl 95
Mt Vernon	Center	French history	33	Ap 93	Jl 93
	"	English language	35	11 N 93	20 N 94
	"	Astronomy	92	27 N 94	25 My 95
	"	German literature	101	17 S 95	....
	Club	Emerson	50	16 S 95	....
	"	Education	57	15 Mr 95	....
	"	Greek hist. & sculpture	67	28 Ja 95	....
New York	Center	Electricity	104	2 Mr 94	18 Ag 94
	"	"	102	11 Ja 95	....
Norwich	"	American history	29	F 93	Jl 93
Ogdensburg	Club	England	103	13 D 94	29 Jl 95
	"	"	103	21 S 95	....

REPORT OF PUBLIC LIBRARIES DIVISION, 1895   209

Summary of use of extension books previous to Oct. 1, 1895
(concluded)

PLACE	Borrowing body	Subject	Vols.	Sent	Returned
Olean	"	Egypt	55	4 Ap 95	4 Ja 96
Oneida	Center ..	Economics	44	11 D 93	30 O 94
	" ..	Amer. colonial hist	55	13 N 94	
	Club	American history	69	16 Mr 95	25 S 95
Oswego	Center ..	English literature	102	2 D 93	15 My 94
Oxford	Club	Six representative Amer writers	78	31 Ja 95	8 O 95
Oswego	Center ..	Greek and Roman life	45	Ja 93	Ap 93
Peekskill	" ..	American history	18	N 92	F 93
Plattsburg	" ..	Zoology	56	Mr 93	Jl 93
Portville	Club	English hist. and lit	59	1 F 95	29 Jl 95
Potsdam	"	Authors and their works	30	26 Jl 95	
Po'keepsie	Center ..	American history	19	F 92	My 92
	" ..	Economics	32	F 93	My 93
Rochester	" ..	English literature	81	Mr 92	Je 92
	" ..	American revolution	3	24 Mr 92	Je 92
Rome	" ..	English literature	65	F 93	Jl 93
	" ..	Economics	50	20 N 93	13 Mr 94
	" ..	American literature	106	5 F 95	16 My 95
	Club	France and Scotland	45	12 O 94	2 My 95
Rushford	Center ..	Discovery of America	36	Ap 93	Jl 93
Salem	Center ..	Colonial history	58	D 92	F 93
	" ..	Studies in Eng. literature	54	6 Ja 94	4 Je 94
Saratoga	" ..	English literature	110	25 Ja 95	3 My 95
	Club	France	63	16 N 94	30 Ap 95
Schenectady	"	Middle ages	25	13 D 94	6 Je 95
Schuylerville	"	Cities of Great Britain, France, Germany	29	3 Ja 95	8 Jl 95
Sing Sing	Center ..	English literature	101	18 S 95	
Skaneateles	" ..	American revolution	31	Mr 92	Je 92
Syracuse	" ..	Romeo and Juliet, the Tempest	32	21 N 94	16 Ag 95
Tarrytown	" ..	English language	30	14 N 92	Ap 93
	" ..	American politics	105	15 Ja 94	16 O 94
	" ..	French history	109	16 N 94	3 My 95
Troy	Club	Ruskin	28	28 Ja 95	16 Ag 95
	"	Pedagogic methods	51	7 Mr 95	10 Je 95
Utica	Center ..	Greek and Roman life	27	Mr 33	Jl 33
	" ..	American history	75	11 O 93	27 D 93
	" ..	Geology of New York	102	16 Ja 94	18 Je 94
	" ..	English novel	104	12 Ja 95	2 My 95
Watertown	Center ..	American revolution	29	Mr 92	Je 92
	Club	Architecture	44	14 Mr 95	13 S 95
Waverly	Center ..	Civil and religious liberty in America	53	30 O 93	2 N 94
	" ..	Roman life	31	10 F 94	2 N 94
	" ..	European history	117	10 N 94	12 O 95
Westfield	Club	American history	100	31 Ag 95	
	"	English literature	35	Ja 92	Ap 92
	"	Astronomy	....	Mr 92	Je 92
	" ..	French history	43	Ja 93	Je 93
Yonkers	Center ..	German literature	60	9 D 93	3 My 94
	" ..	Electricity	47	9 F 94	3 My 94
	" ..	Geology	55	9 N 94	11 Ap 95
	Club	Art	43	28 Ja 95	11 Ap 95

a The public libraries division did not have charge of leading extension libraries till Oct 11, 1895 and the previous records being inadequate some of the entries are approximates

Extension books lent on other applications

PLACE	Borrowing body	Subject	Vols.
Buffalo	Private school	General	112
	University club	Sociology	25
Canajoharie	Union school	Economics	23
Fort Hill	Petition	Fiction	18
Franklin	Union school	Literature	79
Lake Placid	Summer hotel	General	50

GENERAL LIBRARY INTERESTS

Local library subsidies. The influence of the University is felt even in the matter of local subsidies. Many libraries not controlled by the public receive considerable aid from the cities and villages in which they are located. The subsidy laws of 1886 and 1887 imposed conditions which could be met only by the larger libraries.

But § 37 of the University law has made it possible for the smallest library to obtain municipal aid if registered by the regents as maintaining a proper standard and having their certificate of the extent of its approved circulation for the preceding year. The Membership corporations law of 1895, repealing the library subsidy laws of 1886 and 1887, made it necessary for every library to obtain a regents certificate as a condition of municipal aid and requests for registry have greatly increased.

A library trustee, after a trying experience of delay in securing recognition of the library's claims by the city, writes to this office:

The city attorney finally concurred in the report of the legal committee and every one of the 16 councilmen voted for the appropriation. We are to receive the money from the city chamberlain whenever we present the proper certificate of circulation from the regents office.

If any librarian or board of trustees has any doubt of the many great advantages of being registered with the regents it will give me great pleasure to write to him and give him the benefit of our experience. We would never have had this $1000 appropriation but for you and you have aided us materially in many other ways all of which we deeply appreciate.

Library council of the University. At the regents meeting June 5, 1894, it was

Voted, That the New York library association be invited to nominate five experts representing different types of libraries, to serve as a library council with whom the University officers may consult whenever the advice or cooperation of experts may be desirable.

The first council shall be so divided that one person shall go out of office each academic year and a successor shall be nominated by the New York library association or be appointed by the chancellor.

At the meeting of February 28, 1895, it was

Voted, That G: W: Harris, Cornell university library; Robbins Little, Astor library, New York; W: T. Peoples, N. Y. mercantile library; A. L. Peck, Gloversville public library; Ezekiel W. Mundy, Central library, Syracuse, nominated by the New York library association in accordance with the request of the regents, be appointed as the library council of the University for the current year.

Future appointments will be made by the chancellor in accordance with regents ordinances, from a list of three nominations made by the New York library association for each vacancy.

With our regularly organized library division the work of this council will be small compared with states without a salaried staff to look after library interests. It is however a decided advantage to have a carefully selected council to whom we can submit at any time any question on which we wish an expression of the opinion of organized librarianship.

Library legislation. Ch. 559 of the laws of 1895, known as the Membership corporations law, constituting chapter 43 of the general laws went into operation September 1, 1895. Repealing general incorporation laws previously in force it leaves library associations hereafter seeking incorporation no alternative except to apply for charter to the regents of the University.

The same act repealed the library subsidy laws of 1886 and 1887 under which libraries not owned by the public but maintained for their welfare and free use might under certain conditions obtain aid at the rate of about $1000 for 15,000 volumes circulation from the cities or towns in which they were located. § 37 of the University law provides for the payment of local subsidies to such libraries on the more liberal basis of 10 cents a volume of the approved circulation of the preceding year, provided the libraries are registered by the regents as maintaining a proper library standard, and a certificate of approved circulation is given by the University. This is now the only method provided by law by which such subsidies can be obtained.

Not a few at first learning of this change have been disappointed at what seemed the repeal of a beneficent law. On looking into it they have all found however that the new law is much better for all libraries except the very few which might be getting municipal aid for the circulation of books which ought not to be encouraged.

A much more liberal payment is authorized for the books which an impartial expert inspector from the regents office can certify to be worthy such aid. We recall no case in which friends of libraries who looked into the subject carefully have not preferred the later form of the law.

Library legislation in other states. A law of Pennsylvania enacted in 1895 authorizes the school board in any school district of the state, not included in a city of the first or second class, to establish a public library for the free use of the people of the district; the library to be administered by the school board through a board of library trustees appointed by and responsible to them. All public libraries so established are under the supervision and subject to the inspection of the state librarian, who may require from them such reports as he may deem proper.

In Michigan the control of the state library has been given to a library committee consisting of the library committees of the two legislative houses acting with the governor and state librarian. Other libraries in the state may become 'associates' with the right to borrow books from the state library. $2500 was voted to establish a system of 'Michigan traveling libraries.'[a]

In Vermont a library commission has been appointed to aid small towns in founding public libraries by giving $100 worth of books to any town meeting required conditions.

In Wisconsin a library commission was created to advise inquirers, aid library organization and direct the public library movement.

In Montana $1000 was voted for state circulating libraries of 100 volumes each to be lent to communities paying expenses and giving security for safe return within six months. $500 was also appropriated for 1896 and $300 annually thereafter. A commission was appointed to examine the public library systems of other states and report to a subsequent session of the legislature.

---

[a] See also p 189

In New Hampshire a notable step was taken by the legislature in requiring every town to assess an annual tax of about 15 cents on a valuation of $1000, 'to be appropriated to the sole purpose of establishing and maintaining a public library within such town.'

New York library association and New York library club. At a joint meeting held in New York city, Jan. 11-12, 1895 the subjects discussed were;

Library work of the University of the State of New York.
1 Securing facts and statistics.
2 Giving advice and instruction on request.
3 Organizing and chartering libraries.
4 Distributing public library money.
5 Lending traveling libraries.
6 Publishing lists of best books.

Adaptation of libraries to local needs.

Value of a classified arrangement of books.

Principles of selection of books.

Reading for the young, considered with special reference to the opportunities of parents and teachers to control and direct the reading of children. Marked interest was developed in regard to this subject.

An attendance of about 100 was secured at the two business sessions as well as at the dinner given in the evening by the New York library club.

A report of the meeting will be found in the *Library journal* for January 1895.

The New York library association also met at Buffalo May 17-18, 1895. The subjects of discussion were much the same as at the New York meeting, but were presented in some instances by different speakers. A paper on the library situation in western New York was accompanied by a map of the eight western counties, showing the number and kind of libraries in each town, and emphasizing the imperative need of awakening a popular interest in the matter.

There were 40 librarians and teachers in attendance at the three sessions.

A report of the meeting appeared in the *Library journal* for June, 1895.

List of best books of the year. In February, 1895, a list of 232 leading books of 1894 was printed by the New York library association and sent to 600 librarians of New York and other states to obtain an expression of opinion respecting the best 25 books of that year for adding to a village library. The books were arranged in class order with author, title, publisher and price. 156 copies of the list with 25 chosen books marked on each were returned. These votes were summarized and a new list printed with the same books arranged in order of their popularity so ascertained. Out of 232 books only 14 failed to receive a single vote, and six books were named which had not appeared on the original list.

The following books were selected:

RANK		VOTES
1	Ward, *Mrs* Humphry. Marcella. 2 v.	97
2	Kidd, Benjamin. Social evolution.	89
3	Caine, Hall. Manxman.	82
3	Fiske, John. History of the United States.	82
5	Drummond, Henry. Ascent of man.	79
6	Kipling, Rudyard. Jungle book.	77
7	Du Maurier, George. Trilby.	73
8	Brooks, E. S. Century book for young Americans.	65
9	Cary, Edward. George William Curtis. (Amer. men of letters.)	64
10	Century. Cyclopedia of names.	60
11	Larned, J. N. History for ready reference. 5 v.	59
11	Wilkins, M.. E. Pembroke.	59
13	Hope, Anthony. Prisoner of Zenda.	58
14	Pickard, S. T. Life and letters of John Greenleaf Whittier.	53
15	Griffis, W. E. Brave little Holland.	52
16	Blackmore, R. D. Perlycross.	51
16	Doyle, A. C. Memoirs of Sherlock Holmes.	51
18	Abbott C. C. Birds about us.	50
19	Burroughs, John. Riverby.	45
20	Brooks, Noah. Abraham Lincoln.	43
21	Crawford, F. M. Katherine Lauderdale. 2 v.	42
21	Weyman, S. J. Under the red robe.	42

23 **Murray, David.** Story of Japan. (Story of the nations) 41
23 **Warner, C : D.** Golden house. 41
25 **Crockett, S. R.** The stickit minister. 40

Of these 25 books, 12 are classed as fiction
                        3   "   biography
                        3   "   history
                        2   "   social science
                        2   "   natural science
                        2   "   books of reference
                        1 is "   literature

The New York library club held five meetings during the year. The first meeting was at the College for the training of teachers, at which the subject of How teachers shall cooperate with librarians, was discussed. Miss Grace H. Dodge was present and spoke of the benefit to education of this cooperation.

The joint meeting of the club and the state association was held January 11 and 12, at the Y. M. C. A. library as reported above.

The February meeting of the club was held at the Methodist book concern, the occasion was memorable as being the club's first introduction to manila rope paper, of which the Rev. Dr Thomas makes so important a use.

The library of the Y. M. C. A. entertained the club again in March, when the Consolidation of the three great libraries of New York was the subject of discussion. The consensus of opinion favored the site since chosen by the trustees.

The annual meeting was held in May at Columbia college.

Officers for the ensuing term :— *President*, W. F. Stevens, librarian of the Railroad branch of the Y. M. C. A. *Vice-Presidents*, W. A. Bardwell, of the Brooklyn library, Miss E. F. Baldwin, of Columbia college. *Secretary*, Miss Josephine Rathbone of Pratt institute. *Treasurer*, Miss Elizabeth Tuttle of the Long Island historical society. The subject of the meeting was the proposed Bibliography of American literary periodicals, and a committee was appointed to formulate a plan for a general catalogue of such periodicals.

The American library association held its annual conference at Denver and Colorado Springs, Col., Aug. 13–16 and 21, 1895.

147 members were present, of whom 35 were from the eastern states, 39 from the lake states and 67 from the mountain states.

The following papers were of special interest:

Libraries in secondary schools.
International bibliography of scientific literature.
A subject index to science.
Medical books for small public libraries.
Use of periodicals.
Need of additional copyright depositories.
Report of the committee on cooperation.

Four papers treated of the methods employed to discover and exclude improper books.

The closing session at Colorado Springs was specially practical and valuable, presenting a discussion of 'systems of control, support and administration of public libraries' having direct reference to the existing situation in that city, some of whose leading citizens, anxious to secure a public library, were present.

A full report of proceedings is published with the papers in the *Library journal* for Dec. 1895.

Respectfully submitted

MELVIL DEWEY
Director

STATISTICS OF NEW YORK LIBRARIES, 1895

Statistics of libraries. The summary of reports from 723 libraries of 300 volumes or more is given in the following tables. This report is somewhat more complete than the last but still falls short of the desired full presentation of the library resources of the state. Repeated requests have been made for delinquent reports and all materials supplied by the libraries have been used. Evidently the libraries will have to come under the same stringent law that secures so much better reports from the teaching institutions of the University.

Of the libraries to which blanks were sent 222 failed to report. This fact seriously detracts from the value of any comparison with the returns of other years. It does not, however, affect very much the record of the free lending libraries, about which the main interest centers, because libraries of this class have, as a rule, been careful and prompt in making reports as the law required.

Reports are arranged in the general table in alphabetic order of places. The relation of each library to the University is indicated in the sixth column of the general table. In the general summaries the number of reporting libraries 'in the University' and 'not in the University' are placed in parallel columns opposite their respective classes.

SUMMARIES

Date of founding

Libraries founded previous to	1800	6
"	1800–19	12
"	1820–29	18
	1830–39	19
	1840–49	30
	1850–59	46
	1860–69	75
	1870–79	89
	1880–89	110
	1890–95 5½ yrs	145
		550
	No date reported	173
	Total	723

SUMMARIES

	Libraries in University	Libraries not in University	Total
Libraries reporting	514	209	723
Source of charter			
Legislature	3	27	30
General law	13	20	33
Regents	74		74
Belonging to chartered or University institution	424	94	518
Not chartered		68	68
Relation to the University			
Department of the University	1		1
Holding University charter	74		74
Admitted to the University	15		15
Belonging to University institutions	424		424
Registered by the University	4	8	12
Not related to the University		201	201
Class of books			
General	494	177	671
Law	4	13	17
Medical	5	8	13
Theological	5	2	7
Scientific	1	5	6
Historical		2	2
Pedagogic	1		1
Pharmaceutic	3		3
Art	1	3	4
Directory		1	1
Ownership or control			
Public school district	271	27	298
Public district	41		41
Other public	8	6	14
Total public	320	33	353
Government	1	15	16
School	98	13	111
College	50		50
Institutional	5	58	63
Endowed	8	11	19
Membership	27	63	90
Business		1	1
Parish		7	7
Private		5	5
a **Support**			
Endowment or productive property	22	38	60
Taxation	308	29	337
State aid	351	56	407
General funds of the institution	182	143	325
U. S. government		2	2

a Many libraries derive part of their support from each of several sources; many have not reported on support.

SUMMARIES (concluded)

	Libraries in University	Libraries not in University	Total
b Terms of use			
Free to public for reference	29	49	78
" " lending	250	59	309
" limited class for lending	254	84	338
Subscription open to all	5	38	43
" limited	1	5	6
Private		1	1

b Some libraries free for reference are also free to a limited class for lending, and included under both heads.

	No. libs	VOLUMES Added in one yr	VOLUMES Total	Circulation
Libraries of 1000 vols. or more				
Free to public for lending	181	83,278	1,047,123	3,012,694
" only for reference	69	71,371	1,610,628	....
College libraries (all)	50	50,005	1,010,737	....
Law "	20	13,174	289,396	....
Libraries of 10,000 vols. or more				
Free to public for lending	23	47,831	657,752	1,612,330
" only for reference	27	63,273	1,453,932	....
Others	24	53,982	1,100,103	....
Total	74	165,086	3,211,787	....
University libraries	93	33,598	257,576	670,580

Comparative summary 1893-95

	1893	1894	1895	Increase for one year	Increase for two years
No. of libraries	600	704	723	19	123
Volumes added	225,195	246,751	258,741	11,990	33,546
" total	3,851,945	4,133,378	4,392,999	259,621	541,054
a Circulation	3,136,602	3,619,178	4,156,744	537,566	1,020,142

a Including the circulation of subscription libraries and of those free to a limited class.

Date of founding. On this point 550 libraries report. Six of these were founded previous to 1800, as follows:

Columbia college library	1745
New York society library	1754
Union college library	1795
Canandaigua academy library	1795
Cherry Valley academy library	1796
New York hospital library	1796

79 of these libraries were established in the half century between 1800 and 1849. After that date the increase is more rapid. In ten years, 46 libraries; in the next ten years, 75; in the next ten, 89; in the next ten, 110, bringing the record to 1890. In the subsequent five years and a half 145 are reported.

Incorporation. For the first time the source of library charters is given. 30 were granted by the legislature, 33 under general laws and 74 by the regents; 518 libraries out of 723 are the property of chartered institutions or of teaching institutions in the University and 68 have neither charter nor the supervision of a chartered body; 201 reporting libraries are not related to the University in any way except in rendering the required annual report.

Growth. There is an increase over 1894 of 89 libraries 'in the University'. 11 of these are public district libraries, two others are public and 14 are membership libraries, all chartered by the regents within the year.

The number of libraries 'not in the University' is less than the preceding year by 20, the principal falling off being in the institutional libraries largely due to their failure to report. 17 law libraries are reported as against 14 in 1894, and it should be further noted that a few of the most important law libraries in the state are not independent libraries but reported as law departments of general libraries as in the state library at Albany and in Columbia and Cornell university libraries. A list of 20 law libraries in order of size is given in the tables.

The number of libraries sustained by taxation has increased from 296 to 337, and those receiving state aid from 302 to 407. This number includes many school libraries that receive grants from the state, and many that draw from the academic fund as well as those libraries that are aided from the public library money.

The number of free lending libraries in the University has advanced from 229 to 250, while outside the University it fell from 64 to 59, a total increase from 293 to 309. It should be noted, however, that some small district libraries formerly reported as free libraries are, on more careful scrutiny, properly described as free to a limited class.

A more evident sign of growth is seen in the free lending libraries of 1000 volumes or more; the number advancing from 156 to 181; 83,278 books having been added during the year and the circulation increased from 2,665,000 to 3,012,000 volumes. 69 reference libraries have added 71,371 volumes and 50 college libraries have added 50,000 volumes, bringing the total for the colleges up to 1,000,000 volumes.

The summary of libraries of 10,000 volumes or more shows an actual diminution in totals, due to failure to report. But the fact remains that 163,451 volumes were added to 74 such libraries during the year.

59,172 volumes were given to the libraries of the state and 199,569 were bought; showing a total addition of 258,741 volumes, as compared with 246,751 in 1894 and 225,195 in 1893.

The total number of volumes reported is 4,392,999, of which 1,127,199 volumes or about one fourth of all are in the free lending libraries. The total for 1894 was 4,133,378 and that for 1893 was 3,851,945.

The total circulation of the year was 4,156,744 volumes; a decided gain when compared with 3,619,178 in 1894 and 3,136,602 in 1893, or an increase of about half a million volumes each year.

Other points relating to the increase of libraries are given in the following special tables:

Geographic distribution of libraries by counties. This table of free and other libraries in each county with the number of volumes, compares the library returns with the population of the county and states the circulation of the free libraries in proportion to the population and to the volumes in the libraries, assigning to each county and to each group of counties its relative rank in the state. The county of New York has more libraries and more volumes than any other, but in the proportion of volumes to population it is fourth in rank, being surpassed by Tompkins, Albany and Ontario. In the use of free libraries New York is the foremost county in volume of circulation, but ninth in proportion to population and seventh in proportion to the books in those libraries, Fulton leading in the relation to population and Clinton in relation to books. Tables are here given to show the 10 counties that stand first in relation to free libraries.

10 counties with largest free circulation in proportion to population

COUNTY	Rank in 1894	Circulation per 1000 population 1894	Circulation per 1000 population 1895	Population	Circulation of free libraries
1 Fulton	2	1431	1744	38,478	67,125
2 Warren	1	1574	1398	28,618	40,029
3 Orange	3	1243	1236	97,760	120,926
4 Tompkins	30	199	1218	33,612	41,968
5 Herkimer	4	850	1140	47,491	54,174
6 Oneida	12	541	899	123,756	111,330
7 Chautauqua	10	603	866	78,900	68,402
8 Tioga	6	745	763	29,675	22,668
9 New York	8	695	745	1,801,739	1,343,464
10 Westchester	5	795	734	145,106	106,623

Comparing this table with the like record for 1894, we find Tompkins and Oneida appearing for the first time among the first 10 counties, while Genesee and Rockland have fallen out. In Tompkins county the circulation of the large library of the Cornell library association was not reported in 1894 and, this year, it brings the county up to its true place. In Oneida county the circulation of the Utica public library has increased from 55,100 to 82,400. In Rockland county there has been a considerable gain over last year and in Genesee county the loss was very slight, but the standard of circulation for the first 10 counties has advanced from 603 to 734 per 1000 of population.

In 1894, three counties circulated 1000 or more books per 1000 population.

14 counties circulated 500 or more books per 1000 population.

In 1895, five counties circulated 1000 or more books per 1000 population.
20 counties circulated 500 or more books per 1000 population.

Among the 10 leading counties, Chautauqua is in the extreme western part of the state, four, Tioga, Tompkins, Oneida and Herkimer, are central, and the other five are near the eastern line.

10 counties with largest free circulation in proportion to volumes

COUNTY	Rank in 1894	Circulation per 100 vols 1894	1895	Volumes in free libraries	Circulation of free libraries
1 Clinton	45	41	516	1,178	6,084
2 Greene	1	518	495	2,894	14,452
3 Broome	15	256	450	9,650	43,490
4 Ulster	10	293	440	5,259	23,191
5 Kings	5	368	433	89,279	386,610
6 Rockland	2	498	412	5,166	21,328
7 New York	4	402	403	333,233	1,343,464
8 Warren	3	447	371	10,786	40,029
9 Otsego	6	345	357	6,795	24,314
10 Fulton	8	309	336	19,961	67,125

Comparing this table with that of the first 10 counties in 1894 we find that Clinton and Broome appear for the first time, while Orange and Albany have fallen out; Ulster has advanced from tenth to fourth place and the others have fallen back. The minimum of circulation for the 10 leading counties has moved from 293 up to 336 for each 100 volumes.

In 1894 one county circulated 518 volumes for each 100
four counties " 400 volumes or more for each 100
eight " " 300 " " "
23 " " 200 " " "

In 1895 one county circulated 516 volumes for each 100
seven counties " 400 volumes or more for each
13 " " 300 " " "
24 " " 200 " " ..

Ulster county increased its average from 293 to 440 per 100. Clinton county owes its place to the remarkable showing made by the new Plattsburg public library which, with 492 volumes, circulated 5620 and Broome county is indebted to the excellent work done by the city school library at Binghamton which increased its circulation from 28,000 to 43,000 in a year.

The two counties standing first in this comparison have the smallest total circulation of the 10 and by far the smallest number of volumes. It is evident that in a new library with well selected books every volume will be in constant demand.

Comparative summary of free and other libraries and the circulation of free libraries 1893-95

	1893	1894	1895	Increase for one yr	Increase for two yr
No. of free libraries	238	293	a309	16	71
" volumes in libraries		1,049,869	1,127,199	77,330	
" other libraries	362	411	a415	4	53
" volumes in libraries		3,083,509	3,265,800	182,291	
Total no. of libraries	600	704	723	19	123
" volumes	3,851,945	4,133,378	4,392,999	259,621	541,054
Vols. per 1000 population	591	634	674	40	83
Total circ. of free libs	2,293,861	2,766,973	3,146,405	379,432	852,544
" per 1,000 populat'n	352	425	483	58	131
" per 100 volumes		263	279	16	

The comparative summary for the entire state for the last three years shows a gratifying increase in every item noted. With a decided increase of volumes and circulation we find a marked advance in the percentage of circulation when compared with population and volumes. In 1893 the reports showed a free circulation of 352 volumes to 1,000 population. This average advanced to 425 in 1894 and to 483 in 1895. The proportion of circulation to books was not noted in 1893. It was 263 for each 100 volumes in 1894 and 279 in 1895.

Comparative summary of libraries having 10,000 volumes or more 1893-95

	1893	1894	1895	Decrease for one yr
No. of libraries	77	81	74	7
No. volumes	3,080,478	3,267,306	3,211,887	56,519

aAlfred univ lib with 9573 volumes of which 1000 are free for circulation is entered under both free and other libraries

The large libraries. The comparative summary of libraries having 10,000 volumes or more shows a decrease for the year due to failure to report.

74 libraries report 10,000 volumes or more
46 " 20,000 "
13 " 50,000 "
7 " 100,000
4 " 200,000

Two libraries, the state library at Albany and Columbia college library in New York city have during the year passed the mark of 200,000. Columbia college added 24,839 volumes and the state library 15,259. Cornell university added 12,898, making a total of 173,793 volumes in all departments of that library. The Astor library added 9,597 and leads the libraries of the state with 267,147 volumes. Its consolidation with the Lenox library, effected May 23, 1895, adds 86,196 to that number, giving a total of 353,343 volumes for the foundation of the New York public library, with the promise of rapid increase in the future from the added resources of the Tilden trust. One library, that of the General society of mechanics and tradesmen in New York city, passed the 100,000 volume mark; the Newburg free library and the Catholic club library in New York passed the mark of 20,000 and the James Prendergast library in Jamestown passed the 10,000 volume mark within the year.

Comparative summary of libraries of 1000 vols. or more, free for lending, 1893-95

	1893	1894	1895	Increase for one yr	Increase for two yr
No. of libraries	137	156	181	25	44
Volumes added	53,789	87,137	83,278	a3,859	29,489
" total	859,235	1,021,250	1,047,123	25,873	187,888
Circulation total	2,244,572	2,665,269	3,012,694	347,425	768,122
" average per 100 volumes	261	261	287	26	26

a Decrease

Free libraries. A table is given of libraries of 1000 volumes or more free to the public for lending. 181 out of 309 free libraries have reached that size, the largest reporting 102,000 volumes. They contain altogether 1,047,123 volumes, an average of 5785 to each. Additions for the year vary from 0 to 5000, amounting in all to 83,278, an average of 460 to each. Circulation varies from 0 to 626,796 in the year, with a total of 3,012,694, an average of 16,644 to a library and a ratio of 287 for each 100 volumes.

The comparative summary shows a large increase for two years in every item. The last year's gain in the percentage of circulation to the number of volumes, from 261 to 287 per 100, is particularly noticeable.

Free libraries of 1000 volumes or more circulating more than 500 volumes per 100

PLACE AND NAME	Rank in 1894	Circulation per 100 vols 1894	Circulation per 100 vols. 1895	Total volumes	Circulation 1895
1 Ellenville public library	3	823	1,014	1,606	16,292
2 New York, Aguilar free library	1	979	885	28,488	252,227
3 New York, Peck memorial lib.	......	......	840	3,569	†30,000
4 Catskill public library	7	761	819	1,674	13,718
5 Highland Falls, Morgan circ. lib	2	976	800	1,250	10,000
6 New York free circ. lib.	5	794	766	81,785	626,796
7 Shortsville, M. M Buck free lib.	9	614	700	11,500	10,500
8 Glens Falls, Crandall free lib.	6	765	640	6,015	38,529
9 Clinton union school lib.	......	252	630	1,229	†7,748
10 New York college settlement hb.	......	549	615	2,436	†15,000
11 Nyack library	10	586	565	3,372	19,066
12 Fort Plain free library	......	338	550	1,023	5,627
13 Brooklyn, Union for Christian work free lib.	......	539	512	31,483	161,426
14 New York, St Agnes free lib.	......	102	503	1,832	9,225
Branch libraries and libraries less than 1000 volumes					
New York free circ. lib. Harlem branch	......	2,197	2,127	4,482	95,356
New York free circ. lib. George Bruce branch	......	976	892	18,570	165,653
New York free circ. lib. Muhlenberg branch	......	603	843	4,092	34,488
Camden library ass'n	......	......	1,165	819	9,546
Plattsburg public library	......	......	1,142	492	†5,620

The above table gives the record of a few libraries that show a circulation far above the average. From this it appears that, including one library of 492 volumes, and another of 819,

3 libraries circulated 1000 volumes or more per 100
7 " 800 " "
9 " 700 " "
12 600
16 " 500
In 1894, 2 libraries circulated 900 volumes or more per 100
4 " 800 " "
7 " 700 " "
9 600
12 500

Three of the libraries in the table were not included in the report of circulation for 1894 ; the small library that stands second in this respect was not established till July of that year. Three branches of the New York free circulating library, though included in the average of that library, are separately given, to call attention to the extraordinary work done, specially by the Harlem branch, which for two years has kept its average of circulation above 2100 volumes for each 100.

Continuing the comparison of this table with that of last year we find, for the first time, among the first 10 on the list, two New York libraries, the Peck memorial and the College settlement, and the Union school library at Clinton. Ellenville public library has moved from the third to the first place, Catskill public library from the seventh to the fourth and the M. M. Buck free library in Shortsville from the ninth to the seventh. Two more of those that have passed the 500 limit, the Fort Plain free library and the St Agnes free library in New York, made a decided advance on the preceding year. Others in the list show a slight falling off. Two have been left behind.

It should not be supposed that the percentage of circulation is the only test of the quality of library work. It is quite possible that a very large circulation may be obtained for awhile with a very inferior class of books. Circulation can show only the number of persons reached and the frequency with which they are reached. It may mark the degree of public interest, but the quality of the work must be secured and ascertained in other ways not shown in these statistics. But 12 of these 16 libraries are under the visitation of the University; yet all of them are directly known and can be confidently commended. It is to be wished that the mark of interrogation could be spared from some of the figures given in this table, so that the rank could be determined with exactness.

Comparative summary of reference libraries of 1000 volumes or more, 1893-95

	1893	1894	1895	Increase for one year	Decrease for one year
No. of libraries	57	61	69	8	
Volumes added	108,918	81,781	71,371		10,410
" total	1,395,692	1,335,252	1,610,628	275,376	

Free reference libraries. The number of free reference libraries of 1000 or more volumes reporting is 69 as against 61 in 1894 and 57 in 1893. This does not indicate the establishment of new libraries of this class but shows that some libraries heretofore used by subscribers or free to a limited class have been opened for public consultation. 71,351 volumes have been added to the free reference libraries which is 10,000 less than the additions of 1894 and 37,000 less than in 1893. Yet the actual increase in the total of volumes is 275,376, to be accounted for by the addition of whole libraries to the column, as will be seen by the following list:

Libraries first reported free for reference in 1895

New York, N. Y. Society lib.	90,000	vols.
" " Univ. of city of N. Y. lib.	30,196	"
Rochester, Univ. of Rochester lib.	29,700	"
New York, Amer. museum of nat. hist. lib.	29,231	"
" " College of St Francis Xavier lib.	25,000	"
Hamilton, Colgate univ. lib.	23,697	"
Brooklyn, Y. M. C. A. lib.	13,512	"
Kingston, Third jud. dist. law lib.	7,000	
New York, City library	6,200	
Oswego, State normal and training sch. lib.	4,529	
New York, Mott memorial med. and surg. lib.	3,000	"

Seneca Falls, Seneca Falls library ass'n 2,711 vols.
Plattsburg, Y. M. C. A. lib. 2,000 "
White Plains, Westchester co. law lib. 1,950 "
New York, Health dep't lib. 1,501
Gouverneur, Gouverneur reading room ass'n lib. 1,317 "
Watertown, Y. M. C. A. lib. 1,130
Ballston Spa, Saratoga co. law lib. 1,000
New York, St Barnabas free reading room 1,000

It should be noted also that some of the libraries reported in 1894 as free for reference have since become free for circulation and have been transferred accordingly to another table.

Comparative summary of college libraries 1893–95

	1893	1894	1895	Increase for one year	Decrease for one year
No. of libraries	50	55	50	....	5
Volumes added	67,101	64,530	50,005	....	14,525
" total	882,833	992,633	1,010,737	18,104	....

College libraries. The comparative summary shows 50 colleges reporting their libraries; five less than last year. This decrease is due to the dropping out or changes of name of some institutions and consolidation of the reports of departments in other cases. 50,000 volumes were added to these libraries during the year, and the total of books is a little more than 1,000,000.

Law libraries. A table is given of 20 law libraries arranged in order of size. This is not complete. It does not include the consultation libraries of some of the most important courts of the state, provided for the use of the judges nor the library of the attorney-general, nor the valuable law library of Columbia college included in the report of the general library of that institution.

Two libraries reported are under the control of institutions, five belong to colleges and 13 belong to the state. Most of the law libraries are open to the public for reference. 289,396 volumes are in the 20 libraries and 13,174 of these were added within the year.

Libraries in the University. A table of University libraries is given including all that have come into this relation under the University law of 1892. The list does not include the state library, itself a department of the University, the libraries of teaching institutions or libraries only registered as maintaining a proper standard.

It has been practicable to give many details respecting the University libraries that could not be readily obtained for others.

The exact dates of incorporation and admission to the University are supplied, the number of books and their circulation for the year, the number of trustees and the method of their election.

A few that were established late in the year had nothing to report. With the single exception of the Grosvenor library in Buffalo, all in this list are free for circulation. The Grosvenor is forbidden by its charter to lend books.

The number of library corporations in the University is 93. Two of these were originally chartered by act of legislature, 16 were ncorporated under general laws and 75 hold the charter of the regents. 39 of these hold provisional charters indicating that the property, including books, held by each is not yet valued at $1000.

This calls attention to the fact that many small communities are attempting the establishment of free public libraries on a small scale but with the promise of great usefulness and rapid increase with state aid. It is confidently expected that in five years, or before, all these provisional charters will be exchanged for absolute charters implying the possession of $1000 worth of property and books.

The University libraries contain 258,426 volumes including additions of 33,598 within the year. Their circulation for the year has reached the sum of 670,580 volumes. They are located in 39 different counties.

Other items of interest respecting these libraries will be found in the preceding report of the public libraries division.

Library buildings. The library of St Stephens college at Annandale has been moved to its new building which cost $74,000.

Hobart college library at Geneva has added 53 feet to the length of its building which contains stack room for 50,000 volumes, three seminar rooms and other offices. Mrs Agnes Demarest of Buffalo, who gave $15,000 to extend the building, adds $35,000 to maintain the library.

Bay Ridge public library reports that a beginning has been made toward a fund for a new building.

The Brooklyn institute library is located temporarily in the Bedford Park building 185 Brooklyn av. pending the completion of the new museum building for the institute on Prospect hights.

The Brooklyn library on Montague st. has completely reconstructed its building introducing steel columns and girders in place of wood, transferring the delivery department to the ground floor, the reading rooms to the second floor and adding shelving for 60,000 volumes.

A new and costly library building for Pratt institute, Brooklyn, is nearly completed.

Grosvenor public library in Buffalo has moved into its elegant and commodious new building.

The Camden library and the Wellsville public library have moved to convenient rooms provided for them by the village authorities in their respective town halls.

Fort Hamilton free library raised $1000 at a fair which was used in part payment for a house. The library was to be in its new quarters Oct. 1, 1895.

The Gouverneur Reading room association, organized in 1885, was incorporated in February 1895, receiving from Hon. James Smith of Buffalo the gift of a house and lot for library purposes.

Washington Heights free library in New York may use $25,000 of a recent bequest of J. Hood Wright for building purposes.

The Young mens Christian association of New York has bought land for a new branch which will give greatly increased library facilities. $165,000 for this purchase was a bequest of W. H. Vanderbilt supplemented by a gift of $25,000 from Cornelius Vanderbilt.

Newfield public library has bought a building for $225.

Ogdensburg public library has secured a building costing $35,000, the amount being raised by subscription. $23,000 of this sum was given by three persons. The premises constitute one of the finest library properties in the state. They were occupied Aug. 1, 1895.

Reynolds library, Rochester, moved October 1, 1895 to new quarters in the Reynolds mansion which was altered and refitted at a cost of $17,000. A branch reading room for newspapers, popular magazines and the most general books of reference is continued at the rooms formerly occupied by the library.

Jervis library, Rome, has received the residence of the late J. B. Jervis, as part of his bequest for founding a public library. The house was refitted and opened as a library July 15, 1895.

Saugerties public library has moved to new quarters and enjoys improved facilities. The average daily circulation, beginning with 14 one year ago, has increased to 47.

Syracuse central library has moved to its new and convenient quarters in the former school house on Montgomery st.

Oneida historical society in Utica looks for the completion of a new building in the summer of 1896, the gift of the late Mrs Helen M. Williams whose generous intention is now being carried out by her daughters, Mrs T. R. and Mrs Frederick Proctor.

Grinnell library at Wappinger's Falls has added an efficient system of ventilation and several alcoves needed for shelf room.

The following schools have added largely to their library facilities by the use of rooms remodeled and refitted, or by rooms in new buildings.

St Margaret's school, Buffalo	Hobart union school
East Aurora union school	Lyndonville union school
Delaware lit. institute, Franklin	Chamberlain institute, Randolph
Friendship union school	Wilson union school
Gouverneur high school	

At St Joseph's academy in Brasher Falls a library and reading room were fitted up at the expense of the graduates.

At McAuley academy in Keeseville, a like expense was borne by the graduates of 1895.

Gifts and special additions. Bay Ridge public library received through the board of education 600 volumes from public school no. 102 of Brooklyn. The books are stored for the present for lack of shelf room in the library.

The Sherman Jewett Williams memorial library of Buffalo was founded by a student of that name in the high school who died before completing his course of study leaving $5000, the interest of which was to be applied to the founding and perpetuating of a library 'for the boys of Miss Karnes' room to read and enjoy.' The privileges of the library are now extended to the whole school. The equipment includes a complete card catalogue.

Ilion district library received $200 for books from 20 men in sums of $10 each.

Ilion free public library received 145 volumes from Mr G. Clifford Russell, 75 volumes from Mrs Clarence W. Seamens and 30 copies of current magazines each month for general circulation from Mr Clarence W. Seamens. 335 bound government reports were given by the Utica public library. By the will of Mrs Harriet Carleton the library receives $2000 endowment.

Cornell university library, Ithaca, received 4624 volumes by gift, including 1200 given by ex-President White to the White historical library and 1000 added by Willard Fiske to his previous gift of the Dante collection which now numbers over 4000 volumes.

From the king of Siam the library received a copy of the Tripitaka in 39 volumes; from Theodore Stanton about 100 volumes of works in modern literature; and from the Record society of Lancashire and Cheshire a complete set of its publications.

Lockport public library has in its care the Asher B. Evans memorial library of 192 valuable works of reference. Capt. A. V. Reid, U. S. N. is placing in the library a complete set of government records of the war of the rebellion 1861-64 with atlases. The library is a designated depositary of U. S. public documents.

Nassau free library received $46 from a young people's entertainment.

At the Cathedral library in New York deficits are made up by personal gifts from Rev. J. H. McMahon. Two additional branches of this library will be opened September 1895.

Washington Heights free library in New York received $1300 of which $1200 represented monthly payments from the late J. Hood Wright and his wife. By the will of Mr Wright the library will receive eventually $100,000.

Ogdensburg public library received from Mrs Dr Robert Morris $1000 to establish, as a memorial of her son, the Robert Eadie Morris library of mechanics and useful arts.

Oyster Bay People's library has received over 600 volumes by gift.

Jervis library of Rome received from the late J. B. Jervis, beside his beautiful home estate his private library of 2500 volumes and from the family of the late Bloomfield J. Beach, the loan of 2700 volumes for five years. Both of these collections are used for reference only. There are 4000 volumes in the circulating department.

Bryant circulating library of Roslyn reports a legacy of $500.

Wellsville public library has received a large paleontologic chart valued at $100, and the loan of a large case of native animals and birds stuffed and mounted.

Wyoming free library has received 170 volumes and financial aid from the family of Mrs J. C. Coonly of Chicago, Ill.

Arrangement and cataloguing. Jamestown high school is cataloguing its library of 3000 volumes.

Jamestown Y. M. C. A. library is being reorganized.

At the library of the college of the city of New York a new card catalogue is being made.

The libraries of Onondaga academy and of Port Richmond union school have been arranged on the decimal system and recatalogued.

The library of the Woman's Institute of Yonkers has been entirely recatalogued and a new charging system introduced.

Loan libraries. The American seamen's friend society has sent out during the year from their rooms in New York 359 loan libraries of which 136 were new and 223 were refitted and reshipped. The total number of volumes in these libraries was 15,537, and of new volumes 5848, available to 4173 seamen on long voyages.

Miscellaneous. At Pratt institute, Brooklyn, a library training school course of one year is carried on by graduates of the N. Y. state library school.

The Long Island free library, 571 Atlantic av. Brooklyn was attached to the Pratt institute library as the Long Island branch in December 1894.

The Woman's institute of Yonkers has opened a small branch library.

May 23, 1895 the Astor library, New York was consolidated with the Lenox library and the Tilden trust under the name of New York public library—Astor, Lenox and Tilden foundations, with 21 trustees, seven named by each interest. John Bigelow was elected president, Henry C. Potter and John J. Kennedy, vice-presidents, Edward King, treasurer and George L. Rives, secretary.

By an amendment of the city charter Yonkers public library receives $2000 a year instead of $200. A separate reading room has been opened. The library and reading room are open from 9 a. m. to 5 p. m. each day and from 7 to 9 on three evenings of the week.

SUMMARY OF REPORTS OF NEW YORK LIBRARIES
1 July 1894 — 30 June 1895

The following tables are a summary of reports made to the regents under the University law of 1892. All libraries containing 300 volumes or more are included. Libraries are arranged in the alphabetic order of places.

Any item with ⸸ prefixed indicates that it is not a verified statement but the best obtainable estimate.

ABBREVIATIONS

used under   Source of charter
L Legislature
G General law
R Regents
I Belonging to a chartered or University institution

used under   Relation to the University
u Department of the University
o Holding University charter
a Admitted to the University
i Belonging to a University institution
r Registered by the University

used under   Class of books

Gen. General   Hist. Historical
Med. Medical   Ped. Pedagogic
Theo. Theological   Phar Pharmaceutical
Sci. Scientific   Dir. Directory

used under   Ownership or control

Pri. *Private:* belonging to an individual, family or firm and open to the public, if at all, only by courtesy.

Mem. *Membership:* controlled by an association requiring an election for an admission or payment of a fee for the right to vote for trustees; e. g. society, association, club, atheneum and other proprietary libraries. A membership library may be open to the public and supported in part by taxation, but is not controlled by the voters or their representatives.

Bus. *Business*. open to any one who pays the fee, i. e libraries run as a business, like the circulating maintained in many bookstores, and many mercantile libraries, though some of the latter are proprietary libraries.

End. *Endowed:* owned and controlled by the trustees of an endowment, usually a self-perpetuating body. An endowed library may be freely open to the public but is not owned or controlled by it. This does not include libraries belonging to endowed institutions, colleges, schools or churches.

Pub. *Public:* owned and controlled by the public through trustees elected by the voters or appointed by their representatives, but does not include government, school or institutional libraries.

Pub. D. *Public district:* the name given to a school district library when placed in control of independent trustees under laws of 1892, ch. 573, § 7.

Pub. sch. *Public school:* that form of public library organized under the laws in force from 1838-92, if it still remains in control of the school authorities.

Gov. *Government* · owned by the U. S , state or local government; e. g. state, department, court, garrison and similar libraries, but does not include those classed as public, school or institutional.

Inst. *Institutional:* belonging to institutions other than colleges, schools and churches; e. g. hospitals, asylums, prisons, Y. M. C. A., etc.

Coll. and sch. *College and school:* maintained for the use of students and teachers and owned and controlled by the institutions.

Par. *Parish:* owned and controlled by a church.

used under Support

End. Endowment or productive property
Tax. Taxation
St. State aid
Sdy. Local subsidy
G. Gifts
Gen. General funds
Pri. Private

used under Terms of use

F. Free
R. Free for reference only
Fl. Free to limited class
S. Subscription open to all
Sl. Subscription limited
Pri. Private

	Place	NAME OF LIBRARY	Year founded	Source of charter	Relations to University
1	Adams	Adams collegiate inst. lib	1864	I	i
2	Addison	Addison pub. lib	1893	R	c
3	Afton	Union sch. lib	1874	I	l
4	Akron	Union sch. lib	1887	I	i
5	Albany	Albany acad. lib	1813	I	i
6	"	Albany coll. of phar. lib		I	i
7	"	Albany female acad. lib		I	i
8	"	Albany free lib	1891	R	c
9	"	Albany inst. lib	1824	I	...
10	"	Albany law sch. lib	1883	I	i
11	"	Cathedral acad. lib	1874	I	i
12	"	Catholic union lib	1887	I	r
13	"	Christian brothers' acad. lib	1869	I	i
14	"	Diocesan lending lib	1890	I	...
15	"	Dudley observatory lib	1856	I	i
16	"	New York state lib	1818	L	u
17	"	New York state normal coll. lib	†1844	I	i
18	"	Public sch. lib	1871	I	i
19	"	St Agnes' sch. lib	1870	I	i
20	"	St Joseph's acad. lib	1891	I	i
21	"	St Vincent's male orph. asy. S. H. lib	1894	I	...
22	"	Young men's ass'n lib	1833	I	...
23	"	Y. M. C. A. lib	1857	I	...
24	"	Y W C A. lib	1888	I	...
25	Albion	Albion free town lib		G	...
26	"	Albion pub lib	1893	R	c
27	Alexander	Union sch lib	1886	I	i
28	Alfred Center	Alfred univ. lib	1857	I	ir
	"	Alfred univ. lib			
29	Allegany	St Bonaventure's coll. lib	1875	I	i
30	"	St Elisabeth's lib	1882	I	i
31	"	Union sch. lib	1823	I	i
32	Allen's Hill	Allen's Hill free lib. ass'n	1895	R	c
33	Amsterdam	Amsterdam lib. ass'n	1891	G	a
34	"	St Mary's catholic inst lib	1880	I	i
35	"	Union sch lib. dist. no. 8	1892	I	i
36	"	Union sch. lib. dist. no. 11	?	I	i
37	Andes	Union sch. and acad. lib	1893	I	i
38	Angelica	Wilson acad lib	1885	I	i
39	Angola	Union sch. lib		I	i
40	Annandale	St Stephen's coll. lib	1860	I	i
41	Antwerp	Ives sem. lib	1869	I	i
42	Arcade	Union sch. and acad. lib		I	i
43	Argyle	Union sch. lib	1892	I	i
44	Arkport	Arkport pub lib	1894	R	c
45	Attica	Stevens mem lib	1894	...	...

LIBRARIES

Name of librarian or person in charge	Class of books if not general	Ownership or control	Support	Terms of use	NO. ADDED LAST YEAR Given	Bought	Total no. in library	
O. B. Rhodes		Sch	St. G	R.Fl.			1145	1
Mary S. Brewer		Pub. D.	Tax St	F		252	1959	2
		Pub. sch.	Tax St	F			†1000	3
Orson Warren		Pub. sch	Tax St	F		70	668	4
Henry P. Warren		Sch	Gen	Fl			800	5
	Phar	Coll	Gen	Fl			90	6
Lucy A. Plympton		Sch	Gen	Fl			3100	7
John A. Howe		Mem	Sdy St	F	283	287	2634	8
G: R Howell		Inst		Fl			5000	9
Ralph H. Overbaugh	Law	Coll	Gen	Fl		16	1382	10
		Sch	Gen	Fl	17		1567	11
William F. Sullivan		Mem	St. Gen	F	a 20	a 193	a 2049	12
		Sch	Gen	Fl		10	2129	13
Mary Salome Cutler	Theo	Par	G	Fl	21		1087	14
Louis Boss	Sci	Coll	Gen	Fl			2000	15
Melvil Dewey		Gov	St	R.Fl.	3540	b11,719	c208,971	16
William J. Milne		Coll	St	Fl			2900	17
Frances M. Prentice		Pub. sch.	Tax St	Fl	82	480	8237	18
Ellen W. Boyd		Sch	Gen	Fl	50	50	3800	19
		Sch	Gen	Fl	16		1048	20
		Inst	Gen	Fl		25	575	21
Nellie B. Lovejoy		Inst	Fees	S		600	†15,000	22
A. A. Clarke		Inst	Gen	R.Fl.	145	22	3707	23
Alice Newman		Inst	G	R.Fl.	d24	d111	d1526	24
Lillian A. Achilles		Pub	Tax	F	37	26	920	25
Lillian A. Achilles		Pub. D.	Tax	F	50		2950	26
J. Howerth		Pub. sch	Tax St	F		16	1133	27
E. M. Tomlinson		Coll	End St	R. F.	107	23	9573	28
E. M. Tomlinson		Coll	End St	F			1000	
		Coll	Gen	Fl			7313	29
Sr M. Thomasius		Sch	Gen	Fl	12	8	1509	30
Jennie L. Burr		Pub. sch.	Tax St	Fl		56	428	31
Mary B. Allen		Mem	St. Sdy	F	27	86	411	32
Belle Huntley		Mem	St G	F	97	248	2368	33
		Sch	Gen	Fl	14	12	1106	34
J. W. Kimball		Pub. sch	Tax St	Fl		116	565	35
		Pub. sch.	Tax St	F		38	638	36
George N. Sleight		Pub. sch.	Tax St	F	6	2	576	37
John P. Slocum		Sch	St. Fees	R.Fl.	30	215	1676	38
		Pub. sch.	Tax St	Fl			575	39
R. B. Fairbairn		Coll	Gen	Fl	50		†10,000	40
F. E. Arthur		Sch	Gen	Fl	5	3	804	41
		Pub. sch.	Tax St	F		110	504	42
		Pub. sch.	Tax St	F		1	1020	43
Frank Hurlbut		Pub. D.	Tax St	F	100	400	500	44
Laura E. Leland		Pri	G	F		215	6905	45

a For year ending Sept 1895
c Including 19,612 in public libraries division.
b Including 7584 in public libraries division.
d For year ending Jan 1896.

NEW YORK

	VOLUMES NO ISSUED		Days open in year	HOURS OPEN EACH WEEK FOR		RECEIPTS		
	For home use	For use at lib.		Lending	Reading	Invested funds	Local taxation	State aid
1								
2	5614		215	10	10		$150	
3								
4	?1000	?600	186	10	30			
5								
6								
7								
8	6356	?1800	307	59	59		200	$200
9								
10	?	1382	213		66			
11	?80	?	187					
12	2500	?	365	7½	86			150
13		150	160		25			
14	145		365	65	65			
15								
16	a21,486		313	80	80			37,900
17								
18	12,866	?	300	11½	32½		250	820 10
19	500		100	2	84			
20	?152		180	42				
21			365		28			
22	12,961	?	365	72	77			
23	1715	687	365	78	82			
24	3162	?	313	9	64			
25	1655	100	104	8	8			
26	11,142	300	104	8	8		78	
27	?570	?200	200	35	35		10	
28	3857	?5000	214	34	34	$166 11		200
29	?	50	150		3			
30		3400	144		10			
31	864		40	1			53 64	24 74
32	343		66	10				50
33	9669	?	308	39	39			200
34	?	?	69	4				
35	2041		116	1½			100	57 50
36	?	?	200	35	35			182 04
37	926	?	170	1	?		25	25
38	2377	?	195	4	30			103 75
39								
40	?	?	216	12	12			
41	?		35	?	?			
42	?200	?600	200	5			42 85	20
43	160		200	5			8 50	
44	450	?	130	30	30		200	200
45	12,850	?	104	16	16			

a Including 9330 from capitol library.

LIBRARIES (continued)

FROM			PAYMENTS FOR				
Annual dues	Gifts and other sources	Total receipts	Books, serials and binding	Salaries	All other expenses	Total payments	
$2 10	....	$152 10	$239 14	$85	$43 51	$367 65	1
....	....	....	53 55	....	30 63	84 18	2
....	....	....	....	....	....	....	3
....	....	....	....	....	....	....	4
....	....	....	....	....	....	....	5
....	....	....	....	....	....	....	6
....	....	....	....	....	....	....	7
....	$462 87	862 87	310 02	312	218 55	840 57	8
....	....	....	....	....	....	....	9
....	....	....	17 40	130	....	147 40	10
....	? 20	20	? 10	....	....	10	11
....	225 08	375 08	280 89	45 43	48 76	375 08	12
....	....	....	31 50	....	....	31 50	13
....	66	66	16 75	16 10	5	37 85	14
....	....	....	....	....	....	....	15
....	....	37,900	b25,207 45	c26,489 44	d5175 67	56,872 56	16
....	....	....	....	....	....	....	17
....	660 10	1730 20	956 81	....	46 88	1003 69	18
....	100	100	100	....	....	100	19
....	8	8	13 50	....	....	13 50	20
....	....	....	....	....	....	....	21
461	1429 60	1890 60	637 58	1202 58	142 63	1982 79	22
....	872 31	872 31	231 04	600	41 27	872 31	23
....	....	....	....	....	....	....	24
....	2	2	2 75	....	....	2 75	25
....	14 25	92 25	12 65	78	....	90 65	26
....	. 10	. 26	26	....	....	26	27
82 55	387 30	1085 96	112 90	300	139 41	552 31	28
....	....	....	....	....	....	....	29
....	20	20	15 35	....	....	15 35	30
....	....	78 38	53 19	....	....	53 19	31
5	50	105	100	5	1 80	106 80	32
184	1850 01	2234 01	128 03	339	1222 03	1689 06	33
45 35	....	45 35	9 78	....	....	9 78	34
....	1 45	158 95	159 95	....	....	159 95	35
....	....	182 04	182 04	....	....	182 04	36
5	....	55	2	....	....	2	37
25	103 75	232 50	213 27	....	8	221 27	38
....	....	....	....	....	....	....	39
....	....	....	....	100	....	100	40
....	6 80	6 80	3 40	....	....	3 40	41
....	....	62 85	62 85	....	....	62 85	42
....	....	8 50	8 50	....	....	8 50	43
....	100	500	335	....	65	400	44
....	....	....	....	....	....	....	45

b Including $10,209.10 public libraries division   c Including $5133 99 public libraries division
           d Including $2305 22 public libraries division.

	Place	NAME OF LIBRARY	Year founded	Source of charter	Relation to University
46	Attica	Union sch and acad. lib	?1868	I	i
47	Auburn	Cayuga asylum lib		I	
48	"	High sch. lib		I	i
49	"	Seymour lib	1876	G	
50	"	State prison lib	1841		
51	"	Theological sem. lib	1820	I	i
52	Aurora	Cayuga Lake mil. acad. lib		I	i
53	"	Wells coll. lib	1868	I	i
54	Ausable Forks	Union sch. lib		I	i
55	Avoca	Union sch. lib	1871	I	i
56	Avon	Union sch. lib	1881	I	i
57	Babylon	Union sch. lib	1892	I	i
58	Bainbridge	Union sch. lib	1873	I	i
59	Baldwinsville	Baldwinsville free acad. lib	1868	I	i
60	Ballston Spa	Ballston public lib	1893	R	c
61	"	Saratoga co. law lib	1813	L	
62	Batavia	Richmond lib	1853	I	i
63	"	State sch for the blind lib		I	
64	Bath	Davenport lib	1889	G	
65	"	Haverling union sch. lib		I	i
66	Bath Beach	New Utrecht pub. lib	1895	R	c
67	Bath-on-Hudson	No. Greenbush pub. lib. dist. no. 6	1893	R	c
68	Bay Ridge	Bay Ridge free lib	1888	R	c
69	Bay Shore	Union sch. lib	1894	I	i
70	Beedes	Keene Heights lib. club	1888	I	
71	Belfast	Genesee Valley sem. lib	1857	I	i
72	Belleville	Union acad. lib	1826		
73	Belmont	Belmont lit. and hist. soc. free lib	1885	R	c
74	"	Union sch. lib	1889	I	i
75	Bergen	Union sch. lib		I	i
76	Binghamton	City sch. lib	1861	I	i
77	"	Lady Jane Grey sch. lib			
78	"	St Joseph's acad. lib	1862	I	i
79	"	Supreme court lib	1859	L	
80	"	Y. M C. A. R. R. branch lib	1888		
81	Blue Mountain Lake	Christian union soc. lib			
82	Bolivar	Union sch lib		I	i
83	Boonville	Erwin lib and inst	1885	G	a
84	"	Union sch lib	1878	I	i
85	Brasher Falls	Brasher and Stockholm un. sch. lib	1886	I	i
86	"	St Joseph's acad. lib	1891	I	i
87	Brewster	Union sch lib	1889	I	i
88	Bridgehampton	Hampton lib	1876		
89	Brocton	Union sch. lib		I	i
90	Bronxville	School lib. dist. no. 2	1870		

STATISTICS OF NEW YORK LIBRARIES, 1895

LIBRARIES (continued)

Name of librarian or person in charge	Class of books if not general	Ownership or control	Support	Terms of use	VOLUMES NO ADDED LAST YEAR Given	Bought	Total no in library	
Arthur M. Preston		Pub. sch.	Tax St	F	6	5	1746	46
James Seymour jr		Inst	G	Fl	55		555	47
....		Pub. sch.	Tax St	Fl		275	1023	48
Martha A Bullard		Mem End	End	S	64	125	11,980	49
Horatio Yates		Inst	St	Fl		ʔ800	1700	50
Arthur S. Hoyt	Theo	Coll	End	F			22,352	51
....		Sch	Gen	Fl			2565	52
Annie A Wood		Coll	Gen	Fl	391	173	5308	53
....		Pub. sch	Tax	Fl			ʔ500	54
C. E. Button		Pub. sch	Tax St	Fl		11	ʔ400	55
R. J. Wallace		Pub sch	Tax St	F		46	975	56
Frederick H Lane		Pub. sch.	Tax St	Fl	10	655	2906	57
F. W. Crumb		Pub. sch.	Tax St	F		9	1220	58
Emma Y Emerson		Pub. sch.	Tax St	F	2	118	965	59
Harriet B. Curtiss		Pub	St G	F		3	838	60
H. L. Grose	Law	Gov	St	R		ʔ30	ʔ1000	61
....		Pub. sch	Tax St	F	314	250	10,794	62
Gardner Fuller		Sch	St	Fl		20	1470	63
H. L. Underhill		Pri.Mem.	G	F		200	9050	64
S. D. Miller		Pub. sch	Tax St	Fl	3	6	390	65
Julia R. Guyn		Mem	St G	F	919	422	1341	66
William A Cuzner		Pub. D.	Tax St	F	2	199	1259	67
N. DeG Doubleday		Mem	St G	F	87	489	3490	68
Claude A Du Vall		Pub sch	Tax St	Fl		88	650	69
E I H. Howell		Mem	Fees	Fl. S.	50	75	1475	70
Fred W Gray		Pub. sch	Tax St	Fl		91	330	71
Alexander Hadlock		Sch	Gen	F	3		2153	72
Mrs Ella B. Pelton		Mem	St G	F	152	245	1368	73
Alice H. Gorton		Pub. sch	Tax St	F	19	253	902	74
....		Pub. sch	Tax St	Flʔ			496	75
Mrs J. W. Clonney		Pub. sch.	Tax	F	5	580	ʔ9000	76
Mary R. Hyde		Pri		Fl		40	1000	77
Sister M. Joseph		Sch	Gen	Fl		7	457	78
Emma C. M Harris	Law	Gov	St	R		ʔ617	ʔ10,617	79
G. L. Nichols		Inst	G	Fl	3		600	80
Fred W. Smith		Inst	Gen	F			450	81
....		Pub. sch	Tax St	F			588	82
L. W. Fiske		End	End. St	F		291	2496	83
Chas. H. Warfield		Pub. sch	Tax St	Fl	10	40	450	84
Wm. H. Adams		Pub sch	Tax St	F	8	43	ʔ900	85
Sister M. de la Salle		Sch	Gen	Fl	9	43	396	86
....		Pub. sch.	Tax St	F	6	6	314	87
John F. Youngs		End	EndFees	S	2	70	4906	88
....		Pub. sch	Tax	F			500	89
Rebecca E. Young		Pub. sch	Tax. St	F			1413	90

NEW YORK

	VOLUMES NO ISSUED For home use	VOLUMES NO ISSUED For use at lib	Days open in year	HOURS OPEN EACH WEEK FOR Lending	HOURS OPEN EACH WEEK FOR Reading	Invested funds	RECEIPTS Local taxation	RECEIPTS State aid
46	112	?	192	30			$25	
47								
48		?	188		25			$200
49	7033		306	54	54	$1502 96		
50			?	?	?			500
51								
52								
53	?	?	265	45	?			
54								
55	100		190	25	25		20	49 17
56	1394	?	40	?			50 24	75
57	?	?4200	185		14		310	110
58	418	?1000	52	2	15		11 50	
59	4000	100	200	5			150	150
60	6653		213	5				
61			313		?			
62	22,932		300	60	79		1582 73	500
63								
64	11,250		180	10½				
65			187		30		20	20
66	5654		126	36	36			200
67	5079		138	6			147 92	73
68	12,226		306	40	40			200
69	670	?425	?130	7	35			72 33
70	1253	?200	78	58	58			
71		330	185				25	25
72	450	?	200	7½	7½			
73	3371		208	10	10			100
74	1172		193	1¼				
75								
76	43,370	?800	277	26	26		2685 98	
77								
78	?80	?55	200					
79		?	300		48		600	2600
80	472		313	72	72			
81			100	a 1	a 1			
82								
83	6231	151	309	12	42	829		200
84	50	125	190	30	30		25 20	25 20
85	?150	?	172	2	30		15	15
86		?250	193		30			
87	290	75	200	35			?	108
88	903	?40	309	52	52	609 33		
89								
90	1638		52	1	1			

a During the summer 18 hours

LIBRARIES (continued)

From		Total receipts	Payments for			Total payments	
Annual dues	Gifts and other sources		Books, serials and binding	Salaries	All other expenses		
....	....	$25	....	.	....	....	46
....	....	....	....	....	....	....	47
....	....	510 65	$510 65	....	....	$510 65	48
$276 90	....	1779 86	279 57	$842 70	$736 91	1859 18	49
....	....	500	....	....	....	....	50
....	....	....	....	....	....	....	51
....	....	....	....	....	....	....	52
....	$1013 39	1013 39	940 14	....	....	940 14	53
....	....	....	....	....	....	....	54
....	....	69 17	58 34	....	....	58 34	55
....	....	125 24	83 74	....	42 50	126 24	56
....	....	420	419 54	....	....	419 54	57
....	....	11 50	11 50	....	....	11 50	58
....	....	300	194 24	20	....	214 24	59
....	128	128	295 80	120	4 16	419 96	60
....	200	200	....	....	....	....	61
....	96 44	2179 17	591 73	1100	487 44	2179 17	62
....	....	....	....	....	....	....	63
....	....	....	401 03	200	122 34	723 37	64
....	....	40	24 25	....	....	24 25	65
....	922 93	1122 93	371 32	150	298 80	820 12	66
....	4 45	225 37	146	55	2 98	203 98	67
....	988 72	1188 72	462 18	489 29	223 44	1174 91	68
....	48 33	120 66	96 66	....	....	96 66	69
200	100	300	190	84	26	300	70
....	....	50	48 01	....	....	48 01	71
....	....	....	....	....	12 83	12 83	72
....	181 06	281 06	265 41	....	15 65	281 06	73
....	109 30	109 30	₹ 89 55	....	....	₹ 89 55	74
....	....	....	....	....	....	....	75
....	139 50	2825 48	1194 50	760	127 21	2081 71	76
....	....	....	....	....	....	....	77
....	....	....	18 90	....	....	18 90	78
....	....	3200	2494 74	600	....	3094 74	79
....	....	....	....	....	....	....	80
....	50	50	....	40	....	40	81
....	....	....	....	....	....	....	82
....	....	1029	397 60	400	231 40	1029	83
....	....	50 40	50 40	....	....	50 40	84
....	6 57	36 57	36 57	....	....	36 57	85
....	51 60	51 60	38 56	....	10	48 56	86
....	....	₹ 108	7 25	....	....	7 25	87
49 37	12	670 70	174 14	194	193 33	561 47	88
....	....	....	....	....	....	....	89
....	....	....	....	110	....	110	90

NEW YORK

	Place	NAME OF LIBRARY	Year found	Source of charter	Relation to University
91	Brookfield	Union sch. lib	1876	I	i
92	Brooklyn (Laf'ette av.)	Adelphi acad. lib	1869	I	i
93	" 1143 Bedford av	Bedford circ. lib	1876	...	...
94	"	Berkeley inst. lib	1887	I	i
95	" 15 Hicks st.....	Bethel sabbath sch. lib	¶1865	...	...
96	"	Boys' high sch. lib	1895	I	i
97	" 198 Washing'n st	Brooklyn inst. lib	1824	I	...
98	" 197 Montague st	Brooklyn lib	1857	L	...
99	"	Female inst. of the Visitation lib...		I	i
100	" 16 Court house..	Law lib	1850	L	...
101	" Pierrepont st...	Long Island hist. soc. lib	1863	I	...
102	" Joralemon st...	Packer collegiate inst. lib	1846	I	i
103	" Livingston st...	Polytechnic inst. Spicer lib	1891	]	i
104	" 215 Ryerson st..	Pratt inst. free lib	1887	I	i
	" 571 Atlantic av..	Long Island branch	1894	...	...
	" 184 Franklin st .	Astral branch		...	...
105	" 300 Baltic st....	St Francis' coll. lib	1883	I	i
106	"	St John's coll lib		I	i
107	" c Alb & St M.av	St John's home lib	1870	I	...
108	" 67 Scherm'h'n st.	Union for Christian work free lib ..	1871	I	...
109	" 502 Fulton st ...	Y. M. C. A. lib	1854	I	...
110	" Schemerhorn st .	Y W. C. A lib	1888	I	...
111	Buffalo	Buffalo catholic inst. lib	1866	I	...
112	"	Buffalo coll. of pharmacy lib	1886	I	i
113	"	Buffalo hist. soc. lib	1862	I	r
114	"	Buffalo lib	1836	I	...
115	"	Buffalo sem. lib	1851	I	i
116	"	Buffalo soc. of nat. sciences lib	1863	I	...
117	" 329-31 E'l'o'tt st	Buffalo Turnverein lib		I	...
118	"	Canisius coll. lib	1870	I	i
119	"	Erie railway lib. ass'n	1874	...	...
120	"	German Martin Luther.theo.sem. lib.	1854	I	i
121	"	Grosvenor pub. lib	1859	L	a
122	"	High sch. lib	1854	I	i
123	"	Holy Angels' acad. lib	1883	I	i
124	" 2064 Main st....	Inst. of the sisters of St Joseph lib.	1891	I	i
125	" City hall	Law lib 8 judicial dist............		L	...
126	"	Niagara univ. art dep't lib........		I	i
127	"	Niagara univ. med. dep't lib.......	1887	I	...
128	"	N. Buffalo catholic ass'n and lib ...	1886	I	...
129	"	St Margaret's sch. lib...........	1884	I	i
130	" High school ..	Shermun J. Williams mem. lib.....	1894	...	...
131	'	State hospital lib...............	1881	I	...
132	'	Univ. of Buffalo lib	1845	I	i
133	" 86 Delaware av	Women's educ.and indust union lib.	1884	I	r
134	"	Y. M C A. lib	1853	I	r
135	Burdett	Burdett lib. ass'n	1885	I	...

STATISTICS OF NEW YORK LIBRARIES, 1895

LIBRARIES (continued)

Name of librarian or person in charge	Class of books if not general	Ownership or control	Support	Terms of use	NO. ADDED LAST YEAR Given	NO. ADDED LAST YEAR Bought	Total no. in library	
Chas. E. Osborne		Pub sch	Tax St	F			760	91
Mabel A. Farr		Sch	St Gen	Fl	83	171	5836	92
		Bus	Fees	S			4630	93
C. E Hayner		Sch	Gen	Fl			450	94
J W. Dartnell		Par	Gen	Fl			2000	95
D W. E Burke		Pub. sch.	Tax. St	Fl	31	3602	3633	96
Franklin W. Hooper		Inst	End	R	100		15,600	97
Willis A Bardwell		Mem	End.Fees	S	999	2975	120,064	98
		Sch	G	Fl			2040	99
Alfred J. Hooll	Law.	Gov	St	R. Fl	161	1171	17,883	100
Emma Toedteberg		Mem	End. Gen	S	579	963	54,000	101
Hannah J Garahan		Sch	Gen	Fl	54	447	6301	102
Mary H. Chadwick		Coll	End	Fl	10	70	7100	103
Mary W. Plummer		Inst	End	F	562	4507	49,800	104
						150	3350	
							4000	
Bro. Angelo		Coll	Gen	Fl			4070	105
		Coll	Gen	Fl			7000	106
Sister St Mark		Inst	Gen	Fl		35	¶1130	107
Fanny Hull		Inst	Sdy.Gen	F	991	3971	31,483	108
Silas H. Berry		Inst	End. Gen	R. Sl	183	264	13,512	109
Fanny D. Fish		Inst	Gen	R. Fl			ab500	110
Eleanor E. Daire		Inst	Gen	R. S.	¶84	¶317	6332	111
John R. Gray	Phar	Coll	Gen	Fl			110	112
E D Strickland		Mem	St. Gen	R. S.	456	29	8724	113
J. N. Larned		Mem	End.Fees	R. S.	b388	b3282	b76,007	114
		Sch	St. Gen	Fl			1718	115
J. N. Larned	Sci	Mem	Gen	R		1651	3503	116
Frank Keuter		Mem	Gen	Fl	162	88	1850	117
H. A. Hartmann		Coll	Gen	Fl		¶20	¶18,400	118
Sue Dana Woolley		Iust	Fees Gen	Sl	20	100	4000	119
William Grabau	Theo	Coll	Gen	Fl			1853	120
E. P. Van Duzee		Pub	End. Sdy	R	300	570	¶39,000	121
Fra'klın W Barrows		Pub sch	Tax. St	Fl			2438	122
Sister St Mary		Sch	Gen	Fl		84	2049	123
Sr. M. of Sac Heart		Sch	Gen	Fl	25	25	¶1050	124
Irving Browne	Law.	Gov	St	Fl		250	9750	125
	Art	Coll	G	Fl			7000	126
Alvin A. Hubbell	Med.	Coll	Gen	Fl			660	127
Frederick P Kientz		Mem	Fees	R. S.		c78	a1586	128
E. Currie Tuck		Sch	St. Gen	Fl	10	11	981	129
FranklinW Barrows		End	End	Fl	41	252	293	130
Arthur W. Hurd		Inst	Gen	Fl			¶800	131
	Med.	Coll	Gen	R		411	5025	132
Gracia S Benedict		Inst	St Gen	R	80	168	¶1000	133
George R Stair		Inst	St. Gen	R. Fl	53	351	6750	134
Eliza S. Brown		Mem	Fees	S			514	135

a For year ending Dec. 31, 1895. b For year ending Jan. 1, 1895. c For year ending Feb 1885.

NEW YORK

| | VOLUMES | | Days open in year | HOURS OPEN EACH WEEK FOR | | | | RECEIPTS |
| | NO ISSUED | | | | | | | |
	For home use	For use at lib		Lending	Reading	Invested funds	Local taxation	State aid
91								
92	7465	?	162	37½	37½			$171 25
93				78	78			
94								
95	2770		35	1½				
96	?150	?7500	100		30			
97			70		8	$500		
98	90,525	60,000	352	75	88	8349 11		
99								
100	1485	?	300		57	39 71	$5800	3600
101		?	300		78	6026 46		
102		?	200		30			
103	700		?240	40	40	500		
104	202,304	11,429	304	61	75			
	9228	?	317	75	75			
105								
106								
107		?2000		2				
108	161,426	2431	305	63	63		5000	
109	18,808	22,800	365	81	89	275		
110	a24,209	?	306	72	72			
111	13,216	?	?327	75	75	34 58		
112								
113		?	294		48			200
114	128,222	39,582	360	72	77	8250		
115								
116								
117	382	420	300	8	42			
118			300	?12	?12			
119		10,000	300	72	72			
120								
121		?18,000	308		63	1821	4000	
122								
123		4896	365	3	70			
124		?	200		7			
125								
126								
127								
128	1115	?	365	27	27	365 05		
129	?820	?900	164	5	25			
130	?1300	?1500	105	25	25	?200		
131	?520		52	1				
132			310		9	120		
133		?	255		69			200
134	6141	783	313	24	82			200
135	?150		?45	2				

a For ear ending Dec. 31, 1894.

STATISTICS OF NEW YORK LIBRARIES, 1895

LIBRARIES (continued)

	FROM			PAYMENTS FOR			
Annual dues	Gifts and other sources	Total receipts	Books, serials and binding	Salaries	All other expenses	Total payments	
							91
....	$171 25	$342 50	$515 88	$500	$22 63	$1038 51	92
							93
							94
							95
							96
....	....	500	....	†	†500	500	97
$9676 62	434 03	18,459 76	5777 23	9455 08	6593 16	21,825 47	98
							99
2473	....	11,912 71	4878 90	4800	852 93	10,531 83	100
2710	4341 10	13,077 56	2989 63	4927 84	3559 08	11,476 55	101
....	300	300	669 12	800	....	1469 12	102
....	229	502 29	387 51	750	70	1207 51	103
....	....	....	9100	18,612	3050	30,762	104
							105
							106
....	64	64	64	....	....	64	107
....	2270 35	7270 35	3199 80	3995 74	....	7195 54	108
....	2825	3100	878	2172	50	3100	109
....	1350	1350	234 63	†1100	52 95	1387 58	110
1124	†	1159 48	353 43	400	†	753 43	111
							112
....	200	400	83 20	....	48 69	131 89	113
3990	5194 30	17,434 30	7283 44	8000 94	1603 73	16,888 11	114
							115
							116
....	....	....	322	....	....	322	117
†250	300	550	†550	....	....	†550	118
....	....	....	35	....	....	35	119
							120
....	....	5821	1610	2717	1265	5592	121
							122
....	....	....	74 22	....	....	74 22	123
....	....	....	....	....	60	60	124
....	....	....	....	800	....	800	125
							126
							127
164	233 80	762 85	55 33	28 30	396 66	480 29	128
....	....	....	10	....	....	10	129
....	510	710	460	....	†250	710	130
							131
....	....	120	543 98	780	50	1373 98	132
....	250	450	446 05	....	3 95	450	133
213 90	....	413 90	413 90	....	....	413 90	134
†10	†5	†15	....	....	15	15	135

	Place	NAME OF LIBRARY	Year founded	Source of charter	Relation to University
136	Cambridge	Union sch. lib.	1892	I	i
137	Camden	Camden lib. ass'n	1891	R	c
138	Canaan	Canaan pub. lib	1893	R	c
139	Canajoharie	Union sch. lib.	?	I	i
140	Canandaigua	Canandaigua acad. lib	1795	I	i
141	"	Union sch. lib.	1877	I	i
142	"	Wood lib	1868	L	...
143	Canaseraga	Union sch. lib	1877	I	i
144	Canastota	Union sch. lib.	?	I	i
145	Candor	Candor free acad lib	1868	I	i
146	Canisteo	Canisteo acad. lib	1871	I	i
147	Canton	St Lawrence univ., Herring lib.	1865	I	i
148	"	Union sch. lib		I	i
149	"	Woman's lib. ass'n	1891	...	...
150	Carmel	Literary union lib	1881	G	...
151	Carthage	High sch. lib.	?1866	I	i
152	Castile	Union sch lib		I	i
153	Catskill	Catskill free acad. lib	1869	I	i
154	"	Catskill pub. lib.	1893	R	c
155	"	St Patrick's acad. lib.	1892	I	i
156	Cattaraugus	Union sch. and acad. lib.	1887	I	i
157	Cazenovia	Cazenovia sem lib.	1894	I	i
158	Central Square	High sch lib.	1887	I	i
159	Central Valley	Union sch. lib.	1895	I	i
160	Champlain	Union sch. lib.	1890	I	i
161	Charlotte.	Union sch. lib. dist No. 4 (Greece)		I	i
162	Chateaugay	Union sch lib.	1883	I	i
163	Chatham	Union sch. lib.	1884	I	i
164	Cherry Valley	Cherry Valley acad. lib	1796	I	i
165	"	Union sch. lib.	?	...	...
166	Chester	Union sch. lib.		I	i
167	Chittenango	Yates union sch. lib.	1871	I	i
168	Cincinnatus	Cincinnatus acad. lib.	1857	I	i
169	Clarence	Parker union sch lib	1841	I	i
170	Claverack	Claverack acad. and H. R. inst. lib.	?	I	i
171	"	Claverack fr. lib. & read'g. r'm. ass'n	1891	G	a
172	Clayville	Union sch. lib.	1879	I	i
173	Clifton Springs	Clifton Springs fem. sem. lib.	1868	I	i
174	Clinton	Hamilton coll. lib.	1812	I	ir
175	"	Houghton sem. lib.	1861	I	i
176	"	Union sch lib.	1894	I	i
177	Clyde	High sch lib.		I	i
178	Cobleskill	High sch. lib.	?	I	i
179	Cohoes	City library	1856	I	...
180	"	Egberts high sch lib.	1880	I	i

LIBRARIES (continued)

Name of librarian or person in charge	Class of books if not general	Ownership or control	Support	Terms of use	NO. ADDED LAST YEAR Given	NO. ADDED LAST YEAR Bought	Total no. in library	
....	....	Pub. sch	St. Fees.	S ...	....	309	2923	136
Mrs E. C. Case.....	....	Mem....	St. Gen	F ...	24	190	819	137
Nellie F. Bates.....	....	Pub. D..	Tax. St..	F ...	....	....	1555	138
E. P. Abell	....	Pub. sch.	Tax	F ...	19	6	1117	139
....	....	Sch	Gen. ...	R. Fl	....	....	1036	140
H. L. Taylor.......	....	Pub. sch.	Tax. St..	F ...	....	....	3105	141
....	....	Mem....	Fees	S ...	2	11	5068	142
Henry E. Adams ...	....	Pub. sch	St	F ...	....	....	600	143
....	....	Pub sch	Tax. St..	Fl ..	....	101	1250	144
C G. Sanford......	....	Pub. sch.	Tax. St..	F ...	....	....	621	145
Helen B. O'Neil	....	Sch	Gen	Fl ..	....	....	1376	146
Henry P. Forbes ...	....	Coll.....	End. Gen	Fl ..	224	3	11,298	147
Fred C. Foster	....	Pub. sch.	Tax St ..	Fl ..	....	....	900	148
Josephine Paige....	....	Mem....	G. Fees .	S ...	8	149	708	149
Clayton Ryder	....	Mem ...	Fees Gen	R ...	43	7	1720	150
Hattie A. Merrill...	....	Pub. sch.	Tax. St..	F ...	....	....	1200	151
Minnie E Hoagland.	....	Pub sch.	Tax St..	F ...	....	70	470	152
Ed. Harris	....	Pub. sch.	Tax.....	Fl...	....	....	544	153
Emily F. Becker....	....	Pub. D..	Tax. St..	F ...	28	400	1674	154
....	....	Sch	Gen.	Fl...	11	7	1638	155
J. L. Walthart......	....	Pub. sch.	Tax. St..	Fl...	....	754	1929	156
Arthur R. Butler ...	....	Sch.	Gen.	Fl...	....	....	3405	157
George W. Woodin.	....	Pub. sch.	Tax. St..	F ...	....	37	515	158
Edwin Cornell......	....	Pub. sch.	Tax	Fl...	....	....	305	159
W. F. Deans	....	Pub. sch.	Tax St..	F ...	....	89	686	160
....	....	Pub sch	Tax. St..	R.Fl.	....	....	475	161
Edward L Stevens.	....	Pub. sch.	Tax St..	F ...	28	130	1092	162
Ella E. Wagar	....	Pub. sch.	Tax. St..	F ...	3	400	2348	163
....	....	Sch	Gen.	Fl...	....	....	628	164
Sarah W Shipway.	....	Pub. sch	Tax. St..	F ...	....	84	766	165
....	....	Pub. sch	Tax	Fl...	....	....	1100	166
N. P. Avery........	....	Pub. sch	Tax. St..	Fl...	....	12	2757	167
W. E. Gushee	....	Sch	Gen.	R. S.	9	....	438	168
George A. Bolles...	....	Pub. sch.	Tax. St..	F ...	....	30	1500	169
Wm. McAfee	....	Sch	Gen.	Fl...	....	....	1460	170
Augusta J. Crane...	....	Mem.....	St. G. ..	F ...	a 30	a 60	a1000	171
James F. Hubbell..	....	Pub sch	Tax St..	F ...	....	3	531	172
Charles Ayer.......	....	Sch	Gen.	Fl...	....	....	600	173
Melvin G. Dodge...	....	Coll.....	Gen.	F ...	292	606	33,758	174
A. G. Benedict	....	Sch.....	St. Gen.	Fl...	....	....	2248	175
Lizzie Anderson....	....	Pub. sch.	Tax. St..	F ...	....	260	1229	176
Mary E. Ackerman	....	Pub. sch.	Tax. St..	Fl...	1	107	1740	177
W. H. Ryan........	....	Pub. sch.	Tax. St..	F ...	....	....	1560	178
R. A. Ross	....	Pub sch	Tax. St..	F ...	....	109	3757	179
Geo. M. Strout.....	....	Pub. sch.	Tax. St..	Fl ..	....	....	750	180

a For year ending September 1895.

	VOLUMES		Days open in year	HOURS OPEN EACH WEEK FOR		RECEIPTS		
	NO ISSUED							
	For home use	For use at lib		Lending	Reading	Invested funds	Local taxation	State aid
136	3945		155	6				$200
137	9546		156	12		$14 81		200
138	?1200		156	3			$25	
139	1034	83	225	5	30		116 90	
140								
141								
142	?	50	104	22	22			
143	400	500	40	1				
144	?2000	?1600	200	3	25		71 69	110 49
145	419	?200	38	1				
146	?	?	40	3½				
147			123	8		50 50		
148								
149	2550		318	42	42			
150	1800	?	52	5¼	5¼			
151	?2500	100	100	2				
152	100	?	189	5	25		15 50	75
153								
154	13,718		328	18			800	200
155	?	?	?240		?6			
156	?2650	?	40	1			300	300
157								
158	210	?200	40	1			20	20
159							133 98	
160	464	?50	220	30	30		50	50
161	?1000	?1000	200	5				
162	?2250	?400	191	2½	30		100	100
163	?		200	5	10		160 03	132 57
164								
165	?500		37	1			35	
166								
167			200				10 90	
168		?	200	30	30			
169	50	400	80	14				
170								
171	1500		300	10	72			57 85
172	462	?100	?120	?	?			
173	100	100	245	30	30			
174	3207	?	240	36	36	45		200
175								
176	?7748		52	2			97 50	67 50
177	1690	?	192				89 89	69 89
178								
179	14,613	14,613	248	26	26		274 32	196 19
180								

STATISTICS OF NEW YORK LIBRARIES, 1895 253

LIBRARIES (continued)

FROM			PAYMENTS FOR				
Annual dues	Gifts and other sources	Total receipts	Books, serials and binding	Salaries	All other expenses	Total payments	
$56 46	$29 66	$286 12	$386 08	$75	$1 50	$462 58	136
29	429 49	673 30	181 56	75 40	236 86	493 82	137
....	5 68	30 68	19 42	....	5 97	30 97	138
....	4 39	121 29	58 90	45	16 37	120 27	139
....	....	....	....	....	....	....	140
....	....	....	....	....	....	....	141
50	50	100	10	80	15	105	142
....	....	....	....	....	....	....	143
....	....	182 18	182 18	....	....	182 18	144
....	63	63	....	....	....	....	145
....	....	....	....	....	....	....	146
....	....	50 50	....	120	....	120	147
....	....	....	....	....	....	....	148
....	443 94	443 94	216 67	161 55	157 32	535 54	149
....	25 20	25 20	8 82	10 35	....	19 17	150
....	....	....	....	40	20	60	151
....	9 50	100	100	....	....	100	152
....	....	....	....	....	....	....	153
....	72 05	1072 05	500 63	262	187 65	950 28	154
....	53	53	53	....	....	53	155
....	....	600 42	600 42	....	....	600 42	156
....	....	....	....	....	....	....	157
....	....	40	20	....	....	20	158
....	....	133 98	133 98	....	....	133 98	159
....	....	100	100 52	....	12	112 52	160
....	....	....	....	....	....	....	161
....	28	228	214	18	....	232	162
....	30	322 60	322 60	....	....	322 60	163
....	....	....	....	....	....	....	164
....	22 92	57 92	57 92	....	....	57 92	165
....	....	....	....	....	....	....	166
....	....	10 90	- 10 90	....	....	10 90	167
....	....	....	....	....	....	....	168
....	....	....	....	....	....	....	169
....	....	....	....	....	....	....	170
50	300	407 85	57 85	30	251	438 85	171
....	....	....	? 10	....	....	? 10	172
....	....	....	....	....	....	....	173
....	1750	1995	1495	500	....	1995	174
....	....	....	....	....	....	....	175
....	20	185	135	50	....	185	176
....	....	159 78	139 78	20	....	159 78	177
....	....	....	....	....	....	....	178
....	....	470 51	188 70	....	....	188 70	179
....	....	....	....	....	....	....	180

No.	Place	NAME OF LIBRARY	Year founded	Source of charter	Relation to University
181	Cohoes	St Bernard's acad. lib.	1890	I	i
182	Cold Spring	Haldane union sch. lib.	1892	I	i
183	College Point	Conrad Poppenhusen ass'n lib.	1868	I	i
184	Cooperstown	Union sch. lib.		I	i
185	Copenhagen	Union sch. lib.	1887	I	i
186	Corinth	Union sch. lib.	1892	I	i
187	Corning	Corning free acad. lib.	1860	I	i
188	Cornwall	Cornwall pub. lib.	1895	R	c
189	Cornwall-on-Hudson	New York military acad. lib.	1889	I	i
190	" "	Cornwall-on-Hudson pub. lib.	1895	R	c
191	Cortland	Franklin Hatch lib ass'n	1888	I	...
192	"	State normal sch. lib.		I	...
193	"	Union sch. lib.	1894	I	i
194	Coxsackie	Union sch. lib.	1840	I	i
195	Crown Point	Chapel library	1884	R	c
196	Cuba	Union sch. lib.	?	I	i
197	Dansville	Dansville pub lib.	1893	R	c
198	De Ruyter	Union sch. lib.	?1874	I	i
199	Delhi	Delaware acad. lib.	1820	I	i
200	Deposit	Deposit acad. lib.		I	i
201	Dolgeville	School society lib.	1892	I	...
202	Dryden	Southworth lib.	1883	G	a
203	"	Union sch. and acad. lib.	1871	I	i
204	Dunkirk	Academic sch. lib.	?	I	i
205	"	Dunkirk lib. ass'n	1872	G	...
206	"	St Mary's academic sch. lib.		I	i
207	"	Union sch lib.	1893	...	...
208	Earlville	Union sch. lib.	1892	I	i
209	East Aurora	Union sch. lib.	1883	I	i
210	East Bloomfield	Union sch. lib.	1877	I	i
211	East Chatham	East Chatham pub. lib.	1893	R	c
212	East Pembroke	Union sch. lib.		I	i
213	East Syracuse	Union sch. lib.		I	i
214	Easton	Easton free lib.	1894	G	a
215	Eddytown	Starkey sem. lib.	1842	I	i
216	Elbridge	Munro coll. inst. lib.	1839	I	i
217	Elizabethtown	Elizabethtown lib. ass'n	1884	G	a
218	"	Union sch. lib.	1868	I	i
219	Ellenville	Ellenville pub. lib.	1893	R	c
220	Ellicottville	Union sch. Harmon lib.	1890	I	i
221	Ellington	Union sch. lib.	1871	I	i
222	Elmira	Elmira coll. lib.	1855	I	i
223	"	Elmira farmers club lib.	1869	...	...
224	"	Elmira free acad. lib.	1840	I	i
225	"	N. Y. State reformatory lib.	1876	I	...

LIBRARIES (continued)

Name of librarian or person in charge	Class of books if not general	Ownership or control	Support	Terms of use	NO ADDED LAST YEAR Given	NO ADDED LAST YEAR Bought	Total no in library	
....	.....	Sch	Gen.	Fl ..	10	......	714	181
O. Montrose	.....	Pub. sch.	Tax. St..	F ...	......	200	2000	182
F. Martens	.....	Inst	Gen.	F ...	46	26	2671	183
....	.....	Pub. sch.	Tax St..	Fl ..	......	......	3317	184
Fred A. Green	.....	Pub. sch.	Tax. St..	F ...	16	......	701	185
A. M. Hollister	.....	Pub. sch.	Tax. St..	F ...	......	70	474	186
Leigh R. Hunt	.....	Pub. sch.	Tax.	Fl ..	......	2	1143	187
....	.....	Pub. D..	Tax. St..	F ...	......	......	438	188
C. J. Wright	.....	Sch.	Gen.	Fl ..	......	......	3070	189
Leonora Pope	.....	Pub. D..	Tax. St	F ...	1	......	812	190
Mary E. Hubbard ..	.....	Mem.End	End.Fees	S ...	28	74	3568	191
J. Edward Bank	...	Sch.	St......	Fl ..	......	1600	?4200	192
....	.....	Pub. sch.	Tax. St..	Fl ..	......	?50	?350	193
Geo. W. Fairgrieve.	.....	Pub. sch.	Tax. St..	F ...	6	31	720	194
Herminie Hammond	.....	Pub. D..	Tax. St..	F ...	15	146	1021	195
J. E. Denry	.....	Pub. sch.	Tax. St..	Fl ..	2	133	400	196
Elizabeth Y. Hedges	.....	Pub. D..	Tax. St..	F ..	4	254	2550	197
George W. Lang	.....	Pub. sch	Tax St	F ...	......	50	350	198
Willis D Graves ...	.....	Sch.	St. G....	F ...	7	13	2286	199
Salem G. Pattison ..	.....	Pub. sch.	St. G....	Fl ..	40	85	1565	200
R. Ruedemann	.....	Mem. ...	Gen	F ...	18	......	1792	201
Cora B. Holden	.....	End	End	F ...	......	329	5700	202
W. V. Flaherty	.....	Pub. sch.	Tax St..	F ...	8	......	650	203
Nora J. Hayes	.....	Pub. sch.	Tax. St..	Fl ..	......	92	1057	204
Jessie Underwood ..	.....	Mem. ...	Fees	S ...	36	20	1737	205
....	.....	Sch	Gen.....	Fl ..	......	......	352	206
J. W. Babcock	.....	Pub. sch.	Tax. St..	Fl ..	......	218	941	207
....	.....	Pub. sch.	Tax St..	F ...	2	13	?541	208
Charles Goldsmith ..	.....	Pub. sch.	Tax. St..	F ...	120	298	1944	209
D. B. Williams	.....	Pub sch	Tax. St..	F ...	1	1	900	210
Staunton B. Smith ..	.....	Pub. D..	Tax. St,.	F ...	1	161	632	211
....	.....	Pub. sch.	Tax. St..	Fl ..	......	......	?575	212
Mabel C. Smith	.....	Pub. sch.	Tax St..	Fl ..	......	85	1501	213
Mary Stiles	.....	Mem. ...	St. G....	F ...	3	194	680	214
Frank Carney	.....	Sch	St. G....	F ...	114	180	2317	215
N. Leonard	.....	Sch	End	F ...	?5	......	?1206	216
Elizabeth V. Hale ..	.....	Mem. ...	St. Fees.	F ...	46	33	1421	217
....	.....	Pub sch.	Tax. St..	Fl ..	......	113	620	218
Retta L. Russell ...	.....	Pub. D..	Tax. St..	F ...	1	79	1606	219
C. J Melrose	.....	Pub. sch.	Tax.	Fl ..	10	30	750	220
....	.....	Pub. sch.	Tax. St..	F ...	7	10	531	221
....	.....	Coll	Gen.	Fl ..	50	150	?5000	222
M. B. Heller	.....	Mem. ...	Gen.....	Fl ..	......	......	1500	223
....	.....	Pub sch.	Tax. St..	Fl ..	8	......	1869	224
I. S. Shultz	.....	Inst	St	Fl ..	......	75	3000	225

NEW YORK

	VOLUMES		Days open in year	HOURS OPEN EACH WEEK FOR			RECEIPTS	
	NO ISSUED							
	For home use	For use at lib		Lending	Reading	Invested funds	Local taxation	State aid
181	370		180	5				
182	750	250	225	25			$95	
183	932	530	365	4	78	$197 58		
184								
185	400	100	80	2	2			
186	705	? 190	80	2			50	$50
187		? 6000	191		50		21 50	
188								
189								
190	1150		80	4			50	25
191	7692		307	61	61	400		
192								
193			200		20		112 50	112 50
194	634	? 1200	187	5	42½		49 91	40
195	? 1765		99	4	4		18	200
196	?	?	200	35	35		75	75
197	8085		? 156	? 8			500	125
198	425	? 50	188	5			15	15
199	970	790	76	½				
200	714		39	1				
201	634	?	156	4	3			
202	? 5000		32	10	10	900		
203	200	25	36	1				
204	1428	? 100	80	1			98 24	50
205	2031		104	6				
206								
207	3714	?	? 200	1	? 25		116 17	84 78
208	? 1980	25	40	1	6		10	10
209	8879	? 250	211	80	30		150	150
210	650		52	1				
211	1151	? 400	? 210	25	5		80	96
212								
213	683	900	200	1	30		50	50
214	583		78	3				200
215	484		365	18	21			80
216	13	30	195	40	40			
217	? 1750	?	104	6	6			200
218		?	200		27½		50	42 50
219	16,292		306	24			400	50
220	? 1200		40	1				
221	?	?	? 180	15			30 27	
222		? 4000	236	36	72			
223			? 100	2				
224	? 753	? 2438	185	20	20			
225	67600							

STATISTICS OF NEW YORK LIBRARIES, 1895

LIBRARIES (continued)

FROM			PAYMENTS FOR				
Annual dues	Gifts and other sources	Total receipts	Books, serials and binding	Salaries	All other expenses	Total payments	
							181
....	....	$95	$95	....	....	$95	182
....	....	197 58	108 17	$84	$5 41	197 58	183
....	....	....	....	....	....	....	184
....	$28 50	28 50	....	....	....	....	185
....	....	100	100	....	....	100	186
....	....	21 50	21 50	....	....	21 50	187
....	....	....	....	....	....	....	188
....	....	....	....	....	....	....	189
....	....	75	....	35	....	35	190
$273 45	90	763 45	125 77	450	150 98	726 75	191
....	....	....	....	....	....	....	192
....	....	225	225	....	....	225	193
....	....	89 91	89 91	....	....	89 91	194
....	? 10	228	125 94	....	35 40	161 34	195
....	....	150	150	....	....	150	196
....	34 32	659 32	349 12	88 40	158 77	596 29	197
....	....	30	15	....	....	15	198
....	....	....	13 80	....	....	13 80	199
....	50	50	....	....	....	....	200
100	....	100	....	100	....	100	201
....	....	900	378	75	50	503	202
....	....	....	....	....	....	....	203
....	....	148 24	113 24	25	10	148 24	204
77 36	43 13	120 49	31 25	9	52	92 25	205
....	....	....	....	....	....	....	206
....	....	205 95	200 95	....	5	205 95	207
....	....	20	20	....	....	20	208
....	? 25	325	325 03	40	....	365 03	209
....	....	....	2	....	....	2	210
....	16	192	177 52	....	11 08	188 60	211
....	....	....	....	....	....	....	212
....	9 95	109 95	116 20	25	....	141 20	213
....	47 55	247 55	182 17	12 50	26 68	221 35	214
....	81 50	161 50	161 50	....	....	161 50	215
....	....	....	....	....	....	....	216
57 33	34 43	291 76	56 36	....	23 34	79 70	217
....	....	92 50	92 50	....	....	92 50	218
....	42 75	492 75	102 46	176 60	202 16	481 22	219
....	....	....	93 42	....	....	93 42	220
....	....	30 27	15 27	....	15	30 27	221
....	125	125	125	....	....	125	222
....	....	....	....	....	....	....	223
....	9 30	9 30	9 30	....	....	9 30	224
....	....	....	....	....	....	....	225

NEW YORK

	Place	NAME OF LIBRARY	Year founded	Source of charter	Relation to University
226	Elmira	Y. M. C. A. lib	1858	I	...
227	"	Y. M. C. A. R. R. branch lib	1881		
228	Fair Haven	Union sch. lib	1890	I	i
229	Fairfield	Fairfield sem. lib	1803	I	i
230	Fairport	Classical union sch. lib	1870	I	i
231	Fayetteville	Union sch. and acad. lib	?	I	i
232	Flatbush	School lib			...
233	Flatlands	School lib. dist. no. 1	?		
234	Florida	S. S. Seward inst. lib	1847	I	i
235	Flushing	Flushing inst. lib	?	I	i
236	"	Flushing lib. ass'n	1884	L	...
237	"	High sch. lib	?	I	i
238	"	St Joseph's acad. lib	?1869	I	i
239	Fonda	Union sch. lib	1887	I	i
240	Forestville	Forestville free lib	1864	I	i
241	Fort Covington	Union sch. lib	?	I	i
242	Fort Edward	Fort Edward collegiate inst. lib	1854	I	i
243	"	Union sch. lib	?1870	I	i
244	Fort Hamilton	Fort Hamilton free lib	1893	R	c
245	Fort Plain	Clinton liberal inst. lib	1831	I	i
246	"	Fort Plain free lib	1885	R	c
247	"	Union sch. lib		I	i
248	Frankfort	Union sch. lib	1888	I	i
249	Franklin	Delaware literary inst. lib	1835	I	i
250	Franklinville	Ten Broeck free acad. lib	1867	I	i
251	Fredonia	Darwin R. Barker lib. ass'n	1875	G	...
252	"	State normal sch. lib		I	
253	Friendship	Union sch lib	1891	I	i
254	Fulton	Union sch. lib. dist. no. 1 (Volney)		I	i
255	Fultonville	Union sch. lib		I	i
256	Garden City	St Paul's sch. library	1882	...	...
257	Geneva	Classical and union sch. lib	1839	I	i
258	"	De Lancey sch. lib	?1868	I	i
259	"	Hobart coll. lib	1822	I	i
260	Gilbertsville	Gilbertsville acad. lib	1838	I	i
261	"	Gilbertsville free lib	1891	G	a
262	Glen Cove	Glen Cove pub. lib	1894	R	c
263	Glen Haven	Glen Haven pub. lib	1893	R	c
264	Glenham	Union sch. lib. dist. no. 3	?	...	...
265	Glens Falls	Crandall free lib	1892	R	c
266	"	Glens Falls acad. lib		I	i
267	Gloversville	Gloversville free lib	1880	G	i
268	"	High sch. lib	?	I	i
269	Goshen	Union sch. lib	1889	I	i
270	Gouverneur	High sch. lib	1828	I	i

STATISTICS OF NEW YORK LIBRARIES, 1895

LIBRARIES (continued)

Name of librarian or person in charge	Class of books if not general	Ownership or control	Support	Terms of use	VOLUMES NO ADDED LAST YEAR Given	Bought	Total no. in library	
Rufus Stanley		Inst	Gen	Fl			3000	226
C. L. Shattuck		Inst	G	Fl			450	227
G. A. Jacobs		Pub. sch.	Tax. St.	Fl	3		350	228
D. D. Warne		Sch	Gen	Fl			3780	229
Elmer G. Frail		Pub. sch.	Tax. St.	Fl	3	167	671	230
Frank J. House		Pub. sch.	Tax. St.	F		119	? 1662	231
							? 5000	232
M. Becker jr		Pub. sch.	Tax. St.	F			1042	233
Arthur J. Clough		Sch	Gen	Fl	10	4	739	234
		Sch	Gen	Fl			1335	235
Eleanor Vanderhoeff		Mem	End	F	254		6000	236
I. J. Chickering		Pub. sch.	Tax. St.	Fl	7		2690	237
Sister M. De Paul		Sch	Gen	FL			3500	238
Charles A Coons		Pub. sch.	Tax. St.	F		151	1171	239
Virginia Hillebert		Pub. sch.	Tax. St.	F		145	1000	240
		Pub. sch.	Tax. St.	Fl		65	? 350	241
		Sch	St. G	Fl			812	242
Laura S. Hubbell		Pub. sch.	Tax. St.	F	2		1300	243
Callie M. Mayo		Mem	St. G	F	66	647	2123	244
Cornelia E. Gayler		Sch	Gen	Fl	260		3508	245
Mrs Ellen Koepping		Mem	St. G	F		50	1023	246
R. H. Bellows		Pub. sch.	Tax	Fl	126	24	674	247
W. L. Weeden		Pub. sch.	Tax. St.	F	20	75	600	248
Charles H. Verrill		Sch	St. G	Fl	10		1871	249
Hamilton Terry		Pub. sch.	Tax	F	260	2	? 1400	250
Isabelle B. Greene		Mem	End. Fees	R. S.	203	195	3893	251
Franklin N. Jewett		Sch	St	Fl		1156	? 3000	252
		Pub. sch.	Tax. St.	Fl		14	777	253
B. G. Clapp		Pub sch	Tax St.	F		9	1246	254
H. Evart Bolton		Pub. sch.	Tax. St.	F	12		573	255
D. C. Sayers		Sch	Gen	Fl			1100	256
W. H Truesdale		Pub. sch.	Tax St.	F	56	350	4154	257
M. S. Smart		Sch	Gen	Fl		15	565	258
Charles D. Vail		Coll	End. Gen.	R. Fl	852	223	31,417	259
		Sch	Gen	Fl			800	260
Mrs Carrie Cloud		Mem	End. St.	F	19	166	1049	261
G. Arthur R. Dalton		Pub. D.	Tax. St.	F	43	204	1495	262
Dora M. Greene		Pub. D.	St G	F	109	167	560	263
William G. Siddell		Pub. sch.	Tax. St.	Fl		15	315	264
Gertrude Ferguson		End	E. T. St.	F	37	414	6015	265
D. C. Farr		Sch	Gen	F			3981	266
A. L. Peck		Mem. pub	E. Sdy. St	F	180	907	12,361	267
		Pub. sch.	Tax. St.	Fl		50	673	268
		Pub. sch.	Tax. St.	F			1062	269
John C. Bliss		Pub. sch.	Tax. St.	Fl		3	799	270

NEW YORK

	Volumes: No. issued: For home use	For use at lib	Days open in year	Hours open each week for: Lending	Reading	Receipts: Invested funds	Local taxation	State aid
226	...	...	...	...	...	...	...	...
227	54	...	300	78	78	...	...	...
228	...	...	192	...	5	...	...	...
229	...	...	...	...	...	...	...	...
230	1207	...	140	4	...	...	$75	$75
231	520	?	48	1	...	...	70 89½	70 89½
232	...	...	...	...	...	...	...	...
233	500	? 100	200	1	...	...	10	10
234	...	500	210	...	18	...	...	...
235	...	...	177	?	...	...	...	...
236	12,882	...	313	18	18	$472 50	...	...
237	...	...	180	5	26	...	...	...
238	...	...	...	...	...	...	...	...
239	? 1500	? 400	200	3	32½	...	50	50
240	1200	1000	104	2	...	...	78 20	78 20
241	100	25	100	½	...	...	95	40
242	...	...	...	...	...	...	...	...
243	4500	100	120	8	8	...	...	...
244	4500	...	156	15	15	...	...	200
245	1175	? 600	195	7½	27½	...	...	...
246	5627	...	156	8	...	...	...	...
247	708	...	50	2	...	...	...	...
248	1188	?	40	1	6	...	...	50
249	300	100	150	4	5	...	...	...
250	? 75	? 150	190	1	15	...	...	...
251	3840	?	120	22½	22½	27 67	25	...
252	...	...	...	...	...	...	...	...
253	6000	200	...	2	...	...	...	5
254	1900	1000	195	3	35	...	8 06	...
255	? 450	? 600	40	1	30	...	...	...
256	300	...	252	21	84	...	...	...
257	7150	6272	212	37½	37½	...	465	74 11
258	...	...	170	30	30	...	...	...
259	3503	?	313	18	82	...	...	...
260	...	...	...	...	...	...	...	...
261	3445	...	358	43	43	233	...	200
262	949	...	85	3	...	...	200	200
263	899	...	104	2	...	...	...	100
264	270	...	180	2½	...	...	25	24 09
265	38,529	?	300	9	9	907	500	200
266	...	...	...	...	...	...	...	...
267	59,695	3753	308	72	72	240 47	2000	...
268	...	?	200	...	30	...	46 99	35 85
269	...	...	...	...	...	...	...	...
270	?	?	188	30	30	...	25	25

STATISTICS OF NEW YORK LIBRARIES, 1895

LIBRARIES (continued)

FROM			PAYMENTS FOR				
Annual dues	Gifts and other sources	Total receipts	Books, serials and binding	Salaries	All other expenses	Total payments	
							226
							227
	$3	$3					228
							229
	1 23	151 23	$151 23			$151 23	230
		141 89	141 89			141 89	231
							232
		20					233
							234
							235
	295 50	768		$352	$414	766	236
	124 09	124 09					237
							238
		100	171 35			171 35	239
		156 40					240
		135	135			135	241
							242
				25	1 50	26 50	243
$251 50	8	459 50	217 20	96	100	413 20	244
			16		150	166	245
	152 85	152 85	88 97		170 41	259 38	246
			100			100	247
		50	100			100	248
							249
							250
176 25	416 35	635 27	238 49	124 33	66 61	429 43	251
							252
		5	10		15	25	253
		8 06	8 06			8 06	254
							255
							256
	139 07	678 18	282 08	300	96 10	678 18	257
	15	15					258
	4604 15	4604 15	561 51	1325 08	940 04	2826 63	259
							260
2	12 45	447 45	182 44	204	70 35	456 79	261
	37 45	437 45	200 07		232 82	432 89	262
	85	185	129 82	10	45 18	185	263
		49 09	48			48	264
	111 99	1718 99	954 69	395 65	318 67	1669 01	265
							266
	2336 16	4576 63	994 08	2066 99	1306 58	4367 55	267
		82 84	82 84			82 84	268
							269
		50	16 50			16 50	270

NEW YORK

	Place	NAME OF LIBRARY	Year founded	Source of charter	Relation to University
271	Gouverneur	Reading room ass'n	1885	G	
272	Gowanda	Union sch. lib	?1876	I	i
273	Granville	Union sch. lib		I	i
274	Greene	Union sch. lib	1860	I	i
275	Greenport	Union sch. lib		I	i
276	Greenville	Greenville acad. lib	1816	I	i
277	Greenwich	Union sch. lib		I	i
278	Groton	Union sch. lib	1869	I	i
279	Hamburg	Union sch. lib		I	i
280	Hamilton	Beta Theta Pi fraternity lib	1846		
281	"	Colgate acad. lib	1873	I	i
282	"	Colgate univ. lib	1820	I	i
283	"	Union sch. lib	1893	I	i
284	Hammondsport	Union sch. lib		I	i
285	Hancock	Union sch. and acad. lib	1863	I	i
286	Hartwick Seminary	Hartwick sem. lib	1816	I	i
287	Hastings-on-Hudson	Fraser free sch. lib			
288	Havana	Cook acad. lib	1872	I	i
289	"	Havana free lib	1874	R	c
290	Hemstead	Hemstead inst. lib	1836		
291	"	High sch. lib	1840		
292	Herkimer	Union sch. lib		I	i
293	Highland	Union sch. lib	1894	I	i
294	Highland Falls	Morgan circulating lib	1884		
295	Hinsdale	Union sch. lib	?1891	I	i
296	Hobart	Union sch. lib	1893	I	i
297	Hogansburg	Hogansburg acad. lib	1889	I	i
298	Holland Patent	Union sch. lib	?1838	I	i
299	Holley	Union sch. and acad. lib	?1847	I	i
300	Homer	Homer acad. and union sch. lib	1819	I	i
301	Honeoye Falls	Union sch. lib		I	i
302	Hoosick Falls	Union sch. lib	?	I	i
303	Hornellsville	Hornell free acad. lib	?1885	I	i
304	"	Hornell free lib	1868	G	a
305	"	St Ann's academic sch. lib	1894	I	i
306	"	Y. M. C. A. R. R. branch lib	1879		
307	Horseheads	Union sch. lib	?1884	I	i
308	Hudson	High sch. lib		I	i
309	Huntington	Huntington lib. ass'n	1875	G	
310	"	Union sch. lib		I	i
311	Ilion	Ilion district lib	1893	R	c
312	"	Ilion free pub. lib	1893	L	
313	"	Union sch. lib		I	i
314	Irvington	Union sch. lib		I	i
315	Islip	Islip lib. ass'n	1884		

LIBRARIES (continued)

Name of librarian or person in charge	Class of books if not general	Ownership or control	Support	Terms of use	VOLUMES NO. ADDED LAST YEAR Given	Bought	Total no in library	
Jessie E. Paul		Mem	End.Fees	R. S.	a204	a39	a1317	271
Chas. A. Black		Pub. sch.	Tax. St.	Fl		11	?777	272
		Pub. sch.	Tax. St.	Fl		134	550	273
William N. Harris		Pub. sch.	Tax. St.	F		117	1300	274
		Pub. sch.	Tax. St.	Fl			962	275
T. W. Stewart		Sch	Gen	F	5		?500	276
George E. Dorr		Pub. sch.	Tax. St.	Sl			?1660	277
O. W. Wood		Pub. sch.	Tax. St.	F		110	1194	278
Byron H. Heath		Pub. sch.	Tax. St.	F		204	1265	279
G. W: Strobel		Mem	G. Fees	Fl		?	?950	280
Chas. H. Thurber		Sch	Gen	Fl	10	6	1516	281
Ralph W. Thomas		Coll	End. G.	R.Fl.	374	498	23,697	282
Chas. H. Van Tuyl		Pub. sch.	Tax. St.	F		90	800	283
		Pub. sch.	Tax. St.	Fl		36	400	284
Lincoln R. Long		Pub. sch.	Tax. St.	Fl	5		390	285
J. L. Kistler		Sch	End.Gen	Fl	14	5	4495	286
M. P. Dunbar		Pub. sch.	Tax. St.	F		50	430	287
Grace Cook		Sch	End.Gen.	R.Fl.	68		2157	288
E.. P. Hopkins		Mem	Tax. St.	F		78	629	289
E. Hinds		Sch	Gen	Fl	?20	?25	?1000	290
W. S. Newton		Pub. sch.	Tax. St.	F		42	1260	291
A. G. Miller		Pub. sch.	Tax. St.	F		50	302	292
David H. Merritt		Pub. sch	Tax. St.	F		34	634	293
Gertrude P. Parry		End	End	F	25		1250	294
Kate J. Kriegelstein		Pub. sch.	Tax. St.	F		?35	?500	295
Jennie Campbell		Pub. sch.	Tax. St.	F			523	296
Mary Canisius		Sch	St. Sdy.	Fl	20	30	1108	297
Herbert A. Pride		Pub. sch.	Tax. St.	F			1100	298
Jennie A. Cowles		Pub. sch	St. G	F		17	649	299
		Pub. sch.	End. St.	F			?1300	300
C. F. Walker		Pub. sch.	Tax. St.	Fl		136	652	301
Ernest G. Merritt		Pub. sch	Tax. St.	F	24	54	2012	302
W. P. Prentice		Pub. sch.	Tax. St.	F		501	2404	303
Mrs I. A. Charles		End	End. Tax	F	?26	?500	?10,000	304
Belle M. O. Cooke		Sch	St. Gen.	Fl		27	746	305
		Inst	Gen	Fl	2		630	306
		Pub. sch.	Tsx. St.	F			583	307
W. S. Hallenbeck		Pub. sch.	Tax. St.	F			4758	308
A. S. Conklin		Mem	G. Fees.	R. S.	26	153	3738	309
C. J. Jennings		Pub. sch.	Tax	F	17	46	1204	310
Anna H. Perkins		Pub. D.	St. G	F		151	963	311
Anna H. Perkins		Pub.	End.Tax.	F	510	112	7542	312
		Pub. sch.	Tax. St.	F			343	313
		Pub. sch.	Tax. St.	F		201	2396	314
Ella S. Clook		Mem	G. Fees.	S		67	867	315

For year ending November 21, 1895.

NEW YORK

| | VOLUMES | | Days open in year | HOURS OPEN EACH WEEK FOR | | Invested funds | RECEIPTS | |
| | NO ISSUED | | | | | | | |
	For home use	For use at lib		Lending	Reading		Local taxation	State aid
271	2727	1872	304	36	36	....	....	....
272	250	?	180	?	30	....	$9 50	$9 50
273	256	734	180	5	5	....	50	75
274	?900	?	40	1	.. ...	....	25	25
275	....	....	....	....	....	....	....	....
276	?100	?500	200	5	....	....	....	....
277	....	....	....	....	....	....	....	....
278	1200	200	80	?4	?4	....	184 17	13 55
279	838	?	188	2	30	....	50	....
280	....	....	200	30	30	....	....	....
281	....	....	222	30	36	....	....	....
282	3035	3841	a273	50	50	$1250	....	....
283	2187	?	200	5	30	....	105 15	....
284	?50	?300	189	6	6	....	25	25
285	221	?	192	1	30	....	....	....
286	?400	?	?190	?10	10	10	....	....
287	305	....	47	2	....	....	10	10
288	509	1207	234	22	22	80 50	....	....
289	4548	....	155	4½	....	....	100	....
290	....	....	....	....	....	....	....	....
291	30	160	80	1	6	....	25	25
292	540	100	200	6	35	....	50	50
293	890	500	210	15	30	....	50	25
294	10,000	56	147	15	15	....	....	....
295	?	?	52	1	....	....	30	24 74
296	279	....	30	1	....	....	7 27	....
297	....	?600	144	....	20	....	....	....
298	?	?	52	2	2	....	....	....
299	2000	....	40	1	....	....	....	33 35
300	?2500	....	92	3	....	40	....	122 77
301	....	....	80	2	....	....	51 65	53 08
302	4382	....	220	30	....	....	140	....
303	560	?2240	200	25	30	....	281 34	250
304	30,321	?	309	21	21	....	1500	....
305	100	22	193	6	30	....	....	56
306	499	?140	313	72	72	....	....	....
307	....	....	....	....	....	....	....	....
308	....	....	....	....	....	....	....	....
309	3130	?250	306	36	36	....	....	....
310	?	?	195	25	25	....	25	....
311	471	?	307	51	54	....	....	200
312	36,891	?	307	51	54	63	1022 75	....
313	....	....	....	....	....	....	....	....
314	1204	....	76	4	....	....	50	25
315	?1381	....	103	2	....	....	....	....

a Including 88 days open for public use during summer vacation.

STATISTICS OF NEW YORK LIBRARIES, 1895

LIBRARIES (continued)

FROM			PAYMENTS FOR				
Annual dues	Gifts and other sources	Total receipts	Books, serials and binding	Salaries	All other expenses	Total payments	
$24 40	$565 31	$589 71	$95 05	$208	$461	$764 05	271
		19	19			19	272
	25	150	117 50			117 50	273
		50	50			50	274
							275
	18	18					276
							277
		197 72	107 49		76 65	184 17	278
		50	181 83			181 83	279
							280
			8 42			8 42	281
		1250	1082 83	1210 50	302 50	2594 83	282
		105 15	105 15			105 15	283
	25	75	83 36			83 36	284
	25 80	25 80	5			5	285
	10	20	10	10		20	286
		20					287
97 50	88 65	266 65	60 65	200		260 65	288
	10	110	93 36		69 69	163 05	289
							290
		50	50			50	291
		100	100			100	292
		75	25		50	75	293
			60	640	250	950	294
		54 74	35			35	295
		7 27	7 27			7 27	296
	208	208	213			213	297
							298
	33 35	66 70	53 75			53 75	299
	122 77	285 54	273 46		4	277 46	300
	44 42	149 15	149 15			149 15	301
		140	50	90		140	302
		531 34	566 34	15		581 34	303
	90 29	1590 29	643 66	425	453 29	1521 95	304
	63 20	119 20	119 20			119 20	305
			9			9	306
							307
							308
200 66	207 57	408 23	142 31	125	209 56	476 87	309
		25	33 36			33 36	310
	200	400	246 41			246 41	311
14 50	248 74	1348 99	150 44	876 58	459 66	1486 68	312
							313
		75	25	50		75	314
40 50	127 59	168 09	55 61	13 50	90 54	159 65	315

	Place	NAME OF LIBRARY	Year founded	Source of charter	Relation to University
316	Islip	Islip pub. lib.	1882	...	...
317	"	St Mark's parish house lib.	1891	I	...
318	Ithaca	Cascadilla sch. lib.		I	i
319	"	Cornell lib. ass'n	1864	L	...
320	"	Cornell univ. lib.	1868	I	i
321	"	High sch. lib.	1875	I	i
322	Jamaica	Union sch. lib.	?	I	i
323	Jamestown	High sch. lib.	?	I	i
324	"	James Prendergast lib. ass'n	1880	L	a
325	"	W. C. A. lib.	1882	...	...
326	"	Y. M. C. A. lib	1885	I	r
327	Johnstown	Union sch lib.	1869	I	i
328	Jordan	Free acad. lib.		I	i
329	Jordanville	Jordanville pub. lib.	1893	R	c
330	Joshua's Rock	Mountainside free. lib.	1894	R	c
331	Keene Valley	Keene Valley pub. lib.	1891	R	c
332	Keeseville	McAuley acad. lib	1891	I	i
333	"	Union sch. lib.		I	i
334	Kenwood	Female acad. of the Sacred Heart lib	1861	I	i
335	Keuka College	Keuka inst. lib.	1890	I	i
336	Kinderhook	Kinderhook acad. lib.		I	i
337	Kingston	Free acad. lib.	?	I	i
338	"	Third jud. dist. law lib.		L	...
339	Knowlesville	Union sch. lib.	1890	I	i
340	Lake George	Lake George free lib.	1895	R	c
341	Lake Placid	Lake Placid pub. lib.	1884	R	c
342	Lancaster	Union sch lib.		I	i
343	Lansingburg	Lansingburg acad. lib		I	i
344	"	Union sch lib. dist. No. 1		...	...
345	Le Roy	Le Roy lib. ass'n	1874	...	...
346	"	Union sch. lib.	1891	I	i
347	Leonardsville	Leonardsville lib. ass'n	1883	...	...
348	Liberty	Liberty pub. lib.	1894	R	c
349	Lima	Genesee Wesleyan sem. lib.	1830	I	i
350	Lisle	Union sch. and acad. lib.	1868	I	i
351	Little Falls	Union sch. lib.	1845	I	i
352	Little Valley	Union sch. lib.		I	i
353	Liverpool	Liverpool pub. lib.	?	R	c
354	Livonia	Union sch. lib	1893	I	i
355	Lockport	Lockport pub. lib.	1893	R	c
356	"	St Joseph's acad. & ind. fem. sch.lib.	1866	I	i
357	"	Y. M. C. A lib	1887	I	...
358	Long Island City	Union sch. lib		I	i
359	Lowville	Lowville acad. lib	1808	I	i
360	Lyndonville	Union sch. lib.	1889	I	i

LIBRARIES (continued)

Name of librarian or person in charge	Class of books if not general	Ownership or control	Support	Terms of use	VOLUMES NO ADDED LAST YEAR Given	VOLUMES NO ADDED LAST YEAR Bought	Total no. in library	
Chas. A. Codman...		Pub. sch	Tax. St..	F ...	16	13	856	316
Mrs J. H. Smith....		Par	Gen	F ...		145	619	317
....		Pub. sch.	Tax	Fl ?			430	318
S. H. Synnott......		End.....	End.....	F ...		116	a18,591	319
G. W: Harris........		Coll.....	End. Gen	R. Fl	4786	8112	173,793	320
H. W. Foster........		Pub. sch.	Tax. St..	Fl...		87	711	321
....		Pub. sch.	St. G....	F ...		448	2645	322
Calista S. Jones		Pub. sch.	Tax. St..	F ...	36	7	? 3128	323
M. E. Hazeltine....		End.....	End. St..	F ...	76	857	10,045	324
Mrs J. H. Clark		Inst.....	Gen	Fl...	87	20	560	325
Chas N. Ramsey...		Inst.....	St. Gen..	F ...	84		1270	326
W: S. Snyder		Pub. sch	Tax. St..	F ..	303	573	7069	327
....		Pub. sch.	Tax St..	F ...			1239	328
E. A. Bell..........		Pub.....	Tax. St..	F ...	1	123	689	329
Esther Coffin		Mem	St. G....	F ...	? 137	? 200	337	330
G. E. Perry.		Mem	St. G....	F ...	97	283	870	331
M. Joseph Carr.....		Sch	St. Gen..	Fl ..	58		582	332
Emily Hallock		Pub. sch.	Tax. St..	F ...		? 90	? 1350	333
Sarah Jones.........		Sch	Gen	Fl ..		36	3602	334
....		Sch	St.......	Fl ..			1257	335
....		Sch	Gen	Fl ..			400	336
....		Pub. sch	Tax. St..	F ...			1527	337
F B. Westbrook....	Law.	Gov	St	R .		? 200	? 7000	338
J. H. Filer..........		Pub. sch.	Tax. St..	F ...		19	360	339
Mrs Ione Bowman..		Mem	St. G....	F ...	15	95	453	340
....		Pub. D..	Tax. St..	F ...	45	200	1103	341
Burt B Farnsworth		Pub. sch.	Tax St..	Fl ..		160	? 400	342
C T R Smith......		Sch	Gen	F ...			590	343
W. J Shelliday		Pub. sch.	Tax	F ...	84		1887	344
Catharine Cameron.		Mem	G. Fees..	S ...	56	44	1600	345
Millicent B. Hopkins		Pub. sch.	Tax	Fl ..		49	1141	346
E E. Hinman		Mem	Fees	S ...			522	347
Nettie A Ward.....		Pub. D..	St. G....	F ...	25	102	1027	348
A. C Works		Sch	Gen	Fl ..	10		4500	349
Josephine C. Meade		Pub. sch.	Tax	Fl ..			369	350
....		Pub. sch	Tax St..	F ...			1320	351
Grace E. Hall		Pub. sch.	Tax St..	Fl S.	11	2	449	352
C T F. Lyon		Pub. D..	Tax. St..	F ...		118	719	353
Chas S Williams...		Pub sch	Tax. St..	R Fl		230	700	354
Emmet Belknap....		Pub. D..	Tax. St..	F ...	8	196	5330	355
Sister Marie Joseph.		Sch	Gen	Fl ..		50	? 1100	356
Walter O. Shults ..		Inst.....	Gen	F ..			325	357
....		Pub. sch.	Tax. St..	F ...			512	358
Susan M. Armstrong		Sch	St G....	F ...	? 20	369	4504	359
Albert C. Mayham .		Pub sch.	Tax St..	Fl ..			679	360

a For year ending December 1894

	VOLUMES		Days open in year	HOURS OPEN EACH WEEK FOR		RECEIPTS		
	NO. ISSUED							
	For home use	For use at lib		Lending	Reading	Invested funds	Local taxation	State aid
316	769		45	1			$12 97	$9 60
317	2324		300	30	30			
318								
319	32,858		300	36				
320	12,437	79,826	309	76½	76½	$15,050		
321		?	190		32½		224 60	150
322	12,154		215	15	15			200
323	7936	8961	176	10	30		645 90	25
324	49,194	?5000	279	57	58	5108		200
325	?266		365	84	84	30		
326			312	60	72			
327	6500	6000	200	35	35		300	200
328								
329	2189		156	4				50
330	?1500		275	90				200
331	1381		150	10	10			205
332		2653	192		48			62 50
333	?300	?50	200	30				
334			120	?	?			
335								
336								
337								
338								
339	236	126	80	2	25		19 60	20 60
340				3	3			125
341	2818	305	231	3	3			200
342	678	?	40	1			100	58
343								
344			48	6				
345	2640		104	10				
346	400	?	40	1	30		51 12	
347	283		104	4				
348	2299	?	?92	3	3			55
349	450	2000	160	7	7			
350	950		38	3				
351	2267	?40	130	7½			113 75	
352	468		42	2			25	105 23
353	2991	658	52	4	4			
354	?1100	?250	114	¾				
355	15,371	?4000	299	36	36		500	135
356	?100		?100	?				
357	67	?15	313	78	78			
358								
359	491	?	140	3	35			
360	240	1200	200	5	30		10	15

STATISTICS OF NEW YORK LIBRARIES, 1895

LIBRARIES (continued)

FROM			PAYMENTS FOR				
Annual dues	Gifts and other sources	Total receipts	Books, serials and binding	Salaries	All other expenses	Total payments	
		$22 57	$22 57			$22 57	316
			155	$240		395	317
							318
							319
	$15,890	30,890	17,350	12,690	$850	30,890	320
		374 60	374 60			374 60	321
	200	400	287 45	120		407 45	322
		670 90	120 90	550		670 90	323
		5308	888 27	2140	1265 73	4294	324
		30	30			30	325
			88 38			88 38	326
		500	400	100		500	327
							328
	56 50	106 50	101 80		4 70	106 50	329
	193	393	139 38		20	159 38	330
$6	210 69	421 69	238 26	52	99 59	389 85	331
	91	153 50	73 96		12	85 96	332
							333
							334
							335
							336
							337
				600		? 600	338
		31 20	31 20			31 20	339
		125	85 02		36 91	121 93	340
	74 46	274 46		100 50	8 89	109 39	341
	25 00	183	183			183	342
							343
							344
71 75	100 81	172 56		54	45	99	345
		51 12	51 12			51 12	346
?	15	15			5	5	347
	99 73	154 73	81 04	51 25	15 53	147 82	348
							349
							350
		113 75	13 75		100	113 75	351
	40	170 23	260			260	352
			100 67	25		125 67	353
	2	2	? 150			? 150	354
	85 92	670 92	270 60	300	52 08	622 68	355
1		1	25			25	356
							357
							358
							359
		25					360

	Place	NAME OF LIBRARY	Year founded	Source of charter	Relation to University
361	Lyons	Union sch. lib	?1840	I	i
362	McGrawville	Union sch. lib	1864	I	i
363	Madalin	Tivoli pub. lib	1894	R	c
364	Malone	Village sch. dist. lib	1852	I	i
365	Manlius	St John's mil. sch. lib	1869	I	i
366	"	Union sch. lib		I	i
367	Marcellus	Union sch. lib	1892	I	i
368	Margaretville	Union sch. lib	1894	I	i
369	Marion	Marion collegiate inst. lib	1854	I	i
370	Maspeth	Union sch. lib	1872		
371	Massena	Union sch. lib		I	i
372	Matteawan	Howland circulating lib	1872		
373	Mayville	Union sch. lib	1867	I	i
374	Mechanicville	Union sch. lib		I	i
375	"	Y. M. C A. R. R branch lib	1887		
376	Medina	Union sch. lib. dist. no. 12			
377	Mellenville	Mellenville pub. lib	1893	R	c
378	Mexico	Mexico acad lib	1826	I	i
379	Middle Granville	Union sch. lib		I	i
380	Middleburg	Union sch. lib		I	i
381	Middleport	Union sch. lib	1891	I	i
382	Middletown	Public sch. lib	1879		
383	"	State homeo. hosp. Bolles mem. lib	1891	I	
384	"	Wallkill free acad. lib	1887	I	i
385	Mineville	Union sch. lib	1892	I	i
386	Mohawk	Mohawk pub. lib	1893	R	c
387	Montgomery	Union sch. lib		I	i
388	Monticello	Union sch. lib		I	i
389	Moravia	Powers lib	1880	I	
390	"	Union sch. lib		I	i
391	Morris	Union sch. lib		I	i
392	Morristown	Morristown pub. lib	1894	R	c
393	Morrisville	Madison co law lib	?	L	
394	"	Union sch. lib		I	i
395	Mt Morris	Union sch. lib	1866	I	i
396	Mt Vernon	Union sch. lib			
397	Nanuet	Nanuet pub. lib	1894	R	c
398	Naples	Union sch. lib	1860	I	i
399	Nassau	Nassau free li b	1893	R	c
400	New Berlin	Union sch. lib	1880	I	i
401	New Brighton	Sailors' snug harbor lib	1833	I	
402	New Hartford	Union sch. lib	?	I	i
403	New Paltz	State normal and training sch. lib	1885	L	
404	New Rochelle	New Rochelle pub. lib	1893	R	c
405	New York city	Acad. of Mt St Vincent lib	1847	I	i

STATISTICS OF NEW YORK LIBRARIES, 1895

LIBRARIES (continued)

Name of librarian or person in charge	Class of books if not general	Ownership or control	Support	Terms of use	VOLUMES NO ADDED LAST YEAR Given	Bought	Total no. in library	
T. H. Gardner		Pub. sch.	Tax. St..	F ...	¶ 90	206	2163	361
C. M. Bean		Pub. sch.	Tax. St..	Fl ..	37	24	333	362
Frank O. Green		Pub. D..	Tax. St..	F ...		134	426	363
D. H. Stanton		Pub. sch.	Tax. St..	F ...	84	146	5035	364
....		Sch	Gen	Fl ..			700	365
Arthur E. Neeley		Pub. sch	Tax. St..	Fl ..	5	68	¶ 1037	366
B. N. Strong		Pub. sch.	Tax. St..	Fl ..	15	¶ 100	¶ 605	367
....		Pub. sch.	Tax. St..	F ...			721	368
....		Sch	Gen	Fl ..			553	369
Arthur C. Mitchell		Pub. sch.	Tax. St..	F ...			1000	370
....		Pub. sch.	Tax. St..	Fl ..			524	371
I. N. Badeau		Mem	End.Fees	S ...		151	5907	372
Thomas E. Lockhart		Pub. sch.	Tax. St..	F ...			¶ 947	373
S. B. Blakeman		Pub. sch.	Tax. St..	Fl ..			500	374
Mirza Bross		Inst	Gen	F ...	63	87	850	375
Mary E. Phelps		Pub sch.	Tax	F ...	11	5	1176	376
Mary I. Miller		Pub. D..	St. G....	F ...	1		338	377
Melzar C. Richards		Sch	Gen	Fl ..	10		1793	378
....		Pub. sch.	St. G....	Fl ..	6		350	379
H. H. Snell		Pub. sch.	Tax. St..	Fl ..			998	380
Eugene G. Hughez		Pub. sch	Tax. St..	F ...			¶ 700	381
Mary K. Van Keuren		Pub. sch.	Tax. St..	F ...	1	150	6891	382
W. B. Ewer		Inst	St. Gen..	Fl ..	10		2200	383
G. T. Townsend		Pub. sch.	Tax. St..	Fl ..		108	546	384
C. Kellar		Pub sch	Tax. St..	Fl ..		37	605	385
Helen L. Smith		Pub. D..	Tax. St..	F ...		111	815	386
Reuben Fraser		Pub. sch.	St. G....	F ...	5		909	387
W. W. Miller		Pub. sch.	Tax. St..	F ...		50	560	388
M. E. Kenyon		End	Fees	R. S.	4		3712	389
....		Pub. sch.	Tax. St..	Fl ..		26	755	390
....		Pub. sch.	Tax. St..	F ...		100	700	391
W. L. Avery		Pub	St. G....	F ...	10	95	310	392
A D. Kennedy	Law.	Gov	St	Fl ..		22	718	393
....		Pub. sch	Tax. St..	F ...	5		397	394
Ida Kelsall		Pub. sch.	Tax. St..	F ...	3	64	1000	395
Mary Irwin		Pub. sch	Tax. St..	F ...			4893	396
Emory Rikert		Pub. D..	Tax. St..	F ...		60	771	397
E. C. Clark		Pub sch	Tax	F ...			1435	398
Clarinda Merchant		Mem	St. G	F ...		53	478	399
....		Pub. sch.	Tax. St..	F ...			626	400
G D. Trask		Inst	Gen	Fl ..		25	3850	401
A. M Scripture		Pub. sch.	Tax	F ...		5	600	402
K. A. Gage		Sch	St	Fl ..		146	2771	403
Mary E. Huntington		Pub. D..	Tax. St..	F ...	22	760	2714	404
....		Sch	Gen	Fl ..			¶ 4970	405

| | VOLUMES | | Days open in year | HOURS OPEN EACH WEEK FOR | | Invested funds | RECEIPTS | |
| | NO. ISSUED | | | | | | | |
	For home use	For use at lib		Lending	Reading		Local taxation	State aid
361	? 1200	?	40	1	?		$125	$125
362	?	?	200		45		35 13	35 13
363	2258	1030	236	40	40		38 75	72 38
364	11,130	? 1590	265	30	30		1000	100
365								
366	1396	75	40	1			33 36	33 36
367	? 600		187	8	8		25	25
368								
369								
370		200	200	5	25		25	25
371								
372	6917		309	66½	66½	$500		
373								
374								
375	300		312	72	72			
376	2328	204	142	4			30	
377	266		190	30				
378	225	150	200	2	30			
379			30	1				
380								
381								
382	27,192	?	285	21	21		500	
383	5000		104	6				
384		?	192		26¼		98 05	98 05
385	760	? 600	200	4	30		25	25
386	1885		156	3			135 93	62 50
387	200	600	200	6	6			76
388	200		196	5			36 49	36 49
389	372		104	7	7			
390	344		80	2			25	25
391	? 1000		200	2			85	
392	1833		156	3				20
393								
394	189	?	190	1	30		75	
395	1042		52	2			50	53 65
396	15,786		96	2½				
397	780	300	140	15	5		40	40
398	75	300	200	10				
399	3612		150	4				
400								
401	12,949		307	24				
402	45		40	1			5	
403								
404	10,018		306	18			3,500	200
405								

LIBRARIES (continued)

FROM			PAYMENTS FOR				
Annual dues	Gifts and other sources	Total receipts	Books, serials and binding	Salaries	All other expenses	Total payments	
	$25	$275	$262 60	$25		$287 60	361
		70 26	70 25			70 25	362
	46 93	158 06	145 31		$12 75	158 06	363
	28 16	1128 16	520 56	250	357 60	128 16	664
							365
	9	75 72	74 72		1	75 72	366
	56	106	? 106			? 106	367
							368
							369
		50					370
							371
$398 50	198 61	1097 11	316 15	130	634 91	1081 06	372
							373
							374
	31 50	31 50	64			64	375
		30	30			30	376
	270	270					377
							378
							379
							380
							381
	92 12	592 12	298 69	401 96	291 87	992 52	382
							383
		196 10	238 15			238 15	384
		50	50			50	385
	4 55	202 98	142 33	52	8 65	202 98	386
	5	81			81	81	387
	15	87 98	72 39			72 39	388
42 75	27 50	70 25		26	10	36	389
		50					390
		85	135			135	391
	21 93	41 93	87 53	2 50	4 40	94 43	392
							393
		75	75			75	394
	54 35	158	84 74	50	35	135 09	395
							396
		80	50 48		29 52	80	397
							398
	167 24	167 24	50 15	15	81 60	146 75	399
							400
			260			260	401
		5	2 34			2 34	402
							403
	47 82	3747 82	785 70	517	1,015 61	2,318 31	404
							405

NEW YORK

	Place	NAME OF LIBRARY	Year founded	Source of charter	Relation to University
406	New York 197 E. B'way.	Aguilar free lib................	1886	G	...
	" " " "	"			
	" 113 E. 59th st....	"			
	" 624 Fifth st......	"			
407	" Bible house......	Amer. Bible soc lib..............	1816	I	
408	" 11 W. 29th st....	Amer. geographical soc. lib........	1852	I	
409	" 111-115 W.38th st	Amer inst. lib...............	1829	I	
410	" 13 Burling slip...	Amer. inst. of mining engineers lib.	1871	I	...
411	" 77th st and 8th av	Amer. museum of nat. hist. lib.....	1869	I	...
412	" 76 Wall st........	Amer. seaman's friend soc. lib......	1858	I	...
413	" 144,146 E. 86th st.	Aschenbroedel verein lib..........	1860	I	...
414	" 7 W. 29th st	Ass'n of the bar of the city of N.Y. lib.	1870	I	...
415	" 34 Lafayette pl..	a Astor library.................	1849	L	...
416	" 395 Broome st....	Broome st. free library............	1885	I	...
417	" 123 E. 50th st....	Cathedral lib....................	1888	I	...
	" " "				
	" 44 Second av	Church of the Nativity lib.........			
	" 141 E. 43d st.....	St Agnes' church lib			
	" 308 E. 78th st....	St Monica's lib			
418	" 120 W. 59th st ...	Catholic club lib	1871	I	...
419	" City Hall.........	City library	1847		
420	" 209 E. 23d st.....	Coll. of phar. of city of N. Y. lib.....	¶1831	I	i
421	" Lex. av. & 23d st.	Coll of the city of New York lib...	1852	I	i
422	" 30 W. 16th st.....	Coll. of St Francis Xavier lib	1847	I	i
423	"	Coll. of veterinary surgeons lib. ...		I	i
424	" 95 Rivington st..	College settlement lib.............	1888	I	...
425	" 65th st. and 1st av.	Colored home and hosp lib.........	1881	I	...
426	" 143d st. & Am. av.	Colored orphan asylum lib	1869	I	...
427	" 41 E. 49th st.....	Columbia coll. lib.................	1754	I	i
428	" 7th st. cor 4th av	Cooper union lib	1857	I	i
429	" 286 Rivington st.	DeWitt mem. free lib.............	1882	I	...
430	" 289 E. 14th st....	Eclectic med. coll. lib..............	1865	I	i
431	" 120 Broadway....	Equitable life assurance soc. law lib.	1876	I	...
432	" 23 W. 44th st	Geneal. and biog. soc. lib	1869	I	...
433	" 18 E. 16th st.....	Gen. soc. of mech. and tradesmen lib.	1820	I	...
434	" C'la sq. W.20th st	Gen theological sem. lib..........	1817	I	i
435	" 137 2d av.........	German hosp. and dispensary lib ...	¶1857	I	...
436	" 55 Marion st......	Grammar sch. No. 21, Holbrook lib.			
437	" 32 W. 123d st.....	Harlem lib	1825	L	...
438	" 301 Mott st	Health dep't lib..................	1866		...
439	" 203 Mulberry st..	House of detention for witnesses lib.	1875		...
440	" 44 2d st..........	La Salle acad. lib.................	1848	I	...
441	" 895 5th av.......	Lenox lib	1870	L	...
442	" 156th & St A's av.	Liter. Gesellschaft of Morrisania lib.	1883	G	...
443	" 203 E. 57th st....	Maimonides free lib	¶1855	I	...
444	" G. B'v'd c.W.131st	Manhattan coll lib	1863	I	i
445	" 12 W. 31st st	Mechanical engineers lib	1890	G	...

a Consolidated May 23, 1895, with the Lenox lib and the Tilden Trust under the name of New York pub lib Astor, Lenox and Tilden foundations.

LIBRARIES (continued)

Name of librarian or person in charge	Class of books if not general	Ownership or control	Support	Terms of use	VOLUMES Given	VOLUMES Bought	Total no in library	
Pauline Leippziger.		Mem	St. Sdy	F		4171	28,488	406
						2461	15,099	
						1436	11,006	
						274	2383	
Edward W. Gilman	Theo	Inst	G	Pri	85	195	5141	407
George C. Hurlbut		Mem	G. Gen	R. S.		579	26,164	408
George Whitfield jr.	Ind	Mem	Gen	R	53	12	13,818	409
R. W. Raymond	Sci	Mem	Gen	Fl	160		2620	410
A. Woodward	Sci	Mem	Gen	R		1149	b 29,231	411
W. C. Stitt		Inst	G	Fl		c 5848	c 15,537	412
Max Pergament		Mem	Gen	Fl			3500	413
William J C Berry.	Law	Mem	Gen	Sl	2038	1130	48,873	414
Robbins Little		End	End	R	1494	8103	267,147	415
Alexander J. Kerr		Par	Gen	F			2314	416
Agnes Wallace		Par	G	F	297	634	17,594	417
							14,297	
							1522	
							825	
							950	
Edward J. McGuire.		Mem	Gen	Fl		1108	20,907	418
Philip Baer		Gov	Tax	R	78		† 6200	419
W. C. Davie	Phar	Coll	Gen	R			4623	420
Chas G. Herbermann		Coll	End.Tax	Fl	122	814	29,342	421
E. Spillane		Coll	Gen	R.Fl.		100	25,000	422
		Coll	Gen	Fl			† 500	423
Amy P. Hall		Iust	G.Gen	F	† 600		2436	424
Thos W. Bickerton	Med	Inst	Gen	Fl	25	3	† 1200	425
		Inst	Gen	Fl			725	426
George H. Baker		Coll	End. G	Fl	5892	18,947	203,000	427
L C. L. Jordan		Inst	Gen	R	368	626	35,870	428
Malcolm R. Birnie		Inst	Gen	F	133		2681	429
C. W. Brandenburg.	Med	Coll	Gen	Fl			2058	430
Thomas Campbell	Law	Inst	Gen	Fl		350	14,366	431
Richard H. Greene		Mem	Fees	Sl	309		3313	432
Jacob Schwartz		Mem	End. Sdy	F	b 707	b 3972	b 102,019	433
Edward H. Jewett	Theo	Coll	Eud. G	R.Fl	d 781	d 205	d 25,900	434
Hermann G. Klotz	Med	Inst	Gen	Fl	8	123	5462	435
Joseph Bernhardt		Pub. sch.	G	Fl			1038	436
George M Perry		Mem	End Fees	R. S.	315	638	† 18,550	437
Roger S. Tracy	M. S.	Gov	Gen	R	13	10	1501	438
Tennis V. Holbrow.		Inst	G	Fl			600	439
Bro. E. Victor		Sch	Gen	Fl	5		827	440
Wilberforce Eames.	A. H.	End	End. G	R	2675	1408	† 86,196	441
Philip J. Moog		Mem	Gen	Fl		e 136	e 1129	442
J Bacharach		Mem	Gen	F	e 1563	e 392	e 43,510	443
Bro. Blimond		Coll	Gen	R.Fl	58	42	† 8155	444
Emma C. Griffin	Sci	Mem	Gen	R		40	3500	445

b For year ending Dec 1894 *c* For year ending Mar 1895 Loan libraries sent on ships.
d For year ending April 21, 1895 *e* For year ending Nov 1894.

NEW YORK

	VOLUMES		Days open in year	HOURS OPEN EACH WEEK FOR		RECEIPTS		
	NO ISSUED							
	For home use	For use at lib.		Lending	Reading	Invested funds	Local taxation	State aid
406	252,227		360	68	91	$1401 19	$9999 98	$200
	141,477							
	85,424							
	25,326							
407								
408		?	274		48			
409	23	? 2000	304	51	51			
410					48			
411								
412								
413	4500		313	18				
414			365		112			
415		214,029	274		48	45,790 06		
416	2034		144	15	78			
417	51,814	1907	230	11				
	39,552							
	2886		111	6				
	4330		160	8				
	5044		94	5				
418	180	?	365					
419		? 1495	300		32			
420								
421	?	?	269	41	41	2008 02	1552 80	
422	5000	100	365	10	84			
423								
424	? 15,000		52	?8	?8			
425								
426								
427	53,471		306	86	86	30		
428	319,868	329		93				
429	7299		140	15		?	?	
430								
431			306		60			
432		?	313		18	447 62		
433	254,371	4750	304	78	78			
434	?	?	287	46	46	3 60		
435	60	?	305	18	18			
436								
437	42,969	?	305	81	81	1911 10		
438	?	?	305	38	38			
439			365					
440	30	?	200	35	35			
441		31,144	309		42	17,655 81		
442	315		25	?				
443	41,852	17,878	351	66	66			
444	50	1,045	? 275	12	70			
445		4500	313		72	2200		

STATISTICS OF NEW YORK LIBRARIES, 1895

LIBRARIES (*continued*)

From Annual dues	Gifts and other sources	Total receipts	Payments for Books, serials and binding	Salaries	All other expenses	Total payments	
....	$2250 44	$13,851 61	$4583 42	$6398 09	$4121 90	$15,103 41	406
....	....	....	....	....	....	....	
....	....	....	....	....	....	....	
....	....	....	....	....	....	....	407
....	....	....	1563 31	....	....	1563 31	408
....	....	....	235 43	600	900	1735 43	409
....	....	....	200	....	....	200	410
....	....	....	....	....	....	....	411
....	....	....	....	....	....	....	412
....	....	....	....	....	....	....	413
....	....	....	....	....	....	....	414
....	....	45,790 06	23,809 13	17,393	7,125 96	48,328 09	415
....	....	....	....	....	....	....	416
....	1590 18	1590 18	2073 01	....	1611 70	3684 71	417
....	....	....	....	....	....	....	
....	....	....	....	....	....	....	
....	....	....	....	....	....	....	
....	....	....	....	....	....	....	418
....	....	....	....	....	....	....	419
....	....	....	....	....	....	....	420
....	....	3560 82	1894 69	1350	....	3244 69	421
....	....	....	....	....	....	....	422
....	....	....	....	....	....	....	423
....	25	25	40	....	....	40	424
....	10	10	10	....	....	10	425
....	....	....	....	....	....	....	426
....	57,879 50	60,879 50	29,486 33	21,343 60	1200	52,029 93	427
....	....	....	1807 37	4899 50	121 43	6828 30	428
....	?	?	....	300	?	? 300	429
....	....	....	....	....	....	....	430
....	....	....	1507 15	....	....	1507 15	431
$1180	1146 37	2773 99	45 80	120	1570 51	1736 31	432
....	....	15,726 31	6198 07	8209 52	1318 72	15,726 31	433
....	673 44	1033 44	673 64	500	....	1178 64	434
705	....	705	409 16	....	25 09	434 25	435
....	....	....	....	....	....	....	436
1369	475 88	3755 98	1502 05	2435 50	2040 47	5978 02	437
....	....	....	114 50	....	....	114 50	438
....	....	....	....	....	....	....	439
....	....	....	....	....	....	....	440
....	58,617 20	106,273 01	14,436 16	18,176 35	10,700 10	43,312 61	441
156 84	....	156 84	130 34	....	26 50	156 84	442
....	2319 40	2319 40	1051 43	676	124 44	1851 87	443
120	....	120	102 75	....	....	102 75	444
900	625	3725	350	1100	2275	3725	445

	Place	NAME OF LIBRARY	Year founded	Source of charter	Relation to University
446	New York 213 W. 54th st	Med. coll. and hosp. for women lib..		I	i
447	" Clinton Hall	Mercantile lib.........................	1820	L	...
448	" 13 Astor pl	Metropolis law sch. lib...............	1891	I	i
449	" Cen. p'k op E 82d	Metropolitan museum of art lib	1880	I	...
450	" Governor's island	Military service inst. lib	1878		...
451	" 64 Madison av ...	Mott memorial med. and surg. lib..	1867	L	...
452	" 226 W. 42d st	N. Y. free circulating lib...........	1880	L	...
	" 49 Bond st........	Bond st. lib......................			...
	" 135 2d av	Ottendorfer lib...................			...
	" 226 W. 42d st	George Bruce lib			...
	" 251 W. 13th st ...	Jackson square lib			...
	" 18 E. 125th st....	Harlem lib			...
	" 49 W. 20th st	Muhlenberg lib...................			...
453	" 8 W. 16th st	N. Y. hospital lib.................	1796	I	...
454	" 412 9th av	N. Y. inst. for the blind lib	1831	I	...
455	" 116 P.O. b'ld'g...	N. Y. law inst. lib.................	1828	I	i
456	"	N. Y. law sch. lib.................	1891	I	i
457	" Pk.av.c E 68th st	N. Y. normal coll. lib	1886	I	...
458	" 67 University pl .	N. Y. society lib....................	1754	L	...
459	" 63 2d st..........	Olivet lib..........................		I	...
460	" 87 W. 77th st....	Peck mem. lib.....................	1893		...
461	" 303 E 20th st....	Post grad. med. sch. and hosp. lib..	1882	I	i
462	" 53 5th av	Presb. bd. of for. missions lib		I	...
463	" 135 E. 15th st....	Prison ass'n lib....................	1846	I	...
464	" 361 Madison av..	Railroad men's building lib	1887	I	...
465	" 259 W. 69th st...	Riverside free lib..................	1894	I	...
466	" 121 W. 91st st ...	St Agnes' free lib	1893	R	c
467	" 38 Bleeker st	St Barnabas' free reading room			...
468	" 207 E. 16th st....	St George's free circ. lib	1893	I	...
469	" Fordham	St John's coll. lib...................	1846	I	i
470	" 120th st. west....	Teachers coll. Bryson lib...........	1887	I	i
471	" 11 University pl..	Trow directory lib.................	1872		...
472	" 700 Park av	Union theological sem. lib	1836	I	i
473	" University h'g'ts.	University of the city of N. Y. lib...	1831	I	i
	" 29 Univer. b'ld'g.	Univ. of city of N. Y. law lib...		I	i
474	" 32 E 26th st.....	University club lib	1879	I	...
475	" 26 Delancey st...	University settlement lib	1892	I	...
476	" c 156 st. & Am.av	Washington heights free lib........	1868	G	...
477	" Foot E. 76th st...	Webster free circulating lib........	1894	I	r
478	" 19 Clinton pl	Woman's lib.......................	1865		...
479	" 321 E. 15th st....	Women's med coll.of N.Y. infirm. lib.	1884	I	...
480	" 52 E. 23d st......	Y. M. C. A. lib.....................	1852	I	...
481	" 7 E. 15th st......	Y. W C. A. lib.....................	1870	I	r
482	N. Y mills	School dist. no. 4			...
483	Newark	Union sch. lib	†	I	i
484	Newark Valley	Union sch. lib......................	1887	I	i
485	Newburg	Mt St Mary's acad. lib	1887	I	i

LIBRARIES (continued)

Name of librarian or person in charge	Class of books if not general	Ownership or control	Support	Terms of use	NO. ADDED LAST YEAR Given	NO. ADDED LAST YEAR Bought	Total no. in library	
....	....	Coll.....	Gen.....	F'...	......	......	900	446
W. T. Peoples......	......	Mem	Fees	S ...	a467	a5089	a246,514	447
Abna C. Thomas....	Law.	Coll.....	Gen.....	Fl...	......	......	1380	448
Wm. L. Andrews...	Art..	Inst.....	End Gen.	Fl...	276	142	4269	449
J. C. Bush	......	Inst.....	Gen	Fl ..	......	......	? 7000	450
J. W. S. Gonley....	Med.	Mem	End.....	R ...	......	......	3000	451
Arthur E. Bostwick.	......	Mem	End.Sdy	F ...	......	b4925	b81,755	452
....	......	....	....	......	......	......	19,572	
....	......	....	....	......	......	......	22,224	
....	......	....	....	......	......	......	18,570	
....	......	....	....	......	......	......	12,849	
....	......	....	....	......	......	......	4482	
....	......	....	....	......	......	......	4092	
Frank P. Foster....	Med.	Inst.....	Gen	F ...	2213	374	? 26,000	453
Wm. B. Wait	......	Inst.....	Gen	Fl ..	......	110	? 3000	454
Wm. H. Winters ...	Law.	Inst.....	Fees	S ...	116	1606	43,301	455
Bernard H. Arnold .	Law.	Sch	Gen	Fl ..	......	1584	1619	456
Edith Rice.........	......	Mem	G	Fl ..	115	129	4400	457
Wentworth S.Butler	......	Mem	End.Fees	R. S.	c248	c1255	cf90,000	458
Lizzie F. Baker	......	Par	G	F ...	7	83	2580	459
Edward H. Boyer ..	......	Pub. sch	End. G ..	F ...	165	200	3569	460
....	Med.	Coll.....	Gen	Fl ..	90	......	? 1000	461
W. H. Grant	......	Inst.....	G. Gen ..	Fl ..	......	......	? 6000	462
Samuel M Jackson.	......	Mem	G. Gen ..	R ...	42	......	908	463
W. F. Stevens......	......	Iust.....	G. Gen ..	Fl ..	120	168	6661	464
Kate Kaufman	......	Inst.....	G. Gen ..	F ...	352	80	1100	465
Anne L. Gibson	......	Mem	St. G....	F ...	294	568	1832	466
H. Myer	......	Iust.....	G	R ...	11	......	? 1000	467
Emma A. Bays.....	......	Par	Gen	Fl ..	......	? 10	4000	468
Joseph Twinge.....	......	Coll.....	Gen	Fl ..	100	150	34,650	469
Liljan Denio	Ped.	Coll.....	St. G....	R.Fl.	357	504	6566	470
....	Dir..	Pri......	Fees.....	R. S.	......	......	? 563	471
Chas. R. Gillett	Theo	Coll.....	End......	R.Fl.	d234	d537	d70,716	472
L. J. Tompkins	......	Coll.....	Gen.....	R.Fl.	350	200	30,196	473
L. J. Tompkins	Law.	Coll.....	Gen.....	Fl ..	......	......	9100	
Lyman H. Bagg....	......	Mem	Gen.....	Fl ..	277	671	12,325	474
Helen Moore	......	Inst.....	G	F ...	......	......	? 1986	475
A.R VanHoevenberg	......	Mem	G	F ...	71	614	10,063	476
Wm. Stone Booth...	......	Inst.....	St. Sdy..	F ...	820	381	5276	477
M. J. Kemp	......	Inst.....	Gen.....	Fl ..	......	......	? 1500	478
Cora Thompson	Med.	Coll.....	Gen.....	Fl ..	14	33	1171	479
R. B. Poole	......	Iust.....	End. G..	R ...	e542	e863	e?42,500	480
Sarah W. Cattell...	......	Inst.....	St. Gen.	R.Fl.	......	e1708	e22,897	481
John Parry.........	......	Pub. sch.	End.T.St.	F ...	......	210	851	482
....	......	Pub sch	St	R.Fl.	......	......	1750	483
Bertha Benedict....	......	Pub. sch.	Tax. St..	F ...	......	......	476	484
Sr. M. Emmanuel...	......	Sch	St. Gen..	Fl ..	......	20	484	485

a For year ending Nov 1894. *b* For year ending Oct. 1895. *c* For year ending Mar. 1895.
d For year ending April 1894. *e* For year ending Dec. 1894.

| | VOLUMES | | Days open in year | HOURS OPEN EACH WEEK FOR | | RECEIPTS | | |
| | NO ISSUED | | | | | | | |
	For home use	For use at lib		Lending	Reading	Invested funds	Local taxation	State aid
446								
447	130,988	45,885	306	63	75	$1030 30		
448								
449						292		
450								
451		?	300		84			
452	a626,796	a27,665	361	77	77	4968 24	$23,333 34	
	98,687	3052						
	145,443	10,947						
	165,653	5123						
	87,169	7580						
	95,356	963						
	34,488							
453			300	42	42			
454			246	2	84			
455			306	13	13			
456		?	213		54			
457	4069	? 2000	185	37	37			
458	27,070	? 900	307	54	69	6608 13		
459	6227	40	237	28	78			
460	? 30,000	?	186	25	25	208		
461		?	300		72			
462								
463			305		48			
464	13,036		365	98	98			
465	5242		200	30	30			
466	9225	33	283	26	26			$200
467		? 2500	250		18			
468	8835		208	7				
469	6000	5000	200	5	6			
470	10,750	?	285	44	54			200
471								
472	?	?	220	38	38	4584		
473		?	175		48			
474		?	365		130			
475								
476	22,552	? 1880	305	63	63			
477	18,825	50	352	42	42		625	200
478		100	307	42	42			
479	2307	?	194	27	27	250		
480		? 49,090	365		89	5400		
481	63,818	?	300	73½	73½			200
482	320		? 20	2		159 51	36 35	10
483	?	?	40	3	3			
484	368	160	40	½				
485	? 130	304	180	2	5			30

a For year ending Oct. 1895.

STATISTICS OF NEW YORK LIBRARIES, 1895 281

LIBRARIES (continued)

From			Payments for				
Annual dues	Gifts and other sources	Total receipts	Books, serials and binding	Salaries	All other expenses	Total payments	
$15,764	$9370 04	$26,164 34	$8193 23	$7654 23	$9094 66	$24,942 12	446 447 448
....	708 69	1000 69	1031 30	....	163 49	1194 79	449 450
....	....	1200	....	?	?	1200	451
3785	11,105 28	43,191 86	7388 84	18,763 60	14,752 45	40,904 89	452
			1409 81	3597 14	2601 48	7608 43	
			1423 83	4045 01	3031 26	8500 10	
			1903 53	4270 97	2657 79	8832 29	
			1113 16	3292 57	1835 23	6240 96	
			999 63	2430 45	1629 25	5059 83	
			538 88	1127 46	339 48	2005 82	
			205 29			205 29	453 454
13,000	....	13,000	....			....	455
....	2785 35	2785 35	2766 35	....	19	2785 35	456 457
3112	378 54	10,098 67	3139 37	4840	1383 72	9363 09	458 459
....	740	948	....			....	460
....	....	....	8			8	461 462 463
....	1800	1800	617	1200	....	1817	464
....	907 47	907 47	85 82	720	....	805 82	465
....	580 30	780 30	411 37	400	162 50	973 87	466
....	....	....	109 48	....	8	117 48	467
48	350	398	19 50	300	76	395	468
190	....	190	425 50	....	....	425 50	469
....	2200	2400	1290	....	1174 80	2464 80	470
....	....	....	....			....	471
....	100	4684	1182 21	2442 50	215 41	3840 12	472
....	....	....	400	2070	?	2470	473
....	4614	4614	2611	1800	204	4615	474 475
540	1379 02	1919 02	632 98	715 25	587 60	1935 83	476
....	995	1820	400	840	580	1820	477 478
38	....	288	83 93	....	....	83 93	479
....	3790 71	9190 71	3697 57	5014 50	394 14	9106 21	480
....	1359	1559	1209 86	2323 60	?	3533 46	481
....	....	205 86	174 26	12	9 60	195 86	482
				20		20	483 484
2	30	62	60	....	....	60	485

NEW YORK

	Place	NAME OF LIBRARY	Year founded	Source of charter	Relation to university
486	Newburg	Newburg free lib	1852	L	...
487	"	Second judicial dist. law. lib	1885	L	...
488	Newfield	Newfield pub. lib	1894	R	c
489	Newport	Union sch. lib	1876	...	...
490	Niagara Falls	De Veaux sch. lib		I	i
491	"	Niagara Falls pub. lib	1895	R	c
492	Niagara University	Niagara university lib	1864	I	i
493	Nichols	Union sch. lib	1873	I	i
494	North Brookfield	Union sch. lib	1885	I	i
495	North Chili	A. M. Chesbrough sem. lib	?1870	I	i
496	North Cohocton	Union sch. lib	1892	I	i
497	North Parma	North Parma pub. lib	1893	R	c
498	North Tarrytown	Union sch. lib	1876	I	i
499	North Tonawanda	North Tonawanda pub. lib	1893	R	c
500	" "	Union sch. lib	1893	I	i
501	Northville	Northville lib	1893	I	i
502	Norwich	Union sch. lib	1873	I	i
503	Norwood	Union sch. lib	1886	I	i
504	Nunda	Union sch. lib	1876	I	i
505	Nyack	Nyack lib	1879	G	a
506	"	Union sch. lib		I	i
507	Oakfield	Cary collegiate sem. lib		I	i
508	"	Union sch. lib		I	i
509	Ogdensburg	Ogdensburg pub. lib	1893	R	c
510	"	St Mary's acad. lib	1891	I	i
511	Olean	Forman lib	1871	G	...
512	"	High sch. lib		I	i
513	Oneida	Union sch. lib		I	i
514	Oneonta	Oneonta pub. lib	1892	R	c
515	Onondaga Valley	Onondaga acad. lib		I	i
516	Orchard Park	Union sch. lib	1878	I	i
517	Oriskany	School lib dist. no 12		I	i
518	Oswego	City lib	1893	I	...
519	Oswego	City sch. lib	?	...	...
520	"	High sch. lib	?1885	I	i
521	"	State normal and training sch. lib		I	r
522	"	Y M. C A. R. R. branch lib	1887	...	...
523	Ovid	Union sch. and acad. lib		I	i
524	Owego	Owego free lib	1848	I	i
525	Oxford	Oxford acad. lib	?	I	i
526	Oyster Bay	People's lib	1893	R	c
527	Painted Post	Union sch lib	1868	I	i
528	Palatine Bridge	Union sch. lib	1857	I	i
529	Palisades	Palisades lib. and reading room	1891	...	...
530	Palmyra	Class. union sch. lib		I	i

LIBRARIES (continued)

Name of librarian or person in charge	Class of book if not general	Ownership or control	Support	Terms of use	VOLUMES NO ADDED LAST YEAR Given	Bought	Total no. in library	
Chas. Estabrook....		aPub. sch	bTax. St.	F ...	149	515	20,329	486
George A. Price.....	Law.	Gov.....	St.......	Fl ..		657	4084	487
Dora M Ham		Mem	Tax. St..	F ..	6	116	488	488
William H. Cone...		Pub. sch	Tax St..	F ...		42	520	489
....		Sch	Gen.....	Fl .			† 1300	490
		Pub. D..	Tax. St..	F ...		37	3641	491
Luke A. Grace......		Coll	Gen.....	Fl ..	400	100	7000	492
C. Juliet Laning ...		Pub. sch.	St G....	F ...			† 470	493
E. J. Bonner.......		Pub sch.	Tax. St	Fl ..		18	550	494
....		Sch	G	Fl ..		356	1961	495
Susan Bushnell		Pub. sch	St. G....	F ...	3	48	367	496
E. B. Murphy......		Pub	St G....	F ...	2	234	648	497
Nathan H. Dumond		Pub. sch	Tax. St .	F ...		317	817	498
....		Pub. D..	Tax St.	F ...	51	345	1825	499
Clinton S. Marsh...		Pub sch	Tax St..	Fl ..	2	69	520	500
B. C. Van Ingen....		Pub sch	Tax	F ...	6	† 70	531	501
Mina B Blackman..		Pub. sch.	Tax. St.	Fl ..	1000		3846	502
Edwin F. McDonald		Pub. sch.	Tax. St..	R Fl.	2	10	662	503
....		Pub sch.	Tax. St..	Fl ..			604	504
Helen L. Powell....		Mem	St Sdy..	F ...	58	283	3372	505
Ira H Lawton.....		Pub sch	Tax. St..	R.Fl.			1321	506
....		Sch	Gen	Fl ..			880	507
A. M. McIlroy......		Pub. sch.	Tax. St.	F ...		138	570	508
Fred Van Dusen....		Pub.....	Tax. St..	F ..	196	310	5005	509
....		Sch	Gen	Fl ..		8	665	510
Ella P. Hazlett		Mem	End.Fees	R. S.	c 8	c 138	c 4550	511
Anna E.. Foote.....		Pub sch	Tax St..	Fl ..	2	28	1980	512
Mrs J. C. Ayres ...		Pub. sch	Tax. St..	R.Fl.	200	344	2062	513
Alva Seybolt.......		Pub D .	Tax. St..	F ...	99	460	4235	514
D. H. Cook		Pub sch	Tax. St..	F ...		200	1000	515
A. K. Hoag........		Pub. sch	Tax. St..	Fl ..	6	129	716	516
....		Pub. sch.	Tax	Fl?..			375	517
Robert S. Kelsey ..		Pub.....	End......	R		† 275	13,350	518
Robert S. Kelsey...		Pub.....	Tax......	F		115	6149	519
C. W. Richards		Pub. sch	Tax. St.	Fl ..	2		433	520
S. Augusta Smith ..		Sch	St. Gen..	R.Fl		576	4529	521
J. G. Watson.......		Inst.....	Fees Gen	R.Sl.	2		603	522
Lewis H. Clark jr...		Pub. sch	Tax. St..	Fl ..	† 12	† 90	1652	523
J B Worthington .		Pub. sch	Tax	F		200	6200	524
Herbert P. Gallinger		Sch	St. Gen..	Fl ..	13	32	1605	525
Herbert F Phillips.		Mem	St. G....	F ...	† 75	† 45	650	526
Alvin Z. Pierce.....		Pub. sch.	Tax	F ...			410	527
George H Hoxie ...		Pub sch.	Tax. St..	F ...	8	239	947	528
Emma J. Quidor ...		Mem	Fees Gen	F ...	118	5	1023	529
S. Dwight Arms....		Pub. sch	Tax St..	F ...	15	215	2579	530

a Incorporated under special act, Mar 30, 1877 Is in charge of board of education
b Tuition fees from non resident pupils are appropriated to purchase of books.
c For year ending April 1895

NEW YORK

	VOLUMES		Days open in year	HOURS OPEN EACH WEEK FOR		RECEIPTS		
	NO ISSUED							
	For home use	For use at lib.		Lending	Reading	Invested funds	Local taxation	State aid
486	67,556	†	292	72	72	....	$3150	$207 19
487	....	....	313	.....	72	....	....	2600
488	370	....	52	3	.....	....	....	100
489	250	50	200	12	12	$29 44	15	15
490	....	....	.....	.....	.....	....	....	....
491	9467	....	145	36	.....	....	600	200
492	1000	† 5000	365	1	.....	....	....	....
493	129	....	190	2½	.....	....	....	....
494	† 400	† 50	† 60	2	.....	....	....	11
495	†	†	† 270	† 70	† 70	....	....	....
496	† 500	† 25	40	10	5	....	30	55
497	2787	....	104	18	.....	....	....	125
498	3560	....	72	2	.....	....	65 61	90 61
499	5293	....	300	12	.....	....	200	200
500	154	† 7000	193	35	35	....	....	....
501	930	† 500	40	1	.....	....	† 50	....
502	2000	....	80	3	.....	....	175	241 35
503	300	620	250	2	30	....	25	25
504	....	....	.....	.....	.....	....	....	....
505	19,066	150	306	58	58	....	1200	....
506	2500	550	195	5	5	....	....	....
507	....	....	.....	.....	.....	....	....	....
508	814	....	80	4	.....	....	100	20 50
509	14,289	....	260	15	15	....	....	200
510	300	8000	189	.....	.....	....	....	....
511	6923	†	305	42	42	414 13	....	....
512	† 3500	†	200	35	35	....	300	300
513	6976	500	120	4	20	....	250	250
514	19,369	800	307	18	18	....	300	200
515	400	25	200	2	45	....	100	125
516	....	551	187	30	.....	....	....	32
517	....	....	.....	.....	.....	....	....	....
518	....	4738	300	.....	39	250	....	....
519	9896	....	300	39	.....	....	525 88	184 45
520	† 200	† 2000	200	25	25	....	23 50	....
521	6535	† 4500	260	60	60	....	....	528 10
522	879	† 30	365	.....	89½	....	....	....
523	†	†	† 40	† 1	.....	....	30 61	25
524	17,100	....	89	8	.....	....	....	....
525	615	†	192	2	30	....	....	19 18
526	2160	†	305	60	60	....	....	350
527	118	26	40	1	.....	....	....	10
528	† 1100	† 400	110	3	30	....	73 67	145 59
529	1482	†	204	11	11	....	....	....
530	2073	†	40	1	.....	....	20	125

LIBRARIES (continued)

FROM		Total receipts	PAYMENTS FOR			Total payments	
Annual dues	Gifts and other sources		Books, serials and binding	Salaries	All other expenses		
....	$1619 07	$4976 26	$1755 41	$2490	? $730 85	$4976 26	486
....	....	2600	2600	....	....	2600	487
....	56 48	156 48	99 82	6 25	19 25	125 32	488
....	....	59 44	59 44	....	....	59 44	489
....	....	....	....	....	....	....	490
....	....	800	98 86	152	353 70	604 56	491
$7	225	232	225	....	....	225	492
....	....	....	....	....	....	....	493
....	5 25	16 25	16 25	....	....	16 25	494
....	? 170	170	? 150	....	? 20	? 170	495
....	....	85	45	....	....	45	496
....	121 48	246 48	219 76	52	5 60	277 36	497
....	....	156 22	324 74	45	37 25	406 99	498
....	....	400	400	100	....	500	499
....	....	....	72 42	....	....	72 42	500
....	....	50	? 50	....	....	50	501
....	66 35	482 70	457 70	25	....	482 70	502
....	....	50	51	....	....	51	503
....	....	....	....	....	....	....	504
....	....	1200	590 64	312 50	389 53	1292 67	505
....	....	....	....	....	....	....	506
....	....	....	....	....	....	....	507
....	....	120 50	108 84	....	....	108 84	508
304 50	36,928 32	37,432 82	534 63	250	35,446 69	36,231 32	509
....	....	....	3	....	....	3	510
220 48	136 02	770 63	816 12	....	....	816 12	511
....	....	600	138 07	100	49 89	287 96	512
....	....	500	487	100	....	587	513
....	74 80	574 80	476 19	288 75	32 65	797 59	514
....	50	275	275	....	....	275	515
....	44 35	76 35	64 25	....	....	64 25	516
....	....	....	....	....	....	....	517
....	1100	1350	431 13	431 54	389 23	1251 90	518
....	....	710 33	107 50	452 92	....	560 42	519
....	....	23 50	23 50	....	....	23 50	520
....	....	528 10	528 10	....	270 20	798 30	521
100	....	100	....	....	....	....	522
....	....	55 61	55 61	....	....	55 61	523
36 87	....	36 87	352 87	250	14 15	617 02	524
....	31 18	50 36	50 36	....	....	50 36	525
5	524 93	879 93	238 69	48	225 42	512 11	526
....	....	10	14	....	....	14	527
....	50 54	269 80	267 80	....	2	269 80	528
50	500	550	? 27 50	200	322 50	550	529
....	125	270	208 65	20	....	228 65	530

	Place	NAME OF LIBRARY	Year founded	Source of charter	Relation to University
531	Parish	Union sch. lib		I	i
532	Patchogue	Union sch. lib	?1870	I	i
533	Peekskill	Drum Hill union sch. lib		I	i
534	"	Field lib	1887	L	...
535	"	Mil. acad. lib		I	...
536	"	Worrall Hall lib		I	i
537	Penn Yan	Penn Yan acad. lib	1859	I	i
538	Perry	Union sch. lib	1857	I	i
539	Peterboro	Evans acad. lib	1851	I	i
540	Phelps	Union and class. sch. lib	?1846	I	i
541	Philadelphia	Union sch. lib		I	i
542	Philmont	Philmont pub lib	1893	R	c
543	Phoenix	Union sch lib	?	I	i
544	Pike	Pike sem lib	1856	I	i
545	Pine Plains	Pine Plains free lib	1874	R	c
546	" "	Seymour Smith acad. lib	1879	I	i
547	Plattsburg	D'Youville acad. lib	1871	I	i
548	"	High sch. lib		I	i
549	"	Plattsburg pub. lib	1894	R	c
550	"	State normal sch. lib		I	...
551	"	Y. M. C. A. lib	?	I	...
552	Pocantico Hills	Pocantico Hills lyceum	1891	G	a
553	Pompey	Pompey acad. lib	1811	I	i
554	Port Byron	Union sch. & acad. lib	1860	I	i
555	Port Henry	Sherman free lib	1887	R	c
556	" "	Union sch. lib		I	i
557	Port Jervis	Port Jervis free lib	1892	R	c
558	" "	Union sch lib	1892	I	i
559	Port Leyden	Union sch. lib	1893	I	i
560	Port Richmond	Union sch. lib	?	I	i
561	Portville	Union sch. lib	1881	I	i
562	Potsdam	State normal & training sch. lib	1869	I	...
563	Poughkeepsie	Hudson river state hosp. lib		I	...
564	"	Hudson river state hosp. med. lib		I	...
565	"	Poughkeepsie lib	1873	I	i
566	"	Vassar coll. lib	1865	I	i
567	Prattsburg	Franklin acad. lib	1823	I	i
568	Pulaski	Pulaski acad. lib		I	i
569	Randolph	Chamberlain inst. Helen Culver lib		I	ir
570	Rhinebeck	Starr inst. lib	1862	I	...
571	"	Union sch. lib		I	i
572	Richfield Springs	Union sch. lib	1886	I	i
573	Rochester	Central lib	1862	...	...
574	"	Court of appeals lib	1849	L	...
575	"	Nazareth acad. lib	1873	I	i

STATISTICS OF NEW YORK LIBRARIES, 1895

LIBRARIES (continued)

Name of librarian or person in charge	Class of books if not neral	Ownership or control	Support	Terms of use	NO. ADDED LAST YEAR Given	NO. ADDED LAST YEAR Bought	Total no. in library	
W. F. Canongh		Pub. sch.	Tax. St.	Fl		71	598	531
W. E. Gordon		Pub. sch.	Tax. St.	F		46	928	532
John Millar		Pub. sch.	Tax. St.	F		1	369	533
S. B. Hasbrouck		End	End. G.	F		166	6177	534
		Sch	Gen	Fl			1200	535
		Sch	Fees	Fl			551	536
H. K. Armstrong		Pub. sch.	Tax. St.	F			1575	537
Etta Chamberlain		Pub. sch.	Tax. St.	F	10	20	1060	538
		Sch	Gen	Fl	4		341	539
D. D. Edgerton		Pub. sch.	Tax. St.	F		15	857	540
J. G. Peck		Pub. sch.	Tax. St.	Fl			345	541
C. F. Randall		Pub	Tax. St.	F		189	810	542
Adeline M. Avery		Pub. sch.	Tax	F		1	628	543
R. H. Whitbeck		Sch	St. G	F		10	400	544
C. E. Cole		Pub	Tax. St.	F		228	2028	545
A. Mattice		Sch	Gen	Fl	9		460	546
Sister Edgar		Sch	Gen	Fl		85	935	547
Emma L. Berry		Pub. sch.	Tax. St.	Fl	5	99	1891	548
Ernest S. Hall		Pub	Tax. St.	F	27	465	492	549
Anne J. O'Brien		Sch	Gen	Fl		300	1959	550
J. H. Carson		Inst	Gen	R. S.			2000	551
Joseph H. Acker		Mem	St. Gen.	F	178	214	1126	552
		Sch	St. G	F			381	553
W. L. Harris		Pub. sch.	Tax. St.	F	3		†950	554
Mrs C.L.Huntington		End	End.T.St	F	a 8	a 507	a 4414	555
Alice M. Gilliland		Pub. sch.	Tax	Fl			586	556
Mary K. Newman		Pub. D.	Tax. St.	F	24	754	6124	557
		Pub. sch.	Tax. St.	Fl			336	558
Rose E. Burrows		Pub. sch.	St. G	Fl		26	547	559
O. H. Hoag		Pub. sch.	Tax. St.	F		106	982	560
		Pub. sch.	Tax. St.	Fl	6	35	882	561
P. B. Stowell		Sch	St	Fl		†150	†5000	562
H. Lounsbury		Inst	St	Fl		381	381	563
	Med.	Inst	St	Fl		12	334	564
John C. Sickley		Pub. sch.	Tax	F	b 136	b 439	b 18,963	565
Frances A. Wood		Coll	Gen	Fl			22,000	566
		Pub. sch.	Tax. St.	F		5	1890	567
		Sch	Gen	Fl			600	568
E. A. Bishop		Sch	End. St	F	83	198	1281	569
Samuel Drury		Inst	End	F		114	4220	570
		Pub. sch.	Tax. St.	F		13	664	571
J. Anthony Bassett		Pub. sch.	Tax. St.	Fl	111	2	709	572
Milton Noyes		Pub. sch.	Tax. St.	F	85	3856	23,941	573
R. D. Jones	Law.	Gov	St	R	30	170	16,200	574
Sister M. Ursula		Sch	Gen	Fl	1	107	2298	575

a For year ending Sept 1895   *b* For year ending Dec 1894

NEW YORK

	VOLUMES NO. ISSUED		Days open in year	HOURS OPEN EACH WEEK FOR		RECEIPTS		
	For home use	For use at lib.		Lending	Reading	Invested funds	Local taxation	State aid
531	?500	164	52	1	.....	.....	$51 50	.....
532	?	?	?200	2	.....	.....	25	$24
533	.....	?215	193	5	.....	.....	25	25
534	?22,200	?	296	36	36	$718 94	.....	.....
535	.....	.....	.....	.....	.....	.....	.....	.....
536								
537	?150	.....	40	1	.....	.....	25	25
538	750	25	150	1	.....	.....	.....	.....
539	?	?	200	.....	.....	.....	.....	.....
540	200	300	200	5	.....	.....	42 04	24 11
541	120	82	10	2	.....	.....	.....	.....
542	2903	?	210	3	30	.....	.....	91 45
543	1121	25	80	1	.....	.....	.....	.....
544	.....	.....	190	30	30	.....	.....	.....
545	?	?	365	98	98	.....	187	187
546	?	?	200	10	25	.....	.....	.....
547	.....	935	242	.....	28	.....	.....	.....
548	2110	.....	200	1½	.....	.....	150	.....
549	?5620	.....	?156	8	8	.....	400	200
550	.....	.....	.....	.....	.....	.....	.....	.....
551	?	?	313	72	72	.....	.....	.....
552	1050	?200	156	5	5	.....	.....	200
553	10	100	195	?	.....	.....	.....	.....
554	45	?	186	25	.....	.....	.....	.....
555	8835	98	306	24	24	600	372	200
556	.....	.....	200	.....	35	.....	25	.....
557	13,578	?	300	36	36	.....	450	450
558	.....	.....	.....	.....	.....	.....	.....	.....
559	1250	?	40	1	.....	.....	.....	25
560	?2000	.....	34	2	.....	.....	20	66 60
561	?	.....	200	30	30	.....	20	28
562	?	.....	180	.....	45	.....	.....	.....
563	.....	.....	.....	.....	.....	.....	.....	.....
564	.....	.....	.....	.....	.....	.....	.....	.....
565	37,586	?8120	306	60	60	.....	3647 38	.....
566	.....	.....	.....	.....	.....	.....	.....	.....
567	?	?	185	2	.....	.....	1 70	.....
568	.....	.....	.....	.....	.....	.....	.....	.....
569	850	400	200	36	39	60	.....	200
570	6448	.....	305	49	49	875	.....	.....
571	188	?400	196	25	25	.....	25	24 10
572	400	.....	175	2	30	.....	5 75	.....
573	85,734	?	282	54	54	.....	5240	1223 01
574	.....	.....	300	.....	60	600	.....	3000
575	?2000	?	40	4	25	202 22	29	75

LIBRARIES (continued)

Annual dues	Gifts and other sources	Total receipts	Books, serials and binding	Salaries	All other expenses	Total payments	
....	....	$51 50	$51 50	....	....	$51 50	531
....	....	49	32 39	....	....	32 39	532
....	....	50	17	....	....	17	533
....	$54 65	773 59	203 55	$345	$84 95	633 50	534
....	....	....	....	....	....	....	535
....	....	....	....	....	....	....	536
....	....	50	31 55	....	28	59 55	537
....	25	25	66	....	....	66	538
....	....	....	....	....	....	....	539
....	....	66 15	26 15	....	40	66 15	540
....	....	....	....	....	....	....	541
....	92 33	183 78	184 81	....	....	184 81	542
....	....	....	2 50	....	....	2 50	543
....	....	....	....	....	....	....	544
....	....	374	245 57	75	41 10	361 67	545
....	....	....	....	....	....	....	546
....	....	....	52	....	....	52	547
....	....	150	146 80	....	3 20	150	548
....	206 52	806 52	382 56	110	155 47	647 03	549
....	....	....	....	500	....	500	550
....	....	....	....	....	....	....	551
$46 50	21 68	268 18	226 18	5	37	268 18	552
....	....	....	....	....	....	....	553
....	....	....	2 50	....	....	2 50	554
....	7 85	1179 85	532 56	268	107 06	907 62	555
....	....	25	....	....	....	....	556
....	25 23	925 23	901 72	a500	b266 05	1667 77	557
....	....	....	....	....	....	....	558
....	12 42	37 42	....	....	....	....	559
....	30 60	117 20	101 20	....	16	117 20	560
....	....	48	48	....	....	48	561
....	....	....	....	....	....	....	562
....	....	....	....	35	....	35	563
....	....	....	....	....	....	....	564
....	....	3647 38	907 40	1968 38	771 60	3647 38	565
....	....	....	....	....	....	....	566
....	....	1 70	1 70	....	....	1 70	566
....	....	....	....	....	....	....	568
....	278 67	538 67	210 30	....	148 91	359 21	569
....	....	875	125 89	311	304 03	740 92	570
....	....	49 10	36 50	....	....	36 50	571
....	....	5 75	5 75	....	....	5 75	572
....	96 54	6559 55	4656 74	2240	163 62	7060 36	573
....	....	3600	2693	1200	12	3905	574
....	12	318 22	218 22	100	....	318 22	575

a Paid by bd. of educ   b $250 rent paid by bd. of educ.

19

	Place	NAME OF LIBRARY	Year founded	Source of charter	Relation to University
576	Rochester	Reynolds lib	1884	L	
577	"	Rochester free acad. lib	1857	I	i
578	"	Rochester theological sem. lib	1851	I	i
579	"	Univ of Rochester lib	1850	I	i
580	"	Wagner mem. Lutheran coll. lib	1891	I	i
581	Rockville Center	Rockville Center pub. lib	1894	R	c
582	Rome	Jervis lib. ass'n	1895	G	a
583	"	St Peter's acad. lib	1873	I	i
584	"	Y. M. C. A. lib	1872	I	r
585	Rondout	Ulster acad. lib		I	i
586	Roslyn	Bryant circ. lib	1878	G	
587	Round Lake	Round Lake inst. lib	1890	I	i
588	Rushford	Union sch. lib		I	i
589	Rushville	Union sch. lib	1868	I	i
590	St Johnsville	Union sch. lib	?	I	i
591	St Regis Falls	Union sch. lib	1891	I	i
592	Salamanca	Union sch. lib		I	i
593	Salem	Washington acad. lib	1891	I	i
594	Sandy Creek	High sch lib	1872	I	i
595	Sandy Hill	Union sch. lib	1871	I	i
596	Saratoga Springs	4th jud. dist. law lib		L	
597	" "	St Faith's sch. lib	1892	I	i
598	" "	Saratoga athenaeum lib	1885	G	
599	" "	Temple Grove sem. lib		I	i
600	" "	Union sch lib	1867	I	i
601	Saugerties	Saugerties pub. lib	1894	R	c
602	Sauquoit	Union sch. lib	1843		
603	Savannah	Union sch. lib	1892	I	i
604	Savona	Union sch. lib		I	i
605	Schenectady	Schenectady free pub. lib. ass'n	1894	R	c
606	"	Union class. inst. lib	1855	I	i
607	"	Union coll. lib	1795	I	i
608	Schenevus	Union sch lib	1880	I	i
609	Schoharie	Union sch. lib	1835	I	i
610	Schuylerville	Schuylerville pub. lib	1894	R	c
611	Sea Cliff	Sea Cliff pub lib	1895	R	c
612	Seneca Falls	Mynderse acad. lib	1867	I	i
613	"	Seneca Falls lib. ass'n	1891	G	
614	Sherburne	Union sch. lib	?1866	I	i
615	Sherman	Union sch. lib	1869	I	i
616	Shortsville	M. M. Buck free lib	1890		
617	"	Union sch. lib		I	i
618	Sidney	Sidney pub. lib	1895	R	c
619	Silver Creek	Union sch. lib	?1840	I	i
620	Sinclairville	Sinclairville free lib	1870	R	c

LIBRARIES (continued)

Name of librarian or person in charge	Class of books if not general	Ownership or control	Support	Terms of use	NO ADDED LAST YEAR Given	Bought	Total no. in library	
Alfred S. Collins		End	End	F	a453	a2280	a31,237	576
John G. Allen		Pub. sch.	Tax. St	Fl		95	2290	577
Howard Osgood	Theo	Coll	End	Fl	251	391	28,034	578
H. K. Phinney		Coll	End	R.Fl.	760	455	29,700	579
....		Coll	Gen	Fl			750	580
Elmer S. Redman		Pub. D	Tax. St	F		436	? 1425	581
M. Elizabeth Beach		End	End	F	1839	2266	b 9315	582
Sister Holy Family		Sch	Tax Gen	Fl	4	6	640	583
H. E. Huie		Inst	St. G	R	35	72	2881	584
....		Sch	Gen	Fl			1165	585
J. H. Bogart		Mem	G. Fees	S			1025	586
James E. Weld		Sch	Gen	F	25	10	2025	587
H. J. Walter		Pub. sch	Tax	F	2	14	313	588
E. J. Rowe		Pub. sch	Tax. St	Fl	10		300	589
F. Yale Adams		Pub. sch	Tax St	Fl	8	9	611	590
....		Pub. sch.	Tax. St	F			? 600	591
Alice L. Pickett		Pub. sch.	Tax. St	F		137	1287	592
M. E. Baker		Sch	End Gen	F		430	4000	593
R. H Snyder		Pub. sch.	Tax St	F	8	30	700	594
George A. Ingalls		Pub sch	Tax St	F	11	148	1251	595
J. P. McCall	Law	Gov	St	R		? 228	? 4511	596
....		Sch	Gen	Fl			1350	597
Elizabeth Brazee		Mem	G. Fees	S	? 100	? 100	? 5000	598
....		Sch	G	Fl			1585	599
....		Pub. sch	Tax	F			400	600
Fred N. Moulton		Pub. D	Tax. St	F		429	1492	601
....		Pub sch	Tax	F			? 350	602
H N. Tolman		Pub sch	Tax. St	F	45	71	544	603
A. O. Tucker		Pub. sch	Tax. St	F		7	356	604
....		Mem	Tax. St	F			? 3000	605
Chas. S. Halsey		Pub. sch.	Tax. St	Fl	3		534	606
Wendell Lamoroux		Coll	Gen	Fl	209	223	30,736	607
Anna Lane		Pub sch	Tax St	Fl	5	95	390	608
Solomon Sias		Pub. sch	Tax St	F		40	744	609
O H. Burritt		Pub D	Tax. St	F			770	610
John Forster		Mem	St. G	F	529		529	611
....		Pub. sch	Tax. St	Fl		13	1517	612
Miss Watling		Mem	G. Fees	R S			2711	613
Mary A. Sholes		Pub. sch	Tax. St	F			2000	614
Lida R. Waldorff		Pub. sch	Tax St	F	25	1	1000	615
Sara Buck		Pri	G	F		200	? 1500	616
W. D. Hewes		Pub. sch	Tax. St	Fl		4	532	617
Ethel A. Case		Pub D	Tax. St	F		150	1137	618
J. M. McKee		Pub. sch.	St. Fees	F	17	96	1536	619
Mrs A. E. Fife		End	St.G	F		100	1450	620

a For year ending Sept 1895   b 5190 volumes are free for reference only

	VOLUMES		Days open in year	HOURS OPEN EACH WEEK FOR		RECEIPTS		
	NO. ISSUED					Invested funds	Local taxation	State aid
	For home use	For use at lib		Lending	Reading			
576	15,107	9,743	244	52	72	$36,757 68		
577			188				$150	$150
578	†	†	255½	35½	35½			
579	†	†	290	39	39	1875		
580								
581	4325	10	102	4	4		100	200
582								
583	140	500	60	2	4		37	
584	1332		313		78			47
585								
586	340		104	12	172	4 46		
587	†	†	190	30				
588	117		200	5			10 50	
589			200				10	
590	663	†	186	5	25		13	13
591								
592			40	6	†		150	150
593	2876	468	156	15	15	1464 75		
594	500	100	200	12	5		35	35
595	2343		30	2½			100	100
596								
597								
598	† 5000	†	300	48	48			
599								
600								
601	6009	†	158	12	12		443 35	200
602								
603	†	†	200	† 1		21 33		
604	496	392	192	35			15	25
605								
606	390	300	180	5	25		6	6
607		†	216		57			
608			200	†				55
609	†	† 270	195	30	30		30	8 50
610								
611	1316	† 10	141	13	30			200
612	650		200	2	30		111 15	61 05
613								
614	† 450	† 50	† 30	1¼				
615	1775	50	200	1	30		13	
616	10,500	† 50	† 313	16	72			
617	150		80	2				24 11
618	4147	700	224	6	6		130	30
619	2291		80	1				202 50
620	2006		131	11				200

STATISTICS OF NEW YORK LIBRARIES, 1895

LIBRARIES (continued)

FROM			PAYMENTS FOR				
Annual dues	Gifts and other sources	Total receipts	Books, serials and binding	Salaries	All other expenses	Total payments	
....	$2787 78	$39,545 46	$5553 28	$2564 40	$24,951 28	$33,068 96	576
....	....	300	† 310	....	....	† 310	577
....	....	....	2020 42	....	600	2620 42	578
....	....	1875	598 36	800	40	1438 36	579
....	....	....	....	....	....	....	580
....	160 20	460 20	416 04	41 50	15 50	473 04	581
....	42,058 34	42,058 34	....	....	....	....	582
....	....	37	26 50	....	....	26 50	583
....	47	94	94	....	....	94	584
....	....	....	....	....	....	....	585
$23	723 75	751 21	39	....	248 28	287 28	586
....	† 20	20	20	....	....	20	587
....	....	10 50	10 50	....	....	10 50	588
....	....	10	....	....	....	....	589
....	....	26	13	....	....	13	590
....	....	....	....	....	....	....	591
....	....	300	286 25	25	59 50	370 75	592
98 88	60 60	1624 23	360 32	445	786 08	1591 40	593
....	20	90	35	....	....	35	594
....	4 74	204 74	395 23	....	22 91	418 14	595
....	....	....	....	....	....	....	596
....	....	....	....	....	....	....	597
700	200	900	270	300	275	845	598
....	....	....	....	....	....	....	599
....	....	....	....	....	....	....	600
....	9 60	652 95	406 42	75	149 73	631 15	601
....	....	....	....	....	....	....	602
22 10	....	43 43	43 43	....	....	43 43	603
....	....	25 15	25 15	....	....	25 15	604
....	....	....	....	....	....	....	605
....	....	12	12	....	....	12	606
....	300	300	85	900	....	985	607
....	55	110	110	....	....	110	608
....	....	38 50	8 50	....	30	38 50	609
....	....	....	....	....	....	....	610
....	587	787	....	90	488 79	578 79	611
....	....	172 20	122 20	50	....	172 20	612
....	....	....	....	....	....	....	613
....	....	....	....	....	....	....	614
....	50	63	13	10	50	23 50	615
....	....	....	160	120	25	305	616
....	....	24 11	3 85	....	....	3 85	617
....	74 75	234 75	212 25	22 50	....	234 75	618
....	99	301 50	138 37	....	5 40	143 77	619
....	23 77	223 77	111 96	52	250	166 46	620

NEW YORK

	Place	NAME OF LIBRARY	Year founded	Source of charter	Relation to University
621	Sinclairville	Sinclairville ladies' lib.	1889		
622	"	Union sch. lib.	1881	I	i
623	Sing Sing	Mt Pleasant acad. lib	1820	I	i
624	"	Prison library			
625	"	Sing Sing pub. lib	1893	R	c
626	Skaneateles	Skaneateles lib. ass'n	1877	G	
627	"	Union sch. lib		I	i
628	Smithville Flats	Smithville union sch lib		I	i
629	Solvay	Union sch. lib.	1894	I	i
630	Somers	Somers library	1875		
631	Southampton	Union sch. lib.	?	I	i
632	Spencer	Union sch. lib.	1875	I	i
633	Springville	Griffith inst and union sch. lib.		I	i
634	"	Springville pub. lib	1893	R	c
635	Stamford	Stamford sem. and union sch. lib.	1875	I	i
636	Stanfordville	Christian biblical inst. lib	1868		
637	Stapleton	Staten Island acad. lib	1886	I	i
638	Stillwater	Union sch. lib	1873	I	i
639	Syracuse	Acad. of Sacred Heart lib		I	i
640	"	Central library	1855	R	c
641	"	Court of Appeals lib.		L	
642	"	High sch. lib	?	I	i
643	"	St John's catholic acad. lib	1887	I	i
644	"	St. inst for feeble-minded child. lib.	1856	I	
645	"	Syracuse univ. lib.	1870	I	i
646	"	Univ. coll. of med. lib	1872	I	i
647	Tarrytown	Union sch. lib. dist. no. 1 (Greenb'g)	?	I	i
648	Theresa	Union sch. lib.	1894	I	i
649	Ticonderoga	Union sch lib	?1885	I	i
650	Tompkinsville	Sch. lib. dist. no. 1	1872		
651	Tonawanda	Tonawanda pub. lib.	1893	R	c
652	Trenton	Barneveld lib. ass'n	1877	G	
653	Troy	Catholic male orphan asylum lib.		I	
654	"	Children's neighborhood lib	1894	R	c
655	"	High sch. lib	1863		i
656	"	La Salle inst. lib.	1878	I	i
657	"	Marshall infirmary lib	?1858	I	
658	"	Rensselaer polytechnic inst. lib.	1824	I	i
659	"	St Peter's acad. lib	1886	I	i
660	"	Troy acad. lib	1834	I	i
661	"	Troy female sem lib.	1821	I	i
662	Trumansburg	Trumansburg pub. lib.	1893	R	c
663	Unadilla	Union sch. lib.	1850	I	i
664	Union	Union sch. lib.	?	I	i
665	Union Springs	Oakwood sem. lib.	1859	I	i

LIBRARIES (continued)

Name of librarian or person in charge	Class of books if not general	Ownership or control	Support	Terms of use	NO. ADDED LAST YEAR Given	NO. ADDED LAST YEAR Bought	Total no. in library	
H. J. Chase		Mem	G. Fees	S	25	52	683	621
....		Pub. sch	Tax. St	Fl			361	622
A. T. Emory		Sch	Gen	Fl			12,000	623
John C. S. Weills		Inst	St	Fl		500	4800	624
J. Irving Gorton		Pub. D	Tax St	F	18	236	3537	625
Lydia A. Cobane		Mem	End Fees	S	a 112	a 44	a 8271	626
H. F. Miner		Pub. sch	Tax. St	Fl			1558	627
A. M. Baker		Pub. sch	Tax. St	F		60	505	628
....		Pub. sch	Tax. St	R			500	629
....		Mem	G Fees	S	10	23	1515	630
F. A. Johnson		Pub. sch	Tax St	Fl		87	†300	631
S. K. Marsh		Pub. sch	Tax St	F		6	518	632
Robert W. Hughes		Pub. sch	Tax. St	Fl		93	1160	633
Robert W Hughes		Pub. D	Tax St	F	88	195	†1634	634
Hattie F. Hubbell		Pub. sch	Tax St	F	29	19	2275	635
Lester Howard		Sch	Gen	Fl	150		2250	636
Susan Hill Yerkes		Sch	St Gen	F	43	57	5569	637
Willis U. Hinman		Pub. sch	Tax. St	F		71	971	638
....		Sch	Gen	Fl			3000	639
Ezekiel W. Mundy		Pub	Tax. St	F	257	1736	26,300	640
T. S. R. Morgan	Law	Gov	St	Fl		460	18,675	641
M. Louise Pattison		Pub. sch	Tax. St	Fl		204	†1431	642
Mary Cronin		Sch	Gen	Fl	23	20	1349	643
J. C. Carsons		Inst	Gen	Fl		6	361	644
Henry O. Sibley		Coll	Gen	Fl			45,661	645
F. W. Marlow	Med	Coll	Gen	Fl			†1,200	646
....		Pub. sch	Tax. St	F			2,369	647
Mrs W. C. Partee		Pub. sch	Tax. St	F		15	†340	648
....		Pub. sch	Tax	Fl			585	649
....		Pub. sch	Tax	F		23	891	650
Mrs F. J. Diamond		Pub D	Tax St	F		178	1,350	651
....		Mem	G. Fees	R	15		3,400	652
....		Inst	Gen	Fl			722	653
E. M. Fairchild		Mem	St. G	F	†12	†235	571	654
James T. McKenna		Pub. sch	Tax. St	Fl	10	150	490	655
....		Sch	St. Gen	Fl	15	140	1,835	656
....		Inst	Gen	Fl		3	1,753	657
John H. Peck		Coll	Gen	Fl			†5,000	658
Sister Mary S. H.		Sch	St. G	Fl	6	10	680	659
Maxcy & Barnes		Sch	Gen	Fl			1,059	660
Emily S. Wilcox		Sch	Gen	Fl	3		2,218	661
E. E. Scribner		Pub. D	Tax. St	F	33	6	†804	662
Adelaide A. Allen		Pub. sch	Tax. St	R.Fl		32	765	663
Ernest E. Smith		Pub. sch	Tax. St	Fl	10	105	762	664
Isaac Sutton		Sch	Gen	Fl	20	15	†1,315	665

a For year ending Feb 21, 1895.

NEW YORK

	VOLUMES		Days open in year	HOURS OPEN EACH WEEK FOR		RECEIPTS		
	NO ISSUED								
	For home use	For use at lib		Lending	Reading	Invested funds	Local taxation	State aid
621	↑ 2500		104	11		$12 13		
622								
623	↑ 700		200	↑ 6				
624								
625	13,716	↑ 3000	204	35	35		$234 20	$125
626	6260		306	70	70	140 50		
627	↑ 1400		200	1	↑			
628			195	35				
629								
630	604	↑	104	4				
631	↑ 1200	↑ 2800	? 180	¾	40		59 75	59 75
632	500	↑ 600	190	1			10	
633	↑		200	30	30			
634	6820		310	6	6		349 19	200
635	634		67	1½			25	25
636			175	↑ 25	↑			
637	↑ 3600	↑	200	25	25			100
638	1760		80	3	6		29 08	25
639								
640	44,585	↑ 8850	177	67	72		8954 58	734 39
641								
642	↑ 50	↑ 300	200	23¼	23¼			135
643		1349	190	5	15			
644								
645								
646								
647								
648	1685		56	6				28 50
649								
650	826		60	2		25		
651	1587	↑	↑ 260	10			200	100
652	↑ 650	↑	104	12	12	100		
653		262	52	2				
654	8370		↑ 300	24	24			200
655		↑	200	20			114 93	114 93
656	↑ 950	↑ 2000	200	30				110
657								
658								
659	↑ 300	↑ 180	220	20				
660								
661			200		40			
662	2340	↑	130	3	35		25	
663	800		200	3	30		56	56
664	1055	↑	190	10	30			58 90
665	↑ 225		↑ 216	↑ 60				

LIBRARIES (continued)

From			Payments for				
Annual dues	Gifts and other sources	Total receipts	Books, serials and binding	Salaries	All other expenses	Total payments	
....	$36 64	$48 77	$50 01	$25	$4 50	$79 51	621
....	....	....	....	....	....	....	622
....	....	....	....	....	....	....	623
....	....	....	....	....	....	....	624
....	....	359 20	259 20	100	....	359 20	625
$444	587 18	1171 68	173 26	720	257 40	1150 66	626
....	....	....	....	....	....	....	627
....	....	....	22 35	....	....	22 35	628
....	....	....	....	....	....	....	629
33 23	3 72	36 95	23 91	11 50	80	36 21	630
....	....	119 50	119 50	....	....	119 50	631
....	....	10	10	10	....	20	632
....	....	....	127 09	....	....	127 09	633
....	....	549 19	320 99	75	142 36	538 35	634
....	1 95	51 95	55 50	....	33 69	89 19	635
....	....	....	....	....	....	....	636
....	103 32	203 32	30	100	....	130	637
....	....	54 08	52 28	....	1 80	54 08	638
....	....	....	....	....	....	....	639
....	....	9688 97	2981 83	3615 13	3092 01	9688 97	640
....	....	....	....	1800	....	1800	641
....	....	135	135	....	....	135	642
....	....	....	75	200	....	275	643
....	....	....	127 56	....	....	127 56	644
....	....	....	....	....	....	....	645
....	....	....	....	....	....	....	646
....	....	....	....	....	....	....	647
....	49 80	78 30	57	40	....	97	648
....	....	....	....	....	....	....	649
10	....	35	....	....	....	....	650
....	....	300	178 10	75	32 20	285 30	651
25	....	125	77	....	43	120	652
....	....	....	....	....	....	....	653
....	340	540	†218	156	†61	435	654
....	....	229 86	....	....	....	....	655
18	110	238	235	....	....	235	656
....	....	....	10	....	....	10	657
....	....	....	....	....	....	....	658
....	....	....	92 11	....	....	92 11	659
....	....	....	....	....	....	....	660
....	....	....	....	....	....	....	661
7 50	....	32 50	90	....	....	90	662
....	....	112	112	....	....	112	663
....	42	100 90	140 71	....	3 80	144 51	664
....	....	....	....	....	....	....	665

	Place	NAME OF LIBRARY	Year founded	Source of charter	Relation to University
666	Union Springs	Union sch. lib.		I	i
667	Utica	Catholic acad. lib		I	i
668	"	Mrs Piatt's sch. lib	1875	I	i
669	"	Oneida hist. soc. lib	1876	I	
670	"	Utica free acad. lib.		I	i
671	"	Utica pub. lib.	1893	R	c
672	"	Utica state hosp. med. lib	1843	I	
673	Valatie	Union sch. lib		I	i
674	Vernon	Union sch lib. dist. no. 7	1839	I	i
675	Victor	Union sch. Clark lib	1891	I	i
676	Walden	Union sch lib.	?	I	i
677	Walton	Union sch. lib.	?1868	I	i
678	Wappinger Falls	Grinnell lib ass'n	1867	G	
679	"	Union sch lib. dist. no. 2	?		
680	Warrensburg	Union sch lib.		I	i
681	Warsaw	Union sch. circ. lib	?	I	i
682	"	Union sch. ref. lib.	1892	I	i
683	Warwick	Warwick inst. lib	1847	I	i
684	Waterford	Waterford pub. lib	1895	R	c
685	Waterloo	Union sch. lib.		I	i
686	Watertown	High sch lib.		I	i
687	"	St Joachim's acad. inst. lib		I	i
688	"	Y. M. C. A. lib	1869	I	
689	Waterville	Waterville pub. lib.	1874	R	c
690	Watkins	Watkins acad. & union sch. lib	1863	I	i
691	"	Watkins lib.	?1869		
692	Waverly	High sch. lib.	?	I	ir
693	Webster	Union sch. lib.	?1876	I	i
694	Weedsport	Union sch lib	1877	I	i
695	Wellsville	Wellsville pub. lib.	1894	R	c
696	West Albany	Y. M. C. A. R. R. branch lib.	1877		
697	West Point	U. S. military acad. lib			
698	West Troy	Sch. lib. dist no. 5 (Watervliet)	1856		
699	"	Sch. lib. dist. no 9 (Watervliet)	?1854		
700	" c. 7th & 5th av	Union sch. lib. (Watervliet)	1889		
701	"	Watervliet arsenal post lib.	1840		
702	West Winfield	West Winfield free lib.	1894	R	c
703	Westbury	Green Wood pub lib.	1884	R	c
704	Westchester	Sacred Heart acad. lib.	1883	I	i
705	"	Union sch. lib. dist. no. 1.		I	i
706	"	Union sch. lib. dist. no 3	?	I	i
707	Westfield	Union sch lib.	?1868	I	i
708	Westport	Westport lib ass'n	1885	G	a
709	"	Union sch lib		I	i
710	White Plains	Westchester co. law lib		L	

LIBRARIES (continued)

Name of librarian or person in charge	Class of books if not general	Ownership or control	Support	Terms of use	NO. ADDED LAST YEAR Given	NO. ADDED LAST YEAR Bought	Total no. in library	
....	....	Pub. sch.	Tax	Fl ?..	....	....	825	666
....	....	Sch.	Gen	Fl ..	....	....	1720	667
....	....	Sch.	Gen.....	Fl...	? 20	? 300	6000	668
M. M. Bagg........	Hist.	Mem	Gen.....	RFl.	80	....	6336	669
....	....	Pub. sch.	Tax	Fl...	....	....	1148	670
Louisa S Cutler....	....	Pub.....	Tax. St.	F ..	684	2914	17,936	671
Rees P. Pughe.....	Med.	Inst.....	St.....	Fl...	....	213	6388	672
....	....	Pub. sch.	Tax. St..	F. ..	....	....	1169	673
E. R. Adams.......	....	Pub. sch.	Tax. St..	Fl...	....	48	675	674
....	....	Pub. sch.	Tax. St..	Fl...	....	....	1000	675
....	....	Pub. sch.	Tax. St..	F ...	16	14	1100	676
J. R. Fairgrieve....	....	Pub sch.	Tax. St..	Fl...	20	....	? 1500	677
E. A. Howarth.....	....	Mem End	End Fees	S....	4	8	5640	678
S. Mansfield.......	....	Pub. sch.	Tax. St..	Fl...	....	16	391	679
B. F. Record.......	....	Pub. sch.	Tax. St..	Fl...	4	72	? 1050	680
Ella Cameron......	....	Pub. sch.	Tax. St..	F ...	3	270	3143	681
Irving B. Smith....	....	Pub. sch.	Tax. St..	Fl...	29	76	482	682
M. L. Wright......	....	Pub. sch.	Tax. St..	Fl...	....	20	1270	683
Mrs Sarah Boughton	....	Pub. D..	Tax. St..	F....	....	187	1366	684
....	....	Pub. sch.	Tax. St..	Fl...	....	....	1193	685
Eugene W. Lyttle..	....	Pub. sch.	Tax. St..	Fl...	....	650	700	686
....	....	Pub. sch.	Tax	Fl...	....	....	409	687
....	....	Inst.....	Gen.....	R.Fl.	10	....	1130	688
Thomas E. Hayden.	....	Pub. D..	End. St..	F ...	2	4	1158	689
S. S. Johnson......	....	Pub. sch.	Tax. St..	Fl...	14	99	975	690
W. L. Norton......	....	Pub. sch.	Tax. St..	F....	....	....	? 2000	691
P. M. Hull........	....	Pub. sch.	Tax. St..	F....	....	340	1812	692
Mittie J. Smith....	....	Pub. sch.	Tax. St	Fl...	....	29	452	693
....	....	Pub. sch.	Tax.....	F. ..	....	....	300	694
Mrs Ida K. Church.	....	Pub.....	St. G....	F. ..	184	157	1425	695
S. T. Fraser.......	....	Inst.....	Gen.	Fl...	....	400	1700	696
P. S. Michie.......	....	Gov.	U. S	Fl...	552	518	38,085	697
....	....	Pub. sch.	Tax. St..	Fl...	....	83	1621	698
Maggie B Costello..	....	Pub. sch.	Tax.	Fl. .	....	....	? 550	699
....	....	Pub. sch.	Tax. St..	Fl. .	....	10	350	700
George W. Burr....	....	Gov.	U. S....	Fl. .	....	....	900	701
A. J. Merrell	....	Pub. D..	St. G....	F. ..	12	295	1412	702
Mary G. Wood.....	....	Pub. D..	Tax. St..	F. ..	....	22	217	703
John A. Ritter.....	....	Sch.	Gen.....	Fl...	....	? 50	? 850	704
....	....	Pub. sch.	Tax. St..	F. ..	....	....	1150	705
Hannah M. Findlay.	....	Pub. sch.	St......	F. ..	....	....	1495	706
A. N. Taylor	....	Pub. sch.	Tax. St..	F. ..	25	....	2500	707
....	....	Mem.....	St. G....	F. ..	15	8	1426	708
F. V. Lester.......	....	Pub. sch.	Tax. St..	F. ..	....	57	482	709
F. F. Miller.......	Law.	Gov.	St......	R. ..	....	....	? 1950	710

| | VOLUMES NO. ISSUED || Days open in year | HOURS OPEN EACH WEEK FOR || Invested funds | RECEIPTS ||
	For home use	For use at lib.		Lending	Reading		Local taxation	State aid
666								
667								
668			200		?			
669			?300	?		$6 64		
670								
671	82,421	?	308	67	67		$8500	$350
672								
673			108	21				
674			200	?			15	75
675								
676	1250	235	200	3	30		15	
677	?820	?4000	40	1				
678	?7000	?400	309	42	42	611 03		
679		?						12 70
680	?400	?	?200	?5	?		25 89	25
681	5945		92	8			202	150
682		?	190		?		25	25
683	1500		190	1				
684	1672		44	4			75	50
685								
686	942	?	190	30	30		?375	?25
687								
688			313	42	72			
689	?1350		52	1½		30	196 49	200
690	?500	?150	187	5				
691	?200		116	2				
692	4150	100	250	30	30		218 11	200
693	400	800	?80	2	30		10	46 90
694								
695	?3357	?	156	6				200
696	3500		365	89				
697	5652		314	60	60			
698	4211		75				50	25
699		?550	195		27½			
700	660	45	200	4	20		25	25
701	?500	?200	365	70	70			
702	3620	?400	160	3	3			177 24
703	197	?	?160	?30	?		5	15
704		413	?200	?1	?6			
705								
706	457		84	2				
707	?4000	?100	40	1				
708	5590		68	12	12			
709	?500	?100	180	5	7		75	75
710			313		48			

STATISTICS OF NEW YORK LIBRARIES, 1895   301

LIBRARIES (continued)

FROM			PAYMENT FOR				
Annual dues	Gifts and other sources	Total receipts	Books, serials and binding	Salaries	All other expenses	Total payments	
							666
							667
							668
$306		$312 64			$485 98	$485 98	669
							670
	$284 18	9134 18	$4871 01	$2948 70	2661 37	10481 08	671
			338 88			338 88	672
							673
		90	90			90	674
							675
		15	15			15	676
	20	20					677
	171 05	782 08	211 12	180	383 49	774 61	678
		12 70	12 70			12 70	679
	2 02	52 91					680
	5 94	357 94	255 23	52	41 75	348 98	681
		50	50 07			50 07	682
			29 96			29 96	683
		125	18 70	25	69 42	113 12	684
							685
		? 400	? 400	30	1	431	686
							687
							688
		426 49	2 75			2 75	689
	133 56	133 56	83 56	50		133 56	690
					36	36	691
	20	438 11	358 11		80	438 11	692
	36 90	93 80	? 2			2	693
							694
	227	427	154		50 37	204 37	695
	500	500	500			500	696
	2000	2000		1000		1000	697
		75	73 93			73 93	698
							699
		50	64			64	700
	20	20	20			20	701
	188 62	365 86	261 55		93 53	355 08	702
	10 54	30 54	29 33		1 21	30 54	703
	92	92	60			60	704
							705
				100		100	706
							707
26	136 71	162 71	35 32	106 50	39 03	180 85	708
	19	169	136 93			136 93	709
				30		30	710

NEW YORK

	Place	NAME OF LIBRARY	Year founded	Source of charter	Relation to University
711	White Plains..........	White Plains acad. lib.	†	I	i
712	Whitehall	Union sch. lib		I	i
713	Whitesboro	Union sch. lib	1892	I	i
714	Whitney's Point.......	Union sch. lib		I	i
715	Willard...............	Willard state hosp. lib.............	1892	I	...
716	Williamsville..........	Union sch. lib		I	i
717	Wilson	Union sch. lib..	1845	I	i
718	Windsor..............	Union sch. lib	1837	I	i
719	Worcester	Union sch. lib		I	i
720	Wyoming.............	Middlebury acad. and union sch. lib.		I	i
721	"	Wyoming free circ. lib. ass'n... ...	1889	G	...
722	Yonkers	Womans inst. lib....................	1880	G	a
723	"	Yonkers pub. lib....................	1893	B	c

LIBRARIES (concluded)

Name of librarian or person in charge	Class of books if not general	Ownership or control	Support	Terms of use	NO. ADDED LAST YEAR Given	Bought	Total no. in library	
Minnie F. Griffin		Sch	Tax. St..	Fl. .		95	718	711
W. W Howe		Pub sch.	Tax. St..	F. ..			?1600	712
		Pub. sch.	Tax. St..	Fl. ..			500	713
E. P. Carr		Pub sch.	Tax. St .	Fl. S.	4	19	345	714
Theo. H. Kellogg		Inst	St.	Fl. .	72	113	1700	715
W. M. Peirce		Pub. sch.	Tax. St..	Fl. .	5		872	716
H. C. Hustleby		Pub sch.	Tax. St..	F. ..		250	754	717
William S. Murray		Pub sch	Tax. St..	F. ..			650	718
		Pub. sch	Tax. ...	Fl. .			480	719
Fred B Waite		Pub. sch.	Tax. St..	Fl. .			1260	720
Lucretia Miller		Mem	G.	F. ..	a170		a1060	721
Mary S. F. Randolph		Inst	St. Gen..	F. ..	194	188	2381	722
Helen M. Blodgett		Pub. D..	Tax. St..	F. ..	48	191	10,403	723
					59,172	201,204	4,392,999	

a For year ending Sept. 1895.

NEW YORK

| | VOLUMES | | Days open in year | HOURS OPEN EACH WEEK FOR | | RECEIPTS | | |
| | NO. ISSUED | | | | | | | |
	For home use	For use at lib.		Reading	Lending	Invested funds	Local taxation	State aid
711	2912		80	4			$165 12	$25
712			15	1½				
713								
714	?1100	?	165	1	36		23 06	
715								229 96
716	491	?	?35	1				
717		?	200	30	30		200	200
718	120	25	40	1	1			
719								
720	25	?500	200	30	30			
721	2340	50	260	30	30			
722	5497		274	75	75			200
723	31,192	?	262	50	50		250	200
	4,156,744	1,205,197						

LIBRARIES (concluded)

FROM			PAYMENTS FOR				
Annual dues	Gifts and other sources	Total receipts	Books, serials and binding	Salaries	All other expenses	Total payments	
		$190 12	$115	$50	$25 12	$190 12	711
							712
							713
	$5 35	28 41	28 41			28 41	714
		229 96	239 96			229 96	715
							716
		400	400			400	717
							718
							719
							720
	67 48	67 48	1 75	26	28 10	55 85	721
	234 38	434 38	161 45	214 50	58 43	434 38	722
	29 71	479 71	441 08		18 75	459 83	723
		$935,759 76				$773,699 17	

GEOGRAPHIC DISTRIBUTION OF

The figures in italics and those prefixed to totals

COUNTY	Population	LIBRARIES			
		FREE		OTHER	
		No.	Volumes	No.	Volumes
New York........	1 / 1,801,739	9 16	1*1 333,233	2 61	1 / 1,564,999
Kings	2 995,276	6 2 89,279	18 2 276,749
Queens	8 141,807	10 14 18,187	6 28 10,650
Suffolk	20 63,572	4 48 3,607	7 21 14,329
Richmond	25 53,452	3 32 7,442	1 42 3,850
Westchester	7 145,106	15 5 41,670	8 15 23,584
Rockland	43 33,726	3 43 5,166	1 51 1,321
Vicin N Y city..	2 1,432,939	8 41 2 165,351	6 41 8 330,483
Orange	11 97,760	9 6 38,915	11 8 52,219
Putnam	59 14,230	2 53 2,314	1 48 1,720
Dutchess	16 78,342	5 10 26,301	10 9 47,678
Ulster	12 87,652	4 41 5,259	3 27 10,936
Sullivan	47 31,860	2 54 1,587	.....	....
Delaware	34 45,488	6 31 7,518	3 44 3,761
Greene	49 31,141	3 50 2,894	2 52 1,183
Columbia.......	35 45,205	8 21 11,610	2 46 1,860
South E. counties	7 431,678	4 39 5 96,398	7 32 8 119,357
Rensselaer.....	9 128,923	6 33 6,797	8 23 13,757
Albany	5 167,289	4 24 10,061	25 3 271,485
Schenectady	24 57,301	1 49 3,000	2 13 31,270
Schoharie	42 34,194	2 55 1,304	1 54 998
Montgomery....	33 46,081	7 29 7,837	5 33 6,464
Fulton..........	39 38,478	3 13 19,961	1 56 673
Saratoga	13 86,254	8 30 7,694	6 22 13,946
Washington	32 46,458	6 25 9,851	5 34 6,295
Middle E. counties	4 604,978	5 37 7 66,505	4 53 2 344,888
Warren	54 28,618	4 22 10,786	1 53 1,050
Hamilton	60 5,216	1 59 450	.....	....
Essex...........	46 33,110	8 20 12,087	7 39 4,953
Clinton	31 46,601	2 57 1,178	4 32 6,785
Franklin........	38 39,817	3 35 6,727	2 50 1,458
St Lawrence....	56 26,542	3 37 6,215	10 16 22,269
Jefferson	18 70,358	3 47 3,693	6 40 4,533
Lewis	51 30,248	2 42 5,205	1 57 547
Northern counties..	9 280,510	7 26 9 46,341	9 31 9 41,595
Herkimer	29 47,491	11 15 16,278	1 43 3,780
Oneida	10 123,756	12 3 70,143	13 12 32,761
Madison	37 42,206	5 51 2,848	11 11 37,768
Onondaga	6 150,808	8 7 33,472	14 6 85,849
Oswego.........	17 70,970	5 27 9,238	7 17 21,906
Cayuga.........	21 62,816	5 11 24,379	11 14 30,088
Seneca	58 16,861	.....	....	5 31 8,773
N. central counties.	5 514,908	1 46 3 156,358	1 62 6 220,925

STATISTICS OF NEW YORK LIBRARIES, 1895

LIBRARIES BY COUNTIES
show the rank of each county or section

					CIRCULATION OF FREE LIBRARIES					
TOTAL			Volumes per 1000 population		Total		Per 1000 population		Per 100 volumes	
No.		Volumes								
5	77	1 *1*	1,893,232	1 *4*	1,053	1 *1*	1,343,464	1 *9*	745	1 *7*	403
	24	*2*	366,028	*28*	367	*2*	386,610	*25*	388	*5*	433
	16	*19*	28,837	*48*	203	*16*	34,748	*32*	245	*28*	191
	11	*31*	17,936	*39*	282	*47*	3,093	*50*	48	*47*	85
	4	*41*	11,292	*46*	211	*41*	6,426	*42*	120	*46*	86
	23	*11*	65,254	*20*	449	*5*	106,623	*10*	734	*18*	255
	4	*52*	6,487	*50*	192	*26*	21,328	*15*	632	*6*	412
4	82	2	495,834	8	346	2	558,828	6	389	2	337
	20	*9*	91,134	*7*	921	*3*	120,926	*3*	1,236	*13*	310
	3	*57*	4,034	*38*	283	*52*	1,040	*46*	73	*50*	44
	15	*10*	73,979	*5*	994	*12*	46,480	*18*	570	*32*	176
	7	*34*	16,195	*52*	184	*21*	23,191	*31*	264	*4*	440
	2	*59*	1,587	*60*	49	*49*	2,499	*45*	78	*35*	157
	9	*42*	11,279	*43*	247	*40*	6,956	*39*	152	*45*	92
	5	*56*	4,077	*54*	130	*32*	14,452	*23*	464	*2*	495
	10	*38*	13,470	*37*	297	*39*	7,020	*38*	155	*49*	60
7	71	8	215,755	7	499	4	222,564	2	515	5	230
	14	*26*	20,554	*54*	159	*25*	21,443	*35*	167	*12*	317
	29	*3*	281,546	*2*	1,682	*18*	27,680	*36*	165	*16*	275
	3	*16*	34,270	*13*	598						
	3	*58*	2,302	*59*	67						
	12	*37*	14,301	*36*	310	*9*	19,380	*24*	420	*19*	247
	4	*25*	20,634	*16*	536	*8*	67,125	*1*	1,744	*10*	336
	14	*24*	21,640	*42*	250	*36*	11,090	*41*	128	*42*	144
	11	*35*	16,146	*32*	347	*38*	10,462	*33*	225	*44*	106
3	90	3	411,393	4	680	7	157,180	9	259	4	236
	5	*40*	11,836	*24*	413	*15*	40,029	*2*	1,398	*8*	371
	1	*60*	450	*58*	86						
	15	*32*	17,040	*18*	514	*22*	22,939	*13*	692	*29*	189
	6	*50*	7,963	*53*	170	*42*	6,084	*40*	130	*1*	516
	5	*49*	8,185	*47*	205	*34*	13,380	*28*	336	*25*	198
	13	*20*	28,484	*57*	107	*31*	16,272	*16*	613	*17*	261
	9	*48*	8,226	*56*	116	*45*	4,635	*48*	65	*43*	125
	3	*54*	5,752	*51*	190	*54*	891	*53*	29	*53*	17
9	57	9	87,936	9	313	9	104,230	7	371	3	244
	12	*27*	20,058	*22*	422	*9*	54,174	*5*	1,140	*11*	332
	25	*8*	102,904	*9*	832	*4*	111,330	*6*	899	*34*	158
	16	*14*	40,616	*6*	962	*43*	4,781	*43*	113	*33*	165
	22	*7*	119,321	*10*	791	*10*	52,519	*27*	348	*36*	156
	12	*18*	31,144	*21*	438	*33*	13,627	*34*	192	*39*	147
	16	*12*	54,467	*8*	867	*51*	1,141	*54*	18	*55*	4
	5	*47*	8,773	*17*	520						
1	108	4	377,283	3	732	3	237,572	4	461	9	151

GEOGRAPHIC DISTRIBUTION OF

The figures in italics and those prefixed to totals

COUNTY	Population	LIBRARIES			
		FREE		OTHER	
		No.	Volumes	No.	Volumes
Tompkins.......	*44* 33,612	6	*8* 27,427	3	*5* 174,934
Cortland........	*55* 28,271	1	*56* 1,300	5	*30* 8,889
Chenango	*40* 37,602	6	*36* 6,651	2	*37* 5,451
Otsego..........	*26* 50,361	4	*34* 6,795	8	*26* 11,584
Broome	*22* 62,793	2	*26* 9,850	8	*19* 15,715
Tioga...........	*52* 29,675	6	*23* 10,097	......	......
Chemung.......	*30* 47,223	1	*58* 583	6	*20* 14,819
8 cen. counties	8 289,537	7 26	8 62,503	7 32	5 231,392
Schuyler	*53* 28,815	2	*52* 2,629	8	*45* 3,646
Yates	*57* 20,801	2	*46* 3,892	2	*49* 1,557
Steuben	*14* 82,468	9	*9* 26,936	7	*38* 5,085
Allegany	*36* 43,131	*a* 6	*39* 5,883	*a* 6	*25* 12,069
Livingston	*41* 37,010	3	*44* 4,525	3	*36* 5,804
Ontario	*27* 48,718	7	*19* 12,362	7	*10* 40,218
Wayne	*28* 48,259	3	*40* 5,306	3	*41* 4,043
Monroe.........	*4* 200,056	3	*4* 55,826	11	*7* 83,483
W cen counties ...	6 509,258	6 35	4 117,359	5 42	7 155,905
Orleans.........	*50* 30,762	5	*38* 6,055	1	*55* 679
Genesee	*45* 33,436	3	*18* 12,497	6	*35* 6,162
Wyoming	*48* 31,218	8	*16* 15,288	2	*47* 1,742
Cattaraugus	*23* 61,774	4	*45* 4,468	10	*18* 20,567
Chautauqua	*15* 78,900	11	*12* 23,907	9	*24* 12,584
Erie	*3* 347,328	6	*28* 8,361	29	*4* 204,602
Niagara	*19* 64,378	6	*17* 12,575	4	*29* 9,920
West counties....	2 647,796	2 43	6 83,151	2 61	4 256,256
Total	6,513 343	*a* 309	1,127,199	*a* 415	3,265,200

a Alfred univ lib with 9573 volumes of which 1000 are free

LIBRARIES BY COUNTIES (concluded)
show the rank of each county or section.

	TOTAL		Volumes per 1000 population		CIRCULATION OF FREE LIBRARIES					
No.		Volumes			Total		Per 1000 population		Per 100 volumes	
9	5	202,361	1	5,960	14	41,968	4	1,218	37	153
6	44	10,189	30	360	48	2,500	44	88	27	192
8	39	12,102	35	321	50	1,768	51	47	51	26
12	29	18,379	29	364	20	24,314	21	482	9	357
10	21	25,365	26	403	13	43,490	13	692	3	450
6	45	10,097	33	340	23	22,666	8	763	23	224
7	36	15,402	34	326	..	....	..	....	..	....
8	58	6	293,895	2	1,015	8	136,706	3	472	7	212
5	53	6,275	45	217	44	4,748	37	164	31	180
4	55	5,449	41	261	55	634	52	30	54	16
16	17	32,021	27	388	11	49,309	17	597	40	145
11	30	17,952	23	416	35	12,157	30	281	24	206
6	43	10,329	40	279	37	10,521	29	284	21	232
14	13	52,580	3	1,079	29	18,918	25	388	37	153
6	46	9,349	49	193	46	3,273	47	67	48	61
14	6	139,309	11	696	6	103,628	20	517	30	185
6	76	.7	273,264	5	530	5	203,188	5	399	8	173
6	51	6,734	44	218	30	17,361	19	564	14	286
9	28	18,659	14	558	19	24,316	11	727	26	194
10	33	17,030	15	544	24	22,297	12	714	40	145
14	22	25,035	25	405	53	925	55	14	52	20
20	15	36,491	19	462	7	68,402	7	866	14	286
35	4	212,963	12	613	28	19,174	49	55	22	229
10	23	22,495	31	349	17	30,198	22	469	20	240
2	104	5	339,407	6	523	6	182,673	8	282	6	219
	723		4,392,999		674		3,146,405		483		279

for circulation is entered under both free and other libraries.

Libraries having 10,000 volumes or more arranged in order of size

	Place	NAME OF LIBRARY	Control	Use	No. vols.
1	New York	Astor library	End.	R	267,147
2	"	Mercantile library	Mem	S	246,514
3	Albany	N. Y. state lib.	Gov.	R.Fl.	208,971
4	New York	Columbia coll. lib	Coll.	Fl	203,000
5	Ithaca	Cornell univ. lib.	Coll.	R.Fl.	173,793
6	Brooklyn	Brooklyn lib.	Mem	S	120,064
7	New York	Gen. soc. of mech. and tradesmen lib	Mem	F	102,019
8	"	Society lib.	Mem	Sl.	90,000
9	"	Lenox lib	End.	R	86,196
10	"	N. Y. free circulating lib.	Mem	F	81,785
11	Buffalo	Buffalo lib	Mem	R. S.	76,007
12	New York	Union theological sem. lib	Coll.	R.Fl.	70,716
13	Brooklyn	L. I. historical soc. lib	Mem	S	54,000
14	"	Pratt inst. lib	Inst.	F	49,800
15	New York	Ass'n of the bar of the city of N. Y. lib	Mem	Sl.	48,873
16	Syracuse	Syracuse univ lib	Coll.	Fl	45,661
17	New York	Maimonides lib	Mem	F	43,510
18	"	N. Y. law inst lib	Inst.	S	43,301
19	"	Y. M. C. A. lib.	Inst.	R	42,500
20	Buffalo	Grosvenor pub. lib.	Pub.	R	39,000
21	West Point	U. S military acad. lib	Gov.	Fl.	38,085
22	New York	Cooper union lib.	Inst.	R	35,870
23	"	St John's coll. lib	Coll.	Fl	34,650
24	Clinton	Hamilton coll. lib.	Coll.	F	33,758
25	Brooklyn	Union for Christian work lib.	Inst.	S	31,483
26	Geneva	Hobart coll. lib	Coll.	R.Fl.	31,417
27	Rochester	Reynolds lib.	End.	F	31,237
28	Schenectady	Union coll. lib	Coll	Fl	30,736
29	New York	Univ. of city of N Y lib.	Coll.	R.Fl.	30,196
30	Rochester	Univ. of Rochester lib.	Coll.	R.Fl.	29,700
31	New York	College of city of N. Y. lib.	Coll.	Fl.	29,342
32	"	Amer. museum of nat. hist. lib.	Mem	R	29,231
33	"	Aguilar free lib.	Mem	F	28,488
34	Rochester	Rochester theological sem lib.	Coll.	Fl.	28,034
35	Syracuse	Central lib	Pub.	F.	26,300
36	New York	Amer. geographical soc. lib	Mem	R. S.	26,164
37	"	N. Y. hospital lib	Inst.	F.	26,000
38	"	Gen. theological sem lib.	Coll.	R.Fl.	25,900
39	"	St Francis Xavier coll. lib	Coll.	R.Fl.	25,000
40	Rochester	Central lib	Pub. sch.	F.	23,941
41	Hamilton	Colgate univ. lib.	Coll.	R.Fl.	23,697
42	New York	Y. W. C. A. lib.	Inst.	R.Fl.	22,897
43	Auburn	Auburn theological sem. lib.	Coll.	F.	22,352
44	Poughkeepsie	Vassar coll lib.	Coll.	Fl.	22,000
45	New York	Catholic club lib.	Mem	Fl.	20,907
46	Newburg	Newburg free lib	Pub. sch.	F.	20,329
47	Poughkeepsie	Poughkeepsie lib.	Pub. sch.	F	18,963
48	Syracuse	Court of Appeals lib.	Gov.	Fl.	18,675
49	Ithaca	Cornell lib. ass'n	End.	F.	18,591
50	New York	Harlem lib.	Mem.	R. S.	18,550
51	Buffalo	Canisius coll lib.	Coll.	Fl.	18,400
52	Utica	Utica pub. lib.	Pub. D.	F	17,936
53	Brooklyn	Law lib.	Gov.	R.Fl.	17,883
54	New York	Cathedral lib.	Par.	F	17,549

STATISTICS OF NEW YORK LIBRARIES, 1895 311

Libraries having 10,000 or more, etc. (*concluded*)

	Place	NAME OF LIBRARY	Control	Use	No vols.
55	Rochester....	Court of Appeals lib.............	Gov.....	R....	16,200
56	Brooklyn	Brooklyn inst. lib..............	Inst.....	R ...	15,600
57	New York....	Amer. Seamen's friend soc. lib	Inst.....	Fl...	15,537
58	Albany	Young men's ass'n lib..........	Inst.....	S....	15,000
59	New York....	Equitable life assurance soc. law lib	Inst.....	Fl...	14,366
60	New York ...	Amer. inst. lib	Mem	R ...	13,818
61	Brooklyn	Y. M. C. A. lib	Inst.....	R. Sl.	13,512
62	Oswego.......	City lib........................	Pub.....	R....	13,350
63	Gloversville .	Gloversville free lib	Mem.Pub	F....	12,361
64	New York ...	University club lib	Mem	Fl...	12,325
65	Sing Sing...	Mt Pleasant acad. lib	Sch	Fl...	12,000
66	Auburn.......	Seymour lib....................	Mem.End	S....	11,980
67	Canton	St Lawrence univ. Herring lib.	Coll	Fl...	11,298
68	Batavia	Richmond lib...................	Pub. sch.	F....	10,794
69	Binghamton .	Supreme court lib	Gov.....	R ...	10,617
70	Yonkers	Yonkers pub lib................	Pub.....	F....	10,403
71	New York ...	Washington Heights free lib ...	Mem	F ...	10,063
72	Jamestown ..	James Prendergast lib. ass'n....	End.....	F ...	10,045
73	Annandale ..	St Stephen's coll. lib	Coll.....	Fl...	10,000
74	Hornellsville.	Hornell free lib	End.....	F ...	10,000
		Total			3,211,787

Libraries of 1000 volumes or more, free to the public for lending, arranged in order of size

	Place	NAME OF LIBRARY	Control	Volumes Added	Volumes Total	Circulation	Circulation per 100 vols.[a]	
1	New York	Gen. soc. of mechanics and tradesmen lib	Mem	4679	102,019	254,371	*62*	249
2	"	N. Y. free circulating lib	Mem	4925	81,785	626,796	*6*	766
3	Brooklyn	Pratt inst. lib	Inst	5069	49,800	202,304	*77*	406
4	New York	Maimonides lib	Mem	1955	43,510	41,852	*111*	96
5	Clinton	Hamilton coll. lib	Coll	898	33,758	3207	*147*	9
6	Brooklyn	Union for Christian work free lib	Inst	4962	31,483	161,426	*13*	512
7	Rochester	Reynolds lib	End	2733	31,237	15,107	*128*	48
8	New York	Aquilar free lib	Mem	4171	28,488	252,227	*2*	885
9	Syracuse	Central lib	Pub	1993	26,300	44,565	*91*	169
10	New York	N. Y. hospital lib	Inst	2587	26,000			
11	Rochester	Central lib	Pub. sch	3941	23,941	85,734	*35*	370
12	Auburn	Auburn theo. sem. lib	Coll		22,352			
13	Newburg	Newburg free lib	Pub. sch	664	20,329	67,556	*42*	332
14	Poughkeepsie	Poughkeepsie lib	Pub. sch	575	18,963	37,586	*80*	198
15	Ithaca	Cornell lib. ass'n	End	116	18,591	32,858	*87*	176
16	Utica	Utica pub. lib	Pub. D	3598	17,996	82,421	*20*	459
17	New York	Cathedral free circ. lib	Par	931	17,594	51,814	*48*	294
18	Gloversville	Gloversville free lib	Mem. Pub	1087	12,361	59,695	*17*	483
19	Batavia	Richmond lib	Pub. sch	564	10,794	22,932	*75*	212
20	Yonkers	Yonkers public lib	Pub	239	10,408	31,192	*47*	299
21	New York	Washington Heights free lib	Mem	685	10,063	22,552	*69*	224
22	Jamestown	James Prendergast lib. ass'n	End	933	10,045	49,194	*15*	489
23	Hornellsville	Hornell free lib	End	1526	10,000	30,321	*46*	303
24	Rome	Jervis lib. ass'n	End	4125	9315			
25	Bath	Davenport lib	Prn. Mem	200	9050	11,250	*101*	124
26	Binghamton	City sch. lib	Pub. sch	585	9000	43,570	*18*	481
27	Ilion	Ilion free pub. lib	Pub. sch	622	7543	36,891	*15*	489
28	Johnstown	Union sch. lib	Pub. sch	876	7069	6500	*114*	91

[a] Rank of each library is given by figures in italics.

29	Attica	Stevens mem. lib	Pri	215	6905	12,950	85	186
30	Middletown	Middletown pub. sch. lib	Pub. sch	151	6891	27,192	30	394
31	Owego	Owego free lib	Pub. sch	200	6300	17,100	55	275
32	Peekskill	Field lib	End	166	6177	22,200	38	361
33	Oswego	City sch. lib	Pub	115	6149	9896	77	160
34	Port Jervis	Port Jervis free lib	Pub. D	778	6124	13,578	8	221
35	Glens Falls	Crandall free lib	End	451	6015	38,529	74	640
36	Flushing	Flushing lib. ass'n	Mem	254	6000	12,882	115	214
37	Dryden	Southworth lib	End	329	5700	5000	123	87
38	Stapleton	Staten Island acad. lib	Sch	100	5569	3600	50	64
39	Lockport	Lockport pub. lib	Pub. D	204	5380	15,871	39	288
40	New York	Webster free circ. lib	Inst	1201	5276	18,825	71	356
41	Malone	Village sch. dist. lib	Pub. sch	180	5095	11,130	53	221
42	Ogdensburg	Ogdensburg pub. lib	Pub	506	5005	14,289	63	285
43	Mt Vernon	Union sch. lib	Pub. sch		4893	15,786		322
44	Hudson	High sch. lib	Pub. sch		4758			
45	Lowville	Lowville acad. lib	Sch	389	4504	491	144	10
46	Port Henry	Sherman free lib	End	515	4414	8835	79	200
47	Oneonta	Oneonta pub. lib	Pub. D	569	4235	19,369	22	457
48	Rhinebeck	Starr inst. lib	Pub. sch	114	4220	6448	95	152
49	Geneva	Classical union sch. lib	Pub. sch	406	4154	7150	88	172
50	Salem	Washington acad. lib	Sch	430	4000	2876	118	71
51	Glens Falls	Glens Falls acad. lib	Sch		3981			
52	Cohoes	City lib	Pub. sch	109	3757	14,613	32	388
53	Niagara Falls	Niagara Falls pub. lib	Pub. D	37	3841	9467	57	260
54	New York	Peck mem. lib	Pub. sch	365	3669	30,000	3	840
55	Sing Sing	Sing Sing pub. lib	Pub D	254	3537	13,716	51	287
56	Bay Ridge	Bay Ridge free lib	Mem	576	3490	12,226	40	350
57	Nyack	Nyack library	Prib	341	3572	19,086	17	565
58	Warsaw	Union sch. circ. lib	Pub. sch	273	3143	5945	83	189
59	Jamestown	High sch. lib	Pub. sch	43	3128	7986	61	253
60	Canandaigua	Union sch. lib	Pub. sch		3105			
61	Schenectady	Schenectady free pub. lib	Mem	50	3000	11,142	34	377
62	Albion	Albion pub. lib	Pub. D	783	2950	10,018	36	369
63	New Rochelle	New Rochelle pub. lib	Pub. D	133	2714	7299	56	272
64	New York	De Witt mem. lib	Inst	72	2681	932	134	34
65	College Point	Conrad Poppenhusen ass'n lib	Inst	448	2671	12,154	20	459
66	Jamaica	Union sch. lib	Pub. sch	520	2645	6356	65	241
67	Albany	Abany free lib	Mem		2634			

Libraries of 1000 volumes or more, free to the public, etc. (continued)

	Place	NAME OF LIBRARY	Control	VOLUMES Added	VOLUMES Total	Circulation	Circulation per 100 vols.a
68	New York	Olivet church lib	Par	90	2580	6227	65
69	Palmyra	Palmyra class. union sch. lib	Pub. sch	230	2579	2073	117
70	Dansville	Dansville pub. lib	Pub. D	258	2550	8085	44
71	Westfield	Union sch. lib	Pub. sch	25	2500	?4000	92
72	Boonville	Erwin lib. and inst	End	291	2496	6231	62
73	New York	College settlement lib	Mem	?600	2436	?15,000	10
74	Hornellsville	Hornell free acad. lib	Pub. sch	501	2404	560	139
75	Irvington	Union sch. lib	Pub. sch	201	2396	1204	126
76	Yonkers	Women's inst. lib	Inst	382	2381	5497	68
77	Tarrytown	Union sch. lib. dist. no. 1 (Greenburg)	Pub. sch		2369		
78	Amsterdam	Amsterdam lib ass'n	Mem	345	2368	9669	26
79	Chatham	Union sch. lib	Pub. sch	403	2348	?	408
80	Eddytown	Starkey sem. lib	Sch	494	2317	484	142
81	New York	Broome st. free lib	Par		2314	2034	115
82	Delhi	Delaware acad. lib	Sch	20	2286	970	130
83	Stamford	Stamford sem. and union sch. lib	Pub. sch	39	2275	634	138
84	Lyons	Union sch. lib	Pub. sch	296	2163	?1200	125
85	Belleville	Union acad. of Belleville lib	Sch	3	2153	450	142
86	Fort Hamilton	Fort Hamilton free lib	Mem	713	2123	4500	76
87	Albany	Catholic union lib	Mem	213	2049	2500	102
88	Pine Plains	Pine Plains free lib	Pub	228	2028	?	
89	Round Lake	Round Lake inst. lib	Sch	36	2025		
90	Hoosick Falls	Union sch. lib	Pub. sch	78	2012	4382	73
91	Cold Spring	Haldane union sch. lib	Pub. sch	200	2000	750	131
92	Sherburne	Union sch. lib	Pub. sch		2000	?450	139
93	Watkins	Watkins lib	Pub. sch		?2000	200	144
94	New York	University settlement lib	Inst		?1986		
95	Addison	Addison pub. lib	Pub. D	252	1959	5614	52
96	East Aurora	Union sch. lib	Pub. sch	418	1944	8679	23

a Rank of each library is given by figures in italics.

STATISTICS OF NEW YORK LIBRARIES, 1895   815

97	Prattsburg	Franklin acad lib	Pub. sch			
98	Lansingburg	Union sch. lib. dist. no. 1	Pub. sch	5	......	
99	New York	St Agnes free lib	Mem	84	9225	14	503
100	North Tonawanda	North Tonawanda pub. lib	Pub.	863	5293	49	290
101	Waverly	High sch. lib	Pub. sch	396	4150	54	284
102	Dolgeville	School soc. lib	Mem	340	634	133	35
103	Attica	Union sch. and acad. lib	Pub. sch	18	112	149	6
104	Catskill	Catskill pub. lib	Pub.	11	13,718	4	819
105	Fayetteville	Union sch. and acad. lib	Pub.	428	520	136	31
106	Springville	Springville pub. lib	Pub. D.	119	6820	24	417
107	West Troy	Sch. lib. dist. no. 5 (Watervliet)	Pub. sch	283	4211	58	259
108	Ellenville	Ellenville pub. lib	Pub. sch	83	16,292	21	1014
109	Whitehall	Union sch. lib	Pub. sch	80			
110	Penn Yan	Penn Yan pub lib	Pub. sch		?150	147	9
111	Silver Creek	Union sch lib	Pub. sch	113	2291	97	149
112	Kingston	Free acad. lib	Pub. sch		50	152	3
113	Clarence	Parker union sch. lib	Pub. sch	30	10,150	7	700
114	Shortsville	M. M. Buck free lib	Pri.	200	949	124	63
115	Glen Cove	Glen Cove pub. lib	Pub.	247	457	137	30
116	Westchester	Union sch. lib. dist. no. 3	Pub. sch		6009	29	402
117	Saugerties	Saugerties pub. lib	Pub. D.	429	2006	99	188
118	Sinclairville	Sinclairville free lib	End	100	75	150	5
119	Naples	Union sch. lib	Pub sch		5590	31	392
120	Westport	Westport lib. ass'n	Mem	23	3357	67	235
121	Wellsville	Wellsville pub. lib	Pub	341	1638	107	115
122	Bronxville	Sch. lib. dist. no. 2	Pub. sch		3620	59	256
123	West Winfield	West Winfield free lib	Pub. D.	307	?75	150	5
124	Frankinville	Ten Broeck free acad. lib	Pub. sch	263	3371	64	246
125	Belmont	Belmont lit. and hist. soc. free lib	Mem	397	1672	102	122
126	Waterford	Union sch. lib	Pub. sch	187	?300	140	22
127	Keeseville	Union sch. lib	Pub. sch	?90	1587	105	117
128	Tonawanda	Tonawanda pub. lib	Pub. sch	178	5654	25	414
129	Bath Beach	New Utrecht pub. lib	Pub.	1341	2267	90	171
130	Little Falls	Union sch lib	Pub. sch		4500	41	346
131	Fort Edward	Union sch. lib	Pub. sch	2	?900	120	69
132	Greene	Union sch. lib	Pub. sch	117	?2500	82	192
133	Homer	Homer acad. and union sch. lib	Pub. sch				

aCamden lib ass'n with 819 vols. and Plattsburg pub. lib with 492 are not included in this table. The first circulated 3546 vols. at the rate of 1165 per hundred and the other 5680 at the rate of 1149 per hundred.

Libraries of 1000 volumes or more, free to the public, etc. (concluded)

	Place	Name of library	Control	Volumes Added	Volumes Total	Circulation	Circulation per 100 vols.[a]
134	Salamanca	Union sch. lib	Pub. sch	137	1287		
135	Randolph	Chamberlain inst. Helen Culver lib	End. Sch	281	1281	850	66
136	Jamestown	Y M. C. A. lib	Inst.	84	1270		121
137	Hamburg	Union sch. lib	Pub. sch	204	1265	838	66
138	Hemstead	High sch. lib	Pub. sch	42	1260	30	2
139	Bath-on-Hudson	N Greenbush pub. lib. dist. no. 6	Pub. D	201	1259	5079	403
140	Sandy Hill	Union sch lib	Pub. sch	159	1251	2343	187
141	Highland Falls	Morgan circ. lib	End	26	1250	10,000	800
142	Fulton	Union sch. lib. dist. no. 1 (Volney)	Pub. sch.	9	1246	1900	152
143	Jordan	Jordan free acad. lib	Pub. sch		1239		
144	Clinton	Union sch. lib	Pub. sch	260	1229	7748	630
145	Bainbridge	Union sch. lib	Pub. sch	9	1220	418	34
146	Elbridge	Munro coll. inst. lib	Sch.	15	1206	13	1
147	Huntington	Union sch lib	Pub sch	63	1204		
148	Carthage	High sch. lib	Pub sch		1200	2500	208
149	Groton	Union sch. lib	Pub. sch	110	1194	1200	100
150	Medina	Union sch. lib. dist. no. 12 (Ridgeway & Shelby)					
151	Fonda	Union sch. lib	Pub. sch	16	1176	2328	197
152	Valatie	Union sch. lib	Pub. sch	151	1171	1500	128
153	Waterville	Waterville pub. lib	Pub. D.		1169		
154	Westchester	Union sch. lib. dist. no. 1	Pub. sch	6	1158	1850	116
155	Sidney	Sidney pub. lib	Pub. D.		1150		
156	Alexander	Union sch. lib	Pub. sch	150	1137	4147	362
157	Pocantico Hills	Pocantico Hills lyceum	Mem	16	1133	1570	50
158	Canajoharie	Union sch. lib	Pub. sch	393	1126	1050	98
159	Lake Placid	Lake Placid pub. lib	Pub. D	26	1117	1094	92
160	Holland Patent	Union sch. lib	Pub. sch	245	1103	2818	255
					1100		

[a] Rank of each library is given by figures in italics.

STATISTICS OF NEW YORK LIBRARIES, 1895

161	New York	Riverside free lib	Inst.	432	1100	5242	*19*	476
162	Walden	Union sch. lib	Pub. sch	30	1100	1250	*108*	113
163	Gilbertsville	Gilbertsville free lib	Mem	185	1094	3445	*45*	314
164	Chateaugay	Union sch. lib	Pub. sch	158	1092	2250	*78*	206
165	Goshen	Union sch. lib	Pub. sch		1063			70
166	Perry	Union sch. lib	Pub. sch	30	1060	750	*119*	200
167	Wyoming	Wyoming free circ. lib. ass'n	Pub.	170	1060	2840	*79*	47
168	Flatlands	Sch. lib. dist. no. 1	Pub. D		1042	500	*129*	223
169	Liberty	Liberty pub. lib	Pub. D	127	1027	2299	*70*	550
170	Fort Plain	Fort Plain free lib	Mem	50	1023	5627	*12*	144
171	Palisades	Palisades lib. and reading room	Mem	123	1023	1482	*98*	172
172	Crown Point	Chapel library	Pub. D	161	1021	1765	*88*	15
173	Argyle	Union sch. lib	Pub. sch	1	1020	160	*144*	
174	Afton	Union sch. lib	Pub. sch		1000			
175	Alfred	Alfred union lib	Coll		1000	?3857	*33*	385
176	Claverack	Claverack free lib. and reading room	Mem	90	1000	1500	*98*	150
177	Forestville	Forestville free acad. lib	Pub. sch	145	1000	1200	*104*	120
178	Maspeth	Union sch. lib	Pub. sch		1000			
179	Mt Morris	Union sch. lib	Pub. sch	67	1000	1042	*109*	104
180	Onondaga	Onondaga acad. lib	Pub. sch	200	1000	400	*131*	40
181	Sherman	Union sch. lib	Pub. sch	26	1000	1775	*86*	177
	Total			83,278	1,047,123	3,012,694		287

Libraries of 1000 volumes or more, free only for reference arranged in order of size

	Place	Name	Control	Volumes Added	Volumes Total
1	New York	Astor lib	End	9597	267,147
2	Albany	N. Y state lib	Gov	15,259	208,971
3	Ithaca	Cornell univ lib	Coll	12,898	173,793
4	New York	N. Y. Society lib	Mem	1503	90,000
5	"	Lenox lib	End	4083	86,196
6	Buffalo	Buffalo lib	Mem	3670	76,007
7	New York	Union theo. sem. lib	Coll	771	70,716
8	"	Y. M. C. A lib	Inst	1405	42,500
9	Buffalo	Grosvenor pub. lib	Pub	870	39,000
10	New York	Cooper union lib	Inst	994	35,870
11	Geneva	Hobart coll. lib	Coll	1075	31,417
12	New York	University of city of New York lib	Coll	550	30,196
13	Rochester	Univ. of Rochester lib	Coll	1215	29,700
14	New York	Amer. museum of nat. hist. lib	Mem	1149	29,231
15	"	Amer. geog. soc. lib	Mem	579	26,164
16	"	Gen. theo. sem lib	Coll	986	25,900
17	"	Coll. of St Francis Xavier lib	Coll	100	25,000
18	Hamilton	Colgate univ lib	Coll	872	23,697
19	New York	Y. W. C. A. lib	Inst	1708	22,897
20	"	Harlem lib	Mem	953	18,550
21	Brooklyn	Law lib	Gov	1332	17,883
22	Rochester	Court of Appeals lib	Gov	200	16,200
23	Brooklyn	Brooklyn inst. lib	Inst	100	15,600
24	New York	Amer inst lib	Mem	65	13,818
25	Brooklyn	Y. M. C. A. lib	Inst	447	13,512
26	Oswego	City lib	Pub	275	13,350
27	Binghamton	Supreme court law lib	Gov	617	10,617
28	Alfred	Alfred univ. lib	Coll	130	9573
29	Buffalo	Buffalo hist soc. lib	Mem	485	8724
30	New York	Manhattan coll. lib	Coll	100	8155
31	Kingston	Third jud. dist. law lib	Gov	?200	?7000
32	Buffalo	Y M. C. A. lib	Inst	404	6750
33	New York	Teacher's coll Bryson lib	Coll	861	6566
34	Brooklyn	Y. W C A. lib	Inst		6500
35	Utica	Oneida hist. soc. lib	Mem	80	6336
36	Buffalo	Buffalo cath inst lib	Inst	401	6332
37	New York	City lib	Gov	78	6200
38	Buffalo	Univ of Buffalo	Coll	411	5025
39	New York	N Y coll of pharmacy	Coll		4623
40	Olean	Forman lib	Mem	146	4550
41	Oswego	State Normal and training sch. lib	Sch	576	4529
42	Saratoga Spr	4th jud. dist. law lib	Gov	228	4511
43	Fredonia	Darwin R Barker lib. ass'n	Mem	398	3893
44	Huntington	Huntington lib ass'n	Mem	179	8738
45	Moravia	Powers lib	End	4	3712
46	Albany	Y. M. C. A. lib	Inst	167	3707
47	Buffalo	Buffalo soc of nat. sciences	Mem	1651	3503
48	New York	Mechanical engineers lib	Mem	40	3500
49	Trenton	Barneveld lib. ass'n	Mem	15	3400

Libraries of 1000 volumes or more, free only for reference, etc. (concluded)

	Place	NAME	Control	Volumes Added	Volumes Total
50	New York	Mott memorial med. and surg. lib	Mem		3000
51	Rome	Y. M. C. A. lib	Inst	107	2881
52	Seneca Falls	Seneca Falls lib. ass'n	Mem		2711
53	Havana	Cook acad. lib	Sch	68	2157
54	Oneida	Union sch. lib	Pub. sch.	544	2062
55	Plattsburg	Y. M C A. lib	Inst		2000
56	White Plains	Westchester co law lib	Gov		¶ 1950
57	Newark	Union sch. lib	Pub. sch.		1750
58	Carmel	Literary union lib	Mem	50	1720
59	Angelica	Wilson acad. lib	Sch	245	1676
60	Buffalo	N. Buffalo cath. ass'n lib	Mem	78	1586
61	Albany	Y. W. C. A. lib	Inst	135	1526
62	New York	Health dep't lib	Gov	23	1501
63	Nyack	Union sch. lib	Pub. sch.		1321
64	Gouverneur	Gouverneur reading room ass'n	Mem	243	1317
65	Adams	Adams collegiate inst. lib.	Sch		1145
66	Watertown	Y M. C. A. lib	Inst	10	1130
67	Canandaigua	Canandaigua acad. lib	Sch		1036
68	Ballston Spa	Saratoga co. law lib	Gov	¶ 30	¶ 1000
69	New York	St Barnabus free reading room	Inst	11	1000
		Total		71,371	1,610,628

College libraries arranged in order of size

	Place	Name	Volumes Added	Volumes Total
1	New York	Columbia college	24,839	203,000
2	Ithaca	Cornell university	12,898	173,793
3	New York	Union theo. sem	771	70,716
4	Syracuse	Syracuse university		45,661
5	New York	St John's college (Fordham)	250	34,650
6	Clinton	Hamilton college	898	33,758
7	Geneva	Hobart college	1075	31,417
8	Schenectady	Union college	432	30,736
9	New York	University of city of New York	550	30,196
10	Rochester	University of Rochester	1215	29,700
11	New York	College of city of New York	937	29,342
12	Rochester	Rochester theo. sem	642	28,034
13	New York	General theo. sem	986	25,900
14	"	St Francis Xavier college	100	25,000
15	Hamilton	Colgate university	872	23,697
16	Auburn	Auburn theo. sem		22,352
17	Poughkeepsie	Vassar college		22,000
18	Buffalo	Canisius college	?20	18,400
19	Canton	St Lawrence univ. Herring lib	227	11,298
20	Annandale	St Stephen's college	50	10,000
21	Alfred	Alfred university	130	9573
22	New York	Manhattan college	100	8155
23	Allegany	St Bonaventure college		7313
24	Brooklyn	Brooklyn polytechnic inst	80	7100
25	"	St John's college		7000
26	Buffalo	Niagara univ. art dep't		7000
27	Niagara univ.	Niagara university	500	7000
28	New York	Teacher's college. Bryson lib	861	6566
29	Aurora	Wells college	564	5308
30	Buffalo	Univ. of Buffalo med. dep't	411	5025
31	Elmira	Elmira college	200	5000
32	Troy	Rensselaer polytechnic inst		5000
33	New York	College of pharmacy of city of N. Y.		4623
34	"	N. Y. normal college	244	4400
35	Brooklyn	St Francis college		4070
36	Albany	N. Y. state normal college		2900
37	New York	Eclectic medical college		2058
38	Albany	Dudley observatory lib		2000
39	Buffalo	German M. Luther college		1853
40	Albany	Albany law school	16	1382
41	New York	Metropolis law school		1380
42	Syracuse	Syracuse medical college		?1200
43	New York	Woman's med. coll. of N. Y. infirmary	47	1171
44	"	Post graduate med. sch. and hosp	90	?1000
45	"	Medical college and hospital for women		900
46	Rochester	Wagner memorial Lutheran college		750
47	Buffalo	Niagara univ. med. dep't		660
48	New York	College of veterinary surgeons		?500
49	Buffalo	College of pharmacy		110
50	Albany	College of pharmacy		90
		Total	50,005	1,010,737

Law libraries arranged in order of size

	Place	NAME	Control	Added	Total
				\multicolumn{2}{c}{VOLUMES}
1	Albany........	N. Y. state law lib.a........	Gov.....	1676	53,584
2	New York.....	Ass'n of the bar of the city of N Y. lib...............	Gov.....	3168	48,873
3	"	N Y. law inst. lib...........	Inst.....	1722	43,301
4	Ithaca	Cornell univ. law lib b......	Coll.....	662	23,403
5	Syracuse	Court of Appeals lib.......	Gov.....	460	18,675
6	Binghamton...	Law lib.....................	Gov.....	1332	17,883
7	Rochester.....	Court of Appeals lib........	Gov.....	200	16,200
8	New York	Equitable life assurance soc. law lib....................	Inst.....	350	14,366
9	Binghamton...	Supreme Court lib..........	Gov.....	?617	?10,617
10	Buffalo.	Law lib. 8th judicial dist....	Gov.....	250	9750
11	New York.....	University of city of N. Y. law lib...................	Coll.....	....	9100
12	Kingston......	3d judicial dist. law lib.....	Gov.....	200	7000
13	Saratoga Spr..	4th judicial dist. law lib	Gov.....	?228	?4511
14	Newburg......	2d judicial dist. law lib.....	Gov.....	657	4084
15	White Plains..	Westchester co. law lib.....	Gov.....	....	?1950
16	New York.....	N Y. law sch. lib...........	Coll.....	1584	1619
17	Albany........	Albany law sch. lib.........	Coll.....	16	1382
18	New York.....	Metropolis law sch. lib......	Coll.....	....	1380
19	Ballston Spa...	Saratoga co law lib........	Gov.....	?30	?1000
20	Morrisville	Madison co. law lib.........	Gov.....	22	718
		Total	....	13,174	289,396

a Included in New York state library.
b Included in Cornell university library.

*Libraries in the

No.	Post-office	County	NAME	Incorporated By b	Date
1	Addison	Steuben	Addison public library	R	9 F 98
2	Albany	Albany	Albany free library	R	21 Je 98
3	Albion	Orleans	Albion public library	R	9 F 98
4	Allen's Hill	Ontario	Allen's Hill free circ lib ass'n	Rp	26 F 95
5	Amsterdam	Montgomery	Amsterdam library ass'n	G	8 O 91
6	Arkport	Steuben	Arkport public library	Rp	5 Jl 94
7	Ballston Spa	Saratoga	Ballston public library	Rp	9 F 93
8	Bath Beach	Kings	New Utrecht free library	R	28 F 95
9	Bath on-Hudson	Rensselaer	North Greenbush dist no 6 public library	Rp	21 Je 98
10	Bay Ridge	Kings	Bay Ridge free library	R	21 Je 98
11	Belmont	Allegany	Belmont lit. and hist. soc. free lib	R	9 F 98
12	Boonville	Oneida	Erwin library and institute	G	6 Je 85
13	Buffalo	Erie	Grosvenor public library	L	11 Ap 59
14	Camden	Oneida	Camden library ass'n	Rp	7 Jl 91
15	Canaan Four Corners	Columbia	Canaan public library	Rp	21 Je 93
16	Catskill	Greene	Catskill public library	R	9 F 98
17	Claverack	Columbia	Claverack free lib and reading room ass'n	G	23 Mr 91
18	Cornwall	Orange	Cornwall public library	Rp	26 F 95
19	Cornwall on-Hudson	Orange	Cornwall on-Hudson public library	Rp	26 Je 95
20	Crown Point	Essex	Chapel library	Rp	12 D 94
21	Dansville	Livingston	Dansville public library	R	13 D 98
22	Dryden	Tompkins	Southworth library ass'n	G	— Ap 83
23	East Chatham	Columbia	East Chatham public library	Rp	9 F 93
24	Easton	Washington	Easton library ass'n	G	— — 79
25	Elizabethtown	Essex	Elizabethtown library ass'n	G	8 O 84
26	Ellenville	Ulster	Ellenville public library	R	21 Je 93
27	Fort Hamilton	Kings	Fort Hamilton free library	R	13 D 93
28	Fort Plain	Montgomery	Fort Plain free library	R	5 Je 94
29	Gilbertsville	Otsego	Gilbertsville free library	G	8 My 91
30	Glen Cove	Queens	Glen Cove public library	Rp	12 D 94
31	Glen Haven	Cayuga	Glen Haven public library	Rp	13 D 98
32	Glens Falls	Warren	Crandall free library	R	9 F 93
33	Havana	Schuyler	Havana free library	Rp	5 Je 94
34	Hornellsville	Steuben	Hornell library ass'n	G	6 Ap 68
35	Ilion	Herkimer	Ilion district library	R	13 D 98
36	Jamestown	Chautauqua	James Prendergast library ass'n	L	29 Ja 88
37	Jordanville	Herkimer	Jordanville public library	R	21 Je 94
38	Joshua's Rock	Warren	Mountainside free library	Rp	5 Jl 93
39	Keene Valley	Essex	Keene Valley public library	Rp	13 D 98
40	Lake George	Warren	Lake George free library	Rp	26 F 95
41	Lake Placid	Essex	Lake Placid public library	R	12 D 94
42	Liberty	Sullivan	Liberty public library	Rp	5 Je 94
43	Liverpool	Onondaga	Liverpool public library	Rp	21 Je 93
44	Lockport	Niagara	Lockport public library	R	9 F 98
45	Madalin	Dutchess	Tivoli public library	Rp	5 Je 94
46	Marathon	Cortland	Peck memorial library ass'n	G	12 D 98
47	Mellenville	Columbia	Mellenville public library	Rp	21 Je 93
48	Mohawk	Herkimer	Mohawk public library	Rp	13 D 98
49	Morristown	St Lawrence	Morristown public library	Rp	5 Je 94
50	Nanuet	Rockland	Nanuet public library	Rp	12 D 94
51	Nassau	Rensselaer	Nassau free library	R	9 F 98
52	New Rochelle	Westchester	New Rochelle public library	R	5 Jl 94
53	New York	New York	St Agnes free library	R	5 Je 94
54	Newfield	Tompkins	Newfield public library	Rp	12 D 94
55	Niagara Falls	Niagara	Niagara Falls public library	R	26 F 95
56	North Parma	Monroe	North Parma public library	Rp	9 F 98
57	North Tonawanda	Niagara	North Tonawanda public library	R	13 D 98
58	Nyack	Rockland	Nyack library	G	10 S 90
59	Ogdensburg	St Lawrence	Ogdensburg public library	R	13 D 93
	Oneonta	Otsego	Oneonta public library	R	9 F 98
	Oyster Bay	Queens	Oyster Bay peoples library	Rp	12 D 94
60	Philmont	Columbia	Philmont public library	Rp	13 D 98
62	Pine Plains	Dutchess	Pine Plains free library	R	26 Je 95
64	Plattsburg	Clinton	Plattsburg public library	Rp	5 Je 94

a Not including the State library or the 424
b R incorporated by regents
 L "   legislature
 G "   under general law

University, June 30, 1895

Admitted	YEAR ENDING JUNE 30, 1895— VOLUMES			TRUSTEES	
	Added	Total	Circulation	No.	Elected by	No.

Admitted	Added	Total	Circulation	No.	Elected by	No.
9 F 93	252	1959	5614	3	District	1
21 Je 93	590	2634	6856	10	Contributors of $1 previous year	2
9 F 93	50	2950	11,142	9	Members of bd of educ trustees ex officio	3
28 F 95	118	411	843	5	Corporation	4
26 Je 95	845	2368	9669	19	Corporation	5
5 Jl 94	500	500	451	6	Bd. of education	6
9 F 93	3	638	6653	5	Village	7
28 F 95	1341	1341	5654	7	Corporation	8
21 Je 93	201	1259	5079	3	Bd. of education	9
21 Je 93	576	3490	12,296	9	Corporation	10
9 F 93	397	1368	2371	5	Society	11
8 F 94	291	2496	6231	5	Corporation	12
5 Je 94	870	39,000	....	3	Mayor and common council	13
7 Jl 91	214	819	9548	5	....	14
21 Je 93	....	1555	? 1200	5	School district	15
9 F 93	428	1674	13,718	3	Bd of education	16
5 Je 94	90	1000	1500	11	Corporation	17
28 F 95	....	438	....	5	Bd of education	18
26 Je 95	1	812	1150	5	Bd. of education	19
12 D 94	161	1021	? 1765	5	1 for life, 3 by bd of ed sc. prin ex officio	20
13 D 93	258	2550	8085	5	Bd of education	21
12 D 94	299	5790	? 5000	7	Corporation	22
9 F 93	162	639	1151	3	School district	23
28 F 95	197	680	583	7	Corporation	24
26 Je 95	79	1421	? 1750	6	Corporation	25
21 Je 93	78	1606	16,292	5	School district	26
13 D 93	712	2128	4500	6	Corporation	27
5 Je 94	50	1028	5827	8	Contributors of $1, previous year	28
12 D 94	185	1094	3445	8	Corporation	29
12 D 94	247	1495	949	5	3 by sch dist. 2 by bd of educ.	30
13 D 93	276	580	899	5	District	31
9 F 93	451	6015	38,529	17	Henry Crandall	32
5 Je 94	78	629	4548	5	Corporation	33
21 Je 93	? 526	? 10,000	30,221	9	Corporation	34
12 D 93	151	963	4710	5	Managers of- Ilion pub.-lib. are trustees ex officio	35
5 Je 94	968	10,045	49,194	7	Corporation	36
21 Je 93	124	669	2189	5	School district	37
5 Jl 94	337	337	? 1500	7	Corporation	38
13 D 93	390	870	1381	9	Association	39
28 F 95	110	453	....	5	Corporation	40
12 D 94	245	1108	2818	5	District	41
5 Je 94	127	1027	2299	5	Bd of education	42
21 Je 93	118	719	2091	3	School district	43
9 F 93	204	5830	15,871	3	Bd of education	44
5 Je 94	134	426	2958	3	School district	45
26 Je 95	....	....	....	5	Corporation	46
21 Je 93	1	338	266	3	School district	47
13 D 93	111	815	1885	3	District	48
5 Je 94	105	210	1833	5	Corporation	49
2 D 94	60	771	780	3	School district trustees	50
9 F 93	58	476	3612	12	Association	51
5 Jl 94	782	2714	10,018	5	Bd of education	52
5 Je 94	862	1882	2225	5	Corporation	53
12 D 94	122	488	370	6	5 by lib ass'n pres bd of ed ex officio	54
28 F 95	37	3641	9467	5	3 by bd of ed mayor and pres of bd of ed ex officio	55
9 F 93	236	648	2787	5	Village trustees	56
13 D 93	396	1695	5983	5	Bd of education	57
5 Je 94	341	2372	19,056	11	Corporation	58
13 D 93	506	5005	14,239	5	Mayor	59
9 F 93	550	4235	19,369	5	School district	60
12 D 94	120	650	2160	7	Corporation	61
13 D 93	189	810	2908	3	District	62
26 Je 95	228	2028	?	5	Town auditors, trustees ex officio	63
5 Je 94	498	498	? 5620	13	Village trustees	64

libraries belonging to teaching institutions
p Provisional charter

*Libraries in the

No.	Post-office	County	NAME	INCORPORATED By b	Date
65	Pocantico Hills	Westchester	Pocantico Hills lyceum	G	29 Mr 98
66	Poplar Ridge	Cayuga	Hazard library ass'n	G	31 D 89
67	Port Henry	Essex	Sherman free library	R	13 D 86
68	Port Jervis	Orange	Port Jervis free library	R	29 S 92
69	Rockville Center	Queens	Rockville Center public library	Rp	5 Je 94
70	Rome	Oneida	Jervis library ass'n	G	13 D 94
71	Saugerties	Ulster	Saugerties public library	R	5 Je 94
72	Schenectady	Schenectady	Schenectady free public library	R	12 D 94
73	Schuylerville	Saratoga	Schuylerville public library	Rp	12 D 94
74	Sea Cliff	Queens	Sea Cliff public library	Rp	12 D 94
75	Sidney	Delaware	Sidney public library	R	26 Je 95
76	Sinclairville	Chautauqua	Sinclairville free library	R	12 D 94
77	Sing Sing	Westchester	Sing Sing public library	R	9 F 93
78	Springfield Center	Otsego	Springfield free library	Rp	26 Je 95
79	Springville	Erie	Springville public library	Rp	13 D 92
80	Syracuse	Onondaga	Syracuse central library	R	13 D 96
81	Tonawanda	Erie	Tonawanda public library	R	13 D 96
82	Troy	Rensselaer	Troy children's neighborhood library	Rp	12 D 94
83	Troy	Rensselaer	Young women's ass'n of the city of Troy	G	15 Je 85
84	Trumansburg	Tompkins	Trumansburg public library	Rp	21 Je 93
85	Utica	Oneida	Utica public library	R	21 Je 96
86	Waterford	Saratoga	Waterford public library	R	23 F 95
87	Waterville	Oneida	Waterville public library	R	23 F 95
88	Wellsville	Allegany	Wellsville public library	Rp	5 Je 94
89	West Winfield	Herkimer	West Winfield free library	Rp	12 D 94
90	Westbury	Cayuga	Green Wood library	Rp	21 Je 93
91	Westport	Essex	Westport library ass'n	G	16 N 87
92	Yonkers	Westchester	Woman's institute of Yonkers	G	23 O 92
93	Yonkers	Westchester	Yonkers public library	R	9 F 93

a Not including the State library or the 494
b R incorporated by regents
  L   "   " legislature
  G   "   under general law

University, June 30, 1895 (concluded)

Admitted	YEAR ENDING JUNE 30, 1895— VOLUMES			No.	TRUSTEES Elected by	No.
	Added	Total	Circulation			
12 D 94	392	1126	1050	9	Corporation	65
26 Je 95	....	850	....	6	Corporation	66
13 D 93	515	4418	8835	7	According to Sherman deed of trust	67
29 S 92	778	6124	13,578	5	School district	68
5 Je 94	436	?1425	4325	8	Bd of education	69
28 F 95	4125	9815	....	9	Corporation	70
5 Je 94	429	1492	6009	8	Bd of education	71
12 D 94	....	?3000	....	7	5 by corporation, mayor and sup't of schools ex officio	72
12 D 94	....	770	....	3	Bd of education	73
12 D 94	529	599	1316	5	Sea Cliff improvement ass'n	74
26 Je 95	150	1137	4147	5	Bd of education	75
12 D 94	100	1450	2006	6	Corporation	76
9 F 93	254	3537	13,716	3	School district	77
26 Je 95	....	....	....	3	Springfield library ass'n	78
13 D 93	288	?1634	6890	3	Bd of education	79
13 D 93	1993	26,300	44,585	7	5 by mayor, mayor and sup't of schools ex officio	80
12 D 93	178	1350	1567	3	Bd of education	81
12 D 94	?247	571	8370	5	Corporation	82
12 D 94	....	....	....	5	Corporation	83
21 Je 93	39	?804	2340	6	Bd. of education	84
21 Je 93	3598	17,986	82,421	7	5 by corporation, mayor and chm school com ex officio	85
28 F 95	187	1366	1672	3	Bd of education	86
28 F 95	6	1158	?1350	8	Bd of education	87
5 Je 94	341	1425	?3357	7	Village trustees	88
12 D 94	307	1412	3690	5	Bd of education	89
21 Je 93	22	217	197	3	School district	90
21 Je 96	23	1426	5590	6	Corporation	91
5 Je 94	382	2381	5497	7	Corporation	92
9 F 93	239	10,408	31,199	5	Bd. of education	93
Total ...	33,598	267,576	670,580			

libraries belonging to teaching institutions
p Provisional charter

INDEX

The superior figure tells the exact place on the page in ninths; e. g. 282² means two ninths of the way down page 282. Dates are printed in italics.

A. M. Chesbrough seminary library, statistics, 282³-85.
Abbreviations, library reports, 236²-37.
Academy of Mt St Vincent library, statistics, 270⁹-73.
Academy of Sacred Heart library, Syracuse, statistics, 294⁵-97.
Adelphi academy library, statistics, 246²-49.
Admissions, libraries and institutes, 177¹, 180², 185⁷.
Agriculture, traveling library, on 200².
Aguilar free library, statistics, 274²-77.
American Bible society library, statistics, 274³-77.
American geographical society library, statistics, 274²-77.
American institute library statistics, 274³-77.
American institute of mining engineers library, statistics, 274³-77.
American library association, conference, 215²-16.
American museum of natural history library, statistics, 274³-77.
American seamen's friend society, libraries loaned by, 234⁸; statistics of library, 274³-77.
Applications for traveling libraries, blanks, 189⁹-93⁶.
Apportionment of public library money, 185⁸-88⁶.
Aschenbroedel verein library, statistics, 274³-77.
Astor library, 225⁴, 235²; statistics, 274⁴-77.

Astral branch library, Brooklyn, statistics, 246⁴-49.

Barneveld library association, statistics, 294⁷-97.
Batavia state school for the blind library, statistics, 242⁵-45.
Bay Ridge public library, fund for new building, 231¹; gift to, 232⁹; statistics, 242⁸-45.
Beach, B. J., gift to Jervis library, 234².
Bedford circulating library, statistics, 246²-49.
Berkeley institute library, statistics, 246²-49.
Best books for farmers, circular, 200⁴.
Best books of *1894*, 214¹-15³.
Beta Theta Pi fraternity library, statistics, 262³-65.
Bethel sabbath school library, Brooklyn, statistics, 246²-49.
Blanks, *see* Forms.
Books, injuries to, 196⁴; losses from traveling libraries, 197⁷-98³; list of best books of *1894*, 214¹-15³. *See also* Traveling libraries; Volumes.
Borrower's agreement for traveling library, form, 193¹.
Brooklyn institute library, temporary location, 231²; statistics, 246²-49.
Brooklyn library, improvements, 231³; statistics, 246²-49.
Bryant circulating library, gifts to, 234³; statistics, 290⁴-93.
Buildings, libraries, 230⁹-32⁹.

REPORT OF PUBLIC LIBRARIES DIVISION, 1895 327

Business corporations, loan of traveling libraries to, 190[3]; application blank, 193[1].

Camden library, new rooms, 231[5]; statistics, 250[2]-53.
Canisius college library, statistics, 246[7]-49.
Capitol library, volumes bought for, 197[7]; report, 206[1]-7[3].
Carleton, Mrs Harriet, gift to Ilion free public library, 233[4].
Cary collegiate seminary library, statistics, 282[5]-85.
Cascadilla school library, statistics, 266[2]-69.
Cathedral academy library, Albany, statistics, 238[4]-41.
Cathedral library, New York, gifts to, 233[3]; statistics, 274[4]-77.
Catholic academy library, Utica, statistics, 298[2]-301.
Catholic male orphan asylum library, Troy, statistics, 294[7]-97.
Catholic union library, Albany, statistics, 238[4]-41.
Cayuga asylum library, statistics, 242[2]-45.
Cayuga Lake military academy, library, statistics, 242[3]-45.
Chamberlain institute library, improvements, 232[6]; statistics, 286[2]-89.
Chapel library, Crown Point, statistics, 254[4]-57.
Charters granted, libraries, 176[1], 185[7]; source, 220[4].
Christian biblical institute library, statistics, 294[5]-97.
Christian brothers academy library, Albany, statistics, 238[4]-41
Christian union society library, statistics, 242[6]-45.
Circular, on proper standard for public libraries, 184[2]-85[2]; on best books for farmers, 200[4].
Circulation, 180[4]-82[8], 221[7], 222[3]-24[2], 226[5]-28[1], 307-9, 312-17.

Classical union school library, Palmyra, statistics, 282[9]-85.
Clinton liberal institute library, statistics, 258[5]-61.
Clubs, loan of traveling libraries to, 190[2], 207[4]-10[1]; application blank, 192[3].
Colgate academy library, statistics, 262[4]-65.
Colgate university library, statistics, 262[4]-65.
College libraries, 229[4]; arranged by size, 320.
College of pharmacy of the city of New York library, statistics, 274[5]-77.
College of St Francis Xavier library, statistics, 274[6]-77.
College of the city of New York, reorganization of library, 234[5]; statistics, 274[5]-77.
College of veterinary surgeons library, statistics, 274[6]-77.
College settlement library, New York, statistics, 274[6]-77.
Columbia college library, statistics, 274[6]-77.
Conrad Poppenhusen association library, statistics, 254[3]-57.
Cook academy library, statistics, 262[5]-65.
Coonly, Mrs J. C., gifts to Wyoming free library, 234[5].
Cooper union library, statistics, 274[6]-77.
Cornell library association, statistics, 266[3]-69.
Cornell university library, gifts to, 233[4]; statistics, 266[3]-69.
Cortland state normal school library, statistics, 254[4]-57.
County distribution of libraries, 221[8]-42[2], 306-9
Crandall free library, statistics, 258[8]-61.
Darwin, R. Barker library association, statistics, 258[6]-61.
Davenport library, statistics, 242[5]-45.

De Lancey school library, statistics, 258⁷-61.
Delaware academy library, statistics, 254⁵-57.
Delaware literary institute library, improvements, 232⁶; statistics, 258⁶-61.
Demarest, Mrs Agnes, gift to Hobart college, 230⁹-31¹.
Des Moines, H. Parmelee library company, traveling libraries, 189⁴.
De Veaux school library, statistics, 282³-85.
DeWitt memorial free library, statistics, 274⁷-77.
D'Youville academy library, statistics, 286⁵-89.
Diocesan lending library, Albany, statistics, 238⁴-41.
Drum Hill union school library, statistics, 286³-89.
Dudley observatory library, statistics, 238⁴-41.

East Aurora union school library, improvements, 232⁶; statistics, 254⁷-57.
Eastman, W; R. libraries inspected by, 171⁵-74⁶.
Eclectic medical college library, statistics, 274⁷-77.
Economics, traveling library on, 198⁷.
Egberts high school library, statistics, 250⁹-53.
Equitable life assurance society law library, statistics, 274-77.
Erie railway association library, Buffalo, statistics, 246⁷-49.
Erwin library and institute, statistics, 242⁶-45.
Evans academy library, statistics, 286⁴-89.
Extension library, form for application, 192³; number of volumes, 197⁷; growth, 207⁴; statistics, 208-10.

Farmers, books for, 200².
Female academy of the Sacred Heart library, Kenwood, statistics, 266⁵-69.

Female institute of the Visitation library, Brooklyn, statistics, 246³-49.
Field library, statistics, 286³-89.
Fiske, Willard, gift to Cornell university library, 233⁴.
Forman library, statistics, 282⁶-85.
Forms, for inspectors memoranda, 174⁷-75⁹; certificate of registry, 183⁵; of applications for traveling libraries, 190⁶-93⁶; for receipt of traveling library, 193⁸.
Fort Hamilton free library new building, 231⁵; statistics, 258⁵-61.
Franklin academy library, statistics, 286³-89.
Franklin Hatch library association, statistics, 254⁴-57.
Fraser free school library, statistics, 262⁵-65.
Fredonia state normal school library statistics, 258⁶-61.
Free libraries, circulating, 226-28¹; apportionment, 185⁸-88⁶; arranged by counties, 306-9; arranged by size, 312-17;
 reference, 228⁴; apportionment, 186³; arranged by size, 318-19.
Friendship union school library, improvements, 232⁶; statistics, 258⁶-61.

Genealogical and biographical society library, statistics, 274-77.
General theological seminary library, statistics, 274⁷-77.
Genesee Valley seminary library, statistics, 242⁶-45
Genesee Wesleyan seminary library, statistics, 266⁷-69.
German Martin Luther theological seminary library, statistics, 246⁷-49.
Gifts to libraries, 232⁹-34⁵.
Gouverneur high school library, improvements, 232⁷; statistics, 258⁹-61.
Gouverneur reading room association, gifts to, 231⁶; statistics, 262²-65.
Green Wood public library, statistics, 298³-301.

Griffith institute and union school library, statistics, 294⁴-97.
Grinnell library, building improvements, 232⁵; statistics, 298⁴-301.
Grosvenor public library, not circulating, 230⁴; new building, 231⁴; statistics, 246⁷-49.

H. Parmelee library company, Des Moines traveling libraries, 1894.
Haldane union school library, statistics, 254²-57.
Hamilton college library, statistics, 250⁸-53.
Hampton library, statistics, 242⁹-45.
Harlem library, statistics, 274⁸-77.
Harmon library, statistics, 254⁸-57.
Haverling union school library, statistics, 242⁸-45.
Herring library, statistics, 250²-53.
Hobart college library, building, 230⁹; gifts, 231¹; statistics, 258⁷-61.
Hobart union school library, improvements, 232⁶; statistics, 262⁶-65.
Holy Angels' academy library, Buffalo, statistics, 246²-49.
Houghton seminary library, statistics, 250⁸-53.
Howland circulating library, statistics, 270⁴-73.
Hudson river state hospital library, statistics, 286⁷-89.

Ilion district library, gifts to, 233²; statistics, 262⁹-65.
Ilion free public library, gifts to, 233²; statistics, 262⁹-65.
Incorporations, see Charters.
Inspection of libraries, 171⁵-74⁶.
Inspectors' memoranda, form for, 174⁷-75⁹.
Institute of the sisters of St Joseph library, statistics, 246²-49.
Institutes, admissions, 177³, 180².
Ives seminary library, statistics, 238²-41.

James Prendergast free library, statistics, 266²-69.

Jamestown high school library cataloguing, 234⁵; statistics, 266²-69.
Jamestown Y. M. C. A. library, reorganization, 234⁵; statistics, 266⁴-69.
Jervis, J. B. gifts to Jervis library, 234².
Jervis library, quarters, 232²; gifts to, 234²; statistics, 290²-93.

Keene Heights library club, statistics, 242⁶-45.

Lady Jane Grey school library, statistics, 242⁷-45.
La Salle academy library, statistics, 274⁸-77.
La Salle institute library, statistics, 294⁸-97.
Law libraries, 229⁷; arranged by size, 321.
Legislation, libraries, 210³, 211⁵-13².
Lenox library, 225⁴, 235²; statistics, 274⁹-77.
Librarian's agreement for traveling library, form, 191¹.
Libraries, founding and control, 178⁷-79⁶, 220⁴; date of founding, 217⁶, 220¹; geographic distribution, 221⁸-24², 306-9; growth, 180⁴-82⁸, 220⁶-21⁸; summary of reports, 236-325; proper standard for, 183⁹-85²; having 10,000 volumes or more, 225¹,310-11; in the University, 230; number under state control, 185⁷; alphabetic list, 322-25. See also Capitol library; College libraries; Free libraries; Law libraries; Reference libraries; School district libraries; Tables; Traveling libraries.
Library associations, influence in founding libraries, 178⁸; meetings, 213², 215³-16.
Library council of the University, 210⁹-11⁵.
Library training school, Pratt institute, 234⁹.

Literarische gesellschaft of Morrisania library, statistics, 274⁹-77.
Literary union library, Carmel, statistics, 250⁴-53.
Loan libraries, American seamen's friend society, 234⁸.
Lockport public library, additions to, 233⁶; statistics, 266⁸-69.
Long Island free library, branch of Pratt institute library, 235¹; statistics, 246⁴-49.
Long Island historical society library, statistics, 246⁴-49.
Lowville academy library, statistics, 266⁹-69.
Lyndonville union school library, improvements, 232⁶; statistics, 266⁹-69.

M. M. Buck free library, statistics, 290⁹-93.
McAuley academy, room for library, 232⁶; statistics of library, 266⁵-69.
McMahon, J. H., gift to Cathedral library, N. Y., 233⁸.
Madison county law library, statistics, 270⁷-73.
Maimonides free library, statistics, 274⁹-77.
Manhattan college library, statistics, 274⁹-77.
Marshall infirmary library, statistics, 294⁸-97.
Mechanical engineers library, statistics, 274⁹-77.
Mercantile library, statistics, 278²-81.
Michigan, adopts traveling library system, 188⁹ 89⁴; library legislation, 212⁶.
Middleburg academy and union school library, statistics, 302⁴-5.
Middletown state homeopathic hospital library, statistics, 270⁶-73.
Military service library, statistics, 278³-81.
Mrs Piatt's school library, 298³-301.
Montana, traveling libraries, 212⁶; library legislation, 212⁶.

Morgan circulating library, statistics, 262⁶-65.
Morris, Mrs Dr Robert, gift to Ogdensburg public library, 234¹.
Mott memorial medical and surgical library, statistics, 278²-81.
Mt Pleasant academy library, statistics, 294²-97.
Mt St Mary's academy library, statistics, 278⁹-81.
Mountainside free library, statistics, 266⁴-69.
Munro collegiate institute library, statistics, 254⁸-57.
Mynderse academy library, statistics, 290⁸-93.

Nassau free library, gift to, 233⁷; statistics, 270⁸-73.
Nazareth academy library, statistics, 286²-89.
New Hampshire, library legislation, 213¹.
New Paltz state normal school library, statistics, 270⁹-73.
New Utrecht public library, statistics, 242⁵-45.
New York Y. M. C. A. library, new branch, 231⁷.
New York library association, meetings, 213².
New York library club, meetings, 213³, 215³.
New York military academy library, statistics, 254³-57.
New York public library, 225⁵, 235².
New York state library, statistics, 238⁵-41.
New York state normal college library, statistics, 238⁵-41.
New York state reformatory library, statistics, 254⁹-57.
Newfield public library, building, 231⁸; statistics, 282³-85.
Niagara university library statistics, 246³-49.
North Greenbush public library, district no. 6, statistics, 242⁵-45.

Oakwood seminary library, statistics, 294²-97.
Ogden memorial library, name changed to William B. Ogden free library, 178⁶.
Ogdensburg public library, new building, 231⁸, gifts to, 234¹; statistics, 282⁶-85.
Olivet library, statistics, 278⁵-81.
Oneida historical society library, new building, 234⁴; statistics, 298³-301.
Onondaga academy library, rearrangement, 234⁶; statistics, 282⁷-85.
Organizations, libraries, 176¹, 220⁴.
Oswego state normal school library, statistics, 282⁸-85.
Oyster Bay people's library, gift to, 234², statistics, 282⁹-85.

Packer collegiate institute library, statistics, 246⁴-49.
Parker union school library, statistics, 250⁷-53.
Parmelee library company, 189⁵.
Peck memorial library, statistics, 278⁵-81.
Pennsylvania library legislation, 212⁸.
People's library, Oyster Bay, gift to, 234²; statistics, 282⁹-85.
Plattsburg state normal school library, statistics, 286⁵-89
Polytechnic institute, Brooklyn, Spicer library, statistics, 246⁴-49.
Port Richmond union school library, rearrangement, 234⁶; statistics, 286⁷-89.
Potsdam state normal school library, statistics, 286⁷-89.
Powers library, statistics, 270⁷-73
Pratt institute free library, new building, 231⁴; training school, 234⁹; statistics, 246⁴-49.
Presbyterian board of foreign missions library, statistics, 278⁵-81.
Prison association library, statistics, 278⁶-81.
Property; of admitted institutions, 180⁴; of registered libraries, 185⁴.

Public libraries division, summary statement, *1894-95*, 188³.
Public library money, appertionment, 185⁹-88³.

Record society of Lancashire and Cheshire, gifts to Cornell university library, 233⁶.
Reference libraries, 228²-29³; apportionments, 186²; arranged by size, 318-19.
Registrations, libraries, 177⁴, 176³; conditions, 182⁹-85⁶.
Reid, Capt. A. V., gift to Lockport public library, 233⁶.
Rensselaer polytechnic institute library, statistics, 294⁸-97.
Reports of libraries, summaries, 236-325
Reynolds library, new quarters, 232¹; statistics, 290²-93.
Richmond library, statistics, 242⁵-45.
Riverside free library, statistics, 278⁶-81.
Russell, G. C., gift to Ilion free public library, 233³.

S. S. Seward institute library, statistics, 258³-61.
Sacred Heart academy library, Westchester, statistics, 298⁸-301.
Sailors, libraries for, 234⁸.
Sailors snug harbor library, statistics, 270⁹-73.
St Agnes free library, New York, statistics, 278⁶-81.
St Agnes school library, statistics, 238⁵-41.
St Ann's academic school library, statistics, 262⁷-65.
St Barnabas free reading room, statistics, 278⁶-81.
St Bernard's academy library, statistics, 254²-57.
St Bonaventure's college library statistics, 238⁷-41.
St Elisabeth's library, statistics, 238⁷-41.

St Faith's school library, statistics, 290⁶-93.
St Francis college library, statistics, 246⁴-49.
St George's free circulating library, statistics, 278⁷-81.
St Joachim's academic institute library, statistics, 298⁶-301.
St John's catholic academy library, statistics, 294⁶-97.
St John's college library, Brooklyn, statistics, 246⁵-49.
St John's college library, New York, statistics, 278⁷-81.
St John's home library, statistics, 246⁵-49.
St John's military school library, statistics, 270³-73.
St Joseph's academy library, Albany, statistics, 238⁵-41.
St Joseph's academy library, Binghamton, statistics, 242⁷-45.
St Joseph's academy library, Brasher Falls, room, 232⁷; statistics, 242⁸-45.
St Joseph's academy library, Flushing, statistics, 258⁴-61.
St Joseph's academy and industrial female school library, Lockport, statistics, 266⁹-69.
St Lawrence university, Herring library, statistics, 250²-53.
St Margaret's school library, improvements, 232⁶; statistics, 246⁸-49.
St Mark's parish house library, statistics, 266²-69.
St Mary's academic school library, Dunkirk, statistics, 254⁶-57.
St Mary's academy library, Ogdensburg, statistics, 282⁶-85.
St Mary's catholic institute library, Amsterdam, statistics, 238⁸-41.
St Patrick's academy library statistics, 250⁵-53.
St Paul's school library, statistics, 258⁷-61.
St Peter's academy library, Troy, statistics, 294⁸-97.

St Stephen's college library, new building, 230⁹; statistics, 238³-41
St Vincent's male orphan asylum.
Sacred Heart library, Albany, statistics, 238⁵-41.
Saratoga county law library, statistics, 242⁴-45.
Saugerties public library, new quarters, 232³; circulation, 232³; statistics, 290⁶-93
School authorities, influence in founding libraries, 178⁶.
School district libraries, transfers, 176².
Seamens, C W., gift to Ilion free public library, 233³.
Seymour library, statistics, 242²-45.
Seymour Smith academy library, statistics, 286⁵-89.
Sherman Jewett Williams memorial library, 233¹; statistics, 246²-49.
Siam, king of, gift to Cornell university library, 233⁵.
Smith, James, gift to Gouverneur reading room association, 231⁶.
Southworth library, statistics, 254⁵-57.
Stanton, Theodore, gift to Cornell university library, 233⁵.
Starkey seminary library, statistics, 254⁸-57.
Starr institute library, statistics, 286⁶-89.
Staten Island academy library, statistics, 294⁵-97
Statistics of New York libraries, *1895*, 217-325. *See also* Tables.
Stevens memorial library, statistics, 238⁹-41.
Study clubs, loan of traveling libraries to, 190⁹, 207⁴-9⁹; application blank, 192³.
Subsidies to libraries, 182⁹-83⁹, 210⁸, 211⁷.
Summer hotels, loan of traveling libraries to, 190⁸, 210²; application blank, 193¹.
Supreme court library, Binghamton, statistics, 242⁷-45.

Syracuse central library, new quarters, 232[2]; statistics, 294[5]-97.
Syracuse state institution for feeble-minded children library, statistics, 294[6]-97.

Tables, charters admissions and registrations, *1895*, 176-77; chartered libraries, founding and control of, *1891-95*, 179[1]; college libraries, 229[4], 320; free libraries, 226[4], 312-17; circulation in free libraries, 224[3], 226[4]; geographic distribution of libraries, 222[3], 223[3],306-9; growth of libraries, *1894-95*, 181-82; law libraries, 321; libraries in the University, 322-25; libraries of 10,000 volumes or more, 224[9], 225[7], 310-11; reference libraries, 228[2], 318-19; summaries of library statistics, 217[6]-19, 224[5]; summary of public libraries division, *1891-95*, 188[3]; transfers, *1895*, 178[1]; traveling libraries, 201-5; use of extension books, 208-10.

Taxpayer's application for traveling library, form, 191[3].
Teachers college, Bryson library statistics, 278[7]-81.
Temple Grove seminary library, statistics, 290[6]-93.
Ten Broeck free academy library, statistics, 258[6]-61.
Tivoli public library, statistics, 270[2]-73.
Transfers, libraries, 178[1].
Traveling libraries, application blanks, 189[9]-93[6]; eligible borrowers, 189[9]-90[4]; circulation, 200[1], 201-5; rules for circulation, 195[7]-96[3]; directions for care of, 194[2]-95[7]; extension books, 197, 207[4]; statistics of extension books, 208-10; H. Parmelee co., 189[5]; lost books, 197[7]-98[3]; Michigan, 188[2]-89[4], 212[5]; Montana, 212[8]; number of readers, 200[1]; receipt postal card, form, 193[6]; report, 188[7]-210[2]; sales, 197[7], 199[1]; statistics of use, 199[7]-200[2], 201-5; subject libraries, 197[5],

198[7], 200[2], 204[7], 205[6]; number of volumes, 196[9]-97[8], 198[4]; young peoples libraries, 198[5]. *See also* American seamen's friend society.
Trow directory library, statistics, 278[7]-81.
Trustees, 178[7], 179[4]-80[2]; application for traveling library, form, 190[6]; agreement for traveling library, form, 191[9]-92[3].

Ulster academy library, statistics, 290[3]-93.
Union classical institute library, statistics, 290[7]-93
Union college library, statistics, 290[7]-93.
Union for Christian work free library, statistics, 246[5]-49.
Union theological seminary library, statistics, 278[7]-81
United States military academy library, statistics, 298[7]-301.
University club library, statistics, 278[8]-81.
University of Buffalo library, statistics, 246[9]-49.
University of Rochester library, statistics, 290[2]-93.
University of the city of New York library, statistics, 278[7]-81.
University settlement library, statistics, 278[8]-81.
Utica public library, gift to Ilion free public library, 233[4].

Vanderbilt, Cornelius, gift to Y. M. C. A., New York, 231[7].
Vanderbilt, W. H., gift to Y. M. C A., New York, 231[7].
Vassar college library, statistics, 286[8]-89.
Vermont, library legislation, 212[7].
Volumes, number in public libraries division, 196[9]-97[8], 198[4]; number in libraries of state, 221[6].

Wagner memorial Lutheran college library, statistics, 290²-93.
Wallkill free academy library, statistics, 270⁶-73.
Washington academy library, statistics, 290⁵-93.
Washington Heights free library, gifts to, 231⁷, 233⁹; statistics, 278⁸-81.
Watervliet arsenal post library, statistics, 298⁸-301.
Webster free circulating library, statistics, 278⁸-81.
Wells college library, statistics, 242³-45.
Wellsville public library, new rooms, 231⁵; gift to, 234⁴; statistics, 298⁷-301.
White, A. D., gift to Cornell university library, 233⁴
William B. Ogden free library, Ogden memorial library, becomes, 178⁶.
Williams, Mrs H.. M., gift to Oneida historical society, 232⁴.
Williams, S. J., memorial gift to Buffalo high school, 233¹.
Wilson academy library, statistics, 238⁸-41.
Wilson union school library, improvements, 232⁶; statistics, 302³-5.
Wisconsin, library legislation, 21.7.

Woman's institute library Yonkers, admitted, 180²; rearrangement, 234⁷; branch library, 235²; statistics, 302⁴-5.
Woman's library, New York, statistics, 278⁸-81.
Woman's library association, Canton, statistics, 250⁴-53.
Women's educational and industrial union library, Buffalo, statistics, 246⁹-49.
Women's medical college of N. Y. infirmary library statistics, 278⁸-81.
Wood library, statistics, 250⁸-53.
Worrall Hall library, statistics, 286⁹-89.
Wright, J. H. gift to Washington Heights free library, 231⁶, 233⁹.
Wyoming free library, gifts to, 234⁴; statistics, 302⁴-5.

Yates union school library, statistics, 250⁷-53.
Yonkers public library, support, 235⁴; hours of opening, 235⁴; statistics, 302⁴-5.
Young men's association library, Albany, statistics, 238⁵-41.
Y. M. C. A. libraries, *see name of place*.
Young peoples libraries, 198⁵.
Young women's association, Troy, 180².

University of the State of New York

Object. The object of the University as defined by law is to encourage and promote education in advance of the common elementary branches. Its field includes not only the work of academies, colleges, universities, professional and technical schools, but also educational work connected with libraries, museums, university extension courses and similar agencies.

The University is a supervisory and administrative, not a teaching institution. It is a state department and at the same time a federation of 668 institutions of higher and secondary education.

Government. The University is governed and all its corporate powers exercised by 19 elective regents and by the governor, lieutenant-governor, secretary of state and superintendent of public instruction who are *ex officio* regents. Regents are elected in the same manner as United States senators; they are unsalaried and are the only public officers in New York chosen for life.

The elective officers are a chancellor and a vice-chancellor, who serve without salary, and a secretary. The secretary is the executive and financial officer, is under official bonds for $10,000, is responsible for the safe keeping and proper use of the University seal and of the books, records and other property in charge of the regents, and for the proper administration and discipline of its various offices and departments.

Powers and duties. Besides many other important powers and duties, the regents have power to incorporate, and to alter or revoke the charters of universities, colleges, academies, libraries, museums, or other educational institutions, to distribute to them funds granted by the state for their use; to inspect their workings and require annual reports under oath of their presiding officers; to establish examinations as to attainments in learning and confer on successful candidates suitable certificates, diplomas and degrees, and to confer honorary degrees.

They apportion annually an academic fund of $106,000, part for buying books and apparatus for academies and high schools raising an equal amount for the same purpose, and the remainder on the basis of attendance and the results of instruction as shown by satisfactory completion of prescribed courses for which the regents examinations afford the official test. Each school of academic grade also receives $100 yearly. The regents also expend annually $25,000 for the benefit of free public libraries.

Regents meetings. Regular meetings are held on the third Thursdays of October, December and March, and in June during convocation week. The executive committee, consisting of the chancellor, vice-chancellor and the chairmen of the six standing committees, meets the third Thursday of each month from October to June.

Convocation. The University convocation of the regents and the officers of institutions in the University, for consideration of subjects of mutual interest, has been held annually since 1863 in the senate chamber in Albany. It meets the last Wednesday, Thursday and Friday of June. Though primarily a New York meeting, nearly all questions discussed are of equal interest outside the state. Its reputation as the most important higher educational meeting of the country has in the past few years drawn to it many eminent educators not residents of New York, who are most cordially welcomed and share fully in all discussions. It elects each year a council of five to represent it in intervals between meetings. Its proceedings, issued annually, are of great value in all educational libraries.

Departments

1 Administrative (Regents office) — including incorporation, supervision, inspection, reports, legislation, finances and all other work not assigned to another department.

Duplicate division. This is a state clearing house, to which any institution in the University may send books or apparatus which it no longer requires, and select from it in return an equal value suited to its locality and needs.

2 Examination—including preacademic, law, medical, dental and veterinary student, academic, higher, law, medical, dental, veterinary, library, extension and any other examinations conducted by the regents, and also credentials or degrees conferred on examination.

The examinations are conducted as the best lever for securing better work from teachers and more systematic and continuous study from students, and as the best means of detecting and eliminating inefficient teachers or methods. They cover 140 subjects and required last year 913,500 question papers (exclusive of bound volumes), and are held the week ending the last Friday in January and March and the third Friday in June, in the 564 academies and high schools in the University and also at various central points where there are 10 or more candidates.

3 Extension—including summer, vacation, evening and correspondence schools and other forms of extension teaching, lecture courses, study clubs, reading circles and other agencies for the promotion and wider extension of opportunities and facilities for education, specially for those unable to attend the usual teaching institutions.

Public libraries division. To promote the general library interests of the state, which through it apportions and expends $25,000 a year for the benefit of free public libraries. Under its charge are the traveling libraries for lending to local libraries or to communities not yet having permanent libraries.

The most important factor of the extension movement is provision of the best reading for all citizens by means of traveling, home and capitol libraries and annotated lists through the public libraries division

4 State library—including general, law, medical, and education libraries, library school, bibliographic publications, lending books to students and similar library interests.

Library school. The law authorizes the state library to give instruction and assistance in organizing and administering libraries Students receive from the state library staff, in return for services rendered to the library during their two years' course, careful training in library economy, bibliography, cataloguing, classification and other duties of professional librarianship.

5 State museum—including all scientific specimens and collections, works of art, objects of historic interest and similar property appropriate to a general museum, if owned by the state and not placed in other custody by a specific law; also the research department carried on by the state geologist and paleontologist, botanist and entomologist, and all similar scientific interests of the University.

University of the State of New York

Extension Bulletin

No. 17 March 1897

REPORT OF EXTENSION TEACHING DIVISION, 1895

	PAGE		PAGE
Statistics of regents centers, 1895	340	Progress outside of New York (con'd)	
Comparative statistics, 1891-95	346	North Dakota	364
Sunday Bible classes	346	California	365
Extension teachers	346	Scotland	365
Lecturers added	346	Cambridge, England	366
New courses offered	358	London	367
Names withdrawn	359	Oxford	368
Free lectures to the people, New York city	359	Austria	369
		France	370
Progress outside New York	360	Norway	370
Maine	360	Sweden	371
Massachusetts	360	Denmark	371
Connecticut	360	Belgium	371
Philadelphia	361	Australia	372
New Jersey	361	Institutes in New York	372
Washington, D. C.	361	Brooklyn institute of arts and sciences	372
Florida	362	Young woman's association, Troy	373
Cincinnati	362	Yonkers woman's institute	374
Chicago	362	Institutes outside New York	377
Michigan	363	American institute of civics, Washington, D. C.	377
Wisconsin	363		
Minnesota	364	Wells memorial institute, Boston	377
Iowa	364		
Missouri	364	Index	379

Regents

ANSON JUDD UPSON, D. D., LL. D., L. H. D., *Chancellor*
WILLIAM CROSWELL DOANE, D. D., LL. D., *Vice-Chancellor*
FRANK S. BLACK, B. A., Governor
TIMOTHY L. WOODRUFF, M. A., Lieutenant-Governor
JOHN PALMER, Secretary of State } *Ex officio*
CHARLES R. SKINNER, M. A., LL. D., Sup't of Pub. Inst.

In order of election by the legislature

YEAR
1873 MARTIN I. TOWNSEND, M. A., LL. D. - - Troy
1874 ANSON JUDD UPSON, D. D., LL. D., L. H. D. – Glens Falls
1877 CHAUNCEY M. DEPEW, LL. D. - - - – New York
1877 CHARLES E. FITCH, LL. B., M. A., L. H. D. – Rochester
1877 ORRIS H. WARREN, D. D. - - - – Syracuse
1878 WHITELAW REID, LL. D. - - - - New York
1881 WILLIAM H. WATSON, M. A., M. D. - - – Utica
1881 HENRY E. TURNER - - - - Lowville
1883 ST CLAIR MCKELWAY, LL. D. - - - – Brooklyn
1885 HAMILTON HARRIS, Ph. D., LL. D. - - - Albany
1885 DANIEL BEACH, Ph. D., LL. D. - - - – Watkins
1888 CARROLL E. SMITH, LL. D. - - - Syracuse
1890 PLINY T. SEXTON, LL. D. - - - – Palmyra
1890 T. GUILFORD SMITH, M. A., C. E. - - Buffalo
1892 WILLIAM CROSWELL DOANE, D. D., LL. D. - – Albany
1893 LEWIS A. STIMSON, B. A., M. D. - - - New York
1894 SYLVESTER MALONE - - - - – Brooklyn
1895 ALBERT VANDER VEER, M. D., Ph. D. - - Albany
1897 CHESTER S. LORD, M. A. - - - - – Brooklyn

Elected by the regents

1888 MELVIL DEWEY, M. A., *Secretary* - - - – Albany

University of the State of New York

Extension Bulletin
No. 17   March 1897

REPORT OF EXTENSION TEACHING DIVISION, 1895

To the regents of the University of the State of New York

I have the honor to report as follows for the year ending September 30, 1895:

During the year, the following seven centers have been formed: Lowville, Buffalo Y. M. C. A., Fairport, Geneva, Saratoga Springs, Sing Sing and Clyde. The Salem center planned a course in electricity, to be given by Calvin W. Rice, of the General electric company at Schenectady, but owing to Mr Rice's illness arrangements could not be completed and it was then too late to make other plans. A course in American literature by Prof. James R. Truax of Union university has been arranged for next year. Silver Lake assembly had several courses of lectures in connection with its summer school, but did not register a full extension course of 10 lectures

In almost all cases in which extension work has been abandoned, one of the main causes has been loose local organization. Often in spite of a strong desire on the part of many citizens to continue extension courses, they are given up because circumstances compel those who have taken the lead in managing the center to abate their efforts, and there are no others whose relation to the work thus far conducted induces them to take the responsibility of carrying it forward. Some centers whose outlook at the beginning was most promising have thus lapsed through the mistaken efforts of friends whose strong interest prompted them to assume so much of the responsibility and care, that no others were in training to take up their work when needed.

A summary of the reports received for 1895 follows:

Statistics of regents centers 1895

Centers	Subject	Lecturer	No. of lectures	Avg Att: Lectures	Avg Att: Class	Students' club	Total no. of papers written	Examined	Passed	Passed with honor
Albany	Political methods	J. W Jenks	10	255	224	..	37	7	7	5
Buffalo	Electric engineering	A. L Arey	10	275	..	..	..	..	..	..
Buffalo (Y M C A)	Money, banking and the silver question	G: M. Forbes	10	212	182	..	153	15	12	8
Clyde	Early Christian church	J. J. Thom	10	22	17	..	..	..	..	..
Dobbs Ferry	Civil and religious liberty in America	C E. Fitch	10	73	..	..	..	..	..	..
Fairport	Labor and capital	H E Webster	10	128	79	..	..	..	..	..
Geneva	English literature	M. H. Turk	10	74	..	..	..	..	..	..
Gloversville	Economics / Modern authors	A L Peck	..	..	..	{6/9}	6/9	..	..	..
Lockport	Development of the nation	W H Mace	10	170	86	7	104	2	2	1
Lowville	Civil and religious liberty in America	C L. Fitch	10	117	19	..	18	..	..	..
Mt Vernon	Astronomy	J. K. Rees	10	97	..	..	..	..	..	..
	French literature	Adolphe Cohn	10	89	..	..	..	..	..	..
New York (American Institute)	Electricity	Specialists	11	64	25	..	242	17	17	10
Oneida	Early American history	G: W: Smith	10	209	..	..	..	..	..	..
	American colonial history	G W. Smith	8	105	97	..	..	..	..	..
Rochester	Money, banking and the silver question	G: M. Forbes	10	292	247	..	28	1	1	1
	American literature	J. H. Gilmore	10	260	187	..	88	9	8	4
	Art of photography	Charles Forbes	10	94	75	..	..	..	..	..
	Civil war	W. H. Mace	10	187	148	..	177	12	12	9
	Life in old Florence	Mrs H. B. Montgomery	10	205	152	..	94	6	6	4
	Labor and capital	H. E. Webster	10	57	57	..	..	..	..	..
Rome	American history	W K Wickes	5	121	..	..	..	..	..	..
	American literature	J H Gilmore	5	163	68	..	..	..	..	..
Saratoga	English literature	J. R. Truax	10	148	78	..	52	15	9	2
Syracuse	Romeo and Juliet and the Tempest	Mrs J K Curtis	10	..	..	..	..	8	8	8
Tarrytown	French history	Adolphe Cohn	10	144	43	..	16	2	2	2
Utica	English novel	W: H Crawshaw	10	110	45	..	..	..	..	..
Waverly	European statesmen	C E Fitch	5	129	42	..	23	..	..	..
Yonkers	Geology	W B Scott	10	142	25	..	..	6	5	3
	Architecture	A D F Hamlin	5	67	..	..	..	..	..	..

Of the 29 courses given during the year seven were on literature, seven on American history, six on economics, three on science and one each on architecture, photography, the Early Christian church, European statesmen, Life in old Florence and French history.

Albany again secured Prof. J. W. Jenks of Cornell and showed its appreciation by large attendance at classes both before and after the lecture. The discussions had an added interest because of the part taken by some of the state and city officials. Prof. Jenks' great tact in bringing his audience into sympathy with him was noticeable both at the class and aftermeeting. Those who had no intention of saying anything on entering the classroom found themselves taking an active part in discussions under the genial influence of the leader's appreciative attention. At the aftermeeting similar skill was shown in treating questions or remarks apparently of little general interest, some of the most unpromising statements often leading to discussion in which all students present were keenly interested.

In December a committee was appointed to increase the center's usefulness. This committee will first attempt to develop interest in establishing a free public library for Albany.

Prof. G: M. Forbes of Rochester university reported specially satisfactory paper work in his course on money at the Y. M. C. A. center at Buffalo. 30 members of the class were enrolled for paper work; the quality of the papers was unusually good and in some cases brilliant. A very large amount of collateral reading was also done.

After finishing the course on money, some members of this center joined with the original Buffalo center in attending the course on electricity by Prof. A. L. Arey of Rochester. This was Prof. Arey's third course on the subject before this center, which is composed of electric workers. During the first two years the character of the work was general and somewhat elementary but this year a 20-weeks course was given dealing with more technical problems.

The course at Clyde on the 'Early Christian church' consisted of weekly meetings during the entire year, when a lecture was given followed by class discussions on the extension plan. At Geneva the secretary of the center, Prof. Milton H. Turk of Hobart conducted the first course. The first lecture was made free, and several who would not otherwise have been interested were in this way led to take the course.

At Gloversville the work is conducted by the energetic librarian, Mr A. L. Peck, who gives up every evening in the week to educational work in connection with his library. Two courses were taken, one on economics based on Prof. Jenks' syllabus no. 1, the other on modern authors, following the plan outlined in Miss A. M. Spence's syllabus no 14. Besides these two courses and two study clubs there is in connection with the library a class in American reading, following the required course outlined in the regents academic syllabus, a quiz club of boys and girls of the intermediate grades, and a boys' debating club.

The course at Lowville on Civil and religious liberty in America by Regent Charles E. Fitch, concluded with a banquet in his honor. The president, Rev. J. Westby Earnshaw was toast master. The University of the State of New York was responded to by Regent Henry E. Turner. Mrs J. W. Earnshaw toasted 'Our lecture course and lecturer' to which a response was given by the lecturer.

The Columbia college center, which has studied electricity since its organization, has become affiliated with the American institute of New York and changed its name to the American institute extension center. The work is still under direction of W H. Freedman of Columbia.

The lecturers and subjects of the course were:

Joseph T. Monell, Principles of continuous current dynamos and motors.

W: H. Freedman, Continuous current dynamos, Incandescent lighting; Electric railways; Alternating currents.

Holbrook Cushman, Measurement of resistance.

G. F. Sever, Continuous current motors, Incandescent light.

L. H. Laudy, Secondary batteries; Arc light.

C: T. Rittenhouse, Systems of wiring

After finishing its course on American colonial history by Prof. (now president) G: W: Smith of Colgate the Oneida center voted to have a second course of 10 weeks with the same lecturer and subject. A study club was also formed in connection with the center, and a second traveling library sent to the club for special study among its members.

The Rochester center continues to hold first place, this year increasing the number of courses to six. In connection with his course on money, Prof. Forbes prepared a valuable syllabus on the subject which has been widely called for. The course on photography by Dr Charles Forbes was given by request and supported by special subscription. Prof. Mace's course on the civil war was the fourth he has given in Rochester on American history. The subjects of his other courses were the Revolution, the American constitution and the Development of the nation. The civil war syllabus like his others, contains a full analysis of each topic, with an appendix of reprints of original documents.

The Saratoga center was the outgrowth of a demand for educational work in which all could join. A public meeting was held on Dec. 18, at which Sec. Melvil Dewey of the University presented the plan of extension work in an hour's address and as a result a center was at once formed. Prof. J. R. Truax of Union repeated here the course given at Salem last year, with an equally appreciative audience

Last year was the third year of the study of Shakspere, with Mrs J. K. Curtis, at the Syracuse center. The subjects were *Romeo and Juliet* and the *Tempest*. The syllabus, like others of Mrs Curtis, is specially adapted to study clubs as it consists largely of suggestive questions. Five lectures are given to each play followed by general discussions and a quiz by the lecturer.

The report of the secretary of the Utica center follows:
The board of managers met several times during the summer of 1894, in the effort to arrange two courses of lectures for the year. It was decided to have Prof. J. W. Jenks of Cornell and Prof W K Terrett of Hamilton, but both lecturers were obliged to cancel their engagements and the fall course had to be abandoned The board at this time voted to avoid the danger of superficial study by fixing on some one large subject and urging at least one course in some branch of it each year. English was finally chosen. and it was agreed to begin with English literature, taking only one period at a time and treating recent periods first.

Prof Crawshaw of Colgate university was engaged for his course of 10 lectures on the English novel and lectures were given weekly, from January 14 to March 18 inclusive. They were thoughtful criticisms of the authors and works considered The lecturer spoke with ease and fluency, using sufficient rhetoric for his purpose, but aiming chiefly at clearness and brevity, after the manner of the classroom lecturer. Each lecture was followed by an appropriate reading well chosen as an illustration of some point made that evening. The average attendance at the lectures was 110. Members of the center found them both pleasant and profitable. A series of appreciative resolutions, prepared by a committee of which Regent Watson was chairman, was unanimously passed.

Nine classes, each lasting half an hour, were held before the lectures The average attendance was 24. Prof Crawshaw conducted the classes with spirit, and students spoke rather more freely than has been usual. At the beginning of the hour, questions were asked by the students on the lecture of the previous week and were answered by the lecturer, who strove to stimulate discussion. He then asked questions and suggested topics for thought and writing. Points suggested by papers received were also taken up The paper record was not large, for Uticans are as yet disposed to think of extension courses as pleasant, connected lyceum lectures, not too expensive, and a good review of school work for those who need to review the subjects chosen It is the desire of the board to emphasize, so far as may be, the possibility of serious work This is no easy matter when all members are so busy. Unfortunately, no one could this year give an evening each week to a students' club and therefore none was formed

The after class was held after seven of the lectures Written questions were handed to the lecturer, who in his answers expanded the topics suggested. The average attendance was 55.

The traveling library lent by the state was placed in the public library. Books were drawn out during the course for three days at a time, and after the last lecture, for a week at a time. Three a day, on an average, were taken out during the course, but the librarian says that the books were used much more in the library than out of it. The public library also was used to a considerable extent on subjects suggested by Prof. Crawshaw Even before the course began, a decided increase was seen in the demand for critical works on the novel.

Prof. Crawshaw gave without charge at the end of the course, an extra lecture on the scenes made famous by the lives and works of English novelists These he described briefly, giving an account of a vacation tour among them, and passing over as much ground as possible. The lecture was illustrated by stereopticon views. Each ticket holder was given two tickets for this additional lecture, which was a most agreeable finale to the course.

Two courses have been arranged for next year: the first, of 10 lectures on electricity by a teacher admirably qualified and popular in Utica, Prof. George C. Hodges of the Utica academy; the second, of 10 lectures on American poetry, by Prof. J. H. Gilmore of Rochester university.—IDA J. BUTCHER, *Secretary*

Early in October, the Yonkers center sent a circular to all likely to be interested in university extension inviting attendance at the annual meeting of the society, when the program of the year would be submitted for discussion by the executive committee. Members of the center are termed managers, and the circular enjoined the recipient, over the signature of the officers of the center, to enrol himself in that capacity. The names of officers and managers of the center followed.

As a result a course on geology by Prof. Scott was decided on, which has been called one of the most successful ever given in Yonkers. This was followed by Prof. A. D. F. Hamlin's architecture course for which a specially valuable collection of books was sent.

The annual report of the Yonkers center follows:

The annual meeting of the board of managers of the Yonkers society for university extension was held on Thursday evening, Nov. 7, 1895, in the parlor of the Woman's institute. The president, Prof. A. V. Williams Jackson, presided. After extending a welcome to the members of the board on the opening of this the fifth year of the society's existence, Dr Jackson reviewed in brief the educational work accomplished by the association during the last four years. His report showed that, in the eight courses of study which had been pursued, 72 regular lectures had been delivered, and in addition to these a series of more than 30 extra class sessions had been held. This gives a total of over 100 special lectures which the society, since its inception, has tendered to the community. Letters encouraging the work of the association were read.

The yearly report of the secretary, J. Harvey Bell, was then presented; it outlined the special line of study which had been followed during the past year. The report on students' clubs was next submitted, by Miss Mary Marshall Butler for the women's division, and by Peter J. Elting for the men's division.

A detailed account of the finances for the fiscal year ending Oct. 1, 1895, was laid before the society by its treasurer, George P. Butler, whose books showed a slight surplus after all the expenses of the past year had been paid. The president voiced the sentiment of the meeting in expressing the hope that, by drawing attention to the treasurer's report, larger financial support might be given during the coming year, so as to increase the educational advantages which the society is offering.

The election of officers and managers for the ensuing season then took place. The following officers were chosen: A. V. Williams Jackson, president, Norton P. Otis, first vice-president, John Kendrick Bangs, second vice-president; J. Harvey Bell, secretary; F. W. R. Eschmann, treasurer.

The following standing committees for the year were appointed· on students clubs; (two divisions, for men and for women), on membership and finance, on entertainment, auditing committee.

The executive committee thereupon, announced that the courses of lectures which had the preference for the first term of the coming season were English literature or English history, and that the choice for the second term favored a course on Great leaders of political thought or on science in the department of physics, electricity or chemistry.

In conclusion, a unanimous vote of thanks was extended to the trustees of the Woman's institute for the use of the lecture hall during last year, and for the hospitable invitation again for the coming year. The managers then adjourned, expressing the hope that they may receive the hearty support and cooperation of the community in the educational work that is being done by university extension in our midst.

Besides the courses already reported, 12 university extension courses were last year given in connection with the Teachers college at Morningside hights, New York city. The lecturers and subjects with the average attendance at classes is here given·

Lecturer	Subject	Average attendance at classes
Pres. Walter L. Hervey	Philosophy of education	10
Clarence E. Meleney	Science and art of teaching	14
Angeline Brooks	Kindergarten (mother's class)	19
John F. Woodhull	Chemistry and physics	30
Anna A. Shryver	Geology	21
Frank T. Baker	English literature	15
Helen Kinne	Cooking	27
Mary S. Woolman	Sewing	17
Charles A. Bennett	Manual training (woodworking)	8
J. F. Lewis	Modeling	7
John H. Mason	Constructive drawing	3
Ida S. Robinson	Freehand drawing	15

Two unregistered courses of 5 lectures have been given at White Plains one by Prof. Charles Sprague Smith of New York city, on art and the other by Prof. Adolphe Cohn of Columbia on French history. Prof. Cohn gave a talk on university extension at the request of the managers who are organizing an extension center to begin work in 1895–96.

The lectures in the course on 'Civil and religious liberty in America' were given by Regent Charles E Fitch at Canandaigua, though there was no organization as a registered extension center.

A comparative view of the work accomplished during the first four years is shown, so far as statistics can be relied on, in the following table, giving summaries of the annual reports since the organization of the department in 1891.

Comparative statistics, 1891-95

YEAR	No. of active centers	No. of courses	Total attendance at lectures	Total attendance at classes	% of total attendance at class	Total no. of papers written	No. of examinations	ANSWER PAPERS Written	Accepted	% accepted	% of total attendance taking examination	% of class attendance taking examination
1891-92..	10	12	28,600	10,200	36	1,610	11	135	119	88	.4	1.3
1892-93..	25	34	35,670	13,190	39	2,562	21	157	141	90	.4	1.
1893-94...	20	31	50,489	22,581	45	1,270	13	106	94	89	.2	.5
1894-95....	21	29	37,594	17,673	47	1,029	12	100	89	89	.26	.56

Sunday Bible classes. As was pointed out in the last report, extension methods of teaching are well adapted to Bible study Sunday schools in the same place, using the International or other lessons in common, would increase interest in Bible work by uniting in supporting an extension course on the general history of the period including the life and character of the author of the special book studied

Such subjects as Messianic prophecy, the meaning and authorship of the Old testament prophecies, study of the New testament with the historic setting of each book, can seldom be satisfactorily included in Sunday school courses except by a plan of this kind. The traveling library which would be supplied for such study would be a valuable aid and the examination at the end would serve as an incentive to some who would not otherwise be willing to give to these topics the same hard study as to secular subjects.

Extension teachers. The university lists now include 154 lecturers offering 277 courses. 35 lecturers and 57 courses have been added during the year, six names and nine courses have been dropped A complete record of changes follows

LECTURERS ADDED

Perley Dunn Aldrich, 123 East av Rochester, N. Y.
 Instructor in vocal music, author *Vocal economy*
 Development of the art of music. 1 Introductory, beginnings of music, 2 Rise of opera and oratorio, 3 Bach and his predecessors, 4 Handel and early English music, 5 Haydn and his time, 6 Mozart; 7 Beethoven, 8 Schubert, Schumann, Franz and Chopin; 9 History of opera from Gluck to Wagner, 10 Wagner and the music of the future.

Peter T. Austen, Ph. D., F. C. S. *Professor of chemistry*, Brooklyn polytechnic institute, Brooklyn, N. Y.

Ph. B. Columbia school of mines 1873; Ph. D. Zürich 1876; instructor in chemistry, Dartmouth college 1876–77; professor of chemistry, Rutgers 1877–91; professor of chemistry, Brooklyn polytechnic institute 1891—; department editor of the *Brooklyn manufacturer* 1895—; member of American, German, English, French, Russian and other chemical societies; fellow American association for the advancement of science; contributor to the *Textile colorist* of Philadelphia and the *Druggists' circular* of New York; author *Kurze einleitung zu den nitroverbindungen* (Leipsic, 1876), Pinner's *Organic chemistry*, revised and translated (1893), *Chemical lecture notes* and numerous papers.

Introduction to the study of chemistry: 1 Chemical and physical changes. Chemistry defined. Classification of sciences. Elements and compounds; 2 Indestructibility of matter. Chemical attraction. Air. Oxygen. Ozone. Heat; 3 Law of definite proportions. Combining weights. Nitrogen. Water. Hydrogen. Weight unit; 4 Water, occurrences and effects. Drinking water, pollution and purification; 5 Atomic theory. Destructive distillation Ammonia Ice machines. Nitric acid. Chlorin. Disinfection. Hydrochloric acid; 6 Carbon and its compounds. Coal gas. Choke damp. Cycle of matter. Combustion, 7 Air, formation and composition. Pollution of air. Ventilation; 8 Bromin. Iodin. Fluorin. Sulfur and its compounds, 9 Phosphorus. Arsenic. Antimony. Silicon Potassium family. Calcium family; 10 Magnesium family. Copper family, 11 Aluminum family. Iron family. Manganese. Chromium. Uranium. Bismuth; 12 Lead family. Chemistry of food.

Edward W. Bemis, M. A., Ph. D., 1472 N. Halsted st. Chicago, Ill

B A. Amherst 1880; M. A. 1884; Ph. D. Johns Hopkins 1885; Professor of history and economics, Vanderbilt university 1889–92; associate professor of political economy, University of Chicago 1892–95; associate editor of the Sociological department of the *Bibliotheca sacra*, 1896– ; member British economic association, American economic association, American historical association, American statistical society; author *Municipal gas in the United States, History of cooperation in New England and the middle states*, contributor to scientific journals.

Present social problems: 1 Evolution of labor from cottage to factory. Effects of machinery; 2 Labor organizations, 3 Factory legislation; 4 Our public school system, 5 Immigration, 6 Cooperation and profit sharing; 7 Problem of the unemployed and of industrial crises; 8 Municipal monopolies of water, light and street railroads; 9 Taxation reforms; 10 Present monetary problems.

A. L. Benedict, M. A., M. D. *Lecturer on botany*, Dep't of pharmacy, lecturer on digestive diseases, Dental dep't, University of Buffalo, Buffalo, N. Y.

B. A. University of Michigan 1887; M D. University of Buffalo 1888; University of Pennsylvania 1889; M. A. Ohio Wesleyan university 1891; instructor in therapeutics, Medical dep't, University of Buffalo 1891- ; lecturer on botany, Dep't of pharmacy, University of Buffalo 1890- ; lecturer on digestive diseases, Dental dep't, University of Buffalo 1892-

Botany 1 The root, 2 The stem; 3 The bud and the arrangement of leaves, 4 The leaf, 5 Physiology and chemistry of plant life, 6 The flower, general consideration and arrangement, 7 Calyx and corolla, 8 Reproductive organs (microscopic demonstration), 9 Pollination and fertilization, 10 Fruit and seed.

Physiology and hygiene 1 Framework of the body; bones and ligaments; 2 Government of the body; brain, spinal cord, nerves; 3 The obedient organs; muscles, glands, etc ; 4 The thoroughfares of nutrition; heart, vessels, blood, lymphatics; 5 Purifying organs; lungs, kidneys, liver; 6-7 Digestive organs, 8 Oxygen, water and other food; 9 Mysterious organs; thyroid, thymus, spleen, adrenals, 10 Vegetable and animal foes; bacteria, amoeba, contagion and infection.

Charles J. Bullock, Ph. D. *Instructor in economics*, Cornell university, Ithaca, N. Y.

B. A. Boston university 1889; Ph. D. University of Wisconsin 1895; Jacob Sleeper fellow, Boston university 1893-94; fellow and instructor in economics, University of Wisconsin 1894-95, lecturer, Extension dep't, University of Wisconsin 1894-95; instructor in economics, Cornell 1895- ; member American economic association, American statistical association, American academy of political science; author *Finances of the United States*, 1775-89.

Economic questions, socialism, money 1 History and functions of money, 2 Credit and credit money; 3 Theory of money; 4 Monetary history of the United States, 5 Bimetallism, 6 History of early socialism, 7 Industrial revolution and laissez-faire; 8 Modern socialism, 9 Critical examination of socialism; 10 Practicable social reform.

Marie Louise Burge, 132 Montague st. Brooklyn, N. Y.

Special student at Vassar 1885-87; secretary Psychology dep't, Brooklyn institute of arts and sciences, 1894- .

Poetry: 1 Sonnets of Shakspere, 2 Dante's *Divine comedy;* 3 Poems of Thomas Gray, 4 Pope's *Essay on man,* 5 Old English ballads.

Biography: 1 Life work of Voltaire; 2 Boswell's *Life of Johnson;* 3 Writings of Johnson, 4 Bourrienne's *Napoleon;* 5 Emerson's estimate of great men.

Albert Isidore Calais, B. ès L. *Instructor in French*, Norwalk military academy, Norwalk, Conn.

B.ès L. University of France; French lecturer. University of Adelaide, South Australia 1893-95; author Wellington college *French exercise book*, Wellington college *French reader*, *French phrase book*, *Exercises on longer syntax*. *Lectures in French or English*

Molière 1 Molière and his time; 2 Les précieuses ridicules, 3 Le misanthrope; 4 L'avare, 5 Les femmes savantes, 6 Le bourgeois gentilhomme; 7 Le tartuffe, 8 L'école des femmes; 9 Les fourberies de Scapin, 10 Le malade imaginaire.
French literature of the 18th and 19th centuries.

George Rice Carpenter, B. A. *Professor of rhetoric and English composition*, Columbia college, New York.

B. A. Harvard 1886; university student in Paris and Berlin 1886-88; graduate student, Harvard 1888-89; instructor in English, Harvard 1889-90, associate professor of English, Massachusetts institute of technology 1890-93; professor of rhetoric and English composition, Columbia 1893- ; vice-president Dante society, Cambridge, Mass.; editor Latham's *Dante's eleven letters*

Dante· 1 Medieval Italy, 2 Predecessors of Dante; 3 Dante's life; 4 Minor works, *Divine comedy*. hell; 6 Purgatory, 7 Paradise, 8 Ethical teachings of the *Divine comedy*, 9 *Divine comedy* as a work of literary art, 10 Italian renaissance.
Italian renaissance. 1 Medieval Italy; 2 Main trend of the Italian renaissance, 3 Dante, 4 Petrarch and the scholarly movement, 5 Boccaccio and the popular movement, 6 Ariosto, 7 Tasso, 8 Culture of the renaissance and its influence on church and state, 9 Art of the Italian renaissance, 10 Influence of the Italian renaissance on English literature.

Livingston Farrand, M. A., M. D. *Instructor in psychology and anthropology*, Columbia college, New York.

B. A. Princeton 1888, M. A. 1891; M D Columbia 1891; instructor in psychology and anthropology, Columbia 1893- ; member American psychological association, New York academy of sciences.

Anthropology· the development of culture 1 Anthropology as a science Man and the lower animals, 2 Animal intelligence, 3 Origin of man various theories, 4 Antiquity of man, 5 Races of man; 6 Primitive culture · theories of its development; 7 Evidences of progression in culture. Doctrine of 'survivals in culture', 8 Origin of language. speech and gesture language; 9 Primitive arts; 10 Primitive beliefs.

Mrs Mary H. Flint, 126 Waverly place, New York.
History and development of architecture 1 Egyptian architecture, 2 Grecian architecture; 3 Roman architecture; 4 Byzantine and Mohammedan architecture, 5 Romanesque architecture; 6 Gothic architecture in France, Spain and Germany; 7 Gothic architecture in England and Italy; 8 Renaissance architecture; 9 Modern architecture, 10 Landmarks of architecture.

Mrs Emma Gottheil, 571 Park av. New York.
Officier d'Académie (France); director French schools of the Alliance Israelite universelle in the east 1878-85.

French writers of the 19th century: 1 Les precurseurs du 19 siècle; 2 Chateaubriand; 3 Madame de Stael et d'autres femmes écrivains du 19 siècle; 4-5 Les romanciers du 19 siècle; 6-7 Les poetes du 19 siècle, 8-9 Le theatre du 19 siècle; 10 Gustav Flaubert.

Harold Griffing, Ph. D. 729 Amsterdam av. New York.
B. A. Columbia 1890, Ph. D 1895, prize fellow in letters, 1890-91, university fellow in philosophy, 1891-93; author *On sensations from pressure and impact*, 1895, contributor to *Philosophical review, Psychological review*.

Psychology of to-day· 1 Scope and methods of the new psychology, 2 Mind and body, 3 Our senses, 4 Seeing and thinking; 5 Memory and attention, 6 Feeling and action, 7 The time it takes to think and how it is measured, 8 Hypnotism and double consciousness, 9 Hallucinations, 10 The new psychology and education

John Grier Hibben, M. A., Ph. D., *Assistant professor of logic*, Princeton college, Princeton, N. J.
B A , M A., Ph D. Princeton, assistant professor of logic, Princeton 1891 —; contributor to *North American review, International journal of ethics* and *Psychological review*.

Ethics.   Psychology   Logic.

Henry M. Hobart, B. S. General electric co. Schenectady, N. Y.
B. S Massachusetts institute of technology 1889.

Electricity

REPORT OF EXTENSION TEACHING DIVISION, 1895   351

George C. Hodges, *Instructor in sciences,* Utica free academy, Utica, N. Y

Special student, Stevens institute, Hoboken, N. J., instructor in sciences, Utica academy 1881—, member American chemical society

Electricity up to date   1 Nature's forces and physical nomenclature, 2 Stationary electricity, or electrostatics, 3 Moving electricity, or electrokinetics; 4 Magnets and magnetism, 5 Electricity by induction, 6 Electric communication, 7 Dynamos and motors; 8 Physical effects of the current, 9 Chemical action of the current; 10 Future of electricity.

William Cranston Lawton, *Professor of Greek and Latin,* Adelphi academy, Brooklyn

B A. Harvard 1873; professor of Greek and Latin literature, Bryn Mawr 1892-94; lecturer at Columbia and staff lecturer of the American society for extension of university teaching 1894-95; professor and director of Greek and Latin, Adelphi academy, Brooklyn 1895—; secretary Archaeological institute of America 1890-94; member American philological association; author *Three dramas of Euripides* 1889, *Folia dispersa* 1895, numerous essays, reviews, poems in *Atlantic monthly, Nation, Lippincott's magazine, Journal of education,* etc

Homer and his school   1 The *Iliad* as a work of art, 2 Womanhood in the *Iliad,* 3 Closing scenes of the *Iliad,* Plot of the *Odyssey,* 5 The underworld in Homer and other poets, 6 A Homeric girl (Nausicaa); 7 Lost poems of the epic cycle, 8 Old Boeotian days (Hesiod's works and days), 9 Hesiod's *Theogony,* 10 Homeric hymns.

Poetry and romance in New England.   1 Literary conditions in New England, 2 Emerson; 3 Hawthorne life and lesser works, 4 Hawthorne· the great romances, 5 Longfellow life, lyrics and sonnets; 6 Longfellow: greater works, 7 Lowell; 8 Hosea Biglow, 9 Whittier, 10 Holmes   retrospect and prospect

Montague R. Leverson, M. A., Ph. D., M. D.   Fort Hamilton, L. I, N Y.

M. A., Ph D University of Göttingen 1872, M D Baltimore medical college 1893, author *Copyright and patents or property in thought, Natural history of a cause under English and English derived legal procedure, Rational system of legal procedure, A simple, speedy and inexpensive code of procedure, Rational schools vs national schools, Common sense or first steps in social economy, Uses and functions of money, Silver problem solved, American system of education, Thoughts on institutions of the higher education, War clouds and how to disperse them*

Legislative science.

Thomas F. Lucy, M. D. 215 Mt Zoar st. Elmira, N. Y.

M. D Eclectic medical college 1881; member Elmira academy of science; honorary and corresponding member Torrey botanical club, Columbia college.

Relation and unity of the animal and vegetable kingdoms.

Frank Morton McMurry, Ph. D., *Professor of pedagogics and Dean of the faculty*, School of pedagogy, University of Buffalo, Buffalo, N. Y.

Student at Ann Arbor, Mich 1881-82; principal of schools in Illinois 1883-86; student at universities of Halle on the Saale and Jena 1886-89; Ph D. Jena 1889; principal of Grammar school, Chicago 1889-90; professor of pedagogics and training teacher, State normal school, Normal, Ill. 1891-92; student at Geneva, Switzerland and at Paris 1892-93; professor of pedagogy, University of Illinois 1893-94; principal of Franklin school, Buffalo 1894-95; professor of pedagogics and dean of the faculty, School of pedagogy, University of Buffalo 1895— .

Pedagogy 1 The new education, 2-3 Apperception, 4 Correlation of studies or concentration, 5-7 Formal steps of instruction, or the principles underlying method in the classroom, 8 Literature; 9 Geography; 10 Elementary science.

Mrs Helen Barrett Montgomery, B. A. Rochester, N. Y.

Life in old Florence 1 Florentine history, its sources, development, 2 Florentine government, 3 Private life, 4 Dante and his times, 5 *Divina commedia*, 6 The work-a-day world; 7 Department of public works: a contrast, 8 The Medici, 9 Savonarola; 10 Michel Angelo Buonarroti.

M. V. O'Shea, B. L. *Professor of educational psychology and child study*, School of pedagogy, University of Buffalo, Buffalo, N. Y.

B. L Cornell 1892; professor of psychology, ethics, pedagogy, physical culture and director of practice school, State normal school, Mankato, Minn. 1892-95; professor of educational psychology and child study, School of pedagogy, University of Buffalo 1895— ; vice president National association for child study 1893-95; member Illinois society for child study, National Herbart society; author articles in *Atlantic monthly*, *Popular science monthly*, *Educational review*, etc ; editor *Cornell magazine* 1891-92

Educational psychology 1 Connections and relations of mind and body; 2 Habit, physical and mental, how formed, how overcome; 3 Influence of physical types, conditions and activities on the intellect, emotions and will; 4 Physical expression; its relation to mental activities and its tendency to shape disposition, 5 Heredity vs environment in determining personality, 6 Imitation and suggestion in shaping personality; their influence in the experiences of daily life; 7-8 Intellectual activities: kinds, connections and methods of training; 9 Emotions and will; relation to intellectual activities, methods of training, 10 Moral character; means of cultivating.

Child study   1 History, problems and methods of child study; 2 Physical growth and development of children through the period of adolescence, 3 Early intellectual life of the child; 4 Mental growth and development; 5 Children's emotions, 6 Children's games and plays, their intellectual, moral and physical significance, 7 Children's imagination and lies, 8 Reasonings of children; 9-10 Means of studying children by parents and teachers.

Burleigh Parkhurst, 11 E. 14 th st. New York.

Special student at Harvard 1880-82; student at Art Students league, New York 1883; director Fine arts dep't Jacksonville academy, Ill. 1883-85; student at Amsterdam 1885; student at Paris 1886-87; artist decorator of interiors, New York 1890-95; member New York water color club; author *Sketching from nature.*

Modern decoration and its origin (stereopticon). 1 Decorative idea; 2 Origin and development of decorative forms; 3 Color in decoration; 4 Mosaics; 5 Stained glass and painted windows; 6 Decorative paintings and painters; 7 Wall coverings, 8 Interiors and furniture, 9 The modern decorator, 10 Originality and development.

Painting from the painter's point of view: 1 Picture making and picture makers, 2 Primitive picture making; 3 Development of color, 4 Decorative painting and painters, 5 Old masters and modern painters; 6 English painters of the 18th century, 7 The school of 1830, 8 Modern Dutch school, 9 Preraphaelite and impressionist; 10 Evolution of landscape.

Salem G. Pattison, M. A.   *Principal* Adams collegiate institute, Adams, N. Y.

B. A Wabash college 1888; M A. Cornell 1891; instructor in Wabash college 1886-89, professor of history and Latin, Taylor university 1891-92, president Carthage collegiate institute, Mo. 1892-94; principal Adams collegiate institute 1895-; member American historical society

Early struggles of the republic: 1-5 Military: 1 Causes of the revolution and the war of 1812; 2 Struggle for independence; 3 Efforts to rend the union, 4 Elements of strength on land and sea; 5 Two characteristic Americans, Washington and Jackson and their relation to the first two wars; 6-10 Constitutional: 6 Evolution of the American constitution; 7-8 Battles over the constitution in state conventions; 9 Unsuccessful proposals to amend the constitution 1787-1816; 10 Tendencies of legislation from 1787-1816.

Ismar J. Peritz, M. A. *Instructor in Semitic languages and archeology*, Syracuse university, Syracuse, N. Y.

M. A. Harvard 1893; member American oriental society.

Semitic history and archeology· 1 Semitic peoples in history; 2 Assyria; 3 Babylonia, 4 Phenicia, 5 Syria, 6 Arabia; 7 The Hebrews, 8 Judaism; 9 Modern Judaism, 10 Modern Semitic studies and problems.

Albert Schneider, M. D., M. S. *Fellow in botany*, Columbia college, N. Y.

M D College of physicians and surgeons, Chicago 1887; B. S. University of Illinois 1894, M S. University of Minnesota 1894; assistant state geologist of Minnesota summer of 1892; scholarship in botany, University of Minnesota 1892-93, member Minneapolis academy of natural science, ordentliches Mitglied der deutschen botanischen Gesellschaft; contributor to American and German scientific periodicals and transactions.

Botany 1 The cell and its function; 2 Tissues and their function, 3 Organs and their function, 4 Forms of organs and organ systems, 5 Origin, position and function of leaves; 6 Reproduction, 7 Chemism and physiology of growth; 8 External influences in their relation to plant life, 9 Movements in plants; 10 Classification of plants.

W. B. Scott, Ph. D., *Professor of geology*, Princeton college, Princeton, N. J and Wagner institute, Philadelphia, Pa.

B A. Princeton 1877; Ph. D. Heidelberg 1880; professor of geology, Princeton 1880- , Wagner institute 1892- , fellow Geological society, Zoological society, Linnean society, London, Geological society of America; author of numerous scientific papers.

Geology 1 Dynamics, igneous agencies; 2-3 Igneous agencies; 4 Atmospheric agencies, 5 Aqueous agencies; 6 Organic agencies, 7 Introduction to historical geology, 8 Eozoic and paleozoic eras, 9 Mesozoic era; 10 Cenozoic era.

Zoologic geography and historical geology: 1-5 Zoologic geography 1 Introductory, 2 North America; 3 Europe and Africa, 4 Oriental and Australian regions; 5 South America and the Antarctic continent; 6-10 Historical geology. 6 Introductory, 7-9 Hoofed animals; 10 Flesh-eaters (carnivora).

James H. Stoller, M. A. *Professor of biology*, Union college, Schenectady, N. Y

B. A. Union 1884, M. A. 1887; instructor in natural history, Union 1884-89; student at University of Munich 1886-87; professor of biology, Union 1889—; bacteriologist for New York state board of health, 1892—; member American association for the advancement of science; author of various reports, contributor to scientific journals.

Principles of biology : 1 Protoplasm or living matter ; 2 The organism or living matter in the living body : cells, tissues, organs, systems, 3 The organism in relation to its physical environment: food, assimilation, waste, 4 Life-history of the organism : growth, development, decay, 5 The organism in relation to its kind or the life of the species reproduction, heredity, 6 The species in relation to its environment variation, natural selection; 7 The species in its derivational relationship to other species: evolution; 8 Relationships of species now living classification, 9 Relations of species now living to their environments: distribution, 10 Past history of species fossils.

Bacteriology 1 What are bacteria ; 2 Sketch of the history of bacteriology, 3 Bacteria in their economical relations ; 4 Bacteria in their relations to disease, 5 Sanitation as based on bacteriology.

Ralph Stockman Tarr, B. S. *Assistant professor of dynamic geology and physical geography*, Cornell university, Ithaca, N. Y.

B. S. Harvard; assistant in geology, Harvard 1890-91; assistant professor of dynamic geology and physical geography, Cornell 1892—; fellow Geological society of America; member Geological society of Washington, Boston society of natural history, National geographic society; author *Economic geology of United States*, *Elementary physical geography* and various geologic articles.

Physical geography of the land (physiography) : 1 Statement of the principles of physiography, 2 History and development of river valleys, 3 Waterfalls with Niagara as the central topic; 4 Lakes including a history of the Great lakes, 5 Glaciers of the world, 6 Effect of glaciation in New York, 7 Lake and ocean shores; 8 Mountains, 9 Volcanos, 10 Relation of man to the earth.

Glacial geology (stereopticon) · 1 Development of glacial theories, 2 The Greenland and Antarctic glaciers; 3 Alaskan and other valley glaciers; 4 Ways in which glaciers work; 5 Continental glaciers of America and Europe ; 6 Glacial deposits : moraines, boulder clay; 7 Glacial deposits kames, terraces ; 8 Effect of glaciers in forming lakes, gorges and waterfalls, 9 Man and the glacial period; 10 Cause of the glacial period.

Sarah Sumner Teall, Fayette park, Syracuse, N. Y.

Colonial history. 1 General introduction; 2 Pilgrim mothers; 3 Landing and settlement of the pilgrims at Plymouth, 4 Puritan women, 5 Dames of old Virginia, 6 Life in Virginia, 7 Social and domestic life of the Dutch in New Amsterdam; 8 Social and domestic life of the English in New York; 9 Domestic life in Pennsylvania, 10 General view of the country on the eve of the war of the revolution.

James J. Thom, B. D. Clyde, N. Y.

* Student at University of Glasgow 1879–82; Colgate university 1888-90; B. D. Rochester theological seminary 1892, graduate student, University of Chicago 1892-93; president, School of expression and elocution 1883-85; author *Elementary principles of the art of expression, Elementary principles of hermeneutics, Sociology of the laws of Moses.*

Art of expression: 1 General knowledge required; 2-3 Mental and moral training required; 4-5 Expressive speech; 6-7 Expressive signs; 8-9 Expressive script; 10 Will power and psychic influence.

Biblical, scientific and practical sociology · 1-3 Sociology of Moses, David and Christ, 4-6 Sociology of the modern schools: German and French, English, American, 7-9 Charities of Europe, England, America, 10 General summary and review.

Universal history 1 Mythological age, 2 Golden age of Greece and Rome, 3 Age of Jesus Christ; 4 Fall of the Roman empire; 5 Rise of the Christian church as an organization, 6 Barbarians of the east, 7 Rise of France; 8 Rise of England; 9 Rise of Germany; 10 Rise of the new world.

Early Christian church

Dean A. Walker, B. D., M. A., Ph. D. *Professor of English Bible,* Wells college, Aurora, N. Y.

B. A. Yale 1884, B. D. 1889, M. A. 1890; Ph. D. University of Chicago 1895; instructor Hopkins grammar school, New Haven, Conn. 1884-85; professor of languages, Colorado college 1885-86; instructor and principal, Preparatory dep't, Syrian protestant college, Beirut, Syria 1889-92; lecturer University extension dep't, University of Chicago 1893-95; professor of English Bible, Wells college 1895— ; author articles in *Old testament student* and *Biblical world.*

Messianic prophecy 1 Character, functions and work of the Hebrew prophets, 2 Messianic hopes in Amos and Hosea; 3 Isaiah's Messianic prophecies in the reign of Ahaz, 4 Messianic prophecies of Isaiah and Micah in the days of Hezekiah; 5 Messianic

REPORT OF EXTENSION TEACHING DIVISION, 1895   357

prophecies of Jeremiah and Ezekiel, 6-7 The servant of Jehovah;
8 Deutero-Isaiah's pictures of the restoration of Zion; 9 Postexilic and apochryphal development of the Messianic idea; 10
Unfolding and fulfilment of the Messianic ideals.

Old testament prophecy · 1 Oral prophecy; 2 General outlines of
written prophecy; 3 Times of Amos and Hosea; 4 Amos' message for his times, a book study of the prophecy of Amos; 5 Hosea's
message for his times, a book study of the prophecy of Hosea;
6 Isaiah's statesmanship and the Syro-Ephraimitic war; 7 Isaiah
and the Assyrian invasion; 8 The reformation under Josiah, 9
Jeremiah and the fall of the monarchy; 10 Ezekiel and the exiles.

History and institutions of Islam: 1 Mohammed; 2 The Qurân and its
institutions, 3 Earlier califs· Abu Bekr, Omar, Othman, 4
Later califs; 5 Ottoman Turks; 6 Turkey in the 19th century.

Mrs Ellen Hardin Walworth. Saratoga Springs, N. Y.

Principal boarding and day school for girls, Saratoga Springs 1879-85;
member American historical association, Association for the advancement
of natural science, New York historical society; corresponding secretary Saratoga historical society; president Shakspere society, Art and
science field club, author, *Battles of Saratoga;* editor *American monthly
magazine*

Parliamentary law, studies in legislative and executive powers of
government with practice in parliamentary rules: 1 Parliamentary
procedure in clubs and societies and boards of trustees; 2 Organization of meetings, duties of president and secretary, 3 Motions
to amend, commit, reconsider, quorum; 4 Motions, to table, to
postpone indefinitely, previous questions; 5 Committees, committee of the whole, voting financial management, incorporation,
duties of treasurer; 6 How laws are made; 7 How laws are
executed; 8 Distribution of legislative powers in U. S. government; 9 Concentration of executive powers in U. S. government;
10 Judicial power in U. S. government.

Harrison E. Webster, LL. D.   5 Sumner park, Rochester, N. Y.

President Union university 1888-94

Labor and capital: 1-2 General political economy; 3 Production
and distribution; 4 Capital and interest, 5 Wages, 6 Taxation;
7 Protection and free trade; 8 Trusts, unions, lockouts, strikes;
9 Communism, socialism, anarchism; 10 Conclusion.

Physiology and anatomy 1 The human skeleton, 2 Muscular system, 3 Food and digestion; 4 Heart, blood and circulation; 5 Lungs and respiration, 6 Brain and nervous system; 7 Secretion and excretion; 8 The senses; 9 Hygiene and exercise, 10 Life and death.

Gerald M. West, M. A., Ph. D. Garnerville, Rockland co. N. Y.

B A. Columbia 1888, M. A. 1889, Ph. D. 1890; fellow in anthropology, Clark university 1890-91, assistant, 1891-92; docent in anthropology, University of Chicago 1892-96; assistant dep't of ethnology, World's Columbian exposition 1891-93; curator of physical anthropology Field Columbian museum 1894; lecturer on anthropology, Massachusetts institute of technology 1892; member, New York bar 1889, American statistical association, American folk-lore society; author numerous papers.

Origin and development of the human race: 1 Introductory; 2 Man and ape; 3 Origin and age of the human species; 4 Appearance and distribution of man; 5 Formation of human races; 6 Man; fossil and modern, 7 Psychological characters; 8 Aryan question; 9 Is there an Aryan race? 10 Semites and Hamites.

James Wood, M. D. 263 Liberty st. Newburg, N. Y.

M. D. Bellevue hospital medical college; member Kings co. medical society, Long Island medical society, Brooklyn central clinical society, Post graduate clinical society of N. Y., New York academy of anthropology, Brooklyn institute of arts and sciences; author of numerous pamphlets and addresses on dietetics, hygiene and food stuffs; contributor to medical and scientific journals; associate editor of the department of dietetics, *American medico-surgical bulletin* of N Y.

Food and dietetics: 1 Food, its nature, origin, purpose and classification; 2 Food stuffs of vegetable origin; 3 Animal foods; 4 Beverages and condiments, 5 Cooking, preservation and preparation of foods; 6 Digestion and assimilation, 7 Economy in the selection of food; 8 Economy in the use of food; 9 Relation of alimentation to disease; 10 Food in health and disease.

NEW COURSES OFFERED

Mrs Jessie K. Curtis, B. A. 111 Waverly place, Syracuse, N. Y.

Julius Caesar · 1 Outline of Roman history; 2 Historical account of the chief contemporaries of Caesar; 3 The Caesar of history, 4 Introduction to the drama of *Julius Caesar*, 5 The insufficiency of worldliness, 6 Seeming self-sufficiency of worldliness; 7 Nemesis to the 'world-spirit', 8 Degeneracy of worldliness; 9 Nemesis to worldly ideals; importance of divinity; 10 Summary of *Julius Caesar*.

Romeo and Juliet and the *Tempest* 1 Love seeking the beloved; 2 Love joined to love, 3 Hate triumphant; the lovers separated; 4 Love tested, 5 The power of love; 6 Nature under control of the intellect; 7 Imagination uncontrolled by intellect, 8 Intellect controlling love and hate; 9 Rewards and punishments, 10 Restoration complete, freedom for all.

Charles Sprague Smith, M. A. Carnegie building, 56th st. and 7th av. New York.

Lakes of Switzerland (illustrated). 1 The northern lakes: the olden time; 2 Lake of the four forest cantons, William Tell and the birth of Swiss liberties; 3 Alpine lakes; Swiss folk-lore, 4 Lakes of Zürich and Geneva; literary footprints.

Outre Mer (illustrated): 1 Italian days; 2 Castles in Spain, 3 Land of William Tell; 4 In the footsteps of the Norsemen; 5 Forest of Fontainebleau and its art interpreters.

Swiss history (illustrated).

NAMES WITHDRAWN (*see* previous reports)

Hjalmar Hjorth Boyesen, Ph D. Professor of Germanic languages and literatures, Columbia college, N. Y. Died October 4, 1895.
Henry White Callahan, M. A. Boulder, Col.
Arthur Kaiser, Ph. B. Died 1894.
Charles H. Levermore, Ph. D. Adelphi academy, Brooklyn, N Y.
Lewis Swift, Ph. D. California.
Ulysses G. Weatherly, Ph. D. Indiana.

Free lectures to the people, New York city. The report of the seventh year of the Free lectures to the people of New York city shows an increase in attendance and in number of lectures which suggests that the lecture course is increasing the literary interests of a large number of citizens. Lectures were given at 16 different places, making four more than last year. The course began Nov. 8, 1894 and closed March 30, 1895. 35 lectures were delivered at each hall. The total attendance was 224,118 an increase of 53,750 over the preceding year. The subjects included physiology and hygiene, natural science, travel, history, civics, art and literature. Several courses of from two to four lectures were given and the present plan provided for increase in the number and length of these courses each year.

Progress outside New York

Notes compiled from university extension periodicals and official circulars and reports

Maine. Colby university is the recognized center of extension teaching in Maine. During the year two courses were given at Waterville, one on Systematic theology before the Minister's institute, the other on Italian painting. As preliminary work, a course of four lectures was given at Fairfield and many single lectures through the state. With Dr Nathaniel Butler, formerly director of the extension division of the University of Chicago, as the new president of Colby university, farther advance may be expected.

Massachusetts. The Lowell free lectures of Boston, for which a bequest of $237,000 was left in 1830 by John Lowell, continue to include the most important branches of natural and moral science. By provision of the will no money may be used for buildings though part may be used for rent No one is admitted without a ticket but these are given to applicants at a designated time and place as advertised in the daily journals of the city. The lectures are given in Huntingdon hall in the Massachusetts institute of technology. Besides the lectures, free instruction in drawing is given to mechanics in the Lowell school of practical design.

Connecticut. Encouraging progress is shown in Connecticut where at the beginning of the year only two centers, Hartford and New London, were established, but during the year New Haven, Waterbury and Meriden have completed organization and carried on several courses. The Hartford center, organized as the Society for education extension, is conducting the Hartford school of sociology (*see* Extension report for 1894, p. 143), lecturers in the school are specialists from the leading universities and the degree of bachelor of sociology will be conferred on completion of the three years' course of study. All lecture courses of the school are open to the public and form part of the extension work of the Hartford center. Courses in Elizabethan drama by Prof. Phelps of Yale, Literature of the age of Queen Anne by Prof. Winchester and French literature of the 19th century by Prof Kuhns were given during the year Another feature of the work is the practical lecture courses on agricultural subjects given before the Granges.

The government of the Connecticut society is vested in a council consisting of two representatives from each university, college and professional school in Connecticut and one delegate from every active extension center. The American society also has a representative in the executive committee.

Philadelphia. 24 new local centers were established in the fall of 1894, and 55 lecture courses were announced. An extension department was created at Beacon college, Kensington, Philadelphia of which Dr E: T Devine was made advisory secretary. The Pennsylvania railroad employees formed a center at their Y. M. C. A. building in West Philadelphia and a course on the American railway was given by Dr Emory R. Johnson of the Wharton school of finance W. Hudson Shaw of Oxford, England, gave seven courses in the Philadelphia centers and others in centers outside of Pennsylvania.

Dr Edmund J. James has resigned the presidency of the American society to become Director of the Extension department in the University of Chicago, succeeding Dr Nathaniel Butler, who resigned to become president of Colby university, Brunswick, Maine.

The publication of the journals *University extension* and the *University extension bulletin* was discontinued and a new journal the *Citizen* is now issued dealing mainly with the general problems of civic education and social progress, but including a special department for university extension. The program of the third session of the summer meeting which is an important work of the society included politics, biology, psychology, music, mathematics and Greek life and thought.

New Jersey. The membership of the Newark university extension society increased from 270 members the first year to 476 the second, The work of the year consisted of three courses · Old Italian and modern French painting, by Prof. J. B Van Dyke of Rutgers, English drama, by Prof. A. V W. Jackson of Columbia and Astronomy, by Prof. R. W Prentiss of Rutgers.

Regent Charles E Fitch gave his course on Civil and religious liberty in America, at Passaic, with appreciative audiences The syllabus printed by the New York department was bought for use by the center.

Washington, D. C. The trustees of the Columbian university have established extension courses in the Corcoran scientific school. The lecturers are either professors in the Columbian university or are specially approved by the university. Besides the usual extension methods of class, paper work, etc., 'class courses' have been adopted. These consist usually of 10 weekly meetings with the lecturer, who acts as instructor and leader of discussions, in preparation for these classes text-books are used. The fee varies according to the number of members in the center or class.

The courses for 1894-95 were: English literature given at Georgetown hights, American literature, at All Souls' church; Personality in literature, at All Souls' church, History of art, at Waugh chapel.

Florida. A department of university extension has been organized at the John B. Stetson university, De Land. In connection with this, a center was formed at Jacksonville and a course in Political economy given. The lecturer's fee for six lectures in addition to expenses is $60.

In addition to lectures and classes offered in literature, art, science, history, civics and economics, correspondence study will be conducted. The fee is $4 for four weeks tuition in a study of academic grade and $6 for studies of college grade.

Cincinnati. The special feature of extension work in Cincinnati has been the Saturday classes for teachers held in the university buildings. The work was organized in September 1891, at the request of a committee of teachers Three courses of 30 lectures each were given in Experimental chemistry, Medieval and modern history, Critical and exegetical study of the *Aeneid*. The total attendance was 80. During 1892-93 a larger number of subjects was offered including analytic geometry, astronomy, English literature, Greek archeology and history, Hebrew and Horace, and the attendance increased to 171.

In 1893-94 instruction was given in six subjects with a total attendance of 257. In 1894-95, 14 courses were offered.

At the same time special Saturday classes were conducted by teachers in the Cincinnati high schools in college preparatory subjects. The fee for each course of 10 or 12 exercises is $4, of 20 exercises, $7; of 30 exercises, $10. All the facilities of the university are placed at the service of the classes.

The Teachers' club of which Prof W. O Sproull, dean of the university is president, has undertaken the formation of evening classes in college studies.

Students in regular courses must be prepared for college, and on completion of the required work will receive the degree of B. A., B. L. or B S.

Chicago. The extension lecture staff of the University of Chicago for 1894-95 numbered 100, including 7 extension professors, 7 extension instructors, 27 university professors, 20 university instructors, 17 graduate students and 22 non-resident lecturers. In spite of this number however, the demand for lecturers in some subjects was greater than could be supplied. Of the 117 registered extension centers 92 were active during the year. 128 courses were given in the following places: Chicago 29, Illinois (outside of Chicago) 45, Indiana 12, Ohio 1, Michigan 23, Wisconsin 1, Minnesota 3, Iowa 11, Missouri 2, California 1.

In the class-work division 102 courses in 21 departments were given with an enrolment of 2193. The average number in a class was 22.

In the correspondence-teaching division there were 64 courses in 17 departments with an enrolment of 368 students.

The second annual university extension conference was held in three sections: at South Bend, Ind., May 10–12; Joliet, Ill., May 17–19; Clinton, Ia., June 7–9. Delegates from centers in Michigan, Indiana, Illinois and Iowa were in attendance Day sessions were devoted to discussion of measures for increasing the efficiency of extension teaching and extending it more widely. In the evening public addresses were given to illustrate university extension methods.

Nathaniel Butler, director of the university extension division has resigned to become president of Colby university Jan. 1, 1896 and Prof. Edmund J James of the University of Pennsylvania and president of the Philadelphia extension society, has been appointed to succeed him.

A university extension club similar to the English association of lecturers was organized for the purpose of bringing together the lecturers and class-instructors of the extension division. Monthly meetings are held at which lectures are delivered and the details of university extension methods explained and discussed.

Michigan. In connection with the biweekly course on Social life in the American colonies, at Flint, Mich., by Francis W. Shepardson, staff-lecturer of the University of Chicago, lectures by a member of the center have been given on the subject during the intervening week. The plan has been highly successful, doubling the number of lectures and increasing interest in the students association.

Wisconsin. The University of Wisconsin, the first institution in the northwest to take up extension work, now offers 31 courses of six lectures, the fee for each being $90 and expenses. Those who comply with the requirements of class and paper work and pass the examinations, receive certificates which are credited on the university records with the value of one-fifth studies for one term. In practice, this results in excusing the holder from certain synoptic courses, intended to give a general knowledge of subjects which are not studied more fully

Minnesota. Two extension centers flourish in St Paul, one in the city and the other in West St Paul. A committee appointed by the High school alumni association has charge of the center in St Paul, though the University of Minnesota supervises the work, provides the lecturers and gives credit for one fourth of a term's work at the university to those who pass the examinations.

During the year two courses in English literature and three courses on the French language were given; of the latter, one was for beginners, another for intermediate work and the third for advanced students. Each French course consisted of 20 weekly lessons, the fee being only $1.50. The books studied in the advanced class were the same as those read at Harvard in the sophomore year. A course on wages was given and the price reduced to 75 cents in order to induce the working classes to attend.

Iowa. Since 1892 lecture courses have been given in 26 different centers by professors from the state university, Cornell and Iowa colleges As yet, however, it has not been possible largely to introduce university extension methods. The section of the second annual extension conference of the University of Chicago held at Clinton in June, was an effort to advance extension interests in this state. University extension, in general, and the relations of the local secretary to the work, were discussed by F. W. Shepardson and R: G. Moulton of Chicago university and representatives from the Iowa centers. The closing address was given by Pres. Harper on Why should I study the Bible?

Missouri. A center was formed at Hannibal in 1893 and lectures given by Prof. M. S. Snow of Washington university, St Louis. In 1894-95 two courses of six lectures each were given; one on American statesmen and great historic movements by F W. Shepardson of Chicago and the other on American literature by Miss Augusta Chapin. A number of single lectures were also given, some by members of the local center.

One of the results of this movement was the formation of a Woman's club, which held special evening meetings to which the extension course tickets gave admission.

The center has planned to take up the study of English history and literature for the next two years, after which courses in French and German history and literature will be arranged.

North Dakota. Extension work in North Dakota has made little progress owing to the distance between large towns, the confining nature of the professors' work at the university and financial difficulties. In the winter of 1894-95, the state university offered 36 lectures to be given separately or in courses to towns maintaining a public high school. The subjects included political and social science, history, literature, pedagogy, science, European travel and life at some of the great English, German and American universities.

California. During the year courses were given by professors of Leland Stanford jr university, at Oakland, San Jose, Riverside, Eureka, Stockton, San Francisco, Sacramento and Portland, Oregon The university does not attempt to organize local centers but its professors are willing to respond to demands for lecture courses and to undertake work in teachers institutes.

Extension courses were also given in San Francisco and Oakland by lecturers from the University of California Attendants at the courses who pass the examinations receive certificates from the university. In connection with the College of agriculture, extension work is carried on at farmers institutes which are held wherever arrangements are made by local societies. To these the university sends representatives without cost to the localities.

Scotland. Dr R. M. Wenley, secretary of the Glasgow university extension board attributes the causes of the slow progress of extension work in Scotland to the conditions of popular life and to the university organization. Owing to the wide diffusion of popular education and lack of entrance examinations at the university till within the last two years, the need for extension teaching has not been imperative. In the autumn of 1884, three extension courses were delivered in the Philosophical institution, Glasgow. In 1885, Queen Margaret gild, now the woman's department of the University of Glasgow, took up extension work and carried it on for three years, when it was placed under the control of the university, and the Glasgow university extension board established.

The following table is a summary of the reports since 1888:

Year	No of courses	Attendance
1888-89	17	1400
1889-90	17	1100
1890-91	8	680
1891-92	8	1065
1892-93	9	1400
1893-94	7	400
1894-95	10	600

In 1888, the Edinburgh university association and the University of St Andrews organized extension work but not meeting with success this was practically abandoned in 1892, though occasional courses have been given, specially at Perth where a University education society has been formed and still supports local lectures.

At present the success of the work depends on Glasgow university which has received a bequest of £60,000 for extension purposes and on the summer school at Edinburgh which owes its origin and success to the efforts of Prof. Patrick Geddes. The scientific coordination of studies is a specialty of this summer meeting, particular attention being paid to educational methods for the training of the student as a man and a citizen.

Cambridge, England. During the last year, Mr Arthur Berry, secretary of the Cambridge syndicate, resigned and Dr R. D. Roberts, secretary of the London society for the last eight years, was appointed as his successor. Dr Roberts in his report of the year's work, notes the decrease in the number of active centers and attributes this falling off in part to the restriction of the county council aid to purely technical courses In connection, however, with the Norfolk county council the work was of great value. The lectures, which are on botany, were designed to prepare instructors in elementary schools to teach science in evening classes. After reviewing the present critical condition of the extension system, the secretary recommends several steps which seem most urgent:

1 That the syndicate should seek to obtain a permanent fund of £25,000 or secure the immediate establishment of four or five lecturing fellowships for superintendent lecturers of £200 a year.

2 That representations should be made to the government through the lord president of the council and the vice-president, urging the importance of either widening the scope of the technical education act so as to enable local authorities to aid any form of education (above primary) desired in the locality, or by some other means render it possible for courses of teaching in literature, history and economics as well as in science, to be established and maintained permanently. This might be specially urged on the ground of the importance of training for citizenship

3 That a diploma should be established for external students obtainable in a scheme of work involving both the higher local examination and the local lectures.

The grades of certificates now issued are:

1 Terminal certificate, awarded after examination in a course of not less than 12 lectures and classes.

2 Sessional certificate, awarded for a complete session's work, including at least 24 lectures and classes.

3 Vice-chancellor's certificate of systematic study, awarded to students who obtain four sessional certificates satisfying certain conditions and pass an examination conducted by the syndicate on the subject matter of certain courses.

4 Affiliation certificate, obtainable only at affiliated centers under special conditions.

Recognizing the value of coordination in organizations engaged in educational work, Cambridge has appointed A. W. Clayden principal of the Exeter technical and university extension college to be superintendent lecturer for the district of Devon and neighboring centers. If a fund large enough to yield an income of £1000 can be obtained, provision can be made for extending farther the important work of superintendent lecturers, who reside in the districts of which they have charge.

Another step toward bringing local centers into closer touch with each other is the formation of the Cambridge university extension local secretaries union. The first meeting was held at Cambridge, February 8–9 with an attendance of 18 secretaries, whose discussions of important points were of interest and value to the syndicate.

Exeter technical and university extension college. Local appreciation of this extension of Cambridge university is evident from the increase in the number of students from 428 in 1893 (the year of opening) to 924 in 1895. On July 19, a new wing of the college was opened by the chancellor of the university.

London. The report of the London society for the extension of university teaching for 1894–95 shows an increased number of sessional certificates awarded, indicating a growing regard for sequence in study. In 1889-90, 12 sessional certificates were awarded and in 1894-95, 303. The proportion of students earning certificates increased from 10.1% of the total attendance in 1893-94 to 11.9% in 1894–95.

In connection with the technical education board of the county councils, seven courses were given to audiences made up largely of working men. Eight classes for study of Greek were held during the year and 10 of the 19 candidates were successful in the examination.

An association of London local centers has been formed which has already done valuable work in grouping and federating centers. Owing to the remarkable growth of the work, it has been necessary to create the new office of chairman of the council, to which Canon G. F. Browne has been elected. Sir John Lubbock was appointed president of the society, succeeding Mr G. T. Goschen who has held the position since the establishment of the society in 1876 and Dr C. W. Kimmins succeeded Dr R. D. Roberts as secretary

In order to bring different extension societies into closer relationship, a standing committee has been appointed consisting of the chief secretaries of the Oxford, Cambridge, London and Victoria societies. As a result of this cooperation the *Oxford university extension gazette* and the London *University extension journal* have been replaced by the new *University extension journal* published by a joint editorial committee of the four societies.

Oxford. The most noteworthy event of the year at Oxford has been the withdrawal of Mr M. E. Sadler from the position of secretary to the Oxford university extension delegacy after 10 years of service, to become director of special inquiries and reports in connection with the national education department. A movement is being made to commemorate his long connection with extension work by founding a summer meeting scholarship for working men. Mr Sadler's successor is J. A. R. Marriott, an Oxford lecturer and a member of the university extension delegacy since its formation in 1892.

During the year 1894-95, 1544 lectures were given in 160 centers by 29 lecturers. The number of lectures given in centers organized by county councils was 260, one half the number given in 1893-94, while the number of courses on subjects not eligible for aid from county councils increased from 130 in 1893-94 to 142 in 1894-95. Technical instruction committees of the county councils are working with the local colleges and institutes and these take the place of local centers for technical instruction under state aid. The total attendance of 20,809 or an average of 129 at each course shows a slight increase over last year. The class attendance was 6134 and the number of paper writers, 1939.

To aid students in centers unable to maintain 12-lecture courses, it has been decided to issue certificates after an examination in the subject matter of two courses of six lectures each.

Farther conditions are that the courses shall be delivered in successive sessions and in educational sequence and that during the intervening period the students shall carry on a course of study in a students association or in a class recognized by the university.

In March 1895, Mr Wells and Mr Horsburgh were appointed district directors of extension teaching. Their duties will be to cooperate with local committees in organizing and developing the work and to keep the delegacy informed of conditions at the centers.

The *Oxford university extension gazette*, one of the most satisfactory extension periodicals, was in September merged into the new *University extension journal*. (see p. 368)

Bournemouth. The Bournemouth students association has for four years issued a monthly journal containing items of interest to local extension students. This paper is on file in the N. Y. extension department and those interested in the English work will find here much of value which is not duplicated elsewhere. The June number contains a report of the Southern counties federation conference at Reading and reprints a valuable paper by W. M. Childs on the opportunity of students associations for historical research In recommending the study of local history to students associations Mr Childs shows that it is a desirable subject of study for three reasons: 1) contact with original materials is more stimulating than the use of books already prepared; 2) acquaintance with local history would vitalize and color knowledge previously gained of the national history; 3) material thus gained would prevent some inaccuracies in future compilations of local histories. The *Gazette* also contains valuable papers on local organizations, the financial problem and other topics of interest to extension organizers.

Reading university extension college. During the year the college was incorporated and the government vested in three bodies, the court of governors, the council and the academic board. Four departments have been established, the literary and normal department and the departments of natural science, agriculture, and fine and applied arts. The board of agriculture has increased the annual grant for the department of agriculture from £150 to £500. Diplomas in agriculture will hereafter be granted by the delegacy. In connection with the college, the British dairy institute has been established and is managed by a joint committee representing the college and the dairy farmers' association Buildings for the new institute are now being erected.

A course of 12 popular lectures attended by an average of nearly 1000 persons was given during the year, and five courses of 12 lectures each in Greek, English and French literature, history and geography. The attendance in the several departments of the college was 620.

Austria. State aid for university extension has been secured in Austria by an annual appropriation of 6000 florins. In 1889-90 the attendance at the single lectures conducted by the *Volkbildungs verein* (Society for promoting culture) in Vienna reached 36,000. Short lecture courses were then tried with success and later the principles of extension teaching including class and paper work and examinations were introduced. At the same time the free courses were continued. In 1890–91, 15 were given for seven of which the society paid. The financial crisis interfering with rapid development of the work, Dr L. Hartmann in 1894 succeeded in interesting some professors at the University and secured state aid. If the courses given in Vienna are successful, state aid will probably be granted to other Austrian universities.

France. On August 30 and 31 and September 1, 1895, an educational congress was held at Havre consisting of 400 delegates of educational societies from France, Algeria, Tunis and Egypt. It was summoned by the Société havraise d'enseignement par l'aspect, a society established in 1880 to promote the use of the magic lantern by schools and in popular lectures. The subjects discussed at this conference have a close connection with university extension They were:

1 Courses of adult instruction;

2 Popular lectures in industrial and rural centers;

3 Illustration of lectures;

4 *Patronages scolaires*, including 'all institutions and private endeavors whose aim was to follow and protect — physically, intellectually and morally — children and adolescents of both sexes before, during and after school age.' As a result of this conference, a course of 12 lectures has been given at Charleville in the Ardennes, though on unrelated subjects. At Lucheux, a course of 16 weekly lectures is in progress which approaches more nearly to the university extension plan than any yet arranged in provincial France.

The work of two societies, the National association for popular lectures and the Republican association for popular lectures has done much to prepare the way for state aid for adult education. The higher council of public instruction has recently decided to vote 100,000 francs to establish lecture courses on the extension plan.

Norway. The beginnings of university extension in Norway are found in the Society for the enlightenment of the people. This was followed a few years later by the Society for promoting the welfare of Christiania, which gave weekly lectures for working classes. In 1880, a Workman's academy was opened in Stockholm and in 1884 a similar institution was organized in Christiania. These institutions are now conducting extension lectures and in addition summer courses are given at the University of Christiania.

Sweden. The chief feature of university extension work in Sweden is still the summer school at Upsala. Short courses of lectures have been given at Gefle and at the continuation schools but the system of local lectures has not yet been organized on a large scale.

Denmark. A system of popular high schools exists in Denmark which resembles the university extension system in its object of educating adults. These schools have existed for 50 years and owe their origin to Bishop Grundtvig, the leader of reform in Denmark. Bishop Grundtvig's original plan of establishing one large high school on a grand scale was not carried out, but later by effort of the people there arose minor schools in different parts of the country, founded by private means and owned by individuals or local societies

The principle that intellectual influence must be personal governs the mode of instruction, which is mainly oral. Books play a subordinate part The aim of the school is to prepare students for teaching in its broadest sense, and history is the principal study. This is taught in such a way as to arouse and exercise religious feeling by portraying the character of different ages and people.

Instruction is given in elementary subjects: the Danish language, writing, arithmetic, drawing and surveying; also physics, geography, botany and zoology. Lectures are delivered on the human body and its functions Needlework is taught in all schools and in some instruction is given in slòjd. No examinations are given.

The schools are all in the country districts and the students for the most part belong to the peasantry. The winter session of five months is for the young men and the summer session of three months for women. The attendance is about 6000. The students board at the school and have free access to the home of the superintendent and the teachers.

An outgrowth of the high schools is the lecturing societies or clubs found in all parts of the country. The lecturers are usually the principals and teachers of the high schools. Every autumn, meetings lasting several days are held at the several high schools and are largely attended.

Belgium. A university extension society was formed in Gand in 1892 by professors and students of the university of Gand. Lectures, however, constituted the only part of the work. M Léon Leclère, a professor at the Free university of Brussels, attracted by this work in Gand, made a study of the extension movement and together with some professors and students succeeded in establishing the University extension society of Brussels, modeled after the English plan. In 1893-94, 13 local committees were formed and 25 courses or 183 lectures were delivered, most of them in smaller towns such as Ardennes, Charleroi, Hasselt and others. Courses were given in history, sociology, zoology, physiology and hygiene, public law, paleontology and agricultural chemistry. The attendance varied according to the locality, from 75 in Quevancamps to 450 in Brussels.

The educational results were not altogether satisfactory; papers were written at only one center. In January 1895 an important extension conference was held in Brussels at which it was decided that the extension system including classes, paper work and examinations should be adopted instead of allowing the work to drift into mere lecture courses. 35 courses were offered in 1894–95 by the lecturers from the Université libre de Bruxelles.

The establishment of a new university in Brussels differing in theory and practice from the old university has led to the formation of a rival extension society called the Extension of the free university.

Australia. Eight centers were established in Victoria in 1891 and 10 courses were given with an attendance of 1382 students. In 1892 the centers increased to 13 with 19 courses and 2018 students. In 1893 owing to the financial crisis which was specially formidable in Australia, only nine courses were given in seven centers with 1018 students in attendance. In December 1894 five centers were active.

In New South Wales the work is practically supported by state aid. The work in Queensland is governed by a council consisting mainly of university men, but the appointments of lecturers are confirmed and examinations conducted by the Sydney board, with which the Queensland board is affiliated. Three courses were given in 1893, and seven were provided for in 1894. Lack of satisfactory railroad accommodations in Australia is a serious drawback to farther progress of university extension, and aid from the government or private generosity must also provide extension traveling libraries before university extension can become a vital factor in the educational system of Australia.

Institutes

Brooklyn institute of arts and sciences. The opening meeting of the year was held Oct. 1, 1894, when an address was given by the Hon. S. D. McCormick of Kentucky. An increased number of evening lectures was given during the year and to accommodate the large number attending the concerts, it was arranged to have each concert given both in the afternoon and evening.

The schools of fine arts, architecture, political science and biology were provided with a larger number of instructors and greater facilities for work.

The following appointments to the presidency of departments were made:

Archeology, Prof. W. H. Goodyear Microscopy, Horace W. Calef
Chemistry, Robert G. Eccles Mineralogy, Wallace Goold
Domestic science, Emma O'Conro Pedagogy, Prin. Almon G Merwin
Geography, James S. Kemp Photography, W. H. Cooper

The department of law was organized in June, 1895 with a membership of 127. The regular meetings will be held on the fourth Monday evening of each month. The work of the department will include occasional addresses on questions of general public interest relating to law, papers on legal questions of local and professional interest presented by members at the regular meetings and courses of lectures in special branches.

Following is the list of lecturers and subjects of the institute extension courses:

Prof. T. W. Rhys Davids, Literature and religion of India
Prof. Thomas Davidson, Dante
Mme R. J. H. Gottheil, French literature, Victor Hugo
Dr Caskie Harrison, Some fundamental principles of Latin syntax, a course for the benefit of teachers of Latin and advanced students
Dr Edward Southworth Hawes, Homer
Prof. William Cranston Lawton, Literary study of Homer
Rev. Charles Leisz, Göthe
Prof. Secondo Marchisio, Poets and literature of Italy
Dr Albert C. Perkins, New testament Greek
Mrs Abby Sage Richardson, Shakspere
Prof. Menco Stern, Faust and the origin of the Faust legend

Young womans' association, Troy. This organization, started in 1883, is adding each year educational features which give it the character of an institute. The attendance at the classes increases, specially in English, penmanship, typewriting and stenography. A large number have availed themselves of the opportunity to learn plain sewing, dress making and millinery.

The class in vocal culture has done excellent work, a number having passed the first examination of the American tonic sol-fa association of New York and received certificates. The Girls' friendship club, a branch of the New York association of working girls' clubs, has been formed and is composed of members of the board, members of the association and a few outside friends. It aims to secure by cooperation means of self-support, opportunities for social intercourse and the development of higher aims among its members. During the year several lectures, practical talks and entertainments are given

The institution has been granted a charter by the University of the State of New York and the library is now open to the women of Troy for five hours each day.

Yonkers woman's institute. The following tables give a summary of the work done during 1894-95.

YONKERS WOMAN'S INSTITUTE CLUB CLASSES 1894-95

Subject	Instructor	Evening	Lessons	Pupils	Total	Average	Teachers	Committee and visitors
Calisthenics Practice	Mrs Morris	Monday Friday	30 21	44 29	645 252	21 12	30 ..	328 105
Plain sewing	Miss Johnson	Monday	31	19	248	8	31	10
Cookery	Miss Wilson	Monday Tuesday	30 30	18 21	390 311	13 11	30 30	27 23
Choral	Miss Hollister	Tuesday	10	8	40	4	10	5
Millinery	Miss Charlton	Tuesday	26	11	125	5	26	5
Dressmaking	Miss Schenck	Tuesday	20	20	180	9	20	...
Dressmaking	Mrs Jones and assistants	Thursday	34	40	340	10	85	...
Home decoration	Miss Johnson	Friday	23	43	230	10	23	25
Lend-a-hand volunteers		Thursday	17	13	107	6	23	...
Current events volunteers		Thursday	21	15	168	8	21	...

YONKERS WOMAN'S INSTITUTE DAY CLASSES 1894-95

Subject	Instructor	Time	Total no of Lessons	Total no of Pupils	Students Total	Students Average	Attendance Instructors	Pianist	Visitors
Calisthenics	Mrs Morris	Monday a. m.	8	6	28	3	8	8	..
Dressmaking	Miss Schenck	Wednesday a. m.	22	23	148	6	22	..	..
Cookery	Miss Gookin	Saturday a. m.	15	16	119	8	15	..	..
Invalid cookery	Miss Wilson	Friday p. m.	12	9	96	8	12	..	10

The character of the Yonkers Woman's institute club can be judged in part from the following classifications, based on the occupations, nationality and church connection of members:

Occupation	Nationality	Church connection
35 At home	152 Americans	20 Baptists
9 Clerks	8 English	32 Episcopalians
1 Companion	8 German	2 Friends
24 Domestic service	35 Irish	7 Lutheran
12 Dressmakers	1 Norwegian	2 Jewish
1 Designer	4 Scotch	8 Methodist
3 Fernbrook carpet factory	1 Swede	1 Norwegian
10 Hat factory	209	20 Presbyterians
45 Moquette factory		1 Reformed
1 Milliner		116 Roman catholics
1 Medicine factory		209
1 Librarian		
10 Stenographers		
2 School		
4 Seamstresses		
43 Tapestry factory		
6 Teachers		
1 Trained nurse		

209

Eight special entertainments including a concert were given for the club during the winter.

The Woman's exchange reports a balance of $38.60 in the treasury.

The Employment bureau registered 26 applicants and 23 received work. In the Domestic employment bureau there were 237 applicants, 164 of whom were placed.

The library reports 2381 volumes and 678 borrowers, 354 of whom registered during the year. 5497 volumes were drawn, of which 85% were fiction Borrowers are classified as follows.

Occupation	Nationality	Church connection
286 At home	533 Americans	70 Baptists
75 At school	1 Dutch	94 Episcopalians
6 Bandbox factory	46 English	14 Hebrews
1 Bookkeeper	2 French	12 Lutherans
184 Carpet factory	43 Germans	63 Methodists
20 Dressmakers	36 Irish	104 Presbyterians
13 Domestics	2 Italian	1 Friend
32 Hat factory	12 Scotch	273 Roman catholics
1 Hair-dresser	2 Swiss	23 Reformed
2 Librarians	1 Spanish	13 Unitarians
3 Milliners		11 None
5 Medicine factory	678	
5 Nurses		678
1 Rubber factory		
14 Stenographers		
16 Stores		
5 Silk factory		
9 Teachers		
678		

Approximate aggregate attendance for year, 1894-95

Library and reading room....................		7,373
Institute club classes pupils................	2761	
teachers.....................	285	
Committees and visitors for classes............	549	
Attendance at entertainments...................	1520	
Attendance at lunch..	4672	
Number of baths taken	815	
Special classes: Lend-a-hand......................	130	
Current events......................	189	10,921

Employment bureau. applicants and employers........ 386
Trustees.. 110
Institute classes: pupils............................. 391
teachers........................... 65 451
University extension lectures and classes............. 1,895
Institute lectures, meetings, etc...................... 905
Entertainments in Institute hall (rentals)............. 2,435
Public school classes: cookery....................... 2550
kitchen garden................. 133 2,683
Miscellaneous attendance.............................. 3,500

Total.. 30,659

Institutes outside New York

American institute of civics, Washington D. C. The American institute of civics was incorporated by congress in 1886, its object being to promote systematic study of great questions of the day and thus to inculcate a broader view of the privileges and duties of citizenship. The work is carried on through several departments: school work in general, a business school, a college department, a department of legislation and an extension department. The principal work of the latter is the formation of clubs for study of current events, specially by an intelligent reading of daily and weekly newspapers The weekly journal *Public opinion* is sent free for one year to each registered club. This forms a means of communication between the club and the central organization, as it contains each week a page devoted to the interests of the club work. An annual fee of $3 is payable by each club, and this also entitles clubs to special rates on subscriptions to American periodicals.

Wells memorial institute, Boston. Evening classes and free lecture courses have been for 16 years offered to the working people of Boston by Wells memorial institute. The courses for 1894-95 included classes and lectures in elementary and advanced mechanical drawing, elocution, practical electricity, elementary and advanced courses, steam and steam engines and a special course on the Organization of labor by Robert A. Woods, of Andover house. The 20 weekly lectures on electricity were attended by 150 men and the course on steam by 68 men, mostly engineers. Members must be working people not less than 18 years of age The annual fee is $1. The membership for the year 1894-95 was 1537 and 1302 members registered for the classes of instruction.

The Instruction committee is considering the desirability of arranging university extension courses in languages, literature and history.

This brief summary of teaching carried on outside the schools and colleges, indicates how general is the feeling that education must be prolonged beyond youth and extended to those outside the aristocracy of culture. Agencies for such instruction are now so numerous that they excite little surprise and it is only by comparison with the opportunities for such study offered 25 years ago, that realization of the advance in popular opinion can be gained. Though progress in many places seems slow and the appreciation of the populace slight in proportion to the efforts made in their behalf, still the steadily increasing extension of educational advantages is a cause for great encouragement to those who see the need and recognize the opportunity for beneficial and permanent results.

Respectfully submitted
MELVIL DEWEY, *Director*

INDEX

The superior figure points to the exact place on the page in ninths; e. g. 365⁴ means four ninths of the way down page 365. Dates are printed in italics.

Agriculture, courses in, 360⁹, 365⁴; study at Reading university extension college, 369⁶.

Albany center, report, 340⁸–41³; statistics, 340; plan for establishing free library, 341³.

American institute extension center, report, 342¹; statistics, 340.

American institute of civics, report, 377⁴.

Arey, A. L., course at Buffalo, 341⁴.

Australia, extension movement in, 372⁵–73².

Austria, extension movement in, 369⁹–70².

Belgium, extension movement in, 371⁸–72⁴.

Biblical study, extension courses, 346³; traveling libraries for, 346⁵

Boston, extension lectures, 360³; Wells memorial institute, report, 377⁷.

Bournemouth students' association, 369².

Boys' debating club at Gloversville, 341⁸.

Brooklyn institute of arts and sciences, report, 372⁸–73⁷.

Brussels, university extension society, 371⁹–72⁴.

Buffalo center, report, 341⁴; statistics, 340.

Buffalo Y. M. C. A. center, formation, 339⁵; report, 341³, statistics, 340.

Butcher, I. J, report on Utica center, 343¹–44².

Butler, Nathaniel, extension work in Maine, 360²

California, extension movement in, 363², 365².

Cambridge (Eng.) extension movement in, 366³-67⁶, local secretaries' union, 367⁴, cooperation with other societies, 368².

Canandaigua, extension course, 345⁸.

Centers, reports, 339-45, reasons for discontinuance of certain, 339⁷; formed during year, 339⁵; statistics, 340¹, 346¹, use of traveling libraries, 342⁵, 343⁷; unregistered 345⁷, 367⁸;

in England, efforts toward affiliation, 367⁴, 367⁸, reasons for discontinuance, 366⁴.

Certificates, issued by Cambridge syndicate, 366⁸-67², by London society, 367⁷, by Oxford extension society, 368⁷; by University of California, 365⁴; by University of Wisconsin, 363⁹.

Chapin, Augusta, course at Hannibal, 364⁷

Charleville, extension movement in, 370⁶.

Chicago, extension movement in, 362⁹–63⁷.

Christiania, extension movement in, 370⁸.

Cincinnati, extension movement in, 362⁴.

Citizen, 361⁵.

Club of extension lecturers, 363⁶. *See also* Boys' debating club; Girls' friendship club; Study clubs; Teachers' club; Woman's club.
Clyde center, formation, 339⁵; report, 341⁵; statistics, 340.
Cohn, Adolphe, course at White Plains, 345⁷.
Colby university, extension work, 360¹.
Columbia college center, *see* American institute extension center.
Conference on extension work, 363².
Connecticut, extension movement in, 360⁵-61².
Corcoran scientific school extension movement, 361ª-62².
Courses, during *1895*, 340¹; unregistered 345⁷.
Crawshaw, W: H., course at Utica, 343².
Curtis, Mrs J. K., courses at Syracuse, 342⁹.

Denmark, high school system, 371².
Dobbs Ferry center, statistics, 340.

Edinburgh university, *see* University of Edinburgh.
England, extension movement in 366²-69⁹.
Eureka, extension movement in, 365².
Exeter technical and university extension college, 367⁵.
Extension centers, *see* Centers.
Extension courses, *see* Courses.
Extension movement, progress in New York state, 339-59; progress in other states, 360-65; progress in foreign countries, 365-73; state aid to, in Austria, 369²-70².
Extension teachers, *see* Lecturers.

Fairfield, Me., extension work, 360².
Fairport center, formation, 339⁵; statistics, 340.
Farmers, courses for, 360⁹, 365⁴.
Fitch, C: E., course at Canandaigua, 345⁸; at Lowville, 341⁹; at Passaic, 361⁸.

Flint, Mich., extension movement in, 363⁷.
Florida, extension movement in, 362².
Forbes, Charles, course at Rochester, 342⁶.
Forbes, G: M., course at Buffalo Y. M C. A., 341³; at Rochester, 342⁶.
Foreign countries, extension movement in, 365⁶-73.
France, extension movement in, 370²
Freedman, W: H., manager of course at American institute extension center, 342².

Gand, extension movement in, 371⁸.
Geneva center, formation, 339⁵; report, 341⁶; statistics, 340.
Gilmore, J. H., proposed course at Utica, 344².
Girls' friendship club, 373⁹-74².
Glasgow, extension movement in, 365⁷.
Gloversville center, report, 341⁷; statistics, 340.

Hamlin, A. D. F., course at Yonkers, 344⁴.
Hannibal, extension work in, 364⁶.
Hartford, extension movement at, 360⁶.
Hodges, G: C., proposed course at Utica, 344².

Illinois, extension movement in, 362⁹-63⁷.
Indiana, extension movement in, 363².
Institutes, reports, 372⁸-77.
Iowa, extension movement in, 363², 364⁴.

Jackson, A. V. W., course at Newark, 361⁷.
Jacksonville, extension movement in, 362².
Jàmes, E. J., resignation as president of American society, 361⁴; director of extension division in University of Chicago, 363⁵.
Jenks, J. W., course at Albany, 340²-41².

Johnson, E. H., course in Philadelphia, 361[3].

Kuhns, Prof., course at Hartford, 360[8].

Lecturers, during *1895*, 340[1]; added since 1 Oct. *1894*, 346[8]–59[5]; withdrawn from list, 359[5]; club, 363[6]; at American institute extension center, 342[2]; at Teachers college, 345[4].

Leland Stanford jr university, extension work in, 365[2].

Lockport center, statistics, 340.

London, extension movement in, 367[7]–68[2]; cooperation with other societies, 368[2].

Lowville center, formation, 339[5]; report, 341[9]; statistics, 340.

Lucheux, extension movement in, 370[6].

Mace, W: H., course at Rochester, 342[6].

Maine, extension movement in, 360[1].

Marriott, J. A. R., secretary of Oxford extension society, 368[4].

Massachusetts, extension movement, 360[3].

Meriden, extension movement, 360[6].

Michigan, extension movement, 363[2], 363[7].

Minnesota, extension movement, 363[2], 364[1].

Missouri, extension movement, 363[2], 364[6].

Mt Vernon center, statistics, 340.

New Haven, extension movement, 360[6].

New Jersey, extension movement, 361[6].

New London, extension movement, 360[6].

New South Wales, extension work, 372[6].

New York city, free lectures, 359[7]. *See also* American institute extension center; Teachers college extension center.

New York state, progress of extension movement, 339–59.

Newark, extension movement, 361[6].

North Dakota, extension movement, 364[9]–65[2].

Norway, extension movement, 370[8].

Oakland, extension movement, 365[2].

Ohio, extension movement, 362[4], 363[2].

Oneida center, report, 342[4]; statistics, 340.

Oregon, extension movement, 365[2]

Oxford, extension movement, 368[2]–69[1]; cooperation with other societies, 368[2].

Oxford university extension gazette, 368[2].

Passaic, extension movement, 361[8].

Peck, A. L., course at Gloversville, 341[7].

Pennsylvania, extension movement, 361[2].

Perth, extension movement, 366[2].

Phelps, Prof , course at Hartford, 360[8].

Philadelphia, extension work, 361[2].

Portland, Or., extension movement, 365[2].

Prentiss, R. W., course at Newark, 361[7].

Public opinion, 377[5].

Queensland, extension work, 372[6].

Reading university extension college, 369[5].

Riverside, extension movement, 365[2].

Rochester center, report, 342[5]; statistics, 340.

Rome center, statistics, 340

Sacramento, extension movement, 365[2].

Sadler, M. E., withdrawal from extension work, 368[3].

St Andrews university, *see* University of St Andrews

St Paul, extension movement, 364[1].

Salem center, work, 339[6].

San Francisco, extension movement, 365[2].

San Jose, extension movement, 365[2].

Saratoga Springs center, formation, 339[5]; report, 342[7]; statistics, 340.

Scotland, extension movement, 365³-66³.
Scott, W· B , course at Yonkers, 344⁴.
Shaw, W. H., courses given by, 361³.
Shepardson, F W., course at Flint, 363⁷, at Hannibal, 364⁷.
Silver Lake assembly, extension work, 339⁷.
Sing Sing center, formation, 339⁵.
Smith, C: S., course at White Plains, 345⁷
Smith, G. W:, course at Oneida, 342⁴.
Snow, Prof., course at Hannibal, 364⁶.
State aid to university extension in Austria, 369⁹-70².
Statistics, of extension centers, 340¹, 346¹; of extension work in Scotland, 365⁸; classes at Yonkers woman's institute, 374-75.
Stereopticon views at Utica, 343⁹.
Stockholm, extension movement in, 370⁸
Stockton, extension movement in, 365².
Study clubs, at Gloversville, 341⁸; at Oneida, 342⁴.
Subjects during *1895*, 340¹.
Sunday schools, courses in Bible study, 316³.
Sweden, extension movement, 371¹.
Syracuse center, report, 342⁹; statistics, 340.

Tables, statistics of extension centers, 340¹, 346¹; of extension work in Scotland, 365⁸; classes at Yonkers woman's institute, 374-75.
Tarrytown center, statistics, 340.
Teachers, *see* Lecturers.
Teachers' club at Cincinnati, 362⁸.
Teachers college, extension work, 345⁴.
Traveling libraries, use at extension centers, 342⁵, 343⁷, for Bible study, 346⁵.
Troy, Young women's association, report, 373⁷-74².
Truax, J. R., proposed course at Salem, 339⁶, course at Saratoga, 342⁸.
Turk, M. H., course at Geneva, 341⁶

University extension, 361⁵.
University extension bulletin, 361⁵.
University extension journal, 368²
University of California, extension work, 365³.
University of Chicago, extension work, 362⁹-63³
University of Edinburgh, extension work, 366¹.
University of Glasgow, extension movement, 365⁷, 366⁹.
University of Minnesota, extension movement, 364².
University of St Andrews, extension work, 366¹.
University of Wisconsin, extension work, 363⁸.
Unregistered courses, 345⁷.
Upsala, summer school, 371¹.
Utica center, report, 343¹-44²; statistics, 340
Van Dyke, J: B., course at Newark, 361⁷.
Victoria, extension movement, 372⁵; cooperation with other societies, 368².
Vienna, extension movement in, 369⁹-70²
Washington, D. C., extension movement, 361¹-62².
Waterbury, extension movement, 360⁶.
Waterville, Me., extension work, 360².
Waverly center, statistics, 340.
Wells memorial institute, report, 377⁷.
White Plains, extension courses, 345⁷.
Winchester, Prof., course at Hartford, 360⁸.
Wisconsin, extension movement, 363², 363⁸.
Woman's club, at Hannibal, 364⁸.
Woman's institute of Yonkers, report, 374³-77³.
Yonkers center, report 344²-45³; statistics, 340.
Yonkers woman's institute, report, 374³-77³.
Young women's association, Troy, report, 373⁷-74².

University of the State of New York

Object. The object of the University as defined by law is to encourage and promote education in advance of the common elementary branches. Its field includes not only the work of academies, colleges, universities, professional and technical schools, but also educational work connected with libraries, museums, university extension courses and similar agencies.

The University is a supervisory and administrative, not a teaching institution. It is a state department and at the same time a federation of more than 800 institutions of higher and secondary education.

Government. The University is governed and all its corporate powers exercised by 19 elective regents and by the governor, lieutenant-governor, secretary of state and superintendent of public instruction who are *ex officio* regents. Regents are elected in the same manner as United States senators; they are unsalaried and are the only public officers in New York chosen for life.

The elective officers are a chancellor and a vice-chancellor, who serve without salary, and a secretary. The secretary is the executive and financial officer, is under official bonds for $10,000, is responsible for the safe keeping and proper use of the University seal and of the books, records and other property in charge of the regents, and for the proper administration and discipline of its various offices and departments.

Powers and duties. Besides many other important powers and duties, the regents have power to incorporate, and to alter or revoke the charters of universities, colleges, academies, libraries, museums, or other educational institutions; to distribute to them funds granted by the state for their use; to inspect their workings and require annual reports under oath of their presiding officers; to establish examinations as to attainments in learning and confer on successful candidates suitable certificates, diplomas and degrees, and to confer honorary degrees.

They apportion annually an academic fund of about $250,000, part for buying books and apparatus for academies and high schools raising an equal amount for the same purpose, $100 to each nonsectarian secondary school in good standing and the remainder on the basis of attendance and the results of instruction as shown by satisfactory completion of prescribed courses for which the regents examinations afford the official test. The regents also expend annually $25,000 for the benefit of free public libraries.

Regents meetings. The annual meeting is held the third Thursday in December, and other meetings are held as often as business requires. An executive committee of nine regents is elected at the annual meeting to act for the board in the intervals between its meetings, except that it can not grant, alter, suspend or revoke charters or grant honorary degrees.

Convocation. The University convocation of the regents and the officers of institutions in the University, for consideration of subjects of mutual interest, has been held annually since 1863 in the senate chamber in Albany. It meets Monday, Tuesday and Wednesday after the fourth Friday in June.

Though primarily a New York meeting, nearly all questions discussed are of equal interest outside the state. Its reputation as the most important higher educational meeting of the country has in the past few years drawn to it many eminent educators not residents of New York, who are most cordially welcomed and share fully in all discussions. It elects each year a council of five to represent it in intervals between meetings. Its proceedings, issued annually, are of great value in all educational libraries.

University of the State of New York

Departments

1 **Administrative** (Regents office) — including incorporation, supervision, inspection, reports, legislation, finances and all other work not assigned to another department.

Duplicate division. This is a state clearing house, to which any institution in the University may send books or apparatus which it no longer requires, and select from it in return an equal value suited to its locality and needs.

2 **Examination**—including preacademic, law, medical, dental and veterinary student, academic, higher, law, medical, dental, veterinary, library, extension and any other examinations conducted by the regents, and also credentials or degrees conferred on examination.

The examinations are conducted as the best lever for securing better work from teachers and more systematic and continuous study from students, and as the best means of detecting and eliminating inefficient teachers or methods. They cover 140 subjects and required last year 913,500 question papers (exclusive of bound volumes), and are held the week ending the last Friday in January and March and the third Friday in June, in the 576 academies and high schools in the University and also at various central points where there are 10 or more candidates.

3 **Extension**—including summer, vacation, evening and correspondence schools and other forms of extension teaching, lecture courses, study clubs, reading circles and other agencies for the promotion and wider extension of opportunities and facilities for education, specially for those unable to attend the usual teaching institutions.

Public libraries division. To promote the general library interests of the state, which through it apportions and expends $25,000 a year for the benefit of free public libraries. Under its charge are the traveling libraries for lending to local libraries or to communities not yet having permanent libraries.

The most important factor of the extension movement is provision of the best reading for all citizens by means of traveling, home and capitol libraries and annotated lists through the public libraries division

4 **State library**—including general, law, medical, and education libraries, library school, bibliographic publications, lending books to students and similar library interests.

Library school. The law authorizes the state library to give instruction and assistance in organizing and administering libraries. Students receive from the state library staff, in return for services rendered to the library during their two years' course, careful training in library economy, bibliography, cataloguing, classification and other duties of professional librarianship.

5 **State museum**—including all scientific specimens and collections, works of art, objects of historic interest and similar property appropriate to a general museum, if owned by the state and not placed in other custody by a specific law; also the research department carried on by the state geologist and paleontologist, botanist and entomologist, and all similar scientific interests of the University.

University of the State of New York

Extension Bulletin
No. 18 March 1897

PUBLIC LIBRARIES No. 5

A LIBRARY OF 500 BOOKS AND 35 PERIODICALS
SELECTED IN 1897 FOR THE

State Commission in Lunacy
FOR USE IN THE
New York state hospitals

	PAGE		PAGE
Note....................................	3	Literature (*continued*)	
State commission in lunacy..........	4	Fiction.............................	12
Reference books.....................	5	Travel.............................	16
Religion.............................	6	General...........................	16
Social science, customs, legends....	6	Europe............................	16
Natural science.....................	7	Asia and Africa..................	18
Botany and zoology.............	8	North America...................	19
Useful arts..........................	8	South America and Oceanica....	20
Hygiene, domestic animals, sailor life	8	Biography........................	21
Art, music, sports...................	9	Collective biography............	21
Literature...........................	9	Individual biography............	21
Collections of poetry............	9	History...........................	23
Individual poets.................	9	History of America..............	24
Essays, miscellany...............	10	Periodicals.......................	26
Humor: collections..............	11	Monthly..........................	26
Individual authors..............	11	Fortnightly.......................	26
		Weekly...........................	26

ALBANY
UNIVERSITY OF THE STATE OF NEW YORK
1897

Lp15m-F97-4000

Price 5 cents

Regents

Anson Judd Upson, D D., LL. D., L. H. D., *Chancellor*
William Croswell Doane, D. D., LL. D., *Vice-Chancellor*
Frank S. Black, B. A., Governor
Timothy L. Woodruff, M. A., Lieutenant-Governor } *Ex officio*
John Palmer, Secretary of State
Charles R. Skinner, M. A., LL. D., Sup't of Pub. Inst.

In order of election by the legislature

YEAR
1873 Martin I. Townsend, M. A., LL. D.   —   —   Troy
1874 Anson Judd Upson, D. D., LL. D., L. H. D.   — Glens Falls
1877 Chauncey M. Depew, LL. D. — — — — New York
1877 Charles E. Fitch, LL. B, M. A., L. H. D. —   Rochester
1877 Orris H. Warren, D. D. — — — — — Syracuse
1878 Whitelaw Reid, LL. D. — — — — New York
1881 William H. Watson, M. A., M. D. — —   — Utica
1881 Henry E. Turner — — — — — Lowville
1883 St Clair McKelway, LL. D. — — —   — Brooklyn
1885 Hamilton Harris, Ph. D, LL. D. — — — Albany
1885 Daniel Beach, Ph. D., LL. D. — — — — Watkins
1888 Carroll E. Smith, LL. D. — — —   Syracuse
1890 Pliny T. Sexton, LL. D. — — — — Palmyra
1890 T. Guilford Smith, M. A., C. E. — — — Buffalo
1892 William Croswell Doane, D. D., LL. D. — — Albany
1893 Lewis A. Stimson, B. A., M. D. — — — New York
1894 Sylvester Malone — — — — — Brooklyn
1895 Albert Vander Veer, M. D., Ph. D. — — Albany
1897 Chester S. Lord, M. A. — — — — Brooklyn

Elected by the regents

1888 Melvil Dewey, M. A., *Secretary* — — — — Albany

NOTE

In the following list books are arranged by classes. Except in fiction and individual biography the numbers of the *Abridged decimal classification* are prefixed with book numbers taken from the revised Cutter tables. In fiction the book numbers stand alone and in individual biography they follow the letter 'B' which indicates the class.

The name of the publisher and the price follow the title of each book. Periodicals and reference books are in separate lists.

This book list may be used as a catalogue by making a distinct mark opposite the name of each book contained in a given library.

Additional copies of the list may be obtained from the **Public libraries division, University of the State of New York, Albany, N.Y.**

MELVIL DEWEY
Secretary of the University

Albany, March 1, 1897

limited to six or eight weeks, no university should permit its summer students to elect more than one, or at most two subjects each summer. By this policy, and with the aid of well equipped libraries and laboratories the work of summer students can be continued at a grade not below that which the institution would expect of its regular students. The tendency seems to be toward specializing at each summer school and so offering opportunities all over the country for real study and help in some subject each year.

The present report contains in tabulated form the reports of the sessions of 1896 of all the summer schools from which reports could be obtained. Preceding these tables, more detailed information regarding some of the more important summer schools has also been given, with a summary of such announcements of 1897 sessions as have been received. New York schools are arranged in order of founding, others are in the same order under the state or country in which they are located. When no other authority is assigned the facts are taken from official circulars and announcements.

SCHOOLS IN NEW YORK

CHAUTAUQUA

The Chautauqua schools open July 3. The session of the school of pedagogy continues four weeks; the other schools, six weeks. The collegiate department consists of the schools of English language and literature, modern languages, classical languages, mathematics and science, social sciences, psychology and pedagogy, sacred literature, music, fine arts and expression, physical education and practical arts.

The assembly department offers daily lectures and entertainments and embraces 16 clubs and classes. Over 60 lecturers have been engaged. Among the chief topics are the following:

Early German literature, Prof. J. H. Worman

Problems of German literature in the 18th century, Dr N. I. Rubinkam

History of the labor movement, Prof. Graham Taylor

Monuments of ancient Rome and Italy, Mr Percy M Reese
The domestic institution; development and problems, Prof. Charles R. Henderson
Some questions of municipal life, Mr Jacob A. Riis
History of popular education, Prof. Herbert B. Adams
Problems in child study, Pres. G. Stanley Hall
The child in home, Sunday-school and society, Pres. W. L Hervey
A group of contemporary novelists, Mr Leon H. Vincent
In the footsteps of English authors, Mr Elbert G. Hubbard
Recent tendencies of American art, Mr A. T. Van Laer

Two cheap 30-day excursions will be run from New York to Chautauqua at $10 for the round trip; one July 2 and one Aug. 2.

NATIONAL SUMMER SCHOOL

This school has been organized as a joint stock association with a capital stock of $25,000 divided into 1,000 shares of $25 each. The object is not to make money but that in case of losses, the burden may not fall too heavily on one person.

The number of speakers has been reduced but not the number of lectures as experience has shown that better results are gained when only one person lectures on the same subject.

One of the most interesting courses announced is that in history by Wilbur F. Gordy. Several historical pilgrimages will be made, the first to Lake George along the old military road first opened by Sir William Johnson's men in 1775; the second to the cave in Glens Falls made famous by Cooper's *Last of the Mohicans;* the third will follow in reverse order the line of march taken by Burgoyne in 1777 and the last, by trolley car, will help the student to understand the reasons for Burgoyne's failure in 1777 to cut off New England from the other states.

The school opens July 20 for three weeks. At the close there will be an excursion to Lake George, Au Sable, Montreal and Quebec. Details of the courses are given in the announcement circular which may be obtained from the manager, Sherman Williams, Glens Falls, N. Y.

SILVER LAKE

The session of 1897 will be held July 20-Aug. 19. The summer school under the auspices of Genesee Wesleyan seminary of which Dr J. P. Ashley is president offers a variety of studies in languages, practical business, art, etc. Special attention will be given this year to the department of music under direction of L. B. Dana of Warren, Ohio. B. B. Brown of Yale divinity school remains in charge of the department of physical training. The kindergarten, classes in Bible study, special instruction in temperance and missionary work are also valuable features.

C. L. S. C. round tables will be held daily for two weeks. Rev. Ward Platt, 226 Averill av., Rochester, N. Y. is the superintendent of instruction.

BIOLOGICAL LABORATORY OF BROOKLYN INSTITUTE

The eighth session of the laboratory at Cold Spring Harbor, L. I. opens July 6 and closes Aug. 28.

Instruction will be given in the following subjects: Elementary botany and cryptogamic botany by D. S. Johnson of Johns Hopkins university; elementary zoology by Prof. H. T. Fernald of State college, Pa.; invertebrate embryology and bacteriology by Prof. H. W. Conn of Wesleyan university who is the general director of the laboratory. The laboratory fee including one course of instruction is $20, for each additional course, $5.

NATURAL SCIENCE CAMP

The eighth season opens June 30 and closes Sept. 1. The following is the list of instructors: T: W. Fraine, taxidermy; G. W. Herrick of Harvard university, entomology; C. K. Sarle of Rochester university, geology; W. Jones, Saunders' gallery, Rochester, photography; W: J. Roach, athletics and boxing; H. B. Woolston of Yale university, swimming; D. D. Gifford, horseback riding. The classes in the various sciences are described as walks and talks with the instructors. No text-books are used. Instruction will be given in the use of cameras of all kinds, in developing negatives and in making positives, and in outdoor portraiture.

Members of previous camps will be entitled to wear a service stripe on each arm for each camp which they have attended. The address of the director, A. L. Arey, is 229 Averill av. Rochester, N. Y. till after June 25 when he will be at the camp, Canandaigua, N. Y.

ST JOHN'S SCHOOL

St John's school at Manlius is a high grade school founded in 1869 by the bishop of central New York. It has a military department directed by an officer of the U. S. army. The school is open during the summer and furnishes an ideal summer resort for boys. All are expected to take light physical exercise, and swimming, fishing and boating parties are organized in charge of teachers. A simplified daily military routine is established. To those who wish to study every facility is offered for the best work. An excursion is planned each year and that for 1897 will be decided by vote of the school.

The charges for the three months' session are $100; for shorter periods, $10 per week. William Verbeck is superintendent of the school.

CATHOLIC SUMMER SCHOOL OF AMERICA

The sixth session will be held at the assembly grounds, Cliff Haven, N. Y. on Lake Champlain, July 11-Aug. 28. Courses of lectures will be given by Rev. J. F. Loughlin, Chancellor of Philadelphia, a specialist in church history; Rev. J. H. McMahon of the Cathedral, New York, on the liturgy of the church; Rev. E: A. Pace of the Catholic university, on mental development; Rev. E. T. Shanahan, of the same university, on Scholastic philosophy and Rev. F. W. Howard of Columbus, Ohio, on Social science.

Moslem vs Greek is the subject of a course by Rev. C: W. Currier of Baltimore and Philosophical questions dealing with topics in educational literature will be discussed by Rev. J. A. Doonan of Philadelphia.

Conferences on practical Sunday-school work will be directed by Rev. D. J. McMahon of New York. A reception will be given to Rev. Thomas J. Conaty, rector of the Catholic university and formerly president of the summer school. New York, Brooklyn,

Boston, Buffalo and Rochester have taken steps toward erecting cottages on the assembly grounds.

CORNELL UNIVERSITY

Cornell university extends the same facilities for work to the summer school students as to the regular university students. The session opens July 5 and closes Aug. 14. Special work may be taken under guidance of the instructors, but students are advised to take only one or two courses. The following courses are announced and will be given without regard to the number of students applying.

Greek, 2 courses
  Study and teaching of Attic Greek
  Teachers' course in Homer
Latin, 2 courses
German, 4 courses
  Elementary course
  Schiller's *Wilhelm Tell*, Heine's prose
  Prose composition, conversation and syntax
  Göthe
Romance languages, 6 courses
  French, elementary and advanced
  French conversation, elementary and advanced
  Elementary Italian
  Elementary Spanish
English, 4 courses
  English composition
  English prose
  Old English
  Middle English
Elocution, reading and speaking
Economics
  Principles of economics
  Economic history of the U. S.
Mathematics, 13 courses
  Elementary and higher algebra

Plane and solid geometry
Higher algebra
Trigonometry
Analytic geometry, 2 courses
Calculus, 4 courses
Differential equations
Astronomy
Physics, 9 courses
　General physics, 2 courses
　Laboratory work in general physics
　Experimental physics
　Advanced laboratory work in electricity and magnetism
　Dynamo laboratory practice, 3 courses
　Laboratory work in general physics and applied electricity
Chemistry, 7 courses
　General chemistry
　Qualitative analysis, 3 courses
　Spectroscopic qualitative analysis
　Quantitative analysis
　Technical gas analysis
Botany, 3 courses
Drawing and art, 5 courses
　Drawing
　Painting in oils or water colors
　Modeling
　Perspective
　History and theory
Mechanical drawing and designing, 3 courses
Experimental engineering, 2 courses

Matriculated students of the university may receive the same credit for summer courses approved by the university faculty as for the same amount and kind in the university but not more than 10 university hours in one summer session will be credited. The credit will be based on the regular examinations held at the beginning of the fall term.

Students not matriculated will receive certificates of attendance.

Summer law school. The session opens July 5, 1897 and continues six weeks. The subjects studied will be contracts, torts, crimes, corporations, real property, wills, equity and evidence. Special attention is paid to the needs of students preparing for the bar examinations The fee for the course is $35.

NEW YORK UNIVERSITY

New York university will hold its third summer session during the summer of 1897. Instruction is offered in mathematics, chemistry, biology, physics, psychology, history, German, French, economics, pedagogy and physical training. The courses will be given by professors and instructors of the university, in the new buildings of the undergraduate college at University hights, New York city. The equipment at University hights, including libraries, reading-rooms, laboratories, recitation halls, residence halls, and gymnasium, will be available for the work of the summer session. The session will begin July 5 and end Aug. 13, except the pedagogy courses, which will begin July 12 and end Aug. 20. The summer courses are offered for the benefit of teachers and others who are unable to attend during the regular college year. Experience shows that much can be accomplished in six weeks by students who confine their attention to one or two subjects. The lectures are given during the first five days of the week, leaving Saturdays free for those who wish to visit the various points of interest in and about the city.

The new buildings of the undergraduate college are beautifully situated at University hights, in the northern part of New York city, 12 miles from the lower end of Manhattan island. The grounds, which cover 25 acres, lie on a high ridge, overlooking the Harlem, the palisades of the Hudson, and Long Island sound. This ridge of land with its low temperature and favorable breezes renders University hights a most inviting spot for a summer school. It would be difficult to find a location better adapted for summer work. The campus is not within the limits of the city except in a legal sense. It is surrounded by large family estates whose beautiful parks, drives and walks add to the attractive scenery so characteristic of the Hudson river region. University hights is easily and quickly reached by the New York Central railroad, from the Grand central station at 42d st. The university campus is 10 minutes' walk from Morris hights station.

Charles Butler hall and the new East hall, the residence halls of the college, will be open during the summer session. Except where two occupy the same room or where a suite of rooms is preferred, there will be a uniform price of $3 per week, and a choice of rooms will be granted in order of application. Diagrams and prices of rooms can be obtained from the secretary. Students are advised to secure their rooms in advance. This may be done by making a deposit of $5, which will be considered as part payment for the rooms. Students will find it to their advantage to live on the campus. Much time will be saved, and the social life centering in the residence halls will be found pleasant. Board will be furnished in one of the college buildings under the supervision of a committee of the faculty. The price will be $4.50 per week.

By vote of the faculty of the college and the faculty of the School of pedagogy, work done in the summer session will be accepted as counting toward a degree, when it is equivalent to the work required in the corresponding courses in the University college or the School of pedagogy. Those not candidates for degrees may obtain certificates if they desire them. This year the courses in pedagogy will begin July 12 and end Aug. 20, a week later than the other courses, to give opportunity, for those who wish, to attend the meetings of the National educational association. Students attending these courses retain their rooms for the additional work at the end of the regular session without extra charge. Only graduates of colleges or of normal schools, advanced course, are eligible for enrolment in the School of pedagogy.

Tuition fee for each student will be $25, with an additional fee of $5 for each laboratory course. The tuition fee admits to all courses which the student may elect subject to the approval of the faculty. As a rule, students are advised to confine their courses to one subject, but they are free to attend occasional lectures of special interest in other departments.

All correspondence should be addressed to Professor Charles B. Bliss, New York university, University hights, New York city.

NEW YORK STATE LIBRARY SCHOOL

The first summer session of the New York state library school was held in July and August, 1896. The number of students was limited to 20, but two others took part of the work. Of these 22, all but one were engaged in library work, and 10 were in N. Y. libraries. At the examinations, 14 passed, four of these with honor.[a]

On account of the American library association's trip to Europe this summer, and also the extra labor involved in moving the Library school from the third to the fifth floors of the capitol, the second session of the summer school will be postponed till July and August, 1898.

TEACHERS COLLEGE, NEW YORK

The attendance at the first session of the School of manual training in 1896 was so much larger than had been expected that the school will be continued, July 7-Aug. 11, with an improved course and a larger teaching staff. The number of students last year was 53, including graduates of colleges and such institutions as Drexel institute, Pratt institute and Teachers college. In addition to the regular course in manual training for elementary schools, free-hand drawing and painting, mechanical drawing, forging, wood-joinery, wood-turning, pattern making and wood-carving, there will be a course of lectures and conferences on Mondays, Wednesdays and Fridays from 11:15 to 12:15. Prof. J: F. Reigart, of Teachers college, will give five lectures on Teaching as a fine art. The following are the subjects: 1) The teacher as an artist; 2) The nature and elements of creative power; 3) Development of creative power; 4) Principles of criticism; 5) Principles applied to government and instruction.

The remainder of the course will be on subjects of particular interest to teachers of drawing and manual training. Subjects suggested by the daily lectures and work in the shops and studios will be selected for conferences.

Persons intending to become students should notify the director, Charles A. Bennett, before June 15, stating what course they intend to take.

---
[a] Above 90%

FRENCH RECREATION CLASS FOR GIRLS

An opportunity for the daily study of French is offered by Mlle Debray-Longchamp at her summer home in the Adirondacks on the west shore of Lake Placid. College preparatory work may also be done. The expenses for the 14 weeks beginning June 21 including tuition, books, stationery, use of piano, chaperonage, board, laundry and traveling expenses from New York to Lake Placid and return is estimated from $225 to $300 according to studies pursued. For farther information address Mlle Debray-Longchamp, 105 W 74th st., New York.

OTHER AMERICAN SCHOOLS

GREENACRE

The Greenacre lectures, at Eliot, Maine, four miles from Portsmouth, N. H., were organized in 1894, the object of the movement being to afford opportunity for rational rest and recreation, together with courses of lectures on vital topics which should stimulate the higher nature and enlarge the horizon of life. The lectures are supported by voluntary contributions, no specific charge being made for the work. Many of the ablest thinkers in America have participated in the programs from year to year freely giving their services for the sake of the benefits derived from the work.

The lectures will be given as usual during 1897, in a series of conferences on the following topics:

July 1— 5, Peace and arbitration
     6—11, Education in home and school
    12—18, Literature and art
    19—25, Evolution
    26—31, Electricity and invention
Aug. 1— 7, Ideals in business life
    8—14, Psychology
   15—21, Sociology
   22—28, Nature
   29—Sept. 2. Comparative religion

MONSALVAT SCHOOL OF COMPARATIVE RELIGION

Auxiliary to the Greenacre work, a school for the comparative study of religions was inaugurated in 1896, and will be continued during the month of August, 1897, with the following corps of instructors and general subjects of study:

History and philosophy of religion and Christian origins, Dr Lewis G. Janes, M. A. (Brown university) director of the Cambridge conferences

Religion, ethics and psychology of Buddhism, Anagárika H. Dharmapála, Ceylon

Vedanta philosophy and religions of India, Swâmi Sâradânanda, India

Zoroastrianism and the religion of the Parsis, Jehranghier D. Cola, Bombay

Religion of the Jains, Virchand R. Gandhi, India

Religions of China, Rev. F. Huberty James, England, 16 years missionary in China

The fees for this instruction are voluntary. Members of the school or attendants of any of these courses of lectures will be required to enroll themselves, and are expected to pay a small sum on entering. For the further compensation of the teachers, the pupils may contribute such sums as they may desire to bestow for that purpose.

For programs and full particulars, address the director, Dr Lewis G. Janes (prior to July 1) 9 Clifton place, Brooklyn, N. Y.; (during July and August) Greenacre, Eliot, Maine.

GREENACRE SCHOOL OF LITERATURE

During the month of July class lectures on literary topics will be given as follows:

Philosophy and poetry of Ralph Waldo Emerson, Charles Malloy

Religion of the poets, Rev. William Norman Guthrie

Indian dramas, the Swâmi Sâradânanda

For farther information address Charles Malloy, Waltham, Mass.

GREENACRE SCHOOL OF MUSIC

Class lessons in vocal and instrumental music, harmony and voice-culture will be given under the direction of Miss Mary H. Burnham, of New York.

For farther information concerning the Greenacre work, address Miss Sarah J. Farmer, Eliot, Maine.

NORTHFIELD CONFERENCES

The opening Bible conference of the series held at Northfield, Mass. each year will meet June 25-July 4. The World's student Christian federation will hold its first convention at Northfield in connection with the American intercollegiate Y. M. C. A. conference. Among the speakers will be Pres. Patton of Princeton and Dr Henry Van Dyke of New York.

The Y. W. C. A. conference, July 9-20 is reported under the International Y. W. C. A. conferences.

The general conference for Christian workers opens July 29 and closes Aug. 16. During July and August a Y. M. C. A. encampment is open.

HARVARD SUMMER SCHOOL

The following courses will be given at the session which begins July 6 and ends Aug. 14.

English, 5 courses
    Composition, 2 courses
    Anglo Saxon
    Chaucer
    English literature of the 18th century
German, 2 courses
French, 2 courses
Latin, for teachers
Greek, for teachers
History and government, 3 courses
    American history
    Civil government
    Opportunities in research

Education and teaching including history and principles of education; psychology for teachers; organization, management and supervision of schools

Methods of teaching algebra and geometry to beginners

Mathematics, 4 courses
  Solid geometry
  Trigonometry
  Plane analytic geometry
  Calculus

Engineering, 2 courses
  Topographical surveying
  Railway engineering

Physics, 2 courses

Chemistry, 4 courses
  Fundamental principles of chemistry
  Qualitative analysis
  Quantitative analysis
  Organic chemistry

Botany

Geology, 3 courses
  Elementary geology
  Geologic field work, 2 courses

Geography, 2 courses
  Elementary physiography
  Geography of the U. S.

Physical training, 2 courses

Courses at the medical school

Courses at the dental school

    The courses are intended primarily for teachers but a few of the more elementary meet the needs of beginners and may be counted toward a degree. A catalogue giving full information of all courses may be obtained from Montague Chamberlain, 16 University hall, Cambridge, Mass.

HARVARD SUMMER SCHOOL OF PHYSICAL TRAINING

The same courses will be given as last year an account of which was given in the last report. The session will begin July 6 and end Aug. 7. Students intending to take the course are recommended to take a moderate amount of systematic physical exercise and to make a study of Gray's *Anatomy*, Waller's *Human physiology* and Appleton's *School physics*.

SAUVEUR COLLEGE OF LANGUAGES AND AMHERST SUMMER SCHOOL

The 22d session will be held at Amherst college July 5-Aug. 13. Changes are noted in the departments of German and Latin, Prof. Arnold Werner-Spanhoofd and Mrs Sofie de Beyersdorff being in charge of the German and Prof. E. D. Merriman of the Latin. There will be classes for adults in French, German, Italian, Spanish, modern and ancient Greek, Latin and English literature, and two classes in French for children. There will be each day seven hours of French, six of German, three of Latin, three of Greek, two of Italian, one of Spanish and two of English literature. Classes meet daily from 8 a. m. to 1 p. m. except on Saturdays which are devoted to recreations and excursions.

In addition to regular courses, Dr Sauveur will give a course of six lectures in French; Dr Bernhardt, two courses in German, one a discussion of the American poets, novelists and humorists as viewed by German critics, the other a description of Kaulbach's six great historical frescos in the Royal museum of Berlin with stereoscopic illustrations; other lectures will be given by the directors of the various departments.

W. I. Fletcher, librarian of Amherst college, offers the same course in library economy with such changes as have been suggested by the previous years' experience. Miss Hitchcock of Smith college remains in charge of the art department.

The tuition for all the studies and lectures of the school of language is $20 for adults and $6 for children. In the other departments the tuition varies according to the subject.

MARTHAS VINEYARD SUMMER INSTITUTE

The work as usual consists of an elementary and a high school course in the school of methods and 19 courses are offered in the academic department.

The school opens July 12. The school of methods closes July 30. The oratory, drawing and vocal music departments close Aug. 6, the other academic departments, Aug. 13.

The school is known as one of the oldest, largest and broadest summer schools for teachers in the U. S. The attendance in 1896 was over 725 from 40 states, territories and provinces.

H. E. HOLT NORMAL INSTITUTE OF VOCAL HARMONY

The 14th session will be held in Lexington, Mass. beginning July 13 and closing with graduating exercises July 30. Nearly 100 pupils attended the session of 1896 and 17 students were graduated. Francis W. Parker says, 'What Grube has done for number, Delsarte for elocution and Ritter for geography, Prof. Holt is doing for music in our schools.'

MASSACHUSETTS INSTITUTE OF TECHNOLOGY

During June and July the following courses will be given if a minimum number of students apply before a fixed date·

1 Mechanical drawing and descriptive geometry

2 Mathematics· analytic geometry

3 Architecture
   Shades and shadows
   Elementary design

4 Chemistry
   Analytical chemistry
   Organic analysis, reactions and preparations
   Principles of organic chemistry
   Water analysis and air analysis
   Gas, oil and sugar analysis

5 Biology
 General zoology
 Physiology and hygiene
 Bacteriology and the micro-organisms of fermentation

6 Physics
 Mechanics, light and electricity
 Heat
 Physical measurements
 Electrical testing

7 European history

8 Modern languages
 French
 German

9 Mechanism

10 Shopwork
 Woodwork
 Forging
 Chipping and filing
 Machine-tool work

SCHOOL OF APPLIED ETHICS

No session will be held this year and the future plans are not as yet announced.

CLARK UNIVERSITY

Most of the courses offered for the fifth session, July 19-31, are entirely new and it is announced that the school is now a school of psychology, physiology, anthropology and pedagogy. The work is intended specially for:

1 University students desirous of learning features of the new psychology, some of which are not now accessible anywhere else.

2 University students of pedagogy, or of other departments, who may desire a general survey of modern psychology, education, etc.

3 Professors of pedagogy, normal school principals and instructors.

4 School superintendents and principals.

5 Writers of school text-books and publishers.

The work in biological psychology, presented by Pres. G. Stanley Hall will, it is believed, open a new field in education. The course of greatest interest will be the study and teaching of nature devoted to topics of chief importance in primary and secondary education.

Special attention has been given to child study for the last three years and it is now proposed to conclude this line of work for the present by gathering up all the results thus far obtained and applying them to actual studies and methods of school and college work by subjects and by grades.

Dr Edmund C. Sanford will give a course in psychology which is a survey of the most important results of recent psychological investigation illustrated by apparatus and class experiments; and two special courses of one week each, one an illustrative course in pedagogic measurements, the other a practical course of simple experiments.

Dr C. F. Hodge will give 12 lectures on Outlines of general biology for public school grades and the high school, with laboratory work and demonstrations. This course is coordinate with those of Pres. Hall.

Dr Adolf Meyer will give 10 lectures on the Principles of neurology and Mr Colin C. Stewart, a laboratory course corresponding with and illustrating Dr Meyer's course.

Dr W: H. Burnham offers two courses in pedagogy, six lectures on the History of education and six on the Hygiene of instruction.

Dr A. F. Chamberlain announces a new course on Anthropological aspects of childhood presenting child study from the points of view of folk thought and modern anthropological science.

The evening lectures, which are free to summer school students, are as follows:

Dr G. Stanley Hall, 1) Specialization, 2) Some fundamental religious affirmations warranted by psychology and other sciences; Dr E. C. Sanford, 1) Mind and body, 2) Physiology and psychology of color; Dr C. F. Hodge, Treatment of alcohol physiology in universities and medical schools compared with its teaching in our common schools; Dr Adolf Meyer, On mental hygiene in the light of a study of nervous and mental diseases; Dr W. H. Burnham, Training of teachers; Dr A. F. Chamberlain, 1) Divinity of childhood, 2) Attitude of primitive people towards nature.

For information address Mr Louis N. Wilson, clerk of the university, Worcester, Mass.

COTUIT SUMMER SCHOOL

The Cotuit summer school which offers a college preparatory course to students will hold its third session from July 7 to Sept. 15. New classes will be formed Aug. 11. Applications should be addressed to Prin. Charles E. Fish, Waban school, Waban, Mass. till June 25; after that to Cotuit, Mass.

UNIVERSITY EXTENSION SUMMER MEETING

The fifth summer meeting conducted by the American society will be held in Philadelphia July 6-30, 1897.

In Department A, Medieval life and thought, the courses will be in sequence with those of the last two years in Greek life and thought and Roman life and thought.

The lectures this year will cover the literature, history, philosophy, religion, education and architecture of the period in as complete a way as possible. Prof. Jewett will give a course of five lectures on Arabic history, Prof. Cheyney, five lectures on the Formation of the English constitution and Prof. D. C. Munro, three lectures on the Influence of the crusades. In the department of literature Prof. Lang will treat of Romance literature, Dr C. G. Child of Early English literature. The Constitution of the medieval church will be the subject of five lectures by Prof Shanahan and Life in the English monasteries will be considered by Dr Fairley. Medieval philosophy and Medieval education will be considered respectively by Prof. Shanahan in 10 lectures and Prof. D C. Munro in five lectures. English local institutions will be the subject of five lectures by Prof. Andrews of Bryn Mawr, Architecture by Mr Pilcher, and Medieval science by Prof. Magie.

Psychology, child study and kindergarten will embrace a course of 20 lectures by Prof. Lightner Witmer of the University of

Pennsylvania, on Modern problems and theories in psychology; five lectures by Prof. J. M. Baldwin, of Princeton, on Mental development; five lectures by Prof. E. B. Titchener, of Cornell, on Psychology of attention; five lectures by Mr R. P: Halleck, on the Education of the central nervous system; five lectures by Miss Laura Fisher, Boston, on the Psychological significance of the kindergarten. Laboratory courses will be given by Prof. A. F. Witmer on the Structure and function of the nervous system and the sense organs, a demonstration course in the Psychology of sensation and perception, by Prof. Lightner Witmer and Mr Albert L. Lewis, a course in Child psychology by Prof. Lightner Witmer and Mr Oliver Cornman, a course in Advanced psychology by Dr Edgar A. Singer jr and Mr Albert L. Lewis. There will be also a psychologic clinic and training school, the practice kindergarten and educational conferences.

Department C is a series of round table conferences, in which will be considered the pedagogic aspects of the various subjects brought up in the other departments. Professors Hart and Davis of Harvard, Prof. Bronson of Brown, Mr Edward Everett Hale jr and others will take part.

Departments D and E will be conducted on the plan of the regular college class, for the benefit of beginners and more advanced students in mathematics and Latin. In the Department of music, courses on harmony and counterpoint are offered by Prof. Hugh A. Clarke, of the University of Pennsylvania.— DANA C. MUNRO, *Director*

LEHIGH UNIVERSITY

A summer school of surveying will be held at Lehigh university South Bethlehem, Pa. for four weeks beginning June 21. Three courses are offered:

1 Land and town surveying, corresponding to the course given to civil engineering students in the second term of the sophomore year, and open to students who have completed the freshman year or to any one having a good knowledge of geometry and trigonometry.

2 Topographical surveying, corresponding to the civil engineering course in the first term of the junior year and open to all who have completed course 1 or its equivalent.

3 Geodetic surveying, corresponding to the senior course in civil engineering and open to all who have completed courses 1 and 2. Examinations are held at the close of the session and certificates are given. The fee is $15.

PENNSYLVANIA SUMMER SCHOOL

The Pennsylvania summer school at Huntingdon, the only professional summer school for teachers in Pennsylvania, will hold its third annual session July 12-30, 1897. Huntingdon is on the banks of the Juniata river in a beautiful mountain valley noted for its historic associations. The Juniata college buildings which will accommodate 200 students with rooms and board are used by the school.

The school aims to give teachers an opportunity to review and keep in touch with recent educational advances and also to take up more advanced lines of professional work. There will be a general course in Educational philosophy by different members of the faculty and special courses in biology and microscopy, child study, drawing and painting, geography, grading and management of rural schools, history and civil government, history of education, literature, methods of teaching and school management, music, natural science, physical culture, photography, psychology, reading and elocution, supervision and high school management.

Round table conferences on pedagogic subjects will be held every afternoon when there are no lectures and there will be evening lectures and musical and literary entertainments. The tuition is $15 and board for the term $10. The secretary is Miss Amanda Landes, Millersville, Pa.

NATIONAL SCHOOL OF ELOCUTION AND ORATORY

The National school of elocution and oratory of Philadelphia will hold a summer session of four weeks, beginning July 8 in connection with the Pennsylvania Chautauqua at Mt Gretna, Pa.

JEWISH CHAUTAUQUA SUMMER SCHOOL AND ASSEMBLY

The Jewish Chautauqua society being the department of Jewish studies in the Chautauqua literary and scientific circle has been in existence about three years. It has created a series of reading courses in Jewish history and literature with nearly 1500 readers in all parts of the United States, Canada and British India.

The following are the courses of readings for circles and individual readers:

1 Young folks' reading union, arranged by Miss Diana Hirschler, intended for post-confirmants, or boys and girls from 15 to 18 years of age. This is a two years' course in fiction and history, in a series of interesting programs for semi-monthly meetings. Members who complete the two years' course will receive a certificate. This course leads up to the regular Chautauqua courses in Jewish history and literature. Membership fee, 25 cents per annum

2 Bible course. In answer to an urgent and wide-spread demand, Rev. Dr Henry Berkowitz, Chancellor of the Jewish Chautauqua society, has prepared a guide for Bible reading, entitled 'The open Bible,' and arranged in accordance with the Chautauqua system of education. Part 1 covers the entire range of Bible history. Membership fee, 50 cents.

'The open Bible,' part 2 contains the books of the Bible not treated of in part 1, and the Apocrypha. (In preparation)

3 Courses in post-biblical history and literature, arranged by Prof. Richard J. H. Gottheil

a Comprising the era from Ezra and the return of the Jews from Babylon (537 B. C. E.) to the origin of Christianity. Membership fee, 50 cents.

b On the origin of Christianity and the compilation of the Talmud. Membership fee, 50 cents.

c The Jews during the crusades and their Golden era in Spain.

4 General Chautauqua course. A four years' course of readings in history, literature, science and art of a high school or academic grade. Membership fee, 50 cents per annum.

5 Special courses of reading on a wide range of subjects arranged by men and women of acknowledged leadership in their departments.

The first summer assembly ever projected by Jews and for the presentation of Jewish thought will be established by this society at Atlantic City, N. J. Daily sessions will be held beginning July 23 and closing Aug. 8, 1897.

At the opening meeting Sunday July 25 an address will be delivered by the Chancellor, Dr Henry Berkowitz of Philadelphia. Fraternal greetings will be extended to delegates of the various national organizations for education among the Jewish people, as follows:

Council of Jewish women, Mrs Hannah Solomons, president, Chicago

Sabbath school union of America, Rabbi William Rosenau, Baltimore

Jewish publication society, Dr Charles Bernheimer, secretary, Philadelphia

Hebrew union college, Rev. Charles Levi, secretary of the faculty, Cincinnati

Theological seminary, Dr S. Morias, president, Philadelphia

National farm school, Rev. Dr Krauskopf, president, Philadelphia

Central conference of American rabbis, Dr M. H. Harris, New York

A series of popular evening lectures will be held. Among the speakers named are Dr R: J. H. Gottheil of Columbia university, New York, Hon. Simon Wolf, Washington, D. C. and Mr Leo N. Levi of Galveston, Texas

Chautauqua circles will be conducted in Bible study by the chancellor, Dr Berkowitz, based on his syllabus entitled 'The open Bible,' and by Mr George A. Kohut of New York.

Chautauqua circles in post-biblical history will be conducted by Prof. R: J. H. Gottheil of Columbia university, author of the syllabuses in that subject. His topic will be the Rise of Christianity and the origin of the Talmud. Dr M. H. Harris of New

York will lead a circle in the study of Jewish history, from the return of the Jews from Babylon to the rise of Christianity.

The first teachers institute for Jewish Sabbath school teachers will be held. Complimentary tickets are issued to all these teachers throughout the land. Dr Henry M. Leipziger of New York will be in charge. A series of practice lessons will be conducted in primary work by Miss Ella Jacobs of Philadelphia, in biblical history by Dr William Rosenau of Baltimore, in Psalms by Dr M. H. Harris of New York.

There will be a series of talks to teachers (syllabuses will be provided) on Bible ethics and how to teach the subject, by Dr K. Kohler of New York; on Jewish Sabbath school pedagogics by Dr Louis Grossman of Detroit; Principles and methods of teaching by Dr H. M. Leipziger of New York.

Lectures on the following special topics will be given:

Palestine illustrated with stereopticon views by Prof. Richard Gottheil; Family life in biblical law, Mr David W. Amram, Philadelphia; Fundamental principles in teaching, Miss Henrietta Szold, Baltimore.

Practical problems will be discussed, among these, Sabbath school organization by Dr Lee K. Frankel of Philadelphia; the Bond between the home and school by Mrs Rebekah Kohut of New York, Sabbath school libraries by Dr Charles S. Bernheimer, Philadelphia.

Divine services will be held and sermons preached by Dr Joseph Krauskopf, Philadelphia, Rev. E. N. Calisch, Richmond, Va., Stephen S. Wise, New York, I. L. Leucht, New Orleans, Joseph Silverman, New York and Rev. S. Hecht, Milwaukee.

The Young folks reading union, a preparatory course for boys and girls will hold sessions under the guidance of Miss Diana Hirschler, Philadelphia, Rabbi Charles Fleisher, Boston, and Isaac Hassler, of Philadelphia.

Social entertainments will also be held. A season ticket at one dollar admits to all sessions.

A complete prospectus is to be had by addressing Lee K. Frankel, director of the Jewish summer assembly, P. O. Box 825 Philadelphia, Pa.

UNIVERSITY OF VIRGINIA
Summer law lectures

Prof. R. C. Minor and Prof. W. M. Lile of the university faculty have conducted the summer lectures since the death of Prof. John B. Minor, the founder, in 1895. Hon. John M. Harlan, associate justice of the U. S. supreme court, delivered a course of lectures before the school in 1896 which was so favorably received that he has been persuaded to become one of the regular faculty of the summer school. The courses now offered will be of benefit to the following classes: 1) those just beginning their professional studies who expect to attend a full course of law; 2) those who propose to pursue their studies privately; 3) those desiring a review preparatory to collegiate work or as candidates for admission to the bar; 4) young practitioners who, lacking the advantage of systematic instruction, find their progress slow, painful and unsatisfactory; 5) those who wish a knowledge of law as a part of a liberal education.

Four classes are announced this year.

Class 1 mainly, though not exclusively, for advanced students, includes 36 lectures by Prof. Minor on common law pleading and practice, real estate and law of corporations.

Class 2 consists of 36 lectures by Hon. John M. Harlan, on constitutional law and federal practice.

Class 3 consists of 36 lectures by Prof. Lile on elementary law, principal and agent, husband and wife, parent and child, guardian and ward, personal property, wills.

Class 4, for Virginia students and practitioners only, includes 25 lectures by Prof. Lile on Virginia statutes.

A special course of 25 lectures, on evidence and mercantile paper is offered by James B. Green, law instructor in the university, beginning July 1.

Special attention is given throughout the course to the bibliography of law and the student is taught how to use text-books and cases in tracing principles and in preparing briefs. No credit is given in the university for summer work.

The dates are as follows: Class 1, July 1-21, Aug. 11-31; class 2, July 1-Aug. 11; class 3, July 21-Aug. 31; class 4, July 21-Aug. 20.

Summer school of physical training

The course will cover both theory and practice, theory only so far as to give the best results in the shortest period of time.

Anatomy, physiology, hygiene and organic training will be studied and an outline of future reading suggested. The practical side will be developed beyond theory.

New features of the work are the introduction of field and track athletics.

The exercise hall is the Fayerweather gymnasium with a floor space of 12,000 feet. The school opens July 1 for eight weeks. The fee for the entire course is $40.

WAKE FOREST COLLEGE

The first summer session of this college will be held at Wake Forest, N. C. June 28-July 23. No preparation is required for entrance and the elective plan will be followed. Instruction will be given mainly by lectures and so far as time will allow will be the same as in the regular college courses. Prof. W: H. Page will give a course of lectures for teachers on the science and art of teaching and school management.

A pastors' institute will be held at the same time as the summer school. Six lectures will be given on the Book of Genesis, Bible doctrines, Preparation and delivery of sermons, Old testament history, Gospel of Matthew and Book of Romans and four lectures on Pastoral duties and Baptist history. A class in New testament Greek will be formed.

The summer school fee is $5, and the pastors' institute entrance fee, $3.

Summer law school

The law school will begin June 21 and continue 10 weeks. In each of the two classes, junior and senior, 50 lectures will be given.

CATHOLIC WINTER SCHOOL OF AMERICA

The Catholic winter school of America held its second session at New Orleans, La. March 4-20. The opening religious services were held in the Cathedral of St Louis Sunday, Feb. 28 when Most Rev. Archbishop Martinelli, Apostolic delegate to the U. S. celebrated pontifical mass. The school was formally opened in Tulane hall, March 4, in the presence of a large audience and many bishops and clergy. The lectures were of a high character and the second session was considered a decided success.

SOUTHERN STUDENTS CONFERENCE

The Southern students conference meets for the purpose of training the leaders of college young men's Christian associations in Bible study and methods of Christian work by students for students. The conference at Knoxville is designed specially for the students of the south and is similar to the conferences under the same auspices at Northfield, Mass., Lake Geneva, Wis. and Casadero, Cal.

The plan of work includes normal Bible classes, conferences on methods of Y. M. C. A. work, addresses on biblical subjects and for the purpose of deepening the spiritual life of the students, conferences on foreign missions. The afternoons are devoted to recreation and athletics.

Among the speakers and teachers for 1897 are Rev. C. I. Scofield, East Northfield, Mass, C. T. Studd, Cambridge university, England, Dr W. R. Lambuth, Nashville, Mr L. D. Wishard, New York, Rev. R. J. McBryde, Lexington, Va., A. C. Harte, Mobile, H. W. Luce, New York and W. H. Morriss, Baltimore.

NORTHERN INDIANA NORMAL SCHOOL

The first session was held in 1877 with an attendance of 300. At the session of 1896 the attendance reached 2000. There will be classes in the departments of mathematics, natural science, language, literature, history, pharmacy, music, vocal and instrumental, drawing and painting, phonography, typewriting, penmanship and commercial work. Special advantages are offered in literature for the study of the origin, growth and development of American and English literature with English and American authors.

There will also be a class in Shakspere, reading five of his best plays and a class in preparatory literature for college entrance for 1897-98 as arranged by the Association of colleges for the English classics.

There will be a teachers' training class and special attention will be given to professional work in pedagogy, psychology, child study and kindergarten.

The school opens June 8 for a term of 10 weeks. Catalogues may be obtained from the president, H. B. Brown, Valparaiso, Ind.

WHEATON COLLEGE

The fourth summer session will be held in the college buildings, Wheaton, Ill June 28-Aug. 6, 1897. The school is intended to meet the needs of teachers and others who desire to rest by liberalizing study. As many teachers prefer other lines of study than those which occupy their attention throughout the year, the work offered is not primarily such as is done in the public schools. A single study is recommended to students and it is expected to accomplish as much in the six weeks as is ordinarily done in a 13 weeks term. Courses are offered in all the departments of the college and credit will be given in the college for summer school work. Recitations and lectures occupy one hour each. Evenings are given up to lectures, readings, musicales and social gatherings. Wheaton is 25 miles west of Chicago and Saturday excursions to Chicago and various points of interest are planned. The fee for the first course is $5 and for each additional one $2.50. Board for the term is $24.

ILLINOIS STATE NORMAL UNIVERSITY

A summer institute will be held at normal for three weeks beginning July 12. Instruction will be given in all the various lines of professional work taught in the institution. The subjects are pedagogy, geography and history, biologic sciences, physical sciences,

English literature, Latin and German, English grammar, mathematics, school law, reading and physical culture and art. A practice school will be in session in the morning to illustrate the work of the various grades.

BAY VIEW SUMMER UNIVERSITY

The college and school of methods of which Miss M Louise Jones of the Kansas state normal school is principal offers elementary and academic courses in kindergarten, primary and grammar grade work, Sloyd drawing, school music, elementary science, literature, history, civil government, mathematics, botany, physics, chemistry, French, German and Latin. Dr Arnold Tompkins, University of Illinois and Pres. Walter L. Hervey, Teachers college, will give courses in pedagogy, psychology and school management. The Bible school will be conducted by Dr F. K. Sanders, Yale university; the art school by J. H. Vanderpool, Chicago art institute; school of oratory by Prof. A. H. Merrill, Vanderbilt university; school of physical culture by Miss L. E. Phoenix, Oswego state normal, N. Y. and the conservatory of music by Mr Wilson G. Smith, Cleveland, O   Over 40 popular assembly lecturers have been engaged.

The school opens July 13 and closes Aug. 17. For descriptive circulars address J. M. Hall, Flint, Mich.

UNIVERSITY OF MICHIGAN

The courses offered by the summer school July 7-Aug. 18 are classified as preparatory courses for university work, special courses for teachers and advanced courses.

Students regularly matriculated in the university may receive credit according to the following rules: 1) No student shall receive more than six hours credit for work done during one session; 2) Not more than 12 hours credit may be secured to count toward a degree. A full course consists of 30 lessons, one hour a day, five days in the week. The fee for one course is $15, two courses, $25, three courses $30.

The law school will open July 5 for an eight weeks session. The methods of instruction combine the lecture, the text-book and the case system. An examination will be held on each subject when closed.

A course of free lectures and entertainments is given each year.

SECRETARIAL INSTITUTE AND TRAINING SCHOOL OF YOUNG MEN'S CHRISTIAN ASSOCIATIONS

Since last year the Western secretarial institute at Lake Geneva has been consolidated with the Y. M. C. A. training school in Chicago under the name Secretarial institute and training school of young men's Christian associations.

The dates for the different programs of 1897 are as follows:

June 18-27 College students conference

July 2-13 Y. W. C. A. summer school

July 14-Aug. 13 Summer school for secretaries and physical directors

Aug. 1-14 Institute program

The camp is open to members and guests from July 1 to Sept. 1.

Chancellor W. F. McDowell of the University of Denver, Prof. J. M. Coulter of Chicago university, Dr R. A. Torrey of Chicago Bible institute, John R. Mott of New York and S. M. Sayford of Boston will take part in the college conference.

WISCONSIN SUMMER SCHOOL OF LIBRARY SCIENCE

Miss Cornelia Marvin, instructor in reference work and bibliography at the Armour institute, Chicago, will conduct the summer school of library science which is held at Madison, Wis. under the auspices of the University of Wisconsin summer school. The session opens July 5 and closes Aug. 13. The instruction which is by lecture, demonstration and laboratory work will follow the treatment of a book through all processes in the library from the accession department till it has been classified, catalogued, loaned, repaired and rebound. The principles of cataloguing of the Dewey decimal classification and the Cutter expansive classifications will receive special attention.

COLUMBIAN CATHOLIC SUMMER SCHOOL

The courses of lectures announced for the third session which will be held at Madison, Wis. July 11-30 are as follows: Religion and politics, Christian antiquities of Rome, Dante, Holy Scripture, Political economy, literature, law, Early missions after the pioneers, psychology, theosophy, and masterpieces of Christian art.

DES MOINES SUMMER SCHOOL OF METHODS

The growth of the summer school of methods since the first session in 1890 has been marked. It is permanently established and further progress is expected this year. The session opens July 5 and closes July 30.

The general outline of work is as follows:

PROFESSIONAL TRAINING

1 Primary and kindergarten methods
2 Methods in intermediate and grammar school work in all branches, including music, drawing and nature study
3 Lectures on school supervision, science of teaching and the art of teaching and managing
4 Lectures on psychology and history of education

ACADEMIC INSTRUCTION

1 A thorough review of all the common branches
2 Rhetoric, literature, civics and economics
3 Algebra, geometry and astronomy
4 Elocution and physical culture
5 Physical geography, physics, botany, geology
6 Penmanship, drawing and vocal music. An examination for state certificates is held at the close of the session

DRAKE UNIVERSITY SUMMER LATIN SCHOOL

The session of nine weeks is devoted entirely to the study of Latin thus enabling students by concentration to cover the work of 36 weeks of Latin as ordinarily pursued. The school opens June 21 and closes Aug. 20. The first year class studies Collar and Daniell's *First Latin book*, 7 weeks and Caesar, book 2, two weeks; the second year class spends five weeks reading three books of Caesar and four weeks on four orations of Cicero; the third year, class spends 7 weeks on six books of Virgil and two weeks on 2000 lines of Ovid. The writing of Latin is made prominent in the first two years and metrical reading and mythology, in the third year. The Roman method of pronunciation is taught.

A series of lectures will be given on the practical value of Latin and its importance as a means of culture and discipline. The fee for the course is $15.

KANSAS STATE NORMAL SCHOOL

The object of this summer school is to enable teachers to secure professional training and a college education by attending a series of summer sessions. A complete record of all work done is kept.

Students are advised to take only two studies. In botany and zoology from four to five hours a week are required to be spent in the laboratories. The fee is $10 for the first study and $3 for each additional study. A nine weeks session is held beginning June 11, 1897.

FAIRMOUNT CHAUTAUQUA

The Fairmount Chautauqua announces its second session at Kansas City, Mo., June 1-12 More attention will be given to school work than last year and an attractive Chautauqua assembly program has been arranged with the usual conferences and round tables.

GREELEY SUMMER SCHOOL

Joseph F. Daniels, art instructor in the state normal school, Greeley, will give a course of 16 lectures on form study and drawing in public schools. The topics are: 1) Forms of expression and correlation; 2) Projections, orthographic and perspective; 3) Theory of color; 4) Use of color; 5) Light and shade; 6) Historic ornament; 7) Decorative design; 8) How to judge a picture; 9) How to decorate a school room; 10) Blackboard drawing, specially for the country school; 11) History of art; 12) Practical things; 13) Esthetics The remaining lectures are reserved for consideration of problems arising during the course. The course ticket is $4.

LELAND STANFORD JR UNIVERSITY

Courses open to matriculated students in the university, to teachers and others qualified for the work will be given at the university beginning May 31. The subjects are Greek, Latin, German, French, English, history, mathematics, physics, chemistry, civil engineering, electrical engineering and music. The fees are $15 for a six weeks course and $20 for an eight weeks course.

Hopkins seaside laboratory. The laboratory is at Pacific Grove on Monterey bay. The sixth session will open June 7 and close July 17. Courses by instructors from the biological departments of the university will be given in elementary zoology and botany, advanced invertebrate zoology, vertebrate embryology and the physiology of marine forms. The fee including laboratory materials and supplies is $25.

INTERNATIONAL Y. W. C. A. CONFERENCES

Four conferences are announced for the summer of 1897. The first will be held at Asheville, S. C. June 15-25 in the Normal and collegiate institute, directed by Miss Eva Seevers. Mornings are devoted to conference and Bible study, afternoons to rest and recreation and evenings to vesper services and public meetings.

The Lake Geneva conference will be held at Y. M. C. A. camp, Lake Geneva, Wis. July 2-13 with Miss Eva Seevers as leader. The Northfield conference at Northfield, Mass. will be held July 9-20 with Miss E. K. Price as leader. The fourth conference will be held at Mills College, Cal July 13-23 with Miss Florence Simms as leader.

The registration fee is $5 except for the Mills College conference which is $3.

For farther information address Miss Carrie B. Wilson, 1004 Champlain bldg. 126 State st. Chicago, Ill.

FOREIGN SCHOOLS
SUMMER SCHOOL OF SCIENCE FOR THE ATLANTIC PROVINCES OF CANADA

The session of 1897 will be held at Yarmouth, N. S. on the Atlantic coast, July 7-22. Besides the science classes there are classes in civics, vocal and physical culture; English literature, the study for this year being a number of Robert Browning's poems; kindergarten principles, music (tonic sol-fa notation), and psychology.

Class instruction is given for the most part between nine and three o'clock leaving the remainder of the afternoon for field work, etc. Advanced classes in the different subjects will be formed providing students send their names and subject to the secretary not later than May 1. There is an additional fee of $2 for advanced work.

NEFF COLLEGE OF ORATORY

The summer session of the Neff college of oratory of Philadelphia will be held in Toronto, July 5-Aug. 14 in the Young woman's Christian guild hall, 19 and 21 McGill st. Daily lectures will be given by the president, Silas S. Neff, on the fundamental principles of the new oratory and the new education, including interpretation of literature and of nature, extempore speech, conversation, authorship, etc. There will be exercises in declamation, recitation, oratory, voice culture, rhetoric, reading, dramatic culture, Bible and hymn reading, delivery of sermons and psychology.

Classes will be in session five days in the week from 9 a. m. to 12 m. The tuition for the full course is $40. Circulars may be obtained from the president, 1414 Arch st. Philadelphia, Pa.

EDINBURGH SUMMER MEETING

The 11th summer meeting at Edinburgh will be held this year at University hall, Aug. 2-28. Courses will be given by Prof. Patrick Geddes, Prof. Charles Zeublin of Chicago, Dr John G. Robertson, Miss Glidden of Pratt institute, Brooklyn, and others. The studio of the Old Edinburgh school of art will be open to students of fine art during the meeting.

OXFORD SUMMER MEETING

The eighth summer meeting will be held at Oxford July 31-Aug 25, 1897. The main courses of study will be the history, literature, art and economics of the revolutionary epoch, 1789-1848 and will be a continuation of those given at the previous meetings. The list of lecturers on these subjects includes among many well known names the lord bishop of Ripon, Canon Gore, Prof. R: G. Moulton, Rev. W. H. Shaw, Rev. P. H. Wicksteed, Justin McCarthy and M. E. Sadler. Lectures will be given in French on Chateaubriand, Victor Hugo, Balzac, George Sand and others and there will also be a class in French, in the original authorities for the study of the French revolution.

Science work will include daily lectures on chemistry, botany, elementary physics, anthropology, zoology and bacteriology if a sufficient number of applications for each course are received on or before July 15. The science lectures are intended to occupy the whole of each morning.

Other courses are the history and theory of education with special reference to child-study and the kindergarten method, a special class in the English language intended primarily for foreigners, history of architecture with special reference to the buildings of Oxford and its neighborhood and if there are a sufficient number of applications, classes in Greek, Latin, French language and literature.

Canon Scott Holland will deliver a course of six lectures on St John's gospel and other theological lectures and special sermons will be given. The London ethical society has arranged for six lectures on the Theory of virtue and the virtues by Prof. W. R. Soley of Aberdeen.

A course of manual training for the certificates of the city and gilds of London institute will be given specially for teachers at the Oxford city technical school. The fee for the 20 lessons is £1.

All correspondence should be addressed to J. A. R. Marriott, University extension office, Examination schools, Oxford.

LECTURES TO CLERGY

The lectures to clergy of the Church of England will be given this year at Cambridge, July 19-31.

The subjects for the first week are St Mark's gospel, History and doctrine of ordination, Christian life and thought in the sub-apostolic age, Relations between England and the papacy to the reformation; for the second week, Some points in the theology of the *Psalms, Epistle to the Galatians*, Types of apostolic teaching in the book of *Acts*, Growth of English nonconformity and its differentiation into dissent.

Other lectures will be given by the dean of Ely, Archdeacon Wilson, Prof. Clifford Allbutt, Rev. J. A. Kempthorne and Rev. W. H. Frere.

NATIONAL HOME READING UNION

No summer meeting will be held this year owing to the Diamond jubilee celebrations in June and July but it is hoped to arrange conferences of special interest to Union readers in connection with the Oxford summer meeting and the Women's educational section of the Victorian era exhibition.

JENA

A general continuation course consisting of general physiology, physiologic psychology, hygiene, philosophy and pedagogy will be held in Jena Aug. 2-14.

A special course for natural science teachers of secondary schools consisting of astronomy, botany, physics and zoology will be held Aug. 2-14.

There will be an elementary and an advanced course in German language and literature for foreigners Aug. 2-21.

Other courses are the history of religion, civilization and art. The secretary is Hugo Weinmann, Spitzweidenweg 4, Jena.

ALLIANCE FRANCAISE

The vacation courses in French conducted by the Alliance française at the Ecole coloniale, Paris, will be given in two series in July and August 1897.

The courses offered are the same as last year consisting of an advanced and an elementary course in each series with 12 lessons on the institutions of France and 12 lessons on the history of French art studied from the works of art in the museums and galleries of Paris and the neighborhood.

The examination in July for the advanced diploma will be on the following works: La Fontaine, *Fables*, (first six books); Bossuet, *Sermon sur la mort;* Molière, *Tartufe;* Beaumarchais, *Le marriage de Figaro;* Hugo, *Les Burgraves*. The works for the August examination are Racine, *Andromaque;* La Bruyère, *Caractères, ch. 1: Des ouvrages de l'esprit;* Mme de Lafayette, *La princesse de Clèves;* Leconte de Lisle, *Les poèmes antiques*. The session of 1896 was most successful with an attendance of 326 students, 31 of whom received the advanced diploma and 17 the elementary diploma.

UNIVERSITY OF GENEVA

The vacation courses of modern French which were organized in Geneva in 1892 will be held in 1897 in two series, a summer course, July 17-Aug. 30 and an autumn course Oct. 1-20. Prof. Bernard Bouvier of the faculty of letters and science is director. The program consists of courses on contemporary French literature, analytical reading of modern French authors, improvisation and discussion, style, methods of teaching French, French syntax and idioms, elocution and pronunciation. A special course of lectures will be given during each series.

SUMMER CONFERENCES AND CONVENTIONS OF 1897

MAINE

American institute of electrical engineers. A general meeting will be held at Greenacre, Eliot, Me., beginning July 26, this date being the 50th anniversary of the electrical discoveries of the late Prof. Moses G Farmer.

CONNECTICUT

American board for foreign missions. The 88th annual meeting will take place in New Haven, Oct. 12-15. Dr R. S. Storrs will deliver the president's address.

NEW YORK

The Home missionary society of the congregational church will meet at Saratoga, June 1-3.

The International missionary union will meet at Clifton Springs, June 9-15. Many prominent in missionary work are expected to take part in the conference.

Music teachers national association. This convention will be held in the Grand central palace, New York city, June 24-28. There will be conferences on Music in the college and university, Prof. G: C Gow of Vassar college, chairman; Public school music, training and popular music culture, Mr Frank Damrosch, chairman; Methods and results in music schools, Mr C: H. Morse, Brooklyn, chairman; and a conference of musical journalists, Mr L. E. Elson of Boston, chairman. Handel's *Messiah* will be given by eminent soloists and a chorus of 1500 voices under the direction of Mr Frank Damrosch.

University convocation. The 35th University convocation of the State of New York will be held in the senate chamber, Albany,

Monday, Tuesday and Wednesday, June 28-30. The first session will open with the Chancellor's annual address. The second session will be devoted to the discussion of science teaching, with a paper by Prof. William Morris Davis of Harvard university on the Present trend of geography; the subject of the third session is Athletic and oratorical contests; of the fifth and sixth sessions the American university and the American college. On Tuesday evening (fourth session) Pres. James H. Canfield of Ohio state university will give an address on The state and education.

The New York summer institutes under direction of the state department of public instruction will be held at Chautauqua, Thousand Island Park and Glens Falls, July 12-30, and will be conducted respectively by Isaac H. Stout, Welland Hendrick and Percy I. Bugbee. There are two departments, the Professional training department, embracing psychology and principles of education; and the Drill and review department, which prepares for the state or the uniform examinations in all subjects except the languages. These institutes are free to residents of the state.

Brotherhood of the kingdom. The annual conference will be held at Marlboro on the Hudson, Aug. 2-7. Religion and social questions of the day will be the subjects under discussion.

Brotherhood of St Andrew of the protestant episcopal church. The first international convention will be held in Buffalo, Oct. 13-17. Delegates from all the brotherhoods in the different national churches are expected to attend and an invitation has been extended to all the Anglican bishops. There will be sermons and addresses by many noted clergymen and laymen among whom are the lord bishop of Rochester, Eng., Rev. Charles Gore, D. D., canon of Westminster, London, Very Rev. Vincent Rorison, D. D., dean of St Andrew's, Scotland and Right Rev. Henry C. Potter, D. D., bishop of New York.

National woman's Christian temperance union. The national convention will be held at Buffalo, Oct. 29-Nov. 3, thus permitting many of the delegates to the World's W. C. T. U. convention at Toronto, closing Oct. 26, to be present. Lady Henry Somerset will deliver the annual sermon.

PENNSYLVANIA

The American library association will meet in Philadelphia, June 21-25. For two of the sessions a double program has been arranged, one for those specially interested in college and advanced library work, the other for less experienced librarians, treating of elementary library practice.

Those who are to attend the international conference in London, arranged by the Library association of the united kingdom, will leave Philadelphia June 25 and those taking the American post-conference trip to Delaware Water Gap and vicinity, June 26.

TENNESSEE

Tennessee centennial. The exposition which commemorates the centennial of the state of Tennessee will be opened at Nashville May 1 and close Oct. 1. Nashville has contributed a half million dollars toward the general expenses and most of the states have made liberal appropriations for exhibitions. A special educational building for the exhibit of school work of all grades has been erected, but so much space has been called for that it has been found necessary to put some of the exhibits in the Commerce building. The Nashville schools will make the most elaborate display. Vanderbilt university, Peabody normal college, the University of Tennessee and many other colleges and private schools have arranged exhibits. The offering of medals and diplomas has aroused considerable emulation.

The International convention of the Baptist young people's union of America will be held in Chattanooga, July 15-18.

OHIO

The American bar association meeting will be held in Cleveland, O. Aug. 25-27. Hon. James M. Woolworth of Omaha, Neb. will present a summary of the important legislation of the year.

MICHIGAN

Scotch-Irish conference. The ninth annual conference of the Scotch-Irish in America will be held in Detroit, June 10-13. Many prominent speakers will deliver addresses.

National Y. P. C. U. of the universalist church will hold its annual convention in Detroit, July 6-13. This organization is similar to the Epworth league of the methodist church and numbers 450 local societies.

The **American institute of architects** will meet in Detroit, Sept. 28-30.

WISCONSIN

The **National educational association** meets this year in Milwaukee, July 6-9. The president of the association is Hon. Charles R. Skinner, superintendent of public instruction of New York state. A rate of one fare for the round trip is offered by the railroads till Aug. 31. The North American child-study association which was tentatively organized at the child-study conference in Chicago, May 1, 1897, will hold its first regular meeting during the session of the N. E. A. and adopt a permanent constitution and by-laws. At the close of the general sessions there will be a conference of the new library department of the N. E. A. The following announcement of the president, Melvil Dewey, is taken from the May number of *Public libraries*.

Library department of the N. E. A.—The greatest gathering of educational workers in the world will be in session in Milwaukee July 9-13. It is the first year of the newly established library department, and it is specially important that those interested should make a strong effort for a successful library meeting. Discussions are not to deal with cataloguing, classification, and other details of library economy, but with those matters in which teachers and educational administrators of the country are most directly concerned. The field is not merely that of the pedagogic or of the general school library, but covers the whole question of reading as a factor in education, both for the young in school and for adults throughout life. Librarians will probably not attend this meeting in such numbers as they do their own national conventions, but it would be a strange neglect of the finest opportunity yet offered for needed cooperation if the representative workers in American libraries were not at Milwaukee ready to do all in their power to help the great body of teachers to increase and put to practical use their new interest in libraries and reading.

I append a list of topics which have been proposed for discussion, with the request that any one interested will suggest other topics, or name speakers who can put into a few minutes a great deal of inspiration or information of practical value. There will be little room for long papers, but we hope for many pithy, helpful little speeches.

Suggested topics: Teachers' and pupils' reading; the proper function of the national and state libraries as part of the American educational system; what they might do to assist the schools and libraries throughout the country; state lending libraries for teachers; help to the evolution of book borrowing into book owning; the function of the schools in training readers for the public library; history of the public library movement; state aid to libraries; the classroom a preparation for popular education through libraries; education outside the classroom; the influence of the teacher in determining the reading of the next generation; is it the duty of a community to provide books for public use? how to make sure of good books in our libraries; book receptions; home libraries.

A definite program will be announced before the meeting, and the active cooperation of all interested is cordially invited.

MINNESOTA

The American missionary association, an organization of the congregational church, will meet in Minneapolis, Oct. 19-21.

CALIFORNIA

The Christian endeavor convention will meet this year in San Francisco, July 7-12. Open meetings will be held in six of the largest churches and one meeting each in Oakland and Alameda.

CANADA

The International conference of charities and corrections will hold an important conference at Toronto, July 7-14.

Epworth league. The third conference of the Epworth league will be held in Toronto, July 15-18.

The British association for the advancement of science will meet in Toronto, Aug. 18. Sir John Evans treasurer of the Royal society of London will preside. It is expected that the most eminent British, American and European scientists will be present at this meeting. The 10 sections of the society are mathematics and physics, chemistry, geology, zoology, geography, economics and statistics, mechanical science, anthropology, physiology and botany.

Woman's Christian temperance union. The World's convention of the W. C. T. U. will be held at Toronto, Oct. 23-26. Miss Willard will preside and there will be reports from the superintendents of the various lines of work and evening mass meeting.

The American institute of instruction of which Albert E. Winship of the *Journal of education* is president will meet in Montreal, July 9-12.

RUSSIA

The International geological congress will meet in St Petersburg, Aug. 17 (29) for a five days session. The difference between the Russian calendar and our own should be remembered.

This brief summary of summer meetings now offering opportunities for study or conference on topics of particular interest, will make apparent the increasing recognition on the part of busy men and women, that recreation may be advantageously combined with some kinds of mental progress. It is with the purpose of directing inquirers to the meeting which is best adapted to their needs, that this bulletin is issued.

Respectfully submitted,
MELVIL DEWEY
Director

STATISTICS 1896

Reports of 1896 sessions only are included in the following tables. Schools whose first session is in 1897 are reported in their proper places in the pages preceding.

In the column headed Subjects of study, 'Chautauqua assembly topics', means the subjects commonly taught at the various Chautauquas; e. g. physical culture, elocution, art, music, W. C. T. U. methods, Sunday-school normal subjects, kindergarten, cooking, with sometimes the addition of lectures on literature or science. Schools which give instruction in the common branches usually include courses in methods of teaching each subject. A normal course is a course specially for teachers and includes method work and subjects commonly taught at normal schools.

College preparatory topics include those taught in high schools implying that the work is with special reference to college entrance requirements.

EXPLANATION OF ABBREVIATIONS

? preceding statements means approximately

a=assembly
anat=anatomy
bact=bacteriology
Bib=Bible study
biol=biology
chem=chemistry
econ=economics
eloc=elocution
Fr=French
geod=geodesy
geol=geology
hist=history
histol=histology
inst=institute
kind=kindergarten
lang=language
lib. econ=library economy

lit=literature
mater. med=materia medica
math=mathematics
mech. eng=mechanical engineering
mus=music
norm=normal
p c=physical culture
path=pathology
ped=pedagogy
photog=photography
phys=physiology
psych=psychology
s. m=Summer meeting
s s=Summer school
sci=science
stenog=stenography
surv=surveying

… Statistics of

	NAME	Place	Year founded	Opening
1	Aberdeen normal summer school	Aberdeen, Miss		
2	Acton Park assembly	Acton Park, Ind	1882	28 Jl
3	Alabama Chautauqua assembly	Talladega, Ala	1894	2 Jl
4	Alma college summer school	Alma, Mich	1889	29 Je
5	Am. inst. norm. meth. East. session		1890	
6	Am. inst. norm. meth. Western session		1891	
7	Amer. society univ exten. s. m	Philadelphia, Pa	1893	6 Jl
8	Art academy summer school	Cincinnati, O		
9	Asheville conf. Internat. Y W. C. A	Asheville, N. C	1895	12 Je
10	Atlanta assembly	Atlanta, Ga	1893	
11	Atlantic prov of Can. s. s. of science	Parrsboro', N S	1887	9 Jl
12	Avalon college summer school	Trenton, Mo		
13	Baker university summer school	Baldwin, Kan	1893	
14	Bay View summer university	Bay View, Mich	1885	8 Jl
15	Baylor female college s s	Belton, Tex		
16	Beatrice Chautauqua assembly	Beatrice, Neb	1887	16 Je
17	Belle Island summer school of art	South Norwalk, Conn	1894	Je
18	Berlitz summer school of languages	Asbury Park, N. J		1 Je
19	Black Hills assembly	Black Hills, S. D	1890	
20	Bowdoin college summer courses	Brunswick, Me	1895	
21	Brooklyn inst. biological laboratory	Cold Spring Harbor, N. Y	1889	6 Jl
22	Buffalo summer school of pedagogy	Buffalo, N. Y	1896	13 Jl
23	Business college summer school	Des Moines, Ia		
24	Butte summer school	Butte, Mont		
25	Caen holiday course for teachers	Caen, France	1894	
26	California univ. physical laboratory	Berkeley, Cal		
27	" s. s. of marine biology	San Pedro, Cal	1892	
28	Cambridge summer meeting	Cambridge, Eng	1890	30 Jl
29	Carthage col summer school	Carthage, Ill		
30	a Cascadilla summer school	Ithaca, N. Y	1891	
31	Catholic s. s of America	Plattsburg, N. Y	1892	12 Jl
32	Catholic winter school of America	New Orleans, La	1895	4 Mr
33	Catskill school of art	Napanoch, N. Y	1891	21 Je
34	Cayuga Lake summer school	Ithaca, N. Y	1894	20 Jl
35	Central New York summer school	Tully Lake, N. Y	1892	21 Jl
36	Central Tennessee college s. s	Nashville, Tenn		
37	Chautauqua col. of liberal arts	Chautauqua, N. Y	1875	11 Jl
38	Chicago commons s. of social econ	Chicago, Ill	1894	27 Ap
39	" "	"	"	8
40	Chicago kindergarten col. s. s of ped	"	"	30 Je
41	Cincinnati summer school	Cincinnati, O	1895	
42	Clarion Chautauqua assembly	Strattonville, Pa	1889	17 Je
43	Clark university summer school	Worcester, Mass	1892	13 Jl
44	Clinton classical school	Peekskill, N. Y	1895	25 Je
45	Col. of agriculture & mechanic arts s. s	Kingston, R. I		

a Discontinued

summer schools, 1896

Closing	Students	Visitors	States	Countries	Subjects of study	
					Normal course	1
15 Ag					Chautauqua assembly topics	2
26 Jl					Chautauqua assembly topics	3
10 Ag					General	4
					Music, drawing, penmanship, p. c	5
					Vocal music, drawing	6
31 Jl	237				General	7
					Art	8
22 Je	63	15	9	4	Y. W. C. A. topics	9
					Chautauqua assembly topics	10
24 Jl	75			Can	Sci. Eng. lit. mus. eloc. econ. kind. psych.	11
					Normal course	12
					General	13
12 Ag	832		11		General	14
						15
28 Je					Chautauqua assembly topics	16
O					Art	17
28 Ag					Languages	18
					Chautauqua assembly topics	19
					Chemistry, physics, biology	20
17 Ag	25				Science	21
24 Jl	123		18	Can	Methods, psychology, child-study	22
					Business	23
					Normal course	24
					French language and history	25
					Physics, chemistry	26
					Biology	27
24 Ag					General	28
					College preparatory and normal course	29
						30
16 Ag	882		20	Can. Eng.	General	31
20 Mr					General	32
					Art	33
10 Ag					Methods, sci. lang. music, mathematics	34
12 Ag					General	35
					Preparatory and normal course	36
21 Ag					General	37
1 My					Social science	38
8					Social science	39
11 Jl	60	40	17		Kindergarten methods	40
					General	41
1 Jl					Chautauqua assembly topics	42
25 Jl	?300				Pedagogy, psychology, child-study	43
3 S					College preparatory	44
					Agriculture and shop work	45

UNIVERSITY OF THE STATE OF NEW YORK

Statistics of

	Lecturers	Lectures	Recitations	EXTENSION COURSES Subjects	EXTENSION COURSES Lecturers	Buildings	FEES Entrance	FEES Full course	FEES Single course
1									
2									
3									
4						Alma college		$ 5	
5								55	$15
6								25	15
7	35	†237				Univ. of Pa.		15	5
8									
9	13	41				Hotel		5	
10									
11	14	140						2 50	1
12									
13						University		15	5
14	43					5		12	6
15									
16									
17								8–15 a mo.	
18									
19									
20						College		20	10
21	6	115				6			20
22	13	112						10	
23									
24									
25									
26									
27									
28								£1 10s	
29									
30									
31	21	78	6			5		$10	
32								10	1
33								15 a mo.	
34						Ithaca high school		6	
35						3		4–5	
36									
37						13		a	
38									
39									
40	10					Chic. kind. col.		12	
41									
42									
43						University		20	12
44								100	
45									

a Fees vary in each department

Summer schools, 1896

FEES Single lecture	SECRETARY Name	Address	
	J. H. Phillips, director	Aberdeen, Miss	1
	Mrs J. D. Gatch	Lawrenceburg, Ind	2
	Rev. S P. West, sup't		3
	J. T. Northon	Alma, Mich	4
	F. D. Beattys	31 E. 17th st. New York	5
	Robert Foresman	262 Wabash av. Chicago, Ill	6
$.50	D. C. Munro, director	111 S. 15th st. Philadelphia, Pa	7
	J. H. Gest	Cincinnati, O	8
	Miss C. B. Wilson	1004 Champlain bldg, 126 State st. Chi. Ill.	9
	Rev. W. Shaw, pres		10
.50-1	J. D Seaman	Charlottetown, P. E. Island	11
	F. A. Z. Kumler, pres	Trenton, Mo	12
	G. W. Martin	Baldwin, Kan	13
.25	J. M. Hall	Flint, Mich	14
	C. P Fountain	Belton, Tex	15
	A. R. Dempster, pres		16
	J. H. Boston	203 Montague st. Brooklyn, N. Y	17
	Berlitz & Co	1122 Broadway, New York	18
	E. E Clough, pres		19
	L. A. Lee	Brunswick, Mo	20
	F. W. Hooper	502 Fulton st. Brooklyn, N. Y	21
.50	F. M. McMurry	School of pedagogy, Buffalo, N. Y	22
	Angus McKinnon	Des Moines, Ia	23
	J F. Davies, sup't	Butte, Mont	24
	J. Richards	Gram. sch. Stoke Newington, Lon. N. Eng.	25
	E. R. Drew	Oakland, Cal	26
	W. E. Ritter	2222 Durant av. Berkeley, Cal	27
	R. D. Roberts	Syndicate bldgs, Cambridge, Eng	28
	W. W. Troup	Carthage, Ill	29
	C. V. Parsell	Ithaca, N. Y	30
.25	W. E. Mosher	Youngstown, O	31
.25	A. H. Fleming	938 Royal st. New Orleans, La	32
	Miss H. S. Peck	100 Willow st. Brooklyn, N. Y	33
	F. D. Boynton	Ithaca, N. Y	34
	T. H. Armstrong	Friendship, N. Y	35
	M. W. Dogan	Nashville, Tenn	36
	W. A. Duncan	Syracuse, N. Y	37
	Miss M. E. Colman	140 N. Union st. Chicago, Ill	38
	"	"	39
	Mrs J. N. Crouse, director	10 Van Buren st. Chicago, Ill	40
	W. C. Washburne	Cincinnati, O	41
			42
.50	L. N. Wilson	Worcester, Mass	43
	Robert McCord	Peekskill, N. Y	44
	J. H. Washburn	Kingston, R. I	45

Statistics of

	NAME	Place	Year founded	DATE Opening
46	Colorado s. s. of sci. phil. and lang.	Colorado Springs, Col.	1892	
47	Columbia college summer schools	Various places	1877	
48	Columbian catholic summer school	Madison, Wis	1894	
49	Columbian university summer school	Washington, D. C.	1894	
50	Connecticut s. s. for teachers	Norwich, Conn	1891	a
51	Connecticut valley assembly	Northampton, Mass.	1887	14 Jl
52	Cook county normal summer school	Chicago, Ill	1893	13 Jl
53	Cooper memorial college s. s.	Sterling, Kan.		
54	Cornell university summer school	Ithaca, N. Y.	1892	6 Jl
55	Summer law school	"		6 Jl
56	Coronado Beach summer school	Coronada Beach, Cal.	1895	
57	Cotuit summer school	Cotuit, Mass.	1895	8 Jl
58	Cours de vacances de l'alliance française.	Paris, France	1894	2 Jl
59	Cumberland univ. summer law school	Lebanon, Tenn	1896	
60	Cumberland valley assembly	Harrisburg, Pa.	1886	21 Jl
61	Denison university summer school	Granville, O.		
62	Denver normal and prep. school	Denver, Col.	1893	14 Je
63	De Pauw university summer school	Greencastle, Ind.	1896	
64	Des Moines s. s. of methods	Des Moines, Ia.	1890	6 Jl
65	Detroit Lake interstate assembly	Detroit Lake, Minn.	1893	21 Jl
66	Devils' Lake assembly	Devils' Lake, N. D	1892	1 Jl
67	Dickinson college summer law school	Carlisle, Pa.		
68	Doane college summer school	Crete, Neb.		
69	Drake univ. summer Latin school	Des Moines, Ia.	1891	22 Je
70	Earlham college summer school	Richmond, Ind	1893	
71	Eastern Maine assembly	Northport, Me.	1893	
72	Eastern New Eng Chautauqua	Ocean Park, Me.	1881	20 Jl
73	Edinburgh summer meeting	Edinburgh, Scotland	1887	3 Ag
74	Emory college summer school	Oxford, Ga.		
75	Epworth Park assembly	Bethesda, O.		5 Ag
76	Fairmount Chautauqua	Kansas City, Mo	1896	30 My
77	Florida Chautauqua	De Funiak Springs, Fla.	1886	18 bF
78	Franklin college summer school	Franklin, Ind		
79	Gates college summer normal	Neligh, Neb		
80	Gearhart Park Chaut. assembly	Gearhart Park, Or.		
81	Geneva univ. vacation courses	Geneva, Switzerland	1892	15 Jl
82	" "	"		1 O
83	Georgia Chautauqua assembly	Albany, Ga.	1888	
84	Georgia univ. s. s. of mathematics	Athens, Ga.		
85	Glenmore sch. for the culture sci.	Keene, N. Y.	1891	
86	Grand Rapids kindergarten train. sch.	Grand Rapids, Mich	1892	6 Jl
87	Greenacre assembly	Eliot, Me.	1894	1 Jl
88	Greer normal college summer school	Hoopeston, Ill		
89	Grindelwald conference	Grindelwald, Switzerland.	1892	
90	H. E. Holt norm. inst. of vocal har.	Tufts college, Mass.	1883	14 Jl

a No session in 1896
b 1897

summer schools, 1896

Closing	Students	Visitors	States	Countries	Subjects of study	
					General	46
					Mining, geol. surv. geod. biol. mech. eng.	47
					General	48
					General	49
					General	50
24 Jl					Chautauqua assembly topics	51
3 Ag	632		29		General	52
					General	53
15 Ag	190				General	54
17 Ag					Law	55
					Science, literature, normal course	56
16 S	20				College preparatory	57
31 Ag	326			17	French language, lit. institutions, art, eloc.	58
					Law	59
31 Jl					Chautauqua assembly topics	60
					General	61
16 Jl	239		9	Can.	General	62
						63
31 Jl	177		6		General	64
30 Jl					Chautauqua assembly topics	65
13 Jl					Chautauqua assembly topics	66
					Law	67
					Music	68
17 Jl	45		6		Latin	69
					General	70
					Chautauqua assembly topics	71
7 Ag					Chautauqua assembly topics	72
29 Ag					Social science	73
					College preparatory	74
18 Ag					Chautauqua assembly topics	75
14 Je					Chautauqua assembly topics	76
17 Mr					Chautauqua assembly topics	77
					Eng. hist. math. chem	78
					Normal course	79
					Common branches	80
28 Ag	159				French language and literature	81
21 O	50				"	82
					Chautauqua assembly topics	83
					Mathematics	84
					Social science	85
29 Ag	56		10	Can.	Kindergarten	86
2 S	75–500			4	Social science	87
						88
					Christian sociology	89
31 Jl	?100				Vocal harmony	90

Statistics of

	Lecturers	Lectures	Recitations	Extension Courses Subjects	Extension Courses Lecturers	Buildings	Entrance	Fees Full course	Fees Single course
46								$10	$5
47									
48								5	
49									
50									
51									
52						Normal school		12	3
53									
54	23					University		25	20
55						University		35	
56									
57	5							15-25	
58	13	158						150 fr.	1 fr.
59									
60									
61									
62	15					Normal school		$10	
63								10	
64	14								
65									
66									
67									
68									
69	4		270			University		15	
70									
71									
72						5		2	
73	19	160				4		£3 3s	10s 6d
74									
75									
76	8	49				Assembly building		$2	
77						Assembly buildings		3.50	
78									
79									
80									
81								30 fr.	
82								15 fr.	
83								$2	
84									
85									
86	5	33	101					15	
87									
88									
89									
90								20	

summer schools, 1896

FEES		SECRETARY	
Single lecture	Name	Address	
$.50	P. K. Pattison	Colorado Springs, Col.	46
	W: H. H. Beebe	Columbia college, N. Y	47
.25	H. J. Desmond	Wisconsin bldg, Milwaukee, Wis.	48
	H. L Hodgkins, director	Columbian univ. Washington, D. C.	49
	C: D. Hine	Hartford, Conn	50
	Dr W. L. Davidson	Cuyahoga Falls, O	51
	W. S. Jackman, manager	6916 Perry av. Station O, Chicago, Ill	52
	S. A. Wilson	Sterling, Kan	53
	D. F. Hoy	Ithaca, N. Y	54
	"	"	55
	Daniel Cleveland	San Diego, Cal	56
	C: E. Fish, principal	Cotuit, Mass	57
1 fr.	P. Foncin	45, rue de Grenelle, Paris, France	58
	A. B. Martin	Lebanon, Tenn	59
	A. A. Line, sup't	Carlisle, Pa	60
	W. A. Chamberlin	Granville, O	61
	Fred Dick, principal	Denver, Col	62
	H. A. Gobin	Greencastle, Ind	63
	C. W. Martindale	Webster City, Ia	64
	Dr S. J. Hill, pres.		65
	Dr Eugene May, sup't		66
	Dr William Trickett, dean	Carlisle, Pa	67
	H. B. King	Crete, Neb	68
	C. O Denny	1090 25th st. Des Moines, Ia	69
	J. J. Mills	Richmond, Ind	70
	G. D. Lindsay, pres.		71
$.25	E. W. Porter	85 Central st. Peabody, Mass	72
	T. R. Marr	Outlook Tower, Univ. hall, Edinb'h, Scot.	73
	W. A. Candler	Oxford, Ga	74
	Rev. D. C. Osborne, sup't		75
	N. S. Doran	618 Wyandotte st. Kansas City, Mo	76
.25	T. F. McGourin	De Funiak Springs, Fla	77
	W. S. Stott	Franklin, Ind	78
	Rev. W. Griffiths	Neligh, Neb	79
	H. S. Lyman	Astoria, Or	80
	Prof. Bernard Bouvier	10, Bourg-de-Four, Geneva, Switzerland.	81
	" " "	" "	82
	H. M. McIntosh	Albany, Ga	83
	C: M. Snelling	Athens, Ga	84
	Thomas Davidson	Keene, N. Y	85
	Clara Wheeler	117 Barclay st. Grand Rapids, Mich	86
	Miss S. J. Farmer	Eliot, Me	87
	J. E. W. Morgan	Hoopeston, Ill	88
	Henry Riches	5 Endsleigh Gardens, Lond. N. W. Eng.	89
	Mrs H. E. Holt	Box 109, Lexington, Mass	90

Statistics of

	NAME	Place	Year founded	Opening
91	Hackley Park assembly	Hackley Park, Mich	1891	
92	Harvard s. s. of physical training	Cambridge, Mass	1887	3 Jl
93	Harvard university summer school	"	1874	6 Jl
94	Hedding assembly	East Epping, N H	1886	27 Jl
95	Hempstead institute	Hempstead, L. I, N. Y	1837	15 Je
96	"	Littleton, N H		18 Je
97	Hopkins seaside laboratory	Pacific Grove, Cal	1892	15 Je
98	Hull house college extension s. s.	Rockford, Ill	1891	6 Jl
99	Illinois medical college summer school	Chicago, Ill		
100	Illinois state normal univ. summer inst.	Normal, Ill		
101	Illinois university summer school	Urbana, Ill	1894	
102	Summer school of biology	Havana, Ill	1896	Je
103	Illinois Wesleyan univ. summer school	Bloomington, Ill		
104	Indiana state normal school	Terre Haute, Ind	1894	29 Je
105	Indiana university summer school	Bloomington, Ind	1890	16 Je
106	aIowa Chautauqua assembly	Colfax, Ia		
107	Iowa school of the kingdom	Grinnell, Ia	1895	b
108	Island Park assembly	Rome City, Ind	1878	29 Jl
109	Jena holiday course for teachers	Jena, Germany	1893	3 Ag
110	Johns Hopkins univ marine zool. lab	Beaufort, N. C	1879	
111	Kentucky Chautauqua assembly	Lexington, Ky	1886	30 Je
112	Knox college summer school	Galesburg, Ill	1894	
113	L. A. U. K. summer school	London, Eng	1893	15 Je
114	Lake Forest college summer session	Lake Forest, Ill	1895	6 Jl
115	Lake Geneva conf. Inter. Y. W C. A.	Lake Geneva, Wis	1891	30 Je
116	Lake Geneva students conference	"	1891	
117	Lake George assembly	Lake George as'bly, N Y		
118	Lake Madison Chautauqua schools	Madison, S D	1891	30 Je
119	Lakeside summer school	Lakeside, O	1877	13 Jl
120	Lancaster assembly	Lancaster, O		29 Jl
121	Lehigh univ. s. s. of surveying	South Bethlehem, Pa		22 Je
122	Leland Stanford jr university	Stanford University, Cal	1894	1 Je
123	Lincoln normal university	Lincoln, Neb	1892	15 Je
124	Long Beach Chaut. assembly and s. s.	Long Beach, Cal	1884	12 Jl
125	cLong Beach summer parliament	Long Beach, L. I., N Y	1894	
126	Long Island Chautauqua	Point o'Woods, L. I, N. Y.	1894	1 Jl
127	Long Pine assembly	Long Pine, Neb	1886	17 Jl
128	Louisiana Chautauqua	Ruston, La	1892	1 Jl
129	Maine state college summer school	Orono, Me	1895	13 Jl
130	Marienfeld summer camp	Milford, Pa	1896	30 Je
131	Marine biological laboratory	Woods Holl, Mass	1888	1 Je
132	Marthas Vineyard summer institute	Cottage City, Mass	1878	13 Jl
133	Mass. inst. of technology s. school	Boston, Mass	1888	
134	Metropolitan normal art s. s	New York, N. Y		13 Jl
135	Michigan agricultural college	Agricultural College		

a Discontinued. Succeeded by Midland Chautauqua assembly
b No session in 1896
c Discontinued

summer schools, 1896

Closing	Students	Visitors	States	Countries	Subjects of study	
					Chautauqua assembly topics	91
8 Ag	104	2,000	26	3	Physical culture	92
14 Ag	624				General	93
15 Ag					Music,art,French,Bible,cookery, kind p.c.	94
1 S	15		1	4	College prep. & business course, music	95
18 S						96
	25				Botany, zoology	97
12 Ag	100				Science, language, needlework	98
					Medicine	99
					General	100
					General	101
Ag					Biology	102
					†General	103
6 Ag					General	104
14 Jl					General	105
						106
						107
12 Ag					Chautauqua assembly topics	108
23 Ag	108				German lang. and hist. pedagogy, sci.	109
					Marine zoology	110
10 Jl					Chautauqua assembly topics	111
					General	112
20 Je					Library economy	113
15 Ag	35				General	114
9 Jl	300	14	17	4	Y. W. C. A. topics	115
					Bible	116
					Chautauqua assembly topics	117
14 Jl	150	25			General	118
15 Ag	50				Chautauqua assembly topics	119
6 Ag					Chautauqua assembly topics	120
20 Jl					Surveying	121
15 Jl					General	122
6 Ag	125				General	123
	469	?600				
10 Ag	?120	?3,000			Chautauqua assembly topics	124
						125
1 O	50	500			General	126
28 Jl					Chautauqua assembly topics	127
8 Ag					Chautauqua assembly topics	128
30 Jl	158				General	129
1 S	15		3		College preparatory	130
1 O					Zoology, botany	131
17 Ag	700		40		General	132
					General	133
10 Ag						134
					Agriculture	135

Statistics of

	Lecturers	Lectures	Recitations	EXTENSION COURSES Subjects	Lecturers	Buildings	Entrance	FEES Full course	Single course
91									
92	30	190				Hemenway gymnasium		$50	$25
93						University			20
94									
95	4					Institute		60	
96								85	
97						2		25	
98	12								
99									
100						University		10	
101						University		10	
102									
103									
104						Normal school	10	10	10
105						University		10	5
106									
107									
108						5		2 50	
109	14	174	12				5 m'rks		15 marks.
110									
111									
112								10	$5
113	7	8							
114	6		1360			College		20	20
115	12	43				Tents		5	
116								5	
117									
118	6	84	56			Assembly buildings	$3	3	1
119	5	30	30			7		5	3
120									
121						University		15	
122	17					University			15-20
123	27	29				University		8	
124	10	18	210			Long Beach tabernacle	2 50		5
125									
126	8					2	3		10
127									
128									
129	10	95				College	1		
130	3					Timber camp		150	
131						4		50	
132	40						1		15
133									25
134									
135									

summer schools, 1896

FEES	SECRETARY		
Single lecture	Name	Address	
....	Dr H. W. Bolton, pres	....	91
....	Dr D. A. Sargent	Cambridge, Mass...............	92
....	M. Chamberlain	"	93
....	O. S. Baketel, sup't...........	....	94
....	L S. Hinds..................	Hempstead, L. I., N.Y..........	95
....	"	"	96
....	O. P. Jenkins...............	Stanford University, Cal........	97
....	Miss Jane Addams	Hull House, Chicago, Ill	98
....	Dr H. H. Brown	Chicago, Ill	99
....	J: W. Cook, pres.............	Normal, Ill	100
....	David Kinley.............	Urbana, Ill	101
....	S A Forbes..................	"	102
....	Wilbert Ferguson.............	Bloomington, Ill	103
....	R. G. Gillum..........	Terre Haute, Ind...............	104
....	S. C. Davisson...	Bloomington, Ind	105
....	....	....	106
....	G D. Herron, prin	Grinnell, Ia...................	107
....	C. S Stroup..................	La Grange, Ind	108
....	Hugo Weinmann	Spitzweidenweg 4, Jena, Germany	109
....	W: K. Brooks................	Baltimore Md..................	110
....	Dr W. L. Davidson, sup't	Cuyahoga Falls, O	111
....	J: H. Finley.................	Galesburg, Ill	112
....	W. E. Doubleday............	48 Priory road, Lond. N. W. Eng	113
....	Malcolm McNeill.............	Lake Forest, Ill................	114
....	Miss C B. Wilson............	1004 Champlain b'g, 126 State st. Chic.Ill.	115
....	C. C. Michener..............	40 E. 23d st. New York........	116
....	D. S Sanford, pres	Lake George assembly, N. Y....	117
....	H. E. Kratz.................	Sioux City, Ia.................	118
....	S. R Gill...................	Lakeside, O...................	119
....	W. V. Dick, sup't............	....	120
....	T: M. Drown, pres............	Lehigh univ. South Bethlehem, Pa......	121
....	O. L. Elliott.................	Stanford University, Cal.......	122
....	E. P. Wilson................	Normal, Neb..................	123
$.25-.50	G: R. Crow..................	1012 W 7th st. Los Angeles, Cal.	124
....	S. H. Berry.................	502 Fulton st. Brooklyn, N. Y..........	125
....	Howard Conklin.............	Patchogue, N. Y...............	126
....	....	....	127
....	....	....	128
....	Mrs E A. Balentine..........	Orono, Me....................	129
....	Dr C. H Henderson.........	Chestnut Hill, Philadelphia, Pa........	130
....	Mrs A. P Williams...........	23 Marlboro st. Boston, Mass...........	131
....	A. C. Boyden.................	Bridgewater, Mass....................	132
....	H. W. Tyler................	Mass. inst. of technology. Boston, Mass..	133
....	L. S. Thompson.............	12 Park st. Jersey City, N. J............	134
....	L. G. Gorton	Agricultural College, Mich.....	135

Statistics of

NAME	Place	Year founded	Opening
136 Michigan university summer school....	Ann Arbor, Mich.........	1894	29 Je
137 Summer school of law	"	"	29 Je
138 Midland Chautauqua assembly........	Des Moines, Ia..........	1896	10 Jl
139 b Mid-summer school.................	Owego, N. Y.............	1891	......
140 Minnesota university summer school ..	Minneapolis, Minn.......	1891	27 Jl
141 Mississippi Chautauqua assembly.....	Crystal Springs, Miss.....	1895	16 Jl
142 Missouri state Chautanqua...........	Sedalia, Mo.............	1887	26 Je
143 Missouri univ. s. s. of languages......	Columbia, Mo............	......	8 Je
144 Summer school of science .	"	1895	1 Je
145 Monona Lake assembly...............	Madison, Wis............	1880	21 Jl
146 Monongahela college summer school ..	Jefferson, Pa............	......	......
147 Monsalvat sch of comparative religion	Eliot, Me................	1896	6 Jl
148 Montana summer school.............	Helena, Mont...........	1891	......
149 Monteagle summer schools...........	Monteagle, Tenn.........	1882	31 Je
150 Morningside college summer school....	Morningside, Sioux City, Ia	......	......
151 Mount Union college s. s....	Alliance, O..............	......	......
152 Mountain Chautauqua assembly.......	Mountain Lake Park, Md.	1883	5 Ag
153 National home reading union..........	Chester, Eng............	1889	27 Je
154 National Prohibition Park	Prohibition P'k, S. I., N Y.	1891	......
155 National summer school	Glens Falls, N. Y.........	1882	14 Jl
156 Natural science camp................	Canandaigua, N. Y.......	1890	1 Jl
157 Naval academy preparatory school....	Annapolis, Md............	......	......
158 Nebraska Chautauqua assembly.......	Crete, Neb..............	1882	3 Jl
159 Nebraska normal college s. s..........	Wayne, Neb.............	......	......
160 Neff college of oratory...............	Toronto, Canada.........	1893	13 Jl
161 New Eng. Chaut. Sunday-school a.....	So Framingham, Mass....	1879	20 Jl
162 New Hampshire coll. s. s. of biology...	Durham, N. H...........	1894	6 Jl
163 New Hampshire summer institute.....	Plymouth, N. H.........	1893	......
164 New York university summer courses.	New York...............	1895	6 Jl
165 Normal school of gymnastics..........	Milwaukee, Wis..........	1895	29 Je
166 North Carolina university s. school....	Chapel Hill, N. C.........	1894	......
167 Summer law school....	"	......	......
168 Northeast Georgia Chaut assembly...	Demorest, Ga	1893	24 Jl
169 Northern Indiana normal school.......	Valparaiso, Ind	1877	......
170 Northern New Eng. Sunday-school a..	Freyeburg, Me..........	1882	28 Jl
171 Northfield conf. Internat. Y. W. C. A.	E. Northfield, Mass.......	1893	10 Jl
172 Oberlin s. s. of Christian sociology....	Oberlin, O...............	1895	......
173 Ocean Grove assembly...............	Ocean Grove, N. J.......	1884	6 Jl
174 Ohio university summer school........	Athens, O...............	......	......
175 Ohio Wesleyan university s. s.........	Delaware, O.............	......	......
176 Olivet summer review school	Olivet, Mich.............	......	......
177 Summer school in Latin........	"	......	......
178 Oregon summer school..............	Eugene, Or..............	......	......
179 Ottawa Chautauqua assembly.........	Ottawa, Kan.............	1878	15 Je
180 Oxford lectures to clergy.............	Durham, Eng............	......	13 Jl

b United with National summer school

summer schools, 1896

Closing	Students	Visitors	States	Countries	Subjects of study	
7 Ag	231				General.	136
21 Ag					Law.	137
24 Jl					Chautauqua assembly topics.	138
						139
21 Ag	1200		5		General.	140
26 Jl					Chautauqua assembly topics.	141
4 Jl					Chautauqua assembly topics.	142
28 Jl					Eng. Latin, French.	143
11 Jl					Biology, physics, chem'y, phys. phys.geog.	144
31 Jl					Chautauqua assembly topics.	145
					Normal course.	146
31 Jl	20-80			4	Religions	147
					Normal côurse.	148
25 Ag					General.	149
					General.	150
					General.	151
25 Ag					Chaut. assembly topics, stenog photog...	152
6 Jl					Science, history.	153
						154
3 Ag	500		28	Can	Pedagogy, common branches	155
26 Ag					Science, taxidermy, sketching, photog.p c.	156
					Preparatory	157
15 Jl					Chautauqua assembly topics.	158
					Normal course	159
20 Ag	40			Can. U. S.	Oratory, voice culture.	160
1 Ag					Chautauqua assembly topics	161
1 Ag					Botany, entomology, zoology	162
					General.	163
14 Ag	60		6		General.	164
8 Ag	35		12		Gymnastics, anat. phys. psych.	165
					General.	166
					Law	167
30 Ag					Chautauqua assembly topics.	168
	2,000				General	169
15 Ag					Chautauqua assembly topics.	170
20 Jl	280	45	18	3	Y. W. C. A. topics.	171
					Christian sociology	172
16 Jl					Chautauqua assembly topics.	173
					General	174
					Languages, mathematics, history	175
					General.	176
					Latin	177
					General.	178
26 Je					Chautauqua assembly topics.	179
25 Jl					Theology	180

88 UNIVERSITY OF THE STATE OF NEW YORK

Statistics of

	Lecturers	Lectures	Recitations	EXTENSION COURSES Subjects	Lecturers	Buildings	Entrance	FEES Full course	Single course
136						University		$30	$15
137						University		35	4–8
138									
139									
140	45					University	$1	a 5–6	
141									
142									
143						University			10
144						University		b	
145								2	
146									
147	9	54							
148									
149							5		4
150									
151									
152									
153								£1	
154									
155	22					Pub. sch & Y. M. C. A		$20	7–14
156								64	
157									
158									
159									
160	4	4	21			Univ of Toronto		40	
161						4.		2 50	
162						Thompson hall		10	
163									
164	10	390	360			University		25	
165	10					Normal school		30	15
166	17					University	1	5	
167									
168								1 50	
169								10	
170						2		2	
171	15	43				Northfield sem		5	
172									
173						3.			
174									
175									
176									
177									
178									
179									
180								£1	15s

a Free to Minnesota students
b Free to Missouri teachers

summer schools, 1896

Single lecture	FEES	SECRETARY Name	Address	
		E. H. Mensel	28 Monroe st. Ann Arbor, Mich	136
		E. F. Johnson	31 N. University av. Ann Arbor, Mich..	1`7
				138
		G: R. Winslow	2 Bevier st. Binghamton, N. Y	139
		D. L. Kiehle	Univ. of Minnesota, Minneapolis, Minn.	140
		Bishop C. B. Galloway	▼	141
				142
		Miss Mary Iglehart	Columbia, Mo	143
		M. L. Lipscomb, prin.	"	144
		J. E. Moseley	Madison, Wis	145
		Dr S. T. Wiley	Jefferson, Pa	146
		Miss S.. J. Farmer	Eliot, Me	147
		R. G. Young	Helena, Mont	148
		J. I. D. Hinds	Lebanon, Tenn	149
		G. W. Corr	Sioux City, Ia	150
		T. P. Marsh.	Alliance, O	151
		Dr W. L. Davidson, sup't	Cuyahoga Falls, O.	152
		Miss M. C. Mondy	Surrey House,Vic. emb't, Lon. W.C. Eng.	153
		C. L. Haskell	West New Brighton, S. I , N. Y	154
		J. A. Holden	Glens Falls N. Y	155
		A L. Arey	229 Averill av. Rochester, N. Y	156
		R L. Werntz	Annapolis, Md	157
		W. Scott, D. D., sup't		158
		J. M. Pile	Wayne, Neb	159
	.50	S. F. Neff, pres	1414 Arch st. Philadelphia, Pa	160
		G· H. Clarke	Malden, Mass	161
		C. M. Weed	Durham, N. H	162
		Fred Gowing	Concord, N. H.	163
		C: B. Bliss	University hights, New York city	164
		W. A. Stecher	3d and Chestnut st. St Louis, Mo.	165
		E. A. Alderman	Chapel Hill, N. C	166
		John Manning	"	167
	.25	A. A Stafford	Demorest, Ga.	168
		H. B. Brown, pres	Valparaiso, Ind	169
	.25	N. W. Edson	First national bank, Portland, Me	170
		Miss C. B. Wilson	1004 Champlain b'g,126 State st. Chic. Ill.	171
		Z. W. Holbrook	475 Dearborn av. Chicago, Ill	172
		B. B. Loomis	Canajoharie, N. Y	173
		Eli Dunkle	Athens, O.	174
		J. H. Grove	Delaware, O	175
		C. G. Wade	Olivet, Mich	176
		G: N. Ellis	"	177
		C. H. Chapman	Eugene, Or.	178
		Sandford Topping	Ottawa, Kan	179
		Rev. Dr Robertson	Bishop Hatfield's hall, Durham, Eng.	180

90   UNIVERSITY OF THE STATE OF NEW YORK

Statistics of

	NAME	Place	Year founded	DATE Opening
181	Pacific Grove Chaut. assembly	Pacific Grove, Cal.	1878	8 Jl
182	Peabody summer school	Troy, Ala	1890	
183	Peabody summer normal school	Lake Charles, La.		
184	Pennsylvania Chautauqua	Mt Gretna Park, Pa.	1892	8 Jl
185	Pennsylvania summer school	Huntingdon, Pa.	1895	14 Jl
186	Petoskey normal summer school	Petoskey, Mich.		
187	Piasa Bluffs assembly	Alton, Ill.	1887	23 Jl
188	Port Leyden summer school	Port Leyden, N. Y.	1891	
189	Prang summer school	Chicago, Ill.		
190	Purdue univ. sum. school of chemistry	Lafayette, Ind.		
191	Rock River assembly	Dixon, Ill.	1888	14 Jl
192	Rocky mountain Chautauqua assem'y	Glen Park, Col.	1886	15 Jl
193	Round Lake summer inst.	Round Lake, N. Y.	1887	21 Je
194	Eastern N Y. s. s. for teachers	"	1894	15 Jl
195	St John's school	Manlius, N. Y.	1891	Je
196	Saratoga summer lectures	Saratoga Springs, N. Y.	1895	
197	Union college summer school	"	1896	6 Jl
198	Sauveur col. of lang & Amherst s. s	Amherst, Mass.	1876	6 Jl
199	Secretarial inst. & train. s. Y. M. C. A.	Lake Geneva, Wis.	1884	15 Jl
200	College students conference	"	1890	19 Je
201	Institute program	"	1884	1 Ag
202	School of applied ethics	Plymouth, Mass.	1891	a
203	Shasta assembly	Shasta, Col.	1895	
204	Shinnecock Hills sum. school of art	Southampton, L. L, N. Y.	1890	1 Je
205	Silver Lake assem'y and sum. univ.	Silver Lake, N. Y.	1887	17 Jl
206	Soper summer school of oratory	Chicago, Ill.		
207	Southern Oregon Chaut. assembly	Ashland, Or.	1893	8 Jl
208	Southern students conference	Knoxville, Tenn.	1892	19 Je
209	Spirit Lake Chautauqua assembly	Spirit Lake, Ia.	1893	2 Jl
210	State normal summer school	Emporia, Kan.	1891	
211	Stryker summer normal	Stryker, O.		
212	Summer review school	Wahpeton, N. D.	1895	
213	Summer school of methods	Dover, Del.	1892	
214	Summer school of pedagogy & review	Benton Harbor, Mich.		
215	Summer school of science	Kingston, Canada	1894	7 Jl
216	Summer vacation meeting	Keene, N Y.	1894	
217	Table Rock assembly	Table Rock, Neb.	1896	1 Jl
218	Teachers college s. s. of manual training	New York	1896	6 Jl
219	Terrell college summer school	Decherd, Tenn.		
220	Texas Chautauqua assembly	Georgetown, Tex.	1888	
221	Throop polytechnic summer normal s.	Pasadena, Cal.		
222	Tri-state normal college sum. school	Angola, Ind.		
223	Tuskegee summer assembly	Tuskegee, Ala.	1895	
224	University summer normal	University, Miss.		
225	Upsala summer meeting	Upsala, Sweden	1893	

a No session in 1896

summer schools, 1896

Closing	Students	Visitors	States	Countries	Subjects of study	
21 Jl					Chautauqua assembly topics	181
......					Normal course	182
......					Normal course	183
4 Ag					General	184
28 Jl	68		4		General	185
......					General	186
20 Ag					Art, music, kindergarten	187
......	52		10	N. Y.	Preparatory for teachers examinations	188
......					Art	189
......					Chemistry	190
30 Jl					Chautauqua assembly topics	191
5 Ag					Chautauqua assembly topics	192
15 Ag					Lang. mus. ora. Bib. hist. art, kind	193
13 Ag					General	194
8					Optional	195
......						196
14 Ag					General	197
14 Ag	220		18	5	Lan. sci. Eng. lit. lib. econ. art. math. p. c.	198
15 Ag	55	? 200	15	Can.	Y. M. C. A. topics, physical culture	199
29 Je	305	? 25	17		Bible, missions, Y. M. C. A. topics	200
14 Ag	? 25	? 100	2		Bible, Y. M. C. A. topics	201
......						202
1 O					Chautauqua assembly topics	203
20 Ag					Art	204
......					General	205
......					Oratory	206
17 Jl					Chautauqua assembly topics	207
28 Je	139		20	11	Y. M. C. A. topics	208
17 Jl					Chautauqua assembly topics	209
......	240			Kan	General	210
......					Normal course	211
......					General	212
......					Normal course	213
......					General	214
9 Ag	22		1	Can	Science	215
......					Nature	216
14 Jl					Chautauqua assembly topics	217
8 Ag	53		10	Can	Manual training, drawing, painting	218
......					General	219
......					Chautauqua assembly topics	220
......					Drawing, sloyd	221
......						222
......					Theology, domestic economy, pedagogy	223
......					General	224
......						225

92   UNIVERSITY OF THE STATE OF NEW YORK

Statistics of

	Lecturers	Lectures	Recitations	EXTENSION COURSES Subjects	Lecturers	Buildings	Entrance	FEES Full course	Single course
181						2			
182									
183									
184									
185						Juniata college		$15	$5
186									
187									
188	3		180			Union school		3	
189									
190									
191									
192						4		2 50	
193						6			
194								9	3
195								100	
196									
197	12					High school	1		15
198	15					Amherst college		20	20
199	12	200	180			6	3		1
200									
201									
202									
203									
204								32-80	
205			160			9	5		1-10
206									
207						1	25	1 50	
208	17							6	
209									
210	11					Normal school			10
211									
212									
213									
214									
215	4					4			4-6
216									
217									
218	8					College			25
219									
220								4	
221									
222									
223									
224									
225									

summer schools, 1896

FEES	SECRETARY	
Single lecture	Name	Address

....	Mrs E. J Dawson	San Jose, Cal........................	181
....	E. R. Eldridge	Troy, Ala...........................	182
....	John McNeese, sup't..........	Lake Charles, La....................	183
....	Rev E. S. Hagen.............	Lebanon, Pa...	184
$.25	Miss Amanda Landes	State normal school, Millersville, Pa....	185
....	M. O. Graves.................	Petoskey, Mich......................	186
....	L. Halleck, pres..............		187
....	C. D. Hill....................	Port Leyden, N. Y...................	188
....	W. S. Mack	Chicago, Ill........................	189
....	W. E. Stone..................	Lafayette, Ind......................	190
....	Rev. W: H. Hartman	Dixon, Ill...........................	191
.25	T. M. Priestly, pres...........	University Park, Col.................	192
....	Rev Dr William Griffin, pres..		193
....	W U. Hinman	Stillwater, N. Y.....................	194
....	William Verbeck, sup't.......	Manlius, N. Y......................	195
....	D. F. Ritchie.................	98 Circular st. Saratoga Springs, N. Y...	196
....	E: E. Hale Jr.................	762 Nott st Schenectady, N. Y...	197
.50	Miss F. M. Henshaw..........	Amherst, Mass......................	198
....	J: W. Hansel.................	709 Association bldg, Chicago, Ill......	199
....	"	"	200
....	"	"	201
....	S B. Weston	1305 Arch st. Philadelphia, Pa....	202
....	Thomas Filben		203
....	W: M Chase, director........	51 W 10th st. New York.............	204
....	Rev. Ward Platt	226 Averill av. Rochester, N. Y.........	205
....	H: M. Soper..................	Chicago, Ill........................	206
.25	Mrs C R. Minkler	Ashland, Or........................	207
....	H P. Andersen, treasurer.....	Asheville, N. C.....................	208
....	F. W. Barron.................	Spirit Lake, Ia.....................	209
....	E. L. Payne..................	Emporia, Kan......................	210
....	C. C Biglow	Stryker, O.........................	211
....	L. H. Allen	Wahpeton, N. D....................	212
....	C. C. Tindal..................		213
....	G. J. Edgecumbe	Benton Harbor, Mich	214
....	William Mason...............	School of mining, Kingston, Canada....	215
....	E. E. Moore..................	109 E. 45th st. New York.............	216
....	Rev. John Gallagher, sup't....		217
....	C· A. Bennett................	Teach. col. Morningside, W. 120th st. N.Y.	218
....	J. W. Terrell.................	Decherd, Tenn......................	219
....	George Irvine	Georgetown, Tex	220
....	C: H. Keyes..................	Pasadena, Cal	221
....	L. M Sniff...................	Angola, Ind	222
....	B T Washington.............	Tuskegee, Ala	223
....	Wickliffe Rose, director.......	University, Miss	224
....	H. J. Hjarne.................	Univ. of Upsala, Sweden	225

UNIVERSITY OF THE STATE OF NEW YORK

Statistics of

	NAME	Place	Year founded	DATE Opening
226	Ursinus summer school	Collegeville, Pa.		
227	Utah university summer school	Salt Lake City, Utah	1894	15 Je
228	Vanderbilt university summer school	Nashville, Tenn	1893	
229	Vashon college summer normal	Burton, Wash	1896	
230	Virginia summer school of methods	Charlottesville, Va	1889	22 Je
231	Virginia university s. s. of law	University station	1870	1 Jl
232	Sum. sch. of medicine (private)	"	1891	1 Jl
233	Sum. class in chem (private)	"	1888	1 Jl
234	Sum. sch of physical training	"		
235	Viroqua assembly	Viroqua, Wis	1895	16 Ag
236	Viroqua summer school	"		
237	Wabash college summer school	Crawfordsville, Ind		
238	Waseca Chautauqua assembly	Waseca, Minn	1885	3 Jl
239	Washington and Jefferson college s	Washington, Pa		
240	Waterloo Chautauqua assembly	Waterloo, Ia	1892	25 Je
241	Wellesley summer school	Wellesley, Mass	1895	8 Jl
242	Western normal college s. s.	Shenandoah, Ia		
243	Western reserve univ summer school	Cleveland, O	1895	
244	Sum. school of theology	"	1895	
245	Wheaton college summer school	Wheaton, Ill	1879	28 Je
246	Willamette Valley assembly	Willamette Valley, Or	1894	7 Jl
247	Winfield Chautauqua assembly	Winfield, Kan	1891	16 Je
248	Wisconsin summer school	Madison, Wis	1887	6 Jl
249	Sum sch. of library science	"	1895	6 Jl
250	Wooster university summer school	Wooster, O		
251	World's student conference	Northfield, Mass	1866	

summer schools, 1896

Closing	Students	Visitors	States	Countries	Subjects of study	
					College preparatory and normal course	226
17 Jl	87		3		General	227
	40				General	228
					Normal course	229
17 Jl	482		6		Pedagogy, common branches	230
1 S	89		22		Law	231
1 S	18		ⲉ		Anat. chem. phys. histol. bact. mater. med.	232
1 S	11		6		Chemistry, toxicology	233
					Physical training, theory and practice	234
20 Ag					Chautanqua assembly topics	235
					Normal course	236
					General	237
23 Jl					Chautauqua assembly topics	238
					College preparatory	239
10 Jl					Chautauqua assembly topics	240
19 Ag					Natural hist. hist. Ger. Fr. Greek, Latin	241
					Normal course	242
					General	243
					Theology	244
6 Ag					General	245
17 Jl					Chautauqua assembly topics	246
26 Je					Chautauqua assembly topics	247
14 Ag					General	248
14 Ag	25				Library science	249
					College preparatory and normal course	250
					Bible	251

Statistics of

	Lecturers	Lectures	Recitations	EXTENSION COURSES Subjects	EXTENSION COURSES Lecturers	Buildings	FEES Entrance	FEES Full course	FEES Single course
226									
227	8	325	75			University			$5
228	17	34	410			University	$1		15
229									
230	22					Public school	a5	$5	
231	3					University		65	40
232	5	120				University		115	25
233	1	32				University		50	
234						Fayerweather gym		40	
235									
236									
237									
238									
239									
240						2	3	3	
241	5					College			12–20
242									
243						Adelbert college		20	10
244						"			
245						College			5
246									
247						3	1	1	50
248						2		15	
249								15	
250									
251									

a To Virginia teachers $3

summer schools, 1896

Fees (Single lecture)	Secretary Name	Address	
	Rev. H T. Spangler, pres	Collegeville, Pa	226
	H. C Lewis	Univ. of Utah, Salt Lake City, Utah	227
	W. C. Banhaw	Vanderbilt univ. Nashville, Tenn	228
	A C Jones	Burton, Wash	229
	W. A. Jenkins	Portsmouth, Va	230
	R C. Minor	University station, Charlottesville, Va	231
	Dr W. A. Lambeth	University station, Charlottesville, Va	232
			233
	Dr W A. Lambeth	University station, Charlottesville, Va	234
	Rev. J. S. Parker		235
	Howard Miller	Viroqua, Wis	236
	Prof. H M. Kingery	Crawfordsville, Ind	237
	Rev H C. Jennings, sup't	Mankato, Minn	238
	Prof Schmitz	Washington, Pa	239
$.50	F J. Sessions	Waterloo, Ia	240
	Dr Helen L. Webster	Wellesley, Mass	241
	J. M. Hussey, pres	Shenandoah, Ia	242
.50	F M. Warren	Adelbert college, Cleveland, O	243
	C F. Thwing	Adelbert college, Cleveland, O	244
	Prof D. A. Straw	Wheaton, Ill	245
	Col R. A Miller, pres		246
.25	J. C Miller, sup't		247
	E. A Birge	Madison, Wis	248
	"	"	249
	J. G. Black	Wooster, O	250
	C. S Cooper	40 E 23d st. New York	251

INDEX

The superior figure points to the exact place on the page in ninths; e. g. 73[6] means six ninths of the way down page 73. Dates are printed in italics.

Abbreviations, explanation of, 73[6].
Albany, convocation at, 67[9]–68[3].
Algebra, see Mathematics.
a Alliance francaise, 66[5].
American bar association, meeting of, 69[7].
American board for foreign missions, 67[5]
American institute of architects, 70[1].
American institute of electrical engineers, convention, 67[3].
American institute of instruction, meeting of, 71[8].
American library association, meeting of, 69[1].
American literature, at Northern Indiana normal school, 58[1].
American missionary association, meeting of, 71[3]
Amherst summer school, see Sauveur college of languages and Amherst summer school.
a Anatomy, at Summer school of physical training, 56[2]
Anthropology, at Clark university 47[7]; at Oxford summer school, 65[1].
Architects, meeting of American institute, 70[1].
Architecture, at Massachusetts institute of technology, 46[7]; at University extension summer meeting, 49[9]; at Oxford summer meeting, 65[2].
a Art, at Chautauqua, 32[7], 33[3]; at Columbian catholic summer school, 61[1];

Art — continued
at Cornell university, 37[6]; at Edinburgh summer meeting, 64[6]; at Greeley summer school, 62[6]; at Greenacre summer school, 41[7]; at Illinois state normal university, 59[1]; at Jena summer school, 66[4], at Sauveur college of languages and Amherst summer school, 45[9]; at Silver Lake, 34[2]
Asheville, Y. W. C. A. conference at, 63[4].
Astronomy, at Cornell university, 37[3]; at Des Moines summer school of methods, 61[6]; at Jena summer school, 66[3].
Athletics, at Natural science camp, 34[8], at Summer school of physical training, 56[3]; at Southern students conference, 57[6]
a Bacteriology, at Biological laboratory of Brooklyn institute, 34[6]; at Massachusetts institute of technology, 47[2]; at Oxford summer meeting, 65[1].
Baptist young people's union of America, convention, 69[7].
Bar association, meeting, 69[7].
a Bay View summer university, 59[2].
a Bible study, at Columbian catholic summer school, 61[1]; at Jewish Chautauqua summer school and assembly, 52[5]–54[7]; lectures to clergy, 65[7]; at Northfield conferences, 43[3]; at Oxford summer meeting, 65[3]; at Silver

a See also Summer schools, statistics.

Bible study — *continued*
　Lake, 34³, at Southern students conference, 57⁴; at Wake Forest college, 56⁷
a Biological laboratory of Brooklyn institute, 34⁴
a Biology, at Clark university, 48⁵; at Illinois state normal university, 58⁹; at Massachusetts institute of technology, 47¹; at New York university, 38³; at Pennsylvania summer school, 51⁶.
Board, price of, at New York university, 39⁴; at Pennsylvania summer school, 51⁶; at Wheaton college, 58⁸.
Boating, at St John's college, 35⁴.
a Botany, at Bay View summer university, 59³, at Biological laboratory of Brooklyn institute, 34⁵; at Cornell university, 37⁶; at Des Moines summer school of methods, 61⁷; at Harvard summer school, 44⁶; at Hopkins seaside laboratory, 63²; at Jena summer school, 66²; at Kansas state normal school, 62⁴; at Oxford summer meeting, 65¹.
Boxing, at Natural science camp, 34⁸
British association for the advancement of science, 71⁶.
Brooklyn institute, biological laboratory, 34⁴.
Brotherhood of St Andrew of the protestant episcopal church, conference, 68⁶.
Brotherhood of the kingdom, conference of, 68⁵.
Browning's poetry, at Canada summer school of science, 63⁹
Buffalo, conventions at. 68⁶
a Business methods, study of, at Silver Lake, 34²; at Greenacre summer school, 41⁸.

Calculus, *see* Mathematics
California, conferences in, 71⁴
Cambridge, lectures to clergy at, 65⁶.
Canada, conferences in. 71⁵.

Canada, summer school of science, *see* Summer school of science for the Atlantic provinces of Canada.
a Catholic summer school of America, 35⁵–36¹. *See also* Columbian catholic summer school.
a Catholic winter school of America, 57¹.
Certificates, state, examination for, 61⁷.
Chattanooga, convention of Baptist young people's union, 69⁷.
Chautauqua, teachers summer institute at, 68²
Chautauqua assembly topics, explanation of term, 73².
Chautauqua summer school, 32⁶–33⁴; collegiate department, 32⁷; assembly department, 32⁸; lecturers, 32⁸. *See also* Fairmount Chautauqua.
a Chemistry, at Bay View summer university, 59³; at Cornell university, 37⁵; at Harvard summer school, 44⁵; at Leland Stanford jr university, 63¹; at Massachusetts institute of technology, 46²; at N. Y. university, 38³; at Oxford summer meeting, 65¹.
a Child-study, at Chautauqua, 33²; at Clark university, 48²; at Northern Indiana normal school, 58²; at Oxford summer meeting, 65²; at Pennsylvania summer school, 51⁶; at University extension summer meeting, 49⁹–50⁵
Child-study association, meeting of, 70³.
Christian endeavor convention, 71⁴
Church history, at Catholic summer school of America. 35⁷; at University extension summer meeting, 49⁷.
Civics, at Harvard summer school, 43⁹; at Pennsylvania summer school. 51⁶, at Bay View summer university, 59³; at Des Moines summer school of methods, 61⁶; at Canada summer school of science, 63⁹.
Civilization, study of, at Jena summer school, 66⁴

a See also Summer schools, statistics

a Clark university, summer school, 47⁷-49².
Classical languages, *see* Languages
Clergy, lectures to, 65⁶.
Cleveland, meeting of American bar association, 69⁷.
Cliff Haven, Catholic summer school of America at, 35⁵-36¹.
Clifton Springs, meeting of International missionary union at, 67⁶.
Cold Springs Harbor, Biological laboratory of Brooklyn institute at, 34⁴.
College preparatory topics, explanation of term, 73⁵.
College students conference, 60³.
Colleges, summer work, 31⁸-32³.
a Columbian catholic summer school, 60⁹-61¹
Commercial work, at Northern Indiana normal school, 57⁹.
Conferences, summer, of *1897*, 67³-71⁹.
Connecticut, conventions in, 67⁵
Constitutional history, at University extension summer meeting, 49⁷.
Conventions, summer, of *1897*, 67³-71⁹
Convocation of University of state of New York, 67⁹-68².
a Cornell university, summer school, 36²-38²; law school, summer term, 38¹
a Cotuit summer school, 49².

Degrees, conferred by New York university, 39⁵.
Dentistry at Harvard summer school, 44⁸.
a Des Moines summer school of methods 61².
Detroit, conventions in, 69⁹-70¹
Diplomas, of Alliance francaise, 66⁹
Domestic institution, study of at Chautauqua, 33¹.
a Drake university summer Latin school, 61⁸-62²
a Drawing, at Bay View summer university, 59³; at Cornell university, 37⁵; at Des Moines summer school of methods, 61⁴, 61⁷; at Greeley summer school, 62⁷; at Marthas Vine-

Drawing — *continued*
yard summer institute, 47²; at Massachusetts institute of technology, 46⁷; at Northern Indiana normal school, 57⁹; at Pennsylvania summer school, 51⁶.
a Economics, at Chautauqua, 32⁹, at Columbian catholic summer school, 61¹; at Cornell university, 36³; at Des Moines summer school of methods, 61⁶; at New York university, 38³.
a Edinburgh summer meeting, 64⁵.
Education, study of, at Catholic summer school of America, 35⁸; at Chautauqua, 33²; at Clark university, 48⁷: at Des Moines summer school of methods, 61⁵; at Greenacre summer school, 41⁷; at Harvard summer school, 44¹; at Oxford summer meeting, 65²; at Pennsylvania summer school, 51⁶; at University extension summer meeting, 49⁶. *See also* Pedagogy.
Educational association, meeting of, 70².
Electricity, at Greenacre summer school, 41⁸; at Massachusetts institute of technology, 47² *See also* Physics
Eliot, (Me.) summer school at, 41⁵; American institute of electrical engineers, convention at, 67³
a Elocution, at Cornell university, 36³; at Des Moines summer school of methods, 61⁷; at Illinois state normal university, 59¹; at Martha's Vineyard summer institute, 46²; at National school of elocution and oratory, 51⁹; at Neff college of oratory: at Pennsylvania summer school, 51⁷.
Embryology, at Biological laboratory of Brooklyn institute, 34⁶; at Hopkins seaside laboratory, 63⁹.
a Engineering, at Cornell university, 37⁸; at Harvard summer school, 44³; at Leland Stauford jr university, 63¹

a See also Summer schools, statistics

Engineers, electrical convention, 67³.
England, summer meetings in, 64⁷-66⁹.
a English, at Chautauqua, 32⁷; at Cornell university, 36⁷; at Harvard summer school, 43⁷; at Leland Stanford jr university, 63¹; at Oxford summer school, 65².
English grammar, at Illinois state normal university, 59¹.
a English literature, at Canada summer school of science, 6.3⁹; at Chautauqua, 32⁷, 33⁸; at Harvard summer school, 43⁷; at Illinois state normal university, 59¹; at Northern Indiana normal school, 58¹; at Sauveur college of languages and Amherst summer school, 45⁵; at University extension summer meeting, 49⁷.
Entertainments, at Jewish Chautauqua summer school and assembly, 54⁸; at University of Michigan, 60¹.
a Entomology, at Natural science camp, 34⁸.
Epworth league, conference, 71⁵.
Ethics, at Oxford summer meeting, 65⁴.
Evolution, at Greenacre summer school, 41⁸.
a Fairmount Chautauqua, 62⁵.
a Fees, at Biological laboratory of Brooklyn institute, 34⁶; at Canada summer school of science, 64²; at Drake university summer Latin school, 61²; at Greeley summer school, 62⁶; at Hopkins seaside laboratory, 63²; at International Y. W. C A. conferences, 63⁷; at Kansas state normal school, 62⁴; at Lehigh university, 51²; at Leland Stanford jr university, 63²; at Neff college of oratory, 64⁴; at New York university, 39⁸, at Oxford summer meeting, 65⁵; at Pennsylvania summer school, 51⁶; at St John's school, 35⁵; at Sauveur college of languages and Amherst summer school, 45⁹; at Summer school of physical training, 56⁴; at University of Michigan, 59⁹;

Fees — continued
at Wake Forest college, 56⁸; at Wheaton college, 58⁷.
Fishing, at St John's school, 35⁴.
Foreign summer schools, 63⁸-67³.
a French, at Alliance francaise, 66⁵; at Bay View summer university, 59³, at Cornell university, 36⁶, at Harvard summer school, 43⁶; at Leland Stanford jr university, 63¹; at Massachusetts institute of technology, 47⁴; at New York university, 38²; at Oxford summer meeting, 65³; at Sauveur college of languages and Amherst summer school, 45⁵; at University of Geneva, 66⁹-67¹. See also Languages.
a French literature, at Oxford summer meeting, 64⁹, 65²; at University of Geneva, 67¹.
a French recreation class for girls, 41¹.
French revolution, study of, at Oxford summer meeting, 64⁹.
Genesee Wesleyan seminary, summer school conducted by, 34¹.
Geneva university, see University of Geneva.
Geography, at Harvard summer school, 44⁷, at Pennsylvania summer school, 51⁶; at Illinois state normal university 58⁹. See also Physical geography.
Geological congress, International meeting of, 71⁹.
a Geology, at Natural science camp, 34⁸; at Harvard summer school, 44⁶; at Des Moines summer school of methods, 61⁷.
Geometry, see Mathematics.
a German, at Bay View summer university, 59³; at Cornell university, 36⁵; at Harvard summer school, 43⁸; at Illinois state normal university, 59¹; at Jena summer school, 66⁴; at Leland Stanford jr university, 63¹; at Massachusetts institute of technology, 47⁴; at New York university, 38²; at Sauveur college of

---

a See also Summer schools, statistics.

German—continued
languages and Amherst summer school, 45⁴. *See also* Languages.
German literature, at Chautauqua, 32⁹; at Jena summer school, 66⁴.
Glens Falls, summer school at, 33⁴; teachers institute at, 68².
Grammar, at Illinois state normal university, 59¹.
Great Britain, summer schools in, 64⁵– 66²
a Greek, at Cornell university, 36⁴; at Harvard summer school, 43⁸; at Leland Stanford jr university, 63¹; at Oxford summer meeting, 65³; at Sauveur college of languages and Amherst summer school, 45⁵. *See also* Languages.
a Greeley summer school, 62⁶.
a Greenacre school of literature, 42⁸.
a Greenacre school of music, 43¹.
a Greenacre summer school, 41⁵.

a H. E. Holt normal institute of vocal harmony, 46⁴.
a Harvard summer school, 43⁶–44⁹.
a Harvard summer school of physical training, 45¹.
Historical pilgrimages, from National summer school, 33⁶.
a History, at Bay View summer university, 59³; at Chautauqua, 33¹; at Harvard summer school, 43⁹; at Illinois state normal university, 58⁹; at Leland Stanford jr university, 63¹; at Massachusetts institute of technology, 47³; at National summer school, 33⁶; at New York university, 38³; at Northern Indiana normal school, 57⁹; at Oxford summer meeting, 64⁸; at Pennsylvania summer school, 51⁶; at University extension summer meeting, 49⁵.
Home missionary society of congregational church, convention, 67⁶.
a Hopkins seaside laboratory, 63².
Horseback riding, at Natural science camp, 34⁸.

Huntingdon, Pennsylvania summer school at, 51³.
Hygiene, at Massachusetts institute of technology, 47¹; at Summer school of physical training, 56²; at Jena summer school, 66².

Illinois state normal university, 58⁸– 59².
Instructors, *see* Lecturers.
International conference of charities and corrections, 71⁵.
International convention of the Baptist young peoples union of America, 69⁷.
International geological congress, meeting of, 71⁹.
International missionary union meeting, 67⁶.
a International Y.W.C.A. conferences, 63⁵.
Italian, at Cornell university, 36⁷; at Sauveur college of languages and Amherst summer school, 45⁵. *See also* Languages.

a Jena summer school, 66².
a Jewish Chautauqua summer school and assembly, 52¹–54⁹.

Kansas City, Fairmount Chautauqua at, 62⁵.
a Kansas state normal school, 62³.
a Kindergarten methods, at Bay View summer university, 59²; at Canada summer school of science, 63⁹; at Des Moines summer school of methods, 61⁴; at Northern Indiana normal school, 58²; at Oxford summer meeting, 65²; at Silver Lake, 34³; at University extension summer meeting, 49⁹–50⁵.
Knoxville, Southern students conference at, 57⁴.

Labor movement, study of, at Chautauqua, 32⁹.
Lake Geneva, Western secretarial institute at, 60²; Y. W. C. A. conference at, 63⁵.
Lake Placid, summer school at, 41².

a See also Summer schools, statistics.

*Languages, at Chautauqua, 32⁷; at Massachusetts institute of technology, 47⁴; at New York university, 38³; at Northern Indiana normal school, 57⁹; at Sauveur college of languages and Amherst summer school, 45⁴; at Silver Lake, 34². See also French; German; Greek; Italian; Latin; Spanish.

*Latin, at Bay View summer university, 59³; at Cornell university, 36⁴; at Drake university summer Latin school, 61⁸-62²; at Harvard summer school, 43⁸; at Illinois state normal university, 59¹; at Leland Stanford jr university, 63¹; at Oxford summer meeting, 65³; at Sauveur college of languages and Amherst summer school, 45⁴; at University extension summer meeting, 50⁷. See also Languages.

Law, meeting of American bar association, 69⁷.

Law courses, at Columbian catholic summer school, 61¹; at Cornell university, 38¹; at Summer law school, 56⁹; at University of Michigan, 59⁹; at University of Virginia, 55²-56¹.

*Lectures, at Bay View summer university, 59³; at Biological laboratory of Brooklyn institute, 34⁵; at Catholic summer school of America, 35⁶; at Chautauqua, 32⁶-33³; at Clark university, 48¹-49²; to clergy at Cambridge, 65³; at Edinburgh summer meeting, 64⁶; at Greenacre school of literature, 42⁸; at Jewish Chautauqua summer school and assembly, 52³-54⁶; at Monsalvat school of comparative religion, 42²; at Natural science camp, 34⁷; at Oxford summer meeting, 64⁸, 65³; at Sauveur college of languages and Amherst summer school, 45⁴; at Secretarial institute and training school of young men's Christian associations, 60⁵; at Silver Lake, 34²; at Southern stu-

Lectures — *continued*
dents conference, 57⁶; at University extension summer meeting, 49⁶-50⁷; at University of Michigan, 60¹; at University of Virginia, 55¹; at Wake Forest college, 56⁵.

*Lectures to clergy, 65⁶.
*Lehigh university summer school, 50⁸-51³.
*Leland Stanford jr university, 62⁹-63³.
Lexington, Mass., summer school at, 46⁴.
Library association, *see* American library association.
Library department of the N. E. A., 70⁴-71³.
*Library economy, at New York state library school, 40¹; at Sauveur college of language and Amherst summer school, 45³; at Wisconsin summer school of library science, 60⁶.

*Literature, at Bay View summer university, 59³; at Chautauqua, 33³; at Columbian catholic summer school, 61¹; at Des Moines summer school of methods, 61⁶; at Greenacre school of literature, 42⁸; at Greenacre summer school, 41⁷; at Northern Indiana normal school, 57⁹, 58¹; at Pennsylvania summer school, 51⁶; at University extension summer meeting, 49⁵. See also English literature; French literature; German literature; Sacred literature.

London, international conference of librarians in, 69³.

Maine, convention held in, 67³.
Maulius, summer school at, 35².
*Manual training, at Teachers college, 40⁴; at Massachusetts institute of technology, 47⁵; at Oxford summer meeting, 65⁵.
Marlboro, conference of Brotherhood of the kingdom at, 68⁵.
*Marthas Vineyard summer institute, 46¹.
*Massachusetts institute of technology, 46⁸-47⁵.

---
a See also Summer schools, statistics.

a Mathematics, at Bay View summer university, 59³; at Chautauqua, 32⁷; at Cornell university, 36⁹; at Des Moines summer school of methods, 61⁶; at Harvard summer school, 44²; at Illinois state normal university, 59¹; at Leland Stanford jr university, 63¹; at Massachusetts institute of technology, 46⁷; at New York university, 38³; at Northern Indiana normal school, 57⁹; at University extension summer meeting, 50⁶.
a Medicine, at Harvard summer school, 44⁸.
Michigan, conference in, 69⁸–70¹.
Michigan, university of, see University of Michigan.
Microscopy, at Pennsylvania summer school, 51⁶.
Military department of St John's school, 35³.
Mills college, (Cal) Y. W. C. A. conference at, 63⁵.
Milwaukee, meeting of National educational association, 70¹–71³.
Minneapolis, meeting of American missionary association, 71³.
Minnesota, conferences in, 71³
Missionary work study of at Silver Lake, 34³
Missions, at Southern students conference, 57⁶; at Columbian catholic summer school, 61¹; conferences, 67⁵, 71³
Modern languages, see Languages.
a Monsalvat school of comparative religion, 42¹.
Municipal government, study of at Chautauqua, 33².
a Music, at Bay View summer university, 59³; at Canada summer school of science, 63⁹, at Chautauqua, 32⁷; at Des Moines summer school of methods, 61⁴; at Greenacre school of music, 43¹; at Leland Stanford jr university, 63¹, at Northern Indiana normal school, 57⁹, at Pennsylvania summer school, 51⁷; at Silver Lake,

Music — continued
34²; at University extension summer meeting, 50⁶. See also Voice culture.
Music teachers national association, convention, 67⁷.
Nashville, Tennessee centennial exposition at, 69⁴.
National educational association, meeting of, 70².
a National home reading union, 65⁹–66¹.
a National school of elocution and oratory, 51⁹.
a National summer school, 33⁴
a National woman's Christian temperance union, convention, 68⁸.
National Y. P. C. U. of the universalist church, convention, 69⁹–70¹.
a Natural science camp, 34⁷–35².
a Nature study, at Greenacre summer school, 41⁹; at Clark university, 48¹, at Des Moines summer school of methods, 61⁴.
a Neff college of oratory, 64².
Neurology, at Clark university, 48⁶.
New Haven, meeting of American board for foreign missions at, 67⁵.
New Orleans, Catholic winter school of America at, 57¹.
New York city, convention of music teachers national association at, 67⁷
New York college for the training of teachers, see Teachers college
New York state, conferences, in, 67⁶–68⁹.
New York state summer institutes for teachers, 68³.
a New York state library school, summer session, 40¹.
a New York university, summer school, 38³–39⁹; situation, 38⁷
Normal course, explanation of term, 78⁴.
North American child study association, meeting of, 70³
a Northern Indiana normal school, 57⁸–58⁴.
a Northfield conferences, 43³, 63⁵.

a See also Summer schools, statistics.

Ohio, conferences in, 69⁷.
Oratory, *see* Elocution.
a Oxford summer meeting, 64⁷-65⁶.
Pacific Grove, laboratory at, 63².
Painting, at Cornell university, 37⁷; at Pennsylvania summer school, 51⁶: at Northern Indiana normal school, 57⁹. *See also* Art.
Paris, Alliance francaise, 66⁵.
a Pedagogy, at Chautauqua, 32⁷; at Clark university, 47⁷; at Des Moines summer school of methods, 61²; at Harvard summer school, 44¹; at Illinois state normal university, 58⁹, at Jena summer school, 66²; at Marthas Vineyard summer institute, 46¹; at New York university, 38²; at Northern Indiana normal school, 58²; at Pennsylvania summer school, 51⁵ at Teachers college, 40⁷; at Wake Forest college, 56⁷.
a Penmanship, at Northern Indiana normal school, 57⁹; at Des Moines summer school of methods, 61⁷.
Pennsylvania, conferences in, 69¹.
a Pennsylvania summer school, 51³.
Pharmacy, at Northern Indiana normal school, 57⁹.
Philadelphia, University extension summer meeting at, 49⁵; National school of elocution and oratory at, 51⁹; library convention in, 69¹
Philosophy, at Catholic summer school of America, 35⁷; at University extension summer meeting, 49⁸, at Jena summer school, 66².
Phonography, at Northern Indiana normal school, 57⁹
a Photography, at Natural science camp, 34⁸; at Pennsylvania summer schools, 51⁷.
a Physical education, at Canada summer school of science, 63⁹; at Chautauqua, 32⁷; at Des Moines summer school of methods, 61⁷; at Harvard summer school, 44⁷; at Harvard summer school of physical training,

Physical education — *continued*
45¹; at Illinois state normal university, 59¹; at New York university, 38²; at Pennsylvania summer school, 51⁷; at St John's school, 35³; at Silver Lake, 34³; at Summer school of physical training, 56².
a Physical geography, at Des Moines summer school of methods, 61⁷.
Physical sciences, at Illinois state normal university, 58⁹.
a Physics, at Bay View summer university, 59³, at Cornell university, 37³, at Des Moines summer school of methods, 61⁷, at Harvard summer school, 44⁴, at Jena summer school, 66³; at Leland Stanford jr university, 63¹; at Massachusetts institute of technology, 47², at New York university, 38²; at Oxford summer meeting, 65¹.
Physiology, at Massachusetts institute of technology, 47¹; at Clark university, 47⁷, at Summer school of physical training, 56², at Jena summer school, 66².
Political economy, *see* Economics
Politics at Columbian catholic summer school, 61¹.
a Psychology, at Canada summer school of science, 63⁹; at Catholic summer school of America, 35⁷, at Chautauqua, 32⁷, at Clark university, 47⁷, 48⁴; at Columbian catholic summer school, 61¹; at Des Moines summer school of methods, 61⁵; at Greenacre summer school, 41⁹; at Harvard summer school, 44¹, at Jena summer school, 66²; at Neff college of oratory, 64⁴; at New York university, 38³, at Northern Indiana normal school, 58³; at Pennsylvania summer school, 51⁷; at University extension summer meeting, 49⁹-50⁵.

Reading, *see* Elocution.
a Religions, study of, at Greenacre summer school, 41⁹: at Monsalvat

---
a See also Summer schools, statistics.

Religions — *continued*
school of comparative religion, 42[2];
at Jena summer school, 66[4].
Revolutionary epoch, study of at
Oxford summer meeting, 64[8].
Rhetoric, at Des Moines summer school
of methods, 61[6].
Romance languages, at Cornell university, 36[5]. *See also* French.
Round tables, at Silver Lake, 34[3]; at
Fairmount Chautauqua, 62[6]
Russia, conferences in, 71[9].

Sacred literature, at Chautauqua, 32[7].
a St John's school, 35[2].
San Francisco, Christian endeavor convention at, 71[4].
Saratoga, meeting of Home missionary society of congregational church at, 67[6].
a Sauveur college of languages and Amherst summer school, 45[5].
School law, at Illinois state normal university, 59[1]
a School of applied ethics, 47[6].
School of expression, at Chautauqua, 32[7].
a Science courses, at Bay View summer university, 59[3]; at Biological laboratory of Brooklyn institute, 34[5], meeting of British association, 71[5]; at Canada summer school of science, 63[9]; at Chautauqua, 32[7], at Cornell university, 37[3]; at Des Moines summer school of methods, 61[7], at Harvard summer school, 44[4]; at Hopkins seaside laboratory, 63[2]; at Jena summer school, 66[3]; at Kansas state normal school, 62[3], at Massachusetts institute of technology, 46[8]–47[3]; at Natural science camp, 34[7]; at New York university, 38[3]; at Northern Indiana normal school, 57[9]; at Oxford summer meeting, 65[1], at Pennsylvania summer school, 51[7]; at University extension summer meeting, 49[9]
Scotch-Irish conference, 69[9].

Scotland, summer meeting in, 64[5].
a Secretarial institute and training school of Young men's Christian associations, 60[2].
Shakspere study, at Northern Indiana normal school, 58[2].
a Silver Lake summer school, 34[1].
a Sloyd, at Bay View summer university, 59[3].
a Sociology, at Chautauqua, 32[7]; at Catholic summer school of America, 35[7]; at Greenacre summer school, 41[9]. *See also* Economics.
a Southern students conference, 57[3].
Spanish, at Cornell university, 36[7]; at Sauveur college of languages and Amherst summer school, 45[5]. *See also* Languages.
State certificates, examination for, 61[7].
Statistics of summer schools, 73–97.
Summer institutes for teachers, 68[3].
a Summer law school, 56[9].
a Summer school of physical training, 56[2].
a Summer school of science for the Atlantic provinces of Canada, 63[8]–64[2].
Summer schools, increasing number, 31[6]; at colleges and universities, 31[8]–32[3]; statistics, 73–97.
Sunday-school work, study of, at Catholic summer school of America, 35[9].
a Surveying, at Lehigh university, 50[8]–51[2].
Swimming, at Natural science camp, 34[6]; at St John's school, 35[2].
a Taxidermy, at Natural science camp, 34[7].
Teachers, summer school for, at New York university, 38[5]; at Wheaton, college, 58[5], at Kansas state normal school, 62[3], summer institutes for, 68[3]. *See also* Lecturers.
a Teachers college summer school, 40[4].
Teachers examinations, preparation for, 91[3].
Teaching, *see* Pedagogy.

a See also Summer schools, statistics.

Temperance instruction, at Silver Lake, 34³; at Clark university, 48⁹–49¹.
Tennessee, conferences in, 69⁵.
Tennessee centennial, 69³.
a Theology, at Columbian catholic summer school, 60⁹–61¹.
Theosophy, at Columbian catholic summer school, 61¹
Thousand Island Park, teachers institutes at, 68³
Toronto, Neff college of oratory at, 64², conferences in, 71⁵.
Trigonometry, see Mathematics.
Tuition, see Fees.
Typewriting, at Northern Indiana normal school, 57⁹.

Universities, summer work, 31⁸–32³.
University convocation of the state of New York, 67⁹–68³.
a University extension summer meeting, 49⁴–50⁷.
a University of Geneva, summer school, 66⁹–67³.
a University of Michigan, summer school, 59⁷–60¹.
University of the city of New York, see New York university.
a University of Virginia summer school of law, 55¹–56¹

Virginia university, see University of Virginia.
a Voice culture, at Marthas Vineyard summer institute, 46²; at H. E Holt normal institute of vocal harmony, 46⁴; at Northern Indiana normal

Voice culture — continued
school, 57⁹; at Des Moines summer school of methods, 61⁷; at Canada summer school of science, 63⁹.
a Wake Forest college summer school, 56⁵.
Western secretarial institute, consolidated with Y. M. C. A. training school in Chicago, 60³.
a Wheaton college, summer session, 58⁴.
Wisconsin, conference in, 70²–71³.
a Wisconsin summer school of library science, 60⁶.
Womans Christian temperance union, convention, 68³, 71⁷.
World's student Christian federation, convention, 46⁵.
Yarmouth, Canada summer school of science at, 63⁸–64².
Young folks reading union, at Jewish Chautauqua summer school and assembly, 52³, 54⁸.
Y. M. C A. students conferences, 43², 57³, Secretarial institute and training school of, 60²; training school of Chicago, consolidated with Western secretarial institute, 60³.
Y. W. C. A. summer school, 60³; conferences, international, 63³
a Zoology, at Biological laboratory of Brooklyn institute, 34⁵; at Hopkins seaside laboratory, 63³; at Jena summer school, 66²; at Kansas state normal school, 62⁴; at Massachusetts institute of technology, 47¹; at Oxford summer meeting, 65¹.

---

a See also Summer schools, statistics.

University of the State of New York

Object. The object of the University as defined by law is to encourage and promote education in advance of the common elementary branches. Its field includes not only the work of academies, colleges, universities, professional and technical schools, but also educational work connected with libraries, museums, university extension courses and similar agencies.

The University is a supervisory and administrative, not a teaching institution. It is a state department and at the same time a federation of more than 800 institutions of higher and secondary education.

Government. The University is governed and all its corporate powers exercised by 19 elective regents and by the governor, lieutenant-governor, secretary of state and superintendent of public instruction who are *ex officio* regents. Regents are elected in the same manner as United States senators; they are unsalaried and are the only public officers in New York chosen for life.

The elective officers are a chancellor and a vice-chancellor, who serve without salary, and a secretary. The secretary is the executive and financial officer, is under official bonds for $10,000, is responsible for the safe keeping and proper use of the University seal and of the books, records and other property in charge of the regents, and for the proper administration and discipline of its various offices and departments.

Powers and duties. Besides many other important powers and duties, the regents have power to incorporate, and to alter or revoke the charters of universities, colleges, academies, libraries, museums, or other educational institutions; to distribute to them funds granted by the state for their use, to inspect their workings and require annual reports under oath of their presiding officers; to establish examinations as to attainments in learning and confer on successful candidates suitable certificates, diplomas and degrees, and to confer honorary degrees.

They apportion annually an academic fund of about $250,000, part for buying books and apparatus for academies and high schools raising an equal amount for the same purpose, $100 to each nonsectarian secondary school in good standing and the remainder on the basis of attendance and the results of instruction as shown by satisfactory completion of prescribed courses for which the regents examinations afford the official test. The regents also expend annually $25,000 for the benefit of free public libraries.

Regents meetings. The annual meeting is held the third Thursday in December, and other meetings are held as often as business requires. An executive committee of nine regents is elected at the annual meeting to act for the board in the intervals between its meetings, except that it can not grant, alter, suspend or revoke charters or grant honorary degrees.

Convocation. The University convocation of the regents and the officers of institutions in the University, for consideration of subjects of mutual interest, has been held annually since 1863 in the senate chamber in Albany. It meets Monday, Tuesday and Wednesday after the fourth Friday in June.

Though primarily a New York meeting, nearly all questions discussed are of equal interest outside the state. Its reputation as the most important higher educational meeting of the country has in the past few years drawn to it many eminent educators not residents of New York, who are most cordially welcomed and share fully in all discussions. It elects each year a council of five to represent it in intervals between meetings. Its proceedings, issued annually, are of great value in all educational libraries.